THE
HOLOCAUST
AND
HISTORY

THE
HOLOCAUST
AND
HISTORY The Known, the Unknown, the Disputed, and the Reexamined

EDITED BY
Michael Berenbaum and Abraham J. Peck

Published in association with the
United States Holocaust Memorial Museum
Washington, D.C.

Indiana University Press
Bloomington and Indianapolis

The assertions, arguments, and conclusions contained herein
are those of the authors. They do not necessarily reflect the
opinions of the United States Holocaust Memorial Council
or the United States Holocaust Memorial Museum.

© 1998 by Michael Berenbaum and Abraham J. Peck

The paper used in this publication meets the minimum requirements
of American National Standard for Information Sciences—Permanence of Paper for Printed Library Materials, ANSI Z39.48-1984.

MANUFACTURED IN THE UNITED STATES OF AMERICA

Library of Congress Cataloging-in-Publication Data

The Holocaust and history : the known, the unknown,
the disputed, and the reexamined / edited by Michael Berenbaum
and Abraham J. Peck.
p.   c.m
"Published in association with the United States
Holocaust Memorial Museum, Washington, D.C."
Includes index.
ISBN 0-253-33374-1 (cl : alk. paper)
1. Holocaust, Jewish (1939–1945)—Congresses.
I. Berenbaum, Michael, date.   II. Peck, Abraham J.
III. U.S. Holocaust Memorial Museum.
D804.18.H66   1998
940.53'18—dc21   97-40030

2 3 4 5 03 02 01 00 99 98

CONTENTS

Part 8
The Axis, the Allies, and the Neutrals   421

Part 9
Jewish Leadership, Jewish Resistance   585

PREFACE

From its earliest conception as a living memorial to the victims of the Holocaust, the United States Holocaust Memorial Museum was envisioned as more than a Museum. Education, scholarship, and commemoration were at the core of the Museum's mission.

Thus, alongside the development of the Museum, plans were undertaken to create what was then called the United States Holocaust Research Institute—since 1996 called the Research Institute—to function as the scholarly division of the United States Holocaust Memorial Museum, an international resource for the development of research on the Holocaust and related issues, including those of contemporary significance.

Since the field of Holocaust studies is diverse, the work includes a variety of approaches by scholars from different disciplines: history, political science, philosophy, religion, sociology, literature, psychology, music, architectural history, even chemistry and engineering, as well as other disciplines.

The Museum, with its widely praised permanent exhibition, opened in April 1993. Because so many of the Research Institute's staff were involved in the creation of the Museum's permanent exhibition and could not change positions until their tasks were complete, the Institute's opening was delayed until December, when an international conference was convened. Invited to this gathering of scholars were three generations of men and women from five continents and from almost all of the European countries who have devoted their lives to the study of the Holocaust. Among them were senior scholars born before World War II who experienced the Holocaust directly or indirectly as young men and women. Some were survivors, others were refugees. Some had spent the war years in safety either in Palestine or the United States, others were in Germany or in one of its allied countries. These scholars were pioneers in a field. Often they had begun their studies before the scholarship of the Holocaust had gained any academic legitimacy. They had worked in isolation for years, out of the limelight, as Raul Hilberg was to say.

They were joined by a second generation of scholars, those with no living memory of the events they study. Born after the war, they are the first post-Holocaust generation. They came to their studies when the field was in its infancy. Often self-taught and self-motivated, they built on the legacy of their more senior colleagues and saw the evolution of the field to prominence. Unexpectedly, they had seen interest in the Holocaust expand into many domains of contemporary culture, popular as well as scholarly.

They were joined by a third generation of scholars that entered an expanding field of both historical and contemporary significance. These young scholars were at the beginning of their careers, asking new questions, developing new insights, learning new things. They were offered an opportunity to present the first fruits of their learning. They were unencumbered by the personal memories that haunted the senior generation. The material they studied, though, was haunting; so too, the event.

It was felt that the best way to launch the Research Institute was to take stock of the field, to consider where it had been and where it must go. An appropriate title was found: "The Holocaust: The Known, the Unknown, the Disputed, and the Reexamined." And various formats were created: scholarly lectures, panels, discussions. The offerings of the opening conference were both wide and deep. Consideration was given to the perpetrators, the victims, and the bystanders, but also to rescue and resistance—armed combat and spiritual defiance. Each of the countries of combat was considered, those of the Allies and the Axis as well as of the neutral countries. Each of the phases of the Holocaust was examined, from definition to expropriation, ghettoization, deportation, and the death camps. Consideration was given to liberation and displaced persons' camps and the efforts of survivors to rebuild their lives after the war as well as to the role of the Holocaust in contemporary culture in Israel, Germany, and the United States.

Consideration was also given to when the decision to kill was made and to the distance between the decision and the implementation of the Final Solution. Scholarly debate was intensified. Questions as to the uniqueness of the Holocaust were raised anew. The role of antisemitism and racism and the interrelationship between Nazi racism and antisemitism were examined afresh. The debate as to the nature of the killers, their motivations, and the scope of their behavior was considered, foreshadowing the scholarly debate; were the killers ordinary men, as Christopher R. Browning argues, or were they ordinary Germans, as Daniel Jonah Goldhagen maintains?

New fields of inquiry were launched and new works were unveiled. Robert-Jan van Pelt gave an architectural history of the Auschwitz concentration camp and its relationship to the town and to regional planners. His insights as an architectural historian added even to the most seasoned understanding of the camp. This presentation later found expression in the volume he coauthored with Deborah Dwork, *Auschwitz: 1270 to the Present,* and because the bulk of the paper was published there it is not reprinted here. Steven T. Katz argued passionately and persuasively for the uniqueness of the Holocaust, condensing the insights of his proposed three-volume study, *The Holocaust in Historical Context.* Henry Friedlander presented the findings of his work for *The Origins of Nazi Genocide: From Euthanasia to the Final Solution* regarding the character and biographies—intellectual and personal—of the physicians who staffed the T4 programs.

Because this work seeks to present the state of Holocaust studies on the brink of the twenty-first century, scholarly readers will see the origins and the impact of many scholarly works, some of which have emerged and some of which will emerge. For the more general reader, *The Holocaust and History* does what it sets out to do. It examines what has been understood from the ashes, what cannot be understood—or is not yet understood. It considers what has been misunderstood, where our insights have taken us, and where they have failed. It offers a distinctive view of an emerging field of study. And it bestows upon the Institute that sponsored the conference the challenges of shaping the field and nurturing an area of scholarship on the eve of maturity.

Michael Berenbaum
Abraham J. Peck

ACKNOWLEDGMENTS

I

Words of gratitude are in order.

As Director of the Research Institute at its inauguration and for its first three years, I have taken the liberty of writing this section alone to acknowledge the major role played by my coeditor, Abraham J. Peck, in organizing the conference and in coediting this work. Collaborating closely with the Academic Committee of the United States Holocaust Memorial Council, he reconceptualized the program time and again to encompass major trends in the field; he identified appropriate scholars and brought off the conference with dignity and an openness that appropriately launched the United States Holocaust Research Institute. Thank you!

I am grateful to Alfred Gottschalk, Chancellor of the Hebrew Union College–Jewish Institute of Religion, who has chaired with distinction the Academic Committee that is the Research Institute's governing body. He has served the Museum in so many ways, as chairman of our Education Committee, then of the Academic Committee, and even for a time as Acting Chairman of the United States Holocaust Memorial Council. He offers wisdom, insight, and guidance, the freedom to achieve major goals, and the advice that empowers accomplishment.

Members of the Academic Committee served as the steering committee for this conference. They included scholars of international repute, survivors, and chairs of the Council's major committees.

I am grateful to Yehuda Bauer, The Hebrew University, Jerusalem; Charles Blitzer, Woodrow Wilson International Center for Scholars; Randolph L. Braham, City University of New York and Rosenthal Institute for Holocaust Studies; Willard Allen Fletcher, University of Delaware; Yisrael Gutman, The Hebrew University, Jerusalem; Raul Hilberg, University of Vermont; Jehuda Reinharz, Brandeis University; as well as Benjamin Meed, Hadassah Rosensaft, Julius Schatz, and Helen Fagin, who chaired the Council's Content, Archives, Collections, and Education committees respectively. Many of these men and women have toiled for the Museum since the inception of the idea. Blessed are those who dream great dreams and see them reach fruition.

Benton Arnovitz is the able Director of Academic Publications. Having worked on books alone and with colleagues, I now know the pleasure of working with a highly skilled professional who does not say an extra word and does not permit an extra word to be written. He was assisted by Aleisa Fishman, who has juggled her graduate studies and Research Institute assignments with skill and grace. She does so much, so well. Michael Gelb recently joined the academic publications staff and worked well to bring this work to completion.

So much that is done at the Research Institute is possible only because of the excellent labors of Wesley Fisher, who, as Deputy Director, was a full partner and able colleague and friend.

This will be the final work that I have produced with my assistant Deirdre McCarthy, who for two years worked with me side by side with dedication and competence. We were assisted by able and energetic interns: Billy Mann of Yale, Trisha O'Connell of Holy Cross, Joshua Grey of the University of Massachusetts, Amherst; and Ian Reifowitz, Jennie Diamond, Julie Hock, James Seidl, and Marjorie Weinstein. Throughout their time at the Museum, they were always of service, organized, intelligent, diligent, and skilled.

I wish to express gratitude to Council Chairman Emeritus Harvey M. Meyerhoff and former Vice-Chairman William Loewenberg, during whose tenure the conference was planned, and Chair Miles Lerman and Vice-Chair Ruth Mandel, during whose tenure the conference was held.

So, too, my gratitude to my distinguished colleagues Jeshajahu Weinberg, who directed the Museum during its creation and supported the conference and the creation of the United States Holocaust Research Institute, and to all other Museum Council members and staff, who are now stewards of the Museum's mission.

This book is the second that the Museum has published with Indiana University Press. We are blessed with an able editor, Janet Rabinowitch. We are grateful to her and to press director John Gallman for the partnership that we have developed that has enabled the scholarship of the Research Institute to come forth. When we published our first work with Indiana University Press it was our hope that it would be the first of many.

May the Research Institute go from strength to strength.

Michael Berenbaum
Los Angeles, California

II

I grew up in a home where the Holocaust permeated every aspect of our private and public existence.

At home I cannot remember a time when my father did not speak of his experiences. My days and nights were filled with stories of the ghetto and the camps. As I have written elsewhere, the sadistic SS men and doctors were much more real to me than the shadow figures of my fourteen murdered aunts and uncles, who had names but little else to tell me about how they lived and how they died.

The stories that I will pass on from my father are the stories I heard from him as a young boy. I remember them still today. They were stories of how ordinary men and women became possessed by an evil that poisoned their very souls. Doctors, engineers, military leaders were all devoted to cleansing the earth of "lives unworthy of life." My father told me things about them, how they thought and what they felt, things that I had never read or heard anywhere else. I heard of the destruction of the Sinti and Roma camp in the Litzmannstadt (Łódź) Ghetto—my father was only a few hundred feet away when the so-called Gypsy camp, rife with disease, was set ablaze. I learned from him of the other victims chosen by the Nazis—political prisoners, gays, communists, and Russian prisoners of war—victims he had encountered in camps such as Buchenwald and Theresienstadt, only two of the many in which he was incarcerated during the fourteen months between his deportation from Łódź in March 1944 and his liberation by Soviet troops on May 8, 1945. I knew about these victims long before they became the subject of study.

I will continue to pass on the lessons that my father asked me to draw from his sufferings—the place of Jews in the world, the role of Christian and racial anti-semitism in the Holocaust, about those few who sought to help Jews, and the many more who did not.

In many respects, the opening conference of the Research Institute and the publication of this book are but two more efforts of mine to pass on those lessons taught to me by my father.

I have been associated with the United States Holocaust Memorial Museum for more than a dozen years, first as deputy chair of its committee on archives and library and then as a special consultant to the Research Institute.

I would like to thank my wife Jean and children Abby and Joel for their patience in living with an often remote and stressed husband and father. I would also like to thank my staff at the American Jewish Archives in Cincinnati for their total devotion to my frenzied calls for help during preparations for the publication of this book.

Abraham J. Peck
Houston, Texas

Part 1

Probing the Holocaust

WHERE WE ARE, WHERE WE NEED TO GO

The theme of the inaugural conference of the United States Holocaust Research Institute was "The Holocaust: The Known, the Unknown, the Disputed, and the Reexamined." For the opening session, three of the world's most distinguished scholars, men of international reputation, were invited to explore that question. One was American, one German, and one Israeli. These senior scholars had been working in the field for almost half a century; they were acknowledged pioneers whose works had stood the test of time. When they began their efforts, they were often alone; now assembled before them were three generations of scholars, their students, and their students' students. Thus, it was time to take stock of how the field had developed and where it must go in the future. A younger Canadian scholar, whose work had placed the Holocaust in its historical context some half dozen years earlier, was invited to comment.

Appropriately, the first to speak was Raul Hilberg, whose magisterial work, *The Destruction of the European Jews*, was written in virtual isolation and in opposition to the academic establishment nearly four decades earlier. It has since come to define the field and to shape the insights of scholars into how Germany perpetrated the Holocaust. In his remarks and again in this essay, entitled "Sources and Their Uses," Hilberg, the dean of Holocaust historians, addresses his fellow Holocaust researchers and concludes appropriately, when the question posed is where we stand today, with the simple answer—in the "limelight."

But such a status was not always seen as being attainable. Holocaust studies took a long time to enter the academic and lay consciences. Hilberg is not satisfied simply to reflect on the success of Holocaust studies. He evaluates the sources that exist in the field and the problems inherent in using some or all of them. He also discusses the new archival resources in Eastern Europe, closed for nearly a half century to Western scholars. Rather than address the achievements of past scholarship, he seeks again to shape the future of the field.

Israeli historian Yehuda Bauer contends in "A Past That Will Not Go Away" that the Holocaust has become a cultural code—the paradigmatic symbol of evil in Western civilization. Thus, whether desired or undesired, the memory of the Holocaust will not fade. He sets out to dismantle the arguments of those who would mystify the Holocaust and treat it as an event that permits no comparison. He does the same with those who would universalize the Holocaust and deprive the event of its particularity. Toward the former, Bauer contends that mystification of the event imparts no meaning. The victims were even deprived of their martyrdom; few chose their death, they were chosen to die because of the accident of their birth to Jewish parents. One cannot argue for uniqueness unless singularity is established in comparison with other events, Bauer argues.

Toward the universalists, Bauer contends that the Jews were the only victims of Nazi Germany chosen for total annihilation for purely ideological reasons; as a perceived satanic force, Jews were as central to Nazi ideology as they were to the birth of Christianity. He attacks Jewish revisionists—not Holocaust-deniers, who are often inappropriately called revisionists—who view the Jewish role during the Holocaust through the prism of contemporary Jewish power. They have internalized, Bauer argues, the antisemitism of their oppressors; for the sad fact is that during the Holocaust, Jews were absolutely powerless. Similarly, he dismisses Ernst Nolte's efforts to see the origin of the concentration camp in the Soviet Gulag and Arno Mayer's attempt to portray Bolshevism and Marxism as the Nazis' central ideological enemy.

He concludes with a plea for the importance of oral history. The Nazis tried to murder the murdered, Bauer contends. Oral history can establish the experience of the victims.

In his contribution, "The Holocaust: Where We Are, Where We Need to Go," German historian Eberhard Jäckel recounts the development of Holocaust historiography in the first half century since the event. Gerald Reitlinger wrote his early work *The Final Solution* in 1953, yet well into the 1960s there was no scholarly debate of note. For a time, the murder of the Jews was viewed primarily through the prism of antisemitism, which Jäckel sees as of only limited value. The question, Jäckel argues, is not why the Nazis were antisemites but why they committed murder. Only in 1977 did the focus shift to German decision making, when Martin Broszat asked how and by whom the decision to kill all the Jews had been made. In short time, two schools of thought developed: the intentionalists, who viewed the Holocaust as Hitler's determined and premeditated plan, which he implemented as the opportunity arose; and the functionalists, who viewed the Final Solution as an evolution that occurred when other plans proved untenable.

Jäckel outlines his own position, which sees the evolution of Nazi anti-Jewish policy in the rivalry between its principal architect, forty-one-year-old Heinrich Himmler, and his subordinate, thirty-seven-year-old Reinhard Heydrich. Heydrich understood Hitler's own commitment to the annihilation of the Jews and he tried to outdo—and perhaps therefore to outdistance—Himmler in implementing this policy. The direction of future research is clear, Jäckel argues. Pure functionalism has been discarded; so, too, intentionalism in its purest form—"the Holocaust was initiated by Hitler." Conditions permitted and facilitated its implementation. These must be explored.

As a commentator to Hilberg, Bauer, and Jäckel, Canadian scholar Michael R. Marrus reminds his readers that we are at an early moment in Holocaust historiography. The Holocaust has become historicized, he argues. "It has entered into the mainstream of historical understanding" and is therefore subject to the same rules of evidence, interpretation, and exposition as the other great issues historians consider. While this may disturb some, it is a healthy development for historians. Marrus argues that the Holocaust is well on its way to being incorporated into history in the way that the French Revolution has become a reference point for understanding its era. He bemoans the personal assaults on historians that challenge their motivation for research and personalize their historical conclusions. He reminds us that we have enough to do trying to get history itself correct. Leave motivation to the psychologists and biographers.

And finally, he argues that future Holocaust historiography will be driven less by new sources than by new questions asked by contemporary graduate students and their students' students.

I.

RAUL HILBERG

Sources and Their Uses

When the question is posed about where, as academic researchers of the Holocaust, we stand today, the simple answer is: in the limelight. Never before has so much public attention been lavished on our subject, be it in North America or in Western Europe. This focus has been sharpened by the construction of museums like the United States Holocaust Memorial Museum in Washington or the Jüdisches Museum in Vienna, to mention just two that were opened in 1993. Interest in our topic is manifest in college courses, which are developed in one institution or another virtually every semester; or conferences, which take place almost every month; or new titles of books, which appear practically every week. The demand for output is seemingly inexhaustible. The media celebrate our discoveries, and when an event in some part of the world reminds someone of the Holocaust, our researchers are often asked to explain or supply a connection instantaneously.

Our academic life was not always so public. There was a widespread taboo between the occurrence of the catastrophe and the current wave of interest. Nor was this hiatus an accident. In Germany the perpetrators—and there were many—did not want to hear what they had done. In the whole Western world the bystanders—and there were many more—did not want to be told what they had not done. For several decades both groups were to a large extent protected from exposure, even while the Cold War or the Israel-Arab conflict preempted the headlines. Under these conditions, the early researchers who insisted on concerning themselves with the Holocaust were engaged in a revolt against silence, and their writing, to the extent that it emerged in print, was perceived as an implied, if not explicit, set of accusations directed at Nazis, the Jewish councils, the United States Department of State, the Pope, indeed anyone who was suspected to have been aware at the time of the Final Solution that a whole people was threatened with annihilation.

Even now the Holocaust stands as an abyss in history, and it is noted for a paucity of heroes. There is little to celebrate and there are few individuals, let alone organizations, that can be praised without reservation. The conclusions of our researched monographs are almost always dismal. What may be offered is at most a warning, a "never again"; but the "lessons" are overwhelmingly negative. The participants and witnesses may be aging, dying, or dead, but a pallor still envelops this past. All we can usefully do is penetrate the fog and excavate the details of this happening, collating them and describing them in the time-honored manner of social scientists examining a phenomenon.

But what details? Our knowledge depends on sources, and it is precisely in this regard that we have reached a turning point. The principal materials with which we have worked are preserved in two piles: 1) the recollections of contemporaries, which in the main can be found in raw oral history, court testimony, and memoir literature, and 2) written contemporaneous records, which are official or private documents, such as orders, reports, letters, memoranda, diaries, and the like. We can already see that we are coming to a natural end in our effort to build the pile of personal accounts. Granted, one may still obtain a secondary input from descendants who have something to pass on or say about their deceased elders, but on the whole the collecting of these data is almost over.

In the matter of remembered history, one should begin to ask what we have and of what use it is. If we treat the statements of witnesses as information about places, names, or dates—the sort of chips that are part of a much larger mosaic—then we will inevitably associate them with documents. That kind of investigation involves any one of three different objectives.

First, we might look at testimony to understand a document. Most often, we are going to find such explanations in judicial proceedings. Inasmuch as no document really speaks for itself, lawyers have wisely consulted the authors or recipients of records in question. An example is an affidavit by Hans Globke of the Reich Interior Ministry, in which he identified all the decrees he had written. Another illustration is a set of statements made to German prosecutors by Richard Korherr, who had been the SS statistician. Korherr furnished important indications of the sources on which he relied to compile his statistical report on the annihilation of European Jewry. Outside the courtroom, in his Argentinean memoirs, Adolf Eichmann revealed that he had drafted the famous three sentences that constituted Göring's authorization to Heydrich, dated July 31, 1941, to proceed with a Final Solution. At his trial, Eichmann talked about the Wannsee Conference, the official summary of which he had drafted with corrections by Heydrich. And so on.

Because many documents were destroyed during the war, there are now conspicuous gaps in the official wartime correspondence. In lieu of records, we must therefore exploit testimony. One of the major subjects of our interest is the creation, operation, and liquidation of the Belzec-Sobibor-Treblinka complex. Here and there we have found some remaining documents about these camps, but much of the little that we know comes from statements of witnesses. Thus a Polish locksmith literally gave us the key to the origins of Belzec when he testified about the dates of its construction.

There are also times when we want to acquire knowledge about events that were never recorded in the first place. We listen to Eichmann when he relates what he heard from Heydrich, who was informed by Himmler about a crucial decision by Hitler to annihilate the Jews of Europe physically. How many of us have not daydreamed of questioning Heydrich and Himmler in person?

In sum, therefore, the use of recalled events for the reconstruction of a history is important but limited. The accounts may be unreliable. Some of the witnesses, particularly if they were actual or potential defendants, withheld or plainly lied about the facts. At other times, a participant or survivor no longer remembers a procedure or a face but mistakenly insists on the accuracy of the recollection. We are all aware of these pitfalls. But what if we are interested in the witnesses themselves, their own experiences, what it is that they remember, and the structure or style of their testimony? If we are going to study the lives or personalities of all these contemporaries, our problems will be different, but not easier. First and foremost, we must recognize that notwithstanding the existence of tens of thousands of statements, not everyone has spoken.

A scarcity of memoirs is most noticeable when we deal with perpetrators. They wrote very few books and in some cases, when they did, left out what we want to know. The most lofty of these writers was Albert Speer. Note what he did not cover: his plans to reserve Jewish apartments in Berlin for bombed-out Germans, his inspection trip to Mauthausen, and his approval of building materials for 300 barracks in Auschwitz. The fewest perpetrators looked at themselves in the mirror, and some of those who did were SS men who had seen or worked in death camps and who had burned the proverbial bridge behind them. In the main, however, our principal sources about these men are their personnel records or similar items. This is to say that in the perpetrator realm, documents must be substituted for testimony.

Generally, when Holocaust testimony is mentioned, it is automatically associated with statements or memoirs of survivors. This understanding is certainly not misplaced, because there is a mountain of such materials. Yet these accounts represent only a small minority of the victims. One cannot interview the dead, and the survivors are not a random sample of the communities that once existed in Europe. Moreover, there are two major groups of survivors, and the large majority of those who come to our notice emerged from camps or woods. These individuals happened to have been younger, healthier, more independent, more alert, more realistic, and more prone to make ultrarapid decisions, than the general Jewish population from which they came. Few of them held positions of responsibility for entire families or communities, and the testimony they volunteer is naturally restricted in content to the encounters that such people would have had. One may analyze what they say, as Lawrence Langer did, but apart from the rare occasions when they are in a courtroom, the survivors may not be cross-examined or openly contradicted. Homage takes the place of interrogation, and we make do with what we gratefully receive. To be sure, we pay a small price for our forbearance. As the mathematician Bronowski once observed: if you want a pertinent answer, you must ask an impertinent question.

There are studies that are based on the accounts of camp survivors and those of fugitives in partisan groups or alone in hiding. Concentration camps were the subject of a book by the sociologist Wolfgang Sofsky, published in 1993. It is what the author calls a dense description of life in the camps and emphasis is placed on the "order of the terror," which is to say, on the stratification of the inmates as determined by the German managers of the system. Sofsky, who drew on accounts by Jewish and, importantly, non-Jewish inmates, produced a book that is itself an example of order, but by analysis and summation. More numerous are publications about resistance, not only because resisters who survived were willing to discuss their tribulations and activities, but also because such accounts have had a receptive audience. Also noteworthy is the growing literature about good samaritans, from Raoul Wallenberg on down. Again, it is survivors who furnished the details about this altruism, and once more a ready readership wishes to be uplifted by these books. The only question we do not pose rigorously enough is the purely numerical one: How typical was resistance? How many helpers were there in a given population and who, precisely, was helped?

We think much less about a second group of survivors, who have not been particularly anxious to tell their stories and from whom relatively little has been heard. These people were privileged members of their communities. In Vienna, postwar prosecutors initiated proceedings against Robert Prochnik, a young man born in 1915 who worked under Rabbi Benjamin Murmelstein in deportation matters, both in Vienna and in Theresienstadt. Prochnik, in Paris, sent a remarkable twenty-seven-page statement to the court through his lawyer in 1954. He outlined the manner in which deportation lists were compiled in the Theresienstadt ghetto. The Jewish ghetto administration, he said, had to make the choice. The responsibility for selection was shared by more than one hundred people. In addition to the deportation rosters, there were two other kinds of lists, which contained the names of privileged people. One way to be privileged was to be deemed essential for the operation of the ghetto; the other was to be chosen as worthy by one of the Landsmannschaften, that is, a group of ghetto inmates from a particular city, for having contributed something to the home community. Jews on a deportation list who were hiding in the ghetto were tracked down, said Prochnik, to avoid substituting privileged families for the missing. Of 140,000 people who passed through Theresienstadt, about 17,000 were still there on May 9, 1945. They, too, were survivors, if not all that well known. In June, before the dissolution of Theresienstadt, Prochnik received a certificate of appreciation and gratitude as a "responsible, thorough, and reliable" civil servant. It was signed by three Jewish Theresienstadt dignitaries. The top signature was that of Rabbi Leo Baeck.

We know, of course, that Theresienstadt was not an isolated case. Such maneuvers occurred in the Netherlands and Hungary, as well as in other countries, and it is understandable that those who were saved did not discuss their history in great detail after the war or that the academic discussion of these situations and the people involved in them has been muted.

One should think that there should have been an attempt to solicit the stories of the immediate neighbors of the victims to discover something about their lives, their thoughts, and the general atmosphere of the time. Claude Lanzmann featured a few of these individuals in his *Shoah*, interviewing villagers particularly in the vicinity of the former camps, and Gordon Horwitz made them the central subject of his book about the environs of Mauthausen; but the cities, where most Jews had lived, have slipped through the net. We may safely assume from various census data that the maximum number of Jews who could successfully hide in a city was approximately 3 percent of the non-Jewish population, and that city was Paris. Yet we have only partial, disconnected information about city conditions; and the reactions of non-Jews to confiscations, ghettoization, deportations, or shootings must now be gathered almost entirely from documents. The opportunity to question these people has been forfeited.

Will we forgo the collection of vital documents as well? Here we can speak of a second change, but one which is a new beginning: the relatively sudden opening of dozens of archives in the countries behind the former Iron Curtain. Less dramatic perhaps, but not altogether unimportant, is also the gradual accession for public use of collections that have hitherto been confidential in the West: the archives of a private organization here or of a public agency there. Sight unseen, we can make one point with certainty: a huge increase of information is awaiting us. Microfilming these materials should be a top priority in our academic planning. The paper of the Second World War is brittle, and with neglect it will become a scrapheap. If we delay or curtail this effort, we will diminish the possibilities of future discoveries forever.

But what is going to be the result of this research, if it can be conducted in full? What will be written in the next few decades? It has always been true that, freed from political constraints or imperatives, a researcher will be powerfully influenced by the availability of material, and more specifically the concentration of particular sources in one place. During the 1940s and 1950s the introduction of documentary items taken from central agencies of the Third Reich in the Nuremberg trials encouraged writing about the Holocaust as a whole. It is during that early period that a telescopic view of the event emerged. Before long, Auschwitz was elevated as a symbol, Eichmann became a concept, and the Einsatzgruppen were entered as a part of our vocabulary. By and by, non-German institutions, such as the Jewish councils or the Office of Strategic Services were uncovered. Recently, our investigations have been devoted increasingly to microscopic examinations of localities, offices, persons, or single events. What is most characteristic about this work is its variety. We must and do look for records everywhere.

The latest thrust has been in the making for some years and it has already produced valuable monographs. Examples—and they are only examples—of this growing library are the recent book by Christopher Browning about the operations of the 101st Police Battalion in Poland, the new monograph by Walter Manoschek about the destruction of the Jews of Serbia, a substantial study by Jean-Claude Favez of the role of the International Red Cross, the investigations by Jean-Claude Pressac and Robert-Jan van Pelt of the architectural history of the Auschwitz-Birkenau complex, or a biography by Ulrich Herbert of Werner Best, who played several roles in the German Reich, the last as the Plenipotentiary in Denmark.

The continuing accretion of documentary collections will open further possibilities for such detailed projects. Now that the records in the former German Democratic Republic of the Reichsvereinigung der Juden in Deutschland, the first of the Jewish councils, are available for public use, it would be surprising if researchers would not attempt to dissect that organization on the basis of footnoted facts. The former Soviet archives at the republic, oblast, or municipal levels abound with records of local collaborators—another topic which has not yet received full treatment. Documents from Romania offer opportunities for studying a wartime regime that is second only to Germany in the killing of Jews, and so on.

Much in the new essays and monographs has already transformed our thinking. Totalitarianism, the catch word of an ignorant era, is an empty shell. Ideology and even antisemitism are obsolete crutches that we are silently throwing away. What, after all, is antisemitic about the railways? "Orders" are often hard to find and there is no "obedience" without them. We now know that the members of the 101st battalion were ordinary men, that the Jewish councils were bureaucratic entities, and that Auschwitz was a camp in search of a mission. Not that these discoveries are making our task any easier. Now that we stand more securely on the ground of empirical knowledge, we know that yesterday's proffered explanations do not work, but this realization does not mean that we have the answers. The ascertained fact of a perpetrator's normal childhood or normal education will, if anything, complicate our thinking. A normal Adolf Hitler who went to the same school as Ludwig Wittgenstein is a bigger problem than a lunatic in charge of automatons.

The new documentation will greatly expand our knowledge and it will crystalize some of our questions. It will not, however, resolve every issue or fact, particularly one issue that is on top of our list: the genesis of annihilation. Holocaust history turns on this question above all. The newly opened archives, apart from the one in Potsdam, do not contain many records of central German administration. At best, the collections in these depositories are only remote reflections of developments in Berlin. Hence we will still be wrestling with the problem. At the moment the latest words on the subject are those of Philippe Burrin and Götz Aly. Yet Burrin's synthesis, published in 1989, and Aly's treatise of 1995 will not be the last of their kind. As the fragmentary items already in our possession are rearranged and reinterpreted, a more refined model will emerge, one in which the very notion of decision making will be reevaluated. We have always thought of the process as having been developed in decisive steps, but we have not sufficiently examined the steps in a decision. In this quest, at least, there are no small facts. Everything, including Göring's appointment calendar and Himmler's telephone log, is major.

The explosive increase of our documents will result in studies of much richer texture. The researcher will step out of an archives and write about a cluster of towns or a particular operation. Given the hundreds of books that will be produced, not a few of them with highly dramatic contents as well as significant implications, we should look forward to a new level of attainment. Yet it is precisely our success in this endeavor that could harbor a danger. Without much awareness we isolate our subject from its broader context and we remove it from meaningful comparisons.

Context means an understanding of the era and the multiplicity of events in which the Holocaust was embedded. If personnel in the occupied eastern territories or in Auschwitz were heavily supplemented with Ethnic Germans, which happens to be the case, then the whole subject of what "Ethnic German" meant acquires importance. If one half of the drama was played out on Polish soil, and it was, then we should note and refer to the situation of Poles in more detail. If labor became an issue, notably during the second half of the war, as it did, then we should thoroughly understand relocations of industry and shortages in the labor supply. And so on, at great length.

Comparison is an ever larger field. Specifically, it entails an analysis of the structural characteristics of various processes against various peoples in different areas and on different continents. Clearly the investment in such projects is all but prohibitive, and even then the results would necessarily be limited. The problem is the disparate supply of source material. One need look only at the discrepancy of detail between studies of the Armenian fate in 1915 and that of the Jews in the Second World War. Even the German assault on the Gypsies, the only ethnic group besides the Jews who were shot or gassed on principle, is at this point underresearched. It may be that the case of Huguenots offers a convenient "control group," but what about East Timor? What happened there? And so forth, literally around the whole world.

Comparative analysis is also politically sensitive. Once the word "Holocaust" entered into circulation, the Jewish catastrophe in Nazi times came to be likened to all manner of things. To some Orthodox Jews, it is yet another trial sent down to His People by God. To the media and several interest communities it is a door opened to any killing, direct or indirect, of any group, including animals. To Ernst Nolte, like some of the defense attorneys in the Nuremberg trials, it is but a variant in a continuum of political actions, differing from them only because of the added contrivance of the gas chambers. No wonder that there should be a fear that comparison will lead directly to submergence. Yet if the attempt to find commonalities and differences is too much of a burden for academic researchers, we will have only a flow of amateurish publications and political messages from all quarters. That would be an unfortunate but inevitable consequence of our current popularity.

NOTE

This essay describes the situation as of the end of 1993. The author has added a reference to Götz Aly's important study of 1995.

2.

YEHUDA BAUER

A Past That Will Not Go Away

About two decades ago, Professor Robert Alter of California published a piece in *Commentary* that argued that we had had enough of the Holocaust, that a concentration of Jewish intellectual and emotional efforts around it was counterproductive, that the Holocaust should always be remembered, but that there were new agendas that had to be confronted. He and others have argued, rightly, that the Holocaust is not to be confused with Jewish history or Jewish identity. Elie Wiesel has expressed the view that with the passing on of the generation of Holocaust survivors, the Holocaust may be forgotten, misinterpreted, or misused. No doubt some of these arguments have validity today as well, but the memory is not going away; on the contrary, the Holocaust has become a cultural code, a symbol of evil in Western civilization. Why should this be so? After all, there are other genocides: Hutu and Tutsi in Rwanda, possibly Ibos in Nigeria, Biharis in Bangladesh, Cambodia, and of course the dozens of millions of victims of the Maoist purges in China, the Gulag, and so forth. Yet it is the murder of the Jews that brings forth a growing avalanche of films, plays, fiction, poetry, TV series, sculpture, paintings, and historical, sociological, psychological and other research. Contrary to pessimistic prophecies, the flood is increasing, not decreasing. Some of it, it is true, is kitsch. Some is not, however. And we must never forget that massive interest in the Holocaust in the United States and Canada arose from the 1978 NBC series *Holocaust*, a kitschy production if there ever was one. Do we then *have* to have kitsch to help produce real interest, real scholarship, real art? Social historians will have to map out these developments and attempt to find answers that will clarify the whys and the wherefores.

The United States Holocaust Memorial Museum in Washington, D.C., which has become the central symbol of public memory of the Holocaust in America, must be American—it addresses, primarily, the population of this country and it has to answer the question why an event that took place far away from here, to people who were not Americans, should be commemorated on the Washington Mall, in a governmental framework, with the active involvement of American Presidents and the American Congress. The answer must, of necessity, include the international side of the museum's raison d'être, the fact that it must be compared to other instances of genocide, and that it is of world importance. If it were not, there would be little interest in having it. On the other hand, the central concern of the Holocaust Museum must be the specific Jewish tragedy. If it were to be ignored, then the whole effort would disintegrate into a diffuse universalistic babble.

We still have no overall histories of the Holocaust in a number of European countries (such as Germany, Poland, the USSR); we still lack a great deal of knowledge regarding the "how" of the Holocaust. However, we should increasingly be concerned with the "why." True, we cannot begin to answer the very difficult "why" questions without studying the "how," and we are, most of us, still very much engaged in the latter. But a study of German, or for that matter, Jewish, or other, bureaucracies or social structures will not answer the question as to what motivated them, except perhaps marginally. Bureaucracies, as Raul Hilberg has so clearly shown us, do have a momentum of their own and can organize death trains using the principles of the organization of children's summer outings. But that does not answer the question why they do the one rather than the other. Nor are efforts such as that of Zygmunt Bauman in his *Modernity and the Holocaust* of great help: Bauman argues that the reason why the Holocaust occurred was the spread of industrial, technological civilization. But modernity, whatever the definition of the concept, did not affect only Germany, and in any case, it does not explain why the Jews were the victims. I believe that the study of the social consensus formed by ideologies and attitudes transmitted over historic time produces the possibility of answering the "why" questions. Nazified society, Nazi leadership, and parts of the Nazi intelligentsia, at the very least, believed in a pseudoreligion that demanded action. It is possible, and it has been done in part, to trace the origins of these ideologies and show how they developed a murderous consensus.

There is a recent vogue that claims that antisemitism does not explain the Holocaust; that is, in my view, totally misleading. No one claims that there is a straight line from traditional antisemitism to its Nazi form, nor does the background to the Nazi murder project consist only of antisemitism. But the disconnection between the two raises a very simple question: if there is no connection between antisemitism and the Holocaust, then why, pray, did the Nazis murder Jews and not bicycle riders? There is, quite clearly, both a strong element of continuity and also a *novum* of a nationalistic-racist character in Nazi antisemitism. Against the background of the crisis of modern Western society, against the background of political and economic dislocations, as well as of the specific impact of these crises on German society, Nazi antisemitism was the central motivation that drove the regime into the murder of the Jews. They could do it, as the British historian Ian Kershaw explained some years ago at a conference in Haifa, not necessarily even because of the identification of the German society with murderous antisemitism, which was the program of the governing elite, but because of the identification with the regime as such of vast masses of the German people, and especially the intelligentsia, who became the transmission belt from the elite to the rest of the population. To argue for a disconnection between antisemitism and the Holocaust makes absolutely no sense at all.

However, if we want to answer these "why" questions, there are a number of important preliminary issues that have to be addressed. We are still battling with the problem of the definition of the very subject we are dealing with. Let us be clear: the Holocaust, Shoah, Churban, Judeocide, whatever we call it, is the name we give to the attempted planned total physical annihilation of the Jewish people, and its partial perpetration with the murder of most of the Jews of Europe. The problem whether this is unique in more than the banal sense that every historical event is unique is still a topic of sharp disagreement, and I have stated my position too often to have to detail it here: to me, the uniqueness lies in the motivation of the murderer, the quest for an annihilation that sentenced all people born of three or four Jewish grandparents to death for the crime of having been born, for purely illusionary, ideological, abstract, "universal" reasons, in order to do away with a mythical, non-existent Jewish world conspiracy; but it was also unique because of the unique place of the Jews in the history of Western civilization; in other words it was the result, though by no means a necessary result, of a long historic process.

A theory is being offered that as the Nazi policy of murder of German mental and other patients deemed to suffer from hereditary illnesses, the so-called euthanasia program, the murder of many Gypsies, and the murder of the Jews were all based on so-called racial, that is, hereditary or genetic principles, that they are all part of the Holocaust. But Nazi policy toward Italians, Romanians, and Japanese was also based on racist principles, and I would suggest that there is a world of difference between problems that Nazis had with the "purity" of their own "race" and the social irritant they saw in the Romani people, whom they accused of being hereditary asocial criminals, on the one hand, and the universal threat to Nazi humankind they saw in the Jews. The attitude to Jews was a central pillar of Nazi ideology, and it could, in the end, be solved only by total murder. The attitudes to the Gypsies was not a central part of Nazi ideology, and to the best of my knowledge there never was a plan to murder all the Gypsies. The T4 program of murder of the handicapped was a derivative of internal German-Nazi concerns. To equate these issues is, I think, to confuse them. It does not do any service to the cause of the Romani people to mix them up in the same analytical framework with the Jews by defining the Holocaust as pertaining to both Gypsies and Jews. The Roma (Gypsies) must be recognized as a legitimate ethnic entity, with its own cultural, political, and economic rights. Unlike the Jews, they are still, after the defeat of Nazi Germany, discriminated against, persecuted, reviled. They must receive compensation for what was done to them by the Nazis, and by post-Nazi society. The suffering of each Gypsy was exactly the same as the suffering of a Jew, a Pole, or anyone else. But the motivation of the perpetrator was different, the place of the different victims in the historical development of so-called Western civilization was different, and therefore the steps to be taken to right the radical evil that was done are different also.

Let me now turn to something else, namely the various forms of Holocaust denials. Apart from the gutter writings of American, French, and other Nazi intellectuals who deny the Holocaust totally, and whose antics have been analyzed so well by Deborah Lipstadt's recent *Denying the Holocaust*, there is perhaps the even more threatening phenomenon of relativization and falsification that is lapped up by a public eager to have this horrible business laid to rest by trivializing it one way or the other. In Germany, Berlin historian Ernst Nolte continues his untenable propagation of myths about the Nazis who supposedly copied the death camps from the Soviet Gulags, arguing that what the Nazis did was no different from Allied war crimes such as the firebombing of Dresden, or the Stalinist or Maoist purges. The purpose is clearly to free German society from bearing any particular responsibility for World

War II generally, and the Holocaust in particular; for Germans, as the late German conservative politician Franz Josef Strauss said, to walk tall again. Nolte has found imitators, in Germany and elsewhere, including the United States. And when a Holocaust survivor such as Arno J. Mayer of Princeton University (in his book *Why Did the Heavens Darken?*) popularizes the nonsense that the Nazis saw in Marxism and bolshevism their main enemy, and the Jews unfortunately got caught up in this; when he links the destruction of the Jews to the ups and downs of German warfare in the Soviet Union, in a book that is so cocksure of itself that it does not need a proper scientific apparatus, he is really engaging in a much more subtle form of Holocaust denial. He in effect denies the motivation for murder and flies in the face of well-known documentation. There are others like that. The great German historian Andreas Hillgruber, who unfortunately became, toward the end of his life, identified with the Nolte group, unwittingly so, I believe, and unwillingly, but very significantly nevertheless, made clear the relationship between Hitlerian antibolshevism and antisemitism as far back as 1972. Hitler saw bolshevism as an expression of the corrupt and destructive Jewish spirit; his enemy was the power that in his view had created bolshevism and was using it to achieve world domination. "The communist," says a Nazi document of 1937, "is an enemy of the people, and nothing else but an instrument of Judaism, which finds here (in communism) a tool for the achievement of its aim: world supremacy."[1]

There is yet another, internal Jewish and very basic issue at hand, which arises when one contemplates, for instance, Emil Fackenheim's recent statement that the victims of the Holocaust were *kedoshim*, holy persons, because they were Jewish martyrs, killed because of their Jewishness, and hence suffering just like their ancestors had suffered, for the Sanctification of the Name. I believe this hides the fact that there is no meaning to the Holocaust, because the only meaning it could have would be a Nazi meaning: for the Nazis there was a purpose in the killing, murder was meaningful. For the Jews it was totally meaningless. They had done nothing to earn the deadly enmity of Nazi antisemitism. Their faith—as far as they were observant in any sense—was not at issue. They were ordinary people, victims of murder; this does not make them holy, it makes them victims of a crime. People were taken from their homes or hiding places and murdered, for no apparent reason but the consensual will of a murderous society. This is extremely difficult to accept, because the conclusion is that the deaths of our dear ones were meaningless, and I must admit that I resisted this conclusion for years. The argument usually is that the meaning lay in the innumerable instances of sacrifice, as when children sacrificed their lives to try to save their parents or, more often, the other way around, or friends for their friends, or just Jews for other Jews. Rebels chose one kind of death over another. But Jews generally did not have the option to either live or choose sacrifice for some purpose, holy or otherwise, as they had had throughout their history, though some Jews at least went to their deaths in the manner of their forefathers, believing they were dying for the Sanctification of the Holy Name.

One of the most terrible things the Nazis did was to deprive the victims of a last satisfaction that their death might have some meaning. There is a perfectly understandable tendency to ritualize the Holocaust so that it may acquire some meaning, and of course there are meanings we ascribe to it post factum. This is in fact what we do when we argue that the meaning lay in the sacrifices, in the Sanctification of the Name, or in armed rebellions, and so on. For us, with our constantly changing understanding of the past, there are good reasons to derive this or that so-called "lesson" from the Holocaust, meanings that make sense for us, but they are quite extraneous to the event and its contemporaries, and they are bound to change over time. Many of these meanings, as Professor Saul Friedlander has pointed out many times, including in his book *Kitsch and Death*, are distorted, because they are based on a misuse of the Holocaust and provide the kitsch that society apparently needs. In Israel, for instance, governments of the Right and the Left viewed the PLO, or alternatively, the Israeli army on the West Bank, as Nazis; President Bush spoke of Saddam Hussein as a Hitler; senseless comparisons were made elsewhere—but in all these cases real comparability is missing, and there is a clear misuse of the Holocaust for political purposes.

There is also, as we know well, artistic and cultural misuse—low-culture films, sensationalist television series, pop artists who have no idea what they are ranting about, and much more.

I would like to make a suggestion to explain why this should be so. I believe that it is, on the one hand, the instinctive rather than the cognitive understanding that the murder of the Jews was unique, in the sense that I tried to outline before; that never before in human history has a well-organized state, representing a social consensus, tried to murder, globally, every single member of an ethnic or ethno-religious group as defined by the perpetrator, for purely ideological reasons that bore not the slightest relation to reality. There is the dim understanding that the Nazi rebellion against civilization and the murder of the Jews that resulted from it form a universal threat to every person everywhere.

On the other hand, it was the character of the victim, the peculiar history and presence of the Jews that lay at the basis of this. The Jews provided one of the basic pillars for what we call Western civilization. The others, the Greeks, the Romans, are no more, but we are still very much around. A Nazi rebellion against the civilization from which they sprang almost *had to* target the Jews for destruction.

In Christian mythology the quintessential Jew was crucified to atone for human-ity's sins, and when the people of the crucified Messiah are murdered, the image seems to return. The Jews have to suffer, be victimized, that is their role in Christian history. When they do, it is seen as their peculiar gift to Christian and post-Christian society; it is natural. When they resist, rebel, and successfully establish their own political independence in their original land, they fall out of their role. An increasing number of concerned Christians totally reject these traditional antisemitic images of the Jews, and see with horror that their society has not changed much and that the Holocaust is the crucible through which their faith has to pass. Anti-Jewish attitudes, as well as pro-Jewish ones (which sometimes are the other side of the same coin) are projected through a fascination with the Holocaust.

Among many Jews in Western countries, especially in North America, there are opposite attitudes toward the memory of the Holocaust: one is to universalize the Holocaust to the extent that people include in it the fate of the Gypsies, of Poles, Czechs, Russians, Ukranians, Serbs, and the German handicapped. This is of course welcomed by those non-Jews who would like to escape from dealing with this unpleasant subject of the Jews and bury it in vague, stupid phrases such as the famous "man's inhumanity to man." They, and many Jews, in effect deny the specificity of the Jewish fate: they refuse to see that the Nazis were not out to murder all the Gypsies, Poles, Russians, etcetera, and that the Nazis did not consider these and other nations and ethnic groups to be global, indeed universal threats to the kind of Nazi humanity to which they aspired. There was terrible mass murder committed against all of these, and proportionately more against the Gypsies than anyone else; and Nazi policy toward the Gypsies and the Poles can only be defined as genocidal. The Jews had the dubious distinction of being the only ethnic group that was destined for total physical annihilation for purely ideological reasons, as a satanic force in human society that had to be completely eradicated. That is what the Nazi project to kill the Jews was all about, and all these universalizing attempts seem to me to be, on the Jewish side, efforts by their authors to escape their Jewishness They are expressions of a deep-seated insecurity; these people feel more secure when they can say "we are just like all the others." The Holocaust should have proved to them that the Jews were, unfortunately, not like the others. Obviously it did not.

The other attitude is the opposite one: a disappointed, ethnically exclusive turning inward, a denial that the Holocaust has anything to do with general Nazi policies, or with other genocides, a denial of the possibility of comparing it to the Armenian, Gypsy, Polish, Cambodian, or other disasters, in our century or in past ages. Those who hold this attitude forget, of course, that you cannot argue for a uniqueness of the Holocaust if you do not compare it to other similar events. They refuse to see in concerned Gentiles, and concerned Christians, their natural allies; they want to go it alone. They close themselves in, in a traditional and totally counterproductive Jewish gesture of defiance toward the world, whether they are ultra-orthodox, or even if they are avowed liberals or secularists. Their attitude is clearly counterproductive because in the end it deprives the Holocaust of all universal implications, and removes it from the concern not only of non-Jews but also of Jews who see themselves as both intensely Jewish and also active in the affairs of the societies in general, indeed of the world at large.

True, one of the problems of the specificity of the Holocaust and of the universal concerns it arouses are the ambivalent attitudes of Christians and Christianity to Jews and Judaism in the wake of the Holocaust. Christians have to learn to live with the self-definitions of Jews, and with Jewish bitterness at Christianity for having provided the background from which the anti-Christian, secular, and racist version of Christian antisemitism sprang; they have to live with the terrible question about the validity of a faith that bases itself on Jewish texts and worships a Messiah who came from the Jews, sacrificed himself to expiate humanity's sins, and whose people, nineteen hundred years after that act, were murdered by baptized Gentiles, as Franklin Littell and others have taught us. Jews, on the other hand, have to recognize that the Hebrew Bible provides texts that call for genocide, that there were Christian Gentiles—not enough of them by a very, very long way, but they existed—who saved Jews and some sacrificed their lives to do this. Jews must recognize, too, that in this quest for a common humanity some Jews and some Christians, and hopefully more and more of both, are in the same boat, and that there have been crucially important first steps by some very central Christian denominations to change theology and attitudes to the Jews—from the Vatican's *Nostra Aetate* in 1965 to the Protestant Rhineland Synod in Germany in 1980, to the Polish Catholic declaration of January 1991, and beyond. First steps, to be sure, hesitant steps, to be sure, but steps nevertheless. Jews have to realize that unless the Holocaust is internalized by Christians and Gentiles generally—and this can only happen if Jews do not lock themselves into precocious groups trying to protect the memory of the Holocaust from Christian invasion—both sides can only lose, and the heathens will have an out for their antisemitism and their denial of the Holocaust.

There is another, major issue on the historical agenda, within the Jewish world. The event was so overpowering that specifically Jewish forms of denial have become endemic. These are rooted in a terrible, overwhelming self-accusation. It is said, in effect, that we know that the Nazis murdered the Jews but that we have to move beyond that and ask who *really* was responsible—who could have rescued but did not? The answer is—the Jewish leadership, who had the means, the intelligence, the political clout, and the unlimited funds, but did not rescue because of a mixture of political wrongheadedness, cold disregard for Jewish lives, Zionist prejudices, and stupidity. Or else, and this is the Jewish orthodox argument, because Jews had angered God by not following His commands, either because their leaders were reform Jews, or nonbelievers, or Zionists, or anti-Zionists, or because they were stupid enough to make the Nazis angry.

Israeli secular, liberal writers such as Tom Segev, in his best-selling *The Seventh Million*, have argued that Ben-Gurion and his colleagues were unfit to guide the Jewish people; they were puny, narrow-minded individuals, bent only on achieving a Jewish independence in Palestine in order to enhance their power. He concludes that they misunderstood the Holocaust and failed to do anything of importance to rescue Jews. In *The Blue and the Yellow Stars of David*, which was published before Segev's book, Dina Porat had already responded to such arguments as these by presenting a balanced picture of the Palestine Jewish leadership. Though they are lacking in historical basis, the arguments presented by Segev find a ready audience among a people traumatized by the Holocaust and incapable of accepting the sad fact that the Jews during the Holocaust were absolutely powerless. There are other authors in Israel who follow Segev's line; in the United States, there was an effort by a so-called Commission of Inquiry, headed by New York professor Seymour Finger, to do the same for the American Jewish leadership. Journalists and historians of the Jewish left and right, liberals and conservatives alike, joined and are still joining in the witch-hunt against the Jewish leadership of the 1930s and 1940s. There are balanced accounts, that do not fall into the trap of a hagiographic defense of Stephen Wise and Nahum Goldman, or of Ben-Gurion or Moshe Sharett, for that matter. Such balanced accounts can be read in the works of David S. Wyman, Henry L. Feingold, Ariel Hurwitz, and others, with all the disagreements between these authors. But the popular and mistaken Jewish perception is that of a leadership that betrayed the Jews of Europe.

The Jewish ultra-orthodox world, and some in the orthodox camp as well, argue for the same conclusions, but from different premises. Everywhere, among secularists as well as orthodox, the explanations and analyses are an often unconscious continuation of the ancient model of Jewish explanation for disasters that befell the Jews. In past centuries, such disasters were always explained as having been caused by the sins of the Jews themselves. They were the result of divine wrath caused by nonobservance of the Torah. Applied to the Holocaust by orthodox and ultra-orthodox commentators, the explanation is threefold, and contradictory: first, that all history is directed by God, and that He is the source of both good and evil, hence the Holocaust is the work of the deity. His intent is educational, that is, to cause the Jews to mend their ways (see, for instance, the late Lubavicher Rebbe's outpourings on this in *Mada Ve'emunah* [Kfar Chabad, Israel, 1980, pp. 115 ff.]); second, that humans cannot understand the reasons that cause the deity not to prevent the Holocaust—this argument holds whether the writers believe that God "hid His face" or not, because even if God hid His face He is still all-powerful, all-knowing, and just; third, that although we cannot know why God did what He did or desisted from doing what He could have done, we do know that it was a punishment for misbehavior, largely due to the growth of the Reform movement, and/or Zionism (in the case of the famous Hungarian ultra-orthodox rabbi, Issacher Teichthal, the opposite is the case: the anti-Zionism of his own group is said to have been the cause of the Holocaust). Zionism is accused of rebelling against the nations of the world in order to establish a Jewish state, in contravention of God's command and in contravention of the rule that Jews should await the coming of the Messiah. The wartime leadership therefore, writers like Moshe Shenfeld or Yoel Teitelbaum argue, knowingly sacrificed the Jews of Europe in order to create their sinful state in Palestine. To my mind, these are forms of a tragic Jewish antisemitism.

Balanced historical accounts present well-grounded descriptions of whole Jewish societies whose reactions to the Holocaust were very problematic. This is true especially for Palestine, where Jews were engaged in everyday pursuits, including Purim balls and party political bickering, while the Holocaust was going on. Why this happened is rarely asked, and the psychological problems of a society that is powerless to help its immediate relatives who are the victims of a massive murder program are rarely addressed. Serious commentators still speak in terms of accusations bearing a moral tinge and not in terms of contextual explication.

Some of these constructs, political, ideological, and/or religious, really reflect the internalization of antisemitism by Jews. Like antisemites, these writers believe, or pretend to believe, that the Jews during the Holocaust were capable of preventing it because they had unlimited financial and political resources at their command; and it was a matter either of ill will or incompetence that they did nothing to rescue the victims. This leads to a form of denial, derived—as I have just pointed out—from Jewish tradition, that says that the Holocaust is really the fault of the Jews themselves, thus fully agreeing with the arguments of some of the neo-Nazi deniers.

There is quite possibly a sort of parallel with other societies that were involved with World War II. However, in these societies, such as the American, accusations against the wartime leadership sound quite different, because there there were real power bases and real options from which leaders or groups chose. The Jewish case is different in that the options of the leaders were severely circumscribed, though not completely absent.

The fact that the books of these Jewish historical revisionists, as I propose to call them, sell considerably better than the tomes produced by those who call themselves serious historians, and that the Jewish revisionists, or at least some of them, have access to television screens, is not only due to their talents but also to the willingness of the Jewish public to listen to their message. This is not surprising, because traumatized Jewish society seeks ready answers to its questions, and what the Jewish revisionists say will be in accord with traditional explanations: it was really our own fault. When we come to deal with our future agenda, especially those of us who work on Jewish history, we must be careful to devote energy and time to a balanced description of the Jewish reaction of the time. The leaders then were powerless, and we have to teach the unpalatable truth that even the Western powers, between 1941 and 1944, could not have saved the Jews even had they wanted to, which demonstrably they did not. The millions were doomed, and rescue could have been marginal at best, though the margin might have been of tremendous importance, for what is a margin in terms of human lives? Thousands? Tens of thousands? We cannot talk of these things in terms of numbers only, forgetting that each number represents the whole world of a human being.

I admit that my personal starting point, my bias if you will, is formed by my overriding interest in the fate of the Jews, their communities, their reactions. It is influenced no less by the desire to know *what* was destroyed, not only how and by whom. Russian, Ukranian, and Belorussian archives have many of the answers. But you may ask—why document another village, another town, another group of partisans? Do we not have enough already?

As with other major historical questions, here too we have to go beyond the historical craft (after all, history is not a science, but the art of telling the story of the past according to certain sets of agreed rules). We all have biases, which have to be reconciled with the overarching demand for objective writing. Clearly, responsible scholars are against antisemitism and view the Holocaust with horror while affirming democratic rule. These are also "biases," and they do occasionally have to be stated, because there are people who write with an antisemitic bias, deny the Holocaust altogether or in part, and do not favor democratic rule. But there are other biases as well, derived from training, tradition, or what have you. There are colleagues who deal primarily with the aspects of the perpetrators, or of the bystanders. I belong to those whose starting point is Jewish life before, the Jewish tragedy during, and Jewish life after the Holocaust. I do believe, in addition, that this is not a bad vantage point from which to view the event as a whole, and deal with perpetrator and bystander. The philosophy behind this is that the Holocaust happened to the Jews, and that it was unique. In my view the threat to the Jewish people that arose in Germany could have arisen elsewhere as well, and we are dealing with the whole of Western culture during the last hundred or so years when we discuss the perpetrators; it developed in Germany, which is a good reason to examine German society in particular. But without understanding Jewish history, all this remains very abstract. There is simply no way of comprehending the Holocaust unless one realizes who the Jews were and are, and why they became the chosen victim of an ideology that wanted to rebel against what we call "Western civilization," utilizing the most modern achievements of technology and science to do so. I think it is a good idea to start with the Jews. That will lead us to the universal implications, including of course the centrally important moral aspects of the Holocaust. I do not claim that this is the only way to approach the subject, but it is one of the more legitimate ones.

Let me now deal with another, methodological issue: there is a huge amount of documentation available on the perpetrator, and some people may conclude that the documentation is reliable—after all, Germans produced it, didn't they? But when we look closer, we find that quite a number of the decisions that really mattered were not even written down, because that was the way the Third Reich operated. Let me remind you of the discussion in Göring's office on November 12, 1938, after Kristallnacht. We are lucky to have a stenographic protocol, because otherwise we would have missed the crucial point: Göring mentions three direct interventions of Hitler, between November 9 and 11, to clarify to his loyal Hermann exactly what he wants done on the Jewish question—concentrate the whole thing under Göring, get the Jews out of the German economy, negotiate with the Western powers about deporting them to Madagascar. The decision was taken orally, in a face to face meeting, by phone, and by a directive from Bormann in Hitler's name, which Göring mentions but which has not survived. Hitler acted, personally and directly, to lay down the line on the Jewish question, and there is no document extant, except for Göring's account at that meeting. Things were handed down orally, and only by a lucky chance do we occasionally find echoes of that procedure in the form of documentation.

And the famous Wannsee protocol? We know today that it is a doctored protocol, that the discussion was much more explicit. Documents were often written to hide things, not to explicate them; not always, to be sure, but at several rather crucial points. We cannot rely solely, or even mainly, on German documentation as the oracle that will give us a true picture.

Jewish documentation, too, is not very impressive. Yes, there are some protocols of Judenräte, but these were also tailored for the Germans who would or might read them. There are diaries, not too many of them; there are German and Polish documents about Jews; there are the Ringelblum and Mersik archives. However, much of the Jewish documentation was destroyed, especially in Eastern Europe, together with the Jews. The Nazis tried to murder the murder. So the main source is oral testimonies. There are colleagues who argue that these are unreliable. But tell me please: when German criminals appear in postwar trials or write memoirs, are they reliable? When testimonies become published memoirs of statesmen and participants, are they universally to be disregarded? I would argue that when we have ten independently recorded, converging and comparable testimonies, they are more reliable than a document about the same situation written by some German or Jewish source, or by a Polish bystander. And for most Jewish communities destroyed by the Nazis there is very little or no written documentation. But there are converging testimonies.

The documentation of the victims and their communities is important not only for Jews but for everyone; it is of vital importance to know what happened to the victims, and how they reacted. How do people react when they are confronted with wholesale and near-inescapable murder? How do they behave? How do they see their enemies? How do they view the bystanders? Were the Judenräte just tools in Nazi hands, or did many of them try, in a large number of different ways, to preserve and save what could be saved? We know the result, but that is only one part of the story. I want to know the life before the death—I know before I ever start to investigate that they were killed. Did the resisters offer a real alternative to the besieged communities in which they tried to operate? What were the real options of leadership groups? What was resistance like, unarmed and armed; what were the moral and physical conditions of armed resistance? Who helped, and who did not? What did the spiritual leadership of the victimized group have to say, and what does that say to us today?

The East European archives may have some answers we do not know. There is a distinct possibility that we may find out more about a large number of Jewish communities, their life and death, their lack of resistance or their resistance, and their relationship with their non-Jewish neighbors. I would suggest that this is one of the priorities, not necessarily the only one, but to me a very important one, indeed.

Finally, some basic considerations. We want to document every Jewish community, because the Jews today are the heirs of those who were killed, and we have to know who these people were, how they lived, and how they died. This is not just a matter of filial piety or ethnic patriotism. An attempt was made to extinguish a small people with a very central place in Western civilization. It was done by a regime that drew its inspiration from Western civilization against which it rebelled and which it wanted to replace, globally, by a hierarchically ordered, racist society. The central, main victims were the Jews, for historical reasons. The rediscovery of as many communities as possible is, in a way, a victory over the Nazi project of cultural, as well as physical, annihilation. That victory, if it is achieved, is universalistic, not sectarian Jewish, because what was lost there was a peculiar Jewish variant of universal civilization. In the final analysis, the Holocaust is a combination of the unique and the universal; it is the uniqueness, and the fact that it happened to a certain people, at a certain time, for distinct reasons, that makes it so real, so threatening, so universal. Hence the fact that the Holocaust has become a cultural code; hence the fascination with the Holocaust; hence its universal aspects.

NOTE

1. National Archives T-175/432; quoted in Heinze Hoehne, *Der Krieg im Dunkeln* (Berlin: Ullstein, 1988), p. 283.

3.

EBERHARD JÄCKEL

The Holocaust

WHERE WE ARE, WHERE WE NEED TO GO

The contemporaries of the murder of the European Jews, now known as the Holocaust, are often divided into three categories: the perpetrators, the victims, and the bystanders. These three categories can also be applied to subsequent reactions to the Holocaust. Reactions in Germany, the country of the perpetrators, were bound to be different from those of the Jews in Israel and elsewhere, and from those in the rest of the world, which differed according to whether the countries in question were or were not affected by the Holocaust.

While such a division is appropriate for political, social, and cultural reactions, that is, for lawmaking, public debates, and education, it seems surprisingly less appropriate for scholarship and historiography, and it is totally inappropriate when applied to research. In the field of Holocaust research, there were and are no national schools of thought, not even, as may be expected, in Germany.

Research on the Holocaust began strikingly late everywhere; even more astonishing, it began internationally almost at the same time. It seems that the first results of serious research did not begin to appear until 1953. In that year the first comprehensive study, by Gerald Reitlinger, was published in England.[1] In the same year the Knesset in Israel passed the law establishing Yad Vashem as a memorial and a research institute. And in that year in Germany the *Vierteljahrshefte für Zeitgeschichte* were inaugurated with the first volume containing Kurt Gerstein's report on the mass gassings. It was also in 1953 that Hermann Graml's book on the November 1938 pogrom saw publication for the first time.

There had not been much scholarly historiography before 1953. Looking at Reitlinger's bibliography one is surprised to see how short the list is. Apart from Léon Poliakov's *Bréviaire de la haine*, which had been published in 1951,[2] and a larger number of what he called "survivor narratives," there had been almost no historical work on the Holocaust in the eight years that had elapsed between 1945 and 1953, and of course even the term Holocaust was not yet applied to the event.

Let me recall another coincidence. Whereas in 1961 Raul Hilberg's monumental study was finally published in the United States,[3] Wolfgang Scheffler's comprehensive introductions, admittedly much less monumental, had already come out in Germany the previous year and were widely distributed by a government agency for political education.

It is true, of course, that while Reitlinger's book had been translated into German in 1956, Hilberg's book was not translated until 1982. But it seems once more that this was not a special case of German reluctance to face the enormous crime committed, as it used to be said, in the German name. For it is equally true that Hilberg's book was not translated into any other language until 1988, when it was published in French.

While in the 1960s and 1970s the stream of historical publications grew steadily, there was still almost no scholarly debate on the Holocaust. Hilberg certainly had sparked a stormy controversy, which was particularly vehement in Israel, but his interpretation, derived from Franz Neumann, was not discussed profoundly by his fellow historians.

The absence of scholarly debate on the Holocaust appears even more surprising when compared to other historical events of central importance. The origins, for example, of the French Revolution or the First World War were already being discussed heatedly while these events were in progress, and mountains of controversial works appeared immediately after their termination.

As to the origins of the murder of the European Jews, the only explanation invariably given over the years was antisemitism. It was taken for granted that it had produced the Holocaust and that it must have been particularly violent in Germany. Consequently, research was focused mainly on antisemitism.

Rehearsal for Destruction, the title of P. W. Massing's famous book, became the catchword.[4] It was not until 1977 that historians finally began to discuss the origins proper, not in terms of antisemitism but in terms of decision making. Strangely enough, the discussion was provoked by David Irving who, in his book *Hitler's War*, had denied that Hitler had ordered the extermination of the Jews and maintained that it had been carried out by some of his subordinates behind his back, without his knowledge, until 1943. Even stranger, Irving's book had been published first in Germany in 1975, but the outrageous passages had been suppressed by his German publisher so that the shocking thesis became known only when the English version appeared in the United States in 1977.[5] This, in turn, provoked Martin Broszat's famous article on "Hitler and the Genesis of the 'Final Solution.'"[6] While refuting Irving's assertions, he admitted that historical research had so far indeed neglected the question of when, how, and by whom the murder of the Jews had been initiated.

I shall not reproduce in detail the arguments exchanged in the course of the debate. I shall, however, venture to make two more general statements in this respect. Broszat's article marked a turning point. It opened the first scholarly debate on the origins of the Holocaust, and it incorporated no national undertones whatsoever. On the contrary, the debate was international from its very outset.

Provoked by an English writer, the debate was launched by a German historian. It became a real dispute when Christopher Browning, an American historian, responded to Broszat in 1981. The topic was discussed by Saul Friedlander, Yehuda Bauer, and many others at an international conference held in Stuttgart in 1984. A further contribution to it was made by the Swiss historian Philippe Burrin in 1989.[7]

The opposing parties in the debate about the origins of the Holocaust have become known as the "intentionalists" and the "functionalists." The terms, which initially did not refer to the origins of the Holocaust but to the nature of the Nazi regime in general, were coined by the English historian Tim Mason at a conference organized by the German Historical Institute at Cumberland Lodge outside London in 1979.[8] Briefly summarized, the intentionalist position is—or was—that it had been Hitler's premeditated intention to kill as many Jews as possible ever since the 1920s and that he implemented his plans when the opportunity arose during the war. The functionalists, on the other hand, were unwilling to attribute such a decisive influence to a single person. They argued that the anti-Jewish measures taken by the Nazis were steadily intensified until they finally and almost automatically culminated in the mass killings.

Christopher Browning took a middle position, which he summarized in a review of Burrin's book as follows: "Hitler played a key role in the decision-making process but not out of premeditation. Frustrated by the failure of previous solutions (emigration and expulsion), he opted for the Final Solution in the 'euphoria of victory' of midsummer 1941."[9]

What Philippe Burrin offered modifies this position. He agrees with Browning that Hitler made the final decision out of frustration. But that frustration was not, he suggests, determined by the failure of previous solutions but by the imminent failure of the war. In his famous threat, pronounced in the Reichstag on January 30, 1939, Hitler announced that, if international Jewry succeeded in provoking another world war, its result would be the "destruction of the Jewish race in Europe." According to Burrin, this meant that if the world were to accept Germany's territorial expansion without seriously resisting, he (Hitler) would be satisfied with the expulsion of the Jews.

Indeed, when in 1939 and 1940 he was winning easy victories, Hitler talked a great deal about resettling the Jews either in the East of Poland or in Madagascar. But when in August 1941 the Soviets prevented him from marching easily into Moscow and when the United States began giving the Soviets aid, he opted for mass killings. The murder of the European Jews was, then, at the same time an act of expiating the spilt German blood and above all an act of revenge, taken in advance, for defeat. Once more I shall not discuss these arguments in detail. Suffice it to say that I agree with Browning's reply that he remains "respectfully unconvinced." This is not the place for continuing the debate. Instead I want to draw some more general conclusions as to where we are and where we need to go in future research.

The first merit of the debate is that it has finally disconnected research on antisemitism from research on the Holocaust. Research on antisemitism will continue to be very useful in that antisemitism certainly was a fundamental precondition since it created the atmosphere that made the crime possible. Or, in rather simpler terms, without antisemitism Hitler could not have become an antisemite, and without being an antisemite he would not have decided on the Final Solution.

But the really pertinent question is not why the Nazis were antisemites but why they committed murder. There is no direct line from antisemitism to the Holocaust for the very simple reason that antisemitism had existed for centuries and yet had never before led to such murderous destruction.

Traditional antisemites had at most strived to remove the Jews from their country. Never before had they invaded foreign and remote countries and either killed the Jews there or deported them for the sole purpose of killing them. The Nazis had certainly started by persecuting the Jews in Germany. But the Holocaust was a fundamentally different affair. Its real meaning and its uniqueness cannot be grasped fully unless it is taken into account that, in the end, of all the Jews murdered, approximately 98 percent were not German Jews. That is what was unprecedented, what requires an explanation.

The second merit of the debate is that it has finally drawn the attention of researchers to the central point. We need to know how the murder was initiated and implemented. Several answers have been supplied over the years, some, of course, long before the debate on decision making started.

The present state of research permits us to discard all answers denying that a relevant decision was made and that it was made by Hitler. That is not to say, of course, that he was the only person responsible. It is evident beyond doubt that he could not have implemented the murder without the help of many others, individuals and governments alike. This, of course, also remains a vast field of research.

It seems equally evident that Hitler took the initiative. Both Browning and Burrin have asked why. The answer has been: out of frustration, although for different reasons. However, the arguments put forward so penetratingly have demonstrated that this particular question cannot be answered with certainty. I think that in the end it is impossible to discern Hitler's most intimate reasoning. We may establish what his intentions were—what his planning was, when and how he made a decision, and when and how and by whom it was executed. But we cannot establish why, at a given moment, he made one decision instead of another. In the Nazi state, decisions were not arrived at in conferences or cabinet meetings where the arguments for and against would be put on the table, discussed, balanced, and registered in a protocol. Hitler never disclosed his real motives. Everything he said (and in this instance we don't even know what he said) was meant only to motivate his subordinates.

I think, therefore, that it is impossible to know why he made a certain decision. The answer can only be conjectural. We should limit our efforts to finding out when and how a decision was made.

Hitler had, of course, to offer reasons for something which in itself was totally unreasonable. He had to justify what was totally unjustifiable. What should he say to Himmler when the latter once more intimated what he had given Hitler in writing in 1940, namely, that the physical extermination of a people was both "un-Germanic and impossible"? Or to Göring when he said it was more important that "we win the war"? That was irrefutable. It forced Hitler to invent pretexts. But it is very unlikely that they were his real reasons. It even seems likely that he had no reasons at all but merely instinctive hatred. All we may be able to establish is when and how the decision was made. These are the questions on which we should concentrate, even though Browning has admittedly already offered some very good answers to them.

Once more, we would have to take our point of departure from the structure of the Nazi state. How were decisions made in other fields where the documentation is better? It becomes increasingly evident, for example, that Hitler already wanted to unleash the war in 1938 even if it meant war with Britain and France. He was opposed by all his advisors because they were convinced that such a war was unwinnable. He was prevented from starting the war in 1938 and again in March 1939, but he succeeded in September. He succeeded because he kept his advisors apart, playing one off against the other. He alone had a complete picture of the situation.

This model could and should be applied to the Final Solution. There is some evidence that Hitler wanted to initiate it as early as September 1939 but failed. He tried again early in 1941 and succeeded when Heydrich's Einsatzgruppen started the killings in June. It seems to me that he succeeded because he played off Heydrich against Himmler. It was their rivalry that enabled Hitler to do what he had wanted to do for a long time.

When Heydrich had become Chief of the Security Police he had reached a rank second only to Himmler. There was no further promotion possible except to Himmler's place. Certainly Heydrich was very ambitious. He was young, thirty-seven in 1941, but Himmler was his senior by barely three and a half years. He was forty-one in 1941 and thus could go on to be Reichsführer SS and Chief of the German police for another twenty-five years or so, until a time when Heydrich would also reach the age of retirement.

It seems likely to me that Heydrich was striving for a supreme authority independent of Himmler's, and that he did so by fulfilling Hitler's anti-Jewish desires better than Himmler. My argument is that in the Jewish question Himmler was less determined than Hitler, that Heydrich sensed this difference in determination and decided to outdo Himmler in this area, not because he was more anti-Jewish but because he recognized that outdoing Himmler was an effective means of winning Hitler's favor and getting a promotion.

There is much evidence for my argument. I shall limit myself to demonstrating one instance only. It is a particularly crucial one: the decision to deport the Jews in Germany.

In August 1941 Hitler was still hesitating. When Heydrich had proposed to evacuate the Jews from the Altreich, Hitler had refused for the time "during the war." Göring also refused when Heydrich repeatedly proposed to mark the German Jews. But Heydrich kept insisting. He joined hands with Goebbels in order to exert influence on Hitler.

The final decision must have occurred in mid-September 1941. Let me just enumerate the elements of what we know and postpone the interpretation for the time being. On September 18 Himmler wrote to Arthur Greiser, Reichsstatthalter in the Warthegau in the incorporated Polish territories: "The Führer wishes that the Altreich and the Protectorate should be emptied and liberated of the Jews, proceeding from West to East, as soon as possible." On September 22, 23, and 24 Himmler and Heydrich were with Hitler at his headquarters. After this it was announced that Heydrich, in addition to his previous duties, was to carry out the duties of the Reichsprotektor in Bohemia and Moravia and that he was promoted to the rank of SS-Obergruppenführer. It was his first promotion since June 1934. He now had a rank that corresponded to that of general in the army and state secretary in the government administration. And he had a territory such as only Reichsministers or Gauleiters had hitherto received.

On September 23 Goebbels, who was also at the Führer's headquarters during these days—but not present at the talks with Himmler and Heydrich—learned from Heydrich what he noted in his diary: "The Führer is of the opinion that the Jews must gradually be taken out of the whole of Germany. The first cities to be made free of Jews now are Berlin, Vienna, and Prague."

On September 30 Heydrich's representative in Vienna informed the leader of the Israelite Religious Community there that the first transport would leave on October 15. It did indeed leave Vienna on that day, followed by the first transport from Berlin on October 18. The deportations from Germany had begun.

If we try now to connect these pieces of information we can state the following series of decisions. On or shortly before September 18: evacuation "as soon as possible." On or shortly before September 23: evacuation "now." This is confirmed by the fact that the evacuations were implemented immediately afterwards.

In this context Heydrich was promoted both to acting Reichsprotektor and Obergruppenführer. We have a photocopy of the latter appointment. It was typewritten on Hitler's letterhead and signed by him in handwriting. The line "Berlin, den" was crossed out and replaced in Himmler's handwriting by "Führer-Hauptquartier, 24.IX.41."

Why had Himmler personally, and not some secretary, added the modification? My tentative answer is: Because nobody else was present. Why was nobody else present? Because the matter discussed at that particular meeting was top secret. Thus, it could not have been the meeting regarding the situation in the Protectorate (when Karl Hermann Frank was also present) but a meeting specifically about the Final Solution.

It is, of course, possible that Heydrich was made acting Reichsprotektor because the situation in the Protectorate required it and that he was promoted to Obergruppenführer because he was to have that rank in his new capacity. But it is also possible (and that is my tentative interpretation) that he received the double appointment as a reward for his position on the Final Solution at the very moment when its implementation had finally been decided.

What was the military situation during these days? Was it marked by frustration or by the euphoria of victory? I quote from Franz Halder's diary. September 18: "satisfactory progress east of Kiev." September 19: "Operations in the South are progressing with delightful speed." On that day indeed Kiev was taken. September 20: "The crisis of encirclement begins." September 21: The enemy is apparently withdrawing. September 22: Preparations for attack on the Crimea. September 23: Nothing new in the South. September 25: Local progress on the Crimea. I would deduce that the situation was tense but not frustrating. It seems to me that Hitler, after much hesitation, had finally crossed the threshold to the Final Solution during these days and that he had conferred the task upon Heydrich, who shortly after proclaimed himself to be Judenkommissar for Europe. Of course, I cannot prove that my interpretation is correct nor can I develop my whole argument here. Many more elements of information would have to be taken into account.

But I am quite confident that this is the direction in which we need to go. We need to assemble meticulously all the elements at our disposal, including those which at first sight are not directly relevant to the Final Solution. Then a mosaic may become visible, perhaps a panorama, from which we can deduce more general and more convincing conclusions.

We have reached a point at which we can look back to quite some progress in research. The purely functionalist approach has been more or less invalidated. The

Holocaust was initiated—initiated by Hitler. There were, of course, conditions under which it was implemented. We are far from having explored all of these, even further from having assembled them into a coherent picture. But we have reached a point where we have found the way that we need to go.

NOTES

1. Gerald Reitlinger, *The Final Solution: The Attempt to Exterminate the Jews of Europe, 1933–45* (London: Vallentine, Mitchell & Co.; New York: Beechhurst Press, 1953).

2. Leon Poliakov, *Bréviaire de la haine: Le IIIe Reich et les Juifs* (Paris: Calmann-Levy, 1951).

3. Raul Hilberg, *The Destruction of the European Jews* (Chicago: Quadrangle Books, 1961).

4. Paul W. Massing, *Rehearsal for Destruction: A Study of Political Anti-Semitism in Imperial Germany* (New York: Harper and Brothers, 1949).

5. David Irving, *Hitler's War* (New York: Viking Press, 1977), pp. 12–15.

6. Martin Broszat, "Hitler und die Genesis der 'Endlösung': Aus Anlass der Thesen von David Irving," *Vierteljahrshefte für Zeitgeschichte* 25/4 (October 1977): 739–75.

7. Philippe Burrin, *Hitler et les juifs: genèse d'un génocide* (Paris: Editions du Seuil, 1989); Burrin's study has been translated into English as *Hitler and the Jews: The Genesis of the Holocaust*, trans. Patsy Southgate (London: Edward Arnold, 1994), pp. 23–24.

8. Tim Mason, "Intention and Explanation: A Current Controversy about the Interpretation of National Socialism," in *Der Führerstaat: Mythos und Realität*, ed. Gerhard Hirschfeld and Lothar Kettenacker (Stuttgart: Klett-Cotta, 1981), pp. 21–40.

9. See the review by Christopher R. Browning in *American Historical Review* 96 (1991): 1226.

4.

MICHAEL R. MARRUS

The Holocaust

WHERE WE ARE, WHERE WE NEED TO GO——A COMMENT

Let me invite you to imagine circumstances different than they are. Suppose that we are in Paris, France. We are not in the 1990s, but at some time in the mid-nineteenth century. As scholars, our minds are focused not on the destruction of European Jews but rather on the French Revolution, which, like the Holocaust now, was then being assessed from the vantage point of half a century.

A conference of distinguished scholars has been assembled, and the first panel sets out to chart "Where we are, where we need to go." To the assembled company this evening in Paris, papers are presented by three eminent historians. They are: Jules Michelet, head of the historical section of the National Archives and professor at the Collège de France; the Count Alexis de Tocqueville, writer, traveler and soon-to-be government minister; and François Guizot, one-time professor, historian, and states-man, and head of the French government during most of the 1840s.

These three historians are called upon to assess the state of research on the French Revolution and to suggest future directions. In response, each of these dwells upon themes with which he has been preoccupied: the "interdisciplinary" Tocqueville focuses on origins, the perils of over-centralization, and the link between economic trends and the collapse of the Bourbon monarchy's reform program; the patriot Michelet, renowned for glorious abstractions, reminds his audience of the volcanic upsurge of the French people after 1789 and the importance of collections at the National Archives; and the liberal monarchist Guizot, a great admirer of the British experience, suggests that his audience consider comparative history in order to understand more fully the progress of liberty through political change.

The evening is a chef d'oeuvre of historical recapitulation and a splendid occasion for all the invited professionals to remember. Still, a few graduate students, gathered at the back of the splendid hall are heard to grumble as they go out into the night: "*Eh bien*, the *patron* really let them have it *ce soir*. He really told us where we should go from here, what themes we should pursue. Nevertheless, I think I'll work on something a little bit different." And so, indeed, they do. Four generations later the students of students of these students have reached the age of retirement, and how different is their work from that of their progenitors of the mid-nineteenth century! The study of origins now links regional studies with machine-assisted investigations of the tax system; gender and family studies now dominate much of social history;

and devotees of comparative history construct models of political development and challenge the notion of revolution itself.

Tocqueville, Michelet, and Guizot are respected for their inspiration, their erudition, and their remarkable original contributions. However, these historians are now read, more often than not, to discover how the historiography got to its present point and to puzzle over the preoccupations people had in the mid-nineteenth century as they contemplated their momentous past.

What is the point of this imaginative exercise? There are several. Most obviously, my reference to the three illustrious Frenchmen is a way of acknowledging the esteem with which we view the work of the distinguished senior colleagues whose writings appear here. No one can tell whether their advice on new directions will be taken, or what will last or not last among the historical paradigms for which they have been responsible over the years. But whatever current or future criticism holds, professors Bauer, Jäckel, and Hilberg will remain foundation stones for my own and so many others' thinking about the Holocaust. Even if we agree or disagree with their opinions, we refer regularly to their work when we develop our own hypotheses.

Second, my reference to the rich historiography of the French Revolution is a way of underscoring a point that is implicit in all three papers: the Holocaust, like the French Revolution, has become historicized. It has entered into the mainstream of historical understanding and is subject to the same rules of evidence, interpretation, and exposition as the other great issues historians examine. Some consider it painful to hear historians demystify the Holocaust. They do not like to see historians resist the notion—as Yehuda Bauer does, for example—that the victims were *kedoshim*, or holy persons, rather than ordinary people. This type of historical analysis, however, is a normal and healthy development, just as it was when our three French historians fashioned their arguments in a way that spoke to the historical culture of their era.

The other side of the coin is that the history of the Holocaust has finally "arrived"; it has been incorporated into the history of our time in the way that the French Revolution was considered by the mid-nineteenth century as a major reference point for the understanding of that era. Each of our essayists has been prominently involved in professional discourse on this subject. The result of their labors, together with those of so many others, is that the Holocaust has come out of the dark shadows and, to paraphrase Raul Hilberg, into the limelight. Our collective responsibility is to avoid the distortions of inaccuracy, vulgarization, and banalization that can easily result.

My third point concerning my French Revolution analogy considers how literally our younger colleagues will take directives from these three distinguished scholars about what postures to adopt on some current controversies and "where we go from here." I have a distinct feeling that the best graduate students will go their own ways, and will surprise us with what they unfold. "History," said the celebrated Dutch historian Pieter Geyl, "is an argument without end." The last thing we would want for Holocaust history is its becoming a broken record, repeating the same agendas over and over again. Accordingly, we must expect that theses will generate antitheses, that one way of looking at matters will be challenged by a new approach. Nothing could be worse for Holocaust history than stilling argument and producing an official orthodoxy. Tocqueville, Guizot, and Michelet would never have tolerated it; nor, I am sure, would Bauer, Hilberg, and Jäckel.

In studying the Holocaust, historians have been challenging theories for decades, far longer than Eberhard Jäckel suggests when he refers to Martin Broszat's famous 1977 attack on David Irving. For example, a firestorm of criticism on the subject of Jewish reactions to Nazi persecution greeted Raul Hilberg's *The Destruction of the European Jews*. The debate on the Judenräte, focused by Hannah Arendt's reporting for the *New Yorker* in 1961 and carried to a new level by Isaiah Trunk's *Judenrat* in 1972, is another important milestone. Reference to these contests serves to recall as well the name of Philip Friedman, both a survivor and a historian of the Holocaust. He insisted that historians examine not only the perpetrators but also the Jews as "the bearer(s) of a communal existence."[1]

Historians are known for challenging established theories and creating their own. More than forty years ago, Hannah Arendt's *The Origins of Totalitarianism* pointed out a path on which research on antisemitism can become, as Jäckel terms it, "disconnected" from research on the Holocaust. While not ignoring antisemitism, Arendt pondered the way in which modern industrial society developed terrible new means of domination, drove entire peoples outside the framework of humanity, routinized terror, and conducted massive assaults on human individuality. For Arendt, what was remarkable about Nazism was not its antisemitism but the machinelike processes of persecution and murder it created, inspired not only by the project of robbing Jews of their lives but of stripping them of their human individuality as well.

Since Arendt's work was published, many others have pondered the Nazis' murder of European Jewry from this vantage point. Karl Dietrich Bracher, for example, studied the way in which Nazism perpetrated the "impersonal, bureaucratic 'extermination' of a people classified as a species of inferior subhumans, as 'vermin,' a problem which the farmer Himmler handled as though it were a biological disease."[2] Raul Hilberg's own work on the Holocaust may be understood as part of the wider discourse on totalitarianism in our time. For Hilberg, the central image of the Nazi apparatus is also a machine—the European-wide "machinery of destruction" which treads upon its victims, following its own logic of expropriation, concentration, deportation, and, finally, mass murder. Antisemitism plays a role in the process but does not serve as a full explanation for the events which unfolded. Study of the Holocaust demands a sense of balance, proportion, and due weight to the various factors involved.

This is the vantage point from which I assess Yehuda Bauer's compromise. He attempts to steer a path between those who "universalize the Holocaust" to the point of denying "the specificity of the Jewish fate," and those, on the other hand, who turn all their interpretative tools inward, rejecting all possibility of comparison with other genocides or persecutions. In the effort to strike this balance, Yehuda Bauer has an important role to play in Holocaust history. Indeed, his 1978 essay "Against Mystification: The Holocaust as a Historical Phenomenon" is one of the milestones in this effort. However, among his arguments that I do not find persuasive are allusions to the motivations of researchers: Jews seeking to deny their Jewishness because of fundamental insecurities (in the case of universalizers), or angry Christians seeking validation of their traditional identities through a morbid, exploitative or distorted picture of the Holocaust. These assessments may be right or they may be wrong. In any case, there are enough balanced, well-grounded cases for "universalization" and for specificity to command the attention of all of us. Let us leave motivations to the psychologists and biographers; we have enough to do trying to get the history itself correct.

In this regard I have to wonder about Bauer's sweeping dismissal of journalist Tom Segev, in which the author is taxed with seeing "Ben-Gurion and his colleagues [as] unfit to guide the Jewish people . . . puny, narrow-minded individuals, only out to achieve a Jewish independence in Palestine which would enhance their power." It may be that I missed this emphasis in the English edition of *The Seventh Million*. The latter has, to be sure, some hard things to say about the leadership of the Yishuv during the Holocaust. But Segev also recounts how, early in 1943, Ben-Gurion went to Haifa to see one of the refugees from Nazi-occupied Europe who managed to reach Palestine, a young woman who was a witness of the Holocaust in Poland: "He was deeply disturbed, to the point of tears," Segev writes. "'I can't escape from the nightmare,' he wrote afterwards. For three hours the girl told him of the horrors she had suffered and, said Ben-Gurion, 'no Dante or Poe' could imagine such things. He felt helpless, he wrote. It was a rare outburst of emotion on his part—he seldom spoke of the suffering of individuals—and even here he quickly regained his composure: 'The sun is rising in all its might and one must go on with one's work.'"[3] An imbalanced portrait overall, perhaps; but "puny, narrow-minded . . . unfit to lead the Jewish people" is an overly harsh assessment. I simply don't see it. While no doubt kinder to Ben-Gurion, more finely grained in his assessment and certainly more appreciative of his Zionist leadership and political genius, his biographer Shabtai Teveth makes essentially the same point when he refers to his subject's determination to "turn a disaster . . . into a productive force."[4]

One suspects that part of the problem here is a reflection of the historicization of the Holocaust and thus the encounter between scholarship and popular history. The dangers professional historians see in a popularization is the neglect of the basic building blocks of historical inquiry, namely recollections or documents. Raul Hilberg rightly draws our attention to the avalanche of documentation from former Soviet-bloc countries that is about to come crashing down around the heads of Holocaust historians. This extraordinary hoard of material will be at least as significant for Holocaust studies as was the opening of the ULTRA and MAGIC archives for the study of Allied policy during the Second World War.

I resist, however, the notion that future studies of the Holocaust will be driven by new sources, rather than by new questions. The documentation on the French Revolution has been freely available for generations. Yet despite this, there has recently been a veritable flood of new books on the French Revolution. Fundamentally, what keeps the subject alive as an intellectual discourse is that the itch to understand is a never-ending process. So long as our historical culture is pluralistic and open, so long as our intellectual life is free and challenging, new questions will rain down on Holocaust history. Count on the next generation to frame different

Part 2

Antisemitism and Racism in Nazi Ideology

All students of the Holocaust agree that antisemitism and racism were important factors in Nazi ideology. Yet beyond this most simple consensus is an ongoing debate. Was antisemitism primary or merely secondary to Nazi racism? Was antisemitism shared by ordinary Germans in what Daniel Jonah Goldhagen has depicted as the movement from "eliminationist" antisemitism to "exterminationist" antisemitism, from the desire to eliminate Jews from German society to the decision to murder all Jews. Other students of the Holocaust such as Sybil Milton and Henry Friedlander see antisemitism as one important, but not all-important, component of Nazi racism, which was ideologically committed to the creation of a master race and hence to the elimination of what it deemed "life unworthy of living" among the Germans—mentally retarded, emotionally disturbed, and physically handicapped Germans, along with Gypsies (Sinti and Roma) and Jews. In the essays that follow, the role of antisemitism is explored. In subsequent sections, Nazi policy toward those Germans whom they deemed unworthy of living is considered, as are Nazi policies toward diverse victims groups, to gain a more complete understanding of the interrelationship between Nazi antisemitism and racism.

A distinguished interpreter of German public opinion during the Second World War, David Bankier focuses on the seeming contradiction in Nazi policy with respect to the "Final Solution to the Jewish problem" in "The Use of Antisemitism in Nazi Wartime Propaganda": Why did the Nazis keep such a tight lid on the actual destruction of European Jewry, vowing to take the secret to their graves, while at the same time prophesying time and again that Germany was involved in a great race war in which Jewry had to be exterminated?

Bankier concludes that publicizing the extermination of the Jew to the German public became a substitute for a quickly fading military victory, especially after 1943. The publicity was designed to galvanize the population, to enforce continued adherence and group loyalty. The Nazis also sought to convince the German population that it, too, was responsible for the Nazi efforts to destroy European Jewry and sought to frighten the population by describing Jewish acts of revenge against the entire German people, and not just the Nazi leadership, should the war end unsuccessfully.

In "The Holocaust: A Very Particular Racism," Steven T. Katz develops part of the hypothesis of his major work, *The Holocaust in Historical Context*. Katz argues that Nazi racism had a biologistic premise that conceived of society in terms of health and disease. Under Nazism, social and political realities were described as healthy or diseased, even pathological or cancerous. This was common to all manifestations of Nazi racism. Yet the Nazi program against the Jews was unique. Other racial groups—Slavs and Blacks among them—were deemed inferior people, destined for conquest or servitude, yet they remained within "the parameters of common humanity." The Jews alone were slated for annihilation. They were portrayed as the eternal enemy of the German people. In the words of Himmler: "All Jews within our grasp are to be destroyed without exception." Unlike the euthanasia program that targeted people based on some personal, biological attributes, all Jews were targeted by virtue of their group membership. Thus under Nazism, Katz argues, "racism became metaphysical and the destruction of the Jews essential for the preservation of the German nation, if not their salvation."

In "Antisemitism and Racism in Nazi Ideology," Walter Zwi Bacharach distinguishes Nazi antisemitism from more traditional forms of antisemitism. The politicization of antisemitism was apparent from 1848 onward when Bruno Bauer first raised the "Jewish Question." As early as 1919, Hitler's ideas regarding antisemitism were radicalized. He said: "the final goal of antisemitism must be total removal of the Jews." Furthermore, Hitler viewed his task in missionary terms: "By defending myself against the Jew, I am fighting for the work of the Lord."

Nourished by the negative image attached to the Jew by Christian theology, radicalized antisemitism, with its underpinning of race doctrine, was given a biological basis. Traditional antisemitism was intermingled with a universal mission to create a new world based on racial purity.

Bacharach describes Nazi policy toward non-Jews as opportunistic and inconsistent, a cynical weapon subject to manipulation. With regard to the Jews, the policy was systematic and consistent. Jews became the central theme of racist policy. As Nazi antisemitism became political, it turned theory and ideology into a lethal practice.

In "Antisemitism, the Holocaust, and Reinterpretations of National Socialism," Omer Bartov examines the history and what one might call the politics of the interrelationship between the three phenomena. He deals with each phenomenon separately and in the end suggests that all three must be seen as intersecting in part because each was a manifestation of modernity.

With regard to antisemitism, two disparate views have predominated. Antisemitism is perceived either as a permanent aspect of diaspora life since the exile, or as firmly rooted in nineteenth-century European society, reaching its culmination in the Holocaust and thoroughly discredited thereafter. For Orthodox Jews, Gentiles always threatened Jews; for Zionists, the circumstances of exile—statelessness and powerlessness—were the root cause of antisemitism and the prescription for its end were an army and a flag. The Holocaust only fortified these perceptions.

Bartov demonstrates how naming the event shapes its perception. The term "Holocaust," as used by the English-speaking world, connotes a sacrificial meaning. Greek in origin, the word means a burnt offering offered whole unto the Lord. Yiddish-speaking Jews used the word *churban*, destruction, to signify the Holocaust. More recently, the word *Shoah* has been used by Israelis to signify destruction, seemingly directly related to natural disasters (a natural outgrowth of exile). Historian Lucy Dawidowicz called the Holocaust "the War against the Jews," and perhaps she was right. The planned destruction of an entire people was a war the Nazis came close to winning. The Nazis euphemistically called the murder of the Jews the "Final Solution to the Jewish Problem." Contemporary Germans speak of the destruction of the Jews, while the French universalize the term by speaking of genocide. Perhaps, Bartov argues, the event itself remains unnamed.

As others have argued, the intentionalists see a direct link between the three phenomena. Antisemitism was the core and essence of the Nazi movement. The

National Socialist state was bound to carry out the threat and intentions of its propagandists. Structuralists, elsewhere termed functionalists, have argued for an indirect and limited influence. National Socialism cannot be explained as a political manifestation of antisemitism alone—it was not a main engine of the movement.

Recent studies of National Socialism have tried to separate it from both antisemitism and the Holocaust, but to no avail. Bartov argues that in understanding all three as a manifestation of modernization, we can reintegrate and understand anew antisemitism, the Holocaust, and National Socialism.

5.

DAVID BANKIER

The Use of Antisemitism in Nazi Wartime Propaganda

I

An inquiry into the use of antisemitism in wartime propaganda may well begin with the question: Why is it that the Nazis withheld information on the one hand about what they were actually doing to the Jews, while announcing their intentions on the other? Why is it that while the Nazis described the role of the Jews in world politics in demonic proportions, they remained tight-lipped on the question of how they themselves were implementing the Final Solution in occupied Europe? The Nazi press was filled with onslaughts against the Jews as an international force that supported world revolution and incited others to attack Germany; at the same time, only crumbs of concrete information were given to the public about the actual treatment of the Jews by the Nazi state.

The handling of the deportations is a case in point. In December 1941 the world press referred to the forthcoming deportation of Jews to the area of the General Government, but the German media avoided mention of the matter. All that the Nazi-controlled press said to its readers was that the solution to the Jewish problem would be achieved through overseas colonization under international control.[1]

To be sure, the attention of the German press was directed toward routine anti-Jewish measures taken by other countries. For example, Goebbels ordered extensive commentaries on Romania's antisemitic laws in the fall of 1941, but nothing was said about the deportations of Jews from Germany, which had just begun.[2] This was by no means coincidental. Examination of the press instructions of the Ministry of Propaganda and the directives of Hitler's press officer Otto Dietrich indicates that German and foreign journalists stationed in the Reich were explicitly ordered to refrain from addressing the topic. For example, Otto Dietrich's press directive of October 2, 1943, instructed the media not to mention the antisemitic measures adopted by the Germans in Denmark.[3]

This policy explains the pains that the Nazis took to avoid public discussion about what was really happening to the Jews. The Nazis had learned a valuable lesson from the public uproar against the euthanasia killings in the summer of 1941; the animated discussion about the campaign to remove crucifixes from Catholic schools; the unexpected adverse reactions to the imposition of the yellow badge in September 1941; and the unrest among certain groups of Berlin's population during the early deportations a month later. They could not take for granted total public support for each and every policy measure, and they therefore decided not to raise thorny issues which could boomerang and provoke unnecessary public debate. This was probably also the main reason that in April 1942 Goebbels called off the show trial of Hershel Grynspan—so that the question of Jewish deportations would not be raised in court. He did so even though all preparations had been completed and Hitler had ordered the trial to start in November 1941.[4]

It goes without saying that if a policy of silence was adopted with regard to deportation, it would have applied to a greater degree to the early news about the mass murder of Jews in Russia and to the Allied announcement of the Nazi plan to annihilate European Jewry. When the Allies began publishing and broadcasting news about the extermination in December 1942, Goebbels could hardly overestimate the importance of their campaign. On December 8 he stated that the fate of the Jews in Poland was a delicate (heikel) matter which had best be left alone. Sensing, however, that silence could be interpreted as consent, he resorted to a diversionary counteraction. On December 13, while commenting in his diary on the Allied broadcast about the extermination, he wrote that Germany would not discuss the subject publicly. Instead, he set in motion a propaganda offensive against the Allies which emphasized their alleged atrocities, giving particular prominence to British repression of the nationalist movements in India, Iran, and Egypt. In his press conference on December 16 he maintained that

> a general hullabaloo about atrocities is our best chance of getting away from the unpleasant subject of the Jews. Things must be so arranged that each party accuses every other of committing atrocities. This general hullabaloo will then eventually result in this subject disappearing from the agenda.[5]

To this effect the German Foreign Office enlisted the cooperation of the Grand Mufti of Jerusalem, Haj Amin El Husseini. The Nazis advertised his speech of December 18, 1942, in which, while addressing a rally in Berlin, he had declared that the United States and Britain, in conjunction with the Jews, were crushing all Arab and Islamic protests with terror, blood, and fire. To the same end Subhas Chandra Bose, a leader of the Indian nationalist movement who had found asylum in Berlin, was also conscripted to the propaganda effort on December 22 and was asked to counter the Allied "atrocity propaganda" with an account of the "barbaric" nature of British rule in India.[6]

This strategy of neutralizing Allied propaganda and discrediting it by highlighting Allied crimes was repeated in the spring of 1943. In view of the USSR's disclosure of the mass graves in Rostow, Goebbels orchestrated a campaign centered on the Russian killings of Polish officers in the Katyn forest.

None of this is surprising since, as we all know, the Final Solution was a secret state matter. On November 18, 1941, while the Einsatzgruppen were shooting Jews in Russia, Alfred Rosenberg briefed German journalists, saying that the biological extirpation (biologische Ausmerzung) of all Jews in Europe had begun. The Jews of Europe were to be pushed beyond the Ural mountains or exterminated in another way, yet the press was to give no details apart from the common phrases on "Bolshevism and its destruction." And a month later, on December 14, 1941, when Rosenberg discussed with Hitler a speech he intended to give, Hitler concurred that he should not mention the annihilation of the Jews.[7]

If the activities of the extermination squads were to be kept secret, that of the gassing centers was to be even more so. Abundant evidence attests to the efforts to conceal the extermination camps. SS Sergeant-Major Walter Burmeister, for instance, who was employed in setting up Chelmno, testified in his trial that in the autumn of 1941 Herbert Lange had summoned him to his office and told him that he had been placed in a special unit to carry out a secret job of which he should never speak. He signed his commitment to secrecy and never referred to what he saw in Chelmno, not even to his closest relatives.[8] Likewise, Kurt Gerstein, who wrote in his report that he had been told by Odilo Globocnik in Lublin: "This whole affair is one of the most secret matters at the moment, in fact one can say the most secret. Anyone who talks about it will be shot on the spot."[9] Offenders were punished, of course, but not as severely as Globocnik had indicated. The Gebietskommissar of Glebokie, Paul Hachmann, for example, was simply not promoted for spreading the "most repulsive rumors" about the execution of Jews.[10]

What was the purpose of secrecy? First, it was expedient to conceal from the victims the fate intended for them so as not to alarm them and in order to minimize resistance. Second, there is evidence that concealment was also a calculation of prudence, out of concern for the success of the operation and its rapid completion. It should be sufficient to cite Viktor Brack, who was in charge of establishing Belzec. In his letter to Himmler on June 23, 1942, Brack quoted Globocnik, who had ordered that the Reinhard action annihilating Polish Jewry be put into high gear and completed as soon as possible lest they be caught in the middle and the program be halted.[11]

What was said in the propaganda for foreign countries? The letter sent by Himmler to "Gestapo" Müller in November 1942 shows that it was vital to conceal the killing from the outside world in order to prevent its utilization in anti-German propaganda and to avert Allied retaliation. Himmler alluded to Stephen Wise's public campaign on the extermination of Jews and asked Müller to make sure that no trace be left of the corpses of the murdered Jews so as to avoid public discussion about the fate of the Jews evacuated to the East.[12]

Propaganda for the West was aimed merely at convincing all ears that the Nazis were struggling to defend the values of Western civilization and that the Western Allies were fighting not only for a cause which was not their own but against their own interests. Indeed in mid-1943, 80 percent of foreign broadcasts were devoted to the Jewish question. The reason is plain. Hitler had made it clear several times that antisemitism was the best stud in the Nazi stable and that the Jewish theme was particularly relevant after four years of war, when people sought, whether consciously or not, a scapegoat on which to lay blame. The more the Jew was attacked, he said, the more he would defend himself and occupy the center of attention. The objective of generating discord around the Jewish problem would thus be achieved and antisemitic sentiment would increase. Small wonder then that, as soon as Goebbels was informed of an alleged rise in anti-Jewish feelings in England, he instructed his propaganda apparatus to exploit the anti-Jewish atmosphere by launching an antisemitic radio campaign.[13] Ideological and utilitarian motivations were thereby intertwined in the antisemitic propaganda broadcasts aimed abroad. The Nazis were convinced that the Jews were the mythical power that united the disparate enemies of Bolshevism and capitalism, the glue in fact, that held the Allied coalition together. Consequently, they believed the Allies could be split if they were made to realize this. The means used in this fight against the Jews, however, were never revealed.

Finally, extermination had to be concealed also from the German public. It was not enough to tell the population, as Himmler told the SS, that despite the mass murders they remained decent. A good many Germans, the Nazis believed, were still shackled by Christian morality and, until their reeducation was complete, the grand scheme could not be uncovered.

When was the secret to be revealed? Although the Nazis were convinced that they were performing a deed of virtue, they knew that it had to be denied in their own lifetime. Dr. Herbert Linden, the liaison official between the Reich Interior Ministry and the euthanasia project, asked Globocnik whether it was proper to bury the corpses instead of burning them, since a generation might arise which would not approve of the entire affair. To this Globocnik replied: "If there is ever a generation so weak that it does not understand this momentous deed then the whole of National Socialism will have been in vain. On the contrary, bronze tablets ought to be buried, on which it is recorded that we had the courage to carry out this great and vital work." According to him, Hitler concurred with this view.[14] Himmler, on the other hand, made it clear that, notwithstanding their pride in what they were doing, the secret could not be revealed to the present generation. Addressing SS officers in October 1943, he stated: "Perhaps, at a much later time, we can consider whether we should say something more about this to the German people. I myself believe that . . . we should now take this secret with us to the grave." Even the SS, he said, could not understand more than the facts as such. Only distance could provide the proper perspective, perhaps only after decades of utter defamation.[15]

Out of the same motives, it was equally important to employ coded language. As we know, the removal of written evidence and the use of euphemisms in criminal activity serves to tighten discipline and mitigate moral accountability. This seems to be the reason that even the coded term Endlösung was prohibited in documents intended for general circulation where its over-use made its real meaning obvious. Other euphemisms—such as working camp, resettlement, transit camps, bathing installations—added to the secrecy, fulfilling yet another highly important psychological function: they diminished responsibility, leaving it to the interlocutor to understand what he wished, thereby further reducing the unpleasantness of the whole operation and removing any remaining scruples. Finally, doubts were handled by routinization: the maintenance of strict bureaucratic routine became a defense against questioning the nature of the act.[16] To complement all this, the entire operation was camouflaged by destroying all evidence, erasing all traces of the gas chambers and crematoria, planting trees and settling Ukrainian farmers on the sites of the killing factories.

II

At first glance, we seem to be dealing with a paradox, for contrary to what has been said till now, while a cloud of secrecy shrouded the entire annihilation program and all details were withheld, the extermination of the Jews was publicized in declarations printed in the Nazi press and announced over the German radio. And, unlike the euphemistic language used in official documents, the declarations on the fate awaiting the Jews of Europe were neither cryptic nor veiled, but were direct official statements issued by the top Nazi leadership.

Hitler's pronouncements in this context are common knowledge. From January 30, 1939, he publicly proclaimed more than half a dozen times that the Jews would be annihilated, and we must discount the possibility that his threats were explosions of uncontrolled rage. They were deliberately calculated declarations.[17] To begin with, it is clear from the film of his speech in the Reichstag on January 30, 1939, that his threat to the Jews was read from a written text. Second, from November 8, 1942, until September 10, 1943, Hitler did not personally address large meetings but had others read his proclamations. Thus, for example, his "prophecies" of the annihilation of the Jews from February 24, 1942, and March 21, 1943, were read by Gauleiter Wagner and by Hermann Esser from prepared texts; the mention of the extermination of the Jews was therefore deliberate. Nor was it only Hitler who enjoyed the prerogative of revealing what was in store for the Jews. There is abundant evidence that the theme was addressed also by other top leaders of the Third Reich.

At the opening of the Frankfurt Institute for Research of the Jewish Question in 1941, Walter Gross, Director of the Office for Race Policy in the Nazi Party, delivered a lengthy lecture that was couched in the typical language of the Nazis' ideological universe. Expressing his forecast of what was in store for the Jews in terms of cosmological and anthropological laws, he criticized the previous attempts that had been made to physically destroy the Jews. Those, he lamented, had been unsystematic and often followed by indifference, toleration, and even pity. With the advent of Nazism, he continued, a transition from history to destiny had been achieved and since the conventional, inconsistent antisemitic methods had helped Jewry to survive, only the Nazi approach, which viewed history as inexorable laws of nature, could spotlight Jewry as subject to earthly death. He worded his conclusion in unambiguous terms: "As far as the historical presence of the Jew in Europe is concerned, we believe that the hour of his death has irrevocably arrived."[18]

Nor were such declarations restricted to closed Nazi forums. On the contrary. The magazine *Volk und Rasse*, in a typically Nazi militarization of politics, wrote in May 1942 that the entire nation, led by the government, was enlisted in achieving the Nazi goals in the present war and, since all were engaged in a battle against a demonic enemy, all action had become legitimate. The writer implied that everyone was responsible for national existence, yet no one was responsible for the means used to achieve it. The article ended with an unequivocal statement: "A proper understanding of Jews and Judaism cannot but demand their total annihilation."

An analysis of Robert Ley's argumentative strategies, revealed by his discursive syntax, also points to conscious manipulation in the manner in which the Final Solution was proposed to the general public. In *Der Angriff*, a popular weekly magazine with a circulation of some 300,000, he wrote: "For centuries Jews found their sanctuary in the East . . . today the German Army stands on the soil which was the basis of Jewish world domination . . . once this is occupied and former mistakes acknowledged, Germany will draw the necessary conclusion." Two days later he left no doubt as to this conclusion. In the same weekly he wrote: "The war will end with the extermination of the Jewish race." In another article in the widely read *Das Reich* he made an identical prediction: "The Jews will pay with the extermination (Ausrottung) of their race in Europe."[19]

No less explicit were Goebbels's speeches and broadcasts in that same week of June 1942, when he referred to the future mass extermination of European Jews, employing a similar stratagem: blaming the Jews for the outbreak of the war, which had forced the Nazis to react, he transferred responsibility for the annihilation to impersonal justice. In this fashion, he actually informed his readers of what was happening and at the same time let them believe in their innocence.[20]

In connection with the renewed antisemitic campaign of the spring and summer of 1943, these utterances appeared both in written form and in public speeches. On the tenth anniversary of the German Labor Front, Robert Ley addressed six thousand party activists and one thousand representatives of nineteen countries, stating in a blend of fanatic belief and rhetorical tactics: "Judah, Capitalists and Bolsheviks, listen, we want Judah to be exterminated, and Judah will be so. . . . That we know, we swear, we will not abandon the struggle until the last Jew in Europe has been exterminated from the face of Europe."[21] In March 1944 Ley further reminded his audience that mankind would not rest until Judah and its Bolshevism were completely annihilated and exterminated (vollkommen vernichtet und ausgerottet).[22]

The question is why the Nazis announced their murderous policy to the German population while withholding information on that policy's execution.

III

Until the end of 1941 the Nazis would generate antisemitic waves that both preceded and accompanied anti-Jewish measures. For example, during the imposition of the yellow badge in September 1941, instructions were issued to intensify the antisemitic propaganda.[23] From 1942 on, however, the Jewish issue was also used to rally the population when the leadership sensed that it was losing public support, to elicit cooperation when the hard facts of the war countered the propaganda and induced public insecurity about the eventual outcome of that war. As the tide of battle edged closer to Germany the Nazis emphasized that the war was becoming a struggle for survival; propaganda centered on the question "What will the Jews do if we were to lose?" This is clearly seen, for instance, from a juxtaposition of the SD surveys on public mood in December 1941 and the antisemitic campaign launched at the time,[24] or from treatment of the Katyn affair in 1943, when the press was told to announce on the front page that the GPU killing squads were composed of Jewish commissars.[25] There is no doubt that these offensives influenced fanatical Nazis. The pogrom mood created in Bochum by Goebbels's February 18, 1943, speech against the few remaining Jews in that area clearly shows that antisemitic harangues definitely worked for true believers, inciting them to action.[26]

Some others, however, concluded that attacking Jews was merely a diversionary tactic adopted by the government to compensate for defeat and they openly criticized the antisemitic initiatives. The journal *Wille und Macht*, in response, took issue with Germans who, it wrote, did not understand the need to solve the Jewish question.[27]

This was also the reason that Robert Ley decided to respond to those who asked: "Why go on bothering about the Jews? We are doing them a great honor, tilting at windmills and becoming ridiculous Don Quixotes with our hatred of them; let us give it up at last."[28] For the majority, however, for reasons that I have explained elsewhere,[29] the anti-Jewish drive met with disinterest. A Swedish journalist stationed in Germany was right when he noted that since the Jews had disappeared, no one was interested in their fate.[30] It was this majority that had to be politically resocialized and made to share in the Nazi objectives, particularly when things went wrong.

The redoubled effort to convince the population to go on fighting underlies the heightened antisemitic propaganda from 1942 on. The Nazis were fanatics and, as George Santayana has said, fanatics always step up their efforts as the goal recedes. We all know that the more distant victory became, the more the Nazis increased their efforts to annihilate the Jews, because the Jews were not only an object of hate but also an emotional valve for Nazi frustration. As recently discovered documents in Russian archives indicate, it was no mere accident that the killing of Jews escalated as Soviet counterattacks increased.[31] Neither is it a coincidence that the open statements on extermination were issued in a context of failure rather than euphoria.

On October 9, 1941, Hitler's spokesman, Otto Dietrich, rushed to announce to the foreign press representatives in Berlin that following Timoshenko's military defeat, Russia was finished. At the end of November, however, Guderian informed Hitler that it was his soldiers who were finished. Instead of crushing the Red Army and conquering Moscow before Christmas as promised, the Germans faced a major counteroffensive when, on December 5, the Russians brought in fresh divisions from Siberia. On December 8, with Germany's troops exhausted and freezing, the Nazis were forced to announce the end of the campaign on the eastern front. Hitler's strategy had clearly failed and his prestige had taken a bad beating; by early 1942 the losses exceeded the German casualties incurred on the eastern front during the whole of World War I, and German troops were demoralized, haunted by the knowledge of Napoleon's defeat. Hitler's assessment of the situation is captured by his graphic description to Goebbels, to whom he confided that in the first three weeks of January he had to work hard to raise the morale of his generals, in his words: "to inflate the rubber men who had lost their air."[32] After having belittled Russian resistance for weeks, the media began to reveal the bitter truth. In his speech of January 30, Hitler could not admit that the subhuman Russians were beating the "master race," so, instead, he blamed the winter, reassuring his audience that the front would hold despite the enemy's numerical superiority and that the events of 1918 would not be repeated.

This was the background for the announcements concerning the extermination of the Jews. The more frustrated Hitler became as total victory eluded him, the greater his urge to achieve the attainable aspects of Nazi doctrine. The reassurance to be derived from eliminating the Jews was aimed at restoring confidence in ultimate victory, no matter what. Similarly, on September 30, 1942, as the raids on German cities and the failure to take Stalingrad aggravated public pessimism, he reminded his audience of the two prophecies he had made: first, that the Jews would be exterminated, and second, that Germany would win the war. Since it was common knowledge that the first prophecy was being fulfilled, he was asking the public to trust him that the second one would be as well. Likewise, on February 24, 1943, after the Stalingrad military disaster, Hitler's proclamation to the public read: "My forecast—that in this war not the Aryans but the Jews will be exterminated—will come true." In a way, this was a reply to the Soviet announcement that an entire German army had been smashed and further advances were being made on the Leningrad and Kharkov fronts.[33]

In the interest of truth we should not rule out the possibility that the announcement of the annihilation of the Jews was a sort of "moral victory" made by a man possessed by insane revenge—a man whose hopes had been dashed. In my opinion, however, there was more to it than that. His threats from 1942 on were more than attempts to restore a narcissistic self-esteem. The threats were a rationalization to pave the way for extermination, coupled with a Machiavellian attempt to involve all Germans in the crime. Its political function was twofold. On the one hand, in order to bolster his position, Hitler promulgated and thus enforced behavioral codes. On the other, he tested public loyalty by revealing the lengths to which he expected Germans to go. The phrasing, however, was devious so as to leave people guessing about what was happening to the Jews. Hitler had already said in late 1941 that public rumor of a plan to kill the Jews was not a bad thing, because terror was salutary.[34] By the same token, his New Year's message did not contradict the Allied statement about the plan to exterminate the Jews; he merely claimed that it was a war of self-defense against international Jewry.

His "prophecies" employed a technique of implicit presuppositions, that is, to say without saying, so that the listener became responsible for what he understood from the statement. Vagueness was deliberate because it enhanced uncertainty and the lack of detail averted public discussion.[35] Parenthetically, it is safe to say that this stratagem of imposed guesswork was employed also by Goebbels in his February 18, 1943, speech on total war when, in speaking of what was happening to the Jews, he referred to the "vollkommener und radicalster Ausrott . . . schaltung des Judentums." This seeming indiscretion was apparently intentional, leaving the listeners to speculate on what was actually happening to the Jews.[36]

In analyzing this strategy, it appears to be significant that Hitler delivered his threats against the Jews in the form of prophecies. As a prophet he demonstrated not only charisma and the ability to bend history to his will, but also a measure of unaccountability. He became an agent of deterministic forces, and the lack of control over circumstances neutralized moral responsibility. Hence, after extermination had begun, prophecy served as a retrospective alibi—what was happening had already been predicted and there was no criminal intent.

Furthermore, to lend an air of truth to his words, he employed two tactics in his discourses: first, he never used the first person singular, which could have tainted his words with subjectivity (this he did in private talks), but rather stressed factual neutrality. It was not a personal opinion but objective reality, absolute certainty. Closely linked to this was the absence of a precise space or time frame, which made his words dogmatic assertions. And finally, certainty granted the statement a ring of scientific truth.[37]

This attempt to enlist the population as accomplices in the Nazi crimes was closely related to the policy of instilling the conviction that there was nothing to lose. By 1943 the SD reports provided factual testimony that only a minority still believed in victory. Total war, which was a direct continuation of the idea of a Volksgemeinschaft, became an increasingly mobilizing and integrative factor and was exploited as a means to involve everybody in the perpetration of Nazi deeds. Goebbels noted in his diary in January 1943 that there was no reason for the population to live in peace cut off from what was happening in war.[38] Socializing the population in the war effort was an instrument of consciousness-raising because they, too, were trapped by guilt. Small wonder, then, that the need to engage the population became particularly urgent in the confidence crisis during and after Stalingrad, because the existence of the Nazi regime depended on success. The regime itself had generated this dependency with its promises, hence the tension between the promises and expectations on the one hand and the actual reality of defeat on the other, which made the need for legitimation greater still. Since there were no victories to compensate for the losses, the emphasis was placed on a community of fate united by crime.

A sentence from Hitler's speech of August 1, 1923, encapsulates his belief in the functionalism of the criminal bond to tie the population to the system. "There are two things which can unite men," he said, "common ideals and common criminality. . . . It matters not whether these weapons of ours are humane; if they gain us our freedom, they are justified before our conscience and before our God."[39]

The second discursive tactic, particularly in wartime, stemmed from the Nazis' awareness of the political advantages of ruling over a population that had nothing to lose. Albert Speer recalled that in 1944 Hitler had reacted to the Allied bombings by saying: "These air raids don't bother me. I only laugh at them. The less the population has to lose, the more fanatically it will fight."[40] It is also in this connection that Jodl's advice to Hitler should be viewed. At the end of the war Jodl said: "Burn all bridges in order to arouse the people to even stronger combativeness."[41]

It is noteworthy that the message conveyed by Allied propaganda contributed to the diffusion of this belief in the population. In the early war years, the British had been apprehensive that propaganda focused on indiscriminate Allied retribution could boomerang and stiffen resistance. The Allied nations, they emphasized, had issued a death sentence on Hitler and the Nazi regime but not yet on the German people. Russian broadcasts also warned Germans to dissociate themselves from Hitler and the Nazis if they wished to escape sharing the impending doom. Until mid-1943 BBC broadcasts contained distinctions between the criminal Nazi leadership and the German people, but after that date the Allies changed their tactics and repeatedly emphasized that the Nazi crimes were being committed in the name of the entire German people. The Allies also emphasized that the longer the population tolerated this, the longer would be the account against them, including moral responsibility for the atrocities involving the German nation.[42]

To counter this line the Nazi media took two steps: it supplied moral justification for what was being done in order to ease the public conscience and at the same time warned that it was too late to abandon ship. Stressing the consensus experienced in a popular war, German propaganda emphasized that nobody need feel guilty about fighting a total war because it was a struggle for survival that demanded the most drastic measures. The reassurances, however, were coupled with a propaganda campaign centered on the theme "if should we lose," aimed at eliciting cooperation and raising awareness of the consequences of defeat. The signals sent out to the population were that too many outrages had been committed in the name of the German people to allow any understanding to be reached with the democracies.

Typical of this course of action were the warnings issued by Paul Wegener, Gauleiter of the Weser-Ems district. In order to strengthen his hold over the party's rank and file and create an esprit de corps, he emphasized the horrors the Germans could expect in case of defeat. He reproached the party activists: "Everything was very much all right as long as the ship made '*Kraft durch Freude*' trips; at present, however, when it is sailing in stormy waters, people have turned blue and green with sea-sickness and wish to get off, but those who want to disembark now will be the first to be drowned."[43] Another case in point is Ley's reminder to party leaders in Cologne that every National Socialist had burnt his bridges upon joining the party.[44] Finally, the *Hakenkreuz Banner* on August 1, 1943, summed up this psychological manipulation: "There is no Party member who has not come to the sober conclusion that, in the event of a plutocratic victory, he and his comrades would be the first to be liquidated by Jewish hangmen. By taking the National Socialist oath we consciously burnt our bridges. These bridges have been burnt behind the entire German people. It is victory or death."

These warnings were also directed at the general public. The Nazis had helped to generate a sense of being a victim and to counterbalance guilt feelings by turning the war into an act of self-defense. However, Goebbels's speeches in Munich in October and in Wuppertal in November of 1942 also bear the stamp of an increasingly important theme in his post-Stalingrad propaganda, namely that the victims were fighting for their very existence and faced possible annihilation. German propaganda devoted its efforts toward convincing the nation that, should Germany lose the war, the Allies would destroy the entire German people, and therefore only two alternatives remained: perish or win the war at all costs. On November 15, 1942, in *Das Reich*, Goebbels wrote that there was no turning back, and in his notorious speech of February 18, 1943, he gave the unvarnished truth, admitting that Germany had underestimated the Russians and that the Germans were fighting for their very existence, for their families, women, and children, thereby making total war the only alternative to total destruction. The danger which was threatening the Reich and Europe, he warned, eclipsed all previous world dangers. It is in this context that we must regard the public announcements on the extermination of European Jewry. They came to complement the awareness that not only were Germans victims, fighting for their very existence, but that they had done things that made retreat impossible.

Following a talk with Göring, Goebbels noted in his diary: "The Reichs-marschall knows perfectly well what is in store for us all if we weaken. On the Jewish question especially, we took a position from which there is no escape. That is a good thing. A movement and a people who have burned their bridges fight with much greater determination than those who are still able to retreat."[45] In *Das Reich* of

November 11, 1943, he wrote: "We destroyed the bridges behind us, we can't—but we also don't want to—go back." There is evidence that other Nazis also understood that even if they wished to, they could not leave. Thus, for example, Globocnik, when drunk, confessed that he would have liked to get out, but he was in too deep and he had to win or perish with Hitler.[46]

The leadership carefully allowed these feelings to spill over onto other people who were not directly involved in the Final Solution, including the general public, as a test of loyalty. A telling instance of the connection between the rumors about what was happening to the Jews and the attempt to incriminate everybody in the Final Solution is furnished by Göring's speech on Harvest Thanksgiving, October 4, 1942. As he accorded high decorations to farmers, his broadcast resorted to the typical Nazi forms of manipulation: seduction and intimidation. He understood that people had to be ensnared by being shown that a leader merely helped realize popular hopes and wishes. To seduce his audience he alluded to the enslavement of the Poles and Russians in order to feed the Germans. He made it clear, however, that the need had been satisfied through ruthless means and that the realization of these wishes exacted a price. The price had already been paid and there was no going back. Consequently, the ensuing intimidation was an unequivocal and direct warning:

> And this I would also like to tell the German people and engrave it in their hearts: what the fate of the German people would be if we don't win this war. . . . If the war is lost, you are exterminated. The Jew with his unvanquished hatred stands behind these ideas of extermination. . . . This is not the Second World War, this is the great race war. . . . Let no one deceive himself with the belief that he can come and say 'I was always a good democrat under the vulgar Nazis.' The Jew will give you the same answer whether you say you where the greatest Jew-lover or Jew-hater. He will treat both equally because his vengeance is for the entire German people. There must be no rift, no lack of confidence *nor should one babble idiotic rumors*. Also he who chats out of stupidity implicates himself. [Italics mine—D.B.][47]

A report on the public mood written during the same week as Göring's speech leaves no room for doubt as to the rumors he had in mind. The report sent that week to the party chancellery stated:

> In the course of the work on the Final Solution of the Jewish question, the population in various parts of Germany has recently begun to discuss the 'very harsh measures' against the Jews, especially in the Eastern territories. Inquiries have revealed that these discussions—often distortions and exaggerations—stem from stories told by soldiers on leave from units fighting in the East, who themselves were able to witness such measures.[48]

In mid-1943 the propaganda continued to insist that the Jews would never accept a distinction between those who supported the Nazis and those who were coerced into following them and, as the following evidence shows, there is no doubt that the message did not fall on deaf ears. The impression that the whole nation was incriminated in overstepping moral boundaries along with their leaders and would therefore suffer the same fate as they is evident in the report of a perceptive Swedish correspondent who returned from Berlin. "Goebbels has allowed so much information on German crimes to filter through," he commented, "that everyone is conscious of shared responsibility and guilt, and afraid of personal retaliation."[49]

A similar assessment was furnished a few months later in December 1943 by an Italian officer formerly attached to his country's embassy in Berlin. He, too, noticed that the official propaganda included Nazi crimes as a group unification factor and that frankness and realism were methods employed not only to create a false sense of popular participation but to actually shift responsibility onto the people. He informed U.S. intelligence that what the Nazis said carried the implicit message of what they did in order to nurture a sense of guilt in the population. And since the Germans feared the consequences of what had been done, Hitler exploited their apprehensions in his propaganda.[50] Finally, according to documents in the files of the psychological warfare branch of the U.S. Army, many Germans suspected that the Nazis were continuing to fight because they no longer had anything to lose. Through the interrogation of deserters, for example, Allied intelligence learned that people believed that Hitler was carrying on with the war because he had gone too far with the atrocities committed against political opponents and Jews, and he was afraid of being brought to account for his deeds.[51]

At the end of the war and in the face of defeatist trends, when no more seduction could be offered, only intimidation remained. In 1945 the party tried to bolster German morale by stressing the responsibility of the entire German people for the war and its consequences, and a steady campaign was conducted to this end in the press, in the speeches of Gau- and Kreisleiter, and at party evening courses. It was pointed out that Hitler was no dictator and that time and again his policy had been borne out by the people, initially at elections and then later by plebiscites showing a one hundred percent majority for the Führer. In this connection the population was reminded that they had supported the party's aims from the beginning and that many of them thereby had enriched themselves.[52]

This line, of enforcing collective responsibility on those who would shift the blame for what had happened onto others who should be made to pay, was clearly articulated in the *Schwarze Korps* of January 25, 1945. The article "Lambs of Innocence" referred to the words of Omar Bradley, who had allegedly affirmed in early December that the Americans were not fighting only against Hitler and his supporters but against the whole German nation. "He is right," affirmed the paper, "these lambs of innocence thoroughly enjoyed and benefited from economic prosperity due to National Socialism. . . . They had no objection to Aryanizing Jewish shops and businesses and thus taking part in the general boom."[53] It was too late for them to claim innocence. Public cooperation was enlisted by driving home the realization that all that had been done by the Nazis had been done for the sake of the people. Thus, by sharing in the responsibility for Nazi policy, all Germans had become hostages in the attempt from above to ward off desertion.

In conclusion, a comprehensive analysis of the available data shows that the cooperative nature of the crimes had an equalizing effect beyond the active participants in the killing operations. Publicizing the extermination to the population served a function for the Nazi regime because it became a substitute for military victory; it became a sort of moral success to cover up military disasters and divert public attention from them. Second, the crime was revealed in order to galvanize the population, enforce continued adherence and group loyalty, and prevent desertion. This became especially important from 1942 onwards when the announcement that Jews were being exterminated served as a group unification factor to preclude desertion and force the Germans to continue fighting. Germans were fed the knowledge that too many atrocities had been committed, especially against the Jews, to allow for an understanding to be reached with the Allies.

NOTES

1. Helmut Sündermann, *Tagesparolen: Deutsche Presseweisungen 1939–1945* (Leoni am Starnberger, 1973), p. 259. See also Ephraim Maron, "The 'Press Policy' of the Third Reich on Jewish Questions and Its Reflection in the Nazi Press and in Liberal Papers," doctoral diss., University of Tel Aviv, 1991, vol. 2, pp. 307–13.

2. Bundesarchiv Koblenz (hereafter BAK), NS 18 alt/62.

3. Sündermann, *Tagesparolen*, p. 256. To the best of my knowledge, this was also the policy of the collaborationist press. In France, for example, nothing was mentioned about the massive roundup of Jews in July 1942. All that *Au Pilori* disclosed to its readership was that "the Jewish race was going to disappear in an absolute fashion." See Ph. Burrin, "Qui savaient les collaborationnistes?" in Stéphane Courtois and Adam Rayski, *Qui savait quoi? L'extermination des Juifs, 1941–1945* (Paris, 1987), p. 77.

4. BAK, NS 18 alt/622; Louis P. Lochner, ed., *The Goebbels Diaries* (New York, 1974), p. 193. Hershel Grynspan was extradited to Germany in July 1940 and the Nazis held him in jail while they prepared a show trial. That trial was never held and what happened to Grynspan is unknown.

5. Willy A. Boelcke, *The Secret Conferences of Dr. Goebbels 1939–1943* (New York, 1970), p. 309.

6. Ibid., pp. 308–11; Lochner, *Goebbels Diaries*, p. 274; Michael Balfour, *Propaganda in War 1939–1945: Organizations, Policies and Publics in Britain and Germany* (London, 1979), pp. 303–304.

7. Christopher R. Browning, *Fateful Months* (New York, 1985), pp. 110–11; Richard Breitman, *The Architect of Genocide: Himmler and the Final Solution* (New York, 1991), p. 219; Eberhard Jäckel, *Hitler in History* (London, 1984), p. 159. The instructions to the press also forbade mentioning the situation of the Jews in the East or quoting from German newspapers that appeared in the occupied territories.

8. Eugen Kogon et al., eds., *Nationalsozialistische Massentötungen durch Giftgas: Eine Dokumentation* (Frankfurt/M., 1983), pp. 113–14.

9. Jeremy Noakes and Geoffrey Pridham, eds., *Nazism 1919–1945* (Exeter, 1988), vol. 3, p. 1149.

10. BAK, R43 II/649b. Civilians who vented rumors about the killing of Jews were condemned to death, not because of what they said about the Jews, but because they were spreading defeatist propaganda and undermining the belief in Hitler. See, for example, the July 13, 1943, sentence against a craftsman in Wiesbaden who said, among other things, that Jews were poisoned with gas; on September 15, 1943, against a dentist in Hanover who said that one million Jews had been murdered; or the sentence on October 2, 1943, against an inhabitant of Liegnitz (Walter Wagner, *Der Volksgerichtshof im nationalsozialistischen Staat* [Stuttgart, 1974], pp. 287, 295, 304).

11. *International Military Tribunal*, vol. 1, NO-205, p. 721.

12. Akten des persönlichen Stabes des RFSS, BAK, NS 19/neu 1686.

13. BAK, NS 18/188. On the value of antisemitism in Hitler's foreign propaganda, see September 10, 1943, BAK, NS 18/225 and ADAP, D, 4, p. 293.

14. Noakes and Pridham, eds., *Nazism*, vol. 3, p. 1150.

15. Speech to Reich leaders and Gauleiters on October 6, 1943, in *Heinrich Himmler: Geheimreden 1933 bis 1945*, ed. Bradley F. Smith and Agnes F. Peterson (Frankfurt/M., 1974), pp. 170–71. See also the memorandum of Franke Gricksch presented as evidence in the Treblinka trial, Institut für Zeitgeschichte, Munich, Zs 1931/Akz 4083/68, printed in Gerald Fleming, *Hitler and the Final Solution* (Oxford, 1986), pp. 147–53.

16. Raul Hilberg, *The Destruction of the European Jews* (Chicago, 1961), pp. 658–62.

17. Hitler referred to his Jewish policy in his public speeches of January 30, 1941; January 30, 1942; February 24, 1942; September 30, 1942; November 8, 1942; February 24, 1943; and March 21, 1943. See Max Domarus, *Hitler, Reden und Proklamationen 1932–1945* (Wiesbaden, 1963).

18. Walter Gross, "Die Rassenpolitischen Voraussetzungen zur Lösung der Judenfrage," *Weltkampf* (April–September 1941), p. 52.

19. "Die Macht der Idee!" *Der Angriff*, May 24/25/26, 1942; "Terror, Mord und Hunger," *Der Angriff*, June 14, 1942; *Das Reich*, June 6, 1942.

20. See Goebbels's "Der Luft und Nervenkrieg," *Das Reich*, June 14, 1942. Goebbels's articles in *Das Reich* were read over the radio on Friday evenings and sometimes rebroadcast on Sundays. See also Carin Kessemeier, *Der Leitartikler Goebbels in den NS-Organen "Der Angriff" und "Das Reich"* (Münster, 1967).

21. Quoted in *Jewish News* 23 (June 2, 1943), p. 134.

22. Robert Ley, "Von Moses bis Stalin," *Der Angriff*, March 19, 1944. Cf. Goebbels's articles "Das Jahr 2000," *Das Reich*, January 21 and February 25, 1945.

23. October 27, 1941, BAK, NS 18 alt/622. See also the instructions of August 21, 1941, to highlight all anti-German utterances of Jews as a step preparatory to the expected marking of Jews (Uwe D. Adam, *Judenpolitik im Dritten Reich* [Düsseldorf, 1972], p. 336).

24. On the public mood at the end of 1941, see Heinz Boberach, *Meldungen aus dem Reich* (Herrsching, 1984), vol. 18, pp. 3069ff.; Kurt Pätzold and Erika Schwarz, *Tagesordnung: Judenmord. Die Wannsee Konferenz 20. Januar 1942* (Berlin, 1992).

25. April 22, 1943, BAK, NS 18/188; June 9, 1943, ibid., NS 18/225; March 15, 1943, ibid., NS 18/224; NS18 alt/622, and the instructions to highlight the Jewish question in the anti-Bolshevik drive, ibid., NS 18/224.

26. Ralf G. Reuth, *Joseph Goebbels* (Munich, 1990), p. 520.

27. *Wille und Macht* (September–October 1943).

28. Robert Ley, "Der Jude bedeutet den Tod," *Der Angriff*, June 6, 1943.

29. David Bankier, *The Germans and the Final Solution* (Oxford, 1992), pp. 145–51.

30. *Central European Observer*, August 20, 1943, p. 244. Cf. "Die Juden sind unser Unglück," *Der Stürmer*, February 18, 1943.

31. Yad Vashem Archives, 03/4646.

32. Reuth, entry for January 20, 1942, vol. 4, p. 1735.

33. Ernst Kris and Hans Speier, *German Radio Propaganda* (Oxford, 1944), p. 44.

34. H. R. Trevor Roper, *Hitler's Table Talk, 1941–1944* (London, 1973), p. 87.

35. On Hitler's prophecies, see his speech on November 8, 1935, in Norman H. Baynes, *The Speeches of Adolf Hitler* (London, 1942), p. 136; Hannah Arendt, *The Origins of Totalitarianism* (New York, 1969), p. 348; Kris and Speier, *German Radio Propaganda*, p. 108.

36. See the transcription of his speech in *Goebbels Reden 1939–1945*, Helmut Heiber ed. (Düsseldorf, 1972), vol. 2, p. 183. To the best of my knowledge the thesis of a guilt bond was first suggested by Ernst Kris, "The Covenant of the Gangsters," *Journal of Criminal Psychopathology* 4 (1943): 445–58. See also Leo Alexander, "War Crimes and Their Motivation," *Journal of Criminal Law and Criminology* 39 (1948): 298–326; Hannah Arendt, "Organisierte Schuld," in *Sechs Essays* (Heidelberg, 1948); Leon Poliakov, *Harvest of Hate* (Syracuse, 1954), pp. 110–11; and more recently Shlomo Aronson, "Die dreifache Falle: Hitlers Judenpolitik, die Alliierten und die Juden," *Vierteljahrshefte für Zeitgeschichte* 32 (1984): 29–65; Jörg Bohse, *Inszenierte Kriegsbegeisterung und ohnmächtiger Friedenswille: Meinungslenkung und Propaganda im NS* (Stuttgart, 1988), p. 80. For a different view, see Erich Goldhagen, "Obsession and Realpolitik in the 'Final Solution,'" *Patterns of Prejudice* 12 (1978): 1–16.

37. In talks with Bormann he spoke in the first person: "If I win this war I shall put an end to the Jewish world power, I'll deal it a death blow"; "I have exterminated the Jews" (*Hitlers politisches Testament: Die Bormann Diktate von Februar und April 1945* [Hamburg, 1981], pp. 43, 66, 69). I wish to thank Isidoro Blikstein, José Fiorin, and Diana Luz Pessoa de Barros of the Department of Linguistics of the University of São Paulo for their comments on my analysis of Hitler's discursive tactics. See also José Luiz Fiorin, *O Regime de 1964: Discurso e ideologia* (São Paulo, 1988); Dominique Maingeneau, *Nouvelles tendences au analyse du discours* (Paris, 1987); and Oswald Ducrot, *Dire et pas dire* (Paris, 1991).

38. Entry of January 23, 1943, Reuth, vol. 4, p. 1878

39. Baynes, *Speeches*, vol. 1, p. 75–76.

40. Albert Speer, *Spandau: The Secret Diaries* (New York, 1976), p. 221.

41. Leon Poliakov, *Harvest of Hate* (London, 1956), p. 111.

42. Balfour, *Propaganda*, p. 302; Conrad Pütter, *Rundfunk gegen das "Dritte Reich"* (Munich, New York, 1986), p. 94.

43. Research Department, Foreign Office, Memoranda on Axis-controlled Europe, December 14, 1943, PRO, FO 371/34440.

44. DNB, May 29, 1943.

45. Entry of March 2, 1943, Lochner, *Goebbels Diaries*, p. 299.

46. Henry V. Dicks, *Licenced Mass Murder* (Sussex, 1972), p. 203.

47. Rede des Reichsmarschalls Hermann Göring zum Erntedanktag im Berliner Sportpalast am 4. Oktober 1942, Berlin 1942. The argument that in the context of a total war between Jewry and Germany no one would be able to escape if Germany lost the war was also employed by Himmler in his address to SS generals on November 8, 1938. See Himmler, *Geheimreden*, p. 38.

48. "Vertrauliche Informationen der Parteikanzlei, October 9, 1942," reprinted in *Das Dritte Reich: Seine Geschichte in Texten, Bildern und Dokumenten*, ed. Heinz Huber and Artur Müller (Munich, 1964), vol. 2, p. 110.

49. *Central European Observer*, August 20, 1943.

50. December 1943, National Archives, Washington, D.C., RG 226/ 54577, box 623.

51. Ibid., RG 226, 60576, box 703.

52. Ibid., RG 226, OSS 190 E Bern 86; Bern OSS OP 31.

53. "Unschuldslämmer," *Schwarze Korps*, January 25, 1945, p. 5.

6.

STEVEN T. KATZ

The Holocaust

A VERY PARTICULAR RACISM

Our understanding of the Nazi state as thoroughly racist has increased dramatically over the past decade. In Europe, Israel, and the United States, scholars have produced impressive, informed studies of most of the major aspects of the instantiation of racial theory in the Third Reich. So we have important examinations of the development of modern racism;[1] of women under Nazism;[2] of the treatment of the insane in Hitler's Reich, with its profound corruption of medical science and practice, mislabeled by its murderous practitioners as a program of "euthanasia";[3] we also have studies of the persecution of homosexuals[4] and of the deadly campaign against the Gypsies.[5] And, of course, a mountain of material exists on the genocidal war against the Jews, a subject with which everyone is familiar. In sum, this explosion of scholarship on all aspects of racial theory and practice as incarnate in Hitler's Reich certainly justifies the title of Michael Burleigh and Wolfgang Wippermann's overview of the German polity between 1933 and 1945, *The Racial State*.

Given this prior scholarship, it is unnecessary to speak in generalities. Instead, I wish to develop, to pick up and decode, the particular theme of Nazi antisemitism—both as it is continuous with, as well as distinctive from, other aspects of Nazi racial theory and practice. In order to do so it is important to begin with an understanding of the larger premise that undergirds the entire Nazi enterprise, and the specific distinctions that attend this elemental starting point. The larger premise to which I refer is the biologistic one that conceives of society in terms of health and disease. This concept derives from a curious mix of anthropological, linguistic, biological, sociological, Darwinian, and philosophical notions, with some considerable debt to romantic theories of the state and society. From this emerged the false model of human society as an "organic" reality in which hereditary and genetic forces putatively played a role similar to that played by heredity and genetic factors in the health of an individual. Accordingly, the language of medicine and medical-racial hygiene was extended to apply to society at large, now understood in terms of primal racial characteristics. As such, social and political issues were reframed in the discourse of medicine. Social and political realia were now described, for example, as "healthy" or "diseased," as well as in a related vocabulary that freely utilized diagnostic categories such as the "pathological," the "cancerous," and the "degenerate." Indeed, it was this distinctive universe of ideas that provided the doctrinal base for Nazism's racial engineering in the name of a "healthy social order."

So one was justified, upon taking power in 1933, in passing laws to protect the German state, and still more the Aryan people, from further degeneration from within and contamination from without. And this led to *two* types of action. Although both had their roots in the biological, medical, and racial dogmas to which I have already alluded, they were quite different policies. These differing, albeit complementary, policies I shall call "pseudoeugenic" programs and "pseudoracial" programs. The former cover actions such as the forced sterilization and/or murder of cripples, the asocial, the incurable, the elderly, homosexuals, and the chronically sick. The latter cover actions against Gypsies, Slavic peoples, blacks, people of mixed race, and, with certain additional differentiations that I will yet come to, Jews.

The need to make the distinction between those marked out and persecuted on the grounds of "pseudoeugenics" versus those marked out and persecuted on the grounds of "pseudoracism" resides in this decisive fact: all those whom I identify as victims of misconceived eugenic theory were Aryans (and Christians). They were not identified as belonging to a different, inferior, or dangerous racial group. That is, they were not "racial enemies" in the same sense as were Slavs, blacks, or, most specifically, Jews; nor were they "racial criminals" by definition as, for example, were Jews. Whatever the bureaucratic and ideological links between the so-called "euthanasia" program between 1939 and 1941 (i.e., in personnel and techniques) and the "Final Solution to the Jewish Problem," the two programs are phenomenologically— not morally—different. And this not least in that the "euthanasia" program was not wholly a prioristic (as was Nazi antisemitism). Note, for example, the requirement that adults targeted by the T4 program had to be independently evaluated by three physicians. One need have no illusions about the morality of this activity to recognize that this procedure is disjunctive with the process and principles followed in the murder of the Jewish people—they were exterminated solely by definition—nor was it, in actuality or by definition, racial, if by "racial" we mean something like "in opposition to an alternate racial group or people."

Moreover, according to eugenic theory, "superior" qualities did not, per definitionem, reside only in certain races but could be found across races—at least so the eugenics formulation of those such as Francis Galton, the founding high priest of the eugenics movement. According to this theoretical reading, "inferior" qualities resided in all groups and races, and hence selective breeding and "population management" was a requirement for all peoples bent on "race improvement." One may rightfully be astonished at the sociobiological mumbo jumbo of Galton, and of those such as Wilhelm Schallmeyer, whose works [*Verehung und Auslese: Grundriss der Gesellschaftsbiologie und Lehre vom Rassedienst* (Jena, 1903), and *Beiträge zu einer Nationalbiologie* (Jena, 1905)] were influential treatises on the theme.[6] It is nevertheless imperative to recognize that Schallmeyer, for example, saw his thesis as universally applicable to all peoples. Moreover, he denied there were any untainted racial groups left in Europe, and dismissed Aryan racial theories as unscientific ideologies. And his fellow eugenicist, Alfred Plötz, earlier counted the Jews as parallel to the Aryans in being one of nature's naturally superior races.[7] In addition, the metaphysical power imputed to Jews by Nazism—a decisive factor in its Judeophobia—was totally absent from eugenic speculation about "inferior" races. Many well-known eugenicists did slide over into an all too easy alliance with Nazism, for example, Karl Pearson, Galton's English disciple; and eventually Alfred Plötz and Eugen Fischer enthusiastically embraced Hitler's racial policies of the 1930s. Yet this human failing was not a logical consequence of eugenic theory. Racial biological theorists would find eugenics an ally but only by "adapting" it according to their own a priori metaphysics that, in actuality, had distinctive conceptual roots. Most important, and analytically decisive vis-à-vis classification, the eugenicists "were not concerned with stigmatizing an inferior race as the villains in the drama of survival."[8]

In connection with the specific discussion of the status of the Jews, it is significant that many early eugenicists did not believe that their theorizing entailed antisemitism, or even that the Jews were a separate race—taking into account the considerable blond populace—or that Jews were inherently inferior. It therefore behooves us to take great care in describing and categorizing these eugenic theories (and theorists), however much we may (and should) disagree with their diagnoses and prescriptions. These pre-Nazi eugenicists are not simply to be equated with, even as mere precursors of, Nazi racial murderers. This conclusion is justified by a close review of the official literature and programs of both the British Eugenics Education Society and its German equivalent. Neither preached racial conflict or the adoption of genocidal policies toward inferior races. The mystification of racial thought essential to the ideology of parasitological racism, which led in turn to Einsatzgruppen and death camps, was not integral to eugenic doctrines. The former, however, often was combined with the latter after 1933 by individual practitioners and by the Nazis in general.

It is also relevant to recognize that the insane, alcoholics, the feebleminded, the epileptic, and the blind, deaf, and dumb are not a group—a people—in the same sense as are Jews and Gypsies. Then, too, though these individuals—always identified as individuals—were perceived as constituting a "health" danger, according to the dominant metaphysical-political ideology, they lacked the mythic power, qua individuals, as well as the larger Manichean mythographic placement associated with Jews.

Moreover, and this is important, it is this phenomenological characteristic, that is, the fact that it was "eugenically unfit" Aryan Christians who belonged to the racial-religious majority who were being murdered, that led to nationwide hostility to this program. That antipathy resulted in the official cessation of this activity on August 24, 1941, after approximately 93,000 persons had been killed under its provisions. (We now know that this killing did continue, if in a more oblique and limited fashion, after 1941.) Here we should understand that this significant opposition involved many influential factors—including genuine moral sensibilities, personal connections with victims, self-interest ("I too will be old and sick one day"), and utilitarian and economic motives given the costs of caring for the sick and elderly[9]—that simply did not apply in the war against those "Others" distinguished by pseudoracial attributes.

This is not to deny the implications, and consequences—the 300,000 to 400,000 people sterilized[10]—of the Law for the Prevention of Progeny with Hereditary

Diseases, of July 14, 1933, and its later emendations, supplemented by Führer orders, and still further legislation. Among those additional steps were Himmler's decree on "the preventive fight against crime" of December 14, 1937, and the amendments to paragraph 175 of the criminal code, dealing with homosexuals, introduced in 1935. Nor is it to underestimate the horrific actions perpetrated under the T4 program, for example, the murder of 70,000 mental patients, and the further acts undertaken under the November 24, 1933, Law against Dangerous Habitual Criminals. But it is to comprehend that these criminal proceedings, particularly the T4 actions, were all intra-Aryan undertakings, undertaken according to Nazi dogma, to "protect the health of the Aryan race" rather than to protect the Aryan bloodstock from the distinctive, alternative threat of external racial poisoning. Reproduction by the mentally ill, by vagrants, drunks, criminals, prostitutes, and other "asocials," was, to those holding Nazi views, a cause for concern, but such reproduction constituted a crime that was racial in a sense other than that utilized when one speaks of the inter-racial crime of miscegenation. It should be noted that even under the T4 program "Jewish inmates of institutions in Germany did not have to meet the ordinary criteria for medical killing [mental deficiency or schizophrenia, length of hospitalization, capacity to work, and the like]. The total extermination of this group of asylum inmates was the logical consequence of the 'radical solution' of the Jewish problem being embarked upon."[11] That is, even in the context of the "euthanasia" program, Jews were treated differently.

Contrast this internal, racial-hygienic, pseudoeuthanasia policy with the complementary, but separate, pseudoracial policy of the Third Reich. In this specific context, that is, in relation to non-Aryan peoples, the asserted danger is *racial*. It is racial in the sense most usually associated with that particular notion—the putative competition and conflict between different *types* of persons defined by their inherited, genetically derived group identities (including the contended negative consequences of miscegenation). Gypsies, Slavs, blacks, Mischlinge, and Jews are *not* Aryans. The threat they represent to Aryan blood is not that of a "diseased gene" within the otherwise "healthy" Aryan body, but rather that of a racial admixing that will—if enacted—eventuate in the disappearance of a "pure" Aryan biological community, with all the sociopolitical and normative consequences that such racial "pollution" would produce.

As a rule, these "racial" groups, except in the case of the Jews, were defined as inferior people within the parameters of a common humanity.[12] Their "inferiority" (and this is the key factor) marked them out for conquest, deculturation, and helotization—their permanent reduction to the status of a quasi-slave population in the service of Aryan masters. The actual policy implemented vis-à-vis the conquered Slavic peoples is the clearest example we have of this programmatic design. Despite erroneous claims to the contrary, the Slavic peoples, once politically decapitated, once their intellectual and sociopolitical elites were eliminated, were *not* targeted for total physical eradication. To put it more directly, they were *not* subject to a fully genocidal assault.

This brings us to our third division, that is, our second branch of the "pseudo-racism" category: the Jews. The Jews clearly were perceived as constituting a different type of structural-racial-metaphysical threat to the Nazi racial design than did the sick, the insane, and the elderly on the one hand, and Gypsies, Slavs, and blacks on the other. Working backwards from the fact—and it is a fact—that only the Jewish people were marked out for total annihilation, we need to ask: Why? Why the Jews? Why were they alone the target of an uncompromising, unmediated, all-inclusive program of extermination.

In beginning to answer this central question, one broad if elemental truth should be recognized at the outset: Hitler's "Jew" is *not* rooted in empirical realities, in how things are in the world. Rather, and seminal, his "Jew" is an inversion, a doctrinally generated distortion of objective historical and sociopolitical conditions both Jewish and non-Jewish. Economic and political events, for example, the economic crises of the 1920s and 1930s, Germany's defeat in World War I, the liberal politics of the Weimar Republic, the Russian Revolution, the development of Marxism, modernist cultural movements, and the spread of syphilis in Europe, provide the cover for Hitler's paranoid explanations; they do not cause them. Conversely, these diverse events are not actually accounted for by the Führer's "explanations." Therefore, to look for reasons for Hitler's antisemitism in the sense of causes, for example, in inflationary or depressionary spirals, upward or downward mobility, political change or instability, Marxist ideology or Christian morality, as many scholars are wont to do, is to miss the most elemental point: no primary cause(s) of this sort exists. Hitler's depiction of the "Jew" and the centrality of this stereotype in his Weltanschauung is, at root, mythic. Or, put another way, Hitler's hatred would exist (did exist) and would continue to exist, no matter what Jews did or did not do. Thus, as he was murdering millions of Jews, nearly two-thirds of all the Jews of Europe, he was ranting about "Jewish power"—some power!

That Hitler's antisemitism was of a mythic variety certainly did not make it inefficacious or reduce it to solipsistic fantasy, as the history of the war years reveals. Indeed, it was precisely the inviolability of the stereotype, the lack of any possibility of disconfirmation, that contributed to the metahistoric, cosmic claims so important to Nazi rhetoric. The destiny of the Jew, and the fate of his pollution-ridden contact with others, was not a contingent, malleable factor that belonged to the empirical realm, but was an absolute, unchanging feature of the ontologically primitive skeleton of historical being itself. As Himmler told Rudolf Höss, the commandant of Auschwitz, "Jews are the eternal enemy of the German people, and must be exterminated. All Jews within our grasp are to be destroyed without exception."[13] The cancerous, oppositional nature of the Jew was a first principle of racial metaphysics, an a priori postulate of Hitler's (and others') conceptual universe. Hence, when one seeks to decipher Hitler's antisemitism and the enacted racial program of the Third Reich, one should not err in thinking that what is decisive is biology or race of any immanent, even if pseudoscientific, sort. Racism (antisemitism) is, in this milieu, a category of metaphysics. Parenthetically, as a corollary of its mythicality, I would also note that Nazism, in contradistinction to all the rhetoric of breeding and race, employed religion, at least in part, to define, according to its own Nuremberg formulations, "who is a Jew." Therefore, one must avoid a reductionist, "quasi-empirical" sense of the "war against the Jews" that would suggest this confrontation represented an authentic racial—as compared to a metaphysical—war.

One needs to understand that blood, that is, race, is a key element in Hitler's discourse, but it receives its valence from a more comprehensive metaphysical-mythological structure. "Those who see in National Socialism nothing more than a political movement," Hitler observed—and, we might add, scholars who erroneously decipher Nazism as primarily an expression of class struggle or nationalism, or even racism, understanding this latter term narrowly—"know scarcely anything of it. It is more even than a religion: it is the will to create mankind anew."[14]

I fully recognize that this is not the standard language of racism, nor the usual mode of the scholarly analysis of racial theory. But then Hitler's extraordinarily vile Manichean anti-Jewish discourse—the "Jew as the personification of the devil,"[15] the "Jew as the symbol of evil,"[16] the Jew "as parasite upon the nations,"[17] the Jew "as vampire,"[18] Jewish victory as meaning only suffocating "in filth and offal"[19]—does not describe in any meaningful sense an actual racial view. Rather, Hitler's language gives elementary expression to a radical, if bizarre, transcendental doctrine that employs the notion of race, in its own peculiar version, to express a larger systematic comprehension of the historical and metahistorical order. As such, to decipher it correctly requires a hermeneutic method that is appropriate. By this I mean one that confronts and decodes the axiological propositions made, and thus, in turn, requires an appreciation of the overarching Judeophobic form of the whole from which individual normative propositions flow in a nonreductionistic manner, as well as an understanding that these assertions and prescriptions are *metaphysical* proposals and recommendations, even if phrased in part in the idiom of blood and race.[20]

In this, Hitler's antisemitism differs from his other "pseudoracial" beliefs. Not that his other "pseudoracial" convictions make any more sense when they are depicted and understood in less metaphysical (and mythic) terms. Nor should one forget that these complementary views of other non-Aryan peoples are also intrinsically connected with his larger metaphysical program. But there is something distinctive about Nazi antisemitism, about antisemitism within the conceptual and practical parameters of Nazism, that marks it out from the other hateful, violent forms of eugenic and racial diagnosis that existed within the Third Reich.

NOTES

1. See, for example, Peter Weingart, Jürgen Kroll, and Kurt Bayertz, *Rasse, Blut, und Gene: Geschichte der Eugenik und Rassenhygiene in Deutschland* (Frankfurt/M., 1988); Hans-Walter Schmuhl, *Rassenhygiene, Nationalsozialismus, Euthanasie: Von der Verhütung zur Vernichtung "lebensunwerten Lebens," 1890–1945* (Göttingen, 1987); Paul Weindling, *Health, Race, and German Politics between National Unification and Nazism, 1870–1945* (Cambridge, 1989); the many wonderfully suggestive contributions of George Mosse; and William H. Schneider's valuable research on French racial views, *Quality and Quantity: The Quest for Biological Regeneration in Twentieth-Century France* (New York: Cambridge University Press, 1990).

2. On this important topic consult Gisela Bock, *Zwangssterilisation im Nationalsozialismus: Studien zur Rassenpolitik und Frauenpolitik* (Opladen, 1986); Renate Bridenthal, Atina Grossmann, and Marion Kaplan, eds., *When Biology Became Destiny: Women in Weimar*

and Nazi Germany (New York, 1984); the contributions to the following wide-ranging collections: *Frauengruppe Faschismusforschung,* and *Mutterkreuz und Arbeitsbuch* (Frankfurt/ M., 1981); Maruta Schmidt et al., eds., *Frauen unterm Hakenkreuz* (Berlin, 1983); Rita Thalmann, *Frauensein im Dritten Reich* (Munich, 1984); Renate Wiggershaus, *Frauen unterm Nationalsozialismus* (Wuppertal, 1984); Claudia Koonz, *Mothers in the Fatherland: Women, the Family and Nazi Politics* (New York, 1986); and Jill Stephenson, *Women in Nazi Society* (London, 1976).

3. Some of the relevant studies are: Alexander Mitscherlich and Fred Mielke, eds., *Medizin ohne Menschlichkeit: Dokumente des Nürnberger Ärzteprozesses* (Stuttgart, 1948, reprinted Frankfurt/M., 1989); Klaus Dörner, "Nationalsozialismus und Lebensvernichtung," *Vierteljahrshefte für Zeitgeschichte* 15 (1968): 121ff.; Karl Dietrich Erdmann, "'Lebensunwertes Leben.' Totalitäre Lebensvernichtung und das Problem der Euthanasie," *Geschichte in Wissenschaft und Unterricht* 26 (1975): 215–25; Lothar Gruchmann, "'Euthanasie' und Justiz im Dritten Reich," *Vierteljahrshefte für Zeitgeschichte* 20 (1971): 235–79; Kurt Nowak, *Euthanasie und Sterilisierung im Dritten Reich: Die Konfrontation der evangelischen und katholischen Kirche mit dem "Gesetz zur Verhütung erbkranken Nachwuchses" und der "Euthanasie" Aktion* (Göttingen, 1987); Ernst Klee, *"Euthanasie" im NS-Staat: Die "Vernichtung lebensunwerten Lebens"* (Frankfurt/M., 1983); Achim Thom and Horst Spaar, eds., *Medizin im Faschismus* (East Berlin, 1985); Gisela Bock, *Zwangssterilisation im Nationalsozialismus* (Opladen, 1986); Heidrun Kaupen-Haas, *Der Griff nach der Bevölkerung* (Nördlingen, 1986); Christian Gansmüller, *Die Erbgesundheitspolitik des Dritten Reiches* (Cologne, 1987); Hans-Walter Schmuhl, *Rassenhygiene, Nationalsozialismus, Euthanasie* (Göttingen, 1987), Götz Aly et al., *Aussonderung und Tod: Die klinische Hinrichtung der Unbrauchbaren. Beiträge zur nationalsozialistischen Gesundheits- und Sozialpolitik,* 2nd ed. (Berlin, 1987), vol. 1; idem, *Reform und Gewissen. "Euthanasie" im Dienst des Fortschritts. Beiträge zur nationalsozialistischen Gesundheits- und Sozialpolitik* (Berlin, 1985), vol. 2; Robert Jay Lifton, *The Nazi Doctors: A Study in the Psychology of Evil* (London, 1986); Benno Müller-Hill, *Murderous Science: Elimination by Scientific Selection of Jews, Gypsies, and Others, Germany 1933–1945* (Oxford, 1988); Robert Proctor, *Racial Hygiene: Medicine under the Nazis* (Cambridge, MA, 1988); Paul J. Weindling, *Health, Race and German Politics between National Unification and Nazism 1870–1945* (Cambridge, 1989); Dorothea Sick, *"Euthanasie" im Nationalsozialismus am Beispiel des Kalmenhofs in Idstein im Taunus* (Frankfurt/M., 1983); Manfred Klüppel, *"Euthanasie" und Lebensvernichtung am Beispiel der Landesheilanstalten Haina und Merxhausen: Eine Chronik der Ereignisse 1933–1945* (Kassel, 1984); Gerhard Kneuker and Wulf Steglich, *Begegnungen mit der Euthanasie in Hadamar* (Rehberg-Loccum, 1985); and Dorothee Roer and Dieter Henkel, eds., *Psychiatrie im Faschismus: Die Anstalt Hadamar 1933–1945* (Bonn, 1986).

4. Among the most important works are Burkhard Jellonek, *Homosexuelle unter dem Hakenkreuz: Verfolgung von Homosexuellen im Dritten Reich* (Paderborn, 1990), and Richard Plant, *The Pink Triangle: The Nazi War against Homosexuals* (Edinburgh, 1987).

5. The anti-Gypsy campaign has been analyzed in detail by Wolfgang Günther, *Zur preussischen Zigeunerpolitik seit 1871 . . .: Eine Untersuchung am Beispiel des Landkreises Neustadt am Rübenberge und der Hauptstadt Hannover* (Hanover, 1985); Rainer Hehemann, *Die "Bekämpfung des Zigeunerunwesens" im Wilhelminischen Deutschland und in der Weimarer Republik 1871–1933* (Frankfurt/M., 1987); Tilman Zülch, ed., *In Auschwitz vergast, bis heute verfolgt: Zur Situation der Roma (Zigeuner) in Deutschland* (Reinbek, 1979), pp. 64–88; Wolfgang Wippermann, *Das Leben in Frankfurt zur NS-Zeit,* vol. 2: *Die nationalsozialistische Zigeunerverfolgung* (Frankfurt/M., 1986); Benno Müller-Hill, *Murderous Science: Elimination by Scientific Selection of Jews, Gypsies, and Others, Germany 1933–1945* (Oxford, 1988); Donald Kenrick and Grattan Puxon, *Sinti und Roma: Die Vernichtung eines Volkes im NS-Staat* (Göttingen, 1981); and Reimar Gilsenback, "Die Verfolgung der Sinti—Ein Weg, der nach Auschwitz führte," in *Feinderklärung und Prävention, Beiträge zur nationalsozialistischen Gesundheits- und Sozialpolitik,* vol. 6 (Berlin, 1988), pp. 11–41.

6. For more details, see Sheila Faith Weiss, *Race Hygiene and National Efficiency: The Eugenics of Wilhelm Schallmayer* (Berkeley, 1987).

7. Alfred Plötz, *Der Tüchtigkeit unserer Rasse und der Shutz der Schwachen* (Berlin, 1895).

8. George Mosse, *Toward the Final Solution: A History of European Racism* (New York, 1978), p. 80.

9. The argument was also made that hospital beds were needed for soldiers and others injured in the war, for example, after the mass bombing of Hamburg in 1943. Accordingly, Robert Proctor has argued that the "fundamental argument for forcible euthanasia was economic"; see Robert Proctor, "Nazi Doctors, Racial Medicine and Human Experimentation," in George J. Annas and Michael A. Groden, *The Nazi Doctors and the Nuremberg Code: Human Rights in Human Experimentation* (New York, 1992), p. 24.

10. Lifton, *Nazi Doctors*, p. 27, cites a figure of 200,000 to 350,000.

11. Lifton, *Nazi Doctors*, p. 77.

12. The constraints of the present format preclude taking up the complexities inherent in each particular case. However, I would argue, if space allowed, that this rule applied in the main, with suitable nuances, even to the Gypsies in their generality. I intend to analyze the complex circumstances of the Gypsies under Nazi domination more fully in volume 3 of my *Holocaust in Historical Context* (New York: Oxford University Press, forthcoming).

13. R. Höss, *Commandant of Auschwitz: The Autobiography of Rudolf Höss* (Cleveland, 1959), pp. 205–206.

14. Hitler as reported in Hermann Rauschning, *Gespräche mit Hitler* (New York, 1940), pp. 231–32.

15. *Mein Kampf*, p. 324.

16. Ibid.

17. Ibid., p. 327.

18. Ibid.

19. Ibid., p. 302.

20. I well understand that the materials here cited are all from Hitler, and the early Hitler at that. A fuller, more complete analysis of this elemental issue would therefore necessarily require a broader documentation not only from the later, post–1933, and particularly post–1939 Hitler, but also from other leading and middle-rank members of the Nazi hierarchy, as well as evidence that these views were implemented bureaucratically and juridically throughout the Third Reich. Obviously such an effort is beyond the scope of this paper. However, let my schematic and preliminary comments here serve as an indicator of the relevance of this subject. A fuller presentation and analysis will be provided in volume 3 of my *Holocaust in Historical Context*, forthcoming.

7.

WALTER ZWI BACHARACH

Antisemitism and Racism in Nazi Ideology

Before elaborating on antisemitism, racism, and Nazi ideology, including the interaction among them, let us clarify the meaning of each phenomenon. Regarding antisemitism, a letter written by Ernst Richter, addressed to Professor Friedrich Heer, the Roman Catholic scholar who attacked Christianity for its wrongdoings to the Jews, is quite illustrative:

> Filled with dismay by your article about the Jews—and with satisfaction at the indigna-tion it has aroused everywhere—I am writing to you to protest most vehemently against the purpose of your arguments, which is to force the peoples of the earth even more under Jewish domination, and even to press the church into its service. Who are you, sir, that you cannot acknowledge what is acknowledged by millions of right-thinking people everywhere? And this you call, in defiance of all the facts, "the cancer of Christianity!"?
>
> Sir, what are you, perhaps you are yourself a Jew, or part-Jewish, so, that with typical Jewish blindness to your own failings, you profess not to recognize this "infamy"? Or have you been bribed with Jewish money to work against all ideas of Right and Justice, for the subjugation of all peoples under the Jewish yoke? We have no wish to eliminate the distinctions which God in His wisdom made between the various peoples, nor to tolerate amongst us parasitic agitators, such as the Jews in fact always have been. God has not only asked us, He has commanded us to fight against wrong. And that is why we ask Christ, our beloved immortal King, to deliver us from our and His enemies, and to destroy all efforts to betray us forever to our murderers.[1]

This letter contains the classic topics of traditional Jew-hatred. I will return to its origins shortly.

Regarding racism, I do not want to deal with the history and origins of race theories and the emergence of racism in the Western world, since George L. Mosse has already done so.[2] What is of specific concern to us is Nazi racism. It was Hitler who linked Jew-hatred with racism. For the moment, it will suffice to listen to his credo: "The racial question gives the key not only to the world, but to all human culture";[3] "And all occurrences in world history are only the expression of the race's instinct of self-preservation, in the good or bad sense."[4]

Nazi ideology should be equated with what Hitler called "Weltanschauung." In this, modern research has followed Eberhard Jäckel's analysis, which is still valid today.[5] Hitler stated in *Mein Kampf*:

Every philosophy of life, even if it is a thousand times correct and of highest benefit to humanity, will remain without significance for the practical shaping of a people's life, as long as its principles have not become the banner of a fighting movement.[6]

And in another passage he wrote:

For the philosophy is intolerant; it cannot content itself with the role of "one party beside others," but imperiously demands, not only its own exclusive and unlimited recognition, but the complete transformation of all public life in accordance with its views.[7]

We may pose this question: In what way is the traditional Jew-hatred a challenge to the Nazi *Weltanschauung* that promotes the primacy and self-preservation of the German race?

Reinhard Rürup stated that since the Hellenistic period we have not been able to talk of a continuity of an "eternal antisemitism" (ewigen Antisemitismus).[8] Although he admits that "for centuries Jews were oppressed, isolated, hated and despised," Rürup contends that there was no "Judenfrage," no Jewish problem. Jews did not constitute a problem that profoundly needed to be solved. Only in the late eighteenth century was a Judenfrage established.[9]

According to his analysis, Jews in earlier ages were economically exploited and a Judenpolitik was initiated by German princes and feudal lords, but there was no Judenfrage.[10] Rürup's distinction between antisemitism and Judenfrage is essentially correct. Antisemitism was prevalent in German history, but the Judenfrage was a modern phenomenon that became widespread after the 1842 publication of Bruno Bauer's brochure *Die Judenfrage*. It was no longer attributed to a particular nation or state but now reflected a world problem, as Alex Bein has postulated in *Die Judenfrage: Biographie eines Weltproblems*.

Antisemitism and the Judenfrage became one in modern times. Antisemitism underwent a process of universalization. Ernst Nolte, in his study *Three Faces of Fascism*, commented that:

It must not be forgotten that every significant ideology of the 19th century had its own brand of antisemitism. Liberal antisemitism accused the Jews of anti-historical rigidity, intolerance and "national separateness." In socialist thought the Jews stood for the chief exemplifiers of the capitalist spirit and its "mamonism." What conservatives disliked most about the Jews was their spirit of unrest, their tendency toward revolution.[11]

All these theories and ideologies were manifestations of universal ideals and outlooks, hence also "their" particular brand of antisemitism became universal.

Hitler's Antisemitism

Adolf Hitler was born in 1889 in Braunau, Austria. He moved in 1908 to Vienna and became acquainted with the so-called "Jewish Problem." In 1913, he moved to Munich. Upon returning to Munich from his stint with a Bavarian regiment of the German Army during World War I, he stated in his first political document, in 1919, that the final goal of antisemitism must be "the total removal of the Jews." In 1921, he became the chairman of the National Socialist German Workers' Party, the NSDAP. His efforts to bring down the government in 1923 failed, and he was sentenced in 1924 to five years imprisonment. In Landsberg prison, he dictated *Mein Kampf*. In 1928 he wrote another book, *Das zweite Buch* (published in 1961), in which he delivered the grounds for his racist antisemitism, which became so central in his Weltanschauung and political activities.[12]

If we examine Nazi ideology and the movement as a whole and its relationship to Hitler's personality, we face the basic question as defined by Karl D. Bracher: To what degree does a biography of the "Leader" disclose the nature and essence of National Socialism? Could we—should we—simply speak of Hitlerism?[13] Hitler was the driving force of antisemitism in the Nazi movement, not only by setting the ideological tone but also by elevating his intense personal antipathy to an affair of state. Hitler alone defined the Jewish menace.[14] This clear link between Hitler's antisemitic ideology and antisemitic practice is further examined in the studies of Helmut Krausnick, Karl D. Bracher, Eberhard Jäckel, Andreas Hillgruber, and Gerald Fleming.

Other historians, popularly known as functionalists, do not see such a clear connection. For example, Karl Schleunes stated that "during the early years of the Third Reich no one in the Nazi movement, from the Führer down, had defined what the substance of a solution to the Jewish problem might be."[15] The psychohistorical efforts to explain Hitler's antisemitism exclude the possibility of discussing the problem historically. In Hitler's case, the weakness of these efforts, evaluated from other angles, has already been exposed by Bracher.[16] Hitler's case, as any other one, would be looked at as a general human complexity, ignoring its specific unique personal-historic development. In both volumes of Hitler's *Mein Kampf*, we read the following:

> Was it possible that the earth had been promised as a reward to this people which lives only for this earth? . . . If with the help of his Marxist creed, the Jew is victorious over the other peoples of the world, his crown will be the funeral wreath of humanity and this planet will as it did millions of years ago move through the ether devoid of men. Hence today, I believe, that I am acting in accordance with the will of the Almighty Creator: by defending myself against the Jew, I am fighting for the work of the Lord.[17]

And in the second volume:

> If our people and our state become the victim of this bloodthirsty and avaricious Jewish tyrant of nations, the whole earth will sink into the snares of this octopus; if Germany frees itself from its embrace, this greatest danger of nations may be regarded as broken for the whole world.[18]

Eberhard Jäckel has emphasized another "new" aspect in Hitler's antisemitism, namely, the universal-missionary trend. The adversary in the struggle of the Jews, Hitler proclaims, was not this or that nation, but all nations, the principle of nation as such, the law of nature and history. Hence, the Jews were not an enemy of the German nation alone, but of all mankind; their elimination was not only a national task but a universal task.[19]

German Antisemitism Before Hitler

As to German antisemitism before Hitler, it will suffice to refer to Fritz Stern's monumental study *Gold and Iron*. Stern scrutinized the history of antisemitism during the Bismarck era. He noted the fact that German liberalism was weaker than, and ideologically different from, its Western counterparts, and that the German Bür-gertum never acquired the self-confidence and historic importance of the French or British bourgeoisie. This meant that the Jewish community did not have a liberal shield that would defend its rights as part of a code of universally recognized human rights. Stern also stressed the peculiarity of German nationalism, characterized by its aggressiveness and xenophobia. The resonance to antisemitism among the leading classes of society was greater in Germany than elsewhere.[20]

In latter-day studies of the German cultural, economic, social, and religious antisemitism of nineteenth-century scholars such as Lagarde, Marr, and Treitschke, one finds that the "Jewish Question" was raised loudly.[21] Stern stressed that the core of all variations of antisemitism was the belief that the pariahs had become the true power in the new Germany.[22] Gradually, the antisemites converted the particular into the general and "leaped," to use Stern's words, from fact to fantasy.[23] The German nation encountered the forces of modernism while barely united from above by Bismarck. Industrial capitalism and the rise of the industrial worker put the middle class, the Bürgertum, in fear of rising socialism. The Jew was identified with capitalism, with socialism, and with modernism. He was perceived as the visible threat to the middle class.

George L. Mosse has described the "middle-class morality," the upholding of middle-class ideals, of German society. It was this class, frightened by the upheaval of modernism, that sought to uphold the importance of family life and moderation. The Nazis claimed to protect such middle-class respectability, that part which found its expression in those clean-cut young men who marched down the street.[24] Hitler wanted to reestablish these values in Germany by destroying the Jewish part of the middle class—the part that was thought to have corrupted the class as a whole.[25] Richard F. Hamilton's recent study *Who Voted for Hitler* has demonstrated that the middle class was the base of Hitler's support. Its motivation was, according to Jäckel, fear of future misery.[26] The fear of the Jew, who was believed to endanger middle-class ideals in Kaiser Wilhelm's time, continued to stir the anxiety of the middle class, who voted for and identified with Hitler's antisemitism. The anti-Jewish attitude of the middle class was a dominant and continuous element in modern German society.

The Jews were viewed as powerful, mortally dangerous enemies. The myth of Jewish might was disseminated by German antisemites in nineteenth-century Ger-man society. The image of the powerful, destructive Jew, however, originated in Christianity. Christian responsibility has been belittled, minimized, and sometimes overlooked, when dealing with modern—even anti-Christian—antisemitism. Ac-cording to Christian belief, the election of the Jewish people manifests itself in the Jewish people's riches and wealth. The Jewish Messiah, as represented in the Christian catechism, symbolizes the earthly king who became mighty because of his wealth. Out of this misconception the legend of the "mighty Jew" was born.[27]

When secularism began, from the seventeenth century forward, to shape the Zeitgeist in Europe, a distorted, ambivalent image of the Jew—rich in money but poor in political power—prevailed. International Jewish domination substituted for religious Messianism. In Hitler's eyes, Marxism-Bolshevism appeared as the illegitimate child of Judaism-Christianity.[28] The idea of Jewish power became the keystone for Hitler's obsession with the mighty Jewish Chosen People. It took Hitler to connect the Jews with what he termed the "deeper" struggle in the world and to proclaim that there could not be two chosen peoples. For him, Germans were God's people, and the world was now composed of two opposing entities—men of God and men of Satan.[29]

Hitler's Ideology of Race

Concerning Hitler's ideology of race, it should be noted that racist antisemitism is anti-Christian and pagan in its essence; it is the antithesis of the transcendental religious outlook. But it is, as Hitler well knew, nourished by the absolutely negative image attached to the Jew by Christian theology. Even if the power and influence of the Church diminished over the generations, the negative image attached to the word "Jew" retained its ideological moorings.[30]

"Parasitology"—the Jew as a parasite, according to Hitler's antisemitism—became crystallized in Hitler's ideas through the political pragmatism that aspired to conquer "living space" (Lebensraum) in Eastern Europe in order to sustain the existence of the Aryan race, the German people. In the spirit of Carl Schmidt's "friend-foe" theory, Hitler presented the Jew as antithesis, as parasite, as counterrace (Gegenrasse), as a corrupter of nature embodying every anti-Nazi element.

Hitler portrayed the Jew as the carrier of the concepts of internationalism, democracy, and pacifism, which were the "three plagues of humanity . . . that had killed the nations' race value."[31] The struggle against these three principles became, in Hitler's hands, the foundation and motivational force of his political programs, both internal and external. Traditional antisemitism served as an ideological nucleus for Nazi racial doctrine. Through this doctrine, he portrayed his ideological and political enemies in a harmful, mighty, flesh-and-blood image—the image of the blemished Jew—that perverted the character of nature itself.[32]

By relying on traditional antisemitism, Hitler played upon themes of continuity in German history. The uniqueness of pre-Hitler antisemitism was expressed in its rebuttal of the Jewish essence. This nationalistic view sought to exalt and give precedence to "Germanism" (Germanentum), and, therefore, focused less on the Jew himself.[33]

Hitler and the Nazis reversed the order of priorities. Hitler demonstrated the greatness of Germans—in a down-to-earth manner, not through exclusive theories. With the aid of military power and marches of conquest and oppression, he proclaimed German greatness while denouncing the Jew and portraying him as a real enemy; the evil Jew became the central theme of his racist policy. He incorporated the Jew's negative image, the continuation and the result of classic Jew-hatred, as a convenient basis and concrete goal within his operational plans. Hitler's method in particular, and that of the Nazis in general, did away with all litigation and all public ideological or legal debates with the Jews. The ideological components of Nazi antisemitism introduced nothing new compared to its predecessors. The innovation is not in the internal content, but in the functional character.

Nazi sources confirm the assumption that we must clearly distinguish between general Nazi racism and Nazi anti-Jewish racism. The first appeared as an opportunistic, arbitrary, and cynical weapon, which even Nazi activists were prepared to take lightly. In contrast, Nazi racial antisemitism was a consistent, calculated Weltanschauung and was well-anchored in Hitler's practical plans. Götz Aly and Susanne Heim, in several articles and finally in their book *Vordenker der Vernichtung: Auschwitz und die Deutschen Pläne für eine neue Europäische Ordnung*,[34] have presented their thesis, as summarized by Christopher R. Browning, that

> the economic and social planners of the German occupation in Eastern Europe saw in the mass murder of the East European Jews the means of solving a problem of overpopulation that blocked the path to economic modernization.[35]

Browning disagrees with several of their claims: that the cooperation and consensus among the "planning intelligentsia" transcended the polycratic rivalries of the Nazi regime, that these planners strove for a Final Solution long before 1941, that working upward from below they had a major impact on the decision-making process, and that without their input the racial hatred of the regime would not have gone beyond pogroms and massacres.[36]

Taking into account the consistency of Nazi racial antisemitism, it is impossible to overlook the deeply rooted Jew-hatred that directed Nazi policy (infused by Hitler's racist Weltanschauung) against all Jews, not only those of Eastern Europe. Therefore, the idea of some economic planning, of "politics of overpopulation," distorts the historical truth.[37]

It is equally difficult for me to accept the thesis offered by Sybil Milton in her article "Gypsies and the Holocaust" that

> the preoccupation with antisemitism as a central motivation in Nazi policy has resulted in Michael Marrus's failure to include Gypsies in his recent analysis of the historiography of the Holocaust, although literature is available.[38]

This is not the place to deal with the polemic that emerged between Yehuda Bauer and Sybil Milton as a result of her article.[39] What is of concern is her remark that "Nazi pejorative attacks against the Gypsies as 'asocial and criminal' were seldom perceived as unambiguously racist."[40]

This is explicitly my emphasis in these reflections. Because Nazi non-Jewish racial policy was of an inconsistent nature, manipulative and opportunistic, as I will show, the Gypsies did not appear as the "counterrace" (Gegenrasse) in Hitler's and the Nazi's Weltanschauung. The racial enemy was the Jew.

The Nazi Revolution: Radical Political Antisemitism

Some examples from Nazi sources will clearly establish the flexibility and inconsistency with which a general theory of race was maintained. Hitler outlined his concept of race in his conversations with Hermann Rauschning. The credibility of these conversations has rightly been challenged. Still, the late Martin Broszat spoke of an "inner authenticity" characterizing Rauschning's stance and report.[41] Although his conversations are not to be accepted in a primary and strict sense, they deliver a genuine insight into Hitler's racist Weltanschauung. Hitler said:

> In the scientific sense there is no such thing as race. But you, as a farmer and cattle-breeder, cannot get your breeding successfully achieved without the conception of race. And I as a politician need a conception which enables the order, which has hitherto existed on a historic basis, to be abolished, and an entirely new and anti-historic order enforced and given an intellectual basis . . . and for this purpose the conception of race serves me well. It disposes of the old order and makes possible new associations.[42]

Scrutinizing Hitler's words reveals the following assertions: racism was not seen as a science by Hitler, since the politician "needs a conception" to implement his political aims. In other words, the politician needs a myth. The concept of race is imposed on the empiric-historic factor (the old order) in order to arrive at a new, anti-historic regime.

The innovation in Nazi racism is the politicization of this racial theory. In their first year in power, Nazi zealots in the ranks interpreted and implemented Nazi racial theory. For example, Professor Tirala of the Institute for Race Hygiene in Munich approached Hans Schemm, the Minister for Culture, with the suggestion that seven hundred to eight hundred illegitimate children born to German women from Moroccan soldiers in the years 1918–1919 be sterilized by means of x-radiation. He argued that they had to prevent "the corruption of the German race." The answer he received (through Dr. Walter Gross) was unequivocal; he was forbidden to take any private action, since such action was liable to involve Germany in "the greatest complications regarding foreign policy." He was also informed that determination of this matter must remain in the hands of the "responsible political institutions."[43] The opportunism is clearly uncovered when questions arise concerning the Nazi stand with regard to foreign elements who were not Jews. The Nazis, of course, knew that Germany's potential allies included races that did not belong to the "Nordic blood" group. What racial policy was to be applied in their case? If they were to be considered inferior in terms of blood origin, their political loyalty was questionable from the start. To extricate themselves from this dilemma, one Nazi declared:

> Politics is not an idea but the realization of ambition. . . . Politics is a matter of what is practical, thus, under certain circumstances, it will not recoil from doing what seems correct even by devious means. . . . I must adapt myself to changing conditions and must accordingly formulate the political racist concept every time.[44]

The racist ideas in Nazi political manifestos were to be adapted to the changing conditions of everyday reality. Therefore, when non-Nordic elements allied with the Nazis needed to be taken in account, it would be best "not to overdo songs of praise to blond hair and blue eyes . . . otherwise the non-Nordic blood would be insulted" (Sonst schnappen die nicht-Nordischen ein!).[45] A second example may suffice.[46] Racist ideology decreed that German soldiers had to keep their distance from women of "foreign blood," but the "natural drives" (satisfaction of the German soldiers' sexual urges) shoved the doctrine aside to such an extent that the suggestion was put forward to "delay the explanation of these matters until after the war."[47]

Just how far the principles of blood purity and preservation of the race were allowed to lapse can be deduced from what occurred at the front. In many cases, the "natural drives," in fact, put the race theory out of mind. The leadership was confronted with incontrovertible facts, and they became part of declared policy. Heinrich Himmler admitted to army officers that, while on Russian soil, German soldiers had sired "between a million and a million-and-a-half children." This problem, he claimed, had aroused Hitler's concern. The solution Himmler suggested was "to take children of 'value' away from their mothers and bring them to the German Reich, and if the mothers were of 'racial value' they could also be brought."[48] The fact that such a relationship existed testifies to the extent of the lack of or relative weakness of racial consciousness among many in the ranks of the SS in everyday life.

Relationships with Jewish women were out of the question. That is what was particular to Hitler and Nazism as expressed in the relationship between racism and antisemitism. Hitler imposed his racial theory on antisemitic concepts that had long been in existence. By this method he turned the negative image of the Jew into a satanic image, which was interpreted as the consequence of necessity; the image was one of an essentially parasitic entity. He concluded chapter 11 of his *Mein Kampf* as follows:

> Now begins the great last revolution. In gaining political power the Jew casts off the few cloaks that he still wears. The democratic people's Jew becomes the blood-Jew and tyrant over peoples. . . . The end is not only the end of the freedom of the peoples oppressed by the Jew, but also the end of this parasite upon the nations. After the death of his victim, the vampire sooner or later dies too.[49]

Hitler dreamed of a new Nazi regime that would arise out of a war-to-the-end against the "old regime," which he described as the regime of the parasitical Jew. He took the negative image of the Jew from the early anti-Jewish traditions. The Nazis fortified this image with absolute racist doctrine, and this was the reason why they employed such a vast number of racist slogans in everything related to the Jews. As Bracher has argued: "If a revolutionary is defined by his ability to combine a radical concept of change with the capacity to mobilize the necessary forces, then Hitler can even be called the prototype of a revolutionary."[50]

The Nazi revolution was an anti-Jewish revolution. It did not invent hatred for Jews, but it radicalized and activated an antisemitism that was already existent—an antisemitism that was, in fact, dominant and continuous in German history. The innovation in Nazi anti-Jewish policy could be summarized as follows: Nazi anti-semitism became political. It turned theory and ideology into practice. In Hitler's words, "There is no making pacts with the Jews; there can only be the hard: either-or. I for my part decided to go into politics."[51] Such a verdict was never passed on other enemies of the Nazis.

Eugen Fischer, professor of anthropology and the first Nazi rector of the University of Berlin, expressed the view that scientists must be the infrastructure of politics. The Nazi achievement was that "the Führer, Adolf Hitler, for the first time in the history of mankind, translated the recognition of the biological foundation of a race-nation, heredity, and natural selection into deeds. . . . German science placed the tools in the politician's hands."[52]

Hitler radicalized traditional antisemitism by underpinning it with the race doctrine and giving it a biological basis. The Jew was conceived of as an unnatural outgrowth. His disappearance from this world should be a blessing for humankind.

Hence, Hitler's antisemitism, originating from German-Austrian tradition, was intermingled with his vision of a universal mission to create a new world order based on what he called race purity. Yet, Hitler was not the first to universalize antisemitism.

Christianity and Antisemitism

Christianity strove to de-Judaize the world, portraying Judaism as a world evil. The difference between Christianity and Nazism was not in the attitude toward Jews but in proposed solutions. Hitler's was final. Nazi anti-Jewish racism was the ultimate, uncompromising climax of antisemitism. It was focused on the Jew, because antisemitism had, during the ages, only one target: not the Semite, but the Jew, and the Jew alone.

The uniqueness of Nazi racism lies in its consistent radicalizing—through biological slogans—of traditional antisemitism. Adolf Hitler knew where to turn when he sought to explain and justify his antisemitism. The process of transition from traditional Christian anti-Jewishness to Nazism is heightened when one is aware of the similarity between them. Both needed an enemy, an antitype. They were required, in order to survive and justify their existence, to translate the image of the Jewish enemy as created by prejudice into the everyday, mundane Jewish enemy antagonist. Hitler openly asserted that he learned this tactic from the Catholic Church.[53]

The central components of the Christian view of the Jew and Judaism were used as the basis for consolidation of the anti-Jewish ideology of the Nazis. The Nazis perceived the Jew to be the foe of the Christian God and the enemy of the Aryan type. The negation of Judaism was essential for the justification of Christian superiority. Hitler sought to bring about the salvation of the German-Nordic race by destroying Judaism. Nazi ideology was able to base its attacks on the Jews on prejudices shaped by Christian theology. The Jew was regarded by both ideologies as a powerful, omniscient enemy and threat to world order.

The sufferings of the Jews in world history are anchored in these facts. Even if Christianity did not call for the death of the Jews, since it had "theological need" for them, one cannot ignore the fact that this was an a posteriori need. Degradation of the Jews was the substitute for their extermination. Christianity could not demand the killing of the Jews, even though this act was the logical outcome of the principles we have noted, since their extermination would have cast doubt on the Christian demand to be considered the legal heir of the Jewish creed: "No jury would agree to grant a legacy to someone who won it through murdering the testator."[54]

The difference between Hitler and Christianity is that the latter chose the path of degradation of the Jew out of its own particular interests, while Hitler humiliated and murdered as well. The tragedy is that substantiation for both policies can be found in Christian theology.

NOTES

1. Friedrich Heer, *Gottes Erste Liebe. Die Juden im Spannungsfeld der Geschichte* (Frankfurt/M., 1986 [1st ed. 1976]), p. 19.

2. George L. Mosse, *Toward the Final Solution: A History of European Racism* (New York, 1978).

3. Adolf Hitler, *Mein Kampf*, trans. Ralph Manheim (Boston, 1971), p. 339 (hereafter *M.K.*).

4. Ibid., p. 296.

5. Eberhard Jäckel, *Hitlers Weltanschauung: Entwurf einer Herrschaft* (Tübingen, 1969).

6. Hitler, *M.K.*, p. 380; I believe Manheim's translation "Philosophy of life" is misleading. The German term "Weltanschauung" should remain unchanged, as Hitler's opinions are in no way a philosophy.

7. Ibid., p. 454.

8. Reinhard Rürup, *Emanzipation und Antisemitismus* (Göttingen, 1975), p. 74.

9. Ibid., pp. 75–76.

10. Ibid., p. 76.

11. Ernst Nolte, *Three Faces of Fascism* (New York, 1966), p. 332.

12. Eberhard Jäckel, *Encyclopedia of the Holocaust* (New York, 1990), p. 672.

13. Karl D. Bracher, "The Role of Hitler: Perspectives of Interpretation," in *Fascism: A Reader's Guide*, ed. Walter Laqueur, 2nd ed. (London, 1979), p. 196.

14. Michael R. Marrus, *The Holocaust in History* (London, 1987), p. 17.

15. Karl Schleunes, *The Twisted Road to Auschwitz* (Chicago, 1992), p. 257.

16. Bracher, "Role of Hitler," p. 207.

17. Hitler, *M.K.*, pp. 64, 65.

18. Ibid., p. 623.

19. Jäckel, *Hitlers Weltanschauung*, p. 68. See also idem, *Hitler in History* (Hanover, 1984), pp. 47–48.

20. Fritz Stern, *Gold and Iron: Bismarck, Bleichröder and the Building of the German Empire* (New York, 1977), p. 462.

21. Ibid., p. 495.

22. Ibid.

23. Ibid., p. 497.

24. George L. Mosse, *Nazism: A Historical and Comparative Analysis of National Socialism* (Princeton, 1978), p. 44.

25. Ibid., p. 43.

26. Jäckel, *Hitler in History*, p. 19.

27. Edmund Kroenes, *Homiletisches Reallexikon: Zum Handgebrauch für Prediger und Religionslehrer* (Regensburg, 1856), vol. 3, p. 49: "Die Juden damaliger Zeit waren voll irdischen, fleischlichen Sinnes und vom Stolze aufgeblasen. Sie betrachteten sich als das auserwählte Volk dem allein ein Messias verhässen wäre und schauten aus ihrer erträumten Höhe mit Verachtung auf die übrigen Völker herab."

28. Adolf Hitler, *Monologe im Führer-Hauptquartier 1941–1944: Die Aufzeichnungen Heinrich Heims*, ed. Werner Jochmann (Hamburg, 1980), p. 41.

29. Hermann Rauschning, *Hitler Speaks* (London, 1940), p. 238. On Rauschning's credibility, see note 41.

30. Jacob Katz, *From Prejudice to Destruction: Antisemitism 1700–1933* (Cambridge, MA., 1980), p. 321: "Antisemites wished to perpetuate the inferior position of Jews, or even reinstitute some features of their pre-emancipatory situation. Thus, even if they negated the Christian motives responsible for the creation of the situation, anti-Semites still took it as the basis of their operation. There is a patent historical continuity between the two phases of the Jewish predicament."

31. M. Domarus, ed., *Hitler, Reden und Proklamationen, 1932–1945* (Würzburg, 1962), pp. 70–71.

32. Rauschning, *Hitler Speaks*, pp. 233–34; Jäckel, *Hitlers Weltanschauung*, pp. 131–32.

33. Werner Jochmann, "Struktur und Funktion des Deutschen Antisemitismus," *Schriftenreihe Wissenschaftlicher Abhandlungen* 33, Leo Baeck Institute (Tübingen, 1976): 389–408.

34. First ed. Hamburg, 1991; 2nd ed.Frankfurt, 1993.

35. Christopher R. Browning, "German Technocrats, Jewish Labor, and the Final Solution: A Reply to Götz Aly and Susanne Heim," in *The Path to Genocide: Essays on Launching the Final Solution* (New York, 1992), p. 59.

36. Ibid., p. 64.

37. Hermann Graml, "Rassismus und Lebensraum: Völkermord im Zweiten Weltkrieg," in *Deutschland 1933–1945: Neue Studien zur Nationalsozialistischen Herrschaft,* ed. Karl D. Bracher, Manfred Funke, and H. A. Jacobsen (Bonn, 1992), pp. 440–51.

38. Sybil Milton, "Gypsies and the Holocaust," *History Teacher* 24/4 (August 1991): p. 376.

39. Yehuda Bauer–Sybil Milton Correspondence concerning "Gypsies and the Holocaust," *History Teacher* 25/4 (August 1992): 513–21.

40. Milton, "Gypsies," p. 377.

41. Martin Broszat, "Enthüllung? Die Rauschning-Kontroverse" (1985), in *Nach Hitler: Der schwierige Umgang mit unserer Geschichte* (Munich, 1988), pp. 263–65.

42. Rauschning, *Hitler Speaks*, p. 229.

43. Bundesarchiv Koblenz, NS 12/748.

44. Directives for propaganda work concerning race policy, September 1935, Institut für Zeitgeschichte (IFZG), IFZG/Ma/115917407/4.

45. IFZG/MA1159/17426.

46. I have dealt in depth with this issue in my book on Nazi racism; see Walter Zwi Bacharach, "Racism—The Tool of Politics," in *Monism toward Nazism* (Jerusalem, 1985) (in Hebrew).

47. Regulations governing relations between foreign residents and German girls, IFZG/MA/666.

48. Himmler's speech, September 16, 1942, IFZG/MA/312, p. 11.

49. Hitler, *M.K.*, p. 326.

50. Bracher, "Role of Hitler," p. 206.

51. Hitler, *M.K.*, p. 206.

52. Eugen Fischer, *Zeitschrift für Morphologie und Anthropologie* 34 (1933).

53. Rauschning, *Hitler Speaks*, pp. 58, 60, 234; Jochmann, *Monologe*, p. 321.

54. David Flusser, *Jewish Sources in Early Christianity: Studies and Essays* (Tel Aviv, 1979), p. 449 (in Hebrew).

8.

OMER BARTOV

Antisemitism, the Holocaust, and Reinterpretations of National Socialism

There is a common tendency to view the Holocaust as a well-ordered plot, in which antisemitism led to Nazism, Nazism practiced genocide, and both were destroyed in a spectacular, "happy" end. This is a tale that most university students and film-goers, book readers and television viewers would like to believe. It breeds complacency about our own world. It refuses to acknowledge that the Holocaust is a story without a clear beginning, and with no resolution. It is for this reason that one finds it such a difficult period to teach; we strive to provide our students with a more comforting, rational, logical, palatable explanation for an event that would otherwise threaten to undermine our civilization's fundamental values and beliefs. And yet we know that would be false; the story has not been resolved, its plot has not been revealed. Ultimately, the world we live in is the same world that produced (and keeps producing) genocide.[1]

I would like to examine several aspects of the postwar discourse on antisemitism, genocide, and Nazism. I will begin by discussing some characteristic features of the scholarly interpretations and popular images of each of these three phenomena, noting the extent to which these debates were molded over time by chronology, geography, ideology, and changing sociopolitical as well as cultural circumstances. I will then attempt to assess the implications of the differing views on the relationship between the causes, essence, and consequences of the Holocaust for the study and deeper understanding not only of the event itself, but also of the nature of modernity. This will then lead me to a final discussion of some aspects of Nazism that the above-mentioned causal model tends to underestimate, though they were both crucial to the theory and practice of genocide and are still very much present in our own society. By touching briefly on the role of the medical and legal professions in the formulation and realization of National Socialist policies, I will thus argue that the world in which we live is still anything but free from the profound contradictions of modernity that made Auschwitz possible.

Antisemitism

Roughly speaking, we can contrast two basic perceptions of antisemitism. One views it as a permanent aspect of Jewish life in the Diaspora since the Exile—perhaps even before. The other views it as a political/ideological/social phenomenon firmly rooted in late-nineteenth-century European society and by and large discredited, except in some of the more remote corners of "Western civilization," following 1945. Each of these interpretations will define the phenomenon itself differently so as to be able to fit it into its own understanding of antisemitism's historical context.

The former views anti-Jewish sentiments as a cluster of religious, social, economic, and political prejudices. The latter stresses the difference between traditional anti-Jewish feelings and actions among the Christian population of Europe, seen as primarily related to religious differences and social exclusion (as well as economic activity), and modern, political, demagogic, "scientific" antisemitism, rooted in a combination of new racial theories, modernization and its effects on society, and nationalism, sometimes invoked along with imperialism and colonialism.[2]

Though the representatives of these two interpretations of antisemitism have often clashed bitterly with each other, and have indeed come from wholly different ideological backgrounds, they have generally agreed on the role played by their various versions of antisemitism both in the rise of Nazism (or totalitarianism) and in the genocide of the Jews (or also of other categories of human beings by totalitarian regimes). The proponents of perpetual antisemitism are thus comfortable within the framework of a historical interpretation that explains everything—even the seemingly inexplicable—and which, while professing a grim, perhaps permanent pessimism, at least provides one with a sense of stability associated with any historical "law." Similarly, the supporters of contextualized antisemitism who view it as part and parcel of modernity, the nation state, industrialization, and mass society, can also employ their (more complex) interpretation as a tool for understanding what would otherwise seem to defy reason. Since modern society does not seem to be on the way out, postmodern fears or aspirations notwithstanding, this latter view also offers a measure of comforting (albeit explosive) stability in a highly fluid and bewildering environment.[3]

Supporters of the traditional view of anti-Judaism seem to come from two very different camps, the Orthodox and the Zionist. For the Orthodox it is a given that the Gentiles are constantly threatening the Jews, as has been the case, from their perspective, ever since biblical times. For the Zionists, who had rebelled against the Orthodox world, it is just as obvious that the Gentiles would always be against the Jews, with the important qualification that the best defense against this situation is not prayer or trust in God but statehood.[4] For both these groups the Holocaust, however catastrophic it surely was in personal human terms, serves the ideological (or theological) purpose of fortifying their understanding of Jewish fate and history. The Zionists obviously could say that had the Jews lived in a state of their own, none of this would have happened (or at least things would have happened differently). The Orthodox have argued that the Holocaust not only proved the biblical truth that all the Gentiles are against the Jews but also that the only way to continue *Jewish* existence after the catastrophe is to go back to the old ways, since that would be the real victory of the Jews over all their foes.[5]

Some of the most brilliant (Jewish) minds who have written on antisemitism as generated by its socioeconomic and ideological context (including the role played by the Jews themselves within Gentile society) have been accused of suffering from that modern disease of "Jewish self-hatred."[6] Yet Hannah Arendt, the main target of such attacks by both Diaspora Jews and Israeli Zionists holding the traditional view, in fact argued that antisemitism was a major factor in the appearance and spread of totalitarianism. However, there have been interpretations of antisemitism that have indeed minimized its role either in the genocide of the Jews or generally in the emergence of totalitarian regimes of one kind or another. Among other factors the difference between these interpretations has to do with their chronological distance from the event, as well as the personal and national perspective. Thus, for instance, during World War II German antisemitism was not often invoked as a major motivating element in the fight against Nazism, not least due to actual or suspected antisemitic sentiments among the populations of the Allies. In the Soviet Union, Marxist interpretations of fascism excluded antisemitism a priori as a substantial factor. After the end of the war and the discovery of the death camps, antisemitism seemed for a while to be the key to explaining the barbarization of German society. But the rhetoric of the Cold War and its insistence on the similarity between Stalinism and Hitlerism replaced antisemitism with totalitarianism. In turn, in the 1960s, refashioned leftist theories of fascism saw class tensions, late capitalism, and imperialism as much more central than antisemitism.[7]

Personal factors were often also crucial in discussing antisemitism. Jews who had been persecuted as Jews by the Germans and their collaborators had no time for interpretations that relegated anti-Jewish sentiments to a secondary place. Conversely, Germans who had lived through the period performing their various duties without much contact with actual Jews beyond perhaps some faint memories of prewar neighbors, or who had encountered the term Jew as an administrative abstraction, could not accept arguments that made Nazi Germany appear to have been mainly populated by rabid antisemites. Hence also the often exaggerated differentiation made between Jewish and Gentile historians writing on Nazism; for some reason critics assume that the latter can achieve greater detachment and objectivity than the former.[8]

Detachment and empathy also seem to be related to chronological distance, with the result that in recent years it has become much easier for some historians to view antisemitism as relatively unimportant in explaining twentieth-century politics and ideology, while calling for greater empathy with those whose own fate had allegedly been obscured by the overemphasis on Jews in previous scholarly work.[9] It is of course a manifestation of the cunning of history that just as the distance from 1945 allows one to speak about *that* past with more detachment (or to call for new subjects of empathy), the present seems to provide one with an ever-growing array of instances where racial and religious prejudice and hatred are gaining political importance.

In the political arena, antisemitism has been abused by all. Israeli governments have sought to legitimize their policies by accusing their critics and enemies of antisemitic sentiments;[10] German governments have sought renewed international respectability by well-orchestrated public proclamations of philosemitic feelings.[11] Both the Left and the Right in Europe have accused each other (not without reason) of harboring antisemitic ideas. Indeed, since 1945 antisemitism, like fascism, has become a term of abuse hurled at one's enemies, while not altogether disappearing both as a private sentiment and as a loosely concealed public platform. Given the growing chronological distance from the Holocaust, it is not unreasonable to expect that at some point in the future antisemitism will regain some of its lost influence, not least by seeping in from those parts of Europe where the collapse of communism left the public open to the rejuvenation of old prejudices.[12]

The Holocaust

In speaking about the Holocaust we may also begin with a basic distinction between the eschatological and the scholarly interpretation. At the same time, however, we should note that in spite of the clear differences, there exists in fact a measure of overlap between these two points of view. Just as what might appear to be a purely academic explanation may reveal, at a closer look, some deeply ingrained, often irrational and inexplicable beliefs and sentiments, so too the eschatological interpretation of the second half of the twentieth century will tend to employ arguments and evidence taken from scholarship and science in order to fortify its own interpretative universe. Hence we must bear in mind that when applied to an event such as the Holocaust—that is, to a disaster carried out by human beings that nevertheless threatens constantly to escape reason or wholly to undermine the very concept of humanity—even this fundamental distinction remains highly tenuous, since the rules of logic or systems of belief on which it is based are constantly overwhelmed by the nature of the abyss they seek to explain.[13]

Let us leave aside the eschatological view since it is, at least by definition, self-contained and foolproof. The constant flux in the secular interpretation of the Holocaust, its many shifts between detachment and sentimentality, harshness and doubt, and ultimately extreme open-endedness, demonstrates that by and large the secular universe is a less secure one than the theological. But more specifically, it shows that the Holocaust as an event, by its very extremity, indeed by its apparent alienation from its modern, progressive, optimistic, scientific, and rational context, has become a threat to our own post-Holocaust secular world. That is both because of what it was, and because of our helpless inability to grasp it as a whole. It is the protean nature of the event, its refusal ever to be tied down to any single meaning and definition, that makes it appear so horrifying even at a distance of two generations.

The secular interpretation of the Holocaust is thus in some respects more difficult than the eschatological. The religious strive to justify God, but since God's justice is inherent to their existence, their struggle is one of belief, not of reason; and once God has been justified so has Man, who is after all only a tool in God's hands. Secularists strive to justify Man, or Man's civilization, but they remain men even if they cannot justify humanity. Yet survival as men in a world devoid of humanity, while possible (as opposed to religious existence in a world devoid of God, which is ultimately a contradiction in terms), is the secular equivalent of Hell. The difficulty of coping with this predicament can be seen not merely on the abstract level, but also more specifically in the various attempts to come to terms with the event.

The Event: in much of the English-speaking world, it is called the Holocaust.[14] This is a highly evocative term since it carries with it the connotation of sacrifice, without specifying who sacrificed whom for what. If the Jews were the victims, the Nazis the slaughterers, what then was the purpose of the sacrifice? Interestingly, the term is used indiscriminately by secular scholars (as well as intellectuals, the media, politicians, laymen, even survivors), signifying once more the overlap between history and myth, the rational and the metaphysical, empiricism and belief. Some use the surprisingly more neutral Hebrew term "Shoah," meaning great disaster, and applied also to such natural catastrophes as floods and earthquakes. The French have, until recently, preferred the more precise term "génocide," which is exactly, though not completely, what the event was about. Since Claude Lanzmann's film entitled *Shoah*, French intellectuals have tended to use that Hebrew-language term. The Germans use the no less precise but more troubling term "Judenvernichtung," more disturbing both because it was exactly the same term which the Nazis themselves used and because "destruction of the Jews" evokes a scientific, methodical, detached, clinical operation, whereas an alternative term such as, for instance, "murder of the Jews," would have provided it with a sorely lacking moral dimension.[15]

The various terms used by different groups and nationalities are not the result of mere linguistic coincidence, though at the same time they are also not to be taken as signifying clear and obvious divergences in interpretation and understanding. The fact is, after all, that the different terms are used also by Jews who speak the languages mentioned here, and though they may not be unaware of their significance, they usually, though not always, tend to accept them. Nevertheless, I would argue that the names given to the Event (itself a term employed by one historian loath to use any other)[16] are of some importance. A multiplicity of names for an event, an object, a phenomenon, may signify a confusion as to its essence, an unease with its presence, fear and anxiety at calling it *what it really is*. The Jews had a name for their God but were allowed neither to write nor to pronounce it. They therefore gave their God many other names, which were, however, never *ha'shem ha'meforash*, the name of God pronounced in full. God was unthinkable, therefore His name was unpronounceable to the extent that He was called simply "the Name" (*ha'shem*). Hence the divine entity, whose name was unpronounceable, became a name denoting an entity whose features were inconceivable.

The multiplicity of names for the mass murder of the Jews is to some extent the obverse side of God's multiplicity of names. In both cases the thing itself cannot be given a name, or rather, its name cannot be pronounced, for pronouncing it would bring an end to all things. Instead, many other names are given, yet with the knowledge that none of them precisely describes the phenomenon that it tries to evoke. Only in the one case we are speaking about Heaven, in the other about Hell.

Because we are speaking about a nameless, yet multinamed Hell, the choice of ersatz names is indicative of the conscious and unconscious motivations of those who employ them. "Holocaust" is a name that provides the event with meaning, and that meaning carries deep religious, Judeo-Christian connotations. Though this may have been the reason for its wide acceptance rather than for the initial choice of the term among English-speakers, it is appropriate to nations that had not experienced the event at close quarters and yet are culturally susceptible to providing meanings (whether concrete and empirical or mythic and metaphysical) to phenomena, and intolerant of things inexplicable. If the Holocaust cannot yield a good historical explanation (and many would argue that it can), then at least it must be given a meaning; if it was mass murder, then it must be given some sacrificial value; if it was genocide then it must have had some purpose for humanity. Indeed, the very use of the term "Holocaust" already provides us with a meaning even before we begin to articulate it. In a society such as that of the United States, where the secular and the religious are so closely intertwined, Holocaust means sacrifice, God, purpose. The Jews (were) sacrificed for the good of Humanity. Now one can turn to the details with less trepidation.

The term Holocaust arrived in Germany in the wake of the screening of the American television series of the same name.[17] It was a strange path to take, as bizarre as the effect of this Hollywood rendering of genocide on German society's perception of its Nazi past. The ambivalent attitude of Germans toward both the event and the film is neatly reflected in the confusion between the two whenever the word "Holocaust" is employed. "Judenvernichtung" (or "Endlösung," the official Nazi term for the "Final Solution of the Jewish problem") thus remains the definitive term, even though not all the Jews were actually "destroyed." For German speakers the term seems natural, since it describes the event with unadorned clarity, not to say brutality. Nevertheless, it has the effect of creating detachment, both personal and moral; it has a bureaucratic ring, an administrative dimension, a military neatness; hence it also appears neutral. When one's neighbor is murdered next door, one does not say that he was destroyed, not even in German. When the population of Hamburg or Berlin or Dresden burned to death by hundreds of thousands, one did not say they were destroyed—either then or now. The cities were destroyed, the houses were destroyed, even the artworks were destroyed, but the people died, or were killed, or were murdered. The Jews, however, were destroyed, even in the most recent German scholarship on the event.[18] *Holocaust* is a sentimental American series; "Judenvernichtung" is a detached, objective, reliable, scholarly term. Coming to "terms" with, or "overcoming" the past, that great German problem, calls for an appropriate word to denote its darkest chapter, a term perhaps not consciously chosen (rather adopted directly from the SS) but somehow wonderfully malleable to the uses to which it is put.

The French term "génocide" has the same clinical and precise connotations as "Judenvernichtung." But while the latter refers to a specific group, the former is more general (although one American historian with French connections has proposed the term Judeocide).[19] The Germans are concerned with the destruction of the Jews, both because it is that which is best remembered by others, and because focusing on that enables them to set aside the larger numbers of people "destroyed" who were not Jews, such as Russians, Poles, Gypsies, and so forth. The French have no qualms about calling the thing by its name, genocide, yet prefer to maintain their distance from it not merely by employing a legalistic terminology but by connecting it with all other genocides. While during the war the English and Americans were on the opposing side of genocide, and the Germans at its very center, the French hovered on the periphery. According to the French perception of the war, all kinds of terrible things happened, such as occupation, collaboration, resistance, destruction, and genocide. It was a terrible (but also heroic) time, and everyone suffered terribly (though some behaved more heroically than others).[20] Thus while the Germans, even when they present themselves as victims, can nevertheless not escape "their" Juden-vernichtung, the French see the genocide of the Jews as the counterpart of their lot under the occupation (though the Résistance remains on a somewhat higher level, since it actually fought against the Nazis instead of being "passively" killed).[21] Genocide therefore becomes detached both because it provides a commonly accepted definition (of any instance of mass killing), and because this specific instance is not seen as a specifically French affair. Precisely because, unlike the American and English case, mass murder took place at a greater geographical proximity and with wide-ranging French collaboration, it becomes necessary to define it accurately and unsentimentally and to associate it with one's own sacrifices, rather than with one's complicity.[22] In English one can speak of "Holocaust" since one had nothing directly to do with it and ostensibly fought against it; in French that would not do, for it would diminish the sacrifice of the Résistance and increase the guilt of the nation as a whole.[23]

In Israel, as well as among some non-Israeli scholars and artists (and most recently also in France and to some extent in Germany), the Hebrew word "Shoah" is used to describe the Holocaust. Modern Hebrew uses the word *shoah*, that is, disaster, in many others contexts as well, such as "nuclear disaster" (*shoah gar'init*), "air disaster" (*shoah avirit*), "natural disaster" (*shoat teva*), and so forth. The term "Shoah" is an accurate description of the genocide of the Jews from a Jewish perspective, since it evokes the fact that this was indeed a disaster for the Jewish people. It is free from any religious connotations, and yet is not as detached as the French and German terms. At a second look, however, the very fact that it is often associated with natural disasters, or with spectacular man-made catastrophes, makes it particularly useful within the Israeli/Zionist context (while when used in other languages it has the benefit of having no associations at all since it is a foreign term whose connotations are unknown). Associating the Holocaust with a natural phenomenon such as the eruption of a volcano would mean that just as it is impossible to prevent the volcano from erupting, but possible to move one's house to a safer location, so too it was impossible to prevent the Nazis (or Gentiles) from trying to kill the Jews, but *was* possible to recreate a Jewish national existence in a way that would have both hampered fulfillment of such aims and made death more honorable, since it would have come only after organized military resistance (and here we hear echoes of the Résistance). Hence while not a Holocaust in the sacrificial sense, the Shoah has a didactic aspect in that it is claimed that it provides ample proof for the view that the Jews, who lived on the edge of a volcano, refused to heed the warnings of the Zionists and consequently perished. The event itself is taken therefore almost as a given, as a natural law, as anything but surprising. If not ordered by God, it was at least a historical inevitability. If it did not justify God, it legitimized the Jewish state. After the Holocaust, Zionism needed none of the pre-Holocaust justifications; it seemed *natural* (to Zionists) that Jews must live in their own land, just as it seemed *natural* that the Gentiles would try to murder them, especially if they did not achieve statehood.[24]

Ironically, Israel as a state behaves like any other state, and expects to be treated in this manner by the international community. That means that although the Shoah was seen as a manifestation of the old Jewish sentiment that the "whole world is against us" (another irony since this ancient belief was mobilized to change the conditions that prompted it), the state of Israel, which seemed the obvious, *natural*, and most positive conclusion to be drawn from the Shoah, largely set this sentiment aside. Nevertheless, Zionism has always retained remnants of this anxiety, to the extent that one might say that the peace process now unfolding in the Middle East was made possible also (though certainly not only) by the disintegration of traditional Zionism in Israeli society. At the same time, one must point out that for Israelis "the Disaster" (*ha'shoah*) is distinct from any other catastrophe and still dominates much of the political, intellectual, and cultural discourse in the country. The role played by the Shoah in the formation of Israeli identity cannot be overestimated and can only be compared to, or be seen in an uneasy partnership with, the Arab-Israeli conflict.[25] A people that chose to call one of the central events in its recent history the Disaster is naturally prone to paranoia, anxiety, hysteria, and manifestations of brutality. It also either consciously or unconsciously chose thereby to ignore or repress some of the most glaring aspects of the Disaster from which it sprang into national existence.

National Socialism

Despite appearances of uniformity both during its existence as party and regime, and in the decades following its demise, Nazism has always meant different things to different people. For some it was an ideology, a political movement, a creed, an aspiration, an explosion of hopes and frustrations; for others it was an abomination, a manifestation of humanity's darkest side, the embodiment of Evil, hell on earth. There were (and are) those who viewed it as a hodgepodge of inarticulate nonsense manipulated by a crafty, ambitious, and ruthless clique, or as an insignificant, if unpleasant blip on a thousand years of German culture, most likely a foreign import from Asiatic barbarism, combined perhaps with the depraved ideas of decadent *fin-de-siècle* French intellectuals; others have claimed it was the culmination of German history since Luther, or a merely extreme example of the capabilities of the German character. Just as during its political existence Nazism managed to attract people from different social and educational origins, not least due to the ambiguity of its message and its refusal, or inability, to put down any written dogma, so too after its demise it has been open to the most contradictory interpretations (and uses).[26]

Such interpretations of National Socialism are, to be sure, not innocent of national, ideological, as well as personal biases. They also reflect the changing perspectives of different generations, as well as the political circumstances under which they were formulated. Arguably the most extreme interpretations of Nazism were put forth by those most remote from its actual manifestations and those closest to its very center. Thus, immediately after the war deterministic historical essays were written by English and American scholars who sought to prove that German history had taken the "wrong turn" some four hundred years before Hitler appeared on the scene, making the final emergence of Nazism only a matter of time.[27] In the Federal Republic of Germany attempts were made at the time to understand "how it could have happened" (to the nation of Goethe and Schiller), and theories were promulgated according to which Nazism was the equivalent of foreign conquest by a group of gangsters, or at least the forceful imposition on the nation of culture of a combination of narrow militaristic interests, fanatical political extremists, deluded conservatives, and mob leaders.[28] Curiously, this latter version of Nazism had more than a little in common with that which emerged in the German Democratic Republic, where Nazis (or rather fascists) and Germans were kept strictly apart, to the extent that a "real German," a "man of the people," could not have been, by definition, a fascist, and a fascist could not have possibly been a "real German." Being fascist (or Nazi) was thus almost the same as being a foreign implant or a member of a dying class (just as in the 1960s anyone who disagreed with one's politics was by definition a fascist, or a communist).[29]

A more profound trend in the analysis of the origins of National Socialism developed in the 1960s, initiated perhaps first and foremost by exiles from the Third Reich. These were men and women who had been raised in the fold of "German culture" but, following the Nazi "seizure of power," were forced to flee the nation to which many of them were deeply attached. Here a more serious attempt was made to link Nazism to earlier periods in German history, and especially to the late nineteenth century, or, in some cases, to the birth and development of German nationalism some hundred years earlier.[30] This brand of analysis, which was taken up by German scholars as well, was seen by many of their colleagues as an unwarranted attack on some of the more glorious chapters of German national history.[31] Besmirching the Kaiserreich by seeing in it Nazi roots was not popular in a nation that found it hard enough to accept that its more recent past was a very dark one indeed. The French had their *Belle Epoque*, and the Germans wanted to retain theirs as well, driven by an even more urgent need to mythologize the pre-1914 era than were the French, whose own inglorious period of occupation and collaboration was hard enough to swallow.

With the debate over the origins of Nazism having exhausted itself during the 1970s, attention turned back to the National Socialist regime itself. Here one might note two major clusters of interpretations: first, intentionalism versus functionalism (or structuralism), and second, comparability versus uniqueness.[32] However, both controversies were arguably driven by the same need to "come to terms" with, or "overcome," the past, during a period of renewed German self-assertion that already anticipated reunification (without anyone expecting it to come quite so soon). Because many of the most interesting and stimulating works of research in this period came from Germany, and because some of the major non-German scholars writing on National Socialism were obviously influenced by their German colleagues—if not indeed coached by them—it is difficult to distinguish here between national biases, although the psychological motivation of individuals often differed substantially. Moreover, this trend was evident not only in scholarship, but also in film, literature, theater, and, of course, political discourse and media preoccupations.[33]

Both clusters of debates were, as such, not new at all. Questions regarding the function and importance of Hitler's position in the Third Reich, as opposed to the bureaucratic and administrative structure and inner logic of the modern (totalitarian) state, were raised even before the end of the war.[34] Nevertheless, there was a new twist to the debate. The functionalist interpretation began as an attempt to discredit the previous conspiratorial theories about the Nazi state and to show that large sectors of society had actually been involved in running the "Hitler state." Yet the same interpretation ended up drawing a highly depoliticized picture of the Third Reich, where nobody was actually responsible for, let alone guilty of, anything, since everyone was involved as a smaller or bigger cog in a monstrous, faceless, and ultimately uncontrollable machine. Rather than being a human creation, the structure was thus presented as having molded the men who worked for it (a representation of past realities somewhat akin to the terrifying visions of the future constructed by Fritz Lang, Franz Kafka, and many other artists of the interwar period).[35]

Similarly, the issue of the uniqueness of (the evil nature of) the Third Reich was anything but new. In fact, this question was raised already, by the regime itself, during if not indeed even before the Nazi "seizure of power." The favorite contender for the position of originator of evil, violence, brutality, inhumanity, and so forth, was naturally enough always the Soviet Union, which served this useful purpose from its very inception to its somewhat pathetic demise.[36] Other long-standing competitors for this title were colonialism and imperialism (with the British concentration camps during the Boer War an understandably popular choice), the North American annihilation of the Indians,[37] and the Turkish attempted genocide of the Armenians. Interestingly, in the search for comparable genocides during the mid-1980s, the Turkish massacre of the Armenians was invoked once more, while millions of Turkish "Gastarbeiter" and their families who had lived for many years in the Federal Republic were being denied German citizenship.[38] Other, more recent cases of mass slaughter were also mentioned, with the Right's most frequent choice being naturally enough the mass murder committed by the Khmer Rouge in Cambodia.[39] Nevertheless, Soviet Russia was always seen as the most pertinent example, both because it shared a so-called totalitarian character with the Third Reich and because of the direct relationship between the two, whereby both indeed learned a great deal from each other in techniques of control and manipulation, brutality and massacre, expansion and domination. The mutual fear (tinged with awe, at least in the case of some individuals such as Hitler and several of his generals) between the two regimes, and the nightmarish visions of their expected fate under the other's domination, span a history that begins as early as the Freikorps of the immediate post–1918 period and reaches beyond the recent revisionist tirades of Ernst Nolte and his supporters.[40]

Intention and structure, similarity and uniqueness, these are issues of crucial importance to all parties involved in the debate over the nature and implications of Nazism. Yet they are slippery concepts, whose clarification often leads one in precisely the opposite direction from that originally intended. If, for instance, we can show that structure played a major role in the formulation and implementation of policies in the Third Reich, and draw the (not necessarily self-evident) conclusion that we have thereby diminished the importance of both ideology and individuals, we may find ourselves inadvertently also raising questions as to the nature of postwar German society and the extent to which the bureaucratic, legal, administrative, and educational structures on which it is founded differ markedly from their predecessors. After all, would this not be one of the implications of emphasizing long-term, slow-changing socioeconomic structures? Similarly, if we show to our own satisfaction that the Third Reich was just as evil, murderous, and totalitarian as other nations at other times, or that at least it had strong competitors for the title of "Evil Empire," what are the consequences to be drawn from this finding? Does it reflect on human nature, or the nature of modernity, on capitalism or imperialism, on totalitarian ideologies, or on Western civilization? Does it in any way alleviate the burden of guilt borne by those who perpetrated evil?

Paradoxically, uniqueness becomes relative in this context. Nazism was unique to the Germans; no one else came up with quite the same idea, or carried it out in quite the same manner. Similarly the Holocaust was unique to Nazism, as it was to the Jews, which is why many Jews insist so strongly on maintaining its uniqueness. Although the Jews had experienced many horrific massacres in the past, the Holocaust was unprecedented in their experience. But then the massacre of the Armenians was unprecedented for them, and has remained unique to *their* experience. And if the Nazi genocide of the Jews had certain unique characteristics (and it certainly did), those are not diminished by comparison with other cases of genocide or mass killings.

Reinterpretations of National Socialism and the Holocaust are often bound together. In recent years, however, new work has appeared in Germany that focuses on the relationship between Nazism and modernity.[41] Here we find arguments according to which Nazism was not only produced to a large extent by a crisis of modernity,[42] but, at the same time, actually ushered in the modernization of German society.[43] According to such arguments, this was achieved not merely by a ruthless attack on the traditional order so as to create the basis for authoritarian rule, nor by the destruction Hitler had brought upon his people (as has been argued before),[44] but also by positive policies and actions carried out during the Nazi regime, which created the infrastructure later used by the Federal Republic to transform postwar German society. In this literature, the Holocaust is rarely discussed, in spite of the fact that it featured at least one unique aspect of modernity, namely, the invention of death factories.[45] Calls for a search for more positive aspects even in the darkest period of German history intensified during the 1980s, accompanied by the demand for a greater degree of empathy with the historical protagonists of the period and a lesser emphasis on moralizing rhetoric.[46] Now a younger generation of German scholars has begun heeding the advice of its elders (often in unexpected ways) by proclaiming detachment (from the horror) and empathy (with the perpetrators and the bystanders, as well as with the fate of the nation as a whole). This may be much less than a Rankean revolution, but it can no longer be viewed as a mere fad.

Some bizarre and disturbing echoes of this new view of the past can be heard in present-day Germany, whether among certain more respectable political circles or among extremist groups of one variety or another. That German historians have not only been influenced by the changing climate of public opinion but have actually anticipated it is an interesting finding especially as regards a nation whose scholars normally prefer to isolate themselves from current affairs. The extent to which this reemergence of the German Mandarins from their ivory tower has led some scholars to call for a "historicization" and "contextualization" of the past, and the relationship between this trend and a more blatant kind of revisionism à la Ernst Nolte is still an open question.[47] One may only wonder whether the growing sensitivity of German scholars to the effects of their findings and interpretations on the public's sense of national identity and historical heritage is such a happy event after all.

Interpretations

By and large, we can speak of two models of interpretation of the relationship between antisemitism, the Holocaust, and National Socialism. The first, which has been labeled intentionalist, assumes a direct and causal link between these three elements. According to this view, antisemitism and especially its modern political, pseudoscientific version, was the core and essence of the Nazi movement, and hence the Nazi state was inevitably bound to end up carrying out the threats and intentions of its propagandists, that is, the physical annihilation of the Jews.[48] (The personalized version of this interpretation sees Hitler as the focus of both the long-term impact of antisemitism and of its direct link with the Final Solution).[49] The second, which has been termed functionalist, hypothesizes a weaker, more indirect relationship between these three phenomena. Hence antisemitism is seen as an independent field of inquiry, while its impact on the rise of Nazism is not thought to have been of crucial importance. National Socialism, for its part, is regarded as a much more complex phenomenon than merely the political manifestation of antisemitism alone. Indeed, it is argued, antisemitism did not function as its main engine and motivation, nor was it the most attractive feature of the Nazi movement as far as its supporters were concerned.[50] Finally, the Holocaust is understood not as the inevitable consequence of the Nazi regime, and certainly not as the premeditated goal of Nazi policy makers, but rather as the result of a specific juncture of circumstances and conditions during the war, combined with the structure of the state and the regime as they evolved during the prewar years.[51]

Although the old debate between intentionalists and structuralists has lost much of its ardor, and proponents of both have been moving toward a middle position, some elements of the debate have been lost sight of in the fray and have not been recovered. Indeed, instead of leading to a more comprehensive analysis of the complex relationship between widely differing elements that led to a general crisis in Western civilization (whether *inherent* to it, or its *aberration*), we have witnessed a growing fragmentation, specialization, and preoccupation with details and an attendant reluctance to draw more general conclusions. Hence the issue of antisemitism was first separated from that of Nazism and the Holocaust; then specialists of National Socialism concentrated on detailed studies of such aspects of the Nazi period as daily life (to the exclusion of the victims of the regime); and finally Holocaust experts concentrated increasingly on the mechanics of the "Final Solution," the decision-making process, the role of bureaucrats on different levels, and so forth.

Hence we can speak now of another, perhaps more subtle division between two discourses on what has been called the "Zivilisationsbruch" (shattering of civilization) of Auschwitz, its causes, context, and implications.[52] While on the one hand we find detailed studies of minor episodes in the history of the Holocaust, the Third Reich, or antisemitism, on the other hand we find more or less acute generalization on the meaning of the event. What seems to be lacking is an attempt to tie together the different strands that lead to and from Auschwitz, to trace both the origins and the consequences, to employ the knowledge collected so meticulously by scholars and yet not to get lost in the details and lose sight of what it is that one is actually confronting.

That a close relationship exists between the elements mentioned above, not only in the historical past but also as regards its reconstruction, is evidenced by the fact that reinterpretations of any one of the factors I have noted seem to have a direct effect on the whole interpretative edifice. This was demonstrated as early as 1950 by Hannah Arendt, whose reinterpretation of antisemitism formed the basis of a new explanatory model of totalitarianism, whatever its faults and merits. Conversely, the more extreme functionalist arguments have not only postulated a weak and ineffective Führer,[53] they have also relegated antisemitism to a relatively irrelevant role in the implementation of genocide against the Jews (a view which *is*, of course, directly related to Arendt's analysis of Eichmann, his function and personality).[54] The recent interest in the "Alltagsgeschichte" of the Third Reich has, on the other hand, had contradictory consequences, either demonstrating the extent to which German society was Nazified, thanks not least to preexisting racist and political prejudices, or, conversely, by presenting a picture of normality and resistance to extremity by a stubborn adherence to old routines, beliefs, and loyalties.[55] By the same token a comparison between the films *Heimat* and *Nasty Girl*, for instance, reveals how differently the daily life of a small community can be portrayed in recent German representations of the past.

It would be foolish to deny that there are vested interests involved in the different presentations of the relationship between the constituting elements of the Holocaust, as well as their continuing impact. Germany is now in the process of both detaching itself from the Nazi past and accepting it (or at least a version of it) with less discomfort than ever before. Jews in many countries, including Israel, find this process painful, yet they too are showing signs of being ready to accept that the past is gradually receding from them. Scholars everywhere are sharing this sense of growing detachment, and welcome it, while searching for new and different ways of approaching a heavily researched area. Intellectuals and writers, filmmakers and media people, are still drawn to this seemingly unprecedented example of man-made extremity but are simultaneously showing signs of impatience with old representations and are searching for new, ever more disturbing ways of dealing with the period.

It is more than sheer irony that while the debate over the study and representation of unprecedented inhumanity continues, we are constantly exposed to new examples of human cruelty and depravity, to scenes of rape and massacre, torture and mutilation. What is the relationship between *this* and the past? What does the killing in the former Yugoslavia, for instance, with all its links to the Nazi occupation and the indigenous fascists, tell us about the roots of the Holocaust? What does our understanding of the relationship between racial prejudice, brutal political systems, international indifference, and mass killing, teach us about the future?

All this notwithstanding, and in spite of the similarity between the Holocaust and other mass murders in history, the case before us is unfortunately not only more complex but also more disturbing and threatening. For while we might believe that, given the humanizing effects of education and democratization, both prejudice and abuse of power might be curbed, few of us would contest the need for, or in any case the inevitability of, continued advance in the fields of science and technology. Yet it was in conjunction with the development of modern science and technology that the mass killing of the Jews (along with many other categories of human beings targeted by the Nazis) took place. It is this aspect of the relationship between antisemitism, the Holocaust, and National Socialism that still must be explored.

Modernity

It would seem that our main difficulty in confronting the Holocaust is due not only to the immense scale of the killing, nor even to the manner in which it was carried out, but also to the way in which it combined the most primitive human brutality, hatred, and prejudice, with the most modern achievements in science, technology, organization, and administration. It is not the brutal SS man with his truncheon whom we cannot comprehend; we have seen his likes throughout history. It is the killing squad commander with a Ph.D. in law from a distinguished university, in charge of organizing mass shootings of naked women and children, whose figure frightens us. It is not the disease and famine in the ghettos, reminiscent perhaps of ancient sieges, but the systematic transportation, selection, dispossession, killing, and distribution of requisitioned personal effects that leaves us uncomprehending, not of the facts but of their implications for our own society and for human psychology—not only the "scientific" killing and its bureaucratic administration; not only the sadism; but rather that incredible mixture of detachment and brutality, distance and cruelty, pleasure and indifference.[56]

Hence the genocide of the Jews, its causes, and its context must be seen as part and parcel of a phase in European civilization that blended modernity and pre-modernity into an often dangerously explosive mixture (though, of course, also a highly creative one, not only in the science of murder). This potent, stimulating but frequently lethal potion, made of ancient prejudices, hatreds, and violent instincts, on the one hand, and of organizational techniques, methods of production, and resource exploitation, on the other, opened the way for the mobilization of individuals whose natural inclinations, talents, and abilities would have been rendered quite harmless in a premodern era, yet within the context of a barbarous modernity cast them in the role of great executioners.[57]

The Holocaust can then be seen as the culmination (but neither the beginning nor the end) of a process begun at some point around the middle of the nineteenth century and still continuing, whose first paroxysm of violence was the so-called Great War, and whose subsequent repercussions can be seen among the millions of victims of the post–1945 era. It is characterized by the missile-wielding religious fanatic, or the cool-headed scientists directing a slave colony of rocket builders, the brutal guard with a given quota of bodies to be disposed of on a daily basis, and the official busy with his schedules of trains bringing anonymous masses of passengers to destinations from which they never return. It is also characterized by two types of professionals so essential to the fabric of modernity: the physician and the lawyer.

Modern society cannot be imagined without these two figures. They represent the greatest achievements of human and political science. Humanity's physical well-being is in the hands of the doctors, and its sociopolitical organization in the hands of the lawyers. Even if we manage to conduct most of our lives out of the hospital and away from the courtroom, it is our awareness of their existence that makes us modern people. Take the doctors away from us and society would be struck by epidemics returning it to bygone periods of fear and ignorance, mysterious death and rampant disease. Take away the legal system that binds together the modern nation-state and the international system, and our lives would slip back into a chaos reminiscent of Hobbes's nightmare.

It is precisely because of our complete dependence on these two professions, and our awareness that they represent the essence of our modern existence, that their participation in the construction and implementation of an evil (mistakenly) per- ceived by us as primeval, as a reversion to a premodern, if not antimodern world, is so disturbing. For it is by observing this fact that we come to understand that the seeds of modernity also contain the potential of moral perversion, then as now.

The point is not, of course, that doctors and lawyers collaborated with a dicta- torial or murderous regime due to opportunistic reasons or human weakness. Indi- vidually, they were and are as human as the rest of us and should not be expected to behave any better than soldiers, politicians, university professors, journalists, writ- ers, train drivers, or sewage workers. The point is, rather, that they were crucial for the *construction* of the system to which they then yielded—that without them things could not possibly have gone so far, or would not have taken that path at all.

In order to legitimize themselves in a modern world, antisemitism, Nazism, and genocide all needed two crucial elements: a scientific stamp and a legalistic sanction. Antisemitism could not have achieved the support of both the masses and the elite, the mob and the school teachers, without being made part of an elaborate racial theory allegedly tested and proven by the most prominent authorities in the fields of human science. In this sense too, and not only the organizational one, the so-called euthanasia of the mentally ill and physically handicapped, and the genocide of the Jews, cannot be seen separately from one another. Eugenics was a science that ruled that some forms of life were undeserving of life. The regime at hand merely had to draw the practical conclusions and carry out the death sentence. National Socialism, which harped incessantly on notions of purity of race, would have been the laughing- stock of Germany had its scientists shown the imbecility of this idea. Instead, it was the scientists who gave an academic garb to racism, or rather, who invented scientific racism as a modern version of pure and simple prejudice and fear of the other. Finally, the Holocaust, the systematic "extermination" of human beings, would have been unthinkable without the medical profession's "detached" evaluation of these human beings not only as inferior and therefore unworthy of life, but as positively dangerous to the national Aryan body and therefore doomed to quick and efficient, yet of course wholly unemotional, elimination. This is what makes the Holocaust central to our era, for it was founded on a scientifically sanctioned, indeed ordered, brutality.[58]

The same can be said about the legal profession. Unlike its predecessors, the modern state must function within a legal system if it does not wish to disintegrate from within under the pressure of contradictory economic, social, and political forces, each pulling in its own particular direction. Chaos is inadmissible, hence everything must be done in the name of the law. At the same time, once things *are* done in the name of the law, it no longer matters what they are, for they *are* legal, and any further scrutiny of their nature is unnecessary, indeed, may be construed as subversive. The law, however, is open to interpretations, and these are given to the legal profession. Hence both the formulation (in varying degrees, depending on the political system) and the interpretation of the law are highly dependent on the members of the legal profession. They represent man-made law (that is, state order), just as the physicians represent biological law (that is, natural order). Between the two is the span of modern man's existence.

Hence modern antisemitism would be inconceivable without the collaboration, indeed the active participation of the legal system. The biologist can say who is a Jew in "scientific" terms. Yet the Jew remains irrelevant to the state until the lawyer defines him legally. A Jew is a person with such and such characteristics that can be determined in such and such a manner. Modern state antisemitism is distinguished from traditional antisemitism precisely by its combination of biological and legal definitions. National Socialism as a political system could not have survived without constant and active support from the legal machinery of the state, as well as new legal theories justifying the rule of the Führer and written by the greatest legal experts of the period. Finally, the Holocaust could not have taken the course it did without constant legal advice, support, legitimation, and participation, which not only smoothed the relations between the various agencies concerned with the implementation of the Final Solution, but also eased the consciences of the individuals involved. There is nothing more calming to a man involved in actions that seem inherently dubious than being told by an expert that they are quite legal. Thus, while the doctors sanctioned murder, the lawyers legalized crime. It is a legacy with far-reaching consequences.[59]

In conclusion, it would seem that quite apart from the causal ties between antisemitism, National Socialism, and the Holocaust, what distinguishes them and puts them all in the same context is that they were extreme and yet characteristic outgrowths of modernity. Late nineteenth-century notions of progress and improvement were not wholly false. In many ways the life of the individual has improved. But the association of material improvement and moral progress was based on a misunderstanding of the inherent nature of modernity. In the modern world certain organizations, professions, and institutions have immense power over the life and mind of the individual. Yet the power of knowledge and direction, though associated with moral sanction, does not imply any elevation in the quality of morality. Indeed, in many ways it may work in the opposite direction, since its legitimation is only its own power, the extent of its own knowledge, not recognizing any other limits or sanctions. The scientist who reaches the "scientific" conclusion that some people deserve life more than others sees this as a truth that no one in the world can refute. "Scientific" laws about humanity will tend to become moral judgments. The individual scientist may decide to keep these "findings" to himself precisely because he perceives their moral implications, but by doing so he will be acting against the essence of his own profession, of scientific "progress," and sooner or later another member of his profession will apply the allegedly value-free rules of science more rigorously, whatever their social, political, and moral implications. The same can be said about the legal profession, whose business is man-made laws. Laws are not expressions of some metaphysical moral order. If the scientist "finds" certain categories of people to be inferior, and the state rules that they should be eliminated, the role of the lawyer is to make sure that the law pertaining to this case be as well formulated, as clear and all-encompassing as possible. Once the law is there, the interest of the legal profession is that it be followed, just as it is the interest of the scientist that the natural law he has discovered be obeyed.

In the modern state, the discovery of laws in nature, the enactment of laws for society, the construction of bureaucratic and administrative systems that would ensure the teaching, imposition, and enforcement of these laws on the citizenry, can be achieved with greater efficiency than at any other point in the past. In the absence of any binding religious commitment or authority, it is the makers and formulators of natural and civil laws who define the limits of our existence, and it is the administration and technical capacities of the state that impose them on us. We have nowhere else to turn, for there is no other sanction or institution. And because we know now the barbaric essence in modernity, its potential of scientifically and legally sanctioned, state-controlled evil, we enjoy our liberty and freedom as citizens of Western civilization with a sense of fear and foreboding.

NOTES

1. See, for example, Berel Lang, *Act and Idea in the Nazi Genocide* (Chicago, 1990), pp. 3–29; Frank Chalk and Kurt Jonassohn, eds., *The History and Sociology of Genocide: Analyses and Case Studies* (New Haven, 1990); Leo Kuper, *Genocide: Its Political Use in the Twentieth Century* (New Haven, 1981).

2. For the first version see, for example, Robert S. Wistrich, *Antisemitism: The Longest Hatred*, 2nd ed. (New York, 1992); Shmuel Almog, ed., *Anti-Semitism through the Ages*, trans. N. H. Reisner (Oxford, 1988); Leon Poliakov, *Histoire de l'antisémitisme*, 4th ed., 2 vols. (Paris, 1991). Somewhere between the two poles, see, for example, Shmuel Ettinger, *Modern Anti-Semitism: Studies and Essays* (Tel Aviv, 1978 [in Hebrew]); Jacob Katz, *From Prejudice to Destruction: Anti-Semitism, 1700–1933* (Cambridge, MA., 1980). On the second version, see, for example, Hannah Arendt, *The Origins of Totalitarianism*, 6th ed. (London, 1986), esp. part 1, pp. 3–120; Peter Pulzer, *The Rise of Political Anti-Semitism in Germany and Austria*, 2nd rev. ed. (Cambridge, MA, 1988); Moshe Zimmermann, *Wilhelm Marr: The Patriarch of Antisemitism* (New York, 1986). For a brief survey, see Patrick Girard, "Historical Foundations of Anti-Semitism," in *Survivors, Victims, and Perpetrators: Essays on the Nazi Holocaust*, ed. Joel E. Dimsdale, (Washington, D.C., 1980), pp. 55–77. See also the important volume edited by François Furet, *L'Allemagne nazie et le génocide juif* (Paris, 1985); and a shorter English translation: *Unanswered Questions: Nazi Germany and the Genocide of the Jews* (New York, 1989).

3. See, for example, the excellent study by Zygmunt Bauman, *Modernity and the Holocaust*, 2nd ed. (Ithaca, 1991).

4. For a forceful presentation of the Zionist view, see Abraham B. Yehoshua, *The Wall and the Mountain: The Unliterary Reality of the Writer in Israel* (Tel Aviv, 1989 [in Hebrew]). See also Dina Porat, *The Blue and the Yellow Stars of David: The Zionist Leadership in Palestine and the Holocaust, 1939–1945* (Cambridge, MA, 1990); Anita Shapira, *Land and Power: The Zionist Resort to Force, 1881–1948*, trans. William Templer (New York, 1992).

5. For a survey of the emancipation of European Jewry, which led to the secularization

and assimilation of growing numbers, see Jacob Katz, *Out of the Ghetto: The Social Background of the Emancipation of the Jews 1770–1870* (New York, 1978). On the relationship of this process to modern antisemitism, see Reinhard Rürup, *Emanzipation und Antisemitismus* (Göttingen, 1975); Arthur Hertzberg, *The French Enlightenment and the Jews: The Origins of Modern Anti-Semitism*, 2nd ed. (New York, 1990). On antisemitism and religion, see Gavin I. Langmuir, *History, Religion, and Antisemitism* (Berkeley, 1990). For alternative views of history among some German Jewish intellectuals, see Stéphane Moses, *L'Ange de l'histoire: Rosenzweig, Benjamin, Scholem* (Paris, 1992); and Gershom Scholem, *On Jews and Judaism in Crisis: Selected Essays*, ed. Werner J. Dannhauser (New York, 1976). For an outsider's post-Holocaust view of antisemitism in a philosophically detached mode, see Jean-Paul Sartre, *Réflexions sur la question juive* (Paris, 1954).

6. See, for example, the critique of Hannah Arendt in Ettinger, *Modern Anti-Semitism*, pp. x-xi; and Walter Laqueur, "Hannah Arendt in Jerusalem: The Controversy Revisited," with comments by William S. Allen and David Schoenbaum, in *Western Society after the Holocaust*, ed. Lyman H. Letgers (Boulder, CO: 1983), pp. 107–29. Compare also with Norman Cohn, *Warrant for Genocide: The Myth of the Jewish World-Conspiracy and the Protocols of the Elders of Zion*, 2nd ed. (London, 1970); and Yehuda Bauer, *The Holocaust in Historical Perspective*, 2nd ed. (Seattle, 1980), pp. 30–49.

7. One example of a work that minimizes the role of antisemitism in the rise of Nazism is Sarah Gordon, *Hitler, Germans, and the "Jewish Question"* (Princeton, 1984). For evaluations of the importance of antisemitism by historians see, for example, Lucy S. Dawidowicz, *The Holocaust and the Historians* (Cambridge, MA, 1981), esp. pp. 22–87; Michael R. Marrus, *The Holocaust in History*, 2nd ed. (New York, 1989), esp. pp. 9–13; Ian Kershaw, *The Nazi Dictatorship: Problems and Perspectives of Interpretation*, 2nd ed. (London, 1989), esp. pp. 82–106; Richard Levy, *The Downfall of the Antisemitic Political Parties in Imperial Germany* (New Haven, 1975). See also the most recent vehement defense of the centrality of antisemitism in explaining the Holocaust: Daniel J. Goldhagen, *Hitler's Willing Executioners: Ordinary Germans and the Holocaust* (New York, 1996). For a more measured view postulating the existence of "redemptory antisemitism," see Saul Friedlander, *Nazi Germany and the Jews*, vol. 1: *The Years of Persecution, 1993–1934* (New York, 1997).

8. This is implied in Kershaw, *Nazi Dictatorship*, p. 82, and stated more strongly in Martin Broszat's correspondence with Saul Friedlander, included in Peter Baldwin, ed., *Reworking the Past: Hitler, the Holocaust, and the Historians' Debate* (Boston, 1990), esp. p. 106. See also Saul Friedlander, *Memory, History, and the Extermination of the Jews of Europe* (Bloomington, 1993). On the memory of the past, see, for example, Judith Miller, *One, By One, By One: Facing the Holocaust* (New York, 1990), esp. pp. 13–60; Bernt Engelmann, *In Hitler's Germany: Everyday Life in the Third Reich*, trans. Krishna Winston (New York, 1986); Lutz Niethammer, ed., *"Die Jahre weiss man nicht, wo man die heute hinsetzen soll": Faschismuserfahrungen im Ruhrgebiet* (Berlin, 1983). A haunting recent book on the memory of the Holocaust is Lawrence L. Langer, *Holocaust Testimonies: The Ruins of Memory* (New Haven, 1991). On official attempts to represent memory, see the recent book by James E. Young, *The Texture of Memory: Holocaust Memorials and Meaning* (New Haven, 1993).

9. I refer here to such prompting from widely differing, yet not unrelated quarters. See, for example, Martin Broszat, "A Plea for the Historicization of National Socialism," in Baldwin, *Reworking the Past*, pp. 77–87; Ernst Nolte, "Between Historical Legend and Revisionism? The Third Reich in the Perspective of 1980," and idem, "The Past That Will Not Pass: A Speech That Could Be Written but Not Delivered," in *Forever in the Shadow of Hitler? Original Documents of the Historikerstreit, the Controversy Concerning the Singularity of the Holocaust* (Atlantic Highlands, NJ, 1993), pp. 1–15, 18–23; Andreas Hillgruber, *Zweierlei Untergang: Die Zerschlagung des Deutschen Reiches und das Ende des europäischen Judentums* (Berlin, 1986); Arno Mayer, "Memory and History: On the Poverty of Remembering and Forgetting the Judeocide," *Radical History Review* 56 (1993): 5–20; and Charles S. Maier, "A Surfeit of Memory? Reflections on History, Melancholy, and Denial," *History and Memory* 5/2 (1993): 136–52.

10. The most conspicuous instance of this was of course Menachem Begin's pronouncement during the Israeli siege of Beirut in 1982. On the debate in the Israeli press, see Tom

Segev, *The Seventh Million: The Israelis and the Holocaust*, trans. Haim Watzman (New York, 1993), pp. 399–403. Also, see Moshe Zuckermann, *Shoah in the Sealed Room: The "Holocaust" in Israeli Press during the Gulf War* (Tel Aviv, 1993 [in Hebrew]).

11. See Frank Stern, *The Whitewashing of the Yellow Badge: Antisemitism and Philosemitism in Postwar Germany*, trans. William Templer (Oxford, 1992). See also Moshe Zimmermann and Oded Heilbronner, eds., *"Normal" Relations: Israeli-German Relations* (Jerusalem, 1993 [in Hebrew]).

12. Reports of growing antisemitism in Russia, as well as in East European countries formerly under Soviet domination, seem to confirm this fear; nor is the growing tide of neo-fascist organizations in Central and Western Europe to be ignored, even if it does not present a danger to the regime, since it may represent an extreme version of more widespread public xenophobia in many countries confronting new economic hardship and the "threat" of foreign immigration. See the recent book by Michael Schmidt, *The New Reich: Violent Extremism in Unified Germany and Beyond*, trans. Daniel Horch (New York, 1993). See also Ian Buruma, "Outsiders," *New York Review of Books* (April 9, 1992): 15–19; Frank Stern, "German Unification and the Question of Antisemitism," *International Perspectives: American Jewish Committee* (May 1993).

13. The recent volume edited by Saul Friedlander, *Probing the Limits of Representation: Nazism and the "Final Solution"* (Cambridge, MA, 1992), tries to confront some of the issues related to this problem.

14. On the origins of the term, see Marrus, *Holocaust in History*, pp. 3–4.

15. Other terms used frequently in Germany to denote the Holocaust are "Final Solution," the official Nazi term for the genocide of the Jews, and "Auschwitz," which stands for the whole industrial killing machine rather than the specific death and concentration camp, as well as industrial works and slave barracks contained within the Auschwitz complex. For those who do not know what Auschwitz was, the term evokes neither genocide nor Jews but at worst a concentration camp somewhere in the East.

16. Peter Haidu, "The Dialectic of Unspeakability: Language, Silence, and the Narratives of Desubjectification," in Friedlander, *Probing the Limits of Representation*, p. 279.

17. On the reception of the film *Holocaust* in the Federal Republic of Germany, see Anton Kaes, *From Hitler to Heimat: The Return of History as Film* (Cambridge, MA, 1989), pp. 28–35. On film and the Holocaust, see Ilan Avisar, *Screening the Holocaust: Cinema's Images of the Unimaginable* (Bloomington, 1988). See also Yosefa Loshitzky, ed., *Spielberg's Holocaust: Critical Perspectives on Schindler's List* (Bloomington, 1997); Eric L. Santner, *Stranded Objects: Mourning, Memory, and Film in Postwar Germany*, 2nd ed. (Ithaca, 1993); and Gertrud Koch, *Die Einstellung ist die Einstellung: Visuelle Konstruktionen des Judentums* (Frankfurt/M., 1992).

18. The term "Vernichtung," annihilation, so popular in the Third Reich, is often employed by German historians writing on the period. Though German scholars sometimes use quotation marks when employing Nazi terms (such as "Führer," "Third Reich," "Final Solution," etc.), the effect of a stream of publications bearing titles lifted out of Nazi discourse is quite disturbing and may well have consequences for the German reading public very different from those intended by the authors. See, for example, Wolfgang Schneider, ed., *"Vernichtungspolitik": Eine Debatte über den Zusammenhang von Sozialpolitik und Genozid im nationalsozialistschen Deutschland* (Hamburg, 1991), a book that raises many other problematic issues on the relationship between modernization and annihilation policies; Peter Jahn and Reinhard Rürup, *Erobern und Vernichten: Der Krieg gegen die Sowjetunion 1941–1945* (Berlin, 1991), which focuses more on the war in the USSR but also raises the problematic issue of demographic policies in the East; and the Piper Verlag collection *"Historikerstreit": Die Dokumentation der Kontroverse um die Einzigartigkeit der nationalsozialistischen Judenvernichtung* (Munich, 1987), a compilation of the main contributions to the German historians' debate of 1986. The term "Judenvernichtung" was changed to "Holocaust" in the English translation of this volume. See *Forever in the Shadow*, n. 9. However, since this essay was originally written, two new German works have referred to "Judenmord" and "Massenverbrechen" in their titles. See Thomas Sandkühler, *"Endlösung" in Galizien: Der Judenmord in Ostpolen und die Rettungsinitiativen von Berthold Beitz 1941–1944* (Bonn, 1996), and Dieter

Pohl, *Nationalsozialistische Judenverfolgung in Ostgalizien 1941–1944: Organisation und Durchführung eines staatlichen Massenverbrechens* (Munich, 1996).

19. See Arno J. Mayer, *Why Did the Heavens Not Darken? The "Final Solution" in History* (New York, 1988), for example pp. vii, 3.

20. See, for example, Jean-Pierre Azéma, *1940 l'annee terrible* (Paris, 1990).

21. See the brilliant treatment of this issue in Alain Finkielkraut, *Remembering in Vain: The Klaus Barbie Trial and Crimes against Humanity*, trans. Roxanne Lapidus (New York, 1992); also see Erna Paris, *Unhealed Wounds: France and the Klaus Barbie Affair*, 2nd ed. (New York, 1986); Pierre Vidal-Naquet, *Assassins of Memory: Essays on the Denial of the Holocaust*, trans. Jeffrey Mehlman (New York, 1992). For some literary treatments of the period see, for example, Jean-Paul Sartre, *Iron in the Soul*, trans. Gerard Hopkins (Harmondsworth, 1984 [1949]); Michel Tournier, *The Ogre*, trans. Barbara Bray (New York, 1972); Marguerite Duras, *The War: A Memoir*, trans. Barbara Bray (New York, 1986).

22. Recently the German genocide of the Jews has been compared by one writer to the genocide of the population of the Vendée by the Jacobins. See Reynold Secher, *Juifs et Vendéens: d'un génocide a l'autre, la manipulation de la mémoire* (Paris, 1991).

23. On the difficulties of the French with the memory of the period, see Henry Rousso, *The Vichy Syndrome: History and Memory in France since 1944*, trans. Arthur Goldhammer (Cambridge, MA, 1991). On collaboration, see Robert O. Paxton, *Vichy France: Old Guard and New Order, 1940–1944*, 2nd ed. (New York, 1975); Michael R. Marrus and Robert O. Paxton, *Vichy France and the Jews* (New York, 1983). For French scholarship on collaboration and opinion during the "black years," see, for example, Pascal Ory, *Les collaborateurs 1940–1945* (Paris, 1976); Pierre Laborie, *L'Opinion française sous Vichy* (Paris, 1990); Henri Amouroux, *Quarante millions de pétainistes, juin 1940–juin 1941* (Paris, 1977); and, most recently, Philippe Burrin, *France under the Germans: Collaboration and Compromise*, trans. J. Lloyd (New York, 1996). On the memory of resistance, see Émile Malet, *Résistance et mémoire: D'Auschwitz à Sarajevo* (Paris, 1993).

24. See Segev, *Seventh Million*; Shapira, *Land and Power*; Porat, *Blue and Yellow Stars*. The ultra-Orthodox use the terms "churban," "gzerot," or "pur'anut." See also Moshe Halbertal, "Speak, Memory," *New Republic* (October 18, 1993): 40–47, esp. p. 45; Sidra DeKoven Ezrahi, *By Words Alone: The Holocaust in Literature* (Chicago, 1980), pp. 10–15; David G. Roskies, *Against the Apocalypse: Responses to Catastrophe in Modern Jewish Culture* (Cambridge, MA, 1984), pp. 41–43.

25. On Israeli attempts to come to terms with the memory of war, see the fascinating study by Emmanuel Sivan, *The 1948 Generation: Myth, Profile and Memory* (Tel Aviv, 1991 [in Hebrew]), and now his article "To Remember Is to Forget: Israel's 1948 War," *Journal of Contemporary History* 28 (1993): 341–59. For further information on history, memory, and myth in Israel, see Yael Zerubavel, *Recovered Roots: Collective Memory and the Making of Israeli National Tradition* (Chicago, 1995).

26. Probably the best introduction to the historiography of the Third Reich is Ian Kershaw, *Nazi Dictatorship*.

27. See, for example, William Montgomery McGovern, *From Luther to Hitler: The History of Nazi-Fascist Philosophy* (London, 1946). See also A. J. P. Taylor, *The Course of German History* (London, 1945). On the demerits of the thesis about German history having "failed to turn," see David Blackbourn, "The Discreet Charm of the Bourgeoisie: Reappraising German History in the Nineteenth Century," in *The Peculiarities of German History: Bourgeois Society and Politics in Nineteenth-Century Germany*, ed. David Blackbourn and Goeff Eley, , 5th ed. (Oxford, 1992), esp. pp. 159–65.

28. See, for example, Max Fechner, ed., *Wie konnte es geschehen* (Berlin, n.d.). The best known examples of this type of literature are Friedrich Meinecke, *Die deutsche Katastrophe* (Wiesbaden, 1946); and Gerhard Ritter, *Das deutsche Problem* (Munich, 1962), originally published under the title *Europa und die deutsche Frage* (Munich, 1948).

29. See, for example, Dietrich Eichholz and Kurt Gossweiler, eds., *Faschismusforschung: Positionen, Probleme, Polemik* (Berlin [East], 1980). See also Wolfgang Wippermann, "The Post-War German Left and Fascism," *Journal of Contemporary History* 11 (1976); Jörn Rüsen, "Theory of History in the Development of West German Historical Studies: A Reconstruc-

tion and Outlook," *German Studies Review* 7 (1984): 14–18; Konrad Kwiet, "Historians of the German Democratic Republic on Antisemitism and Persecution," Leo Baeck Institute *Year Book* 21 (1976): 173–98; Otto Dov Kulka, "Major Trends and Tendencies in German Historiography on National Socialism and the 'Jewish Question' (1924–1984)," Leo Baeck Institute *Year Book* 30 (1985): 215–42.

30. See, for example, Fritz Stern, *The Politics of Cultural Despair: A Study in the Rise of the Germanic Ideology*, 2nd ed. (Berkeley, 1974 [1961]); George L. Mosse, *The Crisis of German Ideology: Intellectual Origins of the Third Reich* (New York, 1964); Walter Laqueur, *Young Germany: A History of the German Youth Movement,* 2nd ed. (New Brunswick, NJ, 1984 [1962]).

31. See especially Fritz Fischer, *Germany's Aims in the First World War* (London, 1966 [1961]); H. W. Koch, ed., *The Origins of the First World War: Great Power Rivalry and German War Aims,* 2nd ed. (London, 1977); Hans-Ulrich Wehler, *The German Empire 1871–1918,* trans. Kim Traynor (Leamington Spa, 1985 [1973]).

32. On the first, see the pathbreaking essay by Tim Mason, "Intention and Explanation: A Current Controversy about the Interpretation of National Socialism," in Timothy W. Mason, *Nazism, Fascism, and the Working Class,* ed. Jane Caplan (Cambridge, 1995), pp. 212–30. The debate on uniqueness relates to the so-called "Historikerstreit." Apart from the Piper Verlag collection and Baldwin's edited volume cited above, see also Charles S. Maier, *The Unmasterable Past: History, Holocaust, and German Nationalism* (Cambridge, MA, 1988); Richard Evans, *In Hitler's Shadow: West German Historians and the Attempts to Escape from the Nazi Past* (New York, 1989); Hans-Ulrich Wehler, *Entsorgung der deutschen Vergangenheit? Ein polemischer Essay zum "Historikerstreit"* (Munich, 1988); Dan Diner, ed., *Ist der Nationalsozialismus Geschichte? Zu Historisierung und Historikerstreit* (Frankfurt/M., 1987).

33. Apart from the book by Kaes cited above, see Judith Ryan, *The Uncompleted Past: Postwar German Novels and the Third Reich* (Detroit, 1983); Ezrahi, *By Words Alone;* Saul Friedlander, *Reflections of Nazism: An Essay on Kitsch and Death* (New York, 1984); Susan Sontag, "Fascinating Fascism," and "Syberberg's Hitler," in her *Under the Sign of Saturn,* 7th printing (New York, 1981), pp. 73–105, 137–65; Dan Diner, *Der Krieg der Erinnerungen und die Ordnung der Welt* (Berlin, 1991).

34. See most especially Franz Neumann, *Behemoth: The Structure and Practice of National Socialism 1933–1944* (New York, 1944).

35. Martin Broszat was the leader of the multivolume project on everyday life in Bavaria; see the concluding essay in the final volume, Martin Broszat and Elke Fröhlich, *Alltag und Widerstand: Bayern im Nationalsozialismus* (Munich, 1987); and Martin Broszat, *The Hitler State: The Foundation and Development of the Internal Structure of the Third Reich,* trans. John W. Hiden (London, 1981 [1969]). The other main proponent of structuralism is Hans Mommsen; see especially his "National Socialism: Continuity and Change," in *Fascism: A Reader's Guide,* 2nd ed., ed. Walter Laqueur (Harmondsworth, 1982), pp. 151–92. Also, see the excellent essay by Mary Nolan, "The *Historikerstreit* and Social History," in Baldwin, *Reworking the Past,* pp. 224–48.

36. See, for example, Jürgen Förster, "The German Army and the Ideological War against the Soviet Union," in *The Policies of Genocide: Jews and Soviet Prisoners of War in Nazi Germany,* ed. Gerhard Hirschfeld (London, 1986), pp. 15–29.

37. One cannot help feeling that in yet another ironic twist, typical this time of the United States, the indigenous peoples of North America were renamed Native Americans only after they were reduced to a harmless, hopeless, and wretched marginal minority.

38. See Roger Brubaker, *Citizenship and Nationhood in France and Germany* (Cambridge, MA, 1992), chapter 8; Ulrich Herbert, *Geschichte der Ausländerbeschäftigung in Deutschland 1880 bis 1980* (Bonn, 1986).

39. Benedict Kiernan, "Genocidal Targeting: Two Groups of Victims in Pol Pot's Cambodia," in *State Organized Terror,* ed. P. T. Bushnell et al. (Boulder, CO: 1991), pp. 207–26.

40. For the psychology of the Freikorps and their visions of war and violence, see Klaus Theweleit, *Männerphantasien,* 3rd ed. (Reinbek bei Hamburg, 1987), 2 vols. Ernst Nolte hoped to put an end to the debate with another book: *Das Vergehen der Vergangenheit: Antwort an meine Kritiker im sogenannten Historikerstreit* (Berlin, 1987), which contains, inter alia, two

interviews with Nolte conducted by Israeli journalists and published there, as well as an article he wrote especially for an Israeli daily trying to explain his position. See also Alan Bullock, *Hitler and Stalin: Parallel Lives* (London, 1991).

41. A good introduction is Thomas Childers and Jane Caplan, eds., *Reevaluating the Third Reich* (New York, l993).

42. Detlev J. K. Peukert, *The Weimar Republic: The Crisis of Classical Modernity*, trans. Richard Deveson (New York, 1992).

43. See, for example, Rainer Zitelmann, *Hitler: Selbstverständnis eines Revolutionärs* (Stuttgart, 1987); and Michael Prinz and Rainer Zitelmann, eds., *Nationalsozialismus und Modernisierung* (Darmstadt, 1991).

44. See mainly Ralf Dahrendorf, *Society and Democracy in Germany,* 2nd ed. (New York, 1979 [1965]), pp. 381–96; and David Schoenbaum, *Hitler's Social Revolution: Class and Status in Nazi Germany 1933–1939* (New York, 1966).

45. A related debate, however, focuses primarily on the extent to which the Final Solution was perceived by Nazi bureaucrats as an economically rational measure, aimed at modernizing Eastern Europe. This is the thesis argued by Götz Aly and Susanne Heim, *Vordenker der Vernichtung: Auschwitz und die deutsche Pläne für eine neue europäische Ordnung* (Hamburg, 1991). It has been criticized by Ulrich Herbert, "Labour and Extermination: Economic Interest and the Primacy of *Weltanschauung* in National Socialism," *Past & Present* 138 (1993): 144–95; and by Christopher R. Browning, "German Technocrats, Jewish Labor, and the Final Solution: A Reply to Götz Aly and Susanne Heim," in *The Path to Genocide: Essays on Launching the Final Solution* (Cambridge, 1992), pp. 59–76, a book that generally presents a series of theses that effectively demolish the Aly/Heim argument. See also Schneider, "*Vernichtungspolitik*," which is wholly devoted to a debate on the Aly/Heim thesis. A much more convincing argument has recently been made by Götz Aly in his new massive study, *"Endlösung": Völkerverschiebung und der Mord an den europäischen Juden* (Frankfurt/M., 1995).

46. See Broszat, *Historicization*; Hillgruber, *Zweierlei Untergang*; Michael Stürmer, "History in a Land without History," in *Forever in the Shadow*, pp. 16–17.

47. See in this context Saul Friedlander, "Reflections on the Historicization of National Socialism," pp. 64–84; and his introduction to Gerald Fleming, *Hitler and the Final Solution* (Berkeley, 1984), esp. pp. x, xii–xxxiii. Fleming's book is a striking example of intentionalist history.

48. One of the best representatives of this view is Lucy S. Dawidowicz, *The War against the Jews, 1933–1945*, 10th ed. (New York, 1986 [1971]).

49. Apart from Fleming, *Hitler and the Final Solution*, see also Eberhard Jäckel, *Hitler's World View: A Blueprint for Power*, trans. Herbert Arnold, 2nd ed. (Cambridge, MA, 1981 [1969]). The personalizing revisionist view is presented in David Irving, *Hitler's War* (London, 1977). The standard biographies, all more or less intentionalist (though not necessarily emphasizing Hitler's role in the Holocaust), are Konrad Heiden, *Der Führer: Hitler's Rise to Power*, trans. Ralph Manheim (Boston, 1969 [1944]); Alan Bullock, *Hitler: A Study in Tyranny*, 2nd rev. ed. (New York, 1964); Joachim C. Fest, *Hitler*, trans. Richard and Cara Winston, 3rd ed. (Harmondsworth, 1982 [1973]). See also William Carr, *Hitler: A Study in Personality and Politics* (London, 1978); Eberhard Jäckel, *Hitler in History* (Hanover, NH, 1984); Ian Kershaw, *Hitler* (London, 1991).

50. Apart from Gordon, *Hitler, Germans, and the "Jewish Question,"* see also Theodore Abel, *Why Hitler Came into Power*, 2nd ed. (Cambridge, MA, 1986 [1938]), esp. pp. 154–65; and Peter H. Merkl, *Political Violence under the Swastika: 581 Early Nazis* (Princeton, 1975), esp. pp. 498–527.

51. See especially Martin Broszat, "Hitler and the Genesis of the 'Final Solution': An Assessment of David Irving's Theses," *Yad Vashem Studies* 13 (1979): 61–98; and Hans Mommsen, "The Realization of the Unthinkable: the 'Final Solution of the Jewish Question' in the Third Reich," in Hirschfeld, *Policies of Genocide*, pp. 97–144.

52. See Dan Diner, ed., *Zivilisationsbruch: Denken nach Auschwitz* (Frankfurt/M., 1988).

53. Apart from Mommsen, *National Socialism*, and Broszat, *The Hitler State*, see also Edward N. Peterson, *The Limits of Hitler's Power* (Princeton, 1969).

54. Hannah Arendt, *Eichmann in Jerusalem: A Report on the Banality of Evil*, rev. and

enlarged ed. (New York, 1977 [1963, rev. 1965]). This trend was noted already in Dawidowicz, *Holocaust and the Historians*, esp. pp. 22–67 and 152–55. The new interest in Nazi eugenic policies has also tended to downplay antisemitism as such in favor of broader Nazi biological policies that included the mentally and physically handicapped as well as women. See especially Claudia Koonz, "Eugenics, Gender, and Ethics in Nazi Germany: The Debate about Involuntary Sterilization, 1933–1936," and Detlev J. K. Peukert, "The Genesis of the Final Solution from the Spirit of Science," both in Childers, *Reevaluating the Third Reich*, pp. 66–85 and 236–52, respectively. See also Gisela Bock, "Racism and Sexism in Nazi Germany: Mother-hood, Compulsory Sterilization, and the State," in *When Biology Became Destiny: Women in Weimar and Nazi Germany*, ed. Renate Bridenthal et al. (New York, 1984), pp. 271–96.

55. Apart from Broszat, *Alltag und Widerstand*, and Nolan, *Historikerstreit and Social History*, see Detlev J. K. Peukert, "Alltag und Barbarei. Zur Normalität des Dritten Reiches," in *Ist der Nationalsozialismus Geschichte?* ed. Diner, pp. 51–61 (Peukert is critical of this approach); Klaus Bergmann and Rolf Schörken, eds., *Geschichte im Alltag–Alltag in der Geschichte* (Düsseldorf, 1982); Ian Kershaw, *Popular Opinion and Political Dissent in the Third Reich* (Oxford, 1983); and idem, *The "Hitler Myth": Image and Reality in the Third Reich* (Oxford, 1987).

56. We have now become used to thinking of Auschwitz as an inhuman death machine where there was no room for individual brutality and which was relatively insulated from its environment. A recent excellent study corrects both these misconceptions: Gordon J. Horwitz, *In the Shadow of Death: Living Outside the Gates of Mauthausen* (New York, 1990). But see also Wolfgang Sofsky, *The Order of Terror: The Concentration Camp*, trans. William Templer (Princeton, 1997), which presents a picture of the camps as insulated from their environment; and Tzvetan Todorov, *Facing the Extreme: Moral Life in the Concentration Camps*, trans. Arthur Denner and Abigail Pollack (New York, 1996), which argues for the possibility for a moral existence in the camps. On the psychology of those involved in genocide, see also the penetrating study by Raul Hilberg, *Perpetrators Victims Bystanders: The Jewish Catastrophe 1933–1945* (New York, 1992). On the indifference of the Allied governments to reports on genocide and/or their refusal to believe the veracity of such news, see, for example, Martin Gilbert, *Auschwitz and the Allies* (New York, 1981); Bernard Wasserstein, *Britain and the Jews of Europe 1939–1945*, 2nd ed. (Oxford, 1988); Walter Laqueur, *The Terrible Secret: Suppression of the Truth about Hitler's Final Solution*, 3rd ed. (Harmondsworth, 1982); Walter Laqueur and Richard Breitman, *Breaking the Silence* (New York, 1986). See also the disturbing account of Polish wartime policies in David Engel, *In the Shadow of Auschwitz: The Polish Government-in-Exile and the Jews, 1939–1942* (Chapel Hill, NC, 1987); and idem, *Facing a Holocaust: The Polish Government-in-Exile and the Jews, 1943–1945* (Chapel Hill, NC, 1993).

57. Here I tend to agree with Detlev Peukert's arguments as presented in his *Weimar Republic* and his article "The Genesis of the 'Final Solution' from the Spirit of Science." However, it is quite true that Peukert's insistence on the "biological politics" of Nazism is open to criticism on two counts: first, it underplays the role of antisemitism and specifically of anti-Jewish policies in the Third Reich; and second, it generalizes "biological politics" to include much of the West and thereby minimizes Germany's centrality in the development and implementation of this concept. Peukert's studies also undermine Marxist class analysis and considerations of economic factors in evaluating fascism and generally imply a complete abandonment of the fascist paradigm. This in turn would make Nazi Germany unique as regards other fascist (or "totalitarian") regimes, on the one hand, and contextualize it as part and parcel of the Western modernist project in general, on the other. Hence this analysis may turn into an apologetic blurring of boundaries and categories. See especially Charles S. Maier, Foreword, and Tim Mason, Appendix, "Whatever Happened to 'Fascism'?" both in Childers, *Reevaluating the Third Reich*, pp. xi-xvi and 253–62, respectively.

58. See especially Michael Burleigh, *Death and Deliverance: "Euthanasia" in Germany 1900–1945* (Cambridge, 1994); Michael Burleigh and Wolfgang Wippermann, *The Racial State: Germany 1933–1945* (Cambridge, 1991); Michael Kater, *Doctors under Hitler* (Chapel Hill, NC, 1989); Robert N. Proctor, *Racial Hygiene: Medicine under the Nazis* (Cambridge, MA, 1988); Robert J. Lifton, *The Nazi Doctors: Medical Killing and the Psychology of Genocide* (New York, 1986); Ernst Klee, *"Euthanasie" im NS-Staat: Die "Vernichtung lebensunwerten Lebens"*

(Frankfurt/M., 1983); idem, *Dokumente zur "Euthanasie"* (Frankfurt/M., 1985); idem, *Was sie taten – was sie wurden: Ärtze, Juristen und andere Beteiligte am Kranken- oder Judenmord* (Frankfurt/M., 1986); Paul Weindling, *Health, Race and Germans between National Unification and Nazism 1870–1945* (Cambridge, 1989). See also Geoffrey Cocks, *Psychotherapy in the Third Reich: The Göring Institute* (New York, 1985). On the involvement of other kinds of scientists, see Michael Burleigh, *Germany Turns Eastwards: A Study of Ostforschung in the Third Reich*, 2nd ed. (Cambridge, 1989); and Alan D. Beyerchen, *Scientists under Hitler: Politics and the Physics Community in the Third Reich* (New Haven, 1977).

59. See Ingo Müller, *Hitler's Justice: The Courts of the Third Reich*, trans. Deborah L. Schneider (Cambridge, MA, 1991 [1987]). Also see Joseph Bendersky, *Carl Schmitt: Theorist for the Reich* (Princeton, 1983); Dan Diner, "Rassistisches Völkerrecht: Elemente einer nationalsozialistischen Weltordnung," *Vierteljahrshefte für Zeitgeschichte* 1(1989): 23–56. On a related issue, see Manfred Messerschmidt and F. Wüllner, *Die Wehrmachtjustiz im Dienste des Nationalsozialismus* (Baden-Baden, 1987); and Manfred Messerschmidt, "German Military Law in the Second World War," in *The German Military in the Age of Total War*, ed. Wilhelm Deist (Leamington Spa, 1985), pp. 323–35. On the fate of German legal institutions after the collapse of the Third Reich, see James Tent, *Mission on the Rhine: Reeducation and Denazification in American-Occupied Germany* (Chicago, 1982).

Part 3

The Politics of Racial Health and Science

German antisemitism cannot be viewed apart from previous manifestations of "the longest hatred." So too, Nazi science and its practice of "eugenics" and so-called "euthanasia" must be seen in the context of German science and of the practice of eugenics during the Nazi era in other countries, most especially the United States. Benno Müller-Hill's "Human Genetics and the Mass Murder of Jews, Gypsies, and Others," is a chilling examination of genetics as a genocidal force. Müller-Hill traces the influence of the 1921 genetics textbook by Erwin Baur, Eugen Fischer, and Fritz Lenz on Adolf Hitler, who read it in prison, where it formed some of the core ideas of *Mein Kampf*.

These geneticists were quite prominent in the German scientific community. Fisher was later to become rector of the University of Berlin where he dismissed Jewish faculty. He was, as described by Müller-Hill, a polite but deeply committed antisemite who called for a law prohibiting sexual relations between Jews and Germans on scientific grounds. Lenz considered Hitler "the only living politician who really understands what genetics and eugenics is all about." Under Nazism, these geneticists received what they requested. Their careers advanced, the laws they advocated were passed. For example, passage of the 1934 law for sterilization resulted in its implementation on some 200,000 people in the first three years and perhaps twice that number before 1939. Müller-Hill cautions that international reaction was quite positive. After all, blacks and whites were not allowed to marry in the United States. Under Nazism, every university had a chair in genetics.

Initial calls for sterilization were supplemented by those of scientists such as Franz Kallmann, who called for the procedure to be applied to all heterozygotes carrying the putative recessive gene for schizophrenia—some twenty percent of the population. Ernst Rüdin called for sterilization of asocials and petty criminals, and Robert Ritter's institute at Berlin's National Institute of Health clarified the status of Germany's thirty thousand Gypsies.

Müller-Hill traces the career of Josef Mengele, who was a postdoctoral fellow at Frankfurt University, where he published a paper on inheritance of facial abnormality. His teacher later headed the Kaiser Wilhelm Institute, from which Mengele was called to Auschwitz. A grant application was made asking for support of Mengele's work in Auschwitz. After the war, little happened to geneticists—aside from Mengele, who had to flee. Most later denied Nazi connections and were regarded as legitimate—often distinguished—scientists.

As to contemporary implications of this misapplication of science, Müller-Hill cautions that genes have not been discovered that form the bases of intelligence, schizophrenia, and manic depression, and that if one leaves genetics to forces of the market place, and if science abandons its clients and becomes linked with ideology, this can become an essential component of mass murder.

Annegret Ehmann's "From Colonial Racism to Nazi Population Policy: The Role of the So-Called Mischlinge" traces the origins of Nazi policy toward "mixed-breed" individuals or "mongrels" back to its origins in German colonial policy. She views the evolution of Nazi policy as rooted in colonialism and in the frantic effort to prevent the interbreeding of pure Aryan stock with first colonials, and then later with Jews or Gypsies (Roma and Sinti). Holocaust research, Ehmann argues, has devoted very little attention to the history of the persecution of the Mischlinge, yet this special case reveals elements of Nazi racial ideology. In a wide-ranging article that traverses German colonial policy, anthropology, racial theory, and biology, she argues that the inner logic of the "Final Solution to the Jewish Question" would have led inevitably to a final solution for the Mischlinge as well.

Stefan Kühl's "The Cooperation of German Racial Hygienists and American Eugenicists before and after 1933," traces the interrelationship between American and German geneticists. Conventional historical accounts often attempt to portray the German movement as aberrant and the capitulation of German science as the result of Nazi domination. Kühl rejects these notions and argues that there was close cooperation and mutual admiration between the Americans and the Germans. He argues that historians have tended to obscure the issue of international collaboration, failing to provide a more detailed account of the differences and similarities that emerge when one compares national eugenics movements and Nazi racial policies.

Kühl contends that the American eugenics movement supported and legitimized the principles of Nazi eugenics. Leading American eugenicists were enthusiastic about the implementation of their practical proposals. In a sense, Hitler adopted their ideology. Since the turn of the century, German eugenicists had admired the Americans. Between 1907 and 1930, more than half of the American states had passed mandatory sterilization laws of one sort or another. After the Nazi rise to power, the admiration went the other way. The American eugenists thought that the Nazi laws were well conceived and consistent; they were rewarded for their admiration with honorary degrees from distinguished German universities, toasts of cooperation, and status in international organizations.

Kühl dismisses as too simplistic the conventional distinctions between hard science and pseudoscience. Instead, he insists that science be viewed as socially constructed within the historical context of the 1920s. In the early 1930s, cooperation strengthened. By the time the war approached, American attitudes toward Nazi Germany had deteriorated. There had been a change of climate in the United States, weakening the position of those advocating a scientific basis for anti-black and anti-Jewish racism.

9.

BENNO MÜLLER-HILL

Human Genetics and the Mass Murder of Jews, Gypsies, and Others

Genetics is a young science. It begins with the rediscovery of Mendel's work in 1900. The chemical nature of the genetic material, DNA, only became known in 1944. The synthesis, sequence analysis, manipulation, and reintegration of DNA into the germ line of plants and animals has only become possible in the last twenty years. Genetics is indeed a young and beautiful science.[1] I am not going to consider here its productive aspects. I am going to focus exclusively on the history of human genetics as a genocidal force. This is about tears, blood, and the murder of Jews and others.

The reader may ask, why does a scientist who is running a genetics laboratory write on this topic? The answer is as follows: a dozen or so years ago, when I gave some lectures on the history of genetics, I suddenly realized there was a blank spot. I read *Hitler's Professors* by Max Weinreich, a devastating description of the active involvement of the German universities in the policies of Nazi Germany.[2] Reading the introduction I stumbled over the sentence, "Two groups deserve the place of honor among those who made their scholarship subservient to Nazi ends: the physical anthropologists and biologists, and the jurists." I later learned that the "physical anthropologists and biologists" were human geneticists. At that time all textbooks of genetics that dealt with the history of this science included only three or four lines at most about its history in Nazi Germany. There were also no special monographs, not even articles about this topic. With the exception of a book by a German anthropologist on the race concept,[3] there was almost nothing about it.

It happened that I had a sabbatical at that time and so I devoted half a year to looking into this dark past. I read all the German journals and books from this period and I talked to almost everyone still alive who had been active as a human geneticist in Germany during those years. It was most disturbing to find the science of human genetics deeply involved in Nazism. I published a short book and some essays on the topic.[4] Some other books appeared at the same time or later. Now eugenics as a medical topic is a field that has been covered by historians of science,[5] but I have some doubt that geneticists, psychiatrists, and historians have taken proper notice.[6] History is of no interest to the young scientist who is trying hard to solve a particular problem. And science is alien to the historian.

The story begins in 1921 when the first textbook on human genetics appeared in Germany. There were three authors, Erwin Baur, Eugen Fischer, and Fritz Lenz,[7] and it was an excellent book. It contained every detail about human genetics known at the time and it had a large section on eugenics. At that time eugenics was based on the conviction of almost all human geneticists that most important behavioral or psychological traits are genetically inherited. They knew of course that there is nurture, but they thought nature to be much more important. They were convinced that there are inferior people with low intelligence, some of them with a tendency to crime, who are breeding much much faster than superior people. All blacks and some whites supposedly belong to this inferior group. The eugenicists were convinced that European and American culture would simply disappear from this planet if this process went unchallenged. Restrictive marriage laws, as they existed in the United States or as they had existed in the German colonies, and sterilization were discussed as the best negative measures. Suitable tax laws were considered to encourage the breeding of the intelligent. It might be noted here that to marry was out of the question for a German "Privatdozent" (assistant professor) since he had no salary; the German authors of the eugenic texts certainly took their own situation into account.

Baur/Fischer/Lenz sold well. Its publisher was generally very successful. He published medical, political, nationalistic, and antisemitic books. His name was Julius Lehmann. Two years later, in 1923, the second edition of the textbook came out. In the same year Hitler tried his unsuccessful *Putsch*. During the *Putsch* Hitler went into hiding for some hours in the house of his friend, the publisher Lehmann. Then Hitler had to go to jail, actually to a very nice jail, for nine months. And Lehmann, the publisher, sent him, without charge of course, his interesting new books—among them a copy of the new edition of the Baur/Fischer/Lenz. Hitler read it. If one reads *Mein Kampf* carefully, which he wrote during his time in jail, one finds there a large section about what one may call human genetics and about eugenics.

A few words about the authors, Baur, Fischer, and Lenz, are in order here By training Baur was a psychiatrist, but he had given up that profession and had gone into plant genetics. Hermann Muller, the greatest American geneticist of the 20s and 30s, called Baur "the leading geneticist of Europe" and the textbook, in his review of the English edition in 1933, the "best work on the subject"; but he was rather critical of the section on races by Eugen Fischer.[8] Fischer was a professor of anatomy who was deeply interested in anthropology and human genetics, and Fritz Lenz, his student, was then a young assistant professor of human genetics in Munich. Fischer had made an impressive career. He had published a book in 1913 on his studies of the descendants of white men and black women in one of the German African colonies, now Namibia.[9] He, as most of his international colleagues, though not Muller, was deeply convinced of the intellectual inferiority of all blacks. And he had witnessed with approval, like so many of his German colleagues, the genocidal policies of the German colonial government.[10]

When in 1926 the International Eugenics Congress was held in Rome, Fischer wrote the official memorandum, which suggested that eugenics was extremely important for the Italian fascist state. He presented it during the congress to Mussolini but Italy had no experts in the field and Mussolini therefore saw no use for it. One year later, Fischer became the director of the newly founded Kaiser Wilhelm Institute of Anthropology, Human Genetics, and Eugenics in Berlin. He was also president of the International Congress of Genetics, which was held in Berlin the same year.

Fischer, Baur, and Lenz and their colleagues looked for political allies to put their eugenic program into effect in Germany. It so happened that they could not find any political allies in the 20s, that is, all democratic parties were opposed, in one form or the other, to sterilization. There were always some eugenicists in one or the other party, but the parties themselves were adamantly against the proposals the eugenicists made; the proposals were for involuntary sterilization of all those who were unfit, that is, inferior, and marital laws. It so happened that the only party favorable to such proposals were the Nazis. They were even more attracted by the race concept proposed by Fischer, who proposed that the white Nordic race was the highest and the black race the lowest. They liked his stand against mixing of the races, although they found his racial antisemitism too little outspoken.

After the Nazis won a rather large portion of the votes in the 1930 elections, Lenz promptly wrote a review of *Mein Kampf* in a German scientific journal read by human geneticists.[11] The bottom line of the review was that Hitler was the only living politician who really understood what genetics and eugenics is all about. In the following two years the situation changed, the Nazis gained more and more power, and in 1932 the party headquarters wrote official letters to Fischer and Lenz and some others, asking them if they would like to collaborate on racial hygiene. They replied that they would be delighted to collaborate with the Nazis on racial hygiene but, of course, they wanted to keep their scientific independence.

So came 1933 and the geneticists got what they wanted. Fischer, who was a most respected scientist, had just been elected rector of Berlin University in the last free election. He had not been the candidate of the Nazis. As rector, he wrote in the following two years the letters in which he dismissed his Jewish colleagues. He said and wrote in his traditional speech as rector that these dismissals were painful but necessary.[12] He saw them in connection with a general eugenic cleaning of Germany. He was what I may call a polite but deeply convinced antisemite. He stated in 1933 that marriage and sexual intercourse between Jews and non-Jewish Germans were, from a scientific point of view, unwanted. He asked for a law outlawing them.[13] He applauded the Nuremberg Laws as scientifically necessary when they were pronounced. The general public relies on the opinion of scientists in such matters. If famous experts and scientists applaud, nothing can be wrong whatever the conscience may say. To act as a most convincing witness for the antisemitic propaganda had indeed become the role of the German human geneticist. In 1941 Fischer applauded the never-realized plan to sterilize all Germans who had one Jewish grandfather or grandmother. He was a guest of honor when this plan was announced to the public.[14] Until 1942 Fischer did not say that Jews were inferior, he said they were different. He simply asked for apartheid or "Trennung" for Jews in order to save German culture. In 1942 he said in print that Jews belong to a different species.[15] This metaphor allows mass murder. I may add here that he, like all his German colleagues who were antisemitic, liked the term "racial hygiene": racial hygiene was eugenics plus more or less antisemitism.

The eugenicist delivered to the Nazis what the Nazis needed most: trust and respect. When scientists and medical doctors say antisemitic actions are all right and a scientific necessity, they cannot be wrong. In return the eugenicists got from the Nazis what they had asked for: a law which foresaw the involuntary sterilization of all the feeble-minded, alcoholics, schizophrenics, the manic depressives, and members of a few other very small groups, the genetically blind and deaf and the people suffering from Huntington's chorea. This law went into force on January 1, 1934. We know the exact number of people who were sterilized in the first three years. In the first three years about 70,000 people were sterilized every year, so altogether in these first three years 200,000 people were sterilized. From that, we can extrapolate that by 1939, about 350,000 to 400,000 people had been sterilized. They were all sterilized against their will. Many tears and a lot of blood were spilled. One percent of the patients, some 3,500 people, mainly women, died from an operation they certainly did not ask for. All these decisions were made by medical doctors trained in human genetics.

How did the international community of eugenicists comment on the sterilization law? The reaction was positive.[16] Finally a large country had taken the necessary steps for an orderly and legal process of sterilization. This general agreement ended with the Nuremberg Laws in 1935. That blacks and whites were not allowed to marry or to have intercourse in some southern states of the United States could easily be defended and accepted among eugenicists. But that German Jews were not allowed to marry or have intercourse with Germans could not be made acceptable whatever the German geneticists said about scientific soundness and necessity. It did not help either that the German eugenicists claimed that the Nuremberg Laws were more lenient than some of the similar U.S. laws against blacks. From then on eugenics lost its support in the international scholarly world.

I should add that the human geneticists really got all they wanted: every medical school in Germany got a chair and an institute of human genetics. So all medical doctors got an education in scientific antisemitism. These institutes usually had various names, they were often called institutes for "Rassenhygiene" (racial hygiene), but they were essentially chairs for human genetics. The German human geneticists now considered themselves to be at the frontier of human genetics. It would be misleading to think that all that was published in Germany after 1933 was no science. It was at first normal human genetics as it was done elsewhere. For example, Fischer, who had become director of the Kaiser Wilhelm Institute for Anthropology in 1927, got a large three-year grant from the Rockefeller Foundation in 1932 for his work on twins. The Rockefeller Foundation certainly did not invest its money in bad science.

To many of the human geneticists, and these were often psychiatrists, the numbers and the groups to be sterilized were much too small. I will quote the case of Franz Kallmann. He gave a talk in 1935 in Germany, where he asked for the sterilization of all "heterozygotes" who carried the putative recessive gene for schizophrenia.[17] Now, if one assumes that there are about one percent schizophrenics, one expects about twenty percent heterozygotes in the population. That is a massive number. To sterilize twenty percent of the German population! Lenz immediately responded that this was irresponsible, one should keep one's fingers off it. It is interesting that this was Kallmann's last speech in Germany; indeed he had to leave

Germany. He seemed to have forgotten that he had Jewish parents. He later became a respected professor for psychiatric genetics ("Kallmann's disease" is named for him) in New York. He continued to publish as he had before, and I may just add briefly that after 1945 he was the most prominent witness for the defense of Ernst Rüdin (see below). Kallmann declared that the sterilizations were all legitimate and that nothing was wrong with them.

Several groups were not covered by the law. One group that was forgotten was colored people. It was a very small group in Germany, about six hundred children of white German mothers and French colored soldiers who were stationed in Germany after 1918. The sterilization of all these children was supervised by expert human geneticists, among them Fischer, who looked at every child and decided whether it was or whether it was not colored. They were all sterilized in 1937, illegally, with police pressure on their mothers.

Then there was a large group that was particularly dear to a professor of psychiatry in Munich, Ernst Rüdin, originally a Swiss citizen. He had been elected president of the International Eugenics Society in 1932 in New York. Rüdin and some other geneticists pointed out to Nazi officials that a most important, large group had been forgotten in the sterilization program: people who in German may be called "asozial." I read this term to mean someone who is antisocial or a petty criminal. The number in this group was estimated to be about one million persons in Germany. The Ministry of the Interior really loved the idea of a new law: a group of two medical doctors (psychiatrists) and one police officer would decide whether a particular person was an antisocial person and should thus be a) sterilized and b) transferred to a concentration camp. This was formulated as a law by the Ministry of the Interior as early as 1937 and proposed several times. It never became reality. Why did it never become reality? Because the Department of Justice, of course, thought that if the law passed, what would the judges still have to do? So there was a bitter fight between the Department of Justice, which was totally against this law, and the Ministry of the Interior, which was for this law and which was supported by all geneticists and particularly by Rüdin. Though the law never became reality, there was one subgroup in among one million people that suffered a particular fate, and these are the Gypsies.

A special institute was set up in 1937 as part of the National Institute of Health (Reichsgesundheitsamt) in Berlin, which was headed by the psychiatrist Robert Ritter. It was supposed to clarify the status of every single Gypsy living in Germany. There were about 30,000 Gypsies in Germany and Austria. The idea of the screen was the following: the Gypsies had come to Europe from India around the year 1400. The small founding group was composed of pure Indians and thus Aryans. But in the following centuries they had interbred with all the criminal scum of Europe, and so most of the Gypsies of the time were supposedly the descendants of European criminals. There were perhaps a very, very few pure Gypsies. The pure Gypsies should be saved, all the others should be sterilized and put into concentration camps. In essence, this was carried out. The mass of German Gypsies, 20,000 of them, were shipped to Auschwitz in 1943 . To the last child they died there of hunger, infections, and the last group by gas. On the other hand, six families of pure Gypsies were officially saved.

The German human geneticists delivered scientific antisemitism to all medical students, but they had nothing to do with defining particular Jews as Jews. This was done by analyzing the certificates of baptism of every person back to 1800 and by the general census of 1939. The role of the geneticist was to defend the antisemitic measures as scientifically sound. But an active role began for the human geneticists in 1941. At that time the possibility of leaving Germany was practically nonexistent for Jews. All Jews, including those who had only a Jewish father, were now shipped to concentration camps. More than one thousand persons had the saving idea, or what they thought to be the saving idea, to claim that their legal father was not their biological father. So these cases had to be decided scientifically as paternity cases by the human geneticists. I have asked all the German human geneticists who are still alive whether they did these tests as true scientists or whether they cheated in favor of at least some of these otherwise doomed, desperate people. All of the German geneticists told me they had done it as pure science. I may add that their Austrian and French colleagues were, fortunately, corrupt—they took money and faked the results. Corruptness under criminal conditions is always a sign of a certain humanity.

During the war two major events happened that opened up the possibility for research. One event was the murder of the psychiatric patients, the other the mass murder of the Jews. Psychiatric patients were extensively used, before they were murdered, for experiments and after their violent death for analysis. I am not going to focus on these crimes. I am going to focus on one particular case of the use of prisoners of concentration camps for medical experiments. To do so, I will have to go back in time. Fischer had a collaborator at the Kaiser Wilhelm Institute whose name was Otmar von Verschuer. Von Verschuer in fact did the twin studies that attracted the Rockefeller money in 1932. Von Verschuer left the Berlin institute and became professor of human genetics (racial hygiene) at Frankfurt University in 1935. There he accepted a postdoctoral assistant, Josef Mengele. Mengele was productive during those few prewar years; he published fundamentally new results on the inheritance of a facial abnormality, he reviewed books, and he wrote a meeting report.[18] In fact, he was on the list of people to go to the International Congress in Edinburgh in 1939, but for some reason he was unable to attend. In 1940 he joined the SS. In October 1942, his teacher, von Verschuer, became the successor of Fischer as director of the Berlin institute. Mengele was wounded in the USSR in the same year. He was sent to Berlin to recover and worked there for half a year as a guest in von Verschuer's institute. In April 1943 Mengele was offered the possibility of going to Auschwitz as a camp doctor, and he accepted. It is reasonable to assume that he was asked by his superiors and not forced to accept; he could very well have said he preferred to go to the front.

In the spring of 1943, exactly at the time when Mengele left his institute to go to Auschwitz, von Verschuer wrote the introduction to the second revised edition of his textbook on racial hygiene: "It is still wartime. The combined force of our people is united in the fight for victory and for a new future in Germany and in all of Europe. In the spiritual (sic!) fight for this goal, in the praxis of population and race politics, solid knowledge of racial hygiene is most important." And what did he write about the Jews?

The historical attempts to solve the Jewish question can be ordered in three groups:

1. the absorption of the Jews tried by the West Goths in Spain;
2. the locking up of the Jews in the ghetto, which was the main solution from the fifth to the nineteenth centuries in Europe; and
3. the emancipation of Jewry which happened in the nineteenth century. Each of these attempts has failed. The challenge today is the new, total solution of the Jewish problem.[19]

So Mengele went to Auschwitz and began his experiments with Jewish and Gypsy twins. He selected routinely on the selection ramp, and he was thus responsible for the deaths of several hundred thousand people. Immediately after Mengele went to Auschwitz, von Verschuer submitted grant proposals to the *Deutsche Forschungsgemeinschaft* to finance the scientific work his assistant, Mengele, would do in Auschwitz.[20] The grant proposals and the reports for these grant proposals survived the war. In one of his reports von Verschuer wrote that Mengele had collected twins of various races and that their sera were analyzed in Berlin by a scientist by the name of Günther Hillmann. Hillmann was then a graduate student. He did not work in von Verschuer's institute but at the institute of a colleague, Adolf Butenandt, the Nobel prize winner and later president of the Max-Planck-Gesellschaft. Hillmann analyzed the blood from Auschwitz in Butenandt's institute. I asked Butenandt about that in 1983 and Butenandt told me he did not know. After the war, Hillmann, who became the first president of the German society for clinical chemistry, did not reveal that he had ever touched this blood. Von Verschuer wrote and said repeatedly that he had only a very vague connection with Mengele, who was not his assistant. He did not know what Mengele was doing in Auschwitz; he had no idea what was going on in Auschwitz. Butenandt signed a memorandum praising von Verschuer as a great scientist and academic teacher and stating that Mengele might not have known what really happened in Auschwitz.[21]

We now have entered the period after the war. To summarize, almost all of the German geneticists got away with it. Only Mengele had to go to South America. They all said they did not know anything, they had nothing to do with the relevant matters, they were no antisemites. The international community was not interested in finding out the truth. In 1947, H. J. Muller, then president of the Genetics Society, sent Max Delbrück to Germany to find out what was going on. Delbrück gave a talk on his phage work in the Harnack House in Berlin, 300 yards from the institute where Mengele and von Verschuer had been active; Delbrück wrote home to Muller that everything was all right: those people who did good genetics had nothing to do with the Nazi system. After the war Lenz became professor at Göttingen University and von Verschuer became professor and dean at Münster University. Fischer was retired but active. He was asked to write a chapter for a book series, "The Creators of Our Time," on the anthropology of the twentieth century. There he stated that the Nazis had badly misused eugenics. But eugenics, he wrote, was beyond reproach: "You do not accuse Christianity because you think that the Inquisition was a crime."[22]

When UNESCO published its 1952 booklet "The Race Concept—Results of an Inquiry," the German geneticists were of course asked for their expert opinion. The key points of the UNESCO booklet were as follows:

Available scientific knowledge provides no basis for believing that the groups of mankind differ in their innate capacity for intellectual and emotional development."

There is no evidence that race mixture produces disadvantageous results from a biological point of view. The social results of race mixture whether for good or ill, can generally be traced to social factors.[23]

Indeed, the two statements were *not* based on any new empirical studies. The old studies were debunked without comment. Only one German geneticist, Hans Nachtsheim, agreed and signed after some hesitation. Von Verschuer chose to be silent; the other German geneticists (Eugen Fischer, Fritz Lenz, Karl Saller, Kurt Scheidt, and Hans Weinert) disagreed. Lenz suspected that the whole statement was part of a now modern anti-antisemitism and noted that this ideology was unscientific. Moreover, Lenz observed that the statement "runs counter to the science of eugenics." Weinert stated: "In defense of prohibiting marriage between persons of different races, I should like to ask which of the gentlemen who signed the statement would be prepared to marry his daughter, for example, to an Australian aborigine."[24] Such is the story of the German human geneticists. The question is what one should learn from it.

I think before one begins to consider conclusions, one should consider a few things. First, the logic of genetics placed Jews, Gypsies, and the insane on a similar level when the value system of the Nazis was applied to the three groups. There was just one other category of persons who were murdered similarly without interrogation: the political commissars of the Red Army. For them no genetic argument prevailed. The same was true for all those who were condemned to death for political reasons.

From a Jewish point of view it always seemed questionable, or even absurd, to connect their murder with the murder of the insane and the Gypsies. The Gypsies, it was thought, had failed to develop any notable culture or religion that could be compared with the magnificent Jewish culture or religion, and similarly, the insane could not be compared to the Jews. However, a deep similarity exists between the three groups if one looks at them with the eyes of the Nazis: the Gypsies considered themselves, and were considered by Jews, to be the direct descendants of Noah's indecent son, Ham. Thus they may be considered to be on the cultural level of the Jews *before* Abraham and Moses, that is, to be a poor nomadic tribe without a country. They carried—in the eyes of the Nazis—the crime genes of the lowest European class; the Jews carried—again according to the Nazis—the crime genes of a higher order. The similar, terrible fate of both groups, of the culturally most highly developed Jews and the most lowly Gypsies, may revive the old Jewish idea that mankind goes back to one father.

But what about the insane? The major group to be murdered were the schizophrenics. I think this is remarkable: the psychiatric theory claimed that the schizophrenic carries a divided mind or two minds. Jewish (and Christian) religion always valued conscience as another part of the soul that questions the daily deeds. This other part of the soul (conscience) has been condemned as pathological by psychiatry. According to the psychiatrist, the insane have precisely the symptoms of such an excessive division of the soul or, as the psychiatrist prefers to say, of the mind. Thus the insane (schizophrenics) are accused exactly of something that is one of the central beliefs of Judaic religion: conscience, which was praised by Moses as I and I. Seen this way it suddenly makes sense to place the insane and Jews together.

According to classical psychiatry, the brain is a biological machine which, at its best, functions without constantly questioning itself. It is of deep irony that the psychiatrist Robert Jay Lifton[25] tried to explain the psychic stability of the Nazi mass murders by "doubling" a new type of split in the mind. No, it was exactly the opposite, the happy murderer was just a person who killed in himself the last traces of conscience, that is, of a split mind or soul.

Another thing to remember is that genetics has grown tremendously. At the time when all this happened nothing was known about the genotype, there was no DNA. Now, of course, knowledge about DNA is growing and growing and more and more genotypes are being determined. But I think the knowledge about behavioral phenotypes is not much better now than it was then. This statement may enrage some of the people who work in this field, but I repeat that the progress in defining these phenotypes has been infinitely slower than the progress in DNA manipulation. It is easy to separate nature and nurture if one regards physical traits. It took just a few years to show that pellagra is caused by the absence of a particular molecule (a vitamin) and that it is not a genetic disease as was proposed by Charles Davenport, the U.S. eugenicist who earlier identified Huntington's chorea as a genetic disease. One can simply feed the patients vitamin B and this makes the Pellagra disappear. This cannot be done easily in the case of intelligence, schizophrenia, or crime: it is impossible to nurture a child or grown-up with knowledge that may make the damage caused by absent or wrong knowledge disappear. I repeat: the genes have not been discovered in the cases of intelligence, schizophrenia, and manic depression. This is one point. Another point is that we all now live here in the Western world in more or less stable democracies and there are obviously barriers that prevent such a thing as happened in Germany from happening again. There is no democratic state now that claims explicitly that the individual is nothing and the population (das Volk) is everything. This claim simply does not exist anymore.

But I think there exists something else which one should keep in mind. What did these German geneticists do? They abandoned their patients and their clients. They simply looked away when thousands and thousands of them were abused, mutilated, or murdered. If one leaves genetics completely to the forces of the market I could imagine a development where something different but similar could happen.[26] It is not happening now. But I could imagine that in a few years there could be massive stigmatization of people who have the wrong genotypes with regard to insurance, employment, and general acceptance. I think it is important that the general public and the politicians ask for laws that make this impossible. I cannot phrase such a law, for mine is not a training in law. I think experts should think about what should be done and discuss this with geneticists.

This is one aspect. There is another aspect of what went wrong in Germany: there was a fusion, an amalgamation of science and ideology. And if science gets fused with an ideology, then science itself goes downhill. So quite a few papers were published then which were rather bad science. But what is ideology and what is science? Science tells you how things are and predicts how things will be. Ideology or religion tells us how they should be. The two should be carefully separated. Science should never tell you how things should be. But what should tell you how things should be? If I say, listen to your conscience or to your religion, you may think this does not mean anything. And if I say, read what the Christians call the Old Testament, this may sound even more esoteric. Thus I would like to present an example.

In the mid-1920s a Jewish associate professor of pharmacology, Philipp Ellinger, and a young, non-Jewish assistant professor in anatomy, August Hirt, began a most fruitful cooperation at Heidelberg University.[27] They developed the first intravital fluorescence microscope, which could be used for the observation of living cells. It was patented and sold by Zeiss-Jena.[28] In 1932 Ellinger became Professor of Pharmacology at Düsseldorf Medical School. One year later he was fired because he was a Jew. Hirt entered the SS in 1933. A non-Jewish associate professor at Berlin University, Otto Krayer,[29] was chosen as Ellinger's successor. Krayer wrote back to the ministry that his conscience told him that he could not accept the position: Ellinger had been fired for no valid reason. Krayer was immediately fired himself. He emigrated and finally became professor at Harvard Medical School.

Hirt became professor in Frankfurt and in 1941 at the newly founded German University in Strasbourg. He published only a few papers in science during these years. But he became known later for two cases of mass murder: in August 1943 he asked for and received 115 *typical* Jews and Asiatics from Auschwitz. Eighty-six of them were killed upon arrival in the local concentration camp, Natzweiler, close to Strasbourg, for his anatomical-anthropological collection. After the killings he stored the corpses in his institute. He did not proceed to work on them. In 1942 he killed another fifty prisoners of the Natzweiler camp and wounded another hundred severely when testing antidotes against a particular chemical warfare poison. The severely wounded prisoners were killed elsewhere. Hirt committed suicide shortly after the end of the war. He had a postdoctoral assistant during those years in Strasbourg, Anton Kiesselbach, who later became Professor of Anatomy at Düsseldorf Medical School. In the years 1963–1964, Kiesselbach was its elected rector. One year later the Düsseldorf Medical School offered Krayer an honorary doctorate. Krayer refused after some hesitation. What made Krayer behave as an honest man when almost none of his colleagues did so? We do not know. Nothing prepared him. He was a Protestant by education, his parents had an inn in a south German village. If we remember the example of Krayer as an honest man, things may be ordered again.

Finally there is a case that I would like to mention in which the borders between science and ideology have been crossed. In the United States there has been an attempt to install a program that sets as its goal the search for the gene or genes that cause crime and violence in (black or Hispanic) slums.[30] Crime is evil, thus a sign of negative value. Is there possibly a mutated gene that determines a value? If geneticists and their psychiatric allies believe there is such a gene for crime, then they have again fused, amalgamated, ideology and science whatever they may say. I see Rüdin and Fischer smile. They said it all along: there is a gene for antisocial behavior. I predict this will lead to a very bad end, particularly if the geneticists are successful in finding it. The psychiatrists will treat the criminal babies and children as biological machines with drugs and not with love. Whoever reduces others to machines may turn himself into a machine. Then we will again envisage the abomination of genetics as evil religion. But this time it will happen in the United States and everywhere else. Beware!

NOTES

I would like to thank Frederick Kasten and Boris Magasanik for bringing to my attention Philipp Ellinger and Otto Krayer.

1. D. J. Kevles and L. Hood, eds., *The Code of Codes: Scientific and Social Issues in the Human Genome Project* (Cambridge: Harvard University Press, 1992).

2. M. Weinreich, *Hitler's Professors: The Part of Scholarship in Germany's Crimes against the Jewish People* (New York: Yiddish Scientific Institute, 1946). No German translation exists.

3. K. Saller, *Die Rassenlehre des Nationalsozialismus in Wissenschaft und Propaganda* (Darmstadt: Progress-Verlag, 1961). No English translation exists.

4. B. Müller-Hill, *Tödliche Wissenschaft: Die Aussonderung von Juden, Zigeunern und Geisteskranken 1933–1945* (Reinbek: Rowohlt Verlag, 1984). This study has been published in English as *Murderous Science: Elimination by Scientific Selection of Jews, Gypsies, and Others, Germany 1933–1945*, trans. G. Fraser (Oxford: Oxford University Press, 1988). Also, "Genetics after Auschwitz," *Holocaust and Genocide Studies* 2 (1987): 3–20; "Psychiatry in the Nazi Era," in *Psychiatric Ethics*, ed. S. Bloch and P. Chodoff (Oxford: Oxford University Press, 1991), pp. 461–72; "Eugenics: The Science and Religion of the Nazis," in *When Medicine Went Mad: Bioethics and the Holocaust*, ed. A. L. Caplan (Totowa, NY: Humana Press, 1992), pp. 43–52; with U. Deichmann, "Biological Research at Universities and Kaiser Wilhelm Institutes in Nazi Germany," in *Science, Technology, and National Socialism*, ed. M. Renneberg and M. Walker (Cambridge: Cambridge University Press, 1994), pp. 160–83.

5. R. J. Lifton, *The Nazi Doctors: Medical Killing and the Psychology of Genocide* (New York: Basic Books, 1986); R. N. Proctor, *Racial Hygiene: Medicine under the Nazis* (Cambridge: Harvard University Press, 1988); P. Weindling, *Health, Race, and German Politics between National Unification and Nazism, 1870–1945* (Cambridge: Cambridge University Press, 1989); M. H. Kater, *Doctors under Hitler* (Chapel Hill: University of North Carolina Press, 1989); P. Weingart, J. Kroll, and K. Bayertz, *Rasse, Blut und Gene. Geschichte der Eugenik und Rassenhygiene in Deutschland* (Frankfurt/M.: Suhrkamp Verlag, 1988).

6. To the best of my knowledge there is only one article with a specifically genetic point of view; see M. Teich, "The Unmastered Part of Human Genetics," in *Fin de Siecle and Its Legacy*, ed. M. Teich and R. Porter (Cambridge: Cambridge University Press, 1990), pp. 298–324. I know of only one American book that deals specifically and in detail with psychiatry and psychiatrists in Nazi Germany, and this book was written by a former patient, not by a psychiatrist; see L. Lapon, *Mass Murderers in White Coats: Psychiatric Genocide in Nazi Germany and the United States* (Psychiatric Genocide Research Institute, P.O. Box 80071, Springfield, NY, 1986).

7. E. Baur, E. Fischer, and F. Lenz, *Grundriss der menschlichen Erblichkeitslehre und Rassenhygiene* (Munich: J. F. Lehmanns Verlag, 1st ed., 1921; 2nd. ed., 1923; 3rd. ed., 1927; 4th. ed., 1936).

8. H. J. Muller, "Human Heredity," *Birth Control Review* 17 (1933): 19–21. Reprinted in H. J. Muller, *Studies in Genetics: The Selected Papers of H. J. Muller* (Bloomington: Indiana University Press, 1962), pp. 541–45.

9. E. Fischer, *Die Rehoboter Bastards und das Bastardisierungsproblem beim Menschen* (Jena: Verlag von Gustav Fischer, 1913).

10. J. Swan, "The Final Solution in South West Africa," *Quarterly Journal of Military History* 3 (1991): 36–55.

11. F. Lenz, "Die Stellung des Nationalsozialismus zur Rassenhygiene," *Archiv für Rassen- und Gesellschaftsbiologie* 25 (1931): 300–308.

12. E. Fischer, *Der völkische Staat biologisch gesehen* (Berlin: Junker und Dünnhaupt Verlag, 1933).

13. E. Fischer, "Ärztliche Eingriffe aus Gründen der Eugenik," *Archiv für Gynäkologie* 156 (1933): 117–28.

14. *Weltkampf* 1 (Munich, 1941).

15. E. Fischer, *Le problème de la race et la législation raciale en Allemagne* (Paris: Cahier de l'Institut Allemand, 1942), pp. 81–109: "les tendences morales et toute activité des Juifs bolchéviques décèlent une mentalité si monstrueuse que l'on ne peut plus parler que d'infériorité et d'être d'une autre espèce que la nôtre."

16. A. Myerson, J. B. Ayer, T. J. Putnam, C. E. Keeler, and L. Alexander, *Eugenical Sterilization; a Reorientation of the Problem,* Report of the Committee of the American Neurological Association for the Investigation of Eugenical Sterilization (New York: Macmillan, 1936); W. W. Petr, "Germany's Sterilization Program," *American Journal of Public Health* 24 (1934): 187–91.

17. F. Kallmann, "Die Fruchtbarkeit der Schizophrenen," in *Bevölkerungsfragen. Bericht des Internationalen Kongresses für Bevölkerungsfragen Berlin, 26.8–1.9.1935,* ed. H. Harmssen and F. Lohse (Munich: J. F. Lehmanns Verlag, 1936).

18. J. Mengele, "Zur Vererbung der Ohrfistel," *Der Erbarzt* 8 (1940): 59–60; "Tagung der Gesellschaft für physische Anthropologie," *Der Erbarzt* 5 (1937): 140–41; Lothar Stengel von Rutkowski, *Grundzüge der Erbkunde und Rassenpflege* (Berlin: Verlag Langewort, 1939); G. Venzmer, "Erbmasse und Krankheit," *Der Erbarzt* 8 (1940): 214.

19. O. von Verschuer, *Leitfaden der Rassenhygiene* (Leipzig: Georg Thieme Verlag, 1st ed., 1941; 2nd ed., 1943/44).

20. Research proposals of O. von Verschuer to DFG: Bundesarchiv Koblenz R 73–15342.

21. A. Butenandt, M. Hartmann, W. Heubner, and B. Rajewsky, "Denkschrift betr. Herrn Prof. Dr.med. Otmar von Verschuer September 1949." I thank Professor Butenandt for a copy.

22. E. Fischer, "Die Wissenschaft vom Menschen: Anthropobiologie im XX. Jahrhundert," in *Gestalter unserer Zeit,* vol. 4, *Erforscher des Lebens* (Oldenburg: Gerhard Stalling Verlag, 1955), pp. 272–87.

23. "The Race Concept: Results of an Inquiry," in the series The Race Question in Modern Science (Paris: UNESCO, 1952).

24. Ibid.

25. See Lifton, *The Nazi Doctors.*

26. B. Müller-Hill, "The Shadow of Genetic Injustice," *Nature* 362 (1993): 491–92.

27. F. H. Kasten, "Unethical Nazi Medicine in Annexed Alsace-Lorraine: The Strange Case of Nazi Anatomist Professor Dr. August Hirt," in *Historians and Archivists: Essays in Modern German History and Archival Policy,* ed. G. O. Kent (Fairfax: George Mason University Press, 1991), pp. 173–208.

28. F. H. Kasten, "The Development of Fluorescence Microscopy up through World War II," in *History of Staining,* ed. G. Clark and F. H. Kasten, 3rd ed. (Baltimore: Williams and Wilkins, 1983), pp. 147–85.

29. A. Goldstein, "Otto Krayer," National Academy of Sciences, *Biographical Memoirs* (Washington, D.C.: National Academy Press, 1987), vol. 57, pp. 151–225.

30. R. Stone, "HHS 'Violence Initiative' Caught in Crossfire," *Science* 258 (1992): 212–13.

10.

ANNEGRET EHMANN

From Colonial Racism to Nazi Population Policy

THE ROLE OF THE SO-CALLED MISCHLINGE

The central objective of the National Socialists, as stipulated as early as the 1920 party platform, was to exclude from German citizenship and membership in the German people all those who were not of "German blood," without consideration for religious belief. These people should, at best, be tolerated under the Fremdengesetz (Foreigner Act) with the status of guests. The further immigration of all non-Germans was to be prevented, while those having immigrated after August 2, 1914, were to be forcibly repatriated.[1] These proposals were aimed primarily at Jews but also included other "Fremdrassige" (persons of foreign "race"), such as Gypsies and Negroes.[2]

The ideas of the National Socialists were not, however, intrinsically new. Resistance to "miscegenation," and "fighting intermarriage with non-Aryans" were mottos previously heard in the rallying cries of the Alldeutscher Verband (Pan-German League) founded in 1894, and of the Deutschbund, two of the many völkisch associations propagating Pan-Germanism, German colonial claims, and racial ideology during the time of the kaiser.

For the followers of völkisch racial ideology—a community of conviction reaching far beyond the bounds of the NSDAP—not only were the *members* of the Jewish religious community members of an "alien people," but so too were those unaffiliated or baptized, as well as those descending from Judeo-Christian marriage, that is, all those of "Jewish descent." The most fanatic apostles of racial purity demanded that Germany should be free of all Jews, in what would amount to an abrogation of all the achievements in integration that had followed the passing of the Emancipation Act of 1812.[3]

Holocaust research has, until now, devoted very little attention to the history of the persecution of the so-called Mischlinge and mixed-marriage partners since most of these people survived; and given the gigantic scale of the murder of the European Jews, attention to the fate of these other groups affected by the racist population policy has receded into the background. After 1945 this fact was even used, with exculpatory intent, to fabricate a theory maintaining that the executive administration—powerless to stop the persecution of Jews—led a fight against the Nazi Party for a "humane" settlement of the "Mischling problem" and therefore saved many lives.[4]

Similarly, the churches emphasized their rescue operations involving the Mischlinge and mixed-marriage partners, insofar as baptized Christians were involved. Neither account stands up to close examination.

Instead, the conflicting attitudes of even the Confessional Church toward the "Judenchristen" (Judeo-Christians) demonstrate the strength of the influence on these circles of the racial hygiene theories generally accepted at the time.[5] With respect to the persecution and murder of Christian Gypsies, 90 percent of whom were regarded as Mischlinge, as well as the forced sterilization of the Christian children referred to as "Rhineland bastards," there is no known activity by the church to defend or protect these people.

Historiographers of the Holocaust emphasize antisemitism as the ideological basis and driving force behind the mass murder. As a result, central issues relating to Nazi population policy remain unresolved. It is necessary to establish more clearly the ideological connection between the fate of those persecuted and murdered on biological grounds and the genocide of the Jews.[6]

In regard to the fate of the Jews, it is argued that the antisemitism practiced by Nazis differed in quality from the persecution and racially motivated murder of other victims, such as Gypsies, sick people, social outcasts, Slavs, or even the "colored people" in the German colonies. Antisemitism was indeed a major motive but only part of a more extensive concept of racism underlying Nazi population policy, which in turn is rooted in the specifically German notion of the nation and Volk.

While the French and American concepts of nation are characterized by free political decision making, civil rights, and the cosmopolitan idea of human rights, membership in the German nation is based upon inheritance, with "blood" as a metaphor for ethnic or genetic descent. Under international law, this principle corresponds to the *ius sanguinis* as opposed to the *ius soli* of modern democracies. Since, of course, one cannot change one's origin, the continued adherence to this principle means that even naturalized foreigners are regarded as "aliens." The retention of the principle of descent as primary requirement for obtaining German citizenship therefore continues to provide a hotbed for racist discrimination.

If we depart now from the worn paths of research on the topic of antisemitism, it is appropriate to look at the neglected lines of tradition in the history of Germany and the history of sciences (e.g., anthropology, ethnology, medicine) that shaped both Nazi racism and corresponding administrative practice to an equally significant extent. The issues of Rassenkreuzung (interbreeding/race crossing), the Mischlinge, and mixed marriage serve as examples in the following look at the largely unknown chapter of racism practiced between 1884 and 1914 by the colonial administration in the German colonies. Nazi ideology, "race science," and population policy were profoundly influenced by the renowned proponents of colonial-era science. Although these men are often mistakenly described as pseudoscientists, it is nonetheless necessary to examine their influence.

The crucial point for a historian is not so much to establish whether the science of the time was correct or incorrect, but rather to ask in which political, social, and cultural context research questions were asked, and what interests lay behind the promotion of particular lines of research. During the colonial era there was an interest in securing domination over the supposedly inferior colonial population.

European colonialism during the second half of the nineteenth century played a central part in the development of so-called scientific racism. Arthur Gobineau's influential work "Essay on the Inequality of Human Races" was, among other things, an attempt to justify, in a speciously rational manner, the subjugation and exploitation of the peoples of Asia and Africa by claiming the biological and cultural superiority of the European "Aryan Hochrasse" over "inferior races" such as the "Semites and Negroes."[7] The standard applied to measure "superiority" and "inferiority" was the Central European, preferably "Nordic" man of middle-class origin.[8]

Historians of the Holocaust have until now disregarded the text passage in the Wannsee minutes referring to the treatment of so-called mixed-marriage partners and Mischlinge, even dismissing it as irrelevant.[9] On January 20, 1942, when Reinhard Heydrich presented the fully elaborated program of the Final Solution to those public authorities who were expected to cooperate in implementing the deportation of European Jews eastward, he informed the authority representatives of measures already agreed upon and underway, and discussed unresolved problems. Only one outstanding issue remained for the deliberating board: to determine the category of persons intended for extermination, that is, to go beyond the definition of the term "Jew" of the "Nuremberg Laws" of 1935 and their application in Germany and the occupied areas. On this point—the definition and registration of those to be designated as "Jewish"—divergent opinions had existed since 1933 among the officials working at various government and party levels: "To desk-bound Jew-persecutors, the Mischlinge and mixed marriages had become a continuously troublesome issue with which they had been unable to come to terms."[10]

The imprecise term "non-Aryan" was used between 1933 and 1935 but proved impractical for foreign policy reasons. The definition of "Jew" was laid down not by the party's ideological rabble-rousers, but by administration lawyers guided by the Nuremberg Laws, the Law for the Protection of German Blood and German Honor, and the Law of German Citizenship. Though it operated with the term "Rassejude," the criterion applied was the religious affiliation of parents and grandparents. With this, people with two grandparents of Jewish origin could be defined as "Halbjude" (half-Jew) or "Mischling of the first degree," while people with one Jewish grandparent were defined as "Vierteljude" (quarter-Jew) or "Mischling of the second degree" and therefore as a Reich citizen subject to various restrictions. The Nuremberg Laws, however, could also be applied to other categories of Mischling, as well as to Gypsies and Negroes.[11]

Holocaust scholarship has so far given scant attention to the origins of the notions used in the Nuremberg Laws of September 15, 1935—conceptions such as "Mischlinge of the first and second degree" or "bastard," and the notion of the "mixed marriages" but also of "Rassenschande" and "protection of German blood." It is necessary to look at these origins in terms of etymology and the history of ideology and law.

We find them as early as the time of the Kaiser in the public discussion of colonial problems and eugenics, in newspaper articles, and in professional medical and anthropological journals. These concepts borrowed from botany, zoology, and matrimonial law were, even then, part of the official jargon used by colonial civil servants. The 1898 edition of *Brockhaus*, the major German encyclopedia, notes under the heading "Mischling": "anthropological type, ref. colored people," and evaluates the intermarriage between American Indians and Negroes in the following way: "In most instances, the colored races in America have inherited solely the shortcomings of their colored parents' character, rarely one of the advantageous sides to it."[12] The term "mixed marriage" is used as early as the 1840s for interdenominational marriages between Protestants and Catholics. Generally speaking, prior to the introduction of civil marriage in 1875, marriage between Jews and Christians could be concluded only by the conversion of one of the spouses to the religion of the other. This meant, virtually without exception, the conversion of the Jewish partner to Christianity.

With the advent of German colonialism in 1884, the notion "mixed marriage" was already used in the sense of "Rassenmischehe" (racially mixed marriage) and designates colonial mixed marriage between whites and colored natives, since the— exclusively colored—wives were missionized Christians.

In addition, the same *Brockhaus* encyclopedia entry "Mischling" refers to the terms "bastard," "hybrid," "bastardization," "hybridization," "cross-breeding," providing a definition: "offspring of different races of the same kind, also called 'Blendlinge.'" Under "Bastard" one reads: "in civil life a child of illegitimate birth/born out of wedlock, semantically originating in Middle English and Old French. Offspring of different species (horse, donkey), in part fertile, or infertile." And finally, associated with these terms of opprobrium is the reference: see "Hottentots."

The following characteristics were attributed to the Mischlinge:

1. Biological inferiority resulting from alleged impaired fertility;
2. Disharmonies in the phenotypic appearance;
3. Preponderantly negative character traits;
4. Torn by inner conflicts.

At the time, not only physiological characteristics were considered immutable genetic traits, but also psychological traits. Early geneticists believed that "miscegenation" entailed, in the vast majority of cases, the "pauperization" of the genetic traits of the "superior" (white) race. Only when closely related races interbred might "betterment" occur in exceptional cases. This, however, would not last, since in the next generations the "worse side" would become dominant.[13]

This latter "Entmischung" (de-mixing) thesis was propounded by the renowned director of the Berlin Museum of Ethnology and professor of anthropology, Felix von Luschan. The thesis stipulated that notwithstanding a "Blutsmischung" during many generations, perfectly pure types will reemerge from mixed marriages, a "fact" Luschan claimed to have observed in the Hottentots and in Near Eastern "Semitic and pre-Semitic types," thus attributing to them a hereditary dominance.

Hitler also believed in this thesis, namely, that even after many generations, a pure-blooded type of the "inferior race" is apt to Mendelize out of the parent generation.[14] To the last days of the Nazi Reich, race scientists continued their dispute with party representatives regarding the "final solution of the Mischling question"— in other words, the best method by which the Mischlinge could disappear, either by murder or gradual extinction through sterilization.

Though the Freiburg anthropologist Eugen Fischer (1874–1967), a disciple of von Luschan, admitted that he had very little understanding of the "Entmischung thesis" he accepted it in his work *The Rehoboth Bastards and the Bastardization Prob-*

lem in Man, which was based on investigations carried out in 1908 in German South West Africa.[15] Fischer had made an anthropological study of 310 members of the so-called Rehoboth Bastards, offspring of white Boer, or German, fathers and "colored" mothers, in the German colony that is today Namibia. Using genealogical sources, photographs, charts of eye and hair color, and head and body measurements, he set out to ascertain whether the "interbreeding of peoples of different races engenders a new race, a mixed race." He also wanted to determine which "racial characteristics" were dominant, and finally, "whether and how the new environment affects an emigrated race." Moreover, he was particularly interested in "whether the fertility of Mischlinge is impaired."[16]

His "bastard study," published in 1913, concluded with recommendations for practical colonial policy. Twenty years later, his study was to have even more far-reaching consequences for the Mischlinge in the Nazi Reich than for the mixed marriages and Mischlinge in the colonies.[17] It was used as the principal argument for the scientific substantiation of the Nuremberg Laws.[18]

Fischer himself had already included comparisons with other Mischlinge in his study of bastards, such as an examination of "Jewish mixed marriages and Mischlinge" in England, India, China, and Abyssinia. Though Fischer passed a mostly favorable judgment on the German colonial bastards, he demanded a strict prohibition of mixed marriage. The advent of a "mixed race" was to be prevented on grounds that had become ideological. He wrote:

> Without exception, each European people that has assimilated the blood of inferior races has paid for this absorption of inferior elements by intellectual, spiritual and cultural decline. . . . Only one thing matters to the patriot anthropologist: not whether Mischlinge are born, but that they should remain natives at all costs.[19]

As to the treatment of Mischlinge already existing in the German colonies, he recommended the following:

> So accord them just the measure of protection they require as a race which is inferior to us, in order to continue their existence: nothing more, and only as long as they are of use to us. Otherwise survival of the fittest, that is, to my mind, in this case, extinction. This point of view sounds almost brutally egotistical, but whoever thinks through thoroughly the notion of race cannot arrive at a different conclusion.[20]

It is remarkable that he makes this statement after the genocide of the Hereros in autumn 1904, and in spite of the fact that the "bastards" had remained loyal to the colonial powers in the colonial wars of 1904–1907.

The imperial colonial commissioner for German South West Africa from 1903 to 1906 was Dr. Paul Rohrbach, a member of the National Liberal Party and a follower of Friedrich Naumann, probably the most outstanding advocate of specifically German imperialism. In his textbook *German Colonial Economy* (1907) we find a justification for the colonial genocide, which can be interpreted as the anticipation of the "euthanasia" concept advocating the extermination of "life unworthy of life"; he writes that "in order to secure the peaceful White settlement against the bad, culturally inept and predatory native tribe, it is possible that its actual eradication may become necessary under certain conditions." The extermination program of

General von Throtha, he maintained, was a mistake from an economic point of view. It was, however, not a question of "annihilating the power of resistance" but "actually wiping out the tribe," since the "Hottentots were considered useless in the larger economic sense and therefore there was no interest in preserving the race." Even missionaries had denied the tribes any viability for the future.[21]

Eugen Fischer's "bastard study" favoring colonialism was one of the factors leading to his career as director of the Kaiser Wilhelm Institute for Anthropology, Human Genetics, and Eugenics in Dahlem, Berlin. This foundation opened the gates of the international scientific community of geneticists to Germany. After 1933 he and the other staff of the institute would put themselves at the service of the Third Reich.[22] While Fischer, in true colonial lord style, still had access to "human research material" in South Africa, the loss of the colonies meant that Mischlinge were no longer available as research objects to ascertain processes of heredity. Fischer's disciple, Otmar von Verschuer, therefore applied himself to the study of twins, and that became the primary method used in human genetics.[23] This situation did not change until 1933, when the racist population policy—which had become state doctrine—made it possible to single out "carriers of miscegenation characteristics." In addition, the prospect of winning back former colonies gave fresh impetus to Fisher's anthropological-genetic colonial research.

Fischer was not the only scientist with a colonial past to give enthusiastic support to the Nazi race policy. Nor was he the only one to influence, because of his academic reputation, the next generation of physicians, anthropologists, and ethnologists. One of the most noteworthy of those so influenced was the physician Ernst Rodenwaldt (1878–1965). He worked as a doctor from 1910–1913 in colonial service in Togo, then from 1921 to 1934 in the Dutch colonial medical service. He continued in the vein of Eugen Fischer's "bastard study" with his own study of the "half-breeds of Kisar." After 1933, Reichsärzteführer (Reich Physician Leader) Gerhard Wagner sponsored him for a chair at the Hamburg Institute for Tropical Medicine, since he had eminently distinguished himself as a racial fanatic. In 1933 he became coeditor of the infamous serial *Archiv für Rassen- und Gesellschaftsbiologie*. In 1934, Rodenwaldt—himself an expert on "Mischling questions"—wrote an article for a publication in honor of Fischer entitled "Of the Mental Conflict of the Mischling," in which he applied the well-known prejudices concerning colored Mischlinge to "Jewish Mischlinge":

> He never sleeps, interfering in all human relationships, undermining trust, even within his own family, when one of the partners is of pure blood. . . . Miscegenation is a risk for every human community. Since no one can estimate its consequences, the mixing of races is irresponsible. A people interbreeding without restraint with a people racially removed will see its numbers of self-assured leader personalities dwindle.[24]

In 1939, in an article on eugenics and colonial policy, he held that no Mischling child should ever obtain the legal status of a citizen of the Reich.[25]

The anthropologist and ethnologist Otto Reche (1879–1966), a racist of the first order, worked between 1906 and 1924 at the Hamburg Museum of Ethnology. He took part in a South Seas expedition during 1908 and 1909. An anthropological study of "natives" and a collection of skulls and skeletons of about 800 individuals for the Hamburg museum was the scientific yield. For his work, Reche was awarded a medal of honor from the city government. He lectured in Hamburg at the Institute for Colonial Sciences and, from 1919, at the university. From 1924 to 1927 he directed the Institute of Anthropology and Ethnology at the University of Vienna, where he developed an anthropological-genetic method of establishing paternity. This method was recognized by the courts in 1926 and used after 1933 for descendancy tests. From 1927 to 1945 he lectured at Leipzig University. He was the author of a "scientific expert" memorandum dated September 24, 1939, on methods to prevent "bastardiza-tion" as well as to advance ethnic cleansing in Eastern Europe under German occu-pation. The document was presented to Himmler for approval.[26]

Another member of the first generation of eugenicists was Philalethes Kuhn (1870–1937), who worked in the colonial service between 1896 and 1914 as a phy-sician and member of the Schutztruppe Deutsch-Südwest. He took part as a military officer in the campaign against the Hottentots and Hereros in 1897 and 1898, and in the annihilation war waged against the Hereros from 1904 to 1907. After 1914 he qualified in Strasbourg to lecture in hygiene, and in 1926 became a professor at the University of Giessen. In 1933, in collaboration with the fanatical Nazi and "Gypsy researcher" Heinrich Wilhelm Kranz, he published the eugenic manual *From German Ancestors for German Grandchildren.*[27]

The physician and anatomist Theodor Mollison (1874–1952) carried out field research in German East Africa in 1904 and lectured from 1926 to 1941 at the University of Munich. In a 1937 letter to Franz Boas, who had emigrated from Germany to the United States, where he had risen to the rank of Nestor of American anthropology, he gave a pertinent description of the sentiments of his aforementioned colleagues:

> If you think that we scientists do not join in the call "Heil Hitler," you are very much mistaken. We, the German scientists, are very much aware of what we owe to Adolf Hitler, last but not least the purification of our people from foreign race elements, whose way of thinking is not the one we have.[28]

Josef Mengele took his first doctor's degree under Mollison with a paper on anomalies of the jaw detected on Melanesian skulls possibly stemming from the spoils of Otto Reche. Even the "Gypsy researcher" Sophie Ehrhardt obtained her doctorate under Mollison.

Notably, the German medical profession showed enthusiastic support from the outset for German imperialism. Upon the foundation of the Deutscher Kolonialverein in 1884, 258 physicians were already members. By 1903 their number had risen to fifteen hundred.[29] The enthusiasm of the medical profession for colonialism was as much due to the general popularity of Darwinian theory as to the paucity of job prospects for physicians that had prevailed since the turn of the century.[30]

What factors favored this affinity between German nationalism and racism? The answer lies in that special German way of nation-state development—the völkisch notion of the state and the resulting traditional acceptance of class and legal in-equality by large parts of the middle classes. The majority of these people rejected the idea of equality that was the basis of the French and the American revolutions. The acceptance of basic inequality was a fundamental condition for National Socialism to find such willing supporters.

The myth of unity and purity (ethnic homogeneity) and the condemnation of interbreeding (with "aliens") are two central motives in the body of German national thought. One is tempted to speak of some sort of cultural code which engenders these specific forms of rejection of everything non-German. We can find elements of racist reasoning, such as claims of the "superiority" of the German people and the "inferiority" of other peoples, as early as in political romanticism. Even great minds such as Immanuel Kant, Johann Gottlieb Fichte, and Goethe were filled with prejudice against Jews. Kant spoke of the "vampires of society"; Fichte recommended that they should be either decapitated or sent back to Palestine. Goethe, minister in the Grand Duchy of Weimar, spoke out vehemently against the Emancipation Acts of 1812. He took the view that Jews, as a "foreign nation," should be left in their marginal position as outsiders. He flew into a rage particularly when, in 1823, mixed Jewish-Christian marriages were permitted by law for a short time. Goethe considered them a "moral danger to the German family."[31]

Particularly revealing trains of thought concerning early völkisch racism can be found in the work of Ernst Moritz Arndt, the harbinger of German nationalism. As early as 1815, he argued that "mishmash and bastardization are the main source of ruin and the greatest calamity for a people," a proposition that, one century later, Fischer tried to scientifically corroborate. Greece and Rome, he held, perished due to interbreeding with the foreigners they had hauled into their land from all over, with the result that there was "no more people, only rabble." The Germans, Arndt continued, were fortunately not bastardized by foreign peoples and had not become Mischlinge. Instead, they had stayed, more so than other nations, in their native purity.[32] And this, he believed, was how things should stay:

> The importation of Jews from foreign parts into Germany should be absolutely banned and prevented, since they are a thoroughly alien people and since I desire to keep the Germanic tribe as far as possible pure from foreign elements. A benevolent ruler fears the foreign and the degenerate, whose incessant influx and mingling in is apt to poison and spoil the pure and magnificent germs of his noble people.[33]

According to Arndt, "those varieties born out of the interbreeding with foreigners will invariably turn back to the bad and the ignoble. Only the mixing of the equal will enrich the species." Since Negroes and Mongolians were a worse anthropological type than the Germanic, they could not be improved, even through interbreeding. The bastards, Arndt argued, were lacking in the harmonic, the secure and the brilliant, and no capable person would ever emerge from them.[34]

One century later, we again meet these stereotyped ideas about bastards/Mischlinge in nearly identical form in the debates held in the German Reichstag, in the daily newspapers, and in the anthropological and eugenics publications treating the "question of the mixed marriages and Mischlinge in the German dependencies." They were, however, simultaneously applied to mixed Jewish-Christian marriages since the difference in creed had long since lost its significance and the supposed "racial difference" between so-called Aryans and Semites was in keeping with the spirit of the time.

The Reich's 1870 Reichsrecht Code did not stipulate a bar to marriage on grounds of racial difference. Nevertheless, marriages between white men and black women were unwelcome from the outset. Since 1890, colonial marriage registrars had refused to officiate at "mixed marriages"; however, by traveling to the British Cape Colony it was possible to contract a legal marriage. On September 23, 1905, a decree issued by Governor von Lindequist banned mixed marriage in German South West Africa. His rationale was the generally "dangerous mixing of blood," which would lead, with six children per couple, to several hundred Mischlinge within two generations. Given this great risk, the government had to see to it that "these bastards would not have equal rights with German citizens."[35]

The ban on mixed marriages was decreed for German East Africa in 1906, while the retroactive annulment of legally contracted marriages in German South West Africa and Cameroon followed in the next year. In 1908 mixed marriages were banned in Togo, with the same ban applied in Samoa in 1912. In 1908 the ban on mixed marriages was integrated, as Article 17, into the Colonial Home Rule Act, with an amendment stipulating that white husbands be punished through the deprivation of civil rights and disfranchisement. Both the "protection of German blood and honor" as formulated in the Nazi Marriage Act of 1935 were already elements of the colonial restraints on marriage.

The question of mixed marriage was clearly connected to the issue of citizenship. Marriage should not entitle "native" women and Mischlinge to German citizenship. In 1913, Governor Duke Adolf Friedrich von Mecklenburg even prohibited Mischling children from bearing German names. The ban was later extended to the African population in general. With this measure, the Mischlinge, who were in any case on an equal legal footing with the rest of the population, no longer stood out socially, except by the color of their skin. It was argued that "Mischlinge having European blood and name easily feel like Europeans and desire to be treated as such."[36]

Between 1910 and 1912, the governor of German South West Africa, Theodor Seitz, drafted far-reaching Mischling decrees, which eventually went so far as to prohibit intercourse with native women "as an offence against racial sentiment." Such a ban was not implemented, however, since there were not sufficient European women available to substitute. The majority of colonists refused to abandon cohabitation with African women.[37]

Though the number of mixed marriages in the colonies was trifling—in 1912 there were just 166 mixed marriages in the German colonies, of which 47 were in German South West Africa—the mixed marriage and Mischling question remained a continuous subject of scientific and public discussion, reaching a climax in the Reichstag debates of May 1912.

It was not only the nationalists and the antisemites who drew analogies concerning Jewish-Christian mixed marriage in this hotly debated question. Physicians and anthropologists dealt extensively with the subject of Rassenmischung (miscegenation) even in liberal scientific publications. The eugenic discourse at the time of the Kaiser was a predominantly middle-class and scholarly subject, with even Jewish scientists joining in the discussion. The sexologist Max Marcuse (1877–1967) and the physician and statistician Felix Theilhaber (1884–1956)[38] chiefly investigated the fertility and large fall in birthrate of German Jews. German Jews exhibited a far lower birthrate than gentile Germans. For more than twenty years, Marcuse specialized in the "mixed Jewish-Christian marriage." His efforts to prove that a low birthrate and high divorce rate were due not to "racial incompatibility" but to psychological and social difficulties, can probably also be explained by the fact that he perceived the risk that arose for German Jews when people argued using analogy.

In his 1912 essay on the "Eastern Jews," he even went so far as to refer to them as "racially foreign" and dangerous. Their interbreeding with the German people, he wrote, was unwanted. Therefore, the Polish border should be closed to prevent their arrival. German Jews were not to merge with the German people through mixed marriage.[39]

To counter the constantly reiterated claim that "racial difference" lay behind the low birthrate in mixed Jewish-Christian marriages, he referred to Fischer's study, which had not been able to establish reduced fertility in Mischlinge. He devoted special attention to the refutation of the outrageous suggestion that Mischlinge were degenerate, put forward by the political economist and historical economist Werner Sombart: Jewish Mischlinge were "intellectually and morally unstable, morally depraved or ended up mentally deranged and then committed suicide."[40]

There were, however, also opponents of the racial theories and racist colonial policy, though they formed a minority. In the Reichstag, the Social Democrats and the Center Party unsuccessfully challenged the ban on mixed marriage in the colonies by raising the issue of human rights. The German practice, they said, was without parallel among modern civilized nations. And indeed, no other colonial power codified and implemented a ban on mixed marriage.

A central principle of colonial policy was at stake: according to the renowned colonial lawyer von Stengel, the "inferior" members of the "foreign race" should, from the outset, be separated from the governing white population. This was advocated not only on the grounds of the supposed injuriousness of "miscegenation" but because "the birth of a mixed race in a colony carries a risk of the mother country losing the colony":

> If the Mischling population is large enough, it will seek to tear itself free from the mother country, convinced that the rule of the foreign race will thus be removed. If the Mischlinge are less numerous, they still pose the threat of siding with the natives and assuming a leadership role in the event of an uprising.[41]

To substantiate this argument, Stengel referred to the "Mischling states" of Haiti and Liberia. This argument can be found in virtually all Nazi pamphlets on this subject and, in a similar version, even in the Wannsee minutes.

Von Stengel also argued by analogy with respect to the Jews. He stated that

> the difference between races, especially evident in the difference in psychological disposition and character, could not be overcome through either education, conversion to Christianity or equality before the law. One only need remind the reader of how the contrast between Aryans and Semites makes itself felt, in all nations, again and again, despite the so-called emancipation of the Jews.[42]

The Nationalists had no intention of allowing the colonies to repeat the consequences of Jewish emancipation in the Reich. After the loss of the colonies, the utopian biological schemes regarding population policy shifted to the domestic level. In the Weimar Republic, a group of five hundred to eight hundred German Mischlinge, referred to as "Rhineland bastards" or "black blemish on the Rhine," became the object of violent racist attacks. The fathers of these children were African and Asian soldiers with the French, British, Belgian, and American occupation forces stationed in the Rhineland from 1920 to 1927. Even during the war, Germany had called the deployment of "colored units" a "danger to European culture and civilization."[43]

From 1920 the authorities turned their attention to these children. Immediately after the Nazis came to power they were registered as the first group of Mischlinge. On March 11, 1935, the "committee of experts on population and race policy" discussed two options for getting rid of them: sterilization or elimination from the German living space, in other words deportation to Africa. The latter solution was dismissed since it would damage foreign relations.[44] Sterilization, not applicable under the 1934 act for the "prevention of progeny afflicted with a hereditary disease," was decreed in secret. In 1937, following an anthropological examination by committees delegated to the Rhineland, some four hundred children were subjected to forced sterilization in Bonn and Cologne hospitals. Eugen Fischer and his research assistant Wolfgang Abel were advisors, as was Heinrich Schade, an assistant of Professor von Verschuer. Another group of undesired Mischlinge were the German Gypsies, the Sinti, already registered as "socially conspicuous." From a total of thirty thousand, twenty-nine thousand were subjected to an anthropological evaluation by the racial biology research center (Rassenbiologische Forschungsstelle) of the public health service (Reichsgesundheitsamt) in Berlin. Dr. Ritter and his assistants Eva Justin and Sophie Ehrhardt took charge. Eva Justin took her degree in 1943 with a paper on "Gypsy Mischlinge." When the test series was completed, the thirty-nine children involved were deported to Auschwitz. Only four of them survived. Eugen Fischer was one of the supervisors involved in this project.

The fate of the Gypsy Mischling children of Mulfingen has similarities with the fate of a group of "Jewish Mischlinge of the first degree" put into reformatory schools. Between June 1943 and April 1944 these children were "hospitalized" at a special "educational ward for Jewish Mischlinge" at the Hadamar state mental institution and euthanasia center, where they were killed. There was, however, no "research" carried out on these children.[45]

From 1933, genealogists, parish registrars, and statisticians dealt with the registration of the Jewish Mischlinge. In 1933 no exact statistics about the Jewish Mischlinge—mostly Protestant Christians—were available. The genealogist Wilfried Euler had worked since 1932 on Ahnenstammkarteien (genealogical card indexes) for the NSDAP Party headquarters in Munich. From 1933 he worked in the Reich Ministry for Internal Affairs. Here, in the "office of the expert for racial questions" he worked under Dr. Achim Gercke on the genealogical and statistical registration of mixed marriages and Mischlinge. To Euler are owed the first numbers concerning Mischlinge when the Nuremberg Laws were prepared. He estimated the number of Jews and Judenmischlinge at 1.5 million. He searched for all those having any Jewish ancestors at all, that is, back to the seventeenth century.[46] Euler was so fervent in tracking down "mixed kinship" between Aryans and Jews that he made himself unpopular in the process. In 1935, after Gercke had been made to hand over his function to Dr. Kurt Mayer (later director of the Reichssippenamt) Euler moved to Munich, where he was associated with Walter Frank's Institute for Research into the

Jewish Question. Here, in 1936, he was officially assigned to compile "global statistics on Jewish baptism and mixed marriage in Germany."[47] He devoted special attention to the question of Rückkreuzung and the "penetration of Jewish blood into the leadership ranks of the nobility and of science, business, and politics." In 1937 Euler published the first results in the institute's paper with a genealogical study on the offspring of the Mendelssohn family.[48] This was a large-scale research project. Voluntarily, and without payment, societies devoted to local and regional history, as well as genealogical societies, contributed to the work. Even the churches took part in the denunciatory hunting down of Mischlinge. In Berlin for example, the Protestant Church card-indexed under the direction of the parish registrar—Karl Themel, chairman of the German Genealogical Society—all the parish registers of Greater Berlin up to 1800. From this—based upon the entries of baptisms for Jews, Gypsies, Turks, and Moors/Negroes—a card index of persons of foreign race (Fremdstämmigenkartei) was compiled. A duplicate went to the Reichsstelle für Sippenforschung. In 1937, the Reich Church Minister made available the records concerning the baptism of Jews from the consistory archives. Without the eager and willing help of genealogists and parish registrars in the registration and demarcation of the Rassenmischlinge and converts, the implementation of NS race policy would have been made considerably more difficult since the majority of the Mischlinge could not have been identified by either their religion, name, or physical traits.[49]

Anthropological institutes also depended upon the contribution of the genealogists, though they would rather have disregarded them since they were competitors in scientific research. The Reichssippenamt, however, invariably relied upon genealogical sources in establishing Ariernachweise (certificates of Aryan origin). After 1940, Euler extended his research to include Italy, France, and England, and in 1942 published a comprehensive genealogical study of the Verjudung (spread of Jewry) in the British upper class. This study contributed to wartime propaganda when it appeared as an illustrated article in the *Illustrierter Beobachter* under the heading "Who Rules England?"[50] At his own instigation, his research assignment was enlarged to cover the "safekeeping of historic and anthropological material in Jewish cemeteries in Germany," since, he argued, the dissolution of these cemeteries was immediately imminent, which Euler knew perfectly well. Tombstone inscriptions were to be recorded and skeletons to be exhumed, "in order to perform anthropological studies upon them." If the latter was carried out it has yet to be ascertained, but tombstones were recorded in Vienna, Hamburg, Berlin, and in other cities.[51]

Eugen Fischer and Otmar von Verschuer were among this institute's circle of experts. In a 1937 lecture Verschuer pointed out the eminent significance for biological research of exact genealogical registration of the Mischlinge and mixed marriages.[52] After the special registration of Jews, Gypsies, and other Fremdvölkische had begun in 1935/36, a Volkstumskartei (card index) was compiled based upon the primary material of the census taken in 1939 in Berlin-Dahlem. This card index of all non-Aryans in the German Reich contained the name, date, place of birth, residence, profession, and "degree of Mischling (Mischlingsgrad)."

In 1939 Eugen Fischer also conferred a doctorate upon Alexander Paul for his study of the Jüdisch-deutsche Blutmischung (Jewish-German blood mixing). This paper was written using dossiers of the Reich Ministry for Internal Affairs, which mainly held data concerning "illegitimate Mischlinge." It drew the conclusion that the provisions of the Nuremberg Laws should be tightened for Mischlinge of the first degree and be extended to cover those of the second degree as well. All those tested, it was argued, exhibited signs of "genetic inferiority." The Mischlinge should thus be counted as belonging among the Jewish people. The German people would have to categorically refuse the integration of these children in the "community of blood" (Blutsgemeinschaft).

This paper was published in 1940 in *Der öffentliche Gesundheitsdienst* (public health service), a publication for medical officers. Paul, who was also a playwright, wrote a didactic play entitled *Sons-in-Law* in 1935, commissioned by the Reichsausschuss für Volksgesundheit (Reich board of public health). It was first performed on October 13, 1935, in Hamburg's Thalia Theater and was intended to propagate the Nuremberg Laws. By 1938 the play had been staged 1150 times in various towns.[53] The drama is set in a German vicarage. The clergyman's two daughters marry the wrong men: one of them is a baptized Jewish Mischling, the other the carrier of a hereditary disease. Both daughters soon become unhappy in marriage. The son-in-law afflicted with the hereditary disease becomes mentally deranged; a child is not viable and dies. The Jewish Mischling, after marriage, reveals himself to be a sexual libertine and deceiver. The father, after having been enlightened about genetics by his brother, a senior medical officer, realizes that he has brought disaster upon his daughters through his Christian "humanitarian delusions."

For the relationship between colonial experience and Nazi racism, certain Free Corps leaders, revered by the Nazis as "colonial heroes," also play a part. One well-known example is Reichsritter Franz von Epp, a highly decorated, conservative general who participated in all the colonial wars—even in the extermination campaign against the Hereros—and who, as leader of a free corps, helped smash the Munich Räte Republic. Epp was one of the earliest and most influential supporters of the NSDAP, making the *Völkischer Beobachter* the mouthpiece of the party. On May 5, 1934, Hitler appointed Epp director of the Kolonialpolitisches Amt of the NSDAP. Hitler was among the soldiers of Epp's volunteer corps, as were the Reichsgesundheitsführer Gerhard Wagner and Karl Astel. The latter was appointed president of the Thüringisches Landesamt für Rassewesen (Thuringia Administrative Office for Race Questions) in 1933, and in 1934 was made director of the Institute for Human Genetic Engineering and Hereditary Research (Institut für menschliche Züchtungslehre und Vererbungsforschung) in Jena. Astel, a fanatical racist, participated in the so-called Final Solution of the Jewish Mischling Question in 1943/44 in an advisory role.[54]

Further members of Epp's free corps included the later state secretary in the Reich Ministry for Internal Affairs, Dr. Wilhelm Stuckart. He coauthored virtually all the fundamental racist laws against Jews. He also commented, together with Hans Globke, on the Nuremberg Laws and participated in the Wannsee conference. His area of special interest was the "mixed marriage and Mischlinge." Though Epp's relations to Hitler and the NSDAP were somewhat strained, this was certainly not attributable to differences in race ideology, but rather to colonial policy objectives. The colonial empire of which Hitler dreamed did not lie overseas but in Eastern Europe.

Also involved in the genocide in German South West Africa was General Paul von Lettow-Vorbeck (1870–1964), known as the "Hero of East Africa." Even the naval officer Hermann Ehrhard participated in the crushing of the Herero uprising and later became a free corps commander as well. From his free corps emerged the murderers of Walther Rathenau and Ernst von Salomon, who wrote the screenplay for the *Carl Peters* film of 1941 with its star cast and lavish production. The role of the Germanic colonial hero was played by Hans Albers. The film must be interpreted as propaganda preparing for the conquest of the Soviet Union, which was to be colonized.

Another member of the Ehrhard corps was Rudolf Höss, who was later commander of Auschwitz.[55] The function of these colonial activists, as models for the shaping of leading National Socialists in terms of their racist ideas, requires thorough investigation. The passage in the notorious Wannsee minutes concerning the treatment of so-called mixed marriages and Mischlinge appears in a different light when viewed against this background. That the mass murder of Mischlinge discussed at the Wannsee Conference was not committed should not lead one to conclude that this group would have been spared in the long run. The treatment of mixed marriages and Mischlinge by the German bureaucracy from 1933 onward shows how resolutely the path leading to the second phase of the extermination policy—the "final solution of the Mischling and mixed marriage question"—was pursued. From 1942, the measures taken against Mischlinge were increasingly tightened.

The proposal to sterilize the Mischlinge offered at the Wannsee Conference of January 20, 1942, came, logically, from the relevant agency in charge of these matters in the Reich Ministry for Internal Affairs. It was not a tactical move by the bureaucrats against the party in order to save Mischlinge from the Final Solution, as later claimed by the Department of Justice in order to exonerate not only Globke and Stuckart but also Franz Massfeller. The prospect of the mass sterilization of Mischlinge was by no means unrealistic. Stuckart and Massfeller were very well acquainted with the state of sterilization techniques.[56] There were two follow-up conferences to the Wannsee Conference, one on March 6, 1942, and one on October 27, 1942. Since, even then, party and executive administration could not reach a consensus regarding basic bureaucratic issues, the solution to the problem was, in spring 1943, deferred to the period following the final victory for reasons of war and pragmatic, political, and administrative considerations. Still, there was far from a standstill in activities leading toward the Final Solution of the Mixed Marriage and Mischling Question. On the contrary, these activities were resolutely pursued. This can be clearly seen by the action of April 1943, when by order of the Reich Ministry for Internal Affairs, forty-two under-age "Mischling children of the first degree" from Bavaria, Berlin, Brunswick, the Rhineland, Hesse, Thuringia, Lorraine, and Upper Austria were remanded to the Hadamar state mental institution. There, thirty-nine of them were killed between June 1943 and April 1944 on the pretext of mental deficiency. The real reason was that they, as Jewish Mischlinge, entailed expenses for the State. Other preparatory measures for the Final Solution of the Mischling Question included the mustering out of Mischlinge of the first degree from the German Armed Forces. This measure, first decreed in secret on April 8, 1940, was again decreed by the OKW (Oberkommando der Wehrmacht) on September 25, 1943.[57] A decree from the

Führer on February 20, 1944, directed that, as from April 1, 1944, the party chancery was to be involved in processing all Mischling matters in order to guarantee uniformity of action.[58]

As a next step, all male Mischlinge of the first degree and Aryan husbands living in mixed marriages were sent to the labor camps of the Todt organization in October 1944. This was immediately followed, via a newsletter on November 7, 1944, by the instruction to all authorities to report and remove "Mischlinge and persons related to Jews by marriage" from leading posts in the civil service, insofar as any of them remained. This measure affected also the "Mischlinge of the second degree" classified as being "of German blood," together with their husbands. The authorities were obliged to report back and performed this duty painstakingly.

The reasons advanced for this measure were the events of July 20, which were bound to cause these civil servants to have conflicts with the National Socialist Weltanschauung "due to their blood-related and relational Weltanschauung."[59] Earlier equalization and special license permits were to be rescinded. Finally, in February 1945, Jewish partners in existing mixed marriages were deported to the Theresienstadt concentration camp. It was because the final victory was prevented by the Allied forces that these persons were to a large extent saved from the Final Solution, not, as Raul Hilberg claims, because they were more German than Jewish.[60] Even the classification of Mischlinge followed the inner "logic" of Nazi race ideology, with the Jewish Mischlinge classified above the Rhineland bastards and the Sinti. With the two latter groups, no consideration had to be taken of their social environment. The Jewish Mischling children murdered in Hadamar were, again, the socially weakest of the Jewish Mischlinge. No protest was to be expected here, unlike the one encountered in February 1943 in Berlin, following the so-called Fabrikaktion, when it was suddenly announced that the Jewish spouses in protected mixed marriages were to be deported.

The so-called Final Solution of the Jewish Question was not the ultimate objective of Nazi race policy. National Socialist policy aimed at creating a national society that was hierarchically structured according to biological criteria and that was genetically and ethnically pure.

This society would grant no right of life to the sick, or to those failing to come up to the required standards, or to racial Mischlinge. Nothing less than a complete ethnic "cleansing of the German living space" was required.[61] From east of the river Weichsel to the Urals a gigantic colonial empire was to be created. Only the "able" among the "inferior Fremdvölkische," as they were termed in administrative German at the time, would have been allowed to serve the economic interests of the Pan-German Reich as slave labor. Nicolaus Sombart, in his book on Carl Schmitt, the theoretician of the NS Führer state, comments upon the antisemitism and racism of German men of the ilk of Schmitt, Fischer, Verschuer, and others:

> To state things very succinctly, perhaps the following can be said: The Holocaust has nothing to do with Jews as they actually are. In reality, it is a profoundly German issue. It is the final, belated, and typical answer of the Germans [i.e., men—A.E.] to the French Revolution.[62]

NOTES

1. Program of the NSDAP of 1920; cf. W. Mickel, W. Kampmann, and B. Wiegand, *Politik und Gesellschaft*, vol. 2 (Frankfurt/M., 1972), p. 121.

2. A. Gütt, H. Linden, and F. Massfeller, *Blutschutz- und Ehegesundheitsgesetz* (Munich, 1936), p. 16.

3. Note on a meeting of officials of the Reich Ministry of the Interior, Reich Ministry of Economics, and party executives of September 29, 1936, Bundesarchiv Koblenz (hereafter BAK), 18/5514, quoted from U. Büttner, "'Nichtarier'-'Judenmischlinge'-'Privilegierte Mischehen': Die Verfolgung der christlich-jüdischen Familien im Dritten Reich," *Acta Universitatis Wratislaviensis* 1169 (Wroclaw, 1991): 139–40: in the May 1934 *Cottbusser Anzeiger*, NSDAP Gauleiter Wilhelm Kube stated that a person with 10 percent Jewish blood is a Jew.

4. Dr. Hans M. Globke's evidence for the Nuremberg trial concerning Reich Minister of the Interior W. Stuckart, quoted from R. Strecker, ed., *Dr. Hans Globke, Aktenauszüge-Dokumente* (Hamburg, 1961), pp. 103–104. See also R. Vogel, *Ein Stempel hat gefehlt* (Munich, 1977), pp. 14–15, defending Globke as a "rescuer of Jews"!

5. Compare the critical reappraisal of the Confessional Church by W. Gerlach, *Als die Zeugen schwiegen: Bekennende Kirche und die Juden* (Berlin, 1987); for political reasons, this 1970 dissertation was not published until 1987.

6. J. A. S. Grenville, "Die Endlösung und die 'Judenmischlinge' im Dritten Reich," in *Das Unrechtsregime: Internationale Forschungen über den Nationalsozialismus. Festschrift für W. Jochmann*, ed. U. Büttner et al. (Hamburg, 1986), vol. 1, pp. 91–92.

7. The abolition of slavery also triggered interest in studies on "race." Rediscovery of Gregor Mendel fundamentally shaped the ideas about race crossing; cf. W. B. Provine, "Geneticists and the Biology of Race Crossing," *Science* 182 (November 1973): 790–96 (German trans. in *Unterricht Biologie* 72/73 [August–September 1982]: 28–34).

8. Eugen Fischer, *Die Rehoboter Bastards und das Bastardierungsproblem beim Menschen* (Graz, 1961; orig. ed. Jena, 1913), p. 296, referred to

> not the worker or the peasant, but the great number of individuals of extraordinary capability. They possess energy, fantasy, the ability to combine, associate, be creative, they are self-confident, don't waver, act fast, have a good, homogeneous, consequent character, are faithful to their principles. These are men who, create values, who organize our politics, industry, technology, science and strategy. Only certain races possess these qualities, colored races totally lack this potential.

9. Commentaries by E. Jäckel and Y. Bauer in the Dutch television film "De Wannsee-Conferentie," AVA (Netherlands, 1992), and by S. K. Pätzold and E. Schwarz in *Tagesordnung Judenmord: Die Wannsee-Konferenz am 20. Januar 1942* (Berlin, 1992), pp. 53ff., emphasized this matter for the first time as one of the four important topics of the conference and the only open question. The intention was to cease limiting the Final Solution by the definitions of the Nuremberg Laws.

10. Ibid., p.45.

11. Cf. W. Stuckart and H. M. Globke, *Kommentare zur deutschen Rassengesetzgebung*, volume 1 of the *Reichsbürgergesetz, Gesetz zum Schutz des deutschen Blutes und der deutschen Ehre, Gesetz zum Schutz der Erbgesundheit des deutschen Volkes* (Munich, 1936), pp. 52–53; Gütt, Linden, and Massfeller, *Blutschutz*, pp. 15–16:

> The first decree concerning the Law for the Protection of German Blood and Honor of 14/11/1935 fills the still remaining gaps by specifying under clause 6 that a couple cannot enter into matrimony if offspring endangering the purity of the German blood are to be expected from it. This principle offers the opportunity to prevent not only the penetration of Jewish blood but also that of other alien blood, i.e., Negro, Gypsy, or bastard blood.

12. *Brockhaus Enzyklopädie* (1898), vol. 6, p. 575. The pejorative but still current term "mulatto" from Latin *mulus*, mule, can be found in contemporary dictionaries as a synonym for "bastard," that is, "Mischling with one Caucasian and one Negro parent"; see *Brockhaus* 1991, p. 164. This racism found expression as late as 1952 in a dissertation by W. Kirchner,

Eine anthropologische Studie an Mulattenkindern in Berlin unter Berücksichtigung der sozialen Verhältnisse, Institut für natur- und geisteswissenschaftliche Anthropologie at Berlin Dahlem, a successor institute to the former Fischer KWI. The thesis relies on literature deriving exclusively from the colonial and Nazi periods.

13. F. von Luschan on the Mischling question, opening speech at the 43rd meeting of the Anthropological Society, in *Zeitschrift für Sexual-Probleme* 9 (1913): 33–35; see also Provine, *Geneticists*, pp. 28–29. For influential studies on race mixing, see F. Galton, *Inquiries into Human Faculty* (London, 1883); P. Näcke, "Die 'inadäquate' Keimmischung," *Zeitschrift für die Gesamte Neurologie und Psychiatrie* (Berlin, 1912); C. B. Davenport, "The Effects of Race Intermingling," *Proceedings of the American Philosophical Society* 56 (1917); A. Mjöen, "Harmonische und unharmonische Kreuzungen," *Zeitschrift für Ethnologie* 52 (1921); Herman Lundborg, "Die Rassenmischung beim Menschen," *Bibliographica Genetica* 8 (1931).

14. H. Picker, *Hitlers Tischgespräche im Führerhauptquartier* (Stuttgart, 1976), p. 79.

15. Cf. Fischer, *Rehoboter Bastards*, p. 302.

16. Ibid., p. 137: "Anthropology today pursues new and promising objectives, special emphasis has to be put on the research about Rassenmischlinge at home and abroad!"

17. Fischer's assertion that he had proven the Mendelian hereditary laws with regard to man was not questioned. *Brockhaus* 1988, vol. 7, p. 334, still affirms this. Fischer's disciples cite his "bastard study" as a classic (see note 8); the foreword reprint omits only the chapter on the "political role of the bastard"; F. Vogel characterizes it as meticulous, empirical, and surprisingly free of prejudice in "Sind Rassenmischungen biologisch schädlich?," in *Rassen und Minderheiten*, ed. H. Seidler and A. Soritsch (Vienna, 1983), pp. 11–12.

18. See BAK, R 18/ 5313, pp. 3–4, and commentaries in Stuckart and Globke, *Kommentare*, pp. 5, 12; and Gütt, Linden, and Massfeller, *Blutschutz*, pp. 343–44; the latter also treat American state legislation prohibiting mixed marriages and concerning eugenic sterilization.

19. Fischer, *Rehoboter Bastards*, pp. 302–303.

20. Ibid.

21. P. Rohrbach, *Deutsche Kolonialwirtschaft*, vol. 1: *Südwest-Afrika* (Berlin, 1907), pp. 350ff.; see also J. M. Bridgeman, *The Revolt of the Hereros* (London, 1981), pp. 60–66.

22. See B. Müller-Hill, *Tödliche Wissenschaft* (Hamburg, 1984), trans. G. R. Fraser as *Murderous Science: Elimination by Scientific Selection of Jews, Gypsies, and Others in Germany, 1933–45* (Oxford: Oxford University Press, 1988).

23. See A. Bergmann, G. Czarnowski, and A. Ehmann, "'Menschen als Objekte human-genetischer Forschung und Politik im 20. Jh.' Zur Geschichte des Kaiser Wilhelm Instituts für Anthropologie, menschliche Erblehre und Eugenik in Berlin-Dahlem (1927–1945)," in *Der Wert des Menschen: Medizin in Deutschland 1918–1945*, ed. C. Pross and G. Aly (Berlin, 1989), pp. 134–35.

24. *Zeitschrift für Morphologie und Anthropologie* 34 (1934): 371–72.

25. "Nationalsozialistische Rassenerkenntnis als Grundlage für die koloniale Betätigung des neuen Europas," *Deutsche Kolonialdienst* 7 (1939): 180. See also Berlin Document Center (hereafter BDC), E. Rodenwaldt; on Rodenwaldt, see *Der Spiegel*, no. 46, November 11, 1993, p. 238. The present Institute of Hygiene of the German Army at Koblenz bears Ernst Rodenwaldt's name to honor him posthumously as a pioneer of "tropical medicine."

26. BDC file O. Reche; BAK, R 153/288, unpaginated, "Leitsätze zur bevölkerungs-politischen Sicherung des deutschen Ostens," September 24, 1939; Mechthild Rössler and Sabine Schleiermacher, eds., *Der Generalplan Ost. Hauptlinien der nationalsozialistischen Planungs- und Vernichtungspolitik* (Berlin, 1993), pp. 351ff.

27. See biography of P. Kuhn in *Reichshandbuch der deutschen Gesellschaft* (1930–1931).

28. BDC, T. Mollison.

29. W. U. Eckart, "Imperialistische, rassenbiologische und revisionistische Aspekte in der deutschen Tropenmedizin zwischen 1884 und 1940," unpublished lecture ms (conference at Bielefeld, 1986), p. 2.

30. N. Kampe, *Studenten und "Judenfrage" im Deutschen Kaiserreich* (Göttingen, 1988), pp. 61–62.

31. Johann Wolfgang von Goethe, "Gespräch mit F. v. Müller am 23.9.1823," Artemis-

Ausgabe 23, p. 298, cited in L. Graf von Westphalen, *Geschichte des Antisemitismus im 19. und. 20. Jahrhundert* (Stuttgart, 1982), pp. 13ff.; see also A. Muschg, "Mehr Licht für ein Ärgernis. Goethe und die Juden. Eine Rede, gehalten im Goethehaus Frankfurt," *Frankfurter Allgemeine Zeitung*, September 26, 1987.

32. E. M. Arndt, "Phantasien zur Berichtigung der Urteile über künftige deutsche Verfassungen," first published in *Wächter*, 1815, and in *Schriften für und an seine lieben Deutschen*, pt. 2 (Leipzig, 1845), pp. 321–462.

33. E. M. Arndt, "Ein Blick aus der Zeit auf die Zeit, 1814," cited in Westphalen, *Geschichte des Antisemitismus*, p. 16.

34. Arndt, "*Phantasien.*"

35. BAK, R 151, FC 5180, cited from C. Essner, "'Wo Rauch ist, da ist auch Feuer' – Zu den *Ansätzen eines Rassenrechts für die deutschen Kolonien,*" in *Rassendiskriminierung, Kolonialpolitik und ethnisch-nationale Identität*, ed. Wilfried Wagner et al., papers delivered at the 2nd International Colonial History Symposium,1991 Berlin, Münster, and Hamburg (1991), pp. 146–47. See also Bundesarchiv Potsdam, RKA 10.01/5417: *Mischehen und Mischlinge 1906–12.*

36. P. Sebald, *Togo 1884–1914 – Eine Geschichte der deutschen "Musterkolonie" auf der Grundlage amtlicher Quellen* (Berlin, 1988), pp. 268–69.

37. Essner, "'Wo Rauch ist,'" p. 155.

38. F. Theilhaber, *Der Untergang der deutschen Juden* (Berlin, 1911).

39. M. Marcuse, "Die christlich-jüdische Mischehe," *Zeitschrift für Sexual-Probleme* 8 (1912): 748. See also idem, "Die Fruchtbarkeit der christlich-jüdischen Mischehe," *Abhandlungen aus dem Gebiete der Sexualforschung* 2/4 (1919/20); and idem, "Der Zeugungswert der Mischehe," *Archiv für soziale Hygiene und Demographie* 1/4 (1926).

40. Marcuse, "Christlich-jüdische Mischehe," p. 740.

41. Carl von Stengel, "Zur Frage der Mischehen in den deutschen Kolonien," *Zeitschrift für Kolonialpolitik, Kolonialrecht und Kolonialwirtschaft* 10 (1912): 739–80.

42. Ibid., p. 773.

43. R. Pommerin, *Sterilisierung der Rheinlandbastarde – Das Schicksal einer farbigen deutschen Minderheit 1918–1927* (Düsseldorf, 1979), p. 10.

44. Memorandum of the meeting of the Arbeitsgemeinschaft II Sachverständigenbeirats für Bevölkerungs- und Rassenpolitik, March 11, 1935; and paper given by W. Gross (head of the Rassenpolitisches Amt der NSDAP), "Wege zur Lösung der Bastardfrage," Politisches Archiv des Auswärtigen Amtes, Inland I Partei 84/4, pp. 3–4. Gross also discussed the equally necessary sterilization of Jewish and Mongolian Mischlinge (p. 5); according to him, even sterilized bastards would still be a danger for the German public because of their "unrestrained sexual instinct" (p. 8).

45. R. Gilsenbach, "Wie Lolitschai zur Doktorwürde kam," in *Feinderklärung und Prävention – Kriminalbiologie, Zigeunerforschung und Asozialenpolitik*, Beiträge zur Nationalsozialistischen Gesundheits- und Sozialpolitik, vol. 6 (Berlin, 1988), pp. 101–34; and catalogue of the memorial exhibition at Hadamar, "Verlegt nach Hadamar" – Die Geschichte der Euthanasie-Anstalt (Kassel, 1991), pp. 136–43.

46. The number of approximately 300,000 first- and second-degree Mischlinge by 1933 may be realistic. We have no exact statistics before the census of 1939.

47. H. Heiber, *Walter Frank und sein Reichsinstitut zur Geschichte des neuen Deutschlands* (Stuttgart, 1966), pp. 466ff.

48. W. Euler, "Die rassische Rückkreuzung des Judenmischlings," *Mitteilungen über die Judenfrage*, no. 2, February 15, 1937, pp. 115–17.

49. K. Themel, *Wie verkarte ich Kirchenbücher?* (Berlin, 1936); and G. Aly and K. H. Roth, *Die restlose Erfassung – Volkszählen, Identifizieren, Aussondern im Nationalsozialismus* (Berlin, 1984), pp. 70–71.

50. W. Euler, "Das Eindringen jüdischen Blutes in die englische Oberschicht," in *Forschungen zur Judenfrage*, vol. 6, pp. 104–252; and photo series in *Illustrierter Beobachter*, January 15 and 22, 1942.

51. Heiber, *Walter Frank*, p. 472.

52. O. von Verschuer, "Was kann der Historiker, der Genealoge und der Statistiker zur

Erforschung des biologischen Problems der Judenfrage beitragen?" in *Forschungen zur Judenfrage*, vol. 2 (Hamburg, 1937), pp. 216–22.

53. BDC file A. Paul; idem, *Schwiegersöhne – Ein Schauspiel in drei Aufzügen* (Leipzig, 1937).

54. BAK, NS 19/1047.

55. The father of Hermann Göring, Dr. Heinrich Göring, was commissioned by Bismarck as first Reich Commissioner of German South West Africa from 1885 to 1890. The uncle of SS-General Erich von dem Bach-Zelewski (1899–1972), Emil von Zelewski, commanded colonial troops in German East Africa. He was killed in 1891 in battle against the Wahehe tribe. Von dem Bach-Zelewski participated in the suppression of the Warsaw Ghetto uprising. The Stroop report about the "liquidation" includes a photo of Polish auxiliary troops with the caption "Polnische Askaris," the colonial term for auxiliary troops.

56. G. Bock, *Zwangssterilisation im Nationalsozialismus: Studien zur Rassenpolitik und Frauenpolitik* (Opladen, 1986), p. 454.

57. H. von Kotze, ed., *Heeresadjutant bei Hitler 1938–1943: Aufzeichnungen des Majors Engel* (Stuttgart, 1974), pp. 121–22, note 375.

58. BAK, NS 6/346, Bl. 95.

59. Bundesarchiv Potsdam, Reichskanzlei 07.01/1793, Bormann to Lammers, November 2, 1944.

60. R. Hilberg, *Die Vernichtung der europäischen Juden* (Frankfurt/M., 1982), p. 302.

61. Wannsee Protocol in Pätzold and Schwarz, *Tagesordnung Judenmord*, p. 103.

62. N. Sombart, *Die deutschen Männer und ihre Feinde. Carl Schmitt – ein deutsches Schicksal zwischen Männerbund und Matriarchatsmythos* (Munich, 1991), p. 291.

II.

STEFAN KÜHL

The Cooperation of German Racial Hygienists and American Eugenicists before and after 1933

The bureaucratized and systematic killing of religious and ethnic minorities and of mentally handicapped people in Nazi Germany is historically unique. But the mentality that made these mass murders possible is not limited to the period 1933 to 1945, nor to Nazi Germany. The Nazi extermination programs must be understood within a historic context—a context that extends beyond the period 1933 to 1945 and beyond the territories dominated by Nazi Germany. However, the killing of religious, ethnic, and social minorities by the Nazis cannot be explained by focusing only on racism and antisemitism. The ideology of race struggle was a necessary, but not sufficient, condition for the Nazi genocide.[1] Without the underlying racist ideology, neither Auschwitz nor the murder of handicapped people in Hadamar would have been possible.

Only in recent years have historians and sociologists attempted a detailed examination of how eugenics, racial hygiene, racial anthropology, psychiatry, human genetics, and population science contributed to the formation of this racist ideology. Important historical studies about racist science in the United States, Canada, Brazil, Argentina, Great Britain, France, Italy, and Spain have illustrated both the similarities to and differences from the development of racial hygiene, anthropology, population science, and psychiatry in Germany. However, we often still find a very simple matrix. Historians writing about eugenic movements in various national contexts have either emphasized similarities and continuities to Nazi race policies, or they have argued that certain aspects of eugenics should be distinguished from these policies. Here we see repeated an oversimplified discussion that long dominated the controversy about the German racial hygiene movement as an ideological forerunner to Nazi race policies.[2]

Why this disparity between excellent studies about eugenics in different countries and overly simplistic descriptions of the relationship of these movements to Nazi race policies? The reason is to be found in the limits of a national perspective. By focusing on eugenics as a national movement and a national science, historians have tended to obscure the issue of international collaboration and have failed to provide a more detailed account of the differences and similarities of national eugenics movements vis-à-vis Nazi race policies. Although important recent studies mention that eugenics was an international phenomenon, their national narrative has not allowed for detailed insights into the workings of transnational cooperation.[3] My research seeks to correct this deficiency by providing a transnational perspective as it explores the relationship of the American eugenics movement to Nazi race policies. First, I reject the claim that the German scientific community accepted and supported Nazi race policies only because of its subjugation to a totalitarian state. Second, I hope to provide new insights into an important controversy about eugenics in the United States. The interpretations of American historians still differ on whether and to what extent the eugenics movement in the United States supported the Nazis.[4] I will illustrate the degree to which American eugenicists supported, and thereby helped legitimize, Nazi race policy. In the discussion that follows, a distinction will be made between different concepts of race improvement within the eugenics movement, and there will be an exploration of how ideas about race shaped different reactions to Nazism. Although reactions varied significantly, I would argue that all reactions were structured by the inherently racist presumptions embedded within eugenics ideology. I will then describe how the connection to Nazi Germany influenced the standing of the American eugenics movement within the scientific community and how eugenicists' support for Nazi race policies played a role in the transformation of the American eugenics movement. Finally, I will offer suggestions regarding future research strategies.

The Legitimation of Nazi Race Policies
by the American Eugenics Movement

Nazi eugenics' measures—including sterilization, marriage restrictions for unwanted members of society, and government subsidies for people defined as "valuable"—corresponded with the goals of eugenicists all over the world. Indeed, eugenicists understood Nazi race policies as the realization of their own scientific goals and political demands. In 1934, Leon F. Whitney, secretary of the American Eugenics Society, expressed his admiration for the German sterilization law. "Many far-sighted men and women in both England and America," he stated, "have long been working earnestly toward something very like what Hitler has now made compulsory."[5]

American eugenicists recognized that Hitler's steps toward improving the "German race" represented not only the implementation of their practical proposals but, even more important, the adoption of their basic ideology. Regardless of nationality or affiliation within the eugenics movement, all eugenicists urged governments to be "eugenically minded" in matters of political programs and social organization.[6] The world, they argued, should operate according to scientific biological principles.[7] Nazism implemented this kind of thinking on an unprecedented scale. At the 1936 meeting of the International Federation of Eugenic Organizations, Falk Ruttke, the ideologist of race for the Nazi state, explained how the German government had designed all measures of racial welfare according to the scientific results of eugenics. To him this represented the consistent "adaptation of biological knowledge to states-manship."[8] The deputy leader of the Nazi Party, Rudolf Hess, expressed the same thought in even simpler terms: "National Socialism is nothing but applied biology."[9]

Thus, the appeal of National Socialism for eugenicists was strong: for the first time, their ideas had become the basis for the organization of an entire state. The *Eugenical News* announced that "nowhere else than in Germany are the findings of genetics rigorously applied to the improvement of the race."[10] In the other important eugenics journal in the United States, the *Journal of Heredity*, Paul Popenoe, a California member of the board of directors of the American Eugenics Society, praised Hitler for basing "his hopes of biological regeneration solidly on the application of biological principles of human society."[11]

The year 1933 marked a turning point in the relationship between German and American eugenicists. In the 1920s, German eugenicists had admired the influence American eugenicists exerted on various U.S. policies. Between 1907 and 1930, more than half of the American states passed sterilization laws, chiefly comprised of measures mandating the sterilization of handicapped persons and criminals.[12] Nazi propaganda expressed admiration for such measures and referred to the "U.S. model" as a major influence on the development of their own race policy. In 1935, the *Rassenpolitische Auslandskorrespondenz* declared that, in terms of race policies, Germany had acted as a "good disciple of other civilized societies."[13] Adolf Hitler declared several times that the United States had made great achievements with their race policies. He studied carefully the American sterilization laws and praised the U.S. Immigration Restriction Act as excluding "undesirables" on the basis of hereditary illness and race.[14]

Although sterilization was never as widely implemented in the United States as in Nazi Germany, German racial hygienists and Nazi race politicians frequently called attention to the fact that sterilization measures in some parts of the United States were more radical than those in Nazi Germany. However, they criticized the United States for using sterilization as a form of punishment. Furthermore, they contrasted the arbitrary character of sterilization practices in the United States with the comprehensive nature of the Nazi program and with the latter's elaborate decision-making process. On the other hand, American eugenicists were proud of their influence on legislation in Nazi Germany. They recognized that the German Law to Prevent Hereditary Sick Offspring was influenced by the California sterilization law and designed after the American Model Eugenical Sterilization Law, which Harry H. Laughlin developed in 1922.[15] The transmission to Germany of information about the legislation and medical implementation of sterilization in the United States was one reason why the Nazi government could pass the sterilization law in Germany only six months after coming to power. In a letter to the Reich Ministry of the Interior in Berlin, Fritz Sauckel, administrator in the Thuringian Ministry of the Interior, explained that German legislators had to rely on reports from foreign countries because of a lack of experience in their own country.[16] In a speech at the Conference of the International Federation of Eugenic Organizations in 1934, the Nazi race politician Ruttke explained that, prior to the passage of the German sterilization law, the experience of other countries had been studied in great detail. He claimed that the German sterilization law was the first to be based on a systematic analysis of practices and discussions abroad.[17]

Detailed analyses of the sterilization measures in California played a particularly important role in the construction of the German law. Both before and after 1933, Paul Popenoe and his colleagues in the California sterilization movement regularly informed German racial hygienists about new developments in California, the state responsible for nearly half of all sterilizations in the United States. Maria Kopp, an American eugenicist visiting Germany in 1935, reported that Nazi race politicians often stated that without information regarding sterilization in California, it would have been impossible to implement the comprehensive German sterilization program.

In view of such recognition, it is not surprising that Popenoe and the California eugenics movement strongly supported the Nazi sterilization law. Popenoe saw in this law the consistent application of the principles developed by the California movement. After the German sterilization law became effective in January 1934, he jubilantly announced that the law encompassed "the largest number of persons who had ever been included in the scope of such legislation at any one time."[18] He called the German law well conceived and argued that it could be considered superior to the sterilization laws of most American states.

Support for the Nazi sterilization law was not limited to California eugenicists. In a letter to the state government of Virginia in 1934, Joseph DeJarnett, a leading member of the Virginia sterilization movement, argued that there were too few sterilizations in Virginia. In urging the government to extend the sterilization law, he argued that "the Germans are beating us at our own game."[19] Leon F. Whitney, author of an important book about sterilization policy, was similarly full of praise for Hitler's race policies. In a note sent to several newspapers in 1933, Whitney, speaking for the American Eugenics Society, claimed that Hitler's sterilization policy had demonstrated the Führer's courage and statesmanship.[20] Though he harbored doubts about the German government's ability to implement fully the sterilization law, he described the measures as evidence that "sterilization and race betterment are . . . becoming compelling ideas among all enlightened nations."[21] Harry Laughlin, a leading figure in both the American Eugenics Society and the Eugenics Research Association, described the Nazi sterilization law as the "most important legislation of this kind, which was ever achieved by a nation."[22]

Why was the eugenics movement in the United States so enthusiastic about the Nazi sterilization law? In the view of American eugenicists, the Nazi government had avoided mistakes that were made in the formulation of sterilization laws in various American states. The German government, they believed, enjoyed the advantage of introducing a nationwide, well-conceived law, far superior to the heterogeneous and inconsistent measures that prevailed in the United States. Furthermore American eugenicists saw the Law to Prevent Hereditary Sick Offspring as firmly grounded in scientific research. After returning from her study tour through Germany, Kopp reported: "The German Law is based on 30 years of research in psychiatric genealogy which was undertaken under the leadership of Dr. Ernst Rüdin at the Kaiser Wilhelm Institute of Psychiatric Research in Munich."[23]

American eugenicists believed the German law was so well developed legally that abuses would be nearly impossible. *Eugenical News* claimed that "to one acquainted with English and American laws, it is difficult to see how the new German Sterilization Law could, as some have suggested, be deflected from its purely eugenical purpose."[24] The American eugenicists were particularly impressed by the clear definition of hereditary illness and the polished legal and bureaucratic system that supported the sterilization law. They pointed to the establishment of special Hereditary Health Courts and appellate courts as safeguards for individuals who faced the prospect of sterilization.

Laughlin, a well-known promoter of sterilization and immigration laws in the United States, was an enthusiastic supporter of Nazi Germany. He used his position as assistant director of the Eugenics Record Office in Cold Spring Harbor in New York State to organize the dissemination of Nazi race propaganda to the American public. He was impressed by the modern methods of Nazi race propaganda, especially by the use of films as a persuasive medium in propagating eugenic goals.

In 1936 he purchased an English-language version of the movie *Erbkrank: A Hereditary View*, one of the main propaganda films of the Racial Political Office of the NSDAP, in order to show it at the Carnegie Institution in Washington. Laughlin described the movie as confined to the "problem of hereditary degeneracy in the fields of feeblemindedness, insanity, crime, hereditary disease and inborn deformity." Although the film propagated the notion that Jews were particularly susceptible to feeblemindedness, mental deficiency, and moral deviancy, Laughlin asserted in the *Eugenical News* that the picture contained "no racial propaganda of any sort." The film's sole purpose, he argued, was to "educate the people in the matter of soundness of family-stock quality—physical, mental and spiritual—regardless of race."[25]

Impressed by the film's powerful effect on the audience at the Carnegie Institution, Laughlin decided to use a slightly altered version of *Erbkrank* to help inform the wider American public about race betterment. He raised money to fund the distribution of the film's edited version, entitled *Eugenics in Germany*, to churches, clubs, colleges, and high schools. The millionaire Wickliffe Draper and his Pioneer Fund undertook to finance the distribution of the Nazi movie. In cooperation with the Eugenics Research Association, the Eugenics Record Office sent a flier advertising the film to biology teachers in three thousand high schools. The Pioneer Fund, the Eugenics Record Office, and the Eugenics Research Association anticipated a favorable response because of the attractive medium and the low cost to viewers.[26] Although plans for national distribution were never realized, the Nazi press reported that *Erbkrank* had been a success in the United States. In a Nazi newspaper, an article entitled "Racial Political Propaganda on the German Model Receives Great Attention among American Scientists" reported that the movie had made an "exceptionally strong impression" on American eugenicists.[27]

The National Socialist government was conscious of the important role that Laughlin played in propagating Nazi race policies outside Germany and rewarded him in 1936 with an honorary doctorate from the University of Heidelberg. He thanked Carl Schneider, professor of racial hygiene and later scientific adviser in the mass killing of handicapped people, for awarding him such a "high honor," one that "stands for the highest ideals of scholarship and research achieved by those racial stocks which have contributed so much to the foundation blood of the American people." Laughlin wrote Schneider that he considered the conferring of the degree as evidence of a common understanding of German and American scientists. Both scientific communities, Laughlin proclaimed, were in agreement concerning the practical application of those "fundamental biological and social principles" that would determine the racial health of future generations."[28]

The 1935 Congress for Population Sciences in Berlin marked the apex of international support for Nazi race policies. The International Union for the Scientific Investigation of Population Problems [IUSIPP], an organization closely connected to its eugenic counterpart, the International Federation of Eugenic Organizations, had already initiated plans in 1931 for the conference to be held in Berlin. The International Union did not alter its plans, even after it recognized that the Nazi government would use the Congress for its own purposes. The president of the IUSIPP, Raymond Pearl, remained committed to Berlin as the conference site, although he feared that population science would be politicized.[29] Pearl, a professor at Johns Hopkins University, was initially a eugenics enthusiast who had become critical of that discipline in the late 1920s and veered toward population science.[30] His position regarding Nazi policies was ambiguous. Although he criticized the Nazi appropriation of eugenics and population sciences for political purposes, he defended the Nazi aim of forcing German Jews out of university positions. Pearl honored the president of the Population Conference, the German racial hygienist Eugen Fischer, as a distinguished and broad-minded scientist. He accepted Fischer's invitation to serve as vice president of the conference as "a great honor." As it turned out, however, Pearl was unable to attend the conference.[31]

Instead, two other American eugenicists jointly served as vice presidents of the Berlin conference: Harry Laughlin and Clarence G. Campbell. Laughlin, too, could not go to Berlin. Nevertheless, he accepted the honorary position of vice president and contributed a paper.[32]

Clarence G. Campbell, president of the Eugenics Research Association, served as the senior representative of the American eugenics movement at the Berlin conference. He delivered a lecture, "Biological Postulates of Population Study," in which he stressed the accomplishments of eugenics during the previous decades and underscored the importance of Nazi race policies for other nations. He claimed that from a synthesis of the work of several non-German eugenicists, Adolf Hitler had been able to construct comprehensive race policies that promised to be "epochal in racial history" and set a pattern that other nations and other racial groups had to follow.[33] At the end of the conference Campbell presented a toast, "To that great leader, Adolf Hitler!"[34]

After his return to the United States, Campbell attempted to garner support among colleagues for the race policies in Nazi Germany. "Anti-Nazi propaganda with which all countries have been flooded," he lamented, "has gone far to obscure the correct understanding and the great importance of the German race policies."[35] In an article in *Eugenical News*, the official organ of the Eugenic Research Association, the Galton Society, the American Eugenics Society, and the International Federation of Eugenic Organizations, Campbell claimed that Nazi race policies had gained the "enthusiastic support and cooperation of practically the entire German nation." He argued that evidence of public support by "racially valuable families" could already be seen in Germany's increasing birthrate: "Where American families desire another motor-car, when they can afford it, German families desire another child."[36] Campbell's enthusiastic support for German race policies was exceptional. Campbell's statements, however, represent only the most extreme example of collaboration; Nazi race policies were widely supported by the American eugenics movement as a whole. Until 1940, the two major scientific journals of the American eugenics movement published only positive articles about eugenics measures in Nazi Germany. The three major national societies for eugenics in the United States—the American Eugenics Society, the Eugenics Research Association, and the Galton Society—all reacted positively to eugenic policies under the Nazis.

Variations within the American Eugenics Movement

Despite the widespread enthusiasm for Nazi race policies by American eugenicists, historical scholarship has traditionally argued that only a small group of eugenicists supported Nazi race policies and that this group was increasingly marginalized and discredited within the scientific community.[37] Historians such as Kenneth M. Ludmerer and Daniel J. Kevles have differentiated between two groups within the eugenics movement: "mainline" and "reform" eugenicists. Mainline eugenicists who lent support to Nazi race policies, they argue, attempted to improve the white race by eliminating the "inferior" elements and by preventing miscegenation with other races. On the other side, these historians argue that reform eugenicists separated themselves from Nazism and mainline eugenicists by pleading for selection on an individual rather than a racial basis.[38] Some historians, who employ the distinction between reform and mainline eugenics, emphasize the two groups' relationship to science as the key differentiating factor. They stress the fact that reform eugenicists were knowledgeable about the latest developments in genetics and were in step with modern scientific thought. Mainline eugenicists and Nazi racial hygienists, on the other hand, are viewed as having appropriated "pseudoscience" to support strongly biased political positions.[39]

My interpretation differs from that conventional historical scholarship on eugenics. I will argue below that it is too simple to separate the activists of the American Eugenics Society into two groups, one supporting and one opposing Nazi race policies. Furthermore, I disagree that the relationship of eugenicists to science can be used as an adequate delineating factor. Such a distinction between "science" and pseudoscience fails to recognize that science is socially constructed within a particular historical context and that both science and pseudoscience share a common basis. Eugenicists perceived themselves as both scientists and social activists, believing that there should be a close relationship between their science and its political implementation. Indeed, the overwhelming majority of eugenicists favored only an analytical distinction between "pure" and "applied" eugenics.

I propose that a more useful way to distinguish between strands in the eugenics movement is to emphasize differing conceptions of race improvement. All eugenicists believed that it was possible to distinguish between inferior and superior elements of society, but not all traced inferiority directly to a racial basis. I argue, however, that any attempt to designate a group as inferior, combined with a political agenda of genetic improvement for a certain racial group, constitutes racism.

This understanding of eugenics relies on a new, broader conception of racism.[40] Historian Gisela Bock has shown that Nazi race policies extended beyond ethnicity and skin color, and she therefore distinguishes between two forms of racism: eugenic and ethnic. Ethnic racism represents "classical racism," the application of hierarchical standards to the taxonomy of human racial groups. Eugenic racism is the demarcation of certain elements within a particular race as inferior, followed by attempts to eliminate these elements through discriminatory policies.[41]

Based on this broader perception, a few historians have argued that any attempt to distinguish between mainline and reform eugenicists is extremely problematic. Focusing on the American Eugenics Society, historian Barry Mehler has pointed out that the borders between these two groups were highly fluid and that it is difficult to situate firmly individual eugenicists in one camp or the other.[42] While I agree with these points, I also believe it is essential to retain an appreciation for the differences among various branches of the American Eugenics Society. Specifically, I see the need to distinguish among three groups: orthodox eugenicists, racial theorists, and reform eugenicists.[43] Differing concepts for race and race improvement serve as the basis of my differentiation.

Orthodox eugenicists dominated the eugenics movements in the United States, Scandinavia, and Germany up to the early 1930s. They believed in white superiority yet argued that the white race also needed further improvement. They explained the inequality of races as resulting from superior adaptation by some groups in the struggle for existence. Whites, in other words, were viewed as more advanced than others in the evolutionary process. Orthodox eugenicists, represented by figures such as Laughlin, Davenport, and Whitney, thus agreed in principle with the ethnic as well as the eugenic racism implemented in Nazi Germany. Although most Orthodox eugenicists were themselves antisemitic, they were careful not to be too blatant in supporting Nazi discrimination against the Jews. They feared that Nazi antisemitism would dominate the perception of eugenics in the United States and would overshadow more "acceptable" measures, such as sterilization, marriage restrictions for handicapped individuals, and special support for the procreation of "worthy" couples. Orthodox eugenicists sought to redirect public attention to these "exemplary" eugenic measures and tried to minimize the antisemitism of Nazi Germany, especially after the passing of the Nuremberg law against "miscegenation" in 1935.[44]

The group of eugenicists who voiced the strongest support for Nazi Germany was clustered around the racial theorists Madison Grant, Lothrop Stoddard, and Clarence G. Campbell. American racial theorists were closely allied with orthodox eugenicists in the various national eugenics societies. Racial theorists, however, based their ideology on the assumption of the French racial philosopher Arthur Comte de Gobineau that races are innately unequal. Their belief in Nordic superiority was combined with a strong antisemitic bias.[45] Grant, Stoddard, and Campbell were more explicit than the orthodox eugenicists in voicing their support not only for eugenic racism in Nazi Germany but also for racism directed at ethnic and religious minorities.

Reform eugenicists grouped around Frederick Osborn, Roswell H. Johnson, and Ellsworth Huntington—all of whom served at different times as president of the American Eugenics Society—distanced themselves from the blatant ethnic racism of the racial theorists and National Socialists. They argued that biological differences among groups were negligible compared to the much more significant differences existing among individuals. After 1930 reform eugenicists gained increasing influence in the United States.

Roswell H. Johnson, a member of the board of directors of the American Eugenics Society from 1928 onward, laid the ideological basis for reform eugenicists. Focusing his attack on Madison Grant, Johnson criticized the notion that all members of one race were in principle superior to those of other races; he labeled such views "ultra racist."[46] In contrast to racial anthropologists and National Socialists, he developed a concept of "overlap racism." His premise was that "in mental traits some races do differ in a significant degree, although the overlap is so great that individual differences outrank social differences in importance." In other words, although races differed in quality, the high quality individuals of a lesser race might be superior to low quality individuals of a higher race. Still, Johnson also believed that the chances of finding a superior human being were higher among whites than among members of other races. This concept of overlap racism shaped the specific position of reform eugenicists on Nazi race policies. Johnson regretted that the enormous progress of the eugenics movement under Hitler "suffered by being linked with anti-Semitism." He feared that the "excellent eugenic program" adopted by the Nazis would be nullified by the "dysgenic" consequences of discrimination against ethnic minorities. The persecution of hereditarily "superior" Jews would cause Germany to remain behind the attainment that would otherwise have been theirs.[47]

Frederick Osborn also combined criticism of Nazi's Nordic arrogance and their discrimination against Jews with enthusiasm for the eugenics measures in Nazi Germany. In 1937, he praised the Nazi eugenics program as the "most important experiment which has ever been tried." Despite his doubts that compulsory sterilization could obtain better results than voluntary sterilization, he called the German sterilization program "apparently an excellent one."[48]

The simultaneous criticism of antisemitism and enthusiastic support for the Nazi eugenic program by American reform eugenicists was possible only because the proponents refused to recognize the inseparable connection between eugenic and ethnic racism in Nazi Germany. Again and again, reform eugenicists stressed that the eugenics measures of Nazi Germany needed to be evaluated independently of its totalitarianism and antisemitism.[49] Thus, reform eugenicists did not equate the eugenics measures of Nazi Germany with National Socialism, and they believed that Nazi antisemitism had nothing to do with the eugenic concept of race improvement. In their minds, the fact that the two things were linked together in Nazi Germany was merely an unfortunate coincidence.

Nazi Race Policies and Their Influence on the Transformation of American Eugenics

The reaction of the eugenics movement to Nazi race policies must also be seen within the context of the larger scientific community in the United States. In the 1930s, important scientific and political groups grew more skeptical about the prejudicial policy of the eugenics movement toward ethnic minorities. The scientific basis for the discrimination against blacks and Jews was questioned by prominent figures such as the socialist geneticists Hermann J. Muller and Walther Landauer, the liberal geneticist L. C. Dunn, and the anthropologist Franz Boas. In the scientific community, Muller, Landauer, and other geneticists enjoyed increasing prestige stemming from the research successes and growing importance of genetics. In contrast to Boas and Dunn, who were in principle critical of eugenics, Muller and Landauer represented a group of socialist, often antiracist eugenicists who were primarily responsible for coordinating the scientific critique against Nazi race policies. Although socialist eugenicists argued in general that there was no evidence for intellectual differences among races, they believed that the human race as a whole should be improved by supporting the procreation of "capable" individuals and preventing the reproduction of "inferior" persons.[50] Socialist eugenicists, as well as critics such as Boas and Dunn, therefore centered their criticism on the ethnic racism of Nazi Germany. They concentrated their attacks on dismantling the scientific basis of Nazi antisemitism, the ideology of Nordic superiority, and the Nazi policy prohibiting so-called miscegenation. They argued that the Nazis abused science for their political purposes and based their ideas and policies on pseudoscience.

The conflict between critical American scientists and Nazi racial hygienists escalated during the preparations for the Seventh International Congress for Genetics in 1939. Prior to the conference, which was originally to be held in Moscow, thirty American geneticists sent a resolution to the general secretary of the conference, the Soviet geneticist Solomon G. Levit. They demanded a special section to discuss differences between human races, the question of whether theories of racial superiority had any scientific basis, and whether eugenics measures could lead to definite improvements in human society. Leading American geneticists signed the resolution. Even some reform eugenicists, such as Clarence C. Little, president of the American Eugenics Society between 1928 and 1929, and Robert C. Cook, editor of the *Journal of Heredity*, also signed.[51]

The government of the Soviet Union canceled the conference because of its new policy against genetics. The conference was then postponed until late August 1939 and relocated to Edinburgh. Although the conference closed early due to the outbreak of the Second World War, leading socialist eugenicists and geneticists succeeded in preparing a resolution against Nazi race policies, the so-called Genetico Manifesto.[52] The manifesto was prepared and supported primarily by scientists from the United States. It demanded effective birth control and the emancipation of women, stressed the importance of economic and political change, and condemned racism against ethnic minorities. The manifesto, however, still reflected a eugenic ideology. The Genetico Manifesto clearly demonstrated that the scientists who opposed Nazi race policies did not do so because of opposition to its eugenic orientation. The manifesto signatories were critical of discrimination against ethnic, social, and religious minorities but continued to advocate an individualistic concept of race improvement.[53]

The struggle within the scientific community in the United States concerning the correct position on Nazi race policies was not between a liberal group of anti-eugenics "real" scientists and a group of reactionary, racist "pseudoscientists." Rather, it was primarily a struggle between scientists with differing conceptions of race improvement and differing positions on how science, economics, and policies should be used to realize their goals.

In the 1920s, American orthodox eugenicists held prestigious positions as professors at universities and as members of leading research institutes, where they received support from major foundations. Their influence extended into the highest political levels of the state and federal governments. The important role they played as scientific experts in shaping immigration policy, health administration, and sterilization laws indicates the extent of their influence in political decision-making processes. By the 1930s, however, orthodox eugenicists had lost a large part of this influence. A number of factors contributed to their demise: public criticism of blatantly antisemitic statements of eugenicists such as Laughlin, discoveries in genetics that contradicted the scientific basis of orthodox eugenicists, and the demand for a stronger sociological approach to the problems of modern society.[54] Critics outside the eugenics movement heightened the distrust by pointing out connections between orthodox eugenics and Nazi racial hygiene. The increasing radicalization of Hitler's race policies provided critics with a vivid illustration of the potential dangers of orthodox eugenicists' racism.

Through their comprehensive and uncritical support of Nazi race policies, orthodox eugenicists made their own standing in the United States dependent partly on the reputation of Nazi Germany. As Nazism grew more unpopular with the American public, orthodox eugenicists were no longer able to distance themselves from Nazi race policies. Laughlin, for example, was ousted from influential political and scientific positions. The Carnegie Foundation, sponsor of the major institutional base of orthodox eugenics, the Eugenics Record Office, accused it of producing political propaganda.[55] One demand was that the Eugenics Record Office cut its close ties to the *Eugenical News*, the journal that played a central role in support of Nazi race policies. Even after it adopted a more restrained strategy, criticism directed at the Eugenics Record Office continued. Finally, in 1939, the Carnegie Foundation forced Laughlin to retire as assistant director. The office closed on December 31 of that year.

Historians have tended to interpret the difficulties of orthodox eugenicists in the 1930s as a crisis of eugenics as a whole. I question this assumption. A recent study concerning sterilization in the United States has proven that eugenically motivated cases of sterilization increased during the 1930s—the same period in which the institutionalized eugenics movement was undergoing redefinition.[56] The transformation of eugenics should not be viewed as a decline but rather as a shift in power from eugenicists with strong notions of Nordic superiority and antisemitism to socialist eugenicists and the reform wing within the American Eugenics Society. Furthermore, the 1930s witnessed the diffusion of eugenic ideas into other scientific fields, such as population science and psychiatry.

The confusion within the American Eugenics Society in the 1930s made it ripe for a transformation into a more sociologically oriented movement. The changes took place peacefully, without an intense internal power struggle and without undermining the solidarity among the different wings of the eugenics movement. The growing influence of reform eugenicists within the American Eugenics Society did not result in the exclusion of orthodox eugenicists such as Laughlin and Davenport, who remained models for younger professionals. The "friendly takeover" of eugenics societies by reform eugenicists opened the movement to new genetic discoveries, new sociological methods, and the question of overpopulation. However, the core of eugenics ideology—the distinction between superior and inferior genetic groups—remained intact. What changed was the definition of "inferior" and "superior" groups. The leaders of the American Eugenics Society after 1935 did not entirely renounce the notion that there were differences among races but adopted a reformist outlook that argued for selection on an individual basis.[57]

Reform eugenicists enjoyed greater influence partially because they had been more careful not to ally themselves with the Nazi regime. Initially, they had stressed the positive features of the German eugenics program. Unlike orthodox eugenicists, however, they were able to separate themselves from Nazi Germany by disavowing both antisemitism and totalitarian "excesses." Their critical position toward these features of Nazism enabled the eugenics movement, dominated by reform eugenicists, to survive the 1940s without being held accountable for their support of Nazi Germany. Successful reform eugenicists began to conceal their previous support for the eugenics measures of Nazi Germany.

When relations between the eugenics movement in the United States and German racial hygienists began to cool in the late 1930s it was not because American eugenicists recognized the negative consequences of the implementation of eugenics principles. Rather, a combination of different factors was at work: gradual recognition by the public and the scientific community that antisemitism was the core concept of Nazi race policies; a power shift inside the scientific community of the United States toward a group of progressive, socialist eugenicists and geneticists; and the rapid decline in the late 1930s of the reputation of Nazi Germany within the United States.

Conclusion

Relations between German and American eugenicists reached a state of crisis after the outbreak of World War II. Prior to 1939, Nazi propaganda claimed that Germany had no interest in going to war against nations that belonged to the same "white Nordic stock." American eugenicists who believed this reacted with surprise when the Nazis initiated aggression against nations of similar racial composition. Nazi aggression obviously strained relations between Germany and the American eugenics movements. Nevertheless, during the years 1939 to 1941, connections between the two were not severed completely. American eugenicists such as T. U. H. Ellinger and Lothrop Stoddard still visited Germany to study Nazi race policies. Exchange of information through letters also continued. The complete break between German and American eugenicists occurred with the entrance of the United States into the war against Germany and Japan. After December 7, 1941, the day of the Japanese attack on Pearl Harbor, all contact between the German and American eugenics movements ceased.

After 1945, American eugenicists' reactions to the Nazi radicalization of eugenics continued to depend on whether the former belonged to the orthodox or reformist wings of the movement. Orthodox eugenicists ignored the excesses of the Nazis. They continued to view the eugenics measures in the 1930s as exemplary, and they referred with pride to the important role the United States had played in the development of this policy. As late as the 1970s, Marian S. Olden, the leading figure in the Association for Voluntary Sterilization, and Leon F. Whitney, secretary of the American Eugenics Society, proudly recalled their support of Nazi race policies.[58]

Historical investigation can demonstrate the continuity of this kind of research and can remind us of the past consequences of scientific racism. The radicalization of eugenics ideology among the Nazis and the consequent discrimination, sterilization, and elimination of millions of human beings defined as "inferior" stands as an indictment of scientists who helped to mold and legitimate this process. Obviously, the actions of eugenicists in the United States and Nazi Germany were not identical. Indeed, American scientists did not take part in the mass sterilization of hundreds of thousands of persons, did not participate in the selection of tens of thousands of handicapped people for the Nazi gas chambers, and did not use the bodies of murdered handicapped people and Jews for scientific experimentation. But the ideology that paved the way for and served to legitimate applied racism in Germany was by no means limited to German scientists. Rather, it was the result of a long history that condoned attempts to distinguish scientifically between "inferior" and "superior" members of humankind.

Further research must show how these scientific attempts extended beyond national scientific and political movements. Eugenics not only existed in many countries; eugenicists from different national backgrounds cooperated internationally in formulating and propagating eugenics policies. The international congresses for eugenics in the early decades of the twentieth century played a central role in organizing eugenics on an international level. The international societies for eugenics and racial hygiene provided a forum for this international cooperation, serving as an arena for debate and exchange of information.

Focusing on the international eugenics movement shows us that racism was not always linked to nationalism. In the International Federation of Eugenic Organizations, an important group promoted the cooperation of all "white" nations in international politics. They urged an end to military conflicts between nations of similar "superior" racial stocks, arguing that such conflicts would only help racially different nations and the "inferior elements" within their own populations. The engagement of eugenicists in developing an ideal, eugenically influenced world order, their favoring of restrictive migration policies, and their position regarding so-called miscegenation shows that racism could be combined with a certain vision of internationalism.

On an international level, we can observe the process of differentiation of views on eugenics among various branches of science, and later the diffusion of eugenic thinking into other sciences. While a group of orthodox eugenicists tried to stabilize the eugenics movement, another group of eugenicists moved into other scientific fields, though largely without abandoning the core of their eugenic ideology. The development and differentiation of human genetics, population science, clinical psychiatry, and mental hygiene was closely connected with the decline of organized eugenics. The diffusion of eugenics first took place on an international level and was then followed by a similar process in various national contexts.

One main purpose of the international eugenics movement was to exert influence—through scientific experts—over national and international policy decision-making. The International Federation of Eugenic Organizations tried to influence migration policy, mailed resolutions about the potential dysgenic effects of war to governments, and attempted to influence the Italian population policy under

Mussolini. After 1933, with the establishment of Nazi race policies in Germany, the International Federation played an important role in supporting these policies. This positive reaction was due to the fact that the International Federation of Eugenic Organizations represented the more radical eugenicists' position. Critics of Nazi race policies, who generally continued to propagate their eugenic ideology, organized themselves outside the eugenics organization.[59] In sum, my case study of the American support of Nazi race policies shows that the tendency of scientific racism to enter into a symbiosis with political racism did not stop at the boundaries of the Third Reich. By examining different concepts of race improvement, we can work out some fundamental differences between American eugenicists and their position toward Nazi race policies. By adopting an international perspective, we can gain important insights into cooperation among national eugenics movements. Concerning Nazi racism, such a focus can help us to understand to what extent Nazi race policies prior to World War II constituted a "Sonderweg," and to what extent they were part of an international history of scientific and political racism.

NOTES

1. Hermann Lübbe, "Rationalität und Irrationalität des Völkermords," in *Holocaust: Die Grenzen des Verstehens: Eine Debatte über die Besetzung der Geschichte*, ed. Hanno Loewy (Reinbek: Rowohlt, 1992), p. 89.

2. Studies focusing on the eugenics movement as an ideological forerunner to the policy in Nazi Germany include George L. Mosse, *The Crisis of German Ideology: Intellectual Origins of the Third Reich* (New York: Grosset and Dunlap, 1964); idem, *Toward the Final Solution: A History of European Racism* (London: J. M. Dent, 1978); Günther Altner, *Weltanschauliche Hintergründe der Rassenlehre des Dritten Reiches: Zum Problem einer umfassenden Anthropologie* (Zürich: EVZ, 1968); Daniel Gasman, *The Scientific Origins of National Socialism: Social Darwinism in Ernst Haeckel and the German Monist League* (New York: American Elsevier, 1971); and Patrick von Mühlen, *Rassenideologien: Geschichte und Hintergründe* (Berlin: J. H. W. Dietz, 1977). Studies that attempt to separate the history of social Darwinism and the early eugenics movement from the later radicalization of Nazi racial hygiene include Sheila F. Weiss, *Race Hygiene and National Efficiency: The Eugenics of Wilhelm Schallmayer* (Berkeley: University of California Press, 1987); Alfred Kelly, *The Descent of Darwin: The Popularization of Darwinism in Germany, 1860–1914* (Chapel Hill: University of North Carolina Press, 1981); and Loren R. Graham, "Science and Values: The Eugenics Movement in Germany and Russia in the 1920s," *American Historical Review* 82 (1977): 1135–64.

3. For Germany, see Gisela Bock, "Racism and Sexism in Nazi Germany: Motherhood, Compulsory Sterilization, and the State," *Signs: Journal of Women in Culture and Society* 8 (1983): 400–21; idem, *Zwangssterilisation im Nationalsozialismus: Studien zur Rassenpolitik und Frauenpolitik* (Opladen: WDV, 1986); Peter Weingart, Jürgen Kroll, Kurt Bayertz, *Rasse, Blut und Gene: Geschichte der Eugenik und Rassenhygiene in Deutschland* (Frankfurt/M.: Suhrkamp, 1988); Robert Proctor, *Racial Hygiene: Medicine under the Nazis* (Cambridge: Harvard University Press, 1988); and Paul Weindling, "The 'Sonderweg' of German Eugenics: Nationalism and Scientific Internationalism," *British Journal of the History of Science* 22 (1989): 321–33. For the United States, see Barry Mehler, *A History of the American Eugenics Society: 1921–1940*, Ph.D. diss., University of Illinois, 1988. For Canada, see Angus McLaren, *Our Own Master Race: Eugenics in Canada, 1885–1945* (Toronto: McClelland & Steward, 1990).

4. See Robert Proctor, "Eugenics among Social Sciences: Hereditarian Thought in Germany and the United States," in *The Estate of Social Knowledge*, ed. JoAnne Brown and David K. van Keuren (Baltimore: Johns Hopkins University Press, 1991), p. 178.

5. Leon F. Whitney, *The Case for Sterilization* (New York: Frederick A. Stocks, 1934), p. 7.

6. Report of the Sub-Committee on Ultimate Program for the Eugenics Society of American, introduction, Jennings Papers: Eugenics Society of America, American Philosophical Society (hereafter APS) Philadelphia.

7. See Herbert S. Jennings, *The Biological Basis of Human Nature* (New York: W. W. Norton, 1930), p. 203.

8. Falk Ruttke, "Erbpflege in der deutschen Gesetzgebung," *Der Erbarzt* 3 (1936): 113.

9. Rudolf Hess at a mass meeting in 1934. See Robert Lifton, *The Nazi Doctors: Medical Killing and the Psychology of Genocide* (New York: Basic Books, 1986), p. 31. Robert Proctor has shown that the expression was coined by Fritz Lenz in 1931. See Fritz Lenz, *Menschliche Auslese und Rassenhygiene (Eugenik)*, 3rd ed. (Munich: Lehmann, 1931), and Robert Proctor, "Nazi Biomedical Technologies," in *Lifeworld and Technology*, ed. Timothy Casey and Lester Embree (Washington, D.C.: Center for Advanced Research in Phenomenology and University Press of America, 1989), p. 23.

10. *Eugenical News* 20 (1935): 100.

11. Paul Popenoe, "The German Sterilization Law," *Journal of Heredity* 25 (1934): 257.

12. In 1930, twenty-five states had passed sterilization laws. In 1938, twenty-nine states had such laws. See Human Betterment Foundation, *Human Sterilization Today* (Pasadena: Human Betterment Foundation, 1939).

13. "Das Ausland als Vorbild für die deutsche Rassengesetzgebung," *Rassenpolitische Auslandskorrespondenz* 2/4 (1935): 1.

14. Adolf Hitler, *Mein Kampf*, 1924; trans. and with an introduction by D. C. Watt (London, 1974), p. 400. On the fact that Hitler studied American sterilization laws with great interest, see Otto Wagener, "Hitler aus nächster Nähe," in *Aufzeichnungen eines Vertrauten 1929–1932*, ed. Henry A. Turner (Frankfurt/M.: Ullstein, 1978), p. 264.

15. *Eugenical News* 18 (1933): 89; Roswell H. Johnson, "International Eugenics," Ph.D. diss., University of Pittsburgh, 1934, p. 120. Marie E. Kopp, "A Eugenic Program in Operation," in *Summary of the Proceedings of the Conference on Eugenics in Relation to Nursing*, ed. Frederick Osborn, unpub., American Eugenics Society Papers, Conference on Eugenics in Relation to Nursing, APS Philadelphia; Laughlin's Model Law in Harry H. Laughlin, *Eugenical Sterilization in the United States* (Chicago: Psychopathic Laboratory of the Municipal Court of Chicago, 1922), pp. 446–47.

16. Fritz Sauckel to the Reich Ministry of the Interior, April 4, 1933, Bundesarchiv Koblenz, R 43 II/717.

17. Falk Ruttke, "Erbpflege in der deutschen Gesetzgebung," *Ziel und Weg* 4 (1934): 601.

18. Paul Popenoe, "The Progress of Eugenic Sterilization," *Journal of Heredity* 25 (1934): 19–25.

19. Joint Committee on Voluntary Sterilization, *Report of the Departmental Committee on Sterilization*, pamphlet (n.p.: June 1934), p. 5; quoted in Daniel J. Kevles, *In the Name of Eugenics: Genetics and the Uses of Human Heredity* (Berkeley: University of California Press, 1985), p. 116.

20. Davenport Papers, Leon F. Whitney, "Memoirs," 204, APS, Philadelphia.

21. Leon Whitney, *The Case Sterilization* (New York: Frederick A. Stocks, 1934), p. 137.

22. Laughlin's enthusiastic opinion regarding the German sterilization law was published in "Amerikanische Anerkennung für das deutsche Sterilisationsgesetz," *Der Angriff*, July 26, 1933.

23. Kopp, "Eugenic Program," p. 4.

24. "Eugenical Sterilization in Germany," *Eugenical News* 88 (1933): 89.

25. Harry H. Laughlin, "Eugenics in Germany: Motion Picture Showing How Germany Is Presenting and Attacking Her Problems in Applied Eugenics," *Eugenical News* 22 (1937): 65–66.

26. See the letter from Laughlin to W. P. Draper, December 9, 1938, Laughlin Papers, Kirksville, Missouri. See also Frances Janet Hassencahl, "Harry H. Laughlin: 'Expert Eugenics Agent' for the House Committee on Immigration and Naturalization, 1921 to 1931," Ph.D. diss., Case Western Reserve University, 1970, pp. 355–56.

27. "Rassenpolitische Aufklärung nach deutschem Vorbild: Grosse Beachtung durch die amerikanische Wissenschaft," press agency report of the NSK, March 19, 1937, and notes, in *Ziel und Weg* 7 (1937): 361, and in *Volk und Rasse* 12 (1937): 150.

28. Laughlin to Schneider, May 16, 1936, Laughlin Papers, Kirksville, Missouri.

29. Population science in the 1920s, 1930s, and 1940s was based on a eugenics ideology. I use "population science" only in discussing the actions of organizations that described their purpose either as the promotion of population science or as population policy.

30. For information on Raymond Pearl's shift from a eugenicist to a main representative of early population science who preserved a eugenic ideology, see Garland E. Allen, "Old Wine in New Bottles: From Eugenics to Population Control in the Work of Raymond Pearl," in *The Expansion of American Biology*, ed. Keith R. Benson, Jane Maienschein, and Ronald Rainger (New Brunswick: Rutgers University Press, 1991), pp. 231–61.

31. Pearl to Sir Charles Close, British eugenicist and population scientist and leading member of the IUSIPP, on December 11, 1934, Pearl Papers, IUSIPP, APS Philadelphia.

32. Harry H. Laughlin, "Studies on the Historical and Legal Development of Eugenical Sterilization in the United States," in *Bevölkerungsfragen: Bericht des Internationalen Kongresses für Bevölkerungswissenschaft Berlin, 26 August–l September 1935*, ed. Hans Harmsen and Franz Lohse (Munich: J. F. Lehmann, 1936), pp. 664–75. Laughlin to Fischer, July 31, 1935, Laughlin Papers, Kirksville, Missouri.

33. Clarence G. Campbell, "The Biological Postulates of Population Study," in *Bevölkerungsfragen*, ed. Harmsen and Lohse, p. 602.

34. Quote in Kevles, *In the Name of Eugenics*, p. 347.

35. Clarence G. Campbell, "The German Racial Policy," *Eugenical News* 21 (1936): 25.

36. Ibid., pp. 28 and 26, respectively.

37. Mark H. Haller, *Eugenics: Hereditary Attitudes in American Thought* (New Brunswick: Rutgers University Press, 1963), p. 174; and Kenneth M. Ludmerer, *Genetics and American Society* (Baltimore: Johns Hopkins University Press, 1972), p. 174. Both were distinguished eugenicists critical of the Nazi race policies of eugenicists who did not see that the eugenic measures of the Nazi government represented a "perversion of the true eugenic ideal as seen by well-meaning men deeply concerned about mankind's genetic future" (Ludmerer, *Genetics*, p. 117). More recently, Kevles made the distinction between a small group of Nazi supporters and a larger group of eugenicists who criticized Nazi policies (Kevles, *In the Name of Eugenics*, p. 118).

38. Ludmerer, *Genetics*, and Kevles, *In the Name of Eugenics*. For the application of this distinction to Scandinavian eugenic movements, see Nils Roll-Hansen, "Geneticists and the Eugenics Movement in Scandinavia," *British Journal for the History of Science* 22 (1989): 335–46. For Great Britain, see Geoffrey R. Searle, *Eugenics and Politics in Britain, 1909–1914* (Leyden: Nordhoff International, 1976). Sheila F. Weiss applied a similar concept to the racial hygiene movement in Germany before 1933 in "The Race-Hygiene Movement in Germany, 1904–1945," in *The Wellborn Science: Eugenics in Germany, France, Brazil and Russia*, ed. Mark B. Adams (New York: Oxford University Press, 1990), pp. 8–68.

39. See Ludmerer, *Genetics*, pp. 148–50. Some recent scholarship also uses this distinction; see, for example, Nils Roll-Hansen, "The Progress of Eugenics: Growth of Knowledge and Change in Ideology," *History of Science* 26 (1988): 293–331.

40. Bock, *Zwangssterilisation*, p. 63. See also idem, "Antinatalism, Maternity, and Paternity in National Socialist Racism," in *Maternity and Gender Policies: Women and the Rise of the European Welfare State, 1880–1950s*, ed. Gisela Bock and Pat Thane (London: Routledge, 1991), pp. 233–55. For the United States, see Garland Allen, "The Misuse of Biological Hierarchies: The American Eugenics Movement, 1900–1940," *History and Philosophy of the Life Sciences* 5 (1983): 105–28; and Robert Proctor, *Racial Hygiene*; and Mehler, *History*.

41. Bock, *Zwangssterilisation*, p. 65.

42. Mehler, *History*, p. iii.

43. See the shift in my terminology as compared to Kühl, *Nazi Connection*, p. 72. Because reform eugenicists were the "mainline" after 1945, I prefer the more accurate term "orthodox eugenicist" to "mainline eugenicist."

44. In a speech at the conference of the American Eugenics Society in 1937, Kopp tried to shift emphasis away from the antisemitic measures of the Nuremberg Laws to what she saw as the more important marriage restrictions placed on the mentally and physically handicapped (Kopp, "Eugenic Program," p. 5). Similarly, Laughlin, in an article promoting the previously mentioned propaganda film *Erbkrank*, claimed, despite a long passage in the film about the connection between Jewishness and a disposition for mental illness, that "there is no racial propaganda of any sort in the picture" (Laughlin, *Eugenics in Germany*, pp. 65–66).

45. Arthur Comte de Gobineau, *The Inequality of Human Races*, trans. from the French edition of 1853–1855 by A. Collins (London: Heinemann, 1915). For a discussion concerning the close relationship of racial theorists to the organized eugenics movement in the United States, see Ludmerer, *Genetics*, pp. 64–66, and Hans-Peter Kröner, "Die Eugenik in Deutschland von 1891–1914," doctoral diss., University of Münster, 1980, p. 31. The more distant relation of German racial theorists to the racial hygiene movement is treated in Hans Jürgen Lutzhöft, *Der Nordische Gedanke in Deutschland 1920 bis 1940* (Stuttgart: Klett-Cotta, 1971), pp. 163–64; and Günter Mann, "Rassenhygiene-Sozialdarwinismus," in *Biologismus im 19. Jahrhundert*, ed. Gunther Mann (Stuttgart: Ferdinand Enke, 1973), pp. 73–77.

46. Johnson, *International Eugenics*, pp. 199–212, citation from p. 212.

47. Ibid., pp. 184–85 and 227.

48. Osborn, *Summary of the Proceedings of the Conference on Eugenics in Relation to Nursing*, February 24, 1937, American Eugenics Society Papers: Conference on Eugenics in Relation to Nursing.

49. For example, before the Annual Meeting of the American Eugenics Society in May 1938, Osborn lamented the fact that the public opposed the "excellent sterilization program in Germany because of its Nazi origin" (Annual Meeting of the American Eugenics Society, May 5, 1938, Osborn Papers, I, 10, APS Philadelphia).

50. Often historians have not distinguished between socialist eugenicists and reform eugenicists. They have categorized all eugenicists who criticized the Nordic arrogance of orthodox eugenicists and National Socialists as either socialist or reform eugenicists. This approach, however, fails to recognize differences in the concept of race improvement held by the two groups. Their different reactions to Nazi race policies further illustrates that the single distinction between reform eugenicists and orthodox eugenicists does not cover the whole spectrum. See Donald K. Pichens, *Eugenics and the Progressives* (Nashville: Vanderbilt University Press, 1968); Michael Freeden, "Eugenics and Progressive Thought: A Study in Ideological Affinity," *Historical Journal* 22 (1979): 645–71; Diane Paul, "Eugenics and the Left," *Journal of the History of Ideas* 45 (1984): 567–90; and Michael Schwartz, *Sozialistische Eugenik* (Bonn: J. H. W. Dietz Nachfolger, 1995).

51. Letter from Jennings to S. G. Levit, April 2, 1936, Jennings Papers, Levit, APS Philadelphia.

52. Historians of eugenics differ widely in their interpretation of the Manifesto. Ludmerer, *Genetics*, p. 129, called it a "condemnation" of eugenics. Roll-Hansen, "Progress of Eugenics," p. 312, saw in it "a pitiful formulation of the position of reform eugenics." Paul, "Eugenics and the Left," p. 583, claimed that the Genetico Manifesto is the "statement of a socialist eugenic position." In my opinion, the content of the resolution, as well as the analysis of the signatories, confirms Paul's position.

53. The Genetico Manifesto was widely published and, for example, was printed in the *Journal of Heredity* 30 (1939): 371–73.

54. See Garland E. Allen, "The Eugenics Record Office at Cold Spring Harbor, 1910–1940: An Essay in Institutional History," *Osiris*, n.s., 2 (1986): 250; Kröner, *Eugenik*, 32; Kenneth M. Ludmerer, "American Geneticists and the Eugenics Movement 1905–1935," *Journal of the History of Biology* 2 (1969): 350–54.

55. See Allen, "Eugenics Record Office," pp. 225–64.

56. See Phillip R. Reilly, *The Surgical Solution: A History of Involuntary Sterilization in the United States* (Baltimore: Johns Hopkins University Press, 1991), p. 96.

57. See Frederick Osborn, "Implications of the New Studies in Population and Psychology for the Development of Eugenic Philosophy," *Eugenical News* 22 (1937): 106. See also ibid., "Memorandum on the Eugenics Situation in the United States," Osborn Papers, I #2, APS Philadelphia.

58. Marian S. Olden, *History of the Development of the First National Organization for Sterilization* (Gwynedd, 1974), p. 65. See also Whitney Papers, Autobiography, 204, APS Philadelphia.

59. For more details, see Stefan Kühl, *Die Internationale der Rassisten: Der Aufstieg und Niedergang der internationalen Bewegung für Eugenik und Rassenhygiene im zwanzigsten Jahrhundert* (Frankfurt/M.: Campus Verlag, 1997).

Part 4

The Nazi State

LEADERSHIP AND BUREAUCRACY

The following five essays examine the role of Nazi leadership in creating and implementing the Final Solution. The first two essays examine the evolution of the Nazi plan for the systematic annihilation of all Jews—men, women, and children. The next two essays depict the evolving role of business and the bureaucracy in the murder of the Jews, and the final essay is a plea for understanding that leadership does not operate in a vacuum. German policies enjoyed the complicity if not the support of the legal, medical, and academic profession as well as of the clergy. Otherwise, they would not have come to fruition.

For years the shadow of Reinhard Heydrich has loomed over the process and instigation of the Final Solution. We know that it was Heydrich who dominated the eventful Wannsee Conference in January 1942, a meeting at which all departments of the Third Reich were asked to participate fully in an evolving plan for the complete elimination of European Jewish life.

But how did the plan evolve and when? In perhaps the fullest portrayal yet written of Reinhard Heydrich's step-by-step development of the Final Solution, Charles W. Sydnor, Jr., incorporating newly found documentation, traces In "Executive Instinct: Reinhard Heydrich and the Planning for the Final Solution," Heydrich's involvement in the plan to destroy European Jewry in the months after the November pogrom of 1938.

For Sydnor, there is no doubt that the mark of Heydrich was on most of the major anti-Jewish planning during this period. Heydrich was the consummate Nazi, "Hitler's ideal," as Sydnor describes him. It was his energy, his ruthless one-dimensional drive for results, his flair for "executive instinct," that is, always being prepared for a superior's query with a plan, short-range, medium-, and long-range, which allowed him the freedom to focus solely on the solution of the Jewish Question in Europe.

Sydnor is convinced that as early as mid-January 1941, Reinhard Heydrich "had prepared and had placed before Hitler . . . a draft proposal—as a plan and therefore as an option—for the extermination of the European Jews."

Richard Breitman sharpens the debate among historians with his essay, "Plans for the Final Solution in Early 1941." Piecing together detailed and diverse sources, Breitman argues strenuously that the plan for the Final Solution was already in place by early 1941.

Breitman offers what lawyers term the "cumulative preponderance of evidence." By December 8, 1940, Hitler had approved Operation Barbarossa. In March 1941, Eichmann announced to rival bureaucrats that the Führer had already entrusted to Reinhard Heydrich plans for the final evacuation of Jews. Breitman is specific about when that action had taken place—eight to ten weeks earlier, in mid-January 1941. As early as January 2, 1941, Heydrich indicated that Himmler had approved concentration camps of diverse scales of severity. Inmates "in 'protective custody' clearly capable of rehabilitation, for example, were to be sent to Dachau, Sachsenhausen, and 'Auschwitz I.'" Breitman notes that at that time there was only one camp at Auschwitz; Heydrich certainly knew of plans for the expansion of Auschwitz. On January 21, Theodor Dannecker, a close colleague of Eichmann, disclosed that "the Führer wanted a final solution of the Jewish Question after the war in all parts of Europe ruled or controlled by Germany."

Breitman stresses the "linguistic continuity" among knowledgeable RSHA (Reich Security Main Office) officials in the articulation of policy. The burden of proof, he suggests, is on the dissenters; they must demonstrate that in early 1941 these words did not mean what they meant by July of that year.

There was a flurry of activity in late January 1941, culminating on the thirtieth of the month in Hitler's reiteration of his prophecy from January 30, 1939. By March, Camp Commandant Rudolf Höss had received orders from Himmler to expand Auschwitz. By June, actual implementation had begun.

Breitman thus dismisses as ludicrous earlier suggestions by scholars that the Final Solution was the plan of last resort—either after other schemes had been tried and found wanting, or after an unfortunate escalation of persecution under the "pressure of a war-to-the-death" on the Eastern front.

Peter Hayes concludes his chapter on "State Policy and Corporate Involvement in the Holocaust" by enhancing Ian Kershaw's oft-quoted remark that the "road to Auschwitz was fueled by hatred, but paved with indifference." Not just by indifference, Hayes adds, but by self-interest. He depicts the circumstances in which the Nazis came to power. The economic condition of Jews in Germany had been declining for two decades, both in prominence and in distinctness. The number of enterprises owned by Jews declined as did the relative presence of Jews on boards. The lower middle class was the source of envy directed at Jews, not big business, at least at the beginning. In fact, during the pre–1933 years and well into 1935, corporate executives did not favor a strong anti-Jewish policy. They feared its impact on the German economy. Thus, Hitler avoided antisemitism in speaking to corporate executives. In the early years, at upper levels of German economic life, fewer competitors grasped the possible gains; surprisingly little acquisitiveness was exhibited. Even well into 1937, large industry continued to observe the established rules of business.

The major change occurred in November of 1937, one year before Kristallnacht. Afterwards, governmental pressure increased, corporate resistance to cooperation diminished, and the willingness and capacity of buyers to make fair share offers shrank. Preparation for the war began in earnest and so too did the determination to remove Jews from the economy. As preparation for war increased, more firms hitched their success to Nazi policy. Thus, in the process of Aryanization, two major German banks chased big profits; while they were involved in only 15 percent of the takeovers, they were engaged in 73 percent of all loans for Aryanization.

Hayes observes that personal ambition and corporate competition produced a striking decline in human sympathy once the Nazi regime made unmistakable its determination to dispossess Germany's remaining Jews. Corporate self-interest took over during the war—almost every major firm was linked into the military economy and not a few succumbed to the temptation to employ slave labor and reap the full benefits.

In "The Civil Service and the Implementation of the Holocaust: From Passive to Active Complicity," Hans Mommsen describes how, as the Nazi state evolved, the role of the civil service became secondary, yet indispensable. In the early years, civil servants would only rarely deliberately circumvent discriminatory legislation against Jews. They were far more active in protecting a Catholic priest ostracized by the Nazi regime. Some Nazis were admitted into the civil service, yet their presence did not destroy the homogeneity of the civil servants. It was the party faithful who adapted to the ways of the bureaucracy, not vice versa. So Martin Bormann's efforts to unite party and state failed for a time.

The activists felt duped by bureaucracy, which permitted them a larger role in anti-Jewish policy. Thus, antisemitism was both tolerated by the bureaucracy and encouraged as an outlet for party radicalism. The competition between party and bureaucracy served to foster anti-Jewish legislation since the civil service was far more interested in the cloak of legality. As momentum was achieved, the civil service became the indispensable instrument for implementing the Final Solution—active players and complicitous throughout.

Franklin H. Littell has, for nearly four decades, been the conscience of American Christendom. As he points out in "The Other Crimes of Adolf Hitler," "the rabbis of old taught that had the Gentiles realized the meaning of the destruction of the [Second] Temple they would have mourned it more than the Jews. . . . when the baptized realize the meaning of the Holocaust, they will mourn it more than the Jewish people."

Littell wishes to puncture the myth that Nazi Germany's various crimes can be attributed simply to the madness of Adolf Hitler, and this includes the preparations and processes of carrying out the Final Solution. We must be aware, he believes, that the corruption of Germany's professions—academic, medical, legal, and religious— was already underway long before National Socialism asked them to join in committing unspeakable crimes against the Jewish people, among other targeted groups. Littell asks if those same professions in America and elsewhere have learned the lessons that the Holocaust has taught us so that they will recognize injustice and potential tyranny when it seeks to seduce them for evil purposes.

12.

CHARLES W. SYDNOR, JR.

Executive Instinct

REINHARD HEYDRICH AND THE
PLANNING FOR THE FINAL SOLUTION

Adolf Hitler's racial and ideological antisemitism was the foundation of his political life and career. His obsession with destroying international Jewry was fundamentally important to the development of Germany's internal policies and to the Third Reich's diplomatic and military strategy. The specific anti-Jewish measures that were the harvest of this hatred were of paramount interest to Hitler from the boycott of April 1933 to the dictation of his political testament in April 1945. The destructive anti-Jewish policies of Nazi Germany, whether publicly announced, unofficially implied, or secretly implemented, resulted from decisions that were strategically driven and were the products of planning. For Hitler, diplomacy, war, and the conquest of living space for the Nazi millennium were inseparably linked to what he called "the merciless struggle against the Jews."[1]

By focusing upon the activities of the subordinates Hitler called upon to carry out Germany's anti-Jewish policies, especially during periods when the Führer exercised critical strategic options, we may learn more about how the regime undertook the preparations and approached the decisions that led to the destruction of the European Jews. This is particularly true in the case of the man charged with the administrative planning and operational direction of the Final Solution to the Jewish Question, Reinhard Heydrich.

We have long known a great deal about Heydrich's career in the SS and the police. The essential features of his working relationships with Heinrich Himmler, Hermann Göring, and with Hitler are fairly well documented. In many respects, he was the ablest and most energetic Nazi operative of radical ethnographic policy. He could be relied upon absolutely to carry out the most brutal orders and inhuman measures required to achieve Hitler's racial and ideological objectives.[2]

An earlier and accurate appraisal depicts Heydrich as a figure of conventional intellect, an unoriginal and lackluster personality who possessed social abilities and communications skills barely adequate to the stature of a major persona exercising vast authority in one of the world's great powers.[3] While this is true, it is well to remember that in the Nazi cosmos even a dwarf star—if determined—could shine brightly. Other traits were to make him a major figure in modern history.

Where Heydrich excelled and stood apart from, if not above, every other major figure of the Nazi era was in the exercise of certain qualities that both Hitler and Himmler valued as indispensable and irreplaceable. Heydrich possessed a unique combination of administrative acumen, organizational insight, pragmatic tenacity, and unparalleled ruthlessness. His phenomenal drive and stupendous capacity for work were propelled by an unbounded physical and psychological energy. No one else in the Nazi hierarchy could keep up with him. His relief from the pressures of office, apart from his passion for the cello and chamber music, was in the pursuit of even more strenuous activity; an accomplished equestrian, a world-class fencer, an enthusiastic sports flyer, and a decorated wartime fighter pilot, Reinhard Heydrich looked and acted the role of the versatile, athletic, prototypical leader of the Nordic New Order. He was Hitler's ideal Nazi.[4]

More important were the even rarer capacities Heydrich possessed, abilities that enabled him to interpret, anticipate, plan, and administer Hitler's anti-Jewish policies in the overlapping sequences that culminated in the Final Solution. Taken together, these qualities can be called *executive instinct*. Both Hitler and Himmler, each in their own vernacular, referred to them in reflecting upon Heydrich's abilities.[5]

Executive Instinct

In Reinhard Heydrich, the talent for executive instinct depended upon a number of exceptional traits. First and foremost was acute sensitivity. Heydrich was always and everywhere alert to the wishes and temperament of his superiors. He could anticipate how to respond reflexively to their most important obsessions or objectives and the moods and circumstances that conditioned them. Knowing what mattered most to Hitler and Himmler, Heydrich engaged his own natural appetite for making decisions and applied his energetic and ruthless determination to the tasks of planning and developing options that could enable them to succeed.

Heydrich could trust his own instincts because he was never unprepared. He understood that in the Hitlerian world, failure most often occurred from lack of choice. In any issue of importance to the growing portfolio of critical charges he carried after 1938, and most especially in matters related to anti-Jewish measures, Heydrich was never caught off guard by his superiors by merely having a plan or an idea. He constantly carried the ammunition of thorough preparation, and he was always well-armed with plans—short term, intermediate, and long-range.[6]

In plain language, Heydrich relied on his instincts to figure out what he thought the bosses wanted, and then took the initiative to present them with the possibilities for achieving their goals. He never had to be told anything twice; he never needed justification or explanation for any assignment he received; he never required supervisory follow-up or had to be reminded of deadlines; and there is no recorded instance in which he ever took a problem to Himmler or to Hitler without corresponding recommendations or options for resolving the dilemma. In the daily pressures of administering the Führer state, a subordinate with these qualities was both a rare find and an irreplaceable asset.

Thus, when Hitler talked of getting rid of the Jews "one way or another," Heydrich understood what he meant. He saw clearly how each of the steps in Germany's escalating anti-Jewish policies would define and condition the stages to follow. Furthermore, he grasped without difficulty the evolving relationships among foreign policy, military strategy, and the war against the Jews.

With Heydrich, the capacity for executive instinct meant not only acting by sensing, it also included an uncanny ability to produce bureaucratic enlargement. He could make rope from shoestring. Beginning in January 1939, he expanded the considerable powers he then held as Chief of the Security Police and the Security Service. To these powers he added further responsibilities that tied the key ministries of the state, the agencies of the Nazi Party, and ultimately the armed forces of the Reich to his authority as the Judenkommissar (commissioned by Göring on behalf of Hitler).[7] In these offices, which finally (and fatally) included a brief but spectacularly successful tenure as Hitler's satrap in Prague, Heydrich's executive instincts enabled him to act upon the opportunities presented by the pace and scope of Germany's military successes to initiate unprecedented "final" measures against the European Jews.

In each instance, the anti-Jewish measures he initiated or undertook were not unauthorized. In every case, with the exception of the Jewish deportations under the Nisko and Lublin Plan to resettle all the Jews of the Third Reich in the eastern portion of German-occupied Poland, they were the result of extensive prior planning and preparation.[8]

Evolution of the Final Solution

Heydrich's activities during three critical periods offer interesting insights into the evolution of planning for the Final Solution. Newly discovered documentation tied to Heydrich strongly suggests that he had prepared and had placed before Hitler, no later than mid-January 1941, a draft proposal—as a plan and therefore as an option—for the extermination of the European Jews.

The three periods in question include the time during the Reichskristallnacht (the winter and early spring of 1938–1939) and shortly thereafter; the weeks during and shortly after the German conquest of Poland in 1939; and the seven months that elapsed between the French surrender in June 1940 and the weeks following Hitler's decision to attack Soviet Russia, which was formally signed on December 18, 1940.

The Reichskristallnacht brought radical changes in Germany's anti-Jewish policies. The national pogrom of November 9–10, 1938, and the events that followed it were driven by two factors: the first was Hitler's decision, taken in the summer of 1938, to launch and wage a European war (a decision that preceded the plans to implement it), and the second was Herschel Grynzspan's killing of a German diplomat in Paris, Ernst vom Rath.[9] Since Hitler was determined to start (and did not intend or plan to lose) the war, the decision altered the methods of Jewish persecution from random tactics to concrete strategy. With the concurrence of Göring, Himmler and Heydrich seized the initiative to get anti-Jewish measures off the streets as mob violence. These measures would be transferred into the hands of the SS and police as administrative measures and policy decisions, coordinated under Heydrich's authority as Chief of the Security Police and the SD.[10]

Himmler himself had been a major barometer of the climate for the pogrom. In a secret speech to SS generals the night before the violence, he had predicted a merciless racial struggle to the death—a long war of annihilation between Germany and the Jews.[11] Though he and Heydrich apparently were surprised by the outbreak and extent of the violence, they intervened to keep the destruction at least under police supervision. At the height of the pogrom, in an order as emblematic of his own views as it was of subsequent anti-Jewish policy, Heydrich telegraphed instructions to his police commanders that "Jewish homes and businesses may only be destroyed; they may not be looted."[12]

At the ministerial conference Göring convened in the Air Ministry on November 12, 1938, in order to deal with the economic and financial aftermath of the pogrom, Heydrich was the key participant.[13] He proposed new, sweeping laws to seal Germany's Jews in an inescapable pressure chamber of discrimination and deprivation. He insisted on radical additional measures to accelerate the emigration of Jews from Germany. Additionally, he urged the creation of a new Central Office for Jewish Emigration in Berlin, modeled on the successful prototype his subordinate Adolf Eichmann had established in Vienna. Within ten weeks of the meeting, virtually all of the anti-Jewish measures proposed by the participants had become law by decree or administrative regulation, and the new Central Office in Berlin was operating under Eichmann's direction and Heydrich's authority.[14]

With the precedent established to enlarge his power in Jewish matters, Heydrich took his first cues from the rhetoric of his superiors. Himmler was already on record predicting the destruction of Germany's Jews in the event of war.[15] Göring had come close to saying the same thing in different words during the Air Ministry Conference on November 12.[16]

On January 30, 1939, six days after Heydrich's new Central Office was authorized by Göring, Hitler prophesied to the world from the rostrum of the Reichstag that the event of war would result in the annihilation of the Jewish race in Europe.[17] Since the prophet was already determined to start the war himself, the unconditional importance of the statement as a self-fulfilling prophecy was not lost on one of his most astute followers.

Five days before Hitler's Reichstag speech, Heydrich himself addressed a gathering of senior SS officers on the nature of the Jewish question. An attentive Himmler jotted down notes. According to the cryptic entries, Heydrich developed the theme of the Jews as the eternal subhumanity whom societies in the past had made "the mistake" of driving out. This error, the reconstructed notes indicate, had led only to the eventual return of Jews into society and to new jealousy (problems). Though inconclusive, the document is extremely suggestive, especially in view of the planning activities involving Heydrich or initiated by him during these same months.[18]

The Conference of December 16, 1938

On December 16, 1938, Heydrich had participated in an important gathering at the Ministry of the Interior involving most of the top-level principals whose agencies or ministries would be involved in coordinating anti-Jewish measures under

Heydrich's direction. The participants included Reich ministers Wilhelm Frick (Interior), Walther Funk (Economics), Lutz Graf Schwerin von Krosigk (Finance), Hans Heinrich Lammers (the Reichs Chancellery); the police president of Berlin, Wolf von Helldorf; a number of Gauleiters, senior regional government officials, and mayors from several major cities, including Hamburg. The subject of the meeting was "further possibilities with the Jewish question"; the results were reflected in the expanded, accelerated planning activities in and among the offices involved.[19]

And the meaning of *further possibilities* emerged clearly during a follow-up inter-agency meeting held in the Ministry of the Interior on February 28, 1939. Convened by Bernhard Lösener (Frick's Jewish affairs expert) and attended by representatives from the High Command of the Armed Forces, the Main Office of the Security Police, a surrogate for Kurt Daluege from the Main Office of the Order Police, and Theodor Eicke, the inspector-general of concentration camps, the conferees gathered to develop options for dealing with the Jews in the event of war. The record of the discussion was kept by Dr. Werner Best, then Heydrich's closest subordinate as deputy chief of the Security Police and the SD.[20]

Since it was entirely clear that no Jew could perform military service, there was general agreement that forced labor would be the appropriate alternative. As no productive wartime labor could be expected from Jewish women and children, the discussion focused on how to deal with the estimated 200,000 male Jews between the ages of eighteen and fifty-five who would be available. They would be subject to a special police registration. The participants from the army and the Order Police were asked to collaborate on proposals and report back.[21]

The participants also agreed that these Jews would be employed in segregated labor columns or gangs. Closely guarded by the police and kept well away from any German workers, the Jews would toil at heavy tasks in road construction and in stone quarries. Since they could not be kept in quarters even remotely comparable to German wartime housing, they would be sealed off in special labor camps. On all these points there was general consensus. The major questions requiring further study concerned whether the Jews could be housed in concentration camps or whether the measures would require the construction of additional camps. If the construction of additional camps was indeed required, the questions then became, How many camps would be needed? Where should they be built? Who would guard them? How would the costs be handled among the various institutions affected? And, once built, would the new camps become part of Eicke's concentration camp system? Eicke was requested to have a designee prepare a memorandum analyzing these questions and setting forth specific recommendations.

The conferees also discussed and assented to a recommendation from the Security Police that in wartime it would be both practical and desirable to round up all the Jews when special developments or circumstances made such a step possible. Since wartime circumstances would from time to time require certain Security Police measures to be applied to all Jews in any event, this measure also opened the possibility of a peacetime round-up and internment of the Jews through a special, compulsory police registration.[22]

All of the major points discussed in this interagency meeting, held four months after the Reichskristallnacht and six months before the German invasion of Poland, were refined and developed in the further planning of anti-Jewish measures, and eventually incorporated into the procedures for the Final Solution.

The Outbreak of War

The German assault on Poland and the European war it unleashed created the conditions necessary to fulfill Hitler's prophecy and opened up further possibilities for measures to avoid the mistake Heydrich noted among societies that had permitted Jews to return after expulsion. In the months before the attack, Heydrich's time and energies were absorbed in his work. He was involved in the planning and preparations for the "ethnographic" measures (killing operations) Hitler wanted the SS and police units to carry out in Poland.[23] In addition, he concerned himself with the reorganization of the SS and police agencies into the larger and more centralized Reich Security Main Office (announced officially at the end of September 1939). Finally, Heydrich was busy with providing the steps necessary to fake a Polish attack on the German radio station at Gleiwitz—an "attack" that Hitler used publicly as the pretext for invading Poland.[24]

With thousands of heavily armed SS and police units operating as Einsatzgruppen behind the advancing armies and under his control, Heydrich carried out and observed the results and new possibilities of large-scale killings and the anticipated removal of whole population groups in the newly conquered eastern territories. Records of these assessments, with an indication of the direction in which Heydrich planned to develop further options for harsher steps against the Jews, are contained in the well-known summaries of his weekly RSHA conferences in September 1939.[25]

On September 14, Heydrich gave the new office chiefs in the RSHA important news. He claimed that the Jewish problem the Einsatzgruppen had encountered was of such magnitude that Himmler was preparing recommendations that Hitler himself would have to decide upon, since they could have such far-reaching implications for foreign policy.[26]

On September 21, meeting with the Einsatzgruppen commanders, the RSHA office chiefs, and with Adolf Eichmann present, Heydrich revealed at least some of what he had learned of Hitler and Himmler's thinking about the intended future of the Jews and Poland. The old German provinces would be incorporated into the Reich as Gaue, while further east a dependent state, a kind of no-man's land, would be created with its capital at Kraków. Heydrich also added that in order to achieve "all the necessary ethnographic measures," Hitler would appoint Himmler resettlement commissar.[27] Himmler's first assignment was already set; Hitler had agreed to deport all Jews from the new German provinces and from the old Reich and dump them into ghettos in the new dependent state, from which subsequent deportation possibilities would also exist.[28]

Shortly after the meeting on September 21, Heydrich dictated a top-secret express letter with copies for all the conference participants, for all office chiefs of the Security Police and the SD, for the High Command of the Army, and for the state secretaries in the Reich ministries working directly with the RSHA in Jewish matters—Erich Neumann (Four Year Plan), Wilhelm Stuckart (Interior), Friedrich

Walter Landfried (for both the ministries of Food and Agriculture, and Economics), and the civilian government chiefs in the occupied eastern territories.

Heydrich's subject was the Jewish Question in the occupied areas. For both the total measures to be taken against the Jews and the final goal (das Endziel)—which Heydrich did not define further—Heydrich wrote that the decision would have to be made first about "the final goal," which would be realized over a long period of time and, second, the steps or stages required in the interim to achieve this goal, which would have to be carried through quickly.[29]

The first step toward the final goal, Heydrich continued, was the concentration of all Jews from the countryside into large cities. This had to be carried out rapidly. It also required the selection of the fewest possible cities and concentration points for Jews in the occupied territories, so later measures would be simpler. The only cities chosen, Heydrich directed, should be those at major rail junctions or those astride main railroad lines.

In distinguishing between the planned measures necessary to achieve the final goal, and in stressing that the planned measures would demand the most thorough preparation in both technical and economic respects, Heydrich advised his recipients that the imminent tasks could not then be outlined in complete detail from his office.[30] In summary, the clear implications pointed to further preparations and decisions that had to be made, to the rapid, radical alteration and expanded application of past experience in anti-Jewish policy in wholly new circumstances, and to the absolute requirement for secrecy throughout. Heydrich was not suggesting any decision had been made by Hitler, or by Himmler acting for Hitler, to exterminate the Jews in the East. He was, however, committing the RSHA and the other agencies involved to the planning and preparation for the mass deportation of Jews to Poland—the prelude to extermination as an eventual option for Himmler to present to Hitler.

The Conference of December 16, 1939

The importance of this conference is clearly confirmed in an RSHA document recently discovered by Richard Breitman. Talking points drafted on December 19, 1939, for Dr. Franz Six to use in a scheduled office chiefs' conference were titled "Final Solution of the German Jewish Problem" (Endlösung des deutschen Judenproblems). The document addressed the fundamental question of whether a Jewish reservation should be created in Poland, or whether the Jews should be housed in the future (sic) General Government (ob ein Judenreservat in Polen geschaffen werden soll oder ob die Juden im zukünftigen Gouvernement Polen untergebracht werden sollen).[31]

In the event of a decision to establish the reservation, the document continued, it would be necessary to resolve whether the administration should be in the hands of Germans or Jews, though preferably it would be Jews responsible to German authorities. In any event, the administration would have to remain in the hands of the Einsatzgruppen for as long as it took the Security Police to complete the resettlement of all Jews from the old Reich and Austria, and from Bohemia and Moravia.[32]

The second option, which is not titled, and which could mean "disposal,"[33] points out that "a final decision" (eine endgültige Entscheidung) in this connection would have to deal with the issue of whether Jewish emigration should proceed in the same manner as would be the case in the creation of the reservation. In foreign policy, the document concludes, the reservation would provide good leverage with the Western powers, perhaps facilitating the question of a worldwide solution at the end of the war.[34]

With the fate of the German, Austrian, and Czech Jews clearly tied to the plight of the millions of Polish Jews in RSHA planning, Heydrich moved the disposal option a significant step further two days later. He named Adolf Eichmann head of the new special section for Jewish affairs in the RSHA (Amt IVb4), and deputized Eichmann with full authority to coordinate all Security Police activities for all deportation and resettlement measures in Poland.[35] Three weeks later, on January 8, 1940, Eichmann presided over his first conference with the designated representatives sent by the Reich ministries to discuss the possibilities for Jewish and Polish deportations in the immediate future.[36]

In the preceding months, parallel developments on a higher plain drew Himmler and Heydrich into a series of difficulties that would delay, but not cancel, their planning, preparation, and determination to present the eventual option of mass extermination as the preferred solution to the Jewish question in all territory under German control.

On October 7, 1939, Hitler signed a secret decree that made Himmler head of the RKFDV, the Reich Commissioner for the Strengthening of Germandom, with broad powers to develop and carry out all population and resettlement policies in the conquered eastern territories.[37] Five days later, the Führer executed the documents creating the General Government of Poland, appointed Hans Frank as governor-general, and then summoned the key figures involved in the occupation of Poland to the Reich Chancellery on October 17 to hear his views on the future course of German policy in the East.[38]

Opposition to the Einsatzgruppen

As these developments unfolded, both Heydrich and Himmler came face-to-face with double trouble: serious opposition to what they were doing and planning in the eastern territories. The first problem exploded in a chorus of protests from army commanders in Poland. These officers vigorously objected to the murderous activities of the Einsatzgruppen and the behavior of senior SS and police officials toward Polish civilians—activities that had created widespread unrest in the upper ranks of the army. The furor evoked both indignation and alarm from Heydrich and Himmler. Though supported by Hitler, they nonetheless cautiously sought to repair the damage as the episode lingered, festering into the spring of 1940.[39]

Far more serious were the difficulties the new governor-general of Poland created for Heydrich and Himmler. Hans Frank had a different and much grander view of his domain and its future than either Hitler or Himmler and Heydrich. He did not want millions of Poles and Jews dumped into his territory to compound the already chaotic economic conditions, especially the acute housing, food, and fuel shortages in the midst of the coldest European winter on record. Though careful to avoid even the appearance of opposing Hitler's wishes, the wily Frank pursued the astute strategy of appealing to Göring with the argument that orderly conditions, including no further deportations, would enable the resources of the General Government to contribute to the war economy of the Reich.[40] With Göring's support, in a series of back-and-forth, mate-checkmate moves with Himmler and Heydrich, Frank managed to suspend, then delay, and then reduce the numbers of Jews, Poles, Gypsies, and other undesirables Himmler wanted thrown into the General Government as part of his grandiose vision for a vast resettlement and ethnographic cleansing. It was a racial reordering of the populations in the occupied East.

The bureaucratic shoving match persisted until after January 1941. By that point, Frank had run out of options. Though he would win a last reprieve of several months before mass deportations began, Frank had no choice but to accept the inevitable.[41]

Even before January 1941, strategic planning for both the military and ideological prosecution of the war had changed everything—everything except the consistent, cumulative planning and experimentation Heydrich pursued in the search for practical experience and useful technique to strengthen the option for mass killing as a solution to the Jewish question.

Technology and Methodology for Mass Murder

Heydrich was especially interested in developments in the euthanasia program Hitler secretly authorized in the autumn of 1939.[42] Deputizing his personal physician, SS Doctor Karl Brandt, to help organize the program by recruiting physicians, Hitler vested administrative authority for the medically directed killings in the two key officials in his own Führer Chancellery, Philipp Bouhler and Viktor Brack. The victims were to include the terminally ill and the mentally and physically handicapped and disabled, the "useless eaters" who tied up precious resources and medical facilities and attention urgently needed for wartime purposes.[43]

By late December 1939, euthanasia officials had developed a method for quietly killing the growing numbers of victims being selected from hospitals and asylums throughout Germany. Brandt, Bouhler, Brack, and Reich Health Commissioner Dr. Leonardo Conti observed the first successful carbon monoxide gassing of four victims in a sealed chamber at the Brandenburg euthanasia facility.[44]

Technology and methodology were harnessed in tandem to the task of mass murder. Improvements and refinements followed rapidly; the possibilities seemed infinite. Within a year, six euthanasia gassing facilities were liquidating German victims selected for death from hospitals and asylums from all over Germany.[45] By June 1940, special teams of physicians from the euthanasia program began systematically selecting concentration camp inmates for gassing based on lists prepared by the SS camp doctors. Among those hauled off to be killed under the cover of euthanasia action were German and non-German Jews, inmates unfit for work, and others the SS simply wanted to eliminate. All the camps were combed, some of them several times.[46]

Both Himmler and Heydrich, as well as senior officials and technical specialists in the RSHA, were intensely interested in learning from and assisting in the murders. Heydrich consulted regularly on legal issues and other matters with the growing number of SS doctors involved in the selections and gassings.[47] The RSHA offered technical assistance as the process spread to the occupied eastern territories. In July 1940, Himmler personally authorized the use of a new, mobile gas van developed by the RSHA to kill nearly two thousand mental patients from facilities in East Prussia and the Wartheland. Their transfer and liquidation were handled by a Sonderkommando of the SD.[48]

If the mentally and physically *useless eaters* could be eliminated so efficiently, why not the racially unfit as well? For the RSHA the question was merely rhetorical. By November 1940, euthanasia became a cover for the murder of forced laborers, Polish Jews, half-Jewish children, political prisoners, and adult Gypsies.[49] Despite the secrecy, the success of the euthanasia program and the rapid expansion and pace of the killings attracted growing unofficial and official attention. In mid-December, Himmler advised Viktor Brack to shut down the Grafeneck gassing facility and move its operations elsewhere because of public unrest in the region about what was taking place there.[50] Moreover, there is growing evidence that since mid-1940 Heydrich had been the source of expanding contacts and information exchanges among the RSHA, euthanasia personnel, and officials in both the Four Year Plan and the Ministry of Food and Agriculture, who were busy with their own plans for winning the war and feeding the Reich by starving millions of Germany's enemies to death.[51]

For Heydrich, the enormous importance of the euthanasia program to racial planning, and to further possibilities for the Jewish Question, were obvious long before Brack's personnel were transferred to the extermination camps in the General Government.[52] The surviving records suggest that, early on, he also grasped the possibilities the existing concentration camps offered in wartime for the secret, convenient elimination of political and racial enemies. The measures he directed for the camps became essential operating procedures for the Final Solution.[53]

On September 3, 1939, Heydrich dispatched a circular order stipulating the principles for internal state security to be followed in wartime. The directive was addressed to all the regional offices and all the senior, central office principals in the Security Police, the SD, the Gestapo and the border police, with information copies to all the Higher SS and Police leaders and all the regional civilian governing authorities. It specified the most draconian measures against anyone even suspected of hostility to the Reich and the war effort. The key paragraph ordered the referral of all information on arrested suspects to Heydrich's office for decision, "*because on the basis of higher authority the brutal liquidation of such elements will follow*" (emphasis in the original).[54]

The crucial implementing procedure was ready three weeks later. Gestapo Chief Heinrich Müller, acting for Heydrich, issued detailed guidelines for the "special treatment" (murder) of religious and political enemies, hoarders and profiteers, and those suspected of malicious or subversive acts.[55] The option for "special treatment" applied to those to be arrested under protective custody and to those already in concentration camps. To close the possibility of any remaining loopholes, Müller—again acting for Heydrich—sent out an express letter on October 24, 1939, addressed to all regional offices of the Security Police and the SD, the Gestapo, the Inspectorate of Concentration Camps, and the individual camp commandants, prohibiting the release of any protective custody prisoners for the duration of the war. Given the regimen of suffering inflicted on camp inmates at the time, this was tantamount to a sentence of slow death for many.[56]

The key omission in the procedures was recognized and rectified four months later. On March 9, 1940, Himmler issued a blanket order forbidding the wartime release of Jews held in concentration camps. The only exceptions were to be those Jews who already held release papers by virtue of their completion of all the required formalities necessary to emigrate from German-controlled territory no later than April (a handful of Jews at most). In view of the treatment then accorded all Jews in concentration camps, Himmler's decision by itself made the facilities sealed death chambers for any Jews who were or would be sent to concentration camps.[57]

The order, however, did not stand alone in pointing toward physical destruction as the preferred solution to the Jewish Question. On March 27, in one of his chess moves with Hans Frank, Himmler issued an unpublished order banning any subsequent emigration of Jews from the General Government to Germany, or to any foreign country that might accept them.[58] The practical experience already gained in officially sanctioned mass killing, and the nearly insurmountable international difficulties involved in shipping Jews out of Europe in wartime, combined to increase the pressure for some solution to the Jewish problem other than emigration. The trap was closing rapidly on all Jews who were, or soon would be, under German control. In the aftermath of Germany's victory in the West, Himmler and Heydrich would slam the trap shut.

The conquest of France and the Low Countries, like the destruction of Poland, altered the strategic direction of the war, and with it the dimensions of Germany's Jewish problem. Each military victory enlarged and compounded, rather than reduced or simplified, the Jewish problem that Heydrich and the growing legion of planners and specialists in the RSHA grappled with. Every conquest expanded and reversed overwhelmingly everything previously achieved through forced emigration in peacetime. By July 1940, the earlier successes in pushing out hundreds of thousands of Jews had been dwarfed by the staggering addition of millions more. Additionally, the strategic and territorial extension of the war was not complete in victory, or in the likely addition of millions more Jews who would come under German control until it was. What further planning possibilities could Heydrich bring to bear on a problem getting bigger instead of smaller?

The Madagascar Plan

One option that emerged that summer, a possibility considered more important and taken more seriously by others than by Heydrich, was the Madagascar Plan. Much has been written in the extensive scholarly debate on the Madagascar Plan.[59] The original proposals came out of the German Foreign Ministry, resulting at least in part from Joachim von Ribbentrop's attempts to assert authority over anti-Jewish policy as an issue in German foreign affairs.[60] The RSHA quickly countered with a more extensive, thorough, and carefully prepared draft.[61] The two versions contained common basic features. Presuming the war to be won, and assuming the French would turn the island over to Germany, the millions of European Jews would be packed off by ship to Madagascar, which would become a super ghetto under Heydrich's authority as head of the RSHA. Heydrich's people were to do all the logistical planning, and would handle all transport and shipping arrangements, which would require the use of the postwar merchant fleets of Germany, France, and possibly Great Britain. The staggering financial costs required to move more than three million Jews from all over Europe to Madagascar would be paid through special assessments placed on Jews living in the West. The RSHA version calculated, optimistically, that it would take at least four years to deport more than three million Jews to Madagascar.[62]

The critical issue at that juncture was the question of Heydrich's assessment of the Madagascar Project. No written evaluation from him survives in the record. The corollary evidence, however, suggests the following: First, the Madagascar Project was never *the* plan; it was an option, a contingency, a possibility. It was one planning development among many. Second, it presumed conditions and circumstances Heydrich would have considered totally impractical. He had naval experience; he would have recognized the shipping projections as hopelessly inadequate.[63] Had the RSHA version been taken seriously, he would have insisted on specifics about the European ports to be used for embarkation, railroad routes, arrangements and timetables to get Europe's Jews to the ports, temporary housing or holding provisions for the deportees, police and security arrangements and assigned responsibilities from point to point, and recommendations for assistance from specific ministries and agencies of the Reich. Furthermore, where were the cost estimates for the European and oceanic phases of the project? None of these points were mentioned in either draft of the Madagascar Plan.

Given his years of extensive experience in the economic and financial aspects of forced Jewish emigration from Germany, Heydrich could only have smiled at the notion that American Jews and the Western powers could, or would, pay the travel costs in the Madagascar Plan. Moreover, he had been schooled by his bitter, frustrating experiences in Poland over the previous nine months—with the Army, with Hans Frank, with Göring's officials, and with local civilian authorities. Heydrich was the last man to assume any fewer difficulties with the British navy and the Western powers in shipping millions of Jews across thousands of miles of uncontrolled ocean to Madagascar, than the problems he had in attempting to deport thousands of Jews over hundreds of miles by rail in a region completely under the control of the Reich and his own police and security agencies.

If he needed further convincing, or support for his skepticism, Heydrich received unwitting assistance from an unanticipated source early in August 1940. The hapless promoters of the project in the Foreign Ministry sought to strengthen their case by enlisting outside expert opinion. They hired two consultants to evaluate the Madagascar Project and submit written feasibility studies.[64] Copies of both reports, which were completed by early August, were distributed to officials in the Four Year Plan and to Heydrich's office in the RSHA. The two studies concluded that Madagascar was economically unsuited to support massive resettlement and that the proposal to ship millions of Jews to the island would be impossible to carry out.[65]

The practical residue left from the exercise of Madagascar planning cemented the working relationships in Jewish matters among the officials in the agencies involved: the RSHA, the euthanasia program, the Foreign Ministry, the Four Year Plan, and the

Propaganda Ministry.[66] The Madagascar Project failed to address strategic realities Heydrich had already grasped. Any European solution to the Jewish question was not possible until (and unless) all the European Jews were in German hands. Millions in the East still were not. If and when they were, Germany's strategic disposition would facilitate the option of a "territorial Final Solution"—a more efficient, less expensive, and permanent way of dealing with the Jews once and for all. By August 1940, Heydrich was already thinking in these terms.

A Territorial Final Solution

Some six weeks earlier he had written to Ribbentrop, reminding the Foreign Minister that Jewish policy was the exclusive provenance of the RSHA and stating for the record why the solution to the Jewish Question was a police matter and not a foreign policy issue.[67] Citing his original authority from Göring in January 1939 to direct Jewish emigration from all German territories, Heydrich declared that Jewish emigration had proceeded successfully in the face of great difficulties and despite wartime conditions. "The *total* problem," he continued, "could no longer be solved through emigration since there were three-and-one-quarter million Jews in the areas *currently* under German control [meaning more were expected]. A territorial Final Solution would therefore be necessary." Heydrich closed by requesting to be notified by advance invitation "to any future discussions about the Final Solution to the Jewish Question," in the event they should be initiated by anyone other than himself.[68]

In this context, given all that had come before and in view of what soon would follow, what did Heydrich mean by "a territorial Final Solution," and "the Final Solution to the Jewish Question"? Did he mean Madagascar, or did he mean what, in fact, the Final Solution became: extermination? If Heydrich was not excluding a Madagascar-like endeavor by ruling out emigration, which common sense and the tone of the document suggest,[69] then strategic decisions Hitler reached in the summer of 1940 effectively foreclosed all options except a territorial Final Solution on the continent of Europe.

In addition, significant developments initiated by Himmler, to which Heydrich was privy, pointed toward similar intentions for the Jews. In late May, the Reichs-führer SS secured Hitler's endorsement for his memorandum on the future treatment of the alien populations in the East and the Führer's permission to circulate the document among a select, restricted group of top-level recipients.[70] The Himmler text refers to Jews only once, innocuously and in passing.[71] This is because the paper had a broader purpose. The memorandum served to reassert and reinforce Himmler's authority as head of the RKFDV, the Reich Commissioner for the Strengthening of Germandom, as Hitler's resettlement commissar in the East.

Himmler had timed the approach to Hitler perfectly. The Führer's euphoria as the colossal victory in the West unfolded created just the right climate for grandiose rhetoric about the racial reordering of Europe. Himmler needed a boost to resolve the continuing challenges by the army and Hans Frank to his authority in deportation and resettlement matters in the East. In April 1940, Friedrich Wilhelm Krüger, the Higher SS and Police leader in the General Government, alerted Himmler to a series of difficulties in resettlement matters involving the army, and to Frank's efforts to undermine or remove Odilo Globocnik, the ruthless, energetic SS and Police leader in the Lublin District of the General Government who was loyally devoted to both Krüger and Himmler.[72] On the original of Krüger's letter, Himmler scribbled: "I claim supremacy in resettlement and will assert it during my trip to Lublin."[73]

The reference was to his forthcoming two-day visit to Globocnik on May 5–6, 1940, during which Himmler discussed a range of issues with Krüger and Globocnik and inspected with great interest the SS units and facilities Globocnik commanded.[74] Globocnik was more aggressive and forceful even than Krüger in serving Himmler's interests in the General Government. Also, Globocnik's temperament and abilities resembled the qualities Himmler most admired and depended upon in Heydrich. He could be relied upon to get any job done without question or explanation.[75] Positioned in the most remote and isolated district of the General Government, Globocnik was the right man, in just the right place, to handle the big resettlement task Himmler was contemplating. After returning to Berlin, the Reichsführer SS supplied both Krüger and Ulrich Greifelt, Himmler's deputy as head of the RKFDV, with a terse, unequivocal written directive citing Hitler's decree vesting the SS with supreme authority for all resettlement actions.[76]

As the summer progressed, there were clear signs that the discussion of SS racial policy, including measures against the Jews, had moved in tandem with the onset of strategic planning for war in the East. On August 10, 1940, after Heydrich had received the consultants' reports on the unsuitability of the Madagascar Plan,[77] Himmler convened an extraordinary meeting in the Prinz-Albrechts-Strasse, the only session of its kind recorded in his office calendar for the entire year.[78]

At 11:00 A.M., eleven of the most senior and powerful figures in the SS and police sat down with Himmler for a meeting that lasted well into the afternoon. Because of their office or assignment, all were, or had been, directly involved in or with the planning for and conduct of anti-Jewish measures, racial policy, resettlement questions in the East, the concentration camps, the euthanasia program, and the Einsatzgruppen. The participants included Heydrich (RSHA); SS General Kurt Daluege (Chief of the Order Police); all five Higher SS and Police Leaders from the East: Jakob Sporrenberg, Richard Hildebrandt, Wilhelm Koppe, Erich von dem Bach-Zelewski, and Friedrich Wilhelm Krüger;[79] Ulrich Greifelt (RKFDV); Oswald Pohl (SS Budget and Construction Office and concentration camps); Otto Hoffmann (SS Race and Resettlement Office); and Karl Wolff, the chief of Himmler's office staff. There is no surviving record of what these men discussed.

The date and length of the meeting, as well as the unprecedented gathering of so many SS and police principals in a format Himmler disliked and invariably avoided, suggest a major conference dealing with the most important, sensitive, and far-reaching aspects of racial and resettlement planning and policy. Strong hints about the tone, if not the substance, of the meeting were recorded independently and shortly after the conference by two of the participants. Wilhelm Frick, the minister of the interior, wanted to extend the Nuremberg Race Laws to the annexed territories in the East. Himmler and Greifelt objected to this measure.[80] On August 21 Greifelt wrote to Frick, insisting that there was no need to introduce complicated racial legalities in the East to keep Poles and Jews from breeding, since "a final cleansing of the Jewish Question and the mixed-blood question was foreseen for after the war."[81]

In a file memorandum that he dictated three weeks later, on September 11, 1940, to Lammers, Martin Bormann, and Otto Hoffmann, Heydrich addressed the issue of how best to solve the problem of racial mixing and Germanization in Bohemia-Moravia.[82] After recommending steps to sort out those racially fit to be Germanized from the elements of bad blood in the population, Heydrich rhetorically asked how Bohemia could then be racially cleansed in order to become entirely German. The answer, he concluded, was obvious: "one had to set the imaginary goal of evacuating those remaining Czechs to a currently imaginary government."[83] Little in the meaning was left to the imagination.

In the fall, planning activities directed toward the extermination of the Jews gathered momentum. Himmler received complaints about the masses of useless Jews in Poland who could not work, who were a constant danger, and who had to be dealt with.[84] Heydrich raised the possibility of eliminating the Jewish population in the Warsaw Ghetto through epidemics introduced by SS doctors.[85] There were new signs that Himmler and Heydrich were gaining the upper hand in their shoving match with Hans Frank over Jewish deportations to the General Government.[86] On November 2, 1940, Himmler secretly ordered Globocnik to proceed with the development of an SS preserve in the Lublin District—a self-sufficient, closed zone of SS industrial and construction enterprises, farmsteads, and military and training installations that would serve as the basis for the expansion of SS and police power in the East.[87]

Heydrich kept busy with matters closer to home—internal measures and legal technicalities that needed ironing out before any deportation of Jews from the Reich. He was at least partially preoccupied with plans for even harsher economic and financial measures against the already impoverished German Jews, such as eliminating pension payments, confiscating property, and abolishing the remaining social benefits for German Jews with relatives who had emigrated.[88]

Then, on December 18, 1940, Hitler signed the secret directive ordering the German attack on the Soviet Union in the coming spring.[89] That night, Himmler went alone to the Reich Chancellery for a long, private meeting with the Führer.[90] In the weeks that followed, the pace of activity in Himmler's office, and especially at the RSHA, quickened dramatically. At the RSHA, the planning for the coming racial and ideological war of annihilation proceeded in tandem with interesting—and supporting—parallel preparations.[91]

The Decision on the Final Solution

On December 14, 1940, Herbert Backe, the State Secretary who was the driving force in the Food and Agriculture Ministry, released a confidential report on the European food situation which created a stir throughout the top level of the Reich government.[92] Citing critical shortages in the first wartime continental harvest, Backe drafted far-reaching plans for German rationing and for the wholesale confiscation of foodstuffs from throughout occupied Europe. The goal was to take enough from elsewhere to offset what otherwise would be disastrous shortages in meat and grains available to the German population. Backe further concluded that the longer-term German food shortages could only be solved through an attack on the Soviet Union, followed by wholesale confiscation of Russian foodstuffs and livestock. Even if all the Russian food and agricultural resources became available to Germany and her allies, Backe concluded, the only way to guarantee a blockade-proof Nazi Europe would be to kill off millions of Russians by liquidation, starvation, or deportation.[93] Both Himmler and Heydrich studied the report, which evidently became the basis for Himmler's comments to senior SS leaders some weeks later that the coming war in the East would kill off 30 million people.[94]

By early January 1941, Heydrich was already at work on a massive assignment. His task was the logical extension of two years of activity in planning and preparation. Its delegation was both a recognition and the natural outgrowth of his singular, cumulative experience in the development of anti-Jewish policy and the implementation of anti-Jewish measures. Consistent with his original authority from Göring two years earlier, he had been deputized through Himmler to prepare (for Hitler) proposals for a Final Solution to the Jewish Question. The documentation of the assignment—which was discovered, has been cited, and was generously made available to me by Richard Breitman—is in my estimation powerfully persuasive.[95] Two crucial pieces of evidence, left individually and in separate records by Heydrich subordinates in the RSHA, fit together in mutually authenticating context and are cemented by independent documents Heydrich himself created in entirely different circumstances.

The first document survived from the files of the Paris office of the Security Police and the SD in occupied France.[96] Its author was Theodor Dannecker, a Jewish affairs specialist in the RSHA and close associate of Adolf Eichmann, who had worked in the Central Emigration Offices in Vienna and Berlin before assignment to Paris from the RSHA in the fall of 1940. Assigned the task of creating a Central Jewish Office in Paris to exert RSHA authority in Jewish matters in occupied France and with the Vichy government, Dannecker staked out the strongest possible claim he could, based on what he already knew.[97] In an office memo dated January 21, 1941, Dannecker revealed that Hitler intended to bring about a final solution (endgültige Lösung) to the Jewish Question at the end of the war in all the areas of Europe that would be under German rule or control. The Führer had already assigned Heydrich, through Himmler and Göring, the task of preparing a final solution project (Endlösungsprojekt). On the basis of the extensive experience Heydrich's agencies had in Jewish affairs, and as a result of the long-standing preparatory work already done by the chief of the Security Police, the essential features of the project had been worked out and the plan had already been submitted to Hitler and Göring (that is, before January 21, 1941).[98]

Dannecker went on to stress the magnitude of the task that lay ahead, the success of which would depend upon the most careful and extensive preparations for every phase of the operation—from the continuing tasks involved in totally removing or isolating the Jews to the planning for the individual resettlement actions, which would be carried out in territories still to be determined.[99] Given all that has long been known about the strategy applied to the Final Solution, the process of destruction, the contents of the Dannecker memorandum seem self-authenticating. Subsequent events in Berlin would appear to confirm both the authenticity of the document and the accuracy of Dannecker's timing for Heydrich's completion and submission of the proposal to Hitler.

As Breitman first noted, the conference in the Propaganda Ministry on March 20, 1941, which Goebbels convened to discuss removing Jews from Berlin, was attended by Adolf Eichmann as the RSHA representative.[100] Goebbels proposed going to Hitler with an "evacuation proposal" for the Berlin Jews. Eichmann recognized the potential complications that such a step would cause. Understanding the larger picture, he responded to Goebbels by revealing enough to satisfy the Propaganda Minister.

Eichmann told those present that Hitler had commissioned Heydrich with the "final evacuation of the Jews" (endgültige Judenevakuierung), for which Heydrich had submitted a proposal to the Führer eight to ten weeks earlier (about mid-January). But the proposal, Eichmann continued, could not be carried out for the moment because the General Government was incapable of taking another single Jew or Pole from the old Reich.[101] Eichmann's comments and Dannecker's memo obviously refer to the same plan or written recommendations and thus place Heydrich's draft proposal before Hitler at approximately the same time.

No copy of the Heydrich proposal has been found. The document doubtless did not survive him. The likely tone of the document and some of its probable contents can be reconstructed from several sources. The first are tied together by consistency in language. Eichmann's choice of words on March 20, 1941, Dannecker's language in the memo of January 21, and Heydrich's terminology in the file memo of September 11, 1940, reflect a descriptive uniformity consistent with Heydrich's own earlier expressions in the letter to Ribbentrop of June 24, 1940. The meaning of "final Jewish evacuation" in March 1941 was no different than Heydrich's intentional phrasing of "territorial Final Solution" and "Final Solution to the Jewish Question" in June 1940. Heydrich's thinking and planning, his grasp of evolving developments had, no later than the summer of 1940, been directed toward physical extermination—mass murder—as the only real, final solution that would get rid of the Jewish problem once and for all.

In November 1941 Heydrich spoke to the issue of his long-term perspective with startling and brutal honesty. In an angry letter to Army Quartermaster-General Eduard Wagner, protesting the lack of military cooperation in carrying out anti-Jewish measures in occupied France—that is, blowing up synagogues in Paris—Heydrich reminded the general and the army, in demanding closer cooperation, of his long-standing supremacy in Jewish matters by observing that the "political significance of the measures taken were fully clear to me, since years earlier I was entrusted with the preparation of the Final Solution in Europe."[102]

However carefully the document for Hitler might have been composed, with elliptical phrasing and with the already familiar euphemisms, the tone and language probably would have conveyed the intent of destruction as the result of years of planning and preparation, as the outgrowth of cumulative experience. What specific details might have been identified in the proposal for Hitler to consider? Related sources offer several suggestions.

In all likelihood, many of the features later noted in the Wannsee Protocol could have been outlined[103]—Jewish census data, the combing of Europe from west to east, an outline of the transport requirements, forced labor, the need for full cooperation and assistance from the Reich ministries and from the foreign governments affected, and the plans for emptying the ghettos in accordance with the annotations from September 1939 for the evacuation of the Jews further to the East.[104]

The details of destruction probably would have been left out, as a matter of tact, and because they were not clearly formulated in January 1941. It took the later experience of killing on so massive a scale to refine the ongoing planning and evolving procedures for extermination, just as the practical lessons of experience had proven so valuable in each of the preceding phases of anti-Jewish policy. There could have been at least two exceptions in the identification of detail in what Heydrich prepared for Hitler's review. Whether or not they were actually reduced to writing for the Führer to read, they seem to have been essential to Heydrich's thinking in January 1941.

The first issue, which we know Heydrich recognized, and addressed with his customary energy and determination, was the question of the masses of Russian Jews who would be caught as German armies overran the Soviet Union. These "Ostjuden," the lowest scum below the dregs of subhumanity, who were infected with the additional bacillus of bolshevism (and therefore most lethally dangerous) could be caught and eliminated swiftly by special SS units operating right behind the advancing armies. The most dangerous could be identified, sorted out and liquidated first, and the rest dealt with in extensive mopping-up operations that undoubtedly would be necessary after the Soviet collapse.[105] Given his pronouncements at the time about the nature of the coming struggle in the East, Hitler probably considered this the most fascinating and striking aspect of the proposal for a continental solution to the Jewish problem.[106]

The Categorization of Concentration Camps and Auschwitz II

The larger issue which would not have escaped Hitler's critical scrutiny was the dilemma posed in dealing with the millions of Polish, German, and other European Jews, the great sedentary concentrations who were less isolated from the world than the Russian Jews, and who had been left in place in the countries allied with or overrun by Germany as the war passed them by. Here, too, there are indications of Heydrich's grasp of the issue, and hints of what he may have proposed in January of 1941.

On January 2, 1941, Heydrich sent out an order for the classification of the concentration camps.[107] The camps were to be divided into categories according to the danger posed by the prisoner—a kind of minimum, medium, and maximum security reordering of the concentration camps. In the future, the most dangerous enemies and arrestees would go to the worst camp, which was identified as Mauthausen. In category 2, the camps specified for serious offenders—but not the most severe political risks—were Buchenwald, Flossenbürg, Neuengamme, and Auschwitz II. There was, of course, no Auschwitz II at that time.[108]

The reference to Auschwitz II on January 2, 1941, and in this context, is extremely interesting. Himmler had then not yet conferred with Rudolf Höss, the commandant of Auschwitz, about the expansion of the camp, and did not until two months later.[109] Additionally, there is no explanatory reference in the Heydrich document to Auschwitz II, only a routine mention. The decision to expand Auschwitz with a second camp had therefore already been made—at sometime before the end of 1940.

Had the construction of a second camp at Auschwitz already been discussed in some context before January 2, 1941? Obviously so, and undoubtedly in SS circles that included the recipients of the Heydrich directive: the RSHA principals in Berlin, the Security Police and SD commanders and inspectors in the East, the inspector-general of concentration camps, and all the concentration camp commandants.

Equally interesting is the careful but authoritative phrasing of the directive. Heydrich did not mince words; neither did he overstate or waste them. The opening paragraph does not say Himmler had ordered the classification of the camps by prisoner category; it states explicitly that "the Reichsführer SS has given his permission" for the classification,[110] meaning the proposal came from Heydrich and had been approved by Himmler. Why would a proposal coming from Heydrich, on January 2, 1941, incorporating a reference to Auschwitz II as a concentration camp—the earliest such reference to have been found in the records—have been dispatched when it was, and why by Heydrich rather than Himmler?

Could this mean Heydrich had a special interest or specific reason to be interested in the construction of a second camp at Auschwitz? If Himmler had given his permission for the classification of the camps, he had also already given his permission for the development of Auschwitz II. Does this mean, then, that the initiative for what became Auschwitz II, the Birkenau death camp, originated with Heydrich? It seems possible, and more especially so in view of the recently discovered materials indicating the placement of SS orders for gassing equipment for the Auschwitz main camp in December 1940.[111]

Heydrich had been keenly interested in the euthanasia gassings throughout 1940. He understood and was impressed by results. The achievements experienced in the numbers of victims eliminated, in some cases with RSHA assistance, clearly pointed to the desirability of gassing on an even larger scale in an enterprise as gigantic as a Final Solution would be. Though all the details still had to be worked out in planning and preparation, Heydrich would have grasped the general concept for mass killing as fundamentally sound. The techniques of the euthanasia program applied in a facility as remote, but as adaptable to expansion, and as accessible by rail as Auschwitz, would have been especially convincing as an early recommendation to Hitler for dealing once and for all with all the non-Russian Jews under German control.[112]

The best engineers take a general concept and from it formulate the plans for development, the specifics of design, and the related operating functions that enable the mechanism to work. And the most successful results of the best engineering come from years of planning and pragmatic adaptation. If Hitler was the author of the Final Solution, and Himmler its architect, then Reinhard Heydrich was both its design and construction engineer, whose abilities for transforming general concept into working reality were equaled, if not surpassed, by the brilliance of his qualities of executive instinct.

NOTES

1. The phraseology is in Hitler's "Political Testament," dictated less than twelve hours before his suicide. An English translation is in *Documents on Nazism, 1919–1945*, ed. Jeremy Noakes and Geoffrey Pridham (New York, 1975), pp. 678–80. See also Eberhard Jäckel, *Hitler in History* (Hanover, NH, 1984). For summaries of the historical literature on the Holocaust, see Otto Dov Kulka, "Die Deutsche Geschichtsschreibung über den Nationalsozialismus und die 'Endlösung,'" *Historische Zeitschrift* 240 (1985): 599–640; Michael R. Marrus, "The History of the Holocaust: A Survey of Recent Literature," *Journal of Modern History* 59/1 (March 1987): 114–60; and idem, *The Holocaust in History* (New York, 1987). For differing views of Hitler's role, see Gerald Fleming, *Hitler and the Final Solution* (Berkeley, 1984); Christopher R. Browning, *Fateful Months: Essays on the Emergence of the Final Solution* (New York, 1985); and idem, *The Path to Genocide: Essays on Launching the Final Solution* (Cambridge, 1992).

2. The best work is still Shlomo Aronson, *Reinhard Heydrich und die Frühgeschichte von Gestapo und SD* (Stuttgart, 1971). Other biographies to date include Charles Wighton, *Heydrich: Hitler's Most Evil Henchman* (Philadelphia, 1963); Günther Deschner, *Reinhard Heydrich: Statthalter der Totalen Macht* (Munich, 1980); and Edouard Calic, *Reinhard Heydrich: Schlüsselfigur des Dritten Reiches* (Stuttgart, 1984). On Heydrich and Himmler, and most aspects of their work, the best book in a generation is Richard Breitman, *The Architect of Genocide: Himmler and the Final Solution* (New York, 1991). Condensed documentary biographical details for Heydrich may be found in National Archives of the United States (hereafter NARUS), Record Group 319, Intelligence Document Series No. 921528; and *Archives of the Holocaust: The Berlin Document Center*, vol. 11, ed. Henry Friedlander and Sybil Milton (New York, 1992), pt. 1, pp. 336–41. Original documentation of Heydrich's responsibility for the Final Solution is in the Bundesarchiv Koblenz (hereafter BAK), RSHA/R/58, Heydrich to Walter Schmitt, Chief of the SS Personnel Office, January 25, 1942; and NARUS, T–175, reel 175, frame 2648487, letter of December 31, 1941, from Rudolf Brandt, Himmler's adjutant, to Oswald Pohl, chief of the SS Main Economic and Administrative Office.

3. Aronson, *Reinhard Heydrich*, chapter 1.

4. Hitler was particularly enraged and embittered by Heydrich's assassination, blaming Heydrich's own recklessness and bravado for depriving Nazi Germany—and Hitler—of a man who was invaluable. See *Hitler's Table Talk: Hitler's Conversations Recorded by Martin Bormann* (Oxford [paperback ed.], 1988), p. 512.

5. Richard Breitman and Shlomo Aronson, "Eine Unbekannte Himmler-Rede vom Januar 1943," *Vierteljahreshefte für Zeitgeschichte* 2 (1990): 337–48. The speech, given on the occasion of Himmler's appointment of Ernst Kaltenbrunner as head of the RSHA, is an unusually frank and revealing summary of the Heydrich-Himmler relationship.

6. This is the theme in the extremely important article by Gustav von Schmoller, "Heydrich im Protektorat Böhmen und Mähren," *Vierteljahreshefte für Zeitgeschichte* 4 (1979): 626–45, which documents the extensive, thorough planning Heydrich had undertaken prior to his appointment to Prague.

7. NARUS, T–120/780/372112–372114; Nuremberg Document NG-5764, copy of Göring's letter authorizing the Central Office for Jewish Emigration, and Heydrich's cover letter to Ribbentrop announcing his appointment and requesting cooperation from the Foreign Ministry.

8. This premature, unplanned effort to dump large numbers of Jews into the Lublin area of Poland is treated in Seev Goschen, "Eichmann und die Nisko-Aktion im Oktober 1939: Eine Fallstudie zur NS Judenpolitik in der leztzen Etappe vor der Endlösung," *Vierteljahreshefte für Zeitgeschichte* 1 (1981): 74–96; and in Jonny Moser, "Nisko: The First Experiment in Deportation," *Simon Wiesenthal Center Annual* 2 (1985): 1–30.

9. Gerhard L. Weinberg, *The Foreign Policy of Hitler's Germany*, vol. 2, *Starting World War II* (Chicago, 1980), pp. 313–535; and Anthony Read and David Fisher, *Kristallnacht: The Unleashing of the Holocaust* (New York, 1989), for the events and the aftermath of the pogrom.

10. The thesis is extensively developed and documented in the important recent study by Götz Aly and Susanne Heim, *Vordenker der Vernichtung: Auschwitz und die deutschen Pläne für eine neue europäische Ordnung* (Hamburg, 1991), esp. pp. 27–31, 48–51.

11. BAK, NS-19/H.R. 5, "Gruppenführer Besprechung am 8.11.1938 im Führerheim der SS Standarte Deutschland," pp. 24–27 and 47 of the typescript. Himmler's phraseology anticipates both Hitler's rhetoric in the speech of January 30, 1939, and Himmler's later description of the annihilation of the Jews in his Posen speech of October 4, 1943. Both Himmler speeches are printed in full in *Heinrich Himmler Geheimreden 1933 bis 1945*, ed. Agnes Petersen and Bradley Smith (Frankfurt/M., 1974).

12. NARUS, Record Group 238, Nuremberg Doc. 3051-PS; Nuremberg Doc. 3058-PS is Heydrich's summary report to Göring of November 11, 1938, on the national extent of the damage and casualties resulting from the Reichskristallnacht.

13. NARUS, RG 238, Nuremberg Doc. 1816-PS, partial stenographic record of the conference. The importance of this document, in signaling the radical shift in German anti-Jewish policy, was first described by Robert Wolfe, "Nazi Paperwork for the Final Solution to the Jewish Question," unpub. paper delivered at the American Historical Association conference of 1983.

14. NARUS, RG 238, Nuremberg Doc. 1816-PS; Aly and Heim, *Vordenker*, pp. 27–32. The measures proposed on November 12 and subsequently enacted are listed in *The Policies of Genocide: Jews and Soviet Prisoners of War in Nazi Germany*, ed. Gerhard Hirschfeld (Boston, 1986), pp. 145–56.

15. BAK, NS-19/H.R.5, "Gruppenführer Besprechung," November 8, 1938.

16. In the ministerial conference on November 12, Göring declared to the participants that he had received instructions from Hitler that the Jewish problem was to be settled "one way or another" (so oder so), and announced that in the event of war, there would be "a great reckoning of accounts" (eine grosse Abrechnung) with the Jews; NARUS, RG 238, Nuremberg Doc. 1816-PS.

17. The natural sound portion of this section of the Reichstag speech is in the 1977 documentary, *Adolf Hitler: 1889–1945*, produced by WCVE-TV in Richmond, Virginia.

18. See NARUS, T-175/R84/2515243, for Himmler's notes. Breitman first discovered the document and made it available to me.

19. Aly and Heim, *Vordenker*, p. 31 and note.

20. Zentrale Staatsarchiv, AST, Berlin, copy of the conference summary from the files of the Chief of the Security Police and SD, Amt III, dated March 1, 1939. The document was first discovered by Konrad Kwiet and given to Richard Breitman, who kindly provided me with the copy cited.

21. Ibid.

22. Ibid. Interesting also is the similarity in German phraseology to the later Wannsee Protocol, a copy of which is reproduced in full in *Topographie des Terrors: Gestapo, SS und Reichssicherheitshauptamt auf dem Prinz-Albrecht-Gelände; Eine Dokumentation* (Berlin, 1987), pp. 142–47.

23. Helmut Krausnick, *Hitlers Einsatzgruppen: Die Truppen des Weltanschauungskrieges, 1938–1942* (Frankfurt/M., [Fischer paperback ed.] 1985), pp. 26–65.

24. A brief narrative of the expansion, an organizational chart of the RSHA, and profiles of the office chiefs are in *Topographie des Terrors*, pp. 70–80. For Heydrich's role in the Gleiwitz incident, see Alfred Spiess and Heiner Lichtenstein, *Das Unternehmen Tannenberg* (Munich, 1979).

25. Heydrich's RSHA office chiefs and Einsatzgruppen commanders conferences of September 7, 14, 21, and October 3, and 8, 1939, are in NARUS, T-175/239/2728499ff.

26. NARUS, T-175/239/2728513–2728515, "Amtschefbesprechung am 14.9.1939."

27. NARUS, T-175/239/2728236ff. Hitler signed a secret decree naming Himmler Reich Commissioner for the Strengthening of Germandom (Reichskommissar für die Festigung Deutschen Volkstums) on October 7, 1939. See especially Robert L. Koehl, *RKFDV: German Resettlement and Population Policy, 1939–1945: A History of the Reich Commission for the*

Strengthening of Germandom (Cambridge, MA, 1957). An English translation of the decree is in *Trials of War Criminals before the Nuremberg Military Tribunals*, vol. 13 (Washington, D.C., 1952), pp. 138–43 (hereafter TWC, Green Series). Article 1, paragraph 2 of the decree stipulates that Himmler will "eliminate the harmful influence of such alien parts of the population as constitute a danger to the Reich and the German community," a euphemism for mass deportations and killings.

28. NARUS, T-175/239/2728236ff., "Amtschef und Einsatzgruppenleiter Besprechung vom 21.9.1939." Two days earlier, on September 19, Heydrich had attended a conference called and presided over by Göring in his capacity as head of the Four Year Plan. The conferees included either Reich Ministers or State Secretaries concerned with the economic and demographic aspects of dividing up and exploiting conquered Poland. In the discussion of the fate of the populations in the annexed and occupied territories, Göring stipulated that all Jews living in Germany would be deported to these areas; see Aly and Heim, *Vordenker*, p. 64.

29. NARUS, RG 238, Nuremberg Doc. 3363-PS, "Schnellbrief . . . Judenfrage im besetzten Gebiet," dated September 21, 1939. An English translation is in TWC, Green Series, vol. 13, pp. 133–37.

30. Ibid.

31. NARUS, T-175/R588/705–706, "Sichtpunkte für das Sachgebiet Judentum zur Amtschefbesprechung," dated December 19, 1939.

32. Ibid. The subject of the office chiefs' meeting was "The Final Solution to the German Jewish Question."

33. Breitman, in *Architect of Genocide*, pp. 58, 61, 62, 64–65, has demonstrated persuasively that the American consul general in Berlin, Raymond Geist, who was unusually well connected and well informed, had pieced together an exceptionally accurate picture of the future course of German anti-Jewish policy—that the collective weight of all the measures pointed to the eventual extermination of Germany's Jews. Geist had so informed the State Department. Geist's assumptions at the time are accurately reflected in the record of the interagency meeting of February 28, 1939, cited above, and in the language of the talking points for the RSHA office chiefs' meeting on December 19. And though conclusive documentation is lacking, I am not persuaded that option 2 noted in the talking points does not mean "disposal" rather than "accommodation, or quartering."

34. NARUS, T-175/R588/705–706.

35. *Topographie des Terrors*, p. 126, presents a photographic reproduction of the document entitled "Räumung in den Ostprovinzen"—evacuation into the eastern provinces.

36. Aly and Heim, *Vordenker*, pp. 133–34, notes 25 and 26.

37. TWC, Green Series, vol. 13, pp. 138–43.

38. Breitman, *Architect of Genocide*, pp. 74–79; NARUS, RG 238, Nuremberg Doc. 864-PS is the annotated record of Hitler's major points during the meeting. Those attending were Field Marshal Wilhelm Keitel, Hans Frank, Rudolf Hess, Himmler, Martin Bormann, Wilhelm Frick, Hans Lammers, and Dr. Wilhelm Stuckart, Frick's State Secretary from the Interior Ministry.

39. Krausnick, *Einsatzgruppen*, pp. 60–62; and Breitman, *Architect of Genocide*, chapter 5, pp. 105–15, are the best summaries of the Himmler-Heydrich conflict with the Army commanders. The dispute with the Army posed a particular dilemma for Heydrich, who could not divulge the fact that all SS measures in Poland had resulted from Hitler's directives to kill off the entire leadership of the Polish nation. See Helmut Krausnick, "Hitler und die Morde in Polen: Ein Beitrag zum Konflikt zwischen Heer und SS um die Verwaltung der besetzten Gebiete," *Vierteljahrshefte für Zeitgeschichte* 2 (1963): 196–208.

40. See Breitman, *Architect of Genocide*, pp. 79–82, 93–104, for the most detailed description of the Himmler-Frank conflicts over deportation. See also NARUS, RG 238, Nuremberg Doc. 5322, for the summary record of the big conference Heydrich convened in Berlin on January 30, 1940, to discuss massive resettlements of Jews, Gypsies, and Poles to the East, and Polish forced laborers into Germany. The list of the forty-five participants and an English translation of the minutes of the meeting are in TWC, Green Series, vol. 4, pp. 855–61.

41. The crucial event that temporarily halted Heydrich's deportation measures was the conference Göring convened at his Karinhall estate on February 12, 1940, attended by Himmler, Frank, and all the eastern Gauleiters. In taking Frank's side against Himmler, and in directing a halt to the deportations, Göring's specific criticism of the SS was that the "resettlement of the Jews" had to be more thoroughly planned and prepared, and incorporated into the general policies in the East. See *Trials of the Major War Criminals before the International Military Tribunal at Nuremberg, Germany* (Nuremberg, 1946), vol 36, pp. 299–307 (hereafter TMWC, Blue Series), for the record of the conference; Breitman, *Architect of Genocide*, pp. 98–101; Aly and Heim, *Vordenker*, p. 65.

42. The leading scholar documenting the extensive influences that made the euthanasia program a model for the Final Solution is Henry Friedlander. The preparation of this essay was completed too early to benefit from the publication of his definitive work, *The Origins of Nazi Genocide: From Euthanasia to the Final Solution* (Chapel Hill, 1995). See especially his chapter, "Euthanasia and the Final Solution," in *The Final Solution: Origins and Implementation*, ed. David Cesarani (London, 1993). See also the works by Ernst Klee, *"Euthanasie" im NS-Staat: Die "Vernichtung lebensunwerten Lebens"* (Frankfurt/M., 1985); and Benno Müller-Hill, *Murderous Science: Elimination by Scientific Selection of Jews, Gypsies, and Others in Germany, 1933–1945*, trans. George R. Fraser (Oxford, 1988), esp. pp. 22–65, for the background and general developments; and Robert Jay Lifton, *The Nazi Doctors: Medical Killing and the Psychology of Genocide* (New York, 1986), esp. pp. 45–144, for profiles of participants and the expansion of the killings to the concentration camps; and see also Breitman, *Architect of Genocide*, pp. 89–92, for specific details involving Himmler, Heydrich, and RSHA personnel.

43. Breitman, *Architect of Genocide*, pp. 89–90, 94–96. During a trip Himmler made to Kraków in January 1940, Odilo Globocnik, the SS and Police Leader in the Lublin District of the General Government, regaled Himmler and his entourage with a descriptive account of his liquidation of the inmates of a Polish insane asylum several weeks earlier.

44. TWC, Green Series, vol. 1, pp. 796–98, 800, closing brief in the trial of SS Dr. Karl Brandt.

45. Aly and Heim, *Vordenker*, pp. 265–72; TWC, Green Series, vol. 1, pp. 796–806.

46. TWC, Green Series, vol. 1, pp. 796–800, 805–806, 842–45.

47. Aly and Heim, *Vordenker*, pp. 265–72.

48. Breitman, *Architect of Genocide*, pp. 102–103.

49. TWC, Green Series, vol. 1, pp. 796–99.

50. TWC, Green Series, vol. 1, Nuremburg Docs. NO-660 and NO-018, letter from Himmler to Viktor Brack of December 19, 1940.

51. Aly and Heim, *Vordenker*, pp. 271–72.

52. Yitzhak Arad, *Belzec, Sobibor, Treblinka: The Operation Reinhard Death Camps* (Bloomington, 1987), pp. 16–17, documents the transfer of ninety-two men to the three death camps from the Führer Chancellery euthanasia program.

53. See Helmut Krausnick's chapter on the concentration camps in *Anatomie des SS Staates*, vol. 2 (Freiburg, 1965), esp. pp. 98–115.

54. NARUS, T-580/49/271ff., which Heydrich supplemented on September 20 with a further order specifying more detailed procedures for the arrest and liquidation of especially dangerous suspects; see NARUS, RG 238, Nuremberg Doc. NO-2263, Heydrich to all regional offices of the Security Police and SD, September 20, 1939.

55. NARUS, RG 238, Nuremberg Doc. NO-905, office file copy of specialists' meeting of September 26, 1939, original signed by Müller.

56. BAK, R58/1027, fol. 106 u.R.' file copy of the express letter dispatched by Müller on October 24, 1939.

57. BAK, R58/1027, fol. 128, copy of a file note for Gestapo office IVe5 by Kurt Lindow, dated April 23, 1940, and citing the Himmler order of March 9.

58. Breitman, *Architect of Genocide*, p. 101, citing the dispatch from the U.S. Embassy in Berlin to the Secretary of State, dated March 28, and recounting the information from the daily briefing for the foreign press on March 27.

59. Christopher R. Browning, *The Final Solution and the German Foreign Office: A Study*

of Referat III D of Abteilung Deutschland (New York, 1978); Leni Yahil, "Madagascar—Phantom of a Solution for the Jewish Question," in *Jews and Non-Jews in Eastern Europe, 1918–1945*, ed. Bela Vago and George L. Mosse (New York, 1974); and Philip Friedman, *Roads to Extinction: Essays on the Holocaust* (New York, 1980).

60. The Foreign Office had defined the objective of shipping all the European Jews to Madagascar as an urgent postwar task in a memorandum completed ten days before the first German troops entered Paris. Ribbentrop had then discussed Madagascar in some detail with his Italian counterpart, Count Galeazzo Ciano, at a conference in Munich on June 17, 1940— prompting reaction from Heydrich and the RSHA (NARUS, T-120/780/37218, Foreign Office memo of June 3, 1940, "New and Urgent Tasks of Referat DIII[Inland]"). See also chapters 1 and 2 in Browning, *Final Solution*. NARUS, T-120/780/372104–372105, is the early draft of the Foreign Ministry's Madagascar Plan.

61. NARUS, T-120/780/372056–372071, "RSHA–Madagascar Projekt," which is undated but obviously followed by some weeks the Foreign Office version of the proposal.

62. NARUS, T-120/780/372104–372105 and 372056–372071, the Foreign Office and RSHA versions of a Madagascar Plan.

63. The RSHA version estimated 120 ships would be required to handle the deportations. Each ship would need sixty days for the round-trip voyage from Europe to Madagascar. Two ships would depart Europe every day, carrying an average of fifteen hundred Jews each, or about twenty thousand Jews per week. At that rate, the RSHA version arrived at the estimate of four years to complete the deportation of more than three million Jews to Madagascar.

64. Aly and Heim, *Vordenker*, pp. 257–65, deal extensively with the activities related to the Madagascar Project during the summer of 1940 among the various agencies involved—the Foreign Office, the RSHA, the Four Year Plan, and the Propaganda Ministry. Stressing the wholly unrealistic assumptions in the drafts of the plans, and the growing importance of economic planning for further conquest and exploitation, they conclude that Madagascar was an impractical exercise that served to camouflage the real consensus among all those involved—namely, that the Jews could disappear during the coming war of annihilation that would guarantee the economic future of the Reich.

65. Aly and Heim, *Vordenker*, pp. 262–65. The two expert consultants were Professor Friedrich Schumacher, a geologist from the mining institute at Freiburg in Saxony, and Professor Friedrich Burgdörfer, a population specialist and demographics expert who was then president of the Bavarian office of vital statistics.

66. Aly and Heim, *Vordenker*, pp. 261–63, also document the extensive involvement of principals from the Führer Chancellery—the euthanasia program—in the Madagascar discussions. Viktor Brack met with the Foreign Office planners and offered his own transport organization for use in getting the Jews to the ports. And earlier, on June 23, 1940, Philipp Bouhler, Brack's superior, who was running the euthanasia program, had approached Hitler and been rebuffed in his desire to become the German Governor General of East Africa.

67. NARUS, T-120/780/372047, Heydrich to Ribbentrop, dated June 24, 1940, and addressed to the Foreign Minister as "SS Gruppenführer Joachim von Ribbentrop."

68. Ibid.

69. There was a definite substantive basis for Heydrich's letter to Ribbentrop. That he was reacting critically to what he already knew of the Foreign Ministry's Madagascar proposal— the office memo of June 3—is strongly suggested by his use of statistics, his estimates for the number of Jews that then temporarily constituted the problem. He would not have written such a letter to Ribbentrop simply because he had learned that the Foreign Minister discussed the Jewish Question with Count Ciano on June 17. Nor would he have dispatched such a letter to Ribbentrop without Himmler's consent. Breitman, *Architect of Genocide*, p. 277 note 46, cites documentation suggesting Ribbentrop had instructed the Foreign Office planners to work closely with Himmler's office, which would mean providing Himmler and Heydrich with the office memo of June 3. In all likelihood, Heydrich received and studied the Foreign Office paper of June 3 by no later than the middle of the month, prompting the response to Ribbentrop of June 24.

70. Breitman, *Architect of Genocide*, pp. 117–20, citing Himmler's memorandum and the instructions for its distribution, which are in NARUS, T-175/119/2645113–2645121. In English, the documents are in TWC, Green Series, vol. 13, Nuremberg Docs. NO-1880 and NO-1881, pp. 147–51.

71. TWC, Green Series, vol. 13, Nuremberg Doc. NO-1880, p. 148.

72. NARUS, T-175/128/2654343–2654348, Krüger to Himmler, dated April 15, 1940, and enclosing a top secret report on discussions held on April 4 with representatives from the army about the creation of military training preserves in the General Government, which would require the massive deportation and relocation of Polish civilians. The victory in the West also provided perfect cover for Hans Frank and the SS principals in the General Government to agree upon a massive campaign to exterminate the Polish resistance and all elements in the population hostile to German rule. See NARUS, RG 238, Diensttagebuch des Deutschen General Gouverneurs von Polen, "Polizei–Sitzung am Donnerstag, den 30. Mai 1940."

73. NARUS, T-175/128/2654343.

74. Breitman, *Architect of Genocide*, pp. 103–104; Himmler's itinerary is in NARUS, T-175/112/2637798. The best published summary of Globocnik's activities is the important article by Peter R. Black, "Rehearsal for 'Reinhard'?: Odilo Globocnik and the Lublin Selbstschutz," *Central European History* 25/2 (March 1989): 204–26.

75. Breitman, *Architect of Genocide*, pp. 103–104, 129–30.

76. NARUS, T-175/128/2654341. On July 9, 1940, responding to Krüger's warnings of additional problems that Frank's people were creating for Globocnik, Himmler wrote Krüger that it went without saying that he would never consent to Globocnik's transfer or removal (NARUS, T-175/84/2609848).

77. Aly and Heim, *Vordenker*, p. 263. Officials in the Foreign Ministry were still discussing practical aspects of the Madagascar Project that would prove essential as procedures in the Final Solution. On August 12, Franz Rademacher, the leader of the Foreign Ministry group working on Madagascar, drafted a memo proposing the creation of an inter-European bank for the purpose of appraising, confiscating and utilizing all Jewish property throughout Europe. In addition, the Foreign Office version also urged enacting laws that would strip German Jews of their citizenship from the time and point of origin of their deportation, while simultaneously forcing them to sign over their remaining property to the Reich (NARUS, T-120/780/372104–372105; Aly and Heim, *Vordenker*, p. 66 note 93).

78. NARUS, RG 242, T-581/R38A, is Himmler's appointment book for 1940. Richard Breitman generously provided me with his copies of Himmler's office calendar and first drew my attention to the probable significance of the meeting noted for the morning of August 10, 1940.

79. For concise but thorough biographical information on these five participants, and for the best treatment of the role and activities of all the Higher SS and Police Leaders, see the standard study by Ruth-Bettina Birn, *Die Höheren SS- und Polizeiführer: Himmler's Vertreter im Reich und in den besetzten Gebieten* (Düsseldorf, 1986).

80. Breitman, *Architect of Genocide*, pp. 137–38.

81. Ibid. p. 138, and NARUS, RG 238, Nuremberg Doc. NG-1916.

82. State Central Archives, Prague, Akten des Stellvertretenden Reichsprotektors von Böhmen und Mähren, with a microfilm copy now deposited in the National Archives as NNMN. Though Heydrich wrote this file memorandum a year before his appointment as Reichsprotector in Prague, this copy survived from the files of Karl Hermann Frank, the Higher SS and Police Leader for Bohemia-Moravia in 1940 and a close associate of Heydrich.

83. Ibid., "Aktennotiz, Berlin, den 11. September 1940."

84. Berlin Document Center, SS Personalakte Bach-Zelewski, letter from Erich von dem Bach-Zelewski, the Higher SS and Police Leader in Silesia, to Karl Wolff, Chief of Himmler's office staff, dated September 13, 1940 (hereafter BDC, by individual SS personnel file).

85. Breitman, *Architect of Genocide*, p. 139. Heydrich approached the chief physician of the SS, Dr. Ernst Grawitz, to inquire if the undertaking would be feasible.

86. On October 2, 1940, Hitler had lunch in the Chancellery with Hans Frank, the Gauleiters Baldur von Schirach of Vienna, Erich Koch of East Prussia, and Martin Bormann. Bormann made a record of the conversation. During lunch, Schirach and Koch complained because Frank would not permit deportations of Jews into the General Government. Frank argued back. Hitler took the side of the Gauleiters, declaring he didn't care how dense the population in the General Government became, citing the per square kilometer population statistics for the Palatinate and Saxony as examples. Frank would simply have to take in more Jews. Bormann's record is in TMWC, Blue Series, vol. 39, pp. 425–30. See also Aly and Heim, *Vordenker*, pp. 282–84.

87. BDC, Globocnik SS personnel file, undated cover letter enclosing a report subsequently written for Himmler and citing the order from the Reichsführer SS of November 2, 1940.

88. NARUS, T-175/204/00812–00814, Heydrich's memorandum for Robert Ley, head of the German Labor Front and Reich Minister of Labor, arguing for a number of additional legal and financial measures against the Jews. That same day, Heydrich received an extremely interesting letter from Gottlob Berger, chief of the SS recruiting office, calling attention to confusion over RSHA policy in Belgium. Berger was astonished to learn that an SD officer, he assumed with Heydrich's blessing, had just agreed to work with the Foreign Ministry in developing the pro-German Rexist Party to be led by Leon Degrelle. Berger requested clarification from Heydrich, since he thought they both had agreed that it simply would not be possible to work with the Foreign Ministry and Degrelle in carrying out the great tasks the Führer had assigned Himmler on behalf of the ethnic Germans and the Germanic peoples. NARUS, T-139/36/889–890, also as RG-238, Nuremberg Doc. NG-3481. I am indebted to Richard Breitman for calling this document to my attention.

89. In English, the text of the directive is in *Documents on Nazism, 1919–1945*, ed. Noakes and Pridham, pp. 593–94. As the historian Eberhard Jäckel noted in *Hitler's Weltanschauung: A Blueprint for Power*, trans. Herbert Arnold (Middletown, CT, 1972), pp. 25–46, the decision to attack and destroy the Soviet Union was the critical step Hitler took to weave together closely his long-standing, unchanging objective of winning living space in the East, his ideological goal of annihilating the plague of communism, and his racial obsession to solve once and for all the European Jewish question.

90. Breitman, *Architect of Genocide*, p. 146, for Hitler's and Himmler's activities on December 18, and for Himmler's evening visit to the Chancellery.

91. Aly and Heim, *Vordenker*, pp. 366–70.

92. Ibid., pp. 368–70, for the contents of Backe's report and its release and circulation. Backe's work and abilities were well known to Himmler, and Backe evidently had a friendly relationship with Heydrich. Eleven months earlier, on January 3 and 9, 1940, Backe had visited Himmler's office to discuss matters related to the food situation. Breitman, *Architect of Genocide*, pp. 95 and 271 note 45, documents Backe's visits to Himmler's office.

93. Aly and Heim, *Vordenker*, pp. 368–70; Backe's testimony at the Nuremberg Trials, in TMWC, Blue Series, vol. 36, pp. 135–37.

94. At Nuremberg, Backe confused the time for his briefing of Himmler, placing their discussion in the early spring of 1941. Breitman, *Architect of Genocide*, p. 147, documents the approximate time for Himmler's meeting with senior SS leaders at the Wewelsburg castle as January, meaning the Himmler-Backe meeting had to be earlier, since Himmler quoted the figures Backe estimated for the number of deaths among the alien peoples during the coming war in the east.

95. Breitman's unpublished paper, "Himmler and the Planning for the Final Solution," presented at the annual meeting of the German Studies Association in Bethesda, Maryland, October 2, 1993.

96. "Zentrales Judenamt in Paris," dated January 21, 1941, a copy made from the original of the Dannecker memorandum. The document, which is now deposited with other captured RSHA materials in the Centre de Documentation Juive Contemporaine, Paris, has been reproduced by Dr. Serge Klarsfeld in his book *Vichy-Auschwitz: Die Zusammenarbeit der deutschen und französischen Behörden bei der "Endlösung der Judenfrage" in Frankreich*, trans.

Ahlrich Meyer (Nördlingen, 1989), pp. 361–63. John Fox advised Richard Breitman of the document's existence and significance, and Breitman, in turn, made it available to me. I am indebted to both of them and to Serge Klarsfeld for providing me with a facsimile of the original document.

97. For Dannecker's activities in Paris, see Jacques Adler, *The Jews of Paris and the Final Solution: Communal Response and Internal Conflicts, 1940–1944* (Oxford, 1987), pp. 12, 13, 44, 56, 58–77, and 79–80. Dannecker was obviously abreast of the most advanced planning at the RSHA in Berlin. He spent the late autumn of 1940 and the winter months of 1941 in efforts to complete a Jewish census and to get the Jews organized under a Council of Elders directly responsible to him. He was following the model Heydrich had established for Poland in the express letter to the Einsatzgruppen commanders on September 21, 1939.

98. Dannecker memorandum on the establishment of the Jewish Central Office in Paris, dated January 21, 1941.

99. Ibid. Dannecker wasted no time in planning and preparing for the French phase of the Final Solution. On January 28, 1941, he wrote to the Chief of the Military Government in France, General Otto von Stülpnagel, demanding the army's assistance in the establishment of concentration camps for the 100,000 Jews he estimated were living in and around Paris. He cited as his authority a directive from Himmler and Heydrich of October 30, 1940, ordering the creation of special concentration camps in all the occupied territories for all foreign Jews, as well as for all Jews of German, Austrian, Czech and Polish nationality. This document is reproduced in Klarsfeld, *Vichy-Auschwitz*. pp. 363–64. Since six months earlier, in March 1940, Himmler had forbidden the release of any Jews from concentration camps for the duration of the war; there could have been little doubt as to their eventual fate.

100. Breitman, *Architect of Genocide*, p. 152. The notes from the meeting in the Propaganda Ministry, "Betrifft: Evakuierung der Juden aus Berlin," of March 20, 1941, are in NARUS, T-81/676/5485604–5485605.

101. NARUS, T-81/676/5485604.

102. The quote is from the third page of the letter, Heydrich to Wagner, dated November 6, 1941. Field Marshal Walther von Brauchitsch, then still Commander-in-Chief of the Army, read and initialed Wagner's copy of the letter. This document was provided by the Office of Special Investigations in the U.S. Department of Justice from materials collected by the French government for the postwar investigation and trials of French nationals who had collaborated with the Paris offffice of the RSHA in anti-Jewish violence.

103. The full text in German is reprinted in *Topographie des Terrors*, pp. 142–46; in English, it may be found in *Documents of Destruction: Germany and Jewry 1933–1945*, ed. Raul Hilberg (Chicago, 1971), pp. 89–99.

104. The Heydrich express letter of September 21, 1939, cited in note 29, above.

105. On the planning and preparations for the organization and deployment of Einsatzgruppen in the Russian campaign, see Krausnick, *Hitlers Einsatzgruppen*, pp. 89–150, and the more recent study, Ronald Headland, *Messages of Murder: A Study of the Reports of the Einsatzgruppen of the Security Police and the Security Service* (East Rutherford, NJ, 1992), pp. 11–50. At his postwar German trial, in Hamburg in 1973, Bruno Streckenbach, a subordinate close to Heydrich who was head of Amt I (personnel) in the RSHA, testified that in January 1941, both the personnel and administrative office (Amt II) received orders from Heydrich to begin planning for a huge Einsatzgruppen operation over a broad area. Cited in Krausnick, *Hitlers Einsatzgruppen*, p. 121.

106. See especially the notes recorded for his diary by Colonel-General Franz Halder from the speech Hitler delivered to the assembled commanders of the Armed Forces on March 30, 1941. Hitler noted that the army would have to put traditional values aside and let nothing stand in the way of the extermination of bolshevism, including the complete liquidation of the communist intelligentsia and all the political commissars attached to units of the Red Army. Halder's notes are reprinted in *Documents on Nazism*, ed. Noakes and Pridham, pp. 619–20.

107. NARUS, RG 238, Nuremberg Doc. NO-743, "Betrifft: Einstufung der Konzentrationslager," dated Berlin, January 2, 1941.

108. Ibid.

109. See Breitman, *Architect of Genocide*, pp. 157–58, for the details of Himmler's inspection visit to Auschwitz on March 1, 1941, and the substance of his directives to Höss about the future expansion of the facilities at Auschwitz, including the construction of a huge new camp at nearby Birkenau, allegedly to house some 100,000 expected Russian prisoners of war.

110. "Der Reichsführer-SS und Chef der Deutschen Polizei hat seine Zustimmung zu der Einteilung der Konzentrationslager in verschiedene Stufen," NARUS, RG 238, Nuremberg Doc. NO-743.

111. As detailed in Breitman's unpublished paper presented on October 2, 1993, at the annual meeting of the German Studies Association, citing the Soviet postwar interrogation records of Karl Schultze, an engineer with Topf and Sons of Erfurt, manufacturers of the crematoria at Auschwitz. A partial transcript of the interrogation, with commentary, was published by Professor Gerald Fleming as "Engineers of Death" in the July 18, 1993, edition of the *New York Times*, section E, p. 19.

112. In addition to the works already cited documenting the relationships between the euthanasia program and the Final Solution, see also Ino Arndt and Wolfgang Scheffler, "Organisierter Massenmord an Juden in nationalsozialistischen Vernichtungslagern," *Vierteljahrshefte für Zeitgeschichte* 24/2 (1976): 105–35.

13.

RICHARD BREITMAN

Plans for the Final Solution in Early 1941

In the last fifteen years historians have felled many trees debating whether the Nazi regime had long planned or hastily improvised the Holocaust. This controversy has often focused on a seemingly small matter of timing: determination of the date when the SS moved to a continentwide program of mass murder, which they euphemistically called the Final Solution of the Jewish Question.[1] The date of a decision to embark on the Final Solution is not only of interest in itself but helps us to establish with greater precision the range of influences on, and participants in, the process—in laymen's terms, the causes and the villains.

In some ways, however, the significance of the move to a continentwide program has been overemphasized. As I have argued in *The Architect of Genocide: Himmler and the Final Solution* and elsewhere, the SS adopted the notion of mass murder as a partial solution to the Jewish Question in Germany before the war broke out in September 1939; and it began to implement mass murder against the handicapped and on a smaller scale against Jews during the years 1939–1940. Henry Friedlander has argued convincingly that, with regard to decision making, personnel, and technique, the killing program for the handicapped served as a model for the Final Solution.[2] These early killings, not to mention the assignment of Einsatzgruppen and Order Police battalions to the forthcoming campaign planned against the USSR well before June 1941, more than amply demonstrate the murderous intentions of Hitler, Himmler, and other key Nazi leaders. Premeditated mass murder was neither a last resort after other schemes had been tried and found wanting, nor an unforeseen escalation of persecution under the pressures of a bitter war-to-the-death on the Eastern front.

Still, the move to "cleanse" the entire continent of Jews certainly was a major escalation in the area of implementation. What can we determine about how, when, and why this turn occurred? Can we do better than to look at the date when killing on a huge scale began? Can we trace earlier preparations for genocide?

If we focus on Adolf Hitler, we are drawn to the period beginning in December 1940. On December 18 Hitler formally authorized Operation Barbarossa, the campaign to invade, conquer, and destroy the Soviet Union—his long-sought geopolitical

This essay is a revised version of "Plans for the Final Solution in Early 1941," which appeared in *German Studies Review* 17/3 (October 1994): 483–94.

and ideological goal. His idea of destroying Jewry was at least as longstanding, even if one rejects the view that he had, early in his political career, made an unalterable decision or fixed his mind only upon mass murder. Now a vast military operation in 1941 would provide opportunities and cover for the liquidation of racial enemies in the East. Deciphering Hitler's exact intentions at a given time, however, is both tricky and subjective, given his habit of concealment and his disinclination to give explicit, written orders.

In any case, one of the lessons of the intentionalist-functionalist controversy is that a strictly Hitler-centered interpretation will not convince those who doubt Hitler's involvement or his efficacy. It is necessary to find evidence that others sought to translate Hitler's wishes or goals into reality. Here Götz Aly and Susanne Heim have uncovered important new evidence regarding the role of technocrats—the "planning intelligentsia" in a number of different agencies and organizations early in the war— in the move toward genocide.[3] These men identified practical benefits in the mass murder of the Jews and prepared alternatives for their political superiors. Exclusive focus on the role of mid-level bureaucrats, however, can create at least as many interpretive problems and objections as concentration on Hitler alone.

Among the welter of Nazi organizations, the SS had ultimate control of Jewish policy, and it was a very hierarchical organization. Yet the evidence of motives and activities of its principal figures is dispersed and in some respects fragmentary. There are no full scholarly biographies of Himmler, Heydrich, or Pohl. A general file in Himmler's office or even in the Reich Security Main Office on the Final Solution of the Jewish Question comparable to the folder in the Foreign Office that contained the one surviving copy (out of thirty that were made) of the Wannsee Conference summary did not survive the war. We need, therefore, to reconstruct what was going on at the highest reaches of the SS at the end of 1940 and the beginning of 1941.

Himmler's itineraries, appointments, and office records are important sources in this process. The recent discovery of additional Himmler materials in the Center for the Preservation of Historical Documents in Moscow makes it possible to do a more precise reconstruction of high-level contacts and movements than I have done here. Still, even the Moscow documents have some limitations, and they must be cross-checked against the evidence I have drawn on in this article

Adolf Eichmann, the Jewish specialist in the Reich Security Main Office (RSHA), provided one major clue about SS and RSHA preparations for the Final Solution. In mid-March 1941, during a meeting at the Propaganda Ministry regarding the evacuation of Jews from Berlin, Eichmann announced to rival bureaucrats that the Führer had already entrusted Heydrich with the "final evacuation" of the Jews (endgültigen Judenevakuierung). In this context, Eichmann specifically discussed only German Jews (and those in recently "annexed" Bohemia-Moravia), but his comment may have referred to a general policy that was still secret. Christopher Browning, however, dismisses the notion that Hitler, Himmler, and Eichmann had far-reaching secret plans, and also cautions us about the imprecision of a notetaker in the Propaganda Ministry recording Eichmann's comments.[4]

The wording of Nazi documents was often inexact, but for particular reasons that do not advance Browning's functionalist argument. There is a consistent pattern of veiling measures against Jews (and other victimized groups) with euphemisms. The gassing of mental patients in the General Government during 1940, for example, was described as "evacuation."[5] Whatever Eichmann said precisely in mid-March 1941 very likely understated the lethal implications of RSHA plans. Even so, "final evacuation" is at least evocative.

Eichmann even gave his audience a little background on the timing of the Führer's authorization. Eight to ten weeks earlier [in early to mid-January], Eichmann said, Heydrich had presented a proposal to the Führer that remained unfulfilled only because the General Government of Poland was not yet in a position to receive even one Jew or Pole from the old Reich.[6]

Christopher Browning's interpretation here is that Eichmann was referring simply to the already well-known "third short-range plan" (deporting Jews from Vienna and Poles from the incorporated territories to the General Government) concocted by Heydrich, not some secret and more lethal second plan for deporting German Jews, let alone all European Jews. (Of course, if Heydrich drew up plans that he labeled short-range, he likely had a long-range conception too.) Browning also refers to Hitler's near-simultaneous discussions with Hans Frank and some luncheon comments to Goebbels and Frank on March 18 to maintain that Hitler had made no immediate decisions on Jewish policy and that, for the short-term, "pragmatic considerations about Jewish labor were given priority over 'racial experimentation.'"[7]

Were Hitler, Himmler, and Heydrich capable of developing more radical ideas but concealing them from officials such as Frank and Goebbels? Did they operate in a conspiratorial manner on such matters? Himmler and Heydrich were both practical in the world of espionage and its methods, and as I will demonstrate below, they also practiced secrecy and deception with the Final Solution.

With regard to Hitler, following Friedlander and Gerald Fleming, we can look for guidance to the killing of the handicapped, which the Nazi elite cast as a "euthanasia" program. That was only one of many deceptions practiced by Hitler and the Führer Chancellery to keep the facts about the gassings of handicapped patients from the German public: the use of code names for the participating officials from the Führer Chancellery, the creation of falsified death certificates, and in some places the use of trucks designed to gas their passengers—trucks that were disguised as coffee delivery vehicles.

Hitler had advocated the killing of the genetically deficient well before the war but signed on his own private stationery in October 1939 a general authorization of the program only after it became necessary to protect the bureaucrats in charge and to obtain the collaboration of physicians. This written authorization reached enough people that it caused trouble for Hitler once news of the (unpopular) "euthanasia" killings began to leak out; this difficulty may explain why Hitler apparently did not authorize the Final Solution on paper.[8] By 1941 Hitler and the Führer Chancellery were already experienced, if not adept, at conspiracy to cover up mass murder.

One of the key "euthanasia" conspirators, Viktor Brack of the Führer Chancellery, also had some knowledge of the state of Jewish policy by March 1941. Brack was a well-informed observer, an old acquaintance of Himmler, and a colonel in the SS. In postwar interrogations he certainly tried at times to give testimony favorable to himself, but he had no particular interest in giving false testimony regarding dates. Brack's testimony, combined with one key surviving original document, can help us clarify the meaning of Eichmann's comments at the Propaganda Ministry.

After Brack explained that he and two close colleagues had lobbied for shipment of Jews to Madagascar and mass sterilization of Jews as alternatives to mass murder, American interrogator Fred Rodell summed up:

> Rodell: There was a general program to kill all Jews. To find a way out, your side made two suggestions: 1) that with Madagascar; and 2) sterilization. Was that the sense?
> Brack: Yes, that was the sense. . . .
> Rodell: When was that approximately?
> Brack: It could have been the beginning of [19]41.
> Rodell: What happened as a result?
> Brack: [Both suggestions were rejected. Reichsleiter Philipp Bouhler, head of the Führer Chancellery, said with regard to sterilization] the Führer wanted nothing to do with it. I worked further on this project and made a new approach to the Reich Führer SS.

Brack was then shown a document that he identified as his—a letter of March 28, 1941, to Himmler describing experiments with X-ray sterilization and recommending it as feasible for three to four thousand persons per day.[9] The document provides essential corroboration of Brack's dating of developments on Jewish policy in early 1941. One week after Eichmann's comments at the Propaganda Ministry, Brack was trying, apparently for the third time (Madagascar plus two efforts regarding sterilization), to get approval for an alternative to mass murder. So the general conception of mass extermination as the solution of the Jewish Question appears well advanced by March 1941, which makes good sense. Some preliminary planning had to precede operational decisions in the summer of 1941.

I will now focus upon the period December 1940–January 1941 in an attempt to recreate in chronological order the contacts, climate, and context of policy at the top of the SS. The weight of evidence, which is admittedly and inevitably fragmentary in many places, will show that Himmler and Heydrich were concerned not simply with short-term, limited objectives for newly acquired German provinces, but with broader racial goals fully consistent with Hitler's grandiose rhetoric.

On December 9 Himmler spent the afternoon and evening with Göring at the latter's estate at Rominten, discussing a variety of subjects, such as the war against England and the SS's economic operations in concentration camps. (Although they spent ten hours together, Himmler kept only one page of fragmentary notes.)[10] On December 10 Himmler gave a speech at the meeting of Reichsleiter and Gauleiter in Berlin, of which only his handwritten notes survive. He emphasized the need to make the eastern provinces German by excluding seven of the eight million non-Germans there. He called for merciless German domination and for struggle against the Polish intelligentsia. The General Government, he said, would become a reservoir for seasonal laborers whom Germany could exploit. He mentioned a Jewish emigration (Judenauswanderung) that would leave more space for Poles. Himmler did not specify where Jews would go, but he clearly did not want them to remain in Poland, although Eichmann later, in March 1941, spoke of a *final* evacuation to Poland.

Interestingly, some six weeks before Himmler's speech, the RSHA had banned Jewish emigration from Poland, a fact Himmler apparently did not mention.[11]

Was Himmler perhaps thinking of Madagascar for the Jews? The British fleet lay between the continent and Madagascar. By mid-September 1940 it had became clear that Britain would not submit and that Hitler would not risk an invasion of the British Isles. It did not take a genius to see by late 1940 that Madagascar was not going to work. (Brack's promotion of Madagascar had come before the end of 1940, he said.)[12]

After a brief trip to Braunschweig and to the Netherlands, Himmler then headed to his castle at Wewelsburg, near Paderborn, for several days with the SS elite. At the Nuremberg trials, Erich van dem Bach-Zelewski referred to a speech made by Himmler during this meeting or the next such meeting at Wewelsburg. The Reich Führer SS declared openly that one purpose of the forthcoming campaign against the Soviet Union was to decimate the Slavic population by some thirty million people.[13]

On December 18, the day Hitler signed the orders authorizing Operation Barbarossa, Himmler gave a speech to assembled Waffen-SS commanders in Berlin. He emphasized the interdependence of all parts of the SS, warned against slighting the Death's Head units formed out of the concentration camp guards, and called for unconditional obedience. That evening he went to the Reich Chancellery. There is no record of who else (besides Hitler) was present or exactly what was discussed. On the following day Himmler met with Heydrich, and on the next day, among others, with Oswald Pohl, head of the SS Budget and Construction Office.[14]

On January 2, 1941, Heydrich's office sent out a memo to various RSHA, Security Police, and SD offices announcing that Himmler had approved the establishment of a severity scale within the concentration camp system for different categories of prisoners. Prisoners in "protective custody" clearly capable of rehabilitation, for example, were to be sent to Dachau, Sachsenhausen, and "Auschwitz I." Severely incriminated prisoners who might still possibly be "educated" and rehabilitated would be sent to Auschwitz II and three other camps.[15] There was a particularly unusual element to this announcement: at the time, there was only one camp at Auschwitz. Heydrich already knew that Himmler would soon order an expansion.

A few weeks later Eichmann's close colleague in the Jewish section of the RSHA, Theodor Dannecker, disclosed additional plans. Dannecker had just come to Paris and wanted to establish a Central Jewish Office there to coordinate and control policy for all of France. Although Dannecker found willing allies in Otto Abetz and key German embassy officials, generally uncooperative German military authorities had strong influence in the occupied zone, and there were French officials at Vichy to deal with.[16] Dannecker had to lay out his claim to superior authority.

In a January 21, 1941, memo Dannecker disclosed that the Führer wanted a final solution (endgültige Lösung) of the Jewish Question after the war in all parts of Europe ruled or controlled by Germany. Hitler, through Himmler and Göring, had given Reinhard Heydrich the task of developing a Final Solution project (Endlösungsprojekt). On the grounds of its extensive experience in Jewish matters and "thanks to long-term preparatory work" (dank der seit längerer Zeit geleisteten Vorarbeiten), Heydrich's office had then worked out the essential features of this project, which *now* [my emphasis] lay before the Führer and Göring.[17] We know from

Brack's aforementioned testimony (and common sense) that this plan could not have been the Madagascar Plan. We know that Eichmann (in the mid-March meeting at the Propaganda Ministry) had also spoken of Hitler's authorization of Heydrich, and of Heydrich's submission, in early to mid-January, of a proposal to the Führer. The timing given by Eichmann matches Dannecker's memo perfectly. With two well-informed sources in agreement, we are entitled to conclude that Heydrich had already submitted a proposal; it was in the Führer's hands before the end of January.[18]

Taken together, Dannecker's and Eichmann's comments reveal a great deal. Dannecker specified a continentwide program based on past experience: the SS had long since planned to separate Jews from the surrounding population, make use of adult Jewish males for hard labor, and to kill some Jews.[19] Eichmann spoke of a "final evacuation"; Poland was not to be a transit point. Yet a Jewish "reservation" in Poland would, in Nazi eyes, threaten the security of German occupation forces and settlements in the East.

There was only one logical conclusion—Europe's Jews were to disappear in the East, even if neither Eichmann nor Dannecker spelled out precisely how that would happen. They could hardly afford to be explicit. Even the now famous July 31, 1941, document in which Göring "authorized" Heydrich to proceed against the Jews on a continentwide basis does not go beyond use of the terms "Final Solution" and "total solution" of the Jewish Question.[20]

Browning elsewhere cautiously accepts the logical and lethal implications of the July 31 mention of a Final Solution. He also concludes that in the summer of 1941, probably in July, Hitler authorized the preparation of a plan for the mass murder of all European Jews.[21] In other words, Browning assumes that in July 1941 Heydrich and Göring knew the real or ultimate meaning of Final Solution, whereas in January 1941 Dannecker could not have known it, and in March Eichmann's comments were supposedly not precisely recorded.

By this logic, must we also discount Walter Schellenberg's May 20, 1941, reference to the "surely approaching Final Solution of the Jewish Question?"[22] The well-informed Schellenberg, soon to become the head of the Foreign Intelligence division (Amt VI) of the RSHA, was still in Division IV (Gestapo) in the spring of 1941. In short, there is linguistic continuity here among knowledgeable RSHA officials, and the burden of proof is on him or her who wishes to show that these early 1941 terms did not mean then what they meant in July 1941. There is also independent testimony from 1942 of Hitler's formal authorization, in January 1941, of a plan that it was said would make Germany "judenfrei" before the end of 1942. Dr. Carl J. Burckhardt was told independently by two high German officials, whom he trusted implicitly, that they had both seen such an order. One was said to be a high official in the Foreign Ministry, the other in the War Ministry.[23]

A flurry of events in late January suggests that urgent and important matters were under consideration then. On January 24 Heydrich went out to Göring's estate at Carinhall to give a presentation for more than two hours. Shortly afterwards, Göring left for Berlin, where he met jointly with Himmler and Heydrich. That same evening he left for Berchtesgaden, and the next day he spent the afternoon and much of the evening alone with the Führer.[24] Himmler had been scheduled to leave on a trip to Norway on January 27, but he postponed his departure for one day.[25] The content of these meetings by the key authorities on the Final Solution went unrecorded—or at least no notes of them have survived.

In a speech in the Berlin Sportpalast on January 30, 1941, the eighth anniversary of the Nazi seizure of power, Hitler referred to his prophecy two years earlier: if Jewry brought about another general war in Europe, the result would be the end of the Jewish role in Europe. (This was actually a toned-down summary of a portion of Hitler's January 30, 1939, speech, in which he had forecast the destruction of the Jewish race.) He added that the Jews might have laughed at his prophecy and that they might still be laughing. The coming months and years would show, however, that he had foreseen things correctly. He looked forward to the day when even Germany's current enemies would join the front against international Jewish exploitation and parasitism.[26] Adolf Hitler hardly sounded as if he were giving pragmatic considerations greater weight than racial experimentation.

To look to Goebbels or Hans Frank for evidence of the unformed state of Jewish policy in March 1941 can be misleading. For reasons some of which Browning himself has already adduced in a past dispute with Martin Broszat,[27] Goebbels's diary and (most non-SS sources) do not provide effective insight into emerging SS programs. Recent scholarship has clearly demonstrated the often bitter rivalry between Himmler and other Nazi leaders and their respective agencies. It was not common practice in the SS/RSHA bureaucracy to give other government and party agencies information about SS plans before it was absolutely necessary: Himmler used to react most strongly against such carelessness.[28]

We have a perfect example of how Himmler and Heydrich required secrecy amidst the organizational competition over Jewish policy, though it comes from early August 1941. After the Reich Commissariat Ostland formulated temporary guidelines for the handling of the Jewish problem there, Franz Stahlecker, head of Einsatzgruppe A, issued a blistering critique on the grounds that the Ostland civil authorities were insufficiently radical. In the process Stahlecker revealed that on the Jewish Question the Security Police had received fundamental orders that were not to be spelled out in writing. They were connected, however, he said, with the impending complete purge of Jews from Europe.[29] Such a ban on explicit statements in writing helps to clarify the significance of ambiguous language, euphemisms, and camouflage in early 1941 documents as well. Given Stahlecker's statement, any scholar who requires a signed, detailed, and completely unambiguous blueprint for extermination as the only acceptable evidence of advance planning is creating an artificial standard. Himmler and Heydrich did not operate in this manner.

Did the early 1941 SS plans for a Final Solution go beyond a general conception of liquidation of millions of Jews in the East? Early hints about mass extermination camps located at particular sites surface with Himmler's March 1, 1941, order to Rudolf Höss to establish a larger camp at Auschwitz-Birkenau for "prisoners of war," and Himmler's April 1941 comment that he had a new task in mind for Odilo Globocnik, the man soon put in charge of Operation Reinhard.[30]

But whenever the sites were designated, the commitment to plan carefully emerges quite clearly from Dannecker's January 21, 1941, memorandum in which he mentioned Heydrich's Final Solution project. Dannecker had added that implementation would require a huge effort, the success of which could be guaranteed only through the most careful preparations regarding both the deportations and the "settlement action" (Ansiedlungsaktion) in territory still to be determined.[31] This Final Solution project was to be *anything but improvised.*

To my knowledge, neither Heydrich nor Himmler referred directly to the date of plans for the Final Solution or of Hitler's authorization of it in a form that has reached posterity. But in November 1941, at a time when most of the specialists agree that the Final Solution was well underway, Heydrich did cast some light on whether his mandate was consistent over time. In an irritated letter to Quartermaster-General Eduard Wagner about the noncooperation of military authorities in occupied France with regard to Jewish policy, Heydrich asserted his authority and declared that the "political significance of the measures taken was fully clear to me, since *years earlier* [my emphasis] I was entrusted with the preparation of the Final Solution in Europe" (*Der politischen Tragweite der getroffenen Massnahmen war ich mir voll bewusst, zumal ich seit Jahren damit beauftragt bin, die Endlösung der Judenfrage in Europa vorzubereiten).*[32] At the level of SS plans, there was a tendency to think big, not small, and long-term as well as short-term. That tendency did not start suddenly in the summer of 1941.

The existence of early SS plans for a Final Solution undercuts several different interpretations. Those scholars who had discounted Hitler's fulminations against the Jewish menace as empty rhetoric have to confront the fact that Himmler, Heydrich, Müller, and their subordinates were taking early, if not necessarily irreversible, steps to translate racial utopia into reality. Browning's stress on Hitler's euphoria of victory in July and October 1941 might conceivably help to explain the timing of some SS operational moves, but it would be misleading to deduce much about fundamental motives from anything in July and October; plans were already on the table and in Hitler's hands in January. Finally, the notion that Nazi Germany turned to genocide as a last resort, only after all other plans had been tried and had failed, and after Germany's fortunes in the war had turned bleak, now looks simply ludicrous.

NOTES

I am grateful to James F. Harris, Konrad Kwiet, and Gerald Fleming for their comments on a draft of this article.

1. Konrad Kwiet, "Judenverfolgung und Judenvernichtung im Dritten Reich: Ein historiographischer Überblick," in Dan Diner, ed., *Ist der Nationalsozialismus Geschichte? Zu Historisierung und Historikerstreit* (Frankfurt/M., 1988), pp. 237–64. See also a number of the papers from the Wiener Library's Conference on the Final Solution (January 1992), now published as David Cesarani, ed., *The Final Solution: Origins and Implementation* (London, 1993).

2. Henry Friedlander, "Euthanasia and the Final Solution," in *Final Solution*, ed. Cesarani, p. 2.

3. Götz Aly and Susanne Heim, *Vordenker der Vernichtung: Auschwitz und die deutsche Pläne für eine neue europäische Ordnung* (Hamburg, 1991), as well as numerous articles.

4. Notiz Betrifft: Evakuierung der Juden aus Berlin, March 21, 1941, United States National Archives (NA), Record Group (RG) 242, Microfilm Series T-81/676/5485604.

Christopher R. Browning, *The Path to Genocide: Essays on Launching the Final Solution* (Cambridge, 1992), pp. 93–99.

5. Gerald Fleming, *Hitler and the Final Solution* (Berkeley, 1984), p. 21.

6. Notiz, March 21, 1941, NA RG 242, T-81/R676/5485604.

7. Browning, *Path to Genocide*, pp. 94–99.

8. Friedlander, "Euthanasia," esp. pp. 2–4; Fleming, *Hitler and the Final Solution*, pp. 21–22. Fleming also argues convincingly that Hitler was generally secretive.

9. Interrogation of Viktor Brack, September 13, 1946, NA RG 238, Microfilm Series M-1019/R8/982–85. Brack to Himmler, March 28, 1941, NA RG 238, NO-203.

10. Himmler's notes of meeting, NA RG 242, T-175/R94/2615303.

11. NA RG 242, T-580/R37. On the RSHA decree, see Richard Breitman, *The Architect of Genocide: Himmler and the Final Solution*, 2nd ed. (Hanover, NH, 1992), p. 142.

12. Breitman, *Architect of Genocide*, p. 141.

13. Bach-Zelewski's testimony, January 7, 1946, International Military Tribunal, *Trial of the Major War Criminals before the International Military Tribunal* (Nuremberg, 1947), vol. 4, p. 482. Bach-Zelewski remembered this meeting as having taken place at the beginning of 1941. The most likely alternative to December 1940—Himmler's next gathering at Wewelsburg—is mid-June 1941. See Himmler's appointment book for 1941 at the Center for the Preservation of Historical Documents, Moscow (hereafter Center–Moscow), 1372-5-23. There is now, in 1998, additional evidence to prefer the mid-June date as the occasion for this discussion.

14. Himmler's appointment book, NA RG 242, T-580/R38A. Notes of speech in NA RG 242, T-175/R112/2636892–2636896.

15. NA RG 238, NO-743.

16. See John P. Fox, "German Bureaucrat or Nazified Ideologue? Ambassador Otto Abetz and Hitler's Anti-Jewish Policies 1940–44," in *Power, Personalities, and Policies: Essays in Honour of Donald Cameron Watt*, ed. Michael Graham Fry (London, 1993), esp. pp. 193–95.

17. Dannecker's memo, "Zentrales Judenamt," Paris, January 21, 1941, reprinted in Serge Klarsfeld, *Vichy-Auschwitz: Die Zusammenarbeit der deutschen und französischen Behörden bei der "Endlösung der Judenfrage" in Frankreich* (Nördlingen, 1989), pp. 361–63. I am very grateful to John P. Fox for calling my attention to this document.

18. Precisely how and when this occurred is unclear. Himmler's appointment book does not indicate a meeting with Hitler from January 4 until Himmler left for Norway at the end of the month (Center–Moscow).

19. Breitman, *Architect of Genocide*, esp. p. 64.

20. NA RG 238, PS-710 The original of this document is in Heydrich's SS File, Berlin Document Center. For a published translation, see Raul Hilberg, ed., *Documents of Destruction: Germany and Jewry, 1933–45* (London, 1982), pp. 88–89.

21. Christopher R. Browning, *Fateful Months: Essays on the Emergence of the Final Solution* (New York, 1985), p. 22. Browning's comment on the document is: "However uncertain the origins of the July authorization and however vague the phraseology about the fate intended for the Jews, this much is known. It was signed by Göring, who two weeks later expressed the opinion that 'the Jews in the territories dominated by Germany had nothing more to seek.' Göring did not spell out their fate further, except to say that where Jews had to be allowed to work, it could only be in closely guarded labor camps and that he preferred Jews be hanged rather than shot, as the latter was too honorable a death. An impending mass expulsion of Jews into Russia was neither mentioned nor implied." Regarding Hitler's authorization, probably in July 1941, see Browning, *Path to Genocide*, p. 25.

22. NA RG 238, NG-3104.

23. Paul C. Squire interview with Dr. Carl J. Burckhardt, November 7, 1942, NA RG 84, American Consulate Geneva, Confidential File 1942, 800; Harrison to Undersecretary of State, Personal, November 23, 1942, NA, RG 59, 740.00116 E. W. 1939/653.

24. Hermann Weiss, "Die Aufzeichnungen Hermann Görings im Institut für Zeitgeschichte," *Vierteljahrshefte für Zeitgeschichte* 31 (1983): 366.

25. Himmler's scheduled itinerary, NA RG 242, T-175/R112/2637759. But Brandt's log shows that Himmler remained in Berlin through January 28; NA RG 242, T-580, R39A and Himmler's appointment book for 1941 confirm his departure on January 28 (Center–Moscow, 1372-5-23).

26. Excerpt from the speech in Max Domarus, *Hitler, Reden und Proklamationen 1932–1945* (Munich, 1965), vol. 2, pt. 2, pp. 1663–64.

27. Christopher R. Browning, "A Reply to Martin Broszat Concerning the Origins of the Final Solution," *Simon Wiesenthal Center Annual* 1 (1984): esp. pp. 115–16.

28. Breitman, *Architect of Genocide*, esp. pp. 73.

29. Hermann Graml, "Zur Genesis der Endlösung," in Walter H. Pehle, ed., *Der Judenpogrom 1938: Von der "Reichskristallnacht" zum Judenmord* (Frankfurt/M., 1988), p. 170. This document was discovered by Gerald Fleming in the Riga Archives of the former Soviet Union.

30. Breitman, *Architect of Genocide*, pp. 156–58.

31. See note 17 above.

32. Reprinted by Klarsfeld, *Vichy-Auschwitz*, pp. 369–70. I am grateful to Betty Shave for calling my attention to this document.

Jews dropped, as did the relative presence of Jews on managing or supervisory boards. One need only recall the examples of AEG, Agfa, Kaufhof, Salamander, the Mosse and Sonnemann-Simon publishing houses, and the Commerz and Dresdner banks—over all of which Jewish shareholders or chief executives lost control between 1925 and 1932—to suggest the strength of the trend.[7]

Partly in consequence, the leaders of German big business had little in the way of a collective personal or economic interest in "Aryanization" at the beginning of the Third Reich. Not only were very few of the approximately 100,000 Jewish-owned economic operations in the country of sufficient size or importance to attract the avarice of the nation's major firms, but most of the corporate barons had served with Jews in the war, rubbed elbows with them in professional life, found them loyal and cooperative in cartels and interest groups, had first- or second-hand experience with intermarriage, and had generally come to recognize the absurdity of group vilification.[8] Of course, there were bigots among them, but they were usually of the snobbish rather than the racist type. The prevailing tendency was to complain against allegedly corrupting Jewish influences in cultural rather than economic life, to distinguish sharply between supposedly uncouth immigrant or lower class Jews and the native-born or well-educated ones, and to cite acquaintances and colleagues as exceptions to prevalent derogatory stereotypes. Even the bigots tended to draw a line between acceptable restrictions on the future activities of Jews—usually in the form of some sort of quota system for professional schools and jobs—and impermissable assaults on their current livelihoods and status.[9] Narrow-minded by the standards of our day, the leaders of the nation's largest enterprises were generally moderate, sometimes even liberal, by the standards of their own. Unfortunately, they were also prepared on the basis of such views only to decry discrimination in their own sphere of action and against particular individuals, but not to stand up against the general practice.

The best indications of the attitude of German corporate magnates toward Nazi antisemitism in 1933 are the well-documented scrupulousness with which Hitler long avoided that theme in addressing them and the frequency with which some of them nonetheless took issue with blanket racial persecution in the months surrounding his appointment as Chancellor. Of course, such executives as Albert Vögler, Paul Reusch, Emil Kirdorf, Hermann Bücher, Carl and Robert Bosch, Gustav Krupp von Bohlen und Halbach, and Carl-Friedrich von Siemens usually made their cases in pragmatic terms, since they were not immune to certain forms of prejudice and had learned that arguments from morality and decency cut no ice with the Nazis. They therefore paid some form of lip service to the party's rationales for discrimination before stressing that neither the depressed German economy nor the insecure new Hitler government could afford the material losses that persecution and foreign reprisals to it would entail. As an aged, retired, and long-time party member, only Kirdorf dared, after Hitler's accession, to express his opposition both publicly and in a form that flatly contradicted Nazi propaganda. In a letter published by the *Rheinische Zeitung*, he denounced calls to remove Jews from leading economic posts as a "stab in the back of a large number of men who have served Germany." But, whether prudent or bold in their statements, all of these figures entered the Third Reich believing that personal loyalty and professional duty required them to reject attacks on Jewish entrepreneurs and the dismissal of employees or board members at home or abroad on grounds of their descent.[10]

In the tumultuous early months of 1933, however, these men could neither control events nor speak for all German firms. As zealous Nazis popped up within managements and as labor or consumer representatives and stormtroopers invaded offices, boardrooms, and shareholders' meetings across the country, demands for the removal of Jewish employees, directors, and even owners became a centerpiece of the so-called "National Revolution."[11] The most vulnerable companies knuckled under, especially as the labor courts began sanctioning abrogations of contracts based on concern for the security or sales of an enterprise.[12] Thus, the often heavily in-debted firms that drew the fire of small shopkeepers and the SA (above all, the department and retail chain stores and the breweries), along with the state-owned enterprises and the ones that were dependent on government largesse or goodwill (e.g., the major construction firms, automakers, and the big banks)—all these launched purges that continued into 1934.[13] Under the prevailing conditions, even Carl Bosch of IG Farben, the nation's biggest firm, could not prevent four of the Jewish members of his supervisory board from resigning in early 1933, and he saw no alternative to transfering abroad some Jewish executives whose functions in-volved them with government agencies that refused to work with them.[14] At predomi-nantly Jewish-owned firms that lived off orders from public agencies or organiza-tions, some principal shareholders, such as Alfred Orenstein of the Orenstein & Koppel machine-building firm, could hang on only by handing over their voting rights to a Nazi-approved trustee.[15]

From behind the scenes, nonetheless, some of the nation's leading managers continued to seek means of limiting Nazi depradations. That was the purpose of a project devised under the auspices of Max Warburg, a Jewish banker from Hamburg, and a group of Jewish and gentile businessmen he assembled, including Krupp von Bohlen, von Siemens, Carl Bosch, and Kurt Schmitt, who was the head of the Allianz insurance firm until he became Economics Minister in June 1933. Between April and August of that year, they reached agreement on a plan that they intended "to forward to a responsible office when the participants thought the moment had arrived."[16] Its central feature, a proposal to funnel Jewish young people increasingly into prepara-tion for manual rather than mental labor, especially in agriculture, echoed the ideas various Jewish groups had been advancing since the early 1920s as antidotes to declining urban incomes and enduring German prejudice.[17] Though the scheme met the Nazis halfway by admitting that German Jewry's occupational distribution required some sort of remedy, it also challenged party ideology and intentions in fundamental respects. First, the plan posited that the existing distribution was a product of culture and history, not race and conspiracy, hence that changing it would lessen differences between gentile and Jewish Germans and lay the basis for long-range harmony. Second, the businessmen stipulated that in the meantime each "patriotic non-Aryan" should continue in his profession to "enjoy the same rank and the same respect as every man." Third, the group's final memorandum stressed the indivisibility of "Aryan" and "non-Aryan" economic interests, arguing that attacks on the latter were bound to have adverse effects in both principle and practice on the former.[18]

This Warburg memorandum was never formally delivered, not least because national policy, under the influence of Schmitt and Hjalmar Schacht, the new president of the National Bank, seemed in the latter half of 1933 to turn in the desired direction.[19] The Cabinet at that time specifically rejected various suggested means of pressuring Jewish firms out of business, such as denial of access to assorted forms of credit, to government contracts, and to the stock markets. It also banned inquiries into the ethnic backgrounds of managers and owners doing business with government agencies.[20] As if on cue, the labor courts reversed their earlier willingness to sanction the dismissal of Jewish employees simply because Nazi coworkers or customers demanded it.[21] At the end of the year, the Economics and Interior Ministries jointly issued a decree exempting commercial activities from all racial regulations passed to govern other walks of life during the preceding eleven months.[22] There seemed to be good grounds to hope that the Third Reich would henceforth follow the course recommended by the IG Farben-owned *Frankfurter Zeitung* in June 1934: "Now that German non-Aryans have been excluded from all professions to which the state assigns particular importance in the political and ideological structure, the time must finally come to assure non-Aryans a sphere in which their activities are free and in which they are not regarded by the people as enemies."[23]

These governmental decisions were, however, widely evaded and abused during the ensuing four years. To be sure, on both practical and ideological grounds, the Nazis refrained from a centrally directed and thorough-going offensive against most of the "commanding heights" of Jewish economic activity in Germany and concentrated, more or less surreptitiously, on driving small-scale Jewish proprietors, especially merchants, out of business.[24] Nonetheless, the experiences of the Leonard and Hermann Tietz department store chains and the Ullstein publishing house in 1933–1934 make clear that when the regime invested major Jewish-led firms with political importance, as in the cases of large retail outlets and newspapers, it did not hesitate to insist on prompt Aryanization at confiscatory prices.[25] Nazi officials were only slightly less direct and more patient in targeting Jewish-owned military and civilian contractors.[26] Moreover, the party did not cease checking into the ethnicity of corporate managers and owners or finding ways of harming the business of recalcitrant firms, especially after the Supreme Court cleared the way once more in 1935 for dismissals on "racial" grounds.[27]

Consequently, for several years after the onslaught of 1933 subsided, the policy of large firms toward their Jewish personnel followed a halting, outwardly arbitrary course, which reflected employers' evolving perceptions of their emotional or economic interests. Many major enterprises seem to have used Nazi antisemitism as an excuse for buying out or letting the contracts of less-valued, well-liked, long-standing, or prominent Jewish employees lapse, but to have clung to those who satisfied these standards until political harassment tipped the balance against retention. Thus, individuals defined by the Nuremberg Laws as Jews were still serving on the managing and/or supervisory boards of, for instance, Mannesmann, IG Farben, Rheinstahl, AEG, Waldhof, Feldmühle, and the Berliner Handels-Gesellschaft in early 1938.[28] Even the Nazified Dresdner Bank still had 100 to 150 Jewish employees in Berlin in 1936, and five Jewish directors retained their posts until the period 1938–1940.[29] However, so long as no coordinated opposition on grounds of principle could or would take shape, these examples represented mere holding actions. Unevenly but inexorably Nazi threats to disrupt corporations' production and sales expanded the number of non-Jewish executives who believed that professional duty required abandoning rather than defending non-Aryan colleagues.

In distinct ways, events at the Porzellanfabrik L. Hutschenreuther AG of Selb in Bavaria and the Gesellschaft für Elektrische Unternehmungen (Gesfürel)/Ludwig Loewe AG of Berlin illustrate how the process of attrition functioned. At Hutschenreuther, when party delegates at the plant explicitly demanded the "Gleichschaltung" of the supervisory board in October 1933, the panicky management urged compliance. Franz Urbig, the supervisory board chairman from the Deutsche Bank, which voted over half the firm's stock, thereupon tried to persuade some of the seven Jewish members to resign for the good of the firm. Confronted, however, by the vehement opposition of one such potential victim, Eugen Schweisheimer, he refused to force the issue so long as the composition of the boards at the main rival enterprise left the party no real alternative. But, by November 1934, Rosenthal porcelain had completed its purge, and the party Kreisleiter in Selb had refocused his pressure directly on Urbig, making the issue a test of his bank's power and political loyalty. This had the desired effect. Late in the month, the banker carried out a reorganization that deprived all but one of the Jews of their seats. Reproached once more by Schweisheimer, Urbig defended himself in pragmatic terms no doubt echoed by many gentile business executives at the time:

> No one aspires to do unpleasant things. One tackles them, when one has to or when one wants to avoid the charge of having been blind to events in the wider world. . . . My experiences and observations in diverse professional positions have shown me that one cannot see the matter before us as one wishes to, but only as it—despite all ministerial pronouncements—in reality is.[30]

The gradual exclusion of Erich and Egon Loewe from the company that bore their family's name demonstrates that the party sometimes needed to exert far less overt forms of pressure in order to bring about a change of heart on the part of executives who earlier had maintained solidarity with their Jewish colleagues. In 1936–1937, Kurt Schmitt and Hermann Bücher were the chairmen, respectively, of the supervisory and managing boards of the financially struggling AEG, the German equivalent to General Electric. Having sought to limit any purge of Jews in 1933, they now capitulated to Nazi racism as the price for recapitalizing their firm and acquiring control over the Loewes'. As originally conceived, a deal between the two corporations had involved the purchase of some 25 million marks of new AEG shares by the Gesfürel/Ludwig Loewe AG and the election of representatives of each firm to the other's boards. However, since the authors of the plan and designated representatives of Gesfürel, Erich Loewe and his banker George Solmssen, were both Jews by Nazi definitions, difficulties arose in obtaining the necessary official approvals for the transaction. As a result, in July 1936, Schmitt and Bücher summarily redrafted the proposed arrangements, in the process relegating Loewe to the supervisory rather than the managing board of AEG, excluding Solmssen from either body on "racial" grounds, and taking the occasion to end the terms of three other Jews. That broke the bureaucratic blockade, and ten months later, when both Loewes were driven from the management of Gesfürel by the local DAF (Deutsche Arbeitsfront) organization, Bücher took over undisputed leadership of that firm as well. Though Erich Loewe remained on AEG's supervisory board until early 1938, as did several other Jews, including Solmssen, on Gesfürel's, Bücher and Schmitt clearly had decided that the time for loyalty to persons and principles had passed.[31]

There is no need to review other such cases; between 1934 and 1937, they hardened into a general pattern. Most corporations sooner or later abandoned directors or employees whenever organs of the party or the regime got around to insisting on their removal. Though willing to write glowing references for those forced into retirement, the firms also moved to head off criticism from shareholders and the Nazi press, playing strictly by the book in determining pensions and severance payments. Sometimes a guilty conscience got the better of one executive or another, as when Karl Kimmich of the Deutsche Bank tried to organize a farewell breakfast at Gesfürel for the Loewes in 1937, "in order," as he put it, "that their departure not proceed so unkindly."[32] But these were mere gestures. By 1937, advancement within a major German firm had become out of the question for Jews, and those who remained did so, in effect, on sufferance. Yet something else must be said. In the early years of Nazi rule, one rarely finds in the surviving documents signs of the initiative for removal coming from firms' own managements. So far as can be determined from often surprisingly copious records, the dismissals were largely reactive and generally perceived internally as damaging to business, albeit less so than continuing trouble with the party would have been.

With regard to the other dimension of Aryanization, the acquisition of Jewish-owned companies and shares, an even more ambiguous, hesitant, defensive, and self-interested pattern of corporate behavior also crystallized in the first years of Nazi rule. Only about 30 percent of the major Jewish firms changed hands or went under between 1933 and the end of 1937, compared to over 60 percent of the small businesses, and of these roughly three hundred transactions, just twenty or so amounted to takeovers by German big businesses.[33] One reason for this situation was that the larger Jewish-owned private banks were not subjected to heavy official or financial pressure until near the end of this period, in part because many of their industrial clients stood by them.[34] Thus, of the roughly fifteen such firms Aryanized prior to September 1937, only one (Gebr. Arnhold) could be called a large enterprise, and only it and one other were taken over by a major bank.[35] A second source of the endurance of large-scale Jewish holdings was that the party and state authorities who harassed Jewish owners were willing in many cases to settle for their withdrawal from the managing to the supervisory boards or from both, while leaving their property rights—and usually their incomes and chances of reasserting control someday—intact.[36]

Nonetheless, would-be sellers appear to have greatly outnumbered interested corporate buyers.[37] A clue to why this was so may be provided by IG Farben's files on proferred acquisitions from 1933 to 1937. They indicate that while the firm was not unwilling to consider or to undertake Aryanizations, it generally rejected the handful of possibilities that came its way on the basis of "oft-discussed" but not otherwise specified grounds.[38] Whether most large firms hung back for purely commercial reasons, because of legal worries, or out of principle is impossible to say. In the banking sector, the limited economic attractiveness of the available properties and the likely damage to buyers' international reputations appear to have been inhibiting.[39] What the major enterprises seem *not* to have been doing was merely waiting for better terms; I have not found a single instance of such a firm later making an acquisition that it turned down in this period. In any case, hang back they did, with the result that the vast majority of takeovers in this period fell under two headings: 1) arrangements by which trusted gentile colleagues fronted for the Jewish owners; and 2) shakedowns by party bosses, often in collusion with opportunistic, empire-building, small firms, such as Horten and Neckarmann, or predatory private banks, such as Merck Finck and Richard Lenz.[40]

When one of the approximately one hundred largest German firms was involved, the terms of sale seem to have come closer to what was commercially fair than did most other transfers at the time, let alone later. This situation reflected the desire of buyers during the mid-1930s to shelter at least some of the profits of economic recovery in acquisitions and depreciation rather than in construction of new plants.[41] Thus, when Henkel GmbH of Düsseldorf in August 1934 gave 125 percent and 150 percent of par for two Jewish-owned packets of stock in the Norddeutsche Hefeindustrie AG that were trading at 110 to 112 percent, and when Unilever's principal German subsidiary behaved similarly in November 1935, both the Nazi and the business press attributed their actions to this sort of financial calculation.[42]

Of course, in the period 1933–1937, a few profiteers also emerged from the ranks of German big business. In particular, the Dresdner Bank began setting the standard for rapacity, largely because its conversion during the bank crisis of 1931–1932 into a virtually state-owned operation, coupled with the presence of ten Jews among its fifteen principal officers in 1933, had made it immediately and especially vulnerable to the penetration of Nazi personnel and policies.[43] Even as two Nazi protégés, Karl Rasche and Emil Meyer, were being elevated to the managing board, the bank's internal documents were being furnished to the police for use against Jews, and two junior associates were actively colluding with the Gestapo to strip Ignaz Nacher of his Engelhardt brewery concern, the second largest of its kind in the country.[44] By September 1934, when repeated intimidation ended in the Dresdner's acquisition of Nacher's core holdings at about 85 percent of their face value, the bank already had built up considerable experience at brokering the sale of Jewish stock packets.[45] One of the most blatant examples occurred a year later, when Rasche apparently played the decisive role in finally ousting Alfred Orenstein and other Jews from the management of Orenstein & Koppel, and then, presumably, in reselling Orenstein's shares.[46] The economic and political rewards of such activity proved so irresistible to the still-struggling bank that it opted, sometime late in 1936 or early in 1937, to establish a special section, led by Paul Binder and responsible to Alfred Busch of the managing board, to drum up Aryanization business.[47] Meanwhile, the Dresdner took advantage of the prevailing persecution not only to drive a hard bargain with the Jewish owners of the Gebr. Arnhold Bank's main branch in Dresden, who had been driven to sell out by the harassment of Gauleiter Mutschmann, but also then to renege on some terms of the sale while insisting on refunds concerning others.[48]

More typical, however, of both the motives and methods of takeovers by large firms during this period are the Degussa AG's well-documented Aryanizations of the Chemische-Pharmazeutische Fabrik Bad Homburg AG, the Degea AG (Auergesellschaft) of Berlin, and the Dr. L. C. Marquart AG of Beuel. In each case, pressure from Nazified agencies drove the owners to approach Degussa, with which they already had a business relationship, and Degussa not only paid at least the going and high market price of the selling firms' stock, but also initially retained the Jewish managers and former owners on the payrolls of its new subsidiaries. Similar terms generally characterized the other takeovers in this period by such firms as the United Steelworks, Siemens, and the Deutsche Bank, for which evidence is currently available.[49]

In sum, by late 1937, the leaders of most major German firms had reached arrangements with Nazi antisemitism that ran from the resigned to the callous. If they would not push to dispossess Jews, neither would they stand up for them. Like Hjalmar Schacht, most corporate executives had come to the self-exculpatory conclusion that the best they could achieve would be to draw the process of Aryanization out over a period of ten to fifteen years in order to minimize its unsettling effects on long-time associates, the stock market, and production and exports.[50] In so far as big business had a collective or common practice in the matter, that was it. On the eve of the rapid radicalization of Nazi racial policy that was to culminate in the Kristallnacht pogrom a year later, the only identifiable commercial pressure to drive the remaining Jewish executives and owners from German economic life was not coming from large firms. It emanated from the trade associations of smaller ones, which began seeking relief from tightening supplies of raw materials and foreign exchange by demanding that the allotments to Jewish competitors be cut off and redistributed.

Such agitation from below contributed little, however, to the striking intensification in November 1937 of the economic assault on the Jews. For Hitler, the controlling fact had become the need to ready the nation for a war that might quickly become opportune under any of several conceivable scenarios.[51] Within days of sketching these for his principal advisors at the famous Hossbach conference, he acted on his fantasy of the Jews as a fifth column by making three moves against the remnants of their economic activities: he fired Schacht as Economics Minister; he temporarily replaced him with Hermann Göring, who promptly decreed a series of measures for defining, detecting, and penalizing so-called "Jewish influence" over firms; and he authorized Gauleiter Julius Streicher to launch in Nüremberg during the Christmas season the first organized boycott of Jewish shops in Germany since April 1, 1933.[52] The starting gun for the long-delayed process of large-scale "Aryanization" was sounded at mid-month, when Herbert Göring and Wilhelm Keppler of Hitler's Chancellery summoned the chief agent in Berlin of the industrialist Friedrich Flick and passed the word that the time had come for him to spearhead the takeover of the huge mining operations owned by the Julius and Ignaz Petschek families. Often overlooked in the numerous accounts of Flick's subsequent, often unprincipled acquisitiveness is the revealing way in which it began—at the behest of the highest political authorities and implicitly as a precondition for their future goodwill.[53]

Over the next fifteen months, the onslaught against Jewish firms and executives signaled by these developments proved more far-reaching and cruel than all that had gone before. Such corporate resistance as remained simply collapsed under the weight of new laws that escalated from denying government contracts and raw material allocations to enterprises with Jewish board members, senior managers, and owners, to requiring their removal; from promoting the "voluntary" sale of Jewish-owned firms, to mandating their seizure and sale by the state.[54] By the middle of 1938, virtually all Jewish board members of major firms had lost their posts. As for large companies still owned by non-Aryans, the most that could be achieved was to get them assigned to reliable Christian associates who promised to hold them in trust, as in the cases of the Oppenheim Bank in Cologne or the Schocken Department Store chain of Leipzig, or to block their subordination to Nazi potentates, for example, at the Metallgesellschaft in Frankfurt.[55]

But there was a good deal less of even this sort of help extended to Jewish German entrepreneurs in this period than earlier, thanks largely to changes in the commercial world and its operating environment. By early 1938, newly ascendant enterprises in key industries and managers in many of the more established companies were opting to hitch their individual wagons to the star of Nazi policy, regardless of widespread reservations about it. This development reflected, above all, the implicit pressure exerted by growing state control over the economy. Quasi-public institutions, such as the regional state banks, notably the Badische and Sächsische banks, or the Reichs-Kredit-Gesellschaft and the Bank für Industrie-Obligationen, not to mention the Reichswerke Hermann Göring, stood ready to gobble up what private firms neglected.[56] At the same time, government regulations had become so complete that growth, profits, and market shares depended almost entirely on satisfying the regime, and increased allocations of key materials often could be obtained only by annexing another firm's quotas through acquisition.[57]

In this context, with massive Aryanization a given ordained from Berlin, and with sellers' bargaining positions weakened, many large firms plunged into the scramble for the spoils. Above all, they acted to prevent old or new rivals from coming away with more, and/or to prevent long-standing business ties from being upset by inept new owners.[58] In other words, Aryanization within Germany in 1938, as in the occupied lands later, became an illustration of one of the key motivating methods of Nazism, "the threat in cases of recalcitrance," as Hans Mommsen has put it, "to entrust the dirty work to another."[59]

Pivotal in the resulting goldrush was the response of the great banking corporations, notably the Deutsche, Dresdner, and Commerz banks. Here, too, behavior reflected the dynamics of commercial competition—not only among the big banks, but also between them and other financial sectors. For these firms now discerned in Aryanization a chance to offset two adverse trends of the mid-1930s: their declining relative share of total bank deposits nationwide, and their loss of proceeds from corporate stock issues that the Nazi regime largely had banned in order to funnel capital into government bonds.[60] Consequently, the big banks now competed intensely to collect brokerage commissions that came to .5 percent to 2 percent of the purchase price, to loan the necessary capital, to speculate on blocs of shares, to hold on to the regular business of client firms that were changing hands and/or to secure that of new owners, and even to make their own advantageous acquisitions.[61] The possible immediate rewards of success were exemplified by the 800,000 marks that the Berliner Handels-Gesellschaft and the Deutsche Bank divided for executing Mannesmann AG's takeover of the Hahnsche Werke in April 1938.[62] As an illustration of the proximate stakes, consider the transformation of the Norddeutsche Trikotwerke of Berlin and the Sigmund Göritz AG of Chemnitz into the Venus-Werke. The Deutsche Bank not only acquired some of the stock at 98 percent of par and later resold it at 148–52 percent, reaping some 92,000 marks in this fashion, but also promptly pocketed a fivefold increase in receipts from the new firm's business (from

2,783 Reichsmarks in the second half of 1938 to 12,364 in the first half of 1939).[63] Moreover, when the banks made their own takeovers, the gains showed up as assets rather than income, and sometimes at values greater than the prices paid for them.[64]

In the pursuit of such returns, the behavior of the big banks differed more in degree than kind. Not until January 1938, after the new urgency of the government's insistence on Aryanization became clear, did the relatively laggard and gentlemanly Deutsche bank begin following the Dresdner's example in soliciting lists of Aryanizable firms from its branches, then collating and distributing the results.[65] Although the headquarters still urged regional offices to handle their inquiries and intelligence with great discretion, it also made plain that "it is very important that the new business possibilities arising in connection with the changeover of non-Aryan firms be exploited and that care be taken not to lose old ties as a result of the . . . extremely active competition in this field."[66] Indeed, so large was the field of activity and so vigorous the competition that two leaders of the big banks, Carl Goetz of the Dresdner and Karl Kimmich of the Deutsche, each briefly entertained versions of the long-standing Nazi project for a single "Auffanggesellschaft" or consortium to buy up and resell Jewish-owned property and thus bring order to the situation. But the scheme smacked too much of state intrusion into economic life for the Deutsche Bank's managing board, and hence the rivalry for clients went on.[67]

Thus impelled, the Deutsche Bank had collected data on some seven hundred target firms by July; by the end of October, it had played the role of intermediary or financier in approximately three hundred and thirty Aryanizations; and by the close of the calendar year, it could take credit for assisting in probably seventy-five major takeovers, including those of such substantial firms as Roth-Händle (tobacco), Bachmann & Ladewig (textiles), and Adler & Oppenheimer (leather).[68] The Dresdner Bank meanwhile probably facilitated more, since it was readier to bend the normal requirements of creditworthiness on the part of buyers and, on occasion, to exploit the help of the Gestapo.[69]

How essential the large banks proved to be in takeovers of significant Jewish-owned enterprises is suggested by the surviving data on Aryanizations in the Frankfurt Industrie- und Handelskammer district. Among three hundred cases surveyed, the Dresdner and Deutsche banks were involved in only approximately 15 percent, but they provided 73 percent of the loans needed for all purchases (4.4 out of 6.0 million marks), and 40 percent of the credits extended for the startup costs of the new owners (2.0 out of 5.0 million marks).[70] As a general rule, the larger the capital requirements of a takeover, the greater the likelihood of involvement by one of the large banks. Thus, one may surmise that they played an instrumental role in most of the Aryanizations of the 747 substantial producers and 22 private banks listed by the *Jüdische Rundschau* between January and October 1938.[71]

The downward pressure on purchase prices during this free-for-all attested not only to the number and desperation of the sellers and the illiquidity of some of the largest buyers in consequence of the drives for armaments and autarky, but also to the regime's oversight of the sales.[72] Mistrusting both the Jewish owners and the "big concerns," the relevant party and state agencies strove to prevent either party from "profiting" by transactions. In this context, corporate negotiators had to walk a fine line between offering too much or too little.[73] From April 1938 on, neither the seller nor the buyer could hope for approval of a transaction involving firms organized as limited partnerships (GmbH or KG) unless it excluded any payment for "goodwill" and called for a price that fell roughly midway between (a) the sum of the average profits of the firm over the preceding three years, capitalized at an assumed interest rate (the "Ertragswert"), either before or after deduction of the annual wage paid to the owner; and (b) the worth of buildings, inventory, and supplies on hand (the "Substanzwert"). Any lesser price would result in the assessment of an "equalization payment" by the buyer to the state, any greater one in rejection of the proposed contract.[74] In September, the government further confined any impulse toward generosity by instructing the pertinent control offices to reject requests for price hikes that appeared to result from increased overhead costs stemming from overly generous Aryanization arrangements.[75] In rare instances, usually resulting from the international connections of the seller, some degree of flexibility seemed advisable; thus the Reich was willing to smooth Friedrich Flick's takeover of the Julius Petschek coal fields by permitting a rare and substantial, if not a fair, payment in scarce foreign exchange.[76] Always a possibility, however, was something like the government's reaction to the contract for the purchase of the Moos blouse factory in Buchau, when the responsible officials halved the Reichsmark figure on which the parties had agreed.[77]

Under these circumstances, the acquisitions from the summer of 1938 on were often the equivalent of fire sales, and the buyers knew it. Indicative of what could happen is the takeover by Zellstoff Waldhof AG of the remaining synthetic fiber and paper holdings of the Hartmann Group in September. For a mere 7.5 million marks, Waldhof obtained control over a network of firms in Germany, Austria, Poland, and the Balkans whose core operations had total sales of 42 million marks in 1937, reported assets of almost 26 million, and open and hidden reserves of almost 14 million marks. The price, a Waldhof internal report noted rather proudly, came to 150 percent of the face amount of the Hartmann stock, but only 86 percent of the buyer's estimate of the book value of the Hartmann holdings, 76 percent of the Group's own such estimate and asking price, and 48 percent of Waldhof's calculation of the current, real worth of what it was obtaining.[78] As this case suggests, the closest buyers would or could come to proceeding fairly, which they often did, was to pay more than the book value of a firm's stock, sometimes even the (admittedly, often by now depreciated) market value, or to overpay, which they did less often, for goods on hand or inventory.[79] Their only real choice, however, was *whether* to participate in the feeding frenzy, not on what terms, and that choice came down to a matter of corporate self-interest in the prevailing commercial and political setting.

Ironically, in joining the pillaging, many large firms ended up merely chasing their own tails. The banks, for instance, may have grossed millions from the process of Aryanization within Germany, but they netted far less. For every old debt they saved from default and every new mark they earned or kept their competitors from gaining, they also lost large funds through the liquidation of Jews' deposits. Sooner or later, for example, the state probably siphoned off nearly all of the 35 million marks in non-Aryan accounts at the Frankfurt branch of the Deutsche Bank as of November 1938, via emigration taxes and currency conversion at extortionist rates, the post-pogrom levy on the Jewish population, and the general confiscations from 1941 on.[80] Similarly, some corporate buyers perceived with annoyance what they dared articulate only indirectly: that they had been drawn into a revenue-raising program, one that maneuvered them into putting up the money for a process that turned Jews' fixed assets (plants) into liquid ones (purchase prices), which were then, in stages, taxed away by the regime.

Indeed, the biggest profiteer from Aryanization was indubitably the Nazi state, which eventually raked off 60–80 percent of the price paid for large-scale property transfers within the Reich, and a total of some 3 billion of the 7.1 billion marks in wealth that native and stateless Jews possessed according to the compulsory property declarations of April 1938, not to mention increased tax proceeds on stock transactions throughout 1938–1939.[81] Such receipts proved essential to the German rearmament effort, contributing some 5 percent of the national budget in the final year prior to the Second World War, precisely at a time when laggard sales of government bonds would otherwise have forced a cutback in military expenditures.[82] Moreover, the unleashing of competitive impulses against the Jews assured the regime of something less quantifiable but equally valuable: the fact that the transfers and confiscations occurred without appreciable damage to the German economy. The banks, for instance, found ways of insulating stock market prices from the sudden flood of Jewish-owned shares being sold in 1938–1939.[83] Once more, the carrot-and-stick method of the Third Reich paid off: the opportunity for gain combined with the desire to head off damage from radical hamhandedness mobilized Nazi and non-Nazi business executives alike to try to make the best of the given situation.

All in all, then, by the end of the great Aryanization wave in 1939, which is the less dramatic and frightful part of the history of corporate complicity in the Holocaust, the Nazi regime had succeeded in transforming Jewish colleagues from people whom many of the nation's business magnates had once thought it in their interest to defend, to people whom it was in their interest to exploit. Having done that, the Reich largely cut the major industrial firms out of the extension of Aryanization to the occupied countries, as the state developed ever more comprehensive means of administering the dispossession itself.[84] Intent on rationalizing production by liquidating as many Jewish-owned enterprises as possible and attaching vital remaining units to state-owned enterprises, the responsible offices consistently allotted what was left over to (more or less in descending order) politically well-connected small to mid-sized German firms, resident Germans, and foreign collaborators, leaving only a remnant to major German corporations. As a result, nearly all of their few acquisitions in occupied or satellite lands consisted of prewar subsidiaries or business partner firms in which Jews had been prominent.[85] Only the large German banks could post appreciable gains from Aryanization after 1939, again largely as brokers of assets that had been seized or bought at depressed prices from Jews, a fact of which they were well aware and which they treated as a matter of course.[86]

That does not mean, of course, that the biggest German corporations thus largely ceased to play a role in the persecution of the Jews. For one thing, money remained to be made from numerous ancillary services that the regime continued to seek from the private sector. Degussa AG, for example, earned considerable, though still indeterminable sums after 1939 from its role in the conversion into negotiable ingots of the billions of marks worth of gold and silver taken from Jews.[87] Having acquired on the cheap and purged the largely Jewish-led and owned Böhmische Union Bank of Prague, the Deutsche Bank then allowed that subsidiary to develop a cozy financial relationship with the ghetto camp at Theresienstadt. In July 1944, the BUB listed among its assets some twenty-five million marks from the so-called Emigration and Resettlement accounts of Jews incarcerated there; in October, another in-house tabulation showed fifty-five million marks in outstanding short-term loans at just over 2 percent interest for the administration of the camp.[88] Most infamously of all, there was the sale of Zyklon B gas to the death camps at Auschwitz and Majdanek by the Degesch company, a subsidiary of Degussa and IG Farben. That total receipts on the purchases by the former camp came to only about forty thousand marks serves as a shocking reminder of how cheaply firms could be enlisted in mass murder.[89]

Moreover, after 1939, the transformation of the stance of corporate leaders toward Jews went a vicious step further—to the attitude that it was in their interest to use up the Jews like any other factor of production. Remarkably, the surviving documents provide only a sketchy accounting of the use of Jewish slave labor by major German firms during the war. To be sure, among the hundreds of corporations to which nearly one-half million camp or ghetto inmates were yoked at the end of 1944, the greatest offenders were either the state-owned firms—such as BRABAG, the Hermann Göring works, and Volkswagen—or the munitions and arms makers in the narrowest sense: Dynamit Nobel, Rheinmetall-Borsig, Krupp, Messerschmitt, Heinkel, and Junkers. But by 1943, almost every major firm in Germany was woven into the military economy, so it is not surprising that BMW, AEG-Telefunken, Siemens, Daimler-Benz, and IG Farben were also among the principal exploiters. All of these enterprises put Jewish prisoners to work in existing factories as well as new ones erected near the ghettos and camps.[90] In every case, the laborers went unpaid; their so-called "wages" of three to eight marks per eleven- to twelve-hour day—depending on sex, age, and skills—went directly to the Reich Finance Ministry or agencies such as the Reichskommissariat Ostland, and the companies' additional costs came to some fraction of a mark per worker per day for food and the overhead charge for the unheated, overcrowded, verminous barracks and the surrounding fences in which the workers often were caged. While Nazi offices pocketed the substantial sums, the companies engaged in a literally vicious circle of maltreatment and low worker productivity. Slave labor at IG Farben's factories three miles east of Auschwitz cost the lives of about twenty-five thousand Jewish inmates and earned the Reich some twenty million marks.[91] Though researchers are making progress in this regard, we probably will never be able to get accurate comparable figures for myriad other installations.

If one looks away for a moment from the horrible consequences of corporate enslavement to concentrate on why it happened, the pattern of behavior that emerges nearly duplicates that which characterized the history of Aryanization. Initial rejection by every major company of Himmler's attempts to lease camp labor to them ever since 1934 was followed first—after 1940 in some quarters, after 1943 almost universally—by a conviction that the alternatives to accepting inmate labor had been exhausted, and then by a general rush by firms to get their share. Once more, it appeared, as in the process of Aryanization, that firms were trying to outdo each other in rapacity, and once more, they were. But here, too, the initial impulse to employ Jews compulsorily in German industry came from the Nazi bureaucracy and met with only gradually and unevenly abandoned reluctance on the part of large private firms, save in the cases of the Berlin factories most desperately short of workers, such as Siemens-Schuckert and Schering.[92] Once more, corporate reservations were phrased in pragmatic rather than principled terms, terms abandoned as the Nazi regime restructured the labor market in such a way that nonparticipation came to seem both disloyal and self-destructive, and hence unthinkable to a competitive capitalist.

Almost without deviation, German firms adjusted to the apparent imperatives of a situation in which 11 million workers had been called into uniform, a higher percentage of German women were already working in 1939 than was ever the case in the United States and Britain during the war, and 7.5 million conscripted foreigners appeared insufficient to generate the necessary production.[93] Plants began appealing for workers—at first mostly for construction projects, then increasingly in 1944–1945 for assembly line service—wherever they could be found.[94] Practical, patriotic, and preoccupied men, the responsible executives appear to have asked themselves few, if any, questions about what they were doing. They harkened, instead, to the urges of fear, corporate and professional advancement, and a "neurotic compulsion . . . to do their best in 'the national defensive struggle.'"[95] Having at one time recognized the moral and economic defects of the opportunity the Nazi regime offered, leaders of the nation's major corporations subsequently lost sight of both. And, in the final year of the war, such firms' recourse to labor from concentration camps grew even more insistent and vicious, as managers sought to transfer machinery valuable to postwar survival to underground locations and to keep plants operating as long as possible so as to avoid being called up for military duty.

Revealing as this dispiriting tale of corporate complicity is in its own right, it also holds important implications for our understanding of the readiness of so many Germans, in so many different capacities, to apply themselves to the persecution of the European Jews. The narrative presented here suggests that whatever the dimensions of antisemitism in Germany at the outset of the Third Reich, that ideological predisposition provided, at most, a necessary but not a sufficient condition for the success of the Nazi regime in turning its increasingly murderous intentions into society's collective project.[96] In microcosm, the behavior of German big business reminds us that, if hatred was the fuel that propelled Nazi Germany on the road to the Holocaust, that road was paved, not just by indifference, as Ian Kershaw has remarked, but by self-interest.[97] Had that self-interest been of business's own making, the subject of corporate involvement in the Holocaust could be left to the numerous simplifiers who have taken it up. But the historical record indicates that corporate complicity—like that of a good many Germans in other walks of life—developed over time and in a series of adaptations to prevailing, politically established cues. To say this is neither to create an alibi for big business nor to blur the moral boundaries between perpetrators, collaborators, resisters, and victims. It is to offer a reminder of how dictatorships work—and of how markets can work under one.

NOTES

1. Bundesarchiv, Abteilung Potsdam (hereafter BAP), 31.01, Reichswirtschaftsministerium, no. 8042, Dr. van Hees to Regierungspräsident, Wiesbaden, February 16, 1945.

2. Illustrative of the monographs are Arno Weckbecker, *Die Judenverfolgung in Heidelberg 1933–1945* (Heidelberg: C. F. Müller Juristischer Verlag, 1985); Hans Witek, "'Arisierungen' in Wien," in *NS-Herrschaft in Oesterreich 1938–1945*, ed. E. Talos, E. Hanisch, and W. Neugebauer (Vienna: Verlag für Gesellschaftskritik, 1988), pp. 199–216; Gerhard Kratzsch, *Der Gauwirtschaftsapparat der NSDAP. Menschenführung–'Arisierung'–Wehrwirtschaft im Gau Westfalen-Süd* (Münster: Aschendorff Verlag, 1989); and Stefan Mehl, *Das Reichsfinanzministerium und die Verfolgung der deutschen Juden 1933–1943* (Berlin, 1990). Among the indications of corporate openness are the access given by the Degussa AG for Peter Hayes, "Fritz Roessler and Nazism: The Observations of a German Industrialist, 1930–37," *Central European History* 20 (1987): 58–79; by BMW and MTU GmbH for Zdenek Zofka, "Allach-Sklaven für BMW," *Dachauer Hefte* 2 (1986): 68–78; by the Deutsche Bank for Lothar Gall et al., *Die Deutsche Bank 1870–1995* (Munich: C. H. Beck, 1995); by Daimler-Benz for Hans Pohl et al., *Die Daimler-Benz AG in den Jahren 1933 bis 1945* (Wiesbaden: Steiner, 1986), and Barbara Hopmann et al., *Zwangsarbeit bei Daimler-Benz* (Stuttgart: Steiner, 1994); and by Volkswagen to Hans Mommsen and Manfred Grieger for *Das Volkswagenwerk und seine Arbeiter im Dritten Reich* (Düsseldorf: ECON, 1996). In a somewhat different category is the recent product of access to the holdings of the Siemens-Archiv in Munich: Wilfried Feldenkirchen, *Siemens 1918–1945* (Munich: Piper, 1995).

3. Among the worst offenders to date are William Manchester, *The Arms of Krupp* (Boston: Litttle Brown, 1968), and the publications of the variously subtitled Hamburger Stiftung, for example, Angelika Ebbinghaus, ed., *Das Daimler-Benz-Buch* (Nördlingen: Franz Greno, 1987), Karl Heinz Roth and Michael Schmid, eds., *Die Daimler-Benz AG 1916–1948. Schlüsseldokumente zur Konzerngeschichte* (Nördlingen: Franz Greno, 1987), and the translations, outfitted with new introductions, of the investigative reports drawn up by the Finance Division of the American occupation authorities in 1945–1947: *O.M.G.U.S. Ermittlungen gegen die I.G. Farbenindustrie AG* (Nördlingen: Franz Greno, 1986); *O.M.G.U.S. Ermittlungen gegen die Deutsche Bank* (Nördlingen: Franz Greno, 1985); and *O.M.G.U.S. Ermittlungen gegen die Dresdner Bank* (Nördlingen: Franz Greno, 1986). For a powerful critique of the Stiftung's volumes on Daimler-Benz, see Volker Hentschel, "Daimler-Benz im Dritten Reich," *Vierteljahrschrift für Sozial- und Wirtschaftsgeschichte* 75 (1988): 74–100.

4. The firms encompassed in this essay by the term "big business" are the one hundred enterprises identified in Hannes Siegrist, "Deutsche Grossunternehmen vom späten 19. Jahrhundert bis zur Weimarer Republik," *Geschichte und Gesellschaft* 6 (1980): 92–102, or their successors, plus the principal banks, trading companies, and newly founded or foreign-owned entities as of the mid-1930s.

5. Obviously, while not conceived as a contribution to the debate set off by the publication of Daniel Jonah Goldhagen, *Hitler's Willing Executioners* (New York: Alfred A. Knopf, 1996), this essay can and should be read, in part, as such. I have taken more direct issue with that unfortunate book in "Because They Wanted To," *Jewish Star* (Chicago), June 14–27, 1996, pp. 7–8.

6. See Helmut Genschel, *Die Verdrängung der Juden aus der Wirtschaft im Dritten Reich* (Göttingen: Musterschmidt, 1966), pp. 19–31, 274–87; Donald Niewyk, *The Jews in Weimar Germany* (Baton Rouge: Louisiana State University Press, 1980), pp. 13–20, 41–42; Monika Richarz, ed., *Jüdisches Leben in Deutschland*, vol. 3: *Selbstzeugnisse zur Sozialgeschichte 1918–1945* (Stuttgart: Deutsche Verlags-Anstalt, 1982), pp. 14–25; Sarah Gordon, *Hitler, Germans, and the 'Jewish Question'* (Princeton: Princeton University Press, 1984), pp. 9–15; and Avraham Barkai, *Vom Boykott zur Entjudung* (Frankfurt/M.: Fischer Verlag, 1987), pp. 11–18 (published in English as *From Boycott to Annihilation: The Economic Struggle of German Jews 1933–1943* (Hanover, NH: University Press of New England, 1989]).

7. See Niewyk, *Jews in Weimar Germany*, p. 14; W. E. Mosse, *Jews in the German Economy*

1820–1935 (Oxford: Clarendon Press, 1987), pp. 325–33; idem, *The German-Jewish Economic Elite 1820–1935* (Oxford: Clarendon Press, 1989), pp. 97, 167–68; Hessisches Hauptstaatsarchiv, Wiesbaden (hereafter HHSA), Abteilung 483, no. 10960, Memo to Karl Eckardt, May 22, 1935; HHSA, Abt. 519, no. 131, AR 1, Westdeutsche Kaufhof AG, November 28, 1945; Peter Hayes, *Industry and Ideology: IG Farben in the Nazi Era* (New York: Cambridge University Press, 1987), pp. 28, 55–56; Peter de Mendelssohn, *Zeitungsstadt Berlin* (Frankfurt/M.: Ullstein, 1982), pp. 398–402, 463, 499–500; and Modris Eksteins, *The Limits of Reason* (London: Oxford University Press, 1975), pp. 105–106, 287–88, 301–303.

8. See Barkai, *Boykott zur Entjudung*, pp. 19–21; Wolfgang Benz, ed., *Die Juden in Deutschland 1933–1945* (Munich: C. H. Beck, 1989), pp. 304–305; Mosse, *Jews in the German Economy*, pp. 373–74; idem, *German-Jewish Economic Elite*, pp. 161–85, 338, 339, 342.

9. For examples, see Hayes, "Fritz Roessler and Nazism," *Central European History* 20 (1987): 73, and Paul Kleinewefers, *Jahrgang 1905* (Stuttgart: Seewald, 1984), p. 69.

10. See Mosse, *Jews in the German Economy*, pp. 343, 376–77; Henry Ashby Turner, Jr., *German Big Business and the Rise of Hitler* (New York: Oxford University Press, 1985), pp. 90–91, 94, 129–31, 337, 469–70 note 99; Hayes, *Industry and Ideology*, pp. 83–84, 92–94; Reinhard Neebe, *Grossindustrie, Staat und NSDAP 1930–1933* (Göttingen: Vandenhoeck & Ruprecht, 1981), p. 194; Siemens-Archiv, Munich (hereafter SAA), 4/Lf676, the letter prepared for circulation by Carl-Friedrich von Siemens, April 8, 1933, and his exchange of letters with Fritz Kranefuss, November 28–December 4, 1933; and, on Bücher and Bosch, the letters in BASF-Archiv, Ludwigshafen (hereafter BASF), Sig. W1.

11. See, most recently, Heinz Höhne, *Die Zeit der Illusionen* (Düsseldorf: Econ, 1992), pp. 69–75, 99–102.

12. See the summaries of the decisions of April 27, 1933 (8A AC 265/33) and May 2, 1933 (3 AC 322/23) in *Jüdische Rundschau*, June 20, 1933.

13. In general, see Genschel, *Verdrängung*, pp. 73–76. On Daimler-Benz, see Pohl et al., *Daimler-Benz AG 1933 bis 1945*, pp. 42–45. On the banks, whose troubles during the Depression already had resulted in considerable reductions in the number of Jews among the leading personnel, see Mosse, *Jews in the German Economy*, pp. 331–33, 374–75; Hamburger Stiftung, ed., *Dresdner Bank*, pp. xxvii, xxxii–xxxiii, xxxiv, 86; Christopher Kopper, *Zwischen Marktwirtschaft und Dirigismus: Bankenpolitik im "Dritten Reich" 1933–1939* (Bonn: Bouvier, 1995), pp. 131–39, 220–27; and Harold James, "Die Deutsche Bank und die Diktatur 1933–1945," in Gall et al., *Deutsche Bank*, pp. 334–39. Among the documents that throw light on the purges elsewhere, see Leo Baeck Institute Archives, New York (hereafter LBIA), AR 7177, Hans Schäffer papers, Box 1A, "Einzelfälle von Massnahmen gegen jüdische Angestellte"; Stadtarchiv Frankfurt (hereafter StAF), Amtsgericht, nos. 11195, 11205, and especially 11220: Protocol of the stockholders meeting of July 31, 1934; and Landesarchiv Berlin, Aussenstelle Breite Strasse (ehem. Stadtarchiv) (hereafter LAB (STA)), Rep. 231: Osram GmbH KG, no. 424: Bekanntmachung 33/19, May 19, 1933; no. 449: Liste der wegen nichtarischer Abstammung gekündigten Angestellten, Niederschrift an Dr. Meyer, June 9, 1933; no. 1059: Umbau und Abbau, Verkaufsorganisation. Entlassungen von Nichtariern . . . 1932/33.

14. Hayes, *Industry and Ideology*, p. 93. For similar decisions by the Dresdner Bank and the Commerzbank, see Kopper, *Zwischen Marktwirtschaft und Dirigismus*, p. 223. Such transfers hardly amounted to defiance of government policy. Indeed, in cases of Jewish employees with foreign citizenship, the party favored such transfers; see LAB (STA), 231, no. 449: Knauer of the Reichsleitung in Munich to Osram AG, June 16, 1933.

15. BAP, 80Ba2, 2671/17496, Dir. Wintermantel, Maschinenbau u. Bahnbedarf AG vorm. Orenstein & Koppel, Allgemeines, Bl. 19–20: confidential memorandum, July 4, 1935.

16. See BASF, W 1, Max Warburg to Carl Bosch, May 18, 1933, listing the members of the group, and the first draft of its report, June 19, [1933]; SAA 4/Lf676, the second draft, with a cover letter from Rudolf Löb to C. F. von Siemens, August 5, 1933, from which the quoted words come; and LBIA, Tagebuch Hans Schäffers, 1933, pp. 44, 47–49, 65–67, as well as AR 7177, Box IA, Schäffer to Melchior, August 20, 1933. Avraham Barkai, "Max Warburg im Jahre 1933. Missglückte Versuche zur Milderung der Judenverfolgung," in *Juden in Deutschland.*

Emanzipation, Integration, Verfolgung und Vernichtung, ed. Peter Freimark, Alice Jankowski, and Ina S. Lorenz (Hamburg: H. Christians Verlag, 1991), pp. 390–405, provides a generally accurate account of this episode but requires a few amendments based on the eyewitness information in Schäffer's diary, which Barkai did not consult. The participating executives convened twice, not once—in May as well as June 1933; Carl Bosch *did* attend the second meeting; both Albert Vögler and Kurt Schmitt were kept apprised of what was going on; and, while von Siemens' comments at the meetings fit Barkai's suppositions about the self-interested caution of the executives, those of Krupp and Bosch indicate a determination to keep pressing the government.

17. See Niewyk, *Jews in Weimar Germany*, pp. 21–24.

18. SAA 4/Lf676, the final draft enclosed with Löb to Siemens, August 5, 1933.

19. On the stances of Schmitt and Schacht, see Willi A. Boelcke, *Die deutsche Wirtschaft 1930–1945* (Düsseldorf: Droste, 1983), pp. 118–20, 124–28; Kopper, *Zwischen Marktwirtschaft und Dirigismus*, pp. 227–28, 234–37, 241; Yad Vashem Archives, Jerusalem (hereafter YVA), R-4/27, Wirtschaftsarchiv Baden-Württemberg, Schmitt to Deutsche Industrie- und Handelstag, Berlin, September 8, 1933, and Schacht to Reichwirtschaftskammer Berlin, August 9, 1935; Nordrheinwestfälisches Staatsarchiv Münster (hereafter NWSM), Gauleitung Westfalen-Süd, Gauwirtschaftsberater, no. 139, Schacht's *Schnellbrief* of December 28, 1935; and BAP, 25.01, no. 6789, especially Schacht to the Reich- und Preussisches Ministerium des Innern, November 1, 1935, Bl. 82–84, and the memo by the Volkswirtschaftliche Abteilung of the Reichsbank, January 2, 1936, Bl. 181–90. The best study of Schacht's attitudes and policy is now Albert Fischer, *Hjalmar Schacht und Deutschlands "Judenfrage"* (Cologne: Böhlau, 1995).

20. Boelcke, *Deutsche Wirtschaft*, pp. 118–20. On the enforcement of these and related policies, see YVA, R-4/27, letters from the Treuhander der Arbeit, Karlsruhe, June 1 and 12, 1934.

21. See *Jüdische Rundschau*, August 11 and 15, 1933.

22. Karl A. Schleunes, *The Twisted Road to Auschwitz* (Urbana: University of Illinois Press, 1970), p. 114.

23. Quoted in *Jüdische Rundschau*, July 31, 1934.

24. On the motives behind the policy, especially the ideological grounds for patience, see Peter Hayes, "Profits and Persecution: Corporate Involvement in the Holocaust," in *Perspectives on the Holocaust: Essays in Honor of Raul Hilberg,* ed. James S. Pacy and Alan P. Wertheimer (Boulder, CO: Westview Press, 1995), p. 57; on the policy itself, see Barkai, *From Boycott to Annihilation,* chapters 2–3.

25. See Avraham Barkai, "Die deutschen Unternehmer und die Judenpolitik im 'Dritten Reich,'" *Geschichte und Gesellschaft* 15 (1989): 235 (also in English as "German Entrepreneurs and Jewish Policy in the Third Reich," *Yad Vashem Studies* 21 [1991]: 126–53); and Johannes Ludwig, *Boykott, Enteignung, Mord* (Hamburg: Facta Oblita, 1989), p. 116.

26. For example, the Waffenfabrik Simson, Suhl; see Genschel, *Verdrängung*, pp. 99–104. See also Brandenburgisches Landeshauptarchiv, Potsdam (hereafter BLHA), Pr.Br.Rep. 60: Staatskommissar/Staatspräsident der Hauptstadt Berlin, nos. 505–509; Ausschaltung jüdischer Lieferanten 1932–1937.

27. On party pressure, see LAB (STA), 231, no. 659: Niederschrift über die Sitzung des Gemeinschafts-Auschusses im Werk A, October 25, 1933, and Arbeiterrat Osram GmbH KG, Werk D an Geschäftsleitung Werk D, November 23, 1933; HHSA, Abt. 483, nos. 10957–60: Schriftwechsel zwecks Feststellung, welche Firmen arisch oder jüdisch sind, 1933–1936. On the permissibility of dismissals, see "Reichsgericht zur fristlosen Kündigung jüdischer Vorstandsmitglieder," *Deutsche Allgemeine Zeitung*, October 22, 1935.

28. See Horst A. Wessel, *Kontinuität im Wandel: 100 Jahre Mannesmann 1890–1990* (Düsseldorf: Mannesmann-Archiv, 1990), pp. 210, 212; Hayes, *Industry and Ideology*, p. 127; Jens Heine, *Verstand und Schicksal* (Weinheim: VCH Verlagsgesellschaft, 1990), pp. 49, 217–20, 250–51, 255–58, 275–78; Mosse, *Jews in the German Economy*, p. 379; Hamburger Stiftung, ed., *Dresdner Bank*, p. xxxii; Kopper, *Zwischen Marktwirtschaft und Dirigismus*, pp. 136, 221–23, 243; and on Feldmühle, see *Das Schwarze Korps*, no. 25, June 23, 1938.

29. Kopper, *Zwischen Marktwirtschaft und Dirigismus*, pp. 221–23. On personnel policy at the major banks, see also YVA, O-1: Ball-Kaduri collection of oral testimonies, no. 196, the informative contribution of Richard Glaser, formerly of the Commerzbank, November 18, 1957.

30. BAP, 80Ba2, 4295/18184: Urbig, Porz. L. Hutschenreuther AG, Allgemeines, esp. Bl. 237–39: Urbig to Schweisheimer, November 17, 1934, where the quoted words appear. That Urbig was no antisemite is clear from both a letter he drafted to the local party cell, then thought better of sending (Bl. 217–18) and from his nearly simultaneous defense of Dr. Hofmann of the supervisory board against a racist attack (4332/18168: Urbig, Hutschenreuther Personalia, Bl. 170 and 172–73).

31. BAP, 80Ba2, 3455/16933: Gesfürel, Allgemeines, 1934–1938; 3458/16832: Gesfürel, Aufsichtsrat Protokolle; 3469/16838: Gesfürel Personalia; and 3475/16826: Personalia Erich Loewe.

32. See BAP 80Ba2, 3455/16833, Bl. 260, Kimmich's secretary to Benz, May 28, 1937.

33. See Barkai, *Boykott zur Entjudung*, pp. 86–87, and Barkai, "Deutsche Unternehmer und Judenpolitik," p. 232.

34. See BAP, 25.01, no. 6790, "Verzeichnis der jüdischen Privatbankierfirmen. Stand Ende Mai 1938"; A. J. Sherman, "A Jewish Bank during the Schacht Era: M. M. Warburg & Co., 1933–1938," in *Die Juden im nationalsozialistischen Deutschland 1933–1943*, ed. Arnold Paucker et al. (Tübingen: J. C. B. Mohr, 1986), pp. 170–71; YVA, Sig. O-1, no. 137, A. P. Michaelis, "Die jüdischen Banken in Deutschland von 1933 bis 1938," dated January 1957; and Kopper, *Zwischen Marktwirtschaft und Dirigismus*, pp. 228–29, 231–32.

35. Ibid., pp. 254–55.

36. For two examples, see *Berliner Börsen-Zeitung*, January 15, 1936, p. 10 (on the retirement of Eugen Jacobi from Wolf Netter & Jacobi), and Nordrheinwestfälisches Hauptstaatsarchiv Düsseldorf (hereafter NWHSA), RW 58: Gestapo, Staatspolizeileitstelle Düsseldorf, Bl. 3, no. 55028: Vermerk, Essen, October 10, 1938 (on the withdrawal of the Stern brothers from the boards of M. Stern, Essen).

37. See "Der Verkauf jüdischer Betriebe," *Deutsche Bergwerks-Zeitung*, August 8, 1935.

38. BAP, 80 IG 1: Farbenindustrie AG, no. A149: Beteiligungen 1928–1937, K–Z, esp. Bl. 21–24, 54–55, 64–67, 502–505; and no. A2036: Beteiligungen 1928–1937, A–J, esp. Bl. 274–78, 475–77, 514–16, 523.

39. Kopper, *Zwischen Marktwirtschaft und Dirigismus*, pp. 254–55.

40. See Wolfgang Benz, ed., *Die Juden in Deutschland*, pp. 306–307; and, on the "good cop/bad cop" method frequently applied in the shakedowns, Kurt Pätzold, *Verfolgung, Vertreibung, Vernichtung* (Leipzig: Reclam, 1983), Doc. 56, p. 98. For examples of such opportunistic grabs, see Ludwig, *Boykott, Enteignung, Mord*, pp. 89–92, 128–30, 154–57. For a Nazi attack on sales intended as camouflage, see "Wie Sie Arbeiten," *Der Angriff*, August 10, 1935.

41. For an illuminating contemporary explanation of the motives behind acquisitions in this period, see Degussa-Archiv (hereafter Degussa), Biographische Unterlagen Fritz Roessler, Zur Geschichte der Scheideanstalt, 1933–1936, Abschrift, dated January 1937, pp. 121–22.

42. BAP, 80Ba1: Dresdner Bank, Zeitungsausschnittsammlung, no. 11671: Henkel &. Cie. GmbH, Bl. 4; and "Überführung nichtarischer Firmen in deutschen Besitz," *Völkischer Beobachter*, November 13, 1935.

43. Kopper, *Zwischen Marktwirtschaft und Dirigismus*, pp. 136–39; Hans G. Meyen, *120 Jahre Dresdner Bank. Unternehmens-Chronik 1872 bis 1992* (Frankfurt/M.: Dresdner Bank, 1992), pp. 102–104; and Hamburger Stiftung, ed., *Dresdner Bank*, pp. xxvi and xxxii–xxxv.

44. On the bank's documents, BAP, 31.01, no. 15514, Kurt Daluege to the Reichsinnenministerium, March 30, 1933. On the extortion of Nacher, see Ludwig, *Boykott, Enteignung, Mord*, pp. 11–89.

45. See, for example, the information on Hirsch Kupfer- und Messingwerke, BAP, 80 IG 1, Bl. 475–78, no. A2036, Director Loewy to G. Frank-Fahle, March 1, 1934.

46. BAP, 80Ba2, 2671/17496, Bl. 19–20: confidential memo, July 4, 1935, and Bl. 80, Vorstand to Wintermantel, December 11, 1935; 2673/17490: Wintermantel, Vorstands-

Protokolle, Bl. 1: Meeting of October 18, 1935; 2677/17495: Personalia Alfred Orenstein, Bl. 9: Wintermantel to Auslandsorganisation der NSDAP, September 25, 1935.

47. Kopper, *Zwischen Marktwirtschaft und Dirigismus*, p. 278.

48. Compare the accounts in ibid., pp. 240–41, and Meyen, *120 Jahre Dresdner Bank*, p. 118.

49. For details of these cases, see Peter Hayes, "Big Business and 'Aryanization' in Germany, 1933–1939," *Jahrbuch für Antisemitismusforschung* 3 (1994): 262–64; and Peter Hayes, "Business Professionalism and the Persecution of the Jews," in *From Prejudice to Destruction*, ed. G. Jan Colijn and Marcia Littell (Münster: Lit Verlag, 1995), pp. 145–46.

50. On Schacht's attitudes and actions, see Fischer, *Schacht und Deutschlands "Judenfrage,"* esp. pp. 123, 162, 175, 177, 193, 213; and Kopper, *Zwischen Marktwirtschaft und Dirigismus*, pp. 234–36, 253–54.

51. For a more detailed discussion of Hitler's calculations at this time, see Hayes, "Profits and Persecution," in *Perspectives on the Holocaust*, ed. Pacy and Wertheimer, pp. 59–60. For recent appreciations of the connection between Hitler's foreign and racial policies, see Herbert A. Strauss, "The Drive for War and the Pogroms of November 1938: Testing Explanatory Models," Leo Baeck Institute *Year Book* 35 (1990): 267–78, especially the concluding section (I would emphasize, however, that the pogrom of 1938 was the dramatic culmination, not the beginning, of an interacting shift in policies that dated from November 1937); and Wolf Gruner, "Arbeitseinsatz und Zwangsarbeit jüdischer Deutscher 1938–1939," in *Arbeitsmarkt und Sondererlass*, ed. Götz Aly (Berlin: Rotbuch Verlag, 1991), p. 137. Cf. Fischer, *Schacht und Deutschlands "Judenfrage,"* pp. 197–201, which argues for September 1936 as the real watershed in government Aryanization policy.

52. See Schleunes, *Twisted Road to Auschwitz*, p. 218; Boelcke, *Deutsche Wirtschaft*, p. 211; Hayes, *Industry and Ideology*, pp. 170, 196; and Uwe Dietrich Adam, *Judenpolitik im Dritten Reich* (Königstein i.T.: ADTV, 1979), pp. 176–77. For one contemporary's view that November 1937 marked a turning point in the situation of his own substantial textile firm, see Benz, *Juden in Deutschland*, pp. 308–12.

53. See United States National Archives (hereafter NA), RG238/ T301, Doc. NI-10123, Memo by Steinbrinck on conference with Herbert Göring, November 16, 1937, and Doc. NI-10124, Memo by Steinbrinck on conference with Wilhelm Keppler, November 20, 1937. It is also clear with regard to Flick's Aryanizations of 1937–1938 that he initially sought to retain the Jewish managers of Rawack & Grunfeld (Doc. NI-2627, Memo by Steinbrinck of conference with Oldewage, December 21, 1937); to retain Warburg & Co. as that firm's house bank (Kopper, *Zwischen Marktwirtschaft und Dirigismus*, p. 262); and to leave the Hahn family in possession of a minority of its shares in the Hochofen Lübeck (Doc. NI-1845, Agreement between Flick and Hahn's representatives, December 10, 1937; and Doc. NI-4381, Memo by Steinbrinck of conference with Keppler, February 10, 1938). Flick's *Arisierungspolitik* has yet to receive definitive scholarly treatment. Valuable, but imperfect, accounts are in Gerhard Mollin, *Montankonzerne und "Drittes Reich,"* pp. 184–87; Raul Hilberg, *The Destruction of the European Jews*, rev. ed. (New York: Holmes & Meier, 1985), vol. 1, pp. 115–22; and Genschel, *Verdrängung*, pp. 216–36.

54. See Hayes, *Industry and Ideology*, p. 170; Genschel, *Verdrängung*, pp. 188–89.

55. See Wilhelm Treue, *Das Schicksal des Bankhauses Sal. Oppenheim jr. & Cie. im Dritten Reich* (Wiesbaden: Steiner, 1983), pp. 9–18; Michael Stürmer, Gabriele Teichmann, and Wilhelm Treue, *Wägen und Wagen* (Munich: Piper, 1989), pp. 365–90; E. Rosenbaum and A. J. Sherman, *M. M. Warburg and Co. 1798–1938* (New York: Holmes & Meier, 1979), pp. 157–69; Konrad Fuchs, *Ein Konzern aus Sachsen* (Stuttgart: Deutsche Verlags-Anstalt, 1990); and idem, "Zur Geschichte des Warenhaus-Konzerns I. Schocken Söhne unter besonderer Berücksichtigung der Jahre seit 1933," *Zeitschrift für Unternehmensgeschichte* 33 (1988): 232–52; Hans Achinger, *Richard Merton* (Frankfurt/M.: Waldemar Kramer, 1970); Hayes, *Industry and Ideology*, pp. 201–202. See also the articles collected in StAF, Sig. S2/3223; "Wie Avieny Generaldirektor wurde," *Frankfurter Rundschau*, August 11, 1949; "Es war wie bei einem Kartenspiel," *Frankfurter Rundschau*, August 13, 1949; and "Die Kulissenvorgänge im Fall Avieny," *Neue Presse*, August 13, 1949.

56. For example, see Generallandesarchiv Karlsruhe (hereafter GLAK), Abt. 505: Arisierungen, no. 218, Badische Bank to Badische Finanz- und Wirtschaftsministerium, July 1, 1938. Valuable, in general, on this competitive impulse is James, "Deutsche Bank", pp. 315–408.

57. See Genschel,*Verdrängung*, pp. 146–47; and GLAK, Abt. 505, no. 384, concerning the takeover of L. J. Ettlinger KG of Karlsruhe by the sales subsidiary of Gebr. Stumm GmbH, where the government initially refused to reinstate, then curtailed the iron quotas of the acquired firm out of suspicion that Stumm had taken it over only in order to obtain them.

58. For examples, see Hayes, "Big Business and 'Aryanization'," *Jahrbuch für Antisemitismusforschung* 3 (1994): 270–71.

59. Hans Mommsen, "Zur Verschränkung traditioneller und faschistischer Führungsgruppen in Deutschland beim Übergang von der Bewegungs- zur Systemphase," in *Faschismus als soziale Bewegung*, ed. W. Schieder (Hamburg: Hoffmann & Campe, 1976), p. 176. On the prototypical "Beutezug" in Austria during these months, see Genschel, *Verdrängung*, pp. 160–65; Hayes, *Industry and Ideology*, pp. 219–32; Kopper, *Zwischen Marktwirtschaft und Dirigismus*, pp. 292–314; and Witek, "'Arisierungen' in Wien," pp. 209–10.

60. See James, "Deutsche Bank und Diktatur," pp. 316–20.

61. See ibid., pp. 344–51; and Hilberg, *Destruction*, vol. 1, p. 100. I believe Kopper understates the value of this sort of business to the large banks; see *Zwischen Marktwirtschaft und Dirigismus*, p. 277. On their motivations, see Sächsisches Staatsarchiv Leipzig (hereafter SSAL), Deutsche Bank, Filiale Leipzig, no. 623, Vorstand to Branch Directors, February 11, 1938; and Dresdner Bank, Filiale Leipzig, no. 167, Direktion Berlin to Branch Directors, July 2, 1938; and no. 168, Frankfurt Branch to Leipzig Branch, August 5, 1938.

62. BAP, 80Ba2, 1293/17772, Bl. 146–47, File note by Rösler, April 14, 1938.

63. See Sächsisches Hauptstaatsarchiv Dresden (hereafter SHAD), Firmenbestand 222: Altbanken Chemnitz, no. A4/21/15, A. Reich to Commerzbank Zentrale Berlin, September 1, 1941; and A7/21/46–47, Deutsche Bank Zentrale to Karl Goeritz, March 30, 1938; account reports of March 1 and August 21, 1939. For a similar case of the Dresdner Bank doubly profiting from the Aryanization of the Textil-Syndikat GmbH, see SHAD, Industrie- und Handelskammer Chemnitz, no. 7, IHK to Kreishauptmann Chemnitz, October 3, 1938; and Firmenbestand 222, no. A8/21/60, Bilanzenbericht, December 31, 1938.

64. The principal cases of such expansion were the Dresdner's acquisition of the remaining Berlin operations of Gebr. Arnhold and the affiliated Bleichroeder & Co. and the Deutsche Bank's takeover of the Bankhaus Hirschland of Essen and Mendelssohn & Co. of Berlin. See Kopper, *Zwischen Marktwirtschaft und Dirgismus*, pp. 256–57, 268–72, 273–75; Meyen, *120 Jahre Dresdner Bank*, p. 118; and James, "Deutsche Bank und Diktatur," p. 349.

65. SSAL, Deutsche Bank, Filiale Leipzig, no. 623, Vorstand to Branch Directors, January 14, 1938; Rundschreiben des Filialbüros Berlin, January 25, 1938.

66. Ibid., Vorstand to Branch Directors, February 11, 1938.

67. Cf. Kopper, *Zwischen Marktwirtschaft und Dirigismus*, pp. 275–76, 279; and Hamburger Stiftung, ed., *Dresdner Bank*, pp. xlii–xliv. On the pedigree of these schemes, see LAB (STA), 200–02: Industrie- und Handelskammer Berlin, Zeitungsausschnittsammlung, no. 130/2, *Frankfurter Zeitung* and *Deutsche Bergwerks-Zeitung*, September 24, 1935.

68. Kopper, *Zwischen Marktwirtschaft und Dirigismus*, p. 279; SSAL, Deutsche Bank, Filiale Leipzig, no. 623, Rundschreiben des Filialbüros, March 7, 1938–January 10, 1939; James, "Deutsche Bank und Diktatur," pp. 348–49.

69. SSAL, Dresdner Bank, Filiale Leipzig, no. 167, Direktion Berlin to Branch Managers, July 2, 1938; and C. Lüer to Leipzig Branch, January 5, 1939.

70. Kopper, *Zwischen Marktwirtschaft und Dirigismus*, pp. 279–80.

71. Genschel, *Verdrängung*, pp. 173–76.

72. On the procedural preconditions for the approval of an Aryanization, including the need for sanction from the local NSDAP and DAF, see ibid., pp. 152–60.

73. See ibid., pp. 197–98, 201, and the attack on the Dreiring-Werke for allegedly overpaying in their acquisition of the Seifenfabrik Heilborn, Frankfurt a.d. Oder, "Arisierung—nicht um jeden Preis!" *Das Schwarze Korps*, no. 12, March 24, 1938. On the NSDAP's

determination to prevent Aryanization from increasing concentration in the German economy or benefiting big business, see "Die Ausschaltung der Juden," *Die deutsche Volkswirtschaft*, no. 33, November 21, 1938.

74. See Genschel, *Verdrängung*, p. 98 note 7; LAB (STA), 200–02/ 163/55/53: Zetsche of the Industrie- und Handelskammer Berlin to Polizeipräsidenten Berlin, November 22, 1941; and Hilberg, *Destruction*, vol. 1, pp. 101–102. The terms laid down for acquisitions in Austria, involving "as a general guideline the assessment of 'bad-will,'" were even more stringent; see SSAL, Deutsche Bank, Filiale Leipzig, no. 623, Osterwind to Deutsche Bank, May 4, 1938.

75. "Arisierung und Preise," *Berliner Börsen-Zeitung*, September 7, 1938.

76. To be sure, this was largely because Göring's Four Year Plan office actually ended up with a profit in dollars on the transaction; see NA, RG238/T301, NI-3306, Wohltat's summary of the J. Petschek deal, December 16, 1938. For other instances of official flexibility, see SSAL, Dresdner Bank, Filiale Leipzig, no. 155, concerning the Aryanization of the Hirtenberger Patronen- Zündhütchen- und Metallwarenfabrik by the Wilhelm Gustloff Stiftung/Berlin-Suhler Waffenfabrik in April 1938, which provided for the transfer of some proceeds in British pounds via a loan to the acquiring firm; and GLAK, Abt. 505, no. 1489, on the takeover of the Rhenania Schiffahrts- und Spedition GmbH by the Haniel concern.

77. See YVA, R-4, no. 32, Schlussbericht of the Württemberg Industrie- und Handels-Beratungs- und Vermittlungszentrale GmbH, Stuttgart, October 11, 1938. For a similar instance, see LBIA, AR6160, Collection Henry Ebert, Gauleitung Hessen-Nassau to Ludwig and Arthur Ebert, August 3, 1938.

78. BAP, 80Ba2, 2079/19686: Dr. Sippell, Zellstofffabrik Waldhof, Allgemeines, 1938–1939, Niederschrift. Betr. Projekt eines Erwerbs des Natronag-Konzerns, July 25, 1938; Aktenvermerk by Sippell, September 20, 1938.

79. For an example of such conduct, see HHSA, Abt. 519, no. 131, AR/35, decision of May 29, 1946.

80. James, "Deutsche Bank und Diktatur," *Deutsche Bank, p.* 351.

81. On the means by which the state collected the proceeds, see Hilberg, *Destruction*, vol. 1, pp. 134–38. Note, however, that his estimate of the total revenue has been superseded by the discovery of a postwar tabulation in the files of the Oberfinanzdirektion Berlin; see Mehl, *Reichsfinanzministerium und Verfolgung*, pp. 44, 78, 85, 97. Typical of the fate of the prices paid for large firms was the case of Gebr. Heine, the largest textile mail-order house in Germany at the time of its takeover in 1938–1939. Here the state confiscated some 60–65 percent of the proceeds of approximately 8 million marks from the sellers in the period surrounding their emigration, and probably most of the residual later; see SSAL, Devisenstelle Leipzig, nos. 849–51: Betr. Erlös aus dem Verkauf der Fa. Gebr. Heine. On the increased tax proceeds from the sale to banks and resale by them of stocks collected from Jews after the pogrom of 1938, see *Deutsche Bergwerks-Zeitung*, no. 122, May 28, 1939.

82. See Mehl, *Reichsfinanzministerium und Verfolgung*, p. 186.

83. See Hamburger Stiftung, ed., *Deutsche Bank*, pp. 169–70.

84. See the illuminating accounts of A. J. van der Leeuw, "Der Griff des Reichs nach dem Judenvermögen" and "Reichskommissariat und Judenvermögen in den Niederlanden," in *Studies over Nederland in oorlogstijd*, ed. A. H. Paape (The Hague: Martinus Nijhoff, 1972), vol. 1, pp. 211–36, 237–49.

85. This is the clear pattern of, for example, the nearly complete records of Aryanization in Holland; see Rijksinstituut voor Oorlogsdokumentatie, SvB 44/IIIa: Generalkommissariat für Finanz und Wirtschaft, Protokolle der 29 Planungssitzungen, April 1941–March 1943.

86. For example, see the account in James, "Deutsche Bank und Diktatur," pp. 367–85.

87. See YVA, R-4/26, Krüger of the Reich Economics Ministry to Kommunale Pfandleih-anstalten, August 24,1939; LBIA, AR6305, Ernst Wertheimer family file, letters from the Stadt. Pfandleihanstalt Stuttgart AG to Hans Strauss, June 1, 1948; the documents from 1943–1944 in *Dokumenty i Materialy, Tom III, Getto Lodzkie* (Warsaw: 1946), pp. 156–57, 163; and Karl Heinz Roth, "Ein Spezialunternehmen für Verbrennungskreisläufe: Konzernskizze Degussa," *1999* 3 (1988): 27–30, 35–36.

88. James, "Deutsche Bank und Diktatur," pp. 369, 376; BAP, 80BA2, 11013/60: Zusammenstellungen der liquiden Mittel der BUB, November 30, 1943–January 31, 1945, esp. Bl. 44 and 102.

89. For the figures that serve as the basis for this calculation, see Hayes, *Industry and Ideology*, p. 362.

90. See NA, RG238/T301, NI-382, undated affidavit by Oswald Pohl, head of the SS Economic Administration Main Office. To date, the best point of access to the vexed question of which firms employed how many workers is the material collected for postwar restitution claims, YVA, M-32: Compensation Treuhandstelle, which includes tallies for such entities as Rheinmetall, Krupp, AEG-Telefunken, IG Farben, Siemens, Brabag, Heinkel, Mannesmann, Junkers, and Bochumer Verein, as well as individual documents referring to concentration camp laborers sent to such installations as Degussa's lampblack factory at Gleiwitz (vol. 170). See also Ulrich Herbert, *Fremdarbeiter* (Bonn: Verlag J. H. W. Dietz Nachf., 1985); Joseph Ferencz, *Less than Slaves* (Cambridge: Harvard University Press, 1979); Hayes, *Industry and Ideology*, pp. 343–61; Hamburger Stiftung, ed., *"Deutsche Wirtschaft": Zwangsarbeit von KZ-Häftlingen für Industrie und Behörden* (Hamburg: VSA-Verlag, 1991); Bernard P. Bellon, *Mercedes in Peace and War* (New York: Columbia University Press, 1990); Hopmann et al., *Zwangsarbeit bei Daimler-Benz*, pp. 335–442; Zofka, "Allach-Sklaven für BMW," *Dachauer Hefte* 2 (1986): 68–78; John Gillingham, *Business and Politics in the Third Reich* (New York: Columbia University Press, 1985), p. 125 (on the Ruhr coal industry); Feldenkirchen, *Siemens*, pp. 204–11; and Florian Freund, *Arbeitslager Zement* (Vienna: 1989). According to one estimate, some seven hundred German firms employed camp inmates at one time or another; Barkai, "German Entrepreneurs and Jewish Policy," *Yad Vashem Studies* 21 (1991): 146 note 44.

91. See Hayes, *Industry and Ideology*, pp. 359–60.

92. See Wolf Gruner, "Arbeitseinsatz und Zwangsarbeit jüdischer Deutscher 1938–1939," in Götz Aly, ed., *Arbeitsmarkt und Sondererlass*, pp. 137–55; idem, "'Am 20. April (Geburtstag des Führers) haben die Juden zu arbeiten . . . ,'" in *Faschismus und Rassismus: Kontroversen um Ideologie und Opfer*, ed. Werner Röhr (Berlin: Akademie Verlag, 1992), pp. 148–67; idem, "Terra incognita?—Die Lager für den 'jüdischen Arbeitseinsatz' (1938–1943) und die deutsche Bevölkerung," in *Die Deutschen und die Judenverfolgung im Dritten Reich*, ed. Ursula Büttner (Hamburg: Christians Verlag, 1992), pp. 131–59; Feldenkirchen, *Siemens*, pp. 203–205; and LAB (STA), Rep. 229: Schering AG, vols. 513–14.

93. See Dietmar Petzina, *Die deutsche Wirtschaft in der Zwischenkriegszeit* (Wiesbaden: Steiner, 1976), p. 153; and R. J. Overy, *War and Economy in the Third Reich* (New York: Clarendon Press, 1994), pp. 291–311.

94. On the unfolding of this process, see Reiner Fröbe, "Der Arbeitseinsatz von KZ-Häftlingen und die Perspektive der Industrie, 1943–1945," in *"Deutsche Wirtschaft,"* ed. Hamburger Stiftung, pp. 33–65; and Lutz Budrass and Manfred Grieger, "Die Moral der Effizienz. Die Beschäftigung von KZ-Häftlingen am Beispiel des Volkswagenwerks und der Henschel Flugzeug-Werke," *Jahrbuch für Wirtschaftsgeschichte*, 2 (1994): 89–136.

95. Hans Mommsen, "Zwangsarbeit und Konzentrationslager bei den Volkswagenwerken," in *"Deutsche Wirtschaft,"* ed. Hamburger Stiftung, p. 225.

96. See also the arguments of much excellent recent work emphasizing the eugenics policies that served as important precursors to the separation, then murder of Jews in, for example, Sybil Milton, "The Context of the Holocaust," *German Studies Review* 13 (1990): 269–83; Claudia Koonz, "Genocide and Eugenics: The Language of Power," in *Lessons and Legacies: The Meaning of the Holocaust in a Changing World*, ed. Peter Hayes (Evanston, IL: Northwestern University Press, 1991), pp. 155–77; Henry Friedlander, *The Origins of Nazi Genocide* (Chapel Hill: University of North Carolina Press, 1995); and chapter 11 in this volume by Stefan Kühl.

97. Ian Kershaw, *Popular Opinion and Political Dissent in the Third Reich* (Oxford: Clarendon Press, 1983), p. 277.

15.

HANS MOMMSEN

The Civil Service and the Implementation of the Holocaust

FROM PASSIVE TO ACTIVE COMPLICITY

The role of the German civil service under and as part of the National Social-ist regime varied with time and with respect to the particular administrative realm within which each facet of that civil service functioned. In general, its influence de-clined considerably, while secondary bureaucracies such as those of the SS, or of the Four Year Plan, or, in the later war years, of the Nazi party itself, continuously eroded former administrative competencies. Because the Third Reich never became a stable governmental system but was characterized by growing infighting between compet-ing agencies and power groups as well as by the increasing impact of sheerly personal factors, it is problematic to speak of a "Nazi State" in precise terms.[1]

The civil service, however, did not disappear, and in some fields it was even enlarged; but its ability to participate in the political process gradually diminished because the ministries as such lost any real influence on policy-making. In 1933 the civil service had appeared to prevail against the prospect of party rule and constantly curtailed or retarded the Nazis' power ambitions. But the civil service progressively weakened.[2] In certain respects, however, it could preserve its prerogatives almost unrestricted. Hence, the bureaucratic apparatus of the Ministry of Finance survived the socio-Darwinist power struggle of the Third Reich, although it was compelled to concede to the party treasury, to the completely nazified Ministry of Propaganda and to the SS Main Office, that these organizations need not comply with the civil service salary and career regulations that were mandatory everywhere else.[3]

With respect to persecution of Jews, the civil service proved to be indispensable in carrying out the ever-increasing variety of anti-Jewish measures incessantly de-manded by party radicals. The processes of social segregation, of expropriation, and of deportation, as well as the definition of those who were to be subject to the per-secution, relied heavily on the direct and indirect support of a great variety of administrative bodies including municipal bureaucracies, order police, railway offi-cials, and many others. Continuous ideological impregnation and terrorist intimida-tion were not the only factors that guaranteed correct and sometimes even over-correct implementation of the multitude of anti-Jewish ordinances. No less important was the mechanical fulfillment of orders from superiors, which is symptomatic of any bureaucratic structure. Only occasionally would civil servants deliberately circumvent discriminatory legislation against Jewish fellow-citizens. In contrast, they frequently tried to protect Roman Catholic priests who were ostracized by the regime.[4] The systematic efficiency of German bureaucrats proved to be the main enemy of the Jewish victims, as the example of the German railway system investigated by Raul Hilberg demonstrates.[5]

During the formative years of the regime, the higher civil service succeeded in preventing a direct nazification of the administrative bodies. By taking in some party members, the Deputy Führer claimed to be filling the staffing agencies—the *Personalabteilungen*—with reliable party members. In due course the administrative bodies became superficially nazified. But even where this occurred, esprit de corps often proved to be stronger than party loyalty.

Although at the upper levels Nazi careerists assumed leading positions, the homogeneity of the subordinate administrative apparatus was not seriously challenged. Consequently, Bormann's scheme of achieving a personal union between party and state apparatus on the district level, between Kreisleiter and Landrat, proved to be a complete failure. Most new position holders readily dropped or diminished their party allegiance and acted as loyal defenders of the homogeneity and independence of public administration.[6] Bormann eventually realized that his concept of merging party and state administration on the regional level—the so-called *Mittelinstanz*—was not feasible at all, and in 1938 withdrew his pressure on the Ministry of the Interior. Even the requirement of party membership for every higher civil servant was not generally enforced at law.[7]

Instead of being permitted to interfere in local and regional administration, party functionaries usually were requested to pursue any complaints through channels. Among this input were the so-called *Politische Beurteilungen*, the "expert" evaluations of the political reliability of those who were candidates for promotion. These judgments were directed through the office of the Deputy Führer. Because party agencies were rarely able to react in time to meet deadlines, any objections they might want to lodge lost much of their impact.[8]

Consequently, activist elements in the party frequently felt themselves duped by the bureaucracy and uncharacteristically helpless in the face of an omnipotent state bureaucracy. Symptomatic of this mentality of the so-called political leaders were the notorious complaints against Wilhelm Frick's neoabsolutist style at the Ministry of the Interior.[9] In fact, after the synchronization process in the summer of 1933 was stopped, the administration successfully blocked any further inroads by local and regional party functionaries and showed little inclination to provide jobs for Old Fighters. Yet the goal of remaining the third power center in the Reich, alongside the army and the party, eventually made the bureaucracy an increasingly loyal instrument of Hitler's wishes.[10]

As a consequence of the widespread strongly antisemitic bias of the German upper middle classes, higher civil service officials unanimously adhered to the principle of racial dissimilation that had been propagated by the conservative Tivoli Program in 1892.[11] As long as Nazi policy seemingly remained within those boundaries—and that was the case with respect to most of the anti-Jewish ordinances adopted between 1933 and 1938—the German civil service did not hesitate to comply systematically. They were happy to cooperate in eliminating the alleged pre-ponderance of Jews in the professional and economic realms.[12]

Conflict resulted when party radicals violated formal legality, particularly by "wild" Jew-baiting and other arbitrary actions against Jewish citizens. Consequently, from the very beginning the civil administration tried to direct some varieties of Nazi violence into legal channels.[13] Nevertheless, while party influence in almost all policy fields was severely limited initially, leading officials showed greater leniency with respect to anti-Jewish actions, which they regarded as the equivalent of chil-dren's diseases—unpleasantness that soon would disappear. Johannes Popitz, the Prussian Minister of Finance, said in an interministerial conference in 1935 that anti-semitic actions should be accepted up to a point, but then the rule of the Reichts-staat should be restored.[14] These administrators regarded antisemitism as a safety valve that could be utilized to let off the pressure exerted by party radicals, such as Old Fighters and SA members, as long as the Nazi revolution persisted.[15]

By channeling social revolutionary energies into the antisemitic field, leading officials contributed to a continuously escalating, racially driven antisemitic on-slaught. Although active, rabid antisemites among Nazi followers and even among party members were a rather small percentage,[16] they played a major role within the process of cumulative radicalization. Bureaucratic indifference, therefore, contrib-uted to what Martin Broszat has called a negative selection among the elements of the Nazi Weltanschauung.[17] In fact, ideological goals conflicting with vested social and political interests typically were immediately dropped, whereas racial anti-semitism flourished insofar as it did not directly interfere with specific economic interests. For instance, the expropriation of Jewish landed estates was only partially implemented.

While still guided by a nationalist-conservative mentality, leading governmental circles opened the gates for anti-Jewish radicalization. In the long run their accom-modation of anti-Jewish policies functioned as a spearhead to destroy the legacy of adherence to form and legitimacy that these officials had sought to preserve. At the party convention in September 1935, Hitler had warned that if the state would not comply with the need to solve the Jewish Question, he would lay it in the hands of the party.[18] By complying, the bureaucracy retained important elements of its power. However, the bureaucracy's attempts to formally legalize anti-Jewish policy and thereby prevent one-sided procedures by local party activists were doomed to failure. This was the case at least partly because of Hitler's habit of defending antisemitic hardliners. The Führer curtailed all efforts to bring effective sanctions against party radicals, as even SS-Judge Konrad Morgen had to realize when he tried to stop atrocities in the concentration camps.[19]

In addition, the bureaucracy was of great importance in translating rather vague and somewhat illusionary Nazi goals into operational terms. Bureaucratic attempts to moderate anti-Jewish legislation were marked by a certain ambivalence. For example, Bernhard Lösener's initiative to exempt half-Jews and Jews living in racially mixed marriages rescued many among this group from deportation and liquidation. Yet their exemption had the effect of facilitating the policy of social segregation of the "less assimilated" Jewish population, which was the precondition for later de-portation measures.[20] Had the Nazi party's attempt to incorporate its own "Aryan paragraph" into the Reich citizenship law been successful, the implementation of that law would have been difficult and might have aroused public protest. Bureaucratic attempts to impose any control on Nazi radicalism sometimes helped to prevent public criticism and also gave rise to erroneous expectations on the part of the persecuted that a lasting legal solution would be found.[21]

Christopher Browning has analyzed the mechanisms that rendered the bureaucracy an efficient instrument in speeding up the process of social segregation, expropriation, and discrimination against Jews. Out of this endeavor not to lose the "leadership in the Jewish Question" to the party, as Wilhelm Frick had put the matter at an interministerial conference in 1935,[22] all ministries installed "Jewish desks" through which anti-Jewish legislative activities escalated.[23] As Browning and others have shown, bureaucratic discrimination continued even after most German Jews had already been deported to the East. The competition between party and bureaucracy came to serve as important leverage in fostering anti-Jewish ordinances, and the nonparty efforts originated less in ideological motives than in the aim to achieve bureaucratic efficiency.

Unquestionably, Ministry of Interior officials, together with the judiciary, provided most of the preconditions for effective persecution. Chief among these was the definition of the persecuted group, an indispensable component of the legal framework by which the decrees of the Reich Citizen Law helped lay the groundwork for a policy of genocide. Hans Globke's contribution was important in this respect.[24] The murderous results of their complicity not withstanding, most government officials hesitated to draw such a consequence from their commitment to serve the regime.

Furthermore, officials in the Ministry of the Interior tried to avoid any direct responsibility. One possible exception was State Secretary Wilhelm Stuckart, who did not interfere in Lösener's attempts to preserve half-Jews from inclusion in the genocide. To distance himself and his organization from the measures, Dr. Hans Globke devised the anti-Jewish legislation in such a way that the responsibility for Jews who were transferred into the eastern ghettos lay only with the Gestapo.[25] More difficult was the role of the administrators in the General Government, as Browning's impressive analysis of the conflict between "productionists" and "attritionists" shows.[26]

Where the leading officials in the ministries are concerned, a general evaluation of their reaction to the escalating Jewish persecution is difficult. Browning's typology, distinguishing between the old generation of civil servants and the young careerists, the party infiltrators and the obstructors, appears to be very convincing.[27] But one should avoid dealing with ministerial bureaucracy as a closely interrelated unit. The Nazi regime was characterized by systematic noncommunication even among the high echelons within party and state. Knowledge of the systematic extermination was repressed and seems to have been incomplete even in the resistance movement.[28] This explains why a great many of the leading functionaries later asserted that they had not known what actually took place at Auschwitz.[29]

There is a series of cases that sheds some light on this phenomenon, the most prominent of which seems to be that of the state secretary in the Reich Chancellery, Dr. Wilhelm Kritzinger. Kritzinger was a typical Prussian official who previously had served as an expert on constitutional law in the Ministry of Justice; he was transferred to the Reich Chancellery in December 1937. Hans Heinrich Lammers induced him to enter the party at the same time, and he reluctantly complied, though he was a member of the Confessional Church and had repeatedly supported persecuted Jews. In 1939 he came in conflict with Himmler when Kritzinger tried to obtain reliable information about the anti-Jewish terror being perpetrated by German units in Poland. Kritzinger's queries were denied, and his informants were threatened with incarceration in a concentration camp.[30]

Kritzinger attended the Wannsee Conference as the official delegate of the Reich Chancellery. We have no written report, but we can infer from his remark to his close colleague Leo Killy that the conference ended up like a "Hornberger Schiessen," that is, it yielded no concrete results on the issue of the treatment of half-Jews or on other legal questions.[31] Obviously, Kritzinger did not take Heydrich's somewhat vague announcement of the destruction process at face value. Killy himself, who was partly of Jewish origin and whose wife was half-Jewish, had been exempted from the Nuremberg Laws and treated as a Deutschblütiger after Lammers had successfully intervened with Hitler.[32] The strong esprit de corps that prevailed among the civil servants in the Chancellery prevented Killy from being forced out of office in spite of a late attempt by Bormann to exclude all civil servants of Jewish descent from public service.[33]

It took Kritzinger a couple of months to acquire further information about the ongoing liquidation of European Jews. When he asked Lammers to release him from his position, the latter pointed to Kritzinger's indispensability in the Chancellery's ongoing fight against the party radicals, and he invoked the notorious formula that it was necessary in order to prevent worse from happening—"Schlimmeres zu verhüten."[34] Lammers himself was not adequately informed about the systematic liquidation process.

I see no reason not to believe Lammers's testimony at Nuremberg that Himmler, when questioned about the Final Solution, gave Lammers only delusive answers and expressly denied that mass liquidations had occurred. Conversely, Himmler cynically assured Lammers that the deported Jews were in good shape and were producing military equipment. When Lammers confronted Hitler with the same questions, he got the impression that Himmler had already given notice of Lammers's intention to raise the issue. In any case, Hitler played down the issue, as he would usually do.[35]

Undeniably, Lammers's reaction to the Wannsee Conference, as Dieter Rebentisch pointed out,[36] was rather naive but was symptomatic of that of many leading civil servants. The episode illuminates the curtailed influence of the Reich bureaucracy. Lammers was unable to prevent the destruction process, so he tried to postpone the deportation program in November 1941, before the original schedule of the Wannsee Conference, and instructed his staff to take a purely passive role in future meetings.[37]

The passive attitude, the futile strategy of noncommitment, could not prevent the civil service from becoming deeply involved in the Final Solution. (A conspicuous exception to this approach was that of Foreign Ministry undersecretary Martin Luther, who *actively* supported the criminal policy against European Jewry.)[38] Any brief glance at the activities of Albert Speer as Reichsinspektor für das Bauwesen, the housing and construction program in Greater Berlin, shows the well-functioning system of expropriation of Jewish apartments and property. In dealing with that, the bureaucracy at all levels became directly involved in the ever-growing corruption and blackmail that characterized the Nazi regime.[39]

Any evaluation of the role of the civil service during the Nazi period must conclude that its inherited moral foundations were even more strongly eroded than its institutional structure. The moral indifference that German civil service displayed in the so-called Jewish Question, long before the Final Solution came into being, was a crucial test case for its incorruptibility, and in general the result was extremely negative. The other question was where to draw the line between passive and active complicity in the implementation of the Holocaust. That appears to be not so much a question of the moral perceptions of the individuals as of their respective function within the system. If one could expand Christopher Browning's pioneering study on Reserve Police Battalion 101 to the civil service at large, the results, presumably, would not be too different.

In the recent literature dealing with the timing of the genocide process, there is still some controversy over the role of the bureaucracy. While Raul Hilberg has stressed the crucial importance of the bureaucratic factor, especially with regard to the implementation of the Holocaust on a European scale, Richard Breitman has concluded that there was no anonymous bureaucratic process automatically leading to mass destruction. "To limit responsibility to the men at the top alone is to provide a convenient excuse for all the others involved," Breitman argues, and he rejects emphasizing "the role of the bureaucrats" versus ideological fanaticism.[40] Presenting Himmler as the main architect of the Holocaust, Breitman tends to put the antisemitic obsession in Himmler's political and ideological thought into the foreground. In criticizing those who put some weight on the bureaucratic contingencies, thereby following Hannah Arendt's analysis of Adolf Eichmann's mentality, he apparently overlooks the fact that it was mainly bureaucratic motive that led Eichmann to continue the destruction of the still surviving Hungarian Jews even after Himmler had ordered a halt to the annihilation.[41] In fact, ideological fanaticism and bureaucratic mentality went together in bringing about the murder of millions of European Jews.

Apart from the aspect of the efficiency of a bureaucratic apparatus functioning on the basis of division of labor, the bureaucratic factor in the process of destruction was indispensable in so far as it served as a smokescreen to hide moral objections. Relying on bureaucratic orders and accepting them as legitimate helped to neutralize possible moral apprehension concerning atrocities on a hitherto unheard-of scale. It was not so much ideological indoctrination as the participants' habits of compliance that allowed them to grow accustomed to the constant use of violence under conditions in which they might see themselves as an involuntary part of bureaucratic machinery that acts according to a rationale of its own. This is shown by the reaction or, better, the nonreaction of the German railwaymen involved in the deportations as well as that of the members of the ordinary police who became actively engaged in the mass liquidations in Poland and the Soviet Union. This also holds true for the average municipal agent in charge of distributing former Jewish property or of assembling the addresses of Jewish fellow-citizens in order to facilitate their deportation. Obviously, crime becomes easier if it is committed collectively, and that necessarily involves the existence of bureaucratic procedures. Still, there is no doubt that all this could not have occurred without the antisemitic indoctrination and the growing adaption to an attitude of moral indifference among the German functional elites since the early 1920s.[42]

NOTES

1. Martin Broszat, *The Hitler State: The Foundation and Development of the Internal Structure of the Third Reich* (London, 1981).

2. Jane Caplan, *Government without Administration: State and Civil Service in Weimar and Nazi Germany* (Oxford, 1988), p. 257; Hans Mommsen, *Beamtentum im Dritten Reich* (Stuttgart, 1966), pp. 89–90.

3. Examples in Mommsen, *Beamtentum*, pp. 63–64.

4. Ralph Angermund, *Deutsche Richterschaft 1919–1945: Krisenerfahrung, Illusion, politische Rechtssprechung* (Frankfurt/M., 1990), pp. 124–25. and 145–46.

5. Raul Hilberg, "The Role of the German Railways in the Destruction of the Jews," paper delivered before the American Sociological Association, 1976.

6. "Niederschrift des Hauptamtsleiters Friedrichs im Stab des Stellvertreters des Führers" (1940), in Mommsen, *Beamtentum*, pp. 228–29; cf. Caplan, *Government without Administration*, pp. 168–69.

7. Mommsen, *Beamtentum*, p. 107.

8. Dieter Rebentisch, "Die politische Beurteilung als Herrschaftsinstrument der NSDAP," in *Die Reihen fest geschlossen*, ed. Detlev Peukert and Jürgen Reulecke (Wuppertal, 1981), pp. 107–25; Mommsen, *Beamtentum*, p. 75.

9. The speeches delivered by Rudolph Hess to the leadership corps of the NSDAP at the party convention at Nuremberg on September 8, 1934, and September 14, 1936 (BA NS 26).

10. Peter Longerich, *Hitlers Stellvertreter: Führung der Partei und Kontrolle des Staats-apparates durch den Stab Hess und die Partei-Kanzlei Bormann* (Munich, 1992), pp. 41–42.

11. Wilhelm Mommsen, ed., *Deutsche Parteiprogramme* (Munich, 1960), p. 78.

12. Uwe Dietrich Adam, *Judenpolitik im Dritten Reich* (Düsseldorf, 1972), pp. 64–65.

13. Sarah Gordon, *Hitler, Germans and the "Jewish Question"* (Princeton, 1984), pp. 152, 168–80; cf. Ian Kershaw, "Antisemitismus und Volksmeinung: Reaktionen auf die Judenverfolgung," in *Bayern in der NS-Zeit II: Herrschaft und Gesellschaft im Konflikt*, ed. Martin Broszat and Elke Fröhlich (Munich, 1979), p. 296; Ian Kershaw, "Popular Opinion in the Third Reich," in *Government, Party, and People in Nazi Germany*, ed. Jeremy Noakes (Exeter, 1980), p. 70; Otto Dov Kulka, "'Public Opinion' in National Socialist Germany," *Zion: A Quarterly for Research in Jewish History* 40 (1975): 260–90.

14. Chefbesprechung im Reichswirtschaftsministerium, August 20, 1935 (BA R18/5523).

15. Hans Mommsen, "The Realization of the Unthinkable: The 'Final Solution of the Jewish Question' in the Third Reich," in Hans Mommsen, *From Weimar to Auschwitz* (Princeton, 1991), p. 228.

16. Ian Kershaw, "The Persecution of Jews and German Public Opinion in the Third Reich," in Leo Baeck Institute, *Year Book* 17 (1981): 86–87; M. Müller-Claudius, *Der Antisemitismus und das deutsche Verhängnis* (Frankfurt/M., 1948), pp. 1699–1700; Hans Mommsen, "Die Funktion des Antisemitismus im 'Dritten Reich,'" in *Zerbrochene Geschichte: Leben und Selbstverständnis der Juden in Deutschland*, ed. Dirk Blasius and Dan Diner (Frankfurt/M., 1991), pp. 163–64.

17. Martin Broszat, "Soziale Motivation und Führer-Bindung des Nationalsozialismus," in Martin Broszat, *Nach Hitler. Der schwierige Umgang mit unserer Geschichte* (Munich, 1988), p. 28.

18. Max Domarus, *Hitler: Reden und Proklamationen, 1932–1945* (Munich, 1965), vol. 1/2, p. 525; Adam, *Judenpolitik im Dritten Reich*, p. 128.

19. Heinz Höhne, *Der Orden unter dem Totenkopf: Die Geschichte der SS* (Gütersloh, 1967), pp. 352–53.

20. Adam, *Judenpolitik im Dritten Reich*, pp. 135–36; Bernhard Lösener, "Als Rassenreferent im Reichsministerium des Inneren," *Vierteljahrshefte für Zeitgeschichte* 9 (1961): 163–65.

21. For the reaction of German Jews to the Nuremberg Laws, see Hans Mommsen and Dieter Obst, "Die Reaktion der deutschen Bevölkerung auf die Verfolgung der Juden 1933–1943," in *Herrschaftsalltag im Dritten Reich*, ed. Hans Mommsen (Düsseldorf, 1988), pp. 384–85; see also Dirk Blasius, "Zwischen Rechtsvertrauen und Rechtszerstörung: Deutsche Juden 1933–1935," in *Zerbrochene Geschichte*, ed. Blasius and Diner, pp. 132–33.

22. Chefbesprechung im Reichsministerium des Inneren of May 21, 1935, and letter by Hjalmar Schacht, September 3 (BA R18/2335); Günter Neliba and Wilhelm Frick, *Der Legalist des Unrechtsstaates* (Paderborn, 1992), p. 202, and Adam, *Judenpolitik*, p. 123.

23. Christopher R. Browning, "The Government Experts," in *The Holocaust: Ideology, Bureaucracy, and Genocide: The San José Papers*, ed. Henry Friedlander and Sybil Milton (Millwood, NY, 1980), pp. 183–97.

24. Adam, *Judenpolitik*, pp. 125–29, and Mommsen, *Realization of the Unthinkable*, pp. 231–32.

25. Adam, *Judenpolitik*, pp. 300–301; Rebentisch, *Führerstaat*, pp. 437–38; Mommsen, *Realization of the Unthinkable*, p. 385.

26. Christopher R. Browning, "Nazi Ghettoization Policy in Poland: 1939–1941," *Central European History* 19 (1986): 343–86; see also idem, *Fateful Months: Essays on the Emergence of the Final Solution*, rev. ed. (New York, 1991).

27. Browning, *Government Experts*, pp. 183–84.

28. Hans Mommsen, "Was haben die Deutschen vom Völkermord an den Juden gewusst?" in *Der Judenpogrom 1938: Von der 'Reichskristallnacht' zum Völkermord*, ed. Walter H. Pehle (Frankfurt, 1988), pp. 194–96.

29. Ibid., pp. 197–98.

30. Hans Mommsen, "Aufgabenkreis und Verantwortlichkeit des Staatssekretärs der Reichskanzlei Dr. Wilhelm Kritzinger," in *Gutachten des Instituts für Zeitgeschichte*, vol. 2 (Stuttgart, 1966), pp. 369–70; Dieter Rebentisch, *Führerstaat und Verwaltung im Zweiten Weltkrieg: Verfassungsentwicklung und Verwaltungspolitik 1939–1945* (Stuttgart, 1989), pp. 63–65.

31. Affidavit by Hans Ficker, October 10, 1948 (Wilhelmstrassen-Trial, MG XI, Bl. 24124); Mommsen, *Aufgabenkreis*, p. 381; cf. Rebentisch, p. 439 note 214.

32. Raul Hilberg, *The Destruction of the European Jews* (Chicago, 1961), p. 53, erroneously believes that Killy was actively involved in the genocide; see Rebentisch, *Führerstaat*, p. 437.

33. Dieter Rebentisch, "Hitlers Reichskanzlei zwischen Politik und Verwaltung," in *Verwaltung kontra Menschenführung im Staat Hitlers: Studien zum politisch-administrativen System*, ed. D. Rebentisch and Karl Teppe (Göttingen, 1986), pp. 78–79; and Uwe D. Adam, "Persecution of Jews: Bureaucracy and Authority in the Totalitarian State," Leo Baeck Institute Year Book 23 (1982): 510–29.

34. Mommsen, *Aufgabenbereich*, pp. 397–98.

35. Rebentisch, *Führerstaat*, pp. 439–40; affidavit by Lammers in IMT XIII, Bl. 61ff. and MG XI, Bl. 21470ff.

36. Rebentisch, *Führerstaat*, p. 440; cf. Adam, *Judenpolitik*, pp. 314–15.

37. Ibid., p. 440. Cf. BA R 22/52, Bl. 153, quoted in Mommsen, "Was haben die Deutschen vom Völkermord an den Juden gewusst," pp. 234–35 note 75.

38. Christopher R. Browning, *The Final Solution and the Foreign Office: A Study of Referat D III of Abteilung Deutschland 1940–43* (New York, 1978), pp. 35–36.

39. Susanne Willms, *Der Generalbauinspektor für die Reichshauptstadt und das Berliner Judentum*, doctoral diss., Bochum University, 1997..

40. Richard Breitman, *Architect of Genocide: Himmler and the Final Solution* (New York, 1991), pp. 248–49.

41. Andreas Biss, *Der Stop der Endlösung* (Stuttgart, 1966); Hilberg, *Destruction of the European Jews*, p. 631.

42. See Christopher R. Browning's impressive conclusion in *Ordinary Men: Reserve Police Battalion 101 and the Final Solution in Poland* (New York: HarperCollins, 1992), pp. 188–89, and see p. 167. See also Raul Hilberg's observations in his *Perpetrators Victims Bystanders: The Jewish Catastrophe 1933–1945* (New York, 1992), chapters 2 and 3.

16.

FRANKLIN H. LITTELL

The Other Crimes of Adolf Hitler

Arguing from within the parameters of biblical theology, we will stipulate immediately that the Holocaust was indeed Hitler's major crime. Outside the biblical context, killing Jews is no more significant—except to Jews, of course—than the killing of Russian apparatchiks and POWs. The Bible text cited most often as a warning to those who wish, contemplate, or plan the genocide of the Jews is *Zechariah* 2:8: "he that toucheth you toucheth the apple of his eye."

We are not arguing from a proof text, however, but in the spirit of the Scriptures so ably interpreted by Eric Voegelin in *Order and History*.[1] The dialogue with the Book of History consists neither in the piling up of mountains of "scientific" facts nor in the chronicle of endless cycles of rising and falling civilizations. The giving of the Torah, the Way of Life, came as the sign of a "leap in being," a discontinuity in human affairs. Previously the tribes and peoples had used the gods to bless and assist their purposes: now the God *who is* (Exodus 3:14) created a people to do *His* will.

The dialogue with the past, in which the memory of the Holocaust hovers over our minds like a dark cloud from Chernobyl, is carried on during a drama which has a beginning, a direction, and an end. In that drama, the survival of the Jewish people is fundamental.

The Question of Uniqueness

We shall also stipulate the uniqueness of the Holocaust, although the nature of that uniqueness is in dispute. Nowhere is the contrast between the language of the Enlightenment and the language of the Bible more evident than in the attempt to identify the uniqueness of the Shoah.

In the language of a reasonable universe, the Holocaust's uniqueness is portrayed in terms of the exigencies of modern war, or the inexorable logic of dictatorships, or the disposal of "surplus populations," or the sheer mass of the project, or an explosion of violent ethnic nationalism. In other words, some general principle or abstraction is sought—a rubric under which the Holocaust may be subsumed. This is the way the children of the Enlightenment think: all of the above are attempts to explain the Holocaust in language that a modern, long-out-of-touch-with-the-Bible worldview, can understand.

Such attempts have one merit: they turn the reader away from the most insensitive and inhuman misuse of biblical myth, in which the Shoah is said to be God's punishment upon a reprobate people. This wicked line of preaching and teaching, even more spiritually debasing than the politics of the Holocaust deniers, is beginning to circulate again in the cultural underworld of Christianity, Islam, and Judaism itself.

However, shrinking our confrontation with the Holocaust to fit the confines of a Cartesian or Kantian mode of thought exacts a price that must be rejected as excessive on two counts. First, a premature closure is effected; our necessary wrestling with the spiritual and intellectual meanings of this watershed event is stopped too soon. We begin to give, in effect, answers that we have already memorized to questions that are utterly new and unique. Second, the moral burden is lifted too soon from our consciences—in our present memory of the past, in our awareness of present choices, and in our present commitment to the future.

There remains a core to the Holocaust story that resists rational explanation, a gravitational pull that draws us back again and again to the story and its meaning(s). What glimpses we have into the dark core of a collapsing universe of discourse reveal a terrifying, mysterious, and demonic chaos for which we have no adequate words. Only the poets, the musicians, and the liturgists, whose message travels along the nerves of the right hemisphere of the brain, can help us initially.

Even yet, as the survivors and liberators and rescuers have begun to speak after "forty years in the wilderness," as the sheer mass of the event has come to command the horizons of our past, present, and future, we look above and beyond pedestrian science for help in rising above our impoverished prose in telling the story and searching its lessons.

When we move on to what Richard Libowitz has called the "third phase," from telling the story and interpreting the message to Holocaust pedagogy,[2] we face a parting of the roads; we may deviate to the abstract/propositional/declarative style, or we can hold to the human measure. The human measure will involve ambiguities, mysteries, paradoxes, varying interpretations, and conflicting insights—what in the Hebrew and early Christian world of thought was called *midrash*. The declarative style, of which we have a prime example in the recent encyclical *Veritatis Splendor*, is, on the other hand, life-destroying in both religious and secular formats.

Since Galileo wrote enthusiastically about the "language of the universe"—that is, mathematics—intellectuals and academics have transferred the style of the dialogue with the Book of Nature in an attempt to control the dialogue with the Book of History and the dialogue with the Book of Books. The human being, who is both the observer and the subject observed, escapes the net cast for him—but he carries a good many scars acquired in the process of auto-emancipation.

With a theology whose method of dealing with the Holocaust has everything tidy, a person can go about his business relatively undisturbed. But if he truly confronts the Holocaust, if he allows himself to be addressed by it, he will, like Jacob, walk the rest of his life with a limp. The uniqueness of the Holocaust is not to be expressed in the propositions, abstractions, and generalizations that academics are accustomed to use in order to seem to tame all disorder and render chaos harmless. The Holocaust is a *specific* story to be told, its uniqueness made troublesome by a concrete truth: six million Jews were targeted and systematically murdered in the heart of Christendom by baptized Roman Catholics, Protestants, and Eastern Orthodox who were never rebuked, let alone excommunicated.

Harry James Cargas, who calls himself a "post-Auschwitz Catholic," has called for the posthumous excommunication of Adolf Hitler[3], Roman Catholic—an action that his church could take but that is not available to contemporary Protestants in their painful recollection of Hermann Göring. Cargas's appeal not only points up the moral uniqueness of the alpine event called "the Holocaust," but also points to the core of the problem of the Shoah for those who still profess Christ. This problem is neither technical nor rational but rather existential.

The Uniqueness Is in Moral Significance

The uniqueness of the Holocaust is not in definition but in moral quality. Using the frame of reference of the Enlightenment, there is no essential difference between what happened to the targeted Jewish victims of Nazism and what happened to the targeted victims of Stalinism. It may be unseemly for a German scholar to assert this, but the equation is fixed by the formula used. Nor is there (in general terms) any difference between the fate of the six million and the fate of the other five million who were murdered in the death camps and in the Nazis' other instrumentalities of death.

A sectarian Jewish objection might be raised to this line of thought, since the person inside the targeted group who has lost precious family and friends quite naturally feels his suffering and his losses most keenly. This response reflects human nature and life in its condition of equivocation and paradox, and it evokes sympathy when it comes to our ears as the outcry of those who still suffer. However, it cannot be made useful as a form of communication to those outside the hearing range of personal association: those at a distance today and the generations yet unborn. The sectarian Jewish warp, which has become much more pronounced in the last decade of Holocaust seminars, conferences, and institutes, is in the long run self-defeating.

Furthermore, it is spiritually degrading for a Jew to argue that the loss of Jewish lives is, in principle, any more serious than the pitiful death of Polish intellectuals, Russian prisoners, German pacifists, and Romanian Gypsies. The word about the meaning of Jewish death and survival is given best by believing Gentiles. For Jewish colleagues, the uplifting and transcendent word reflects a spirit carried by the text, "Blessed be Egypt my people, and Assyria the work of my hands, and Israel mine inheritance" (Isaiah 19:25).

Bruno Bettelheim made the point very well in *The Informed Heart*, and also in the essay "Freedom from Ghetto Thinking," when he lamented the "tragic ghetto thinking that so many Jews still see this greatest tragedy in Jewish history only from the perspective of their own history and not from that of world history to which it belongs."[4] When a Jew makes the case against a narrow sectarianism in this way, he is a Jew with universalist principles. When a Gentile argues in similar language for the "principle of universalism," he is usually trying to escape confrontation with the awful specificity of the Holocaust. This is another of the many reasons why partnership—true collegiality between Jewish and Christian and other Gentile scholars of conscience—is imperative in study and discussion of the lessons of the Holocaust.

The Credibility Crisis for Christians

This partnership must have a more substantial common ground than admission of the important but factually marginal consideration that surrounding the Jewish

Holocaust there were a few rescuers and a few liberators of camps. No honest Christian will be able to divert his eyes long from the fact that the overwhelming number of the baptized were perpetrators and spectators. Nor, unless he runs to escape into some mode of denial (in which case his latter end will be worse yet), can he for long avoid facing the credibility crisis in which post-Holocaust Christianity finds itself.

The rabbis of old taught that had the Gentiles realized the meaning of the destruction of the [Second] Temple they would have mourned it more than the Jews. Likewise, when the baptized realize the meaning of the Holocaust, they will mourn it more than the Jewish people.

In the language of the Bible, the Lord has delivered Israel, and in time the Jewish midrashim will no longer use the Holocaust as a means of Jewish self-definition. The Hebrew genius across the generations has been to avoid the necrophilia into which Gentile enthusiasts of Nazism and Stalinism and other false religions and ideologies have sought their identity. In due season it will be understood that a restored Israel and a renewed Jewry in the *galut* are far more central in the Jewish return to history than the agony of the Shoah.

When, however, will the Christians return to history? This question cannot be answered as long as the churches continue to avoid confrontation with the story and the lessons of the Holocaust. Rabbi Irving Greenberg's challenge to Jewish and Christian thinkers has become a classic: no theological claim should be made after the Shoah "that would not be credible in the presence of burning children."[5] The German Catholic scholar Johannes Metz has issued a similar authoritative word to cobelievers: "What Christian theologians can do for the murdered of Auschwitz and thereby for a true Jewish-Christian ecumenism is, in every case, this: Never again do theology in such a way that its construction remains unaffected, or could remain unaffected, by Auschwitz."[6]

Neither individual Christians nor their communities can find a road back, a path that will take them up to Jerusalem again, without the fraternal concern and assistance of Jewish colleagues. For the sake of both communities, the interfaith cooperation that was present when Holocaust studies were launched in the United States must be stubbornly maintained. This means, among other things, that we must avoid structuring conferences on the Holocaust in which the church factor is purely marginal, and that we must resist the bent of university administrators to render Holocaust studies courses harmless by placing them in Jewish studies departments.

For wisdom and not power politics to rule the agenda, all concerned must recognize that the Holocaust is an alpine event in the history of Christianity as well as in Jewish history. On this side of the mountain nothing is ever the same again, but not all Jewish scholars have yet made it over the pass, and comparatively few Christian academics have assailed as yet the icy slopes.

Hitler's Other Crimes

Confronting the lessons of the Holocaust is necessary to cure the malaise of Christendom. Yet to let the impression arise that Hitler's only crime was the genocide of the Jews is dangerous, both politically and spiritually. Even if the German Third Reich had laid no heavier hands upon the Jews than upon other peoples conquered and controlled, the system was guilty of monstrous sins and crimes. By 1932 there were courageous opponents of the NSDAP terrorist movement; in 1933 some already were risking everything to subvert the regime, before the assault on the Jews was well launched. The first million were in the concentration camps before any Jews as such were incarcerated and years before the killing centers were established. Hitler's other crimes should never be slighted, least of all by declared Jews and believing Gentiles (Christians).

The chief wickedness of Hitler was not a crime at all, but a sin—a sin from which monstrous crimes reasonably, even predictably, issued forth. That sin was idolatry, rendering to a finite and temporal power—in the biblical sense of the word a "creature"—an ultimate authority that rightfully belongs only to the Most High. The Führerstaat was an idol of the intellectuals and the Führer was an idol to the masses they betrayed.

Reading that handwriting on the wall, we see again the merit of government that is limited and secular, politics that is problem-solving and pedestrian rather than sacral or ideological. And again we have our minds opened to the benefits of the social model that features cultural pluralism and religious liberty, in contrast to the monolithic and monochromatic model—whether carrying over from the medieval period or artificially (künstlich) induced by a dictatorship. Above all, we see the inevitable end of idols, idolaters, and idolatry.

Before that clarification reaches us, however, we must wrestle to the point of exhaustion with the implications of Christian apostasy and betrayal, the meaning(s) of the treason of the intellectuals, the unhealthy twist that mere majoritarianism can give to the voice of the people. To make sense of the story, we use "Hitler" as a metaphor—the way many Europeans use "Auschwitz" when they mean the Shoah.

The Credibility Crisis of Academe

Were the sins and crimes of which we speak "Hitler's crimes?" To illustrate the point, the claim is frequently made that among Hitler's other crimes were the corruption of the professions and the perversion of professional ethics (Berufsethik, on which German philosophers of ethics have always placed a high value). After the classic works of Max Weinrich and Werner Richter, not to mention the recent studies by Robert Ericsen (theologians), Benno Müller-Hill (doctors), Joseph Borkin (business managers), and Ingo Müller (jurists), no one can deny the debasement of professional ethics associated with the Third Reich.

But did the initiative lie with "Hitler?" The authoritative studies show otherwise. The years when the victors spoke of Hitler and Hitlerism as uniquely German maladies are gone. So too are the days when Germans could attempt to bracket Nazism and its accompanying crimes as an interregnum, a mysterious mushroom growth without roots, an inexplicable interruption in the course of national history—best speedily set aside, ignored, forgotten. The uniqueness of the Holocaust lies elsewhere. The antecedents to the Nazi genocide of the Jews are intelligible, explicable, and susceptible to scientific analysis and explication. The caesura that is the Shoah is religious and moral, not rational.

More than that: the line of development of the terrorist movement that was the NSDAP would have been charted, its style of governance predicted, and its genocidal mode foreseen—had there existed seventy years ago the body of information and analysis of extremist populist movements that is now available. There are lessons to be drawn from study of the Nazi and Holocaust era of Western civilization, none more important than the refinement of an Early Warning System on potentially genocidal movements.

We do not have a science when a narrator reports on some plague that ravages a city or a people. Fundamental to science is predictability. We have a science when a group of specialists can say with certainty that given certain conditions there will be a plague.

We are coming close to that situation today, in the identification of potentially genocidal movements, of terrorist movements that in both theory and practice are outside the political covenant, that say they mean to destroy some republic or democracy, and the constitution—written or unwritten—that guarantees the liberties of its citizens. A fifteen-point identification "grid" has been published, and to it the distinguished scholar of the Armenian genocide Vahakn Dadrian has recently added another basic identifying characteristic: the process by which a single party infiltrates and absorbs the basic functions of the state.[7]

The Credibility Crisis of Democracy

What de Tocqueville called "democracies that are not free" and Jacob Talmon called "totalitarian democracies" have shown the disturbing capacity of spawning populist movements that are disloyal to the constitution of a free nation and destructive of the rights of loyal citizens (including "loyal oppositions"). Following on the identification of potentially genocidal movements there must be developed a network of laws and enforcements that inhibit their development in time, before they become strong enough to induce civil war or come to power.

One has only to remember the extent to which Hitler's policies were reinforced by plebiscites and other "evidences" of overwhelming popular support, or contemplate the way in which in a very short time the injection of tens of millions of dollars has succeeded in creating a Rush Limbaugh cult of racism and verbal assault in recent American politics, to see that "democratic" politics still has a weak flank.

The Three Fronts in Teaching the Lessons

The Third Reich was *not* an inexplicable aberration. The churches were not infiltrated and corrupted. Their corruption—theological and cultural antisemitism, anti-democratic orientation, and lack of formative work among the laity—was well advanced before the Nazi Party was founded with its Article 24, a net for the unwary: "positives Christentum" (encouraging party faithful to deregister from the church tax rolls and register as "gottgläubig," i.e., non-sectarian).

The professions were *not* infiltrated and corrupted: their essential disinterest in morals and ethics and the claims of life itself, their deference to technological "progress" at all costs, was far advanced before the Nazis appeared on the scene. So was their acceptance of euthanasia and the essentials of what became Nazi "biological politics." In one of his several important articles in the field of medical ethics,

Stephen G. Post of Case Western Reserve University has pointed out that in the early 1920s Americans had already engaged in experiments that won the praise of Nazi medics, that medical researchers outside Germany have shown no hesitation in using tainted data from the Nazi experiments on concentration camp inmates, and that within recent years German medics who criticized and/or exposed the Nazi abuses of medicine have been penalized by the German Chamber of Physicians and have found German medical journals closed to them.[8]

Wherever we turn in study of the Third Reich and Nazi genocide we see that the forces and factors were converging toward a point where, when a critical mass was reached, certain consequences would arise. In short, although the Evil itself is a religious and theological mystery, the specific expressions and forms it took during the Third Reich are no more mysterious than any other policies of modern governments.

Among the critical factors, none was more important than the treason of the intellectuals; among the fateful forces, none was more telling than the servile relationship of the universities to corporations and political centers of power. These are not uniquely German factors and forces, nor did they die out with the military defeat and collapse of the German Third Reich.

It is a hard word to hear, especially for those who live in and on *academe*, but one must listen: the Intellektuellen were not dragged reluctantly into murderous enterprises by the Nazi dictatorship: they were among the imaginative inventors of policies the Nazi state in its own time put into practice. Without the universities and their alumni in the professions—those on corporate boards, in the medical institutes and faculties, before pulpits and lecterns, on the floor and on the bench, who sported the degree of "Doktor" so proudly and at every opportunity—the Third Reich and its programs would never have come into being.

The credibility crisis of the modern university, at least in the United States, is shared by Jews and Christians and others of conscience. The credibility crisis of republican structures and democratic self-government is shared by all citizens. The credibility crisis of Christendom, with which this essay began, rests upon those who still claim to be professing Christians. Although the system will not get well without the assistance of Jewish colleagues, the responsibility of taking the first steps rests with Christians.

Our colleagues can assist in putting the Holocaust on a large map, however, to reject what Stafford Cripps many years ago called thinking of "postage-stamp" dimensions, by resisting the natural temptation to treat the Christian factor in Nazism and the Holocaust as purely marginal to the only important story: the fate of the Jewish people.

Major and Minor Strains of Christian Self-Definition

The Holocaust is threatening for Christian self-definition as well as for Jewish. From the time of the family quarrel, there have been two Christian self-definitions. One of them was given by Jesus in summarizing the Torah:

> Thou shalt love the Lord thy God with all they heart, and with all thy soul, and with all thy mind.

This is the first and great commandment.
And the second is like unto it, Thou shalt love thy neighbor as thyself.
On these two commandments hang all the law and the prophets. (*Matthew* 22: 37–40)

The second identity became a minor note with the rise of the Gentile church, and the resentment of the *goyyim* of the priority of the Hebrew component in the Early Church: a definition of Christian belief stained indelibly by theological antisemitism.

In the declining Christendom of the nineteenth century and the first half of the twentieth century, the negative definition came to the fore. Baptized peoples who had since the 1840s steadily fallen away from church attendance and other basic obligations showed many harmful signs of the lack of formation as Christian community. Thus Christendom in dissolution showed itself still capable of sustaining the negative definition.

Long after most of its casual adherents were incapable of producing the "fruits worthy of repentance" of which the Christian apostolic writings speak, long after the good works of sound faith had become the monopoly of specialized and elite societies and orders, the state-church system was still leaving in the bottom of the barrel a wretched residue of vicious religious and cultural antisemitism. Nazi antisemitism was not a product of the antisemitism of Christendom alone, but the overt expressions of modern political antisemitism found rootage and feed in that thick bottom stratum.

The "other crimes of Adolf Hitler," a baptized Christian for whom Cardinal Bertram of Breslau instructed his priests to celebrate a Memorial Mass on May 5, 1945, and for whom a Memorial Mass was said in Madrid until dictator Francisco Franco died, haunt us because they remind us of who we are and where we are. The demonic Hitler of our wartime propaganda and our current subtle escape mechanisms is no great problem to us any more. What haunts us is the realization that when the crucifixion of the Jews was carried out, as "Christian" peoples we were denying that we knew the prisoner, applauding the political wisdom that let a few die for the sake of "peace in our time," and throwing dice to share in the profits.

What We Cannot Forgive

The "crime" that we really cannot forgive "Adolf Hitler" is the truth that he and his regime hold before us in Christendom a mirror in which we must look at ourselves—serving our most cherished Baalim and Ashtaroth (1 Samuel 7:3–4). We who have triumphantly called ourselves "Christian nations" must see ourselves for what we are: idolatrous nations, peoples who have turned aside, a civilization that sorely needs to have its feet set on the high road of righteousness and justice and peace.

When that happens and we have begun truly to absorb the lessons of the Holocaust, our churches and synagogues, our universities and professions, and our parties and political covenants shall be greatly changed.

NOTES

1. Eric Voegelin, *Order and History*, vol. 1: *Israel and Revelation* (Baton Rouge: Louisiana State University Press, 1956), p. 123.

2. Richard Libowitz, "Teaching the Holocaust: End of the Beginning," in *What Have We Learned?: Telling the Story and Teaching the Lessons of the Holocaust,* ed. Franklin H. Littell, Alan L. Berger, and Hubert G. Locke (Lewiston: Edwin Mellen Press, 1993), pp. 277–88.

3. Harry James Cargas, *A Christian Response to the Holocaust* (Denver, CO: Stonehenge Books, 1981), p. 173.

4. Bruno Bettelheim, *The Informed Heart* (Glencoe, IL: Free Press, 1962); idem, "Freedom from Ghetto Thinking," in *Freud's Vienna and Other Essays* (New York: Knopf, 1990), pp. 259–60.

5. See Irving Greenberg, "Cloud of Smoke, Pillar of Fire: Judaism, Christianity, and Modernity after the Holocaust," *Auschwitz: Beginning of a New Era?* ed. Eva Fleischner (New York: Ktav/Cathedral of St. John the Divine/ADL, 1977), p. 23.

6. Johannes Metz, *The Emergent Church* (New York: Crossroad, 1981), p. 28.

7. Vahakn N. Dadrian, "The Secret Young Turk-Ittihadist Conference and the Decision for the World War I Genocide of the Armenians," *Holocaust and Genocide Studies* 7/2 (1993): 173–201.

8. Stephen G. Post, "Tainted Scientific Data: To Use or Not to Use?" in *What Have We Learned?* ed. Littell et al., pp. 203–204.

Part 5

"Ordinary Men"

THE SOCIOPOLITICAL BACKGROUND

Two of the most fundamental and indeed controversial questions of Holocaust scholarship are who were the perpetrators, and what were their motivations? In *Nazi Doctors*, Robert Jay Lifton relates a conversation he had with Elie Wiesel. "Were they beasts when they did what they did or were they human beings?" Wiesel inquired of Lifton about the Nazi doctors, the men who worked at Birkenau conducting "selections" and human experimentation.

Lifton replied that they were "neither brilliant nor stupid, neither inherently evil nor particularly ethically sensitive, they were by no means the demonic figures—sadistic, fanatic, lusting-to-kill [individuals] people have often thought them to be."

Frustrated by the answer, Wiesel retorted, "But it is demonic that they were not demonic!"

In the five essays below, we learn of a variety of murderers—physicians and policemen, soldiers and members of Einsatzgruppen, Germans and non-Germans, as we seek to understand the human beings behind the killing processes.

Henry Friedlander's "The T4 Killers: Berlin, Lublin, San Sabba" explores two fundamental questions: who were the killers and why did they kill. Friedlander begins his analysis with the T4 operations because they were the first of the systematic killing processes and also the training course for the expanded operations of the Final Solution. Through a mixture of specific portraits and general discussion, he depicts the killers as amateurs mastering skills and soon to become efficient killers. Most were lackluster until the Nazi rise to power. Raised in the modest circumstances of the German lower middle class, almost all joined the Nazi Party at an early stage and held minor, not leading, party positions. The jobs they received provided them with access. Thus, they were motivated by career considerations. They wanted to be close to the center of power while still remaining close to home. Some were motivated by material benefits; others were fascinated by the power they possessed, the right to command and to make life and death decisions.

They were selected for loyalty to the party and to the men who recruited them. They in turn hired men of loyalty, often people to whom they were bound by ties of friendship or family relationship. Many possessed managerial and organizational abilities, special skills not as killers but as lawyers and accountants. Each demonstrated a willingness to collaborate. Because they were working with friends and relatives, peer pressure was intense. Their esprit de corps was strengthened in part by their sense of discipline and of history. They had to be hard. They had a sense of participating in "a historic understanding." They were bound by blood and by an oath of silence.

Friedlander admits that ideology is missing from his analysis. Certainly in a study of the T4 managers who began their career killing the handicapped in the so-called euthanasia programs, antisemitism is not identified as a prime motivation. The T4 killers, however, did share the larger racial ideology of the Nazis, demonstrated by their depth of commitment and measure of radicalism.

Christopher R. Browning's "Ordinary Germans or Ordinary Men: A Reply to the Critics" is directed at the criticism leveled against his books. These criticisms are voiced primarily by Daniel Jonah Goldhagen and Israeli critics who suggest that Browning erred in not emphasizing the ideological factor influencing the behavior of the killer—antisemitism—and in not using Jewish sources. Browning tackles his critics directly. He argues that while Lucy S. Dawidowicz and Daniel Jonah Goldhagen emphasize the singularity and centrality of German antisemitism, recent scholarship by Ian Kershaw, David Bankier, and Otto Dov Kulka does not confirm their conclusions. Kershaw has argued that antisemitism was not a major factor in attracting support for Hitler, most especially in the early 1930s. As the regime came to power and during its first years, the majority of Germans accepted legal disemancipation but were alienated by hooliganistic violence. All three scholars have distinguished between the antisemitism of the party, of the true believers, and of the general population.

The general conclusion of these scholars does not sustain the image of an entire population deranged by delusional mass psychosis and in the grips of a hallucinatory lethal view of Jews. Furthermore, Browning argues that to understand the assault against the other victims of Nazis, such as the handicapped, Soviet POWs, and Gypsies, among others, something more than antisemitism must be included. The road to Auschwitz, as Kershaw demonstrated, was built with hatred but paved with indifference.

Browning also argues that the behavior of non-German units in Belorussia and the Ukraine, the rural forces that participated in the second wave of mobile killings, closely paralleled the behavior of Reserve Unit 101. Since these were not German units, the killers could not be called "ordinary Germans." Browning contends that the local police joined the killing units for many reasons: pay, food, release from POW camps, and family exemption from deportation to forced labor. As to his nonuse of Jewish sources, Browning responds that while Jewish testimony is indispensable to establishing chronology, survivor testimony does not really shed light on the "internal dynamics of the itinerant killing units." Some recent works do, however, suggest that as close contact was sustained between killer and victims, a greater variety of behaviors could be observed, and some testimony from Jewish sources, which Browning cites, confirms his conclusions.

Jürgen Förster's "Complicity or Entanglement? Wehrmacht, War, and Holocaust" explores the role of the Wehrmacht in the killing process. In the controversy surrounding a visit to Bitburg, President Ronald Reagan tried to distinguish between German soldiers and members of the SS. Förster concludes with the poignant observation that with regard to the Holocaust, "the Wehrmacht acted in many roles. It was perpetrator, collaborator, and bystander. Only after the war did it claim to be victim." Förster argues that while the portrayal of the army as another of Hitler's victims may assuage the honor of the Wehrmacht, it does no justice to truth.

During the early 1930s, the Wehrmacht responded to the change of political climate by engaging in a process of purification, which intensified after the German entry into Austria and again in 1940. With the commencement of the war in September 1939, the attitude of German forces toward the Polish population was a mixture of racial arrogance, insecurity, and naive trust in methods of force. After the first month, Hitler granted a general amnesty to those who violated military law during the Polish campaign, overstepping ordinary military discipline. Two years later, he issued a seemingly blanket amnesty before the invasion of the Soviet Union, where the military aims were expressed in the most unusual of terms; it was called a "Vernichtungskrieg," a war of destruction,—against an ideology and its adherents. Förster comments that Hitler wanted to "erase the line between military and political warfare before the first shot was fired."

The military feared the disorderly nature of the attacks against Jews and other targets. They feared the barbarization of the troops. They also sought to create some distance between themselves and the SS. Thus, they fought real subordination of the SS under the army because the latter would then become responsible for the execution of political tasks. Still, even "pure military" handling of civilian populations included reprisals, mass killing, and ideological warfare.

It would be a mistake to assume that the relationship between the SS and the Wehrmacht was uniform throughout Eastern Europe. In fact, Förster argues that while in the Soviet Union the Wehrmacht assisted the Einsatzgruppen in their mass killing operations, in Serbia their roles were reversed, with the Wehrmacht as major player and the Einsatzgruppen performing a supporting role.

Dutch historian Guus Meershoek's "The Amsterdam Police and the Persecution of the Jews," is a careful and courageous examination of the entire process of bureaucratic persecution of Jews in the Netherlands as seen from the vantage point of the Amsterdam police. It is bound to be—and intended to be—embarrassing for Dutch historians who tend to describe the persecution by occupying forces rather than Dutch cooperation. But Meershoek is committed both to telling the truth and to describing the persecution of the Jews from the vantage point of the Dutch bureaucracy.

For a long time, the Amsterdam police adopted a conciliatory attitude toward the Nazis to prevent the occupying forces from imposing their demands by force. They tried to keep one step ahead of the occupying forces but were unable to keep pace as the scope and the pace of the Final Solution intensified.

This approach was doomed to failure. Amsterdam police then fell back on their traditional decentralized structure. In the end, the occupying forces directed local police in the round-up of Jews.

What distinguished Amsterdam police behavior from that of their counterparts in other occupied countries and cities was frequent demonstration that they were acting with reluctance. Nevertheless, they still acted to facilitate and thus make possible the deportation of Jews.

Meershoek points out the three major shocks to German expectations that were inflicted by the Dutch people: the February 1941 riot, the response to the 1941 ban on Jews entering public places, and the reaction to the September 2, 1942, order to deport Jews. He describes the bureaucratic means by specifying the internal struggles that in the end led to wholesale compliance. The inspector who protested the loudest was assigned to lead a detachment; he refused and was soon dismissed. Police who were under severe stress during the raids engaged in small-scale revolts, requiring the hands-on presence of the Chief of Constables. Shortly after his death, operations against Jews were taken over by Dutch Nazi Auxiliary police. Meershoek concludes that in Amsterdam, police did not turn to persecution on their own initiative. Yet in the end, after much infighting and maneuvering, they became an indispensable and compliant instrument of the Nazis.

Daniel Jonah Goldhagen's "The Evil of Banality" was almost the lone dissenter in the high praise that was accorded Christopher R. Browning's : *Ordinary Men: Reserve Police Battalion 101 and the Final Solution in Poland*. In dialogue, both Browning and Goldhagen sharpened the points of engagement. Here, in "Ordinary Men or Ordinary Germans?" Goldhagen suggests that there is a difference in their reading of empirical accounts. Browning, he says, understates the brutality of the men and the voluntary nature of their participation in the killings. In German documents, most especially postwar testimony, lying is rampant. Testimony is often self-exculpatory. Goldhagen suggests that the brutality of the killers was far more than merely pragmatic. He asks whether they were ordinary men or ordinary Germans and insists that Browning understates the role of ideology as well as the public antisemitic and racist culture of Nazi Germany—which was anything but ordinary.

Their debate continued with the publication of Goldhagen's controversial book *Hitler's Willing Executioners: Ordinary Germans and the Holocaust*. The Research Institute of the United States Holocaust Memorial Museum again became a site of intellectual engagement when Browning criticized a narrow reading of the sources by Goldhagen. The five essays here demonstrate the complexity involved in understanding the perpetrators and the difficulty involved in reaching simple conclusions.

17.

HENRY FRIEDLANDER

The T4 Killers

BERLIN, LUBLIN, SAN SABBA

Those studying Nazi crimes and Nazi criminals have always asked two fundamental questions: "Who committed these crimes?" and "Why did they commit
them?" I shall attempt to answer these questions by examining the T4 killers.

The term "T4" designated the mass murder of the handicapped; it was euphemistically called euthanasia and was initiated on Hitler's orders in late 1939 and
directed by the Chancellery of the Führer (KdF). To hide this killing operation, the
KdF created various front organizations that operated from headquarters at Tiergar-
tenstrasse 4 in Berlin, therefore known as T4. To accomplish their task, the T4 killers
invented the killing center, using modern industrial methods to accomplish mass
murder. They established and operated six such centers—Brandenburg, Grafeneck,
Hartheim, Sonnenstein, Bernburg, and Hadamar—and murdered there more than
seventy thousand German "Aryan" nationals before T4 decentralized its killings in
August 1941.

The so-called euthanasia program was not the only killing operation involving
the KdF and T4. The KdF was also involved, from the beginning, in the implementation of the Final Solution, the mass murder of European Jews and Gypsies. In 1942
the KdF dispatched selected members of the T4 staff to Lublin to run the killing
centers of Operation Reinhard: Belzec, Sobibor, and Treblinka. Applying the methods
they had invented to kill the handicapped in the Reich, the T4 killers murdered at
least one and three-quarter million human beings in the Lublin camps. After the
completion of Operation Reinhard in 1943, the KdF posted their men as a group to
Trieste. There, in addition to other duties, the T4 contingent created a concentration
camp and killing center in the Risiera di San Sabba, a former rice factory in the San
Sabba district of the city of Trieste.[1]

An analysis of the T4 men is particularly valuable for a variety of reasons. First,
they invented, directed, and operated history's first technological killing operation.
Their project—the first one Nazi Germany implemented—served as a model for all
that followed. Second, most of them were amateurs with no previous killing experi-

ence who mastered their killing profession on the job. Third, as they did not belong to any one paramilitary organization and were secretly recruited from a variety of places, they tell us a great deal about the process of selecting killers. Finally, they first murdered handicapped Germans, and later Jews and Gypsies; we therefore have to look beyond antisemitism for their ideological motivation.

One further introductory comment is warranted. These perpetrators of the Holocaust were dull and uninteresting men. Although they were competent at their jobs, most lacked imagination, had pedestrian minds, and led conventional lives. These facts emerge from their postwar testimonies, and even more clearly from the few surviving personal letters. Their writings were bureaucratic, their speeches were cliché-ridden, and their postwar testimonies evasive, insensitive, and self-pitying.

The chief perpetrators—Hitler and his intimates—set policy, but they left the implementation of mass murder to a group of managers. The careers of the T4 managers were lackluster until the Nazi revolution lifted them from obscurity. An extraordinarily small number of men managed T4: Viktor Brack (chief, KdF office II), Werner Blankenburg (Brack's deputy), Dietrich Allers (second T4 business manager), Hans-Joachim Becker (T4 accountant), Gerhard Bohne (first T4 business manager), Friedrich Haus (T4 personnel officer), Hans Hefelmann (KdF office IIb), Richard von Hegener (Hefelmann's deputy), Adolf Gustav Kaufmann (T4 inspector), Friedrich Robert Lorent (T4 finance officer), Arnold Oels (T4 personnel officer), Fritz Schmiedel (T4 finance officer), Willy Schneider (T4 finance officer), Gerhard Siebert (T4 transport officer), Friedrich Tillmann (T4 office manager), and Reinhold Vorberg (KdF office IId).[2] Five of them—Brack, Blankenburg, Hefelmann, von Hegener, and Vorberg—were officials of the KdF before the killings; the others came on board to help run the killing operation. But even this number is deceptive.

The managers, all born between 1900 and 1910, were unexceptional for men of their age group. Though a few had professional degrees, most had worked in business after high school. None was well established when the Nazis came to power in 1933. Although the professional careers of the T4 managers were ordinary, their past politics proved an advantage under the Nazi regime. Almost all had joined the Nazi movement in their early or middle twenties, prior to Hitler's assumption of power. Several were members of the SA, three also of the SS. Brack, the leader of the group, had the most impressive party connections: his father had delivered one of the Himmler children, and Brack had served as Himmler's driver before he worked for Philipp Bouhler. Several had been junior bureaucrats in the German civil service. Still, these young men held only auxiliary, not leading, party positions.

For these young men, jobs at the Chancellery of the Führer provided access to influence, power, and future advancement. These jobs spelled professional success. In addition, these jobs brought personal benefits. Thus Kaufmann, drafted into the navy, wanted a safe rear area job ("Druckposten") to enable him to visit his sick wife.[3] Becker, who was released from military duty for poor health, did not like his wartime civilian assignment in Danzig and wanted to use his connections to get a better job.[4] Allers had been drafted and was a noncommissioned officer stationed in Poland; he apparently did not like this low status and obtained his appointment at T4 through his mother's intervention with Blankenburg.[5] Oels was unemployed after his discharge from the Waffen-SS following the French campaign.[6] Lorent, who wanted to leave his assigned post in occupied Poland, visited the KdF to get himself another job.[7]

We may ask how these men were selected. Obviously, it was not an open competition. Instead, a variety of factors determined recruitment: party credentials, availability, required skills, and—especially—nepotism. Among the KdF staff, Brack moved from driving Himmler to serving as Bouhler's adjutant; von Hegener was a brother-in-law of Hans Reiter, president of the Reich Health Office; and Vorberg was Brack's cousin. Bohne and Allers came with legal experience. Becker was a cousin of the wife of Herbert Linden, the physician in the health department of the Reich Ministry of the Interior who served as liaison with T4. Kaufmann, Lorent, Haus, Schneider, and Schmiedel were friends or acquaintances of Brack. Linden had met and recruited Tillmann. Oels's Viennese lady friend worked at Hadamar and told him to apply at T4. Siebert was a cousin of Brack and Vorberg.

Most of these men, then, were selected primarily for their loyalty to the party and to those who recruited them, but their technical knowledge, such as office management and accounting, were also qualifications. There is no evidence that those who defined the hiring requirements and who recruited were looking for expertise in killing people. Still, willingness to collaborate in a killing enterprise was a job requirement. Since the men newly hired by T4 were either relatives or friends of the KdF managers and had solid party credentials, we may assume that their willing collaboration was never in question. We know of no instance where a manager recruited by the KdF refused to join. Some left after a short period with T4, of course, but there is no evidence that they did so because they morally objected to their assignment. Rather, they simply moved on to other jobs. The departure of Gerhard Bohne in the summer of 1940 was caused by his opposition to the way the euthanasia killings were implemented, not out of moral concerns about the procedure itself. Bohne criticized the personal behavior of T4 personnel: sexual licentiousness, misuse of resources, and arrogant conduct involving local staff and visiting dignitaries at the killing centers. His aim was to improve efficiency, not to stop the killings. Bohne simply argued that "loose morals soon lead to a general decline of government service."[8]

These men were "Schreibtischtäter," bureaucratic killers, but they were not as distant from the killings as is usually assumed. Almost all visited the killing centers, saw the victims, and watched the gassing. The lawyer Dietrich Allers, the T4 business manager who married a secretary who had worked at Hartheim, visited the T4 killing centers numerous times, as well as the extermination camps in the East; in the spring of 1944 he assumed command of Sonderkommando Trieste. These managers thus knew what they were doing and had seen the final results of their actions.

Why did they agree to manage mass murder? Historians have offered a number of common sense explanations, which they have applied to the managers as well as to the rank and file who did the actual killings: authoritarianism, careerism, duress, and peer pressure.[9]

Duress does not apply.[10] These men maneuvered to get their jobs and left when it became personally convenient. Peer pressure does not apply. Although there was

Kameradschaft, or esprit de corps, there was also a great deal of back-biting and in-fighting. Authoritarianism did play a role, because they all believed in the Führer-prinzip, and they were all the Führer's men. But Hitler had first commissioned Leonardo Conti, State Secretary of Health in the Reich Ministry of the Interior, to manage the killings, and the KdF had maneuvered to get this commission away from him. It was therefore not a direct order to be obeyed but a plum to be sought.

Career considerations were undoubtedly the most important reason why the T4 managers agreed to direct the killings. A job at the KdF placed them close to the center of power. These young men had reached positions commonly considered important and influential. In addition, these jobs involved an assignment that was secret, sensitive, and significant. They operated at the center of events.

A good example of the pride generated by a mixture of careerism and authoritarianism is Hans-Heinz Schütt, a thirty-eight-year-old junior manager who served in the office at Grafeneck and later also in Sobibor. In a letter to his stepbrother on the occasion of the boy's confirmation, Schütt told him that they were living in "an age . . . never previously experienced by a German," also pointing out that "there is only one victor, and this victor will determine the future of Europe, even the entire world. And this victor is Adolf Hitler." In passing, Schütt reveals the reason his job is so attractive: he is "happy and proud," because he is a member of a Sonderkommando "known possibly only to 100 people in this large German Reich."[11]

These jobs also involved other benefits. First, they provided a secure berth at the home front, with no stigma for all and even medals for some. Second, they provided material benefits, including monetary allowances, travel, and expense accounts. Third, they brought power over others, the right to command, and the ability to make life-and-death decisions. T4 managers exercised this power and appeared to others as arrogant men of influence.

One motivation—ideology—is missing from this analysis. Historians have argued that Nazi ideology was an important motivation that led the perpetrators to comply with murderous orders.[12] This argument is usually advanced concerning the murder of Jews and focuses on the antisemitism of the perpetrators. Obviously, antisemitism as a cause is too restrictive when applied to men who started their killing careers murdering German non-Jews. Instead we must point to the larger eugenic and racial ideology of the Nazis, one that included hostility toward the handicapped as inferior ("minderwertig") and toward Jews and Gypsies as aliens. The T4 managers undoubtedly shared this hostility toward those perceived as inferior and alien, as they shared most other tenets of Nazi ideology. After all, they were Nazis.

But most Germans shared these beliefs. Except for political opponents incarcerated in the concentration camps and their sympathizers, most Germans accepted Nazi ideology, at least in part. Yet except for a few fanatics such as Irmfried Eberl and his wife, this ideology served as a necessary justification for most T4 killers but was not the only reason, as mentioned above, that they agreed to carry out the dirty job of killing.

For reasons of space, I must omit physicians, chemists, police officers, and ministerial bureaucrats in analyzing the T4 perpetrators. Unlike Robert Jay Lifton, who has advanced a theory of "doubling" as an explanation, I see no special problems analyzing the physicians. The senior ones had the same motivation as the managers. The junior ones were simply rank-and-file killers with medical degrees.[13]

Rank-and-file members were usually not individually recruited. As T4 was looking for people without supervisory or technical skills to do physical labor, routine office work, and janitorial service, those selected were basically interchangeable. The T4 managers wanted individuals they could trust, but the selection criteria were nevertheless simple; to some extent these rank-and-file members were much like those who had applied to be managers themselves. They selected individuals who were recommended, knew someone already inside the organization, or had party credentials. T4 relied on the bureaucracy to recommend candidates, circulating job announcements for "trustworthy party members" to various party and government offices.[14] Thus the T4 mason Erwin Lambert, who worked for T4 in Germany, Lublin, and Trieste, was recommended by the Labor Front; and August Miete, who later also went to Treblinka and Trieste, was told to apply to Grafeneck by his local Chamber of Agriculture office.[15] T4 also preferred candidates whose friends were already part of the killing operation, thus permitting insiders to vouch for newcomers. This, apparently, was the way Franz Suchomel and Franz Wolf, who later served in Hadamar, Sobibor, Treblinka, and Trieste, entered T4.[16] Most often, however, the news about jobs circulated by word-of-mouth. Thus, for example, Margit Troller heard that the Linz Nazi party regional office was looking for people to fill jobs at an agency outside the city; she applied and was hired as a clerk for Hartheim.[17]

Most rank-and-file staff members were hired on the local level. To staff Hartheim, for example, T4 used the office of Upper Austrian Gauleiter August Eigruber. The job of finding people was apparently given to the regional inspector, Stefan Schachermeyer, who also arranged the necessary paper work. Candidates usually had a brief interview in Linz with T4 representatives from Berlin—Brack, Kaufmann, and others—but most often with the local people, Rudolf Lonauer and Christian Wirth.[18]

This relatively lax selection system was based on the assumption that party members could be trusted, especially if other party members vouched for them. Sometimes, however, they needed to hire someone with special skills—someone who did not have such recommendations. At that point T4 had to investigate. Thus, the electrician Herbert Kalisch was interviewed by the Gestapo before T4 would complete the hiring process.[19]

One Hartheim stoker ("Brenner") can serve as a good example of the truly idiosyncratic nature of the hiring process. The Austrian Vinzenz Nohel, born in Moravia in 1902, was trained as a mechanic but was frequently unemployed. In 1939 he earned 25 RM per week toward the support of his wife and four children and was thus always "looking to earn more money." Although his postwar interrogation does not indicate whether he was a member of the Nazi party, his brother was a long-time party member and SA brigadier general ("Brigadeführer"). Nohel hoped that this brother, who returned to Austria from the Reich after the Anschluss, would help him obtain a better-paying job. At first the brother did not help him. Finally, late in 1939 or early in 1940, his brother invited Nohel to his Linz office, and there the T4's Kaufmann hired Nohel to work in the Hartheim killing center. During his postwar interrogation, Nohel described the hiring procedure: "I went with my brother, and several other men looking for work, to the government building to see a certain Kaufmann. There I was asked about my current wages. They laughed when I told them that I had been earning 25 RM per week. They then told me and the others that we would be sent to Hartheim and that we would earn more money." In Hartheim Nohel was assigned work as a stoker and he remained there until the end. He did receive the promised higher wages: 170 RM per month, plus 50 RM family separation allowance, 35 RM stokers' allowance, and a 35 RM premium for keeping quiet. Further, "because the work [as stoker] was very strenuous and nerve-shattering, we also received a quarter of a liter of schnapps every day."[20]

After the war, many T4 rank-and-file killers claimed that they had cooperated only under duress. But in more than thirty years of postwar proceedings, no proof has emerged that anyone who refused to participate in killing operations had been shot, incarcerated, or penalized in any way, except perhaps through transfer to the front—but this, after all, was the destiny of most German soldiers.[21] Punishment, even incarceration in a concentration camp, was a real possibility only if members of the staff talked about the killings to outsiders. All had to sign an oath of silence. One secretary at Grafeneck was committed to a concentration camp by Viktor Brack because she talked about her work; she was released through the intervention of Werner Heyde.[22] Regardless of the truth and fiction of such stories, punishment had nothing to do with a refusal to participate.

It is appropriate to ask how difficult it actually was to get away. This is hard to ascertain, because virtually no one openly refused. There is, however, testimony that staff members who wanted to leave were told to approach the T4 manager Adolf Kaufmann, who got them discharged within two weeks.[23] The male nurse Franz Sitter from Ybbs volunteered for Hartheim in October 1940 without knowing the details of the job. After Wirth informed him and swore him to secrecy, Sitter decided to refuse. He asked to see Lonauer and demanded to be released. Lonauer tried to talk him out of it, pointing to the "financial advantages" and to the draft deferment. Sitter insisted and was returned to Ybbs. He was drafted in February 1941.[24]

Sitter was the exception to the rule; most staff members, despite any personal reservations, continued to do their assigned work. These men and women worked day after day in a factory with only one product: corpses of murdered human beings. They rapidly developed an atmosphere of licentiousness, an attitude that "anything goes." One constantly used stimulus was alcohol, which was freely distributed by the supervisors. One staff member assigned to Hartheim as a photographer found that the stench of burning flesh made it impossible for him to keep any food in his stomach. Wirth prescribed alcohol, and thereafter the photographer was always drunk.[25]

Reports abounded about drunken orgies, numerous sexual liaisons, brawling and bullying, and the stealing of property of victims.[26] The toleration of such behavior by T4 had led to the resignation of business manager Gerhard Bohne, but the other T4 managers knew that they could not impose too many restrictions on those assigned to the secret killings.[27] After all, the important task was killing, and the job of managers was to assure that the staff members served the killing process. At Hadamar the staff celebrated the cremation of the ten thousandth corpse with a party.

Assembling in the basement crematorium, they covered the corpse with flowers, a staff member dressed as a priest delivered a sermon, the corpse was cremated, and the staff drank beer.[28]

Even more revealing is the story of the Hadamar secretary Ingeborg Seidel. As she told her postwar interrogator, she did her secretarial work with a carton of gold teeth on her desk:

> Gold teeth? They were handed to us in the office whenever there was someone who had gold teeth. Many handed to us? No. They were brought to me in a bowl by one of the stokers. He had a book and I had a book, and we thus confirmed accuracy. We had a little carton, and that is where we kept them until we had accumulated a sufficiently large amount, and we then sent them by courier to Berlin.[29]

Almost one hundred T4 killers were eventually posted to Belzec, Sobibor, and Treblinka. Some of the staff had been stokers, and others had transported, undressed, and led patients to the gas chamber. But many had never been assigned to work with patients or near gas chambers. All of them, however, had been intimately involved in the killing process. One might assume the T4 killers who were selected for further duties in the East were the most dedicated of the T4 staff, those with the greatest killing experience. Yet this was not true, and we may never know why these particular men were chosen. Nothing distinguished them from their T4 colleagues; their background, party affiliation, and T4 jobs did not differ from those of their colleagues who were not posted to the Lublin camps.

Why did these rank-and-file men and women participate in the killings? The reasons did not differ substantially from those that motivated their superiors. Though most were committed to Nazi ideology, there is no evidence that they were particularly fanatic Nazis. Peer pressure probably helped sustain their involvement, especially after posting to the East, but it does not explain their initial willingness to participate. And there is no doubt that they expected material benefits: a safe job, good food and drink, special allowances, and "brownie points" for the future.

When all is said and done, I am still unable to fathom why seemingly normal men and women were able to commit such extraordinary crimes. Neither ideology nor self-interest is a satisfactory explanation for such behavior. Attempts to replicate their actions in the laboratory must fail, even if experiments seem to show, as did the one by Stanley Milgram, that ordinary men anywhere can commit such crimes.[30] But there is a fundamental difference between the antiseptic experimental setting and the grisly reality of the killing centers. The T4 killers confronted real human beings as victims and saw their agony, the blood and gore of the killing process. In Milgram's social science experiment, the subjects might lack the imagination to understand the pain they could inflict, but the Nazi killers, even if they lacked all imagination, could not avoid knowing what they were doing. They understood the consequences of their deeds.

NOTES

1. On the euthanasia killings, see Ernst Klee, *"Euthanasie" im NS-Staat: Die "Vernichtung lebensunwerten Lebens"* (Frankfurt/M., 1983). On the camps of Operation Reinhard, see Adalbert Rückerl, *NS-Vernichtungslager im Spiegel deutscher Strafprozesse* (Munich, 1977). On San Sabba, see *San Sabba: Istruttoria e processo per il Lager della Risiera*, ed. Adolfo Scalpelli, 2 vols. (Milan, 1988).

2. See Berlin Document Center (BDC), dossiers of Allers, Brack, Blankenburg, Becker, Bohne, Hefelmann, von Hegener, Kaufmann, and Lorent. See also Nuremberg Docs. NO-426 and NO-820 (affidavits Brack); National Archives and Records Administration (NA), RG 238, M–1019, roll 8 (interrogations Brack); U.S. Military Tribunal, Case 1 Transcript, pp. 7413–72 (testimony Brack); and Ernst Klee, *Was sie taten–Was sie wurden: Ärzte, Juristen und andere Beteiligten am Kranken- oder Judenmord* (Frankfurt/M., 1986), pp. 34–36, 75–76, 78–79, 81–82, 293–95. On von Hegener, see also correspondence in Bundesarchiv Koblenz (BAK), NL 263, Nachlass Rheindorf, no. 50; ibid., Landeskriminalpolizeiabteilung Mecklenburg, Anklage von Hegener, 5-0/410/47/B1, 5-0/339/49/B1, Schwerin, September 9, 1949; and Zentrale Stelle der Landesjustizverwaltungen Ludwigsburg (ZStL), Slg. Verschiedenes, Bd. 18: Landgericht (LG) Magdeburg, Urteil von Hegener, 11 Kls 139/51, February 20, 1952. On Allers and Vorberg, see also Generalstaatsanwalt (GStA) Frankfurt, Anklage Vorberg und Allers, Js 20/61 (GStA), February 15, 1966, pp. 267ff.; LG Frankfurt, Urteil Vorberg und Allers, Ks 2/66 (GStA), December 20, 1968, pp. 2ff. On Becker and Lorent, see also GStA Frankfurt, Anklage Renno, Becker, und Lorent, Js 18/61 (GStA), Js 7/63 (GStA), Js 5/65 (GStA), November 7, 1967, pp. 79ff., 87ff.; and LG Frankfurt, Urteil Becker und Lorent, Ks 1/69 (GStA), May 27, 1970, pp. 3ff. On Kaufmann, see also GStA Frankfurt, Anklage Kaufmann, Js 16/63 (GStA), June 27, 1966, pp. 3–8, 21–36. See also *Berlin Document Center*, vol. 11, pts. 1–2 of *Archives of the Holocaust*, ed. Henry Friedlander and Sybil Milton, 2 vols. (New York, 1992), pp. xvii, xix, and Docs. 14, 51, 58–61.

3. GStA Frankfurt, Anklage Kaufmann, Js 16/63 (GStA), June 27, 1966, pp. 21, 40–41.

4. GStA Frankfurt, Anklage Renno, Becker, und Lorent, Js 18/61 (GStA), Js 7/63 (GStA), Js 5/65 (GStA), November 7, 1967, p. 80.

5. Gitta Sereny, *Into That Darkness: From Mercy Killing to Mass Murder* (New York, 1974), p. 79. See also GStA Frankfurt, Anklage Vorberg und Allers, Js 20/61 (GStA), February 15, 1966, p. 273.

6. ZStL: interrogation Arnold Oels, Hanover, April 24, 1961.

7. GStA Frankfurt, Anklage Renno, Becker, und Lorent, Js 18/61 (GStA), Js 7/63 (GStA), Js 5/65(GStA), November 7, 1967, p. 88.

8. Cited in Klee, *Was sie taten–Was sie wurden*, p. 73.

9. See, for example, Christopher R. Browning, *Ordinary Men: Reserve Police Battalion 101 and the Final Solution in Poland* (New York, 1991).

10. For a discussion of duress as a defense in postwar trials, see Adalbert Rückerl, *NS-Verbrechen vor Gericht* (Heidelberg, 1982), pp. 281ff. For specific examples of how duress has been argued and applied in postwar proceedings, see Henry Friedlander, "The Deportation of the German Jews: Postwar Trials of Nazi Criminals," Leo Baeck Institute *Year Book* 29 (1984): 201–26.

11. Cited in LG Hagen, Urteil Werner Dubois, 11 Ks 1/64, December 20, 1966, pp. 302–304. Emphasis in original.

12. See, for example, Daniel Jonah Goldhagen in *New Republic*, July 13 and 20, 1992, pp. 49–52.

13. See Robert Jay Lifton, *The Nazi Doctors: Medical Killing and the Psychology of Genocide* (New York, 1986).

14. LG Hagen, Urteil Dubois, 11 Ks 1/64, December 20, 1966, p. 120.

15. On Lambert, see Staatsanwaltschaft (StA) Stuttgart, Verfahren Widmann, Ks 19/62 (19 Js 328/60), interrogation Erwin Lambert, April 26, 1961, continuation May 4, 1961, pp. 20–22; ZStL, interrogations Erwin Lambert, April 3, 1962 and February 12, 1963. On Miete, see StA Düsseldorf, Anklage Franz, 8 Js 10904/59, January 29, 1963, p. 47.

16. ZStL: interrogation Franz Suchomel, February 5, 1963; LG Hagen, Urteil Dubois, 11 Ks 1/64, December 20, 1966, pp. 210–13 (Franz Wolf).

17. Dokumentationsarchiv des österreichischen Widerstandes Vienna (DÖW), E18370/3: interrogation Margit Troller, Linz, June 25, 1946.

18. DÖW, E18370/1: Kreisgericht Wels, interrogation Stefan Schachermeyer, March 11, 1964; DÖW, E18370/2: Volksgericht des LG Linz, Hauptverhandlung Harrer, Lang, und Mayrhuber, Vg 6 Vr 2407/46 (186), July 2–3, 1948, p. 14 (testimony Schachermeyer).

19. StA Stuttgart, Verfahren Widmann, Ks 19/62 (19 Js 328/60), interrogation Herbert Kalisch, Mannheim, January 25, 1960.

20. DÖW, E18370/3: Kriminalpolizei Linz, interrogation Vinzenz Nohel, September 4, 1945.

21. See Herbert Jäger, *Verbrechen unter totalitärer Herrschaft: Studien zur nationalsozialistischen Gewaltkriminalität*, 2nd ed. (Frankfurt/M., 1982), pp. 94ff.

22. Alice Platen-Hallermund, *Die Tötung Geisteskranker in Deutschland: Aus der Deutschen Ärztekommission beim amerikanischen Militärgericht* (Frankfurt/M., 1948), p. 107.

23. GStA Frankfurt, Anklage Kaufmann, Js 16/63 (GStA), June 27, 1966, p. 31.

24. DÖW, E18370/2: Bezirksgericht Ybbs, interrogation Franz Sitter, March 20, 1947.

25. DÖW, E18370/1: Bundesministerium für Inneres, interrogation Bruno Bruckner, Vienna, May 24, 1962.

26. See Platen-Hallermund, *Die Tötung Geisteskranker*, p. 61. See also DÖW, E18370/1: Bundesministerium für Inneres, interrogation Bruno Bruckner, Vienna, May 24, 1962.

27. GStA der DDR (StA Dresden), Verfahren Nitsche, (S) 1 Ks 58/47 (1/47), vol. 5: interrogation Paul Nitsche, May 2, 1947.

28. *Verlegt nach Hadamar: Die Geschichte einer NS-"Euthanasie"-Anstalt*, ed. Bettina Winter et al. (Kassel, 1991), p. 95.

29. Hessisches Hauptstaatsarchiv Wiesbaden (HHStA), 461/32061/7: LG Frankfurt, Verfahren Wahlmann, Gorgass, Huber, 4a KLs 7/47 (4a Js 3/46), Protokoll der öffentlichen Sitzung der 4. Strafkammer, March 3, 1947, p. 32.

30. For the use of the Milgram experiment as a limited explanation of Nazi behavior, see Browning, *Ordinary Men*, pp. 171–73.

18.

CHRISTOPHER R. BROWNING

Ordinary Germans or Ordinary Men?

A REPLY TO THE CRITICS

In the spring of 1992, I published a book entitled *Ordinary Men*, the case study of a reserve police battalion from Hamburg that became the chief unit for killing Jews in the northern Lublin district of the General Government. In general, the book has been quite well-received, but it has not been without its critics in both the United States and Israel. While these critics have accepted the narrative presentation in the book that reveals the mode of operation and degree of choice within the battalion, they have objected to my use of sources, my portrayal of the perpetrators (particularly their motives and mindset) and, above all, the conclusions that I draw—the crux of which is summed up in the title *Ordinary Men*. As one friendly but critical letter-writer suggested, "Might not a preferable title . . . possibly have been Ordinary Germans?"

The argument of my critics for German singularity rests above all upon their assertion of a unique and particular German antisemitism. The letter-writer cited above argued that "cultural conditioning" shaped "specifically German behavioral modes." He continued, hypothesizing that "even many decidedly non-Nazi Germans . . . were so accustomed to the thought that Jews are less human than Germans, that they were capable of mass murder." Non-Germans in the same situation as the men of Reserve Police Battalion 101, he implies, would have behaved quite differently.

Daniel Goldhagen, the most severe critic of what he called my "essentially situational" explanation, put the matter more pointedly. The "Germans' singular and deeply rooted, racist anti-Semitism" was not "a common social psychological phenomenon" that can be analyzed in terms of "mere" negative racial stereotypes, as I had so "tepidly" done. "The men of Reserve Police Battalion 101 were not ordinary 'men,' but ordinary members of an extraordinary culture, the culture of Nazi Germany, which was possessed of a hallucinatory, lethal view of the Jews." Thus, ordinary Germans were "believers in the justice of the murder of the Jews." In their "inflamed imaginations," destruction of the Jews "was a redemptive act."[1]

The issue raised here, namely the appropriate balance of situational, cultural, and ideological factors in explaining the behavior of Holocaust killers, is an important—indeed central—subject that merits further exploration. I would like to approach this issue along two lines of inquiry. First, what has the bulk of recent scholarship concluded about the nature, intensity, and alleged singularity of anti-semitism within the German population at large? Second, what light can comparisons between German and non-German killers of Jews in the Holocaust shed on the issue of "specifically German behavioral modes"?

Let us turn to the first line of inquiry, namely the nature and intensity of anti-semitism within Nazi Germany. Perhaps the most ardent advocate of an interpretation emphasizing the singularity and centrality of German antisemitism was Lucy S. Dawidowicz. In her book *The War against the Jews*, she argued that

> generations of anti-Semitism had prepared the Germans to accept Hitler as their re-deemer. . . . Of the conglomerate social, economic, and political appeals that the NSDAP directed at the German people, its racial doctrine was the most attractive. . . . Out of the whole corpus of racial teachings, the anti-Jewish doctrine had the greatest dynamic potency. . . . The insecurities of post-World War I Germany and the anxieties they produced provided an emotional milieu in which irrationality and hysteria became routine and illusions became transformed into delusions. The delusional disorder assumed mass proportions. . . . In modern Germany the mass psychosis of anti-Semitism deranged a whole people.[2]

A large number of other scholars, however, have not shared this view.[3] Three scholars in particular—Ian Kershaw, Otto Dov Kulka, and David Bankier—have devoted a significant portion of their scholarly lives to examining German popular attitudes toward National Socialism, antisemitism, and the Holocaust.[4] While there are differences of emphasis, tone, and interpretation among them, the degree of consensus on the basic issues is impressive.

While Kulka and Bankier do not pick up the story until 1933, Kershaw argues that prior to the *Machtergreifung*, antisemitism was not a major factor in attracting support for Hitler and the Nazis. He cites Peter Merkl's study of the "old fighters," in which only about one-seventh of Merkl's sample considered antisemitism their most salient concern and even fewer were classified by Merkl as "strong ideological anti-semites." Moreover, in the electoral breakthrough phase of 1929–1933, and indeed up to 1939, Hitler rarely spoke in public about the Jewish question. This reticence stood in stark contrast to the Hitler speeches of the early 1920s, in which his obsession with and hatred of the Jews was vented openly and repeatedly.[5] Kershaw concludes that "antisemitism cannot . . .be allocated a decisive role in bringing Hitler to power, though . . . it did not do anything to hinder his rapidly growing popularity."[6]

For the 1933–1939 period, all three historians characterize German popular response to antisemitism by two dichotomies. The first is a distinction between a minority of party activists, for whom antisemitism was an urgent priority, and the bulk of the German population, for whom it was not. Party activists clamored and pressed, often in violent and rowdy ways, for intensified persecution. The antisemitic measures of the regime, though often criticized as too mild by the radicals, served an integrating function within Hitler's movement: they helped to keep the momentum and enthusiasm of the party activists alive. Despite Hitler's pragmatic caution in public, most of these radicals correctly sensed that he was with them in spirit.

The second dichotomy characterizes the reaction of the general population to the antisemitic clamor of the movement and the antisemitic measures of the regime. The vast majority accepted the legal measures of the regime, which ended emancipation and drove Jews from public positions in 1933, socially ostracized the Jews in 1935, and completed the expropriation of their property in 1938–1939. Yet this same majority was critical of the hooliganistic violence of party radicals toward the same German Jews whose legal persecution they approved. The boycott of 1933, the vandalistic outbreaks of 1935, and above all the Kristallnacht pogrom of November 1938 produced a negative response among the German population. Bankier and Kulka emphasize the pragmatic concerns behind this negative response: destruction of property, foreign policy complications, damage to Germany's image, and general lawlessness offensive to societal notions of decorum. In Kershaw's opinion, the idea that the population discounted virtually any moral dimension is "a far too sweeping generalization."[7] Nonetheless, these historians agree that a gulf had opened up between the Jewish minority and the general population. The latter, while they were not mobilized around strident and violent antisemitism, were increasingly "apathetic," "passive," and "indifferent" to the fate of the former.[8] Antisemitic measures— if carried out in an orderly and legal manner—were widely accepted for two main reasons: such measures sustained the hope of curbing the violence most Germans found so distasteful, and most Germans ultimately agreed with the goal of limiting, and even ending, the role of Jews in German society.

The records of the war years upon which Kulka, Bankier, and Kershaw based their studies were sparser and more ambiguous. Accordingly, the difference in interpretation is greater. Kulka [9] and Bankier[10] deduce a more specific awareness of the Final Solution among the German people than does Kershaw. Kershaw and Bankier advocate a more critical and less literal reading of the SD reports than does Kulka.[11] Kershaw sees a general "retreat into the private sphere" as the basis for widespread indifference and apathy toward Nazi Jewish policy. Kulka sees a greater internalization of Nazi antisemitism among the population at large, particularly concerning the acceptance of a solution to the Jewish Question through some unspecified kind of "elimination," and accordingly prefers the term "passive" or "objective complicity" over "indifference."[12] Bankier emphasizes a greater sense of guilt and shame among Germans, widespread denial and repression, and a growing fear concerning the consequences of impending defeat and a commensurate rejection of the regime's antisemitic propaganda.[13] But these differences are matters of nuance, degree, and diction. Fundamentally, the three scholars agree far more than they differ.

Above all, they agree that the fanatical antisemitism of the party "true believers" was not identical to the antisemitic attitudes of the general population and that the antisemitic priorities and genocidal commitment of the regime were not shared by ordinary Germans. Kershaw concludes that while

> the depersonalization of the Jew had been the real success story of Nazi propaganda and policy . . . the "Jewish question" was of no more than minimal interest to the vast majority of Germans during the war years. . . . Popular opinion, largely indifferent and infused with a latent anti-Jewish feeling . . . provided the climate within which spiralling Nazi aggression towards the Jews could take place unchallenged. But it did not provoke the radicalization in the first place.[14]

Kershaw summarized his position in the memorable phrase that "the road to Auschwitz was built by hatred, but paved with indifference."[15]

Despite his subsequent critique of Kershaw, Kulka's conclusions are strikingly similar. Surveying the SD reports, he notes that "during the war period the unquestionably dominant feature was the almost total absence of any reference to the existence, persecution and extermination of the Jews—a kind of national conspiracy of silence." The few reactions that were noted were "characterized by a strikingly abysmal indifference to the fate of the Jews as human beings. It seems that here, the 'Jewish Question' and the entire process of its 'solution' in the Third Reich reached the point of almost total depersonalization"[16]: "What is known is that the composite picture that the regime obtained from popular-opinion reports pointed toward the general passivity of the population in the face of the persecution of the Jews." While the Jewish Question "might not have been high on the list of priorities for the population at large . . . there were sufficient numbers who chose to give the regime the freedom of action to push for a radical 'Final Solution.'"[17]

Bankier noted the "deep-seated anti-Jewish feelings in German society," but likewise concluded that "on the whole the public did not assign antisemitism the same importance as the Nazis did. . . . The policy of deportations and mass murder succeeded because the public displayed moral insensibility to the Jews' fate." Bankier goes beyond moral insensibility and passivity to argue for a growing schism between the people and the regime:

> From 1941 onwards, the failure of Nazi promises to materialize drove a wedge between the population and the regime. . . . Declining hopes of victory and spiralling presentiments of a bitter end issued in a move to distance themselves from propaganda in general and from the Jewish issue in particular. . . . Ordinary Germans knew how to distinguish between an acceptable discrimination . . . and the unacceptable horror of genocide. . . . The more the news of mass murder filtered through, the less the public wanted to be involved in the final solution of the Jewish question.[18]

The general conclusions of Kershaw, Kulka, and Bankier—based on years of research and a wide array of empirical evidence—stand in stark contrast to the Dawidowicz/Goldhagen image of the entire German population "deranged" by a delusional mass psychosis and in the grips of a "hallucinatory, lethal view of the Jews." If "ordinary Germans" shared the same "latent," "traditional," or even "deep-seated" antisemitism that was widespread in European society but not the "fanatical" or "radical" antisemitism of Hitler, the Nazi leadership, and the party "true believers," then the behavior of the "ordinary Germans" of Reserve Police Battalion 101 cannot be explained by a singular German antisemitism that makes them different from other "ordinary men."

My characterization of the depersonalizing and dehumanizing antisemitism of the men of Reserve Police Battalion 101, which Goldhagen finds too "tepid," places them in the mainstream of German society as described by Kershaw, Kulka, and Bankier, distinct from an ideologically driven Nazi leadership. The implications of my study are that the existence of widespread negative racial stereotyping in a society—in no way unique to Nazi Germany—can provide fanatical regimes not only the freedom of action to pursue genocide (as both Kershaw and Kulka conclude) but also an ample supply of executioners.

In regard to the centrality of antisemitic motivation, it should be noted that German executioners were capable of killing millions of non-Jews targeted by the Nazi regime. Beginning in 1939, systematic and large-scale mass murder was initiated against the German handicapped and Polish intelligentsia. More than three million Soviet prisoners of war perished from hunger, exposure, disease, and outright exe-cution—two-thirds of them in the first nine months after the launching of Barba-rossa but before the death camps of Operation Reinhard had even opened. Tens of thousands fell victim to horrendous reprisal measures. Additionally, the Nazi regime included Gypsies in their genocidal assault. Clearly, something more than singular German antisemitism is needed to explain perpetrator behavior when the regime could find executioners to murder millions of non-Jewish victims.

Let us follow another approach to this issue as well by examining the behavior of non-German killing units in the Ukraine and Belorussia, which carried out killing actions quite similar to those performed by Reserve Police Battalion 101.[19] I will not be looking at those elements that enthusiastically carried out the initial murderous pogroms in the summer of 1941—often at German instigation—and were then frequently formed into full-time auxiliaries of the Einsatzgruppen for the subsequent large-scale systematic massacres. The zealous followers of Jonas Klimaitis in Lithu-ania or Viktors Arajs in Latvia, who eagerly rushed to help the invading Germans kill communists and Jews, are not appropriate counterparts of Reserve Police Battalion 101 for the purpose of cross-cultural comparison.

Instead, I will examine the rural police units in Belorussia and the Ukraine, which did not really take shape until 1942, when they participated in the "second wave" of killing on Soviet territory. Like the men of Reserve Police Battalion 101 in Poland, these policemen provided the essential manpower for the "mopping-up" killings of Jews in small towns and villages and for the "Jew hunts" that relentlessly tracked down escapees.

On July 16, 1941, Hitler made known his desire for accelerated pacification in the occupied Soviet territories. They were to be turned into a "garden of Eden" from which Germany would never withdraw.[20] Nine days later, on July 25, Himmler gave orders for the formation of units to be designated as Schutzmannschaften.[21] During his inspection tour of the Baltic in late July, Himmler spoke about the immediate creation of police formations of Estonians, Latvians, Lithuanians, and Ukrainians to be used outside of their home areas.[22]

While Himmler concerned himself primarily with the formation of battalion-sized police formations, the behind-the-front security divisions and the local Feld-kommandanturen and Ortskommandanturen of the military administration also found themselves confronted with the need to create smaller units of local police for what the Germans called Einzeldienst (precinct service). As early as July 11, 1941, the chief of staff of Rear Army Area Ukraine had approved the formation of Ukrainian police to maintain order and provide protection within the Ukrainian communities.[23] As one Wehrmacht officer subsequently explained: "The vast tasks of the German security forces in the rear army areas require an extensive recruitment of reliable portions of the population to provide help of all kinds."[24]

German army officers of the military administration toured the outlying small towns and villages in their occupation zones and appointed mayors, who in turn helped recruit local police units.[25] One Ortskommandantur noted that the local population was very hesitant to provide manpower to the German-appointed mayors until after the fall of Kiev in late September.[26] As an enticement, each mayor was to offer ten rubles per day to each volunteer as well as free rations to his wife and children. If sufficient volunteers were not forthcoming, the Ortskommandantur was instructed to contact the nearest POW camp concerning the release of Ukrainian prisoners for police service.[27]

Variously called "auxiliary police" (Hilfspolizei), "order service" (Ordnungs-dienst), "citizens' guard" (Bürgerwehr), and "militia" (Miliz), only a minority of these local police forces were initially armed , and only then for special assignments and with limited ammunition (10 rounds per man).[28] In Uman, the Ortskomman-dantur provided weapons for only 20 of 139 Ukrainian police.[29] In Dnepropetrovsk, arms were given to between 100 and 400 auxiliary policemen.[30] In Novi Saporoshje, 50 firearms were provided for 126 police.[31] These local police were to be used for numerous tasks—guard duty, patrol, price and market controls, as well as "guarding Jews" (Judenüberwachung) and "special tasks" (Sonderaufgaben). In the cities where the Einsatzgruppen were organizing large-scale massacres, the Ukrainian police were involved. As one Ortskommandant reported in mid-October 1941, "At the moment a police action against the remaining Jews in Krivoy-Rog is in progress, during which the entire Ukrainian auxiliary police is being put to work. Krivoy-Rog shall become free of Jews."[32] In contrast to the Baltic, however, such participation in Einsatzgruppen mass killings during 1941 seems to have been less widespread in the Ukraine.[33] Other employment of the Ukrainian police was apparently much more mundane. Their use as "errand boys" (Laufburschen) and private servants in the military was apparently so widespread that it had to be explicitly forbidden.[34]

When large portions of the Ukraine were transferred from military to civil administration in mid-November 1941, the army prepared to transfer its plethora of local Ukrainian police units to the Order Police. Rear Army Area South insisted, however, that this transfer was not to take place until these units were no longer militarily indispensable.[35] The transfer of the local Ukrainian police to the Order Police and their renaming as Schutzmannschaften generally occurred in December 1941 and January 1942.[36] Kurt Daluege, head of the Order Police, reported a phenomenal increase in the size of the Schutzmannschaften over the next year—from 30,000 in December 1941 to 300,000 in December 1942.[37] The initial figure may not have included numerous police still under army jurisdiction, but the growth of the Schutzmannschaften was still significant. What must be kept in mind, quite simply, is that the vast majority of the 300,000 Schutzmänner in December 1942 had been in German service for less than a year. They had not yet become policemen during, much less personally involved in, the "first wave" of killing in 1941.

The Order Police were vastly outnumbered by the Schutzmannschaften they recruited, trained, and supervised. This was particularly the case for the German and Ukrainian police scattered throughout the occupied territories in precinct service. For instance, in the district (Generalbezirk) of Nikolayev in the Ukraine, 271 German Schutzpolizei (city police) supervised 700 Ukrainian police at the urban precinct level as well as three "Schuma" battalions, totalling about fifteen hundred men. In the rural areas, 410 German Gendarmerie supervised 4,946 Ukrainian Schutzmänner. The overall ratio was more than 10 to 1. In the neighboring district of Kiev, the ratio was nearly 12 to 1.[38] Approximately two-thirds of the German police, moreover, were not career police but middle-aged reservists conscripted after 1939.[39]

As Lieutenant Deuerlein, the commander of the Gendarmerie outside Brest-Litovsk, complained, 14 of his 22 German police were reservists who had only four weeks of training with weapons and themselves were in need of basic weapons training. Such was the manpower with which he was to train and supervise his 287 Schutzmänner— surely a case of the one-eyed leading the blind.[40]

Recruiting and training remained ongoing problems. Order Police calls for new recruits were issued in the press, over the radio, on placards, and through flyers.[41] In addition to the pay and family rations, one further inducement proved to be the most effective in attracting recruits: the immediate families of Schutzmänner were exempt from deportation to forced labor in Germany.[42] Lieutenant Deuerlein, outside Brest-Litovsk, reported: "Whenever the natives are supposed to be sent to Germany for labor, the rush for employment in the Schutzmannschaft is greater."[43] Nevertheless, he concluded, recruitment went very slowly, and those who did volunteer were "not always good human material."[44]

In summary, the precinct-level Ukrainian police were first organized by the military administration in 1941. They were vastly expanded under the Order Police in 1942, whom they outnumbered in precinct service by at least a 10 to 1 ratio. The local police joined for numerous reasons, including pay, food for their families, release from POW camps, and especially a family exemption from deportation to forced labor in Germany. Although the Germans had difficulty recruiting as many Ukrainian police as they wanted, the Ukrainian police nonetheless numbered in the tens of thousands and constituted a major manpower source for the "second wave" of the Final Solution that swept through the Ukraine in 1942.

There is scant documentation from the precinct level on the day-to-day participation of the auxiliary police in the mass murder of Jews. From the Ukraine one series of police reports survives, from which we can see that the local Schutzmänner and their supervising German Gendarmerie performed precisely the same duties as Reserve Police Battalion 101 in Poland, with one exception—there were no deportations to death camps, only shooting actions. The first series of reports came from Lieutenant Deuerlein, Gendarmerie commander in the countryside surrounding Brest-Litovsk. In October 1942 Deuerlein reported:

> On the 19th and 20th of September a Jewish action was carried out in Domatshevo and Tomatshovka through a Sonderkommando of the SD, in conjunction with a mounted squadron of Gendarmerie stationed in Domatshevo and the Schutzmannschaft. A total of 2,900 Jews were shot. . . . After the Jewish action in Domatshevo and Tomatshovka the Jews living in the region are now almost totally destroyed.[45]

The next month he reported: "Participation in the action against the Jews in the city and region of Brest-Litovsk since October 15. Up until now some 20,000 Jews have been shot." For his anticipated activities in the near future, he added: "Search for bunkers to be found in the area around Brest-Litovsk. . . . Taking care of (Erledigung) the fleeing Jews still found in the region."[46] One month later the "Jew hunt" was still in progress as Deuerlein once again reported on his future activities: "Search for the Jews even now hiding in bunkers in the forests."[47]

The Gendarmerie outpost in Mir, in Belorussia, likewise reported the results of its killing activities to headquarters in Baranoviche. Its commander noted that "560

Jews were shot in the Jewish action carried out in Mir" on August 13, 1942.[48] The Gendarmerie commander in Baranoviche thereafter reported to Minsk:

> I have been given general instructions by the Gebietskommissar in Baranoviche to clear the area, especially the lowlands, of Jews, so far as the forces at my disposal permit. As a result of the major actions which were carried out in the past months, large numbers of Jews fled and joined groups of bandits. To prevent further escapes, I have eliminated Jews who were still living in the towns of Polonka and Mir. Altogether, 719 Jews were shot. In the meantime, 320 Jews who had escaped from the major actions could be recaptured by the Gendarmerie posts and executed after court martial.[49]

Around Mir the Jew hunt continued. On September 29, 1942, a "patrol of the Mir Schutzmannschaft" found in the forest six Jews, who "had fled the previous Jewish action." They were shot on the spot."[50] Six weeks later a forest keeper discovered a Jewish bunker. He led a patrol of three German gendarmes and sixty Schutzmänner to the site. Five Jews, including the former head of the Judenrat of Mir, were hauled from the bunker and shot. "The food"—including 100 kilos of potatoes—"as well as the tattered clothing were given to the Mir Schutzmannschaft."[51]

In short, the role in the Final Solution of the precinct-level police recruited on Soviet territory seems scarcely distinguishable from that of German reserve police in Poland. The precinct-level Schutzmänner were not the eager pogromists and collaborators of mid-summer 1941, just as the German reserve police were not career SS and policemen but post–1939 conscripts. The role and behavior of the Ukrainian and Belorussian auxiliary police in carrying out the Final Solution do not lend support to the notion of "specifically German behavioral modes."

I would like to look into the particular case of the German Gendarmerie in Mir and their Belorussian auxiliaries in greater detail because this case pertains to a further criticism of my book, my alleged misuse of German sources and nonuse of Jewish sources. It has been suggested on the one hand that I was much too gullible and methodologically uncritical in my acceptance of German testimony, particularly that which I cited in support of my portrayal of a differentiated reaction by the perpetrators and a dramatic transformation in character of many of the policemen over time. I argued that most of the men were upset by the initial killing action, and that over time a considerable minority of the men became enthusiastic and zealous volunteers for the firing squads and Jew hunts; that the largest group within the battalion did not seek opportunities to kill but nonetheless routinely contributed to the murder operations in many ways with increasing numbness and callousness; and that a not insignificant minority remained nonshooters while still participating in cordons and roundups. On the other hand, both Goldhagen and a number of my Israeli colleagues have chided me for not using Jewish sources. If I had been more critical of my German sources and more inclusive in my use of Jewish sources, a more reliable image of a uniform and pervasive bestiality, sadism, and even "jocularity," "boyish joy," and "relish" on the part of the perpetrators would have resulted, they suggest.

After working with these German court testimony records for more than twenty years, I would readily concede that the vast bulk of it is pervasively mendacious and apologetic, especially concerning the motivation and attitude of the perpetrators. It was precisely on the basis of my previous experience with German court testimony, however, that I judged the court testimonies of Reserve Police Battalion 101 to be qualitatively different. The roster of the unit survived, more than 40 percent of the battalion members (most of them rank and file reservists rather than officers) were interrogated, and two able and persistent investigating attorneys spent five years carefully questioning the witnesses.

The resulting testimony provides a unique body of evidence that permits us to answer important questions for which previous court records did not provide adequate information. A historian would be wrong to lump this body of evidence together indiscriminately with other court records. Admittedly, these are subjective judgments on my part, and other honest and able historians could reach other conclusions. My critics' dismissal of my use of this particular German testimony as gullible and methodologically unsound, without giving due attention to the special character of these records, ought to be noted, however.

As for the nonuse of Jewish sources, I would make several observations. First, Jewish testimony was indispensable to my study in establishing the chronology for the fall of 1942. What became a blur of events for the perpetrators remained quite distinct days of horror for the victims. Also, while survivor testimony may be extremely valuable in many regards, it does not illuminate the internal dynamics of an itinerant killing unit. It would be difficult for the victim of such a unit to provide testimony concerning the various levels of participation of different perpetrators and any change in their character over time. Where long-term contact between victims and perpetrators did occur, survivors are able to and in fact do differentiate on such issues. Such long-term contact did not occur in the situations that I examined, however. The testimony of survivors and even Polish bystanders of a massacre or ghetto-clearing action by a unit such as Reserve Police Battalion 101 would inevitably focus on the brutality, sadism, and horror of the perpetrator unit, with little differentiation among its individual members. It would indeed support the conclusions of my critics concerning the uniform and enthusiastic behavior of the perpetrators, but that does not make those conclusions correct.

I would note, furthermore, that several survivor testimonies have come to my attention since the publication of *Ordinary Men*. These confirm the conclusions I reached based on perpetrator testimony. First, the memoirs of Sobibor escapee Thomas Blatt relate the following incident.[52] Shortly before the liberation, Blatt and another Jew in hiding were caught by a patrol of three German policemen. Blatt was vouched for by nearby Poles, but one of the policemen took the other Jew into the woods and a shot was heard. Several days later, the other Jew rejoined Blatt. He explained that once he was out of sight of his comrades, the policeman had fired his gun into the ground to give the impression of an execution and then chased the Jew away. In short, the phenomenon testified to by some of the men in Reserve Police Battalion 101, namely that Jews were allowed to escape by certain police when the latter were not being observed by those who might report them, is not without confirmation from a Jewish source. This is, however, precisely the kind of testimony—undoubtedly self-serving and exceedingly difficult to confirm but not thereby necessarily false—that I have been criticized for citing.

A remarkable testimony has recently been published by Nechama Tec in her book about Oswald Rufeisen. It is especially valuable because Rufeisen observed the internal workings of the Mir Gendarmerie post as a translator for the German sergeant in charge.[53] Since some of Rufeisen's testimony so strikingly confirms the dynamics within the reserve police that I portrayed based on perpetrator testimony, I will quote it at length. Tec reports that, according to Rufeisen, there was:

> a visible difference in the Germans' participation in anti-Jewish and anti-partisan moves. A selected few Germans, three out of thirteen, consistently abstained from becoming a part of all anti-Jewish expeditions. . . . No one seemed to bother them. No one talked about their absences. It was as if they had a right to abstain.

Among these middle-aged gendarmes too old to be sent to the front, Rufeisen noted the presence of enthusiastic and sadistic killers, including the second-in-command, Karl Schultz, who was described as "a beast in the form of a man." "Not all the gendarmes, however, were as enthusiastic about murdering Jews as Schultz," Tec notes. Concerning the policemen's attitude toward killing Jews, she quotes Rufeisen directly:

> It was clear that there were differences in their outlooks. I think that the whole business of anti-Jewish moves, the business of Jewish extermination they considered unclean. The operations against the partisans were not in the same category. For them a confrontation with partisans was a battle, a military move. But a move against the Jews was something they might have experienced as "dirty." I have the impression that they felt that it would be better not to discuss this matter.

This is hardly the image of men uniformly possessed of a "lethal, hallucinatory view of the Jews" who viewed their killing of Jews as "a redemptive act."

Finally, I would like to look at a third example of crosscultural comparison that is very suggestive: the Luxembourgers. Reserve Police Battalion 101 was composed almost entirely of Germans from the Hamburg region, including some men from Bremen, Bremerhaven, and Wilhelmshaven, as well as a few Holsteiners from Rendsburg who felt like relative outsiders. In addition, the battalion included a contingent of young men from Luxembourg, which had been annexed to the Third Reich in 1940. The presence of the Luxembourgers in Reserve Police Battalion 101 offers the historian the unusual opportunity for a "controlled experiment" to measure the impact of the same situational factors upon men of differing cultural and ethnic background.

The problem is the scarcity of testimony. Only one German witness described the participation of the Luxembourgers in the battalion's activities in any detail.[54] According to this witness, the Luxembourgers belonged to Lieutenant Buchmann's platoon in first company and were particularly active in the roundups before the first massacre at Józéfów. This was a period in late June and early July 1942 when the trains were not running to Belżec, and Jews in the southern Lublin district were being concentrated temporarily in transit ghettos such as Piaski and Izbica. On the night before the initial massacre at Józéfów, Lieutenant Buchmann was the sole officer who said he could not order his men to shoot unarmed women and children, and who asked for a different assignment. He was designated responsible for taking the work Jews to Lublin and, according to the witness, the Luxembourgers under his command provided the guard. Hence they did not participate in the massacre.

Thereafter Lieutenant Buchmann continued to refuse participation in any Jewish action. However, those in his platoon, including the Luxembourgers, were not exempted. Under the command of the first sergeant, who was a "110% Nazi" and real "go-getter,"[55] the Luxembourgers in particular became quite involved. According to the witness, the company captain took considerable care in the selection of personnel for assignments. "In general the older men remained behind," he noted. In contrast, *"the Luxembourgers were in fact present at every action* [emphasis mine]. With these people it was a matter of career police officials from the state of Luxembourg, who were all young men in their twenties." Despite their absence at Józefów, it would appear that the Luxembourgers became the shock-troops of first company simply because of their younger age and greater police experience and training, the absence of "specifically German behavioral modes" and a singular German antisemitism notwithstanding.

None of the Luxembourgers of Reserve Police Battalion 101 was interrogated by the German investigators. However, two of them, Jean Heinen and Roger Weitor, wrote brief accounts of their wartime service with the German police that were published in Luxembourg in 1986.[56] According to this testimony, the Luxembourgers in question were not career police but prewar volunteers in Luxembourg's army—the so-called "Luxembourg Voluntary Company." After Luxembourg's annexation by Germany, one large contingent of Luxembourg soldiers was assigned to a police unit from Cologne and then sent to Slovenia. When the Luxembourgers were deemed "unreliable" in February 1942, they were disarmed and sent to Innsbruck. From there they were dispersed in much smaller groups among various German cities. Fifteen of them, all between the ages of twenty and twenty-four, were sent to Hamburg in early June 1942. One fell ill there, but fourteen departed with Reserve Police Battalion 101 on June 21 for the Lublin district.

Two aspects of the accounts of Heinen and Wietor stand out. First, they portrayed themselves as victims of both German conscription and the horrors of war. After the withdrawal from Slovenia to Innsbruck, however, Wietor admitted that he had had the choice of leaving the German police but had chosen to remain to protect his parents, as he claimed, from the threat of resettlement. Second, both men portrayed the actions of the Luxembourgers as consistently nonsupportive of the German cause. The local population in Poland could easily distinguish the Luxembourgers from the Germans because the "latter, exclusively reservists, were twice our age."[57] Thus the Luxembourgers were contacted by the Polish resistance, and Wietor claims to have provided them, at great risk to himself, with both information about impending searches and arrests as well as captured guns and ammunition.[58] Heinen claimed that on several occasions Luxembourgers assigned to machine-gun duty did not shoot in action, since machine-gun crews would immediately draw concentrated enemy fire and suffer excessive casualties.[59] Between June 1944 and January 1945, when the front line reached Poland, five Luxembourgers successfully deserted and two others were killed trying to go over to the Russians.[60]

Most notable, given what we know about the battalion's mission in Poland, is that neither account mentions even the presence of Jews, much less the battalion's participation in their mass murder. At most, there is a slight hint behind several comments of Heinen. He notes that although the battalion was engaged in numerous actions, the Luxembourgers did not suffer their first casualty until mid-1943.[61] A tacit consensus for silence among themselves emerged in the postwar period, he concludes: "When we meet one another by accident now, we no longer speak of our tour of duty in Poland, or at most of the great amount of vodka that helped us through many difficult times."[62]

One can make a very strong argument from the silence of German and Luxembourger testimony. The Luxembourgers detailed every aspect of dissident behavior that they could. If they had been among the nonshooters in anti-Jewish actions, would they not have claimed this to their credit in postwar accounts? Many German witnesses could still remember the nonshooters in the battalion twenty years later, though it was not always in their interest to do so. Yet the Luxembourgers attracted no comment whatsoever in this regard. Did the Luxembourgers stir no memories and cause no comment by German witnesses in the 1960s precisely because they were behaving like most of their German comrades in 1942?

I will conclude briefly. If the studies of Kershaw, Kulka, and Bankier are valid and most Germans did not share the fanatical antisemitism of Adolf Hitler and the hardcore Nazis, then an argument based on a singular German antisemitism to explain the murderous actions of low-level perpetrators does not hold up. If the Nazi regime could find executioners for millions of non-Jewish victims, the centrality of antisemitism as the crucial motive of the German perpetrators is also called into question. If tens of thousands of local policemen in Belorussia and the Ukraine—taken as needed by the Germans, who were desperate for help and offered a variety of inducements—basically performed the same duties and behaved in the same way as their German counterparts in Poland, then the argument of "specifically German behavioral modes" likewise fails. Finally, if Luxembourgers in Reserve Police Battalion 101 did not behave differently from their German comrades, then the immediate situational factors to which I gave considerable attention in the conclusion of my book must be given even greater weight. The preponderance of evidence suggests that in trying to understand the vast majority of the perpetrators, we are dealing not with "ordinary Germans" but rather with "ordinary men."

NOTES

1. Daniel Jonah Goldhagen, "The Evil of Banality," *New Republic*, July 13 and 20, 1992, pp. 49–52.

2. Lucy S. Dawidowicz, *The War against the Jews* (New York, 1975), pp. 220–21.

3. Marlis Steinert, *Hitler's War and the Germans* (Athens, OH, 1977); Walter Laqueur, *The Terrible Secret* (Boston, 1981); Lawrence Stokes, "The German People and the Destruction of the European Jews," *Central European History* 6/2 (1973): 167–91; Sarah Gordon, *Hitler, Germans, and the "Jewish Question"* (Princeton, 1984); Robert Gellately, *The Gestapo and*

German Society: Enforcing Racial Policy, 1933–1945 (Oxford, 1990). In contrast, however, see Michael Kater, "Everyday Anti-Semitism in Prewar Nazi Germany," *Yad Vashem Studies* 16 (1984): 129–59.

4. See, by Ian Kershaw, "The Persecution of the Jews and German Public Opinion in the Third Reich," Leo Baeck Institute *Year Book* 26 (1981): 261–89; *Popular Opinion and Political Dissent in the Third Reich: Bavaria 1933–1945* (Oxford, 1983); *The Hitler "Myth": Image and Reality in the Third Reich* (Oxford, 1987); "German Popular Opinion and the 'Jewish Question,' 1939–1943: Some Further Reflections," in *Die Juden im Nationalsozialistischen Deutschland: 1933–1943* (Tübingen, 1986), pp. 365–85. See, by Otto Dov Kulka, "'Public Opinion' in Nazi Germany and the 'Jewish Question,'" *Jerusalem Quarterly* 25 (Fall 1982): 121–44 and 26 (Winter 1982): 34–45; and see Otto Dov Kulka and Aaron Rodrigue, "The German Population and the Jews in the Third Reich: Recent Publications and Trends in Research on German Society and the 'Jewish Question,'" *Yad Vashem Studies* 16 (1984): 421–35. And see David Bankier, "The Germans and the Holocaust: What Did They Know," *Yad Vashem Studies* 20 (1990): 69–98; *The Germans and the Final Solution: Public Opinion under Nazism* (Oxford, 1992).

5. Kershaw, *Hitler "Myth,"* pp. 232–39.

6. Kershaw, "Persecution of the Jews," p. 264.

7. Ibid., p. 279.

8. Ibid., pp. 280–81; Bankier, *Germans and the Final Solution*, pp. 72, 84.

9. Kulka, "'Public Opinion' in Nazi Germany," *Jerusalem Quarterly* 26 (Winter 1983), p. 36.

10. Bankier, *Germans and the Final Solution*, pp. 101–15.

11. Ibid., p. 117; Kershaw, "German Popular Opinion," p. 373.

12. Kulka and Rodrigue, "German Population and the Jews," pp. 430–35.

13. Bankier, *Germans and the Final Solution*, pp. 114–15, 137, 140, 146, 151–52.

14. Kershaw, "Persecution of the Jews," pp. 281, 288.

15. Kershaw, *Popular Opinion*, p. 277.

16. Kulka, "'Public Opinion' in Nazi Germany," pp. 43–44.

17. Kulka and Rodrigue, "German Population and the Jews," p. 435.

18. Bankier, *Germans and the Final Solutions*, pp. 155–56 and pp. 151–52.

19. For a brief overview of the "non-German volunteers," see Raul Hilberg, *Perpetrators Victims Bystanders: The Jewish Catastrophe 1933–1945* (New York, 1992), pp. 87–102.

20. IMT, vol. 38, pp. 86–94 (221-L: conference of July 16, 1941).

21. Bundesarchiv-Militärarchiv Freiburg (hereafter BA-MA), RW 41/4, Daluege to HSSPF, July 31, 1941.

22. Ereignismeldung no. 48, August 10, 1941, in *The Einsatzgruppen Reports*, ed. Yitzhak Arad, Shmuel Krakowski, and Shmuel Spector (New York, 1989), p. 82.

23. BA-MA, 16407/4, "special orders for the treatment of the Ukrainian question," Rückw. H. Geb. 103, July 11, 1941.

24. BA-MA, 16407/8, Rückw. H. Geb. Süd, November 14, 1941.

25. BA-MA, RH 26-45/121, 45th Infantry Division, July 22, 1941; Special Archives Moscow (hereafter SAM), 1275-3-662, pp. 6–13, FK 675 to Security Division 444 via FK 675, August 11, 1941; and pp. 14–16, FK 183 to Security Division 444, August 13, 1941.

26. SAM 11 B/1275-3-662, pp. 38–40, Ortskommandantur II/575 to FK 676, September 25, 1941.

27. Bundesarchiv Koblenz (hereafter BAK), R 94/6, Security Division 454, "special order" concerning Ukrainian auxiliary police, August 18, 1941.

28. BA-MA, 16407/4, Rückw. H. Geb. 103, "special orders" for the treatment of the Ukrainian question, July 11, 1941; SAM, 1275-3-662, pp. 5–8, Oberfeldkommandantur Winniza (FK 675) to SD 444, August 1, 1941; BAK, R 94/6, SD 454, special order concerning the Ukrainian auxiliary police, August 18, 1941.

29. SAM, 1275-3-662, pp. 38–40, OK II/575 to FK 676, September 25, 1941.

30. SAM, 1275-3-666, pp. 13–18, FK 240 monthly report, October 19, 1941.

31. SAM, 1275-3-661, pp. 39–47, FK 676 to SD 444, October 21, 1941.

32. SAM, 1275-3-665, pp. 12–22, FK I/253 to FK 246, October 15, 1941.

33. Dr. Dr. [sic] Otto Rasch of EG C reported that it was not easy to incite pogroms in the Ukraine. It was "deemed important to have men from the militia (Ukrainian auxiliary police force) participate in the execution of Jews." EM no. 81, September 12, 1941. Six days earlier, in Radomshyl, SK 4b shot 1,107 adult Jews, while the Ukrainian militia shot 561 Jewish children. EM no. 88, September 19, 1941. But the Einsatzgruppen in the south do not report the kind of regular participation of local auxiliaries that is reported by Jäger and Lange in the Baltic.

34. SAM, 1275-3-662, pp. 5–8, Oberfeldkommandantur Winniza to SD 444, August 1, 1941; pp. 14–16, FK 183 to SD 444, August 13, 1941.

35. BA-MA, 16407/8, Rückw. H. Geb.Süd, "auxiliary manpower from the native population," November 14, 1941.

36. Zhitomir Archives, 1182-1-2, Generalkommissar Zhitomir to Stadts/Gebietskommissare, December 15, 1941; Nikolayev Archives, 1432-1-1, FK 193 Order no. 34, January 13, 1942.

37. Nuremberg Document NO-286: Daluege report of January 1943.

38. BAK, R 19/122, SSPF Ukraine to RFSS, November 25, 1942.

39. BAK, R 19/464, RFSS to BdO Prague and others, November 17, 1941; R 19/121, RFSS note, November 8, 1941.

40. BAK, R 94/7, Gendarmerie-Gebietsführer Brest-Litovsk, monthly report, December 5, 1942.

41. Zhitomir Archives, 1151-1-21, Generalkommissar Zhitomir, February 24, 1942, to Gebiets- and Stadtskommissare.

42. Zhitomir Archives, 1182-1-35, KdO Zhitomir, May 24, 1943.

43. BAK, R 94/7, Gendarmerie-Gebietsführer Brest-Litovsk, monthly report, November 8, 1942.

44. Ibid., December 5, 1942.

45. Ibid., October 6, 1942.

46. Ibid., November 8, 1942.

47. Ibid., December 5, 1942.

48. Brest Archives, 995-1-7, Gend. Post Mir to Gend. Geb.-führer Baranoviche, August 20, 1942.

49. Brest Archives, 995-1-7, Gend.-Hauptmannschaft Baranoviche to KdG Belorussia (Minsk), September 29, 1942.

50. Brest Archives, 995-1-4, Gend. Post Mir to Gend. Geb.-führer Baranoviche, October 1, 1942.

51. Ibid., November 15, 1942.

52. Thomas Tori Blatt, *From the Ashes of Sobibor: A Story of Survival* (Evanston, 1997), pp. 211–12.

53. Nechama Tec, *In the Lion's Den* (New York, 1992), pp. 102–104.

54. Staatsanwaltschaft Hamburg, 141 Js 1957/62, testimony of Heinrich E., pp. 2167, 2169, 2172, 3351.

55. Christopher R. Browning, *Ordinary Men: Reserve Police Battalion 101 and the Final Solution in Poland* (New York, 1992), p. 151.

56. *Freiwëllegekompanie 1940–1945*, ed. L. Jacoby and R. Trauffler, vol. 2 (Luxembourg: Imprimerie St. Paul SA, 1986), pp. 207–21. I am very grateful to Dr. Paul Dostert, Luxembourg representative on the International Committee for the History of the Second World War, for providing me with this material.

57. Ibid., p. 209 (Heinen testimony).

58. Ibid., p. 221 (Wietor testimony).

59. Ibid., p. 212 (Heinen testimony).

60. Ibid., pp. 212–17 (Heinen testimony).

61. Ibid., p. 209 (Heinen testimony).

62. Ibid., p. 219 (Heinen testimony).

19.

JÜRGEN FÖRSTER

Complicity or Entanglement?

WEHRMACHT, WAR, AND HOLOCAUST

After fifty years of research and writing on the Third Reich, the close relationship between the history of the Holocaust and that of the Second World War is still on the agenda. Although the wartime context points to an evolution of the Nazis' plans for a solution to the Jewish Question, analyses of the Holocaust have ignored important connections with the course of the war. On the other hand, specialists on the Second World War have failed to understand the racial character of the war Hitler unleashed on September 1, 1939. Only when historians of the Holocaust and specialists on the Second World War jointly analyze the totality of Nazi racial and social policy and its murderous implementation inside and outside Germany during the war, and only when general historians of Nazi Germany give as much attention to that period as to the peace years, shall we arrive at an adequate interpretation of both the Third Reich and the Holocaust.[1]

The relationship between the Wehrmacht and National Socialism remains a major bone of contention in Germany, especially concerning the army's involvement in Nazi racial policies.[2] From the Nuremberg trials onward, one popular notion separates the followers from the Führer, the generals from their supreme commander, and the Wehrmacht from the Nazi crimes. For far too long the memoirs of German generals shaped the public image of the Wehrmacht's record in the Second World War. Hitler was dismissed as a bungling amateur in military matters; his illogical aims had supplanted the generals' objective professionalism. The generals presented themselves as having pursued a fundamentally just cause and as having become Hitler's victims. This concept was most cleverly phrased in Erich von Manstein's *Lost Victories* (1958) and Siegfried Westphal's *Army in Chains* (1950). Moreover, with his book *On the Other Side of the Hill* (1951), B. H. Liddell Hart had already provided the generals with a large audience they could address about the campaigns in Europe and Africa and their purely professional role in them.

It was not until the late 1960s that historians began to research the available documents and presented the public with a different picture of *this* side of the hill. The clear linkage between strategy and mass murder in the war policy of the Third Reich makes it impossible to posit a Wehrmacht that remained detached from its political leadership. However, many a veteran not only doggedly perpetuates the myth that the German soldier only did his duty and fought a clean war, but also tries to whitewash the Wehrmacht's shield of honor whenever certain historians of the Militärgeschichtliches Forschungsamt, especially Manfred Messerschmidt, have painted it black.[3]

In 1989, the veterans organization went so far as to openly appeal for donations for their defensive efforts. They expected another onslaught on the German soldierly tradition by the mass media and other publications in connection with the remembrance of the outbreak of the Second World War, an onslaught that they were unable to fight without more money.[4] It is regrettable, then, that Alfred Streim, the renowned lawyer and a man of outstanding merit, published a relevant article in the most vociferous veterans' journal.[5] His one-sided critique of unnamed "biased" historians added fuel to the flames for those who live in the past and interpret any thorough research on the Wehrmacht as defamation of the soldier. The constant lobbying by the veterans in favor of including the tradition of the Wehrmacht as an aspect worthy of inclusion in the education of today's soldiers has had some limited success; former Bundeswehr Chief of Staff, General Naumann, responded to their representatives that despite the "misuse of the Wehrmacht by an evil regime, . . . far the overwhelming majority of the soldiers [who fought in World War II] preserved the honor and dignity of the German soldier."[6] This statement, far too general and not reflecting the results of scholarly research, could easily be understood by the readers of those journals as a "Persilschein," a carte blanche endorsement of initiatives, against what the audience already perceives as the unjust and biased findings of many historians of the Second World War. It was not until the spring of 1997 that the German Minister of Defense, Volker Rühe, disassociated the Bundeswehr's tradition from the Wehrmacht. To say that the Wehrmacht was responsible for innumerable crimes in the Soviet Union, in the Balkans, and in Italy is not to say that every German soldier was a criminal or was equally guilty of the travesties perpetrated in the name of the regime; yet, not every soldier was a mere defender of his fatherland.

The Wehrmacht was certainly one of the finest fighting forces of the war.[7] Yet this definition is clearly superficial, since the Wehrmacht was not merely a superb professional organization misused by Hitler to realize his war aims, but also an integral part of state and society in the Third Reich. The Wehrmacht intentionally formed the "second pillar" of the Führer-state, alongside the National Socialist Party. Since more than 17.3 million Germans, ethnic Germans, and drafted foreigners from occupied countries served in the Wehrmacht it was a people's army. Thus, the history of the armed forces and the history of Nazi Germany have to be viewed as *one* in order to arrive at an adequate interpretation of the Third Reich.[8]

The role and function of the Reichswehr/Wehrmacht was heavily shaped by the 1933 alliance between Hitler and Werner von Blomberg, Minister of Defense and Commander-in-Chief of the Armed Forces. Their common goal was the "Wiederwehrhaftmachung" of Germany. This highly emotional and politicized term has often been misunderstood as meaning solely the military rearmament of Germany. In reality, Wiederwehrhaftmachung meant the complete reshaping of Germany: militarily, economically, socially, and spiritually. While the party was to militarize the nation and eliminate all internal enemies, thereby respecting the military domain, the Reichswehr/Wehrmacht ceased to interfere in domestic politics and concentrated on speedy rearmament and politicizing the troops.

The assumptions and conditions under which Hitler and Blomberg worked until 1938 were heavily influenced by a selective interpretation of the history of the First World War. To them and to other soldiers, the "battle as an inner experience" (*Fronterlebnis*) was not a mere literary convention. It became the pivot for the intentional amalgamation of National Socialism and German soldierly tradition.[9] The Nazis did not *have* to invent the glorification of trench warfare as a communal experience, dismantling social barriers and uniting the whole nation, except for those who (with the help of Bolshevism) had stabbed the victorious army in the back and caused Germany's downfall. Traditional antisemitism within the military had long since found special confluence with the double threat to the German nation-state and its social order, what in 1920 Werner von Fritsch had called "domestic and foreign Bolshevism."

The bond between the movement and the armed forces was the idea of a militarized Volksgemeinschaft as a new national community of blood and destiny, which was needed for the restoration of Germany's position as a major power. Yet the concept of Volksgemeinschaft strengthened not only the ties between Hitler and his generals but also between the Führer and his followers. It gave Germans a sense of "us," a national unity and purpose. The price of belonging was conformity to prescribed social norms and sacrifice for the national cause. The ominous side of Volksgemeinschaft was the purification of the nation from "them." That meant, first of all, Jews. Later, membership was refused to a widening range of persons, from Gypsies to the mentally and physically handicapped, the asocial, vagrants, and wayward or rebellious youth.

The Reichswehr/Wehrmacht united in carrying out Hitler's twin goals of domestic purification and creation of a new leadership cadre based upon racial principles. In June 1933, Blomberg told his subordinate commanders that soldiers were subject to the Aryan clause of the Civil Service Act; this applied to marriages and the recruitment of cadets. When, in December 1933, the military establishment discussed the threefold enlargement of the Reichswehr, the minister of defense made public his intention to take over the Aryan Clause for the future personnel policy of the army.[10] Yet by the end of February 1934, Blomberg decided, on his own initiative as he had told the commanders four weeks earlier, to eliminate from the service Jewish officers, deck officers, NCOs and other ranks.[11] In practice, it turned out that only seventy individuals in the army and navy were affected. Jewish civil servants had already been dismissed.

There was only one protest from within the Reichswehr that expressed fundamental concern. It came from Colonel (GS) von Manstein. Significantly, he mentioned that he approved of National Socialism and its racial principles. Thus, von Manstein neither argued against the qualification by Aryan descent in the future personnel policy of the Wehrmacht nor doubted the necessity of purifying the military professions. Based on a "soldierly sense of what is right and wrong," however, he criticized the retrospective acceptance of the Aryan Clause. In von Manstein's view, it did not make sense to eliminate those who, by their signing up as soldiers, by their willingness to die for Germany, and by their loyalty to the army had proved that they were "Germans" and not "Jews," while at the same time permitting the Wehrmacht to keep those veterans who by their marriage to Jewish women had clearly shown that they lacked the necessary race instinct.[12]

It was not before May 13, 1936, that Hitler, as supreme commander, directly influenced the Wehrmacht's personnel policy. In the wake of the Nuremberg Laws, he demanded that von Blomberg ensure that the Wehrmacht select its professional soldiers "according to the strictest racial criteria, going beyond the legal regulations. The National Socialist view of the state requires the encouragement of the racial idea and the selection of leaders from people with German and related blood."[13] One month later, the Military Law of 1935 was amended accordingly. Conscription was forbidden for "Jews," and Jews of "mixed blood" could not become "leaders." Another wave of purification of the ranks started after the incorporation of the former Austrian contingents into the Wehrmacht.

The Wehrmacht's personnel policy based on blood and merit was radicalized during the war. Successive steps in April 1940, July 1941, September 1942, and June 1944 removed "Jews" and the so-called "50 percent and 25 percent Mischlinge" [literally "mixed breed," in Nazi terminology a person of both Jewish and German gentile ancestry] from the ranks. In October 1943, Hitler ordered the establishment of work battalions made up of "Jewish 'Mischlinge'and close relatives of Jews. Only those liable for military service and not engaged in any other duty vital to the war effort were subject to this obligation. Former officers and noncommissioned officers could not be utilized as leaders."[14] According to a survey of summer 1940, 107 officers in the Bavarian Military District fell into those racial categories.[15] It is interesting that the relevant personnel directives before the wars against France and the Soviet Union show that Jews were given the chance to prove their racial worthiness as Germans by bravery in the face of Germany's enemies. This was an idea that von Manstein had already hinted at in 1934.

Hitler was a revolutionary and a racist. He saw history as a conflict between races and believed that conflict "in all its forms" was inevitable and the "father of all things." It determined the life of individuals and nations. In this ideological context, war took on a very special meaning for Hitler. It was not only the "highest expression of the life force" of a people but also the legitimate and inevitable tool in the hands of its Führer for acquiring the sufficient Lebensraum by which the nation's future would be secured racially, economically, and militarily. War was not a moral issue, a question of right or wrong, but the physical means to a social end: the survival of the Germans. With survival of the race being contingent on military victory, Hitler's politics and strategy became indistinguishable.

By 1938, at the latest, Hitler was master in the Third Reich. He regarded himself as the executor of a historical mission and was not willing to allow the military to exert influence on policy-making. Since there were no bodies such as a war cabinet or joint chiefs-of-staff, it was solely in his hands that the threads came together. The Wehrmacht was politically emasculated and the military establishment reduced to a functional elite.

In January and February 1939, Hitler addressed selected military audiences and the public from the Reichstag. His purpose in those speeches was to explain to his listeners the basic National Socialist principles behind his policies since 1933. The orations were intended to inspire his listeners with particular devotion so that they would follow him with renewed sense of purpose. These speeches did not present the audiences with new ideas. Every listener must have been certain who the racial and political enemies were: Jewry, "the plutocrats," and Bolshevism. Only the open threat to the Jews before the Reichstag in the Kroll opera house on January 30, 1939, and, ten days later, the clear-cut demand for the officer corps to acknowledge him as their supreme ideological leader in the coming racial war stand out for their obvious rhetoric.

The latter, however, did not fall on barren ground within the Wehrmacht. Its commanders had just decided to intensify among the troops the instruction in National Socialist Weltanschauung and national-political objectives. Before there were any coherent pamphlets, the army leadership instructed its officer corps on December 18, 1938, to master National Socialism, to be its standard-bearer, and to act according to these ideas in every situation, as both the political and tactical leaders of their soldiers.[16] From February 1939 onward, the High Command of the Wehrmacht, the OKW, issued the respective "Schulungshefte." Following the essays "The Officer and Politics," "Hitler's World-Historical Mission," "The Army in the Third Reich," and "The Battle for German Living Space," pamphlet no. 5 (except for a short but timely essay titled "Hands off Danzig") dealt almost exclusively with the Jew in German history. In C. A. Hoberg's contribution, the "Final Solution of the Jewish Question in the Third Reich" appears as emigration, with its complete execution only a question of time: "The defensive battle against Jewry will continue, even if the last Jew has left Germany. Two big and important tasks remain: 1) the eradication of all lasting effects of Jewish influence, above all in the economy and in culture; 2) the battle against World Jewry, which tries to incite all people in the world against Germany." Yet the author is certain Hitler will win these battles, since his wisdom is greater than Jewish guile, and the German volk is stronger than World Jewry.

While the troops were instructed along these ideological lines, the military staff prepared for an offensive against Poland, which Hitler initially had ordered by the end of March 1939. In two addresses to senior military commanders, one on May 23 and the other on August 22, 1939, Hitler justified his decision to go to war and argued that Germany had no alternative but to launch a risky immediate attack; otherwise the nation would face certain annihilation sooner or later. It was not Danzig that was at stake. The goal was the destruction of Poland and her human potential in order to gain the necessary territories for the resettlement of Germans. There would be no legal restraints. Only victory mattered, not pity.[17]

The Wehrmacht still planned for a normal war. In his address to the troops on September 1, 1939, Colonel-General von Brauchitsch, however, pointed out that the "young National Socialist Army was going to war believing in the justice of our cause and for a clear goal: the lasting safety of the German Volk and German living space against foreign infringements and claims."[18] The "elimination of all active and passive resistance" was not yet determined in ideological terms. Partisans were to be court-martialed and subsequently shot. Poles and Jews between seventeen and forty-five years of age, that is, who were fit for military service, were to be interned and treated as prisoners of war. In a directive on behavior in enemy territory, von Brauchitsch merely stated that the "attitude of the soldiers of the National Socialist Reich toward the Jews is not worth specific mention."[19] For fighting the racial battle and purifying the acquired living space from all who could infect the German people, Hitler relied on the SS.

Seen from the viewpoint of 1941, the occupation of Poland looks like a test case for Nazi racial policy. Such a view minimizes the conditions created by the war itself as determining factors and overlooks the role the Soviet Union had in Hitler's race and war policy. Though Poland clearly marks an escalation in the persecution of the Jews, the murderous Final Solution was not a concrete aim in 1939–1940. It still meant deportation and ghettoization.

The attitude of the Wehrmacht toward the indigenous population in Poland was a mixture of racial arrogance, insecurity, and naive trust in the use of force: "The life of a non-Aryan was worth very little."[20] Jews were at the bottom of the racial scale. They were considered "a horrible lot. Dirty and scheming."[21] Their deportation from Lódz was settled for General Hans-Gustav Felber, the Chief of Staff of the 8th Army, even before Heydrich's relevant order. The Wehrmacht did not doubt that there was a Jewish Question, but the solution was not considered to be its business.

The army acted ruthlessly, however, against insurgents, and it was responsible for mass executions of prisoners of war and indiscriminate shootings of civilians, among them many Jews. What it did forbid were "wild," or unauthorized, spontaneous measures against Poles and Jews and the participation of Wehrmacht soldiers in executions carried out by the SS. The brutalization of the soldiers began in Poland; the barbarization of warfare itself would begin on Soviet territory. The commanders reacted against the threat to military discipline by multiplying courts-martial. On October 4, 1939, however, Hitler pardoned all military and police personnel who had overstepped military law and justified this by saying that such crimes had been the natural result of bitterness unleashed by Polish behavior toward Germans. This amnesty and the granting to the SS of its own military law on October 17, 1939, were encouragements to further acts of terror.

After October 17, 1939, the top army leaders had clear knowledge of the destructive Nazi program in Poland. They neither objected on principle nor shared their information with the officer corps at large, because they were satisfied to wash their hands of responsibility for the administration of Poland. Yet some local commanders protested the slaughter of Poles and Jews by the SS and/or informed their superiors about crimes they had witnessed.[22] After the mayor of Rypin had made Jews work in freezing cold with bare chests on Christmas day 1939 and later, whipping them, had driven them into the icy river, the chief of staff of Military District XX (Danzig) stated:

> All these instances have not remained unconcealed from the troops, despite the efforts of the responsible military authorities. . . . In addition to vehement indignation over the form of the execution of many measures considered necessary on national-political (*volkspolititischen*) grounds, there is a gradually growing scorn toward the perpetrators [of these actions], which must inevitably lead to an antagonism between the Wehrmacht and the [National Socialist] Party organization represented here, especially the SS.[23]

A man such as Colonel-General Johannes Blaskowitz, who himself defined Jews and Poles as "our arch-enemies in the eastern sphere," became increasingly concerned about the spread of "brutalization and moral debasement" among valuable German manpower.[24] The Commander-in-Chief of the Army, however, blunted those protests when he made himself an advocate of Hitler's program against Poland. What Colonel-General Walther von Brauchitsch did was stress the need to maintain the army's spirit and discipline by keeping its own troops from participation in such acts of violence against the indigenous population.[25] At the same time that the army leadership accepted the "severity" of the SS in carrying out the necessary racial measures in the new territories, it initially criticized the "killing frenzy" of the SS and sought to avoid the brutalization of its own troops. When Himmler made it perfectly clear to the army's top commanders in Koblenz on March 11, 1940, that the SS action had been ordered by Hitler, the apparent discontent of many and the criticism of a few concerning German policy in Poland came to an end.

The army's attention turned to the impending attack on France, for which a plan more promising than the original had been evolved in the meantime. The campaign in the West differed from that against Poland. No Einsatzgruppen crossed the borders with the troops. The military administration's occupation policy disallowed "special measures" against the Jews solely on grounds that they were Jews.[26]

The Führer's triumph in the West acted as an additional impetus for the acceptance of the SS's "unparalleled radical measures for the final solution of the racial struggle (*Volkstumskampf*) which has been waged for centuries along the eastern frontier."[27] Significantly, this characterization was made by Colonel-General Georg von Küchler, commander of the 18th Army, who, ten months earlier, had infuriated Himmler by interceding against SS crimes. This had cost him a field marshal's baton. A few weeks later, the same 18th Army instructed its troops about the "attitude of the German soldier toward the non-German population in the East." One army corps staff informed higher headquarters about its experiences with this instruction. Although a final assessment would depend on the future organization of the General Government, "the attitude of the German soldier towards the Jews is by no means in question. Down to the last man, the standpoint has been taken that it is impossible to mix with this race and that it must be completely disposed of in the German living space one day."[28]

At that time, Hitler already had ordered the Wehrmacht to prepare for an offensive against the Soviet Union. When their preparations for Operation Barbarossa were already far advanced, Hitler defined—first within the small circle of his military advisers and then before a large gathering of senior commanders and their chiefs-of-staff—that this campaign was not a mere conflict between two enemy nation-states and their armies. It would also be a clash of antagonistic ideologies and races. Hitler stated openly that he wished to see Operation Barbarossa conducted not according to military principles but as a Vernichtungskrieg against an ideology and its adherents, Red Army or civilian.[29] Responsibility for the liquidation of enemy cadres was to be shared between the army and the SS. The latter were to eliminate the civilian cadres of the enemy Weltanschauung, and the army was to eliminate the "Jewish-Bolshevik intelligentsia" within the Red Army—the commissars—as well as real or potential carriers of resistance. And these actions were to be carried out *directly* by the troops, without benefit of courts martial. Hitler had declared the Vernichtungskrieg against the enemy per se in the East to be a military necessity. Traditionally illegal measures were now authorized, ostensibly in part to safeguard the operational blitzkrieg concept. The difference between operations White (Poland) and Barbarossa was that in 1941 Hitler wanted to erase the line between military and political warfare before the first shot was fired. The common goal of the army and the SS was the quick break-up of the Soviet regime and the speedy pacification of the conquered territory.

Such guidelines from the supreme ideological leader came neither as a surprise to the army nor were they particularly unwelcome. When Colonel-General Franz Halder, chief of the Army General Staff, noted in his diary the essence of Hitler's address of March 30, 1941, he made a telling side-note: "In the East, severity is mildness for the future."[30] This clearly echoes Hitler's remark of October 17, 1939: "Shrewdness and severity . . . in this racial struggle [would] spare us from having to go into battle again."[31] Three days before the large gathering of generals in the Reich Chancellery on March 30, 1941, von Brauchitsch himself had told commanders that the troops should see the German-Russian war as a "struggle between two different races, and act with the necessary severity."[32]

Although it was Hitler who wanted to transform the military campaign against the Soviet Union into a war of destruction against Bolshevism and Jewry, he left the implementation of his ideological intentions to his own military staff, the OKW, the Army General Staff, and the Reichssicherheitshauptamt. This process constitutes a typical example of what Raul Hilberg has defined as the "mechanism of destruction." The directives that were to give the war in the East its singular character emerged from a routine bureaucratic process within the relevant departments: "Regularization of the Deployment of the Security Police and the SD within the Army," April 28, 1941; "Decree Concerning the Exercise of Military Jurisdiction and Procedure in the Barbarossa Area and Special Measures of the Troops in Russia," May 13, 1941; and "Guidelines for the Treatment of Political Commissars," June 6, 1941. Within the complex of the so-called criminal orders, including their oral interpretations, lies the most obvious connection between the tactical and racial sides of the war against the Soviet Union. On the one hand, the Wehrmacht accepted the idea that the SS was entrusted with "special tasks" within the army's zone of operation and was entitled to take "executive measures" against the civilian population on its own responsibility. An officer of the Naval High Command staff wrote in the margin of the OKW-guidelines of March 13, 1941: "This will have consequences!"[33] The Wehrmacht's own deliberate linkage of military need with ideological goals, of punitive with preventative measures against the actual and alleged resisters, paved the way for the army's joining the SS in striking a fatal blow against those they had identified with the phantom of Jewish Bolshevism.

The military leaders did not simply comply with Hitler's dogmatic views; they were not mere victims of an all-exonerating principle of obedience. The military leaders, too, believed that the threats of Russia and Bolshevism should be completely eliminated. The Soviet Union and Germany were seen as being divided by a yawning chasm, defined in terms of both ideology and race. Thus, Operation Barbarossa assumed an even higher justification than the war against mortal enemy France. The broad image of a Bolshevist enemy combined with the goal of acquiring space and resources in the East proved to be crucial factors for the concept of a war of destruction in that arena. This time the army leadership was willing to let the troops fight the ideological part of the war as well, as Colonel-General Halder noted in his diary on May 6, 1941. Transforming Hitler's views, the High Command drafted its own instructions to restrict military jurisdiction and to allow for the shooting of alleged guerillas; in the same draft it also took the initiative for the execution of captured Red Army political commissars. In making these violations of international law palatable for the troops, the High Command rooted its justification in the linkage of miliary need and a distorted vision of post–1918 German history. As regards Poland, Hitler had pardoned soldiers and SS men *after* the campaign. In the battle against "Jewish Bolshevism," a preemptive amnesty was decreed *before* the first shot was even fired. It was assumed that Jewish commissars would be more convinced communists than others. The fear that these men might disseminate Bolshevik propaganda later in the prisoner of war camps in the Reich was another factor influencing the army leadership to have the commissars shot in the zone of operations. Another factor behind the army's willing acceptance of the Commissar Order was the concept of 'military necessity': the hope for a speedier and less costly advance by removing the naive Russian soldier from his criminal political leadership cadre. The evidence of the bureaucratic origin of the Commissar Order makes it highly unlikely that the decision to murder the Jews can be based on this military directive, as Hans Mommsen claims.[34] The Commissar Order was not intended to move the army "towards acceptance of the general killing of Jews" either, as Richard Breitman asserts.[35]

The final decrees of May 13 and June 6 were issued by the OKW. They had to go through the army High Command. Von Brauchitsch amended both decrees before he passed them on to the troop commanders. On the one hand, he laid the burden for segregating and executing the commissars "inconspicuously" on the shoulders of any officer. On the other hand, he stressed the duty of all superiors to prevent arbitrary excesses of *individual* soldiers against the Soviet population and, thus, a brutalization of the troops. Soldiers were bound by the orders of their officers. "Timely action by every officer must help to maintain discipline, the basis of our successes," wrote Brauchitsch on May 24, 1941.

Concern for the discipline of the troops obviously was deemed more important than scruples about illegal shooting of captive commissars or of civilians who were mere suspects. The whole concept of *ius in bello* was viewed as an irksome obstacle to the war of destruction against the Soviet Union. "Feelings of justice must under certain circumstances yield to military necessity," said General Eugen Müller on June 10, 1941. From such oral instructions to intelligence officers and judge advocates, it becomes evident that the suspension of military jurisdiction was seen as a temporary measure, depending on the course of operations and the pacification of the country. After the experiences in Poland, the army's attempt to preserve the institutional control of violence and prevent the brutalization of the soldiers while calling for ideologically motivated measures against the "deadly enemy of the National Socialist German nation" must be seen as "riding the tiger." The troops themselves were instructed that the battle against the destructive ideology of communism and its adherents demanded "ruthless and vigorous measures against Bolshevik provocateurs, guerrillas, saboteurs, and *Jews,* and the complete elimination of all active and passive resistance."[36]

About the decision-making process for Barbarossa within the SS, we know much less than about that on the military side. We are even less acquainted with what the military leadership knew about the "special tasks" with which Himmler had been entrusted by Hitler. The military had had their experiences with the SS in Poland. They were not to be misled by the euphemistic language that was used to describe the task of the Einsatzgruppen. Therefore, von Brauchitsch had refused their real subordination to the army since the latter then would have become responsible for the execution of political tasks.[37] On the occasion of an oral instruction of intelligence officers in Berlin on June 6, 1941, SS-Colonel Nockemann went so far as to state that, according to an order in his hands, SS forces consisting of twenty-five hundred men were to establish the basis for the final elimination of Bolshevism and would act "with utmost harshness and severity."[38] Significantly, two days before, the chiefs of staff of the armies and army groups had been informed that Himmler and von Brauchitsch had agreed to finally end the disagreement about the legitimized murders in Poland. Thus the official groundwork was laid for the ordained close cooperation between army and SS in smashing "Jewish Bolshevism."

German security policy in the occupied territories of the East was a highly complex matter from the very outset. As in previous operations, the military commanders were empowered to exercise supreme military as well as administrative authority during the initial phase of the invasion. All administrative plans were based on the premise that the army's area of operation would be turned over to civilian authorities in short order. The great difference in the case of Barbarossa was that the campaign did not go according to plan. The Baltic states, the Ukraine, and a large part of Russia remained under military authority. According to an agreement of March 26, 1941, the Einsatzgruppen had been given a free hand to carry out their task of eliminating communist functionaries, Jews, and subversive elements without restraint within the army's zone of operation. The only concession was that military demands retained precedence over "special measures." The army's own plans for military security were determined by the vast expanse of the occupied territories and the shortage of security forces. Therefore, it had welcomed the deployment of order police and Waffen-SS formations not only in the rear areas. Military security was thus often jointly conducted by Army and SS forces, though only rarely with the Einsatzgruppen.

At the beginning of the operations, especially in those territories that the Soviets had occupied after the autumn of 1939, the army consciously aimed at what it perceived as freeing the population from the yoke of Bolshevism and avoiding measures that would make it hostile to the German invader. In fact, the Germans actually received a traditional welcome in some villages. The as yet small number of sabotage incidents allowed for striking a bargain between the interests of the Wehrmacht and the civilian population. Let the latter only be quiet, work, and obey orders, and the Germans' would only combat outright resistance and carry out reprisals chiefly against Jews and communists. Thus in the western parts of the Soviet Union, the Wehrmacht appropriated minorities for its own use as scapegoats.

Yet by the end of July 1941, the army leadership ruled differently. One reason was that Stalin had countered the Wehrmacht's invasion with his own concept of a merciless people's war which, together with the Red Army's fight, would decide the future of socialism. Moreover, the Soviet dictator's appeal for a partisan war behind the German lines, to be led by the Communist Party, played directly into Hitler's hands. He seized the opportunity to mask his extermination program more effectively as a military necessity: to shoot everyone who merely looked suspect. On the other hand, the army leadership believed that their troops had not dealt energetically enough with the partisans' activities. These were reasons for von Brauchitsch to supplement the earlier directives with a special order for the "treatment of enemy civilians and of Russian prisoners of war" in the army group rear areas. He accused supporters of the "Jewish-Bolshevik system" of being responsible for the renewal of resistance in already pacified areas, and justified reprisals and collective punishment instead of taking hostages. The shooting of suspected civilian sympathizers and the destruction of entire villages were seen as appropriate reactions to any instances of sabotage.

The guiding principle was terror: "to crush all will to resist among the population."[39] Pity and softness were considered weaknesses that posed a threat to the German soldier. Since some military commanders and officers still tried to draw a line between ideological warfare and military necessity, Field Marshal Wilhelm Keitel issued his order of September 12, 1941. In reminding them of his guidelines of May 19, 1941, Keitel declared again that the "struggle against Bolshevism demands ruthless and energetic action especially also against the Jews, the main carriers of Bolshevism."[40] Four days later, Keitel informed the military commanders in all occupied areas, not just in the Soviet Union, that the Führer had ordered them to use "everywhere the harshest methods to crush the [communist insurgent] movement within the shortest possible time." In this context, Keitel provided guidelines that demanded from the military occupation forces "unusual severity" to prevent any further spread of rebellion, that in every case, "no matter what the individual circumstances may be, communist origins must be assumed to be present." He considered the summary execution of 50 to 100 'communists' an "appropriate retribution for the life of a German soldier."[41]

One telling example of the close cooperation between the army and the Waffen SS in the area of operations is the mopping up of the Pripyat Marshes. The commander of the rear area of Army Group Center, General Max von Schenckendorff, had charged the SS cavalry brigade under SS-Colonel Hermann Fegelein with this military task. The operation began on July 29, 1941, after Himmler had instructed his men to act harshly against "a racially inferior" population. All male Jews were to be shot, women driven into the marshes. Suffering 17 dead, 3 missing in action, and 36 wounded, Fegelein could proudly report to Himmler that the brigade had shot 699 Soviet soldiers, 1,001 partisans, and 14,178 Jews.[42] In an earlier, differently worded communication of September 3, 1941, Fegelein had informed General von Schenckendorff of the "pacification of the Pripyat Marshes," asserting that the contact between the partisan units was maintained "above all by Jews" and that villages "free from Jews" had in no instance served as partisan bases.[43] This rather dubious assertion served the general's purposes as Schenckendorff's report of August 10, 1941, to the army High Command shows.[44] The practice of Fegelein's Waffen-SS unit was not only recommended to his own security divisions but combating partisans was also defined as a soldierly activity in which commanders could prove their receptiveness and creativity.[45] In addition, von Schenckendorff initiated a joint seminar for combating partisans, held in Mogilev between September 24 and 26, 1941. The desired "exchange of experience" between the army and the SS was led by Lieutenant-Colonel Montua of the Order Police. After lectures by Higher SS and Police Leader Bach-Zelewski on the "apprehension of commissars and partisans," and by Arthur Nebe, leader of Einsatzgruppe B, on "the Jewish question with special reference to the partisan movement," the "correct" screening of the population was demonstrated on the closing day of the course by a live exercise of the 7th Company of Police Battalion 322 in Knjashizy, fourteen kilometers northwest of Mogilev. We read in its war diary:

> The action, first scheduled as a training exercise, was carried out under real-life conditions (*ernstfallmässig*) in the village itself. Strangers, especially partisans, could not be found. The screening of the population, however, resulted in 13 [adult male] Jews, 27 Jewish women, and 11 Jewish children, of which 13 Jews and 19 Jewish women were shot in cooperation with the Security Service.[46]

It was not surprising that participants in such a course, which was repeated in May 1942, returned to their units with this doctrine: "Where the partisan is, there is the Jew, and where the Jew is, there is the partisan."[47]

Three weeks earlier, on September 1, 1941, General von Schenckendorff had handed over White Russia to Gauleiter Wilhelm Kube. Military security in that part of Reichskommissariat Ostland was now in the hands of the commander of the 707th Infantry Division and commandant of White Ruthenia, Major-General Gustav von Bechtolsheim. He was subordinate to Lieutenant-General Walter Braemer, commander of armed forces in the Ostland. On September 25, 1941, Braemer issued "Guidelines for Military Security and Maintenance of Quiet and Order" in his province. Reacting to Keitel's orders of September 12 and 16, Braemer stated that the security of the fighting troops, of the country, and of its economic situation would demand "imperatively to eliminate all factors threatening peace and order." As such factors, he specified "a) Bolshevik soldiers and agents (partisans) dispersed or purposely dropped or left behind in the forests; b) Communists and other radical elements; c) Jews and prosemitic (*Judenfreundliche*) circles." All German organizations and individuals must cooperate with the Wehrmacht and police to eliminate these elements. The guideline for combating partisans must be "speedy, ruthless, and brutal action."[48] Since it was assigned to Braemer, the 707th Infantry Division not only acted according to those guidelines, but its situation reports also reveal initiatives of its own and striking examples of self-fulfilling prophecy in the extermination of Jewish Bolshevism:

> It was noticed with the Jews that they tend to leave their homes in the flat country, probably for the south, whereby they seek to escape the operations introduced against them. Since, then and now, they make common cause with the communists and partisans, the complete extermination of this alien element is being carried out. (Monthly report of October 11–November 10, 1941.)

> The measures introduced against the Jews, as bearers of the Bolshevik idea and as leaders of the partisan movement, have shown tangible results. The massing of Jews in ghettos and the liquidation of Jews who have been found guilty of partisan activity and incitement of the people is being continued and thereby the pacification of the country is being advanced at its best. During this month the raiding parties repeatedly noted and confirmed the association of Jews with the partisan movement. (Monthly report of November 1–November 30, 1941.)[49]

Although the fragmented partisan movement posed no major threat to the German occupation in that area, the 707th Division exacted a tremendous toll in "reprisals." Within four weeks, it shot 10,431 "captives" out of a total of 10,940, while in combat with partisans the division suffered only seven casualties, two dead and five wounded.[50] Among those "captives" were former Soviet soldiers, escaped prisoners of war, and civilians arrested in sweep operations. The combatting of partisans and the slaughter of Jews blended together in the "cleansing" of White Russia. From newly discovered records of the same division we learn that the mass killings of 5,900 Jews by two companies of Police Battalion 11 and their Lithuanian auxiliaries in late October 1941 were carried out under army auspices.[51] The practice of racial extermination and burden-sharing between army and SS in White Russia becomes clearer from Order No. 24 of November 24, 1941:

> 5. Jews and Gypsies: .... As already has been ordered, the Jews have to vanish from the flat country and the Gypsies have to be annihilated too. The carrying out of larger Jewish actions is not the task of the divisional units. They are carried out by civilian or police authorities, if necessary ordered by the commandant of White Ruthenia, if he has special units at his disposal, or for security reasons and in the case of collective punishments. When smaller or larger groups of Jews are met in the flat country, they can be liquidated by divisional units or be massed in ghettos near bigger villages designated for that purpose, where they can be handed over to the civilian authority or SD.[52]

The deliberate blending of ideological warfare with military necessity had taken on a new form in the East by the fall of 1941. The blitzkrieg illusion was gone but not confidence in eventual victory. The Wehrmacht, however, knew that it had to fight a fierce and stubborn enemy at the front. Moreover, the Wehrmacht was now facing a partisan movement better organized and better trained under the leadership of Communist Party officials and functionaries, and the Germans were short of troops in the vast rear areas. The solution was ever more ruthless actions against real and suspected "supporters of the hostile attitude," that is, Jews and communists. This becomes especially clear in the well-known orders of the commanders of the 6th, 11th, and 17th Armies—field marshals Walther von Reichenau and Erich von Manstein[53] and Colonel-General Hermann Hoth. They called for the complete extermination of the Soviet war machine as well as the annihilation of the "Jewish-Bolshevik system."

In terms even more concrete than von Reichenau and von Manstein used, Hoth turned his soldiers' thoughts to German history, to the guilt (as he saw it) of the Jews for domestic conditions after World War I: "The destruction of those same Jews who support Bolshevism and its organization for murder—the partisans—is a measure of self-preservation."[54] Hoth, who had been present in the Reich Chancellery on March 30, 1941, followed his supreme ideological leader and strove to turn Hitler's unequivocal maxims into guidelines for his soldiers. In contrast to the campaign against France, he saw two irreconcilable world views clashing in the East: "German feelings of honor and race, and a centuries-old German soldierly tradition against Asiatic thought and its primitive instincts stirred up by a few, mostly Jewish, intellectuals." This struggle could only be ended by the destruction of one or the other. There was no room for compromise.

Von Manstein concluded his order with an appeal to maintain discipline and to preserve military honor. It seems as if in their struggle for survival against "Jewish

Bolshevism," the German people, "because of their superiority of race and deeds," could reconcile the two ideas of destruction and honor. The orders of von Reichenau, von Manstein, and Hoth had also instructed their soldiers to show understanding for the "necessity of harsh punishment of Jewry." This could only be understood by the troops as justification of the mass executions carried out by Einsatzgruppe C. Thus, these commanders went further with the program of extermination than Field-Marshal Wilhelm von Leeb, who had favored a policy of merely "turning a blind eye" to the savage public pogroms in Kaunas.[55] Many an army commander restricted the scope of his orders: *individual* soldiers were to be prevented from *unauthorized* participation in SS mass executions; neither were army troops to take pictures of the massacres. These commanders' main concern was the maintenance of discipline, though others pitilessly recorded the extermination measures of various SS formations.

The considerable discrepancy between the number of partisans killed and the German casualties on the one hand, and the minor difference between the numbers arrested and those later executed, both point to the dialectical dimension of the Wehrmacht's reprisal policy. The destruction was inspired by ideology but rational in its implementation. Ordinary men performed extraordinary tasks. Proclaimed military necessity provided the bridge. A few examples will make this context clear.

After a mopping-up operation near Mirgorod in the rear area of Army Group South, the 62nd Infantry Division shot the "entire Jewish population (168 people) for associating with partisans" in addition to executing 45 partisans. After a similar operation near Novomoskovsk in the same area, the 444th Security Division reported "305 bandits, 6 women with rifles (*Flintenweiber*), 39 prisoners-of-war, [and] 136 Jews" shot. The 2nd Army informed Army Group Center that in "combating partisans," it had arrested 1,836 persons and shot 1,179 between August and October 1941.[56] The 285th Security Division reported that it had shot nearly 1,500 "partisans, civilians, [and] Soviet soldiers" in or after combat between June 22 and December 31, but it had suffered only 18 casualties—7 dead and 11 wounded. Reflecting more than military operations against partisans, the army's reprisal policy now was closely aligned with Nazi racial policies spelled out in Hitler's formula of July 16, 1941. There were, of course, commanders who tried to draw a distinction between military and police measures and who warned the troops not to consider everyone as their enemy just because he looked like a Bolshevik—in rags, unhygienic, unkempt.[57] But such efforts were futile. The majority of commanders either believed or allowed themselves to be convinced that the war of destruction against the Soviet Union required such harshness. Even opponents of National Socialism, such as Erich Hoepner and Carl-Heinrich von Stülpnagel, were able to combine this attitude with a militant anticommunism.

It was not in the Soviet Union alone that German military commanders of all ranks saw the Jews as especially hostile to the German occupation and acted accordingly. This happened in Serbia, too. In Sabac, "Central European Jewish refugees, mostly Austrians, were shot by troops predominately of Austrian origin in retaliation for casualties inflicted by Serbian partisans on the German Army!"[58] This was done not merely in compliance with the guidelines issued by Keitel on September 16, 1941.

The military commanders in Serbia had carried out so-called reprisal executions against Jews and communists prior to the OKW's instruction, which did not mention Jews explicitly. As long as anti-Jewish measures were "perceived and construed as military measures against Germany's enemies, it did not require nazified zealots (though surely such were not lacking), merely conscientious and politically obtuse soldiers to carry them out."[59] In regard to the relationship between the army and the SS, a distinction should be made between actions in the Soviet Union and in Serbia. In the latter, "the mass murder of the male Jews was accomplished primarily by the German Wehrmacht, though it certainly received willing help from the Ordnungs- and Sicherheitspolizei of the SS";[60] in the former it was the other way round. Babi Yar, the name of a ravine near Kiev, has become the symbol of the support that the Einsatzgruppen received from the Wehrmacht.[61]

How does this documentation fit into the wider historiographical debate on the Shoah and the Second World War? If we agree, as we must, with Wolfgang J. Mommsen that the systematic killing of almost 6 million Jews and the death of more than 3 million Soviet prisoners of war is "one of the darkest chapters of German history,"[62] then we have to accept the fact that the Wehrmacht wrote some pages of this chapter. Another dreadful, but rarely mentioned chapter is its murder of about 6,300 former Italian soldiers in 1943/44.[63] Total exoneration of the Wehrmacht is no more helpful for understanding these chapters in German history than is total condemnation.

The development of the broad pattern of Nazi racism can be viewed both as programmatic and evolutionary—dogmatic and flexible. The transformation and fusion of long-range concepts such as Lebensraum, Volksgemeinschaft, Entfernung der Juden, and Vernichtungskrieg must not be seen only in a post-Barbarossa perspective. "Nazi racial policy was radicalized in quantum jumps"[64] between 1939 and 1941, with war shaping those objectives by its own momentum. The war not only opened up favorable conditions for ideologically fixed aims, but these were themselves the reason for going to war in 1939. The racial end justified the radical means. The symbiosis between ideology and strategy—end and means—was eventually made real in the Vernichtungskrieg against the Soviet Union. The murder of the cadres of the Jewish-Bolshevik system, either by the SS or the army, was decided in connection with the military preparations for Operation Barbarossa.

Backed by the euphoria of victory over Jewish Bolshevism in the summer of 1941, Hitler's two most cherished objectives could be fused: the acquisition of Lebensraum and the elimination of Jewry. The vision of a purified Germanic empire stretching from the Atlantic to the Ural Mountains led first to the decision to completely "cleanse" conquered Russia of Jews, and second, to preparations for the European-wide mass murder of the Jews. If we view the Shoah against the background of the war we can see that the long way to Auschwitz is both a straight path and a twisted road. Between 1939 and 1945, the military followed its supreme ideological and military commander in both fields and moved—as Christopher R. Browning has said—from "abdication of responsibility to outright complicity." With regard to the Holocaust, the Wehrmacht acted in many roles. It was perpetrator, collaborator, and bystander. Only after the war did it claim to be victim.

NOTES

1. See Detlev J. K. Peukert, "Rassismus und Endlösungs-Utopie. Thesen zur Entwicklung und Struktur der nationalsozialistischen Vernichtungspolitik," in *Nicht Nur Hitlers Krieg: Der Zweite Weltkrieg und die Deutschen*, ed. Christoph Klessmann (Düsseldorf: Droste, 1989), pp. 71–81; Sybil Milton, "The Context of the Holocaust," *German Studies Review* 12/2 (May 1990): 269–83; Michael Burleigh and Wolfgang Wippermann, *The Racial State: Germany 1933–1945* (Cambridge: Cambridge University Press, 1991); Michael R. Marrus, "The Shoah and the Second World War," in *The Shoah and the War*, ed. Asher Cohen, Yehoyakim Cochavi, and Yoav Gelber (New York: Peter Lang, 1992), pp. 1–24; and Hans-Heinrich Wilhelm, "Zur Historiographie des deutschen Besatzungspolitik in Russland – Forschungslücken, Proportionierungsprobleme und Tabus," in *Deutsch-russische Zeitenwende. Krieg und Frieden 1941–1945*, ed. Hans-Adolf Jacobsen, Jochen Löser, Daniel Proektor, and Sergej Slutsch (Baden-Baden: Nomos, 1995), pp. 353–87.

2. See Omer Bartov, *Hitler's Army: Soldiers, Nazis, and War in the Third Reich* (New York: Oxford University Press 1991); Jürgen Förster, "Das nationalsozialistische Herrschaftssystem und der Krieg gegen die Sowjetunion," in *Erobern und Vernichten: Der Krieg gegen die Sowjetunion 1941–1945*, ed. Peter Jahn and Reinhard Rürup (Berlin: Argon, 1991), pp. 28–46; Manfred Messerschmidt, "Die Wehrmacht im NS-Staat," in *Deutschland 1933–1945: Neue Studien zur nationalsozialistischen Herrschaft*, ed. Karl Dietrich Bracher, Manfred Funke, and Hans-Adolf Jacobsen (Düsseldorf: Droste, 1991), pp. 377–403; and Theo Schulte, *The German Army and Nazi Policies in Occupied Russia* (Oxford: Berg, 1989).

3. See the relevant articles in *Deutsche Soldatenzeitung* (November 1979); *Deutsche Wochenzeitung* (January 18, 1985); *Criticon* (January/February 1985); *Soldat im Volk* (February 1985); *Alte Kameraden* (March 1985 and August 1991). Another wave of articles against Manfred Messerschmidt and his collaborators was published in *Soldat im Volk* in April and July/August 1993, and in Rüdiger Proske, *Vom Marsch durch die Institutionen zum Krieg gegen die Wehrmacht*, 2nd ed. (Mainz: V. Hase & Koehler, 1997). Hannes Heer's exhibition on Wehrmacht crimes in Belorussia, the Ukraine, and Serbia led to another violent outburst of whitewashing in 1995–1997, especially in Munich.

4. *Das Ritterkreuz* 2 (June 1989), p. 14.

5. *Soldat im Volk* (June 1990), pp. 146–47.

6. *Soldat im Volk* (September 1992), p. 128.

7. Max Hastings, *Overlord: D-Day and the Battle for Normandy* (London: Michael Joseph, 1984), p. 315. Cf. Martin van Creveld, *Fighting Power: German and U.S. Army Performance, 1939–1945* (Westport, CT: Greenwood Press, 1982), p. 163.

8. See Messerschmidt, *Die Wehrmacht im NS-Staat*, p. 403.

9. See von Blomberg's educational directive of May 24,1934, published with an incorrect date in *Nazism 1919–1945*, ed. Jeremy Noakes and George Pridham, vol. 3: *Foreign Policy, War and Racial Extermination* (Exeter: Exeter University Publications, 1988), pp. 640–41.

10. See Hans-Jürgen Rautenberg, "Drei Dokumente zur Planung eines 300.000 Mann-Friedensheeres im Dezember 1933," *Militärgeschichtliche Mitteilungen* 22 (1977): 120, 134 note 126. The relevant document is partly published in *Nazism*, ed. Noakes and Pridham, vol. 3, pp. 632–33, but the reference in the original to marriages has been omitted.

11. *Nazism*, ed. Noakes and Pridham, vol. 3, p. 642.

12. Klaus-Jürgen Müller, *Armee und Drittes Reich 1933–1945: Darstellung und Dokumentation* (Paderborn: Schöningh, 1987), pp. 183–89.

13. *Nazism*, ed. Noakes and Pridham, vol. 3, p. 643.

14. See the meeting of commanders in the Seventh Military District (Munich) on October 18, 1943, in Bundesarchiv-Militärarchiv (Freiburg), RH 53-7/v. 271. In Joseph Walks's commendable edition of anti-Jewish regulations, *Das Sonderrecht für die Juden im NS-Staat* (Heidelberg: C. F. Müller, 1981); similar directives of the SS and the Ministry of the Interior are listed under October and November 1944.

15. Report of the Personnel Department no. 2510/40 of August 10, 1940, in Bundesarchiv-

Militärarchiv, RH 53–7/v. 1120. A study by Mark Ryan Riggs will shed more light on this chapter of racial discrimination.

16. Extracts of both the address of February 10, 1939, and Walther von Brauchitsch's directive on education are cited in Jürgen Förster, "New Wine in Old Skins? The Wehrmacht and the War of Weltanschauungen 1941," in *The German Military in the Age of Total War,* ed. Wilhelm Deist (Leamington Spa: Berg, 1985).

17. Both addresses can be found in *Nazism,* ed. Noakes and Pridham, vol. 3, pp. 736–43.

18. Bundesarchiv-Militärarchiv, RH 53-7/v. 1069. Other commanders reminded their soldiers of the injustice of Versailles.

19. Military Archives (Prague), 2nd SS-Panzer Division (Das Reich).

20. *Das Deutsche Reich und der Zweite Weltkrieg,* ed. Militärgeschichtliches Forschungs-amt, vol. 5/1 (Stuttgart: Deutsche Verlags-Anstalt, 1988), p. 48. See Alexander B. Rossino's article "Destructive Impulses: German Soldiers and the Conquest of Poland," in *Holocaust and Genocide Studies* 11/3 (Winter 1997): 351–65.

21. Note in the diary of Major-General Hans-Gustav Felber of September 20, 1939, in Müller, *Armee und Drittes Reich,* p. 191.

22. See Hans Umbreit, *Deutsche Militärverwaltungen 1938/39* (Stuttgart: Deutsche Verlags-Anstalt, 1977), p. 210.

23. Short report on the development of the domestic situation of January 26, 1940, Bundesarchiv-Militärarchiv, RH 1/v. 58.

24. *Nazism,* ed. Noakes and Pridham, vol. 3, pp. 938–39, dealing with February 6, 1940.

25. See Helmut Krausnick and Hans-Heinrich Wilhelm, *Die Truppe des Weltanschau-ungskrieges: Die Einsatzgruppen der Sicherheitspolizei und des SD 1938–1942* (Stuttgart: Deutsche Verlags-Anstalt, 1981), pp. 103–104, dealing with February 7, 1940.

26. See Sammelmappe Militärverwaltung, clause 6, in Bundesarchiv-Militärarchiv, RH 24-3/218.

27. See Krausnick and Wilhelm, *Die Truppe des Weltanschauungskrieges,* p. 112 (July 22, 1940). Küchler's directive can also be found, with an incorrect date and slightly different wording, in *Nazism,* ed. Noakes and Pridham, vol. 3, p. 941.

28. Communication of September 20, 1940, signed by Chief of Staff, Colonel (GS) Faeckenstedt, in Bundesarchiv-Militärarchiv, RH 24-3/36.

29. Quoted in *Nazism,* ed. Noakes and Pridham, vol. 3, pp. 1086–88 (March 30, 1941).

30. *Generaloberst Halder, Kriegstagebuch,* ed. Hans-Adolf Jacobsen, vol. 2 (Stuttgart: W. Kohlhammer, 1962), p. 337.

31. *Nazism,* ed. Noakes and Pridham, vol. 3, p. 928.

32. Notes of the 1st General Staff Officer of the 18th Army, in Bundesarchiv-Militärarchiv, RH 20–18/71.

33. See the copy sent to the naval high command, ibid., RM 7/985.

34. Hans Mommsen, "The Realization of the Unthinkable—The 'Final Solution of the Jewish Question' in the Third Reich," in *The Policies of Genocide: Jews and Soviet Prisoners of War in Nazi Germany,* ed. Gerhard Hirschfeld (London: Allen & Unwin, 1986), p. 121.

35. Richard Breitman, *Architect of Genocide: Himmler and the Final Solution* (New York: Knopf, 1991), pp. 149–50.

36. "Guidelines for the Conduct of the Troops" of May 19, 1941, in *Nazism,* ed. Noakes and Pridham, vol. 3, p. 1090.

37. *Das Deutsche Reich und der Zweite Weltkrieg,* vol. 4, p. 424.

38. Ibid., p. 425.

39. Order of July 25, 1941, signed for Brauchitsch by General Eugen Müller, in Bundesarchiv-Militärarchiv, RH 22/271.

40. Ibid., 99th Infantry Division, 21400/17.

41. *Documents on German Foreign Policy,* Series D, vol. 12, p. 542.

42. Report of September 18, 1941, in Military Archives (Prague), KdoS RF-SS, box 24, folder 154.

43. Bundesarchiv-Militärarchiv, RH 22/224.

44. Ibid., RH 22/227. Von Schenckendorff had explicitly made a causal connection between the oppression of the Jews and the successful pacification of the area.

45. Order of September 14, 1941, in ibid., RH 22-221/13.

46. Entry of September 25, 1941, in Military Archives (Prague), Pol Rgt, folder 251. Cf. Konrad Kwiet, "From the Diary of a Killing Unit," in *Why Germany?* ed. John Milfull (Oxford: Berg, 1992). See Martin C. Dean, "The German *Gendarmarie*, the Ukrainian *Schutzmannschaft* and the 'Second Wave' of Jewish Killings in Occupied Ukraine: German Policing at the Local Level in Zhitomir Region, 1941–1944," *German History* 14 (1996): 168–92.

47. Testimony in court after the war. See Krausnick and Wilhelm, *Truppe des Weltanschauungskrieges*, p. 248.

48. This order was recently found in the State Archives in Riga and has been cited by Hans-Heinrich Wilhelm, "Motivation und 'Kriegsbild' deutscher Generale und Offiziere im Krieg gegen die Sowjetunion," in *Erobern und Vernichten*, ed. Jahn and Rürup, p. 172.

49. Bundesarchiv-Militärarchiv, RH 26–707/v. 1.

50. Ibid., monthly report of October 10–November 10, 1941.

51. See the communications of the Commander in White Ruthenia of October 10 and November 3, 1941, in *United States Holocaust Memorial Museum Archives* (USHMMA), RG 53. 002M, reel 2, folder 698. The figures are from the above cited monthly report of October 11–November 10, 1941. Cf. Christopher R. Browning, *Ordinary Men: Reserve Police Battalion 101 and the Final Solution in Poland* (New York: HarperCollins, 1992) pp. 19–23.

52. USHMMA, RG 53. 002M, reel 2, folder 698. See also Hannes Heer, "Killing Fields: The Wehrmacht and the Holocaust in Belorussia, 1941–1942," *Holocaust and Genocide Studies* 7 (1997): 79–101; and Jürgen Matthäus, "Reibungslos und planmässig.' Die zweite Welle der Judenvernichtung im Generalkommissariat Weissruthenien (1942–1944)," *Jahrbuch für Antisemitismusforschung* 4 (1995): 254–74.

53. Orders of October 6 and November 20, 1941, in 35, pp. 84–86, and vol. 34, pp. 129–32. See Hans Safrian, "Komplizen des Genozids. Zum Anteil der Heeresgruppe Süd an der Verfolgung und Ermordung der Juden in der Ukraine 1941," in *Die Wehrmacht im Rassenkrieg*, ed. Walter Manoschek (Vienna: Picus Verlag, 1996), pp. 90–115.

54. Order of November 17, 1941, in Bundesarchiv-Militärarchiv RH 20-17/44.

55. See Krausnick and Wilhelm, *Truppe des Weltanschauungskrieges*, pp. 205–209.

56. For this and the following, see *Das Deutsche Reich und der Zweite Weltkrieg*, vol. 4, p. 1055.

57. See the communication of the Commander of the III (tank) Army Corps, General Eberhard von Mackensen, of November 24, 1941, in Bundesarchiv-Militärarchiv, RH 24-3/136. Cf. the "Personal Reflections on the Ukrainian Question" by 1st Lieutenant Dr. Pauls of September 20, 1941, ibid., RH 26-2v.67.

58. Christopher R. Browning, "Wehrmacht Reprisal Policy and the Mass Murder of Jews in Serbia," *Militärgeschichtliche Mitteilungen* 33 (1983): 39; and Walter Manoschek, "Gehst mit Juden erschiessen? Die Vernichtung der Juden in Serbien," in *Vernichtungskrieg. Vebrechen der Wehrmacht 1941–1944*, ed. Hannes Heer and Klaus Naumann (Hamburg: Hamburger Edition, 1995), pp. 39–56.

59. Ibid., p. 39.

60. Ibid., p. 42.

61. See Krausnick and Wilhelm, *Truppe des Weltanschauungskrieges*, pp. 235, 237–38. Kovno may become the symbol of the participation of the Soviet population in the murder of the Soviet and Reich Jews. See Dina Porat, "The Legend of the Struggle of Jews from the Third Reich in the Ninth Fort near Kovno, 1941–1942," *Tel Aviver Jahrbuch für Deutsche Geschichte* (1991): 363–92.

62. Mommsen, "Realization of the Unthinkable," p. 11.

63. See Gerhard Schreiber, *Die italienischen Militärinternierten im deutschen Machtbereich 1943 bis 1945—Verraten – Verachtet – Vergessen* (Munich: Oldenbourg, 1990).

64. Christopher R. Browning, "Nazi Resettlement Policy and the Search for a Solution to the Jewish Question," *German Studies Review* 9 (1986): 519.

20.

GUUS MEERSHOEK

The Amsterdam Police and the Persecution of the Jews

Two weeks after the Amsterdam police began taking part in the nightly round-ups of Jews from their homes, a patrolman sent a letter to the procureur-generaal (chief state prosecutor) in September 1942.[1] Writing under a pseudonym, the patrol-man wrote that he and his colleagues were carrying out orders "with bleeding hearts":

> from the start we were very reluctant to assist in the deportation of Jews who live in our city, but after several nights in which we had to drag elderly, infirm, and wretched men and women from their homes, we have had too much. Many of us consider the assignment to carry out this work as an insult to our Dutch force. . . . Could you ensure that it is speedily brought to an end. Your Honour would show us all a great service in the Justice that we are bound to serve.[2]

The picture that emerges from this letter is confirmed by scanty sources containing information on the motivation of the members of the force to obey orders and their attitude toward these assignments. Although most of them had serious qualms about performing the task, the tradition of submissiveness won the day; occasional protests were too little and too late. How were these unwilling policemen turned into painstaking executors?

The Amsterdam police force was firmly rooted in the local community. The police had a balanced organization and experienced staff who knew the city and enjoyed the confidence of its residents. Most members of the force viewed the German measures with disdain, especially those aimed at Jews. At first, these characteristics of the force restrained its involvement in the persecution of the Jews.

The change in the police role was not a gradual one. On three separate occasions, German authorities broke abruptly with the established forms of contact between the German and the Dutch administrators in order to mobilize the police force for a specific project. Each of these shocks brought about lasting changes in the internal authority of the police. They induced members to enforce anti-Jewish measures and eventually also to assist both in the deportation of Jews and in tracking down Jews who tried to flee.

The very characteristics that initially had hindered police involvement had a fatal effect from that time forward. Victims were rounded up from their homes by repre-sentatives of an institution that they had been accustomed to trust. Moreover, in contrast to their German colleagues, the Amsterdam policemen who carried out the orders were familiar with the city and its Jewish population. They often conveyed to their victims their reluctance. The victims could not but feel that resistance would be pointless. From the perpetrators' point of view, these "all too human" policemen were the best executors.

As indicated, changes in the internal wielding of authority by the Amsterdam police force were brought about on three occasions by shocks caused by changed behavior of the German authorities. This account of the participation of the Amsterdam police force in the persecution of the Jews will focus in particular on the extent to which these changes explain the obedience of the force and the preservation of its normal prewar habits in its new role under German direction. The concluding summary reflects on the potential importance of these findings for research on the German persecution of the Jews elsewhere in Europe.

The Established Order

Before the German invasion, the Netherlands was a stable democracy with a modern, liberal constitution and a decentralized polity with oligarchic features. The government had not been faced with violent disturbances such as war or revolution for more than a century. The Amsterdam city council had been dominated for some time by Liberals and Social Democrats, and as a result of their reforms the city had a modern administration at its disposal. Still, its political culture was predominantly one of traditional, consociational values. While the top levels of administration no longer came from the time-honored merchant families, they still tried to reach compromises that were acceptable for all groups in society. Additionally, they maintained a distance from their own sources of electoral support, and they were convinced that the chief obligation entailed by their position was the maintenance of "authority."[3]

The legal system occupied an important position in the polity. The constitution assigned the highest authority to the existing laws. Legislation was regarded as the ideal instrument for the renewal of society. The police system reflected these values, as the Ministry of Justice and the judicial authorities played a dominant role.

The Amsterdam police force was led by a chief constable who was immediately answerable to the mayor and the chief state prosecutor. When the war broke out, the force employed more than 2,400 people. Seven police stations, each led by a superintendent, were responsible for police duties in a particular area of the city. In addition, there was a headquarters with specialized services. Patrol work was carried out by the lower ranks—patrolmen and their immediate superiors. The whole city was patrolled day and night along predetermined routes. The senior officers (inspectors) handled the charges made by the patrolmen and supervised police work. As a result of the stringent demands imposed on the police by the judicial authorities, the inspectors had a heavy workload and their numbers were relatively large. They had received good training, had quite often joined at the age of nineteen, and were divided from the patrolmen by deep social barriers.

In the 1930s, Chief Constable H. J. Versteeg had drastically reorganized the police force. He had begun to centralize the organization and had improved the administration, raised the level of physical conditioning and knowledge of the law, and introduced technical innovations such as traffic lights. As a result of concentration of authority at the top, the paternal authority that had been wielded by the superintendents in their neighborhoods diminished and the pressure on the personnel on the streets was intensified. However, when Versteeg planned to centralize the organization even further in 1937, the superintendents successfully resisted his initiatives. As a result, three problems arose in the management of the police force. First, Versteeg, who had been accustomed to behaving as a liberal governor and to pay no heed to his reputation, failed to realize that his authority had acquired an anonymous character through the reorganization and aroused insecurity among his subordinates. Second, the increase in the volume of written instructions had led to a bureaucratic regulation of internal conflicts. While Versteeg extended his authority over the patrolmen on the beat, this development undermined his control over what took place. Third, Versteeg lacked essential information because, despite the increasing specialization in the organization, he followed the customary practice of not consulting those below him in rank. By the end of the thirties, the administration of the force had become paralyzed. Versteeg rarely left his desk.[4]

The relatively rapid military defeat of the Dutch armed forces in May 1940 and the flight of the queen and her government to London caused confusion and insecurity both in the administration and among the population. The Dutch were surprised by the initially correct behavior of the German forces. The civil administration was left intact; existing laws remained in force. A few weeks later a Reichskommissariat was set up; its two bridgeheads in Amsterdam were a Beauftragte of the Reich Commissioner and an Aussenstellenleiter of the Sipo (SD). At first, they both watched from the wings. The top-ranking members of the national administration, the secretaries general, who had taken over the responsibility of governing and who maintained contact with the occupying forces, were given legislative powers by the Reich Commissioner. They ensured that the German instructions reached provincial and local government, but they also seized the opportunity, with the aid of the occupying forces, to push through projects previously thwarted by Dutch politicians. These included merging the various police forces and issuing identity cards.[5]

During the last four months of 1940, Reich Commissioner Dr. A. Seyss-Inquart gradually managed to get the general secretaries to eliminate Jews from the administration. He began by presenting every request in a mild form, and once it had been accepted, he came up with more stringently formulated stipulations that were followed with irritation but without protest.[6] The first step was to prohibit the promotion or appointment of Jews. Then came the "Ariërverklaring" (Aryan declaration): all civil servants had to answer the question of whether they were Jewish or not. Finally, all Jews were to be dismissed. The Amsterdam municipal council was notified of the measures in circulars from the Secretary General for Domestic Affairs. Although the national government was not allowed to interfere with municipal personnel policy under Dutch law, the city council implemented the measures punctually. There was no trace of the traditional attachment to its own autonomy.

Fear based on an intuitive awareness of the importance attached to these measures by the German leadership seems to have played a part, but this reaction was above all a return to the ingrained habit of obeying orders, apparently irrespective of where they originated. Under pressure from their colleagues, who called upon them not to take the matter too seriously and to comply, Jewish aldermen declined to protest.[7] Municipal civil servants followed the line adopted by their superiors. None of the Amsterdam civil servants or policemen refused to sign the Aryan declaration, and a similar reaction was displayed by most civil servants in the rest of the country.[8]

The First Shock

This cooperation, which was so advantageous to the occupying forces, was disrupted by the Beauftragte of the Reich Commissioner, Dr. J. H. Böhmcker, in January 1941. This was the *first shock*. Böhmcker instructed the municipal council to investigate the possibility of setting up a ghetto and encouraged Dutch National Socialists to use violence against Jewish customers in inner-city pubs.[9] His intervention met with a reaction different from the response to the Reich Commissioner's measures. Jews and non-Jews joined to defend the former against the acts of violence. The city council did collect the requested information, but instead of passing it on to Böhmcker, the council put pressure on its own national administration to prevent the establishment of a ghetto.

When the acts of violence escalated, Böhmcker closed off the Old Jewish Quarter, which he wanted to transform into a ghetto. This measure and a German round-up of Jewish young men provoked a massive protest by the population, the "February strike," on February 25. By initially adopting a reticent attitude, the police gave the popular movement every opportunity to develop. Lacking leadership and specific demands,[10] the protest had the spontaneous character of a riot, the traditional form of resistance in Amsterdam. Once the collective protest had been violently crushed by the occupying forces in a display of strength, the Reich Commissioner replaced the city council and the chief constable with pro-German Dutchmen. In the end, the Beauftragte failed to achieve his ambition, and a ghetto was not established in Amsterdam. In fact, his own position was seriously weakened for a while. After the strike, the Sipo—under Höhere SS- und Polizeiführer H. A. Rauter—came to prominence. Rauter, who better sensed the final direction of the anti-Jewish policy than Böhmcker, advocated a different approach to the persecution: Jews were forbidden to leave the city for any length of time, and a Zentralstelle für Judische Auswanderung (Central Office for Jewish Emigration) was established.[11]

The new chief constable, S. Tulp (1891–1942), was a retired lieutenant-colonel of the Royal Dutch East Indian Army (KNIL).[12] It was very rare for former members of the armed forces to hold civilian public office in the Netherlands. Tulp had acquired a good deal of experience in the rigid enforcement of law and order during his stint as an infantry commander in the Dutch East Indies, where racial discrimination was an administrative principle and reprisals against specific ethnic groups were common practice.[13] The German actions against the Jews had thus paralleled his own experiences. Dissatisfied with the defense policy of the Dutch government, he had become a member of the Dutch National Socialist Party (NSB) in 1939 after his premature retirement. However, he did not hold a high opinion of the party. He was well disposed toward the SS, which he regarded as a European army in the fight against communism. He had an unbounded admiration for Hitler.[14]

As chief constable, Tulp was under orders not only from the mayor and the chief state prosecutor but also from the liaison officer of the Ordnungspolizei, whom Rauter had seconded to the police force shortly before. However, he soon acted independently, as he had been accustomed to do in the Dutch East Indies, and gradually detached the police force from the Dutch polity. Tulp represented the interests of his organization more vigorously than his predecessor had done, and he was not afraid of conflicts, not even with German authorities. If the Germans were unanimous in their decisions, however, he obeyed unquestioningly. That was the genuine advantage that the German administration had gained with the first shock. It was to be of decisive importance in the persecution of the Jews. In the spring of 1941, the Germans disposed of a Dutch chief constable who was able to discern their essential interests.

Contrary to expectation, Tulp did not get rid of those members of the force who were hostile to the occupiers. Above all, he endeavored to enhance his own authority over his staff and to increase the unity of the force. Insofar as there were other concerns, he was confident that the existing division of powers was favorable to National Socialism. His style of management offered an extraordinary solution to the three problems that had crippled the efficiency of the force under his predecessor. First, unlike Versteeg, he was often on the spot during police actions and energetically defended the interests of the members of his force, even if a member had ended up in the hands of the Sipo for something he had said or done. While the population came into increasingly direct confrontation with German repression, Tulp gave his staff a sense of security. Second, Tulp broke with the conventional administrative procedures. He developed a personal attachment to members of the force in key positions and demanded unconditional obedience in return. In addition, he regularly assembled the entire force in a local theater to address the members personally and to show German films. Finally, as a stranger to the profession, Tulp regularly consulted his subordinates. This made a great impression on the members of the force. Many breathed a sigh of relief at Tulp's style of management. One of them, Inspector B., stated to a colleague at the time: "When the war is over, he [Tulp] must be executed, but with a golden bullet."[15]

Tulp failed to implement the far-reaching transformation of the police force that the National Socialists intended. He left the organization of the force intact and added only new units that operated with a large degree of independence and which were directly under his own authority. Initially these were a Bureau Inlichtingendienst (political investigation department) and a barracks unit, the Politiebataljon Amsterdam; later he added a Bureau Joodsche Zaken (bureau for Jewish affairs). The barracks unit was his favorite, and he drew heavily on his experience in the Dutch East Indies for the establishment of this unit. It consisted of 300 demobilized soldiers. At first, the easy-going atmosphere and tradition of the peace-time Dutch Army predominated in the unit, but within a year Dutch and a few German instructors had introduced an iron discipline similar to that which had prevailed in the Royal Dutch East Indian Army.[16]

In the meantime, the advance that the Sipo, under Rauter, had launched after the February strike had come to a halt. In May 1941 a compromise was reached in the Reichskommissariat, providing that the Aussenstellenleiter and the Beauftragte would share responsibilities for the persecution of the Jews at the local level.[17] It probably was as a result of these changes that Rauter's anti-Jewish measures were not executed. The police force did not receive the usual Ministry of Justice instructions to carry them out and, therefore, did almost nothing to ensure their observance.[18]

All the same, two incidents led to the involvement of the force in the persecution in June 1941. At the request of the Sipo, Tulp provided 247 detectives to arrest some 300 German Jews for interrogation. Afterwards, however, it transpired that they had been deported to Mauthausen in retaliation for a bomb attack on a German office. The population, including the police, by now were aware that the Jews who had been arrested by the German police shortly before the February strike had died in Mauthausen soon afterwards.[19] Tulp, who felt deceived by the Aussenstellenleiter W. P. F. Lages, and saw this as a blow to his prestige among his men, assured the detectives that there would be no repetition of the incident.[20] However, he ran into problems again two weeks later, when the Reich Commissioner announced a regulation prohibiting the opening of shops on Sunday. Forty Jewish shops were affected by this measure in Amsterdam. Tulp instructed his staff to apply the new rules flexibly, and he himself announced in the press that it was possible to apply for exemption from the prohibition. This irritated the Reich Commissioner. The Chief Constable received a reprimand and was forced to modify the instructions to his staff.[21] Three months later it would be seen that Tulp had learned from both incidents.

The Second Shock

Rauter produced the *second shock*. After setting up in the national administration of the Sipo a special bureau for the persecution of the Jews, he promulgated a decree on September 15 which barred Jews from entry to numerous public places and prohibited them from changing their place of residence. The Dutch police were to arrest offenders and hand them over to the Sipo, who were authorized by Rauter to punish them.[22] It was possible to take action against offenders because the municipal registrars recently had issued identity cards, which were specially marked for Jews. Tulp learned of the decree from the newspaper. Without waiting for implementation instructions to come from the Ministry of Justice, he immediately ordered his staff to carry it out to the letter. On his own authority, he reserved one bar and one theater for the Jews in Amsterdam. However, the patrolmen refused to carry out his instructions, even after Tulp had repeated the order. The officers may have removed Jews from public places, but they did not arrest them.[23]

This second initiative by Rauter was foiled, too. Immediately after the promulgation of the decree, Reich Commissioner Seyss-Inquart had visited Hitler and received the assurance that he, not Rauter, would be in charge of actions against the Jews in the Netherlands. He therefore instructed his Beauftragte to draw up a list of additional anti-Jewish measures. He promulgated some of them himself in the form of decrees, while the rest were implemented by the Beauftragte as administrative measures. He deprived the Sipo of the right to punish offenders and emphasized once again that the supervision of the execution of the anti-Jewish measures was the joint responsibility of his Beauftragte and of the Aussenstellenleiter.[24]

Nevertheless, Tulp forged ahead. In October he managed to convince Rauter of the suitability of his force for the implementation of the anti-Jewish measures. He was assured that Aussenstellenleiter Lages would give him immediate and full information on new measures in the future. Thereupon Tulp appointed an officer to serve as liason with Lages and to supervise the execution of the measures by the police force. Furthermore, Tulp obliged the police stations in the city to send him monthly written reports on the execution of these measures, and he held members of the force personally responsible for any failure to arrest offenders. Finally, Lages reserved more bars and restaurants for Jews than Tulp had done on his own authority in September.[25] This enabled the police to enforce the prohibition on Jews frequenting places of this kind. All of these measures were effective.

Beginning in November 1941, the Amsterdam police expelled Jews from a large part of public life. The relatively small number of offenders whom the police handed over to the Sipo were shipped via the transit camp in Amersfoort to Mauthausen, where they soon met the same fate as their predecessors.[26] By December 1941 the situation that Rauter had envisaged when he unleashed the second shock—the social separation of Jews and non-Jews—had become a fait accompli in Amsterdam. It was Tulp who had brought about this situation through his interventions in the organization of the force.

It was most probably in January 1942 that the Reich Commissioner received instructions from Berlin to deport the Jews from the Netherlands. Independently, and at about the same time, the administrative leadership of the Ministry of Justice made a decision with far-reaching consequences for the deportation operation. It decided not to intervene any longer if the Reichskommissariat adopted police measures against the Jews.[27] It was the start of the collapse of the recent forced centralization of the police. Unlike the situation in France, the German police was not faced with a national administration that (temporarily) defended the interests of a part of the Jews, that is, those sharing the nationality of the local authorities.[28] In the Netherlands, the German police was itself able to direct the local police in deportation actions.

In the same month Tulp altered his position in the police system. Without being initiated into the objectives of the German authorities, he had discovered the priorities of the latter by trial and error. His requests with regard to the police battalion and on anti-Jewish measures often met with a positive response. In February 1942, with Rauter as intermediary, he obtained permission from Himmler to arm his battalion with carbines. Thereafter Tulp attempted to form a direct, personal link with a member of the Reichskommissariat. He began to send them signals indicating that he was entirely reliable in political terms and that they could entrust his force with the major police tasks. Though it was not directly relevant to the matter in hand, in various letters to the Reichskommissariat, Tulp stressed that Jews should be singled out in retaliation for acts by the Resistance or for other sabotage. His suggestions were not followed, but the signal came over clearly enough. From April 1942 Tulp and Rauter were on personal terms.[29] At the instigation of Rauter, Tulp joined the Dutch section of the SS.

In the spring of 1942, the actions of the patrolmen against Jews who contravened the anti-Jewish measures were dropping off. One factor may have been the disappearance of the liaison officer who had been appointed by Tulp in October 1941 to supervise these activities (he was dismissed for drinking too much). Nevertheless, the general reluctance of the staff to carry out these actions was probably the decisive factor. In March and April Tulp spurred his men to take more vigorous action, but in vain. It was not until the end of April, when the Jews were obliged to wear a yellow star, that the police operations resumed their former intensity. The police force also increased to around thirty a week the number of (mainly Jewish) offenders who were handed over to the Sipo. After a brief drop in the number of arrests, the figure remained constant at that level. Not every police station began to hand over Jews at the same time. It was not necessarily the case that those in districts where many Jews were living arrested more than other police stations did. It is remarkable that once a police station had arrested more than five Jews in one week, it continued to do so.[30] It is unlikely that we will ever be able to unravel the internal factors behind these statistics. For example it is unclear whether these arrests were carried out by a handful of National Socialist policemen or whether a much larger group was involved.

In October 1941 Rauter had suggested that Tulp set up a bureau for Jewish affairs in his force. He had also mentioned a candidate to lead this bureau: R. W. Dahmen von Buchholz, a fanatical antisemite who had been active in all sorts of extreme right-wing groups for twenty years, had no experience at all in police matters, and was a notorious grumbler.[31] Rauter did not reveal to Tulp what the bureau was intended for and waited without actually appointing Dahmen von Buchholz. It was not until the Reichskommissariat started making preparations for the deportation that he set the wheels in motion. Dahmen von Buchholz was appointed to the rank of superintendent, and Tulp first gave him a few weeks experience in a police station. On June 1, 1942, the new chief started work with ten detectives, most of them National Socialists. Tulp had ensured that a few policemen who were not pro-German were appointed to this bureau to prevent it from acquiring too isolated a position within the force. The main task of the bureau was to track down offenders against a number of new anti-Jewish measures that were intended to make deportation a rapid, thorough, and profitable operation. The detainees were handed over to the Zentralstelle, which generally marked them as criminals and put them on the train to the Westerbork transit camp. Rough treatment was a common occurrence in the Bureau.[32]

Tulp adopted all these measures without knowing that they were for deportation. In late May 1942 he was still repeating to his men that the German leadership would not act to "destroy the Jewish influence" until the war with the Soviet Union was over.[33] On June 19, one week before the Zentralstelle informed the Jewish Council about the deportation, Tulp had heard only rumors of it.[34] Although the new measures made heavy demands on his men, in all his correspondence Tulp never asked Rauter about the purpose of the action.[35]

Tulp was certainly annoyed by the fact that he had not been involved in the preparations for the deportation, and that not he but Aussenstellenleiter Lages was in charge of the execution of the action at the local level. His irritation was not caused by concern about the consequences of the measures for the political system he defended, nor did it reduce his willingness to provide assistance. It is virtually certain that he was in the dark about the fate of the Jews in the ensuing months as well. He knew that they had been given false information about their place of destination, but his previous experience in colonial administration had inured him to such practices.[36]

At first, the Jews who had been selected received a letter in the mail summoning them to report to the Zentralstelle, where they would receive details of when they were to go to the station to be transported. Lages soon noticed that only a few reported, so he had absentees arrested by his own men and by the political investigation department of the Amsterdam police. The summonses were now delivered to the doors of the victims by Amsterdam patrolmen. However, these changes failed to produce the desired effect. Only too frequently patrolmen returned to the police station with the summonses, reporting that they had found no one at home.[37] The first train that left the Central Station as scheduled, on July 14, was thus not filled to capacity. In the succeeding weeks, Lages instructed the Ordnungspolizei to hold round-ups in the streets. If the selected Jews did not show up, he threatened to send the victims of these raids to Mauthausen, which was by now tantamount to a death sentence. This blackmail was counterproductive, and the number of Jews who voluntarily reported dropped even lower.[38] By August it had become clear to the Sipo leadership in the Netherlands that the only way to get the Jews out of their houses was through a large-scale police operation.

The Third Shock

The order to provide men to pick up the Jews from their homes, which Tulp probably received on the telephone from Rauter on September 2, was the *third shock*. Tulp realized how important this order was in the eyes of the German head of police. The fact that he was not informed about the deportation until the last minute seems to have prompted him to carry out orders as precisely as possible. He organized two meetings in a theater to motivate the members of the force personally for the job.[39] He was on the spot every night during the raids. This enabled him to make it clear to his men that he bore responsibility for the operation. It also enabled him to take an active part in its execution, drawing on his experience in the East Indies. His staff could no longer count on protection. Tulp even asked Rauter for additional powers to punish vacillating policemen severely. He kept the German head of police informed about the operation both by telephone and in writing, and Rauter even came to take a look for himself on one occasion.[40]

As usual, the selection of the personnel entrusted with the task of carrying out the raids was in the hands of Inspector B. B., who was born in 1894 in the Dutch Indies, had joined the force in 1920, and in 1942 had reached the rank of Inspector First Class. He was the man who had informally declared that Tulp should be shot with a golden bullet after the war. Inspector B.'s work, which was completely administrative in character, demanded a thorough knowledge of the day to day strength of the force as well as psychological insight. Considerable influence was attributed to him by other inspectors, for whom his decisions had far-reaching consequences.

On September 2, B. went to the Sipo and was told that two inspectors, one sergeant, and eighteen patrolmen, spread over three detachments, were to be ready at 7 P.M. on the first night of the operation. Each detachment was to have a truck and driver at its disposal. The police battalion was also required to supply manpower. B. had obtained the names and addresses of the victims, and with this he could appoint the inspectors to direct the operation. Then he would tell the appropriate police stations in the city how many patrolmen and sergeants they were to supply.

On that afternoon and the following days, B. selected inspectors who had recently joined the force, who were not pro-German, and who worked in the districts where they were to carry out the operation. All were between the ages of nineteen and twenty-five and clearly the most malleable group in the service.[41] In the afternoon they were notified by service telegram that they would be required to carry out "a special operation." Soon afterwards, B. telephoned these inspectors to tell them what the operation entailed and thus to assure himself of their cooperation. The whole force soon got to know the meaning of the unusual formulation.[42]

From the start, the inspectors carried out the round-ups with reluctance. They muttered complaints, but there was no opposition until a few days later, when some ten inspectors had an opportunity to discuss the issue during physical training at the sports field, without their superiors present. Various inspectors who worked in police headquarters and were thus not yet entrusted with the task themselves leveled accusations against those who took part in the round-ups. When B. heard of this, he took an unusual step. He decided that the inspectors who opposed the operation while at the sports field would be the next to be recruited. Tulp agreed to this proposal. On the afternoon of Friday, September 10, the inspector who had protested the loudest, J. van der Oever, was told that he was to lead a detachment that very evening. Despite the enormous pressure brought to bear on him by his colleagues, van der Oever stuck to his refusal, hardened in his resolution after several telephone conversations with his wife. That afternoon he went to see B.'s superior, the National Socialist commander of the Uniformed Branch, J. C. Krenning, and told him that on the basis of his religious convictions, he refused to pick up Jews. To Van der Oever's amazement, Krenning seemed to take a very conciliatory attitude. Van der Oever was immediately suspended from the task. Courteous to his subordinate's face, Krenning reported to Tulp that Van der Oever had openly refused to obey orders. Tulp decided on instant dismissal, the heaviest penalty that the chief constable could apply at that time.[43] Once it had been smothered in the obscurity of the hierarchy, the protest could no longer become a point of crystallization for a wider protest.[44]

The patrolmen and sergeants were not selected by B. but by their own superiors—inspectors from the city police stations. Little is known about their working procedure. The strict demarcation between the higher and the lower ranks barred them from consulting with the patrolmen in making their decisions.[45] There are indications that primarily those patrolmen were selected who were known to abide less strictly by the police regulations; there are also statements that older policemen stepped into the breach for their younger colleagues and volunteered for the distasteful duty.[46] Shortly before 7 P.M., the inspectors received from B. documents bearing the names and addresses of the victims. There was no time to warn friends or acquaintances. The policemen were sent in pairs to remove the Jews from their homes. Contrary to past practice, the inspectors now remained at the police station.[47]

The police officers were under stress during the raids. Although the resistance of the Jews had been largely broken by the previous events, so that the policemen rarely ran up against opposition, the predicament of the victims made an impression on them. Sometimes a Jew jumped out a window when they approached his apartment; sometimes they discovered that a Jewish family had already gassed itself. The Sipo noted few irregularities among the policemen.[48] There are reports of some individual rebellions during the raids. For instance, soon after the war a patrolman commented that during a raid one of his colleagues "was so worked up that he was prepared to open fire on the Grüne Polizei [Ordnungspolizei]. His colleagues simply took him home."[49]

Besides the Ordnungspolizei, both the police battalion and (less frequently) the militia (Orde Dienst) of the Jewish Council were involved in the raids. In Amsterdam the militia was sometimes led by a Jewish inspector who had been expelled from the Amsterdam police force in November 1940. Little is known about the attitude of this unit.[50] The members of the battalion behaved more roughly than the ordinary patrolmen. They often stole from the houses and sometimes mistreated the victims. Although Tulp was aware of these excesses and took action against them, he presented a glowing portrait of his pupils to Rauter:

> You will understand, Gruppenführer, that the weeklong continuous catching of approximately 450 Jews per evening has aroused enormous pity and indignation among the Dutch population. Still, the men of the battalion are respected enough that, for example, in the environment of the Krugerplein where week after week a big crowd watches the catching of Jews, the presence of only two members of the Battalion is enough to prevent any dissent from being voiced, where it was common in Amsterdam in such cases for regular police to find the place out of order all evening and to have a hard job.[51]

After the dismissal of Van der Oever, the police force continued to participate in the round-ups under the leadership of Tulp until October 3, when Tulp fell ill and Krenning had to take over directing the force. No Dutch reports are known that deal with the course of events that evening. Some German reports indicate that the inspectors, without openly refusing duty, used every opportunity to disrupt the action. Processing documents of the victims was a lengthy process, and Jews were allowed to take large amounts of luggage, up to five bags. Consequently, the transport to the police stations stagnated. Everything indicates that Krenning lacked Tulp's authority. At 10 P.M. the German authorities canceled the action.[52] There are no German sources that indicate why they did that. Tulp languished for two and a half weeks, then died on October 22, 1942.

Because of the lack of a suitable replacement for the chief constable, the police force could not be deployed in the raids again. The battalion continued with the raids on its own. This situation prevailed until February 1943, by which time there was no discipline at all, and corruption and abuse were rife. Its activities were taken over by the Vrijwillige Hulppolitie (voluntary auxiliary police), a body of Dutch National Socialists who had volunteered for this work and who were installed in the police barracks. Most of the raids were now carried out by the Ordnungspolizei.

Deportation involved more than just rounding up and dispatching the victims. The homes they left behind had to be guarded, pets removed, and gas and electricity shut off. After the houses had been emptied by the Einsatzstab Rosenberg, they had to be cleaned up and prepared for reuse. Several Dutch organizations were involved in this work, which was usually conducted under police supervision.

Jews who tried to escape deportation by going into hiding created a special problem for the persecutors. Tracking them down was the responsibility of the Bureau for Jewish Affairs and the Central Investigation Department of the Amsterdam police force. The Bureau for Jewish Affairs consisted of some twenty-five detectives at that time. Most of them were antisemites who viewed their victims with scorn and tried to get their less convinced colleagues to adopt the same attitude.[53]

Other motives played a part among the detectives of the investigation department. They were customarily assessed on the basis of the number and type of criminals whom they captured. Tracking Jews was not rated very highly, but since they were a relatively easy prey, a detective could easily boost his score by arresting them. It was, therefore, mainly the less esteemed detectives who were attracted to this kind of work.[54] Both services used informers to hunt down their victims; these were Jews who informed on Jews in hiding in return for postponement of their own deportation. The ordinary detectives usually protected these informers after they had performed their services; those from the Bureau of Jewish Affairs never did that.[55]

In *The Destruction of the European Jews*, Raul Hilberg writes that in the persecution of the Jews, German bureaucrats "displayed a striking pathfinding ability in the absence of directives, a congruity of activities without jurisdictional guidelines, a fundamental comprehension of the task even when there were no explicit communications."[56] Their collective behavior conferred on the persecution a systematic character to which Hilberg refers with the following terms: definition by decree, expropriation, concentration, and annihilation.

In Amsterdam the police had not turned to persecution on their own initiative. The impetus for their participation was provided by the German authorities in a number of confrontations. Although the German interventions did not always achieve the desired result, they caused important changes in the wielding of authority within the police force. As we have seen, these episodes led to the appointment of a chief constable who had acquired his skills in the Dutch colonial army and quickly learned when to obey the German occupier unconditionally. At his initiative, separate mission-dedicated departments were set up with particularly motivated staff members. Although the members of the police force lacked both the "striking pathfinding ability" and the self-assurance of their German counterparts, during these German-induced shocks the new chief and the new units prompted the policemen to take part in the actions. However, it was only a temporary change, and the former pattern was more or less reestablished after a while. But the effect was cumulative. Each successive shock penetrated deeper into the police hiercharchy.

In the end, by the time of the third shock the police force as a whole itself ensured its compliance with German orders. Potential objectors were pressured by their colleagues, and resistance was nipped in the bud by the obscurity of the hierarchy. By this point, the police force had internalized the sense of direction described by Hilberg.

The Historian's Challenge

The challenge to contribute new ideas that might broaden research on the German persecution of the Jews is bound to be embarrassing for Dutch historians. Solid studies of this subject have been published in the Netherlands, and they have been read by a wide audience.[57] However, the style of these works is generally that of the traditional narrative, and the range of focus is narrowed to the German administration, the Secretaries General and the Jewish Council. As a result of work carried out by scholars in the United States, Israel, Germany, and elsewhere, a younger generation of historians has discovered the limitations of this kind of historiography and has begun to pose questions that are new to them (if not to their colleagues abroad). For example, the work of Hilberg has taught us not to become fixated on a few crucial decisions at the top level of the apparatus of persecution, but to examine the entire process of bureaucratic preparation and implementation. My own research into the Amsterdam police is intended not only to fill a gap in what is known about the persecution in the Netherlands, but also to throw light on the role of the Dutch authorities in a fashion more in keeping with standard international academic practice. At the same time, I use research on the history of local political institutions and traditions—studies that are the outcome of an interest rooted in the particularistic political culture of the Netherlands but which have not yet been used in writing the history of the Occupation. One of the themes of my research is the persistence of local political traditions. Since this not only played such a fatal role in the persecution of the Jews in the Netherlands but also seems to have operated elsewhere as well, it may be this aspect of my research that attracts the most attention from other historians.

At first glance the German organization of the persecution and deportation of the Jews in the Netherlands seems to have run like clockwork. The German administrators involved were almost all experienced in persecution elsewhere, the staff of the *Zentralstelle für Judische Auswanderung* had acquired experience in Vienna and Prague, and Seyss-Inquart managed to prevent the execution of anti-Jewish measures from creating discord in the ranks of the German administration. In the Netherlands, the perpetrators were particularly successful. Within a year, approximately 100,000 Jews—more than 70 percent of the Jewish population of the Netherlands—had been transported to the Westerbork transit camp. At that time more than seventy-three thousand Jews had already been sent to death camps.[58] The actual course of the persecution in Amsterdam, however, indicates that the German contribution to the achievement of this result can easily be overrated.[59] Most German authorities were not in a position to deal with the Dutch administration effectively. Often, their brusque interventions did not immediately produce the desired result. In order to gain insight into the effectiveness of the persecution, it is necessary to devote an equal amount of attention to the specific reaction of the indigenous administration. For a long time the Dutch authorities adopted a conciliatory attitude with the aim of preventing the occupying forces from imposing their demands by force. The Dutch administration wanted to retain control, apparently at any price. In their own circles this strategy was referred to as "keeping one step ahead of the occupying forces." This attitude was doomed to failure, which is precisely what happened in the spring of 1942. The Dutch administration now fell back on its traditional, decentralized structure. When the deportation of the Jews began shortly afterwards, the occupiers could direct even the local police force. As a result of the tradition of compromise, the civil service apparatus continued to run smoothly, and it continued to assist the occupying forces until the summer of 1943.

Chief Constable Tulp was an extraordinary character. He was a convinced National Socialist, but he remained to the end an admirer of Dutch Queen Wilhelmina. During the Occupation he wore both his Dutch royalist insignia and the National Socialist wolf trap on his lapel.[60] All the same, he fell in line with the German persecution apparatus with remarkable ease. The conclusions of an article by Christopher R. Browning, in which he compares the behavior of three German officials—Franz Rademacher, Harald Turner, and Hans Biebow—at the beginning of the mass killings confirm Hilberg's picture of the German bureaucrats: these three men were not issued clear instructions, they were not initiated into the new policy by their superiors, and they did not experience the move toward the mass killings as the crossing of an identifiable threshold.[61]

Tulp's behavior is very similar. Initially, he was less aware of the importance attached to anti-Jewish measures by the German authorities; but he learned quickly. As in the case of the three German bureaucrats, signals from above played an important role. The difference between their behavior and Tulp's was that the Dutchman did experience qualitative changes in the operations of the Germans, namely in September 1941 and in the summer of 1942. The radical turn taken by the German persecution of the Jews did not cause him any apparent pangs of conscience, and the confidence demonstrated in his superiors remained unshaken. However, he was forced to modify the picture of Germany's intentions that he presented to his subordinates. And he must have found this difficult. It tarnished his cultivated image as someone who supposedly had been knowledgeable about Germany's plans.

In order to gain insight into the behavior of the ordinary policemen, it is necessary to realize their position in the organization. They were even less able than their superiors to foresee where they were likely to end up. Moreover, they were both accustomed and bound by their membership in the force to follow rules and procedures that did not envisage the possibility of refusal. Nevertheless, they must have been aware of the consequences of their actions all the time. On two occasions they were driven to cross a threshold, with the implementation of the anti-Jewish measures in September 1941 and the raids on Jews in September 1942. In the first case, the initial resistance of the rank and file was apparently quite strong. They had not had a long enough experience of the charisma and unusual management style of their superior officer to obey his orders to execute a task that they found distasteful. It was not until Tulp had placed his men under special supervision and threatened them with sanctions that they gave in. In September 1942, the situation was different; this time the pressure of colleagues was directed against potential conscientious objectors and in support of an unconditional carrying out of orders. The resistance offered by the only objector in September 1942 rested largely on the support that he received, not from his colleagues, but from his wife. This time, Tulp's personal charisma and skill played an important part. The importance can be gauged from the events of October 3, when he was suddenly taken ill: the police operations that night were so severely disrupted by his absence that the raid had to be terminated prematurely.

NOTES

1. The information on which this article is based was collected as part of the research for my doctoral thesis on the operations of the Amsterdam police during the German Occupa-

tion. See G. Meershoek, "De Amsterdamse hoofdcommissaris en de deportatie van de joden," in N. D. J. Barnouw et al., *Oorlogsdocumentatie '40–'45*, Zutphen, 1992, pp. 9–43; and idem, "The Amsterdam Municipality, Its Police Force and the Persecution of the Jews," paper presented at the Amsterdam Conference on Deportation Management and Resistance in Western Europe, November 1992, pp. 44–88.

2. Letter Van der Geus to Feitsma, September 9, 1942, Archives of the Amsterdam chief state prosecutor (PPG), P-907-42.

3. On Dutch consociationalism, see H. Daalder, "Consociationalism, Centre and Periphery in the Netherlands," in *Mobilization, Center-periphery Structures and Nation-building*, ed. P. Torsvik (Oslo, 1981), pp. 181–240. On the modern Dutch polity, see H. Daalder, *Politisering en lijdelijkheid in de Nederlandse politiek* (Assen, 1974); and J. C. H. Blom, *Crisis, bezetting en herstel* (The Hague, 1989). On the local government of Amsterdam, see G. W. Borrie, F. M. Wibaut, *mens en magistraat* (Assen, 1968).

4. Meershoek, "De Amsterdamse hoofdcommissaris," pp. 14ff.

5. G. Hirschfeld, *Nazi Rule and Dutch Collaboration: The Netherlands under German Occupation, 1940–1945* (Oxford, 1988), pp. 132ff.

6. Hirschfeld, *Nazi Rule*, pp. 142ff.

7. Archives of the City of Amsterdam (GAA) 5181-1669-100-171/271. *Gemeenteblad* 1940, II, p. 697, GAA.

8. Archives of the Amsterdam Police Force 5225-OBHC-D6aII-2, GAA.

9. GAA 5181-1941-100-30/64.

10. B. Sijes, *De Februari-staking* (The Hague, 1954). My interpretation of the events differs on two points from that of Sijes: 1) the importance of the plan to set up a ghetto as the cause of the protest; and 2) the character of the movement. It was more of a riot—like the one that took place in Amsterdam in 1934—than a strike.

11. J. Houwink ten Cate, "Heydrich's Security Police and the Amsterdam Jewish Council," *Dutch Jewish History* 3 (1993): 381–93. Initially it was called *Beratungsstelle für judische Auswanderung* (GAA 5181-1670-100-1).

12. Meershoek, "De Amsterdamse hoofdcommissaris," pp. 16ff.

13. Chef van den Generalen Staf (KNIL), *Voorschrift voor de uitoefening van de politieke politioneele taak van het leger* (n.p., n.d.); C. Fasseur, "Hoeksteen en struikelblok. Rasonderscheid en overheidsbeleid in Nederlands-Indie," *Tijdschrift voor geschiedenis* 105 (1992): 2.

14. It is remarkable that a relatively large number of colonial administrators began a new career during the German occupation of the Netherlands. The chief constables appointed by the Reichskommissariat in the cities of Utrecht and The Hague were also former officers in the Royal Dutch East Indian Army. In H. Arendt's *The Origins of Totalitarianism* (New York, 1966 [1st ed. 1951]), p. 207, the author points out interesting correspondences between the colonial form of administration and National Socialist bureaucracies.

15. Interview A (Tulp's warrant-officer), December 2, 1990.

16. Interview B (member of the battalion in 1941, later detective in the police force), March 20, 1990.

17. J. Michman, "Planning for the Final Solution against the Background of Developments in Holland in 1941," *Yad Vashem Studies* 17 (1986): 162.

18. GAA 5225-bur.JDMplein-uitg.corr.-25/4/41-684.

19. L. de Jong, *Het koninkrijk der Nederlanden in de Tweede Wereldoorlog* (The Hague, 1968–1991, vol. 5, p. 566.

20. GAA 5225-tel.-11/6/41; Doc-II, Zuivering Pol.A'dam, statement. E.C.J.Staal, RvO.

21. VO 114/41 d.d.27/6/41, RvO; GAA 5225-tel.-28/6/41-15.44.

22. VO 138/41 d.d. 15/9/41, RvO.

23. GAA 5225-tel.-19/9/41-17.27.

24. De Jong, *Het koninkrijk*, vol. 5, pp. 1026–31.

25. GAA 5225-tel-10/11/41-15.25, 12/11/41-16.40, 15/11/41-14.10. Letter Tulp to Lages, November 3, 1941, in J. H. Heyink, "Kort chronologisch verslag," bijl.13A, in Doc II-363-mp.a, RvO.

26. A. Hiemstra-Timmenga, "Notitie voor het geschiedwerk nr. 97," RvO. Some of the offenders were released in Amersfoort. Men were sent to Mauthausen, women to Ravensbrück. In 1942 some 500 Dutch Jews perished in Mauthausen; in 1941 and 1942 some 100 Dutch Jews died in Ravensbrück.

27. Memorandum, January 24, 1942, in DGvP, AO, 0/90/41, Archives of the Ministry of Justice (MvJ).

28. R. Hilberg, *The Destruction of the European Jews* (New York, 1985 [1st ed. 1961]), p. 637; B. Kasten, '*Gute Franzosen*' (Sigmaringen 1993), pp. 95–104, 166–75.

29. GAA 5225-KHC-1942-38/74.

30. Meershoek, "Amsterdam municipality," p. 72.

31. Doc II-63-mp.a, RvO.

32. Diary 758 d.d. 4/6/42, RvO; cf. GAA 5225-BHC-D6aII-13.

33. S. Tulp, "De politie en de maatregelen inzake joden," *Tijdschrift voor de Amsterdamse Politie*, June 1942. Only available at the library of the Amsterdam Police Force.

34. Letter Tulp to Rauter, June 19, 1942, GAA 5225-KHC-1942-183.

35. This impression was affirmed by his warrant-officer. Interview A., December 2, 1990.

36. While the German bureaucrats unanimously declared that the Jews were being sent to work in Germany, Tulp knew that they were being sent on freight trains to Poland; diary 758, July 7, 1942, RvO.

37. GAA 5225-bur.JDMplein-uitg.corr.-12/7/42-1004.

38. GAA 5225-BHC-V1-15/7/42-15/9/42.

39. Nothing is known about the speeches of Tulp at these meetings.

40. Letter Tulp to Rauter, September 26, 1942, in GAA 5225-KHC-1942-264.

41. One could join the higher ranks of the force after secondary school or after university. One started as an Inspector Second Class. After ten to fifteen years, one could become an Inspector First Class. It took another ten to fifteen years to become Chief Inspector (*hoofdinspecteur*). A lucky few became Superintendent (*commissaris*) after the age of fifty-five. There was only one Chief Constable (*hoofdcommissaris*).

42. Various postwar statements in GAA 5225-BHC-2e Coll.-M5-2, and GAA 5225-tel.-2/9/42-nr.17.

43. Various statements in GAA 5225-BHC-2e Coll.-M5-2. Van der Oever went into hiding with his family. He did not experience any further problems. After the war he rejoined the Amsterdam Police Force. He was not fully accepted by his colleagues and soon afterwards he assumed an administrative position in a magistrate's court.

44. It is worth noting that the patrolman quoted in the introduction addressed his letter to an authority who by 1942 had lost his influence on the police force.

45. Statement J.C., GAA 5225-BHC-2e Coll.-M5-2.

46. Interview B., June 13, 1990.

47. Statement J.C., GAA 5225-BHC-2e Coll.-M5-2.

48. Letter Lages to Tulp, September 7, 1942 in GAA 5225-KHC-1942-252.

49. Report W.F.J., February 22, 1946, in Coll.F.S., ds.28, RvO.

50. G.P.Smis/S.Olij, *Peccavi* (unpublished manuscript), p. 112ff., private collection and Doc I–294A, RvO.

51. Translation of "Sie werden es verstehen, Gruppenführer, dass das jede Woche regelmässig Einfangen von durchschnittlich 450 Juden pro Abend das niederländische Publikum vor Mitleid und Empörung bersten macht. Trotzdem ist der Respekt vor den Männern des Bataillons so gross dass z.B. in der Nähe des Krugerplein, wo abendaus abendein zahlreiche Leute das Einfangen von Juden beobachten, bloss die Anwesenheit von zwei Polizeiagenten des Bataillons genugt um dem aüssern von auch nur einem Misklang vorzubeugen, während es in Amsterdam üblich war dass bei den anderen Polizeiagenten in einem solchen Falle die Platz den ganzen Abend in Berührung gewesen wäre und diese Polizisten alle Hände voll zu tun gehabt hätten" (letter Tulp to Rauter, September 26, 1942, in GAA 5225-KHC-1942-264).

52. J. H. Heyink, "Kort chronologisch verslag," bijl.13n, in Doc II-363-mp.a, RvO.

53. Doc I-311A, RvO.

54. Doc I-896A, RvO.

55. Ibid.

56. Hilberg, *Destruction of the European Jews*, p. 993.

57. For a survey, see H. von der Dunk, "Jews and the Rescue of Jews in the Netherlands in Historical Writing," in Y. Gutman and G. Greif, *The Historiography of the Holocaust Period* (Jerusalem, 1988).

58. G. Hirschfeld, "Niederlande," in W. Benz, *Dimension des Völkermords* (Munich, 1991), pp. 137–65.

59. A balanced survey of the factors that contributed to the large number of victims in the Netherlands is contained in J. C. H. Blom, "The Persecution of the Jews in the Netherlands: A Comparative West European Perspective," *European History Quarterly* 19 (1989): 333–51.

60. The wolf trap was a Germanic symbol to which protective powers were ascribed. The insignia was popular among SS-minded Dutch National Socialists.

61. Christopher R. Browning, "Bureaucracy and Mass Murder: The German Administrators' Comprehension of the Final Solution," in *Comprehending the Holocaust: Historical and Literary Research*, ed. A. Cohen, J. Gelber, C. Wardi (Frankfurt/M., 1988).

21.

DANIEL JONAH GOLDHAGEN

Ordinary Men or Ordinary Germans?

Neither Christopher Browning nor I have enough space in this forum to respond fully to the positions of the other. We cannot here go into a lengthy, detailed examination of the evidence, which in the end would be necessary for us to have a satisfactory exchange of views.[1] So I confine myself to a few more general thoughts. Before beginning, let me say that Browning's views are challenging and helpful. This will, I hope, be the beginning of an ongoing discussion that will help to clarify the issues— not just for Christopher Browning and me, but perhaps also for others, who may not have devoted as much attention to these themes as we have.

Just as Browning has chosen for his response a few of the many criticisms of his account that I have offered, for lack of space I too cannot address every point that he raises. For example, I leave untouched the large and complex subject of how to read the data about German antisemitism, except to say that even the work of the authors that Browning discusses can be read differently. Indeed, David Bankier's book[2] can more plausibly be read to argue the opposite of what Browning asserts. So I confine myself here to clarifying my criticisms—and therefore the differences that separate us—and to responding to Browning's responses.

Let me start by saying that the differences between us are more various than Christopher Browning's response suggests (even though the ones that he discusses are substantial). They can be highlighted by using one central theme as an illustration: the degree of brutality that the members of the battalion inflicted upon the victims, a subject which Browning in his contribution to this volume could touch upon only in passing.

First, there are differences in the *empirical accounts that we would construct*. Although I think that his reconstruction of the battalion's life history is generally admirable—and my appreciation is based on a complete reading of the internally contradictory and, in the end, partial, source material—I do take issue somewhat with his account of what took place. In my view the emphasis is at times misplaced. (Naturally, from the existing material, we all choose what to present and, from that, what to emphasize. But, it need hardly be said that this does not mean that all readings are equally good. Ultimately, each must be explained and justified.) I think that, in his book, Browning generally understates two matters: the degree of brutality of these men—even though I am sure many, upon reading the book, find more than enough—and their general voluntarism in killing.

Second, we have differences on the *evaluation of sources*, which is an exceedingly complex subject that I can but touch on here. There are three points:

First, it is true that Police Battalion 101 contains testimony that is more forth-coming than most of what is contained in many of the records of the Federal Republic's legal investigations. My criticism, by no means ignores this. Contrary to what Browning suggests, I do not lump this testimony with that from the members of other institutions of killing. It should be said, however, that there is honest and revealing testimony in many other cases as well. I do not think that Browning was implying that there was not, yet we should not create such a strong distinction between the testimony of the men of Police Battalion 101 and that of others: some members of each institution are forthcoming and truthful, many are not. We have to think about how we should deal with the individual testimonies of all those who give it, whatever their roles in the events, whatever institutions each was a member of when he or she contributed to mass slaughter.

Second, it needs to be emphasized that lying to minimize physical and cognitive involvement in the mass murder is rampant in perpetrator testimony. There are virtually endless examples, even from the testimony of members of Police Battalion 101. When asked during an interrogation why he had not mentioned a particular killing operation of the battalion, one of its men explained that he kept quiet about it because he thought that others would not mention it.[3]

If we were to accept the perpetrators' self-exculpatory versions of events, then we would frequently have to believe the following: that in a killing operation in which some company in its entirety is known to have participated, only a few of the men killed (with rifles) thousands of Jews, and only a few more were there giving logistical support. We would have to conclude this because only a few admit to having killed. And because not enough killers were engaged in the particular killing operation to have taken so many lives, we would also have to conclude, contrary to what we know, that few Jews died.

It needs to be acknowledged, as Browning does, that such problems exist in the record. Yet it must also be recognized that these prevarications are systematically and explicably motivated. We, therefore, need to face squarely the problems posed by the misleading testimonies, and to discuss how best to avoid being taken in by them.

The Germans, in focusing on the subject of their own brutality, consistently understate its magnitude. This is obvious. Add up all the testimony of survivors on the one hand and, on the other, what the perpetrators say about brutality—either for the Holocaust as a whole, or for any ghetto or camp—and in the sheer quantity and the quality of the brutality, two very different accounts emerge. Who is to be believed? Yes, the survivors often cannot tell much about the individual perpetrators, as in the case of an itinerant unit such as Police Battalion 101. Yet, they still can convey the atmosphere and the general tenor of the perpetrators' deeds, which can be strikingly different from that created by the perpetrators' self-serving portrayal.

As to Police Battalion 101 itself, take Józefów. The killers themselves concede that, after their roundup of Jews in Józefów, Jewish corpses littered the streets and homes of the ghetto. Yet of the more than 200 battalion men who gave testimony (not all of them were involved in the ghetto roundup), only two confess that they killed during the operation. So we have a *demonstrably gross* underreporting of the individuals' own killing and brutality in Police Battalion 101.

Of course, we should not lightly assume and assert that so much more occurred than the perpetrators report; but we must be aware that the perpetrators systematically conceal and enormously underreport their brutality, creating a bias in the records available to us. It is therefore crucial to adopt a skeptical stance toward the perpetrators' accounts—especially their accounts of their motivations—and also to use Jewish sources in reconstructing the events.

Third, another general area of difference is over *matters of interpretation*: What is the significance of the brutality? Christopher Browning thinks that it stems from the pressure to get a difficult job done quickly, to undermanning, and from the consequent *need* to be brutal in order to get results. He writes: "The greater the pressure on the German ghetto clearers in terms of manpower, the greater their ferocity and brutality to get the job done."[4] Brutality, in this view, is a utilitarian response of sorts to objective difficulties. It is functional and pragmatic. No doubt this did occur. But pragmatism cannot be seen as having been the major cause of brutality and cruelty. Once again, Józefów provides a telling example: here the ratio of Germans to Jews was substantially higher than in Międzyrzec, the city that Browning presents almost as a paradigmatic case of pragmatic brutality. So in Józefów there was less pressure on the perpetrators. Yet the brutality in Józefów was itself enormous. As I pointed out in my review of *Ordinary Men,* even in Międzyrzec, the brutality was clearly not merely or principally pragmatic:

> According to survivors—accounts that are entirely absent from this book—the cruelty that day was anything but instrumental. It was wanton, sadistic. At the marketplace the Jews, who had been forced to squat for hours, were "mocked" (*khoyzek gemacht*) and "kicked." And some of the Germans organized "a game" (*shpil*) of "tossing apples and whoever was struck by the apple was then killed." This sport was continued at the railway station, with empty liquor bottles. "Bottles were tossed over Jewish heads and whoever was struck by a bottle was dragged out of the crowd and beaten murderously amid roaring laughter. Then some of those who were thus mangled (*tseharget*) were shot." Afterward the dead were loaded on the train bound for Treblinka, together with the living. Small wonder that in the recollections of the victims—though not in the recollections of the perpetrators, or in this book—these ordinary Germans appeared not as mere murderers . . . but as "two-legged beasts" filled with "bloodthirstiness."[5]

This description highlights the general differences that exist between us in the empirical accounts that we give, in our evaluation and use of sources, and in the way in which we interpret and explain the material.

Let me turn now to the heart of the matter: to say that there were other people—non-Germans—who did do what these Germans did, should not cause us to leap to the conclusion that these Germans were therefore "ordinary men." It may lead us to conclude this, but only after careful investigation.

Sociologically, there is no doubt that almost all of the men of Police Battalion 101 were "ordinary Germans," men of German nationality who were not distinguished by background, personality, or previous political affiliation or behavior as having been men unusually likely or fit to be genocidal executioners. But for them to have been ordinary *men,* then the "German" part of this must have been irrelevant. That would mean that any men (perhaps harboring some "negative racial stereotypes," as Browning terms it in his essay), any men placed in these conditions, in this institution, would have killed Jews when they knew that they did not have to. It is worth emphasizing that the commander of Police Battalion 101 announced to his men before their first killing operation that they did not have to kill. Some of the men accepted his offer, and the others saw that they were not punished.

If my reading of Browning's book is correct, his explanation for the men's essentially having agreed to be mass executioners is mainly a situational one. The men's conception of the deed, which included the identity of the victims, did not contribute to their voluntarism—namely their willingness to kill—in any significant way. Indeed, the book ends with an explicit statement to this effect in the form of a question: "If the men of Reserve Police Battalion 101 could become killers under such circumstances, what group of men cannot?" Browning does not say: what group of antisemites, or what group of men with "negative racial stereotypes," but rather "what group of men." Circumstances are the cause.

Browning gives a situational explanation. In his essay, it appears to me that he is backtracking a bit, discussing the importance of "negative racial stereotypes." Yet in the book, he gives a situational explanation. These men were reluctant killers who, so to speak, did the best that they could in trying circumstances. They were aware of the futility of refusal—the Jews would have been killed by others anyway— and they felt pressure to live up to their obligations to one another. They did it for their buddies.

To the extent that Browning does believe that "negative racial stereotypes" did play a causal role in producing the deaths of so many men, women, and children, it would be interesting to hear from him an elaboration and specification of what that role was *precisely*. I do not think that he elaborates the content of these negative stereotypes. I would also like to learn how "negative" they indeed were. Some "negatives," it need hardly be said, are more negative than others. Did they believe that Jews were stingy and clannish (to take favorite negative stereotypes of the American social landscape), or that they were a major source of Germany's woes and a major threat to the future well-being of Germany? There are enormous differences among the triad of types of antisemitisms—latent, traditional, or deep-seated—which Browning lists as having been the common property of European societies. The differences matter and need to be explained.

Moreover, I would like to learn whether these beliefs—whatever they were— were artifacts of the pressure of war or (as the book suggests) of "race war," or had they been inculcated in these men as *ordinary members of German society*? If the latter, then we might be back to the proposition that they were ordinary Germans and not ordinary men. After all, types of prejudice (that is, specific prejudices against certain groups), the distribution of such prejudices among a given population, and their salience for individuals and a country as a whole, vary greatly from society to society.

I am not claiming that there is something organic about the prejudice of Germany or Germans, and I am not maintaining that these were some kind of "specifically German behavioral modes"—which, I hasten to add, was not my formulation, but that of someone else, and I am not quite sure what it would mean. It just seems to me that we cannot ignore the public antisemitic (and, more broadly, as Henry Friedlander reminds us, racist) culture of Germany—which was anything but ordinary. (I should also make clear that, Browning's melding of our views notwithstanding, I by no means agree with much of Lucy Dawidowicz's formulation. I have never said, and do not hold the view, that the German people were "'deranged' by a delusional mass psychosis.")

Now, it was the case that a widespread and politically potent antisemitism characterized not just Germany but also other peoples in other areas of Europe, particularly in Eastern Europe. The Germans were able to find willing, even enthusiastic helpers in many corners of Europe, again, particularly in parts of Eastern Europe. Browning argues that the Ukrainians whom he discusses should be thought of as analogous to the men of Police Battalion 101. Perhaps. I have not studied them intensively, so I cannot speak definitively about them. Yet from the evidence that he has presented in his paper, I am not convinced that these Ukrainians demonstrate that it is indeed "ordinary men" who did and would be willing to do what these Germans did. In fact, it appears that very little is known about them. As Browning himself acknowledges, we also know next to nothing about the Luxembourgers. What we can say is that Ukraine was anything but a region untouched by antisemitism.

We do know, however, that not all ordinary men were willing to do what the men of Police Battalion 101 did, and did with distinction. Had a battalion of ordinary Danes or ordinary Italians somehow found themselves in the Lublin region and received the same orders from their government *with the same opportunity to have exempted themselves*, would they have slaughtered, deported, and hunted down, with the same efficacy and brutality, Jewish men, women, and children, as these ordinary Germans did? This notion not only strains credulity beyond the breaking point but is also falsified by the actual historical record. The Danes saved their Jews, and before that resisted the imposition of antisemitic measures by the Germans. And Italians, even the Italian military (in Croatia), by and large disobeyed Mussolini's orders for the deportation of Jews to what they knew would be death at the Germans' hands.[6]

Thus, what is more *analytically significant* than finding some other group of ordinary people (if indeed they were ordinary in Browning's sense)—be they Ukrainians, Luxembourgers, or French—who helped the Germans deport and kill Jews, is to find those who did not or even would not have. The refusal or the unwillingness of others to do so demonstrates that the Germans were not ordinary *men*, but that there was something particular about them, which is what must be investigated and specified. That some non-Germans did or might have done the same thing suggests only that we must uncover what they had in common with the men of Police Battalion 101, or recognize that there might be more than one path to becoming party to mass slaughter. After all, there were enormous differences between Germans on the one hand, and on the other Ukrainians (hardly a favored people under Nazism), who worked in German institutions; there were pressures operating on the Ukrainians that did not exist for the Germans, so this may not be such a good comparison after all. Police Battalion 101 is so illuminating, in part, because we know that similar pressures did not exist on its members.

The crucial comparative strategy, therefore, is to establish, first, whether there was something not purely structural about the perpetration of the deed. (That is, did the *identities* of the perpetrators or of the victims matter in any way?) If it was not purely structural, then we need to investigate and specify what it was that brought the perpetrators, whatever their identities were, to contribute to the Holocaust.

We should also not forget that the Jews were—certainly for the Nazi leadership, and for all those ordinary Germans who shared their outlook—a figmental enemy, a people declared by Nazi fiat to be an enemy, a people who themselves harbored no ill for Germany, had no capacity to harm Germany, had no army or weapons to threaten Germany or even substantially to defend themselves. They were a prostrate people who, because of circumstances, could by and large not even battle for their lives, since they were unable to influence their fate by little more than by begging in vain for their lives.

I find it hard to believe that it was ordinary "men" who slew these fearsome, figmental warriors, including the twelve-year-old-child, whose brains were spattered by a point blank shot onto the sidearm of one of the Germans in Police Battalion 101. The laughter and joking of the man who shot the boy—which led me, in reviewing Browning's book, to use the words "jocularity" and "boyish joy" to describe the attitude of only this *one* killer—was, however, not an isolated incident. The bespattered German who reports the laughter added, "I have experienced more obscenities (*Schweinereien*) of this kind. . . ." (This episode is, in my view, among the most revealing contained in the testimony of the men of Police Battalion 101. Yet Browning did not include it in his book. This is a case of important presentational differences between us.)

My unwillingness to believe, my conclusion that it was not "ordinary men" who slaughtered this figmental enemy is not born of some naive notion of human goodness, or of some belief in the peculiarity of Germans of the time. After all, many genocides and mass slaughters have occurred in human history and in the twentieth century. I simply do not believe that the evidence supports a universalistic reading of the perpetration of the Holocaust according to which "ordinary" man, that trans-historical, acultural being, would be willing to kill as these men did, simply for the asking.

Let me conclude by pointing out the most general subject that our disagreements raise. Christopher Browning and I have read the same finite body of material, yet we have very different understandings of it. Much of the future scholarship about the Holocaust will turn not on differential access to sources but on the ways in which we read them. If this is so, then we would all benefit from more self-conscious and explicit methodological discussions. Indeed, it seems to me that a greater focus on methodology is imperative.

NOTES

1. See Daniel Jonah Goldhagen, *Hitler's Willing Executioners: Ordinary Germans and the Holocaust* (New York: Alfred A. Knopf, 1996), chaps. 6–9, 15, for my different interpretation of Police Battalion 101 and of police battalions in general.

2. David Bankier, *The Germans and the Final Solution: Public Opinion under Nazism* (Oxford: Blackwell, 1992).

3. W.Sc., *Investigation of G. et al.*, StA Hamburg 141 Js 128/65, p. 333.

4. Christopher R. Browning, *Ordinary Men: Reserve Police Battalion 101 and the Final Solution in Poland* (New York: HarperCollins, 1992), p. 95.

5. Daniel Jonah Goldhagen, "The Evil of Banality," *New Republic*, July 13 and 20, 1992, p. 52.

6. Susan S. Zuccotti, *The Italians and the Holocaust: Persecution, Rescue, and Survival* (New York: Basic Books, 1987), writes: "Clearly, the immediate factors favorable to Jewish rescue during the Holocaust must be placed in the context of the customs and traditions of individual countries. The most pertinent tradition, of course, is the existence or absence of anti-Semitism. For many reason, modern Italy lacked an anti-Semitic tradition (p. 278)." See also Daniel Carpi, "The Rescue of Jews in the Italian Zone of Occupied Croatia," in *Rescue Attempts during the Holocaust: Proceedings of the Second Yad Vashem Internationl Conference*, ed Yisrael Gutman and Efraim Zuroff (Jerusalem: Ahva Cooperative Press, 1977), pp. 465–506.

Part 6

Multiple Voices

IDEOLOGY, EXCLUSION, AND COERCION

One of the most divisive and persistent academic debates over the past fifteen years has centered around the question of who the victims of the Holocaust were. Is the word "Holocaust" to be confined solely to what the Nazis termed the "Final Solution of the Jewish problem," the systematic, state-sponsored execution of the Jews, or does the Holocaust encompass a mosaic of Nazi victims—Soviet prisoners of war; Jehovah's Witnesses; mentally retarded, physically handicapped, or emotionally disturbed Germans; Roma and Sinti; German male homosexuals; trade unionists; political dissidents; and outspoken clergymen. The following essays do not answer this question definitively, but they do focus attention on the diversity of Nazi victims and the divergent policies aimed at these groups.

In "Neglected Holocaust Victims: The Mischlinge, the Jüdischversippte, and the Gypsies," John A. S. Grenville attempts to reverse the neglect. He believes that the continuing debate over whether to define the Holocaust as a uniquely Jewish tragedy or to include the Gypsies (Sinti and Roma) as well has hampered research into Holocaust history by focusing on certain groups of victims to the exclusion of others.

Grenville is concerned with the differences between Nazi racial theory and reality. Indeed, the question of who was an Aryan and who was not plagued the racial theoreticians of the Nazi state from the very inception of the racial laws. Problems of establishing racial purity of the "full Jew, the full Gypsy," or of the "Aryan" were multiplied when it came to tracing fractional Aryans, or Gypsy or Jewish Mischlinge (products of mixed marriages and their offspring).

Yet the Nazis sought to develop a systematic method of dealing with the Mischlinge and with the Jüdischversippte, Germans married to Jews or to Mischlinge before 1935. Numerous ordinances circumscribed the lives of the Mischlinge and by the end of the war condemned Mischlinge (Grade I) and Jüdischversippte, heretofore spared direct official persecution, to forced labor and deportation. Grenville believes that if Germany had won the war, both groups would have faced sterilization.

Hugh Gregory Gallagher's "'Slapping Up Spastics'" describes the T4 operations— the officially sanctioned program to kill mentally retarded, emotionally disturbed, and physically handicapped Germans during the war. The program was directly authorized by Hitler under the supervision of Dr. Karl Brandt. As the killing process developed, it involved leading figures of the German medical establishment, where details of the operation were well known. Church protests and popular antagonism forced Hitler to formally cancel the program in 1941, but it continued thereafter by the most secretive, clandestine means. Perhaps as many as 200,000 Germans were killed in the operation.

Euphemisms were used to describe the program. They were not difficult to unravel. "Negative population policies" meant mass killing. "Refractory therapy cases" was a less charged way of describing "targeting disabled people for killing." "Specialized children's wards" were children's killing centers, and "final medical assistance" was a polite way of describing murder.

"Humane" considerations were strong when Philip Bouhler, chief of Hitler's chancellery, insisted that the way to death be not only painless but also imperceptible to the patient.

The program's structure, Gallagher argues, made it easier to participate. At no point in the process did the patient receive a death warrant. Similarly, physicians were offering opinions, they were not pronouncing judgments or interacting with the patients. Work was divided so that at no time could it be said that a particular physician was responsible for a patient's death.

Those transporting patients were merely transporting them; they did not see themselves as part of a killing process. Even those operating the gas chambers could claim innocence, for they had no part in the selection process; they were merely following orders, approved procedures.

Having described the T4 process, Gallagher traces the intellectual origins of the idea, the means by which the ideology permitting euthanasia was communicated to physicians, and its echoes in contemporary medical practice. He also traces the consequences of speaking bluntly about the past in German medical practice today.

He cautions that the careful delineation of the economic benefits to the well-being of the Volk—not the rights of the individual—could enable well-meaning, socially conscious debates to slip almost imperceptibly into the devaluation of human life.

Günter Grau's "Final Solution of the Homosexual Question? The Antihomosexual Policies of the Nazis and the Social Consequences for Homosexual Men" is brief yet pithy. German male homosexuals, Grau argues, were subject to persecution and incarceration. Approximately fifty thousand were arrested at one point or another, about one in ten were sent to concentration camps—Grau's figures are low—and many of these men perished in the camps from disease, malnutrition, and nonsystematic murder. The Nazi persecution of lesbians is less well documented and less documentable; simply put, lesbians were not important to the Nazis. Neither were homosexuals in the territories occupied by the Nazis, excepting Austria (which was incorporated into Germany).

Grau argues persuasively that the Nazi attack on homosexuals was worlds apart from the planned total annihilation of the Jews. Grau distinguishes between the publicized antihomosexual ideology of the Nazis and the reality of day-to-day practice. Homophobia was not specific to National Socialism. He details three stages in the Nazi persecution: prior to 1935, when a campaign of terror was instituted and homosexual bars and clubs were closed and changes were introduced into the criminal code; between 1935 and the war, when widespread arrests were made; and wartime persecution that resulted in deportations, capital punishment, and castration. Yet the number of homosexuals actually punished decreases as the severity of the punishment increases. He also dispels the claims of those who exaggerate the role of the Reich Office for Combating Homosexuality and Abortion. With only eighteen people on its staff, there is no evidence that it planned a final solution. Like Rüdiger Lautmann, whose essay follows, Grau stresses the Nazi goal of reeducation, and he notes the continued victimization of homosexuals after the war.

Rüdiger Lautmann's "The Pink Triangle: Homosexuals as 'Enemies of the State,'" details the distinction in goals between the Nazi annihilation of the Jews and Nazi persecution of homosexual men. Again, as with Grau, Lautmann believes that lesbians were of little interest to the Nazis. Lautmann weighs the evidence and estimates the number of homosexuals incarcerated at ten thousand, the middle ground between low estimates of five thousand and higher estimates of fifteen thousand. He describes the particular fate of homosexual men whose middle-class origins left them particularly vulnerable to physical mistreatment and less equipped for manual labor.

Homosexuals were neither fully integrated into the concentration camp community nor did they develop group solidarity. Thus, even though annihilation was not the goal and no "final solution of the homosexual problem" was contemplated, homosexuals died more rapidly and more frequently than political prisoners or Jehovah's Witnesses. Their stigmatization—legal and social—did not end with liberation; laws outlawing homosexual activity were in effect in Germany well after the war. Homosexuals were thus reluctant to bear witness to their experience in the camps, and historians have had greater difficulty discovering and understanding their experience.

Robert Kesting (1946–1997) explores the few cases of blacks incarcerated and persecuted by the Nazis in "The Black Experience during the Holocaust." He contends that a straight line of antiblack thought and action runs through the history of Germany in the late nineteenth and early twentieth centuries. He traces it to German excesses, including what he sees as genocide, in colonial Southwest Africa, following a path to the mention of blacks in the Nuremberg Laws as a minority in Germany with "alien blood."

African-Germans were the victims of sterilization under the Nazis, and blacks from various nations were the objects of medical experimentation by Nazi doctors; they were also prisoners in Nazi concentration camps. Kesting argues that it was only the fact that blacks in Europe were too few to constitute a perceived racial threat equal to that seen to be posed by Jews and Gypsies that kept Nazi racial theorists from paying more attention to them. But the Nazis had already developed plans for a future conquest of Africa that included the implementation of the Nuremberg Laws and perhaps far worse.

22.

JOHN A. S. GRENVILLE

Neglected Holocaust Victims

THE MISCHLINGE, THE JÜDISCHVERSIPPTE, AND THE GYPSIES

The definition of the word "Holocaust" has itself become the subject of controversy.[1] There are the protagonists who assert that it must be confined to the mass murder of the Jews. The United States Holocaust Memorial Museum in Washington has included the Gypsies, also gassed in Auschwitz, who were persecuted and classified racially during the years preparatory to the Final Solution. If birth and unalterable genetic condition as defined by the National Socialists are the criteria for inclusion, why not also the "euthanasia" victims, handicapped Christian Germans? Then homosexuals might be included. It is not my intention here to enter this controversy but rather to demonstrate that it has distracted and hampered our research into Holocaust history whatever our point of view may be. It is distracting because it tends to focus on one group of victims to the exclusion of, and in a kind of competition to, others. All these groups were singled out as a danger to the Volk. Much can be learned from the stages and comparative timing of their subjugation to discrimination and persecution, and whether extermination or some other fate was in store for them.[2]

Nazi ideology was absolute, any influence harmful to the Volk had to be eliminated. What in pseudoscience appeared clear, however, became much more complicated in practice. At first glance the Jews were unique in not requiring any differentiation; they were all condemned regardless of age or gender, professional status or nationality. But in reality it was not as simple as that. Ideologically, not only the half-million German Jews posed the "Judenproblem," but no one knew how many hundreds of thousands more racial Jews there were, offspring of mixed marriages between Christians and Jews. According to the prevailing Nazi theory, a Jew's genetic influence would negatively affect those descended from him or her, even in part, regardless of the fact that generations had elapsed. While therefore what was meant by the Endziel was theoretically absolutely clear, in practice it could never be attained. The Nazi racial definition of Jew was defined, but conversion to Christianity could mask racial identity. How far back would it be necessary to investigate to ensure that an apparently Christian forebear would not turn out to be a concealed racial Jew? While the required investigation into Aryan status mandated in the legislation of 1933 and 1935 stipulated the tracing of ancestry back only as far as grandparents, much more stringent criteria were to be applied to the civil service and others in positions of authority. In carrying out the law of April 7, 1933, civil servants could be retired or dismissed even if all their grandparents were Christians, although such cases were relatively rare.[3] Instructions from the Ministry of the Interior on September 1, 1933, stated that if a grandparent was a baptized Christian and even if the great-grandparent was baptized, the civil servant was to be regarded as non-Aryan; not religion but race was the determinant. As is well known, Heinrich Himmler required proof of ancestry as far back as 1800. The same date was laid down for farmers who owned their land. Higher functionaries of the NSDAP were also supposed to provide proof of Aryan ancestry to 1800. To show their enthusiasm for racial purity other organizations, such as the Reichsschaft of students at institutions of higher learning, followed the lead. Theory and practice differed perforce. On October 17, 1937, Dr. Wilhelm Stuckart, State Secretary of the Ministry of the Interior circulated his response to the Minister of Education that it was unlikely that all students would be able to trace their ancestry to 1800. The difficulty would arise, according to experience, that only half the Volksgenossen were able to trace their ancestry to the required date. According to a memorandum of the Reichsstelle für Sippenforschung, when the functionaries of the NSDAP in Gau Berlin attempted to fulfil this requirement only a quarter could do so.[4]

Problems of establishing racial purity of the full Jew, the full Gypsy, or of the Aryan were multiplied manifold when it came to tracing fractional Aryans or Gypsy or Jewish Mischlinge. The theory was clear, its application relatively straightforward for the majority, but for the remainder, the worrisome minority, scientific racial purity could not be established with certainty because human behavior is capricious and defies the records of the churches and of a bureaucracy even as thorough as the Prussian. There were illegitimacies, and during the nineteenth century and earlier there was considerable migration. Early conversions could not always be traced.

Seeking to cleanse the race by preventing further miscegenation between the German Volk and those races deemed harmful and alien to it caused continuous concern and dispute within the hierarchy after 1933. There was the question of which peoples were "compatible," of artverwandtes Blut; settled Europeans were held by the experts in the mid-1930s to qualify. But this decision of principle soon shifted with the outbreak of war, when Poles and the peoples of the Soviet Union, Russians, and Ukrainians, became racial enemies unless in arbitrary instances judged by their appearance they were deemed capable of Germanization. It was not an exact science after all. Had the Poles opted for alliance with Germany in January 1939, their racial categorization would have turned out differently, as did that of the Slovaks.

Public stigmatization of race incompatibility also had to be opportunistically adjusted according to foreign policy needs. Thus, the Japanese were no longer described as non-Aryan.[5] In Hamburg a senior civil servant of the state government was found in 1933 to have had a Chinese grandmother, his grandfather having served before 1914 in Kiaochow. He was clearly non-Aryan, but after some discussion it appears that his file was simply allowed to gather dust.

Much more immediately serious for the Nazis were international reactions to the persecution of Jews and of Christians classified as Jews or Mischlinge. Economic boycotts posed a danger to the speed of German recovery and to the efforts to reduce unemployment. The acceptance Hitler wanted to win in pursuit of his foreign policy goals also required that leaders abroad judge the discriminatory measures as reasonable. Early in 1933 there was even concern that the League of Nations might define the Judenproblem as a minority question, thus falling within its sphere. After a number of earlier discussions, the Foreign Ministry convened, in November 1934, a meeting with the officials of the Ministry of the Interior then responsible for racial legislation to discuss its harmful effects on Germany's foreign relations. To mollify foreign opinion, Minister of the Interior Wilhelm Frick issued a clumsy public assurance that National Socialist race policy was not based on a value judgment of races but only on their difference. Naturally this convinced no one. In 1935 the Foreign Ministry stressed once more that with each month the repercussions from race policies had become more serious. Deputy Führer Hess thereupon issued the following guideline, no doubt after consultation with Hitler: "Decisions of a racial kind are to be avoided if they threaten relations with foreign nations. The principles and bases (rassenpolitische Grundsätze) in their practical application must be harmonized with foreign policy necessities." While the conclusions specifically excluded decisions concerning Jews and descendants of Jews and referred to Japanese, Chinese, Indians, and foreign nationals, the general sensitivity to foreign reactions is clear. Unfortunately, there was little to fear from the Western nations that mattered most; in the era of appeasement, until the outbreak of war, their governments gave high priority to normalizing, as far as possible, relations with Germany.[6]

The German preoccupation with Mischlinge was based on debate whether acquired characteristics could be inherited. This in turn was confused with the valid scientific findings of Gregor Mendel, a nineteenth-century Austrian monk. In the Nazi literature and discussion papers, the unlovely word "mendeln" came to be commonly used to show how Jewish characteristics would persist, to a weaker or stronger degree, through generations of mixed "racial" genes so that a nearly "pure Jew" might suddenly pop up after many generations of intermarriage with the Aryan or German because he or she could be "mendeled out."

It was taken for granted by Nazi "racial hygiene" experts that the mixing of the racial characteristics of German people with those of incompatible races—there was never any doubt about the harmful effects of admixing traits of Jews, blacks, and Gypsies—would lead to the racial weakening, even ultimate destruction of the German people. The more sophisticated among Nazi scientists and doctors recognized, however, that human heredity did not correspond to the simplicity of mixing the colors of sweet pea plants. The expert Dr. Arthur Gütt of the Ministry of the Interior pointed this out in a September 25, 1935, memorandum that influenced the debate about the drawing up of the Nuremberg Laws. He pointed out that descendants may not show some specific characteristics at all or may exhibit them to a lesser or greater degree than expected. Furthermore, he declared, if a white person and a Negro interbred, no descendants, however many generations later and despite subsequent white marriages, would ever be fully white; they would always show some Negro characteristics. Such a cross therefore did not correspond to the outcome of Mendel's colored sweet peas. The harm done by racial intermarriage could therefore never be completely undone.[7]

Thus a final solution of the race problem—and statistically by far the largest segment of this was the Judenproblem—always meant drawing the line somewhere as far as descendants of mixed marriages were concerned. It entailed absorbing the not quite pure Aryans with the Aryans, diluting them further and further, so to speak. All races of incompatible blood would be affected: the descendants of a few thousand mixed blacks dating from the French occupation of the Rhineland, Gypsies, and above all, Jews and Jewish Mischlinge. There could be no ideal solution but a time would come when the problem simply could be declared to have ceased to exist—the final solution.

How long would that take? By what means could it be achieved? What other considerations would have to be taken into account? It is in regard to the last question that a comparison between Jews, "Negro bastards," and Gypsies becomes so instructive. There were virtually no "pure Negroes" in Germany to be dealt with, so it is unlikely that the option of mass murder ever came within the realm of consideration. Their numbers were small; forced emigration was not an option. If one puts oneself into the mind-set of the Nazi decision-makers, one conclusion is obvious; their reasoning was logical given the false premises on which it was based, and for most of them it was devoid of ethical or humanitarian considerations. As regards the Jews, emigration or deportation were the only options in peacetime. The most undesirable Jews obviously were the youngest and those still of child-bearing age. Consequently, it was entirely logical to favor the Kindertransporte after 1938. The able-bodied would be most likely to be able to emigrate to Palestine and elsewhere. Eventually the Reich would be left with a remainder of the old and sick to deal with, predictably a short-term problem, together with smaller than natural proportions of the able-bodied and children. These would have to be removed in one way or another.

The real long-term problem was presented by the living Mischlinge and by mixed-marriage Jüdischversippte, who would produce more Mischlinge. There could be no final solution if Mischlinge as a distinct group were allowed to perpetuate themselves and increase. Their emigration was a less likely option than for Jews. Who would be prepared to help Germans, possibly even former members of the Nazi Party, for humanitarian reasons? The Nazis counted on world Jewry to mobilize their resources to assist their coreligionists, which they did. The so-called Jüdischversippte, that is Germans married to Jews or to Mischlinge before 1935, were Aryans who constituted a danger to the Volk and an obstacle to a final solution. All this was recognized years before a solution could be decided on and before Hitler judged the time right to enforce it.

In timing the discrimination against Jews, Jewish Mischlinge, Gypsies and Gypsy Mischlinge, "Negro bastards," and Germans married to Jews or Mischlinge, opportunistic considerations were taken into account. Jews and Mischlinge in business would not immediately be replaced at a time when the priority was to revive the economy and reduce unemployment. Where there was an oversupply in certain professions and no shortage of newcomers—doctors, lawyers and university teachers for example—their immediate removal was deemed advantageous, opening opportunities for "good Germans." Even so, before the death of Hindenburg in August 1934 the Nazis moved with some caution. Not only were the well-known exceptions made part of the law, but the dismissed non-Aryan civil servants, provided they had sufficient length of service, received pensions whose payment was confirmed by Hitler even as late as December 1938. This placed them in a situation in which they were better off than the majority of Germans. Nor were they stripped of their titles, a matter of some importance in Germany. The letters a.D. [ausser Dienst], literally "out of service," meaning "in pension," were added after their professional titles, as, for example, in Landgerichtsdirektor a.D. Not only Jews were forcibly retired but also many of those married to Jews and Mischlinge if they refused to divorce, as well as Mischlinge with one or more Jewish grandparents.[8]

The term "non-Aryan" in 1933 did not distinguish between Mischlinge and "full" Jews. Nor was there a separation between Christians and Jews. The non-Aryans, who were descendants of one or two Jewish grandparents, were predominantly Christian. After 1933 it became more and more clear that crude categorization simply as non-Aryans and Aryans would not meet Germany's needs as then perceived and that the non-Aryans would have to be subdivided further. The problem became acute with the reintroduction of conscription in May 1935. Considering the manpower potential in future wars, the Wehrmacht wanted to draw on all possible reserves. While numbers were availabe for persons who stated their religion as Jewish, there were no such censuses for Christians of wholly or partly Jewish descent. Even going back two generations, only for purposes of classification, the estimated number was regarded by the Wehrmacht as unacceptably large. Clearly the same question occupied Hitler, too; through his adjutant responsible for the Wehrmacht, the Führer inquired after the number of non-Aryans, asking that they be categorized as full Jews, half Jews, and quarter Jews. The response on April 3, 1935, stated that no precise figures could be given since the classification in the June 16, 1933, census was by religion, not by race. Accordingly, Mischlinge and converted "full Jews" were not counted as such. If the Saar region was included, the total number of Jews by religion was 503,900, less some 30,000 who had emigrated. Thus 475,000 were still in the Reich. Taking into account the researches and estimates of the Reichsstelle für Sippenforschung and the Rassenpolitisches Amt der N.S.D.A.P., based on very limited evidence, "racial Jews," including the converted, numbered approximately 775,000, and Mischlinge of the first and second degree, 750,000. These non-Aryans together amounted to about 1.5 million. Within the group that might bear arms, men between the ages of eighteen and forty-five, the number worked out at 308,000.[9] The Nuremberg Laws of November 1935 must be seen in light of these figures. The decision to dispense with the "full Jews" by placing them in a Reserve II category on the one hand and permitting Mischlinge of both grades to join active service—provided they were examined and found to be acceptable—exemplifies the opportunistic approach to the question of the German Mischlinge. What it does not do is to define their ultimate fate in the Endlösung.

The racial census taken on May 15, 1939, gives the following well-known total figures: Mischlinge I, 72,738, and Mischlinge II, 42,811. Mischlinge I constituted 0.09 percent of the total population, including Austria, the annexed Sudeten areas and the Saar, and Mischlinge II, little more than half of that tiny percentage; 330,892 "racial" Jews constituted 0.42 percent of the population. Thus, according to the census, there were almost three times as many racial Jews as Mischlinge in the Reich as a whole. Yet in Hamburg the census lists 10,131 racial Jews and 7,788 Mischlinge, revealing a much higher proportion of Mischlinge there, probably due in part to a higher rate of intermarriage in Hamburg, but possibly also because local records were more accurate, according fewer Mischlinge the ability to hide a Jewish grandparent. There must have been many instances in Germany in which the racial Jewishness of a grandparent was genuinely unknown due to a lack of records or to conversion. The Mischlinge together with the Jüdischversippte may have numbered as many as 500,000; 400,000 is probably a reasonable estimate.[10]

Estimates noted the number of German Gypsies at about 22,000 before 1938. Registration and classification as Gypsy Mischlinge was pursued with the same, if not greater, thoroughness and intensity as that applied to Jews and Jewish Mischlinge. Himmler's special interest in the Gypsies combined with criminal police registration of Gypsies long before 1933 permitted much more accurate genealogical research. For practical purposes Hitler drew the line at quarter-Jewish Mischlinge at Nuremberg in 1935. He accepted that cutoff boundary in order to prevent continuous unrest and to avoid affecting thousands more if racial identity were for general purposes to be traced further back. The smaller number of Gypsies permitted a more radical approach in better conformity with "scientific ideology"; even one great-great grandparent deemed to be a gypsy was sufficient to justify discriminating against all descendants who were classified as Gypsy Mischlinge. As Sybil Milton has pointed out, the failure of researchers of the Holocaust to compare and study all racial persecution in parallel has impoverished Holocaust research.

A Reichszigeunergesetz (Reich Gypsy Law) was prepared by Dr. Zindel of the Ministry of the Interior to accompany and supplement the Nuremberg Laws. In March 1936, he produced a memorandum to act as a guideline together with a draft for such a law. According to Zindel, the root of the Gypsy "evil" lay in their nomadic lifestyle, their "racial incompatibility," and their purported criminality. To force settlement on them would only make matters worse from a racial point of view, evidently by leading to more miscegenation. But to establish Gypsy reservations—in 1936 these would have to be inside the Reich—would only create breeding grounds of murder and crime. In any case no German community would welcome a Gypsy reservation as its neighbor. Their numbers were too large to imprison them all. The only workable principle on which a solution could therefore be based, he concluded, was deportation and sterilization; foreign and stateless Gypsies could be deported immediately, and this should be carried out without exception as far as possible. Close control of all Gypsies in the Reich, their registration, identification, and supervision, moreover, were the preconditions of the measures that would have to be taken; dangerous Gypsies were to be held in concentration or work camps. The priority now was to identify and register all Gypsies. The Reich Gypsy Law should lay this down in the first part and prescribe their treatment in the second.[11] At the Reich Health Office's Institute for Racial Protection, Criminal Psychology, and Criminal Biology, much research was done and genealogical trees of all Gypsies living in Germany for the past ten generations had been charted according to a visitor, Dr. Franz Orsos, President of Hungary's National Association of Physicians. This was no doubt an exaggeration as classification continued from 1938 onward. German scientists regarded the "halfbreeds" as particularly dangerous. Public health authorities were asked in 1938 to register all Gypsies and Gypsy Mischlinge with the police and the Deutsche Ärzteblatt in 1938, referred to the coming of an endgültige Lösung, a "final solution," of the Gypsy problem. It was made clear that this lay in the hands of Reichsführer-SS and Chief of German Police Heinrich Himmler.[12] Thus the phrase "Final Solution" did not by any means refer to Jews alone.

However, Gypsy law analogous to the Nuremberg laws was never enacted. Evidently no need was felt to reassure German public opinion by appearing to base this particular persecution on a pseudolegal system. Nor was it necessary to observe great secrecy when the deportations to the General Government (Poland) began in 1940.

The Reich Health Führer, Dr. Leonardo Conti, advocated the sterilization of all Gypsies and Gypsy Mischlinge as the only radical solution that would protect German blood. Whether they were deported after that or whether their capacity for work should then be exploited (ausgenützt) was a secondary consideration as long as they were rendered biologically harmless. A law was unnecessary—only a decree mandating special measures (Sondermassnahmen) would be required.[13] Noteworthy here is how these suggestions anticipated the discussion of what to do with the Jewish Mischlinge two years later at Wannsee. The German Jewish Mischlinge were evidently a far more sensitive problem. By the end of 1941, nearly all of the 30,000 German Gypsies and Gypsy Mischlinge in Grossdeutschland had been registered and placed in one of five categories ranging from full Gypsy to Gypsy with predominantly German blood, and also assigned to one of four clans (Stämme). Registration had been carried out by the criminal police.

Himmler's decree of December 16, 1942, ordering German Gypsies to be deported to Auschwitz, was carried out in 1943 and 1944 with few exceptions; so-called pure Sinti, Sinti-Mischlinge, and socially assimilated Gypsies were excluded, as were those Gypsies still serving in the Wehrmacht. The distinctions made, however, were arbitrary and by no means always observed; few Gypsies would be left in 1945; their mass murder, like that of the Jews, extended to all of Europe under German domination. In any comparisons there were thus both similarities and specific differences relating to each biologically persecuted group. An estimated ten thousand German Gypsies survived, returning from camps or forced labor; this was a proportion of survivors higher than that of German Jews. But the suffering of those who were gassed, upon whom medical experiments were conducted, or who were starved to death in camps did not differ from that of other racial victims. Despite treatment that differed in some respects from that accorded Jews, no one studying the Nazi documents can seriously doubt that their persecution was indeed racial; pure Gypsies and Mischlinge Gypsies were held to be genetically predetermined criminals, and their intermarriage with Germans was forbidden. Although family camps were established, Gypsy mothers, children, and babies were gassed just as Jews were. If persecution was not based on racial theory, why murder children? Why create Mischlinge categories in the first place? Why "privilege" some Gypsies unless a worse fate was intended for the others?

By the time of the Wannsee Conference in January 1942, the question of the German Mischlinge and the Jüdischversippte had become the two immediate problems still needing resolution before it could be claimed that plans for a Final Solution were complete. As far as the Jews were concerned, the "marker" chosen to distinguish those who would have to be biologically separated from the Germans and those who were to be biologically absorbed had originally been laid down by a Führer decision at Nuremberg in September 1935. A further and equally important decision had then been taken that the treatment of the Mischlinge was not to be dependent on any individual examination of their characteristics, that is whether they were predominantly "German" or Jewish. Hitler rightly foresaw that this would have opened the door to possible corruption, widespread local and personal differences, publicity, questioning, and general unrest among millions of Germans. He had conceded such selection only to the Wehrmacht in 1935 because that organization still enjoyed a certain degree of independent power. But he did not overlook this compromise of his will and ordered the Mischlinge and Jüdischversippte out of the armed forces in the spring of 1940, the Gypsies in 1942. At Nuremberg simple definitions and decrees placing quarter Jews on the German biological side and half Jews on the Jewish biological side were intended to bring the Jewish Problem to an end within a measurable period of time. The decision Hitler took regarding the half Jews was logical. As Bernhard Lösener of the Ministry of the Interior had pointed out, they had inherited half of each characteristic, while the party had argued that either German or Jewish could predominate; placing them all on the Jewish line of the divide was the safest decision.[14] As a sop and small safety valve, Hitler and his deputy Führer, Hess, reserved to themselves decisions on whether exceptions could be made and on upgrading the degree of a particular Mischling. In practice there were few exceptions. Furthermore, the principle of biological separation logically had to be extended to forbidden marriages, half Jews with quarter Jews or Germans transgressing the biological divide. And then, logically again, there was a further problem: What was to be done about existing (pre-1935) mixed marriages that would in some cases produce more Mischlinge—half Jews or quarter Jews? The question posed at Wannsee in 1942 was whether these Führer decisions regarding German Jews and Mischlinge should still stand. Furthermore, how were Jews and Mischlinge who were not Germans but who fell under German control in occupied Europe to be defined and treated?

As we have seen, Hitler had insisted on maintaining control of the Mischlinge problem as far as the German Mischlinge were concerned. Cases were referred to him personally for decision. This limited their number drastically. According to the Ministry of the Interior, as of September 1942 the number of German Mischlinge raised to equivalence of Germans was only 394.[15] After instructions from the Reichskanzlei on October 25, 1937, all applications had to be sent directly to State Secretary Lammers, and on November 4, 1938, Lammers informed the Minister of the Interior that no further exceptions were to be granted.[16] Although Hitler's personal decision had permitted one of his favorite conductors, Franz von Hoesslin, musical director of the Wagner Festival at Bayreuth, to continue conducting in Germany without hindrance though his wife had been classified a Jew, when Hoesslin, who also conducted Wagner abroad, requested that the obligatory "J" should not be entered on his wife's passport, this was refused.[17]

After the outbreak of the war, the Jewish problem could be tackled more radically. Hitler had foreseen this before his infamous Reichstag speech of January 1939. He had promised the annihilation of the Jews if a new war should break out—a war for which he would hold international Jewry responsible. In preparation, he had given considerable thought to how to accomplish this without unduly unsettling German public opinion in wartime. His approach was probably more cautious than required. At Nuremberg the first fundamental distinctions between the treatment of different categories of Mischlinge as regards their biological future had been settled in the marriage regulations. In December 1938 more elaborate classifications were added. The occasion was an amendment to the law securing tenancies. Hermann Göring, as head of the Four Year Plan, made it clear in a secret circular of December 28, 1938, that Hitler had taken these decisions himself. As far as Jews were concerned, there was to be no general abrogation of their protection as tenants; instead, they were, as far as possible, to be collected in individual houses. The Aryanization of ownership of houses was to be placed at the end of a list of other Aryanization measures. There was to be no ban on Jews using public transport, and prohibitions on their staying in hotels or eating in restaurants were to be limited only to facilities where party meetings were held. After the outbreak of war, these and many further restrictions were soon introduced. As far as the Mischlinge were concerned, in December 1938 Hitler had acted even more cautiously, differentiating and placing a household with children where the father was German and the wife Jewish in a better position than vice versa. The property of both kinds of household could be transferred to the German partner or Mischling children. They were not to be moved to Jewish quarters since in 1939 Mischling children could serve in the Wehrmacht. Partners in mixed marriages without children where the husband was German, would also be treated in a privileged manner, but not partners in marriages where the husband was Jewish. In the latter case, they were to be treated as Jews unless the wife divorced her husband.[18] The wording made clear that all the considerations given to the status of the Mischlinge and Jews in mixed marriages were temporary. The screw could be turned tighter whenever Hitler regarded it as opportune. But for the time being Hitler thought it wise to tread carefully in the face of the coming war, particularly in family situations where many German relatives might be involved. A large number of decrees followed the outbreak of war, and these laid down in detail under what circumstances exceptions from the general anti-Jewish measures might be allowed for Jews in mixed marriages and Mischlinge. The most important of these was that Jews in the so-called privileged Mischehen (with children who were not religiously Jewish) did not have to wear the Yellow Star as of September 1941.

In October 1941 emigration of Jews from Germany was stopped in readiness for their deportation. Once more Jews living in mixed marriages were excluded. The fate of the other full Jews had been sealed; at the Führer headquarters on October 25, 1941, Heydrich and Himmler were special visitors. It was natural, therefore, that Hitler should raise the issue of the fate of the Jews. His hatred comes through in the record of his table talk, referring to the Jews as a criminal race with "two million dead of the world on their conscience, and now again hundreds of thousands. Let no one tell me that we cannot send them into the morass."[19] The Wannsee Conference had to be postponed, but not the Final Solution.

When the representative of the concerned ministries and authorities met at Wannsee on January 20, 1942, there was no great need to discuss the fate of the Jews who were not in mixed marriages. That was settled. It was more a question of providing information and explaining the full extent of the Final Solution. The future as regards the German Mischlinge, however, was another matter. Hitler had not moved forward since December 1938 with a decision on their fate in the Endlösung. The usual way to secure a decision was to lay proposals before him. So Heydrich at Wannsee concluded that Mischlinge of the first degree were to be treated as Jews except for individually examined cases worthy of separation, and they were to be offered "voluntary" sterilization instead of deportation. Knowing Hitler's decision to place Mischlinge of the second degree biologically with the Germans, Heydrich paid lip service to the Führer's decision but then added that upon individual examination exceptions could be made to decide one's fate.

Then Heydrich created new categories of mixed marriages between Germans and Jews and Mischlinge with the objective of forcibly deporting and killing as many of the latter two groups as possible. State Secretary Stuckart wished to exclude all discretion in these matters: he wanted to forcibly dissolve all marriages between Jews and Germans and to sterilize all the Mischlinge who remained in the Reich. This brutally revived the old Nuremberg controversy—the ministry wanted no provision for examination of individual cases but sought a directive applying to everyone in any particular category. Stuckart preferred the Verwaltungsweg. Heydrich would not object to this, provided the result victimized everyone in these categories. His Wannsee proposal to examine individual cases was an attempt to circumvent Hitler's original Nuremberg decision in favor of second degree Mischlinge, as well as the Führer's later elaboration of the privileged Mischehen. But in 1942, Hitler was still not ready to take the measures put forward by Heydrich and Stuckart. Declaring marriages null and void might lead to a direct confrontation with the German churches—a possibility he wanted to avoid before the war was won. And until 1944 Hitler held to a distinction in the treatment of the Mischlinge: their biological treatment might have included murder in the case of Mischlinge of the first degree but not Mischlinge of the second degree. His distinctions also encompassed persecution and discrimination in every other respect, such as education and permission to enter a profession or the state service. Many new ordinances circumscribed the lives of the Mischlinge; by the end of the war these measures condemned Mischlinge of the first degree and Jüdischversippte to forced labor and deportation.

By 1945 it seemed likely that the first degree Mischlinge and Jews married to Germans were shortly to be condemned to murder or labor-to-destruction, and any of the former who survived, to sterilization. A German victory would have led to the speedy completion of the Final Solution. The "privileged" German Mischlinge of the second degree would in all probability have survived in Germany provided they submitted to sterilization. Such careful distinctions as applied to German Mischlinge did not extend to the East.

No Jew or descendant of a Jewish forebear and no Gypsy or Gypsy Mischlinge could be certain after 1933 what new measures were in store for the following day except that worse nearly always followed. They not only suffered directly from each new step of escalating persecution but after 1938 lived in constant fear of tomorrow. They could count on no protection and were exposed to abuse and the uncaring attitudes of their neighbors, with few notable exceptions. Humiliated at every step, they were outcasts of society and, when they were not deported themselves, became witnesses of the deportation and murder of close relations. They lived in fear that their turn would come next. The few shining examples of sympathy and support from outside the family provided but crumbs of comfort. Fewer were hidden in Germany than anywhere else in occupied Europe. Some German partners of mixed marriages divorced, some for the craven reason of escaping from discrimination, others tragically, in the mistaken belief that this provided better protection for their children. They did not realize that divorce delivered the Jewish partner to the death camps unless they were able to emigrate in time.

In all this moral gloom the shining exception are the loyal spouses who fought for and protected their Jewish husbands or wives and their Mischlinge children, and these were the majority. They were Germans from all walks of life. Then, too, there were the hundreds of partnerships formed—*wilde Ehen*—between young men and women unable to marry because of the Nuremberg Laws who supported each other despite threats from the Gestapo and obvious dangers. Since Jews were deported, or they emigrated, the majority of the secret "marriages," unsanctioned by state or church, that survived the war were between Germans and Mischlinge. There were illegitimate children, too, whose full parentage had to be hidden. That story of persecution and hardship has yet to be told.

NOTES

1. For a good discussion, see Sybil Milton, "The Context of the Holocaust," *German Studies Review*, 13 (1990): 269–83. Where in this essay "German" is used it is in the sense of the Nazi definition, the great majority of the Jews and Mischlinge living in Germany were Germans, of course.

2. The detailed study of the significance of the Mischlinge in Holocaust history is recent, and studies of mixed marriages are even more sparse. Uwe Dietrich Adam, *Judenpolitik im Dritten Reich* (Düsseldorf, 1979) drew attention to the discussion about mixed marriages and Mischlinge at Wannsee and after; two contributions of importance are Jeremy Noakes, "Wohin gehören die 'Judenmischlinge'?: Die Entstehung der ersten Durchführungsverordnungen zu den Nürnberger Gesetzen," and John A. S. Grenville, "Die 'Endlösung' und die 'Judenmischlinge' im Dritten Reich," both in *Das Unrechtsregime*, vol. 2, ed. Ursula Büttner (Hamburg: Christians Verlag, 1986), pp. 69–89, and pp. 91–121, respectively. See also Jeremy Noakes, "The Development of Nazi Policy towards the German-Jewish 'Mischlinge' 1933–1945," Leo Baeck Institute *Year Book* 34 (1989): 291–354; Ursula Büttner, "The Persecution of Christian-Jewish Families in the Third Reich," Leo Baeck Institute *Year Book* 34 (1989): 267–89; W. Cohn, "Bearers of a Common Fate?: The 'Non-Aryan' Christian 'Fate Comrades' of the Paulus Bund 1933–1939," Leo Baeck Institute *Year Book* 33 (1988): 327–66; Ursula Büttner, *Die Not der Juden teilen* (Hamburg: Christians Verlag, 1988), for the most detailed discussion of Mischlinge and "Jüdischversippte." The literature on the Gypsies is also growing; for a discussion of the literature, see Milton, "Context of the Holocaust."

3. Reichsministerium des Innern (hereafter RMI) to Reichsstatthalter, September 1, 1933, Hamburger Staatsarchiv (hereafter HStA), Senatskanzlei, Personalabteilung I 1933 Ja 13.

4. RMI to Minister für Wissenschaft, Erziehung und Volksbildung, October 17, 1935, HStA Senatsakten, Präsidialabteilung 1935 A 35.

5. RMI to Reichsstatthalter, April 18, 1935, HStA Senatsakten, Präsidialabteilung 1935 A 35.

6. Ibid.

7. Memorandum by Dr. Gütt, RMI, September 25, 1935, Bundesarchiv Koblenz (hereafter BAK), R18/5513.

8. Circular Pfundtner, RMI, April 8, 1937, and August 16, 1937 BAK, R18/5515.

9. For the discussion, see Grenville, "Die 'Endlösung' und die 'Judenmischlinge,'" pp. 102–103.

10. Cohn, "Bearers of a Common Fate?" pp. 350–53.

11. Dr. Zindel to Pfundtner, March 4, 1936, BAK, R18/5331. See also Sybil Milton, "Antechamber to Birkenau: The Zigeunerlager after 1933," in *Die Normalität des Verbrechens: Bilanz und Perspektiven der Forschung zu den nationalsozialistischen Gewaltverbrechen. Festschrift für Wolfgang Scheffler zum 65. Geburstag*, ed. Helge Grabitz, Johannes Tuchel, and Klaus Bastlein (Berlin: Hentrich, 1994), p. 248.

12. R. N. Procter, *Racial Hygiene: Medicine under the Nazis* (Cambridge: Harvard University Press, 1988), pp. 140, 214.

13. Dr. L. Conti to Reichssicherheitshauptamt, copy to Pfundtner, January 24, 1940, BAK, R18/5331.

14. The full original text of Lösener's memorandum of October 11, 1935, of which only excerpts have been printed, is to be found at the Hoover Institution Archives at Stanford University in Wiedemann, Adjutantur des Führers, Miscellaneous Files.

15. Noakes, "Development of Nazi Policy," p. 386.

16. State Secretary Lammers, Reichskanzlei to Reichsminister, October 25, 1937, and from Berchtesgaden to RMI, November 4, 1938, BAK, R18/5331.

17. Ambassador Mackensen to Pfundtner, March 31, 1939, and Heydrich to RMI, May 2, 1939, BAK, R18/5331.

18. Hermann Göring, Beauftragter für den Vierjahresplan, to Reichsministers, secret, December 28, 1938, BAK, R18/5519.

19. Werner Jochmann, *Adolf Hitler: Monologe im Führerhauptquartier 1941–1944* (Hamburg: Knaus, 1980), pp. 30–31, 106.

23.

HUGH GREGORY GALLAGHER

"Slapping Up Spastics"

"If the physician presumes to take into consideration in his
work whether a life has value or not, the consequences are
boundless and the physician becomes the most dangerous
man in the state."
—CHRISTOPHER HUFELAND,
eighteenth-century German physician[1]

A Personal Statement

I am a historian, author of *By Trust Betrayed: Patients, Physicians and the License to Kill in the Third Reich*; I am also a severely disabled person, a polio quadriplegic. As such, I am interested in the evolution of social attitudes toward and assumptions about disabled people. It is my conviction that the underlying assumptions that made possible the killing by physicians of upwards of 200,000 disabled German citizens in the 1930s and 1940s are still widely held, not just in Germany but throughout the Western industrialized world. The purpose of the following material, as of my book, is to make the reader aware of these assumptions and of the evil that can arise from their careless application.

Aktion T4 Euthanasia: Summary of Program

In the late 1930s and throughout World War II, physicians of Germany's medical establishment, acting both with and without the acquiescence of the Nazi government, systematically killed their severely disabled and chronically mentally ill patients. Their doctors called these people "useless eaters"—persons with "lives not worth living."

The officially sanctioned killing program was authorized by Hitler in 1939 at the request of leading figures of the German medical establishment. The program was under the direction of the Führer's personal physician, Dr. Karl Brandt. It was called "euthanasia," although most of its victims were neither terminally ill nor in unbearable pain, nor were they anxious to die. The program's proponents advanced various arguments for its justification—compassion, eugenics, economics, racial purity. The official program was halted by Hitler in the summer of 1941 due to a rising wave of protests from disabled people, their families and friends, and religious officials. Even so, many doctors, acting largely on their own counsel, continued killing patients in hospitals and institutions throughout Germany.

Over the course of the official program and the unofficial so-called "runaway" euthanasia that followed it, more than 200,000 German citizens met their death at the hands of their physicians. The mass murder techniques developed in the euthanasia hospitals were later utilized against Jews.

As part of the official program, the medical establishment was informed of the Aktion T4 operation at secret briefings held across the country. At these meetings, the psychiatrists, physicians, and medical professors were fully informed about euthanasia. Euphemisms were used to describe the program: "negative population policies" was mass killing; "refractory therapy cases" were disabled people targeted for killing; "specialist children's wards" were child killing centers; and "final medical assistance" was, of course, murder. There was virtually never a doubt as to what was being discussed.

These doctors were told that the euthanasia program was a part of the "breakthrough campaign" necessary to obtain the new medicine of the Third Reich. This held that medical attention and money should go, on a cost-benefit analysis, to those who can be brought back to full productive health, while the chronically disabled would be removed from society as, said Dr. F. Klein, "I would remove the purulent appendix from a diseased body."[2]

In both the minutes of the Reich Committee for the Scientific Registration of Serious Illnesses of Hereditary or Protonic Origin— a high level physicians' committee that met regularly with the Reich Chancellery—and in the reports of the briefing meetings with rank-and-file physicians, it was fiercely argued that the radical modernization of therapeutic activity could not be achieved without—and, in fact, must go hand-in-hand with—the elimination of these "refractory therapy cases."[3]

There can be no doubt that the existence of the euthanasia program was generally known within the medical community of the wartime Reich.

As long as the program was in effect— whether death came by pill, starvation, or carbon monoxide shower—death came at the hand of a physician. It was program administrator Viktor Brack's firm and oft-stated belief that the "syringe belongs in the hand of a physician."[4]

Philip Bouhler, chief of Hitler's Chancellery, was insistent that a way of death be found that would be not only painless but also imperceptible to the patient. He did not want to frighten the patients, nor make them uncomfortable. These things must be "done according to his orders, and in a dignified and not a brutal fashion."[5]

The original regulations envisioned a "conservative" program with careful review procedures. In operation, however, the program became a matter of killing in wholesale lots. The psychological reasons physicians were willing to participate in these killings are, no doubt, complex. There is, however, an aspect of the structure of the program that made it easier: there was no single point of responsibility—no place in the procedure at which it was possible to say, "here is where the patient receives his death warrant"; no point where it could be said, "*this* physician is responsible for *this* patient's death."

The local practicing physician simply filled out questionnaires as he was required to do. The members of the assessing committee simply gave their individual opinion on each case. Nothing more would happen unless the members were in substantial agreement. The senior review physician simply went along with the committee or else expressed an objection. He was expressing a medical opinion, nothing more. Neither the assessors nor the review physicians ever saw the patient. The transportation staff was involved in transporting patients, but it was no business of theirs where or why the patients were being moved. The staff that ran the centers were simply doing their jobs. Even the physician whose job it was to operate the gas chamber was not responsible for the death of the patients. After all, he played no part in their selection; he knew nothing of their cases. He was only following the procedures laid down by his superiors—carrying out the policy of his government as advised by the most eminent members of the medical profession.

The official, centralized euthanasia program lasted from 1939 through the summer of 1941. After two years of operation, the program's existence was widely known. The churches had raised strong and vocal objections. There had been public demonstrations in opposition to the killings. The German army was deep in the Russian campaign, and Hitler had no wish for public unrest at home. Accordingly, the Führer, in a conversation with Dr. Brandt, without ceremony or discussion, ordered a halt to the euthanasia program.[6]

This did not, however, bring an end to the killing of the disabled and the insane. Physicians across Germany continued to administer "final medical treatment" to patients they considered as having "lives not worth living." The killings continued, but the decision making and the criteria used in these decisions became those of the immediate doctor, rather than the assessor committees and the review professors. The "children's campaign," by which retarded and deformed infants were put to death, proceeded unabated. Even *after* the war, U.S. Army occupation forces found the killing continuing at Kaufbeuren and Eglfing-Haar.[7]

In 1944 as the war came to its climax and Allied bombing of German cities increased, health "czar" Dr. Brandt undertook to evacuate institutionalized patients to the countryside, where approximately twenty thousand are believed to have been killed by their physicians. On the eastern ramparts of Germany—in Danzig, Pomerania, and West Prussia—as well as in Poland, mentally ill patients were simply shot by the local SS and police forces. Physicians, in what was called Operation 14f13, practiced wanton killing of the sick and disabled in the concentration camps. What the Germans referred to at the time as "wild euthanasia" led to additional, widespread, unorganized, and indiscriminate killing. As Klaus Dörner has said, "Unplanned groups and individuals were murdered: welfare wards, asocials, wayward children, healthy Jewish children, or those of mixed blood, homosexuals, political offenders, elderly wards of nursing homes, sick and healthy Eastern workers."[8]

It is not possible to tell with any accuracy how many disabled German citizens were put to death during the Nazi years. No reliable figures exist for the spontaneous killings.

Figures survive for the official centralized T4 killings:

	Facility	1940	1941	Total
A	(Grafeneck)	9,839	–	9,839
B	(Brandenburg)	9,772	–	9,772
Be	(Bernburg)	–	8,601	8,601
C	(Linz)	9,670	8,599	18,269
D	(Sonnenstein)	5,943	7,777	13,720
E	(Hadamar)	–	10,072	10,072
		35,224	35,049	70,273

In the summer of 1991, unexpected verification of these figures was unearthed in the cellar of the headquarters of the Stasi, the former East German secret police. The medical files of the seventy thousand patients, filed alphabetically, were discovered by English scholar Michael Burleigh.[9]

In some of the Nuremberg trial documents, the figure 120,000 is given as the overall number of inmates killed in public institutions. According to Götz Aly and Heinz Roth, this number is on the low side and does not include those who died in such separate programs as the children's operation, random euthanasia, and the so-called "Brandt campaign."[10] Dr. Leo Alexander, who served with the Office of the Chief of Counsel for War Crimes at Nuremberg and who performed the major study of the euthanasia program for the court, has estimated that 275,000 persons were killed.[11] The psychiatrist Fredric Wertham has looked into hospital records. He found, for example, that in 1938 the state of Brandenburg had 16,295 mental patients from Berlin. By 1945, there remained but 2,379 patients. In an institution called Berlin-Buch, out of 2,500 patients, 500 survived. Kaufbeuren in Bavaria had 2,000 patients at the beginning of the war and 200 at war's end. Many mental institutions simply closed their doors because of lack of patients. In 1939, in all of Germany, there were some 300,000 mental patients. In 1946, there were 40,000. This is not to say that all these persons were destroyed by the German state in the course of its euthanasia operation. No doubt some were released. And, of course, the general German war losses were colossal.[12] Nevertheless, it cannot be doubted that the euthanasia program swept out entire wards, emptied entire hospitals. It decimated the entire German population of the severely disabled and the chronically insane.

Scientific and Economic Origins of the Killing

The euthanasia killing program was no Nazi aberration; rather, it was the efficient application through public policy of the theories of leading scientists and philosophers in Western society. Darwin's theories of evolution, combined with the rediscovery of Mendelian law, had encouraged Victorians in the belief that the biological world could be as knowable, as predictable, as Newton's physical world. Proponents of social Darwinism and the "science" of eugenics sought to apply evolutionary and genetic principles, as then understood, to human society and breeding. Eugenicists believed most human characteristics to be inherited. In W. Duncan McKim's book *Heredity in Human Progress*, which was published in 1900, heredity is blamed for, among other things,

> insanity, idiocy, imbecility, eccentricity, hysteria, epilepsy, the alcohol habit, the morphine habit, neuralgias, "nervousness," Saint Vitus's dance, infantile convulsions, stammering, squint, gout, articular rheumatism, diabetes, tuberculosis, cancer, deafness, blindness, deaf-mutism, color blindness.[13]

It is, he said, "the fundamental cause of human wretchedness."[14]

President Theodore Roosevelt spoke for many forward-thinking people when he said "Someday we will realize that the prime duty, the inescapable duty, of the good citizen of the right type is to leave his or her blood behind him in the world. . . .We have no business to permit the perpetuation of citizens of the wrong type."[15]

The impact of Darwinian theory upon German thought was no less strong upon British and American thinking. Darwin cast a long shadow over the development of National Socialism and the Third Reich. The influential book *The Destruction of Life Devoid of Value* was written in 1920 by psychiatrist Alfred Hoche and lawyer Karl Binding.[16] These men were professors of reputation and importance. They argued that the medical profession should participate not only in health-giving, but under certain circumstances, in death-making as well. With a carefully reasoned argument, defining their terms precisely, their analysis concluded that certain people should be exterminated for reasons of racial hygiene purposes. They argued that the retarded, the deformed, the terminally ill, and those who were mentally sound but who were severely damaged by disease or accident should be put to death. They believed that the death should be painless and expertly administered—that is, by a physician. According to their reasoning, the right to "grant death" was a natural extension of the responsibilities of the attending physician.

Binding and Hoche were widely read and vigorously discussed. One of their readers was the young Adolf Hitler, who had read a good deal on eugenics prior to writing *Mein Kampf*. On one occasion, Hitler even allowed his name to be used in advertisements for Hoche's books.[17]

There were numerous other books and articles on the subject. The romantic philosopher Ernst Haeckel wrote several books that sold well for many years. His disciple, Heinrich Ziegler, was a popular writer on such issues and won the important Krupp literary award. The 1920 book *Moral der Kraft* (Morality of terror) by Ernst Mann advocated that disabled war veterans kill themselves to reduce welfare costs.

An exceedingly popular movie in the Germany of the mid-1930s dealt entirely with the issue of euthanasia for the disabled. *Ich klage an* is the story of a young woman suffering from multiple sclerosis. Her husband, a doctor, after lengthy soul-searching, kills his wife in the last reel, as a fellow physician in the next room plays softly and funereally on the piano.

Training films illustrated the unbearable life of the insane, with particularly grisly shots of defective dystonias. These films were used to indoctrinate the staffs of the euthanasia centers, and they were widely shown at meetings of physicians' societies. One was shown at the annual meeting of the Nazi Party in 1935 by Dr. Gerhardt Wagner, leader of the medical delegation.

Although long thought lost, the raw, unedited footage of these training films and their original scripts were also found in the basement of Stasi secret police headquarters in the summer of 1991 by Michael Burleigh. Making use of this material, Burleigh pieced together a documentary film, *Selling Murder: The Killing Films of the Third Reich*, which was broadcast in Britain in November 1991.[18] It is a remarkable experience for the historian who for years has researched the Aktion T4 euthanasia program actually to see in operation the killing center at the Hadamar Psychiatric Hospital. The impact is extraordinary.

In the film script, a "professor" lectures that the "incurably mentally ill" have a "right to die." "Is it not the duty of those concerned," he asks the earnest, note-taking students (described in the script as "today's strong, racially pure and healthy youth"), "to help the incapable—and that means total idiots and incurable mental patients—to their right?"[19]

The economics of euthanasia for the chronically disabled were widely discussed. It was wartime, budgets were sky-high, deficits were extraordinary, and health resources were limited. It was argued that expenditures for long-term care of patients, who might never again be economically productive citizens, made little economic sense in cost-benefit terms, as compared with similar expenditures on improved public health programs to keep the able-bodied healthy. Scarce health care resources were to be rationed.

This thinking was based on the assumption that the life of a disabled person was less valuable to himself, as well as to the state, than that of an able-bodied person. This general devaluation of disabled lives was widespread and extended even to schoolroom textbooks. One text, *Mathematics in the Service of National Political Education*, set the following problem: "If the building of a lunatic asylum costs six million marks and it costs fifteen thousand marks to build each dwelling on a housing estate, how many of the latter could be built for the price of one asylum?" Another asked, how many marriage allowance loans could be given to young couples for the amount of money it costs the state to care for "the crippled, criminal, and insane?"[20]

When the German physicians and medical professors set up Aktion T4, they were instituting a program whose principles had been widely and thoroughly discussed.

Aktion T4 Euthanasia: Impact and Response

After the war, Dr. Karl Brandt, director of the euthanasia program, and Viktor Brack, administrator of the program, were hanged at Nuremberg for war crimes and crimes committed against humanity. Many of the principal T4 physicians fled or disappeared. Occasionally, one has surfaced and faced trial. These trials have been long, drawn out, inconclusive affairs, largely because of the unwillingness of one physician to testify against another.

Other principal physicians simply resumed their medical practice under assumed names. Their presence was known to their peers in the medical community but was not reported. The rank and file of the German physicians, those who had been active in the program and the rest who had raised no objection to it, continued the practice of medicine, albeit no longer killing their patients.

Over the half century since the T4 program, the German medical establishment has never officially acknowledged, seriously examined, or apologized for the killings. A book summarizing accurately the T4 euthanasia evidence accumulated in the Nuremberg trials and written by a young psychiatrist, Alexander Mitscherlich, was published in 1949. It was suppressed, denounced as "irresponsible, . . . lacking documentation." The book was seen as an attack on the "inviolable honor of German medicine." One reviewer said that only a "pervert" would read such a book and called its author a "traitor to his country."[21]

The German medical establishment enjoys, and rightly so, much prestige in society. German physicians have made many important contributions throughout the history of medical science. Unfortunately, the profession has chosen to deal with the euthanasia episode with what amounts to an across-the-board denial. Medical students have been expelled from medical schools for attempting to discuss the matter. It is reported (in a personal communication) that Dr. Harmut M. Hanauske-

Able was no longer able to practice in Germany after publishing a 1986 article on the subject in the British medical journal *Lancet*. In 1967, the courageous Margarete and Alexander Mitscherlich wrote in the foreword to their book *Die Unfähigkeit zu trauern* (published in English as *The Inability to Mourn*):

> Today in many minds, there is a reluctance to accept the facts of history. . . . What happened in the Third Reich remains alive in our subconscious, dangerously so. It will be fatal for us to lose touch with the truth of what happened then. We must struggle to seek out the truth of that era rather than search for improved defenses to hide us from this truth.[22]

It is encouraging that in the 1980s a new, younger generation of historians began to focus their attention on the social history of the Nazi years. In the course of their studies, they have done important research on the Aktion T4 euthanasia program and associated killing—work which is only now being published. These historians include Ernst Klee, Götz Aly, Heinz Roth, Benno Müller-Hill, and Michael H. Kater. Their work documents the known killings and uncovers killings hitherto unknown.

A breakthrough of sorts occurred at the annual meeting of the principal German medical society, the Deutsche Ärtzetag, in 1989. In spite of heavy resistance, the Berlin Chamber of Physicians mounted an exhibition, "The Value of the Human Being," which portrayed the role of German doctors during the Nazi years. In conjunction with the display, articles on medicine in the Third Reich were published in the *Deutsche Ärtzeblatt*, the German equivalent of the *Journal of the American Medical Association*.[23]

In his remarks opening the exhibition, University of Münster medical historian, Richard Toellner is reported to have said,

> The whole spectrum of normal representatives of the medical profession was involved and they all knew what they did. . . . A medical profession accepts mass murder of sick people as a normality, and to a large degree explicitly approves of it as a necessary, justified act for the sake of the community, has failed and betrayed its mission. Such a medical profession *as a whole* has become morally guilty, no matter how many members of the profession directly or indirectly participated in the killing of sick people in *a legal sense*. [personal communication, emphasis added]

This set off a storm of protest, with the chairman of the national organization, Karsten Vilmar, asserting that the majority of doctors had honorably served the medical needs of their patients and were neither aware of nor participants in the atrocities.[24]

The Persistence of Underlying Attitudes

In Germany today, as in the United States, there is a lively, on-going debate over issues of health delivery and medical ethics. Present, like Banquo's ghost, in all these discussions must be the memory, expressed or unexpressed, of the medical killings of the 1930s and 1940s.

We have seen how the rationale in the 1930s was grounded on eugenic "principles," social Darwinism, and a humane concern for persons judged by their doctors to have lives "not worth living." Then, as now, budgets were in deficit, health care resources were limited, and rationing was called for. Careful economic cost-benefit analysis led to the diversion of funds from the treatment of "recalcitrant," long-term chronically ill patients to patients more likely to respond positively to therapy, more likely to return to full productivity. The health and well-being of the Volk as a whole was of greater value than that of the individual unfortunate.

Today in Germany as well as the United States, there are similar economic concerns, similar budget constraints that have an impact on the health care debate. Valid questions are being raised concerning such things as the cost effectiveness and social merits of intensive life support care for the terminal AIDS patient, liver transplants for the chronic alcoholic, kidney dialysis for the aged, the cost of lifetime care for the very high-level neck- and respiratory-involved quadriplegic. Concerns about matters such as abortion, amniocentesis, tracking the genome, "the right to die," euthanasia, and disability rights are both complex and unavoidable. These are brutal issues, inescapably requiring cost-benefit analysis and "quality of life" judgments, implicitly measuring the value of human life in economic terms.

Sometimes these measurements become quite explicit. A troubling example of this can be found in the debate over the cost of care for severely disabled, premature neonates. *Der Spiegel* recently reported about a doctoral dissertation on the subject, which asserted that 7.3 million marks could be saved in the cost of care and special education for "each handicapped child not born." It concluded that as much as 730 million marks could be saved if 100,000 "genetically damaged" babies were aborted.[25]

This study illustrates how well-meaning, socially conscious debate can slip, almost imperceptibly, into the devaluation of the lives of the people being discussed, in this case disabled infants.

Present today in this country and in Germany, just as in the Third Reich, are three underlying assumptions:[26]

Otherness: This is the assumption that we, however our group is defined, are better than the others—Christians are superior to Jews, Germans are superior to Turks, the able-bodied to the disabled, physicians to patients. The superior group, whether "superior" by reason of birth, wealth, education, or status, believes that its perceived superiority gives it the authority to make judgments or take actions affecting the well-being of lesser groups.

Spread: This is the often unconscious assumption that a person, disabled in one way, is therefore disabled in all other ways. Because a child with cerebral palsy may be unstable on his feet, the assumption often made is that he will be unstable in his mental processes. If a disabled person cannot do one thing, it is assumed he cannot do anything—he is useless.

Devaluation: This is the assumption, again often unconscious, that because a person is flawed, he is therefore without value. He is a devalued person, useless; and whether the disabled person is aware of it or not, his is a life not worth living.

Unspeakable acts were committed in the Third Reich because of these assumptions. These same assumptions are alive today and just as dangerous.

A particularly vivid example of this took place at Rehab 88, the fifth international rehabilitation trade fair held at Karlsruhe, Germany, in 1988. On such occasions, physicians, rehabilitation specialists, equipment manufacturers, and the disabled community gather from around the world. The medical experts organizing the professional section of the conference on the rehabilitation of disabled people asked Dr. Hans Henning Atrott to give the keynote speech. Atrott is president of the German Society for Humane Dying. His subject was "Euthanasia (the German translates literally as Active Assistance for Dying): The Final Rehabilitation." It is perhaps not surprising that organizations of disabled persons were outraged that such a talk should be given on such an occasion. They protested to the conference organizers but to no avail. As a last resort, they broke up Atrott's lecture by bursting into the hall in their wheelchairs, dressed in garbage bags, sipping from cans labeled "cyanide," and waving signs that read, "useless lives" and "lives not worth living."[27] Atrott found it all most unfortunate, telling the media that the protest reminded him of Nazi tactics. It was a return, he said, to "terror against different thinking."[28]

In unified Germany, the neo-Nazi bully boys have been abusing disabled people. The Nazi punks call it "slapping up spastics." People in wheelchairs have been spat upon, cursed, and physically attacked. The *Journal of the British Council of Organizations of Disabled People* reported for 1993, for example, that as many as one thousand disabled German citizens had been harassed, physically or verbally, that year. The disabled have been taunted with shouts of "You are wasting my tax money"; "You are a worthless life"; "Under Hitler you would have been gassed."[29]

The *London Daily Mail* reported on a particular case, that of Mr. Guenter Schirmer. Mr. Schirmer, forty-six, had been injured in an auto accident thirteen years earlier. He lived in a small town near Hanover. He was able to move about on his own, making use of a tricycle type of wheelchair. On a visit to Hanover, Schirmer was attacked by a large gang of neo-Nazis, who spat upon him and kicked his wheelchair, all the while taunting him with shouts of "Under Hitler, you would have been gassed!" The abuse reached its climax when Schirmer and his wheelchair were thrown down a subway staircase.

After several episodes of such abuse, Schirmer, depressed, killed himself. In a suicide note to his wife, Schirmer wrote, "The handicapped are unlikely to have a chance ever again in this world. . . . Under Hitler I would have been gassed. Perhaps all these young people are right. Devaluation is contagious."[30]

These young people have been busy. The local Pestalozzi Foundation, which cares for mentally and physically disabled children, reports similar attacks on their clients. Elsewhere, five hearing-impaired boys in Halle were set upon by a gang of punks who beat them so severely they needed hospitalization. Group homes for disabled people have been attacked in Stendal and Quedlinburg.[31]

It is not fair to lay all the blame for such events at the feet of the Nazi youth. On a Blind Awareness Day, blind people of Hanover were passing out pamphlets at a stall in the market place: they were abused and insulted by passersby. Parents of disabled children in Hanover protest that school authorities discriminate against their children, refusing to allow them on school trips. At Spiekeroog, on the North Sea, handicapped children attending a church retreat were made to leave the beach by able-bodied bathers who objected to their disabilities. These same children were denied access to a museum and later were forced off a path because pedestrians refused to let them pass. The handicapped already receive too much help, complained one of the pedestrians.[32]

Most well-known is a case in which a court ordered a 10 percent refund to hotel guests who were made to eat in the same dining room with disabled people in wheelchairs. In making his decision, the judge said he agreed with the plaintiffs that it certainly must have been a "nauseating experience."[33]

Of course, the United States is not exempt. A 1993 study of the National Center on Child Abuse and Neglect found that disabled children, whether physically or emotionally impaired, when compared with able-bodied children, were twice as likely to be physically and sexually abused and three times as likely to be emotionally abused by their primary caretaker. On a personal note, in April 1993 a blind friend of mine was riding up the escalator at the Dupont Circle Metro station in Washington, D.C. Without warning, she was punched in the shoulder from behind, knocked to her knees, and her cane was wrenched from her and hurled down to the bottom of the escalator. "You gays and cripples should all be gassed," her assaulter hissed as he ran off.

In our time, important advances have been made by disabled people. For the first time in recorded history, the disabled have organized to ensure that their voices will be heard and their rights respected. In the United States, the Americans with Disabilities Act has been a giant step forward. In Europe, the European Parliament has created a panel of representatives from the disabled community to monitor and report, on an annual basis, the incidence of attacks on the disabled within the member nations. And at the United Nations, a movement is underway specifically to include disabled people within the terms of the Human Rights Declaration.

These are, of course, major advances. However it is my conclusion that the underlying psychological attitudes and assumptions concerning the worth and place of disabled people in society have not changed very much over fifty years.

The sociocultural upheaval now underway, both in this country and Europe, and the brutal social decisions that cannot be avoided in the allocation of health care, make it vital—as vital as can be—that the martyrdom of the German disabled at the hands of their physicians be examined, widely understood, and not forgotten.

NOTES

1. Cited in Fredric Wertham, M.D., *A Sign for Cain: An Exploration of Human Violence* (London: Robert Hale, 1968), p. 153.

2. See Hartmut M. Hanauske-Able, "Politics and Medicine: From Nazi Holocaust to Nuclear Holocaust—A Lesson to Learn?" *Lancet*, August 22, 1986, p. 271.

3. See Götz Aly and Heinz Roth, "The Legalization of Mercy Killings in Medical and Nursing Institutions in Nazi Germany from 1938 until 1941," *International Journal of Law and Psychiatry* (1984): 148.

4. See Robert Jay Lifton, *The Nazi Doctors—Medical Killing and the Psychology of Genocide* (New York: Basic Books, 1986), p. 7.

5. *Trials of War Criminals before the Nuremberg Military Tribunals under Control Council Law No. 10*, Nuremberg, October 1946–April 1949 (Washington, D.C.: U.S. Government Printing Office, 1951), vol. 1, p. 877.

6. Lifton, *Nazi Doctors*, p. 95.

7. Hugh Gregory Gallagher, *By Trust Betrayed—Patients, Physicians, and the License to Kill in the Third Reich* (Arlington: Vandamere Press, 1995), p. 250.

8. Klaus Dorner, "Nationalsozialismus und Lebensvernichtung," *Vierteljahrshefte für Zeitgeschichte* 5/2 (April 1967): 151.

9. See Rosalie Horner, *St. Louis Post Dispatch*, September 26, 1991, p. 25.

10. Aly and Roth, *Legalization of Mercy Killings*, p. 162.

11. Peter Roger Breggin, M.D., "The Psychiatric Holocaust," *Penthouse* (January 1979): 81.

12. Benno Müller-Hill, *Murderous Science* (Oxford: Oxford University Press, 1988).

13. See Mark H. Haller, *Eugenics: Hereditarian Attitudes in American Thought* (New Brunswick, NJ: Rutgers University Press, 1963), p. 42.

14. Ibid., p. 42.

15. Ibid., p. 79.

16. Karl Binding and Alfred Hoche, *Die Freigabe der Vernichtung lebensunwerten Lebens: Ihr Mass und ihre Form* (Leipzig: Felix Meiner, 1920).

17. Breggin, "Psychiatric Holocaust," p. 81.

18. See Horner, *St. Louis Post Dispatch*, September 26, 1991, p. 26.

19. Ibid., p. 26

20. See Alexander Mitscherlich, *The Death Doctors*, trans. James Cleugh (London: Elek Books, 1962), p. 234. See also Major Leo Alexander, *MC, AUS. Public Mental Health Practice in Germany: Sterilization and Execution of Patients Suffering from Nervous or Mental Disease*, Combined Intelligence Objective Subcommittee, G2 Division, SHAEF (Rear) APO 413. National Archives (1949).

21. Cited in Hanauske-Able, "Politics and Medicine," p. 272.

22. Alexander and Margarete Mitscherlich, *Die Unfähigkeit zu trauern: Grundlagen kollektiven Verhaltens* (Stuttgart: Deutscher Bücherbund, 1967).

23. See Christian Pross, "Nazi Doctors, German Medicine, and Historical Truth," in *The Nazi Doctors and the Nuremberg Code*, ed. George J. Annas and Michael A. Grodin (New York: Oxford University Press, 1992), p. 45.

24. Ibid., p. 46.

25. See "Disabled in Germany Face Antagonism and Violence," *Los Angeles Times*, May 3, 1993, p. 1.

26. The psychosocial origins of these assumptions are both complex and profound, quite beyond the scope of this investigation.

27. See Gallagher, *By Trust Betrayed*, p. 270.

28. Ibid., p. 270.

29. See "Fascists Attack Disabled People," *Journal of the British Council of Organizations of Disabled People* 1 (Winter 1992): 2.

30. See "The Helpless Who Fear They Are Nazis' Next Target," *London Daily Mail*, November 25, 1992, p. 102.

31. See "Fascists Attack Disabled People," *Journal of the British Council of Organizations of Disabled People* 1 (Winter 1992): 2.

32. See "Disabled in Germany," May 3, 1993, p. 1.

33. Ibid., p. 1.

24.

GÜNTER GRAU

Final Solution of the Homosexual Question?

THE ANTIHOMOSEXUAL POLICIES OF THE NAZIS AND THE
SOCIAL CONSEQUENCES FOR HOMOSEXUAL MEN

It is undeniable that historical research in the Federal Republic of Germany has achieved considerable results in the attempt to shed light upon National Socialism. This is what political scientists have said.[1] However, and this needs to be added, it is also undeniable that historical research has excluded or neglected certain issues. These particular issues include questions about the fate of victims of sterilization and of those who were stigmatized as "asocials." Other subjects have suffered a similar lack of attention: forced-labor victims, those persecuted as a result of having contracted forbidden mixed marriages, those killed in the "Euthanasia" program, as well as the question of the effect of Nazism on the social position of homosexual men and women.[2] According to recent estimates, homosexuals in Germany then numbered between 1.5 and 2 million.

Serious controversy about the fate of this group appeared late in scholarly discourse. Even though some essays touched on this topic at the end of the 1960s, research efforts gained prominence only during the second half of the 1970s. Today a range of studies and publications examines different perspectives on National Socialist policies against homosexuals. A number of viewpoints, statements, and hypotheses on the subject will be explored and evaluated here.

In the late 1970s and early 1980s researchers became increasingly interested in analyzing this special topic. Even now, however, there is a widespread notion that the issue is marginal. Research and its dissemination are still the exception in comparison with, for example, the vast number of publications about members of groups that were persecuted for political, religious, and eugenic reasons. A conscious attempt to link the sociohistorical environment for homosexuality and homosexual men and women in the Third Reich to what Dirk Blasius calls the "broader context of historical process,"[3] has not been identified. For the most part, relevant research projects have been treated separately from one another. In reappraising this special part of German history there has been a general lack of conceptualization of the matter as a distinct and important issue.

From the beginning, the process of critical reflection has been connected with the controversy over how to interpret the changes National Socialism wrought in the

social image of homosexuality. The primary concern has been the immediate consequences of Nazi policies, based on that image, for homosexual men and women. For
a long time, any public debate wavered between two extreme evaluations. One camp
asserted that the persecution was not an injustice; others insisted that Nazis had
every intention of physically destroying all homosexuals. The cause for the latter
speculation can be understood in terms of the political interest that inspired its reappraisal of the past. This speculation has been especially encouraged by individuals
and/or groups active in or close to the politically oriented homosexual movement of
the Federal Republic of Germany. They still have one common characteristic: they all
attempt to restore history to the victims, as they say, to "rehistoricize" them, so that
they can regain a forward-looking perspective. They attempt to encourage survivors
to view their fate no longer as a private affair, but to inform future generations about
what happened.

For many years the above reappraisal has been carried out in direct confrontation
with official policy. This is so because the main body of German politicians has long
believed that Nazi proceedings against homosexuals were legally and socially justifiable. They have refused to grant the victims a status analogous to that of others
recognized as persecuted under the Nazi regime. They have declared that the Nazis
acted out of military necessity as well as in line with traditionally widespread sanctions to prevent criminal behavior all of which has meant that homosexuals were
not considered subject to "typical" Nazi injustice.[4] At the same time, this interpretation has evaded any necessity of prosecuting the perpetrators. In this regard, recall
that neither the Nuremberg trials nor those of medical doctors invoked any crimes
committed against homosexual men as such. Even later, there were no publicized
trials either in the Federal Republic of Germany or in the German Democratic
Republic that called to account prosecutors, judges, military officials, or doctors who
were proven to have taken part in such measures.

The most important goal has been to sensitize the public to the fate of this
"forgotten" group of victims. The first autobiographical works by homosexual men
were important milestones in this regard.[5] These works were followed by thematic
exhibitions in large cities, wreath-layings in honor of victims of fascism, and
initiatives to erect memorial plaques in locales that were and are centers of homosexual life and culture. All these endeavors have not only shed light upon the fates of
homosexual men in the Third Reich, but have also led to the inclusion of representatives of homosexual emancipation groups in discussions regarding reparations at
the end of the 1980s. For the first time, homosexual victims of the National Socialist
regime have had their own proponents represent claims for appropriate compensation in parliamentary forums. This is especially important because it is obvious that
in trying to render justice to the victims, the historical dimension was previously
unduly confined. For the contemporary gay and lesbian community, the shadow of
the pink triangle, the antihomosexual stigma that was attached to the gay prisoners
in the extermination camps by the National Socialists, still weighs heavily on German
homosexuals. This opinion derives from the assumption that the majority of homosexual men were exterminated in the concentration camps of the Nazis.

Even today, the view that the Nazis intended a final solution of the homosexual
question dominates a great many publications. Those who put forward this argument also insinuate a well-calculated and long-term program. They claim that with

the openly announced goal of eliminating homosexuality, the Nazis pursued a policy that led to a destructive campaign, a "homocaust" that was similar to the intended extermination of all Jews.[6] According to this theory, any homosexual man who caught the attention of the system would have become, like the Jew, a victim of the mass-murder process. The number of victims is estimated accordingly and amounts to between 100,000 and 1.5 million.[7] An examination of the Third Reich's trial statistics, however, reveals that these numbers are wildly exaggerated. Between 1933 and 1945, about 50,000 homosexual men and youths were sentenced by the Nazi criminal courts. According to the records, about 5,000 of those sentenced were deported to concentration camps after serving their sentences.[8]

In such characterizations of a perceived "final solution" of the homosexual question there surely must be a serious mistake in its proponents' failure accurately to differentiate the high-level programmatic-ideological statements from the actual process of putting anti-homosexual notions into practice. If a parallel is drawn with insufficient care and rigor between Himmler's rhetoric about the elimination of homosexuality and the destinies of individually murdered homosexual men, the National Socialist antihomosexual policy may appear to have been a program for the eradication of all homosexuals. If one differentiates, however, between the publicized anti-homosexual ideology and the reality of the day-to-day practice of persecution, the "final solution" here appears in another light. Himmler's phraseology really did point toward the elimination of homosexuality. Nevertheless, he had in mind the image of homosexuality, to him a form of degeneracy, as it emerged in public life. With his ideology, he did not strive for the extermination of each and every homo-sexual who was caught in the act of committing a "sexual offence." "If Himmler spoke of the homosexual as the bearer of homosexuality, he nearly always used the singular case. This shows that what he had in his sights was the homosexual type, and obviously not the fate of each individual homosexual man taken into custody by the persecuting apparatus," as Burkhard Jellonnek has correctly observed. And further-more: "If a homosexual man could convincingly demonstrate under Gestapo ques-tioning that he was not homosexually active, and if the proof to the contrary did not fall into the hands of the Gestapo, he would escape prosecution. The crucial point was carefully to prove that the subject had engaged in homosexual activity, and not just that he had homosexual inclinations. This was a further difference from the practice of antisemitic persecution, in which it was quite immaterial whether some-one observed the rules of their faith in everyday life or had renounced the Jewish religion altogether."[9]

Furthermore, the assumption that the Nazis had a long-term, social strategy for a "final solution" for homosexuals does not withstand the test of a critical examina-tion. In this context, one must remember that even though the persecution of homo-sexual men during National Socialist rule assumed specific characteristics, it was not a specific feature of National Socialism per se. Since 1871 homosexuality had been punishable under article 175 of the Penal code of the German Empire.[10] There was an efficiently functioning police and justice apparatus in the "Second Reich," as Nazi terminology called it. Thus the antihomosexual policy of the Nazis did not start from zero. Hitler, Himmler, and their companions neither had to work out a special program, nor invent a new law, nor install a new apparatus. The Nazis had to come to power in order to push through what they propagated before "seizure of power": the formation of society according to racist-nationalist (*völkisch*) ideals.

Fewer than twenty relevant regulations, secret commands, and special rules illustrate the Nazis' proceedings against homosexuals. Among these were a prohibition of bars and other sites where homosexuals might assemble and the proscription of certain types of magazines and books. There was a sharpening of penal sanctions (changes to article 175 of the Reich Penal code), the extension of the grounds for compulsory castration, the threat of capital punishment for members of the SS and police, and special regulations dealing with the Wehrmacht and the Hitler Youth.[11] If one attempts to categorize these measures over time, three rather discrete periods can be discerned:

The first phase extends from the "seizure of power" to 1935. It is characterized by the elimination of the institutions and associations that were active in the sexual reform movements, as well as by the first campaign against homosexuals, including an immense propaganda effort in 1934 after the so-called Röhm coup.[12] Terror directed against individuals by police and Gestapo, as well as other deliberately planned actions against homosexuals, their clubs, and their meeting places marked this phase. Finally, alteration of the criminal laws (reinforcement of article 175)[13] marked a definite break with the past.

The second phase lasted from 1935 to the beginning of the war. It was characterized by a significant increase in the number of persons arrested under article 175, the second antihomosexual campaign of the Third Reich, the demagogic so-called "Cloister Trials" of Catholic clerics.[14]

The third phase lasted from the beginning of the war until the collapse of the regime, and it extended physical terror, formally legalized deportations to concentration camps, introduced capital punishment in "especially severe cases," and increased efforts to introduce forced castration.

All of this seems to invite an interpretation of the Nazis' systematic proceedings as increasingly ferocious. Had that been the case, one might have expected that any planned extermination would have been prepared prior to 1939 and, at least partially, realized after 1939. However, looking at the statistics of sentences handed down under article 175, one detects a different tendency. It is true that the number of judgments rather drastically increased up to and during 1938. Afterwards, the records indicate a decrease.[15] The quantitative decline in the number of sentences clearly demonstrates that the proceedings were enforced with reduced determination. This development was influenced by a number of circumstances, mainly by the declining official interest in publicly highlighting the image of any considerable criminal disobedience. Faced with preparations for the war, they became more interested in mobilizing as many males as possible for the Wehrmacht. This actual, if not theoretical, reversal of their course probably also reflected a realization on the part of many officials that persecution had not successfully worked the desired "prevention." In addition, the focus of the Gestapo's responsibilities was redirected after 1938. Thereafter it was increasingly involved in preparation for the extermination of the Jewish people.

In connection with the thesis of the final solution of the homosexual question, evidence forces us to reject speculation that a special institution set up by Himmler in 1936 took a leading part in the persecution policy. The Reichszentrale zur Bekämpfung der Homosexualität und Abtreibung (Reich Office for Combating Homosexuality and Abortion) belonged to a system of fifteen central registration offices that had either been taken over from departments existing before 1933 or founded in 1936 during the course of the reorganization of the Criminal Police. Although its name can be associated with a centrally coordinated function, this institution essentially fulfilled registration requirements. These included recording personal data of convicted as well as suspect persons, registering transvestites and abortionists, and controlling the manufacture and sale of abortion and birth control items. Individual cases called for special operations by squads assigned by the Reichszentrale (e.g., in connection with the so-called Cloister Trials). There is no proof that the Berlin Reichszentrale specifically directed and planned the persecution of homosexuals. With a personnel force of only eighteen employees, that institution would not have been capable of doing such work.

In light of the previously listed measures, the regulations, secret commands, laws, and prohibitions, one can understand that the proceedings in this area were not carried out thoroughly. We can, however, discern a differentiated effort to deter the "homosexual minority" from their sexual practices. The purpose was to integrate them as heterosexuals into mainstream society, or failing that, to force them to do without sex. The main issue was to be "Umerziehung," or reeducation. In tandem, criminal law threatened drastically increased punishments. Together, these measures were supposed to deter homosexuals. Whoever would not respond was liable to deportation to a concentration camp "for reeducation through work." Even so-called incorrigibles, according to Himmler, could be used as workers to the advantage of the public, as long as they were castrated.

Consequently, the sexually active homosexuals who were "caught" were not all lumped together. Rather, the Nazis attempted to find punishments according to the "severity" of the act, punishments that would constitute an appropriate deterrent for the future. For this purpose, the Nazis ultimately devised homemade theories of homosexuality that divided homosexual men into "Hanghomosexuelle" (habitual homosexuals) and "Gelegenheitshomosexuelle" (opportunistic homosexuals), those who seduce and those who are seduced, and so on. "All these particular classifications had two characteristics in common," observed Rüdiger Lautmann, "a wide margin of discretion [in judging] the 'guilt' of a homosexual offender or for determining a sanction, and the assumption of curability is always present."[16]

Offenders who relapsed and those who seduced youngsters were subject to draconian punishments. Criminal records revealed that they were usually deported to concentration camps after serving their sentence.

Although only some homosexuals were physical victims of National Socialist persecution, the day-to-day life of every German homosexual during the Third Reich was deeply affected and influenced by the official repressive policies. Political officials and society together rejected homosexuality. No special forces could protest against the rigorous policies.

Homosexuals were not expected to resist. They were not safe from denunciation that might arise from heterosexual surroundings. Moreover, unlike socialists, communists, and the Jews, they were not able to form a more or less coherent subculture inside or outside the camps and were, therefore, left totally defenseless. Those who did not perish in the camps reacted by conforming to accepted patterns of public behavior. Homosexual men who were older than thirty got married in order to artificially balance their peculiarity with the behavior that society expected. The manner in which the repression and accommodation affected the interacting homosexual subcultures that still existed can be inferred (at least partially) from the trial records. In their behavior many men manifested a split identity.

To date, long-term effects, that is entrenched prejudice and its ongoing expressions after 1945, have generally not been explored. Moreover, we do not know how surviving gay men—and the majority did survive—have psychologically overcome that period and what the consequences were for their sexual identity. In any case, all homosexuals were victims, whether incarcerated in concentration camps, jailed, or untouched by persecution. In the end, the racist Nazi regime had a negative effect on all homosexuals.

NOTES

1. C. Hoffmann and E. Jesse, "Vergangenheitsbewältigung – ein sensibles Thema. Über Geschichtsbewusstsein und justizielle Aufarbeitung," *Neue politische Literatur* 32/3 (1987): 451.

2. The position of lesbian women has to be considered separately. Their situation in the Third Reich can only partly be described in terms of clear-cut criteria of persecution (for more details, see Claudia Schoppmann, *Nationalsozialistische Sexualpolitik und weibliche Homosexualität* (Pfaffenweiler, 1991).

3. D. Blasius, "Das Ende der Humanität. Psychiatrie und Krankenmord in der NS-Zeit," in *Der historische Ort des Nationalsozialismus,* ed. W. Pehle (Frankfurt/M., 1990), p. 52.

4. See, among others, H. G. Stümke and R. Finkler, *Rosa Winkel – Rosa Listen. Homosexuelle und "Gesundes Volksempfinden" von Auschwitz bis heute* (Reinbek, 1981); C. Goschler, *Wiedergutmachung: Westdeutschland und die Verfolgten des Nationalsozialismus (1945–1954)* (Munich, 1992); M. Sartorius, "'Wider Gutmachung' – Die versäumte Entschädigung der schwulen Opfer des Nationalsozialismus," in C. Schulz, *Paragraph 175 (abgewickelt). Homosexualität und Strafrecht im Nachkriegsdeutschland. Rechtsprechung, juristische Diskussion und Reformen seit 1945* (Hamburg, 1994), pp. 88–124.

5. See, for example, W. Harthauser, "Der Massenmord an Homosexuellen im Dritten Reich," in *Das Grosse Tabu,* ed. W.S. Schlegel (Munich, 1967); H. Heger, *The Men with the Pink Triangle* (Boston, 1980); R. Plant, *The Pink Triangle: The Nazis War against Homosexuals* (New York, 1986).

6. L. Crompton, "Gay Genocide: From Leviticus to Hitler," address delivered to Gay Academic Union, New York University, November 1974; F. Rector, *The Nazi Extermination of Homosexuals* (New York, 1981); M. Consoli, *Homocaust. Il nazismo e la persecuzione degli omosessuali* (Milan, 1991).

7. Heger, *Men with the Pink Triangle;* H. Grün, *Zur Situation der Homosexuellen in der Weimarer Republik und im Deutschen Faschismus. Frühlings-Erwachen. Beiträge zur sozialen und sexuellen Befreiung* (Hamburg, 1981).

8. There is much dispute about the numbers; see R. Lautmann, "The Pink Triangle," *Journal of Homosexuality* 6/1 (1981): 141–60; B. Jellonek and R. Lautmann, eds., *Wider das Vergessen. Die Verfolgung von Homosexuellen im Dritten Reich* (Paderborn, 1998).

9. B. Jellonnek, *Homosexuelle unter dem Hakenkreuz* (Paderborn, 1990), p. 219.

10. G. Bleibtreu-Ehrenberg, *Tabu Homosexualität. Die Geschichte eines Vorurteils* (Frankfurt/M., 1978).

11. F. Seidler, *Prostitution, Homosexualität, Selbstverstümmelung. Probleme der deutschen Sanitätsführung 1939–1945* (Neckargmünd, 1977).

12. M. Höhne, *Mordsache Röhm. Hitlers Durchbruch zur Alleinherrschaft 1933–1945* (Reinbek, 1984); O. Gritschneder, *"Der Führer hat Sie zum Tode verurteilt . . .". Hitlers "Röhm-Putsch" – Morde vor Gericht* (Munich, 1993).

13. The tougher provisions under article 175 were a) the amendment to the old version of 175. The concept of "unnatural sex acts" was replaced with the considerably broader one of "sex offense." The former had applied only to intercourse-like acts, a "sex offense" between men now designated any kind of self gratification in the presense of another man. An "offense" was also committed when the member of one male touched the body of another "with sexual intent"; and b) the introduction of a new article 175a. Abuse of a relation of dependence upon service or employment, sex acts with young people under twenty-one years of age, and homosexual prostitution were considered "serious sex offenses" and were punishable by up to ten years' penal servitude.

14. H. G. Hockerts, *Die Sittlichkeitsprozesse gegen katholische Ordensangehörige und Priester* (Mainz, 1971); U. von Hehl, *Priester unter Hitlers Terror. Eine biographische und statistische Erhebung*, Veröffentlichungen der Kommission für Zeitgeschichte, series A, source no. 37 (Mainz, 1984).

15. G. Grau, ed., *Hidden Holocaust? Gay and Lesbian Persecution in Germany 1933–1945* (London, 1995), p. 154.

16. R. Lautmann, "Categorization in Concentration Camps as a Collective Fate: A Comparison of Homosexuals, Jehovah's Witnesses and Political Prisoners," *Journal of Homosexuality* 19/1 (1990): 86.

25.

RÜDIGER LAUTMANN

The Pink Triangle

HOMOSEXUALS AS "ENEMIES OF THE STATE"

Initially I was tempted to give this essay a different title; I thought of calling it "Homocaust." And I still favor that artificial word. It is no mistake. I must, however, apologize for possibly seeming to abuse a concept as sacred as the Holocaust, but I would like to give some reasons for the neologism. Above all, a concept should not be so sacrosanct that it would be blasphemy to discuss it and to modify it.

To me "Holocaust" means a singular policy of genocide against the Jews and, additionally, against the Gypsies (the Roma and Sinti). The other victims of National Socialism have to be categorized and analyzed together under other headings, since there was never such a definite decision to exterminate them. My differentiation does *not* mean that these other victims should not be represented in museums and at conferences. On the contrary: we share the fate of having been the target of a Nazi declaration against their enemies. From all victim groups we have lost relatives and companions. We have lost cultures, traditions, and institutions. We have lost our collective identity—a loss from which Germany still suffers today.

Historical, sociological, and political accuracy demands that each of the victim groups be investigated in its specificity. For me there is no doubt that the fate of the European Jews is the central theme in this research. Victims who were defined by external racial features never had a chance to escape once they had been caught. The Nazis had formulated only one policy toward them: killing (and the Nazis themselves knew precisely that it was murder).

Similarity, Dissimilarity, Interdependence

If we now consider the other victims, there are several similarities and dissimilarities. What is similar is the confrontation with the entire cruelty of Nazi institutions, exercised through the mass media, social control, "deterrence," and segregation. In less abstract terms, there is the propaganda, the Gestapo, the camps. Then there is the similarity of being victims of the Nazis' firm intention to build a new society without the negative presence of democratic elements and of their definite program of coordination (i.e., Gleichschaltung) of all social life, according to the Nazi conception of society. Also similar are the ideological foundations of the politics of purification and leveling. There were racist biological reasons, too, for the persecution of homosexuals and so-called asocial individuals.

But there are several dissimilarities that allow, even call for, the separate analysis of each target group and of its specific fate and structure. The particularities of victimization relate mainly to the social character of the individuals declared to be the "enemy." To a lesser degree, the dissimilarities refer to the implementation of Nazi policies that condemned these groups to exclusion from the new society.

The persecution of homosexuals was aimed at preventing sexual behavior between men and men, not so much at the homosexual as a human being. Same-sex relations, precluding as they do biological reproduction, were antithetical to the demographic goals the Nazis had established for the German nation. In contrast, antisemitic persecution was aimed at the individual Jew in his or her totality. This may offer an initial explanation for the astonishing difference in the numbers of victims in the two groups.

Aryan and Jewish genes were to be prevented from any further mixing, yet Lesbians were encouraged to become mothers, and homosexual men were not disqualified from marriage and fatherhood. Whereas the homosexual population was to be integrated into the labor force and encouraged to participate in physical reproduction, the Jewish population was to be forbidden regeneration. The differences and similarities in the treatment of victim groups do not by any means constitute confusion and contradiction in Nazi policy. Rather, there is a structure of intermeshed coherence. The Nazi reordering of society sacrificed considerable segments of the German national population and culture. Such an inhuman policy proceeded in ways partly arbitrary, partly calculated, but always under the vague rationale of the Nazi program.

In Machiavellian terms, we may compare this situation to a game of chess. There is only one ultimate aim, and there are figures of graded importance. The king plays a symbolic role. The queen possesses the greatest weight. And so the adversary's queen is pursued with every effort. Nazi policy identified Jews as the most important target. By comparison, homosexuals had a minor rank, in this game perhaps the weight of a knight. In the struggle of black against white figures, of fascists against all other human beings, the figures on each side necessarily stood together. Thus, groups of the greatest cultural diversity found themselves part of a collective defense. All heterogeneity aside, these groups merged in the melting pot of collective Nazi hostility. The instruments of social coercion and ostracism were used against them indiscriminately.

There are many confirmations of this peculiar coalition, of the involuntary interdependence of the victim groups. For example, the instrument of the concentration camp was at first developed principally to segregate from mainstream society those perceived by the Nazis to be political and cultural enemies. Shortly after the beginning of the Nazi regime, in the spring of 1933, homosexuals sometimes constituted nearly 10 percent of the prisoners in the camps. After the beginning of World War II, the proportion sank to around one in one thousand.

There is another example of this interdependence of victim groups. According to Nazi propaganda, homosexuality was one of the evils the Jews had brought to the healthy Germanic race. The Nazis made the mistake of conflating the scientific study of sex as it related to gay subjects with the phenomenon of homosexuality itself. Some famous doctors of Jewish descent, especially Albert Moll and Magnus Hirschfeld, had written comprehensive books on homosexuality. Nevertheless, the first nineteenth-century studies of self-declared "men-loving-men"—from those by Graf August von Platen through those by Karl Heinrich Ulrichs—were carried out by non-Jewish Germans.[1] In the 1920s Jewish intellectuals were at least as critical of homosexuality as were others. It may be that their polemic was a bit more cautious, especially Sigmund Freud's, since these Jews had extensive experience of social prejudice.

The Pink Triangle in Statistics

My own empirical studies of the concentration camps began in 1976, when I read an article that touched me deeply: "About the Mass Murder of Homosexuals in the Third Reich." It had been written under a pseudonym in 1967 by the German journalist Reimar Lenz[2] but was still relatively unknown.

The search for more information led to the archives, where I hoped to discover the facts. With two students I spent several weeks at the International Tracing Service in Arolsen, Germany, which is the most important documentation center for individual data. The director and the archivists were a bit astonished when our crew appeared wanting to look for information about homosexual prisoners in the camps. But they knew that in the endless lists of those incarcerated, among Jews, political prisoners, criminals, and others, there was sometimes the term "homo" or "175er" (175 being the paragraph in the German penal code that since 1871 had criminalized male homosexual acts).

According to the experts at the International Tracing Service, pink triangles in more than insignificant numbers were to be found only in the concentration camps Buchenwald, Dachau, Flossenbürg, Mauthausen, Gross-Rosen, Mittelbau, Natzweiler, Neuengamme, Ravensbrück, Sachsenhausen, Stutthof, and a few of the earlier camps. So we made as complete a survey as was possible in the autumn of 1976 of all identifiable homosexual prisoners in Nazi concentration camps. In addition, we looked for memoirs of survivors, and some one hundred volumes, mainly by nonhomosexual authors, were reviewed. Finally, we communicated personally with a small number of surviving men who had worn the pink triangle.

The absolute number of prisoners who wore the pink triangle is uncertain: the reports of "several hundred thousand" that we sometimes encounter can be based only on supposition. Since the concentration camps were, in terms of their economy or administration, hardly run in a rational fashion, there was no unified system of documentation. The total number of inmates who wore the pink triangle will therefore never be fully ascertained, for the documentation on them was kept too unreliably. This was so in spite of the fact that the inmates were subjected to roll calls that often lasted for hours each day. To estimate figures, we consulted the head counts that were taken sporadically and that are now only partially preserved. They record the approximate number and categories of prisoners present on a given day. On the basis of forty such counts (from seven camps between 1938 and 1945 and, as far as possible, at three-month intervals), a tentative and imprecise estimate can be drawn.

The number of homosexual inmates incarcerated at any given moment in any given concentration camp varied (just as, e.g., the number of political prisoners also varied). At times there were only a few—sometimes fewer than ten—but very rarely were there none at all. At other times or in other camps, as many as a few hundred pink triangles were reported. The highest figures known to us at present are as follows: 150 in Dachau in March and September 1938, 194 in Buchenwald on January 2, 1945, and "a few hundred" in Neuengamme.

Conservatively interpreting the evidence uncovered to date, we may hazard the following estimates: immediately following the Nazi seizure of power, there were, at any given time, a total of several hundred homosexual prisoners in the concentration camps; later the figure would rise to around one thousand. On the whole, the number of officially defined homosexual prisoners incarcerated in the camps may have been about ten thousand (though the figure could be as low as five thousand or as high as fifteen thousand).

The total number of deaths in the concentration camps will never be entirely known. For several reasons there is a high rate of uncertainty about the fate of prisoners, and this is especially the case (28%) for the wearers of the pink triangle.

From the information that we could gather, the statistics are as follows: of the homosexual prisoners, 60 percent died, 26 percent were liberated, 13 percent were released, and 0.4 percent escaped. The death rate among homosexuals (60 percent) was nearly one and a half times that of political prisoners (41 percent) and Jehovah's Witnesses (35 percent).

There are some detailed reports concerning the greater probability of death for men wearing the pink triangle. These reports come from heterosexual inmates who had a wider perspective on conditions in the camps. Independent of each other, two authors report on Dachau: "The inmates with the pink triangle never lived long, they were exterminated by the SS with systematic swiftness"; and, "In general these unfortunate creatures did not survive long."[3]

In Sachsenhausen, E. Büge, a political prisoner who worked in the political section of the camp, kept a diary that has been preserved. For the period from April 1940 to June 1942 he records that 345 of the homosexual inmates died (with the frequency increasing yearly). The ultimate death toll is not known; on April 30, 1943, only six men were still alive. H. Lienau, another political prisoner, also reports: "The SS could count themselves satisfied if by nightfall a few of the 175ers had been picked off: but when in January 1943 the number of homosexuals eliminated in one day reached a total of twenty-four, the commandant's office became somewhat disquieted. A pause then ensued."[4]

Of the survival-threatening factors to which the inmates were subjected, the homosexual prisoner appears to have been particularly vulnerable to physical mistreatment by the surveillance personnel (SS and Kapos) and at times to the risk of transport.[5] The differing fates of the various categories of prisoners can be explained sociologically in terms of stratification in the camps and also in terms of social control.

The Social Career of the Homosexual Prisoner

The practice of sending homosexuals to concentration camps dated from immediately after the Nazi seizure of power and not, as is sometimes believed, from after the Röhm affair. Nevertheless, it was a measure that, by virtue of its sublegal nature, was initially applied not so much systematically as with exemplary stringency. In the first years of Nazi power, the police destroyed the most important institutions of homosexual subculture: raids were conducted on homosexual meeting places, especially the bars. Also, the homosexual individual was subjected to terror tactics that were meant to serve as an example. The organs of control formed a chain: police/Gestapo—penal court—prison—Gestapo—concentration camp (SS). The officially cited target groups of such antihomosexual measures were the potential "seducers" of minors and those already penalized as such. Neither of these two criteria were applied in a consistent fashion; "ordinary" homosexuals (i.e., of-age gays consorting with one another) were also prosecuted. The actual target was homosexuals as a group, primarily German homosexuals.

It is possible to view a concentration camp as potentially the purest type of total institution—one that drastically cuts off its inmates from the outside world and subjects them to a formalized routine. Guards oversee the prisoners' integration into the camp organization in accordance with the social status the new members are to assume: humiliation and brutality function as a degradation ceremony.

From the beginning of Nazi rule, homosexual prisoners in the camps had their own insignia, the pink triangle. This small piece of fabric fulfilled its prescribed symbolic function, in the words of one prisoner, by "forming with their colors the walls that separated the prisoners from one another." Yet one must guard against the frequently repeated generalization that all homosexual prisoners were constantly treated in a manner worse than that of their fellow prisoners. Even without such sweeping statements, it can be assumed that as a category the homosexuals in the camps (as in the entire social structure) had a special status. This status cannot, however, be described in negatives or superlatives; that would not only mean being blind to the suffering of other camp prisoners but would prevent a sociologically adequate understanding of the phenomenon of the pink triangle.

The social integration of the pink triangle wearers into the partial society of the camp was neither without difficulty nor was it completely nonexistent. Whether or not the necessity of entering into a relationship with fellow prisoners as well as among themselves was perceived, it was a precarious matter: How could homosexuals arrive at the solidarity that was a prerequisite for survival? Any form of mutual contact would raise suspicion as to sexual intent, as illogical as this might seem in general. The homosexual in the outside world might have been able to bear derision and contempt as a price to be paid for his deviant status; in the camp, however, the transition from moral degradation to physical aggression knew no limits, and there was no relief in knowing one's status was shared.

Work—surely the most crucial part of life in the camps—with few exceptions taxed the prisoners of all categories the hardest. A number of reports mention that pink triangle prisoners were from time to time assigned to the most strenuous work details (e.g., the gravel pits of Dachau from 1934 to 1936, and the underground V-2 works in Nordhausen in the winter of 1943/44). Homosexual prisoners were probably physically less well-equipped for hard manual labor than their fellow prisoners, since a higher proportion of them came from white-collar professions. Proportionally fewer homosexuals entered the camps from manual occupations which, given the operative selection criteria, reduced from the outset their chances of survival. What the SS was primarily looking for were manual workers, while intellectuals, or those who had the appearance of being intellectuals, soon found themselves in a position on the precarious fringe. It was exactly what homosexuals had endeavored to do in daily life—neutralize the stigma imposed on them through education and the pursuit of desk jobs—that betrayed them in the concentration camps. In this process, one can see something of the fate that awaits purely individual adaptation as a behavioral strategy in the face of social injustice.

Work was an area of constant confrontation with the SS. This leads us to one phenomenon relating to the pink triangle that is closed to any balanced analysis, be it of a descriptive or analytical nature, because our powers of empathy and imagination must, of necessity, fail. It is no doubt impossible, except in a fashion that panders to latent sadism, to come to terms with the physical terror inherent in the concentration camp surveillance system. The omnipresence of an aggression against which the prisoner had no defense has already been noted at other stages in a prisoner's career: arrival and integration in camp society, living conditions and status, and work conditions. One of the two forms in which violence at its most brutal was visited upon the prisoner was arbitrariness.

The second form of violence appeared as "procedure," that is, in the form of exemplary punishments that were meted out with inhuman severity. The number of isolated reports of brutality against homosexuals—high in relation to the number of pink triangle prisoners—indicates that this category of prisoner, at least from time to time, was particularly susceptible to these additional punishments. The phenomenon of homosexuality must have been an ideological provocation of strongly conflict-laden intensity for many SS personnel. This conflict, which was made an issue in the question of the continued existence of National Socialist supremacy, was somewhat defused at higher levels of the SS hierarchy by antihomosexual administrative measures, such as incarceration in the camp, while for the lower levels it was dealt with in the form of individualized terror.

Homosexual prisoners were exposed to all these deadly factors to at least the same degree as those in comparable prisoner categories. Their position was exacerbated in the sense that, as wearers of the pink triangle, they were not fully integrated into the "camp community" (to the extent that this was ever possible at all). Nor were they, as a group, able to reach the essential level of solidarity and cohesion. The degree of their social integration, as earlier touched upon, remained far behind that of other groups, with the possible exception of the "antisocials." Much has been written about the solidarity of the green and red triangle groups (the "criminals" and the political prisoners); there is much to be admired in the reports of solidarity among the Jehovah's Witnesses. For the homosexuals—since their special status forbade it— it remained impossible to form a group of even approximately comparable cohesion. Because they lacked the ability to form an organization capable of dealing with conflicts they remained individually isolated. Since they had no special advantages to trade on, they were in general separated from the system of barter and exchange so necessary for survival in the camps. And part of the mechanism of victimization through individual isolation was the lack of external integration, that is, contact with the outside world in the form of communication with family or friends. Prisoners who could not document their contacts with the world at large through letters, food packets, or the like, were particularly vulnerable to being scapegoated by the SS.

Not all homosexual prisoners perished in the camps, although in terms of percentages they did so more frequently than the prisoners in the green and red triangle groups. But comparison of prisoner groups would border on the inhumane if it were conducted as a numbers game or with an eye toward demonstrating some sort of moral superiority resulting from a higher percentage of the severely persecuted. Indeed, as seen against the background of the terrible number of dead in the concentration camps, and viewed as a whole, the number of dead among homosexuals and Jehovah's Witnesses remains proportionally small. What remains indisputable is that the deaths of homosexuals in the concentration camps are a direct consequence, indeed a reflection, of their social situation in Nazi Germany.

Social Stratification in the Concentration Camps

The concentration camp as an institution can be described structurally in terms of its social stratification. Its members had varying degrees of access to influence and chances for life. This resulted in differentiation, a hierarchy among the members based on the degree of participation in power (here, the possibility of exercising physical violence oneself or of dictating terms to others), money, food, shelter, work conditions, time off, and prestige.

The social stratification approach reveals its flexibility and usefulness in the analysis of social structures that are not based primarily on production. The concentration camp is an example of such a social structure. Little has been written on social stratification within the camps; most frequently one encounters analyses of the position and function of the concentration camp within the political and economic system of the Third Reich. Such analyses are surely indispensable, but of themselves they do not adequately explain prisoners' lives and deaths.

Access to the goods and services shaping daily life in the camps was greater for one, lesser for another. This applied not only to the SS in the camps (whose internal relations are not of interest here), it was also the case—in a drastic fashion—for the mass of prisoners. Their resemblance to one another was only partial in the sense that all were behind barbed wire and subject to the whims of the SS. The resemblances cease when one studies their chances to preserve health and life—chances that were directly affected by their social status within the camp. The prisoners' possibilities for dealing with their basic situation can be seen as distributed along hierarchically ordered lines that form part of a pyramid.

At the top of the pyramid were the SS officers who directed the camps; below them were the surveillance officers of the SS, block leaders and security guards of various ranks, even the lowest designated as some sort of "Führer." Below them but, in terms of influence, with certain privileges comparable to those of the lower-ranking surveillance personnel, were the camp "VIPs": camp elders, Kapos who administered a work roster; clothing issue, mail room, kitchen, and infirmary supervisors; a few favored block elders; Kapos of certain work stations and work squads; as well as all personal favorites, such as officers' lackeys and the like. The "middle class" of prisoners consisted of other Kapos, foremen, plant workers, lower-level clerks, and infirmary personnel. Until the overcrowding of the camps this group formed about a quarter of all prisoners. The "masses" of prisoners, without any privileges whatsoever, were comparable to the lower classes in larger social systems. And finally, the "musselmen," that is, prisoners who had withered to skeletal proportions and who had sunk into complete apathy, occupying the place otherwise reserved for outcasts and those with no standing at all.

How the individual prisoner attained his social position in the camp, that is, the process of placement, depended on several factors: a) initiative and input of the affected individual; b) intermediaries who watched out for the interests of the individual; c) agencies that determined the placement of the individual at this or that level; and d) selection mechanisms on the social levels at which placement was attempted.

How all these mechanisms operated so that in the end, every individual occupied a definite social position, depended on the particular social context. In the concentration camp, the number of operative placement agencies was drastically reduced: the directives of the SS administration and the recommendations of the camp VIPs were what counted. Influence from the outside was probably quite rare. Above all, two selection criteria seem to have been operative: the prestige of the color of the triangle on the one hand, and the individual ability to fight for one's personal interests under conditions of *homo-homini-lupus* (survival of the fittest) on the other.

The status that devolved to the wearers of triangles was not always consistent, for it differed from camp to camp and from period to period. Nevertheless, those who were generally on top were the wearers of red and green triangles, that is, political and criminal prisoners. The lowest rank was always occupied by those who wore the yellow triangles, the Jews. Above them, wearers of black triangles (antisocials) were potentially in a worse position, wearers of violet triangles (Jehovah's Witnesses) potentially in a better position. Further differentiation would require more study, as does the fact that the color of the triangle occasionally made no difference in the way a prisoner fared.

The status of the pink triangle was in all the camps clearly negative, always below the red, green, and violet triangles. Even the black and brown triangles (Gypsies) were relatively better off, as the few reports seem to confirm. But again, at the absolute bottom of the hierarchy came the yellow triangles, at least to the extent that they were not supplemented by a pink one.

The value scale of the triangles reflects the ideological priorities of the SS, which on the surface were not much different from the priorities of the prisoners. The partial similarities in the positive or negative assessments of the SS and a majority of the prisoners made triangle color a highly effective agent of social placement. The result was a stratification of prisoners from top to bottom, which assured the efficient functioning of the "divide and rule" principle known from the power structure of the outside world.

The prisoners with the pink triangle were burdened with the general stigmatization of homosexuality; this reduced from the outset their influence on the internal communication and power structures of the camps. As social outsiders, they were only minimally capable of interaction and cooperation. The individualistic, as opposed to collective, strategy of seeing to their own interests, which was already imposed on them in the outside world, could work only further against them in the camps.

Political Background of Antihomosexual Persecution

The persecution of homosexuals has never been a matter of personal antipathy or even collective idiosyncrasy; it must be seen in its political context. The incarceration and liquidation of homosexual men in Nazi concentration camps cannot be regarded as a historical accident. Homophobia seems to be connected intrinsically with fascist government, as is illustrated by all comparable instances in Europe and Latin America. Antihomosexuality in its ideological and administrative practice assures essential features of fascist society: namely, exclusive domination by male groups and the general repression of women. Homophobia preserves these structures against dissolution by behavior-transgressing sex roles, protects them against cognitive and effectual criticism, and stabilizes the Führer hierarchy as well as the relative resilience of fascist power.

This tendency was directed toward males: female homosexuality, and feminist issues in general, were not deemed to be of any importance. In Nazi Germany, homosexuals were defined as "enemies of the state," in consonance with the Nazis view of everyone as either a friend or enemy of their political system.

At least officially, the National Socialists advocated the conventional virtues of moderation and sexual "normality," and they ensured practice of them through numerous sanctions and campaigns. Where expansionism and militarism were taken for granted, violence and war were glorified: the ideal person was strong in mind, body, and deed. In contrast, homosexual men were deemed soft and spineless. For all the truth or untruth of this characterization, fascists were obliged to see in homosexuals the incorporation of certain qualities and behavior, patterns that could be identified and combatted as diametrically opposed to their own ideals of ruthless struggle, moral tenaciousness and patriotic anti-individualism.

Fascist ideology forms the basis for moral totalitarianism, so well expressed in Mussolini's words: "There is no act which escapes moral judgment. . . . This is why life, as the Fascist understands it, is serious, hard, religious."[6] There is no room for homosexuals in this philosophical edifice: female homosexuality is simply not taken seriously, it is brushed aside because of a compulsion to breed children. Gay men, as they are defined—soft and capricious—and as they are—beyond the authorized bounds of sexuality—are explicitly repressed. Fascist ideology holds homosexual desire in the same contempt as other attempts at personal emancipation; the political platform of the NSDAP called for combatting homosexuality, and it did so *before* the Nazi seizure of power.

The final solution of the homosexual problem was not thought to be a biological one. Not even the Nazis had any of the presently fashionable assumptions concerning homosexual genes, homosexual brains, and the like. The Nazis' answer to the problem was a sociocultural one. In this sense it was quite modern. They ignored the Stalinist option: the Soviet Union denied the possibility of homosexuality in the progressive socialist state. Nazi Germany recognized the occurrence of homosexuality and tried to suppress its manifestations. The function of the pink triangle was to make homosexual men abstain from fulfilling their erotic needs.

The true addressees of the pink triangle were homosexual men and women outside the camps. They were required to renounce their desires. Since it was difficult, if not impossible, to catch them all, individual prisoners were used as an instrument to change the behavior of the homosexual population. The political challenge of same-sex love was answered by educational, that is, cultural means—individual correction and general prevention.

Daily Life of Homosexual Men under National Socialism

Fascism completely controlled the conditions of daily life for homosexuals. If the Weimar Republic had represented a high-water mark for tolerance toward homosexual women and men, matters changed quickly in the opposite direction after the Nazi seizure of power. The relationship between death in the camps and life in so-called free society is an area for further investigation.

My research as presented in this chapter is based solely on qualitative material from fifteen interviews, conducted around 1980. In some cases the interviews were conducted during casual, unstructured conversations lasting several hours; in others, the answers were written responses to a printed questionnaire. The interviews were conducted with gay men who survived the Third Reich, some of them after detention in a concentration camp. None of the interviewees were women, since I had no access to lesbians of this generation.

After a few interviews the results were clear enough: no stereotypical notion of "The Homosexual" can be accurate, nor is there any proof that "one route" was taken by all these men. I have written about further details of careers, politics, subculture, collective identity, love, and sexuality in another article.[7]

It would be an all too simple rendering of historical complexities to attribute all the reductions observed in the biographies of the men interviewed solely to National Socialism. That the Hitler regime radically persecuted homosexual men and women and brutally interfered in their lives is a fact as sure as that Hitler was able to seize power only because certain economic, political, and ideological conditions favored it. Antihomosexual tendencies existed before the advent of fascist dominance—kept in check, to be sure, by democratic institutions and by the developing self-organization of homosexuals. The long-standing antihomosexual tendencies in society made their contribution to the rise of fascism.

Under the Nazi regime, homosexuals were cut off from opportunities for personal development, but not exclusively by agencies of the state or the party. Close ties to family and church significantly restricted these men as well, indeed far more than is reported today by people of a comparable age group. "I'm religiously minded, [and] the Bible says: 'woe unto the perverters of youth'" was the comment of H.T. "At the time I was laboring under strong religious illusions and vowed to remain chaste. I kept that up for about three months," said E.C. in reporting on the year 1929. Many of the interviewees—the sample may be a random one—found themselves bound to religion and the church, for example, as members of orders or as students of theology, and this retarded their coming-out process. Contacts with one's family of origin similarly demanded special loyalties. "I didn't want to cause my parents and relatives any shame. I knew how my mother felt about things—for example, from the way she read newspaper reports and got worked up about them. A so-called good reputation was all-important to her. All my relatives, parents, etc., knew nothing. A whole world would have collapsed" (H.T.). A similar duty to consider others has always existed; today, for the first time, it can slowly be dismantled by an appeal to a central core of social feeling and moral decency. Fascism, with its reactionary appeal to the established institutions of obedience, strengthened the sense of duty on a broad level and made innovative behavior in the face of traditional morality even more difficult and improbable than it already was (and still is).

To be sure: most of the interviewees didn't describe the period of the Third Reich as a historically isolated period. Their recollections integrate those years into their life histories. The milestones in their lives are not so much the 30th of January 1933 as the experience of unemployment, not so much the 8th of May 1945 as the experience of being a prisoner of war.

Nevertheless, there is a clear impression of the difference between the Weimar Republic and the Hitler era: "[In the former period] they sort of let us go our own way, there was no great danger. [The peril] arose after '33. After the Röhm Putsch you were actually in mortal danger" (H.Hu.); "Up to 1933 everything was permitted, open: you could dance in the bars, cruise the cottages. I had a mad time" (E.C.). In 1933 this interviewee fled temporarily to France. The tangible progressive development during the Weimar Republic, with its encouraging consequences for the forms of personal, contractual, and social organization, came to an abrupt end. Also abruptly terminated, for years that would extend far beyond 1945, were the development of forms of social behavior by homosexuals among themselves; the development and opening-up of a homosexual subculture; and self-organization and political articulation within the homosexual movement.

The specifically National Socialist sanctions against homosexual men—court-imposed prison sentences at the slightest manifestation of such sexual orientation, often followed by arbitrarily imposed concentration camp sentences—were brought against many thousands of men, to be sure, but they represented only a minority among the homosexuals of the time. For all that, terror was widespread: "Everybody knew that you landed in a concentration camp after sitting out your legal sentence" (R.B.); "The men with the pink triangle—we knew all about that then. Only a few made it out alive, a very few. . . . I knew about Oranienburg at the time, [but] not from first-hand experience; Berlin was full of rumors" (Wil.). Fear became the dominant mode. Many of the interviewees report suicides within their circle of acquaintances; one tells of the suicide of his lover (W.D.).

The potential sanctions affected those involved on all levels: "Even without having been in a concentration camp, the numerous pin-pricks dealt out by those in power in the Thousand Year Reich, as well as the pangs of conscience, could destroy a person physically and psychically, driving one indeed to despair" (B.R.). Since social stigmatization belongs to the group consciousness of homosexuals as the result of uninterrupted historical experience, most were able to adapt quickly to renewed repression. The renewed traditional response included chastity, denying oneself relationships, strict control over what information about oneself was made available to others, as well as a normalization of one's own conduct and previous experience. The main strategy became one of survival, a strategy that defined all central activities.

The more homosexuality became one's chief status in the eyes of the world at large—the sole characteristic defining what a person was—the less homosexual activity could be valued in the life of the individual. At that time, much less than today, it could be a question of homosexuality as a major moving force in one's life. To save their own skin, many took recourse to escapism, looked for the meaning of life and psychic feedback in substitute endeavors: one in music, another in literature, a whole set in the founding of a family: "I've played the 'normal' person until today, have a wonderful wife whom I don't want to compromise" (Wil.); "I live in the world of music" (H.T.); "Sometimes I ask myself what's the most important thing for me— is it music, literature, or is it the sexual? I've never been able to decide" (E.C.). But the pressure to retreat was the least damage that fascism did to homosexuals.

The Liberation: 1945 and After

On June 29, 1956, the Reparations Act for Those Persecuted under National Socialism was made law in the Federal Republic of Germany. Under the provisions of this law, some 50 million marks had been distributed by the mid-1970s.

The German word for the legal principle behind the Reparations Act, "Wieder-gutmachung," suggests literally "a setting things right." This sounds idealistic enough. But under the provisions of the law, "those persecuted" are those whose persecution was for "political opposition to National Socialism or for racial, religious or philosophical reasons." In fact, the law says nothing about the principally illegal nature of all referrals to the concentration camps: it excludes "nonpolitical" catego-ries such as Gypsies, homosexuals, criminals, antisocial elements, and those "who were persecuted for security reasons" (a not insubstantial group, according to some experts). Individuals who fall into the category of the "nonpolitically" persecuted have remained essentially without rehabilitation or compensation.

The Reparations Act hardly did justice to the social reality of the National Socialist system because its narrow definition of the "political" extended only to active, conscious opposition and religious or racial discrimination. For this reason, only part of the number of cases that the Nazi regime itself defined as arising from "opposition" have been accounted for: excluded were those in which latent resistance to the regime consisted of deeds of direct human solidarity, emotional revolt, or opinions or acts that clashed with the Nazi definition of "security."

Those persecuted for "nonpolitical" reasons were of course not always conscious members of the resistance; but they were nonetheless people whose rights to freedom, health, and life were brutally interfered with by the National Socialist regime. The persecution of this relatively large number of people none of whose names are particularly prominent, has never before been thought of as a problem for historians. Perhaps this is because the level of consciousness enjoyed by most historians is a reflection of the public opinion represented by the Reparations Act and narrow definition of political persecution.

It would be interesting to double-check the records of reparations payments to see whether errors were ever made in the assignment of the "nonpolitical" category to the possible enemies of the state. After all, the SS sometimes did act arbitrarily in assigning people to these categories. Could it be that such errors have been rectified and that "members of the nonpolitical opposition" have been reclassified so as to be eligible for compensation? For so-called criminal and antisocial elements there are a very few such cases. But for the group classified as homosexuals there has never even been any point in filing an appeal; they are totally absent from the files.

Just as the stigmatization of homosexuals by no means came to an end, rehabilitation for injuries suffered, even for concentration camp sentences, never took place. Those who were so bold as to apply officially for compensation were unsuccessful. Hz.H.'s application for official compensation in Austria was denied. Our interviewee B.R., himself never arrested, "knows that claims were put forward for compensation on the basis of damage done to personal health, which were all rejected with the reasoning that Paragraph 175 had existed at the time, and the sentence passed was therefore perfectly legal." A decision handed down in this way must have discouraged those affected from fighting through to a successful outcome their morally and legally justifiable claims. One source did not know of a single applicant during his fifteen years as an official at the War Reparations Office in North Hesse.[8] Whereas the War Reparations Law came to apply to more and more categories of the persecuted in the course of time, homosexuals remained ignored; the tightening of the laws under fascism was viewed as being "not typical of National Socialism"; homosexuals remained common criminals.

This was the situation for the first twenty-five years of post-Hitler Germany. Things changed during the following two decades. The Gay Liberation Movement adopted the pink triangle as a symbol with which to fight repression. And for some years there have been public funds to help the surviving members of victim groups formerly ignored by the Reparations Law. Those funds pay a moderate sum if a former camp prisoner is living in poverty. Only a very small number of survivors are entitled to claim this help. On the whole, this was a modest step in the right direction, but it has come too late. Moreover it is restricted to individuals. A policy of collective rehabilitation has not yet been formulated.[9]

NOTES

1. See the important book by Klaus Müller, *Aber in meinem Herzen sprach eine Stimme laut*, published by Verlag Rosa Winkel (Berlin, 1991).

2. Wolfgang Harthauser, "Der Massenmord an Homosexuellen im Dritten Reich," in *Das grosse Tabu*, ed. Willhart S. Schlegel (Munich, 1967), pp. 7–37.

3. R. Schnabel, *Die Frommen in der Hölle* (Frankfurt/M., 1966), p. 53; P. Berben, *Histoire du camp de concentration de Dachau* (Brussels, 1968), p. 19.

4. Heinrich Lienau, *Zwölf Jahre Nacht* (Flensburg, 1949), p. 70.

5. For more details, see Rüdiger Lautmann, "The Pink Triangle," in *Historical Perspectives on Homosexuality*, ed. Salvatore J. Licata and Robert P. Petersen (New York, 1981), pp. 141–60.

6. Quoted in *Theorien über den Faschismus*, ed. Ernst Nolte (Cologne, 1967), p. 206.

7. See Rüdiger Lautmann, "Hauptdevise: Bloss nicht anecken," in *Terror und Hoffnung in Deutschland 1933–1945*, ed. Johannes Beck et al. (Reinbek, 1980), pp. 366–90. English translation available from the author.

8. Letter of Max Mayr (December 28, 1975).

9. For further details see Burkhard Jellonek and Rüdiger Lautmann, eds., *Wider das Vergessen. Die Verfolgung von Homosexuellen im Dritten Reich* (Paderborn, 1998).

26.

ROBERT KESTING

The Black Experience during
the Holocaust

Much has been written about the millions of Jews and the large numbers of others who were persecuted and murdered during the Holocaust, but little has been written about how blacks fared at the hands of the Nazis in Europe, partly no doubt because their numbers were so much smaller. Nevertheless, evidence clearly reveals that a number of African Germans and, later, African Americans and other blacks, were brutally treated.

The fate of these black people ranged from isolation to persecution, sterilization, medical experimentation, torture, and murder. Their stories have been documented in war crimes investigations, archives, and libraries in the United States and foreign countries, and in the testimony of African American witnesses.

In one respect, the Nazis had no need to treat black people the way they treated Jews. No special identification badges were required because the race of the blacks was obvious. As prewar prisoners, concentration camp prisoners, and prisoners of war (POWs), blacks and part blacks (mulattoes) experienced varying degrees of racism. Even in internment camps, black people were commonly set apart. Black people who were arrested by the Gestapo and SS were often tortured or murdered. However, there was no plan for a Final Solution per se. The Nazis felt that the bureaucratic system could encourage most blacks to leave the country, or isolate those who remained.

German Racism

Pre–World War I Germany saw the rise to prominence of social-Darwinism, anthropology, eugenics, and human genetics. Dr. Eugen Fischer was an anatomist and anthropologist who served as the Director of the Kaiser Wilhelm Institute of Anthropology in Berlin-Dahlem from 1927 to 1942 and later became judge on the Superior Genetic Health Court under the Nazi Regime. In 1908, Fischer left on an expedition to study the German colony of Southwest Africa, in particular the so-called Rehoboth Bastards, who were descendants of Boers and Nama ("Hottentots").

His published report of 1913, "The Political Importance of the Bastard" (the 1961 reprint excludes the final chapter), concluded "Negroes, Hottentots and many others are inferior . . . but should be protected as long as they serve [German] needs."[1]

None of this was to be, however. In 1915 the Allies stripped Germany of its colonies. As a result, many among the colonial population, including some interracial couples and their offspring, left those territories for Germany. Some of the most committed racists among them joined the Freikorps, right-wing paramilitary societies that combatted the communists and attacked liberal democracy in postwar Germany. This movement expressed the racism of the Alldeutscher Verband and the Deutscher Bund (right-wing pan-German organizations) and developed an ideology calling for the persecution of blacks.[2] No doubt this ideology influenced those members who later became Nazis.

Following the treaty of Versailles and Allied occupation of the Rhineland, the presence of African colonial troops stimulated racist sentiment. The German state backed racist propaganda depicting African soldiers as rapists of German women and carriers of venereal and other diseases. "Rhineland Bastards," the offspring of these soldiers and German girlfriends or prostitutes, were treated as a threat to the purity of the Germanic race. British occupation authorities endorsed this agitation, concerned that images of black troops ordering whites about at gunpoint might find their way into its own overseas territories, calling into question the "naturalness" of European rule. The Weimar press preceded that of the Nazis in inflaming racism, particularly against mulatto children and their German mothers, but it remained for Hitler to charge in *Mein Kampf* that the "Jews had brought the negroes into the Rhineland with the clear aim of ruining the hated white race by the necessarily resulting bastardization."[3] A January 14, 1933, Jehovah's Witnesses periodical observed—two weeks before Hitler came to power—that "if Negroes were as numerous and progressive in Germany as the Jews, then the Hitlerites would direct their shafts against the negroid race."[4]

But the Nazis were more interested in Africans for purposes of exploitation than genocide. In 1945 Dr. Ernst Rodenwaldt, who in 1940 had been Director of the Institute for Tropical Diseases in Berlin, and who was an "expert" on "Negermischlinge" (mulattoes) in the former German colony of Togo, rendered a report to U.S. Army Intelligence. There had been, he said, a "Negro" prisoner-of-war camp near Stargard; medical experiments had been performed on the captives. The data gathered were used to prepare German officials selected for work in the tropics (some were to go to Cameroon) after the war.

Fischer and other Nazi eugenicists performed medical experiments on blacks, as they did on members of other minority groups. On July 20, 1942, for example, Dr. Ernst Grawitz, SS Chief Physician, reported to Heinrich Himmler that racial blood testing had been performed by Dr. Fischer on the serums of "whites and blacks" in 1938. Perhaps some of the test subjects were Rhineland Bastards, or African Germans. Fischer had performed the same tests on Gypsies and had scheduled similar tests for Jewish inmates at Sachsenhausen in 1942. Grawitz reported that Dr. Horneck, an SS physician who had conducted experiments on negro POWs in France, had achieved similar results. Apparently, the experiments concerned white adaptation to tropical environments.[5] Unfortunately, a 122-page report containing detailed information became detached and is now missing. We do know, however, that part of the plan was for each company of the German occupation troops to have special equipment and a doctor specializing in tropical diseases.[6]

The documentation we do have offers a glimpse of the Nazi plan for "Mittel-Afrika" in their "Grossgermanisches Reich." The MittelAfrika plan called for exploitation of Africa's resources to bolster Germany. The Nazis planned to reconquer the German colonies lost in 1915, add other African territories, resettle or enslave the natives, expropriate African property and land, form a police state under Heinrich Himmler's direction, and adapt the Nuremberg Laws of 1935 for colonial conditions.[7] A Reich and Prussian Ministry of Interior Circular of November 26, 1935, had already included the prohibition of marriages between blacks and whites in Africa. Following passage of the Nuremberg racial laws, commentary recommended blacks as a racially distinctive minority with "alien blood."[8]

On June 20, 1939, Fischer indicated something about the Nazi scheme of things when he stated, "I do not categorize every Jew as inferior, as [are] Negroes, and [thus] do not underestimate the greatest enemy with whom we have to fight."[9] But if blacks were not for Fischer the greatest threat to the "Aryan" race, and though he did allow for some overlap with the Jews, he nonetheless relegated Africans to the lowest anthropological stratum within the world order his party planned.

Persecution

Fortunately, the European black population was small compared to that of the Jews and Gypsies in the period leading up to the Holocaust.[10] But despite their small numbers, even under the Weimar Republic, many Germans considered them a threat to the purity of German blood.

In 1927, the Bavarian Ministry of the Interior recommended sterilization of the Rhineland Bastards, but the suggestion was turned down at Reich level because of the demoralizing effects upon the children's German mothers. In 1933, Dr. Hans Macco published a pamphlet entitled "Racial Problems in the Third Reich," advocating eradication of the "black curse" by sterilization. On April 13, 1933, Hermann Göring, Minister of the Interior of Prussia, ordered a study in Düsseldorf, Cologne, Koblenz, and Aachen to provide accurate statistics on Rhineland Bastards. The material collected was sent to Dr. Wilhelm Abel at the Kaiser Wilhelm Institute of Anthropology; after reviewing the data, Abel appealed to those "in whose hands it lies to prevent their reproducing." By 1937 hundreds of Rhineland mulatto children had been taken into custody by the Gestapo under secret orders. Ultimately, doctors Fischer, Abel, and Heinrich Schade were instrumental in sterilizations and disappearances of, and medical experiments performed on, the children.[11]

Other African German mulatto children were victimized by the Nazi bureaucratic system. Upon completion of their mandatory education, they were ostracized from National Socialist society. Racial discrimination prohibited them from seeking employment, welfare, or housing. They were not allowed to pursue higher education. In 1936, an official of the German Municipal League (*Deutscher Gemeindetag*) in Königsberg sought guidance from other local league officials and from the main office in Berlin about how to resolve the case of "Tom" (last name unknown), a fifteen-year-old mulatto. According to the official, Tom was unable to get a job, and even official efforts to find work for the young man had proven useless because of racial discrimination practiced by employers. He concluded by stating that Tom had been driven to a life of crime.

In 1939 he finally received a reply from Berlin containing an opinion from the Prussian Ministry of the Interior. The letter told him to handle the situation as he saw fit, since the insignificant number of mulattoes did not warrant laws or official guidelines. Other correspondence in the German Municipal League's files contains similar guidance.[12] Not all African Germans, however, were driven to crime.

Repression

Hilarius (Lari) Gilges, an African German dancer who suffered much from the racism of white Germans, joined the KJVD (German Communist Youth League) in 1926. As a performer he founded the leftist actors group "Nordwest Ran," which organized a number of anti-Nazi demonstrations. In 1931, during a labor demonstration, he was arrested and imprisoned for a year. After release he continued agitating against the Nazis. He was arrested by the Gestapo on June 20, 1933, and his body was found under a bridge in Düsseldorf the next day. One of his alleged killers was Karl Wüsthoff, a member of the SS.[13] It was racism that led to Gilges' death: white communists and social democrats (including Jews) were being incarcerated but, at that time, not necessarily killed.

While Joe Lewis, Jesse Owens, Ralph Metcaff, and other black athletes achieved success and fame, thus contradicting Nazi racial propaganda,[14] black entertainers suffered under the Nazis. "Niggerjazz" musicians in Germany and in some of the German occupied territories were denounced in racial propaganda and subjected to discrimination, persecution, and, later, incarceration in the Falkensee concentration camp in Czechoslovakia. In 1943, Valaida Snow, a black female jazz musician, was reportedly jailed in Denmark and Germany by the Nazis.[15]

The Nazi fear of blacks also extended into the ghettos of Poland and other occupied territories. A report in *The Chronicle of the Lodz Ghetto* states that in 1942, members of Precinct VI of the German Gendarmerie inquired whether there were any "Negroes" or mulattoes in the ghetto. The chairman reported that there were no Negroes in there.[16] Perhaps they were looking for black musicians or escaped prisoners of war. Meanwhile, at a conference in 1942, Robert Wagner, Gauleiter of Alsace, announced a policy of expulsion [deportations], which included "Negroes and colored hybrids."[17] Other evidence indicates non-German blacks were incarcerated in internment camps by the Nazis.

The Camps

On April 14, 1942, Josef John Nassy, a mulatto artist born in Surinam (Dutch Guiana) who possessed a counterfeit American passport, was arrested and incarcerated in Beverloo prison (which also served as a transit camp) in Belgium. In November 1942, he was transferred to Internment Lager (Ilag) VII at Laufen, Germany. The camp population consisted of fifty Jews, twelve blacks, and an assortment of white Americans and British nationals. The Jews came from Eastern Europe, while the blacks claimed various nationalities. Despite the common predicament of black and white prisoners, the two groups were segregated in separate barracks. The landscapes and portraits Nassy painted at Laufen will serve as a lasting testament to an otherwise untold story.[18]

Other blacks were incarcerated in Nazi concentration camps. According to a Norwegian survivor of the Grini camp near Oslo, Norway, a negro from South Africa entered the camp with him in 1943. The camp commandant was surprised to see a black "Norwegian."[19] Jean [Johnny] Marcel Nicolas, a Haitian Creole, was arrested by the Gestapo in Paris and charged with collaborating with the French resistance. In 1943, he was sent to Fresnes prison, and soon he was transferred to Royallieu concentration camp near Paris. On January 1, 1944, Nicolas was registered at Buchenwald and was given the number 44451. He was recorded as a "USA"/"H" Haitian. On October 28, 1944, he was transferred to Dora, later Mittelbau. Nicolas was next transferred to the subcamp Rottleberode. Survivor testimonies confirm his attending to the physical maladies of Jewish slave laborers and providing them with forms excusing them from work details. Jewish survivors referred to Nicolas as a "doctor."

On April 4, 1945, approximately 2,000 inmates were marched from Rottleberode to Niedersachswerfen, Germany. The inmates then embarked on two trains ostensibly for another camp. Nicolas was reportedly on one of these trains. After an Allied air attack, the trains had to be abandoned at Mieste and Zienau. At this point Nicolas disappears from history. However, a Supreme Headquarters, Allied Expeditionary Forces (SHAEF) investigation of the "Gardelegen massacre" discovered a "negro" corpse lying inside the Isenschnibbe barn near a door. The victim had been shot in the side of the head and the body partially burned. At the Nordhausen Trial in 1947, a photograph of the corpse was introduced into evidence. It may have been Nicolas; but other survivors of Mittelbau and its subcamps claimed to have seen black inmates, and the unidentified corpse in the SHAEF photograph may therefore be that of another black victim of the Holocaust.[20]

Toward the end of April 1945, two "Negroes" were evacuated from Ploemnitz (Leau) a subcamp of Buchenwald. During the march they were shot by SS guards because they were too weak to keep up. On June 1, 1945, the 21st Army Group submitted to the United Nations War Crimes Commission a report that stated that "Negroes" were used as slave laborers at Neuengamme concentration camp in Germany.[21] During the liberation of Dachau by the 7th U.S. Army, an unidentified American soldier took a photograph of Jean (Johnny) Voste, an African Belgian, who was an inmate of the camp. Voste was born in the Belgian Congo of a Belgian mother.[22]

Furthermore, other black civilians and prisoners of war were incarcerated in Gestapo prisons. Wilhelm Ruhl, a Gestapo guard at the infamous Butzbach prison, testified that African French civilians and prisoners of war and Lieutenant Darwin Nichols, an African American airman, were incarcerated in this facility in March 1945. Ruhl accused other Gestapo guards of deliberately executing some of the black prisoners and burying their bodies in a bomb crater.[23] Black Allied prisoners of war and other black inmates were brutally mistreated in comparison to their white counterparts, particularly when they encountered members of the Gestapo or SS, the enforcers of Nazi racial ideology.

In 1940, Ernst Heming Hardenberg, a member of the SS since 1933 and a physician assigned to the 2nd SS Panzer Grenadier Division "Das Reich" during the French campaign, was tried by an SS court for failure to shoot a wounded African French prisoner of war. He was acquitted of the charges, but the court recommended his removal from the SS. Heinrich Himmler issued the order removing him.[24]

During the war, captured black colonial troops from South Africa and the French colonies were used as slave laborers by the Wehrmacht in engineering battalions constructing military fortifications and repairing roads. Some died of malnutrition and diseases. Not interned in the German POW system, their mistreatment violated the Geneva Convention. Another violation occurred when five African American prisoners of war were forced to serve as drivers for the 116th SS Panzer Division near Petit Halleux, France.[25] One Volkssturm commander ordered his men to "kill all colored prisoners on sight, because they stink."[26]

By April 18, 1945, the military and political situation in Germany had grown steadily worse. Himmler was willing to trade concentration camp inmate lives for promises by the Allies to treat his SS like normal prisoners of war, and as part of the negotiations he asked that "no negro occupation forces be stationed in Germany after the war."[27]

Conclusion

Under the Nazis, there was no central plan to eliminate African Germans and other blacks from Germany and the occupied territories. Even though the 1935 Nuremberg racial laws declared them a minority with "alien blood," their small population, unlike Jews and Gypsies, was not perceived as an immediate threat. The telling exception to the rule was the hundreds of foreign mulattoes from the occupied Rhineland who were rounded up by the Gestapo. African Germans were indeed considered pariahs in the Nazi system. Black internees were subjected to segregation even in the camps. As nonmilitary prisoners, concentration camp inmates, and POWs, blacks experienced varying degrees of racism. Most of their encounters with such Nazi racists as members of the Gestapo and SS, ended in torture and murder.

NOTES

1. Christian Pross and Götz Aly, *The Value of a Human Being: Medicine in Germany 1918–1945* (Berlin: Edition Hentrich, 1991), p. 15.

2. Adolf Hitler was a member of the Franz von Epp Freikorps. Von Epp participated in the near destruction of the Herero people in German Southwest Africa. However, additional research is needed into the complicity of influential Freikorps leaders in atrocities in Africa. See Annegret Ehmann's "Rassistische und antisemitische Traditionslinien," *Sportstadt Berlin in Geschichte und Gegenwart* (Berlin: Sportmuseum, 1993), pp. 131–43.

3. Michael Burleigh and Wolfgang Wippermann, *The Racial State: Germany 1933–1945* (Cambridge: Cambridge University Press, 1991), p. 128.

4. Watchtower Bible and Tract Society, "The German Crisis," *Golden Age: A Journal of Fact, Hope, and Courage* 14/347 (January 14, 1933), p. 210.

5. Letter from Grawitz to Himmler, National Archives Record Group 242, National Archives Collection of Foreign Records Seized, Microfilm Publication T-175, reel 66, frame 25882139.

6. U.S. 7th Army's report on the interrogations of doctors Rodenwaldt and Wesch, and General Lutkenhaus, April 21, 1945, National Archives Record Group 492, Records of the Headquarters, European Theater of Operations, U.S. Army, Assistant Chief of Staff for Intelligence (G-2), MIS-Y, box 73, no. SAIC/X/2.

7. Alexandre Kum'a N'dumbe III, *Hitler voulait l'Afrique: le project du 3e Reich sur le continent africain* (Paris: L'Harmattan, 1980), pp. 1–372; and "Black Africa and Germany during the Second World War," Reports and papers of a symposium, UNESCO (November 1980), pp. 51–74.

8. Wilhelm Stuckart and Hans Globke, *Kommentare zur deutschen Rassengesetzgebung* (Munich and Berlin: C. H. Beck'sche Verlagsbuchhandlung, 1936), pp. 55, 153.

9. Benno Müller-Hill, *Murderous Science: Elimination by Scientific Selection of Jews, Gypsies, and Others; Germany, 1933–1945*, trans. George R. Fraser (Oxford: Oxford University Press, 1988), p. 12.

10. The statistics have not been well researched, but caution is required if Nazi censuses are used. Some figures are in Müller-Hill and Pross and the records of the Deutscher Gemeindetag. My estimate is 1,000 to 1,500 blacks in Germany between 1933 and 1936.

11. Burleigh and Wippermann, *Racial State*, pp. 129–30; Keith L. Nelson, "The Black Horror on the Rhine: Race as a Factor in Post–World War I Diplomacy," *Journal of Modern History* 41 (December 1970): 606–27; Pross and Aly, *Value of a Human Being*, pp. 98–99. Müller-Hill, *Murderous Science*, pp. 10–12, 30, 138.

12. Bundesarchiv Koblenz, R36, file 1442: Deutscher Gemeindetag, 39–47, 52–53, 60–61, and 102–103.

13. Severin Hochberg located a biographical sketch provided by Gilges's mother in 1945. It included a photograph of the dancer circa 1929–1933 in Mahn-Gedenkstätte Düsseldorf Dumond-Lindermann Theater-Düsseldorf. Copies are located in United States Holocaust Memorial Museum (USHMM) Photo Archives.

14. Richard Mandell, *The Nazi Olympics* (New York: Macmillan, 1975), pp. 221–32.

15. Michael Zwerin, *La Tristesse de Saint Louis Swing unter den Nazis* (London: Quartet Books, 1985), pp. 22–23; Szymon Laks, *Music of Another World*, trans. Chester A. Kisiel (Evanston: Northwestern University Press, 1989), p. 13; United States Holocaust Memorial Museum Research Institute (USHMMRI), Record Group 55, Aleksander Kulisiewicz Collection; letter from Jackie Warren-Moore (a reporter) to Sybil Milton, September 7, 1993, USHMMRI, Historian Files.

16. Lucjan Dobroszycki, ed., *The Chronicle of the Lodz Ghetto*, trans. Richard Lourie et al. (New Haven: Yale University Press, 1984), p. 274.

17. Sybil Milton, "German Occupation Policy in Belgium and France," in *A Mosaic of Victims: Non-Jews Persecuted and Murdered by the Nazis*, ed. Michael Berenbaum (New York: New York University Press, 1990), pp. 80–87.

18. Monica Rothschild-Boros, *In the Shadow of the Tower: The Works of Josef Nassy, 1942–1945* (Irvine, CA: Wundermann Foundation, 1989), pp. 7–34. Nassy's paintings are currently in the collections of the United States Holocaust Memorial Museum.

19. Katherine John, *From Day to Day*, trans. Odd Nansen (New York: G. P. Putnam's Sons, 1949), p. 309.

20. Original Buchenwald Register for Male Inmates, 44,001 to 45,000, ca. 1942–1945, National Archives Record Group 238, National Archives Collection of War Crimes Records, book 45, pp. 14, 197. Witness statements of Abraham Stahl, Erhard Richard Brauny, Josef Fischer, Icek Halicewicz, and miscellaneous correspondence of Dora-Mittelbau inmates by nationality, photograph of unidentified black victim by U.S. Army Signal Corps at Gardelegen,

lists of unknown victims buried at Gardelegen, SHAEF Court of Inquiry Report on the Gardelegen Massacre, National Archives Record Group 153, JAG, War Department, War Crimes Division, series 143, file 12-480; and National Archives Record Group 496, JAG, ETOUSA, War Crimes Branch, file 000-50-037.

21. Interrogation of Johannes Volk, First U.S. Army Special Report, National Archives Record Group 332, Records of the Headquarters, ETOUSA, Assistant Chief of Staff for Intelligence (G-2), MIS-Y, box 66; report forwarded by the 21st Army Group to UN War Crimes Commission, entitled "Report on Neuengamme-Hamburg Concentration Camp," National Archives Record Group 153, Records of the Judge Advocate General, War Department, War Crimes Branch, series 143, file 12-427, box 266.

22. Photograph of Jean Voste, black inmate at Dachau, n.d., Dallas Memorial Center for Holocaust Studies. Brief biographical sketch of Voste supplied by Barbara Distel, Director of the Dachau Museum and Archives.

23. Report of Interrogation of Wilhelm Ruhl, National Archives Record Group 338, JAG, ETOUSA, WCB, WCCF 12-1457.

24. Report of Interrogation of Ernst Heming Hardenberg, National Archives Record Group 332, Records of the Headquarters, ETOUSA, Assistant Chief of Staff for Intelligence (G-2), MIS-Y, box 68.

25. Interrogations of Paul Kather and Dieter von der Burg, 1st U.S. Army PWI Report no. 10, National Archives Record Group 332, Records of the Headquarters, ETOUSA, Assistant Chief of Staff for Intelligence (G-2), MIS-Y, box 63.

26. Interrogation of Joachim Jannek, 6824th Detailed Interrogation Consolidated Report no. M. 1033, National Archives Record Group 332, Records of the Headquarters, ETOUSA, Assistant Chief of Staff for Intelligence (G-2), MIS-Y, box 62.

27. "Report of the Headquarters and Headquarters Detachment, Office of Strategic Services, ETO [European Theater of Operations], U.S. Army, Reports Board, April 18, 1945," located in National Archives Record Group 84, Records of the Foreign Service Post, U.S. State Department, Top Secret Correspondence of the U.S. Political Advisor for Germany.

Part 7

Concentration Camps

THEIR TASK AND ENVIRONMENT

In the essays that follow, the concentration camp is examined in its historical development. Auschwitz, as the largest and the most infamous of the camps, will be subject to particular examination, but two small subcamps of Dachau also will be discussed to illustrate the variety and diverse functions of the installations. The interaction between the concentration camps and the surrounding towns will be explored as well.

Auschwitz historian Franciszek Piper offers a comprehensive analysis of that concentration camp in "Aushwitz Concentration Camp: How It Was Used in the Nazi System of Terror and Genocide and in the Economy of the Third Reich." Piper examines the history and function of the facility from its initial construction until its liberation on January 27, 1945.

Piper focuses on the death tolls of the various incarcerated groups and arrives at a figure that differs substantially from other estimates. He also discusses the uses and misuses of Nazi documents concerning Auschwitz and proposes a series of projects necessary to answer important questions about the camp's history and functions—questions that have so far remained unanswerable.

At the conclusion of her paper on "Antechamber to Birkenau: The Zigeunerlager after 1933," Sybil Milton argues that the "decentralized . . . provisional attempt to segregate Sinti and Roma, . . . like the later ghettos in Eastern Europe, served in the end only as transfer stations to the killing centers."

Milton traces the evolution of anti-Sinti and anti-Roma policies in Nazi Germany. Though persecution of these people preceded the Nazi ascent to power, persecution was intensified and codified under the Nazi regime. Initiatives for the persecution of Roma and Sinti often began at the local level and ascended to national policy. As the German civil service moved to implement racial laws, local measures became national measures, police surveillance and arbitrary intimidation intensified. Thus, Sinti and Roma were included as asocials in the July 1933 Law for the Prevention of Offspring with Hereditary Defects, and in the November 1933 Law against Habitual Criminals. Milton cautions: "The first law permitted involuntary sterilization, the later law permitted incarceration in concentration camps." After the Nuremberg Laws of 1935, at least semiofficially, Gypsies along with Jews and blacks were classified as racially distinctive minorities with alien blood. By 1936, they had lost their right to vote in Reichstag elections. Even in Austria they were not permitted to vote on the plebiscite.

In 1936, Gypsies in Berlin were arrested prior to the Olympic games and incarcerated in Berlin at the Marzahn Camp, soon to become the largest Gypsy camp. There they suffered in conditions of marginal sanitation and semistarvation. Still, unlike others in the pre-war concentration camps, the Gypsies remained in family units. Similar camps existed in other German cities such as Düsseldorf and Cologne.

During the prewar period, Sinti and Roma, like the handicapped, were labeled unproductive and inferior. In wartime, such stereotyping was lethal; Sinti and Roma became vulnerable to similar eugenic measures.

While Piper explores the familiar history of Auschwitz, a camp that has come to symbolize the Holocaust, Edith Raim, in "Concentration Camps and the Non-Jewish Environment," has investigated the histories of two of the subcamps, Kaufering and Mühldorf, affiliated with the oldest of the Nazi concentration camps, Dachau.

Both camps were created in the spring of 1944 in response to an effort by Hermann Göring to recapture German air superiority and consequently to avert losing the war.

Göring's plan included the transfer of large parts of German industry underground and the building of a jet fighter vastly superior to any Allied airplane. The entire operation was to be supervised by the Todt Organization.

The Dachau subcamps of Kaufering and Mühldorf utilized mostly Jewish slave labor, mainly from Hungary. Conditions in these installations resembled those in the major concentration camps, and both facilities vigorously pursued the concept of "Vernichtung durch Arbeit" (destruction through labor). At the end of the war at least fifteen to twenty thousand prisoners had died in both camps, neglected by the German population of both places, who took little or no notice of the terrible and inhumane conditions in their midst.

In his pioneering work, "Places Far Away, Places Very Near: Mauthausen, the Camps of the Shoah, and the Bystanders," Gordon J. Horwitz examines not the history and functioning of the concentration camp but its interaction with the surrounding community. Horwitz discusses the psychological and existential state of these archetypal "bystanders." Horwitz finds that the concentration camps often spilled beyond their fortified boundaries. Local townspeople were employed by the camps, supplying goods and services of every sort as well as playing the role of camp "auxiliaries" by helping to hunt and capture escaped prisoners.

And despite the fact that the sights and sounds of the camp often permeated their front windows and doors, many of these townsfolk rationalized all that went on, at best, or denied seeing or knowing anything that went on, at worst. Horwitz's work thus yields new understanding of the frequently asked questions, "What did they know and when did they know it?" He raises anew the question of the role of the bystander.

27.

FRANCISZEK PIPER

Auschwitz Concentration Camp

HOW IT WAS USED IN THE NAZI SYSTEM OF TERROR AND
GENOCIDE AND IN THE ECONOMY OF THE THIRD REICH

Creation of the Camp, Its Physical
Development and Methods of Extermination

Millions of human beings in occupied Europe perished as a result of the
purposeful activities of different agencies of the Third Reich. The Nazi extermination
policy rested on far-reaching plans for the Germanization of Eastern Europe and
demographic restructuring of the rest of Europe.[1] The implementation of these plans
was supposed to lead to the complete annihilation of the Jews and Gypsies and to the
partial elimination of Slavs, most especially the Poles. Concentration camps, and
death camps for Jews, along with an extensive system of court and police institutions
were the tools for implementing these plans. The concentration camps in particular
were the central instrument of terror against the nations of occupied Europe. In the
last phase of the war they were one of the places where hundreds of thousands were
exploited for slave labor.

The largest of these was the Auschwitz-Birkenau camp. Established by the Nazis
in occupied Polish territory, it combined in one complex both types of these camps.

The concentration camp in Oświęcim (renamed Auschwitz by the Germans) was
set up in May 1940 at the initiative of local German police authorities in Silesia, where
mass arrests of Polish nationals had been carried out since the beginning of the
German occupation. As was the case in other parts of occupied Poland, the prisons
quickly became so overcrowded that they could not house all of those whom the
Germans had rounded up. The need for speed precluded building a camp from
scratch, and so the German authorities made use of the prewar Polish army barracks
located on the outskirts of Oświęcim at Zasole.

From its creation in 1940, the facility was systematically expanded so that by
1945 it was a complex of about forty camps and subcamps situated around the
original camp. The area of the so-called "camp businesses" (Interessengebiet) was
administered directly by the commander. It included the original camp and that at
Brzezinka (Birkenau in German), covering forty square kilometers. During the
period of its fastest growth, in the summer of 1944, there were 135,000 people in all
the camps that formed the Auschwitz complex. Because of its rapid growth, as early

as November 1943 the camp was divided into three closely interrelated organizational units: Auschwitz I, including the original camp; Auschwitz II, including the Birkenau camp and subcamps at agricultural and breeding farms; and Auschwitz III, with its headquarters at Monowice, including subcamps at industrial enterprises.

In the first two years of the camp's operation, malnutrition and exhausting labor were the main causes of mass death. Individual murders also played a significant role at that time, although for the most part they were intended to maintain draconian discipline and absolute obedience. The efficacy of such conventional methods of killing is best illustrated by the fate of 10,000 Soviet prisoners of war who were transported to the camp in October 1941. After five months of starvation, hard labor, beatings, and outright killings, only 945 were still alive on March 1, 1942.[2]

On July 28, 1941, the first selection of diseased and disabled was carried out; 575 prisoners were to die in the gas chambers of the "euthanasia" center in Sonnenstein (Germany). Shortly thereafter, experiments began with various kinds of poisons; these were injected into prisoners to cause death. Finally, it was found that the quickest killing agent was phenol, injected directly into the heart, so this method was subsequently used in the camp hospital.

In August and September 1941, several experiments were carried out with Zyklon B (hydrogen cyanide) gas. Previously used as an insecticide, it now was used to carry out mass murder. In this way several transports of Soviet prisoners of war were killed in a mortuary adapted for that purpose at Crematorium I in the main camp.

In Birkenau, in the first half on 1942, two provisional gas chambers with a capacity of 800 and 1,200 people were put into operation in two houses taken from expelled peasants. Until September 1942 the bodies of the gas victims were buried in mass graves; subsequently, corpses were burned in the open air. From March 22 to June 25, 1943, four modern gas chambers and crematoria were put into operation at Birkenau to replace the earlier gas "bunkers." The official capacity of these four crematoria was 4,416 corpses every twenty-four hours.[3] According to survivors of the Sonderkommando, the prisoners who were obliged to work in these facilities, the actual daily capacity was increased to 8,000 by shorter cremation times and incomplete incineration of the bones. From 1942 onward, the majority of Auschwitz victims died in the gas chambers. Most were Jews gassed as families—men, women, and children. Upon their arrival, Jews were subjected to selections, conducted mainly by SS doctors. At first these selections were conducted sporadically; after July 4, 1942, they became routine. Young and healthy people were chosen for labor from the new arrivals; the rest, including almost all the children, were sent directly to the gas chambers. Prisoners able to work were placed in barracks and then registered. After a period of quarantine they were put to work maintaining the camp or in industrial enterprises such as mines, armament factories, and other plants. The prisoners so employed outside Oświęcim were moved to subcamps located close to their work sites. If they became seriously ill, they were returned to Auschwitz-Birkenau.

Non-Jewish prisoners were not subjected to a preliminary selection; as a rule all of them were registered. Between July 1941 and April 1943, after registration, they underwent selections as did the Jews, and those who were weak or otherwise unfit for work were killed by phenol injection or in the gas chambers. Selections of non-Jews, however, were less frequent and less strict.

Characterization of Victims by Nationality, Numbers, and the Proportion in the Balance of Casualties

Jews

Although from 1942 onward Auschwitz-Birkenau remained the place of deportation for Poles and small numbers of representatives of other nationalities, the camp functioned mainly as a center for the mass murder of Jews. The choice of Auschwitz was made in the summer of 1941, shortly after Hitler gave the order to completely annihilate that people. The first phase of this gigantic crime with five to six million victims was the mass execution of Jews by Einsatzgruppen, special execution squads of the German security police and security services in the wake of the German armed forces entering the Soviet Union. Near Mińsk, Kovno, and Riga, the Jews deported from Germany, Austria, and the Protectorate in late 1941 were shot en masse or killed in mobile gas vans.

In line with the plan presented on January 20, 1942, at a conference in Berlin-Wannsee, all the Jews in Europe, numbering over 11,000,000, were to be murdered. Included were those of countries such as Britain, not yet conquered by Germany, of Germany's allies, and of unoccupied neutral countries. Apart from the killing center in Chełmno, in use as of December 1941, the Nazis built three new such centers— Treblinka, Sobibór and Belzec—in 1942 at the eastern border of the General Government of Poland to shorten transport routes. These centers were equipped with special gas chambers designed for the mass killing of thousands. These camps were first and foremost places for the massacre of Polish Jews; Jews from other countries constituted a small percentage of the victims.

A small number of Jews were transported to Auschwitz as soon as the camp opened. Several Jews were in the first transport of 728 prisoners from Tarnów. According to the so-called "registers of newcomers," in the period from May 21 to December 22, 1941, of the total 9,415 arrivals, mostly from Poland, 1,079 were Jews. As objects of special persecution and torment by SS-men and camp functionaries, Jews died quickly. Otherwise, they were hardly noticeable as a separate national group in the camp.

Reichsführer-SS Heinrich Himmler's order from the summer of 1941, several months after his March 1, 1941, inspection of Auschwitz, included that camp in the annihilation campaign against the Jews. To avoid leaving any evidence in writing, Himmler called camp commandant Rudolf Höss to Berlin and verbally informed him of his plan, without the usual presence of the Reichsführer's aide-de-camp. The SS chief's reasons for employing Auschwitz in the operation were that "the existing death centers in the East cannot cope with actions on a large scale," Auschwitz was in a good location for transport, and "the area can be easily isolated and concealed." Since many such sites could have been identified, it seems that the decisive factor was that at Auschwitz there was a preexisting concentration camp with a functioning administrative and technical base.

It can also be hypothesized that in locating the center for the mass killing of the Jews in this relatively new but existent concentration camp, Himmler tried to use the camouflage of the well-known camps of the 1930s to hide the radical purposes of Auschwitz. From 1942 onward, Auschwitz, an actual place on the map, not some abstract place called "East," became the destination for hundreds of transports of Jews dispatched from all over Europe.

The exact date when the slaughter of Jews began in Auschwitz is not known. In their accounts and testimonies former prisoners and SS-men describe a number of cases in which transports of Jews were killed in the gas chambers at Crematorium I, but only in one instance was the autumn of 1941 cited as a date of the arrival of a transport. In a postwar deposition, Commandant Höss stated that he was unable to give the exact date; once he wrote that it may have been in December 1941 or January 1942, in another place he claimed that it was in the spring of 1942, or before the women's camp was established, that is before March 26, 1942.

The first transport of Jews for which the exact date of arrival at the camp is known is the transport of several hundred Jews brought from Bytom, then in Germany, on February 15, 1942.[4] Mass inflow, however, began with the first registered transport of Jewish women from Slovakia, who arrived on March 26, 1942.[5] It was followed by transports from France, the first on March 30, 1942; from Poland on May 5, 1942; the Netherlands on July 17; from Belgium, on August 5; Yugoslavia, on August 18; Theresienstadt in the Protectorate, October 7; Norway, December 1; Greece, March 20, 1943; Italy, October 23; and Hungary, May 2, 1944. According to the minutes of the Wannsee Conference, in January 1942 about five million Jews lived in those countries, excluding the western Ukraine, Byelorussia, and unoccupied France; they were potential victims of Auschwitz.

The territories of Europe involved in the deportation and mass murder of Jews fell, in effect, into four zones:

1. the lands east of the Bug River (Einsatzgruppen zone);
2. the General Government (Central Poland—zone of operations of the death camps of Treblinka, Sobibór, Belzec, and concentration camp Lublin-Majdanek);
3. Polish lands incorporated into the Reich, the so-called Warthegau (Wartheland) (zone of operations of the Chełmno-Kulmhof death camp);[6] and
4. the remaining parts of Central, Western, Southern, and Northern Europe (Auschwitz-Birkenau camp operation zone).

This division did not result from a preconceived schema; rather, it reflected certain practices that allowed for numerous exceptions. The fact that the majority of Austrian, German, and Slovakian Jews were deported to the Soviet Union (Mińsk, Kovno, Riga), to the ghetto in Łódź (Litzmannstadt), or to a number of places in the Lublin area may serve as an example. Moreover, although Auschwitz was, above all, the place where Jews from outside occupied Poland were massacred, a substantial number of Polish Jews (300,000) from the central (General Government), western (Upper Silesia, Zagłębie Dąbrowskie), and northern (Ciechanów and Białystok) regions of occupied Poland also died there.[7] The genocidal role of Auschwitz expanded when, in 1943, other killing centers ceased operations: Chełmno in April, Belzec in June, Treblinka in September, and Sobibór in October. After Operation Erntefest (Harvest Festival), the last mass execution at Majdanek, on November 3, 1943, the Auschwitz camp essentially became, for a time, the only center specifically oriented toward the mass murder of the Jews. An exception was the three weeks the death camp at Chełmno subsequently resumed operations. Until spring 1944 the concentration camps inside the Reich were excluded from the annihilation campaign against the Jews; before that, under Himmler's order of October 1942, Jewish prisoners were to be sent to Auschwitz or Majdanek in order to leave other camps "free of Jews" (Judenfrei).

In the spring of 1944, as a result of economic difficulties and especially a depleted work force, enforcement of the principle of a "Jew-free Reich" was interrupted and Jewish labor was increasingly used in German industry. From that same time, Auschwitz was not only a site of mass murder. Simultaneously it exploited prisoner labor in its subcamps—mainly in Silesia—and it served as a transit point for the Jewish work force withdrawn from the territories threatened by the Red Army offensive. A huge sifting of human material took place there; those who were fit for work were left alive and sent to industrial plants, the rest were murdered and burned. In this way 600,000 people, including some 438,000 Hungarian Jews, 60,000 to 70,000 Jews from Łódź, and prisoners of Majdanek, Płaszów and the Jewish labor camps in the General Government passed through Auschwitz.

Jewish citizens of almost all the countries of Europe, and even from other continents, were in the transports to Auschwitz. Of at least 1.1 million Jews sent there, about one million lost their lives.

Poles

Although the initial reason for creating Auschwitz was the local police problem in Silesia, from the very beginning the camp's reach extended to almost all of occupied Poland. It was one of the main deportation sites for Poles who were sent to concentration camps. The first transport of Polish prisoners—728 of them —arrived from Tarnów on June 14, 1940. Other transports followed: 313 prisoners from Wisnicz on June 20; 23 from Katowice on June 22; 160 prisoners from Kraków on July 18; and 1,666 from Warsaw on August 15. By the end of that year, 7,879 prisoners had been incarcerated, almost all of them Poles. The great majority of them were imprisoned for political reasons, usually in revenge for real or suspected resistance activities. Some of them were arrested preventively as "undesirable" persons known for their patriotism, for their specific prewar social or political activities, or because their social status or education defined them as members of the Polish leadership. Large numbers of these individuals were rounded up in the mid-May to mid-June Extraordinary Pacification Operation (Ausserordentliche Befriedungsaktion), commonly known as the AB-Aktion.

In addition to the political prisoners, Auschwitz also received persons who were caught during so-called round-ups—actions aimed at intimidating the civilian population—as well as the hostages who were shot from time to time in reprisal for resistance actions in the areas they came from. Poles who were sentenced to death by courts-martial or on the basis of police decisions in the course of so-called "special treatment" procedures (Sonderbehandlung) were also executed at the camp. A separate group of prisoners were Poles who were placed in the camp for "reeducation" after violating labor regulations. Unlike other prisoners incarcerated indefinitely, the "reeducation prisoners" were to be imprisoned no longer than eight weeks; even so, about 10 percent of them did not survive. Others had their term of imprisonment prolonged or status changed, and they were held in the camp for an unlimited time. A small number were arrested for ordinary criminal offenses. After the Warsaw Uprising, in August and September 1944, 13,000 men, women and children from Warsaw were confined in that camp.

To the unfulfilled annihilation project against Poles should be added the intended deportation to Auschwitz of tens of thousands of men, women, and children from Zamojszczyzna, a region selected as one of the first bridgeheads of Germanization in eastern Poland. According to this plan, from the beginning of November 1942 three trains, each with one thousand people in category (Wertungsgruppe) IV, the "worst" racial status—were to be sent to Auschwitz weekly.[8] At the last moment, the Nazis abandoned this plan, although at least thirteen hundred prisoners in this group were sent to Auschwitz.

According to our estimates 70,000 to 75,000 Poles of the 140,000 to 150,000 deported to Auschwitz died in the camp.[9]

Gypsies

The third most numerous national group was the Gypsies. As with the Jews, the Germans planned the total elimination of all Gypsy tribes except the Sinti and Lalleri (many members of these tribes were killed later, too). In the territory of the Soviet Union, the Gypsies were shot by the Einsatzgruppen. About 30,000 were killed in Nazi occupied Poland when they were shot on the spot or murdered together with the Jews at killing centers. Gypsies from Western and Central Europe were transported to killing centers and ghettos. Deportations to Auschwitz were based on Himmler's order of December 16, 1942, and the implementation regulations of January 29, 1943, of the Reich Security Main Office. In total, 23,000 Gypsies—men, women, and children—were placed in a separate section of Birkenau, the "family camp," from February 1943 to August 1944. Most of them died of hunger and disease. On August 2, 1944, after the last group of 2,897 was gassed, the Gypsy camp at Birkenau was liquidated. It is estimated that about 20,000 Gypsies perished there.[10]

Soviet prisoners of war

Against international law, prisoners of war were also placed in Auschwitz. In order to keep up appearances, they were initially kept in a separate part of the original camp, called the "POW labor camp." Within the first five months of their stay, from October 1941 to March 1942, of a total 10,000 Soviet POWs, more than 9,000 died of hunger or were killed. By the end of the camp's existence, another 2,000 Soviet prisoners of war had been incarcerated there. Selected prisoners from POW camps were executed at Auschwitz; these prisoners were not registered but were shot or killed in the gas chambers immediately after arrival. It is estimated that at least 15,000 Soviet prisoners of war lost their lives at Auschwitz.

Members of other nationalities

On a smaller scale, Auschwitz also eliminated prisoners of other nationalities: Czechs (including members of the Sokół organization), Byelorussians (5,000 persons, including children, from the area of Mińsk and Vitebsk caught in the antipartisan operation known as the Flurbereinigung), Yugoslavs, French, Germans, and Austrians. Among these last two were political prisoners (including members of the international brigades in Spain), as well as criminal offenders. The latter served as Capos, prison block seniors, and other trusties. It is estimated that 10,000 to 15,000 of 25,000 people other than the Jews, Poles, Gypsies, and Soviet POWs died in the camp.

Considering the dominant proportional victimization of Jews and Poles, the history of Auschwitz can be divided into two periods: the Polish period (1940 to mid-1942), when the majority of the deportees killed were Poles, and the Jewish period (mid-1942 to 1945), when the great majority killed were Jews.

Functions of Auschwitz: Concentration, Hard Labor, and Murder

From 1940 to mid-1942, the Auschwitz camp mainly fulfilled the role of a concentration camp, that is, here the prisoners were killed off only gradually, the main instruments being hunger and hard labor. Execution by shooting, by poison injection, and, from 1941, by gas chamber took place on a relatively small scale.

The use of prisoners as a workforce included assignment to construction detail, industrial enterprises, and the agricultural and breeding farms attached to the camp.

From mid-1942 to 1944, the camp retained its function of concentration, but in addition became the center of the mass annihilation of Europe's eleven million Jews, whose impending murder was announced at the Berlin-Wannsee Conference on January 20, 1942.

The killing center at Birkenau and the concentration camp, as well as all other components of the Auschwitz complex, were interrelated organic parts of one structure. The concentration camp was an administrative and economic base for the killing center, providing the workforce for servicing the ramps, gas chambers, crematoria, storage areas for the stolen property, and for concealing the traces of the crime as well as for various economic enterprises. In turn, Auschwitz as a death center received exhausted prisoners from camp hospitals and slave labor subcamps for final disposal.

Because of its labor and killing potential, Auschwitz played a central role in the Nazi camp system. From summer 1942 to summer 1944, about 20 to 30 percent of all concentration camp prisoners were handled at Auschwitz.

From 1942 onward, a process of specialization can be observed throughout the whole Auschwitz complex. In November 1943 this was institutionally sanctioned when the camp was divided into three organizational units:

1. Auschwitz I (the main camp) served as administrative center for the camp complex. It was the seat of the chief of the local SS garrison, the garrison doctor, the political and employment departments; the main storage areas, workshops, and most enterprises were located there. The prisoners were employed mostly in these units and at the Union Armament Factory.

2. Auschwitz II (Birkenau and farm subcamps) was the center for annihilating the Jews and for killing sick and exhausted prisoners from the whole complex and even other camps.

From the first selections of Jews brought in mass transports, that is, from spring 1942, the camp was to become the main labor reserve and transit point for the whole network of concentration camps. After the POW camp concept was abandoned, these very plans were the justification for expanding the camp on an enormous scale, with a projected limit of 200,000 people. Because the camp had its own needs, and the camps inside the Reich from October 1942 had been closed to Jewish prisoners, whose numbers were constantly increasing in the total workforce, and because of other organizational problems (quarantine, epidemics, security considerations), between 1942 and 1943 the camp fulfilled this role only to a very limited extent.

During that time, Polish prisoners were the only group transferred to camps in the Reich to avert the possibility of contact with other Poles. Employment in the Upper Silesian industrial area was avoided. Therefore, the main contingent of Jewish prisoners was directed to Auschwitz subcamps or employed on the spot operating the execution facilities, sorting the stolen property of the victims, or working at the camp farms or the Union and Zerlegebetriebe armament factories (half of the prisoners remained unemployed or unfit for work). Not until 1944, when Germany found itself in a very critical military and economic situation, were the earlier objections overcome, and Jewish prisoners too were transferred to employment in the Reich.

3. Auschwitz III had as its basic task exploitation of the prisoner workforce; all subcamps at industrial plants in Upper Silesia and the Protectorate of Bohemia and Moravia were grouped under it. Despite the importance of the prisoner workforce, Auschwitz III did not occupy a dominant position within the Auschwitz complex. During the period of its fastest growth, the number of Auschwitz III prisoners did not exceed 30 percent of the Auschwitz camp total. This rose to 50 percent only in the camp's last months as a result of the partial evacuation of Auschwitz I and Birkenau to the Reich; the subcamp prisoners were evacuated just ahead of the Soviet army.

Auschwitz was the most important Nazi death center and concentration camp. Of at least 1,300,000 deportees to Auschwitz, about 900,000 were killed immediately after arrival. The other 400,000 were registered as concentration camp prisoners and given numerical identification. About 200,000 of these died of hunger, disease, and slave labor; many of the remainder were killed by injection or in the gas chambers. Thus at least 1,100,000 died in the camp. Ninety percent of them were Jews. The second largest group were the Poles, followed by Gypsies and prisoners of other nationality. Thus, accepting Raul Hilberg's estimate that 5.1 million Jews died in all camps, ghettos, and execution sites, Auschwitz accounts for 20 percent of Jewish victims. The special nature of Auschwitz is due to its role in the Final Solution and its dual task as a center for immediate mass execution and concentration camp.

This was visible in the treatment of prisoners. If in other camps limits were placed on killing the sick (Glück's regulation of April 27, 1943, limiting "euthanasia" to the mentally ill), and if living conditions were improved by allowing food parcels to be received, in order to prevent too great loss of manpower, in Auschwitz human life had no value. The labor force was maintained through continuous replacement of weak, ill, or exhausted prisoners: unlimited numbers came from an almost uninterrupted stream of new transports of Jews. The prisoners' treatment resulted mainly from Nazi doctrine: political goals (annihilation) had priority over economic goals (exploitation). Regardless of the dramatic deficit in Nazi Germany's workforce, the massacre of Auschwitz prisoners continued virtually until the last days of its existence.

Was the combination of immediate mass execution with the gradual annihilation by work (Vernichtung durch Arbeit) the prototype for a new type of camp that would replace the simple killing centers? No primary German documents permit a definitive answer. The liquidation of the killing centers in Chełmno, Treblinka, Sobibór, and Belzec in 1943, when (in Hungary, France, the Protectorate, Slovakia, Romania, and the General Government) there were still large groups of Jews subject to eventual annihilation, suggests that in the future death centers were to be replaced by the combination camps. Expansion plans for Auschwitz indicate that the most permanent camp facilities were to be the gas chambers and crematoria at Auschwitz II–Birkenau; and brick barracks for prisoners, together with all the auxiliary economic and administrative buildings at Auschwitz I; so mass murder and hard labor were to continue for some time. The most perishable structures were the rapidly erected wooden barracks at Birkenau meant to hold Jews temporarily before transfer to work sites. The conditions in these barracks did not suggest plans to allow prisoners to stay alive for a long time.

There is no question, however, that the system of true killing centers, sites for annihilation with no exceptions or any kind of selection, could if necessary have been restored at any time, if any other nation had been designated for a "Final Solution" (the *Generalplan Ost* gives us grounds for believing that it would have been probably the Poles).

Evidence in support of the possibility of renewed genocide is found in the fact that in June and July 1944 the Chełmno (Kulmhof) death camp resumed operations and that temporary gassing facilities within the Auschwitz-Birkenau complex (Bunker 2), out of use for a year, were brought back into operation. This was not especially difficult, since the killing facilities were simple; any kind of building could be used as a gas chamber after unnecessary holes were bricked up and ventilation installed. A more complicated process was involved if the corpses were burnt in crematoria, but crematoria could be supplemented by burning in the open air, which would have permitted unlimited execution possibilities.

Auschwitz as a Subject of Research

Archival sources

Documentary sources are essential for writing history, marking both the direction and scope of research, and narrowing the latitude for speculation and hypotheses. The essential sources for research on the Nazi concentration camps would in principle include the files of the camp offices and such administrative agencies as the Inspectorate of Concentration Camps, the Reich Security Main Office, and the SS

Central Office for Economy and Administration. These files, however, were largely destroyed since they could have been used in prosecutions after the war.

Auschwitz started to destroy files in July 1944, soon after the concentration camp Lublin–Majdanek, which was located 200 kilometers away, fell to the Russians. The Auschwitz card index, correspondence, and reports to the supreme authorities were taken to the crematoria and burnt. The most valuable documents destroyed included the name lists of Jewish transports, most files of particular camp departments, and registers of incoming prisoners (only records from 1941 and fragments from 1942 and 1943 escaped). Only three documents sent to SS headquarters describe selections from Jewish transports and record both the number of those registered as prisoners and the number sent directly to the gas chambers. The absence of such documents was among the causes of the incorrect estimates of the number of victims of Auschwitz (up to 4 million) after the war. These numbers could be corrected only after copies of the lists of transports and other documents were found in the archives of countries from which Jews were deported to Auschwitz, permitting estimates of the number of deportees as well as information on individual transports. Yet no such lists of Polish Jews were found. On the basis of other documents and the accounts of witnesses to the process of extermination, one may assume that in most cases lists were not written at all during the liquidation of ghettos and transit camps in German-occupied Poland. The transports were formed at random, including anyone the Germans managed to capture at a particular moment. Studies of the liquidation of particular ghettos and Jewish communities are one of the few bases on which the number of Polish Jews deported to Auschwitz can be roughly estimated. The inmates' secret register of assigned camp serial numbers plays an exceptionally important role. The number of 300,000 Jews from Poland deported to Auschwitz is supported by both the research of Frank Golczewski, Martin Gilbert's *Atlas of the Holocaust*, and Danuta Czech's *Auschwitz Chronicle, 1939–1945*. The incomplete documents of the Construction Office permit us to trace with some precision the stages of the building and expansion of the camp, as well as the construction of crematoria and gas chambers, but that is all. In all likelihood, the number of surviving files is only some 5 to 10 percent of the camp's registry (records, documentation, archives).

While the Germans were covering up the traces of their crimes, they left those documents that could testify to their "law and order" and to their "solicitude" for camp inmates. It is striking that they left an extensive set of analyses of blood, urine, saliva, and stool—documents prepared by the Institute of Hygiene in Rajsko. On the surface these might seem evidence of care for the health of inmates. In fact they were a manifestation of formalism and bureaucracy indicating as well the fear that infectious diseases might spread to the SS-men. Analyses revealing infectious diseases often resulted in the gassing of the sick inmates.

It is also surprising that the SS left individual death certificates for the period from July 1941 to December 1943, which testified to the deaths of 87,000 people (4,500 in 1941, 45,616 in 1942, and 36,991 in 1943). There is only one explanation: the documentary citation of disease as the cause of death of all of these people was to be a kind of alibi. Most of all it was to conceal the deaths of hundreds of thousands of people—deaths that were never recorded. The death certificates were written only for prisoners who were registered (i.e., assigned one of the 400,000 serial numbers), and not even for all of them. Death certificates were not prepared for Soviet prisoners of war, and for many Jews, especially after March 1943.

Thus, the researcher has to employ, much more frequently than is otherwise common, indirect sources, including materials of the camp resistance movement (i.e., all kinds of notes and copies of documents illegally written out by prisoners), as well as reports, memoirs, and testimonies by inmates and other eyewitnesses.

Such sources have three functions for research on the history of the camp: they fill gaps in existing camp files; they help to interpret and correct the files; and they constitute the only source of information about certain sides of camp life such as everyday bullying, the psychological life of the inmates, and acts of resistance or self-defence.

Materials of the camp's resistance were closely connected with the fact that Auschwitz was seen by both inmates and the Polish resistance organizations within the occupied country, as historically unique because of the technique of killing, the scale of the crimes committed there, and their ideological motivation. That gave rise to inmate efforts to reveal the crimes to the world and to preserve the memory of the victims. One of the first accounts was Witold Pilecki's report smuggled from the camp to one of the Resistance organizations in Warsaw in November 1940. Other inmates who rallied to the conspiratorial organization "Kampfgruppe Auschwitz" led by Poles Józef Cyrankiewicz and Stanisław Kłodziński, and the Austrian Hermann Langbein. This organization regularly smuggled reports out of the camp; the most important reached the Polish Government-in-Exile in London; others were distributed in occupied Poland or placed in conspiratorial archives "pro memoria."[11]

One of the most valuable documents is the fragmentary newcomers' list containing the date of arrival of the transport, numbers assigned to people from the given transport, and, in many cases, notation of where the transport came from. Thanks to this data, the chronology, course, and to some extent the proportions of deportations to Auschwitz can be reconstructed. Other materials confirm important events such as the first attempt to kill people with Zyklon B and the employment of gas chambers for mass extermination of Jews. Despite some inaccuracy, these materials combined with other sources are a valuable supplement to our knowledge about Auschwitz.[12] Reports of escapees are another valuable source of knowledge. The best-known are accounts of four Jews who escaped in April and May 1944—W. Rosenberg, A. Wetzler, A. Rosin, and C. Mordowicz—as well as the Pole J. Tabeau. The reports were published, in Europe and the United States, during the war.[13] The notes of Jewish members of Sonderkommando working at the burning of bodies are another precious source of information about Auschwitz. Buried in the ground and found after the war, these manuscripts provide unique evidence of the crimes committed in the camp.[14]

As was mentioned above, one of the functions of all these sources is to provide a context in which to interpret the German documents. Nazi usage created a jargon to camouflage their crimes. Murder was called "Sonderbehandlung" (special treatment), "Sonderunterbringung" (special housing), or "Evakuierung" (evacuation). Gas chambers were called "Leichenkeller" (cellars for corpses), shooting was called "umlegen" (overturning), partisans "Banditen," and "Zyklon B" was called "Materialien für Judenumsiedlung" (material for Jewish resettlement). Deciphering the cryptonyms is possible only because of the information included in the memoirs and prisoners' reports.

Subjective aspects of research

The postwar image of Auschwitz was created by Jewish and Polish survivors and scholars—members of two groups who lost most in this camp. The lack of an objective picture of the national structure of the victims of Auschwitz undoubtedly influenced the dissemination of different images of the camp. The number of victims of particular nationalities was not even approximately known until Wellers' work, and that only very divergent, general estimates had been known. The number of Jews was estimated as between 1 and 2.5 million, while estimates of the number of prisoners called "non-Jews" ranged from 100,000 (Gerald Reitlinger), to 300,000 (Raul Hilberg). Undoubtedly, the lack of impeachable sources and, above all, proper statistical comparisons was the main reason for the wide divergences. Both Jewish and Polish researchers were also under the pressure of their own environments. This ethnocentricity influenced their research, sometimes leading them to violate the rules of objectivity.

For Jewish researchers, Auschwitz was the center for immediate extermination of Jews; Auschwitz as concentration camp was treated as a marginal topic, in spite of the fact that half of 400,000 registered inmates were Jews. One can get the impression that for some Jewish researchers the introduction of other nationalities into the history of Auschwitz somehow diminished the genocide of Jews. For Polish research-ers, however, Auschwitz was most of all the place of martyrdom of "citizens" from all of Europe with the matter of nationality remaining in the background. The diver-gence of these two understandings of Auschwitz was intensified by the lack of free access to information, the infrequency of discussion and exchange of opinions among Jewish and Polish scholarly and cultural circles, the rupture in relations between Poland and Israel in 1968, and the anti-Jewish repression that followed in Poland. Jews did not—and often still do not—realize the scale of crimes committed against Poles during the war. They also do not understand the significance of Auschwitz in the consciousness and history of the Polish nation. On the other hand Poles were not—and to some extent are still not—aware of the enormity of the crimes committed against Jews in this camp and what Auschwitz means as the symbol of the Holocaust in the consciousness of Jews all over the world.

All of this has repeatedly given rise to misunderstandings, controversies, acri-mony, and accusations. The controversy about the location of the Carmelite Convent in Oświęcim was a symptom of this mutual misunderstanding. So, too, the three years of discussion about the short text of the inscriptions on the monument in Birkenau. However, the results of both discussions, heated and emotional, resolved the contro-versies satisfactorily for all the participants, changed mutual misperceptions, and brought both sides closer to the objective truth. The rapprochement between members of Jewish and Polish social, religious, political, and cultural circles was made possible, in part, thanks to a far-reaching consensus among scholars who proved in this instance more objective about the subject of their research, in particular research on the national composition of the victims published for the first time by Wellers and the present writer.

For many, the results were a great surprise because they violated the accepted stereotypes. They contributed to a decline in the tension over the Carmelite Convent, and ultimately to its cessation. This was duly noted by one Polish publicist who wrote in 1991:

> The figures . . . have revealed the great quantitative disproportion of the two groups of victims: Jewish victims of Auschwitz 960,000 [and] Poles 75,000. . . . It's time to end disputes and polemics.

Scholarship objectively representing the past can contribute to better understanding between peoples inheriting that past, which is especially important today when revival of animosities built on past myths, misconceptions, and prejudices represents an unacceptable tragedy.

Goals and methods for further research and education

Fifty years of research have established Auschwitz's importance as a historical event. Nonetheless gaps and sometimes even contradictions and discrepancies still survive in the literature, exploited by Holocaust deniers whose goal is to question the very nature of this camp as a center for genocide. This is why research should continue, with the following goals:

1. Locating still-unknown primary sources, especially in archives of the former socialist countries: a survey of such materials should be drawn up and, if possible, computerized. The Auschwitz Museum has made substantial progress in this regard. Since 1991, archival materials have been entered systematically into a data base to protect their contents in the event the documents are damaged and to facilitate their study. The lack of published archival inventories hampers research. The largest quantity of such lists is published in Israel, but they are not always available outside that country.

2. Studies on new subjects or subjects heretofore only superficially examined: detailed work on arrests, deportation, selection, and registration of prisoners of different countries should be carried out, in particular, on Polish, Slovakian, Hungarian, and Yugoslavian Jews. Studies should focus on decision-making, cooperation among various levels of German and local collaborating administrations, and implementation by local authorities. Polish prisoners at Auschwitz still await treatment; the issues here require investigation at many sites—mostly prisons—into the causes and implementation of the deportations. This subject requires surveys of prison archives and analyses of the so-called group transports (Sammeltransporte). There are few histories of the prisons under Nazi rule. The same applies to the Gypsies and prisoners of other nationalities. Lists of the largest possible number of names of prisoners should be included in such works. Data on the less numerous nationality groups—Czechs, Byelorussians, Ukrainians, Germans, Austrians, Yugoslavs, and others—should be assembled precisely. About 70,000 death certificates the Russian authorities have recently transferred to the Auschwitz Museum will play an extremely important role in such research. Another issue that has not been sufficiently clarified is the extent to which communities in various countries, including the

victims—and especially the Jews—were aware of the truth about Nazi intentions.

3. Resolving existing discrepancies: one such question is the number of victims. J. C. Pressac's recently published figures indicate that this question should be discussed further.[15] Discrepancies concerning the murder facilities—the gas chambers and crematoria—and especially their origins, capacity, operational period, and role in the killing process demand serious attention. There is still no consensus on the role of the Polish resistance in informing the world about the crimes being committed at Auschwitz. Over-reliance on outdated works instead of more recent literature, such as the *Auschwitz Chronicle, 1939–1945* by Danuta Czech, or the works the State Museum Auschwitz publishes in its "*Zeszyty Oświęcimskie*" ("*Hefte von Auschwitz*" in the German edition) suggests that a permanent distribution system should be created for publications about Auschwitz, including (at a minimum) the Yad Vashem Memorial Museum in Israel, the State Museum at Oświęcim, and the United States Holocaust Memorial Museum in Washington.

Countering Holocaust deniers

The work ahead requires sensitive attention to the tragedy of the victims and forbids reduction of genocide to a technological process. A minor corollary is that studies of secondary phenomena such as spiritual and cultural life should always be grounded in camp reality, that is, the process of genocide; failure to stress their marginality risks falsifying the historical truth.

Another issue is the question of relativizing Nazi crimes by comparing them with those of Stalinism. Discussion of Nolte's views made this current again, as did discussion of commemorating the victims of the Stalinist camps established at sites of former Nazi camps in Germany. In Poland, the overuse of the name Auschwitz has magnified the scale of repression in the Stalinist camps established at the sites of Auschwitz-Birkenau and its subcamps at Świętochłowice and Jaworzno. In fact, such comparisons relativize German crimes. The same applies to the Gulag in the former Soviet Union. But even in the absence of new research on the Gulag, we may categorically state an important difference between the natures of the Stalinist and Nazi crimes. Stalin's policies repressed or immobilized real or imaginary political opponents, whereas Nazi crimes were based in ideology and their fundamental motivation was the nationality not only of the victims but even their ancestors. They sought to murder the whole target population regardless of age, political views, religion, language, or activities. At least in this respect the crimes against the Jews and the Gypsies had no parallel in all of history.

Responsibility for progress rests upon all researchers. Among institutions, this is a duty primarily of the Auschwitz Museum. In spite of the fact that this is not an academic research institution in a strict sense and the activities of its staff reach far beyond its research work, the museum can boast of a large number of works that have made important contributions to research on the camp's history. In 1995, the Auschwitz Museum published the five-volume monograph, *Auschwitz 1940–1945. Węzłowe zagadnienia z dziejów obozu* (Auschwitz 1940–1945: The most important problems from the history of the camp). Volume 1 presents the establishment and organization of the camp; volume 2 the life and work of the prisoners; volume 3 extermination; volume 4 the resistance movement; and volume 5, the epilogue: liquidation of the camp, prosecution of Auschwitz criminals, and the medical consequences of imprisonment. Currently researchers from the museum are studying the deportation and extermination of Jews from occupied Poland, deportation and extermination of Poles, the life and extermination of women and children, and the activity of IG Farbenindustrie in Auschwitz.

NOTES

1. Alan Bullock, *Hitler: Eine Studie über Tyrannei* (Frankfurt/M.: Fischer Bücherei, 1964), vol. 2, p. 739.

2. Archives of the State Auschwitz Museum (ASAM), D-Au-2, Stärkebuch.

3. Archives Domburg (Germany), ND 4586, letter of June 28, 1943, from Zentralbauleitung Auschwitz to SS-WVHA. ASAM. Microfilm no. 1034. The capacity of the crematorium was projected to reach 60 bodies per hour x 24 = 1440/day.

4. *Kommandant in Auschwitz, Autobiographische Aufzeichnungen von Rudolf Höss* (Stuttgart: Deutsche Verlags-Anstalt, 1961), p. 123 note 3.

5. Sources in the Auschwitz Museum Archives prove that from September 1941 to March 1942, few Jewish transports arrived at Auschwitz. We know exactly the date that one such transport arrived, having left February 15, 1942, from Bytom (Beuthen). The number of 100,000 Jews buried in mass graves, given by Höss, relates to the period from the beginning of mass destruction to September 1942. Compare Yehuda Bauer, "Auschwitz," in *Der Mord an den Juden im Zweiten Weltkrieg* (Stuttgart: Deutsche Verlags-Anstalt, 1985), p. 168.

6. Yitzhak Arad, *Belzec, Sobibor, Treblinka: The Operation Reinhard Death Camps* (Bloomington: Indiana University Press, 1987).

7. Franciszek Piper, *Die Zahl der Opfer von Auschwitz: Aufgrund der Quellen und der Erträge der Forschung, 1945 bis 1990* (Oświęcim: Verlag Staatliches Museum in Oświęcim, 1993). The same number of Polish Jews was established by German historian Frank Golczewski in his essay "Polen," in *Dimension des Völkermords: Die Zahl der Jüdischen Opfer des Nationalsozialismus*, ed. Wolfgang Benz (Oldenburg, 1991), p. 411–97. A higher number— 600,000—was established by G. Wellers; see Georges Wellers, "Essai de determination du nombre de morts au camp d'Auschwitz," *Le monde juif* 112 (1983): 125–59. Jean Claude Pressac's calculations, on the contrary, diminish the number to 150,000; see Jean Claude Pressac, *Les crematoires d'Auschwitz: La Machinerie du meurtre de masse* (Paris, 1993).

8. *Periodical of Central Commission for the Investigation of Nazi Crimes in Poland* 13, Document No. 2, pp. 6ff., telegram of October 26, 1942, from Günther to Krumey relating the deportation of Poles to Auschwitz and Berlin.

9. According to Wellers, of 146,605 Poles and "others," 86,505 died; see Wellers, "Essai," pp. 153, 155; Piper, *Die Zahl der Opfer*, pp. 103, 151, 167.

10. *Memorial Book. The Gypsies at Auschwitz-Birkenau* (London: K. S. Saur Verlag, edited by State Museum of Auschwitz-Birkenau, 1993). In the book, 11,843 deaths in the Gypsy camp are given, the number of death marks in the Gypsy camp register. About 3,000 Gypsies were also killed during the liquidation of the Gypsy camp (the register had already been hidden by the prisoners); another 1,700 Gypsies were killed without registration on March 23, 1943, and approximately another 1,000 Gypsies who had been transferred to Germany were sent back to Auschwitz and gassed; see Danuta Czech, *Kalendarium der Ereignisse im*

Konzentrationslager Auschwitz-Birkenau 1939–1945 (Reinbek: Rowohlt Verlag, 1989), pp. 448, 903, 910.

11. Henryk Swiebocki, "Die Lagernahe Widerstandsbewegung und ihre Hilfsaktionen für die Häftlinge des KZ Auschwitz," *Hefte von Auschwitz* 19 (1995).

12. "Obóz koncentracyjny Oświęcim w świetle akt Delegatury rzadu RP na Kraj," *Zeszyty Oświęcimskie*, special number 1 (1968).

13. "Raporty uciekinierów z KL Auschwitz," *Zeszyty Oświęcimskie*, special number 4 (1992).

14. *Amidst a Nightmare of Crime. Manuscripts of Members of Sonderkommando* (Oświęcim: Panstwowe Muzeum w Oświęcim, 1973).

15. See Pressac, *Les crématoires*. There are some problems in Pressac's book, including the date of the early gassings, the number of Polish Jews deported to Auschwitz, the total number of deported, and others. Many inaccuracies mar the information supplied by computer by Kenneth N. McVay (1993), "HOLOCAUST FAQ: Auschwitz-Birkenau: Layman's Guide," Usenet news, answers.

28.

SYBIL MILTON

Antechamber to Birkenau

THE ZIGEUNERLAGER AFTER 1933

The "apocalyptic fanaticism"[1] of Nazi genocide during World War II resulted in the mass murder of between one-quarter and one-half million Roma and Sinti in German and Axis-occupied Europe. The American prosecution at Nuremberg understood that Sinti and Roma, then referred to as Gypsies, were one of three genetic groups (Jews, Sinti and Roma, and the handicapped) targeted for exclusion, concentration, and annihilation as a result of planned scientific and bureaucratic policy.[2] Captured German records and trial interrogations revealed the parallelism and convergence of Nazi policy against these groups, all defined as alien to the German national community on genetic grounds, what the Nazis called "blood."

The Sinti and Roma, linked as non-Caucasian ethnic minorities to African Germans by their darker skin pigmentation and classified like the Jews as aliens and criminals, were routinely denounced by the xenophobic press and bureaucracy, which called for the "elimination of the Gypsy plague." Like the handicapped, Sinti and Roma were stereotyped as unproductive and inferior and were thus vulnerable to similar restrictive eugenic measures. Sinti and Roma represented only about 0.05 percent of the 1933 German population and were considered socially marginal. They were stigmatized as racial aliens. But while substantial scholarly and survivor literature has covered the fate of the Jews and the handicapped, the fate of Sinti and Roma has received far less attention. Scattered articles and monographs published by small presses about this subject have not, with few exceptions, penetrated the mainstream of Holocaust historiography.[3] For that reason, a full understanding of the totality of the Nazi genocidal program requires a detailed analysis of its anti-Gypsy policies. Lack of space precludes a full discussion of these anti-Gypsy policies, and I shall thus concentrate on the early years from 1933 to 1939.

After Hitler's assumption of power on January 30, 1933, the German civil service moved rapidly to implement the racial legislation championed by the Nazi leadership. This involved the expansion of laws imposed in several states (Länder) during the Second Empire and Weimar Republic—laws that had allowed arbitrary arrest,

An earlier version of this essay appeared in *Die Normalität des Verbrechens: Bilanz und Perspektiven der Forschung zu den nationalsozialistischen Gewaltverbrechen; Festschrift für Wolfgang Scheffler zum 65. Geburtstag*, ed. Helge Grabitz et al. (Berlin: Hentrich, 1994), pp. 241–59. Used by permission. Copyright © 1994 by Sybil Milton.

preventive detention, and registration of domiciled and migratory German Sinti and Roma and the expulsion of foreign and stateless Sinti and Roma. On March 18, 1933, the Cooperative Interstate Agreement to Combat the Gypsy Plague (Länderverein-barung zur Bekämpfung der Zigeunerplage) incorporated and expanded the 1926 Bavarian Law for Combatting Gypsies, Vagabonds, and the Work Shy and its 1927 Prussian counterpart, which had stigmatized Sinti and Roma as habitual criminals, social misfits, and vagabonds.[4] The agreement included provisions that restricted for Sinti and Roma the issuance and renewal of licenses for itinerant trades, thus increasing their poverty and unemployment at a time when municipal welfare payments for the indigent were reduced during the Depression; mandated the supervision of school-age Gypsy children by municipal welfare authorities, removing truants to special juvenile facilities and children unable to speak German to special schools for the retarded; limited freedom of travel to routes designated by the police; and remanded Gypsies who were without proof of employment to workhouses and forced labor camps. The agreement also stipulated that any state could issue addi-tional regulations.[5] The states did not hesitate long. For example, on August 10, 1933, the city-state of Bremen promulgated a Law for Protecting the Population from Molestation by Gypsies, Vagrants, and the Work Shy, and on July 7, 1933, the Düsseldorf district governor (Regierungspräsident) published a Decree to Combat the Gypsy Nuisance.[6]

This interim decentralized patchwork of parallel local decrees provided the prototype for the synchronization and radicalization of measures against Sinti and Roma throughout the Reich after 1935. Although states and provinces had lost their original autonomy under Nazi rule, they were retained as administrative units and could implement policies on their own initiative as long as they did not contravene national policy. Thus, these local measures cumulatively imposed greater police surveillance and arbitrary intimidation on German Sinti and Roma, intensified restrictions on their freedom of movement, and limited their employment. Moreover, the Munich Center for the Fight against Gypsies in Germany, established under Bavarian legislation in 1926, served as the prototype for the Central Office to Combat the Gypsy Menace, which was created in 1936 as a national police data bank on Sinti and Roma. The latter agency was under the jurisdiction of the Central Office of the Detective Forces (Reichskriminalpolizeiamt, or RKPA) and the Reich Ministry of the Interior.[7]

These initial decrees also facilitated the expulsion of stateless and foreign Sinti and Roma, a precursor of subsequent German expulsions and dumping of several racial groups designated "undesirables."[8] Sinti and Roma were included as "asocials" in the July 1933 Law for the Prevention of Offspring with Hereditary Defects and in the November 1933 Law against Habitual Criminals. The first law resulted in their involuntary sterilization,[9] while the second permitted their incarceration in concen-tration camps. The Denaturalization Law of July 14, 1933, and the Expulsion Law of March 23, 1934, initially implemented against Ostjuden, were also used to expel foreign and stateless Gypsies from German soil.

As early as 1933, several Sinti had been arrested and detained in local concentra-tion camps. Two male Sinti were incarcerated for six weeks at Osthofen concentration camp near Worms, and one Düsseldorf Sinto arrested without identity papers and thus deemed to be "endangering public safety" was detained for five months at Brauweiler concentration camp located in a converted provincial workhouse near Cologne.[10] Precise statistics for Sinti and Roma arrested and confined in correctional or penal institutions and in concentration camps during police sweeps throughout the Reich, such as the week-long SA and SS roundup of "beggars and vagabonds" from September 18–25, 1933, are not available, although it is known that Sinti and Roma were among the arrested vagrants and that both groups were regarded as social pariahs in German society.[11]

Following passage of the 1935 Nuremberg racial laws, semiofficial commentaries on these laws classified Gypsies, along with Jews and blacks, as racially distinctive minorities with "alien blood" (artfremdes Blut).[12] The passage of the so-called marriage law, promulgated only one month after the Nuremberg racial laws, had broader ramifications.[13] All marriages required permission from public health offices, and every person had to obtain prior to marriage a certificate from the public health service that offspring would be genetically sound. Marriages deemed detrimental to the hereditary health of the nation were prohibited. It excluded from marriage a group even larger than that affected by the sterilization law.[14] The information thus collected by the public health service grew enormously. The final aim was a comprehensive system of registration to provide eugenic information on all individuals. The state wanted to establish an inventory on race and heredity (erbbiologische Bestandsaufnahme).[15] In any event, on November 26, 1935, an advisory circular from the Reich Ministry of the Interior to all local registry offices for vital statistics prohibited racially mixed marriages between those of German blood and "Gypsies, Negroes, or their bastard offspring."

In the ever-escalating series of interlocking Nazi regulations implementing the Nuremberg racial laws, both Gypsies and Jews were slowly deprived of their rights as citizens. Thus both Jews and Gypsies lost the right to vote in Reichstag elections on March 7, 1936.[16] Similarly, neither Jews nor Gypsies were permitted to vote in the April 10, 1938, plebiscite on Austria's incorporation into the German Reich; this directive was issued in Vienna on March 23, 1938, ten days after the Anschluss.[17]

In 1934, the Nazi Racial Policy Office began to compile, in collaboration with the Gestapo, an "asocials catalog," that is, a comprehensive list of so-called antisocial elements. The Nazi police and health bureaucracies thus continued and expanded the systematic registration of Sinti and Roma as potential criminals, genetically defined, that had already begun during the Weimar Republic.[18] Thus, anthropological and genealogical registration (rassenbiologische Gutachtung) identified Gypsies as "racially inferior asocials and criminals of Asiatic ancestry."[19] Anthropologists, psychiatrists, and geneticists, usually financed by the German Research Foundation, covered the nation to study the hereditary health of twins, families, and small communities, focusing on Sinti and Roma and the handicapped. Dr. Robert Ritter, the leading researcher to specialize in the study of Gypsies, assembled a team of assistants and, after the spring of 1936, commenced the systematic genealogical and genetic investigation of Gypsy families as part of his assignment at the Racial Hygiene and Demographic Biology Research Unit (Rassenhygienische und Bevölkerungsbiologische Forschungsstelle), also known as Department L3 of the Reich Department of Health.[20] Ritter's unit was assigned to register the approximately 30,000 Gypsies and part-Gypsies in Germany (and, later, in incorporated Austria) in order to provide genealogical and racial data required for formulating a new Reich Gypsy Law. Ritter's group aimed to show that among Gypsies criminal and asocial behavior was hereditary.[21]

Moreover, Nazi social policy toward Jews and Sinti and Roma resulted in decreased expenditures for welfare; assistance to the growing number of impoverished Jews had been assigned to the Reichsvertretung der Juden in Deutschland, transformed after 1939 into the Reichsvereinigung der Juden in Deutschland, whereas indigent Sinti and Roma received progressively less financial assistance from municipal authorities.[22] These same local officials subsequently interned Sinti and Roma in so-called Gypsy camps (Zigeunerlager), where national eugenic policies sometimes resulted in the sterilization of individuals deemed racially inferior.

On June 6, 1936, the Reich and Prussian Ministry of the Interior issued a decree containing new directives for "Fighting the Gypsy Plague."[23] This order also provided retroactive authorization for the Chief of the Berlin Police to direct raids throughout Prussia to arrest all Gypsies prior to the Olympic games. A few families were deported to the so-called Rastplatz Marzahn in late May 1936, and 600 Sinti and Roma were arrested in Berlin on July 16, prompting the daily *Berliner Lokalanzeiger* to carry a story about "Berlin without Gypsies." The arrested Sinti and Roma were marched under police guard in horse-drawn caravans or their wagons were pulled as freight on flatbeds to a sewage dump adjacent to the municipal cemetery in the Berlin suburb of Marzahn.[24] Although the presence of both sewage and graves violated Gypsy cultural taboos, Berlin-Marzahn became the largest Gypsy camp. Guarded by a detachment of Prussian uniformed police (Schutzpolizei) with guard dogs, the camp consisted of 130 caravans condemned as uninhabitable by the Reich Labor Service. The hygienic facilities were totally inadequate; Marzahn had only three water pumps and two toilets. Overcrowding and unsanitary conditions were the norm; in March 1938 city authorities reported 170 cases of communicable diseases.

At first without perimeter fences, Marzahn was subsequently encircled by barbed wire. Women were permitted to leave only to make household purchases, since there was no commissary inside the camp. Although extended families had sometimes traveled together in small groups, the large number of stationary caravans converted this camp into an oppressive ghetto with virtually no prospects of escape. Unlike the earlier arrests of Sinti and Roma as individuals, Marzahn was a "family" compound, where the internees were assembled, concentrated, and imprisoned, thus serving also as a transit depot for later deportations.

The Sinti and Roma at Berlin-Marzahn were assigned to forced labor. Further, the Reich Department of Health compelled them to provide detailed data to the police and health bureaucracies for anthropological and genealogical registration. In turn, this data provided the pretext for the denaturalization and involuntary sterilization of the imprisoned Sinti and Roma. The Berlin-Marzahn Gypsy camp provided evidence of a growing interagency cooperation between public health officials and the police, essential for subsequent developments resulting in the deportation and mass murder of German Gypsies.[25] Anthropological measurements of the Roma and Sinti prisoners in Marzahn were made by Gerhard Stein, a student of the Frankfurt race scientist Otmar von Verschuer.

Gerhard Stein specialized in the study of twins, sterilization, and eugenic suitability for marriage. Born in 1910 in Bad Kreuznach, he joined the Nazi party and the SA in 1931 as a Tübingen University student. He completed medical training at the universities of Würzburg, Innsbruck, Tübingen, and Frankfurt, and passed his state medical examination in Frankfurt in 1937. In 1936 and 1937, he worked at Marzahn as a member of Ritter's unit at the Reich Health Office, and in 1938 he spent six months at Professor Verschuer's Frankfurt Institute for Hereditary Biology and Race Hygiene. Stein incorporated the results of his Marzahn research into his 1938 dissertation on "The Physiology and Anthropology of Gypsies in Germany," submitted and accepted by Verschuer at Frankfurt University and published in 1941 as a forty-three-page article with charts and photographs in *Zeitschrift für Ethnologie*.[26] In Stein's first report from Marzahn, written at the beginning of September 1936, he mentioned "the wildness and licentiousness of Gypsies" and commented that "part-Gypsy bastards are generally dangerous hereditary criminals." Although hardly sympathetic to the plight of the Sinti and Roma detainees, Stein did describe the catastrophic poverty at Marzahn and the appalling sanitary conditions.[27]

Official publications rationalized the transfer to Marzahn by using the deliberately misleading and innocuous term "Rastplatz" for the camp, literally translated as "roadside rest stop." The Nazis used the term pejoratively and ironically, transmuting objective usage into caustic terms of contempt to describe the victims and places that their own policies had created.[28] The official justification for the deportation of entire Sinti and Roma families from their legally rented and registered domiciles and caravan parking sites in Berlin was ostensibly the need to control crime and beggars in the capital prior to the 1936 Olympics.[29]

Created for the 1936 Olympics, the Marzahn camp became a permanent place of incarceration for Sinti and Roma. During the war, the detainees were also compelled to work at forced labor in the Sachsenhausen stone quarries and to clear rubble from Berlin streets after Allied air raids. Most were deported to Auschwitz in 1943.

Marzahn was not the only Gypsy camp, although it probably was the largest. After 1935, several municipal governments and local welfare offices pressured the German police to confine a growing number of German Gypsies in newly created municipal Gypsy camps. These camps were in essence SS-Sonderlager: special internment camps combining elements of protective custody concentration camps and embryonic ghettos; they held full families including women and young children. Usually located on the outskirts of cities, these camps were guarded by the SS, the gendarmerie, or the uniformed city police. They became reserve depots for forced labor, genealogical registration, and compulsory sterilization. Between 1933 and 1939, Gypsy camps were created in Cologne, Düsseldorf, Essen, Frankfurt, Hamburg, Magdeburg, Pölitz near Stettin, and other German cities. These camps evolved after 1939 from municipal internment camps into assembly centers (Sammellager) for systematic deportation to concentration camps, ghettos, and killing centers.[30]

In Frankfurt, for example, local officials—including Frankfurt Chief of Police Beckerle, Mayor Krebs, and representatives from the welfare office—expanded existing municipal anti-Gypsy ordinances in the spring of 1936. New measures included police searches of all Gypsy residences three times a week; police checks on all Gypsy identity papers to determine whether any were stateless or foreigners, vulnerable to expulsion; compulsory municipal genetic and genealogical registration; resettlement of all Sinti and Roma found within the city limits in the Frankfurt Gypsy camp; prohibition against renting local camp sites to Sinti and Roma outside the municipal Gypsy camp; and expelling migrant Sinti and Roma upon their arrival in Frankfurt.[31]

Additional measures in Frankfurt further increased police harassment of both domiciled and migrant Sinti and Roma. These directives included restricting the number of new trade licenses issued to itinerant Sinti and Roma, thereby preventing or limiting their employment as knife (or scissors) grinders, horse traders, traveling salespersons, fortune-tellers, musicians, and circus performers; checking school attendance by Gypsy children, truancy to be punished by removal to municipal juvenile facilities; and compulsory registration of all Gypsies detained or arrested by the police. Flight from the Gypsy camp was punishable by automatic transfer to a concentration camp.[32]

At the Düsseldorf Höherweg camp, the Sinti and Roma were compelled to pay six marks monthly for inferior accommodations in barracks that did not even have electricity; they were also barred from receiving either unemployment or welfare assistance. In addition, the camp commandant mandated rigid curfews, prohibited children from playing on the grounds, and banned visits and communications from non-Gypsy relatives.[33] Similar measures were implemented in other municipal Gypsy camps.

The situation in Cologne was similar. On February 28, 1938, the president of the German Association of Cities (Deutscher Gemeindetag) advised the lord mayor of Hindenburg in Upper Silesia:

> In Cologne, the so-called "traveling people," i.e., Gypsies and their bastard offspring, basket and umbrella makers, were relocated together with their caravans to a place on the edge of town. They are no longer permitted to stop at other sites. Welfare support payments, almost exclusively products in kind, are contingent on this.[34]

The Cologne Gypsy camp at Venloer Strasse 888 had opened in May 1935; it served as a model for "Gypsy camps" in other German cities and the German Association of Cities shared experiences and data from Cologne with other towns.

In March 1936, a memorandum prepared for State Secretary Hans Pfundtner of the Reich Ministry of Interior contained the first references to the preparation of a national Gypsy law (Reichszigeunergesetz) and to the difficulties of achieving a "total solution of the Gypsy problem on either a national or international level." The interim recommendations in this memorandum included expulsion of stateless and foreign Gypsies, restrictions on freedom of movement and on issuing licenses for Gypsies with itinerant trades (Wandergewerbe), increased police surveillance, sterilization of Gypsies of mixed German and Gypsy ancestry (so-called Mischlinge), complete registration of all Gypsies in the Reich, and confinement in a special Gypsy reservation.[35] The abortive attempt to create a national policy was successful only with the consolidation of police authority and in the growing coordination of municipal Gypsy camps through the German Association of Cities.

A reexamination of existing historical literature reveals the parallel between the Gypsy camps and the concentration camp system. In addition, Sinti and Roma were also sent to the main German concentration camps. For example, 400 Bavarian Sinti and Roma were deported to Dachau in July 1936. This arrest occurred almost simultaneously with the arrest of Berlin Sinti and Roma and their relocation to Berlin-Marzahn. An additional 1,000 Sinti and Roma, "able to work," were arrested in raids during the week of June 13, 1938, and deported to Buchenwald, Dachau, and Sachsenhausen; women were sent to the Lichtenburg concentration camp in Saxony.[36] These 1938 arrests were authorized under an unpublished decree on "crime prevention" (vorbeugende Verbrechensbekämpfung) issued in December 1937. This decree extended the use of preventive arrest to all persons whose asocial behavior supposedly threatened the common good, irrespective of whether the individual had a criminal record. It was applied to migrant and unemployed Gypsies, so-called asocials, the unemployed, habitual criminals, homeless panhandlers, beggars, and Jews previously sentenced to jail for more than thirty days (including for traffic violations). The arrests were made by Kripo detectives (rather than by the Gestapo) and provided the expanding camp system with potential slave labor.[37]

After the Anschluss, several Gypsy camps were established in Austria, the two largest at Maxglan near Salzburg and Lackenbach in the Burgenland. In addition, Austrian Sinti and Roma were also sent to various concentration camps, including Mauthausen and Ravensbrück. Thus in the summer and fall of 1938 about three thousand allegedly "work-shy" Austrian Sinti and Roma were deported: two thousand male Gypsies above the age of sixteen were sent to Dachau and later remanded to Buchenwald, and one thousand female Gypsies above the age of fifteen were sent to Ravensbrück.[38]

In 1938 and 1939, the Nazi ideological obsession with Gypsies became almost as strident and aggressive as the campaign against the Jews.[39] In August 1938, Sinti and Roma were expelled, ostensibly as military security risks, from border zones on the left bank of the Rhine and, once war had begun, they were prohibited from "wandering" in the western areas of the Reich. In May 1938, Himmler ordered that the Munich bureau of Gypsy affairs be renamed Reichszentrale zur Bekämpfung des Zigeunerunwesens and placed within the RKPA in Berlin. Moreover, on December 8, 1938, Himmler promulgated his decree "Fighting the Gypsy Plague," basing it on Robert Ritter's anthropological and genealogical registration forms (rassenbiologische Gutachtung).

Himmler's decree recommended "the resolution of the Gypsy question based on its essentially racial nature" (die Regelung der Zigeunerfrage aus dem Wesen dieser Rasse heraus in Angriff zu nehmen) and mandated that all Gypsies in the Reich above the age of six be classified into three racial groups: "Gypsies, Gypsy Mischlinge, and nomadic persons behaving as Gypsies." The guidelines for implementation published in early 1939 stipulated that the RKPA assist in the "development of a comprehensive Gypsy law prohibiting miscegenation and regulating the life of the Gypsy race in German space."[40] Comprehensive and systematic residential and genealogical registration of Gypsies by local police and public health authorities was required and photo identity cards were to be issued to all Gypsies and part Gypsies. The implementation of Himmler's decree was comprehensive, leading, for example, to the purge of several dozen Gypsy musicians from the Reich Music Chamber.[41]

The deportation of German Sinti and Roma began shortly after the outbreak of war. On October 17, 1939, Reinhard Heydrich issued his so-called Festsetzungerlass, prohibiting all Gypsies and part-Gypsies not already interned in camps from changing their registered domiciles; this measure was essential for implementing deportations.[42]

In the second half of October, Arthur Nebe, chief of the RKPA (RSHA Department V), tried to expedite the deportation of Berlin Gypsies by requesting that Eichmann "add three or four train cars of Gypsies" to the Nisko Jewish transports departing from Vienna. Eichmann cabled Berlin that the Nisko transport would include "a train car of Gypsies to be added to the first Jewish deportation from Vienna."[43] However, the failure of the Nisko resettlement scheme at the end of 1939 precluded the early expulsion of 30,000 Gypsies from the Greater German Reich to the General Government that was rump Poland.[44] The aborted October 1939 deportation belatedly took place in May 1940, when 2,800 German Gypsies were deported from seven assembly centers in the Old Reich to Lublin.[45] In Austria, the deportations to Poland were planned for the second half of August 1940.[46] The rules concerning inclusion and exemption for Gypsies paralleled the later regulations used in Jewish transports.

The property and possessions of the deported Gypsies were confiscated and the deportees were compelled to sign release forms acknowledging the transfer of their possessions as volks-und staatsfeindlichen Vermögens (under the Law for the Confiscation of Subversive and Enemy Property initially used for the seizure of assets of proscribed and denaturalized political opponents after July 1933).[47] The same confiscatory procedures were also employed during the earliest deportations of Jews, prior to the passage of the 11th Ordinance. The 11th Ordinance, promulgated on November 25, 1941, provided for automatic loss of citizenship, including property rights, for Jews who moved from the Reich, even if the move was involuntary.[48] The deportation of Sinti and Roma from Germany and incorporated Austria was again suspended in October 1940 because the General Government had protested the potential dumping of 35,000 Gypsies as well as the impending arrival of large numbers of German Jews.[49] Again in July 1941, the RSHA halted the deportation of East Prussian Sinti and Roma, probably because of the invasion of the Soviet Union, noting that "a general and final solution of the Gypsy question cannot be achieved at this time." Instead, the RSHA proposed to construct a new Gypsy camp enclosed with barbed wire in the outskirts of Königsberg.[50] Nothing is known about conditions in this last Zigeunerlager, the last special municipal camp for Sinti and Roma before the creation of tbe Gypsy family camp at BIIe in Auschwitz-Birkenau.

The Gypsy camps were parallel structures coexisting with the concentration camp system. Roma and Sinti were confined in these municipal camps for indeterminate sentences in dilapidated housing with marginal sanitation and lack of provisions. The prisoners suffered from verbal abuse by guards and police and physical intimidation by prying anthropologists, physicians, and geneticists researching their genealogy and folklore. The pattern of deporting and holding Sinti and Roma as family units commenced in the municipal Zigeunerlager during the 1930s, continued with deportations during the first year of the war, and ended in the Gypsy "family camp" (BIIe) at Auschwitz-Birkenau. A parallel system existed in the main concentration camps, where thousands of German and Austrian Sinti and Roma were incarcerated. Although prisoners could be transferred at any time from municipal Gypsy camps to concentration camps as punishment for noncompliance with regulations or attempted escapes, most transfers occurred after 1938 to provide forced labor for the concentration camp system. The municipal Gypsy camps were an early, decentralized, and provisional attempt to segregate Sinti and Roma, and, like the later ghettos in Eastern Europe, served in the end only as transfer stations to the killing centers.

NOTES

1. This phrase is found in Norman Cohn, *The Pursuit of the Millennium: Revolutionary Messianism in Medieval and Reformation Europe and Its Bearing on Modern Totalitarian Movements* (New York: Harper Torchbooks, 1961).

2. Telford Taylor, *The Anatomy of the Nuremberg Trials: A Personal Memoir* (New York: Knopf, 1992), p. 103.

3. For a discussion of Roma and Sinti in Holocaust historiography, see Sybil Milton, "The Context of the Holocaust," *German Studies Review* 13 (1990): 269–83; idem, "Gypsies and the Holocaust," *History Teacher* 24, no. 4 (August 1991): 375–87; idem, "Correspondence," *History Teacher* 25, no. 4 (August 1992): 515–21; idem, "Holocaust: The Gypsies," in *Genocide in the Twentieth Century: Critical Essays and Eyewitness Accounts*, ed. William S. Parsons, Israel W. Charny, and Samuel Totten (New York: Garland Publishing, 1995), pp. 209–64; idem, "Sinti und Roma als 'vergessene Opfergruppe' in der Gedenkstättenarbeit," in *Der Völkermord an den Sinti und Roma in der Gedenkstättenarbeit*, ed. Edgar Bamberger (Heidelberg: Dokumentations- und Kulturzentrum Deutscher Sinti und Roma, 1994), pp. 53–60; and idem, "Vorstufe zur Vernichtung: Die Zigeunerlager nach 1933," *Vierteljahrshefte für Zeitgeschichte* 43, no. 1 (January 1995): 115–30. See also Michael Zimmermann, *Verfolgt, vertrieben, vernichtet: Die nationalsozialistische Vernichtungspolitik gegen Sinti und Roma* (Essen: Klartext, 1989), pp. 87–98; Kirsten Martins-Heuss, *Zur mythischen Figur des Zigeuners in der deutschen Zigeunerforschung* (Frankfurt/M.: Haag and Herchen, 1983); and Benno Müller-Hill, *Murderous Science: Elimination by Scientific Selection of Jews, Gypsies, and Others, Germany, 1933–1945*, trans. George R. Fraser (Oxford: Oxford University Press, 1988).

4. See Ludwig Eiber, ed., *"Ich wusste, es wird schlimm"; Die Verfolgung der Sinti und Roma in München 1933–1945* (Munich: Buchendorfer Verlag, 1993), pp. 43–45. For the development of police and psychiatric registration practices in the late nineteenth and early twentieth centuries, see Susanne Regener, "Ausgegrenzt: Die optische Inventarisierung der Menschen im Polizeiwesen und in der Psychiatrie," *Fotogeschichte* 10, no. 38 (1990): 23–38.

5. Karola Fings and Frank Sparing, *Nur wenige kamen zurück: Sinti und Roma im Nationalsozialismus* (Cologne: Landesverband Deutscher Sinti und Roma NRW and El-De-Haus, 1990), p. 3; and idem, *"z. Zt. Zigeunerlager": Die Verfolgung der Düsseldorfer Sinti und Roma im Nationalsozialismus* (Cologne: Volksblatt Verlag, 1992), pp. 17–20, 111.

6. Inge Marssolek and René Ott, *Bremen im Dritten Reich: Anpassung, Widerstand, Verfolgung* (Bremen: Carl Schünemann Verlag, 1986), pp. 334–35; and Fings and Sparing, *"z. Zt. Zigeunerlager,"* p. 19.

7. Runderlass des Reichs- und Preussischen Ministers des Innern betr. "Bekämpfung der Zigeunerplage," June 5, 1936 (III C II 20, no. 8/36), in *Ministerialblatt für die Preussische Innere Verwaltung* 1, no. 27 (June 17, 1936): 783. Reproduced in facsimile in Eva von Hase-Mihalik and Doris Kreuzkamp, *"Du kriegst auch einen schönen Wohnwagen": Zwangslager für Sinti und Roma während des Nationalsozialismus in Frankfurt am Main* (Frankfurt/M.: Brandes and Apsel, 1990), pp. 43–44.

8. For the involuntary expulsion of Russian, Romanian, Polish, and stateless Jews from Germany in 1938, see Sybil Milton, "The Expulsion of the Polish Jews from Germany, 1938," in *Leo Baeck Institute Year Book* 29 (1984): 169–99; idem, "Menschen zwischen Grenzen: Die

Polenausweisung 1938," in *Der Novemberpogrom 1938: Die "Reichskristallnacht" in Wien*, ed. Siegwald Ganglmair and Regina Forstner-Karner (Vienna: Museen der Stadt Wien, 1988), pp. 46–52; and Jacob Toury, "Ein Auftakt zur Endlösung: Judenaustreibungen über nichtslawische Reichsgrenzen 1933–1939," in *Das Unrechtsregime: Internationale Forschung über National-sozialismus*, ed. Ursula Büttner, 2 vols. (Hamburg: Christians, 1986), vol. 2, pp. 164–97. For the expulsion of "Jews, Gypsies, Blacks, foreign racial elements, and the incurably insane" from incorporated Alsace to unoccupied France between July and December 1940, see Sybil Milton, "German Occupation Policy in Belgium and France," in *A Mosaic of Victims: Non-Jews Persecuted and Murdered by the Nazis*, ed. Michael Berenbaum (New York: New York University Press, 1990), pp.80–87.

For the laws and decrees issued concerning the handicapped, see Control Commission for Germany (British Element), Legal Division, British Special Legal Research Unit, "Translations of Nazi Health Laws Concerned with Hereditary Diseases, Matrimonial Health, Sterilization, and Castration (8 Nov. 1945)"; for those issued concerning Jews, see Joseph Walk, ed., *Das Sonderrecht für die Juden im NS-Staat: Eine Sammlung der gesetzlichen Massnahmen und Richtlinien – Inhalt und Bedeutung* (Heidelberg: C. F. Müller, 1981); for those issued concerning Gypsies, see the collection in Staatsanwaltschaft [hereafter StA] Hamburg, Akten des Verfahrens gegen Dr. Ruth Kellermann u.A., file no. 2200 Js 2/84, and in United States Holocaust Memorial Museum Research Institute Archive, Washington, D.C. [hereafter USHMMRI]: Fojn-Felczer collection.

9. "Gesetz zur Verhütung erbkranken Nachwuchses," *Reichsgesetzblatt* [hereafter *RGBl*] 1933, 1:529; English translation in Control Commission for Germany (British Element), "Translation of Nazi Health Laws," 1–5. See also Gisela Bock, *Zwangssterilisation im National-sozialismus: Studien zur Rassenpolitik und Frauenpolitik* (Opladen: Westdeutscher Verlag, 1986), pp. 361–68, 452–56; idem, "Racism and Sexism in Nazi Germany: Motherhood, Compulsory Sterilization, and the State," in *When Biology Became Destiny: Women in Weimar and Nazi Germany*, ed. Renate Bridenthal, Atina Grossmann, and Marion Kaplan (New York: Monthly Review Press, 1984), pp. 279–89; and Hansjörg Riechert, *Im Schatten von Auschwitz: Die nationalsozialistische Sterilisationspolitik gegenüber Sinti und Roma* (Münster: Waxmann, 1995).

10. For Sinti in Osthofen, see Michail Krausnick, ed., *"Da wollten wir frei sein!": Eine Sinti-Familie erzählt* (Weinheim: Beltz und Gelberg, 1993), p. 73. For Sinti in Brauweiler, see Fings and Sparing, *"z. Zt. Zigeunerlager,"* p. 19; and Josef Wisskirchen, "Das Konzentrationslager Brauweiler, 1933–1934," *Pulheimer Beiträge zur Geschichte und Heimatkunde* 13 (1989): 153–96.

11. Wolfgang Ayass, "Die Verfolgung von Bettlern und Landstreichern im National-sozialismus," in *Wohnsitz Nirgendwo: Vom Leben und Überleben auf der Strasse*, ed. Künstlerhaus Bethanien (Berlin: Frölich and Kaufmann, 1982), pp. 405–13; idem, "Die Verfolgung der Nichtsesshaften im Dritten Reich," in *Ein Jahrhundert Arbeiterkolonien, "Arbeit statt Almosen": Hilfe für obdachlose Wanderarme 1884–1984* (Freiburg, 1984), pp. 87ff.; and Fings and Sparing, *"z. Zt. Zigeunerlager,"* pp. 19, 111–12.

12. Wilhelm Stuckart and Hans Globke, *Kommentare zur deutschen Rassengesetzgebung* (Munich: C. H. Beck'sche Verlagsbuchhandlung, 1936), pp. 55, 153; and Arthur Gütt, Herbert Linden, and Franz Massfeller, *Blutschutz- und Ehegesundheitsgesetz*, 2nd ed. (Munich: J. F. Lehmanns Verlag, 1937), pp. 16, 21, 150, 226.

13. "Gesetz zum Schutze der Erbgesundheit des deutschen Volkes," *RGBl* 1935, 1:1246; English translation in Control Commission for Germany (British Element), "Translation of Nazi Health Laws," 33–34.

14. See Gerhard Friese, *Das Ehegesundheitsgesetz*, Schriftenreihe des Reichsausschusses für Volksgesundheitsdienst, no. 17 (Berlin 1938), pp. 9–12 (copy in Österreichisches Staatsarchiv, Allgemeines Verwaltungsarchiv [Vienna: Reichskommissar für die Wiedervereinigung Österreichs mit dem Deutschen Reich, also known as Bürckel Akte, file 2354]).

15. See Götz Aly and Karl Heinz Roth, *Die restlose Erfassung: Volkszählen, Identifizieren, Aussondern im Nationalsozialismus* (Berlin: Rotbuch, 1984), pp. 96ff.; and Sybil Milton and

David Luebke, "Locating the Victim: An Overview of Census-taking, Tabulation Technology, and Persecution in Nazi Germany," *IEEE Annals of the History of Computing* 16/3 (Fall 1994): 25–39.

16. See Walk, ed., *Sonderrecht für die Juden im NS-Staat*, no. 127, p. 156.

17. See Dokumentationsarchiv des österreichischen Widerstandes, Vienna [hereafter DÖW], file 11151; and Elisabeth Klamper, "Persecution and Annihilation of Roma and Sinti in Austria, 1938–1945," *Journal of the Gypsy Lore Society* 5, vol. 3, no. 2 (August 1993): 55–65.

18. See Franz Calvelli-Adorno, "Die rassische Verfolgung der Zigeuner vor dem 1. März 1943," *Rechtsprechung zum Wiedergutmachungsrecht* 12 (December 1961): 121–42.

19. See Heinrich Wilhelm Kranz, "Zigeuner, wie sie wirklich sind," *Neues Volk* 5/9 (September 1937): 21–27.

Heinrich Wilhelm Kranz (1897–1945), an opthalmologist, had joined both the Nazi Party and the Nazi Physicians' League prior to 1933. After his appointment to teach race science (Rassenkunde) at Giessen, he obtained in 1938 the newly created chair for race science at Giessen University. He became the rector of Giessen in 1940. In Giessen he also headed the Race Political Office of the Gau Hessen-Nassau. In 1940–1941, together with Siegfried Koller, he published a three-volume work, *Die Gemeinschaftsunfähigen*, advocating sterilization, marriage prohibition, and compulsory internment in labor camps for "asocials."

For biographical data on Kranz, see Berlin Document Center: Heinrich Wilhelm Kranz file. For a brief history of Ritter's office in the *Reichsgesundheitsamt*, see *Bundesgesundheitsblatt* 32 (March 1989), special issue "Das Reichsgesundheitsamt, 1933–1945: Eine Ausstellung."

20. On Robert Ritter, see Bundesarchiv Koblenz [hereafter BAK], R73, file 14005: Ritter to Deutsche Forschungsgemeinschaft (DFG), February 2, 1938, February 22, 1939, June 25, 1940; Ritter report to DFG and Reichsforschungsrat, January 31, 1944. See also Joachim S. Hohmann, *Robert Ritter und die Erben der Kriminalbiologie: "Zigeunerforschung" im National-sozialismus und im Westdeutschland im Zeichen des Rassismus*, vol. 4 of *Studien zur Tsiganologie und Folkloristik* (Frankfurt/M.: Peter Lang, 1991); and idem, *Feinderklärung und Prävention: Kriminalbiologie, Zigeunerforschung und Asozialenpolitik*, vol. 6 of *Beiträge zur national-sozialistischen Gesundheits- und Sozialpolitik* (Berlin: Rotbuch Verlag, 1988).

21. Robert Ritter, "Die Bestandsaufnahme der Zigeuner und Zigeunermischlinge in Deutschland," *Der Öffentliche Gesundheitsdienst* 6/21 (February 5, 1941): 477–89; idem, "Die Aufgaben der Kriminalbiologie und der kriminalbiologischen Bevölkerungsforschung," *Kriminalistik* 15/4 (April 1941): 1–4; and idem, "Primitivität und Kriminalität," *Monatsschrift für Kriminalbiologie und Strafrechtsreform* 31/9 (1940): 197–210. See also BAK, ZSg 149/22, Ritter reports to the DFG in the Hermann Arnold Collection.

22. BAK, R36, files 1022 and 1023: Deutscher Gemeindetag, Fürsorge für Juden und Zigeuner. The institutionalized handicapped faced similar deteriorating conditions; see Angelika Ebbinghaus, "Kostensenkung, 'Aktives Therapie' und Vernichtung," in *Heilen und Vernichten im Mustergau Hamburg: Bevölkerungs- und Gesundheitspolitik im Drittem Reich*, ed. Angelika Ebbinghaus, Heidrun Kaupen-Haas, and Karl Heinz Roth (Hamburg: Konkret Literatur Verlag, 1984), pp. 136–46.

23. StA Hamburg, Verfahren 2200 Js 2/84: Reich- und Preussisches Ministerium des Innern, Runderlass betr. "Bekämpfung der Zigeunerplage," June 6, 1936 (III C II 20, no. 10/36); also published in *Ministerialblatt für die Preussische Innere Verwaltung* 1/27 (June 17, 1936): 785.

24. See Wolfgang Wippermann and Ute Brucker-Boroujerdi, "Nationalsozialistische Zwangslager in Berlin III: Das 'Zigeunerlager' Marzahn," *Berlin Forschungen* 2 (1987): 189–201; idem, "Das 'Zigeunerlager' Berlin-Marzahn, 1936–1945: Zur Geschichte und Funktion eines nationalsozialistischen Zwangslagers," *Pogrom* 18/130 (June 1987): 77–80; Reimar Gilsenbach, "Marzahn, Hitlers erstes Lager für 'Fremdrassige': Ein vergessenes Kapitel der Naziverbrechen," *Pogrom* 17/122 (1986): 15–17; and Wolfgang Benz, "Das Lager Marzahn: Zur nationalsozialistischen Verfolgung der Sinti und Roma und ihrer anhaltenden Diskriminierung," in Grabitz, Bästlein, and Tuchel, eds., *Die Normalität des Verbrechens*, pp. 260–79.

25. BAK, ZSg 142/23: Report by Gerhard Stein about the Gypsy Camp Marzahn, September 1, 1936, five pages; and Gerhard Stein, "Untersuchungen im Zigeunerlager Marzahn," Frankfurt/M., October 26, 1936, eight pages.

26. Hohmann, *Robert Ritter und die Erben der Kriminalbiologie*, pp. 291–96.

27. BAK, Zsg 142/23.

28. See Henry Friedlander, "The Manipulation of Language," in *The Holocaust: Ideology, Bureaucracy, and Genocide*, ed. Henry Friedlander and Sybil Milton (Millwood, NY: Kraus International, 1980), pp. 103–13.

29. Organisationskomitee für die XI. Olympiade Berlin 1936 e.V., ed., *XI. Olympiade Berlin 1936: Amtlicher Bericht* (Berlin: Wilhelm Limpert Verlag, 1937), vol. 1, pp. 446–48.

30. For Cologne, see Karola Fings and Frank Sparing, "Das Zigeuner-Lager in Köln-Bickendorf, 1935–1958," *1999: Zeitschrift für Sozialgeschichte des 20. und 21. Jahrhunderts* 6/3 (July 1991): 11–40. For Düsseldorf, see Angela Genger, ed., *Verfolgung und Widerstand in Düsseldorf, 1933–1945* (Düsseldorf: Landeshauptstadt Düsseldorf, 1990), pp. 126–33; and Fings and Sparing, "*z. Zt. Zigeunerlager.*" For Essen and Gelsenkirchen, see Michael Zimmermann, "Von der Diskriminierung zum 'Familienlager' Auschwitz: Die nationalsozialistische Zigeunerverfolgung," *Dachauer Hefte* 5 (1989): 87–114; and idem, *Verfolgt, vertrieben, vernichtet*, pp. 18–22. For Frankfurt, see Wolfgang Wippermann, *Die nationalsozialistische Zigeunerverfolgung*, vol. 2 of the four-part study *Leben in Frankfurt zur NS-Zeit* (Frankfurt/M.: Stadt Frankfurt am Main—Amt für Volksbildung/Volkshochschule, 1986); Die Grünen im Landtag Hessen, Lothar Bembenek and Frank Schwalba-Hoth, eds., *Hessen hinter Stacheldraht; Verdrängt und Vergessen: KZs, Lager, Aussenkommandos* (Frankfurt: Eichborn Verlag, 1984), pp. 153–68; and Hase-Mihalik and Kreuzkamp, *Wohnwagen*. For Hamburg, see Rudko Kawczynski, "Hamburg soll 'zigeunerfrei' werden," in *Heilen und Vernichten im Mustergau Hamburg* ed. Ebbinghaus, Kaupen-Haas, and Roth, pp. 45–53.

31. Stadtarchiv Frankfurt, Mag. Akte (Stadtkanzlei) 2203, vol. 1: Minutes of the Frankfurt City Council, March 20, 1936, concerning "Massnahmen gegen das Zigeunerunwesen."

32. Hase-Mihalik and Kreuzkamp, *Wohnwagen*, p. 42.

33. Fings and Sparing, "*z. Zt. Zigeunerlager,*" pp. 36–37.

34. BAK R 36/881, pp. 28–30, containing a letter from Zengerling, President of the Deutscher Gemeindetag in Berlin, to the Lord Mayor of Hindenburg o.S., February 28, 1938, four pages. See also Karola Fings and Frank Sparing, ". . . tunlichst als erziehungsunfähig hinzustellen"; Zigeunerkinder und -jugendliche: aus der Fürsorge in die Vernichtung," *Dachauer Hefte* 9 (1993): 159–80.

35. BAK, R18/5644, pp. 215–27, containing cover letter and six-page memorandum from Oberregierungsrat Zindel to Staatssekretär Pfundtner, "Gedanken über den Aufbau des Reichszigeunergesetzes," March 4 ,1936. The document states: "Auf Grund aller bisherigen Erfahrungen muss jedenfalls vorweg festgestellt werden, dass eine *restlose Lösung* des Zigeunerproblems weder in einem einzelnen Staate noch international in absehbarer Zeit möglich sein wird" (emphasis in the original).

36. For data on the Lichtenburg women's concentration camp, see Sybil Milton, "Women and the Holocaust: The Case of German and German-Jewish Women," in *When Biology Became Destiny*, ed. Bridenthal, Grossman, and Kaplan, pp. 305–307.

37. StA Hamburg, 2200 Js 2/84: Decree of the Reich and Prussian Ministry of the Interior concerning "Vorbeugende Verbrechensbekämpfung durch die Polizei," December 14, 1937, and "Richtlinien," April 4, 1938. For the raids against so-called asocials, see Wolfgang Ayass, "'Ein Gebot der nationalen Arbeitsdisziplin': Die Aktion 'Arbeitsscheu Reich' 1938," *Beiträge zur nationalsozialistischen Gesundheits- und Sozialpolitik* 6 (Berlin 1988): 43–74. For a survey of the concentration camp system, see Henry Friedlander, "The Nazi Concentration Camps," in *Human Responses to the Holocaust*, ed. Michael Ryan (New York: Edwin Mellen Press, 1981), pp. 33–69; Falk Pingel, *Häftlinge unter SS-Herrschaft: Widerstand, Selbstbehauptung und Vernichtung im Konzentrationslager* (Hamburg: Hoffmann and Campe, 1978); and Klaus Drobisch and Günther Wieland, *System der NS-Konzentrationslager 1933–1939* (Berlin: Akademie Verlag, 1993), pp. 284–89.

38. The persecution of Gypsies in incorporated Austria is relatively well documented;

see Selma Steinmetz, *Österreichs Zigeuner im NS-Staat* (Vienna: Europa Verlag, 1966); Erika Thurner, *Nationalsozialismus und Zigeuner in Österreich* (Vienna: Geyer Edition, 1983); Andreas Maislinger, "'Zigeuneranhaltelager und Arbeitserziehungslager' Weyer: Ergänzung einer Ortschronik," *Pogrom* 18/137 (1987): 33–36; and Erika Weinzierl, "Österreichische Frauen im nationalsozialistischen Konzentrationslagern," *Dachauer Hefte* 3 (1987): 198–202. Weinzierl notes on page 199 that although these figures cannot be confirmed from extant fragmentary camp records, 440 female Gypsies from Vienna, Lower Austria, and Burgenland were registered on arrival at Ravensbrück concentration camp on June 29, 1939.

39. See, for example, "Fahrendes Volk: Die Bekämpfung der Zigeunerplage auf neuen Wegen," *NS-Rechtsspiegel* (Munich), February 21, 1939, facsimile in Sybil Milton and Roland Klemig, eds., *Bildarchiv Preussischer Kulturbesitz*, vol. 1 of *Archives of the Holocaust* (New York: Garland, 1990), pt. 1, figs. 150–51; "Die Zigeuner als asoziale Bevölkerungsgruppe," *Deutsches Ärzteblatt* 69 (1939): 246–47; and "Die Zigeunerfrage in der Ostmark," *Neues Volk* 6/9 (September 1938): 22–27.

40. Runderlass des Reichsführer SS und Chef der Deutschen Polizei im Ministerium des Innern, December 8, 1938, betr. "Bekämpfung der Zigeunerplage," *Ministerialblatt des Reichs- und Preussischen Ministeriums des Innern* 51 (1938): 2105–10. See also "Ausführungsanweisung des Reichskriminalpolizeiamts," March 1, 1939, published in *Deutsches Kriminalpolizeiblatt* 12, special issue (March 20, 1939).

41. See National Archives and Records Administration, Washington, D.C., Microfilm Publication T-70, reel 109, frames 3632755–6: Peter Raabe's remarks as President of the Reich Music Chamber published in *Amtliche Mitteilungen der Reichsmusikkammer*, May 1, 1939. The lists of expelled Gypsy musicians were published between February and December 1940. See ibid., frames 3632796–8, containing the list published on February 15, 1940. This material is cited in Alan E. Steinweis, *Art, Ideology, and Economics in Nazi Germany: The Reich Chambers of Music, Theater, and the Visual Arts* (Chapel Hill: University of North Carolina Press, 1993), pp. 126–27, 132. See also the autobiography of Alfred Lessing, *Mein Leben im Versteck: Wie ein deutscher Sinti den Holocaust überlebte* (Düsseldorf: Zebulon, 1993).

42. StA Hamburg, Verfahren 2200 Js 2/84: RSHA Schnellbrief to Kripo(leit)stellen, October 17, 1939.

43. Zentrale Stelle der Landesjustizverwaltungen, Ludwigsburg, Slg. CSSR, vol. 148, pp. 55–57, and vol. 332, pp. 289–300, 306. See also Jonny Moser, "Nisko: The First Experiment in Deportation," *Simon Wiesenthal Center Annual* 2 (1985): 1–30.

44. BAK, R18/5644, pp. 229–30: letter from Leonardi Conti, Secretary of State for Health in the Reich Ministry of the Interior, to the Central Office of the Security Police, Kripo headquarters, and the Reich Health Department, Berlin, January 24, 1940. The letter states:

> It is known that the lives of Gypsies and part-Gypsies is to be regulated by a Gypsy law (Zigeunergesetz). Moreover, the mixing of Gypsy with German blood is to be resisted and if necessary, this could be legally achieved by creating a statutory basis for the sterilization of part-Gypsies (Zigeunermischlinge). These questions were already in a state of flux before the war started. The war has apparently suddenly created a new situation, since the possibility of expelling Gypsies to the General Government is available. Certainly, such an expulsion appears to have particular advantages at the moment. However, in my opinion, the implementation of such a plan would mean that because it is expedient to do this at the moment, a genuine radicalization would not be achieved. I firmly believe, now as before, that the final solution of the Gypsy problem (endgültige Lösung des Zigeunerproblems) can be achieved only through the sterilization of full and part Gypsies. . . . I think that the time for a legal resolution of these problems is over, and that we must immediately try to sterilize the Gypsies and part Gypsies as a special measure, using analogous precedents. . . . Once sterilization is completed and these people are rendered biologically harmless, it is of no great consequence whether they are expelled or used as labor on the home front.

45. Hessisches Hauptstaatsarchiv, Wiesbaden [hereafter HHStA], 407/863. See also Milton, "Gypsies and the Holocaust," pp. 380–81; Zimmermann, *Verfolgt, vertrieben, vernichtet*, pp. 43–50; Hans Buchheim, "Die Zigeunerdeportation vom Mai 1940," in *Gutachten des Instituts für Zeitgeschichte*, 2 vols. (Munich: Institut für Zeitgeschichte, 1958), vol. 1, pp. 51ff.; and Michael Krausnick, *Abfahrt Karlsruhe 16.5.1940: Die Deportation der Karlsruher*

Sinti und Roma; ein unterschlagenes Kapitel aus der Geschichte unserer Stadt (Karlsruhe: Verband der Sinti und Roma Karlsruhe e.V., 1991). The May 1940 deportation was linked to Reinhard Heydrich's instructions to chiefs of police and district governors in Germany in the so-called Umsiedlungserlass of April 27, 1940, for the "resettlement, arrest, and deportation of Gypsies above the age of seventeen from western and northwestern border zones." See BAK, R58/473: Richtlinien für die Umsiedlung von Zigeunern, Berlin, April 27, 1940.

46. See DÖW, file E18518: letter from Kripostelle Salzburg to the Reichsstatthalter Provincial President Dr. Reitter, Salzburg, July 5, 1940. The Gypsies were to be imprisoned in a special camp until deportation; there they would be registered and given medical examinations.

47. United States Holocaust Memorial Museum, Washington, D.C., Fojn-Felczer collection: ruling (Feststellung) of the Reich Ministry of the Interior, Berlin, January 26, 1943, that Gypsies transferred to concentration camps on orders of the Reich Leader SS were defined as enemies of the Reich and, consequently, their property and possessions could be seized.

48. See Henry Friedlander, "The Deportation of the German Jews: Postwar German Trials of Nazi Criminals," Leo Baeck Institute *Year Book* 29 (1984): 212.

49. Werner Präg and Wolfgang Jakobmeyer, eds., *Das Diensttagebuch des deutschen Generalgouverneurs in Polen, 1939–1945* (Stuttgart: Deutsche Verlags-Anstalt, 1975), pp. 93, 146–47 (March 4, 1940), 158 (April 5, 1940), and 262 (July 31, 1940). See also Friedlander, "Deportation of German Jews," p. 209.

50. StA Hamburg, Verfahren 2200 Js 2/84: RSHA Rundschreiben to Kripoleitstelle Königsberg, July 22, 1941.

29.

EDITH RAIM

Concentration Camps and the Non-Jewish Environment

This essay addresses two issues—first, the involvement of the construction organization, Organization Todt (OT), in the Holocaust; and second, the non-Jewish environment of two of the "outer camps" of Dachau in the last ten months of the Third Reich.

As a result of "Operation Big Week"—the intensified Allied bombing in February 1944—German aircraft production had been severely damaged at the beginning of that year. For the first time the aircraft industry had been specifically targeted. Tens of thousands of bombs had hit factories, causing a loss in production of up to two-thirds of former output. These bombings also caused a significant loss of trained manpower and problems in transportation and supply delivery.[1]

Under these conditions the National Socialists were obliged to make drastic efforts to increase armament production. They realized that they had to give special emphasis to the production of fighter aircraft if they were not to lose air supremacy over Germany. Such a situation, they realized, could ultimately lose them the war. For this reason, the fighter staff (Jägerstab) was established on March 1, 1944, with the sole aim of maintaining and increasing the production of fighter aircraft.[2] The chief initiators of the new department were Albert Speer, the armament and war production minister; and Erhard Milch, Secretary of the Air Combat Ministry. Milch played a leading part in the operation of the Jägerstab, although Saur—the secretary to Speer's ministry—was chiefly responsible for the day to day organization. Designed as a temporary expedient, the Jägerstab included members of the aircraft industry and specialists from the armament and air ministries. Göring, the minister of air combat, established three high priority guidelines for the activities of the fighter staff: 1) the immediate repair of damaged factories; 2) decentralization and expansion of existing factories; and 3) the creation of bomb-proof manufacturing sites.[3]

Of these, industrial decentralization, both above and underground, had been discussed since 1943; the most complex project thus far had been the manufacturing of the A4 rocket in tunnels under Kohnstein Mountain, near Nordhausen. However, decentralization alone could not solve the problem of production loss: the protection of factories by means of screening and antiaircraft guns was neither completely efficient nor feasible for a longer term. Besides all of the transportation problems caused by the war, certain parts of industry were so linked together that they could not be spread around the country. Still, despite its high costs, locating key industries underground seemed like a particularly sound solution to the problems confronting the Jägerstab planners.

Hitler himself was thrilled by the idea and ordered the "generous and final transfer of German industry under the surface."[4] Despite the seemingly farfetched nature of the proposal, three million square meters of production area were planned to come into use by the end of 1945. The Reich and the occupied territories were combed for appropriate subterranean spaces such as caves, mineshafts, quarries, car tunnels, and underground tunnels; even beer- and vegetable-storage cellars and the crypts of churches were considered.[5]

In May 1944 there were 200,000 square meters of underground production space; between June and August 1944 this number increased fivefold.[6] The final aim, however, was even more ambitious: eight million square meters. Twenty-seven main centers of aircraft manufacturing were to be divided into 729 production units.[7]

Implementation was the difficult part of these plans. Industry's enthusiasm for subterranean space is easily explicable: it could provide security from Allied bombs for equipment and plant materials. However, despite the vigorous interest of some manufacturers, only a few of the subterranean areas presented satisfactory working conditions. As existing underground locations were both insufficient and rare, the idea of purposely built bunkers began to take shape. The main prerequisites for their location were accessibility by ship or train and the existence of gravel locally for the production of concrete. The structures were to be camouflaged by screening and further protected by antiaircraft batteries. Hitler demanded that construction be given massive support, and the results were to be enormous in scale: 600,000 to 800,000 square meters per bunker, six to eight stories high, partly dug into the earth.[8]

Xaver Dorsch, the construction specialist in Speer's ministry, devised plans to build six bunkers within six months, which pleased both Hitler and Göring greatly. Dorsch and his construction organization were appointed to build the bunkers, and were made responsible to Hitler personally. Speer, however, felt snubbed and could not conceal his skepticism and criticism, prophesying that none of the six bunkers would be finished on time.

Because of the intense chaos of the last months of the war, it is difficult to determine how many bunkers were actually finished. An obsession with secrecy took on absurd proportions; locations were given code names as were the factories and the actual buildings. Of the six bunkers proposed, only four were begun: three near Landsberg, sixty kilometers west of Munich, and one near Mühldorf, eighty kilometers east of Munich. Very quickly, work on two of the bunkers near Landsberg ceased, and only one, Weingut II, was continued. The bunker near Mühldorf was codenamed Weingut I.

The decision to design and build the bunkers for fighter plane production was made very quickly. Within two months, plans, designs, contractors, and responsibilities were settled by Hitler, Göring, and Dorsch.[9] Organization Todt was commissioned to take overall responsibility for the project, although sub-contractors were to carry out the actual work.

The Todt Organization was the most important nonmilitary, war-supporting institution of the Third Reich.[10] It had been founded in 1938 in order to build the Westwall and had grown steadily in importance. Interestingly, apart from the Hitler

Youth, it was the only organization in the Third Reich named after a member of the Nazi elite. A hybrid organization, its structure was patterned after that of the military but it was not part of the Wehrmacht. Its members wore uniforms bearing the swastika, but it was not part of the Nazi Party. The OT was involved in all sorts of construction work, including roads, railroad tracks, bridges, mines, and factories. The group served war aims through the maintenance of essential infrastructure, which allowed the Wehrmacht to fulfill its logistical tasks.

In 1942, the OT was organized in seven task forces, but it operated only in the occupied territories and behind the front. Approximately four-fifths of its workers were foreign nationals. Many others were forced laborers who had been drafted. Russian POWs and German "half-" or "quarter-" Jews were also in its ranks. Mistreatment and discrimination were part of daily life, and imprisonment in so-called OT camps therefore often resembled life in concentration camps.[11]

While the OT was engaged in building the bunkers for the fighter planes, it was given authority to interrupt other projects and take over materials or workers. The task force set up for this project was formed from the remnants of groups that had served in France and Russia. Its head was Professor Hermann Giesler, an architect and personal friend of both Hitler and Speer, who was a brother of the Gauleiter of Munich.

One of the main problems in the building of the bunkers was the shortage of workers. By 1944 the influx of foreign workers had slowed to a mere trickle, and the forced laborers within the Reich were already involved in regular war production or construction projects. Initially, concentration camp prisoners were offered frequently by the SS. But once the SS realized the authority this conferred upon the OT group, it started to pursue its own war production and building projects in order to become even more independent and powerful—thus, limiting private access to the potential workforce in the camps.

Where could the laborers be taken from? One plan was to get them from Italy, and it seems that Mussolini had even agreed to send a few thousand workers to Germany for the sole purpose of building the bunkers. That possibility evaporated with the fall of Mussolini, and the few forced laborers the OT was able to obtain were insufficient.

The biggest contingent of workers available were the approximately 40,000 Jews deported from all over Europe into the camps erected near the construction sites. Their use within the Reich constituted a precedent that needed special authorization by the Führer because the Reich had been officially judenfrei since 1942.[12] So important was the OT project to the regime that ideological reservations were overruled by economic considerations. Jews who would have been killed without any scruples in 1942 or 1943 were now exempted from gassing and instead were deported to Germany. These concentration camp prisoners were survivors of the ghettos and of the concentration and extermination camps, particularly Hungarian Jews who had been spared Nazi persecution until the spring of 1944. However, construction work for the OT hardly gave them a better chance to survive.

The system of concentration camps had vastly expanded in the last one-and-a-half years of the war, covering the Reich and the occupied territories with a network of main and subcamps. Dachau, the oldest concentration camp, was surrounded by hundreds of small camps. The two biggest camps were called Kaufering and Mühldorf after the neighboring village and town. They were founded in 1944 in connection with the work on the bunkers. The Kaufering subcamp system consisted of eleven camps, all numbered with Roman numerals or named after neighboring villages. Some of the camps near Mühldorf were given code names, the others were named after Todt Organization camps.[13] The camps were not founded simultaneously but were built (and abandoned) as needed. No previous planning for the prisoners' accommodation had been made; quite often, when the prisoners arrived, they had no accommodation until they built primitive huts themselves.

Instead of the traditional wooden or stone barracks typical of the main camps, huts and wooden shacks—half sunk into the earth—were used, as well as lean-tos made of plywood. The prisoners slept on wooden planks covered with straw, often sharing a blanket or with none at all. When it rained or snowed, the roofs of the huts leaked and the floors became muddy; the huts soon were infested with lice and other vermin. The only sources of light were two windows on each side of the hut, and the only source of heating was a little oven in the middle of the room. However, prisoners were not even provided with heating material; they had to "organize" it themselves. The onset of even the mildest winter near the Bavarian Alps meant incredible hardship for the prisoners.

The OT displayed the same slack attitude toward the food it had agreed to provide for the prisoners. The SS members who ran the camps ordered rations for both prisoners and SS staff only once a week. This inflexible system was extremely disadvantageous for the prisoners, as new transports often arrived unexpectedly during the week. This meant that they sometimes could not be fed, or that the meager rations had to be divided among an even larger group of inmates. Moreover, rations for sick prisoners were cut.[14]

To aggravate the situation further, the midday meal was not given to the prisoners in the camp but only to those working on the construction site. Some of the sick prisoners tried to drag themselves to the work site to try to get food. In a statement made shortly after the war, an OT director of the Landsberg bunker explained that he had meant well by introducing the arrangement of lunch on the site, since the workers would otherwise have eaten all the food before even coming to work. He also mentioned that a separate sick bay had to be installed at the construction site since so many sick inmates wished to come to work in order to get food.[15]

A former prisoner noted that illness was worse than death; being ill meant being useless—and, therefore, being forced to suffer additional pangs of heightened hunger.[16] The OT's technocratic "philosophy" did not allow even the most basic needs of human beings to be taken into account. Despite providing only minimal facilities for accommodation and food, both OT and the contracted firms expected a maximum amount of work from the prisoners. The Jewish inmates were used for the hardest work, and there was no protective clothing or headgear.

The work consisted of building dams, laying track for railways, cutting wood, and other construction activities. One of the hardest tasks was unloading cement from trucks or railcars, dragging it to and then pouring it into the concrete-mixing machines. To prevent the mixer from clogging, prisoners had to poke the concrete down the funnel. Inmates sometimes fell into the sticky, still-soft concrete and were too weak to get out.

Apart from the murderous everyday work conditions, German OT first-line supervisors often added to the prisoners' misery. Again and again OT management was obliged to forbid the guards to beat the workers from the concentration camps. One of the directors complained about the readiness with which the OT members hit the prisoners with sticks and other instruments to "teach them to work."[17] Victims died regularly as a result mistreatment by OT personnel.

After only a few weeks the wretched state of health of the prisoners came to the attention of even the negligent OT management—only, of course, in the context of poor work performance. The delousing of the prisoners' barracks was recommended, although it was acknowledged that all previous efforts in this regard had been to no avail. The management complained that some prisoners spent much of their time scratching their wounds, which often covered entire limbs. Of course such concern did not spring from humanitarian compassion but economic considerations. With the limited availability of forced laborers, not only the amount of work done every day but also the health of the prisoners had to be considered. In the past, a director complained, the prisoners at the Landsberg construction sites had been mistreated so badly that of 17,600 prisoners interned in the Kaufering camps, only 8,319 were able to work.[18]

Working and living circumstances gradually led to complete physical (and psychological) breakdown. Typhoid fever, typhus, tuberculosis, and other contagious diseases spread rapidly because there were no sanitation facilities available, either in the camps or at the work sites. In one instance, latrines were provided only after the first cases of typhoid fever occurred. In some camps there was not even running water.

According to the contract between the SS and the OT, medicine also should have been provided by the OT itself. Only small amounts were provided by the camp administration, however. Embezzlement by the SS added to the shortage of even the most basic medicines. Prisoners fell victim to diseases that could have been treated with medicines from the OT's well-stocked depot nearby.

The inmates' medics described the desperate situation: the medicine could not be given to the terminally ill, as it would have deprived other prisoners whose lives could still be saved. Even more shocking, prisoners in the Mühldorf camps were subjected by an OT doctor to medical experiments for the treatment of paradentosis.[19] Although it is not known how much prisoners suffered from the treatment (which consisted of intramuscular and intravenous injections), it is certain that, given most prisoners' critical state of health, this therapy was both irresponsible and useless.

The construction contractors often complained that the prisoners' work hours had to be paid for, despite the fact that many were no longer able to work satisfactorily because of their poor health. In response, the OT, always eager to help, requested SS headquarters in Dachau to remove the sick who "only put a strain on the camps" of Kaufering and Mühldorf. In Mühldorf, the OT acted on its own initiative. The OT task force physician, Dr. Erika Flocken, conducted the selection. The notice for the transport of the sick read: "This transport was ordered by the headquarters of Dachau concentration camp and constituted by the OT task force doctor."[20] Two thousand one hundred fifty-seven prisoners who had come to the Kaufering and Mühldorf camps in mid-June 1944 (at the earliest) were in such poor health by September and

October 1944 that they were deemed unfit to work. They were deported to Auschwitz and gassed shortly before that facility ceased gassing operations in November.[21] Since many of these prisoners had gone through Auschwitz before their arrival in the Bavarian outer camps, they must have been well aware of the fate that awaited them.

The OT itself was never held responsible for the criminal treatment of prisoners or for acting as an accessory to murder. Only in the case of the Mühldorf trial—which dealt with OT and contractor staff as well as the SS—were the criminal acts of the OT pointed out. Among the defendants was Hermann Giesler, the former head of OT task force VI; Dr. Flocken; the OT task force doctor, and Griesinger, director of project Weingut I at Mühldorf. Griesinger, however, escaped American custody and was not convicted. Giesler was sentenced to life imprisonment, Flocken to death; both verdicts were shortly thereafter commuted to a few years' imprisonment. In his defense, Giesler tried to blame OT headquarters, the SS, and the contractor, Polensky and Zöllner. He claimed to have made it clear that the OT project was an aberration and to have told Hitler about his reservations; one could not, after all, build on such a scale with Jewish merchants, lawyers, and others unskilled in construction.[22] His statement reflected no remorse, nor any apparent realization of the enormity of the crimes.

The Americans tried to no avail to collect prosecution material for the Kaufering camps, but the SS and OT had evidently destroyed most of the files. When questioned by the American investigators, Dorsch—the person principally responsible for the OT—claimed that he did not remember where the buildings had been located or the circumstances under which they had been constructed.[23]

In summary, the OT was not only responsible for accommodation, nutrition, and medical supervision at its sites but also for the conditions of work. It made decisions even about the life and death of the prisoners since, apart from destruction through work, there was selection and handing over of prisoners for killing in Auschwitz. In some sense the concentration camps were completely run by the OT, since the SS was simply an instrument to terrorize and guard the prisoners.

The SS often had willing helpers in their mass killings, including help from the Wehrmacht and the police for the murders by the SS task forces and support from industry in the program "Vernichtung durch Arbeit." The OT offered itself willingly as an accomplice, taking on the responsibility for thousands of human beings in camps initiated by their giant building projects and ruthlessly committing them to work tasks and selections that killed thousands of prisoners. In the Kaufering camps, between eleven and fourteen thousand of the thirty thousand prisoners died, in Mühldorf more than four thousand of the eight thousand.

The camps were situated near railway tracks, roads, and farmhouses. Sometimes prisoners marched through parts of the towns on their way to work. Although the prisoners worked primarily on the construction sites, they were used also for odd jobs both in Mühldorf and Landsberg, which brought them into close contact with the Germans. For example, they were involved in "clearing up" operations at bombed airfields, and they worked on farms in the surrounding countryside. Former prisoners described the painful sensation that life in Germany was going on normally around them while they had been deported; had lost their families, friends, and neighbors; and were subjected to murderous work and living conditions. Many of the prisoners encountered indifference or even antisemitism in public, although a few kindly people helped by secretly feeding them in farmhouses or passing food to marching columns. A chimney sweeper, commissioned to clean the chimneys of the prisoners' huts in the concentration camp in Kaufering, was able to smuggle medicine and food into the camp. In a few instances, prisoners were able to talk to Germans and tell them about their fate and the fate of their families. Also, during the last chaotic days of the Third Reich, some families offered shelter to prisoners who had fled during evacuation marches.

Despite some very limited assistance from the local population, the prisoners, especially those not able to speak German, were left to their own devices to survive. Particularly outrageous were the machinations of the Landsberg town council, which hoped to use the prisoners' presence indirectly for their advantage. Citing the difficulties of coping with the unpleasant disorder caused by the extensive construction activities, and because the town was called upon to supply some food for the camps, the burgers expected some compensation, requesting that the main railway lines should be connected with Landsberg station. This request was made in a letter from the mayor to Dorsch.[24]

Today there are few traces to tell us of the prisoners' fate. The prisoner-laid tracks leading to the construction sites have long been dismantled. Forests cover many of the construction efforts. The bunkers—one in ruins, one still used as a depot—remain as silent witnesses to slave labor. The prisoners' wooden huts no longer exist. The sites of the former concentration camps are covered with industrial parks, allotments, junkyards, or simply grass. Only cemeteries, many Jewish cemeteries, remain to bear witness to the prisoners' life and death.

However, sometimes prisoners did leave their mark. On one of the pillars in a dynamite production factory near Landsberg there is a charcoal drawing of a rough street map captioned "Budapest 1944." Perhaps a prisoner drew it during one of the short breaks in order to show another prisoner where he had lived, or where a particular building or street had been. We will never know the purpose of that map, or what happened to the prisoner who drew it. Was he deported to Auschwitz in the autumn of 1944? Did he live until the end of the war, only to die of starvation or be shot during the evacuation marches? Was he burnt alive in Kaufering camp IV on April 27, 1945, shortly before the Americans came? Or did he survive and emigrate to Israel?

NOTES

1. See Alan Milward, *Die deutsche Kriegswirtschaft 1939–1945* (Stuttgart, 1966), p. 125.

2. "Anordnung des Reichsministerium für Rüstung und Kriegsproduktion (RMfRuK)" [decree of the Minister for Armament and War Production concerning the founding of the Jägerstab], March 1, 1944, R 50 II/46a, Bundesarchiv Koblenz (hereafter BAK).

3. "Erlass des Reichsmarschall des Grossdeutschen Reiches und Beauftragten für den Vierjahresplan," Hermann Göring, March 4, 1944, BAK, R 50 II/46a.

4. *Protokoll der Führerbesprechung am 5.3.1944* [Minutes of the conference at Hitler's

headquarters, March 5, 1944] R 3/1509, pp. 13–14. Willi A. Boelcke, ed., *Deutschlands Rüstung im Zweiten Weltkrieg: Hitler's Konferenzen mit Albert Speer 1942–1945* (Frankfurt/M., 1969), p. 338.

5. See *Kriegstagebuch der Rüstungsinspektion VII des Reichsministeriums für Rüstungs- und Kriegsproduktion vom Juli 1944*, Bundesarchiv-Militärarchiv Freiburg, RW 20-7/15.

6. See Milward, *Die deutsche Kriegswirtschaft*, p. 127.

7. See United States Strategic Bombing Survey: Aircraft Industry Report (Washington, D.C., 1945), p. 24.

8. *Protokoll der Führerbesprechung am 5.3.1944*, p. 13; Boelcke, *Deutschlands Rüstung*, p. 337.

9. *Brief Hitlers an Speer vom 21.4.1944* [Hitler's letter to Speer, April 21, 1944], BAK, R 3/1576, p. 131; see also BAK, R 3/1637, p. 8.

10. See Franz Seidler, *Die Organisation Todt: Bauen für Staat und Wehrmacht 1938–1945* (Koblenz, 1987).

11. See Hermann Graml, *Reichskristallnacht: Antisemitismus und Judenverfolgung im Dritten Reich* (Munich, 1988), p. 152.

12. See *Protokoll der Besprechung Dorschs mit Hitler am 6./7.4.1944* [Minutes of a conference between Hitler and Dorsch, April 6/7, 1944] as quoted in Albert Speer, *Der Sklavenstaat: Meine Auseinandersetzungen mit der SS* (Stuttgart, 1981), pp. 400–401; and *Protokoll der Besprechung Saurs am 6./7.4.1944* [Minutes of a conference with Saur, April 6/7, 1944], BAK, R 3/1509, pp. 26–27.

13. See Edith Raim, *Die Dachauer KZ-Aussenkommandos Kaufering und Mühldorf: Rüstungsbauten und Zwangsarbeit im letzten Kriegsjahr 1944/1945* (Landsberg, 1992).

14. See letter by Langleist (camp commander of the Mühldorf complex of camps), dated March 8, 1945, vol. 2, microfilm 123a/6 of the Mühldorf trial, Bayerisches Hauptstaatsarchiv, Munich.

15. Statement by Stroh, Case 000-50-105, NARA RG 338. Stroh was responsible for Weingut II, one of the three bunker building sites near Landsberg.

16. See Henryk Goldring, *Di Kulturtreger* (Munich, 1947), p. 61 (in Yiddish).

17. "Vermerk des OT-Stabsfrontführers Buschmann" [note by OT director Buschmann], December 6, 1944, Case 000-50-105, NARA, RG 338.

18. Ibid.

19. See statements of former prisoners during the Mühldorf trial, microfilms 123a/4 and 123a/5, Bayerisches Hauptstaatsarchiv, Munich.

20. See transport lists D-Da-3/2/1, no. 149717, Archiwum Pastwowe Muzeum W Oswiecimiu (State Archives Auschwitz).

21. See transport lists D-Da-3/2/2, nos. 149717 and D-Da 3/2/1, no. 149717 (State Archives Auschwitz).

22. See Giesler's testimony during the Mühldorf trial, microfilm 123a/5, pp. 1378–79, Bayerisches Hauptstaatsarchiv, Munich.

23. See Dorsch's statement during the trial against Milch, Trials of War Criminals before the Nuremberg Military Tribunal, Washington, D.C., 1949–1954, pp. 1369–70.

24. Letter by Landsberg's mayor, Linn, to Dorsch, dated July 11, 1944, 065/1 Wehrmachtsanlagen/OT-Rüstungsbau, archives at Landsberg.

30.

GORDON J. HORWITZ

Places Far Away, Places Very Near

MAUTHAUSEN, THE CAMPS OF THE SHOAH,
AND THE BYSTANDERS

We turn to the world of the ghettos and concentration camps and we imagine we are on a journey to a world apart, a world far away. You and I are not the first to think in these terms. Images of a distant and forbidding realm occupied the thoughts of those who first set foot in these places. One thinks of Jan Karski, envoy of the Polish government-in-exile, on a clandestine journey into the Warsaw ghetto in October 1942. His story, repeated decades later before the camera for Claude Lanzmann's film *Shoah*, was told in print as early as 1944. To enter the ghetto he was led through a doorway and then, by way of a cellar passage, he emerged on the other side, inside the Jewish zone. "Indeed, at that time, the building had become like a modern version of the River Styx which connected the world of the living with the world of the dead."[1] He described the terrifying sight of the persons he encountered inside the ghetto. He found people, "the shadows of what had once been men or women," who "flitted by" crazed with starvation, "enveloped in a haze of disease and death through which their bodies appeared to be throbbing in disintegration." He came upon bodies left unattended, unclothed in the streets because, he was told, their families could not afford to bury them. His guides, a pair of Jewish leaders—"two dejected shadows" who "seemed like apparitions," he had earlier described them—told him not to worry, as the ghetto dwellers, just barely alive, passed before him. "They are dying, that's all," they said, "they are dying." Yet they urged him, above all, to "remember, remember."[2]

Overwhelmed, after a brief stay, he said he had to leave. He described running through the streets of the ghetto, not because he was being pursued, but because he wished to get away; he could stand no more. He returned to the secret passage and entryway and departed. He was on a trip to the land of the dead, and from that realm of the shades he reemerged on the other side of the wall. "It was not a world," Karski said, groping for words to describe this fantastic city within a city that was beyond his imagination. "It was not a part of humanity. I was not part of it. I did not belong there."[3]

Karski was not alone in being initially unprepared to fit the ghettos and the camps into a picture of the world of common experience. When the concentration camps were liberated and open to view, the soldier-liberators and those who came in their wake could hardly believe their eyes.[4] This realm was unlike any known to humankind. Few could enter without experiencing something akin to Karski's reaction to the Warsaw ghetto, seeking as soon as possible to flee. In May 1945 a priest from the Austrian town of Ebensee entered the camp of this name, a subsidiary of Mauthausen, in order to minister to the sick; he confessed he was appalled at the assault upon his senses, the smell of the bodies stacked in or near the crematorium, the wretched odors emanating from bodies still alive, the sight of human wrecks dragging themselves forward, begging for some food, for a warm gesture. Following a stay inside the camp, the priest describes how, once at home, fearing infection, he washed his hands in a strong disinfectant. He could hardly believe that this lovely town of Ebensee where he had been raised, nestled picturesquely amid the hills and lakes of the scenic Salzkammmergut, home to forests and luxurious grazing land, had been simultaneously the setting of this horrific institution, the concentration camp of Ebensee. "This screaming contradiction," as he termed it, had altered the world as he knew it. Prompting the priest's despair was the displacement of long-cherished images of this setting so close to his heart, so evocative of nature and family, by the things he witnessed in the aftermath of the liberation.[5] He was being forced to admit that that place, the concentration camp of Ebensee, was not far away, not distant, but very near.

In the opening sequence of his film, Claude Lanzmann presents his viewers with an image of Simon Srebnik, survivor of Chełmno, seated in a boat. An oarsman, standing, silently ferries him past the Polish village of Chełmno along the placid River Ner, river of ashes, river of time, back to the land of the dead he had miraculously escaped as a child. We are meant to sense, at least at first, the remoteness of this place to which one journeys by water, and whose silence is the absent voice of the dead. That silence is broken by Srebnik's song, a soldier's tune, a song of the executioners, a haunting echo of the killers and a lullaby of death. The last trip by river lies at the heart of one of our oldest and most moving representations of death. But ultimately, the metaphor proves inadequate to describe what happened to people who were forced to journey to these places. For, as we discover, this place far away is not deserted. The villagers of what seems to many of us a place remote in time as well as space are still here, just as they had been when Chełmno was the site of a death camp. We learn that Chełmno was, and that it is still a place on earth, locatable on the map, a place populated by the living as well as by the dead.

Let there be no confusion: these places *were* repellent. They did have about them, quite literally, the sight and stench of death. The camps were a unique synthesis of sordid imaginings and very real exercise of man-made violence and force. They were places into which perfectly whole human beings were driven, held briefly between life and death before being beaten, or hung, or shot, or electrocuted on the wire, or gassed, then burned and blown through a chimney into the sky. The scope of the undertaking alone was enough to create among outsiders a sense of incredulity. That incredulity was one manifestation of a system designed to create a division in society between a normal world, inhabited by the citizenry, and a "phantom world," to borrow Hannah Arendt's phrase, into which the outcasts of society would slip before exiting this world without a trace.[6]

Even so, the project to seal from observation, to isolate the killing from the outside world, to wipe free all traces of lives destroyed and to screen the deeds of the killers, was an imperfect endeavor. In 1938 a concentration camp was built in Mauthausen, a market community on the Danube, fourteen miles east of Linz. For the next seven years the camp spread its shadow over the town and its inhabitants. As the original camp expanded to include a network of more than forty outlying, subsidiary camps, the shadow fell across additional towns and villages that dotted the landscape. The shadow represented torment and death for more than 100,000 individuals swept into the Mauthausen system over seven years. Much of that torment was visible to persons who lived in the vicinity of these camps. They were witness to repeated beatings and shootings. Their eyes saw what few eyes would have wished to see. Assuredly, they were spared the worst of sights: few were given the dubious privilege of witnessing the gassing of inmates. The masters of the camp, the SS, were at pains to keep residents somewhat in the dark concerning the extent and the details of the killing. But it was impossible for them to keep all of their doings a complete mystery to the townsfolk. Rather, they asked of the residents both a discreet silence, a tactful averting of their gaze. Through tacit understanding, though all knew it to be in fact near and present, the camp was to be considered a realm distant and apart.

One of the first notions to be grasped in considering the relationship between a concentration camp and the town and townspeople nearby, is to understand how, in numerous ways, a concentration camp touches upon the affairs of the citizenry. A concentration camp such as Mauthausen can be likened to a new enterprise locating in a given community. The comparison is particularly apt in the case of a camp such as Mauthausen because, quite above and beyond its planned role as a center of torture and death, it was designed as an economic enterprise centering on the extraction of granite from rock quarries, operating for the benefit of an SS-owned and operated corporation, the German Earth and Stone Works. That enterprise profited from the exploitation of slave labor in the form of inmates brought to Mauthausen to be worked to death. The Mauthausen quarry, an imposing and frightful pit whose walls ranged some 300 feet in height round about, was at once an enclave of terror and a work site. For these same quarry operations, for example, local stone masons were needed to carry out skilled tasks as well as to serve as foremen on labor details which where simultaneously under SS guard. During Mauthausen's establishment phase, for example, barracks were built and outfitted, and civilian carpenters were called in from the surrounding communities to do some of the work. In operation, the camp needed basic supplies, and for these it turned to area merchants. Regular food purchases were made from nearby farmers and from an agricultural cooperative located near the railway station. Goods had to be trucked in, and here too a local firm was engaged to provide vehicles and drivers. The camp staff also liked to drink and dine out, frequenting local taverns and restaurants. SS families were housed in the community, and local women took on housekeeping duties, tidying SS residences. Local merchants were a ready source of necessities for the SS and their families. In short, there was on one level a routine, everyday quality to the interaction between the camp and the town.[7]

Still, the nature of contacts, for some, evolved beyond the everyday to a level more direct and sinister. In the early phase of the camp's existence, before such facilities were installed on site, inmates who died at Mauthausen were routinely shipped for disposal to a public crematorium in Steyr, a city to the south of Mauthausen. We are also informed of the case of a small businessman from Linz, owner of a commercial extermination firm, who acted as a supplier of deadly Zyklon-B to the camp.[8] Moreover, a number of local persons representing a variety of trades and professions—ranging from simple mechanics, plumbers, and bus drivers, to secretaries and nurses and doctors—served in the so-called euthanasia center at castle Hartheim, located just west of Linz. Hartheim operated not only as a center for killing, first, by means of carbon monoxide gas, mentally ill and physically infirm patients from Austria and southern Germany, but also, beginning in August 1941, inmates from the concentration camps of Mauthausen and Dachau. Hartheim thus doubled as a killing outpost for Mauthausen, its own gas chamber a forerunner to the gas chamber installed in Mauthausen and operating by the spring of 1942. Local persons, many sharing Nazi party connections, carried out the task of assembling the pipes, the tiles, and the doors of the gas chamber in Castle Hartheim. Custodians kept the physical plant in running order; bus drivers drove the victims to the castle; nurses met the vehicles and escorted the victims inside, readying them for the gas chamber; secretaries carried out correspondence informing loved ones of the death of their relatives in Hartheim, processing false information concerning the cause of death; above all, overseeing these activities, were the doctors. When gassing was completed, local men assigned to the crematory carried out the heavy task of stacking and then disposing of the bodies in the oven they serviced.[9]

Local businessmen not only profitably took on contracts for services rendered to the camp but exploited the availability of cheap labor rented out from the SS slave pool. Beyond this, however, there were opportunities for corruption and enrichment. The adjacent black market included the exchange of rare foodstuffs for valuables seized from the inmates themselves. In particular, items such as watches of silver and gold, skimmed from the treasure house of items taken from the inmates (and in the case of much of the gold, literally routinely wrenched from their teeth), served in Mauthausen and in other camps as items for barter with persons from the local population.[10] Yitzhak Arad recounts extensively instances of this trade at Treblinka. He estimates that easily more than a thousand boxcars of property were loaded and shipped from the camp. But not all of the loot was funneled into the "proper" channels. Rather, some guards had valuables smuggled out of the camp to nearby Malkinia, where they could expropriate it and return with the goods to Germany when on leave. Farmers in the vicinity of Treblinka were said to have been seen with these watches stuffed into their baskets. Guards took advantage of their access to the expanding pile of wealth, providing a windfall for greedy area residents, including "farmers' daughters" near Treblinka who went out with the guards and received these stolen goods.[11] Soon after the war, civilians could be found rooting about the former camp terrain, digging up remains in a frantic search for what was presumed to be buried loot scattered among the human remains. Observing evidence of this treasure hunt, Rachel Auerbach, a Jewish investigator with a team examining Treblinka in November 1945 appropriately described these people as human "jackals and hyenas" who would "drag parts of half-rotted corpses from the earth, bones and scattered refuse in the hope that they may come upon at least a coin or a gold tooth."[12]

The people living round about had to see to it that even should an inmate escape, not only would he be turned away, but turned in by a hostile population. In the event of breakouts, the local citizenry were to be the eyes and ears of the guard corps. In Sobibor, in Treblinka, mass escapes did occur. Nothing is more damning to the reputation of the outside world as is the indifference and, above all, the hostility of persons in the surrounding areas where the escaped prisoners sought assistance. In Poland, Jewish prisoners had to evade denunciations and tip-offs by the local citizenry to the Germans. Few Polish partisans came to their assistance. Some killed escaped Jews on their own.[13]

What is more, just as the German army units were on hand near Auschwitz, in reserve to back up the guard staff in the event of mass escapes,[14] the citizenry living in the vicinity of those camps inside Germany formed a potential auxiliary force to be armed in a similar emergency. In Mauthausen, in fact, on a moonlit night in early February 1945, a group of some four hundred badly weakened Soviet prisoners of war, under sentence of slow death in an isolation barrack in the main camp, miraculously succeeded in scaling one of the walls of the camp. Those who were not immediately cut down by gunfire succeeded in scattering into the countryside. They desperately sought morsels of food and help at the doorways of the local citizenry in Mauthausen and surrounding villages and towns in the area; they begged not to be turned in to the SS. According to the written account of the local police commander, these men, even in their desperate situation, did not do harm to persons or property. They asked only that citizens allow them, for a brief while, to hide in their farm buildings. But a manhunt was immediately called up by the SS and local Nazi party officials. Aged men and teenage boys not yet eligible for army service were assembled and armed to participate. The citizenry had been, in effect, deputized to act as killers. By all accounts, numerous citizens—and not only men, for farm women and women shopkeepers took a hand in this as well—thoughtlessly seized the opportunity to participate in the sport of chasing and killing. In hunting down the inmates—with guns and knives and pitchforks—the local citizenry revealed unmistakably that the surrounding communities were in fact extensions of the camp.[15]

The concentration and extermination camps called forth particular ways of seeing.[16] It is precisely because the camps were in fact constructed so close to populated areas that their designs incorporated elements of disguise and camouflage. Mauthausen was able to take advantage of the natural, semicircular enclosure of its rock quarry, the very center of operations, and to have built for the prisoner compound, assembled on a height overlooking the quarry, thick walls made of stones hauled up from the pit below. In Treblinka, a camp of relatively lighter construction, the SS had to make do with earthen barriers and with wire, but here care was taken to weave foliage into the mesh to obstruct the vision not only of the victims themselves but of anyone looking in on the camp from surrounding fields. At Sobibor and Treblinka the forest was similarly used as a natural barrier to sight. Enhancing these natural shields were a host of improvised and inexpensive additions whose major purpose was to mislead or to conceal from view what went on inside or near the camps. We are reminded that the killers also experimented at Treblinka with the by now familiar stage-set deception of a Potemkin-like village railway station complete with its "fake clock" and "fake ticket windows."[17] The buses that drove the victims to the gassing center at Castle Hartheim had their windows painted over; passengers were to be prevented from looking out, outsiders from looking in. Also at Hartheim a wooden canopy was placed at the entrance where buses pulled up and unloaded those about to be led to their deaths in the gas chamber inside the castle.[18]

There were, of course, euphemisms for murder built into the linguistic codes enforced in the verbal commands and in the correspondence of the bureaucrats. Radically new techniques of distancing were effected for the perpetrators on the scene, however, with the substitution of mobile and fixed gas killing devices for the previously relied upon killing squads, whose victims had been lined up before their eyes. This was critical, because it helped to remove most of the killers from the line of sight.[19] Shoshana Felman, however, in her salient review of the Lanzmann film, suggests that similar restrictions of visual encounters, above and beyond those ingeniously developed to protect the sensibilities of the killers, played a critical role in safeguarding the bystanders from the act of witnessing, helping them, too, to avoid seeing with their own eyes things that in fact were happening within range of their senses. Combined with ruses aimed at deceiving the victims of their fate, deliberately sparing them until the final instant the site of the pit at the edge of a forest or the interior of the sealed gassing room, perpetrators and bystanders, in narrowing their vision, acceded to a process that was designed to make the killing "invisible" and to make of the Holocaust *"an event without a witness,* an event which historically consists in the scheme of the literal *erasure of its witnesses."*[20]

Primo Levi is one of our best guides to the implications of these strategies of visual and other sensory avoidances. It was he who wrote of the "cordon sanitaire" people may draw up around those things they wish not to see; nothing so effectively protects one against later unpleasant memories of a sight or an experience than does not looking at the moment it presents itself before one's field of vision. By not seeing, by turning away, one is already selecting one's memories, screening those memories, and hence screening oneself from unpleasant and potentially bothersome thoughts in the future.[21]

Still, we have come to recognize that the bystanders, to the extent that they participated in this process of blocking disturbing sensations associated with the activities of the camps, did so against a background of numerous, often unavoidable daily contacts with these institutions. We discover that in negotiating such interactions, residents of the communities bordering on the camps often collaborated in narrowing their vision to a minimum. In 1941 a woman whose farm lay on a height above the rock quarry in Mauthausen filed an anguished request with the police after witnessing bodies of inmates who had been shot and left in the open. Indicating that the sight of inmates lying dead at the rock quarry was burdensome to her nerves, she was compelled to ask that the killing be halted or at least done elsewhere and out of sight.[22] The priest from Ebensee who arrived at the end of the war to enter the liberated camp wrote in 1946 that he had spoken with residents of the town, discovering not only women whose nerves suffered because of the unavoidable sights and sounds of persons being beaten, but also farmers who avoided working certain fields too near to the camp, and mountaineers who went out of their way just in order to avoid coming into contact with such "horrifying events."[23]

People had some control over what they saw, and could try to look away, but what of what they smelled? The stench was simply unavoidable for persons living near camps that had operating crematoria, as in Mauthausen and its main subsidiaries in Melk and Ebensee. Smoke respected no absolute boundaries. The unmistakable, sickly sweet odor of burning human flesh was, as townsfolk readily admit, a part of the atmosphere. Read enough testimonies to this effect and one learns that these people, undoubtedly already experts in the vagaries of the local climate, had become veritable specialists in detecting the interaction between wind and cremation fumes.[24] Approximately thirty kilometers from Nuremberg, in the vicinity of the Hersbruck camp, subsidiary to the Flossenbürg main camp, a crematorium whose "chimney stood clear of obstructing terrain features" was available to the sight of "all who traveled the two valley roads to the market town of Hersbruck from the south." As the wife of a local minister noted, "From our house one had a view down the valley to Happurg and beyond. One could see smoke pouring out the chimney on a low brick building. Often when I opened the door in the morning there would be an awful smell. It was always the same. At different times I said to my husband, 'There's that awful smell again.'" Also established in the area were two open pyres, one of which was located on "a hilltop site" fed by "wood being requisitioned from farmers" in the area. Those working their fields came across the sight of bodies being incinerated. Another woman noted, "One evening one of my sons came running into the house and shouted, 'Mama the woods are on fire.' Sometimes the flames were so high that it looked as if the trees were burning. Whenever they were burning bodies the smell was awful, and when the wind brought the smoke toward Molsberg it was terrible."[25]

Characteristically, the SS attempted to explain away the unmaskable odors. The explanations were designed to permit persons to ignore, rationalize, or cancel these sensations by offering a more palatable interpretation. Immediately after the crematorium in Hartheim went into operation a representative of the castle administration assembled residents in a tavern to try to convince people that in fact the heavy smoke was the result of a war-related "chemical treatment" for processing oil for use in submarines.[26] Similarly, the SS at first attempted to explain away open-air cremation at one of the pyres in the Hersbruck area by first restricting access to the area and stating that "an Allied plane had crashed there."[27] For those who wished to believe so, there existed rationales for the burning of bodies in wartime. A woman from Melk who remembered the smoke recalled, "I said, 'uh huh, someone is being burned again.' One smells that you know. That is, I believe none were shot in Melk. They often simply died of hunger or something. They often died of weakness."[28]

To those who looked away, the towns beside the camps embodied goodness and decency. In Mauthausen the local Nazis and camp staffers mingled at recitals, lectures, youth assemblies, sporting competitions, and hunts. Here the executioners found relaxation in local taverns and with some of the local women at private gatherings held in farmhouses. Here resided the wives and children of SS family men; here were the shopkeepers—hairdressers, druggists, grocery owners—whom they patronized. Above all, here resided the decent folk, as opposed to the outcasts and criminals sealed within the walls of the camp. One is pained to read the words of a wife whose husband, a dentist, oversaw the removal and preparation of gold extracted from the teeth of inmates at Mauthausen before shipment to Berlin. In June 1946, pleading for his life, she stated, "He was always a devoted husband who valued his family above anything else and I love him with all my heart." And she continued, "The children are too small to beg for their father. I enclose a picture of the children in the hope that their innocent eyes will plead with you and save their father from death by hanging. Furthermore, I enclose a picture of my husband showing him as a happy family man. Please look at his eyes. You will see in them how good and unselfish he is and that he does not belong among the criminals of Mauthausen."[29] From this to Heinrich Himmler's SS men of 1943 who, in his words, "apart from exceptions caused by human weakness . . . have remained decent fellows" to the defiant remarks of Austrian presidential candidate Kurt Waldheim, defending in the year 1986 "the reputation of a whole generation" against the attack of those who would "make all these people bad people," the upholding of goodness was essential. "We were not doing anything but our duty as decent soldiers, we were not criminals but decent men who faced a terrible fate."[30]

We confront repeatedly a binary vision permitting alternate versions of the self: the perpetrator who is simultaneously the caring family man; the bystander, the honored citizen of a town that is a town like any other save that it also serves a killing establishment. The two sides of the self, however, cannot be neatly separated. Each person trails, close by, his shadow.[31] So, too, the camp, bounded as it was by stone and by wire, patrolled by guards, cast its presence upon the nearby towns, its inmates at once confined within, yet also routinely led through neighboring communities; killing went on within its walls, but not exclusively, and the remains of the dead, let loose, rode the breeze. Lines were sharply drawn, yet never absolute and impermeable.

Not all townsfolk took up instruments to strike directly at the inmates; some of the former took refuge in a spurious neutrality. It was of no small comfort to know that one did not kill; one was not a murderer, one concluded, so long as one's own hand did not strike down a life. But to allow matters to rest at that overlooked the simple fact that the rulers of the concentration camps asked, at a minimum, but one thing of the residents of these bordering communities: not to interfere, so that the SS could proceed with their tasks. In complying, assuming what amounted to an attitude of noninvolvement, they not only made life easier for the executioners but denied the inmates what they most needed: assistance from the outside world. As we know, one can contribute to evil as easily by thoughtlessness as by deed. That lesson is one not readily acknowledged, as the philosopher Mary Midgley is at pains to point out: "If we ask whether exploiters and oppressors know what they are doing, the right answer seems to be that they do not know, because they carefully avoid thinking about it—but that they could know, and therefore their deliberate avoidance is a responsible act."[32]

Throughout the years the bystanders have been reluctant to come forward. Like the perpetrators, they have no reason to speak; what is more, they preferred to forget the past. Have we waited too long to approach them? Claude Lanzmann conducted his interviews in the late 1970s and the early 1980s. It was not too late at that time, but is it too late now? I recall that as a college student I had been influenced greatly by William Sheridan Allen's by now classic history of the rise of the Nazi party in a single German town.[33] But the book I really wanted to read did not exist: a study of a town that was located near a concentration camp. By the time I took the chance on such an undertaking in the succeeding decade, more than thirty-five years had passed since the end of the Second World War. And now the war is half a century behind us, not a great span for most historians; measured against the course of an individual life, however, fifty years is indeed a long time. Many adult witnesses from that era have slipped away, silent in their own lifetimes, and now silent in death. But one of the things my investigation of Mauthausen made me aware of was that there were not only adults but also children who viewed what went on from the periphery of the camps. Indeed, in some instances they were afforded a closer look at things, for the guards were less likely to threaten or chase them away. Born during the years, roughly, 1928–1933, they are only now approaching retirement, or would be just recently retired. In the year 1943, such persons would have been between ten and fifteen years old, certainly old enough, had they lived near one of these places, to have seen the camps. Even someone born as long ago as 1923 would have celebrated in 1993 no more than his or her seventieth year. No, it is not too late. The witnesses are still among us. Or, at the least, they are still in their home towns, many of them. Shall we not ask of them what they saw, what they heard for themselves, and what their parents may have seen and heard and said? And in so doing we can find among them and among later generations valuable allies: local historians, archivists in the Second World War research institutes, Gymnasium teachers who came of age in the 1960s and 1970s. They are a ready resource, often with ties to the towns where the camps were located, helpful in locating contacts in these communities. Peter Sichrovsky's success in interviewing the children of perpetrators and victims underscores the need to speak with the children of the bystanders as well.[34]

In the meantime, we await the development of a new imagination, akin to that "imagination of the heart" which, Karl Jaspers noted, when missing, leaves the individual open to moral "blindness" and "inner indifference toward the witnessed evil."[35] Still, we have before us the example of Jan Karski, a man whose vision was, however painful to him, directed to taking in with his eyes all that he needed to see, that he might bear witness to the crime before the world. He sought out what was human in those he encountered. And in the figure of Szmul Zygielbojm, a Jewish leader with whom Karski spoke when he reached London, we find an example of one who responded to Karski's message with all his heart. With the messenger, Zygielbojm was a man seeking to place himself, a man at a distance, far away in London, with Karski in the ghetto. Zygielbojm pressed his witness for precise descriptions: "He asked me what the houses looked like, what the children looked like."[36] The vision he sought was internal; it was the vision of the mind's eye.

In the year 1944 Arthur Koestler wrote of a man he knew, "a well-known London publisher," who had taken upon himself the task of reporting on the destruction of the Jews. "Before each meeting he used to lock himself up in a room, close his eyes, and imagine in detail, for twenty minutes, that he was one of the people in Poland who were killed. One day he tried to feel what it was like to be suffocated . . . ; the other he had to dig his grave with two hundred others and then face a machine gun, which, of course, is rather imprecise and capricious in its aiming. Then he walked out to the platform and talked. He kept going for a full year before he collapsed with a nervous breakdown. He had a great command of his audiences and perhaps he has done some good," concluded Koestler."[37]

Agonized that year by a recurring dream in which he found himself left to die as others indifferently walked past, Koestler acknowledged that there are degrees of knowing; "I believe in spiral nebulae, can see them in a telescope and express their distance in figures; but they have a lower degree of reality for me than the inkpot on my table. Distance in space and time degrades intensity of awareness."[38] Günther Anders, in his parable of a woman who, from the height of a tower witnesses the death of her child, then exclaims, had she but been down below she would have been overwhelmed, expressed, chillingly, a like notion.[39] But not only does distance diminish perception, "So does magnitude. Seventeen is a figure which I know intimately like a friend; fifty billion is just a sound. A dog run over by a car upsets our emotional balance and digestion; three million Jews killed in Poland cause but a moderate uneasiness. Statistics don't bleed; it is the detail which counts. We are unable to embrace the total process with our awareness; we can only focus on little lumps of reality."[40]

Karski was a rare individual, as were at this time Zygielbojm, Koestler, and the London publisher he mentions. Few were willing to suffer the unpleasant sensation of dwelling on such matters. It was not always the case, Koestler noted. "There were periods and moments in history—in Athens, in the early Renaissance, during the first years of the Russian Revolution—when at least certain representative layers of society had attained a relatively high level of mental integration; times when people seemed to rub their eyes and come awake, when their cosmic awareness seemed to expand, when they were 'contemporaries' in a much broader and fuller sense; when the trivial and the cosmic planes seemed on the point of fusing."[41] We are not there yet; we can only look forward to such a time when sensibilities are more refined, when each of us, in approaching both present and past, learn to have the courage to see, even when, safe within our homes, within ourselves, we "rub [our] eyes and come awake" to sense this world far away close to us, and a part of us.

But in so doing let us acknowledge that we awaken upon this world, not an underworld, and recall that among the rivers that course its landscape are the fabled Danube, which, just east of Linz, bathes the shores of a place called Mauthausen, and lesser ones, among them the River Ner, a body of water as real as the mightiest and proudest of all Europe's riverways, which drinks the ashes of a place called Chełmno.

NOTES

1. Jan Karski, *Story of a Secret State* (Boston: Houghton Mifflin, 1944), p. 329.

2. Karski, *Story of a Secret State*, pp. 325–26, 329–30; Claude Lanzmann, *Shoah: An Oral History of the Holocaust* (New York: Pantheon, 1985), p. 174.

3. Lanzmann, *Shoah*, p. 174.

4. Robert H. Abzug, *Inside the Vicious Heart: Americans and the Liberation of Nazi Concentration Camps* (New York: Oxford University Press, 1985), p. 10.

5. Franz Loidl, *Entweihte Heimat* (Linz, 1946), pp. 15–16.

6. See the discussion entitled "Total Domination" in Hannah Arendt, *The Origins of Totalitarianism*, 2nd enl. ed. (New York: World Publishing, A Meridian Book, 1958; 12th printing 1972), pp. 437–59. The phrase "phantom world" appears on page 445.

7. Gordon J. Horwitz, *In the Shadow of Death: Living Outside the Gates of Mauthausen* (New York: Free Press, 1990), pp. 26–27, 29, 40–41.

8. Ibid., p. 41; Eugen Kogon, Hermann Langbein, Adalbert Ruckerl et al., *Nationalsozialistische Massentötungen durch Giftgas* (Frankfurt/M.: S. Fischer Verlag, 1983), p. 248.

9. See the chapter entitled "The Castle" in Horwitz, *In the Shadow*, pp. 55–82.

10. Ibid., pp. 41, 43–44.

11. Yitzhad Arad, *Belzec, Sobibor, Treblinka: The Operation Reinhard Death Camps* (Bloomington: Indiana University Press, 1987), pp. 158–59, 163.

12. Rachel Auerbach, "In the Fields of Treblinka," in Alexander Donat, ed., *The Death Camp Treblinka: A Documentary* (New York: Holocaust Library, 1979), p. 69. See also Arad, *Belzec, Sobibor, Treblinka*, pp. 371, 379.

13. Arad, *Belzec, Sobibor, Treblinka*, pp. 342–48.

14. Raul Hilberg, "Bitburg as Symbol," in *Bitburg in Moral and Political Perspective*, ed. Geoffrey Hartman (Bloomington: Indiana University Press, 1986), p. 22.

15. Horwitz, *In the Shadow*, pp. 124–27, 131–34.

16. Shoshana Felman speaks of "*three different performances of the act of seeing,*" in which "in effect, the victims, the bystanders, and the perpetrators are here differentiated not so much by what they actually see (what they all see, although discontinuous, does in fact follow a logic of corroboration), as by what and how they *do not see*, by what and how they fail to witness" (emphasis in original) (Shoshana Felman, "In an Era of Testimony: Claude Lanzmann's Shoah," *Yale French Studies* 79 [1991]: p. 42).

17. See diagram and accompanying description of the camp layout in Gitta Sereny, *Into that Darkness: An Examination of Conscience* (New York: McGraw-Hill, 1974; Random House, Vintage Books edition, 1983), pp. 146–47.

18. Horwitz, *In the Shadow*, p. 72.

19. See Pierre Vidal-Naquet, *Les juifs, la mémoire et le présent: II.* (Paris: Editions La Découverte, 1991), p. 233.

20. Felman, "In an Era of Testimony," pp. 44–45.

21. Primo Levi, *The Drowned and the Saved*, trans. Raymond Rosenthal (New York: Summit Books, 1988), p. 31 (also in Hartman, *Bitburg*, p. 135).

22. Horwitz, *In the Shadow*, p. 35.

23. Dokumentationsarchiv des österreichischen Widerstandes, *Widerstand und Verfolgung in Oberösterreich 1934–1945* (Vienna: Österreichischer Bundesverlag, 1982), vol. 2, p. 592.

24. See Claude Lanzmann, "J'ai enquêté en Pologne," in *Au sujet de Shoah: Le film de Claude Lanzmann*, ed. Michel Deguy (Paris: Editions Belin, 1990), p. 214.

25. Elmer Luchterhand, "Knowing and Not Knowing: Involvement in Nazi Genocide," in *Our Common History: The Transformation of Europe*, ed. Paul Thompson with Natasha Burchardt (Atlantic Highlands, NJ: Humanities Press, 1982), pp. 254, 264–65.

26. Horwitz, *In the Shadow*, p. 62.

27. Luchterhand, "Knowing and Not Knowing," p. 255.

28. Horwitz, *In the Shadow*, p. 110.

29. National Archives, RG 153–5–31, vol. 1. Trial record Court Dachau, pt. 5, pp. 1462ff., Case of Walther H., clemency petition dated June 12, 1946.

30. Jeremy Noakes and Geoffrey Pridham, eds., *Documents on Nazism* (New York: Viking Press, 1974), p. 492; James M. Markham, "Waldheim Campaigns to Memories in Borderland," *New York Times*, May 1, 1986, p. 2.

31. See the discussion of "Selves and Shadows" in Mary Midgley's *Wickedness: A Philosophical Essay* (London: Ark Paperbacks, 1986), pp. 113–31; and "Doubling: The Faustian

Bargain," in Robert J. Lifton, *The Nazi Doctors: Medical Killing and the Psychology of Genocide* (New York: Basic Books, 1986), pp. 418–29.

32. Midgley, *Wickedness*, pp. 62–63.

33. William S. Allen, *The Nazi Seizure of Power: The Experience of a Single German Town, 1942–1945*, rev. ed. (New York: Franklin Watts, 1984).

34. Peter Sichrovsky, *Born Guilty: Children of Nazi Families* (New York: Basic Books, 1987).

35. Karl Jaspers, *The Question of German Guilt*, trans. E. B. Ashton (New York: Capricorn Books, 1961), p. 70.

36. Karski, *Story of a Secret State*, p. 337.

37. Arthur Koestler, "On Disbelieving Atrocities," *New York Times Magazine*, January 1944, cited in Arthur Koestler, *The Yogi and the Commissar and Other Essays* (New York: Macmillan, 1967; 1st ed. 1945), p. 93. The publisher, whom Koestler did not identify by name, would be Victor Gollancz. See Ruth Dudley Edwards, *Victor Gollancz: A Biography* (London: Victor Gollancz, 1987), p. 377.

38. Koestler, *The Yogi and the Commissar*, pp. 91–92.

39. Günther Anders, *Der Blick vom Turm* (Munich: Verlag C. H. Beck, 1968), p. 7.

40. Koestler, *The Yogi and the Commissar*, p. 92.

41. Ibid., p. 93.

Part 8

The Axis, the Allies, and the Neutrals

The Holocaust occurred in many different countries and under diverse circumstances. Some countries, such as Romania, Hungary, and Italy, were allied with the Nazis—at least for much of the time. The nature of their relationship with Germany—their "independence," their dependence, their perceptions of German success in the war effort—as well as their own relationship with the native Jewish population influenced the course of the Final Solution in these countries.

Some countries, such as France, were conquered by the Germans and remained subservient to German demands even if nominally independent. Other countries, such as Sweden, Switzerland, and Spain, remained neutral in the war effort and also, it seems, neutral toward the "final solution of the Jewish problem." Some institutions, such as the Vatican, also maintained a quasi- or formally neutral role. And the Allies, who fought a total war against the Axis, did not fight with the same abandon against the Final Solution. In the essays that follow, the fate of Jews in Hungary, Italy, and Romania will be considered. So, too, will the fate of Jews in France and the attitude toward Jews by England, Sweden, Turkey, the Vatican, and the Protestant churches. Some of these essays are by senior scholars who have long dominated the field; others are by young scholars presenting the first fruits of their efforts in an academic forum.

Randolph L. Braham is a distinguished historian of the Holocaust in Hungary. In his retrospective analysis of that subject, an excellent essay that also appears in a somewhat different version elsewhere, he argues that what happened in Hungary was in many respects distinct from the tragedies that befell the other Jewish communities in Nazi Europe. The relationship of Hungarian Jewry to Hungary's ruling aristocratic-conservative elites was for Braham a kind of "Golden Era." Each side used the other for its basic needs—for the Jews, protection against antisemitism; for Hungary's feudal elites, the necessity of Jewish business acumen to bolster economic and, hence, political stability in the nation. For Hungarian Jewry, this relationship proved to be a "fatal flaw."

Even after 1918, when left-wing Jews were part of a socialist Hungarian government and the threat of communism was the greatest fear of Hungary's ruling elites, and through the early 1940s, the great majority of Magyarized, assimilated Jews still believed that they, unlike all other large European Jewish communities, would escape total destruction even if they would be ruined economically.

And Hungary was an oasis, an island of safety for the first four and one-half years of war. Motivated by the constant Hungarian fear of the Soviet Union and the Nazis' continuing pressure to implement antisemitic actions and deportations, Hungary nevertheless resisted imposing the Final Solution on its Jewish population until the overthrow of its regime and the imposition of German rule. Then, with a swiftness unparalleled in the Holocaust, within four months beginning in March 1944, Jews were defined, isolated, ghettoized; from May 15 to July 8, 437,402 Jews were deported to Auschwitz. By the July 9 arrival of Raoul Wallenberg in Budapest, the Jews of the capital city were the last surviving community in Europe.

Meir Michaelis is one of the most distinguished interpreters of the plight of Italian Jews during the Holocaust. In "The Holocaust in Italy: Areas of Inquiry," he presents a succinct but informative discussion of the place of Italian Jewry in the nation from 1870 until the seizure of power by Benito Mussolini; he then investigates the Italian Fascist response to the rise of National Socialism and the place of anti-Jewish thought and action within the Italian Fascist movement.

Michaelis concludes his essay with an extended discussion of the major research problems that continue to cause controversy among historians of the Italian Jewish community in the twentieth century, such as the native roots of Fascist antisemitism; the attitude of the Catholic Church; the attitude of the Italian masses toward the Jewish issue between 1938 and 1945; Italian resistance to genocide in the occupied territories from 1941 to 1943; the personal role of Mussolini as associate, ally, and puppet of Hitler; and the respective roles of the Germans and the Italians in the implementation of the Final Solution on Italian soil.

Jean Ancel is one of the outstanding historians of the Holocaust in Romania. He is also the outstanding expert on the anti-Jewish policies of Marshal Ion Antonescu, the wartime dictator of Romania.

In "Antonescu and the Jews," Ancel traces the evolution of Antonescu's antisemitism and finds that the Marshal's hatred of Jews was fully developed even before his association with Adolf Hitler and the Third Reich. Ancel examines Antonescu's anti-Jewish decrees in the various regions of Romania and concludes that the dictator was responsible for the deaths of at least 350,000 Jewish men, women, and children.

In a wide-ranging discussion, "The Allies and the Holocaust," the distinguished historian of the Second World War Gerhard L. Weinberg concludes that one had to understand that for the Allies, saving Jewish lives was a secondary or even tertiary goal—if it entered into their thinking at all.

Could more have been done by the Allies to rescue Jews? Certainly the creation of quota systems and the careful scrutiny of any potential immigrants to America with regard to their ability to avoid the welfare roles points to the near paranoia with which countries such as the United States and Britain, both in the midst of terrible economic depressions, viewed the arrival of Jewish immigrants.

Weinberg is convinced that the Allies could have done precious little more with regard to rescue and interference. What has been overlooked, according to Weinberg, is the enormous effort made by Germany—including its governmental agencies—to maximize the killing and minimize rescues.

When one understands the fact that the Nazis were committed to destroying all of Jewish life everywhere, it becomes apparent that even if the Allies had bombed concentration camp rail lines, only a few more Jewish lives might have been saved, though Jewish prisoners would have been given a bit more hope of survival.

Susan S. Zuccotti has mastered more than one nation's involvement with the Holocaust. Her works on Italy and France depict the unique fate of Jews in these two countries in a combination of historical overview and personal narratives. In this contribution, "Surviving the Holocaust: The Situation in France," Zuccotti seeks to understand why more than three of four French Jews survived the Holocaust, a figure that is significantly higher than the survival rate of Jews in Belgium and the

Netherlands. Still, both Jewish accounts of the Holocaust in France and the descriptions by a non-Jew are quick to criticize the absence of an organized and substantial French effort to save Jews. These testimonies are often more harsh toward the French than toward the Belgians and Dutch.

In her statistical analysis, Zuccotti discovers that a highly disproportionate number of foreign Jews in France were killed during the Holocaust years. In part, she attributes this to the Vichy authorities' reluctance to go after native French Jews and in part to the superior survival skills of that group, which knew better how to remain in hiding and the best places to do so.

But Zuccotti also attributes the relatively low number of French Jews, both native and foreign, who died during the Holocaust to a kind of "benevolent indifference" that she ascribes to the French nation. That term does not immunize them against charges of complicity and collaboration, but Zuccotti finds the attitude qualitatively different from that demonstrated by the average bystander in other European nations.

Louise London's dissertation in progress is one of the most important studies yet undertaken on the response of the British government and Anglo-Jewish rescue associations to the plight of European Jews fleeing the long grasp of the Third Reich. In "British Responses to the Plight of Jews in Europe, 1933–1945," an overview of her work thus far, London reaches a number of disturbing conclusions: "The wartime ban on humanitarian admissions in the face of deadly persecution was a continuation of peacetime priorities, not a discontinuity," or "for nine out of ten Jews in Europe who wished to escape to Britain before the Holocaust, the answer of the Home Office was 'no.'"

London also evaluates the role of the Anglo-Jewish refugee organizations and finds that their policies often reflected the restrictive immigration policy of the British government. Yet London is also quick to point out that because of these refugee organizations, a larger number of alien Jews were admitted to Britain than might have been the case without their influence.

Paul A. Levine's report on his recently completed dissertation at Uppsala University, Sweden, is an effort to develop a theoretical approach to a particular Holocaust problem and to revise the current understanding of Swedish neutrality during the Second World War as merely the activities of a "bystander."

In "Bureaucracy, Resistance, and the Holocaust: Understanding the Success of Swedish Diplomacy in Budapest, 1944–1945," Levine is most interested in developing the notion of "bureaucratic resistance," a term he feels is applicable to the diplomatic corps of Sweden after 1943. Indeed, his paper also seeks to shift the focus of heroism to include not only Raoul Wallenberg but a large part of the Swedish Foreign Office and its activities on behalf of Jews inside and outside Hungary.

In so doing, Levine believes that he has found a weak spot in Nazi officialdom: "When confronted, perhaps for the first time since the war began, with an official from another sovereign state authorized to make an appeal for mercy, Nazi officials could and did give way."

The indifference if not callousness of Western European nations toward the entire question of accepting refugees from Nazi Germany is well known. Hence, Mark

A. Epstein's discussion of the Turkish government's rescue of dozens of refugee German scholars in "A Lucky Few: Refugees in Turkey" is an important and little known "other side" of the rescue story.

Epstein's investigation of that rescue provides, he believes, an answer to the question: What was a reasonable response by a neutral country (as Turkey was during World War II) to the moral and political challenges of the Nazi regime? Epstein also believes that in the example of Turkey's rescue efforts one may see an early hint (mid-1939) that protests and firmness could indeed yield some results in dealing with the Nazis.

Father John T. Pawlikowski is one of the leading Catholic ecclesiastics in the United States and one of this country's leading scholars on the history of Christian-Jewish relations. In "The Catholic Response to the Holocaust: Institutional Perspectives," Pawlikowski argues that to discuss Vatican policy, during the Holocaust, in terms of its "silence" is misleading and wrong-headed.

Instead, he calls for a more balanced approach to understanding the role of Pope Pius XII and the Catholic Church by examining the role of the Church on a regional basis and the actions of Church representatives on an individual basis.

Yet, Pawlikowski makes clear that he and other historians of this period are not satisfied with the historical accounts presented by Vatican historians. Pawlikowski finds antisemitism at the regional level as well as a conservative Vatican "diplomacy" that surely contributed to the late and restrained efforts on the part of the Vatican to intercede on behalf of the Jews.

Pawlikowski also reiterates the necessity of the opening of the Vatican archives to all scholars interested in researching this period and the role of the Holy Father and the Catholic Church.

Scholarship over the past decade has uncovered the extent of National Socialist racial and genetic thought and its influence on nearly all parts of German society during the Third Reich. The fusion of medicine and race politics has been especially disturbing to those who consider the practice of medicine and the power of physicians to be almost godlike.

But what is one to make of the situation discussed in Doris L. Bergen's essay, "The Ecclesiastical Final Solution: The German Christian Movement and the Anti-Jewish Church," where the Christian churches in Germany, too, found it possible and advantageous to mix Christian theology with Nazi racial thought and antisemitism. According to Bergen, what resulted was "the quest for an explicitly anti-Jewish Christianity."

Bergen's research on the German Christian Movement, whose members, predominantly Protestant lay people and clergy, came to be called the German Christians, challenges the prevailing assumption that the 600,000 members of the German Christian Movement were a marginal force in Germany's Protestant population. German Christians, she maintains, occupied key positions on theological faculties, held regional bishops' seats, and sat on local church councils. Bergen argues that the movement, far from being revolutionary, was rooted in the culture around it and was able to build on familiar trends in German Protestantism.

31.

RANDOLPH L. BRAHAM

The Holocaust in Hungary

A RESTROSPECTIVE ANALYSIS

The Holocaust in Hungary was in many respects distinct from the tragedies that befell the other Jewish communities in Nazi-dominated Europe. This distinction is reflected in the disastrous set of historical circumstances that combined to doom Hungarian Jewry in 1944.

The destruction of Hungarian Jewry that year constitutes one of the most perplexing chapters in the history of the Holocaust. It is a tragedy that ought not to have happened, for by then—on the eve of Allied victory—the leaders of the world, including the national and Jewish leaders of Hungary, were already privy to the secrets of Auschwitz. Moreover, except for a few diehards who still believed in Hitler's last-minute wonder weapons, even the perpetrators realized that the Axis had lost the war.

The last major phase in the Nazis' war against the Jews, the Holocaust in Hungary, is replete with paradoxes. The roots of one of the most startling of these paradoxes can be found in the Golden Era of Hungarian Jewry (1867–1918). It was during this period that a cordial, almost symbiotic relationship developed between the aristocratic-conservative elite and the Jewish elites of Hungary. It was this *very* close relationship, however, that distorted the Jewish leaders' perception of domestic and world politics during the pre-Holocaust era. While the Jewish elites shared the aristocratic-conservative leaders' abhorrence of Nazism and Bolshevism, they failed to recognize that the fundamental interests of the Hungarians were not always identical with those of Jewry. Their myopic views proved counterproductive during the interwar period and disastrous after the German occupation of March 19, 1944.

After its emancipation in 1867, the Jewish community of Hungary enjoyed an unparalleled level of multilateral development, taking full advantage of the opportunities offered by the so-called "liberal" regime that ruled the country during the pre–World War I era. The Hungarian ruling classes—the gentry and the conservative-aristocratic leaders—adopted a tolerant position toward the Jews. They were motivated not only by economic considerations but by the desire to perpetuate their dominant political role in a multinational empire in which the Hungarians constituted a minority. Because of Hungary's feudal tradition, the ruling classes encouraged the Jews to engage in business and industry, so that in the course of time a friendly, cooperative, and mutually advantageous relationship developed between the conservative-aristocratic leaders and the Jewish industrialists, bankers, and financiers—a relationship that was to play a fatal role during the Holocaust. The Jews also took full advantage of their new educational opportunities and within a short time came to play an influential, if not dominant role in the professions, literature, and the arts.

As a consequence of the Hungarian policy of tolerance, the Jews of Hungary considered themselves an integral part of the Hungarian nation. They eagerly embraced the process of Magyarization, opting not only to change their names but also to serve as economic modernizers and cultural Magyarizers in the areas inhabited by other nationalities in the polyglot Hungarian kingdom. The Hungarian Jews, who had no territorial ambitions and naturally supported the group that offered them the greatest protection—as did the Jews of the Diaspora practically everywhere during their long and arduous history—were soon looked upon as agents for the preservation of the status quo by the oppressed nationalities clamoring for self-determination and independence.

The Jews were naturally cognizant of the protection the regime provided against the threat of antisemitism. The prompt and forceful intervention of the government in dealing with anti-Jewish manifestations, however sporadic and local they were at the time, further enhanced the fidelity of the Jews to the Magyar state.

In the course of time the Jews, especially the acculturated and assimilated ones, became ever more assertively pro-Magyar. In many cases this allegiance was not only because of expediency or gratitude for the opportunities and the safety afforded by the aristocratic-gentry regime, but also because of fervent patriotism. As Oscar Jászi, a noted sociologist and social-democratic statesman, correctly observed, "there is no doubt that a large mass of these assimilated elements adopted their new ideology quite spontaneously and enthusiastically out of a sincere love of the new fatherland." Jászi concluded, however, that the "intolerant Magyar nationalism and chauvinism of the Jews had done a great deal to poison relations between the Hungarians and the other nationalities of the prewar era."[1] Paul Ignotus, a noted publicist, echoed these sentiments, arguing that the Jews had become "more fervently Magyar than the Magyars themselves." A similar conclusion was reached by the noted British historian Robert Seton-Watson, whose sympathies clearly lay with the oppressed nationalities. He claimed in 1908 that "the Catholic Church and the Jews form today the two chief bulwarks of Magyar chauvinism."

It was to some extent the political and economic symbiosis between the conservative-aristocratic and Jewish leaderships during the so-called Golden Era that determined their views and attitudes toward both the Third Reich and the USSR during the interwar and wartime periods. While the Hungarian leaders looked upon the Third Reich as a vehicle for the possible satisfaction of their revisionist ambitions, they shared with the Jewish leaders a fear of both German and Russian expansionism and above all a mortal fear of Bolshevism. It was these attitudes and perceptions that guided both leadership groups during the fateful year of 1944 with almost equally disastrous results.

The signs that the commonality of interests ("Interessengemeinschaft") between the two groups was in fact limited, fragile, and based primarily on expediency were clearly visible even before the end of World War I: despite the eagerness with which the Hungarian Jews embraced the Magyar cause and the enthusiasm with which they acculturated themselves, they failed, with relatively few exceptions, to fully integrate themselves into Hungarian society. Their ultimate assimilationist expectations were frustrated, for they were accepted socially neither by the aristocratic gentry, which exploited them politically and economically for the perpetuation of their feudal privileges, nor by the disenfranchised and impoverished peasantry, which—like a large proportion of the industrial workers—often viewed them as instruments of an oppressive regime.

Christian-Jewish relations were further strained by the presence in the country of a considerable number of mostly impoverished Yiddish-speaking Jews who resisted assimilation, let alone acculturation. In contrast to the assimilated Magyarized Jews, these were pejoratively referred to as "Eastern" or "Galician," and almost by definition unworthy of the government's policy of toleration. During the interwar period these Jews became the target of special abuse, for even the "civilized" antisemites regarded them as constituting not only a distinct "biological race" but also an "ideological race" representing a grave threat to Christian Magyars. This perception was shared by Miklós Horthy, the Regent of Hungary, who probably also considered this "threat" when he consented, during his March 1944 meeting with Hitler, to the "delivery of a few hundred thousand workers" to Germany.[2]

The Interessengemeinschaft between the Hungarian ruling classes and the Jews came to an end with the collapse of the Habsburg empire and the dismemberment of the Hungarian kingdom in 1918. The short-lived communist dictatorship that followed soon thereafter had a crucial effect upon the evolution of Hungarian domestic and foreign policy during the interwar period. The brief but harsh period of the proletarian dictatorship headed by Béla Kun left a bitter legacy in the nation at large and had a particularly devastating effect upon the Jews of Hungary. Although the overwhelming majority of Jews had opposed the proletarian dictatorship and perhaps suffered proportionately more than the rest of the population—they were persecuted both as members of the middle class and as followers of an organized religion—popular opinion tended to attach blame for the abortive dictatorship to the Jews as a whole. In part, this was due to the high visibility of communists of Jewish origin in the Kun government and administration; however, it was primarily the consequence of the antisemitic propaganda and anti-Jewish activities of the counterrevolutionary clericalist-nationalist forces that came to power later in 1919—forces dedicated to the reestablishment of the status quo ante.

Driven by the so-called "Szeged Idea" (a nebulous amalgam of political-propagandistic views whose central themes included the struggle against Bolshevism, the fostering of antisemitism, chauvinistic nationalism, and revisionism—an idea that antedated both Italian Fascism and German Nazism), the counterrevolutionaries engulfed the country in a wave of terror that dwarfed in ferocity and magnitude the Red Terror that had preceded and allegedly warranted it. While their murder squads killed a large number of leftists, including industrial workers and landless peasants as well as opposition intellectuals, their fury was directed primarily against the Jews; their violence claimed thousands of victims.

Radicalized by the national humiliation, social upheavals, and catastrophic consequences of the lost war—Hungary lost two-thirds of its historic territory, one-third

of its Magyar people, and three-fifths of its total population—the counterrevolutionaries organized themselves in a variety of ultrapatriotic associations devoted primarily to the successful resolution of the two major issues that came to obsess Hungary
during the interwar period: revisionism and the Jewish Question. In the course of
time these two issues became interlocked and formed the foundation of not only
Hungary's domestic policies but also its relations with the Third Reich.

Following the absorption of historic Hungary's major national minorities into
the Successor States, the Jews suddenly emerged as the country's most vulnerable
minority group. With the transformation of Trianon Hungary into a basically homogeneous state, the Jews lost their importance as statistical recruits to the cause of
Magyardom. In the new, truncated state they came to be exploited for another
purpose: as in Nazi Germany a little later, they were conveniently used as scapegoats
for most of the country's misfortunes, including its socioeconomic dislocations.

In this climate it was no surprise that Hungary—the country in which the Jews
had enjoyed a golden era just a few years earlier—emerged as the first country in post-
World War I Europe to adopt, in the wake of the White Terror, anti-Jewish legislation.
The so-called Numerus Clausus Act (1920), which was adopted in violation of the
Minorities Protection Treaty, restricted admission of Jews into institutions of higher
learning to 6 percent of the total enrollment—the alleged percentage of Jews in the
total population. Although this particular legislation was allowed to expire a few
years later, it sanctified the fundamental principle that was to guide many of the
"civilized" antisemites of the 1930s, who were eager to solve the Jewish Question in
an orderly and legal manner. This principle would be formulated by Gyula Gömbös,
one of the foremost representatives of the Hungarian radical Right, who stipulated
that "the Jews must not be allowed to succeed in any field beyond the level of their
ratio in the population."[3]

At any rate, at that time the Jewish leadership viewed the anti-Jewish measures
of the counterrevolutionaries merely as temporary aberrations caused by the unfortunate outcome of the war and retained its patriotic stance. The leadership not only
embraced the cause of revisionism, but actually protested and rejected all "foreign"
interventions on its behalf, including those by the international Jewish organizations,
as violations of Hungarian sovereign rights. And indeed, their optimism was for a
while reinforced during the 1920s, when Count István Bethlen, a representative of
the conservative-aristocratic group of large landholders and financial magnates who
had ruled Hungary before World War I, headed the Hungarian government.

The appointment of Gömbös as prime minister in October 1932, coinciding with
the spectacular electoral victories of the Nazi Party in Germany, brought the Jewish
Question to the fore once again. It soon became a national obsession that frequently
rivaled revisionism in intensity. Borrowing a page from the Nazis' propaganda book,
the Hungarian radicals depicted the Jews as naturally unpatriotic, parasitically
sapping the energy of the nation, and prone to internationalist—that is, Bolshevik—
tendencies. The propaganda campaign was soon coupled with demands for a
definitive solution of the Jewish Question. The suggestions offered by the radical
Right at the time ranged from legal restrictions on the Jews' professional and
economic activities to their orderly "resettlement" out of the country.

Although expediency and temporary tactical considerations induced Gömbös to "revise" his position on the Jewish Question, his policies prepared the ground for the disaster that was later to strike Hungary and its Jews. He tied Hungary's destiny almost irrevocably to that of Nazi Germany. He not only abandoned Bethlen's reliance on the Western democracies and the League of Nations as a means to correct "the injustices of Trianon," he also brought Hungary's foreign policy into line with that of Nazi Germany and made possible the subsequent penetration and direct involvement of the Reich in practically every aspect of the country's life. This was greatly facilitated by the formidable and potentially collaborationist power base Gömbös established during his tenure. He was able not only to replace the civil and military bureaucracies of the state apparatus with his own protegés, but also—and this was perhaps more crucial—to pack the upper army hierarchy, including the General Staff, with younger, highly nationalistic Germanophile officers. The stage for anti-Jewish excesses to come was further set through the radicalization of the press and the flourishing of ultrarightist political movements and parties.

The spectacular domestic and foreign policy successes of the Third Reich, including the Anschluss with Austria by which Germany extended its borders to those of Hungary, were achieved largely because of the shortsighted appeasement policies of the Western democracies. The Nazi victories induced successive Hungarian governments to embrace the Axis ever more tightly. They became increasingly eager to see Hungary involved in the establishment of the "New Order" in Europe and reaping the benefits of the Nazi revisionist-revanchist policies as an active member of the Axis Alliance. The pro-Reich policy was especially supported by the Germanophile General Staff, the right wing of the dominant Government Life Party, and the industrial-banking establishment, including Jews and converts.

While this policy yielded considerable dividends, enabling Hungary to fulfill parts of its revisionist ambitions at the expense of Czechoslovakia, Romania, and Yugoslavia, it was in the long run disastrous for the country. It was, of course, even more catastrophic for the country's Jews. In retrospect, the policies of the aristocratic-gentry-dominated conservative governments appear to have been quite unrealistic, if not quixotic. Having embraced the Third Reich for its opposition to Bolshevism and its chief bulwark, the Soviet Union, and for its support of revisionism, these governments were soon compelled to come to grips with the ever more influential Right radicals at home. While they despised and feared these radicals almost as much as the Jews—the Hungarian Nazis had advocated not only the need to solve the Jewish Question, but also the necessity to bring about a social revolution that would put an end to the inherited privileges of the conservative-aristocratic elements—the governmental leaders felt compelled to appease them as well as the Germans. In fact, these leaders looked upon the right radicals' preoccupation with the Jewish Question as a blessing in disguise, for it helped deter attention from the grave social-agrarian problems confronting the nation. They were, consequently, ready to adopt a series of anti-Jewish measures. These became more draconian with each territorial acquisition between 1938 and 1941. In addition to passing three major anti-Jewish laws—the third one incorporated some of the basic provisions of the Nuremberg Laws of Nazi Germany—they adopted a discriminatory system of forced labor service for Jews of military age, a unique institution in Nazi-dominated Europe.

These anti-Jewish measures of the various governments, endorsed by the leaders of the Christian churches, were based on the illusions that guided the ruling elites until the German occupation. They thought that by passing laws that would curtail the Jews' economic power and "harmful" cultural influence, they could not only appease the ultrarightists who thrived on the social and economic unrest that plagued the country, but also satisfy the Third Reich and at the same time safeguard the vital interests of the Jews themselves. This rationalization was part of the larger quixotic assumption that Hungary could satisfy its revisionist ambitions by embracing the Third Reich without having to jeopardize its own freedom of action.

The upper strata of Hungarian Jewry, including the official national leadership, shared these illusions, convinced that the Jewish community's long history of loyal service to Magyardom would continue to be recognized and their fundamental interests safeguarded by the ruling elite of the country. They accepted, however reluctantly, many of the anti-Jewish measures as reflecting the "spirit of the times" and as necessary tactical moves to "take the sting out of the antisemitic drive" of the ultrarightists at home and abroad. They tended to concur with the rationalizations of the governmental leaders that the anti-Jewish laws were "the best guarantee against antisemitism and intolerance."[4] In consequence, they were convinced that the safety and well-being of the Jews were firmly linked to the preservation of the basically reactionary conservative-aristocratic regime. And, indeed, as long as this aristocratic elite remained in power, the vital interests of Hungarian Jewry were preserved relatively intact. This remained so even after Hungary entered the war against the Soviet Union in June 1941. The regime continued not only to provide haven to the many thousands of Polish, Slovak, and other refugees, but consistently to oppose the ever greater pressure by the Germans to bring about the Final Solution of the Jewish Question. While the Jews in Nazi-controlled Europe were being systematically annihilated, Hungary continued to protect its 825,000 Jews (including approximately 100,000 converts identified as Jews under Hungary's racial law of 1941) until it virtually lost its independence in March 1944.

The pre-occupation record of Hungary was, of course, not spotless. About 60,000 Jews lost their lives even before the German invasion: over 42,000 labor servicemen died or were killed in the Ukraine and Serbia, close to 18,000 were killed in the drive against "alien" Jews, and about 1,000 were slaughtered in the Bácska area. Nevertheless, Hungarian Jewry continued to dwell in comparative personal and physical safety. There were no restrictions on their freedom of movement and they were treated relatively fairly in the allocation of food. Although the anti-Jewish laws had a particularly severe economic impact on the lower strata of the Jewish population, including both skilled salaried workers and unskilled laborers, the economic situation of the Jews as a whole was relatively tolerable, primarily because of the well-developed communal self-help system. Also, those in business and industry, though their activities were severely curtailed, were usually able to circumvent some provisions of the anti-Jewish laws or take advantage of loopholes. The relatively few industrial magnates, mostly converts, actually benefited from Hungary's armament program and dealings with the Third Reich.[5]

The situation of Hungarian Jewry appeared to improve in 1943 despite the Nazis' relentless war against the Jews in the rest of German-occupied Europe. Following the destruction of the 2nd Hungarian Army near Voronezh and the subsequent defeat of the Germans around Stalingrad early in 1943, the Hungarians began a desperate search for an honorable way out of the war, a search that was intensified after Italy's extrication from the Axis Alliance later that summer. It ultimately led to disaster, primarily because of the irreconcilably conflicting political and socioeconomic objectives the conservative-aristocratic leaders were pursuing.

The Hungarian leaders were eager not only to safeguard the independence and territorial integrity of the country, including the retention of the areas acquired between 1938 and 1941, but also to preserve the antiquated socioeconomic structure of a gentry-dominated society. While they were apprehensive about a possible German occupation, they were above all paralyzed by the fear of the Soviet Union and communism. They viewed the latter as the ultimate evil to which even Nazism, if it proved unavoidable, was preferable. Ignoring the geopolitical realities of the area, they consequently unrealistically tried to solve their dilemma by maneuvering "in secret" for a possible separate peace with the Western powers. Unaware of the realities of the Grand Alliance, they fervently hoped that the Allies would invade Europe from the Balkans and thereby achieve a double military and political objective: the destruction of the Nazi forces and the prevention of Bolshevik penetration into the heart of Europe.

With spies planted in all segments of the Hungarian government, the Germans were fully informed about the nature and scope of the "secret" negotiations between the emissaries of Prime Minister Miklós Kállay and the representatives of the Allies in Italy and Turkey. Reports to the Nazis by their many agents in Hungary about the "treacherous and pro-Jewish" activities of the Kállay government were reinforced by two secret memoranda by Edmund Veesenmayer, the German expert on East Central Europe who later became Hitler's plenipotentiary in Hungary.

Veesenmayer warned the Führer not only about the untrustworthiness of the government but about the "danger" represented by the Jews. He contended that the Jews were "Enemy No. 1" and that "the 1.1 million Jews amount to as many saboteurs . . . who must be viewed as Bolshevik vanguards."[6] In addition, there were weighty military considerations: extrication of Hungary from the Axis when the Soviet forces were already crossing the Dniester would have deprived Germany of the Romanian oil fields and exposed the German forces in the central and southern parts of Europe to encirclement and possibly an immediate and crushing defeat. It was primarily to safeguard their military security interests that the Germans decided to occupy Hungary and prevent it from emulating Italy.

The destruction of Hungarian Jewry, the last surviving large block of European Jewry, was to a large extent the concomitant of this German military decision. Ironically, it appears in retrospect that had Hungary continued to remain a militarily passive but vocally loyal ally of the Third Reich instead of provocatively engaging in essentially fruitless, perhaps even merely alibi-establishing diplomatic maneuvers, the Jews of Hungary might have survived the war relatively unscathed. But the fundamental interests of the Hungarians were in conflict with those of the Jews. While the aristocratic-conservative leaders despised the Nazis, they were grateful for the support of the Third Reich in achieving a great part of their revisionist ambitions and mortally fearful of a Bolshevik takeover. Although most of the Jews shared the Hungarians' abhorrence of both Nazism and Bolshevism, they looked upon the

Soviet Union—a member of the Grand Alliance—as the only realistic savior from the threat represented by the Nazis and their local allies.

The German forces that invaded Hungary on March 19, 1944, were accompanied by a small but highly efficient special commando unit ("Sonderkommando") headed by Adolf Eichmann, which had prepared a number of contingency plans to take advantage of any opportunities to "solve" the Jewish Question that might be provided by the new Hungarian leaders. Two years earlier, Eichmann had been indirectly approached by some high-ranking Hungarian ultrarightists to help "resettle" thousands of "alien" Jews; at that time he had refused to mobilize his deportation apparatus for this small-scale operation, preferring to wait until the Hungarians consented to a total removal of the country's Jews.[7] The occupation provided that opportunity.

It turned out that the Nazis found in Hungary a group of accomplices who outdid them in their eagerness to eliminate the Jews from the country. And indeed, it was primarily the joint, concerted, and single-minded drive by these two groups that made the effectuation of the Final Solution in Hungary possible: neither group could have succeeded without the other. While the Germans were eager to solve the Jewish Question, they could not take action without the consent of the newly established Hungarian puppet government and the cooperation of the Hungarian instruments of power. And the Hungarian ultrarightists, though anxious to emulate their German counterparts, could not have achieved their ideologically defined objectives in the absence of the German occupation.

As a consequence of the occupation, the Hungarian Jewish community, which had survived the first four-and-a-half years of the war relatively intact, was subjected to the most ruthless and concentrated destruction process of the Nazis' war against the Jews. The drive against the Hungarian Jews took place on the very eve of Allied victory, when the grisly details of the Final Solution were already known to the leaders of the world, including those of Hungarian and world Jewry. Informed about the barbarity and speed with which the Hungarian Jews were liquidated, Winston Churchill concluded that it was "probably the greatest and most horrible crime ever committed in the history of the world."[8]

The liquidation of Hungarian Jewry reminds one of a prophecy by Theodore Herzl. In a letter dated March 10, 1903, when Hungarian Jewry was still in the midst of its Golden Era, the father of Zionism cautioned his friend Ernö Mezei, a member of the Hungarian Parliament: "The hand of fate shall also seize Hungarian Jewry. And the later this occurs, and the stronger this Jewry becomes, the more cruel and hard shall be the blow, which shall be delivered with greater savagery. There is no escape."

Was there no escape? The evidence clearly indicates that had Horthy and the clique around him *really* wanted to save Hungarian Jewry, they could have done so. According to the testimony of Veesenmayer and Otto Winkelmann, the former Higher SS and Police Leader in Hungary, in the postwar trial of Andor Jaross, László Baky, and László Endre—the triumvirate primarily responsible for the destruction of Hungarian Jewry—the Final Solution of the Jewish Question was only a *wish*, not an absolute *demand* of the Germans. The Eichmann Sonderkommando, numbering fewer than 200, could not possibly have carried out its sinister plans without the wholehearted cooperation of the Hungarians who placed the instruments of state power at its disposal. As the examples of Bulgaria, Finland, and Romania reveal—and Horthy's own actions of July 1944 clearly indicate—the Regent and his associates could have saved most of the Jews. Unfortunately, they were interested primarily in protecting the assimilated ones, especially those with whom they had good and mutually advantageous business and financial relations; they were almost as eager as the Right radicals to rid the country of the "Eastern-Galician" Jews. It was partially for this reason that Horthy, who considered the imminent Nazi occupation less of an evil than a possible Soviet invasion, had made concessions that proved fatal for Hungarian Jewry. When he met Hitler at Schloss Klessheim the day before the occupation and consented to the "delivery of a few hundred thousand Jewish workers to Germany for employment in war-related projects,"[9] Horthy was apparently convinced that by giving his consent he would not only satisfy Germany's "legitimate" needs but contribute to the struggle against Bolshevism and at the same time get rid of the Galician Jews, whom he openly detested. The Eichmann Sonderkommando and its Hungarian accomplices took full advantage of this agreement to implement the Final Solution program throughout the country, based on the argument that "the Jews will be more productive in Germany if they have all members of their families with them."

Once they were given the green light, the "de-Jewification" experts proceeded with lightning speed. Time was of the essence, for the Third Reich was threatened with imminent defeat. And, indeed, in no other country was the Final Solution program—the establishment of the Judenräte; the isolation, expropriation, ghettoization, concentration, entrainment, and deportation of the Jews—carried out with as much barbarity and speed as in Hungary. Although the "de-Jewification" squads were relatively small, the interplay of many domestic and international factors aided them in the speedy implementation of their sinister designs.

The German and Hungarian agents in charge of the Final Solution program had at their disposal the instruments of state power—the police, gendarmerie, and civil service—and were able to proceed unhindered by any internal or external opposition. The puppet government provided them with legal and administrative cover, and a considerable number of Hungarians proved eager and willing to collaborate for ideological or materialistic reasons. With public opinion having been successfully molded by years of vicious antisemitic agitation, the population at large was at best passive; the bulk of the "proletariat," including the miners and industrial workers, continued the political stance of the 1930s, embracing the Arrow Cross rather than the leftist parties.

Postwar Hungarian historiography notwithstanding, there was no meaningful resistance anywhere in the country, let alone organized opposition for the protection of the Jews. This was especially so in the countryside. It was primarily in Budapest that Christians and a variety of Church organizations were ready to offer shelter to Jews, saving thousands of them from certain death. But by that time late in 1944, the countryside was already judenrein, the Soviet forces were fast approaching the capital, and most Hungarians realized that the Allies were bound to win the war.

The Allies, though fully aware of the realities of the Final Solution, were reluctant to get involved in the Nazis' war against the Jews. When the Western powers were asked, shortly after the beginning of the deportations from Hungary on May 15, 1944, to bomb Auschwitz and the rail lines leading to the camp, they declined, stating among other things that they could not spare aircraft for such "secondary targets." (A few months later, by contrast, they assembled a large armada to destroy another target without real strategic value: the art-laden and refugee-filled city of Dresden.)The Soviet air force, which was strategically in even better position to bomb the death camps and the rail lines leading to them, also did nothing about them. The record of the leftist, mostly pro-Soviet, underground and partisan forces in Hungary, Slovakia, and Poland is no better in this regard. There is no evidence that they engaged in any but the most isolated individual acts of sabotage or resistance to prevent the deportation of the Jews.

During the first phase of the deportations from Hungary, the attitude of the neutral states—Portugal, Turkey, Spain, Sweden, and Switzerland—was fundamentally no more positive. But their position, like that of the Vatican and the International Red Cross, changed when late in June 1944 the Swiss press began to publicize the horrors of the Final Solution in Hungary. Their pressure on Horthy, complementing his concerns over the rapidly deteriorating military situation—by that time the Soviet forces were fast approaching the borders of Hungary and the Allies had successfully established their beachheads in Normandy—advanced the desired result. Horthy halted the deportations on July 7. (In fact, however, the squads continued their operations around Budapest until July 9.) By that date, all of Hungary with the exception of Budapest had been made judenrein. The success of Horthy's belated action is another piece of evidence demonstrating that the German demands for the Final Solution could have been refused or sabotaged even after the occupation. Had Horthy and the Hungarian authorities really been concerned with all their citizens of the Jewish faith, they could have refused to cooperate. Without the Hungarian instruments of power, the Germans would have been as helpless during the first phase of the occupation as they proved to be after early July 1944.

What about the victims, the Jewish masses and their leaders? Though the German invasion of Hungary took place on the eve of Allied victory, when the Hungarian and Jewish leaders were already privy to the secrets of Auschwitz, the ghettoization and deportation process in Hungary was carried out as smoothly as it was almost everywhere else in Nazi-dominated Europe. Helpless and defenseless, abandoned by the Christian society surrounding them, the Jews of Hungary—with the notable exception of some young Zionist pioneers in Budapest—displayed little or no opposition throughout the occupation period. In accordance with well-tested Nazi camouflage methods, the Jews were lulled into acquiescence by assurances that the deportations involved merely their relocation for labor within the country and Germany for the duration of the war. They—and the rest of the world—were further assured that the young and the old were included in the transports only out of "consideration for the close family-life pattern of the Jews."

Under the conditions of relative normality that prevailed until the German occupation, the predominantly assimilated leaders of Hungarian Jewry were quite effective in serving the community. Firmly committed to the values and principles of the traditional conservative-aristocratic system, and convinced that the interests of Jewry were intimately intertwined with those of the Magyars, they never contemplated the use of independent political techniques for the advancement of Jewish interests per se. They took pride in calling themselves "Magyars of the Jewish faith" (*Zsidóvallású magyarok*). The leadership, consisting primarily of patriotic, rich, and generally conservative elements, tried to maintain the established order by faithfully obeying the commands of the government and fully associating itself with the values, beliefs, and interests of broader Hungarian society. Consequently, the national Jewish leaders' response to the exacerbating anti-Jewish measures during the interwar period was apologetic and isolated from the general struggle of European Jewry. Their loyalty to the Hungarian nation, and their attachment to the aristocratic-gentry establishment, remained unshaken. To the end, they followed an ostrichlike policy, hoping against hope that the ruling elite would protect them from the fate of the Jewish communities of the neighboring countries. They did not, of course, expect that Germany would invade an ally and that the anti-Nazi Christian leadership would also be among the first victims after an occupation. Practically until the beginning of the deportations, the national Jewish leadership continued to believe that the Hungarian Jewish community, unlike all other large European Jewish communities, would emerge from the war relatively intact even if economically generally ruined. While tragically mistaken, their belief that they would escape the Holocaust—"megusszuk" (we'll get by), they frequently said in self-assurance—was not irrational. After all, Hungary had in fact been an island of safety in an ocean of destruction for four-and-a-half years of the war.

The Jewish leaders' faith in the Hungarian establishment was not entirely groundless. They personally, along with close to 150,000 of the 247,000 Jews of Budapest (including some 62,000 converts identified as Jews in 1941), were spared the fate that befell those in the countryside because Horthy, under great diplomatic and military pressure, halted the deportations early in July 1944. In addition, many tens of thousands of Jewish males of military age from all parts of Hungary were saved by the armed forces.

This represents still another paradox of the Holocaust in Hungary. The Hungarian labor service system, which was unique in Nazi-dominated Europe, had been the major source of Jewish suffering before the German occupation. Deprived of their dignity and rights, the Jewish labor servicemen were compelled to do hard and often hazardous military-related work under the constant prodding of mostly cruel guards and officers. Particularly tragic was the fate of the tens of thousands of labor servicemen who had been deployed, along with the 2nd Hungarian Army, on the Soviet front and in the copper mines in Bor, Serbia. Yet, after the occupation, the Jewish labor servicemen—unlike the Jews at large, who at first were placed under the jurisdiction of the Germans—enjoyed the continued protection of the Hungarian armed forces. Moreover, many Jewish males were recruited by decent military commanders from the ghettos and concentration centers and thus saved from deportation and almost certain death.[10]

The liberation of the surviving Jews of Hungary itself became a controversial issue after the war, reflecting the traditional conflict in the fundamental interests of the Jews and non-Jews. Credit for the liberation of the Jews of Budapest was claimed by many after the war, including Horthy and his supporters, the Wallenberg myth-makers, and even the SS and the Arrow Cross. It has become politically fashionable and historically prudent not to identify the determining factor in the liberation of the surviving remnant of Hungarian Jewry: the Red Army. The Soviet occupation of Hungary following the crushing defeat of the Germans and their Hungarian allies—the only ones to adhere to the Axis to the end—engendered diametrically opposed perceptions of the postwar era. While for the Jews and the other victims of Nazism and Hungarian fascism the entry of the Soviet forces meant liberation for most Hungarians, it denoted the subjugation of Hungary. Although most Jews suffered perhaps even more than the Christians did under the Soviet-imposed communist regime—they were persecuted on both social and religious grounds—nationalists and their sundry antisemitic Rightist allies continue to identify the system with the Jews. Their most frequently cited "proofs" include the prominent role played by the relatively few communists of Jewish origin in the Béla Kun (1919) and Stalinist (1949–1956) dictatorships and in the postwar law-enforcement agencies, including the secret police. The presence of Jews in these agencies was particularly galling to antisemites, for it had been unthinkable in pre-1945 Hungary.

The conflict over the different perceptions and interpretations of the Holocaust and of the postwar era became particularly bitter after the collapse of communism in 1989–1990. But this chapter in Hungarian history and Hungarian Jewish relations lies beyond the scope of this essay.

NOTES

This essay has appeared in a somewhat different version elsewhere.

1. See Oscar Jászi, *The Dissolution of the Hapsburg Monarchy* (Chicago: University of Chicago Press, 1929), p. 825. See also Randolph L. Braham, *The Politics of Genocide: The Holocaust in Hungary* (New York: Rosenthal Institute for Holocaust Studies, 1994), pp. 5–12.

2. For some details on the Golden Era, see Braham, *Politics*, pp. 1–39.

3. Jenö Lévai, *Zsidósors Magyarországon* (Jewish fate in Hungary) (Budapest: Magyar Téka, 1948), p. 17.

4. Braham, *Politics*, pp. 129–30.

5. For details on the pre-occupation losses of Hungarian Jewry, see ibid., pp. 205–22.

6. "Edmund Veesenmayer's Memorandum to the German Foreign Office dated December 10, 1943," in *The Destruction of Hungarian Jewry: A Documentary Account*, Randolph L Braham, comp. and ed. (New York: World Federation of Hungarian Jews, 1973), pp. 254–84.

7. Ibid., pp. 283–93.

8. For details on the Final Solution program in Hungary, see ibid., chapters 17–22.

9. Ibid., pp. 391, 397–401. See also C. A. Macartney, *October Fifteenth: A History of Modern Hungary* (Edinburgh: Edinburgh University Press, 1997), vol. 2, pp. 234, 239.

10. For details on all aspects of the labor service system, see ibid., pp. 294–380.

32.

MEIR MICHAELIS

The Holocaust in Italy

AREAS OF INQUIRY

Introduction

Although nearly four-fifths of the Jews of Italy survived Hitler's Final Solution to the Jewish Question, the impact of the Holocaust on Italian Jewry was profound. Ever since the end of World War II, it has been the subject of scholarly debate, political controversy, and legal conflict. Some of the accounts by survivors have won fame throughout the Western world, most particularly Primo Levi's *If This Is a Man* (on the author's experiences in Auschwitz). Giorgio Bassani's *The Garden of the Finzi-Continis* (on the persecution and deportation of a prominent family of Ferrarese Jews), and Silvano Arieti's *The Parnas* (on the murder of Giuseppe Pardo Roques, the venerable ex-president of the Jewish community at Pisa, by Himmler's myrmidons).

Of the problems that have emerged in this context and have given rise to controversy, six are particularly important: first, the native roots of Fascist antisemitism; second, the attitude of the Catholic Church, with special reference to the silence of Pius XII; third, the attitude of the Italian masses; fourth, Italian resistance to genocide in the occupied territories from 1941 to 1943; fifth, the personal role of Mussolini as associate, ally, and puppet of Hitler; sixth, the respective roles of the Germans and the Italians in the implementation of the Final Solution on Italian soil.

The controversy over the Holocaust in Italy received a fresh impetus in late 1986 when an Italian journalist, Niccola Caracciolo, conducted a series of televised interviews on aid to Jews during World War II. These interviews provoked sharp polemical reactions from various Italian Jews, including Tullia Zevi, president of the Union of Italian Jewish Communities. Two years later, the fiftieth anniversary of the Fascist race laws was marked by an explosion of articles, books, and pamphlets on the anti-Jewish campaign that set the stage for the Final Solution on the Italian peninsula.

Prior to Hitler's rise to power there was no "Jewish Question" in modern Italy; it is no exaggeration to say that until 1936 there was less antisemitism there than in any of the Western democracies. Hence, before discussing the issues and controversies already mentioned, we shall do well to deal briefly with the historical background.

From Liberalism to Fascism

The emancipation of Italian Jewry, extended to the whole of the peninsula after the capture of Rome in 1870, has been hailed by practically all students of the subject as a unique success in both its positive and its negative aspects—in the perfect equality accorded Italian Jews, and in the progressive erosion of their Jewish identity: "Italy became a byword in the Jewish world for the completeness of emancipation on the one hand, for its deadly corrosive potentialities on the other."[1]

By 1900 Italy's Jews were fully integrated into the surrounding society; they played a prominent part in the political, cultural, and economic life of the country and had access to careers in diplomacy and the armed forces, avenues generally closed to them elsewhere. The first Jewish minister of war and the first Jewish prime minister in Europe were Italians: Giuseppe Ottolenghi (1902–1903) and Luigi Luzzatti (1910–1911). By 1905 eleven Jews were sitting among Italy's elder statesmen in the royally nominated Senate; eighteen years later the number had risen to twenty-six.

Antisemitism on the peninsula was a marginal phenomenon throughout the period. Even the clerical campaign against the Jews during the reign of Leo XIII (1883–1903), in which about forty newspapers and periodicals took part, had little effect on the position of the Jews in Italian life. A. M. Canepa observed:

> It never had the opportunity to coalesce with other antisemitic and antiliberal currents or to pose a threat to republican institutions, as in France during the Dreyfus affair; and in contrast to the situation in the Second Reich, where antisemitism was a vehicle for the integration of the Center Party into the German political establishment, the anti-Jewish campaign of Italian Catholics served only to increase the isolation of the Church from the political life of the country.[2]

Jewish assimilation was facilitated by several factors peculiar to Italy, at least in their convergence: the smallness of the Jewish nucleus (about one-tenth of one percent); the all but total absence of Jewish immigration from Eastern Europe; the laic ideology of the Italian state; the "universalist" nature of Italian nationalism itself; the integration of clerical forces into the Italian political system during the liberal era; the racial affinity between Sephardic Jews (as distinct from Ashkenazi Jews) and Italians; and, last but not least, a curious blend of general respect for the persons and rights of individual Jews with a widespread disregard for Judaism as a religion and as an ethical system, a combination that subtly encouraged irreligion and apostasy among members of the Jewish community.[3]

Countercurrents of Jewish revival began to surface at the end of the nineteenth century. In 1898 Rabbi Giuseppe Sonino of Naples went to Basel to address the second Zionist Congress. In the following year the Collegio Rabbinico, after a lengthy period of semiactivity, was revitalized under the direction of Shmuel Zvi Margulies, a rabbi of Galician origin; and in 1907 the first of a new nexus of Jewish cultural societies, under the name of Pro Cultura, was established by Margulies's disciples in Florence. Four years later a Jewish Youth Congress was held there and the new synthesis between the Italian and Jewish cultures was taken as a basis for action. Margulies also succeeded in rallying some of the most outstanding minds of the younger generation, and an "integral" Judaism, embracing Jewish observances, Jewish culture, and Jewish national solidarity, came to be fairly widespread among the younger intelligentsia. Their mouthpiece was *Israel*, the Zionist weekly founded in 1916 and edited by Dante A. Lattes and Alfonsa Pacifici; Chaim Weizmann rightly considered it "one of the best Zionist papers of the day."[4]

Italian Jewry under Fascism

During the first fourteen years of Fascist rule (1922–1936), the position of the Jews remained ostensibly much what it had been before. Throughout this period, Mussolini aimed at "Fascistizing" his Jewish subjects and at using them as tools of his imperial policies in the Mediterranean and in Africa. Toward this end, in 1931 he set up the Union of Italian Jewish Communities, which was charged with the task of maintaining "spiritual and cultural contacts" with the Jewish communities of other countries. There was latent tension between the regime and the Jews from the outset, mainly due to Fascist suspicions of Jewish particularism, but there was no attempt to create a "Jewish problem" and no specifically Jewish opposition to the dictatorship. If some Jews were among its opponents, others were among its earliest supporters. Such anti-Jewish feeling as existed in Fascist circles was purely political; its main target was "international Jewry," not the "Jewish Italians." In the words of Luigi Villari, the leading Fascist propagandist in the Anglo-Saxon countries: "Antisemitism among the Fascists is the result not of any dislike of the Italian Jews, who are absolutely absorbed into the nation and are good patriots, but of suspicion of the international activities of foreign Jews especially of those representing the great cosmopolitan financial interests of Paris, London, Berlin, and New York, and of dislike of the Russian Bolsheviks, whose leaders are mostly Jews."[5]

The rapprochement between Church and State after Mussolini's rise to power caused alarm among the Jews, the main reason being a law of July 1923, which called for mandatory religious instruction in Italian schools, and the Concordat of February 1929, which restored Roman Catholicism to its place as the state religion. Since the pact with the Vatican lessened the Duce's dependence on the goodwill of the pope, its effect on Fascist policy was to some extent positive. Even so, it established an inequality of religions under the law.[6]

From 1922 to 1936 (and on occasion as late as 1937), the official Fascist attitude toward the Jews was summed up in the phrase: "The Jewish problem does not exist in Italy." The spokesmen of Italian Jewry naturally hastened to subscribe to the official thesis, paying tribute to the magnanimity of the regime and blaming the manifestations of antisemitism on "irresponsible underlings." At first these expressions of regard for the new rulers were mainly a matter of tactics; by 1932, however, even antifascist Jews had become convinced that Mussolini was as good as his word. In April of that year he condemned racism and antisemitism in a talk with Emil Ludwig; two months later he defined the concept of the nation in antiracist terms. The Jews were duly impressed. In an editorial on the tenth anniversary of the March on Rome, *Israel* emphasized the radical difference "between the true and authentic Fascism—Italian Fascism, that is—and the pseudo-Fascist movements in other countries, which . . . often make use of the most reactionary phobias, and especially of the blind, unbridled hatred of the Jews, as a means of diverting the masses from their real problems."[7]

Assimilation continued unabated (in 1938, 43.7% of all married Jews had Gentile spouses), but so did the Jewish revival. The Italian Zionist Federation was not banned, despite Mussolini's aversion to Italians with "dual loyalties"; a nexus of local cultural societies was set up, and *La Rassegna Mensile di Israel*, the literary supplement of *Israel*, attained a standard of excellence matched by few Jewish periodicals in any country; the Zionist publishing house in Florence had an output that, though small, was of very high quality; and Youth Cultural Congresses were held in Livorno and Venice.[8]

However, given the Fascist ideal of the "unitary state," in matters of religion as well as political allegiance, some degree of discrimination against nonconforming elements was inevitable. No Jew ever reached a position of control either in the government or in the Fascist Party; no Jew was ever admitted to the Italian Academy, although the number of outstanding Jewish scholars was high. The number of Jewish senators dwindled from twenty-six in 1923 to six in 1938. On the other hand, Jews continued to be prominent in commerce, in the liberal professions, in the armed forces, and in the academic world. Margherita Sarfatti, Mussolini's Jewish mistress, was also his official biographer; Ugo d'Ancona Achille Loria, and Teodoro Mayer were among his closest financial advisers. Guido Jung, a Catholic of Jewish extraction, served as minister of finance from 1932 to 1935. Three among the major Italian publishing houses—Bemporad, Formiggini, and Treves—were in Jewish hands.[9]

The first deterioration in the position of Italian Jewry occurred after Hitler's rise to power. In 1933 Mussolini could not yet risk antagonizing France and Britain by forming an ideological bloc with Berlin. But if Hitler's antisemitism was a source of embarrassment to him, so was the anti-Hitler crusade conducted by Jewry: while his newspapers were exulting over the triumph of "German Fascism," the spokesmen of Italian Jewry vied with their antifascist brethren abroad in denouncing the German atrocities. He reacted by unleashing an anti-Jewish campaign—the first in the history of modern Italy—in the Fascist press, most particularly in his unofficial mouthpiece, *Il Tevere*. His official mouthpiece, *Il Popola d'Italia*, took up the anti-Jewish theme in a more moderate way. Since "Jewish anti-Fascism" was being increasingly identified with Zionism, the Jewish Fascists established an appropriate weekly organ, *La Nostra Bandiera*, to set themselves off from the Zionists.[10]

After the abortive Nazi putsch in Austria (July 25, 1934) the Jewish issue in Italy receded into the background, overshadowed by the clash between Rome and Berlin that prompted the Duce to join the anti-German coalition known as the Stresa front (April 1935). However, once the invasion of Ethiopia was launched (October 3, 1935), the anti-Hitler front collapsed. True, Mussolini could not change sides overnight: while taking steps to improve relations with Hitler, he continued to play the Western card for all it was worth. In so doing, he naturally took account of Jewry's alleged influence on Western policy toward Italy: Jewish emissaries were sent abroad to warn against the sanction policy and to exploit Zionist aspirations for Fascist ends. His advances toward the Zionists continued until July 1936, the month in which the German and Italian secret services began to cooperate in Spain.[11]

As long as Mussolini pursued a middle course between the democracies and the Reich, he had no motive for attacking the Jews as such. With the beginning of German-Italian collaboration in Spain, however, there was a marked change for the worse. The overtures to the Zionists ceased; Italian propaganda in Palestine now fed on the anti-Jewish feelings of the local Arabs. On September 12, 1936, an anti-Jewish campaign was launched by Roberto Farinacci, the Fascist boss of Cremona; six weeks later, the Rome-Berlin Axis was born. In March 1937 a stir was caused by Paolo Orano's book *Gli Ebrei in Italia*, which equated *italianità* with Roman Catholicism and contested the right of the Jews to retain their own identity. Other Fascist scribes went further, calling for racial measures on the German model. Finally, on July 14, 1938, Mussolini had the press publish a statement, called the Manifesto della Razza (Manifesto of the race), in which the Italian Jews were defined as inassimilable aliens. On August 22, 1938, a new Jewish census identified 55,103 persons as being of the Jewish "race" (the census of 1931 had returned 47,825 persons of the Jewish faith). On September 5, Jewish pupils were excluded from public schools and Jewish teachers were forbidden to teach in such schools or in any scientific or academic institution. Simultaneously, a Directorate-General for Race and Demography was established within the Ministry of the Interior and given the responsibility for co-ordinating racial legislation. On September 7, Jews of foreign birth, including those who had acquired Italian citizenship after January 1, 1919, were ordered to leave the country within six months. For the purposes of the law, Jews were defined as persons "having two Jewish parents even if they profess a religion other than the Jewish." The Declaration on Race followed on October 7. In it the Fascist Grand Council laid down the guidelines for the racial policy instituted in the ensuing months. A law enacted on November 17 prohibited Jews from marrying "Aryans," made it obligatory for them to declare they were Jewish, banned them from military service, and forbade them to tutor an "Aryan" minor. Neither might Jews own a business, land, or buildings above a certain value; employ "Aryan" servants; or hold posts in any public service. The same law specified that Jews with civil or military merits might apply for exemption. They would be allowed to employ "Aryans" and own real estate; the other restrictions, however, would still apply. Subsequent laws progressively reinforced the anti-Jewish measures.[12]

The racial campaign and its swift translation into official policy was a crushing blow to Italian Jewry; over 4,000 sought refuge in baptism, and about 6,000 emigrated. Most of those who remained, however, faced persecution with dignity. The chief communities opened Jewish schools, and various charitable organizations were set up to aid foreign Jewish refugees, who continued to enter Italy despite the race laws. The most important of these, DELASEM (Committee for Assistance to Jewish Emigrants) helped to save thousands of Jewish lives during the war years. The Union of Italian Jewish Communities, after undergoing a profound crisis, regained its authority in 1939 under the leadership of Dante Almansi. After Italy's entry into the war (June 10, 1940) the Fascist authorities took a series of security measures against the Jews. On June 14, all Jewish bank accounts were blocked and stocks owned by Jews were ordered to be registered. On the same day the police began to intern foreign Jews as well as Italian Jews considered "politically dangerous." By September, fifteen internment camps had been set up; living conditions in these camps were harsh, but they had nothing in common with Hitler's extermination camps.[13]

While Jews on the peninsula were punished for the crime of being "Semites," the Jewish issue outside Italy became a test of the Duce's remaining autonomy. This eminently political consideration helps to explain why the Italian-occupied territories in France, Yugoslavia, and Greece became havens of refuge for persecuted Jews, at any rate until Italy's surrender to the Allies.

With the fall of Fascism (July 25, 1943) Italian racial policy lost its point. But the new premier, Marshal Pietro Badoglio, was unwilling to antagonize his "ally" by repealing the anti-Jewish laws. The internment camps were not dismantled, and the lists of Jewish names and addresses were not destroyed; most of these lists subsequently fell into the hands of the SS after September 8, 1943. Thus Mussolini's downfall, far from putting an end to the racial persecutions, merely set the stage for the implementation of the Final Solution on Italian soil.[14]

The Final Solution in Italy

On September 11, 1943, three days after Badoglio's surrender, Field Marshal Albert Kesselring, commander of Army Group South in Italy, declared all Italian territory to be a theater of war under German military control. Italy, in Mussolini's phrase, was thus "reduced from the position of a confederated province to the worse one of a colony," with fatal results for the Italian Jews.

In any assessment of the Final Solution in Italy, we must bear in mind three basic facts. First, there was the geographical distribution of Jews; since the Spanish expulsions, Jewish life had been confined to the north of the country. South of Rome there were very few Jews, and these were liberated by the Allies before the end of 1943. But the expected Allied landings in the Gulf of Genoa failed to materialize, with the result that the area of Jewish settlement from Rome northwards remained under German control until June 1944.

Second, Hitler's decision to restore Mussolini to power. If the creation of the Italian Social Republic had enabled the Duce to regain some measure of independence, many Jewish lives might have been saved. But since he was now virtually a prisoner, his reinstatement had the effect of facilitating the implementation of the Final Solution on Italian soil.

Third, Hitler's change of mind with regard to the projected occupation of the Vatican City. His first thought had been to occupy the Vatican; subsequently, however, under pressure from his entourage, he had agreed to spare the Holy See. Of all the decisions taken by Hitler after the fall of Fascism, this was the only one that benefited the Jews, for it enabled the Church to save a good many Jewish lives.

Immediately after the Italian armistice Hitler began to extend the Final Solution to Italy, without even waiting for the restoration of the Fascist regime. On September 12, Herbert Kappler, head of the Gestapo in Rome, was ordered to round up and deport the Jews of Rome; a few days later the SS initiated a series of pogroms, arrests, and deportations in Northern Italy; that resulted in the death of nearly 400 Jewish men, women, and children.

The history of the Final Solution in Italy can be divided into three periods. During the first (October–November 1943), the SS took advantage of the Italian power vacuum to carry out a series of autonomous actions. During the second (December 1943–mid-February 1944), the Fascists issued a series of anti-Jewish decrees with the object of restoring a measure of Italian sovereignty. During the third (mid-February 1944–April 1945), the SS imposed itself on the directives and policies of the Italians, by now almost totally devoid of autonomy.

During the first phase, operations were directed by Hauptsturmführer Theodor Dannecker. He enjoyed complete autonomy from even the Gestapo stationed in Italy, and he was tied to no fixed headquarters. On October 16, he struck in Rome. One thousand and thirty Jewish men, women, and children were deported to Auschwitz; only seventeen of them later returned. Dannecker's Einsatzkommando then shifted to other cities, including Florence, Venice, Milan, and Genoa.

The Fascist reaction to German interference took the form of an affirmation of autonomy rather than a helpless application of German orders. On November 14, 1943, the Fascist Party Congress at Verona endorsed a Manifesto that defined the Jews of Italy as "enemy nationals" for the duration of the war. On November 30, Mussolini's minister of the interior, Guido Buffarini-Guidi, ordered the arrest and internment of all Jews resident in the Fascist Republic ("even if exempted and irrespective of citizenship") and the immediate confiscation of their property "for the benefit of the indigent refugees from enemy air attacks." On the following day this order was broadcast over the radio, with the result that thousands of Jews went into hiding or fled to the countryside. On December 10, Mussolini's chief of police, Tullio Tamburini, instructed the heads of provinces to exempt certain categories of Jews from internment, including the aged, the sick, the "Aryanized," and those with "Aryan" spouses.

Buffarini's order of November 30 meant that no Jew could move about in public after that date because he or she was liable to arrest by the local police. In the following months, in fact, arrests were effected directly by the central police headquarters of the Fascist Republics. The police searched Jewish households or rounded up the Jews in the style of the SS lightning raids. The victims of the Fascist Jew hunt were crowded into local jails and then interned at Fossoli di Carpi (Modena), the central concentration camp for Jews. This went on until the summer of 1944, when the terms of Italian-German collaboration underwent a radical change.

At the end of January 1944, Dannecker was replaced by Sturmbannführer Friedrich R. Bosshammer, Eichmann's adviser on Italian affairs, who lost no time in making it clear that he had no intention of respecting Fascist laws designed to prevent him from making Italy judenrein. In vain Buffarini protested against the "illegal" deportation of Italian Jews to the East; in vain he requested the commandants of Italian concentration camps not to hand Jewish internees over to the SS. The fate of the Jews in German-occupied Italy was no longer in his hands. By the end of February the Fossoli concentration camp was under direct German administration, becoming a Durchgangslager (transit camp) designed to prepare deportation convoys. Thus, after depriving the Jews of their property and their freedom, the Fascist authorities took part in handing them over to those who would deprive them of their lives. True, Mussolini did not approve of the Final Solution (as late as 1944 he told his German medical adviser that Hitler's treatment of the Jews "did not redound to Germany's honor"); even so, he and his henchmen helped to create the conditions in which the murder of Jews became possible.

At the time of the Italian armistice there were some 44,500 Jews in Italy and Rhodes, about 12,500 of them foreigners. By the end of the war at least 7,860 of these had perished, including 303 who died on Italian soil. Of the 6,746 "Semites" who were deported from the Fascist Republic, 830 survived; of the 1,820 who were deported from Rhodes, 179 survived. In addition there were between 900 and 1,100 victims who have not yet been identified.[15]

Recovery and Reintegration

Although Italy shares with Denmark the distinction of saving the highest percentage of Jewish lives, Italian Jewry suffered a crushing blow. In the words of

Cecil Roth: "On paper, it was possible to reconstitute Italian Jewry as it had been in former days. . . . It was impossible, however, to bring the dead back to life, impossible to cancel the memory of the evil years, impossible to redress the broken spirits. . . . Not only had the habit of Jewish life been interrupted, but in many places its setting had disappeared. . . . Such a blow could not fail to leave a lasting impression."[16]

Once-proud Italian Jewry was no more than a shadow of its former self. Even so, the process of recovery and reintegration started long before the final surrender of all Axis troops in Italy. The first phase of this process was initiated by the Allied military authorities with the abrogation of the racial laws of Sicily on July 12, 1943. It ended with the liberation of Naples by British troops. It was during this period that several thousand Jews interned at Ferramonti Tarsia and other camps in southern Italy regained their freedom.

The second phase, slightly overlapping the first, began on September 9, 1943, the day after Badoglio's surrender, when the Resistenza Armata (the anti-Fascist resistance movement) was born. Jews had played a prominent part in the opposition to Fascism since 1919; they now had their share, and more than their share, in the armed struggle against the Nazi invader and his Italian accomplices. Two to three thousand (out of a total of 30,000 Jews in the half of Italy under the German heel) joined the partisans, and seven of these were posthumously awarded the Gold Medal, the highest Italian decoration for valor. Fighting shoulder to shoulder with their Gentile comrades-in-arms for the liberation of their country, they were once again Italians among Italians, an accepted and respected part of the people from which they had been excluded five years earlier. For most of them it was an unforgettable experience.

The third phase of the process of recovery and reintegration began on June 4, 1944, when Rome was liberated by the American 5th Army, and the Jewish fugitives came out of their hiding places. On the following day the race laws were repealed. There were indescribable scenes of jubilation as Jewish soldiers from Palestine made their first appearance. But Roman Jewry was in a sorry state. Many of the survivors had lost all their possessions, hunger was rampant, and the local Jewish leadership was in disarray. The formidable task of reorganizing the shattered Jewish community now fell to two American officers, Colonel Charles Poletti, Allied Regional Commissioner for Rome, and his Jewish aide, Captain Maurice E. Neufeld. Both Poletti and Neufeld were highly educated and gifted men, but neither of them was familiar with the complex problems of the Jewish survivors in Rome.

On July 7, 1944, a month after assuming his duties, Poletti dissolved the councils of both the Roman community and the Union and forced out the two presidents, Ugo Foa and Dante Almansi, because of their "Fascist past." He then appointed an "extraordinary commissioner" of Roman Jewry, Silvio Ottolenghi, a more genuine Fascist than either Almansi or Foa. To fill the void in spiritual leadership, Poletti reinstated the former chief Rabbi of Rome, Israel Anton Zolli, who had been dismissed from his post as a "deserter" on April 2. Zolli now retaliated by charging Foa with partial responsibility for Dannecker's Judenaktion of October 16, 1945, thus sparking an acrimonious controversy over Jewish collaboration and complicity in the Holocaust—a dispute that has occupied scholars and publicists ever since. Zolli's return to office met with opposition from his constituents; even so, he continued to enjoy the backing of Poletti until February 15, 1945, the day of his conversion to Roman

Catholicism. His place was then taken by his predecessor, David Prato, a much more popular figure, who had been ousted by the Fascists in 1938.[17]

Dante Almansi, whose outstanding leadership had earned him the gratitude of thousands of Italian Jews, was succeeded as president of the Union of Italian Jewish Communities by Giuseppe Nathan, a banker, whose father, Ernesto, had been mayor of Rome and grandmaster of Italian Freemasonry. Nathan had never been an observant Jew, nor was he involved in the community's internecine feuds; but he accepted the post as a moral obligation, feeling himself "bound in a special way after the abominable persecutions, of which we were the victims."[18] His appointment marked the resumption of the corporate life of Italian Jewry as a whole, although another eleven months had to pass before the process of liberation was complete.

Meanwhile, steps were taken to restore Roman Jewry to its former state. On July 13, 1944, a Jewish news bulletin was first issued. On December 7, the Zionist weekly, *Israel*, resumed publication. On January 15, 1945, the Italian Zionist federation was reinstituted; and on January 26, the Rabbinical College was reopened with Zolli as its head. In 1944, when the Jew hunt in the Fascist puppet republic was still in full swing, Nathan commissioned Colonel Massimo Adolfo Vitale, a gallant airman, to set up and direct a search committee for deported Jews, the precursor of the Jewish Documentation Center in Milan.

On April 29, 1945, the Germans signed a document providing for the unconditional surrender of all Axis forces by May 2. After twenty months of anguish, Italian Jewry was finally free to resume its rightful place in Italian society and to reconstruct itself to its own design. But although a beginning had been made, the obstacles to recovery were still formidable.

Areas of Inquiry I: The Roots of Fascist Antisemitism

The Fascist race laws of 1938 surprised and shocked Jewish and Gentile Italians alike. According to an acute British observer, the "non-Aryans" of the peninsula are "struck dumbfounded" by Mussolini's sudden jump from "philo-Semitism" and antiracism to racial antisemitism, "like people stupefied by a bad dream from which they had not yet awakened." The reactions of Italian "Aryans," a great many Fascists included, were not dissimilar:

> True, there are individuals who are profiting personally by the dismissal of Jewish officials, functionaries, and employees and it would be asking too much of human nature to expect such individuals to regard the policy which directly benefits them with wholehearted abhorrence. It must be true also that propaganda on lines which are being slavishly copied from Germany must in the course of time, if it is sufficiently prolonged, have some effect on ignorant minds. The fact remains that at the moment it would be difficult to hear anything outside official circles in defense of the official policy. It is notorious that Italian Jews . . . were almost completely assimilated—so much so that I was constantly hearing of individuals whose Jewish origin had remained unsuspected by their closest associates until a few months ago.[19]

In 1938 it was widely (and comprehensibly) assumed that Mussolini's about-face on the Jewish issue had been forced upon him or at least inspired by Hitler. The ordinary people received it with "resentful shame," because their leader had "stooped to copy the example of German neobarbarism." Pope Pius XI publicly branded it a "disgraceful imitation" of Hitler's Nordic mythology, adding that it ran directly counter to the noblest traditions of the Roman Empire that the Fascists had hitherto professed themselves so anxious to restore. The king of Italy voiced similar views in private, expressing astonishment at the fact that his prime minister should have seen fit "to import these racial fashions from Berlin into Italy." Even members of the Fascist Grand Council, including Marshal Emillio De Bono, one of the Quadrumvirs of the march on Rome, and Giuseppe Bottai, the Duce's minister of education from 1936 to 1943, charged Mussolini with "more or less voluntary" mimicry. At the time, this interpretation was more than shared by the anti-Fascist exiles, who denounced the race laws as an example of "scandalous German interference" and of "Italian servitude." After the war this interpretation was repeated in an apologetic tone by Mussolini's accomplices including Marshal Pietro Badoglio, his successor as prime minister, who claimed that the racial policy had been "imposed" by Hitler and Dino Grandi, his foreign minister from 1929 to 1932, who affirmed that his master had eliminated the Jews in response to an explicit request from his German ally.[20]

In 1938, however, the Fascists insisted that Mussolini's brand of racism was an original Italian creation; all the resources of Fascist propaganda were deployed in a vain attempt to convince the Italians that Fascism had been a racist movement from its very inception. Mussolini himself reminded his lieutenants that he "had spoken of the Aryan race in 1921 and after that always of race." As for the thesis of "direct German interference," he alternately rejected and confirmed it. In 1938, stung to the quick by the charge of mimicry, he claimed that it was the conquest of an empire in Africa rather than the alliance with Berlin that had prompted him to introduce racial measures into Italy.

After World War II, however, various students of Fascism pointed out that the thesis of "direct German interference" was not confirmed by any documentary evidence. A first attempt at a scholarly examination of the problem, based on published sources only, was made in 1960 by this writer who arrived at the unexpected conclusion that Hitler, far from trying to impose his racial obsession on Mussolini, had made a point of refraining from interference in Italian domestic matters. The Duce's decision to break with the Jews was due not to any irresistible foreign pressure but to his recognition of Italy's changed alignment in Europe and more particularly to his desire to cement the Axis alliance by eliminating any strident contrast in the policy of the two powers. These conclusions were confirmed in the following year by Renzo De Felice (who had access to unpublished Italian records), and they are now generally accepted. On the other hand, recent research by two German experts, Jens Petersen and Klaus Voigt, has shed new light on the clandestine anti-Jewish activities of German agents in Italy and on the attempt to exploit the German-Italian cultural accord of November 1938 for anti-Jewish ends. Hence, absence of official intervention should not be confused with absence of German guilt.[21]

Fascist racism was anything but an original creation; Mussolini himself admitted as much when he told one of his underlings that the Race Manifesto was "a conscientious German treatise translated into bad Italian."[22] But while it is true that the Fascist race laws were an Italian variant of the Nuremberg laws, it is no less true that this is not the whole story. Although antisemitism on the peninsula was a marginal phenomenon until 1936, it provided an indigenous tradition to which both

Fascists and anti-Fascists later appealed. And although clerical anti-Judaism had ceased to be a factor in Italian politics long before the march on Rome, Christian prejudices against Jews were deeply ingrained in secular as well as Catholic culture. Nor can the liberal strain of Italian antisemitism be ignored in our context; for liberal intolerance of Jewishness was at the root of the Fascist attitude toward the Jews.

Liberal intolerance was defined as long ago as December 23, 1789, by Clermont Tonnerre: "Everything must be refused to the Jews as a nation; everything must be granted to them as individuals." Legal parity required that the Jews renounce, along with their corporate autonomy, any separate national identity; with their admission to citizenship they had ceased to exist as a nation and all that remained, or should remain, were individual French citizens.[23]

Thus, from its very inception in the Enlightenment, emancipation contained an equivocation. The case for civil and political parity was not argued solely on the grounds of natural equality; rather, the assumption was that legal disabilities were the cause of all that was perceived to be wrong with the Jews (clannishness, materialism, parasitism) and that their removal would lead to assimilation and fusion. Hence the concept of emancipation could more accurately be called "betterment"; the proponents of equality did, in fact, label their projects civic improvement or "regeneration."[24] Betterment of the Jews presupposed the Enlightenment tenet of an initial unity of human nature. But it equally presupposed the negative image of the Jew purveyed by Christian anti-Judaism: "Seen in this light, emancipation involved serious implications for the emancipated in that an ill-defined self-improvement and assimilation were demanded of them, creating a situation in which European Jewry was left open both to charges of incomplete fusion and to self-doubt."[25]

The terms of emancipation in Italy were as severe as those in France. Even so, the Italian case is sui generis. In contrast to both France and Germany, where the liberal camp itself was sharply divided on the issue, Italian liberals were all but unanimous in their support of Jewish rights. It is no coincidence that the three leading figures of the Risorgimento—Cavour, Mazzini, and Garibaldi—were also the leading champions of parity (Cavour's secretary, Isacco Artom, born in the ghetto, was ennobled and elevated to the Senate). However, even in Italy the equivocal legacy of emancipation gave rise to charges of Jewish exclusiveness and dual loyalties after unification. In 1873 these charges attracted national attention when a liberal deputy, Francesco Pasqualigo, opposed the appointment of a Jew to a cabinet post. When accused of religious intolerance, he replied that his objections were purely political:

> My opinion is that the Jews, scattered among other peoples from the days before Christianity, have nevertheless always constituted among themselves a political and religious association; given this, that the interests of their own nation prevail over those of the particular state of which they happen to be citizens; and that the alleged complete identification of their interests with those of the Italian nation (due perhaps to the short period elapsed since their emancipation) has not yet occurred and, according to some, may never come to pass.

On September 28, 1873 Pasqualigo reiterated the attack, bracketing Jews and clericals as a common threat because of their supranational loyalties: "I stick to the facts and say: You are not yet assimilated [connaturati] to the Italian nation; you have indeed been born and raised in Italy, but above all else you are Jews; you are indeed *legally* citizens of the state . . . but in fact you are not Italians; when you become (Italians) and cease to be Jews, I will change my opinion."[26]

Most Italian liberals rejected Pasqualigo's conclusions; but few of them disagreed with his premises. Even philo-Semites, while supporting emancipation and appreciating the Italian patriotism of their Jewish fellow-citizens, had no use for Jewishness, let alone Jewish nationhood. Shortly after World War II, as staunch an opponent of antisemitism as Benedetto Croce urged the Italian Jews to shed their particularism (which he compared to Hitler's racism), adding that failure to do so might give rise to further tragedies.[27]

The triumph of Fascism added a totalitarian dimension to liberal intolerance. Henceforth all Italians, including those of the Jewish faith, owed unconditional loyalty not only to their country but to the Blackshirt movement and its leader.

Prior to the rapprochement between Rome and Berlin, the "totalitarian" solution of the Jewish Question envisaged by the Duce was assimilation, culminating in total fusion: "The frequency of mixed marriages in Italy must be greeted with satisfaction by all who consider themselves good, sincere, and loyal Italians, as it constitutes proof of the perfect civic, political, and above all 'moral' equality between all Italians, whatever their remote descent."[28] Once he decided to throw in his lot with Hitler, however, his "totalitarian" intolerance of minorities was bound to assume an explicitly anti-Jewish character, whatever his private feelings about Hitler's Nordic heresy.

As has been noted, Mussolini had his underlings affirm in 1938 that his race laws were a purely indigenous growth, implicit in Fascism from its inception and rooted in more than three centuries of Italian history. Farinacci went so far as to claim that the racial decrees were no more than a logical application of Catholic principles and a logical continuation of the anti-Jewish policy pursued by former popes.[29] At the time, these claims were dismissed as propaganda; even Fascist hierarchs poked fun at them. After the war, however, similar claims were made by Mussolini's enemies, though for very different reasons. Having dropped the charge of "scandalous German interference," the anti-Fascists now tended to agree with Mussolini's propagandists that Fascism had been antisemitic from the outset. Both sides were staking out political positions. In 1938 the Fascists tried to divert attention from the German origin of their race laws; after 1945, the anti-Fascists were anxious to counter neo-Fascist attempts to whitewash Mussolini by putting the blame for the racial persecutions on the Germans.[30]

The Jewish participants in this debate were likewise addressing current concerns rather than historical events. Faced with the resurgence of antisemitism in Italy since the 1960s, Jewish students of the phenomenon pointed out that liberal intolerance was indeed at the root of the Fascist attitude; all the Duce had done was to carry this intolerance to its logical conclusion.[31]

Since the 1970s this controversy has prompted new historical research analysis. Andrew M. Canepa, an American Catholic of Italian origin and the leading authority on Italian Jewry during the liberal era, published a series of monographs on the Pasqualigo Case, on Christian-Jewish relations after unification, on emancipation and the Jewish response, and on the image of Jewish Italian folklore and literature. This last subject was reexamined by Lynn M. Gunzberg, an American Jewish scholar, in a book published in 1992, in which she traced certain abiding themes that, in her view, reflected the anti-Jewish prejudices of the Italian reading public.[32] The nub of the matter (she argued) was the persistence of anti-Jewish stereotypes: "The . . . words and phrases applied to the Jews remained the same in 1930 as . . . in 1830" ("usurers," "hook-nosed misers," "perfidious plutocrats," "traitors" with "shifty eyes"). True, the anticlerical reaction did affect the portrayal of Jewish characters in Italian novels: in the nineteenth century Jews were depicted as alien and corrosive to Christian society; in the twentieth century they were described as alien and corrosive to the nation—"conversion was no longer sufficient to wash away fundamental Jewish corruption." Gunzberg concluded that "Fascist racial legislation . . . took root in a fertile terrain: the hearts and minds of the mass of Italians."[33]

This conclusion was promptly challenged by other scholars. Canepa pointed out that Fascist racial policy had struck a dissonant note from the start because the "average Italian knew how to distinguish between the Jews of fiction and the Jews of real life." True, Gunzberg's book was "a valuable antidote to an uncritically encomiastic view of Christian-Jewish relations in modern Italy" and "a fascinating and insightful case study of the nature, uses, and evolution of antisemitic stereotypes." She had, however, greatly overstated the pervasiveness and influence of the anti-Jewish undercurrent in the Italian literary tradition. Jewish themes, whether pro- or anti-Jewish, "were a decidedly minor motif in the corpus of paraliterature, at least before the Fascist propaganda machine was put into high gear. A comparative perspective would have revealed the paucity and inconsequence of 'Jew-consciousness' in modern Italian literature as opposed to its German, Austrian, and French counterparts." No less questionable (always according to Canepa) was Gunzberg's assessment of the Italian Nationalist Association, which she viewed as the progenitor of Fascist ideology and of its racist component. Though several nationalist writers did employ anti-Jewish stereotypes, antisemitism was never an integral part of nationalist thought, a feature that distinguished it from similar movements elsewhere: "Indeed, when racist legislation was introduced in 1938, prominent Nationalists-turned-Fascists, such as Luigi Federzoni and Alfredo Goffredo, expressed their dissent from the new government policy and its fabricated underpinnings."[34]

Henry Stuart Hughes, an eminent American historian and an acute student of modern Italian Jewry, made the same point. He agreed with Gunzberg that there were abiding anti-Jewish themes in Italian literature that reflected the prejudices of the reading public and that even Italians of good will had little use for Jewishness, let alone Jewish nationhood. However, a "countercorrective" was in order: what about relations of day-to-day neighborliness that became more frequent as the ghettos opened up and Jews moved to new quarters where neither they nor their Gentile compatriots nourished memories of their past? Was it possible that Christians kept in one part of their minds the shocking things they had read and in another what they knew at firsthand of Jewish neighbors who appeared so much like themselves? Such questions could not be answered in any statistical sense, "but the near-absence of *overt* manifestations of antisemitism in the period from unification to Fascism would suggest growing acceptance and even friendship on the part of the majority." Beyond that, "in Italy the achievement of national independence and unity did not bring in its wake the recrudescence of anti-Semitism that hit Germany in the late nineteenth century and that is visible in East Central Europe today. . . . Whatever fears and antipathies individuals may have harbored, no organized antisemitic movement emerged. Nor did Italian Jews encounter the sort of deadly hatred that flared up in France at the time of the Dreyfus Case. As the public power of religion declined, no major biologically based ideology on the German or French model took its place. Where hostility lurked, it remained muted."[35]

We may conclude, therefore, that Jewish emancipation in Italy, though marred by dark spots and ancestral antipathies, was a success story after all. Traditional prejudices, liberal as well as clerical, did affect the Fascist attitude to the Jews from the outset; even so, Mussolini had only one reason for persecuting them as a race— his ill-fated alliance with a Jew-baiter.

Areas of Inquiry II: The Attitude of the Catholic Church

Ever since the appearance of Rolf Hochhuth's play *Der Stellvertreter* (translated into English as *The Deputy*), the silence of Pius XII in the face of the Holocaust has been the subject of heated controversy. His critics have leveled four main charges against him. Gerald Reitlinger claims that his failure to speak out was motivated not by Christian prudence but by un-Christian cowardice. Guenter Lewy and Renzo De Felice affirm that anti-Jewish prejudice prevented him from viewing the plight of the Jews with a real sense of moral outrage. Hochhuth contends that he could have saved many lives (if not put a stop to the massacre) had he chosen to take a public stand. Cardinal Eugène Tisserant reproached the pontiff with failure to provide moral leadership for his flock. He complained that he had vainly pleaded with him to issue an encyclical on the duty of the individual to follow the dictates of his conscience rather than to blindly execute orders, no matter how criminal. More recently an American priest, Father John Morley, has reached the conclusion that "Vatican diplomacy failed the Jews during the Holocaust by not doing all that it was possible for it to do on their behalf. It also failed itself because in neglecting the needs of the Jews and pursuing a goal of reserve rather than humanitarian concern, it betrayed the ideals it had set for itself."[36]

The first of the above charges—that of "un-Christian cowardice"—is obviously unfounded. As Ciano noted in his diary, the pope "is even ready to be deported to a concentration camp but will do nothing against his conscience."[37] The second charge—that of "anti-Jewish prejudice"—is mainly based on the fact that the Holy See failed to object to the "Jewish statutes" introduced by the Vichy government. But while it is true that Vatican objections to Pétain's anti-Jewish laws were somewhat half-hearted, it is equally true that the pontiff was profoundly shocked by Hitler's policy of genocide. In 1964 it was revealed by Pirro Scavizzi (a military chaplain who repeatedly accompanied an Italian hospital train to the German-occupied East) that Pius XII, on being informed of the mass murders, "cried like a child."[38] The third charge—that a forceful stand by the pope would have saved many lives—ignores the fact that Hitler toyed with the idea of occupying the Vatican City and deporting the pontiff to Germany. The probability is that a public protest by Pius XII would not only have been unsuccessful in halting the machinery of destruction but would have caused a great deal of additional damage—not least to the Jews hidden in the Vatican and the monasteries. (Michael Tagliacozzo, the leading Italian Jewish authority on the Holocaust in Rome, defended the pope's silence on the ground that it deprived Hitler of a pretext for invading these islands of safety, with fortunate results.) The fourth charge—that the pope failed to provide unequivocal moral guidance to his flock—has been raised by those within the church who felt that, in the face of a monstrous evil, it was wrong to be guided by reasons of state.

In sum, Pius XII was a diplomat who thought it his duty to keep silent *ad maiora mala vitanda*. His critics may be right in affirming that, in failing to speak out, he missed an opportunity for regaining stature; but they are wrong in accusing him of cowardice or indifference to human suffering. If he was guilty of an error of judgment, it does not follow that his silence was due to unworthy motives; nor is it likely that a public protest would have saved the life of a single Jew. It should also be borne in mind that the pope had an international duty to be neutral. Any violation of that neutrality would have been fatal, given the physical dependence of the Holy See on Italian good will.[39]

As for the Italian clergy, it is generally recognized that priests, monks, and nuns were in the forefront of those offering help to persecuted Jews, whatever their prejudices against the "Christ killers": "Theirs was an altruism that laypeople may often expect as a matter of course from the religious, but that can never be taken for granted. In Italy, most men and women of the church were a credit to their calling."[40]

Areas of Inquiry III: The Attitude of the Italian Masses

Since 1938, observers of the Italian scene, both Gentile and Jewish, have re-peatedly noted the "philo-Semitism" of the Italian masses. Sir Andrew McFadyean informed the heads of British Jewry in January 1939 that, in spite of Fascist racial policy, antisemitism outside a restricted government circle was "nonexistent." Daniel A. Binchy made the same point eleven months later: "Prudence may have compelled the observance of the letter of the anti-Jewish laws, but their spirit has never been observed and is not observed today. The cruel measures designed to segregate Italian Jews from the social and economic life of their fellow-countrymen have been mitigated as far as possible by the pity and consideration shown by Italians of all classes." When Hitler extended the Final Solution to the German-occupied part of Italy, many Italians quietly rallied to the support of the Jews. The following extracts from the diary of Bernard Berenson, the celebrated Jewish art historian in Florence, shed light on the resistance Eichmann's emissaries had to face:

> January 25th, 1944: . . . I am seeing friends who, unlike myself, have no drop of Jewish blood to taint their views. They are at least as horrified over the treatment of the Jews as I am, and can get it as little out of their minds. . . .
> September 1945: . . . [The Italian people's] sympathies for suffering, whether physical or moral, are wide and warm. . . . Nowhere else have I encountered like generosity and self-sacrifice. . . . Despite alarms and excursions, nobody in any situation gave me away. I learned afterward that some friends deliberately avoided finding out where I was, not to run the risk of betraying it under torture.[41]

After the Holocaust, the spokesmen of Italian Jewry hastened to express their whole-hearted agreement with Berenson's tribute to their Gentile compatriots. The following report, which deals with the years 1944–1945, accurately reflects the prevailing view: "When Rabbi Zolli spoke of the period during which the Nazis had been in control of Rome, he contrasted the good hearts of the Italians with the cruelty of the Germans: 'the whole Italian population has been wonderful to us.' Verification of this impression of the fine attitude and behavior of the Italian people and the Catholic Church came from other sources as well." A subsequent report covering the year 1949 claimed that there was "rather less fear of antisemitism in Italy than in most other countries because the experience of the war and the postwar attitude of the Jewish displaced persons had shown that the Italian people had a high resistance to antisemitism." In December 1956 Sergio Piperno, then president of the Union of Italian Jewish Communities, affirmed in a public speech that the entire Italian people had stood by the Jews during the twenty months of the German occupation. In 1961 Hulda Cassuto Campagnano, a Jewess from Florence, stated at the Eichmann trial in Jerusalem that "every Italian Jew who survived owed his life to the Italians." Similar tributes were paid by such eminent scholars as Henry Stuart Hughes and Renzo De Felice.[42]

Some Jewish activists took a less optimistic view, most particularly Colonel Vitale, who noted as early as 1953 that the Fascist poison had "left traces which are, unfortunately, firmly rooted and which nothing will destroy."[43] In the ensuing years the anti-Jewish prejudices of the Italian people—clerical, liberal, neo-Fascist and leftist—became the subject of concern to Jews and Gentiles alike. The controversy over the "kindly Italians" and "Fascism with a human face" came to a head in 1986 when Nicola Caracciolo extolled Italian resistance to Hitler's policy of genocide. In reply Rossella Fubini, a Jewish activist in Turin, pointed out that antisemitism had been imposed on the Italian people by Mussolini, not by Hitler; that until July 1943 Italian Jewry had been persecuted and humiliated by the Fascists, not by the SS; and that the opposition of the Italian people had been confined to murmured regrets and individual acts of kindness. When Hitler extended the Final Solution to the German-occupied part of Italy, numerous Italians, especially of the lower classes, came to the aid of the victims; but there was another side to the picture that Caracciolo had chosen to ignore.[44]

In the following year this other side—the collaboration and betrayal that led to the death of thousands—was explored by Susan S. Zuccotti, an American Gentile of Anglo-Saxon background, who warned against facile generalizations about the Italian national character. The focus on Jewish survivors and non-Jewish rescuers (she argued) had distracted attention from the other, equally important aspects of the issue: "Does the high number of rescuers in Italy imply that Italians generally are more compassionate and altruistic than other people? Certainly the answer is negative. On the contrary, despite their international reputation as warm and immensely humane people, Italians are not known for the civic virtues of dedication to charity sometimes associated with 'altruism.'" Most Italians rejected Fascist racial policy, opposed the war, and hated German actions. But there were a good many others who followed Mussolini and Hitler to the end: "The Holocaust in Italy was a twisted legacy—a blend of courage and cowardice, nobility and degradation, self-sacrifice and opportunism. In contrast to other countries, perhaps, the worthy behavior outweighed the unworthy, but horror was nonetheless real."[45]

Areas of Inquiry IV: The Italian-occupied Territories

In 1938 the Fascist race laws were hailed as a major ideological triumph of National Socialism in Germany. Hitler himself was greatly pleased and gave public expression to his gratification in a speech at the Nuremberg party rally.[46] In the ensuing years, however, it became increasingly clear that the Duce's conversion to the Nordic gospel had failed to eliminate the divergence of views on the racial issue: though side by side, the two Axis partners never marched in step, and this was reflected in systematic Italian resistance to Hitler's policy of genocide. While Jews were being rounded up and deported all over German-occupied Europe, those of Italian citizenship continued to enjoy complete immunity; what is more, the Italian-occupied territories in Yugoslavia, Greece, and France became havens of refuge for the Jews of those countries.

Why should the Italians have wanted to save foreign Jews? Why should senior servants of the Fascist regime have defied their allies and risked their careers for the sake of strangers who had no claim on them and whose interests were bound up with the defeat of the Rome-Berlin Axis? As has been noted, Mussolini broke with his Jewish subjects in order to eliminate any strident contrast between the two Axis powers. Why, then, did he allow his underlings to sabotage his anti-Jewish policy? And what prompted the latter to act as they did? They had no ties of any kind with the people whom they were shielding from the *furor teutonicus*. None of them had shown a heroic tendency to protest when their Jewish fellow-citizens were ousted from Italian public life. Why, then, did they react differently when their allies de-ported foreign Jews from Croatia, Greece, and France? To put it in another way, was the rescue of Jews in these territories a manifestation of Italian resistance to Ger-man encroachments on Italian sovereignty? Or was it also a genuine expression of spontaneous humanitarianism?

Before assessing the motives of the rescuers, we shall do well to trace the evolution of Italian rescue activities from the occupation of Yugoslavia to the Italian armistice. During the first phase of this evolution (April 1941 to June 1942) the Italian occupiers had to cope with the unsystematic murder of Serbs and Jews by Croat Fascists. Their reaction took the form of spontaneous resistance; by September 1941 this resistance had crystallized into official policy. During the second phase (from June to November 1942) they were faced with systematic murder (Hitler's Final Solution). At first they failed to grasp the true meaning of what the Germans called "resettlement" and "labor service." On November 1, 1942, Carabinieri General Giuseppe Pièche, who had been sent to Croatia to investigate the problem, recom-menced handing over the Jews over to the Croats because that would rid the Italians of elements who were the "eyes and ears of London." But three days later he changed his tune, having meanwhile found out that the Croatian Jews deported from the German zone of occupation had been "eliminated" by means of toxic gas. Thus the policy of obstructing the Final Solution in the Italian-occupied part of Croatia began to take shape.

During phase three (November 1942 to June 1943) the net widened: the Holocaust spread to Greece and France, prompting the Italians to extend their policy of obstruction to those countries. The final phase (July 25 to September 8, 1943) began with the overthrow of Mussolini and ended with Badoglio's surrender to the Allies, after which the Italians lost control of the situation.

Various political and economic arguments were advanced by the Italian authorities to justify their resistance to the policy of genocide. In Croatia, it was maintained that the request for extradition could not be complied with because compliance would deal "a serious blow to the prestige of the Italian Army in all of Croatia and the Balkans," would be interpreted "as a violation of the guarantees given by us . . . to the population of the occupied zone (guarantees explicitly excluding any religious or racial discrimination)," and would have "harmful repercussions also among the Orthodox."[47] In Greece, which the Germans had recognized as part of the Italian sphere of influence, it was necessary to safeguard "the complex of [Italy's] economic and political interests," largely represented by Italian Jews. In Tunisia the Italian Jews had been exempted from the application of the racial laws "in consideration of these interests of ours. Now our point of view is valid for Greece, too, and we expect it to be properly taken into account." In Vichy France Italian prestige was as much at stake as in Croatia; in both countries nominally autonomous governments were eager to cooperate with the German deportation decrees. Italian acquiescence would have reduced their own role to that of mere accomplices.[48]

In addition, it is evident that quite a few of the rescuers acted with an eye on a future reckoning of accounts. Rescuing Jews obviously made sense for those who spun schemes to unlink Italy's fate from Germany's.

All the above arguments are perfectly valid; but all the experts are agreed that they do not fully account for Italian behavior. In the words of Susan Zuccotti: "When all the logical reasons for and against cooperation are weighed and measured, it is apparent that decency, courage, and humanity often tipped the balance." True, the rescuers were "far too few"; even so, they "restored a glimmer of honor to the shabby history of Fascist Italy."[49]

But why the efforts to defend Jews abroad on the part of Italians who had signally failed to defend Jews at home? In any attempt to explain this amazing story, we shall have to consider a variety of factors, the first of which is the absence of a Jewish problem in Italy. The unpopularity of antisemitism at home had an obvious bearing on the willingness of the Duce's subordinates to oppose antisemitism abroad when the right circumstances arose.

Second, Italian intervention on behalf of foreign Jews began in Croatia as early as 1941, during Hitler's run of victory. It was not an anti-German move but a spontaneous reaction to the massacre of Serbs and Jews by Croat Fascists, part of an attempt to maintain order. The political aspect of the problem did not come to the fore until June 1942 when the Italians accidentally found out that a German-Croatian agreement on the deportation of all Jews in Croatia had been signed behind their backs. It was then that the battle was joined between Rome and Berlin for the lives of the Jews.[50]

Third, although the initial steps taken to save Jewish lives were simply part of the general responsibility of the Italian Army, a change occurred as soon as the facts about the Holocaust became known. As has been noted, General Pièche, on learning the truth about resettlement in the East, urged his superiors not to consign the Jews; so did the other Italians in positions of authority.

Finally, Italian resistance to genocide was not part of a plot to overthrow Fascism. The "resisters" were able to act as they did precisely because they were loyal servants of the Fascist regime (at any rate up to a point) who merely refused to carry out orders that they rightly considered objectionable on both moral and political grounds.

But whatever the merits of the rescuers, these tributes to servants of the Fascist regime were a source of embarrassment to Italian Jewry, not only because they distracted attention from the Fascist criminality, but also because they were exploited by neo-Fascist apologists for their own reactionary ends.[51]

Areas of Inquiry V: The Role of Mussolini

Mussolini was the principal architect of both the Axis alliance and Fascism's about-face on the Jewish issue; just as Hitler could have imposed the Final Solution on him long before his downfall, so he himself could have imposed cooperation with Himmler's myrmidons on his "philosemitic" subordinates. His failure to do so therefore calls for an explanation.

Mussolini's own pronouncements on this subject were as contradictory as those on all other subjects; but in the light of the evidence now available it is possible to discern a guiding thread through the maze of inconsistencies. First, he was distrustful of "World Jewry" long before the birth of the Axis; concurrently, he resented the manifestations of Jewish separatism, with special reference to the activities of the Italian Zionists. Until 1936 these private feelings (which were reflected in anonymous diatribes against Zionism and "Jewish high finance") had little effect on his official attitude; but they do go far to explain the ease with which he passed from "philosemitism" to antisemitism. Second, his visit to Germany in 1937 convinced him that here was an ally whom it would be profitable to join and whom it would be dangerous to cross; hence his willingness to sacrifice the Jews on the altar of Axis friendship. Third, while anxious to demonstrate his "total" solidarity with Hitler, he was no less anxious to demonstrate his independence and the "originality" of his racial policy. The reverses of the Italian armed forces in Greece and North Africa had the effect of increasing his dependence on German help. But they also had the effect of increasing his determination to resist German encroachments on Italian sovereignty; and it is in this context that his attitude to the Final Solution has to be assessed. Blasco Lanza d'Ajeta, *chef de cabinet* to Ciano, put the point well when he told a German diplomat that the Duce could not permit foreigners to discriminate between his subjects; nor could he tolerate attempts to use antisemitism as a means of undermining Italy's position in the occupied territories. And while he fully understood the need for security measures, he would never agree to the deportation of Italian citizens to the East.[52]

When, after the Italian armistice, Hitler decided to treat Italy as conquered territory, Mussolini lost control of the anti-Jewish campaign he had unleashed five years earlier. The writ of his puppet government did not run beyond the roadblocks of Gargnano, the hamlet on Lake Garda where he set up his headquarters in October 1943; his attempts to remove the Jewish issue from German hands were therefore doomed to failure from the start. His order to intern the Jews, though designed to restore a measure of Italian sovereignty, had the effect of facilitating the task of

Eichmann's emissaries; so had his decision to denationalize his Jewish subjects and declare them to be "enemy nationals" for the duration of the war. But for willing or unwilling Fascist cooperation with the SS, many more Italian Jews would have survived the Holocaust.

In sum, Mussolini was an opportunist who played his usual double and triple game throughout the period under review. Even so, we cannot but agree with Renzo De Felice that the Fascist brand of racism was in a sense more shameful than its German model; for Hitler at least believed in the guilt of the Jewish victims, whereas Mussolini was perfectly aware of their innocence—as late as 1944 he denied the existence of a Jewish problem in Italy.[53]

Areas of Inquiry VI: Fascist Responsibility for the Holocaust

Although the Italian Social Republic bore no direct responsibility for the deportation and murder of its Jews, it was involved in all the preliminary steps of registering them, tracking them down, rounding them up, and sending them to internment camps. As noted above, these camps functioned as holding pens, from which the Fascists furnished the SS with a steady supply of victims, despite the objections to German interference in Italian domestic affairs.

Research on the vicissitudes of the Jewish deportees from Italy and Rhodes, which had originally been directed by Colonel Vitale (1944–1953), was resumed nineteen years later by the Jewish Documentation Center in Milan, first by Giuliana Donati (1972–1974) and then by Liliana Picciotto Fargion (since 1979), whose magisterial memory book is by far the best account of the Final Solution on Italian soil available to date. It contains not only the most complete list of the victims but also the most comprehensive and accurate analysis of Italian complicity: at least 1,898 arrests (out of a total of 7,013) were carried out by the Italian police during the period under review, in addition to which the Italians collaborated with the SS in at least 312 roundups. True, some Italian officials and policemen sabotaged the anti-Jewish policy they were supposed to implement; but they were the exceptions that prove the rule. Perfunctory, if not zealous, execution of criminal orders was the norm; the bureaucratic machinery for the persecution functioned almost automatically. The Council of Ministers, presided over by Mussolini, decided; the Ministry of the Interior issued orders; the chief of police circulated instructions; the heads of the various provinces passed along their orders and the local police executed them. Everyone could consider himself innocent and refer responsibility to his superiors; everyone was involved, for otherwise the machinery could not have functioned as smoothly as it did. Individual examples of compassion should not and cannot detract from the monstrous bureaucracy that was placed at the service of the SS. Worst of all, hardly any of Hitler's Fascist accomplices were brought to trial after the war.[54]

In France and other Western European countries the Germans were forced to proceed gradually; in Italy, on the other hand, the preparatory phase could be omitted because the ground had been thoroughly prepared by five years of Fascist racial policy. In Western Europe, initial arrests generally focused exclusively on foreign Jews. In Italy, Dannecker's first targets were the Jews of Rome, who traced their roots in that city to ancient times. The great roundup of October 16, 1943, took the victims by surprise because until then the only example of antisemitism clearly visible to them—and beyond which no one dreamed it possible to go—was that of Mussolini, who aimed not at their physical extermination but merely at their elimination from the mainstream of Italian life and, if possible, at their emigration.

The continuous friction between the SS and the Fascist authorities did not prevent the latter from loyally cooperating with the former. And while it is true that nearly four-fifths of the Jews living in Italy succeeded in eluding the grasp of the Germans, and that most of these were saved by Italian "Aryans" of all classes, it is no less true that such successes as Bosshammer was able to achieve were largely due to Italian complicity. Thousands of Jews were arrested and interned by the Fascist police to be deported and killed by Himmler's myrmidons. Others were denounced by the local agents and spies of the Gestapo; as Bernard Berenson noted in his diary on January 25, 1944, "forty new agents were appointed in Bologna to ferret out Jews still in hiding." Yet others were tracked down by Fascist action squads, headed by notorious thugs and Jew-baiters who took advantage of the German occupation to do their worst. Many Jews had their hiding places betrayed by Italian civilians who were actuated either by anti-Jewish prejudice or by greed (the Germans having offered rewards for the denouncement of Jews). In Rome the new chief of police, Pietro Caruso, demonstrated his zeal by launching a hunt for Jews in February 1944; it resulted in the capture of several hundred persons. He even disrespected the sanctuary agreements between the Holy See and the Reich, permitting his men, on February 3, to raid the Basilica of Saint Paul, where they seized six "non-Aryans," two of them Swiss citizens.[55]

In view of all this, we cannot but agree with Leo Valiani, an eminent Italian Jewish historian and one of the leaders of the anti-Fascist resistance during the twenty months of the German occupation, that the Italo-German differences over the Jewish Question were due not to any fundamental ideological difference between the two sister movements but to the diverse histories of the two countries and their conflicting political ambitions. There was a community of destiny between the two regimes and their leaders but no community of interests between the two peoples and no identity of views on any concrete issue, least of all on the racial issue. The Holocaust was firmly embedded in the totalitarian principles common to both dictatorships; but the Italian brand of Fascism was rooted in historical conditions that posed infinitely greater obstacles to the realization of totalitarian aspirations, especially where the Final Solution of the Jewish Question was concerned. The persecution of the Jews on "racial" grounds was unpopular in Italy, not because it ran counter to Fascist ideology but because it was totally out of step with Italian history and traditions. Hitler himself admitted as much when he told Vittorio Cerruti, the Italian ambassador in Berlin, that "the Jewish problem affecting Germany . . . had no counterpart in Italy."[56]

Valiani's interpretation of Fascist antisemitism received support from Piero Caleffi, another veteran anti-Fascist of Jewish extraction and a survivor of a German concentration camp, who affirmed that Mussolini's regime, like Hitler's, aimed at the "destruction of the human personality" and the annihilation of real or imaginary enemies. Caleffi wrote in his memoirs, describing the horrors of life at Mauthausen: "Never as now did I see so clearly the connection between my first sentence and my first beatings, which humiliated my person in 1923 during the first Fascist reaction, and the horrible world in which I now found myself. Consciously or not, the Fascists had been the originators (*anticipatori*) of the extermination camps."[57]

To be sure, there was a difference between originators and executors; Mussolini's will to annihilation was not biological, like Hitler's, but solely political. Even so, the German dictator, in resorting to the mass murder of imaginary enemies, had done more than carry totalitarian principles of Fascism to their logical conclusion.

NOTES

1. C. Roth, *The History of the Jews of Italy* (Philadelphia, 1946), p. 506.

2. A. M. Canepa, "Cattolici ed ebrei nell'Italia liberale (1870–1915)," *Comunità* 22 (April 1978): 109; L. Villari, "Luigi Luzzatti," in *Twelve Jews*, ed. H. Bolitho (London, 1934), p. 123; G. Cogni, *Il razzismo*, 2nd ed.(Milan, 1937), pp. 157–59.

3. A. M. Canepa, "Half-hearted Cynicism: Mussolini's Racial Politics," *Patterns of Prejudice* 13 (November–December 1979): 19.

4. See Roth, *History*, pp. 506–508; E. Toaff, "La rinascita spirituale degli ebrei italiani nei prima decenni del secolo," *La Rassegna Mensile di Israel* 47 (July–December 1981): 63–73; Chaim Weizmann, *Trial and Error* (London, 1949), p. 356.

5. L. Villari, *The Fascist Experiment* (London, 1926), pp. 201–202.

6. Canepa, "Half-hearted Cynicism," p. 27.

7. "Decennale," *Israel*, October 27, 1932. The author of the anonymous article was Alfonso Pacifici.

8. Roth, *History*, pp. 513–14; R. De Felice, *Storia degli ebrei italiani sotto il fascismo*, 3rd ed. (Turin, 1993), p. 17.

9. Roth, *History*, pp. 510–11; idem, "Italian and German Fascism: A Contrast," *Opinion* (May 1933): 14–16; De Felice, *Storia*, pp. 67–68; P. V. Cannistraro and B. R. Sullivan, *Il Duce's Other Woman* (New York, 1993) (on Margherita Sarfatti).

10. M. Michaelis, *Mussolini and the Jews* (Oxford, 1978), pp. 59–61.

11. Ibid., pp. 81–102.

12. Ibid., pp. 107–91.

13. De Felice, *Storia*, pp. 417–33.

14. S. S. Zuccotti, *The Italians and the Holocaust* (New York, 1987), pp. 71–73.

15. Michaelis, *Mussolini*, pp. 342–406, 413–14; L. Picciotto Fargion, *Il libro della memoria. Gli ebrei departati dall'Italia (1943–1945)* (Milan, 1991), pp. 791–875.

16. Roth, *History*, p. 552.

17. W. P. Sillanpoa and R. G. Weisbord, "The Baptized Rabbi of Rome: The Zolli Case," *Judaism* 38 (Winter 1989): 74–91.

18. Ibid., p. 86.

19. Memorandum on the position of the Jews in Italy by Sir Andrew McFadyean, January 25, 1939 (Public Record Office/F. O. 371/23799/R751/10/22). Sir Andrew McFadyean was Joint Treasurer of the British Liberal Party in 1939.

20. De Felice, *Storia*, p. 241; G. Bottai, *Diario 1935–1944* (Milan, 1982), p. 480; Pentad (five anonymous authors), *The Remaking of Italy* (Harmondsworth, 1941). p. 103; P. Badoglio, *L'Italia nella seconda guerra mondiale* (Milan, 1946), p. 92; D. Grandi, *Il mio paese* (Bologna, 1985), p. 444.

21. Michaelis, *Mussolini*, pp. 128–29; De Felice, *Storia*, pp. 247–48; J. Petersen, "Vorspiel zu Stahlpakt und Kriegsallianz: Das Deutsch-Italienische Kulturabkommen vom 23. November 1938," *Vierteljahrshefte für Zeitgeschichte* 36 (January 1988): 41–77; K. Voigt, "Jewish Refugees and Immigrants in Italy," in *The Italian Refuge*, ed. I. Herzer (Washington, D.C., 1989), pp. 141–58.

22. B. Spampanato, *Contromemoriale II* (Rome, 1951), pp. 131–32.

23. A. E. Halphen, *Recueil des lois concernant les Israélites* (Paris, 1854), p. 185.

24. "Bürgerliche Verbesserung" (Ch. W. Dohm, 1781); "régénération" (H. Grégoire, 1789).

25. A. M. Canepa, "Emancipation and Jewish Response in Mid-Nineteenth Century Italy," *European History Quarterly* 16 (October, 1986): 404.

26. A. M. Canepa, "Emancipazione, integrazione e antisemitismo liberale: il caso Pasqualigo," *Comunità* 29 (June 1975): 168, 170.

27. D. Lattes, "Benedetto Croce e l'inutile martirio d'Israele," *Israel*, January 30, 1947; A. Momigliano, *Pagine ebraiche* (Turin, 1987), p. 142.

28. "Matrimoni misti e malinconie inattuali," *Il Popolo d'Italia*, May 29, 1932. Mussolini's authorship of the anonymous article was disclosed by Paolo Orano (*Gli ebrei in Italia* [Rome, 1937], p. 123).

29. R. Farinacci, "La Chiesa e gli ebrei," in *Realtà storiche* (Cremona, 1939), pp. 86–87.

30. See, for example, E. Collotti, *Fascismo, fascismi* (Florence, 1989), p. 58.

31. G. Fubini, *La condizione giuridica dell'ebraismo italiano* (Florence, 1974), p. 120.

32. L. M. Gunzberg, *Strangers at Home: Jews in the Italian Literary Imagination* (Berkeley, 1992), pp. 279–80.

33. Ibid., p. 284.

34. A. M. Canepa, review of *Strangers at Home* in *Studies in Contemporary Jewry* 11(1994): 363–65.

35. H. Stuart Hughes, "The Integration of Italy's Jews: A Contemporary Perspective," paper read at the international conference on Italian rescue activities during World War II, Los Angeles, October 27, 1992 (unpublished).

36. For a detailed assessment, see Michaelis, *Mussolini*, pp. 372–77; cf. J. F. Morley, *Vatican Diplomacy and the Jews during the Holocaust, 1939–1943* (New York, 1980), p. 209.

37. G. Ciano, *Diario 1937–1943*, ed. R. De Felice (Milan, 1980), p. 430.

38. See H. Stehle, *Die Ostpolitik des Vatikans* (Munich, 1975), p. 239.

39. O. Chadwick, *Britain and the Vatican during the Second World War* (Cambridge, 1988), pp. 131–32: "The Italian government could switch off its electric light, its water supply, or even its food. It could refuse its banking facilities and bankrupt the Pope's government. . . . If the Vatican broke its side of the treaty by interfering in Italian politics, Italy had an easy and instant answer."

40. Zuccotti, *Italians*, p. 209; De Felice, *Storia*, pp. 479–83.

41. B. Berenson, *Rumor and Reflection* (New York, 1952), pp. 218, 443.

42. "Italy," *American Jewish Yearbook* 46 (September 18, 1944–September 7, 1945): 233; "Italy," *American Jewish Yearbook* 51 (1950): 310; De Felice, *Storia*, p. 472; G. Romano, "Una testimonianza sul 'capitolo' italiano al processo Eichmann," *Rassegna Mensile di Israel* 28 (March–April 1962): 238–47; H. S. Hughes, *Prisoners of Hope: The Silver Age of Italian Jews 1924–1974* (Cambridge, 1983), pp. 55, 152–55; R. De Felice, "Razzismo e antisemitismo nel XIX e XX secolo," *Nuova Antologia* 128 (January–March 1993): 67.

43. Yad Vashem Archives 031/14–57; M. A. Vitale, "The Jewish Question in Italy after the Fall of the Nazi-Fascist Regime," (n.p., 1953).

44. N. Caracciolo, *Gli ebrei e l'Italia durante la guerra 1940–1945* (Rome, 1986); R. Fubini, "La giustizia e il pietismo: su una recente trasmissione televisiva," *Ha-Keillah* 11 (December 1986): 5.

45. Zuccotti, *Italians*, pp. 283–86.

46. *Reden des Führers am Parteitag Grossdeutschland 1938* (Munich, 1938), p. 26.

47. D. Carpi, "The Rescue of Jews in the Italian Zone of Occupied Croatia," *Rescue Attempts during the Holocaust: Proceedings of the Second Yad Vashem International Conference—April 1974* (Jerusalem, 1977), p. 514.

48. *Relazione sull'opera svolta dal Ministero degli Affari Esteri per la tutela delle Comunita Ebraiche 1938–1943* (n.p., n.d.), pp. 46–47 (Palazzo Chigi to Italian Embassy in Berlin, June 19, 1943); Zuccotti, *Italians*, pp. 97–99.

49. Zuccotti, *Italians*, pp. 99–100; cf. J. Steinberg, *All or Nothing: The Axis and the Holocaust 1941–1943* (New York, 1990), p. 58; M. Michaelis, *Axis Policies towards the Jews in*

World War II, Fifteenth Annual Rabbi Louis Feinberg Memorial Lecture, University of Cincinnati, April 30, 1992, pp. 16, 20.

50. See, for example, M. Shelach, *Heshbon Damin* (Tel Aviv, 1986), pp. 57–59 (with unpublished documents).

51. See, for example, G. Pisanò, *Mussolini e gli ebrei* (Milan, 1967) (on Mussolini as the alleged defender of Hitler's Jewish Victims). Pisanò is a prominent neo-Fascist publicist.

52. Mackensen to Wilhelmstrasse, October 11, 1942 (Foreign Office Library/London/ 5602H/E401595–6).

53. De Felice, *Storia*, p. 462; M. Sarfatti, *Mussolini contro gli ebrei* (Turin, 1994), p. 124; G. Zachariae, *Mussolini si confessa* (Milan, 1948), pp. 169–70.

54. Fargion, *Il libro*, p. 30; idem, "The Jews during the German Occupation and the Italian Social Republic," in *The Italian Refugee*, pp. 109–38; Michaelis, *Mussolini*, pp. 389–90.

55. Fargion, *Il libro*, p. 30; idem, "The Jews during the German Occupation and the Italian Social Republic," in *The Italian Refugee*, pp. 109–38; Berenson, *Rumor*, p. 163; Michaelis, *Mussolini*, pp. 389–90.

56. L. Valiani, "Osservazioni sul fascismo e sul nazismo," *Rivista Storica Italiana* 88 (September 1976): 517. Sir Ronald Graham to Foreign Office, April 3, 1933, on conversation with Mussolini (Public Record Office/F0371/16720/410); cf. M. Michaelis, "The Current Debate over Fascist Racial Policy," in R. S. Wistrich and S. Della Pergola, eds., *Fascist Antisemitism and the Italian Jews* (Jerusalem, 1995), pp. 80–81.

57. P. Caleffi, *Si fa presto a dire fame* (Milan, 1955), pp. 133–34, 135; see also Michaelis, *Mussolini*, pp. 413–14, and De Felice, *Storia*, pp. 460–63.

33.

JEAN ANCEL

Antonescu and the Jews

With his advent to power as the dictator of Romania in September 1940, Ion Antonescu offered the following précis of his attitude toward the Jews: "I don't protect the Jews, because they bear the blame for most of the disasters visited on this country."[1] During his rule Antonescu's anti-Jewish sentiments became even more virulent. In fact, under the influence of contacts with Hitler and the Nazis, this Romanian general, who had been trained in the spirit of French military doctrine and whose contacts with the Jews had been very limited at best, became a full partner of the Nazis in their plan to wipe out the Jewish people. The question that needs to be addressed, therefore, is where Antonescu's views about the Jews originated prior to his advent to power.

Antonescu's Antisemitic Heritage

From the beginning of modern Romanian history, hatred of Jews was a manifest and enduring phenomenon in social, economic, and intellectual life. Antisemitism had become the hallmark of Romanian nationalism and had served as a catalyst in rallying the Romanian people around national causes; anti-Jewish sentiments accompanied the birth of the national collective identity and persisted even after the realization of liberation and unification of all parts of the country.[2]

Members of the ruling class accepted without reservation both home-grown and Western antisemitic theories and ideas. The Romanian intelligentsia, which emerged as a distinct social group in the years preceding and following the establishment of the state in 1854 and which received its education in the West, was familiar with humanist and liberal ideas. Most of them, however, discarded these concepts upon their return to Romania and reembraced traditional hatred and contempt toward the Jews who lived in that country.[3]

In fact, it was precisely members of this stratum of Romanian society who developed the local version of antisemitism, lent it an ideological dimension, and turned it into an integral part of the mindset of the average Romanian official, army officer, teacher, and politician. With time, the country's political and intellectual establishment developed what might be called a schizophrenic attitude toward the West and its values. As followers of a Western, particularly French, system of values, members of Romanian elites endeavored to adopt the spirit and ideas of justice, democracy, and freedom, as well as Western patterns of administration. At the same time, however, the entire establishment was pervaded by antisemitic bigotry.

The ideas that served as guideposts of Antonescu's early policy toward the Jews had been stated as early as 1922 by A. C. Cuza, the leader of the "classical" Romanian antisemitic movement, in his party's manifesto. Cuza stressed that the Jewish Question could be solved only by "removing [the Jews] from the country after an interim stage during which their influence on the Romanian nation will be completely eliminated."[4] Cuza and his associates —most of them professors in the three Romanian universities—were midwives to and subsequently teachers of the new generation with radically antisemitic views. This generation was well exemplified by Corneliu Codreanu, who in 1927 founded a second fascist movement in Romania called the Iron Guard. These new antisemites declared that the "old" methods were no longer appropriate to the character of the issue and could not cope with the scale of the problem as they saw it. The "Legionnaires," as members of the Iron Guard were called, not only embraced in its entirety the religiously-based antisemitism of the Cuza school but rejected altogether Western democratic values, which they regarded as Jewish inventions and an embodiment of a social order created to serve Jewish interests.

Thus the core of the Romanian rendition of fascist ideology consisted not only of hatred of the Jews but also of rejection of the fundamental Western social ideas and concepts that had evolved since the French Revolution: liberalism, tolerance, democracy, freedom of speech, freedom of organization, industrialization, capitalism, public opinion, free elections, competition, and last but not least, civil rights.

Antonescu's State and Its Attitude toward the Jews

"The national-totalitarian regime, the regime of national and social restoration,"[5] as Antonescu himself described it, came into being against the background of the political and social conditions in Romania in the 1930s. Because of its ideological contradictions and its considerable difference from other fascist regimes in Europe, it remains difficult to understand the internal logic of Antonescu's regime or to classify it. Antonescu and his ministers never referred to their regime as fascist. Moreover, Antonescu brutally crushed the Romanian fascist movement, dismantled the apparatus of the Iron Guard, hunted down and rounded up its members, denounced its terrorist methods, and even portrayed it obliquely as subservient to the Nazis.

The political and ideological foundations of Antonescu's regime had been laid earlier by prominent Romanian intellectuals as well as by radical, traditional right-wing and antisemitic movements.[6] Contributing, too, were King Carol, nationalist politicians who either despised the entire democratic system or its implementation in Romania, and nationalist organizations and political parties that had been established in the 1930s.

Dubious Family Connections and "Ties" to Freemasons

To many, some of Antonescu's personal characteristics as leader, "Conducator," of Romania bore a resemblance to those of Hitler. Among these were his conviction that Providence itself had chosen him to restore the country to its old borders, to nurse Romanian society back to health, to solve the Jewish Question, and, in sum, to inscribe a glorious chapter in the history of Romania. One personality trait in particular proved of considerable importance in his decisions in matters of state and in Jewish affairs: he was susceptible to radical changes of mood, outbursts of rage alternating with calm and self-restraint, often in the course of the same conversation. Alexandre Safran, the chief rabbi of Romania, described him thus:

> His face was flushed and pale by turns. His aspect was that of a beast of prey, ready to pounce on me and tear me to pieces. At this point my strength left me and I began whispering Shema Israel. . . . In the course of one meeting he was capable of turning into a completely different person without any warning.[7]

This aspect of Antonescu arguably can be linked to the syphilis he had contracted: a secret German report dispatched to Berlin asserted that "among [Romanian] cavalry officers this disease is as widespread as a common cold is among German officers. The Marshal suffers from severe attacks of it every several months."[8] Another little-known facet of Antonescu's life, which was played down in his official biography, relates to his marriage to a French woman of Jewish extraction. He divorced her while he was still in France as the military attaché. His only child, who apparently died at an early age, was born to him by this woman. His marriage to his second wife, Maria, touched off a storm of political and legal controversy. She, too, had previously been married to a French Jew, a man whom she met in Romania and who was her second husband. After the couple went to France, Maria met Antonescu; Ion Antonescu and Maria married after divorcing their Jewish spouses.[9]

It should be mentioned in this context that Antonescu's father, mention of whom had been excised from all official biographies published during the war, had divorced the Marshal's mother and married a Jewess, Frida Cuperman. After he became Conducator, the Marshal demanded that his stepmother renounce the name Antonescu after her husband's death, but she refused. Wilhelm Filderman noted in his diary that the Cuperman woman had relatives in New York.[10]

Another episode that seems to have influenced Antonescu's attitude to the Jews relates to a charge leveled against him by the Legionnaires. The Iron Guard accused him of harboring sympathies toward Freemasons, maintaining ties with them, and even being a member. In fact, Antonescu was a target of a smear campaign whose reverberations reached Berlin. There is little doubt that these accusations affected some of the measures and decisions of the Romanian leader with regard to the Jews, including his adoption of a plan to physically liquidate Romanian Jewry.

Antonescu the Antisemite

The depth of Antonescu's antisemitic sentiments and views is abundantly attested by his statements. In the early stages of his career he believed—like Cuza—in the notion of a "Jewish invasion" of Romania and in a conspiracy of world Jewry against Romania. He believed that many of his country's debacles and difficulties were caused by Jews and that Jews had taken over its wealth by means known only to them. He also maintained that those Jews whom his regime had adjudged to have "committed crimes" against Romania and the Romanian people—especially those who for one reason or another had been ordered to leave the country but had failed to do so on time—should be put into detention camps. Antonescu held these beliefs even before he was influenced by Hitler and the Nazis. Though not as passionate and obsessive about the subject as the Legionnaires, Antonescu also saw the Jews as evil incarnate. Like his antisemitic predecessors, Antonescu gave little credence to official counts of the number of Jews in the country. The figure of 339,000, as cited in 1940 by the government's bureau of statistics (and which later proved to be approximately fifty thousand too high) seemed to him too low. Antisemites, after all, spoke of millions of Jews in the country: "If no more than this number [existed] our Yid problem wouldn't have been so severe." Like every run-of-the-mill antisemite, he believed that it would be possible to extort money from the Jews by forcing them to do work that purportedly only Romanians were accustomed to do: "We shall put them to work in the fields and right away you'll see the Yids eager to pay up."[11]

Antonescu's antisemitic views, his affiliation with the Romanian traditional right, and, of course, the fascist atmosphere prevailing in much of Europe and in Romania itself—all these caused him to see Jews as less than human and therefore not entitled to the protection of law, freedom of movement, physical security, property rights, and similar guarantees. At this point, however, he was still a long way from promulgating an explicit directive to kill the Jews. What pushed him further in this direction was the influence of Hitler at the time Nazi victory in Europe seemed assured.

Antonescu Adopts the Idea of the Final Solution

On June 12, 1941, at the third meeting between Hitler and Antonescu, this one at Nazi party headquarters in Munich, the Führer revealed to his interlocutor the *second* big secret of the regime, the guidelines for the treatment of Eastern Jews ("Richtlinien zur Behandlung der Ostjuden"), in other words, the plan for their physical liquidation. At their previous meeting on January 14, Antonescu had been honored when Hitler made him privy to the *first* secret, Operation Barbarossa, even though the Nazi leader did not divulge the date of the invasion of the Soviet Union. Hitler's revelations testify to the favor Antonescu enjoyed with the Führer.[12]

Antonescu's practical measures to implement a Romanian final solution in Bessarabia and Bukovina confirm that he knew in advance about the establishment of the Einsatzgruppen and their assignment, and about their coordination with the army. In fact, he adopted the German methods.

Convinced of German victory, Antonescu had returned to Romania and, following Hitler's example, began drafting his own plan for the solution of the Jewish Question in the two regions Romania had been forced to cede to the Soviets in June 1940. On June 19, 1941, he sent a secret memorandum to General Ilie Steflea, in which he said, inter alia: "All the Yids, communist agents and their sympathizers must be identified . . . so that we will be able to carry out whatever orders I may transmit in due time." This resembles the directive Field Marshal Wilhelm Keitel issued to Wehrmacht commanders. The Pretoria (the Pretoria was the civil administration of the army) High Commander (Marele Pretor), General Ion Topor, was given a special order concerning the treatment of Jews, whereas commanders of the Gendarmerie (consemn special) had been told on June 18 about the confidential order on "cleansing the ground" ("curăţirea terenului") in Bessarabia and Bukovina. The order, the text of which has been preserved in its entirety, was read aloud to assembled Gendarmerie officers by General C. Vasiliu on behalf of Antonescu. It speaks of, among other things, the liquidation on the spot of all the Jews in the countryside, incarceration of Jews in ghettoes in urban centers, detention of all persons suspected of being activists of the Communist Party, and the like.[13]

Following the meeting in Berlin, Antonescu reached agreements (Abmachungen) with the Main Office for Reich Security (RSHA) concerning the "removal of Jews from Bessarabia and Bukovina, and also from Transnistria."[14] Reconstruction of the background of agreements between the Germans and the Antonescu regime poses serious difficulties since Romanian archival collections from the period in question remain inaccessible. Most of the documents that deal with the crimes against the Jewish people disappeared from the files even prior to the collapse of the Antonescu regime, whereas the remaining documents were hidden by communist authorities.

Three days before the outbreak of the war in the East, Ion Antonescu ordered the deportation within forty-eight hours of Jews from villages and townships in Romania itself. He required the incarceration of the men, and sometimes also the women and children, in camps in the south of the country.[15] Shortly before the invasion of the Soviet Union on June 21, acting on Antonescu's special orders, the Romanian Secret Service, the S.S.I., set up a special unit modelled after the Einsatzgruppen. On June 29 the pogrom in Jassy broke out; it was carried out jointly by the S.S.I., the Romanian army, and the German troops stationed in town.[16]

If Antonescu's predilection toward a final solution had been reflected in the Conducator's earlier attitude toward the Jews and in his language, after June 1941 his antisemitic outlook assumed an unmistakably Nazi-racist character.

Antonescu, his deputy, and his heads of administration repudiated—initially in closed forums and later publicly—the universal values of morality, humanism, and rule of law. At the same time they gave a free hand to the executors of secret directives and released them from the constraints of the moral values of the "demo-liberal world"—Antonescu's terminology for the Western democracies and the old Romanian regime. In so doing, Romanian leaders appropriated, in effect, the Legionnaire ideology. Its tenets had repudiated the values of humanism and "Jewish morality," had mobilized Orthodox Christianity around its goals, and had set the model of the "new man"—liberated from moral constraints, "virile," "tough," and able to throw off the yoke of "mobilized humanity."[17] On the eve of the war Antonescu expressed his hatred of the democratic system, democratic countries, the League of Nations, a regime based on free elections, parliament, public opinion, politicians, Jews, and so on.[18] The Romanian fascist legacy spoke out in its authentic voice: democracy is to be rejected because it benefits the Jews, gives them civil rights, allows them to express themselves, and undermines the Romanian "national idea" and "ethnic state." Thus the long process of obliterating the Jews from Romanian life, a process that had been set in motion by prominent Romanian intellectuals in the nineteenth century, was completed on the eve of the war by the Antonescu regime.

It is against this background that we should examine the directive of the Romanian administration concerning "cleansing the ground," an order that paralleled the Nazi Final Solution. The directive was made possible not only because of the influence of Hitler on Antonescu but also because of a long process of delegitimation of Jewish existence, of the Jew as human being.

The first stage of "cleansing the ground" was completed in August 1941. At least

100,000 Jews were murdered on Ion Antonescu's orders.[19] According to his deputy, Mihai Antonescu, the objective was to carry out "ethnic and political cleansing" in Bessarabia and Bukovina. At the government meeting of July 8, 1941, Mihai Antonescu called upon the ministers to show implacability and told them "there is no place here for saccharine and vaporous humanitarianism. . . . I do not mind if history judges us barbarians . . .; history will not offer us other moments of grace. We must take advantage of it. . . . If need be—use machine guns."[20]

Ion Antonescu followed the execution of his directives in the operation of ethnic cleansing as closely as if it were a military campaign. He demanded constant updates and reports, requested presentations in the form of graphic charts and tables, convened the Order Council (Consiliul de ordine), whose members were responsible for the operation, and held separate discussions with the governors of Bessarabia, Bukovina, and Transnistria. As was his custom, he gave orders on the spur of the moment. On July 24, five days after his arrival in Kishinev, Antonescu issued an order "to set up camps and ghettos."[21] The Kishinev ghetto, among others, was established in accordance with this order. Traveling to the frontline, Antonescu noticed thousands of Jews concentrated in improvised camps—the surviving remnant of the first wave of mass murder. On July 18 he issued an order to "put to work in hard labor all the Jews in labor and detention camps. In case of escape, one out of ten must be shot. If they don't work properly, they must be denied food and not allowed to receive food or to buy it."[22]

Late in August 1941, in Tighina, a Romanian township on the bank of the Dniester River, Antonescu convened a special council of the governors of Bessarabia and Bukovina, and the governor-designate of Transnistria, who was to assume his duties after the province's occupation. "At this opportunity we received precise instructions regarding the way in which the operation of sending the Jews toward the Bug River would be carried out,"[23] wrote General Constantin Voiculescu. At this time an agreement was reached in Tighina "concerning security and economic management and exploitation of the areas between the Dniester and the Bug rivers, as well as between the Bug and the Dnieper." The agreement was signed by a representative of the Romanian General Staff, General Nicolae Tataranu, and a representative of the Wehrmacht, General Hauffe. Section 7 of the agreement dealt with the fate of the Jews in the camps and ghettos in Bessarabia and Bukovina, as well as those who would survive the sweep of Einsatzgruppe D in Transnistria. "Evacuation of the Jews across the Bug River was not possible at that moment. Therefore, they were to be concentrated in labor camps and put to work until the cessation of hostilities, when it would be possible to move them to the East."[24]

Antonescu attached utmost importance to logistics. The Second Department of the General Staff, which oversaw the deportation, made one of a number of requests to the Gendarmerie to "draw up an accurate situation report about all the Jewish camps and ghettos in Bessarabia and Bukovina."[25]

The directives concerning the conduct of the deportation operation were drawn up by General Ion Topor in accordance with secret verbal instructions from Antonescu that were transmitted, also verbally, to commanders—usually officers of the Gendarmerie—of convoys of Jews. The General Staff of the Romanian army gave orders to "shoot the Jews who are not able to keep up with the pace of the convoys either on account of weakness or because of sickness." The directives also contained a provision whereby two days prior to the departure of each convoy, gendarmes were to be dispatched ahead to prepare, with the aid of local residents, "one pit every ten kilometers for roughly 100 people, in which those executed for lagging behind the convoy could be buried."[26]

On October 6, at a government meeting, Antonescu summed up the operation for "cleansing" Bessarabia: "As for the Jews, I decided to remove all of them once and for all from these areas. The operation is going on. There are still some 10,000 Jews left in Bessarabia and they too will be moved across the Dniester within several days. If circumstances allow me they will be moved across the Ural mountains."[27] Antonescu mentioned the Ural mountains since the Führer had bragged to him that he would be able to push the Soviet army there.

On October 11, three days after the commencement of the deportations from the Kishinev ghetto, the head of the Federation of Jewish Communities, Filderman, addressed an emotional appeal to Ion Antonescu to halt the deportation: "This is death, death for no reason except that they are Jews."[28] Unlike other fascist dictators, who would have left such an appeal without any response, Antonescu replied to Filderman in a long letter in which he justified his policy of extermination, accused the Jews of Bessarabia of collaborating with the Soviet enemy, and saddled the Jews, including the Jews of Russia, with a collective responsibility for the price paid in blood by the Romanian army in the war "on the Dniester, in Odessa, and the Sea of Azov."

On November 11, Filderman received a second letter from Antonescu outlining the Conducator's policy; he stated bluntly that Jews had no place in the "liberated territories" and set several conditions for Jews residing in Romania proper:

> We decided to defend our Romanian rights because our all-too-tolerant past was taken advantage of by the Jews and facilitated the abuse of our rights by foreigners, particularly the Jews. . . . We are determined to put an end to this situation. We cannot afford to put in jeopardy the existence of our nation because of several hundred thousand Jews, or in order to salvage some principle of humane democracy that has not been understood properly.[29]

In his concluding report sent to Antonescu, after he referred to the orders he received from the Conducator, the governor of Bessarabia wrote that the deportation operation was "well organized and carried out in a civilized manner."[30] At this stage of the war, Antonescu no longer hid his intentions from the people. In an open letter published in the press, he addressed one of his supporters: "As long as I live no one and nothing will stop me now from completing the cleansing operation."[31]

Odessa and Transnistria

Transnistria, the land between the Dniester and the Bug rivers, had been placed under the jurisdiction of the Romanian army. The occupation of this territory posed new problems for Antonescu as far as Jews were concerned. For the first time he had an opportunity to rule over "Russian Jews," believed by the Marshal to be carriers of communism and responsible for the Romanian losses he had spelled out earlier to Filderman.

The sweep of Einsatzgruppe D left in Transnistria tens of thousands of Jews; in

Odessa alone, on the day the Romanian army entered the city, 100,000 Jews remained of the total of 180,000 who had lived in the city on the eve of the war.

On October 22, a huge blast rocked the building housing the headquarters of the Romanian army in that city, killing dozens of military personnel, including a general. The headquarters had been located in the former command center of the Odessa N.K.V.D. (Soviet secret police), which had managed to mine several buildings in the city prior to the Soviet retreat. Antonescu concluded that the Jews were to blame, and on the night of the explosion he issued the following order:

> 1. For every Romanian or German officer killed in the explosion 200 Communists will be executed and for every killed soldier 100 Communists. Executions will be carried out throughout the day, October 23.
>
> 2. The Communists in Odessa will be taken prisoner as well as one person from each Jewish family.[32]

In actual fact, almost all of those arrested or executed as communists were Jews. On October 23, some five thousand Jews were shot or hanged on Odessa streets. At the same time Romanian soldiers rounded up tens of thousands of other Jews. A detachment of the 10th Infantry Regiment escorted 20,500 Jews out of the city toward a place called Dalnic. There were nine large storehouses there, each about twenty-five meters long and ten to fifteen meters wide. Most of the Jews were women, children, and the elderly, because most able-bodied men had long since been drafted into the Soviet army and had left the city. Those who couldn't keep pace with the Romanian deportation convoy were shot then and there; the road to Dalnic was strewn with corpses. Jews in groups of forty to fifty were tied to each other, led into antitank ditches from the days of the siege of Odessa, and shot by the soldiers. This method of killing proved inefficient and "wasted" ammunition, and so it was decided to cram the Jews into storehouses. After each warehouse was packed with some two thousand Jews, mostly women and children, the soldiers opened fire on them through openings in the walls made especially for this purpose. But this time too it emerged that after the shooting not all the Jews were dead. The killers threw straw inside, shut the openings, sprayed the buildings with gasoline and kerosene, and set them on fire. The soldiers were given orders to shoot anyone who tried to jump out of the burning buildings.[33]

News of the massacre reached Bucharest on November 10, 1941. The French ambassador reported to the Foreign Ministry at Vichy that Romanian authorities had taken revenge on the Jews: "Following the explosion on October 22 in Odessa, 25,000 Jews were packed into storehouses and shot with machine guns and cannons before the Romanian army units set fire to them."[34] On November 13, at a government meeting, Antonescu casually asked the governor of Transnistria about the results: "Reprisals against the Yids were very severe," said the governor. "Sufficiently severe?" asked the dictator. "Yes, Marshal. Scores were killed and hanged on Odessa Streets," replied Gheorghe Alexianu, and the conversation moved on to other matters.[35]

In 1943, after the defeat at Stalingrad, the Odessa killings were brought up once again, this time following a direct request to the Marshal by Minister of War, General Pentazi, to approve an operation related to the massacre: "The atrocity (*grozăvia*) in Odessa must be concealed. Bodies of these wretches must be removed and scattered about." Antonescu feigned innocence and asked: "What happened, Pentazi? What are you talking about?"[36] Not one among the ministers present dared to remind the Conducator that the reprisal against Odessa Jews was carried out on his orders.

The tragedy of the Odessa Jews did not end with the October 23 massacre, and Antonescu intervened time and again in their fate. Thus he issued an order to the 3rd Army to concentrate all the Jews in a ghetto, and he dispatched a special envoy on behalf of General Staff, Major Ştefănescu to oversee the ghettoization of the Jews and later their deportation.[37] Antonescu himself issued the deportation order through Deputy Chief-of-Staff, General Tataranu:

> General Antonescu decided that all the Yids would be removed from Odessa forthwith in view of the fact that due to [Soviet] resistance at Sebastopol [and because] of manpower shortages in Odessa we are in for an unpleasant surprise. It is possible that because of these Yids a disaster will occur in case the Russians land in Odessa and the environs of the city. Marshal Antonescu said that it is a crime to keep them there. I do not wish to tarnish my operation by such an oversight. Contact the Transnistria authorities immediately, tell them about it, and cooperate with them in carrying out the Marshal's orders without delay. Report on the execution [of these orders].[38]

The General Staff envoy reported on the ghettoization of the Jews, the seizure of their property by the Romanian state, and looting by soldiers and gendarmes. The report reflected the horrible living conditions in the ghetto and the marching of Jews to the railroad station without supplying them with any food, loading them onto cars, transporting them aboard German freight trains to the transit camp at Berezovca, and the death of some of them as a result of hunger and cold. He concluded his report: "All the Jews who reach the [second] ghetto are the elderly . . . children younger than 16, women. . . ."[39] Ion Antonescu feared that these Jews would join with Soviet troops expected to land in the area and together they would strike against Romanian forces stationed in the city. These apprehensions amounted to a "logical" extension of the accusations he earlier had leveled against Russian Jews in his letter to Filderman.

Bodies of the Jews who had died inside the train cars—called "funeral trains" (*trenul-dric*) by Romanian soldiers—were unloaded at railroad stations en route to Berezovca and burned to avoid further spread of the typhus epidemic. The deportation route was marked by huge bonfires.[40]

It is appropriate to ask why a decision was taken to rid southern Transnistria of Jews. The answer, as it eventually emerged, lay hidden in Romanian archives that had been transferred to the former Soviet Union. Only recently accessible to researchers, these documents reveal that in late 1941 the typhus epidemic among the deportees was reaching a peak and began affecting the Ukrainians also. At least fifty thousand Jews were felled by the disease in the harsh winter of 1941–1942; weakened by hunger, cold, lack of sanitation, and by brutal treatment, their bodies proved no match for the raging epidemic. Typhus posed a serious threat also to German and Romanian troops, as well as to inhabitants of the areas south of Transnistria, which included large concentrations of ethnic Germans who were not under Romanian jurisdiction.

For his part Antonescu was also preoccupied with the fate of the seventy thousand Jews from southern Transnistria who had so far been concentrated on the bank of the Bug. At a government meeting on December 16, that is, before he gave the order to deport the Jews from Odessa, Antonescu told his ministers that although he faced some difficulties, a solution was at hand:

> The question of the Yids is being discussed in Berlin. The Germans want to bring the Yids from Europe to Russia and settle them in certain areas, but there is still time before this plan is carried out. Meanwhile, what should we do? Shall we wait for a decision in Berlin? Shall we wait for a decision that concerns us? Shall we ensure their safety? Pack them into catacombs! Throw them into the Black Sea! [As far as I am concerned] 100 may die, 1,000 may die, all of them may die.[41]

At this meeting, which was attended also by the governor of Transnistria, Alexianu, Antonescu gave him carte blanche to rule the area as he saw fit, "as if Romania has been settled there for two million years. We'll wait and see what happens later," added the Marshal. "That's what I wanted to hear," replied Alexianu.[42] For their part the Germans also evinced interest in the fate of seventy thousand Jews who remained stranded on the bank of the Bug. The Jews were placed in cowsheds, pigsties, chicken coops, dilapidated storehouses or in the fields—without undergoing any registration, without food and water, in the harshest winter on record in the twentieth century. The Nazi Gebietskommissar of the Nikolayev district, Obergruppenführer Ewald Oppermann, sent a cable to the prefect of Berezovca, Colonel C. Loghin, in which he reported that the Romanian army "has concentrated 70,000 Jews" along the Bug River, about sixty kilometers north of the town of Nikolayev, that these masses had been left to fend for themselves, and that they were dying of hunger and cold. "The epidemic of typhus has broken out among the Jews," he warned, "who do everything they can to barter articles of clothing for food and thereby endanger also the German area that easily can be reached by the frozen river."[43] The German official asked the prefect to make a quick decision on the fate of these Jews and suggested that they be moved "as far away as possible within the territory of Transnistria" to prevent them from crossing the Bug. Governor Alexianu replied in a cable in German to the governor of Nikolayev; he explained that the Jews had been concentrated there in accordance with the Tighina agreement. Measures were taken, he went on to say, to reinforce the guard force but, for technical reasons, the return of the Jews to Transnistria was not possible at the moment. Romanian authorities in Transnistria hastened to reassure Oppermann by informing him that forceful measures had, in fact, been taken: "We replied to Gebietskommissar Oppermann that we have taken steps to incinerate the bodies of the Jews."[44] The number of seventy thousand Jews, quoted at Antonescu's postwar trial, is corroborated for the first time in these documents. So too is the fact that the decision to execute and burn such a large number of Jews was taken by the Romanians themselves. Still, many details of the operation had been known before the discovery of these archives.

The Bogdanovca camp consisted of forty cowsheds, former property of the local "sovkhoz" (state farm), scattered across one square kilometer. Some forty-eight thousand Jews, most of them from Odessa and about seven thousand from south Bessarabia, were packed into this area. Some eighteen thousand Jews who had been brought from three districts in southern Transnistria together with a few from southern Bessarabia were put into the Domanovca camp. About four thousand Jews, including the sick, the elderly, and women, all described by the gendarmes as unfit for any forced labor, were incarcerated in the Acmecetca camp. It consisted of four pigsties and a long windowless and doorless storehouse; this last building served as living quarters for children who were also brought to Acmecetca—without their parents.

The order to begin executions was transmitted verbally to the prefect of Golta who in turn passed it down to his deputy, Aristide Pădure. The murder was carried out jointly by the gendarmes stationed there, Ukrainian auxiliaries under the command of a Ukrainian-born Romanian named Kazachievichi, and a number of local volunteers. The operation began on the morning of December 21, 1941, the last day of Hanukkah; some four thousand Jews—the sick, invalids, and orphans—were packed into two of the cowsheds and burned alive. The method was the same as used in Odessa: the openings were closed, straw was thrown inside, and the building was doused with gasoline and set on fire. The remaining Jews were lined up in rows of three hundred to four hundred, marched to the woods, stood on the edge of a ravine close to the Bug River, told to undress, and then shot in the neck. Now and then grenades were lobbed into the ravine to finish off those still alive. The massacre went on until the evening hours of December 24, with a recess to enable Christians to celebrate Christmas.

The executions resumed on December 28 and were completed with considerable effort on December 31, just in time for the new year's eve parties. Over the first four days of the operation, thirty thousand Jews were shot or burned to death, while those awaiting their turn remained stranded on the banks of the frozen-over river; some of them set up impromptu shelters in earth pits and employed the frozen bodies of previously murdered Jews for this purpose in their desperation. In the second stage of the operation, eleven thousand Jews were executed before the New Year.[45]

The gendarmes picked two hundred Jews whom they judged to be young and able-bodied, and put them to work gathering the bodies scattered throughout the camp, dragging them to the ravine, and heaving them in. On Christmas Eve, December 24, Prefect Isopescu went on a sleigh ride in the camp area and near the ravine; he was accompanied by guests from Bucharest and relatives whom he had invited for a visit. The two hundred Jews who had been picked to work at obliterating the traces of the carnage were kept for three days in an earth pit; one hundred and fifty of them were shot dead because they grew weak or because the gendarmes decided they didn't work fast enough. One of the survivors, Chaim Kogan, who later emigrated to Israel, described the work he was forced to do for over two months:

> I was in the group that during the initial period worked in gathering the bodies left along the path to the execution site. After several days I was transferred to work in removing several thousand bodies that had been thrown into the pit. We transported the corpses in carts to the ravine where they were burned. After several more days I worked at another pit. . . . The cold was so fierce that the corpses could not be taken out. They made us cut pieces off the corpses and carry them on our backs to the incineration pit. . . . For two full months, January and February, we the survivors worked to exhaustion in burning the bodies. The policemen came and shot 150 of us. We were preparing pyres for burning the corpses: a layer of straw on top of which we laid corpses in a layer 4 meters wide and about 10 meters long. They were piled up to the height of a man. We added some wood at the edges and in the middle and once again a layer of straw and firewood and a row of

corpses. Then fire would be set to the pyre, another pyre would be built and so it went on for two months. We turned our brethren to ashes and in the fierce cold we warmed ourselves by the warmth of their ashes.[46]

The crime committed by Romanians on the banks of the Bug River at Bogdanovca surpassed in its savagery the massacre carried out by the Germans at Babi Yar. The burning of bodies extended into the spring after the thaw and the acrid smell coming from the site indicated that the job was not completed. The camp at Domanovca was liquidated by the same team only after the liquidation of Bogdanovca was completed. At Acmecetca there was no need to shoot anyone: the camp was fenced off with barbed wire and the Jewish prisoners were left to die of hunger. Prefect Isopescu was fond of visiting the place every few days to watch, and he even took photographs of the dying Jews.[47]

Jews of the Regat

From February 1941 to August 23, 1944, the lives of Romanian Jews were dependent solely on the wishes, whims, and moods of Antonescu, as well as upon his assessments of the ways in which Jewish existence might serve Romanian national interests. The balance sheet of this period is not clear-cut and not completely damning. The dictator's ideas concerning the solution of the Jewish Question in Regat and southern Transylvania moved from one extreme to another; at one moment Antonescu was prepared to hand over the Jewish population in Regat to the Nazis, then he would change his mind. The vacillation was repeated. At the same time, however, throughout that period Antonescu's reactions derived from several fundamental antisemitic assumptions that remained constant and were even more passionately upheld as time passed:

—Jews were more numerous than demographers thought;
—Jews exploited Romanians and grew rich at their expense. Antonescu's regime would restore to the Romanian people that which had been taken away from it;
—Jews posed a serious internal threat to society. They had undermined the healthy core of the Romanian people and corrupted Romanian elites;
—Jews were natural allies of Romania's enemies, no matter who they were;
—Jews rule the world.

Antonescu continued the policy of expropriation and enriched the state by billions of lei from Jewish assets. He personally ordered levies, confiscations, compulsory loans, and donations for the benefit of the state and the "charity" managed by his wife—the latter distributed Jewish property to the Romanian poor, as well as to orphans and war widows. Antonescu was behind legislation aimed at pressing Romanian Jews into forced labor squads; he followed their productivity there and dealt severely with overseers who did not treat the Jews with sufficient severity. By the end of his rule most surviving Jews had been completely dispossessed and reduced to penury, while fifty thousand became refugees within Romania proper after they had been expelled from their villages and townships. This expropriation policy was pursued until August 1943. Antonescu succeeded in realizing the great dream of all antisemites: to cleanse the countryside of Jewish presence, thereby releasing the souls of the peasantry from "pollution" through contact.

With the April 1941 arrival of the Nazi advisor for Jewish affairs, Gustav Richter, the approach to the Jewish Question in Romania underwent change. Side by side with the continuing implementation of the policy of Octavian Goga (poet, anti-semite, and prime minister, 1937–1938), which included expropriation of the Jews and an intentional retrogression to the civil rights situation of the nineteenth century, ground was laid for a new policy that threatened the very existence of Jews in the country.

At that time the Nazis were unsatisfied with the anti-Jewish measures that had been taken by the Romanians; those steps lacked the determination necessary, in their view, to deal with the Jewish Question.

On Richter's advice, followed by pressure from the German legation, Romanian authorities set up a central Judenrat, the Jewish Central Office (Centrala Evreilor). They also banned all Zionist activity, carried out a census of "persons of Jewish blood," and launched technical preparations for the deportation of Romanian Jews to the Belzec death camp. In their efforts to further the implementation of the Final Solution in Romania, the Nazis were willing to turn a blind eye to the activities of the corrupt Romanian establishment. One serious factor, however, appears to have escaped Richter and his masters, namely, that without Antonescu's consent the plan could not be put into practice. Its dependence on the Reich notwithstanding, Romania was not an occupied country but an ally. Furthermore, the large-scale massacres of Jews and Antonescu's tenacity in implementing the Final Solution in "liberated" Romanian territory and later in Transnistria aroused admiration among the Nazis and in Hitler in particular. As early as late August 1941, the Führer told Goebbels: "As far as the Jewish Question is concerned, it can now be determined that a man like Antonescu is pursuing much more radical policies in this area than we have done so far."[48]

In June 1942, under the impact of impressive German victories in Russia and following the Romanian army's advance to the Caucasus and its crossing of the Don River, Antonescu agreed to a final solution with regard to Romanian Jews that foresaw their deportation.[49]

On August 31, 1942, ten days before the deportations were to begin, Antonescu gave himself up to an outburst of rage after he had read a detailed survey of the number of Jews and their distribution in Romania. In an effort to prepare public opinion for the operation of deporting Romanian Jews he wrote the following:

> The data on the composition of the urban population must be published so that the country will realize the extent of the danger posed to the economy and development of Romania by the criminal Jewish-Masonic policy represented by the parties in Transyl-vania and the Regat that call themselves "national." By passing this situation on to the successors of the present regime, I shall turn my regime into an accomplice in crime. I shall disregard everyone and every obstacle to cleanse the nation completely of this pest. . . . This decision must be published in its entirety together with the statistics and the present survey . . . before September 10.[50]

The fact that Antonescu's decision was not published in the press indicates that over the following ten days he must have changed his mind: the nationalist in him won over the antisemite. Antonescu yielded to the persuasions of the democratic oppositionists Maniu and Bratianu and took into consideration that Hungary had not deported its Jews. It also appears that he was affected by intervention of members of the royal court circle as well as an official letter from the government of the United States delivered to him via the Swiss embassy. But perhaps the chief consideration at play here was his sincere concern over the fate of northern Transylvania and the link between this national issue and the continuing Jewish existence in Romania. The fact is that he did not yield to the Nazis, who put heavy pressure on him—initially through the German ambassador and later also during his meetings with Hitler and Ribbentropp in April 1943—to follow through on his commitment to deport Romanian Jews.[51] We may conclude with absolute certainty that Antonescu and his regime prevented the Final Solution in the Regat and southern Transylvania. At the same time, however, we must not lose sight of the fact that Antonescu never resigned himself to giving up his dream of ridding the country of its Jews. True, unlike the Nazis he was not bent on murdering the Jews and, as far as he was concerned, he was willing to let them leave Romania to go anywhere else in the world provided they would leave all property behind. In his last public statement on the Jewish issue, delivered on February 4, 1944, Antonescu threatened the survivors and Romanian Jews in general that he would settle the score with them: "I want the Jews to take notice that should they continue to subvert this all-too-tolerant country, they will suffer consequences even more grievous than those they have suffered until now."[52]

In a letter he sent to his Jewish architect, Antonescu outlined the argument that was later adopted by subsequent Romanian regimes. He summed up his relations with and responsibility toward the Jews by saying that what had happened was a world catastrophe and not just a catastrophe of the Jews: "In this war that has been waged across the globe, the Jews cannot escape the suffering, difficulties, and disasters that have befallen the whole world."[53]

As we have seen, Antonescu imbibed his antisemitic prejudices before he became dictator and before his contacts with Hitler and other Nazi leaders. The eventual contacts, however, served only to intensify his hatred toward the Jewish people and toward democratic and liberal values. As did the Legionnaires, he regarded these values as "Jewish inventions" designed to benefit the Jews at the expense of Romanians. Under Hitler's influence and having become convinced that Europe was entering the fascist era and that Germany was poised to win the war in the East, Antonescu adopted the policy of physical liquidation of the Jews with a view toward carrying out ethnic cleansing in the liberated territories and in northern Romania. Once Hitler turned over to his administration a huge part of the Ukraine, Antonescu was in a position to give a free reign to his hatred for "Russian" Jews, and he committed the crime of genocide against them.

In the summer of 1942, Antonescu agreed to deliver Romanian Jews into the hands of Eichman's underlings, even though he knew what lay in store for them; he changed his mind only for reasons of state and not because of any humanitarian considerations. All told, this Balkan dictator remains responsible for the death of at least 350,000 Jews, including 100,000 Ukrainian Jews.[54]

NOTES

1. Ion Antonescu in *Pe marginea prăpastiei* (Bucharest, 1941), p. 165, two volumes of documents published by the Antonescu administration on the crimes of the Legionnaires.

2. For an overview of Romanian Jewry, see Jean Ancel, introduction to Alexandre Safran, *El mul pene ha-se'arah: Yahadut Romanyah bi-tekufat ha-Shoah: Zikhronot*, ed. Jean Ancel (Jerusalem: Yad Vashem, 1990), pp. 4–25 (also available in English as *Resisting the Storm: Romania, 1940–1947: Memoirs* [Jerusalem: Yad Vashem, 1987]; hereafter Safran, *Memoirs*).

3. See Jean Ancel, "The Image of the Jew in the View of Romanian Anti-Semitic Movements:Continuity and Change," *Shvut* 16 (1993): 39–57.

4. A. C. Cuza, *Apel către toți românii* (Bucharest, 1922).

5. Letter dated June 23, 1941, from Antonescu to leaders of the opposition, Maniu and Brătianu, Archivele Statului Bucharest, Archiva Ministerului de Interne, dosar 40.001, vol. 44.

6. N. Crainic, *Programul Statului Etnocratic*, Colecția Naționalistă (Bucharest, 1938), pp. 3–5, 12.

7. Safran, *Memoirs*, pp. 58–59.

8. Raul Hilberg, *The Destruction of the European Jews* (Chicago: Quadrangle, 1961), p. 490. The Nazi intelligence service believed Antonescu was afflicted with leukemia; see W. Hoettl, *The Secret Front* (London: Praeger, 1953), p. 174.

9. Nicușor Graur, *In preajma altei lumi* (Bucharest, 1946), pp. 192–93.

10. Dr. Wilhelm Filderman Archives, P-6/47, p. 72, Yad Vashem Archives (hereafter YVA).

11. Minutes of the government session, October 29, 1940, Arhiva C.C. al P.C.R., Fondul 103, dosar 8212.

12. On these two revelations, see 1) Ambassador Killinger to the Foreign Ministry in Berlin, Bucharest, August 16, 1941, Akten zur deutschen auswärtigen Politik, 1918–1945, Series D 1937–1941, vol. 13 (1970), do. 207, p. 264.; and 2) record of the conversation between Mihai Antonescu and General Rottkirchen, Bucharest, August 28, 1942, in the course of which the early disclosure of the Barbarossa plan in January 1941 was mentioned; see Jean Ancel, ed., *Documents Concerning the Fate of Romanian Jewry during the Holocaust* (Jerusalem: Beate Klarsfeld Foundation, 1986) vol. 9, no. 162, pp. 423–24.

13. Jean Ancel, "The Romanian Way of Solving the 'Jewish Problem' in Bessarabia and Bukovina, June–July 1941," *Yad Vashem Studies* 19 (1988): 207–208.

14. United Restitution Organization (URO), Frankfurt am Main, October 1959, Sammlung, vol. 3, p. 578. Protocol of the conversation between Ribbentropp and Mihai Antonescu, September 23, 1942.

15. Ancel, ed., *Documents*, vol. 2, no. 136, pp. 414–15.

16. Jean Ancel, "The Jassy Syndrome," *Romanian Jewish Studies* 1 (Spring 1987): 33–51; ibid., 2 [pt. 2] (Winter 1987): 35–53.

17. Vasile Marin, *Crez de generație*, 2nd ed. (Bucharest, 1937), pp. 47, 135, 189.

18. Ion Antonescu to Iuliu Maniu, June 22, 1941; Josef Constantin Dragan, *Antonescu, Mareșalul României și Răsboaiele de reîntregire, Mărturii și documente* (Cannaregio Venetia: Editura Nagard, 1988), vol. 2, no. 13, p. 197.

19. Ancel, "Romanian Way," p. 231.

20. Protocol of the government meeting of July 8, 1941, Ancel, *Documents*, vol. 5, no. 3, p. 4.

21. Memorandum by the governor of Bessarabia, Voiculescu, undated report, end of 1941, Ancel, *Documents*, vol. 10, no. 61, p. 137.

22. Order issued by the Interior Minister on behalf of Antonescu, July 18, 1941, Ancel, *Documents*, vol.2, no. 181, p. 468.

23. Voiculescu report, p. 138.

24. Nuremburg Documents, PS-3319; Odessa State Archives 2361/1/1486, pp. 39–40.

25. Ancel, *Documents*, vol. 5, no. 65, p. 73.

26. Report no. 2 by the commission that investigated "irregularities" in the Kishniev

ghetto on Antonescu's orders, undated (end of December 1941), ibid., vol. 5, no. 124, p. 195; see also Carp, *Cartea Neagrǎ*, vol. 3, *Transnistria* (Bucharest, 1947), p. 64.

27. *Procesul Marei Trǎdǎri Nationale* (Bucharest, 1946), p. 246, protocols from the trial of Antonescu and other functionaries of his regime (hereafter *Trial*). On October 17, 1941, Richter reported to Berlin having learned from Leca about Antonescu's order to concentrate for liquidation 110,000 Jews from Bessarabia and Bukovina in two forests near the Bug River. Nuremburg Documents, 3319-PS, copy in Ancel, *Documents*, vol. 5, no. 187, p. 110.

28. Letter from Filderman to Antonescu, October 11, 1941, in Carp, *Cartea Neagrǎ*, vol. 3, pp. 183–84; Ancel, *Documents*, vol. 3, no. 136, p. 224.

29. Second letter from Antonescu to Filderman, signed by his secretary, November 11, 1941, ibid., no. 230, p. 380.

30. Voiculescu report, p. 139.

31. I. Gǎvǎnescu, "Rǎspunsul d-lui Mareşal Antonescu la scrisoarea profesorului," *Curentul*, November 3, 1941; copy in Ancel, *Documents*, vol. 3, no. 219, p. 332.

32. *Trial*, pp. 285–86.

33. Warrant for the arrest of Lieutenant Mǎrculescu Eustaţiu, who commanded one of the companies that carried out the massacre of 16,000 Jews in Odessa; see Ancel, *Documents*, vol. 6, no. 26, pp. 282–83.

34. Report from the French (Vichy) ambassador in Romania to the Foreign Minister, November 10, 1941, ibid., vol. 3, no. 229, p. 276.

35. *Trial*, pp. 64–65, 289.

36. Ibid., p. 289.

37. Odessa State Archives, 2242/1/1486, p. 8.

38. General Staff directive, December 28, 1941, ibid., p. 31.

39. Report by Ştefǎnescu, January 10, 1942, ibid., pp. 8–11.

40. "Trenul-Dric," *Curierul Israelit*, November 11, 1944 (trains were placed at the disposal of Romanian administration by the Nazis).

41. *Trial*, pp. 34–35.

42. Ibid., p. 148.

43. Cable on behalf of the German Commissioner in Nikolayev (German original and Romanian translation, February 5, 1942, Odessa State Archives, 2241/1/1486, pp. 178–79.

44. Internal memorandum and remark in handwriting of the Governor and his office chief saying that measures were taken "to burn bodies of the Jews," February 18, 1942, ibid., p. 199.

45. See the indictment and court proceedings in the trial of the first group of war criminals in 1945 in *Actul de acuzare, rechizitoriile şi replica în prcesul primului lot de criminali de rǎsboi* (Bucharest: Editurea Apǎrarii Patriotice, 1945), pp. 2, 27–28.

46. Testimony of Chaim Kogan in his handwriting, *Bat-Yam*, May 1963, YVA, PKR/V, p. 43. Kogan also testified in the trial in Bucharest in 1945. Of the group of fifty survivors, three others also testifies on the same date: R. Gheza, Leonard Grunstein, Iosif Braunstein.

47. Isopescu also took pictures of the massacres in the two other camps; see *Actul de acuzare*, pp. 29, 30, 61.

48. From Goebbels's diaries, quoted in Gerald Reitlinger, *Die Endlösung* (Berlin, 1960), p. 94.

49. Jean Ancel, "Plans for Deportation of the Romanian Jews and Their Discontinuation in Light of Documentary Evidence, July–October 1942," *Yad Vashem Studies* 16 (1984): 381–420.

50. Internal memorandum from the Prime Minister's office concerning the number of Jews in Romania, submitted to Antonescu; the documents contain comments and decisions in his handwriting, August 31, 1942; see Ancel, *Documents*, vol. 10, no. 91, pp. 210, 215.

51. Andreas Hillgruber, ed., *Staatsmänner und Diplomaten bei Hitler* (Frankfurt/M., 1970), no. 30, p. 233. The conversation with Ribbentropp took place in Salzburg on April 14, 1943.

52. Letter from Antonescu to Clejan, February 4, 1944, in Ancel, *Documents*, vol. 8, no. 13, p. 19.

53. Ibid., p. 19.

54. In his trial Antonescu claimed: "I never took any extermination measure directed against another person. In my house we wouldn't slaughter even a chick. It was the General Staff and not myself who took the steps" (*Trial*, p. 51).

34.

GERHARD L. WEINBERG

The Allies and the Holocaust

In the years before the systematic killing of Jews began, the persecution of Jews by the German government was widely reported in the media of the time as well as followed and described in reports home by the diplomatic representatives of foreign powers stationed in Germany. It is, however, important to recall that at the time practically no one inside or outside Germany anticipated that these measures were steps on the road to mass murder. The actions of the German government were generally understood—perhaps we should now say misunderstood—by both the victims and the bystanders, as a return to the kinds of persecutions and restrictions imposed on Jews in prior centuries, not as steps on the road toward a new policy.

Since these events in Germany coincided in time with the great world depression, it was particularly difficult for Jews to emigrate from Germany—and subsequently German-annexed Austria—to other countries. At a time of massive unemployment and enormous difficulties in financing government relief measures, all countries were reluctant to receive refugees who had been deprived of most of their assets by their former country and would be competing for the already scarce jobs in any new home. The uproars over immigration at a time of economic difficulties that we have witnessed in Europe and the United States in the most recent past should remind us that a time when unemployment was from three to five times as high as it has been in many countries recently was not an auspicious moment for the acceptance of large numbers of refugees.

On the contrary, most states adopted measures to restrict immigration; one of the few steps President Herbert Hoover took to cope with the Depression in the United States was to have regulations issued to make the issuance of visas within the quotas allowed by the existing American immigration legislation dependent on a showing that the individual allowed into the country would not become a public charge. It was this procedural restriction that would greatly hamper filling the available quota during the early years of the Nazi regime. After his reelection in 1936, President Roosevelt felt sufficiently secure politically to insist on a more lenient interpretation of the rules, thereby allowing a substantially greater number of visas to be issued. As a result, the United States accepted about twice as many Jewish refugees as the rest of the world put together, about 200,000 out of 300,000.[1] It must be recalled, however, that at the time the overwhelming majority of Americans opposed the admission of refugees, and that Roosevelt acted in the face of strong and politically damaging criticism for what was generally considered a pro-Jewish attitude by him personally and by his administration.

Great Britain followed a restrictive immigration policy of its own, and the relaxation after the pogrom of November 1938 would have the effect of saving many lives but was at the time intended for, and restricted to, those who had prospects of leaving Great Britain for the United States or another country after what was expected to be a short time. In the 1930s, of course, Britain was also the mandatory power for Palestine. It had partitioned Palestine in the early 1920s into two mandates and had prohibited Jewish immigration into the larger of the two, called Trans-Jordan, from a typically colonialist perspective: seen from London it was the other side of the river.

As is generally known, the British government abandoned its original intention of further partitioning the smaller of the two, now called Palestine, into three parts, a small Jewish unit, a much larger Arab one, and an international zone. Instead the British government issued a general limitation on Jewish immigration—an immigration that was to end entirely not long afterward unless the Arabs approved its continuance—something they were not expected to do. What is not so generally known, or when known is not considered in connection with the infamous 1939 White Paper, is that this step was taken as part of a general reorientation of British policy that was to prove of decisive positive significance for the survival of many Jews.

A most important factor in the decision to close Palestine to Jewish immigration was the belief in London that the troops that had to be stationed there to contain the Arab uprising—at the time the largest deployment of British active duty troops anywhere—were needed in England against the contingency of war with Germany. As the British government turned, in the winter of 1938–1939, from the policy of appeasement to one of resistance to German aggression, the military imperatives of the new policy included not only the first-ever introduction of conscription in peacetime but also the need to transfer troops from Palestine to the home islands so that a new British Expeditionary Force for deployment on the continent against Germany could begin to be formed. Furthermore, any new war with Germany was expected to require the large-scale recruitment and employment of troops from India, large numbers of whom were expected to be Muslim. In this context, the shift from appeasing Germany to very likely fighting Germany entailed a reversal of policy toward the Arabs—a shift from fighting their uprising to appeasing their demands for a cessation of Jewish immigration into Palestine.

I do not want to suggest that there were no other motives, and I certainly am not denying the generally anti-Jewish and pro-Arab attitudes of most of those then in the British Foreign and Colonial offices who had anything to do with the Middle East; but it does seem that this interrelated double-reversal of British policy illuminates a point about most policies of the major powers in the years before and during World War II: the whole issue of the fate of the Jews was entirely marginal to the considerations that drove policy choices.[2] Today, with the Holocaust seen quite properly as one of the defining events of the twentieth century, we are inclined to examine the developments of the period 1933–1945 in a perspective which places that event at the center. To understand the decisions made by leaders and governments at the time, however, we must recognize that for them entirely different issues were dominant. To them, the fate of the Jews was a very marginal consideration—if it entered into their thinking at all; but both enormously negative as well as enormously positive effects on the fate of the Jews resulted from choices that were made completely or almost completely without any regard to those effects.

This point should be kept in mind when we examine one of the most fascinating aspects of the beginnings of the systematic killing of Jews—an aspect that is still shrouded in secrecy and about which we have only the vaguest and most tantalizing hints. Whatever the differences in scholarly interpretation about what those documents tell us about the decision-making process in Germany with regard to the Final Solution, the periodic reports of the Einsatzgruppen, the killing squads that accompanied the German military in the invasion of the Soviet Union, constitute one of the most important sources we have on the early stages of the actual process of mass murder. These reports are too well known to need detailed discussion here. What is not sufficiently taken into account by the existing literature is that the British decoding experts at Bletchley Park had broken the German police code in which similar reports, or summaries of them, together with other regular reports on SS camps were sent to Berlin.

In a book on the subject by Peter Calvacoressi, who worked at Bletchley, Calvacoressi asserts:

> There is a peculiarly horrible example of the links between ciphers of different grades. The basic problem in cryptography is to get randomness. . . . At one point the German cryptographers responsible for finding entirely random settings for an Enigma cipher thought that they had hit on a bright solution. Every day the concentration camps rendered returns giving the numbers of prisoners who had been delivered to the camp that day, the number who had died or been killed, and the number of surviving inmates at the end of the day. These were truly random figures. They were reported in a medium-grade cipher and the recipients passed them on to their Enigma colleagues who used them in determining the settings of a particular Enigma cipher. B[letchley] P[ark] was reading that medium-grade cipher and it realized too that these daily concentration camp returns were being used in Enigma. So these sad, grisly statistics of human suffering and indignity played a part which the piteous victims never dreamed of.[3]

There is more evidence. An Appendix in volume 2 of F. H. Hinsley's *British Intelligence in the Second World War* makes it clear that the British were reading German police ciphers with a high degree of regularity.[4] The messages to which Calvacoressi alludes seem to be the daily returns from the spring of 1942 to February 1943 from Dachau, Buchenwald, Auschwitz, and seven other camps to which Hinsley refers.[5] Furthermore, the messages read at the time included what originally certainly sounded like Einsatzgruppen reports or preliminary summaries of them. Hinsley writes:

> Between 18 July and 30 August 1941 police decrypts on at least seven occasions gave details of mass shootings, in the central sector, of victims described variously as 'Jews,' 'Jewish plunderers,' 'Jewish bolshevists' or 'Russian soldiers' in numbers varying from less than a hundred to several thousand.[6]

The reason that we have had to rely on deductions from these and a few similar comments in the secondary literature is that the original decrypts remained closed to research and, if they survive at all, were intended to be closed to access in perpetuity.

The decision to keep these records closed was, of course, not Hinsley's, but his description of the issue deserves quotation. After explaining that in the published volumes of his official history of British intelligence precise references are provided for documents already open or likely to be made available, even if after a lengthy interval, he continues:

> But it would have served no useful purpose to give precise references to the domestic files of the intelligence-collecting bodies, which are unlikely ever to be opened in the Public Record Office. We have been permitted—indeed encouraged—to make use of these files in our text and we have done so on a generous scale, but in their case our text must be accepted as being the only evidence of their contents that can be made public. This course may demand from our readers more trust than historians have the right to expect, but we believe they will agree that it is preferable to the alternative, which was to have incorporated no evidence for which we could not quote sources.[7]

No sources were cited for the police reports, including quotations from them; at the time of publication, all these documents fell into the category of permanent withholding. In April 1996 the National Security Agency—presumably with the agreement of the government in London—released, through the National Archives, a huge collection of materials pertaining to deciphering operations by the Allies and the Axis before, during, and after World War II. Included among these records is a set of British decrypts of German Ordnungspolizei (order police, regular uniformed police) reports of mass killings of Jews in the newly occupied Soviet territories from July to September 1941. These appear to be some of the documents cited by Hinsley; the set was turned over to U.S. authorities on an as yet unknown date. They demonstrate that not only the notorious Einsatzgruppen but also regular German police units were engaged in the mass slaughter of Jews from the earliest days of the German campaign in the East. What can be learned from future releases of Allied decrypts—such as the concentration camp returns cited by Hinsley and Calvacoressi—remains to be seen. Here is an issue on which scholars in the United Kingdom and the United States might try to work; the need to maintain secrecy about intercepted German World War II concentration camp reports is difficult to understand.

This reference to records of World War II that are still kept secret in Washington and London calls for reference to another group of records also still closed that may turn out to be of interest for research on the Holocaust: the "Floradora" material. These are the decodes of German diplomatic World War II traffic. The point that is too often overlooked is that such intercepts not only shed light on the knowledge of the British and American governments at the time, in this case among other topics about the German program of systematically killing Jews, but that in addition in some cases the intercepts are likely to be the only surviving texts of documents for which the German originals are missing from German archives because of destruction during the war. The United States Holocaust Memorial Museum has made a major effort to locate and microfilm material in the archives of the former Soviet Union pertaining to the Holocaust; perhaps it could try to get at some of the documents that are in British and American archives but are still kept closed as effectively as the Soviet archives once were.

The point of all this is that the governments of the Western Allies may well have known a great deal more about the Holocaust considerably earlier than previously recognized by scholars. This comment is not meant to detract from the fine books dealing with this subject, Walter Laqueur's *The Terrible Secret*[8] and Richard Breitman and Walter Laqueur's *Breaking the Silence*,[9] but to suggest some new avenues for future exploration at a time when the argument that certain records cannot be made accessible to scholars is becoming less and less plausible. Furthermore, there are likely to be all sorts of other important hitherto unknown materials on the Holocaust in these records.

It should always be remembered that during World War II Allied intercepting and decoding capabilities steadily improved—just as the proportion of German records that survives decreases equally steadily each year of the war. For the later portion of the war, therefore, the Allied intercepts are increasingly likely to be the only surviving record. What makes this even more important for scholars of the Holocaust is that one significant side-effect of the strategic bombing offensive was that the disruption of German transportation and communications systems in the last year of the war obliged the Germans to resort to wireless systems for messages that had earlier been entrusted for security reasons to cables, the mail, and messengers and thereby protected against interception and decoding. If and when the remaining Allied intercepts and decodes are opened up, we may expect to learn a great deal more about the later stages of the Holocaust.

To return to the events of 1941 and their relationship to the Allies, we need to consider more carefully than has been the case hitherto the German plans for and Allied measures against German projects in the Middle East and North Africa. In the fall of 1941 German planning, which had originally anticipated a drive into the Middle East in the winter of 1941–1942 as a follow-up to the defeat of the Soviet Union, shifted the timetable to 1942. There was, however, one aspect of this project which, at least in Hitler's thinking, had not changed. In late July he had assured the Croatian minister of defense that all Jews would disappear from Europe; and he had predicted that Hungary would be the last country to give up its Jewish inhabitants. In November he made it clear that the project of killing Jews was by no means confined to Europe. As he explained to the Grand Mufti of Jerusalem, the Jews not only of Europe but everywhere else were to be killed; his expression refers to Jews living outside Europe, those living among "außereuropäischen Völker."[10] Since the Mufti was presumably more interested in the Middle East than, say Australia or Latin America, Hitler spelled out for him that Germany intended the destruction, "Vernichtung" is the word recorded by the interpreter, of Jews living in the Arab world.[11] What this latter term meant at the time was the Jewish community in Palestine and the then still substantial Jewish communities in Syria, Iraq, Iran, the Arabian peninsula, Egypt, and French Northwest Africa. And the Germans were indeed expecting to take over these areas so that, among other things, their Jewish inhabitants could be killed as was already being done in the newly occupied portions of the USSR. As I have just pointed out, German drives from Libya through Egypt into Palestine, across Turkey into Syria and Iraq, and across the Caucasus into the Middle East from the North were already being planned. Because a number of relevant documents on this have been published for years, I would mention only Hitler's draft Directive No. 32 of June 11,

1941, as a prominent example.[12] All this is widely known. Two aspects of this issue have not, however, received the attention they deserve.

First, German interests were not limited to the Middle East and the northeast African route into it. As Norman Goda has clearly demonstrated, Hitler anticipated German control over important portions of Northwest Africa, primarily as a basis for his anticipated war against the United States.[13] The Jewish community of Morocco was thus at risk, as was that of Palestine. Second, the Allied forces that defended Egypt against German advances and those that subsequently landed in Northwest Africa were primarily responsible for the survival of the Jewish population in the Middle East. Certainly no Jewish state in Palestine, however configured, would have emerged had all of the Jews in the then-British mandate been killed during World War II.

There were several preconditions for this success of the Western Allies. One was the decision of President Roosevelt in April of 1941 to open the Red Sea to American shipping, once the British had conquered Italian East Africa, and thus to assist in the defense of Egypt. A second such precondition was Roosevelt's decision of June 1942 to turn over to the British the tanks of America's first armored division so that Rommel's rush into the Middle East could be halted and reversed after the surrender of Tobruk. Though essential to the survival of the Jewish community of Palestine, these decisions were clearly taken without reference to that consideration. The other major precondition was, however, very much connected with the question of the Holocaust, but ironically in a reverse fashion. The British forces that defended the southern approach to Palestine through Egypt were made up to a very substantial extent of troops from India, two-thirds of them Muslim.[14] It is, of course, obvious that these men did not volunteer for the Indian Army in order to defend Jews; but that is, among other things, what they were in fact doing in the North African campaign. Although this cause of British concern over Muslim opinion about Jewish immigration into Palestine is rarely mentioned in the literature, it was clear enough to those in charge of the British war effort. The British 8th Army is always referred to as "British"; that a majority of its soldiers did not come from the United Kingdom is generally forgotten by both writers and readers of history. But it was not forgotten by either their commanders (one of whom came out of the Indian Army himself) or by the authorities in London.

The point that again needs to be emphasized is that the decision of the London government in the summer of 1940 to try very hard to defend the British position in the Middle East—even if that meant leaving her Far Eastern, South Asian, and Southeast Asian positions open to attack by Japan—like most of the other choices made by Britain and the United States that had a profound effect on the course of the Holocaust, was made without reference to it. This may make it a little less surprising that the triumph of that British policy, and the association of the United States with it, in the last months of 1942 and the first months of 1943 would have a double effect on Germany's hopes of killing the world's Jews, one restricting those hopes and the other facilitating a portion of their realization.

The way in which the Allied victory restricted Germany's program should be obvious but is rarely mentioned. The turning of the tide in the war, obvious in the Mediterranean theater in the winter 1942–1943 (I shall turn to the Eastern Front in a moment) meant that Nazi expectations of victory and the slaughter of all the world's Jews had been thwarted. In effect, the Allies had saved about two-thirds of the globe's Jews from the fate the Germans intended for them. On the other hand, the collapse of the Fascist regime in Italy, which was both an expected and an obvious by-product of the Allied victory in North Africa, would open up to the Germans the opportunity to kill many Jews in Italy and in Italian-controlled portions of Europe—Jews who had hitherto been protected by the general unwillingness of the Italian diplomatic and military leadership to cooperate in the German murder program.[15] As is well known, the Germans utilized what they saw as the opportunity opened up by the Italian surrender to try to include the Jews of Italy, the Italian islands in the Aegean, and the Italian occupation zones in France, Yugoslavia, and Greece in their killing program, and many thousands of Jews lost their lives as a result. Although this aspect of the Mediterranean campaign has received the attention it quite properly deserves, one ought not to overlook the fact that literally millions of Jews were saved by the same success of the Allies.

If the choices and decisions of Britain and the United States mentioned up to this point were, on the whole, taken without regard to their positive or negative implications for the Jews whom the Germans intended to kill or were actually in the process of killing, there was one further element in the situation that tended to reinforce the existing inclination to disregard the Holocaust even as it was under way. German propaganda throughout the war years took the line that the Jews had caused the war and either controlled the countries aligned against Germany or influenced those who did exercise power. The expectation that in any new war the Jews would be killed had been part of the phrasing of Hitler's original public declaration on January 30, 1939. This propaganda line was a central one in subsequent years, and for a very good reason: it was correctly believed in Berlin that it was an effective one. Although the antisemitic sentiments of large portions of the British and American public certainly did not extend to any wish for the Jews to be killed, on the other hand any hint that their government was taking major steps to assist the Jews at their time of greatest danger was certain to evoke the strongest opposition.

The Western Powers were losing the war on land until the end of 1942, losing the war at sea until the fall of 1943, and were unable to assure victory in the war in the air until February–March 1944. So at a time when there was in practice very little that could be done to assist Germany's Jewish victims, the leadership in both London and Washington wanted nothing to happen on the home fronts that might discourage their peoples. Victory over the Axis was the first priority, a subject to which I shall return. In the meantime, anything that might be seen as giving substance to the German propaganda line—that the Allies were fighting not for the survival of their own peoples in life and in freedom but for the interests of the Jews—was pushed aside. The Soviet Union, of course, had made it a matter of national policy to disregard the antisemitic policies and actions of the German government. Obsessed with the fatuous notion that fascism was the tool of monopoly capitalism, there was neither understanding of nor reaction to the persecution of Jews by the Nazis at the time—and, one might add, after the war until the collapse of the Soviet system a few years ago. It can, in fact, be argued that the official Communist Party line, sedulously spread throughout the Soviet Union, combined with the Nazi-Soviet Pact of 1939, contributed to the early successes of the German killing program during 1941 in that it led many citizens of the Soviet Union to expect that the Germans would behave in any occupied portions of the country rather the way they had in the preceding war when huge Russian territories had also been under temporary German occupation. By the time people discovered that this was a serious mistake, many Jews who might have made a greater effort to escape the Germans were already dead.

But just as the Soviet policy that had this effect as a terrible by-product was adopted for reasons having nothing to do with the Holocaust, so the major contribution that the Red Army made toward the containment of the German killing program was also unaffected by any consideration for the prospective Jewish victims. Keeping the German army away from a substantial proportion of the Jews living in the USSR as well as contributing to the defeat of Germany's attempt to control the globe obviously made for the saving of Jewish lives inside and outside the country. This point has already been made in connection with the Western Allies, and it certainly must be mentioned once more in this context. And in this context, furthermore, belongs the successful defense by the Red Army of the Caucasus in the late summer of 1942 when it appeared for a moment that the German army might be able to break from the north into the Middle East with its large Jewish communities. The Soviets were mainly concerned about defending their country, and the Western Allies were terrified, to put it mildly, that the Axis might gain control of the oil resources of that region; the survival of the Jews of Palestine, Syria, Iran, and Iraq was, however, as surely due to the Soviets holding the Germans in the Caucasus as to the British holding in the Western Desert of Egypt.

During the course of 1944, as the tide of the war either had turned or was turning clearly in favor of the Allies, two issues related to the Holocaust came increasingly to the fore, and both have received considerable attention since 1945—or rather since serious discussion of the Holocaust began in the 1960s. These two issues were the possibility of rescue and the possibility of interference, that is, the prospects for rescuing Jews threatened by the killing program and/or of interfering with the mechanics of that program by steps such as the bombing of killing centers or the railway routes to them. These issues will be discussed separately, but only with reference to the Western Allies since the Soviet Union had no interest in either of them a priori.

There were some minimal possibilities of rescuing Jews, but they were minimal indeed. The most recent examination of the subject by Shlomo Aronson and Richard Breitman shows quite clearly that whatever the details of the various rescue schemes, there were very tight limits on what could be done.[16] These limits were largely the result of German insistence on the sorts of trades and concessions that were impossible—and that they knew to be impossible—for the Allies to accept. A tiny number were saved in a variety of projects in which Jewish organizations, the War Refugee Board, and various neutral agencies and persons such as Raoul Wallenberg played significant roles; and it is entirely possible that more might have been done. The major obstacle, however, arose from the German side, a point that is too often overlooked.

The fixation on rescue attempts and their very limited success has tended to divert attention from the enormous efforts made by the Germans—including practically every agency of the German government—to maximize the killing and minimize any rescues.[17] This is not to minimize the resistance of the British to most rescue attempts that involved getting the rescued into Palestine, and of the Americans to most rescue attempts that were likely to bring Jewish refugees to the United States.[18] It is in this context that the title of Monty Penkower's book *The Jews Were Expendable* seems entirely appropriate.[19] But such a title should not divert attention from those primarily responsible for the killing: the killers. This is a major aspect too often omitted from consideration of the other issue now frequently discussed, namely the possibilities of interfering with the killing process, primarily by bombing. This question is really appropriate only when considering the period beginning in the summer of 1944, when the Western Allies had finally defeated the German air force, had succeeded in establishing a firm bridgehead in Normandy, and had taken the airfields in central Italy from which airplanes could reach almost any portion of Europe still controlled by the Germans.

What could have been done and should have been done is essentially what the United States recently did with the dropping of air supplies to some isolated portions of Bosnia: the clear and public indication of a policy preference opposed to the established policy of one side, even if there is little or no prospect of providing substantial practical assistance. An excellent example of this from World War II is the attempt by the Allies to drop supplies from the air to the Polish resistance forces that had risen against the Germans in Warsaw. These efforts no doubt showed where the British and Americans stood, and they also certainly helped the morale of those active in the uprising; but the practical effect was virtually nil. Perhaps the effort enabled the Poles to prolong their resistance a few days longer than otherwise would have been possible, but the outcome could not be in doubt.

One further point should be made in this connection. When the Western Allies sent planes to Warsaw, it was done over the strong objections of the commanders in the affected theaters of war. They always had other targets and priorities; this is particularly obvious from the records of the Allied command in Italy. In wartime there are invariably competing demands for all military resources, and the diversion of such resources in the fall of 1944 to the futile effort to assist the Polish uprising in Warsaw was ordered from the top.[20]

One aspect of the debate over the possible bombing of Auschwitz or the railways leading to it has been too readily overlooked. That is the German side. By 1944 the murderers were both hardened and experienced. They were, it should be noted, proud of their activities and what they considered their great accomplishment. The notorious Stroop report on the destruction of the Warsaw Ghetto should be reread from this perspective: it shows men who boasted of what they were doing.[21] They were completely committed to their careers as professional killers, and not only because of their ideological stance. By 1944 it was obvious to all of them that this was their road to advancement and to medals. It is not a coincidence that promotions and decorations invariably occupy such a central place in military and pseudomilitary hierarchies; these are the visible signs of success.

Furthermore, every individual involved in the program to kill all the Jews the Germans could reach knew very well, most especially by the summer of 1944, that this was not only the route to higher rank and higher decorations but the best chance of exemption from conscription if he was still in a civilian position and from far more dangerous duty at the front if he was in uniform. It may be a nasty picture, but these were nasty people. For them, killing Jews, most of whom had no weapons, was vastly preferable to serving at the front, where those with whom one had to deal had plenty of weapons, especially in this stage of the war.

Those active in the killing program had by this time an enormous vested interest in its continuation and in their own participation in it. There are signs that, even in the preceding year, 1943, the vast number of Jews killed in 1941 and 1942 had led those inside the apparatus of murder to search Europe for new categories of victims. Among them were Jews still protected in some way by Germany's satellites and allies; additional grist for the death mills was to be provided by the Sinti and Roma (Gypsies), persons of mixed ancestry (the so-called Mischlinge), and others.[22]

The idea that men who were dedicated to the killing program, and who saw their own careers and even their own lives tied to its continuation, were likely to be halted by a few cuts of railway lines or the bombing of a gas chamber is preposterous. By the summer of 1944 these people had managed by one means or another the deaths of well over four million, and quite probably over five million, Jews; the notion that they lacked the persistence, ingenuity, and means to kill the majority of Hungary's 700,000 Jews defies all reason. It would have required greater exertions and more ingenuity on their part—and would perhaps have produced additional promotions and medals for those who in the face of great obstacles had carried out their Führer's design. On the other hand, interference by the Western Allies would have been an important assertion of policy, would have encouraged desperate victims in their last days and hours, might have inspired a few additional persons to provide aid and comfort to the persecuted, and might even have enabled a tiny number to escape the fate planned for them by the Germans. As it is, the absence of such essentially symbolic action leaves a blot on the record of the Allies and, possibly more effectively than any other development of those horrendous years, gives the lie to the endless stories about the alleged power of the Jews in the world: in the hour of supreme agony, all the Jewish organizations on earth could not get one country to send one plane to drop one bomb.

In connection with the last stage of the war and of the Holocaust, one additional significant aspect of the policy of Britain and the United States needs review. To those who urged more drastic steps to assist the victims of the German killing program, time and again both governments responded that the most important thing was to win the war as quickly as possible. Victory would end the killing, and anything that might delay victory would only hurt, not help, those whom the Germans had marked out as victims. It is frequently claimed that this was not only a silly answer but that there was something mendacious about it because most of Europe's Jews were killed before victory was in fact attained. In future research this issue ought to be given far more careful scrutiny.

Given the determination of the Germans to fight on to the bitter end, and given their equally fierce determination to slaughter Jews to the last moments of the Third Reich, there were, as is well known, thousands of deaths every day into the final days of the war; and many of the surviving camp inmates had been so weakened by hunger and disease that thousands more died even after liberation. In this connection, it might be worthwhile to consider how many more Jews would have survived had the war ended even a week or ten days earlier—and conversely, how many more would have died had the war lasted an additional week or ten days. Whatever numbers one might put forward in such speculations, one thing is, or ought to be, reasonably clear: the number would be greater than the total number of Jews saved by the various rescue efforts of 1943–1945.

Every single life counts, and every individual saved counts. There cannot be the slightest doubt that more efforts could have been made by an earlier establishment of the War Refugee Board and by any number of other steps and actions. The general picture in terms of overall statistics would not have been very different; but the record of the Allies would have been brighter, and each person saved could have lived out a decent life. The exertions of the Allies in World War II saved not only themselves but also the majority of the world's Jews. But the shadow of doubt whether enough was done will always remain, even if there really were not many things that could have been done.

Any examination of the failure to do more must, however, carefully avoid a most dangerous shift in the apportioning of responsibility. It is the killers, whether in an office, a murder squad, or a killing center, who bear the central responsibility for their deeds. Any general distribution of blame, the "we are all guilty" syndrome, only serves to exculpate the truly guilty. And they were not to be found among the Allies.

NOTES

1. An excellent review of the subject in Richard Breitman and Alan M. Kraut, *American Refugee Policy and European Jewry, 1933–1945* (Bloomington: Indiana University Press, 1987).

2. See Bernard Wasserstein, *Britain and the Jews of Europe* (Oxford: Oxford University Press, 1979).

3. Peter Calvacoressi, *Top Secret Ultra* (New York: Pantheon, 1980), p. 15.

4. F. H. Hinsley, *British Intelligence in the Second World War*, vol. 2 (New York: Cambridge University Press, 1981), appendix 5.

5. Ibid., p. 673.

6. Ibid., p. 671.

7. Ibid., pp. x–xi.

8. Walter Laqueur, *The Terrible Secret: The Suppression of the Truth about Hitler's "Final Solution"* (New York: Penguin, 1981).

9. Walter Laqueur and Richard Breitman, *Breaking the Silence* (New York: Simon and Schuster, 1986).

10. *Akten zur deutschen auswärtigen Politik, 1918–1945*, series D, vol. 13, no. 515.

11. Ibid.

12. The text has been published repeatedly; it may be found in Walther Hubatsch, ed., *Hitlers Weisungen für die Kriegführung 1939–1945* (Frankfurt/M.: Bernard und Graefe, 1962), pp. 129–39, and in *Akten zur deutschen auswärtigen Politik, 1918–1945*, series D, vol. 12, no. 617.

13. Norman J. Goda, "Germany and Northwest Africa in the Second World War: Politics and Strategy of Global Hegemony," Ph.D. diss., University of North Carolina, 1991, and "The Riddle of the Rock: A Reassessment of German Motives for the Capture of Gibraltar in the Second World War," *Journal of Contemporary History* 28 (1993): 297–314.

14. Byron Farwell, *Armies of the Raj: From the Mutiny to Independence, 1858–1947* (New York: Norton, 1989), p. 310.

15. Jonathan Steinberg, *All or Nothing: The Axis and the Holocaust 1941–1943* (London: Routledge, 1990).

16. Richard Breitman and Shlomo Aronson, "The End of the 'Final Solution'?: Nazi Plans to Ransom Jews in 1944," *Central European History* 25 (1992): 177–203.

17. Note Jürgen Rohwer, *Die Versenkung der jüdischen Flüchtlingstransporter* Struma *und* Mefkure *im Schwarzen Meer, Februar 1942, August 1944* (Frankfurt/M.: Bernard und Graefe, 1963), pp. 31–45.

18. There is an excellent introduction to this issue in Leonard Dinnerstein, *America and the Survivors of the Holocaust* (New York: Columbia University Press, 1982).

19. Monty Noam Penkower, *The Jews Were Expendable: Free World Diplomacy and the Holocaust* (Urbana: University of Illinois Press, 1983).

20. The full text was first published in *Trial of the Major War Criminals before the International Military Tribunal,* 42 vols. (Nuremberg: The Tribunal, 1947–1949), vol. 28, pp. 628–94.

21. See Neil Orpen, *Airlift to Warsaw: The Rising of 1944* (Norman: University of Oklahoma Press, 1984).

22. On these matters, see the author's introduction, "The 'Final Solution' and the War in 1943," in *Fifty Years Ago: Revolt amid the Darkness* (Washington, D.C.: United States Holocaust Memorial Museum, 1993), pp. 1–15.

35.

SUSAN S. ZUCCOTTI

Surviving the Holocaust

THE SITUATION IN FRANCE

Nearly 76 percent of the Jews of France survived the Holocaust.[1] The statistic may come as a surprise to those familiar with the Dreyfus Affair, the antisemitism rampant in France in the 1930s, and the collaborationist Vichy regime. The French survival rate is, after all, far higher than that of Belgium, about 58 percent, and that of the Netherlands, a staggeringly low 25 percent. Yet neither Belgium nor the Netherlands share France's reputation as an antisemitic society. The French statistic even approaches the 85 percent survival rate of Italy, a country which, rightly or wrongly, is considered to have been "good to its Jews." How are we to understand these figures?

This essay will examine the persecution of the Jews in France during the Shoah in an effort to explain how survival was possible. It will become apparent that although the attitudes and actions of non-Jews were crucial, they were not the sole determinants of Jewish survival. It will also be clear that while comparisons between survival rates in different countries can be instructive, they must be made with caution and with careful attention to a wide and complex range of variables.

There were, in 1940, roughly 330,000 Jews in France. They represented well under 1 percent of the total population. Of these, roughly 195,000 (or 59%) were French citizens and 135,000 (41%) were foreigners.[2] Those whose families had been French for several generations were generally deeply patriotic, highly integrated, and accustomed to full and unrestricted acceptance and participation in the political, economic, and social life of their country. Foreign Jews were often very different. Many were immigrants; between 1906 and 1939, some 150,000 to 200,000 foreign Jews, or twice the number of Jews already living in France at the turn of the century, entered the country in search of a better life. They represented just a small portion of some 2,450,000 foreigners (7% of the population) in France during the 1930s, but with their distinctive dress, language, lifestyles, and neighborhoods, many of them stood out.[3] Like most foreigners during the Depression, they were unpopular among French non-Jews and Jews alike.

After the war, thanks largely to the efforts of Serge Klarsfeld, the names of 73,853 Jews deported from France in seventy-four convoys between March 27, 1942, and August 17, 1944, were discovered and recorded.[4] Of these, only about 1,653 men and 913 women, or 3 percent, survived. To the 73,853 must be added at least 815 Jews arrested in the French departments of the Nord and the Pas-de-Calais under Belgian-based German military occupation during the war and deported from the camp of Malines in Belgium; about 400 wives and children of Jewish prisoners of war deported to Bergen-Belsen on May 2 and 3, and July 21 and 23, 1944; roughly 360 deported from Toulouse to Ravensbrück and Buchenwald on July 30 or 31, 1944; at least 63 deported from Clermont-Ferrand to Auschwitz on August 22; and at least 230 Jews deported individually or with groups of resistance fighters. Of these groups, survivors are sometimes difficult to calculate, but they included at least 219 from the prisoner-of-war families and a handful of others. Thus, Jewish deportees totaled a minimum of 75,721. Survivors numbered about 2,800, and the dead—about 72,921.[5]

There were, as will be seen, other dead. At least 1,100 Jews were executed in France during the war, and an estimated 3,000 died in camps such as Compiègne, Drancy, Gurs, Le Vernet, Noé, Récébédou, and Rivesaltes.[6] The death toll, then, reached at least 77,021. Including the 2,800 who returned, nearly 80,000 Jews had been deported or murdered in France. They represented more than 24 percent of the Jewish community as a whole.

Breaking these statistics down into their native and foreign components is more difficult. From lists of deportees (including survivors) and individuals who died in France, Serge Klarsfeld estimated that about 24,500 were French and 56,500 were foreigners. French victims in turn consisted of about 8,000 born in France to French-born parents (including 6,500 born in metropolitan France and 1,500 born in Algeria); 8,000 naturalized citizens; 8,000 children born in France to foreign Jewish parents but made French by parental declaration; and 500 unaccounted for.[7] If these admittedly approximate figures are valid, one may conclude that, of the 80,000 Jews who were deported from France or died there during the war, roughly 30 percent were French and 70 percent were foreign—percentages significantly different from the proportions of natives and foreigners in the Jewish population as a whole. Also, it seems that about 12.6 percent of all French Jews, including those naturalized at birth and later, and about 42 percent of foreign Jews were deported from France or died there during the war.

These different, if always rough, statistics for French and foreign Jews may be interpreted yet another way if the 8,000 deported children born in France to foreign Jewish parents are placed in the foreign category. They clearly *were* French, by declaration at birth, but they were almost invariably treated as foreigners. Vichy officials, who usually refrained from putting the names of French Jewish adults on arrest lists, carefully specified that most children of foreign Jews were to accompany their parents. Calculating them as *foreigners*, then, about 16,500 Jewish citizens and 64,500 Jewish foreigners were deported or died in France. Thus, about 20 percent of the victims were French and 80 percent were foreign. According to this manner of calculation, about 9 percent of all French Jews and 45 percent of foreign Jews were deported or died in France.

Before considering the manner in which deportations and rescue occurred, it may be useful to review briefly the critical dates and the general administrative structure of France during the German occupation. The German army, of course, invaded the Low Countries on May 10, 1940, definitively ending the "Phony War" that had been going on since the invasion of Poland in September 1939. By June 14, the Germans were in Paris, and some four million French men, women, and children were fleeing toward the south. French Premier Paul Reynaud resigned on June 16, after recommending that President Albert Lebrun call upon Vice-Premier Henri Philippe Pétain to form a government. Pétain's first act as premier was to inform the French people by a radio address at noon on June 17 that he was asking the Germans for a "cessation of hostilities." The resulting armistice between the French and the Germans was signed on June 22.

After the armistice, France was divided into several parts. The three departments in Alsace and Lorraine that had been German between 1871 and 1918 (Moselle, Bas-Rhin, and Haut-Rhin) were annexed to the Third Reich and administered by two Nazi Gauleiter (district leaders). The departments of the Nord and the Pas-de-Calais in northeastern France were placed under the administration of a German military governor based in Belgium. The vast area of France that remained was divided into an occupied and an unoccupied zone, separated by a demarcation line that quickly became a formidable barrier, difficult to cross legally and dangerous to cross illegally. About three-fifths of the country north of the Loire River and extending south in a narrow strip along the Atlantic coast to the Spanish frontier constituted the occupied zone, administered by a German military governor. About forty departments south of the line were unoccupied. This arrangement continued until November 11, 1942, when, after the Allied landings in North Africa, the German army forcibly occupied the entire southern zone except for eight southeastern departments or parts of departments east of the Rhône River that fell to the Italians.[8] After the Italians signed an armistice with the Allies on September 8, 1943, and attempted to withdraw from the war, those departments also came under German control.

By the terms of the armistice, the French government was to have sovereignty over the entire country while acknowledging and respecting the "rights of the occupying power." A formula as difficult to interpret then as it is today, it became the source of continual discussion, friction, and maneuvering—a process in which the Jews of France were often bargaining chips and sacrificial lambs. In effect, the policies of the Vichy regime were enforced in the unoccupied zone, while in the occupied zone they applied so long as they did not conflict with those of the Germans. The armistice imposed several other restrictions upon French sovereignty, such as a limitation on the size of the army in metropolitan France (about 125,000 officers and men), a huge payment for "occupation costs," and an obligation to deliver any refugees from the Third Reich requested by the German government. Hitler was, at this early date, most interested in political refugees, but a dangerous precedent was established.

Less than three weeks after the armistice, on July 9 and 10, the deputies and senators elected to the "Popular Front" Chamber in 1936, along with the senators, agreed by an overwhelming majority to revoke the Third Republic Constitution of 1875 and award Pétain full powers to promulgate a new one.[9] Within the next few hours, the Marshal issued three constitutional acts. The first gave him the title of chief of state, the second declared that the chief of state had a "totality of government power" and was responsible for making and executing all laws, and the third adjourned the Chamber of Deputies and the Senate indefinitely. The so-called Vichy regime, named for the spa in the unoccupied zone that served as the capital of France during the occupation, was ready for business.

Among the many pressing problems facing the new regime was the existence in France of millions of unwanted foreigners. Compounding the "problem" of some 2,450,000 immigrants already in the country before the war, well over a million war refugees poured into France when the Germans invaded the Low Countries in May 1940. Included among the million were at least 40,000 Jews. These refugees naturally had no exit or entry visas and no legal right to remain in France. In addition, most, as citizens or former citizens of the Third Reich, were either enemy or stateless aliens. They were seen as security risks and a potential source of profound economic and social disorder.

Already in the fall and winter of 1939, during the so-called Phony War, the last government of the Third Republic had arrested at least 15,000 mostly male enemy aliens, both Jews and non-Jews, and interned them in miserable camps.[10] Most internees were released before the German invasion, but in May and June 1940 the government attempted to seize *all* male immigrants from the Third Reich and all unmarried or childless married women of specific ages, Jews and non-Jews alike. At least 10,000 of the 40,000 Jewish war refugees from Belgium and the Netherlands were included among the victims. As the Germans advanced through France, most internees were moved south, to miserable camps such as Gurs, Rivesaltes, Saint Cyprien, Rieucros, Le Vernet, and Les Milles, to mention only the largest.[11] Many of the detainees were released or allowed to escape at the time of the armistice, but at the end of 1940, some 40,000 to 50,000 foreigners were still interned in the unoccupied zone. About 70 percent were Jews.[12] Included in their number were many of the 1,400 German Jewish refugees seized and forced into the unoccupied zone when the Nazis occupied Bordeaux. Also included were most of the 6,538 German Jews from Baden-Württemburg, and 1,125 from the Palatinate, expelled from the Third Reich in October 1940 and dumped into southern France.[13]

On July 17, just seven days after receiving full powers, Pétain's government issued its first antiforeign measure. Employment in the public sector was henceforth limited to individuals born of French fathers.[14] The law was applicable, as were all Vichy decrees, in both zones. Laws on August 16 and September 10 similarly regulated the practice of medicine and law, respectively.[15] On July 22, another measure authorized Minister of Justice Raphaël Alibert to establish a commission to review all grants of French citizenship awarded under the liberalized law of August 10, 1927.[16] Within the next three years, the commission reviewed, among others, the cases of 13,839 Jews, revoking the citizenship of 7,055.[17] On August 27, Alibert annulled the Daladier-Marchandeau decree of April 21, 1939, which had prohibited newspaper attacks on individuals based on race or religion. An antisemitic press, often with covert Nazi funding, soon proliferated. Subsequent laws, on September 3 and 27, gave prefects the power to intern individuals considered dangerous to the national security and all male immigrants between the ages of eighteen and fifty-five judged "superfluous in the national economy."[18]

Except for the revocation of the Daladier-Marchandeau decree, these first government measures were aimed at foreigners in general, including foreign Jews, rather than at Jews in particular. That, however, was soon to change. On September 27, a German ordinance applicable only in the occupied zone defined who was to be considered Jewish, prohibited Jews who had fled to the unoccupied zone from returning, called for a census of Jews in the occupied zone, demanded that the word

"Juif" be stamped on identity cards, and required that Jewish shopkeepers place a yellow sign in two languages in their windows reading "Enterprise juive" and "Jüdisches Geschäft"—"Jewish Business."[19] Six days later, on October 3, the Vichy government announced its first Statut des Juifs. The timing suggests that the statute had been in preparation well before the publication of the German decrees in the north. Furthermore, witnesses have testified that the legislation was spontaneous, and not a product of German pressure.[20]

The law of October 3 actually broadened the German definition of a Jew, as it applied in the occupied zone, to include anyone with two grandparents "of the Jewish race" who was also married to a Jew. In addition to the definition, the law specifically excluded Jews from public service, the officer corps of the armed forces, teaching, journalism, theater, radio, and cinema.[21] The day following the statute, a second law specifically authorized prefects to intern, assign to supervised residence, or enroll in forced labor any foreign Jews in their departments, as they saw fit.[22] Another on October 7 deprived the roughly 115,000 Jews of Algeria of the citizenship granted them by the Crémieux decree in 1870.[23]

The months that followed the first Statut des Juifs witnessed a long series of anti-Jewish regulations from both the Germans and the French. The Germans extended the list of occupations closed to Jews and issued decrees for the expropriation of Jewish property. The French responded with their own confiscatory measures. They also created, on March 29, 1941, the Commissariat général aux questions juives (CGQJ), a government bureau of Jewish affairs. With help from Xavier Vallat, the first commissioner, the Vichy regime produced a second Statut des Juifs on June 2, 1941, enlarging yet again the definition of who was Jewish, extending the list of private occupations prohibited to Jews, and requiring a census in the unoccupied zone.[24] Further measures throughout the summer imposed, among others, a *numerus clausus* of 3 percent on Jewish university students and 2 percent on Jewish lawyers and doctors allowed to practice.[25]

Also in early July 1941, Admiral François Darlan, in his capacity as minister of the interior, sent a sinister-sounding circular to all prefects; it read in part, "I have decided that no foreigner of the Israelite race will henceforth be freed from lodging or internment centers if he did not live in France before May 10, 1940. . . ."[26] Thus, most of the Jews from Baden, along with the Jewish (but only the Jewish) refugees who had fled from the German invaders in Belgium, were sentenced to remain where they were, regardless of their past histories as anti-Nazis, their ability to support themselves, or the existence of free family members able to help. Darlan, anxious to get Jewish refugees out of France, emphasized that repatriation or other forms of emigration were to be encouraged, but not freedom within France. Jewish foreigners had been treated differently from other immigrants for several months, but Darlan's circular made the policy official and obligatory. It was to have devastating results in the summer of 1942, when foreign Jews of recent dates of arrival in France were needed to fill deportation trains.

During the first eleven months after the June 1940 armistice, nearly all Jews in both zones of France suffered from the racial laws and several thousand foreigners, mostly Jews, lingered in internment camps in the unoccupied zone. Arrests, however, increased only slightly. Like non-Jews in both zones, Jews could be arrested for political or criminal offenses; unlike others, they could also be seized for minor infractions of the racial laws. They were, however, not yet picked up simply for being Jews. That relative security came to an abrupt end in the spring of 1941. Between May 9 and 14 in Paris, 6,494 Polish, Austrian, and Czech male Jewish immigrants, mostly workers, received a summons from the Prefecture of Police ordering them to report to one of five specified centers. About 3,747 obeyed and were sent to the makeshift internment camps of Pithiviers and Beaune-la-Rolande in the Loiret.[27]

Disaster struck again on August 20, when French police blocked all streets and closed all métro entrances in the eleventh arrondissement in Paris and proceeded to arrest as many male Jews between the ages of eighteen and fifty as they could find, except Americans. About 2,894 men, mostly foreign Jewish workers, were arrested that day, and about 1,000 more, including 200 French Jewish intellectuals, were detained elsewhere in Paris in the days immediately following.[28] By August 25, 4,230 had been sent to Drancy, a transit camp in an unfinished apartment complex on the outskirts of Paris.

A third large raid in Paris followed on December 12. This time the perpetrators were German police, and the victims were 743 carefully selected French-Jewish middle-class professional men.[29] Hoping to assemble 1,000 Jewish hostages in a reprisal action, the Germans also arrested fifty-four foreign Jews caught by chance in the Place d'Étoile, and removed 300 others from Drancy. They sent the unfortunate victims to Compiègne (Oise), about eighty kilometers northeast of Paris. Seventy-three were released on December 20 for health reasons. The others remained in flimsy freezing barracks, without heat, water, or electricity, throughout the winter. On March 19, 178 men over the age of fifty-five left Compiègne for Drancy. Of those remaining, about eighty who were married to non-Jews stayed on, while 558 joined another 554 from Drancy to make up the first French deportation convoy to Auschwitz. The 1,112 men left France on March 27, 1942.[30] Since systematic mass gassings had not yet begun at Auschwitz, all were admitted. One thousand and eight died from exhaustion, starvation, and abuse within five months. An estimated total of twenty-three men survived.[31]

Two months after the first Jewish deportation train, a German ordinance on May 29 imposed the wearing of the yellow Star of David upon all Jews over the age of six in the occupied zone. Then on June 5, 22, 25, 28, and July 17, a terrifying succession of five trains carried most of the victims of the May, August, and December 1941 roundups, and some other Jews, to their deaths in the East.[32] Drancy, Pithiviers, and Beaune-la-Rolande were being emptied, in preparation for new arrivals.

At four in the morning on Thursday, July 16, 1942, about 4,500 carefully organized French policemen, nearly always in teams of at least two, began knocking on doors throughout Paris and the surrounding suburbs. Their targets were 27,388 foreign Jews of specific ages, who were either stateless or from the Third Reich, Poland, or the Soviet Union. Included also were their children under sixteen, even if French born.[33] By the end of the second day of the huge roundup, 12,884 Jews had been detained. These included 3,031 men, 5,802 women, and 4,051 children.[34] The victims suffered awful deprivation in internment until, during the next month and a half, some sixteen deportation trains carried them to Auschwitz. The most appalling and heart-breaking cases involved some 3,500 children under fourteen who were forcibly separated from their parents and deported later, alone. None of them returned.[35]

The July 16 roundup in Paris was the result of a long series of negotiations between German and Vichy officials and was based on the understanding that French Jews would not be included. During those same talks, Premier Pierre Laval and National Police Chief René Bousquet also agreed to deliver 10,000 foreign Jews from the unoccupied zone to the Germans in the occupied zone.[36] Feverish preparations began. Bousquet instructed his regional prefects on August 5 to round up all Jews from specific countries who had entered France after January 1, 1936, whether or not they had been naturalized. Unaccompanied children under eighteen were not to be included, and parents were to be given the option of leaving behind their own children under that age.[37]

The first to go, of course, were 4,620 Jews with the applicable national origins and dates of arrival in France who had been languishing in internment camps, forced residence, or work camps in the unoccupied zone since 1940. Then on August 26, the Vichy government launched a massive coordinated raid throughout the unoccupied zone in an effort to seize other foreign Jews eligible for expulsion.[38] About 6,700 people were arrested, and 5,293 were retained; another 592 were arrested in the next few days.[39] Between August 28 and September 5, 5,259 were delivered to the Germans at Drancy, on seven trains that were as crowded, filthy, and terrifying as any that the Germans themselves organized. By the end of October, the number rose to 6,392, in twelve trains.[40] Most victims waited only briefly at Drancy, before other but very similar trains carried them east to Auschwitz.[41]

While foreign Jews were being assembled, processed, and expelled from the unoccupied zone in August, conditions in northern France remained quiet. Roundups resumed in September, however, again conducted by French police carrying carefully prepared lists of individuals from specific Jewish groups. On September 14 in Paris, the targets were Dutch, Yugoslavian, Latvian, Lithuanian, Estonian, and Bulgarian Jews. More than 200 were caught, from a list of 708.[42] On September 24, also in Paris, the victims were 1,594 Romanians; on September 29, they were Belgians; and on November 5, they were 1,060 Greeks, from a list of 1,416.[43] Similar French-conducted raids against foreign Jews occurred in other French cities. By the end of the year, 42,000 mostly foreign Jews had been deported to Auschwitz in forty-three convoys.[44] Meanwhile, French Jews were picked up individually, for real or alleged political offenses or minor infractions of racial laws or other regulations. Most, however, remained in their homes and moved about the streets quite openly, wearing their stars in the occupied zone but free of any Jewish identification in the south until December 1942.

The year 1943 began with two general indiscriminate roundups. In Rouen between January 13 and 16, French police seized 222 Jews, of whom 170 were French.[45] Then in Marseille between January 22 and 27, German and French police working together captured, among others, 800 Jews, of whom a majority were French. All 800 were ultimately deported to Auschwitz, and none returned.[46] These were special "reprisal" raids, however. The threat to all Jews regardless of nationality that the raids seemed to represent had not yet become the rule.

More typical were two roundups conducted by French police in February. In

Paris on February 10 and 11, French police initiated a raid quite apart from any Nazi order, to arrest enough foreign Jews to replace citizens reportedly about to be deported to Auschwitz from Drancy. The police combed Jewish hospitals, old age homes, children's centers, and orphanages, seizing 1,549 young and old foreigners hitherto exempt from arrest because of their ages.[47] Of the raid and the effort to protect French Jews, SS Colonel Helmut Knochen, chief of the Reich Central Security Office (RSHA) in France, cynically reported, "Obviously both categories of Jews will be deported in this case."[48] That is, of course, exactly what happened.[49] Then on February 20, French police scoured the southern zone in response to a Nazi demand for 2,000 male Jews to deport in reprisal for the killing by partisans of two German officers in Paris. They found the requisite number of foreigners, many of whom had been exempt from expulsion to the north the preceding August, and eased the threat to citizens.[50]

Arrests of Jews continued in a piecemeal fashion throughout the country during the spring and summer of 1943. By now, many Jews had moved from their homes to unregistered addresses. German and French negotiators pressed the Italians, unsuccessfully, for the release of some 20,000 to 30,000 foreign Jews in the Italian zone, and time passed. Germans also demanded that the French denaturalize about 16,000 Jews who had received citizenship after 1927 as a result of a law liberalized in that year. Laval and Pétain agreed, then hesitated, then respectfully declined. Both measures would have made thousands of Jews eligible for arrest and deportation, and eased the pressure on French-born adult Jews.[51]

On September 8, 1943, just as Laval was refusing to abandon recently naturalized Jewish citizens, the Italian armistice with the Allies was announced and the German army occupied the peninsula. The Italian army withdrew from southern France, and the Germans moved in. About 50,000 Jews had sought refuge in the Italian zone, an area of some 15,000 to 20,000 Jewish residents before the war. SS Captain Aloïs Brunner and a specially trained unit of about fifteen German SS police, refusing to wait for the slow-moving French authorities and unwilling to distinguish between Jewish citizens and foreigners, launched their roundup in Nice, unassisted.[52] The result was terrifying, brutal, and relatively ineffective. Without lists, searching for victims who wore no stars and had no identifying stamps on their documents, and with little native cooperation, the Nazis had no way to determine who was Jewish. They seized and searched all suspects, in a manner much more common in Eastern and Central Europe than in France.[53] About 1,800 French and foreign Jews in Nice and the surrounding area, from the local Jewish population of 25,000 to 30,000, were caught and deported. Most did not return.[54] But the others survived, hidden by French non-Jews offended by the undisguised and solely German brutality.

From September 1943 until the end of the war, Nazi Jew-hunting units conducted raids throughout the country, making no distinction between citizens and foreigners. Until the end of 1943, French police did not offer them much help, although certain other units, particularly the Milice, cooperated fully. At the end of December, however, on German insistence, Chief of the Milice Joseph Darnand replaced René Bousquet as national police director. Under Darnand's influence, Pierre Laval permitted French police to participate in Jewish manhunts that were not reprisal actions and made no distinctions between citizens and foreigners. Although

Jews in cities that had already experienced severe raids had hidden by 1944, those in more peaceful or remote areas were less suspicious. In Laon, Saint Quentin, Amiens, Reims, Bordeaux, Poitiers, Troyes, Dijon, and countless smaller cities and towns, the results were devastating. More Jews were arrested in France during the first four months of 1944 than in any comparable period in 1943, including the peak months of the Nice roundup. Unrestricted French cooperation proved decisive.

The manner in which about 80,000 Jews were either deported or killed in France is clear. As in Belgium and the Netherlands, the German occupying forces set up a Jewish Office (Judenreferat) in Paris, as a direct counterpart of Adolf Eichmann's Section IV-B-4 in Berlin. Under the direction of SS Captain Theodor Dannecker until July 1942, and of SS First Lieutenant Heinz Röthke subsequently, specialized Nazi Jew-hunters pressed the Vichy government hard and consistently for deportations. Happy to get rid of unwanted foreigners, anxious to retain control over French police in both zones, and hoping to gain concessions in other fields, Vichy officials co-operated eagerly in measures against foreign Jews, arresting thousands. Discreetly and hypocritically, they ignored mostly German-conducted arrests and deportations of smaller but not insignificant numbers of French Jews.

Much less discreetly, Vichy officials also carried out against all Jews in France measures that seemed comparatively harmless at the time—for example, the several censuses, the constant updating of addresses, and the enforcement of the wearing of the star and the "Juif" stamp on documents. These policies ultimately marked all victims, decisively and irrevocably. Then after a period of real hesitation in the second half of 1943, especially on the issue of Jewish denaturalizations, Pétain and Laval yielded to the demands of the most fanatic French fascists and abandoned foreign and French Jews altogether. While French police may have been increasingly uneasy at the visible effect of such policies on Jewish women and children, they nevertheless continued to carry out orders.

Above all, Vichy officials, with their articulation of antisemitic rhetoric and their enforcement of the racial laws, set a tone throughout the country. Jews were defined as "fair game" for informers and bureaucrats alike. Unlike the case in Denmark and to a lesser extent in Belgium and the Netherlands, French men and women until late August 1942 received no message from their indigenous elites encouraging sympathy for Jews. No leaders suggested that they think for themselves and question prevailing policies.

Much more difficult to understand are the means by which about 76 percent of the Jews in France managed to survive under such pressures. Some of the explanation lies with the physical characteristics of the country. Unlike Belgium and the Nether-lands, France is a large country with extensive tracts of remote, sparsely populated, often mountainous terrain favorable to hiding. Especially after the exodus from the north in May and June 1940, Jews in France found themselves dispersed throughout this vast territory. In addition, France borders Switzerland and Spain, countries that were neutral during the Second World War and received, sometimes reluctantly, at least 50,000 Jewish fugitives from France alone.[55]

Another factor in Jewish survival involves the nature of the German presence and the necessarily gradual escalation of the persecution. In comparison to Belgium and the Netherlands, far fewer German personnel were allocated to France after the armistice in relation to the size and population of the country.[56] German RSHA security agents under the direction of Helmut Knochen, concerned above all with minimizing political dissent and maintaining order, were thus dependent upon help from the French police. To retain that help, and to continue to free German security agents for service in less compliant countries, Knochen had to refrain from antagonizing the French population unnecessarily. Insofar as the Vichy government and the French people cared about the roughly 59 percent of Jews who were French, German security police felt obliged to respect their concern, at least in part and especially in Paris, where roundups had the largest potential audience. The far fewer specialized Jew-hunting police under Dannecker and Röthke did not share Knochen's priorities, but they were formally under Knochen's control. Furthermore, they too needed large-scale French police support for major actions. The comparative failure of their independent action in the Nice roundup in September 1943 demonstrates most clearly their inability to function efficiently without French help.

Knochen's awareness of the sensitivities of French police and his fundamental conflict of interest with Röthke were demonstrated most vividly on September 21, 1942. Röthke informed his superiors of his elaborate plan for a huge roundup the next day in Paris; 5,129 specific, prominent French Jews and their families were targeted. The action was to be followed within a few hours by a thorough police search of six arrondissements and the indiscriminate arrest of all individuals wearing the Star of David, plus their families. The situation, in other words, was to resemble that later regarded as the standard Holocaust condition: any and all Jews could be seized on sight. Three thousand French police were to be mobilized for the raid that very evening, bypassing Vichy police chief René Bousquet and his representative in the occupied zone, Jean Leguay.

Helmut Knochen immediately vetoed the raid. Acting independently, a furious Röthke and two French assistants arrested seventy-six Jews in two apartment buildings on the night originally scheduled for the great roundup. Fifty-eight of the seventy-six were French. But the vast majority of the 5,129 potential victims were spared, at least for a time.[57] In fact, an "open season" on all Jews in Paris never occurred, even in 1944 when Vichy officials had abandoned French Jews elsewhere in the country. A full 30,000 Parisian Jews, mostly citizens, continued to live in the homes where they were registered and to appear occasionally on the streets, wearing the Star of David, until just before liberation.[58] They were the beneficiaries of French police reluctance to arrest French Jews, of Parisian sensitivity to the sight of Germans making such arrests, and of Knochen's dependency upon the French police in general.

The commitment of the Vichy government to protect Jewish citizens must not be overstated or exaggerated here. It was lukewarm at best, and frequently hypocritical. Vichy officials said nothing when Nazi occupiers ordered the arrests of Parisian Jewish professional men in August and December 1941. They did not protest when those same prominent citizens were deported "to the East" in the spring and summer of 1942.[59] Throughout the occupation, thousands of other Jewish citizens were arrested individually, often by French police, for specific real or alleged offenses, and mixed among foreign Jews on the deportation trains. Vichy leaders said nothing. French police served as guards at Drancy and accompanied the trains as far as the

German frontier. Meanwhile, in July 1942 in Paris, Laval and Bousquet consented to, and sometimes even urged, the arrests of Jewish children born to foreigners in France and naturalized at birth. Their citizenship was conveniently overlooked. Then in August 1942 they allowed the expulsion from the unoccupied to the occupied zone of Jews who had entered France since 1936, regardless of their citizenship status. In Rouen and Marseille in January 1943, and in smaller numbers in other French cities except Paris, French Jews were also arrested specifically for deportation, and the government did little. And finally in 1944, Laval abandoned any semblance of state protection of French Jews.

Despite the exceptions, however, protection was not a complete fiction until 1944. French police participation in the huge July 1942 roundup in Paris was based on the explicit understanding that French Jews (with the awful exception of children of foreigners) would not be included. The expulsion by French police in August 1942 of Jews from the unoccupied to the occupied zone involved recent immigrants, *most* of whom were not naturalized. Pétain and Laval's refusal, despite intense German pressure during the summer and early autumn of 1943, to denaturalize Jews who had become citizens since 1927 confirmed the principle of government protection of its citizens. Local French police officials *usually* balked at German orders to round up Jewish citizens, requesting written confirmation of such orders from their Vichy superiors. Such confirmation rarely came before 1944. In Paris itself, as seen, it never came.

The policies and preferences of French officials, then, made a great difference. Without the limited protection they received, many more French Jews would have been deported. Had that protection been extended to foreigners, however, far fewer of them would have died.

Because Knochen needed the French police, a peculiar pattern of persecution emerged by which Jews of specific nationalities became eligible for arrest at different times. Did this gradual enlargement of eligible categories—from Jews from the Third Reich, Poland, and the Soviet Union, to Belgians, Dutch, Romanians, Greeks, Bulgarians, and others—itself affect survival rates? It is difficult to say, for it may have worked both ways. For those caught in any first attack on a national group, of course, it made no difference, but many would have been seized at the beginning of any unexpected indiscriminate roundup also. For those Dutch or Greek or Romanian Jews lucky enough to escape the first attack on their category in Paris, however, the warning was clear—their specific group was endangered, they were undoubtedly on a specific list, they would be next, and it was essential to hide. On the other hand, Jews with nationalities not yet endangered may have been encouraged to postpone hiding a little longer, fatally. Jews in cities not yet affected by roundups seem also to have sometimes remained convinced that "it cannot happen here," until in fact it did.

While the gradual enlargement of eligibility may simply have obscured the danger, however, the slowness of the whole process was surely a factor in overall survival. Every day that passed made a difference. Jews and non-Jews alike had time to learn about the deportation of women, children, and old people incapable of labor and to ponder its meaning. Jews had time to make plans and secure false papers. Non-Jews could reflect and ask themselves whether the official antisemitic and antiforeign rhetoric that they perhaps applauded in the abstract justified the dreadful suffering of human beings that they heard about and sometimes even observed personally. Churchmen of goodwill had time to exercise moral leadership, speaking out against deportation and encouraging alternative attitudes and behavior.[60] And perhaps most important of all, the Allies had time to win victories and convince the French that the Germans were not invincible, the Vichy regime might not last forever, and collaboration might not be the most opportune route to follow.

Time was secured in other ways as well. The existence of an Italian occupation zone in southeastern France between November 1942 and September 1943 secured time for the 50,000 Jews who found shelter there. The prolonged negotiations between German and Vichy officials during the summer of 1943 concerning the denaturalization of Jewish immigrant-citizens bought time that the Nazis might have used to begin roundups on their own. The menace of deportation returned in the Italian zone when the Italians withdrew, and throughout the southern zone when the Nazis, failing to secure denaturalizations, did indeed begin indiscriminate actions on their own. Many Jews were caught unprepared, but each day that had passed without arrests meant fewer arrests overall.

Technical structural factors influenced survival rates, but so too did the nature of the Jewish and non-Jewish populations themselves. Looking first at the Jewish community, the preponderance of French Jews was obviously crucial. French Jews not only benefited from some government protection, but they found it easier to hide when they chose. Most were indistinguishable from non-Jews in language, education, culture, and dress. They could "pass" as non-Jews with less risk to themselves and their protectors. They also had more friends, contacts, and resources.

Among foreign Jews, also, certain factors operated to facilitate survival. Many had been in the country since the 1920s and were partially integrated. These immigrants knew some French, although accents always made individuals targets of suspicion and more difficult to hide. Most had non-Jewish acquaintances, either from their workplaces, among their customers or clients, or among the parents of schoolmates of their children. They were not totally different, isolated, and impoverished, as recent war refugees were.[61] The resultant possibility of finding helpers in hiding gave many immigrant Jews the will and the courage to try.

The size and rootedness of the overall Jewish community also contributed to the emergence of many Jewish social welfare organizations before the war. During the occupation, many of these groups continued to feed and care for those in need, and some engaged in rescue activities. The overall results were mixed. Certainly the continued operation of Jewish welfare agencies, along with synagogues, until well into 1944 provided an illusion of normality and a false sense of security, and discouraged the most reluctant or the least mobile from hiding. Furthermore, tragic mistakes were made: hospitals, children's homes, and orphanages continued to function when they should have dispersed their clients, and they thus became targets of vicious raids.[62]

On balance, however, the contribution of Jewish organizations was most certainly favorable. Along with the tragedies, there were outstanding and brilliant successes. Jewish rescue networks, most of them affiliated with social service organizations such as Oeuvre de secours aux enfants (OSE), Éclaireurs israélites de France (EIF), and Mouvement de la jeunesse sioniste (MJS), placed several tens of thousands of Jews, most of them children, with non-Jewish families and institutions and continued to supply them throughout the occupation. Many young Jewish rescuers paid for their resistance with their lives, but few of the children were caught.[63]

Finally, and perhaps most important, Jewish survival in France depended upon attitudes within the non-Jewish community. The causal relationship functioned on several levels. First, the limited protection offered by the Vichy regime to French Jews was related not only to Laval's definition of the rights of citizens, his wish to maintain a semblance of autonomy, and his growing awareness both of the fate of Jews in deportation and of the probable victors in the war. It was connected also to Laval's understanding of what the French people would tolerate. And while the French had multiple problems of their own and were only secondarily concerned about Jews, they did not like the sight of French police arresting women, children, and French citizens generally. They liked even less the sight of German police doing the same. Especially after the expulsions of foreign Jews from the unoccupied zone in August 1942 but also after Brunner's indiscriminate roundups in Nice in September 1943, French prefect reports to the minister of the interior refer often to the public's unease.[64] Such reports surely influenced Laval's decisions, particularly in the summer of 1943 when he was considering the denaturalization of recently naturalized Jewish immigrants.

Second, of course, Jewish rescuers of their coreligionists depended upon the active assistance of some non-Jews in order to place young children. They also needed, however, at least the passive indifference of the majority in order to move about at all. Few village residents could have been unaware of young "teachers" passing through town with different groups of children each week, or of young women regularly visiting remote regions, carrying baskets of foodstuffs—for their relatives? Excuses were given, but most people were not fooled. Anyone with malice could have investigated and discovered the truth. A few did, but most did not.

Active child-rescuers and their roughly 20,000 to 30,000 clients were not the only ones who depended upon the passive benevolence of the non-Jewish population, however. The 50,000 Jews who escaped into Spain and Switzerland succeeded in part because French men and women who saw them pass did not ask too many questions. The 30,000 Jews who lived openly in Paris wearing their stars succeeded in part because few protested their presence to the police. And the dozens of thousands who survived simply by leaving their homes quietly, unassisted, but illegally, and moving to new unreported residences were equally dependent upon the reactions of their countrymen. They needed to find places to live and explanations for moving. They had to obtain new false documents for residency permits, identification cards, and ration coupons. To avoid suspicion, they had to place their children in school. For all of this, they depended upon neighbors who would not ask too many questions, or, if they found answers, would remain silent. In most cases, they found what they needed to survive.

Benevolent indifference is a condition hardly deserving of praise. Praise, however, is not intended here, for we seek only explanations and understanding. Indifference also, it might be argued, was offered by a French populace that did not necessarily *know* that individual newcomers were Jewish. That, of course, was often the case, but equally often it was not.[65] As historian Lucien Steinberg wrote in 1977, after concluding his own research:

> I would like to emphasize that the majority of the Jews saved in France do not owe their rescue to Jewish organizations. The various Jewish bodies which worked with such great dedication managed to save only a few tens of thousands, while *the others were saved mostly thanks to the assistance of the French population*. In many cases, groups of Jews lived in small villages. Every one of the Jews was convinced that no one in that area knew their true identity: after the war it turned out that everyone knew that they were Jews.[66]

Clearly, the overall Jewish survival rate of 76 percent in France masks an enormous diversity of suffering and a much higher deportation statistic among foreign Jews. Clearly also, the rate must be attributed to a complex interaction of factors. These conclusions point to the difficulties involved in interpreting Holocaust statistics and, particularly, to the need for caution in making comparisons between countries.

Specifically in France, a "high" survival rate does not "prove" the presence of a benevolent non-Jewish population, nor does it suggest the opposite. Nor can we conclude from the statistic alone that French non-Jews were any more or less helpful to the Jews in their midst than were their counterparts in Belgium, the Netherlands, or Italy. We must instead consider in each case a whole set of variables, including the size and topography of each country, the extent of prewar antisemitism, the length and nature of the German presence and control during the war, the degree of Nazi involvement in Jewish deportations, characteristics and responses of the Jewish communities, and the responses of indigenous non-Jewish elites and common citizens. Comparisons between countries may help us to formulate the proper questions. They will not necessarily lead us to the right answers.

NOTES

1. This statistic is documented and examined in greater detail below.

2. See, for example, Serge Klarsfeld, *Vichy-Auschwitz: Le rôle de Vichy dans la solution finale de la question juive en France: 1943–1944* (Paris: Fayard, 1985), pp. 178–80.

3. Jean-Charles Bonnet, *Les Pouvoirs publics français et l'immigration dans l'entre-deux-guerres* (Lyon: Centres d'histoire économique et social de la région lyonnaise, 1976), p. 193. According to Georges Mauco, *Les Étrangers en France et le problème du racisme* (Paris: La Pensée Universelle, 1977), p. 26, the largest groups of foreigners in 1935 were the 850,000 Italians followed by the Spaniards, with 650,000.

4. These names are recorded in Serge Klarsfeld, *Memorial to the Jews Deported from France 1942–1944* (New York: Beate Klarsfeld Foundation, 1983).

5. Ibid., p. xxvii.

6. Ibid., pp. 612–40.

7. Klarsfeld, *Vichy-Auschwitz: 1943–1944*, pp. 180–81.

8. Since June 1940, the Italians, who had declared war on France in May, had held a smaller part of the country in the southeast, including some of the Vallée de la Tarentaise and the city of Menton.

9. Unable to vote were some seventy Communists elected in 1936 but expelled from the

Chamber of Deputies in January 1940, as well as twenty-nine deputies and one senator who had sailed for North Africa on the *Massilia* on June 21, in the hope of continuing the war from there.

10. Michael R. Marrus and Robert O. Paxton, *Vichy France and the Jews* (New York: Basic Books, 1981), p. 65; and Richard I. Cohen, *The Burden of Conscience: French Jewish Leadership during the Holocaust* (Bloomington: Indiana University Press, 1987), p. 16.

11. For descriptions of the camps by internees, see especially Arthur Koestler, *Scum of the Earth* (New York: Macmillan, 1941), and Bruno Frei, *Die Männer von Vernet: Ein Tatsachenbericht* (Berlin: Deutscher Militärverlag, 1961) on Le Vernet; Lion Feuchtwanger, *The Devil in France: My Encounter with Him in the Summer of 1940*, trans. from German by Elisabeth Abbott (New York: Viking, 1941), and Alfred Kantorowicz, *Exil in Frankreich: Merkwürdigkeiten und Denkwürdigkeiten* (Bremen: Schunemann Universitatsverlag, 1971) on Les Milles; and Lisa Fittko, *Escape through the Pyrenees*, trans. from German by David Koblick (Evanston, IL: Northwestern University Press, 1991), and Hanna Schramm and Barbara Vormeier, *Vivre à Gurs: Un camp de concentration français 1940–1941*, trans. from German by Irène Petit (Paris: François Maspero, 1979) on Gurs. Excellent later studies of the camps include André Fontaine, *Le Camp d'étrangers des Milles, 1939–1943 (Aix-en-Provence)* (Aix-en-Provence: Edisud, 1989); *Les Camps en Provence: Exil, internement, déportation, 1933–1942* (Aix-en-Provence: Alinéa et LLCG, 1984); Claude Laharie, *Le Camp de Gurs 1939–1945: Un aspect méconnu de l'histoire du Béarn* (Biarritz: Société Atlantique d'Impression, 1985); and Gilbert Badia, *Les Barbelés de l'exil: Études sur l'émigration allemande et autrichienne, 1938–1940* (Grenoble: Presses Universitaires de Grenoble, 1979).

12. Anne Grynberg, *Les Camps de la honte: Les internés juifs des camps français, 1939–1944* (Paris: La Découverte, 1991), p. 12.

13. For their story, see Laharie, *Camp de Gurs*.

14. *Journal officiel de la république française: Lois et décrets* (hereafter JO) (July 18, 1940), p. 4,537.

15. JO (August 19 and September 11, 1940), pp. 4,735–36 and 4,958.

16. JO (July 23, 1940), p. 4,587.

17. Report of Maurice Gabolde, Keeper of the Seals, to Fernand de Brinon, Vichy representative to the German occupying forces in Paris, recorded by de Brinon, September 8, 1943, Centre de documentation juive contemporaine (CDJC), XXVII–47.

18. JO (September 4 and October 1, 1940), pp. 4,490 and 5,198.

19. The German ordinance defined as Jewish anyone adhering or once adhering to the Jewish religion, or anyone with more than two Jewish grandparents, as also determined by religious affiliation. The German-decreed census was conducted in the occupied zone between October 3 and 19. In the Paris region, 149,734 Jews of all ages, including 85,664 citizens and 64,070 foreigners, officially registered their names, addresses, professions, and places of birth, and received the requisite document stamp. An estimated 10 percent ignored the census. Prefect of Police to Militärbefehlshaber in Frankreich (MBF) (German Military Administration), October 26, 1940, CDJC, LXXIXa-10. About 20,000 Jews lived in the rest of the occupied zone in 1940.

20. See especially the testimony of Henri du Moulin de Labarthète, Pétain's private secretary in 1940, in his *Le Temps des illusions: Souvenirs (Juillet 1940–Avril 1942)* (Geneva: Les Éditions du Cheval Aile, 1946), p. 280.

21. JO (October 18, 1940), p. 5,323. The law provided that exemptions from some of its provisions might be granted, on special application, to Jewish war veterans and individuals of outstanding merit. Few were in fact granted.

22. JO (October 18, 1940), p. 5,324.

23. For the number of Algerian Jews affected, see Joëlle Allouche-Benayoun and Doris Bensimon, *Juifs d'Algérie hier et aujourd'hui: Mémoires et identités* (Toulouse: Édouard Privat, 1989), p. 44.

24. JO (June 14, 1941), pp. 2,475–76. The definition of who was Jewish was expanded to include anyone with two Jewish grandparents who could not produce a baptismal certificate dated before June 25, 1940. About 140,000 Jews registered in the census in the unoccupied

zone; the "Juif" stamp, however, was not required until December 1942, after the Germans had occupied the zone. The census statistic is from CGQJ to Controleur général d'armée, December 2, 1941, CDJC, CXCIII-86. Lucien Lazare, *La Résistance juive en France* (Paris: Stock, 1987), p. 49, estimates that about 180,000 Jews were actually present in the unoccupied zone at the time of the census.

25. *JO* (June 24, July 17, and September 6, 1941), pp. 2,628, 3,000–3,001 and 3,787. Philippe Bourdrel, *Histoire des Juifs de France* (Paris: Albin Michel, 1974), pp. 373–74, estimates that in Paris alone, 250 lawyers and 726 doctors lost the right to practice.

26. Admiral François Darlan, circular to the prefects, July 1941 (no day on document), CDJC, CCXIII-125. Darlan was also vice-premier at this time; Pétain was officially both head of state and head of government.

27. For the number of men who received a summons and the number who responded, see a report from the Paris Prefecture of Police, May 14, 1941, reprinted in full in Serge Klarsfeld, *Vichy-Auschwitz: Le rôle de Vichy dans la solution finale de la question juive en France: 1942* (Paris: Fayard, 1983), p. 15. For a study of the roundup and the fate of the victims, see David Diamant, *Le Billet vert: La vie et la résistance à Pithiviers et Beune-la-Rolande, camps pour Juifs, camps pour chrétiens, camps pour patriotes* (Paris: Renouveau, 1977). Diamant received a summons, but did not report.

28. Prefect of Police to Prefect Delegate of the French Ministry of the Interior to the Occupied Zone Ingrand, Paris, August 21, 1941, reprinted in full in Klarsfeld, *Vichy-Auschwitz: 1942*, pp. 25–26. German military authorities had ordered the French police to conduct the raid, apparently in reprisal for Communist agitation in France following the German invasion of the Soviet Union.

29. For subsequent accounts of the roundup by survivors, see Roger Gompel, *Pour que tu n'oublies pas . . .* (Paris: Mme. S. de Lalène Laprade [private printing], 1980); Jean-Jacques Bernard, "Le Camp de la mort lente: Choses vécues," *Les oeuvres libres*, 227 (1944): 87–127; and Georges Wellers, *L'Étoile jaune à l'heure de Vichy: De Drancy à Auschwitz* (Paris: Fayard, 1973).

30. Georges Wellers, married to a non-Jew, remained at Compiègne and then Drancy until he was deported to Auschwitz late in the war. He witnessed the departure of the first convoy and wrote of it in his *L'Étoile jaune*, p. 118.

31. Klarsfeld, *Memorial*, pp. 1–9.

32. Ibid., pp. 1–56.

33. Exempt within those categories were women about to give birth or with children under two; wives of prisoners of war; Jews with proof that they were married to non-Jews, plus widows and widowers of non-Jews; Jews married to someone of a nondeportable nationality; Jews with special cards from the Union générale des Israélites de France (UGIF), the German-imposed Jewish welfare organization; and the children under age sixteen of the exemptees. See Paris Prefecture of Police, "Consignes pour les équipes chargées des arrestations," July 12, 1942, and "Secret circulaire no. 173–42," July 13, 1942, both reprinted in full in Klarsfeld, *Vichy-Auschwitz: 1942*, pp. 248–56.

34. Paris Prefecture of Police report, July 17, 1942, cited in Klarsfeld, *Vichy-Auschwitz: 1942*, p. 262.

35. Witnesses to the separations of parents and children or to the deportations of the children include Annette Muller Bessmann, "Manuscrit-témoignage," (unpublished document): CDJC, later published in part as Annette Muller, *La Petite fille du Vel d'Hiv: Récit* (Paris: Denoël, 1991); Annette Monod Leiris, quoted at length in Claude Lévy and Paul Tillard, *Betrayal at the Vel d'Hiv*, trans. Inéa Bushnaq (original, 1967; translation, New York: Hill and Wang, 1969), pp. 158–60; Georges Wellers, *L'Étoile jaune*; and Odette Daltroff-Baticle, quoted at length in Klarsfeld, *Memorial*, pp. 166–69. I am grateful to Mrs. Bessmann and Mrs. Leiris for the interviews they granted me in Paris, November 13, 1987, and July 15, 1991, respectively. The convoys are described in Klarsfeld, *Memorial*, pp. 172–235.

36. See especially Major Herbert Hagen, résumé of July 2 meeting, July 4, 1942, CDJC, XXVI-40 (11 pp.), p. 8. SS Major Hagen was chief assistant to SS Brigadier General Karl Oberg, the overall SS and military police commander in France. Laval had been dismissed as vice-

premier in December 1940 and replaced briefly by Pierre-Étienne Flandin and then by Darlan. In April 1942, he returned as full head of government.

37. The countries or areas of origin included Germany, Austria, Czechoslovakia, Poland, Estonia, Lithuania, Latvia, Danzig, the Saar, and the Soviet Union. Specifically excluded within that category were Jews over age sixty; unaccompanied children under eighteen; parents with a child under five; pregnant women; people incapable of being moved; veterans (and their families) of combat or of at least three months' military service with the French army or former allied armies; men or women with French spouses or children, or with spouses from countries other than those eligible for delivery; and adults with jobs in the national economic interest or with a record of special service to France. Bousquet's dispatch is cited in full in Klarsfeld, *Vichy-Auschwitz: 1942*, pp. 318–19.

38. Those eligible were from the same national groups as those expelled earlier in the month, but exemption categories were restricted. The cut-off date for arrival in France for male bachelors between the ages of eighteen and forty was pushed back to January 1, 1933, unless they had served in the military or rendered special services to the country. The age limit for young children and their parents who were to be exempt was cut from five to two, and the option granted to parents to leave their children behind in France was suppressed. See the secret telegram from Bousquet to the regional prefects, August 18, 1942, reprinted in full in Klarsfeld, *Vichy-Auschwitz: 1942*, p. 339.

39. Ministry of Interior report, September 1, 1942, reprinted in full in Klarsfeld, *Vichy-Auschwitz: 1942*, p. 393.

40. Ibid., pp. 158–61.

41. I trace the connection between those expelled from the unoccupied zone and those deported by the Nazis from Drancy to Auschwitz in Susan S. Zuccotti, *The Holocaust, the French and the Jews* (New York: Basic Books, 1993), pp. 118–37.

42. Paris police report, September 12, 1942, reprinted in full in Klarsfeld, *Vichy-Auschwitz: 1942*, pp. 429–30.

43. See especially Heinz Röthke reports, "Festnahme rumänischer Juden," September 24, 1942, CDJC, XXVI-65, and "Festnahme von Juden griechischer Staatsangehörigkeit am 5.11.1942 früh," November 5, 1942, CDJC, XXV-51a. SS First Lieutenant Röthke was chief of the Gestapo's Jewish Office (Judenreferat) in France.

44. Klarsfeld, *Memorial*, pp. xxiii-xxvi.

45. Claude-Paul Couture, *La Déportation raciale en Seine-Maritime de 1940 à 1944* (Rouen: CRDP, 1981), p. 18.

46. Klarsfeld, *Vichy-Auschwitz: 1943–1944*, p. 21; and idem, *Memorial*, pp. 410–25.

47. Paris Prefect of Police report, February 13, 1943, reprinted in full in Klarsfeld, *Vichy-Auschwitz: 1943–1944*, p. 221.

48. Knochen to SS Lieutenant General Heinrich Müller (Gestapo chief in Berlin), "Endlösung der Judenfrage in Frankreich," February 12, 1943, CDJC, XXVI-71 (5 pp.), p. 3.

49. Klarsfeld, *Memorial*, pp. 360–83.

50. SS Lieutenant Colonel Kurt Lischka, aide to Helmut Knochen, report, "Endlösung der Judenfrage in Frankreich: hier: Stellung der Italiener zur Judenfrage," February 24, 1943, CDJC, XXVa-277; and Klarsfeld, *Vichy-Auschwitz: 1943–1944*, pp. 34–35.

51. For details, see Zuccotti, *Holocaust*, pp. 175–80.

52. Brunner was Röthke's aide and director of Drancy after July 1943.

53. For eyewitness accounts of the Nice roundup, see Philippe Erlanger, *La France sans étoile: Souvenirs de l'avant-guerre et du temps de l'occupation* (Paris: Plon, 1974); Léon Poliakov, *L'Auberge des musiciens: Mémoires* (Paris: Mazarine, 1981); Jacques Neufeld, *Le Seuil de l'abîme: Jour après jour: La résistance juive dans le sud-est de la France 1940–1945* (Montreal: Guerin Littérature, 1988); Henri Pohorylès in David Diamant, *250 Combattants de la résistance témoignent: Témoignages recueillis de septembre 1944 à décembre 1989* (Paris: L'Harmattan, 1991), pp. 258–60; testimony of a Jewish rescuer, December 20, 1943, CDJC, CC-CLXVI-64 (4 pp.); and testimony of Dr. A. Drucker, February 15, 1946, CDJC, CCXVI-66, (12 pp.).

54. Klarsfeld, *Vichy-Auschwitz: 1943–1944*, p. 124.

55. Zuccotti, *Holocaust*, pp. 247–59.

56. According to Michael R. Marrus and Robert O. Paxton, "The Nazis and the Jews in Occupied Western Europe," in *Unanswered Questions: Nazi Germany and the Genocide of the Jews,* ed. François Furet (New York: Schocken, 1989), p. 175, there were fewer than 3,000 German civilians at work in occupied France in August 1941, compared with just over 3,000 in the Netherlands. Also according to the same authors, *Vichy France and the Jews,* p. 241, there were just three battalions of German police, or 2,500 to 3,000 men, in France by mid-1942.

57. See Heinz Röthke, report to Helmut Knochen, "Plan für die Verhaftungsaktion am 22.9.1942," September 21, 1942, CDJC, XLIX-43a (3 pp.); and French police report, September 23, 1942, reprinted in full in Klarsfeld, *Vichy-Auschwitz: 1942,* p. 447.

58. Klarsfeld, *Vichy-Auschwitz: 1943–1944,* p. 155; and Klarsfeld, interviews with the author, New York, March 14 and September 28, 1988. Maurice Rajsfus, a historian of the Holocaust who lost his parents in deportation but survived with his sister in Paris, confirmed this phenomenon from his own observation in an interview with the author, Paris, July 2, 1990.

59. One of those deportees was Pierre Masse, a former deputy, senator, and cabinet minister; another was René Blum, brother of former premier Léon Blum.

60. I give examples of churchmen who spoke out against deportations in August and September 1942 in Zuccotti, *Holocaust,* pp. 140–48.

61. The situation may be compared with that in Belgium, where only 6.5 percent of the 57,000 Jews in the country in October 1940 were citizens. A full 30,000 Jews were recent war refugees. More than 42 percent of the Jews in Belgium were deported, despite German-imposed restrictions on SS autonomy within the country, the absence of significant antisemitism before the war, some articulated opposition to persecution of the Jews from indigenous elites, and other factors operating in the Jews' favor. Since most Jews in Belgium in 1940 were foreigners, their deportation rate is not significantly different from that of *foreign* Jews from France (i.e., about 42 to 45%).

62. Among them were the Gestapo raid on April 6, 1944, on the children's home in the village of Izieu, in which forty-four children and seven adults were arrested, and the Gestapo raids between July 21 and 25, 1944, on eight of the eleven UGIF children's homes in the Paris region, in which about 258 children and thirty adults were seized. Nearly all those arrested died in deportation. See Serge Klarsfeld, *The Children of Izieu: A Human Tragedy,* trans. Kenneth Jacobson (original, 1984; translation, New York: Harry N. Abrams, 1985); Antoine Spire, *Ces enfants qui nous manquent* (Paris: Maren Sell, 1990); and, for the Paris raids, reports of UGIF-North President Georges Edinger to CGQJ, July 24 and 27, 1944, at YIVO Institute for Jewish Research, New York, UGIF-111.1.

63. Of the many works on Jewish rescue organizations, see especially Centre de documentation juive contemporaine, *L'Activité des organisations juives en France sous l'occupation* (1st ed., 1947; Paris: CDJC, 1983); Sabine Zeitoun, *L'Oeuvre de secours aux enfants (OSE) sous l'occupation en France: Du légalisme à la résistance, 1940–1944* (Paris: L'Harmattan, 1990), and idem, *Ces enfants qu'il fallait sauver* (Paris: Albin Michel, 1989); Frédéric Chimon Hammel, *Souviens-toi d'Amalek: Témoignage sur la lutte des Juifs en France 1938–1944* (Paris: CLKH, 1982); Alain Michel, *Les Éclaireurs israélites de France pendant la seconde guerre mondiale, Septembre 1939–Septembre 1944: Action et évolution* (Paris: Éditions des EIF, 1984); and Lazare, *Résistance juive en France.*

64. I give several examples of such prefect reports in Zuccotti, *Holocaust,* pp. 154–56.

65. Ibid., for many examples of individuals who lived in villages where nearly everyone knew they were Jewish.

66. Lucien Steinberg, "Jewish Rescue Activities in Belgium and France," *Rescue Attempts during the Holocaust: Proceedings of the Second Yad Vashem International Historical Conference, Jerusalem: April 8–11, 1974* (Jerusalem: Yad Vashsem, 1977), p. 614 (emphasis mine).

36.

LOUISE LONDON

British Responses to the Plight of Jews in Europe, 1933–1945

British policy regarding the plight of the Jews in Europe during the period 1933–1945 was the product of interaction between the government and Anglo-Jewish leaders. The government's legal responsibility for British immigration controls and their enforcement was carried out by the Home Office, the department responsible for matters regarding aliens. Yet the system of control was far from being a government monopoly. In practice it was a partnership between the Home Office and voluntary organizations. From 1933 onwards the most important of these institutions were the new Jewish Refugees Committee and its associated funding bodies. They undertook the financial risks, the responsibilities, and the huge amount of casework generated by the refugee influx. Their leading role in managing refugee immigration was the basis for their contribution to the immigration policy process. Jewish leaders made several important interventions that led the government to adjust the immigration controls on refugees. Leaders of Jewish organizations also expected to have a say in the operation of admissions policy.[1]

The Jewish Refugees Committee was a new organization, but it grew out of a solid tradition of Jewish institutional cooperation with the Home Office controls on alien Jews. This cooperation took place within the framework of the restrictive system of government immigration controls—a system in operation in Britain in 1933. The essential features of this system were that it imposed comprehensive port controls and that it ruled out mass alien immigration for permanent settlement. The admission of aliens, other than for short-term visits, was restricted to those who could support themselves without working or the few who qualified for employment permits. The system dated from 1919–1920, when the right of appeal against refusal of entry contained in the earlier law was abolished. The system therefore enabled the government to exclude any unwanted alien immigration. A legal concession benefiting refugees had also been abolished. Refugees who failed to qualify on normal immigration grounds could gain admission only through the exercise of Home Office discretion on an exceptional, case-by-case basis. Home Office spokesmen asserted that they used their discretion humanely, in a way that maintained the country's tradition of granting political asylum, and that there was therefore no need to alter the law to make it more generous. Thus in early 1933, when the first refugees from Nazi Germany arrived, they faced the possibility of refusal without recourse to any appeal or to any formal mitigation of the system for refugees. If admitted, they could not hope for settlement or for employment, but only for temporary refuge.

Thus, the only scope for the operation of humanitarian considerations was in the exercise of Home Office discretion. How did this system react to the refugee influx? The government's response to the 1933 influx was to leave the restrictive system formally unchanged but to modify it in practice. A parallel process occurred at the level of policy; the government avoided any formal or public adoption of a refugee policy—this, it was feared, would tie the government's hands, generate expectations that it did not wish to satisfy, create structures through which new and unwanted obligations might be forced on the government, and encourage the growth of refugee problems in Europe. Policy nevertheless evolved, but in a way that did not tie down the government. In April 1933 the government refused to comply with a request from Jewish leaders for a general undertaking to admit refugees. The Jewish leaders offered a guarantee on behalf of the Jewish community to provide maintenance and accommodation for refugees admitted to Britain. They promised that refugee support would not be charged to public funds and that they would arrange for their reemigration.[2] The government's response was that in considering individual cases it would take into account the Jewish guarantee. This produced a crucial, informal modification in the way the system worked, which set the pattern for decisions on refugee cases for five years.

In practice the government largely satisfied the humanitarian desire of Jews in Britain that Jews who arrived in search of refuge should not be turned away. The government's willingness to allow Jews to enter and to remain was based on the assumption that the Jewish organization was able and willing to provide for the influx and to contain its impact on Britain. Relatively few Jewish refugees—on average fewer than one per day—were refused admission.[3] Those admitted were subjected to precautionary landing conditions that limited the time for which they could remain and restricted employment. Yet officials often made exceptions for individual refugees—Ministry of Labour officials, for example, stretched regulations to let refugees who had come in as visitors take employment. Among ten thousand or so refugees who remained in Britain at the beginning of 1938, a minority had been allowed to settle; but most were present on a temporary basis. Home Office officials claimed that they had the situation well under control and that the numbers of Jewish refugees did not pose a problem. They relied on the insurance of the Jewish guarantee, plus limited absorption and reemigration, to prevent the development of a Jewish refugee problem in Britain. This equilibrium could be maintained because the demand for admission to Britain was modest. The demand for Jewish emigration from German-controlled territory was as yet limited and Britain offered few prospects. Jewish leaders preferred to direct German Jews to Palestine.

Thus Britain was allocated a minor role in offering refuge to Jews from Europe. Neither Anglo-Jewish leaders nor the government wished to encourage large-scale Jewish refugee admissions to Britain. They therefore worked together to expand opportunities for European Jews to emigrate to other destinations, especially to places to which refugees might reemigrate from Britain.

The Jewish organizations discouraged Jews from coming to Britain and from expecting settlement there. They acted to reduce numbers, through repatriation to Germany as well as reemigration overseas. Britain was thus a country of transit and intended to operate as a small-scale, temporary refuge. However, an elite who could bring wealth with them or who had attained preeminence in their fields might obtain permanent settlement.

With the Anschluss in March 1938, the refugee problem was transformed in scale and urgency. As pressure for admission to Britain mounted, the principles of British policy remained unchanged, but the methods of enforcing them altered. The major change was the swift decision to reimpose a visa requirement on holders of German and Austrian passports in order to stem the flow of refugees. Control without visas could hardly be expected to survive the announcement, immediately after the Anschluss, of the withdrawal of the Jewish guarantee from future arrivals. On March 14, 1938, Otto Schiff, Chairman of the Jewish Refugees Committee, told the Home Office by letter that the Jewish organizations, heavily committed to expenditure on refugees already in the country, were unable to commit themselves to such an unlimited liability. Indeed, the visa requirement and its employment to bar the entry of Austrians was supported by the Jewish organization.[4] Visas became mandatory in May 1938. New Home Office instructions explicitly discriminated, singling out applicants who were Jews or who had "non-Aryan affiliations" for close scrutiny as potential refugees. The new regulations favored the entry of the rich or famous while excluding most of the rest.[5] Yet room for Home Office discretion remained and the Jewish organization was still prepared to guarantee selected refugees to whose admission it had given prior approval. However, the vast majority of Austrian Jews could not qualify for admission. And hopeful and hopeless cases alike were delayed interminably by the administrative chaos caused by overwhelming numbers of applications.

Preselection abroad was now mandatory. Henceforth the Home Office would not countenance any breach of this principle. However, during the year it simplified procedures to facilitate the entry of certain priority categories. These included unaccompanied children, transmigrants, and women who were prepared to come to Britain to satisfy the demand for domestic service. Increasingly, the Home Office delegated to voluntary organizations authority over the selection of refugees for admission, and this course reduced delays. After Kristallnacht the British Cabinet agreed to permit the expansion of temporary refuge. Admissions were accelerated and the numbers increased. The generosity of the non-Jewish public in providing funds and hospitality played a major part in making this expansion possible. Yet in 1939, when it was realized that the American government would not help by speeding up reemigration from Britain to the United States, new Home Office restrictions curtailed admission for transmigrants. Extra requirements for financial sponsorship were imposed on child refugees for a time by the Jewish refugee organization. As war approached in the summer of 1939, increasing financial stringency and the lack of permanent emigration prospects led the nearly bankrupt Anglo-Jewish refugee organization to halt new commitments to refugees and to ask the British government not to authorize further admissions. It's leaders also objected to Adolf Eichmann's accelerated timetable for the expulsion of Jews from Austria.[6]

In Czechoslovakia, under German rule since March 1939, the Gestapo was also pushing for the emigration of the Jewish population. The British organizations refused to undertake responsibility for this. The Jewish organization said that its funds were for German Jews. The nonsectarian British Committee for Refugees from Czechoslovakia and the British government, which was now funding the committee's activities and dictating its policy, prioritized the cases of a limited number of Sudeten German political refugees and refugees from Germany and Austria. They categorized Czech Jews as racial or economic refugees and rejected proposals to allocate substantial British funds or priority visas to assist them, arguing that to do so would be a surrender to Gestapo pressure for the expulsion of Jews and would only encourage further persecution.

This summary of British prewar policy demonstrates that its overriding aim was to minimize the impact of Jewish refugees on Britain—to avoid a refugee problem. British policy was highly restrictive, and admission was equally selective. Financial support or sponsorship was obligatory. Refugees who offered a benefit to Britain and appeared to present no risk might be admitted. The requirement that refuge be temporary narrowed the scope of admission to persons with sponsors and good reemigration prospects. European Jews learned that persecution was in itself no passport to refuge: the individual had also to fit into one of the admission categories.

One of the major goals of my work has been to emphasize the role of refugee organizations in selecting some refugees for entry even as they sought to restrict the admission of others. The Jewish organization gave priority to those who would assimilate easily or would be good candidates for reemigration; in practice, this meant favoring the young and excluding the elderly.[7] The aspirations and insecurities of Anglo-Jewish leaders, combined with their fear of allowing their financial obligations to run out of control, largely explain these efforts to restrict the scale of the influx and to determine its character. I must stress, however, that the Jewish organization's commitment to keeping a firm grip on the influx made the government readier to admit refugees than it otherwise would have been. Indeed, a far greater number entered than either the government or the Jewish organizations had envisaged or desired. Yet for too many Jews in Britain this topic is still off limits, as is any criticism of the British government's record.

In wartime the restrictive principles of prewar policy persisted in relation to reemigration, long-term stay, and new admissions. The Home Office wanted no addition to refugee numbers. On the contrary, it aimed to reduce the number of refugees in Britain through reemigration and achieved a reduction of the total by an estimated thirteen thousand, facilitated by an undisclosed subsidy from the Treasury. Further reductions resulted from deportation of internees in 1940.

By August 1942 the mass murder of Jews then under way in Europe was known within the Home Office. Thereafter, senior officials used this knowledge to support their arguments that the majority of refugee Jews in Britain should be allowed to remain after the end of the war. However, their cabinet minister, Herbert Morrison, disagreed. This issue was left unresolved until late 1948. Meanwhile, the refugees were unable to plan for their future.

Throughout the war, the government treated Britain's national commitment to the war effort as one that precluded humanitarian admission of refugees. There are a few cases of Jews who got in on war-effort grounds. For example, as Western Europe fell to the Germans in 1940, British efforts to deny resources to the enemy led to the admission of leading Belgian Jewish diamond merchants and, of course, the diamonds they had managed to salvage. Since skills in diamond-cutting and polishing were in short supply, refugee Jewish diamond workers were also welcomed for a time. On the other hand, British officialdom also obstructed the admission of Jews with expertise badly needed for the war effort; even physicians were affected. War-effort arguments were the only ones that were supposed to count: they could be used to provide cover for admissions, the motives for which were predominantly humanitarian; they could also provide a handy formula for refusal.[8]

By increasing our understanding of the restrictiveness of prewar and early wartime refugee policy and of the choice not to solve refugee problems in Europe prior to the Holocaust, my work throws light on British failure to act to provide refuge and rescue during the Holocaust period. The wartime ban on humanitarian admissions in the face of deadly persecution was a continuation of peacetime priorities, not a discontinuity. This is easier to explain once we dispense with the myth of an open-handed British response before the war. When we recognize that officially perceived national interest was the overriding criterion, although in wartime it took an altered form, it is easier to see that the scope for humanitarian considerations was always restricted. It is also possible to see more clearly the opportunism of the British approach, which permitted admission in peacetime only if refugees could comply with restrictive immigration policies and tolerated entry in wartime only if a compensating advantage to the war effort was expected.

This understanding of the negative cast of British wartime policy highlights how immigration considerations remained significant. The overwhelming emphasis on the "temporariness" of the solution the British were affording to the refugee problem reflected the government's wish to avoid postwar pressure to offer permanent settlement in British territory to Jews who might refuse to return to the countries from which they had fled. The difficulties imposed on Britain by its war effort were invoked as reasons to rule out even most small-scale assistance to persons outside Nazi control as well as more ambitious efforts to rescue people from the Nazis' clutches. However, it was the fear of pressure to undertake the settlement of homeless Jews once they had entered British territory that remained fundamental to British policy. This was apparent throughout the war, and we see it, for example, in early 1942. At that time, Britain was undertaking arrangements to move refugee Jews from neutral Portugal to the British colony of Jamaica, largely in order to maintain escape routes into Portugal. But British representatives would not let the evacuations proceed until other Allied governments promised to admit such refugees after the war.[9] The fear of being saddled with homeless and stateless Jews was invoked by the British at Bermuda in 1943 and afterwards.[10] This concern to maintain firm control and avoid open-ended commitments to Jews did not merely shape policy, it *was* policy.

There were those within the British establishment who objected to and dissented from the prevailing and consistent rejection of humanitarian considerations during the Holocaust period. This documented dissent, which is particularly apparent among certain senior civil servants, was not entirely without success. In 1944,

Treasury officials working with Sir Herbert Emerson, the British director of the Intergovernmental Committee on Refugees, helped to mount a British contribution to rescue and refuge in Europe in cooperation with the American Joint Distribution Committee. These operations did not entail admission to British territory. They were set in motion largely in response to the establishment in early 1944 of the United States government's War Refugee Board. These British activities were too little and too late to constitute an alternative policy. They existed at the margins of the overall British position of inaction. The instigators of this contribution to rescue explicitly distanced themselves from the lack of generosity shown by the Allied consensus on inaction reached in Bermuda in 1943 and by the "prudent" line taken by the Foreign Office.

These dissenters emphasized humanitarian considerations and acted on them. They got approval for British financial assistance for rescue work, ensuring all the while that the war effort was safeguarded.[11] The fact that this could and did happen suggests that the British ministers and officials who preferred to do nothing chose inaction because of lack of interest rather than because of solicitude for the national interest in winning the war. It is the degree of inaction by the British government, its reluctance to help even in minor ways, that demonstrates the low priority accorded to humanitarian considerations. Arguments based on the impossibility or risks of mounting an effective challenge to the entirety of Nazi power to carry out its program of mass murder—the large problem—were not objections to helping on the margins. They were nevertheless used in this way by the British government.

Yet as we have seen, British policy was not without a humanitarian element. The Home Office in 1938–1939 was reluctant to discuss openly the humanitarian aspects of its policy, apparently fearing attack from the anti-refugee lobby. Indeed, the humanitarian side of refugee policy was largely concealed from public view. It lay in making discretionary exceptions for people who were unable to comply with standard immigration restrictions. It was thus essentially part of a pragmatic British tradition of bureaucratic improvisation: the humanitarian administration of a harsh system by means of discretion. Many refugees whose lives were saved by coming to Britain feel warmth and gratitude toward the Home Office. Those sentiments reflect the knowledge that the Home Office had a choice, and in their case chose to exercise it in their favor. But for nine out of ten Jews in Europe who wished to escape to Britain before the Holocaust, the answer of the Home Office was "no." Those who were allowed in offered Britain many benefits and few risks. The continuation of this opportunistic and calculating approach to the problem as a whole during the Second World War is less difficult to explain than its opposite would have been. In wartime the Home Office had little opportunity for mitigating the harshness of the system. Indeed, in Herbert Morrison the country had a Home Secretary whose approach was harsher than that of his subordinates. With few exceptions, Morrison wanted no more admissions. He was convinced that to allow even refugee Jews then within Britain to remain would be a recipe for outbursts of antisemitism.

This leads to the question of how British attitudes to Jews influenced policy, to the question of the role of antisemitism, which can be touched on only briefly here. Both before and during the war, the government and Jewish leaders believed that there was a limit to the number of Jews who could be admitted to Britain before antisemitic reaction reached a disturbing level. This perceived national limit was usually not quantified as an actual figure. This argument was used by Zionists to press for more admissions to Palestine—a place where both Anglo-Jewry and the government felt Jews could be allowed to settle. Chaim Weizmann, for example, in 1936, used the chemist's image of a solution that becomes saturated once a critical level has been reached.[12] The Home Office felt at the start of the war, with perhaps seventy thousand Jewish refugees in the country, that this threshold had already been exceeded.[13] It was this belief that prevented British wartime leaders from offering even temporary refuge to Jews who might well have nowhere to return to later.

What direction should be taken by research in this field? As the archives of British refugee organizations become more accessible it is possible to study their activities in more depth and to compare them. One issue that needs particular attention is the official response to "non-Aryan" Christians. The major role of Jewish bankers would also benefit from more research and international comparison. British debates about Jewish responses continue. In Britain, work that looks critically and objectively at Jewish responses has received a far from unanimous welcome. If we accept the taboos in this area, whether they concern Jewish responses or criticism of the British government, we compromise the quality of the history we write. These taboos, and the myths they preserve, also get in the way of our doing our duty, as citizens, to make an objective assessment of the refugee policies being carried out on our behalf. Nowadays, the myth of past British openhandedness to persecuted Jews is regularly invoked by the British government to justify its harshness to asylum seekers. Home Secretaries claim that Britain will always help the genuine refugee and only wishes to exclude the bogus. This account of the response to Jews in flight from Nazism tells a very different story. The history of such responses to immigrants and minorities is central to an understanding of our national identity. It also provides a measure of the values and priorities of our society. If we do not like what the analysis reveals, blaming the messenger is no remedy.

NOTES

1. Financial assistance for research for this article was provided by the Harold Hyam Wingate Foundation and the British Academy. Documents in the Public Record Office are quoted with the permission of Her Majesty's Stationery Office.

See Louise London, "British Immigration Control Procedures and Jewish Refugees, 1933–1939," in Second Chance, Two Centuries of German-Speaking Jews in the United Kingdom, ed. W. E. Mosse (Tübingen: JCB Mohr [Paul Siebeck], 1991), pp. 485–517; idem, "British Government Policy and Jewish Refugees 1933–1945," Patterns of Prejudice 23, no. 4 (1989): 27–43; idem, "British Reactions to the Jewish Flight from Europe," in Britain and the Threat to Stability in Europe, 1918–1945, ed. Peter Catterall and C.J. Morris (Leicester: Leicester University Press 1993), pp. 57–73; idem, "Jewish Refugees, Anglo-Jewry and British Government Policy, 1930–1940," in The Making of Modern Anglo-Jewry, ed. David Cesarani (Oxford: Blackwell, 1990), pp. 163–90; idem, "Refugee Agencies and Their Work, 1933–39," Journal of Holocaust Education 4, no. 1 (Summer 1995): 3–17.

2. "Proposals of the Jewish Community as regards Jewish Refugees from Germany," undated, appendix 1 to Sir John Gilmour (Home Secretary), memorandum, "The Present Position in Regard to the Admission of Jewish Refugees from Germany to this Country," April 6, 1933, Public Record Office (hereafter PRO) CAB 27/549.

3. Statistics of landings and refusals are in Aliens Immigration Returns, Home Office, 1932–1939, published in House of Commons Papers.

4. Home Office, Minutes of meeting with deputation, April 1, 1938, PRO HO 213/42.

5. Passport Control Office Circular, "Visas for Holders of German and Austrian Passports Entering the United Kingdom," April 27, 1938, PRO FO 372/3283, T6705/3272/378, f329.

6. Norman Bentwich, "Report on a visit to Vienna," August 17, 1939, Central British Fund for World Jewish Relief (microfilm), Council for German Jewry, Wiener Library, London (hereafter CBF), reel 4, file 25.

7. A speech by Lord Rothschild criticizing this policy was reported in *Jewish Chronicle*, October 28, 1938, pp. 17–18.

8. Fuller treatment of wartime policy will be found in this author's forthcoming monograph, *Whitehall and the Jews: British Immigration Policy, Jewish Refugees and the Holocaust, 1933–1948* to be published by Cambridge University Press.

9. See London, "British Government Policy and Jewish Refugees," p. 33 note 45.

10. Ibid., pp. 37–38.

11. See note 8.

12. Speeches delivered at the Anglo-Jewish Conference, convened by the Council for German Jewry at the Dorchester Hotel, Sunday March 15, 1936, CBF, reel 4, file 15.

13. For the figures, see Sir Alexander Maxwell (Permanent Under Secretary at the Home Office) to AV Hill, April 16, 1943, PRO FO 371/36725, W11797/6711/48.

37.

PAUL A. LEVINE

Bureaucracy, Resistance, and the Holocaust

UNDERSTANDING THE SUCCESS OF
SWEDISH DIPLOMACY IN BUDAPEST, 1944–1945

When Germany occupied Hungary on Sunday, March 19, 1944, approximately 800,000 Jews were living in relative safety there and in the regions of Romania, Slovakia, and Yugoslavia occupied by Germany's erstwhile ally. Little over three months later, more than 400,000 were dead—assembled, deported, and exterminated with astonishing efficiency and rapidity. Yet most of the Jews living in Budapest survived the war.[1] How, in the midst of that German-occupied, collaborationist city, after more than 400,000 of their countrymen and coreligionists had been murdered in the gas chambers of Auschwitz-Birkenau, did they escape?

The reasons are manifold and complicated, but at least some of the tens of thousands of the almost 200,000 Jews who survived owe their lives, directly or indirectly, to Swedish and other neutral diplomats stationed there. Most of the factors that explain this unprecedented example of survival during the Holocaust have been uncovered and analyzed by scholars, most prominently Randolph L. Braham. But careful analysis of the relative success of Swedish diplomacy remains to be done. Most work on Swedish diplomacy in Budapest center upon Raoul Wallenberg, but even these remain inadequate.

The following is an examination of some aspects of what the Swedish government accomplished in Budapest. It does not employ a narrative, empirical point of view, but adopts a theoretical stance by highlighting those elements of Swedish activity that explain how neutral diplomats, stationed thousands of miles from home, were able to save the lives of some Jews. Because the methods used by the Swedes to at least partially obstruct the implementation of the Final Solution in Budapest had in fact already been in evidence prior to 1944, there are reasons to try to fit these earlier episodes into a broader theoretical framework. This construct may be called "bureaucratic resistance." Because Swedish diplomats, in Stockholm and on the continent, repeatedly utilized such tactics to help non-Swedish Jews, the commonly accepted characterization of Sweden as a Holocaust "bystander" is incorrect and should be reconsidered.

Although the remarkable output of research and publication by the first generation of Holocaust scholars has left few substantive issues unexamined and little unknown about the most essential aspects and personalities of this epochal event, most publications have been in narrative form. Often based upon a country or a government's experience during the Holocaust, empirical exposition and secondary analysis have dominated the field. While there are good reasons for this, relatively little theoretical work has been done, a circumstance that appears more striking in light of the social-scientific trend of postwar historiography. Although the theoretical analysis of the role of bureaucracy in both the structure of the Third Reich and the Final Solution is central to our understanding of the Nazi epoch, attempts to impose that theoretical understanding upon particular episodes of the Holocaust have been few. Moreover, no known work attempts to explain how bureaucracy may have contributed to saving Jewish lives.

Yet as professional study of the Holocaust enters its second generation, it seems natural that new approaches be undertaken. Such attempts run a number of obvious risks, both scholarly and (because of the emotional and political demands of this field), personal. But in his 1993 review of the status of Holocaust studies, Michael R. Marrus wrote, "The process of definition itself helps to clarify historical argument . . . and points the way to alternative visions."[2]

It is important to keep in mind the limitations of a theoretical approach to historical understanding, for at best, artificial constructions can serve only as guides to addressing the data. Theory is most useful when it is used not to replace well-grounded analytical narrative but to better illustrate or illuminate analogous episodes. Hans Ulrich Wehler wrote that a theoretical posture is useful only if it "combine[s] a maximum of empirically obtained and verifiable information with as much explanatory power as possible [and covers] a variety of similar phenomena."[3] Emil Fackenheim warns that a theoretical postulate is doomed to remain, "an empty conceit unless it [is] both illustrated and validated by acts . . . that *actually occurred.*"[4]

Resistance as a Theoretical Concept

Analysis of the various forms assumed by resistance against Nazi Germany constitutes a vital element in the historiography of both the Holocaust and the Third Reich.[5] Studies identifying and analyzing manifestations of Jewish and German resistance constitute an increasingly imposing body of work. Yet they have developed to date along parallel but essentially distinct lines. This dichotomy between studies of Jewish and German resistance may well be caused by the need of each group's partisans to highlight events, personalities, and organizations long considered of negligible significance. For the discussants of both Jewish and German resistance, however, the demonstration of active resistance remains an act of great moral import, one whose value lies far beyond mere empirical demonstration. Both groups seek to demonstrate, for political and moral reasons, life during death, moral affirmation during physical negation. Maybe because of this, the literature on Jewish resistance (armed and unarmed) has often been of a more theoretical nature than the rest.[6]

Lost against this background has been a third form of resistance against the Third

Reich's anti-Jewish policies. This was engaged in by neither Jews nor Germans but by third-party protagonists who attempted, at least on some occasions, to stop the Germans from killing (as Christopher R. Browning recently phrased it) "every Jew in Europe on whom they could lay their hands."[7] Analysis of Swedish diplomatic efforts on behalf of Jews during the Holocaust reveals a different kind of resistance than what has been previously defined; here it is characterized as bureaucratic resistance. Working as an officially authorized and ostensibly disinterested third party that sought neither to kill the perpetrators nor overthrow the regime, these resisters sought to exploit their agency to interpose themselves between the aspiring perpetrator and his potential victim. Although at times noted anecdotally in the literature, bureaucratic resistance undertaken by neutral diplomats has hitherto remained undefined and unanalyzed.[8]

Documentary evidence and the secondary literature alike indicate that at least part of the explanation for Jewish survival in Budapest lies in Swedish diplomatic efforts. Precedents can be found in a number of significant episodes in which Swedish diplomats confronted the Final Solution.

Before proceeding, an explicit caveat is necessary. No claim is being made that bureaucratic resistance by a few neutral diplomats during the war might have changed significantly the final outcome of Germany's effort to murder the Jews of Europe; such an assertion would border on historical nonsense. Only political circumstances and actors beyond the ken of those Jews who were slaughtered could have ameliorated the impact of Hitler's wrath. Still, it can well be imagined that such tactics, had they been employed earlier and more often by potential resisters, could have saved at least a few more lives.

Sweden and the Holocaust

Prevailing discourse places those countries and institutions that remained neutral during the war within the category of "bystanders"; Sweden has of course been included, as have, not incidentally, the Western Allies. The "bystander" nations and governments have been excoriated for having contributed to the killings through their failure to understand what was in fact taking place and, even following some measure of comprehension, for their continued lack of a sense of moral and political urgency. However, Sweden, it increasingly appears, does not deserve the sobriquet, "bystander."

Sweden's government chose, over the course of some months, to abandon its neutrality vis-à-vis Germany's racial policy, repeatedly attempted to obstruct implementation of Nazi anti-Jewish policy, and helped a number of Jews who in more normal times would have had no claim to Swedish diplomatic protection. Yet seen from the vantage point of 1938, this significant change could hardly have been predicted. The shift is even more surprising in light of Swedish history, its political culture, and the tenacity that country has long demonstrated in its attempts to maintain an internationally recognized neutrality. Yet there is no question that a bureaucratically informed and quasi-legalistic resistance against national socialist racial policies was conducted from late 1942 forward by representatives of the Swedish government. By repeatedly engaging in such efforts, all of which took place with the government's knowledge and approval, civil servants in Sweden's Foreign Office abandoned all pretense of neutrality toward a critical aspect of Nazi Germany's declared policies.

This shift was gradual and evolved in response to a variety of political, economic, and humanitarian factors. Though some of the motives were less noble than others, Sweden's coalition government chose to act when it judged it feasible and when significant results might be attained. Importantly, throughout the 1930s and early 1940s, Sweden responded to Germany's persecution of its Jewish population in the same disinterested fashion as virtually all other nations. The nation kept its hearts and borders closed. But following the onset of the Final Solution—and Sweden had as good or better information about the killings than most other governments—the cabinet gradually chose to abandon its political and moral indifference. The increasingly effective response evolved from indifference to an activism that saw its greatest results in Budapest in 1944. As information detailing the ongoing Final Solution mounted, the Social Democratic government of Prime Minister Per Albin Hansson grasped the opportunities available to it.

Regardless of the specific motivating factors, the Swedish government's opportunities for resistance and assistance did not surpass those of other Western governments. Indeed, Sweden's evolutionary response to the Holocaust reveals much about the Swedish people's difference from other Western nations and their elected governments. The Swedish government and the officials who made the decision to intervene may be more properly understood as "resisters" than "bystanders."

Interestingly, Sweden's response to the Holocaust has been largely ignored by professional historians, with the important exception of Steven Koblik's pioneering study.[9] From 1942 onward, Sweden's Foreign Office responded to Nazi racial policy with ever more frequent confrontations, beginning with an intervention in November on behalf of a few Norwegian Jews who were able to demonstrate some connection with Sweden. Official lobbying to save isolated individuals increased in early 1943 after the Germans announced to the neutral and satellite governments that all Jews of nationalities previously exempt from deportation were now to be subject to general anti-Jewish measures. The next important episode was Sweden's determined, and eventually public, intervention on behalf of Denmark's Jews in October 1943. Efforts reached unprecedented levels in Budapest after March 1944. Here we can note that the Jews whom Swedish diplomats sought to aid were first Scandinavian, then Western, and finally Central European Jews. Significantly, there appears to be no case in which Swedish diplomats intervened on behalf of Jews from Eastern Europe.

Of course Raoul Wallenberg's story has been told and commemorated innumerable times, but these mostly hagiographic accounts neither adequately examine the background of earlier Swedish acts, nor do they explain how Wallenberg was so individually effective in saving lives. And apart from Koblik's study, the fact that Swedish activities in Budapest were based upon earlier experience has gone unnoted, creating misunderstandings about evolving Swedish policy in Budapest. Indeed, a fuller understanding has been hampered by the emphasis on Wallenberg's genuinely heroic but essentially misunderstood achievements.[10] We need not devalue the potent symbolism of Wallenberg in Holocaust memory and commemoration. One may revise without debunking. Yet it is just as clear that inaccurate myths, however well-intended, are shaky ground upon which to build a theoretical explanation or a lasting and positive collective memory.

Theoretical and Empirical Components of Bureaucratic Resistance

For our purposes, bureaucratic resistance can be understood as tactics of obstruction—based primarily upon the standard norms and accepted praxis of international diplomacy—against the implementation of Nazi racial policy. As Swedish diplomats engaged in their quite normative, "everyday" diplomatic activities, they came to understand that their position gave them a chance to resist the implementation of what has been called the Nazi "logic of destruction."[11] Importantly, their "obstructive capacity" was based not upon individual charisma or even idealistic humanitarianism but solely upon the political position and bureaucratic status of Swedish officials vis-à-vis their German counterparts. For there to be any chance of success, it had to be made clear to the Germans that the Swedish government had a political interest in the safety of those Jews they wished to protect and that failure to respect this interest could have an adverse effect, first on Swedish public opinion, and subsequently on Swedish-German relations.

By conducting affairs in bureaucratic fashion, representatives of the Swedish state proved capable of engaging in a very real form of resistance. Before proceeding further, however, we need to note the critical element of choice. When in fact they might have chosen, as did so many others, not to declare a political interest in non-Swedish Jews, Swedish diplomats in Stockholm and on the continent chose to help.

Bureaucratically informed obstruction was conducted by nations other than the Swedes, the most important case being that of the Italians. In both Italian-occupied areas and in Italy itself, officials also chose to protect Jews being hunted by the Germans, and they often succeeded, at least until the fall of Mussolini's Fascist government in 1943.[12] Several satellite governments aided, at least occasionally, their own Jewish citizens faced with deportation by the Germans.[13] Yet the actions of Allied and satellite governments, even if analogous to the resistance being defined here, represent substantially different cases than the actions of neutral and nonaligned governments; the resistance to Nazi policies conducted by the different types of governments should thus be treated separately.

The employment of diplomatic documents and an irregular and legally dubious process of naturalization emerged from the core of bureaucratic resistance as practiced by the Swedes. Swedish officials knew that in theory all who could claim Swedish citizenship were protected from deportation, and that empirically a Jew could show an official Swedish document to a policeman or bureaucrat as "proof" of the political interest of a protecting power.[14]

The issuance of various types of diplomatic documents to those whose claim to Swedish protection during more normal times would have been tenuous began in Norway, picked up throughout 1943, most prominently in Copenhagen, and was used in an unprecedented fashion in Budapest, where Wallenberg's famous Schutzpass was just one type of document used in a legalistic attempt to shield holders from deportation or even arrest. Others included entry visas, provisional and regular passports, and certificates of protection. In fact, the flood of documents authorized by Stockholm became so unwieldy that Swedish officials there and in Budapest essentially lost track of what they were doing, which led them to start putting those who appealed for protection on lists labeled "stark" (strong) and "svag" (weak).[15]

These documents were able to protect their holders because of the very real gap in Nazi anti-Jewish policy. As is well known, German practice did not treat all Jews the same. Exemptions from deportation, if only temporary, could be based on such things as distinguished service in the First World War, marriage to an Aryan, and labor in essential industries. Most importantly, exemptions were granted to certain Jews based on citizenship in countries which for one reason or another the Germans felt unable to treat as they might have genuinely desired. In fact, the Germans were often forced to compromise and take pragmatic political factors into account when deciding the fate of individual or small groups of Jews. This apparent lack of complete autonomy has often been noted in the literature, but never thoroughly analyzed, although Charles S. Maier cogently observed that

> the conflicting sources of authority . . . allowed oases of relative freedom, interstices where control was not absolute. . . . The war demonstrated that if foreign leaders—even leaders of countries occupied by the Germans—resisted, the Nazis left its Jews relatively undisturbed (if only, it was believed, for a while). In short, Nazi rule depended upon voluntary compliance.[16]

While less evident or likely in (post-Anschluss) Germany itself, in the Reich Protectorate, or in Poland and other occupied areas of the East, this gap in Nazi ideology created possibilities for bureaucratic resistance in the countries that Raul Hilberg has identified as "a vast semicircular arc, extending counterclockwise from Norway to Romania."[17] The gap was based upon concrete political, military, and economic considerations particular to the country in question; yet those governments and statesmen, mostly Western, who might have exploited this opportunity most often ignored its existence. The Swedes, on the contrary, increasingly utilized this life-giving gap.

A second important theoretical point of departure is the very nature of bureaucracy, how it functions, and how its functionaries view their procedures and position. From both a theoretical and an empirical viewpoint, the study and analysis of bureaucracy as an element in the murder of the Jews has long been central. As Browning once put it, "The interpretation of the Final Solution as a bureaucratic and administrative process has not been seriously challenged since the appearance of Raul Hilberg's . . . *The Destruction of the European Jews*."[18] Thirty years of reflection have not dissuaded Hilberg himself from viewing the centrality of modern bureaucracy as the key element in explaining the Holocaust:

> If we examine this event in detail, observing the progression of small steps day by day, we see much in the destruction of Jewry that is familiar and even commonplace in the context of contemporary institutions and practices. Basically, the Jews were destroyed as a consequence of a multitude of acts performed by a phalanx of functionaries in public offices and private enterprises, and many of these measures, taken one by one, turn out to be bureaucratic, embedded in habit, routine and tradition.[19]

Closely aligned with bureaucratic explanations of the Final Solution are functionalist arguments explaining how Nazi Germany came to carry out the Final Solution. Functionalist thinking helps not only because it points the way toward a bureaucratic understanding of the Final Solution but also because its more social-science oriented methodology lends itself to building a theoretical framework. On the other hand, it clearly would not do to build a theoretical framework upon the methodology promoted by "intentionalist" thinking.

Even so, the traditional understanding of bureaucracy is not applied here, for when considering Swedish intervention on behalf of non-Swedish Jews, bureaucracy played a rather different role than is generally understood. Given the right circumstances and motivations, bureaucracy and bureaucrats could play a role in aiding Jews, not only in killing them. Furthermore, instead of exclusively requiring unconditional obedience from functionaries, a bureaucracy can be turned into a system of resistance and obstruction. That a bureaucracy is able to obstruct government policy is hardly a novel notion, but traditionally functionaries obstruct their own government; this was the case in Italy and areas under its control. In the Swedish case the system functioned as a third-party protagonist—open, for the most part legal, and acting strictly according to "habit, form, and tradition." Thus, rather than overturning the traditional, and still illuminating, understanding of the function of bureaucracy in the Final Solution, here we argue that bureaucracy could and did play two roles.

Two elements central to bureaucracy play important roles here: rationality and predictability, and fear. The idea of rational, predictable adherence to rules has been universally accepted ever since Max Weber described institutional behavior. A normally functioning bureaucracy, as Hilberg put it, will be characterized by "habit, routine and tradition." Most scholars agree that traditional German patterns of state and society by no means changed unrecognizably following the National Socialist takeover; Weberian rationality continued after 1933 to characterize most ministries and other agencies, which served the Nazi regime according to patterns of bureaucratic behavior operating long before Hitler came to power.

Because of this, when Swedish diplomats confronted, indeed lobbied, their German counterparts, they could count on their efforts being received according to the customs and rules of bilateral diplomatic behavior. The documentary record of requests, refusals, appeals, and obfuscations amply demonstrates a rational and traditional system at work, one that operated, even when the issue was human lives, according to habit, routine, and tradition.[20]

In one of the few studies of German bureaucracy that extends into the war, Uwe D. Adam confirms that even as their material and political world was falling apart, German bureaucrats maintained the same predictable forms, and that the traditional ethos still prevailed among German officialdom as late as 1944.[21] In his study of Nazi bureaucrats, Fred Katz echoed Weber: because bureaucracies routinize behavior, they can "coordinate the skills of diverse specialists and functionaries in the pursuit of goals that are subdivided into limited discrete tasks," obscuring the ultimate goals of the institution—particularly in a time of chaos and institutional dysfunction such as wartime—and rendering irrelevant "the question of performing good or evil deeds."[22] Another relevant behavior Katz terms "calculative compliance." Pointing out that considerable individual autonomy is as much an element of bureaucracy as the collective elements enforcing control, Katz concluded that the individual within a bureaucracy actually has considerable institutional space for autonomous thought and action:

> The focus on bureaucratic control leaves a crucial component out of consideration. Bureaucrats do have considerable autonomy. . . . Many forms of autonomy are built into the structure of bureaucratic organizations. . . . It is just as basic to the continuing operation of bureaucracies as are the controls. When Nazi bureaucrats said they were merely following orders, they were hiding the fact that they had considerable . . . autonomy.[23]

Persistent rationality plus institutional autonomy equaled opportunity for a third party to interpose himself between victim and perpetrator. If the Nazi functionary had possibilities to choose different courses of action, with the question of "good and evil" irrelevant to some particular choices in regard to the alleged goals of the organization, an appeal by a respected—or at least duly authorized—fellow official could well have an effect. This notion of available choice becomes even more important because functionaries not wishing to be involved in atrocities, either in the field or at their desk, could in fact distance themselves from the killings without retribution.[24] Thus, in spite of the extreme violence of the regime the functionary was a part of, most still retained an ability to think for themselves. The calculus of compliance and rationality becomes particularly complex when no longer overshadowed only by a fear of the regime, but now of culpability in the rapidly approaching postwar world as well. This nexus of factors could be decisive in the decision-making process of the Nazi functionary.

Indeed, these various factors influenced decisions in a mental world characterized, as virtually every study of German bureaucracy has noted, by a lack of ideological commitment to National Socialist racial ideology. As Browning has written, "For the most part . . . the Final Solution would be implemented not by . . . zealots, the 'anticipators,' but rather by the 'normal' bureaucrats, the 'accommodators' who waited for the signal from above."[25] Those bureaucrats who had been easily swayed, "with so little friction and so little formal coordination," toward the institutional goal of mass murder were now ripe to be influenced in the other direction—especially when it was in their self-interest.[26] The lack of ideological commitment was particularly noticeable among the middle-level officials of the German Foreign Office with whom Swedish diplomats most commonly dealt, and who could place their own institutional obstructions in the way of SS or RSHA officials seeking to expedite deportations.[27] These men were more aware than most of Germany's rapidly deteriorating political and military situation following the great defeats of 1943.[28] Bureaucrats who had previously coordinated and directed "evil" were potentially ready to be reoriented toward "good deeds."

One of the leading functionalist historians, Hans Mommsen, has posited two ideas that have influenced my contention that a third form of resistance can be demonstrated theoretically. But while Mommsen explains the internal workings of the Hitler regime and the realization of its plan to exterminate the Jews, his ideas are to be understood essentially in reverse here in order to apprehend their metaphorical contribution to the theory being proposed.

Mommsen has written that the German bureaucracy, in its race (as Hilberg puts it) "to act in accordance with perceived imperatives,"[29] was both influenced and characterized by what the former calls the "removal of inhibitions." Agreeing with other scholars who failed to find ideological commitment amongst those seeking to climb the organizational ladder by contributing to the efficient murder of Jews, Mommsen has argued that

> an essential element in the explanation of the Holocaust was the removal of the inhibitions [of those] involved in the extermination process, and indeed of all those who implemented the Final Solution. This loss of inhibition is not necessarily linked to anti-semitic and racial-biological indoctrination of the persecutors and the on-lookers. . . . Technocratic and subordinate attitudes could be as important as blind racialism or the mere narrating of national socialist anti-Jewish cliches.[30]

This shedding of normative notions of morality and civil decency itself resulted from the drumbeat of propaganda, antisemitic and otherwise. The process accelerated rapidly during the war, and as inhibitions were lost, as one threshold of behavior and policy after another was crossed, each succeeding barrier was overcome in a fashion that would have been unthinkable in an earlier political, social, and psychological culture. Mommsen has persuasively described this process as one of "cumulative radicalization."

And Mommsen, who like most other functionalists adopted Hilberg's four-step explanation of the Nazi process of annihilation, contributed a powerful metaphoric insight with his notion of "cumulative radicalization."[31] Mommsen argued that quite normal bureaucratic personnel and structures became caught up in the process, a precipitously climbing spiral of expropriation, deportation, and annihilation. In the psychological world of government and warfare created by the National Socialists, ascent was unhindered by the moral factors that usually inhibit the wilder fantasies of errant leaders. In the Third Reich, the spiral's climb was fueled by the individual functionary's understanding of "the Führer's will" and by a cynical, nihilistic propaganda of hate.

When confronted with differing yet nonconflicting policy options for "solving the Jewish Question," the German bureaucracy usually opted for radical policies, for murderous solutions previously unthinkable.[32] The borders of this radicalization kept moving ever deeper into a realm of unprecedented, almost surreal violence, a process Mommsen has described as follows:

> This tendency led to a cumulative radicalization, so that extravagant objectives, far away at first, came nearer to immediate realization. In this way, it provided the possibility of anticipating some of the millennial aims of the Third Reich. . . . [Yet their] efforts [were] choked by a torrent of crime, blood and mediocrity . . . impelled by the inhuman consistency of machinery running on, without the slightest relevance to actual political interests and realities.[33]

Viewed metaphorically, political society seems susceptible to general laws of nature. In politics as in physical existence, gravity is one of the most powerful forces governing behavior and action. When the motive force of a moving object—or a political policy—is spent, gravity inevitably takes over and causes the object, or policy, to return, as it were, to earth. Taking Mommsen's paradigm to its logical terminus, one can imagine the spiraling process of "cumulative radicalization" inevitably reaching a terminal point, whence decline is inevitable as a new reality is created.[34]

Hilberg has written that one of the "key phenomena of the bureaucratic destruction process [was the] crucial . . . requirement that the bureaucrat had to understand opportunities and 'necessities,' that he should act in accordance with perceived imperatives."[35] Had the Nazis been victorious, the apogee of violence might well never have been reached until all perceived racial enemies were done away with. As approaching defeat gave rise to growing perceptions of a post-Hitlerian world, the terminal point of the spiral was reached and decline became evident. In this atmosphere an openness to new thinking widened the already existing gaps in the implementation of Nazi racial policy. This is when the tactics of bureaucratic resistance became most possible. As the outlines of the postwar world became sharper, so did the individual's "perceived necessities," creating new opportunities for those intent upon obstructing Nazi racial goals.

When decline became logical and inevitable, other considerations came to be relevant and important. Precisely when the spiral reached its apogee can only be surmised, but we can understand it to have been reached sometime in early 1943, with the cresting of the continent-wide orgy of violence that Browning has called "the core of the Holocaust . . . a short, intense wave of mass murder." This wave crashed over Hilberg's counterclockwise arc, an area where anti-Jewish ideology was more susceptible to dilution than in Eastern Europe. This area coincides, not coincidentally, with the geography and time period when Swedish diplomats began an almost weekly, even daily series of contacts with their German counterparts on behalf of threatened Jews, both Swedish citizens and others. As German efforts to kill Jews lessened slightly, Swedish efforts to help them increased.

It may be further surmised that with the cresting of the wave of violence in early to mid-1943, a new atmosphere began to become evident within the German bureaucracy. Faint at first, the dedication necessary for the German functionary to do his job as skillfully as possible began to decay, and influenced by the critical setbacks of 1943, the spiral of impersonal, state-sponsored violence begun in 1933 finally began to lose some of its momentum. When those staffing the machinery of annihilation could view the future with confidence, all political or moral doubts were swallowed up. But in 1943, the changed military situation began to transform political reality, even for Nazi ideologues.[36] To be sure, killing was still the prime motive when the Germans occupied Hungary in early 1944. However, for the nonideological German bureaucrat, the change of atmosphere made other options conceivable.

Functionaries who had previously acted so conscientiously upon "necessities and perceived imperatives" now understood that the political conditions upon which their loyalties were based had changed. Those functionaries who in 1941–1942 so arrogantly had declared that all matters concerning the Jews of Europe were "internal affairs of the Reich," in 1943–1944 began to perceive a decidedly more menacing reality; and human nature being what it is, those motives that had enabled relatively normal men to engage in mass industrialized slaughter now began to lose their relevance.

German civil society began to withdraw the carte blanche to kill Jews that it had given its bureaucrats; it was a change in attitude that was no doubt stimulated both by the series of defeats that began in North Africa and on the Eastern Front and, closer to home, the civilian casualties caused by the ever-increasing Allied bombing attacks.[37]

Not surprisingly, the change in attitudes evidenced by German bureaucrats influenced the collaborationist functionaries who throughout Europe played such an important role in the Final Solution. Not least in Budapest itself—which must be separated of course from what happened in the Hungarian countryside—this abstract reality became concrete when the bureaucrats and policemen typical of the entire European process of destruction and who had only weeks before so willingly offered their services to the Germans now began to seek alibis "for future eventualities."[38]

German bureaucrats, previously confident they might organize mass murder unhindered, now proved ever more willing to negotiate with neutral appellants. This new reality gave Swedish and other neutral diplomats a different type of ear to talk into, a different mental universe in which to place their appeals on behalf of some foreign Jews.

Swedish Bureaucratic Resistance Made Concrete

Space permits us to examine only a few episodes upon which our theory of bureaucratic resistance is founded. As conducted by Swedish diplomats, bureaucratic resistance against Germany succeeded for two overriding reasons. The bureaucratic elements facilitating resistance have been related. These, however, meshed with the second reason, the political and economic realities of Swedish-German relations. Germany's dependence upon Swedish iron ore, ball bearings, and ball-bearing machinery was considerable, and because of this, Germany could never afford a rupture with Sweden. Indeed, some believe that this dependence enabled Sweden to avoid German occupation, as any military action by Germany would have triggered immediate sabotage of the iron ore mines in the far north.[39]

The onset of the Final Solution in November 1942 in Norway, a nation of critical importance to the Swedes, marks the real beginning of their evolution from indifference to activism. Here, for the first time, the threatened Jews were citizens of a fellow Scandinavian nation, a "broderfolk." This gave them claims to Swedish assistance and sympathy that Jews from Central and Eastern Europe could never make upon the country's political leadership and public opinion. Four elements of the Swedish response are important, for they would be repeated subsequently. First, the government made it clear to the Germans that the few Swedish Jews in Norway must be allowed to return, a demand to which the Germans agreed. Second, the Foreign Office issued an official but unpublicized demarche to Berlin requesting that all other Jews in Norway be allowed to cross the border. The Germans refused to even officially acknowledge this request, but it served an important purpose by establishing Sweden's interest in Jews other than its own citizens. Third, Sweden now indicated an unequivocal willingness to provide shelter for any Jew (or non-Jew for that matter) who could make it across its long, unguarded border. Finally, and most important as a precedent for future tactics, there were the steps energetically undertaken by Swedish diplomats in Oslo to naturalize some Jews whose claim to Swedish citizenship was at best tenuous, and to lobby their German counterparts, in both Oslo and Berlin, for their release from detention. Although most of these attempts at such ex post facto naturalization in Norway were ultimately rejected by the Germans, the Swedes had established a vitally important tactical precedent for what increasingly appeared to be a viable method of protecting a few individuals.[40]

In January 1943 the Germans informed all neutral and satellite governments that those Jews still in occupied Western Europe who claimed citizenship in these countries had until the end of March to return to their respective lands, after which time they would be subject to the same measures as all other Jews, that is, deportation. This German demand led to a prolonged series of contacts by Swedish officials in Berlin to lobby on behalf of a handful of Jews who, the Swedes claimed, qualified for diplomatic protection. Their requests frequently resulted in exemption from deportation, a delay that often meant at least temporary salvation. Of special interest are Swedish efforts to rescue five children, three Dutch and two stateless, already interned in Theresienstadt. All were rather irregularly naturalized by the Swedes, a step the Germans hotly contested. Even though officials of the RSHA, among them Adolf Eichmann, indignantly denied the validity of any such ex post facto naturalization, Swedish diplomats, citing a promise made to them by the since deposed Martin Luther of Abteilung Deutschland, refused to take no for an answer. All five children survived.[41] This tactic of naturalization, or in some cases a resumption of citizenship previously lost, proved one of the most effective methods of bureaucratically obstructing German anti-Jewish measures; it was even imitated by others.

Thus, in spite of German protests, the tactic of claiming protection for foreign citizens, who during more normal times would have had absolutely no claim to such protection, was now even more firmly established. Crucial in this respect is the key requirement of the Swedes making a clear and unequivocal statement of their political interest in the ultimate fate of those Jews concerned.[42]

Sweden's response to events in Denmark in October of 1943 represents both a continuing evolution of these tactics and, possibly more importantly, a significant juncture in the history of the Holocaust. For the first time since Hitler began his persecutions, a sovereign nation publicly offered to help large numbers of foreign Jews. Again, these Danish Jews were citizens of a Scandinavian nation, but the intent of the offer was clear and its historic significance fully understood by contemporaries.

On October 2, in response to rumors of pending deportation and the beginning of arrests in Copenhagen, the Swedish government again officially requested that they be allowed to accept Denmark's Jewish population, offering even to intern them if necessary. Motivated by their own inner conscience, increasingly anxious to court Western public and official opinion after previous pro-German concessions, and abandoning their almost paralyzing fear of German invasion, the Swedes decided to make public their request—and the subsequent German refusal.[43] Drawing on the experience gained during the Norwegian episode, the Swedes issued protective and provisional passports and entry visas in Denmark. The role of Gosta Engzell, a lifelong civil servant whose efforts and attitudes would loom large six months later in Budapest, was prominent in this episode. In an internal report summarizing Sweden's understanding of such legalistic measures, Engzell wrote:

During Jewish deportations from Norway the German occupation authorities adopted a viewpoint based on the principle that Swedish government decisions to grant Swedish citizenship to Norwegian or stateless people could not be legally recognized. From a formal point of view the German standpoint is unquestionably well founded. . . . Nonetheless, in spite of this attitude, in many cases, if the person in question knew that he had been naturalized and this had been confirmed with the German authorities, this led to a forestalling of deportation. Furthermore this made it possible to conduct negotiations concerning the person's release, which sometimes succeeded. In light of this experience it is urgent that all people who have during the last days been granted Swedish citizenship . . . be informed immediately and receive a Swedish passport. In Norway it proved possible to inform even some people who were in hiding.[44]

Less than six months later the Germans occupied Hungary, and in the following days, hundreds, if not thousands of Jews besieged the Swedish Legation in Budapest. Word had spread that the Swedish government would and could protect Jews. From the first day of the occupation, Swedish Minister Ivan Danielsson and Chargé d'Affaires Per Anger had no doubt what the issues were, and they immediately began to consider appeals for help and in a limited number of cases to issue protective papers.[45] Realizing their limitations, Swedish officials were forced to restrict their help to Jews in Budapest, unable to do anything for the hundreds of thousands deported in the short period following the occupation. Importantly, the first measures taken in Budapest were for the most part supported by Stockholm, which authorized the legation to distribute documents to appellants who could "show strong connection to Sweden." Initially this meant persons with either family or substantial business connections in Sweden. Under the press of events, however, the legation interpreted this definition elastically, troubling some officials in Stockholm, but not Gosta Engzell, who formally conferred upon Anger and Danielsson considerable latitude in deciding who was and was not eligible.[46]

From the start, Swedish efforts to impede Nazi racial policy in Budapest were based upon bureaucratic behavior. At least until the Arrow Cross coup of October 15, and afterwards in many cases, the three bureaucracies, Swedish, German, and Hungarian, continued to operate according to "habit, routine, and tradition." The frequent contacts of Swedish officials with their counterparts while assisting Hungarian and stateless Jews remained characterized by rational discourse and diplomatic custom. Swedish training quite correctly told them that if they acted accordingly, their counterparts would respond in kind. These tactics were strikingly effective in 1944 Budapest, and even after chaos reigned on the streets, bureaucratic lobbying saved far more lives than the heroic yet ad hoc activity of Raoul Wallenberg. In the most important effort after the coup, Wallenberg and other neutral diplomats aided many more thousands of Jews by continuing to act, not as heroes, but as diplomats and bureaucrats.[47]

Wallenberg was by all accounts an extraordinarily brave man and fully deserves his image. But he was, in fact, just one link in his country's evolutionary, positive response to the Holocaust. Historical memory aside, however, had he not been an officially authorized, duly accredited diplomat of a neutral country whose government chose to help, all goodwill, bravery, and intent would have gone for naught in the face of the Nazi onslaught against the Jews.

Conclusion

Because the Swedes had successfully engaged in bureaucratic resistance before Budapest, we may conclude that their tactics of obstruction might have worked well elsewhere. But while in the post-Holocaust world we may permit ourselves some scant hope that the world community would not tolerate another continentwide genocide, there is little reason to conclude that more localized killings, even organized genocide, will not take place. Thus, identification of social structures, bureaucratic mechanisms, and even personality types that are able to obstruct or resist remains important. The process of cumulative radicalization that so manifestly affected common functionaries was just that, a process with differing stages of reality and differing moments of compulsion, choice, and inevitability. As long as the concrete reality these functionaries responded to consisted only of the call to more murder, appeals for leniency, morality, and even simple mercy played little part in the decision-making process. But if a potential perpetrator—be he bureaucrat or soldier—is asked to make a decision regarding the fate of a victim after the process of cumulative radicalization has declined, determined intervention by an officially recognized third party can be decisive.

When confronted, perhaps for the first time since the war began, with an official from another sovereign state authorized to make an appeal for mercy, Nazi officials could and did give way. Simply by doing their jobs, by deciding to help threatened civilians, Swedish diplomats did something that few others tried to do. They took advantage of an opportunity that had, in fact, long existed.

Hannah Arendt's concept of the "banality of evil" has for many reasons provoked considerable discussion. One of the more troubling aspects of her thesis is how easy it is for otherwise normal people, whether bureaucrats or middle-aged policemen, to take part in radical violence. Here we have tried to identify, both theoretically and empirically, opportunities for quite normal people, armed with only their conscience and political authorization, to place themselves between the perpetrator and the victim. It is not only evil that may be banal, but good as well.

NOTES

I would like to thank the following for their help: Rutgers University, Omer Bartov, David Fogelsong, and John Gillis; Christopher R. Browning of Pacific Lutheran University; and Torkel Jansson and the participants of his seminar at Uppsala University, Sweden.

1. Randolph L. Braham, *The Politics of Genocide: The Holocaust in Hungary* (New York: Columbia University Press, 1981), vol. 2, pp. 1143–44.

2. See Michael R. Marrus, "'Good History' and Teaching the Holocaust," *Perspectives of the American Historical Association* 31 (May/June 1993): 7–8.

3. See Hans Ulrich Wehler, "Bismarck's Imperialism, 1862–1890," *Past and Present* 48 (1970): 120.

4. Emil Fackenheim, "The Spectrum of Resistance during the Holocaust," *Modern Judaism* 2 (1982): 116.

5. See, for example, the recent supplement to the *Journal of Modern History* 64 (December

1992), "Resistance against the Third Reich." Studies of the forms of Jewish resistance to Nazi racial policies constitute, of course, an increasingly important part of the scholarly literature.

6. See, for instance, Emil Fackenheim, George Kren, and Leon Rappoport, *The Holocaust and the Crisis of Human Behavior* (New York: Holmes & Meier, 1980), esp. chapter 5; Roger S. Gottlieb, "The Concept of Resistance: Jewish Resistance during the Holocaust," *Social Theory and Practice* 9/1 (Spring 1983): 31–49. Michael R. Marrus devotes volume 7 of *The Nazi Holocaust* (hereafter *TNH*) (Westport: Meckler, 1989) to Jewish resistance.

7. Christopher R. Browning, *The Path to Genocide: Essays on Launching the Final Solution* (New York: Cambridge University Press, 1992), pp. 84–85.

8. As noted, the literature on both Jewish and German resistance is vast and growing. But so far as is known, no other historian of the Third Reich or the Holocaust has attempted to define, either from a theoretical standpoint or from available empirical evidence, the actions of neutral diplomats as a third form of resistance.

9. Steven Koblik, *The Stones Cry Out: Sweden's Response to the Persecution of the Jews, 1933–1945* (New York: Holocaust Library, 1988), went a long way toward filling this glaring gap. As a pioneering effort, however, it raises and leaves unanswered many questions. Swedish historians of the Second World War have overlooked their country's response to the Holocaust; see Wilhelm Carlgren's "standard" work, *Svensk utrikespolitik 1939–1945* (Stockholm: Almänna Förlaget, 1973); and Alf Johansson's *Per Albin och Kriget* (Stockholm: Tiden, 1984). Richard Breitman has recently made an important contribution with his study of one particular episode; see "American Rescue Activities in Sweden," *Holocaust and Genocide Studies* 7/2 (Fall 1993): 202–15. An impressionistic description of Sweden's efforts on behalf of Scandinavian Jews was published in the early 1950s by Hugo Valentin, a Swedish-Jewish historian. While still of some value, Valentin's article was not based on documentary material available today; see "Rescue and Relief Activities in Behalf of Jewish Victims of Nazism in Scandinavia," *YIVO Annual* 13 (1953): 224–51.

10. A good example is Michael R. Marrus's brief comment about Raoul Wallenberg: "There is scarcely a better example of how an intrepid, strategically placed individual could capitalize on the standing of a neutral power to effect large-scale rescue" (*The Holocaust in History* [New York: New American Library, 1987], p. 178; see the chapter entitled "Bystanders"). "100,000 Lives Saved" is the almost mantralike refrain in hagiographic representations of Wallenberg. The true number can probably never be determined. The above figure, which includes the approximately seventy thousand Jews crowded into Budapest's short-lived ghetto, is most certainly a considerable exaggeration. According to Randolph L. Braham, Wallenberg had little or nothing to do with forestalling the planned attack against the ghetto; see Braham, *Politics of Genocide*, vol. 2, pp. 873–74 and 883 note 123.

11. Fackenheim, "Spectrum of Resistance," p. 113.

12. Although no one defines Italian obstruction as it is treated here, several scholars have noted analogous behavior by Italian officials; see Jonathan Steinberg, *All or Nothing: The Axis and the Holocaust* (New York: Routledge, 1990); and Lilianna P. Fargion, "Italian Citizens in Nazi-Occupied Europe: Documents from the Files of the German Foreign Office, 1941–1943," *Simon Wiesenthal Annual* 7 (1990): 93–141.

13. On Hungary, see Braham, *Politics of Genocide*, vol. 2, chapter 22; Asher Cohen, "Pétain, Horthy, Antonescu and the Jews, 1942–1944: Toward a Comparative View," in *TNH*, pp. 63–100. On France, see Hillel J. Keival, "Legality and Resistance in Vichy France: The Rescue of Jewish Children," in *TNH*, pp. 482–510.

14. Nathan Eck was one of the first to systematically look at the various types of documents; see "The Rescue of Jews with the Aid of Passports and Citizenship Papers of Latin American States," *Yad Vashem Studies* 1 (1957): 125–52. Since then, the use of diplomatic documents as a means of protection has been noted in many studies but it has not been studied systematically or theoretically.

15. These and hundreds of other Foreign Office documents can be found at Sweden's National Archives, *Riksarkivet, Utrikesdepartments* 1920 ar dossier system, HP 1 Eu vols. 579–83, and HP 21 Eu, vols. 1092–1100. "Weak" and "strong" were penciled designations written by foreign office officials in Stockholm next to names on the lists they received from Budapest;

the notation reflected the connection they felt the individual had with Sweden, leading to a decision whether the individual should or should not receive some sort of help.

16. Charles S. Maier, *The Unmasterable Past: History, Holocaust, and German National Identity* (Cambridge: Harvard University Press, 1988), p. 94. Asher Cohen also points to this gap in Nazi racial policy.

17. Raul Hilberg, *The Destruction of the European Jews* (New York: Holmes & Meier, 1985), vol. 2, p. 543.

18. Christopher R. Browning, "The Government Experts," in *The Holocaust: Ideology, Bureaucracy, and Genocide: The San Jose Papers*, ed. Henry Friedlander and Sybil Milton (Millwood, NY: Kraus International, 1980), p. 183.

19. Raul Hilberg, "The Bureaucracy of Annihilation," in *Unanswered Questions: Nazi Germany and the Genocide of the Jews*, ed. F. Furet (New York: Schocken Books, 1989), p. 119.

20. Both German and Swedish documents reveal the almost surreal formalism bureaucrats are capable of, even when discussing questions of life and death.

21. Uwe D. Adam, "Persecution of the Jews, Bureaucracy and Authority in the Totalitarian State," in *TNH*, vol. 3, p. 379.

22. Fred E. Katz, "The Implementation of the Holocaust: The Behavior of Nazi Officials," in *TNH*, vol. 3, p. 357.

23. Ibid., p. 365.

24. Christopher R. Browning has demonstrated this both with regard to the mid-level functionaries in the German Foreign Office and, more recently, a reserve police battalion; see his study, *The Final Solution and the German Foreign Office* (New York: Holmes & Meier, 1978), pp. 147–54; see also his *Ordinary Men: Reserve Police Battalion 101 and the Final Solution in Poland* (New York, HarperCollings, 1992), p. 57. One reviewer of *Ordinary Men* agrees that German functionaries had ample opportunity to avoid killing Jews: "Not once in the history of the Holocaust was a German killed, sent to a concentration camp, or punished in any serious way for refusing to kill Jews" (Daniel Jonah Goldhagen, "The Evil of Banality," *New Republic*, July 13 and 20, 1993, pp. 49–52).

25. Browning, "Bureaucracy and Mass Murder," p. 142.

26. Ibid., p. 142.

27. See note 41 below.

28. Studies of the German Foreign Office have often noted the lack of ideological fervor of diplomats, even in the Abteilung Deutschland, deeply involved in the Final Solution. See, among others, Browning in the two works on the Foreign Office cited in note 24 above; Paul Seabury's older *The Wilhelmstrasse, A Study of German Diplomats under the Nazi Regime* (Berkeley: University of California Press, 1954); and Milan Hauner, "The Professionals and the Amateurs in National Socialist Foreign Policy," in *The 'Führer State': Myth and Reality,* ed. G. Hirschfeld and L. Kettenacker (Stuttgart: Klett-Cotta, 1981), pp. 305–28.

29. Hilberg, "Bureaucracy," p. 127.

30. Hans Mommsen, "The Realization of the Unthinkable: The 'Final Solution of the Jewish Question' in the Third Reich," most recently published in *From Weimar to Auschwitz*, trans. Philip O'Connor (Princeton: Princeton University Press, 1991), p. 225.

31. Hilberg, *Destruction of the European Jews*, p. 53. Hilberg later wrote, "One step at a time, and each step dependent on the preceding step. The destruction of the Jews transpired in this manner; it had an inherent logic, irrespective of how far ahead the perpetrators could see and irrespective of what their plans were" ("Anatomy of the Holocaust," in *The Holocaust: Ideology, Bureaucracy and Genocide, The San Jose Papers,* ed. Henry Friedlander and Sybil Milton (Millwood, NY, 1980), pp. 86–87.

32. Christopher R. Browning has recently argued that Mommsen was wrong to conclude that anti-Jewish policy always or inevitably chose the most radical solution. This is an important empirical exception. Yet Mommsen's notion remains, it seems to the present author, a powerful heuristic device. See Browning, *Path to Genocide*, pp. 3–58.

33. Hans Mommsen, "National Socialism," in *From Weimer to Auschwitz*, p. 158.

34. Mommsen concentrates upon the prewar period and first years of the war. Theoretical appraisals of bureaucracy in the final years of killing are lacking.

35. Hilberg, "Bureaucracy of Annihilation," p. 127.

36. Peter Black points to this changing situation: "The loyal, somewhat realistic National Socialist was torn between his emotional and psychological need to keep the faith and a desire to insure his own personal survival. . . . The well-publicized intentions of the Allies to try the Nazi leaders for war crimes moved some SS leaders to contemplate an alternate solution to the war, either through flight or negotiation with the enemy" (*Ernst Kaltenbrunner: Ideological Soldier of the Third Reich* [Princeton: Princeton University Press, 1984], pp. 218–19. Chapter 7, "Ideology, Politics and the Search for Peace," is particularly illuminating.

37. Ian Kershaw, *Popular Opinion and Political Dissent in the Third Reich* (Oxford: Clarendon Press, 1983); idem, "The Persecution of the Jews and German Popular Opinion in the Third Reich," in *TNH*, vol. 5, p. 109.

38. This reason was given to German Foreign Minister von Ribbentrop to explain the growing reticence of Hungarian functionaries to cooperate in organizing deportations from Budapest when they had so shortly before been so cooperative in the Hungarian countryside. See Braham, *Politics of Genocide*, vol. 2, p. 808.

39. These issues have long been at the heart of Swedish historiography of the Second World War. Sweden's Social Democratic government feared a German invasion for much of the war, yet German dependence on Swedish iron ore in fact gave Sweden a strong bargaining hand; some evidence suggests that this kept the Germans from contemplating invasion. See Martin Fritz, "Swedish Iron Ore and German Steel, 1939–40," *Scandinavian Economic History Review* 21/2 (1973): 133–44; and John West, "German-Swedish Relations, 1939–1942," Ph.D. diss., University of Minnesota, 1976. For a recent discussion by Swedish scholars of the range of issues surrounding Swedish neutrality, see Bo Hugemark, ed., *I Orkanens Oga 1941— Osaker neutralitet* (Stockholm: Probus, 1992). A rather different view, one that caused Swedish historians to see red, is Maria-Pia Boethius, *Heder och Samvete, Sverige och andra varldskriget* (Stockholm: Norstedt, 1991).

40. Koblik, *Stones Cry Out*, pp. 59–61; Hilberg, *Destruction of the European Jews*, vol. 2, pp. 554–58. When asked by a German official why his government wanted to help Norwegian Jews, a Swedish diplomat in Oslo answered that his government, "wished to 'help the poor Jews, who, after all, are human beings too'" (National Archives [hereafter NA], Washington, D.C.) NG–5217. On Norway, see also Samuel Abrahamsen, *Norway's Response to the Holocaust: A Historical Perspective* (New York: Holocaust Library, 1991).

41. In response to Sweden's legally dubious but effective methods of naturalization, Eichmann complained to Germany's Foreign Office that such attempts to block "standard" Nazi procedure represented an effort to "thwart German Jewish measures through precipitate naturalization of people who had never even been in Sweden." For the German Foreign Office's response to this and similar Swedish attempts to forestall deportation, see Browning, *Final Solution and the German Foreign Office*, pp. 156–58. The Swedish documents are at the Riksarkivet (hereafter RA), Utrikesdepartementet (hereafter UD) 1920 ars dossier system, HP 21 J, vols. 1049–50.

42. Attempts by officials in Stockholm, primarily Gosta Engzell, head of the Foreign Office's Legal Division, to enlarge the categories and numbers of individuals whom they might protect are documented in RA UD 1920 ars dos. system, HP 21 J, vols. 1049–50, and ibid., HP 21 J Ad (Denmark), vols. 1056–57.

43. S. Soderblom to A. Richert, October 2, 1943, RA UD 1920 ar HP 21 J Ad, vol. 1056/ parm II. Arvid Richter was Sweden's highly influential Minister in Berlin and an important influence on Swedish foreign policy. Although reluctant to first make another request as in Norway, and even less sure of the value of publicizing it, he was overruled by Stockholm.

44. Promemoria written by Gosta Engzell, October 8, 1943, RA UD 1920 ar HP 21 J, vol. 1056/parm II.

45. In his second telegram to Stockholm after the occupation, Danielsson reported that, in his opinion, Germany's primary motive was, the "lack of [Hungary's] ability or will to solve the Jewish problem according to the German pattern" (telegram #23, 23 March 1944, RA UD 1920 ar HP 1 Eu [Hungary], vol. 582/parm XXI).

46. These categories were immediately broadened when the Legation received permis-

sion from the Cabinet to issue provisional passports to first, "those who have applied for Swedish citizenship," and very soon after, "for all Jewish people who through us have requested assistance"; see Cabinet to Legation Budapest, tel. #25, 23 March 1944, and Cabinet to Legation, #45, 31 March 1944, both in RA UD 1920 ar, HP 21 Eu, vol. 1094/parm II. By no means did all applicants receive assistance, either those who approached the Legation or those who appealed directly to the Foreign Office in Stockholm on behalf of relatives or friends. In fact, the categories went through many changes, an imprecision fully exploited by Per Anger, and later Raoul Wallenberg.

47. Immediately following the Arrow Cross coup, Gabor Vajna, the newly appointed Interior Minister, issued a directive which, among other things, made officially invalid all the different types of protective documents issued by neutrals. These documents had played an increasingly important role in shielding some people from bands of Arrow Cross hooligans. Yet a few days later, following the determined and aggressive lobbying of Wallenberg and other neutral diplomats, he rescinded the order. See Braham, *Politics of Genocide*, vol. 2, pp. 823–33, and C. A. Macartney, *October Fifteenth: A History of Modern Hungary, 1929–1945* (Edinburgh: University Press, 1956), vol. 2, p. 449.

38.

MARK A. EPSTEIN

A Lucky Few

REFUGEES IN TURKEY

With one notable exception, only specialists on Turkey appear to have given much thought to the fact that about 10 percent of the twelve thousand or so academics who lost their jobs after the Nazis came to power went to Turkey—a surprisingly high percentage given the other possible destinations. Few realize that the University of Istanbul had the highest concentration of refugee professors in a single institution anywhere in the world.

I relate these facts because of the reception of an earlier version of this essay—a reception that seems even more relevant today than it was then. It fell behind what I perceive as a curtain of prejudice toward Turks, and perhaps more broadly toward Muslims, a prejudice that is deeper and wider in Christian Europe than in the United States and that has played a part in the recent conflicts in Bosnia and elsewhere.

After the earlier presentation at a conference on intellectual and academic refugees from Germany, held at an eminent institution, the organizers asked that the text be revised for publication in the volumes that were to present the conference proceedings. I revised my text and sent it to the editors, looking forward to receiving a stack of offprints to be passed out with pride at some future conference. Nearly two years later, while in the United States, I discovered that the volumes had appeared but without my contribution. When I inquired, I was given an apology. The explanation was that the editors had space limitations and therefore had to leave out "marginal" countries.

Since the paper had been very well received at the conference and Turkey was so important in the world of academic refugees and later of Jewish rescue from Europe, I reached a number of rather disturbing conclusions, but their full import probably was not clear to me at the time. One conclusion was that, as a Muslim country, Turkey was simply beyond the comfortable reach of Europe-oriented scholarship. For the most part, we do see the East through the historical eyes of Europeans, hence as an infidel, threatening, morally corrupt place.

This theme is not new or unique, nor do I necessarily agree with the theses of others who write about these issues, especially those who argue that the high concentration of Jews in Oriental studies has skewed the perception against Muslims. I believe that the contrary is the case.

Turkish enlightened self-interest, and a measure of generosity toward individual

Jews and German non-Jews in the 1930s and 1940s, seem to be viewed by many non-Islamicists and non-Turcologists as curious exceptions within a larger picture. Alternatively, these motivations and actions are seen as crass and self-serving, despite the fact that the Turkish record is far more admirable than most.

Relatively recently there appeared a work that praises the role of Turkish diplomats in France, who intervened on behalf of former Turkish and former Ottoman subjects there and saved a goodly number. While other neutral countries also intervened on behalf of their nationals in France, Turkey went so far as to help former Ottoman citizens who had emigrated and whose papers or citizenship had lapsed. Such intervention was hardly necessary. More interesting to me is that some years ago this story was known and essentially dismissed out of hand by Jewish observers for no discernible reason, as noted by Stanford Shaw.[1]

The Turkish experience, both the story Shaw tells and the general behavior of the Turks, mostly lacks the drama of deportations and mass death. Since Turkey remains a relatively distant place, on the "other" side of an historical divide between Christianity and Islam, it receives short shrift at best.[2]

The history of Turkey in relation to the Holocaust is the story of a response to the Nazis that concerns not only the plight of the Jews. Still, were these the issues of a distant, hoary past—even events as remarkable as those of 1492—it might seem a matter of concern to scholars alone. Sadly, in today's world, these matters seem all the more timely.

I believe that the Turkish experience does offer us the answer to an important historical question: What was a reasonable response by a neutral country to the moral and political challenges of the Nazi regime? The Turkish attitude toward the events of the period of Nazi rule is also worthy of careful consideration because of what it implies about contemporary developments that threaten to take on the same character.

When the Nazis seized power in 1933, many German professors, artists, musicians, and others in state-controlled institutions were dismissed from their positions because they were Jews—at least under the terms of Nazi racial definitions—or married to Jews, or they were liberals or communists, or were charged with any of a number of other sins. Many among them were to leave Germany, and of those a most remarkable group found haven and employment in the young Turkish Republic.

The Republic of Turkey was one of the successor states to the Ottoman Empire, a large mass on the map to the southeast of those countries that most of us learned about or describe to students in courses on European civilization. At the height of its power and glory, in the sixteenth century, it stretched from what subsequently become central Yugoslavia and Hungary through the Balkan peninsula, across Anatolia to the present Iraqi-Iranian frontier. It included the Arab lands of the Fertile Crescent, present-day Israel, Saudi Arabia, Yemen, Egypt, much of North Africa, Ethiopia, and occasionally a slice or two of southern Italy.

By the eighteenth century, and certainly in the nineteenth, the Ottoman Empire had fallen into decay and degeneracy, and at the end of World War I, having found itself on the losing side, the "Sick Man of Europe" faced the final stages of the process of partition and division that had long been underway. At the peace conferences following the war, most of the Ottoman provinces would be established as separate countries under British or French mandates granted by the League of Nations. To the Ottomans were apportioned a part of the Anatolian plateau and the area around Istanbul (Constantinople), which was still under Allied occupation.

Under Allied protection, Greek armies quietly invaded Izmir (Smyrna), laying claim to many of the Anatolian coastal areas with Greek populations. In a long and strenuous war, Turkish nationalist forces under the leadership of Mustafa Kemal Pasha, hero of the battle of Gallipoli and probably the only Ottoman general to emerge from World War I with his reputation enhanced, vanquished the Greeks and unified Anatolia under Turkish control. Within a matter of months, the last Ottoman sultan had been stripped of his powers, and a few years later he would lose his title of caliph, leader of the world's Muslims. A nationalist regime under Mustafa Kemal was in control.

In the course of the struggle for independence, Kemal had laid the foundation for ending Ottoman identity: the multireligious, multiracial Muslim empire existed no longer. The heartland that remained was, after an exchange of populations with Greece, relatively homogenous, and Mustafa Kemal set about forging a new, distinctly Turkish identity.

He attempted to achieve a complete break with the Ottoman past, and set as his task the creation of a secular, Western-oriented nation. He moved the capital from Istanbul, with its imperial history and non-Turkish minority groups, to Ankara, a drab town in central Anatolia. Soon he would attempt to break the power of the religious establishment and replace Arabic script with a much more suitable, modified Latin alphabet. He outlawed the veil for women and the fez for men, forcing the adoption of European dress. An attempt was begun, and indeed continues, to purge Arabic and Persian borrowings from Turkish speech. Under his iron-fisted but relatively benevolent rule, a new society was being formed. As part of his scheme he had sought advice regarding the establishment of a modern, European-style university system.

In 1932, Professor Albert Malche of the University of Geneva had been invited by the Turkish government to submit recommendations for university reform in Turkey. He made a series of suggestions regarding reform of the Darülfunun (Abode of Sciences), the old Ottoman university that had been established in the course of Westernizing reforms in the nineteenth century.

For the new Istanbul Üniversitesi, Malche proposed a general overhaul of pedagogic method, particular emphasis on training in foreign languages, a centralized administration, library reform, and a program for conferences and seminars throughout the country in order to spread the influence of the university beyond the campus and outside Istanbul. The problem of providing the necessary faculty for this new approach had not been fully solved, but Malche suggested inviting small groups of academics from various foreign countries.

About that time, in June 1933, Malche received a telegram from Professor Philipp Schwartz, founder of the newly established Notgemeinschaft Deutscher Wissenschaftler im Ausland (Emergency Society of German Academics Abroad), which was based in Zürich.[3] Schwartz believed, quite correctly, that he had something to offer Malche and the Turkish Ministry of Culture.[4] A physician from Frankfurt am Main, Schwartz had taken refuge with his in-laws in Zürich during March 1933, and by

April had established the Beratungsstelle für Deutsche Wissenschaftler (Advisory Bureau for German Academics); the Notgemeinschaft was formed to support the work of the Beratungsstelle.

By July, a month after his telegram to Malche, Schwartz was in direct contact with the Turkish authorities, and in October he made his first trip to Istanbul.[5] When he met with the Minister of Culture and the members of the university reform committee, who asked him to suggest professors in various disciplines to be invited to Turkey, he happily supplied names from his card file.[6]

The Turkish authorities were specific regarding their requirements: they wanted prestigious, well-known academicians with world-caliber reputations. Younger people might be permitted to accompany the professors as assistants. The principle was to be applied almost without exception.[7]

The negotiations over the first contracts, mostly for a five-year term, confirmed that the government was serious in its purpose. The foreigners were to receive salaries two, three, and sometimes four times as high as those earned by their Turkish colleagues.[8] Furthermore, in what serves as a remarkable example of support and courage, the Turkish government would intervene diplomatically on behalf of any professors who had been imprisoned or interned in concentration camps after signing their contracts, considering them as already being in Turkish government employ and thus entitled to the protection of a Turkish civil servant. This actually occurred in a number of cases.[9]

In retrospect, this willingness by a relatively weak, young country seems quite remarkable. While one may argue that self-interest was at stake, seasoned perhaps by a characteristic stubbornness and national pride, it is easy to imagine a government arguing under the circumstances that, especially since the matter concerned foreign nationals, little could be done.

It makes no sense to argue that an incident or two, little known at the time and probably less known more than sixty years later, should have been widely noticed or its full implications understood. But two things are evident. First, a general pattern in Turkish behavior, which to my mind has historical roots, is reconfirmed. Second, it is an early hint that protest and firmness could yield some results in dealing with the Nazis. It is this recurring truth, with many individual examples elsewhere over the years that followed, that haunts us all.

The Turkish government demonstrated the seriousness of its intent in contractual terms as well. Within three to five years, the foreign professors were to have learned to read Turkish, and they were expected, perhaps with assistance, to produce Turkish textbooks for the basic courses in their disciplines.[10] Over time, they were pressured to teach in Turkish as well, but few were ever up to the task.

Since Turkish is so linguistically distant from what most Europeans knew and know, learning it may seem to be an unreasonable expectation. Still, considering the alternatives in the mid-1930s, it hardly seems too high a price to pay for the opportunity to pursue one's chosen profession in a pleasant city beyond the grasp of the Nazis.

It was, of course, a shortcoming of the Turkish vision that they did not choose to seek hundreds, even thousands of other German and European Jews from other disciplines as well. At their meetings, the Turkish Minister of Culture cited to Philipp

Schwartz the events of 1453 and the belief that Byzantine scholars fleeing to Italy from the Ottomans created the Renaissance. However it seems that the full implications of the Turkish opportunity were hidden to the historical and national vision of the time. Still, within a few months agreements had been reached with seventy or so German professors to begin teaching in Turkey. Of these, some fifty to sixty were in Istanbul University and comprised the largest concentration of German emigrant professors in the world.[11]

In the course of the two decades that followed, some would leave and be replaced by others and, in all, about a hundred served in that one university. There were, in addition, assistants and laboratory workers, so the actual number of foreigners was even larger, augmented by members of other faculties in Istanbul and Ankara, and some numbers of businessmen, writers, and others.

On the basis of numbers alone, we can begin to grasp the significance of the role these people would play. It was Norman Bentwich who first suggested that some twelve hundred scholars and scientists were dismissed from German institutions in 1933–1934, some 650 of whom emigrated.[12] When one considers how many of them went to the United States and Britain, where they were spread among numerous institutions, one begins to perceive the impact of a concentrated group of more than fifty.

When Philipp Schwartz arrived in Turkey to negotiate the placement of German scholars, he felt that he had discovered a wondrous land, unpoisoned by the plague that was destroying European life.[13] Many of the immigrants lived in Bebek, a then wooded suburb of Istanbul on the Bosporus, and one of a number of suburbs where the major powers had summer embassies. In Ottoman times the sultan and his court and harem, along with diplomatic and social life, withdrew there to escape the heat of the city.

Other immigrants lived in Kadiköy, on the Asian shore of the Sea of Marmara.[14] One can, perhaps, fantasize about what it must have been like to walk down to the ferry dock, board the boat with newspaper or book in hand, purchase a glass of hot, sweet, deep orange Turkish tea for a penny or two, and settle down for the twenty-minute ride across the Marmara, past the Topkapi Palace and Hagia Sofia, and, look up at the seven hills with fabulous mosques and towering minarets, pull into the dock in the Golden Horn, and then work one's way through the twisting market streets up to the university campus. The ferry trip from Kadiköy or down the Bosporus is certainly the world's most elegant commuter trip.

Once up the hill on the campus, however, problems arose. First, of course, was the understandable resentment of a certain element of the faculty—those who had professorial rank in the old Darülfunun and were kept on in subordinate roles—not to mention those who lost their positions. Nonetheless, there were reforms ordered by Ankara, according to the express wishes of the stern Mustafa Kemal, now known as Atatürk, Father of the Turks. Such commands could not be completely disregarded because of the passive resistance of a few. In fact, a new rector had been appointed to institute the requisite changes. The reform-minded members of the faculty, along with the students, went forth with great enthusiasm, full of belief in building their future and the foundations of a new society.

For the Republic, Atatürk's remarkable and essentially successful policy of Western orientation led not only to the introduction of European dress, the Latin alphabet, and a secular constitution. It also ended an old debate that had dominated Ottoman life since the eighteenth century: Could one be a Muslim and still use Western technology and innovation? It was already irrefutable that the unthinkable had happened, that is, the infidel, Christian West had surpassed Islam technologically. With that question apparently solved, one could act on the consequences.

In this new phase of nationalism, enthusiasm and progressivism, the new professors were worshipped to the point of embarrassment by their students, and by some colleagues as well; for the Germans were the embodiment of what Turkish academicians wished to be. For students, they held the mystical key to modern life, a European education. German universities enjoyed a considerable reputation at the time.

Yet still the problems of where and how to disseminate the collective wisdom they were to propound lay before them. With the exception of a few Orientalists and Turcologists among them, who knew Turkish? One, the chemist Fritz Arndt, had taught for a year at the Darülfunun during World War I and did speak the language.[15] The others had promised under the terms of their contracts to acquire at least a reading knowledge of Turkish. Some of the students, mostly members of the non-Muslim minority groups, knew French; most did not. Turkish was to be the means of communication.

Each professor had been assigned one or more Turkish assistants, usually junior faculty members. Some were lucky enough to have been assigned young holders of doctoral degrees who had received their training in Germany or had elsewhere acquired a good knowledge of German. Most were not so fortunate.

In any case, lectures were in German and were translated sentence by sentence into Turkish. It required of the professors that they organize their thoughts with great precision, a system that functioned well in many cases, but not universally.

As some of the professors acquired enough Turkish to understand the translations while still unable to lecture in Turkish, they perceived errors or shortcomings on the part of their translators, but for reasons of good oriental manners or because of linguistic limitations, were unable to correct the misinformation or clarify the problems. One can only imagine the pleasure of correcting hundreds of handwritten examinations in a language imperfectly mastered, or having to do so with the aid of assistants. The situation, though, was not universally bleak. On the contrary, most of the German professors seem to have taken great pleasure in teaching their Turkish students, whom they found to be intelligent and full of hope and enthusiasm.[16]

There were, of course, the general frustrations that accompanied living in Turkey. In Rudolf Nissen's memoirs one finds the amusing account of his entering the Institute of Surgery and Pathology, which he was to direct and which had been totally remodeled to meet the new demands to be placed upon it. Imagine his discovery that the new laboratories and offices were fully equipped with electrical outlets that did not function because the contractors, presumably in the interests of speed and economy, had neglected to install any wiring![17]

Returning to the problem of resettlement: the Turkish government had been taken aback at the attendant costs, but after long and tortuous negotiations had agreed to pay up to 90 percent of such costs, and should there be a surplus in the budget, to distribute the remainder among the various academicians.

As fate would have it, one professor who had signed a contract committed suicide in Europe before moving to Turkey. Before the sum allotted to him could be distributed among the others, however, a minor university official had forged his signature and taken the funds. No amount of argument could persuade the authorities to make good on the funds—and when it was suggested that the employee be docked a percentage of his monthly salary, they responded that it would be decades before the sum would be repaid.[18]

Despite such frustrations, the German professors were soon established and teaching. The initial difficulties were quickly behind them, but the problems of living in Turkish society were not always uncomplicated, though solutions usually presented themselves. One could not simply breeze into a shoe store or haberdashery and select the desired items, a state of affairs mitigated to some extent by the fact that numerous tailors and shoemakers would produce custom products cheaply within a few days.[19] But life was not simply tailor-made pajamas.

Doubtless, personality played a major role in the quality of relationships. Fritz Neumark records instances of lasting friendships, shared interests in European music, and family outings with Turkish friends and colleagues;[20] but Neumark may be an exception. A baptized Protestant who lost his job for "racial" reasons, he returned to postwar Germany and was instrumental in planning its economic miracle. In the Bundesrepublik he was deeply involved in German-Turkish relations and was an active leader of the Deutsche-Türkische Gesellschaft well into his eighties.

Neumark may be an exception in the context of the Holocaust and victims of the Nazis generally: a Protestant by denomination who returned to Germany. However, he is also one of a rare species in that he found work in his field quickly upon his return and spent the thirties and the war years productively in a safe place.

In general, experiences in Turkey were a bit different, but by the standard of the day, hardly burdensome. Most of the university professors seem to have had cordial and rewarding relationships with their Turkish colleagues, but relatively little contact outside the university and few real friendships.[21] This impression is confirmed by nonacademic German refugees as well, and by nonrefugee Germans who were in Turkey in the years just after the war.

German and Turkish societies were relatively separate from one another, but rarely did the hosts complain about the inability of the guests to assimilate into community.[22] As most of the professors lived in a few neighborhoods along the Bosporus or on the Marmara, their natural tendency to seek each others' company was reenforced. Likewise, language alone, if not cultural differences in general, buffered them and eased them toward nonrefugee Germans and German cultural institutions. Here the relationships were at least as complicated as with the Turks.

During Ernst Fabricius's tenure as German legate in Turkey, a fiction was maintained that the presence of the Jewish and other refugee professors in Turkey enhanced German prestige and was in Germany's interest.[23] Franz von Papen, the German ambassador in Ankara, apparently did not cultivate this view.

Both Nissen and Philipp Schwartz claim that on at least one occasion, in 1933, Nazi flags were removed from the summer embassy in Tarabya, on the Bosporus, because of their refusal to enter a building over which the swastika flew.[24] Late in the 1930s this may have been unthinkable. Still, it is another little reminder of the vulnerability of the Nazis, especially in neutral settings or countries where they hoped to expand their influence. It is also disturbing for its implications about the silence of so many others.

Those professors with school-age children in Istanbul were faced with the problem of whether to send the children to the German school.[25] In the first years a few attended, but soon none remained. The German cultural institutions in Turkey were split along political lines: those on one side of the spectrum, along with the consulate, were the Club Teutonia, German school, and the journalists' club; on the other side were the Archeological Institute, the German hospital, and the Evangelische Gemeinde.[26] Not all refugees were Jews and, indeed, not all the "Jews" were Jews.

In the middle years of the 1930s, events in Germany had an effect on relationships in the Turkish German community as well. Part of the change accompanied the replacement of Fabricius by von Papen in 1939; still, it remained possible for the exiles to renew their German passports. In 1938, as the situation had worsened, attempts were made to stamp "J" in the passports of those considered Jews according to Nazi racial laws; finally, in 1940, the passports of those defined as "non-Aryans" were revoked. The Turkish government, it should be noted, created no difficulties for those without passports.[27] Admittedly it was in the Turkish interest to keep the professors they had hired, but lenient practice seems to have applied to Jewish nonacademics and noncivil servants as well.

Likewise, in the course of the 1930s, other members of the German community—who were not Jewish or politcal refugees in Turkey— came under increasing pressure to break off social relations with "non-Aryans."[28] After 1938, for propaganda purposes, the Auswärtiges Amt (Foreign Office) stepped up attempts to gather information on the activities of the German professors in Turkey.[29] Foreign Minister Joachim von Ribbentrop's brother-in-law had been posted to Ankara, and throughout the thirties had been observing the activities of all German nationals in Turkey.[30]

At this point something must be said about Turkey's position in World War II. Ismet Inönü, a hero of the war of independence, had taken over the government after the death of Atatürk in 1938; for the most part he followed the path of the father of the country. A 1939 treaty with Britain was ignored in favor of neutrality. However, the course of that neutrality was not simple or straightforward, nor did neutrality mean disinterest.

First, there was the traditional Turkish sympathy for Germany and the Germans; it represented more than just a residue of affection based on the military alliance of World War I. Also, the Germans were still part of that magic "Europe" to which Atatürk and the Republic had turned for inspiration,[31] and without giving a false impression, one must say that some elements of Nazi ideology and German life— nationalism, industry, modernity, and discipline—conformed to Turkish ideals and struck a responsive chord. This was especially true after the German invasion of archenemy Russia, which was as feared by the Turks in its communist form as it had been as an imperial power.

Upon the outbreak of the war, most foreigners in Turkish government service, including ministerial advisors, were relieved of those jobs.[32] Nonacademicians came under considerably more pressure than the university professors, especially later in the war. Istanbul, especially, quickly became the battleground of numerous espionage services, both Allied and Axis, and a regular funnel for information and money. With the only Balkan territory not occupied by the Nazis or allied with the Axis, and with free passage through the Bosporus and the Dardanelles guaranteed by treaty, Turkey became a center of intrigue, and a feasible refuge.

There are numerous stories, both individual and collective, dealing with Jewish refugees arriving from various parts of Central Europe. There are stories of individual tragedy, and little was made easy. But for the most part one hears positive stories, interlaced with well-known catastrophes, including the sinking of the *Struma*.

Turkey guarded its neutrality desperately and tried to remain out of the war, yet cooperated with the Allies. There are sufficient accounts of such cooperation—of soldiers and airmen being rescued and aided, of Greek resistance fighters being assisted, and of Jewish refugees managing to enter the country and remain safely— that a pattern is clear, even if there is still no adequate study of Turkish policy, especially as regards the Jews. In addition, refugee and other vessels did pass through Turkish waters regularly and often anchored off Istanbul during their passage elsewhere. It appears that the Turks behaved correctly, or even better than correctly.

From interviews and conversations many years ago in Istanbul with older members of the Jewish community, I heard a variety of accounts. During the war (and in the years 1945–1948) it sometimes happened that significant numbers of Jewish refugees hidden on ships were smuggled off the vessels into Istanbul, slept on the floors of Jewish owned business offices, and returned on board before dawn. Reportedly, this was to minimize potential incidents and public embarrassments should the harbor police and customs authorities come across them while checking passenger lists and vessels. It is inconceivable that the Turkish police, who have a prodigious reputation for counterespionage work, were unaware of this activity. Throughout the war and after, the individual anecdotes suggest that at least those who were clever and those with the means to persuade various authorities survived safely in Turkey.

Late in the war some of the Germans and other foreigners in Turkey came under suspicion of espionage—or perhaps more accurately put, their activities were no longer tolerated—and they were deported. In August 1944, when Turkey finally broke off diplomatic relations with Germany, all Germans except those still permitted in public service, primarily professors, were offered a choice of transport to the Third Reich or internment in central Anatolia. Jews, that is, Volljuden, according to the Nazi definition, were exempted, and families were in some cases split up by this policy. After the end of the war in 1945, all were released.

Unattractive as this particular chapter may seem, it points out some important contradictions and ironies. First, there was the victimization of non-Jewish Germans, some but not all of whom were themselves persecuted by the Nazis; but at least they were offered a choice other than deportation to the Reich. Second, there was the bittersweet sensation of enjoying the privilege that in this particular situation derived from being a "full Jew" according to the Nuremberg Laws. And miserable as the camps were, the recollection of that experience does not seem to have dimmed the general affection that most of these refugees continued to hold for Turkey and the Turks generally.

Having come to the end of the war, we should return briefly to say something of the role of this remarkable group of German academics and intellectuals and their impact on Turkish society. There had been few professionals in Turkey trained after the European manner, whether civil servants, economists, engineers, or others. Hence, the German refugees were engaged not only in teaching on all levels, they produced the basic textbooks in their fields and translations ranging from Plato's *Republic* to modern literature. Neumark, who later played an important role in the planning of the Wirtschaftswunder, was instrumental in founding the *Journal of the Faculty of Economics* in Istanbul, which remains the most important Turkish scholarly journal in its field. Paul Hindemith oversaw the foundation and formation of the Conservatory of Music in Ankara, carrying out his responsibilities in the course of four stays in Ankara and through extensive correspondence.

Among the musicians and dramatists, Carl Ebert, Ernst Prätorius, and Eduard Zuckmayer played fundamental roles in establishing Western music and theater in Turkey.[33] Zuckmayer served as an adviser in the Ministry of Culture and taught music in Ankara until his death in 1972.

Several Turkish government ministries hired German émigrés as full-time consultants, and some of the university professors served as part-time advisers. Alfred Isaac, who taught economics in Istanbul, advised the Ministry of Labor regarding social security insurance and labor relations. Bruno Taut and others served as architects for public projects and taught in institutions such as the Istanbul Technical University. Clemens Holzmeister taught in the State Academy of Fine Arts. The names, of course, go on.

Ernst Reuter, who would later serve as mayor of West Berlin and who taught urban planning in Ankara during his exile, was employed by the Turkish government. Social observer and philosopher Alexander Rüstow taught and advised the government in Ankara, but he also spent considerable time in Istanbul. Rüstow was one of those who learned Turkish extremely well and was well liked in Turkish circles.

Rudolf Nissen, protégé of the Berlin surgeon Ferdinand Sauerbruch at the Charité, is remembered not only for his considerable role in the medical faculty in the years from 1933 until his departure for the United States five years later. More than one Anatolian born in those years bears the forename Nissen. When the popular internist Erich Frank died in 1957, he was given a state funeral, so pervasive were his role and influence.

It is unnecessary to reproduce lists of figures, but one must develop some feeling for the overwhelming presence of the refugee professors. Of twelve institutes of the medical faculty, nine were directed by immigrants, along with six of the seventeen university clinics. There were sixteen professors and thirty others of lower rank.[34]

In the natural sciences the programs in mathematics, astronomy, physics, chemistry, biology, and zoology were all directed and dominated by émigrés. In the humanities, the chairs of philosophy, archeology, Romance languages, Germanic studies, Oriental studies, classical philology, psychology, and Asian languages were held by foreign professors. The exceptions were, not surprisingly, Turcology, history, and other related disciplines.

Foreigners taught in eight of the twelve institutes of the Faculty of Humanities. In the Faculty of Economics, foreigners occupied five of the eight professorships. Widmann calculates a total of fifty-six professors, thirty-five nonprofessorial faculty, and seven assistants—in all, ninety-eight at Istanbul University, three at Istanbul Technical University, and two at the State Academy of Fine Arts.

In Ankara there were twenty-one immigrant academics and artists at the Conservatory of Music; six on the Faculty of History, Geography and Languages; eight physicians in various hospitals; four at the Institute of Agricultural Sciences; two on the Faculty of Social Sciences—all together some forty-one.[35]

As one can see, the scope of disciplines, from Hittitology to the most sophisticated disciplines in the natural sciences, is impressive. That, and the caliber of the people who served in Istanbul and Ankara, is especially impressive when one recalls the situation in Turkey before their arrival.

Not all of the refugee professors renewed their initial five-year contracts. Many received offers from institutions in the United States and Britain, which they accepted. They were replaced by other Germans or, after the *Anschluss*, Austrians, and occasionally a German-speaking Hungarian or Romanian.

After the war the émigrés faced the question of whether to return to Europe or move elsewhere, though most did not leave Turkey immediately. Many went to the United States, a large number to Germany and Austria, and some to other parts of the world. Some remained in Turkey, but their number steadily declined. One or two had married or remarried there and stayed on, but by the mid-1950s most were gone.

And what of their legacy, their impact on Turkish society? It is no exaggeration to say that the German refugee scholars introduced a whole generation of Turks to the ways of the European university and helped lay the foundation of Western-style cultural life in Turkey. Of course, they did not achieve this alone, but rather in conjunction with Turkish colleagues and assistants. It is eloquent testimony to the abilities of the Turks that in five to ten years, Turkish faculty were often able to replace their foreign guests.

The debt to foreign scholars is not unappreciated in Turkey. Throughout the postwar years, in a most Teutonic fashion, the birthdays of many of the German professors were celebrated by their Turkish colleagues and successors. Articles appeared in Turkish professional journals describing the role and activities of the foreign professors, and Festschriften were occasionally published, while some Turks invited their mentors to revisit their former campuses. Throughout the 1950s and 1960s it was difficult to find among Turkish university professors and professionals important figures who had not had some contact with the immigrant professors and who were not affected by them. With the passing of time, of course, the situation has changed.

To broach the question of lasting influence one would have to enter the realm of the hypothetical and speculate regarding the situation that might have prevailed had the emigrant professors not spent the Nazi years in Turkey. Anything more that might be said about the breadth and depth of their influence would be superfluous, and we cannot tell what the situation would have been like had the Turks been left to their own devices. Certainly, had it not been for political considerations in Germany, Turkey would have had to look long and hard to find scholars of the quality of those who were her long-term guests.

This remarkable chapter in Turkish and immigrant history could have been written only in the very special circumstances of the 1930s: the concurrence of the plight of the Germans in the face of Nazi persecution and the quest of the Turks for modernization.[36]

The Turks expected great things; despite their strong nationalism, they were receptive to foreign professors as a means of building a Turkish university system.[37] Still, the lenient treatment of other refugees suggests more than simple self-interest and pedagogical policy. Students of the German Jews and other victims of the Nazis seeking refuge in the 1930s shudder at the insensitivity and inhumanity of the world. After the outbreak of war this inhumanity became even more dangerous, counteracted by individual instances of heroism. In the case of the Turks, we encounter a society welcoming certain refugees on practical grounds, with no particular intention of absorbing and assimilating them.[38] When Minister of Culture Reşid Galip signed the first contract with Philipp Schwartz in 1933, he expressed the hope that the German professors would help bring about a rebirth in Turkey, just as, in his words, the flight of Byzantine Greek scholars to Italy after the Ottoman conquest of Istanbul in 1453 contributed so much to the Italian Renaissance.[39] More appropriately, perhaps, we should recall the haven in the Ottoman Empire offered to Spanish Jews after their expulsion in 1492. In the new nationalist republic, however, there probably was less flexibility for whole communities to simply immigrate and lead a separate life alongside and among dozens of other groups.

It would have been not only a great humanitarian act, but also a brilliant exercise in self-interest if the Turks had done more. Indeed, had they been more sophisticated and more open, had they had a deeper understanding of the impact of 1492 on their own history, they might well have brought immense individual ambition and industry to their country and thereby achieved the rapid economic and Western cultural development they sought.

But in the 1930s the Turks wished to do something for themselves, after centuries of feeling persecuted, patronizingly over-advised, exploited, and eventually partitioned and invaded by foreigners. They hired happily what they could not find at home, European professors, but still they let in some others too.

Perhaps we should give more weight to the fact that, until 1942 or 1943, many in Turkey were inclined to join the Axis, a factor that reduced their willingness to accept many foreign Jews. Still, even if the Turks did not seek opportunities to help, they generally did not simply turn away those who reached their country. No bribe, no amount of begging, no starving infant at a mother's breast was enough to move most of Europe. Some element of common decency was present in Turkey, and apparently emerged more often than not.

It should also be borne in mind that those who managed to enter Turkey and stay, with or without papers, with or without work permits, with or without jobs, were well known to the Turkish police. They were not hidden under floorboards and in barns, converted to a different faith and reeducated. Except when we are stopped for a traffic violation, we tend to forget that sometimes there is virtue in having the police look the other way, or even line their pockets, if that is what it took.

To some degree, however, the receptivity of the Turkish government to foreign professors in general and German professors in particular must be understood in the context of traditional relations between Ottoman Turkey and her non-Muslim minority groups, and of the Ottomans employing foreign advisors of various sorts since the eighteenth century and before. Ironically, the legacy of good relations between Turkey and Germany resulting from the First World War also played a role. Like most foreigners who spend considerable time in Turkey, the refugees felt themselves to be friends of the Turkish people and came to think of the country as a second homeland. Some of their children and grandchildren have become students of Turkish history and culture. In addition, refugee scholars paved the way for a further German cultural presence in Turkey in the 1950s and 1960s.

In some respects, the Jewish refugees among the academic group in Turkey were able to continue their lives as "German" outsiders in a foreign country. Since they were welcomed for various reasons, they did not face the problem of reestablishing themselves, a problem that confronted many refugees elsewhere. Still, significant anecdotal evidence shows that other Jews (and non-Jews), nonacademics and those who were not prominent, who reached Turkey before and during the war, managed to enter and stay without documentation. To that must be added what is known about cases of commendable Turkish intercession in France, Rhodes, and elsewhere, where Turkish self-interest was less evident.

One might venture to guess that in no other country was the impact of refugee academicians so profound as in Turkey. Their concentration in the educational system and cultural institutions was highest in Turkey. The size of the university population whom they served was among the smallest of those lands to which refugees fled, and the educational system probably the least developed. The state that employed them was the youngest. Though one cannot say this with certainty, the esteem in which they were held and the respect that they were accorded were probably greater than anywhere else. The story deserves to be better known. It also serves to underline the irony of what the Turks may have lost by not pursuing a policy of seeking other refugees from Europe. Still, I suspect that in no other country was it possible for refugee Jews to enter and survive in this fashion. And this was made possible by the esteem, and the visa, that a university contract and the patronage of the Ministry of Education offered.

This brings me again to the question I posed earlier. What could one expect of a neutral country at the time of the Nazis? What was the responsibility of any country or people that considered itself civilized, and part of the great monotheistic tradition shared by Muslim, Christian, and Jew? And why have we been reluctant to give more credit for these acts? Even if they did not represent salvation for millions, they do stand in stark contrast to much else that happened in Europe.

This chapter in history should not be construed to be more than it was, nor should undeserved moral characteristics be attached to the explanation. It is not necessarily heroic, though individual acts of considerable courage occurred. Another attitude seems to characterize it. As a whole, the Turks behaved "correctly," and usually "decently." That is worth mentioning when one recalls those times and circumstances. One could wish that other countries, including the United States, had behaved as well when confronted with individuals seeking help or refuge.

It seems to me that the standard to which we hold the behavior of governments may be too high. Few countries take pride and speak openly, even if for their own advantage, of having accepted refugee Jews, whether in 1492 or 1942. How many countries could make such a boast, even if they wished?

In Bosnia we have just witnessed a war along religious lines at the frontier that divided the Turks from Christian Europe. To me, this chapter of history, and its treatment by historians seems at very least worthy of detached examination if our purpose is to seek relevant lessons in the ashes of the Holocaust and the era of the Nazis.

NOTES

1. Stanford J. Shaw, *Turkey and the Holocaust* (New York: Macmillan, 1992). See Shaw's introduction, pp. xiv–xv, and his discussion of the second Yad Vashem Historical Conference in 1974.

2. The question of how Jewish historians and Jewish historiography should deal with these matters is also important. On a recent occasion in Washington, D.C., the rescue of Bulgarian Jews was commemorated in a program sponsored by B'nai B'rith International with the assistance by the Friedrich Ebert Stiftung, the political foundation affiliated with the German Social Democratic Party. On that occasion, the Ambassador of Israel to the United States, Professor Itamar Rabinovitz, himself an Islamicist and scholar of Arab politics, said that there is a natural tendency in the Jewish world generally, and in Irsraeli politics and diplomacy as well, to view countries in light of their role and behavior during the Holocaust. Ambassador Rabinovitz's observation is undoubtedly correct. Still I wonder whether, in the Turkish instance, we, too, have not fallen prey at times to the prejudice that Christian Europe holds, but that does not reflect Jewish historical experience since the Middle Ages.

3. Horst Widmann, *Exil und Bildungshilfe: Die deutschsprachige akademische Emigration in die Türkei nach 1933* (Frankfurt/M., 1973), p. 49.

4. Fritz Neumark, *Zuflucht am Bosporus: Deutsche Gelehrte, Politiker und Künstler in der Emigration 1933–1953* (Frankfurt/M., 1980), pp. 13–14, says that Schwartz's father-in-law, Professor Tschulok, knew of Malche's work and had spoken with him in this regard.

5. Widmann, *Exil und Bildungshilfe*, pp. 53–54.

6. Ibid., p. 56.

7. Neumark, *Zuflucht am Bosporus*, p. 17.

8. Ibid., p. 19, and Ernst Reuter, *Schriften, Reden*, ed. Hans E. Hirschfeld and Hans J. Reichhardt (Berlin, 1972–1975), vol. 2, p. 494, refers to Martin Wagner leaving Turkey in 1938 for a job that Gropius arranged for him at Harvard, where he would earn less than in Ankara.

9. Widmann, *Exil und Bildungshilfe*, p. 57 note 49, cites Philipp Schwartz's unpublished *Memoirs*, pp. 9–10.

10. Neumark, *Zuflucht am Bosporus*, p. 20; Widmann, *Exil und Bildungshilfe*, p. 74; Reuter, *Schriften, Reden*, vol. 2, pp. 513, 583.

11. Neumark, *Zuflucht am Bosporus*, pp. 26–27; Widmann, *Exil und Bildungshilfe*, p. 17; and Rudolf Nissen, *Helle Blätter – dunkle Blätter: Erinnerungen eines Chirurgen* (Stuttgart, 1969), p. 24.

12. Norman Bentwich, *The Rescue and Achievement of Refugee Scholars* (The Hague, 1953), p. 42.

13. Widmann, *Exil und Bildungshilfe*, p. 56, cites Schwartz's *Memoirs*, pp. 6–8.

14. Nissen, *Helle Blätter*, p. 216.

15. Ibid.

16. Ibid., p. 201. Lecture of Philipp Schwartz published in Helmut Müssener, *Die deutschsprachige Emigration nach 1933 – Aufgabe und Probleme ihrer Erforschung* (Saltsjo-Duvnas, Sweden, 1969), p. 273. Reuter, *Schriften, Reden*, vol. 2, p. 473, letter of September 6, 1935, wrote, "Hier will ein Volk unter allen Umständen seine Zukunft selbst in die Hand nehmen, und es steckt unzweifelhaft viel Idealismus, viel Hingabe und auch viel Talent in der Arbeit, die hier geleistet wird" (Here [in Turkey] is a people that wishes to take every aspect of its future in hand, and without doubt much idealism, devotion, and talent are going into the effort). Neumark, *Zuflucht am Bosporus*, p. 140, is not enthusiastic about having had lectures translated.

17. Ibid., p. 131; Nissen, *Helle Blätter*, p. 199.

18. Neumark, *Zuflucht am Bosporus*, pp. 20–21.

19. Ibid., pp. 19–20.

20. Ibid., p. 191.

21. Nissen, *Helle Blätter*, p. 217.

22. Lieselotte Dieckmann, "Akademische Emigranten in der Türkei," in *Verbannung: Aufzeichnungen deutscher Schriftsteller im Exil*, ed. by E. Schwartz and M. Wegner (Hamburg, 1964), p. 125, is quite bitter in her complaints, but such attitudes are rare. Reuter, *Schriften, Reden*, vol. 2, p. 479, letter of January 28, 1937, and p. 483, letter of February 3, 1937, refers to a circle of German friends and does not view this as "colonial life" or express any resentment. Later he would write, "Hier ist eine Assimilierung wohl innerlich nicht gut möglich. Man bleibt immer ein Fremder. . . . Wir werden immer hierher zurückdenken und diesem liebenswerten Volke eine gute Zukunft wünschen" (Here, [complete] assimilation is not really possible. One always remains an outsider. . . . [But] we will always think back and wish this kind people a fine future). (ibid., p. 652, letter of May 11, 1946).

23. Nissen, *Helle Blätter*, p. 226.

24. Ibid., p. 194; Widmann, *Exil und Bildungshilfe*, p. 58 note 52.

25. In Ankara German children were all instructed privately by a German woman married to a Turk; see Reuter, *Schriften, Reden*, vol. 2, p. 468.

26. Widmann, *Exil und Bildungshilfe*, p. 76.

27. Neumark, *Zuflucht am Bosporus*, pp. 182–83.

28. Ibid., pp. 95–96.

29. Nissen, *Helle Blätter*, pp. 243–44.

30. Ibid., p. 203.

31. Bernard Lewis, *The Emergence of Modern Turkey* (London, 1961), pp. 290ff.

32. Neumark, *Zuflucht am Bosporus*, pp. 116, 210; Reuter, *Schriften, Reden*, vol. 2, pp. 247 and passim.

33. See Metin And, *50 Yilin Türk Tiyatrosu* (Istanbul, 1973).

34. Widmann, *Exil und Bildungshilfe*, pp. 91–101.

35. Ibid., p. 167.

36. Bentwich, *Rescue and Achievement*, p. 53; Widmann, *Exil und Bildungshilfe*, pp. 186, 187 note 27, cites Ernst Hirsch, ed., *Dünya Üniversiteleri ve Türkiye'de Üniversitelerin Gelişmesi* (Istanbul, 1950), vol. 1, pp. 459–60.

37. Neumark, *Zuflucht am Bosporus*, p. 166, cites Ali Hasan Yücel, *Pazartesi Konusmalari* (?Istanbul, 1937).

38. In this regard we must also note that, in general, German Jews were not permitted into Turkey; see Reuter, *Schriften, Reden*, vol. 2, p. 500, letter of January 8, 1939.

39. Widmann, *Exil und Bildungshilfe*, p. 56, cites Schwartz's *Memoirs*, pp. 6–8.

39.

JOHN T. PAWLIKOWSKI, O.S.M.

The Catholic Response
to the Holocaust

INSTITUTIONAL PERSPECTIVES

Preface

Since the appearance of Rolf Hochhuth's controversial play *The Deputy* in 1963, most of the attention of researchers focused on the church question in terms of Catholicism has centered on Pope Pius XII. To what extent did he actually attempt to assist the victims of Nazism, particularly the Jews? Should much have been expected from him given the relatively isolated situation in which the Vatican found itself, sitting in the center of Fascist Italy? In the final analysis do any of the adjectives such as "indifferent," "callous," or "discreetly caring" apply to Pius's overall approach? Such questions and other similar ones certainly remain relevant and in need of further discussion.

But the entire emphasis of any examination of institutional Catholicism during the Shoah should not fall solely on the activities of Pius XII. There is equal need to examine how church bodies and Catholic leaders in other parts of Europe were reacting to Hitler's effort to annihilate the Jewish people and to eliminate thousands of the disabled, gay people, Poles, Gypsies, and others, and whether they were affected by Vatican decisions to any significant degree. Likewise we must examine the sense of self-identity prevailing within institutional Catholicism during that critical period, especially in Vatican circles, to see what impact this self-identity (what theologians term "ecclesiology") ultimately exercised on the Vatican's response to the Hitlerian challenge. For whatever the final evaluation of historians regarding Pius XII's tenure as pope, and much remains to be researched in this regard, his deeds will remain buried with him. There is nothing the contemporary church can do but confront the record with full honesty. It cannot rewrite history. It can, however, significantly redefine its understanding of how a religious institution and its leadership ought to respond in the midst of a grave social crisis.

Several years ago, speaking at an International Jewish-Christian Conference in Vienna, historian Michael R. Marrus sounded an apt warning about evaluating historical situations such as that faced by the Vatican during the Nazi era. He argued that a measure of humility must surround any investigation of individual and/or group responses during such difficult periods. Posing such questions as "Why didn't they (i.e., the Pope, American Jews, Churchill, Roosevelt, etc.) do more during the Holocaust?" is dangerously misleading, according to Marrus. For behind it stands the uncontested assumption that we today would in fact act more responsibly. Marrus termed such an assumption "narcissistic."

Another caution that must be sounded has to do with the tendency to generalize about the Vatican or overall Catholic responses to the Holocaust. At the same November 1988 international conference in Vienna, Bernard Lewis strongly urged that this tendency be strenuously resisted. Instead we need to undertake a painstaking country-by-country analysis in Europe (Western, Central, and Eastern), taking into account the church's particular social and political status in each nation. Only such an approach can lead to a truly fair assessment of the Catholic response.

Clearly there are those in the Catholic community, including influential Catholic organizations in the United States, who wish to void any critical scrutiny of the church's activity during the Nazi era and to portray Christians purely as victims. Such a position fortunately has been rejected by an increasing number of responsible Catholic leaders. At the May 1992 meeting of the Vatican-Jewish International Dialogue in Baltimore, for example, Cardinal Joseph Bernardin of Chicago, in the opening plenary address, praised the 400-page report by a panel of historians commissioned and supported by the Cardinal Archbishop of Lyons (France) regarding the diocese's response to the Nazi challenge. He said that "it is only through such candor and willingness to acknowledge mistakes where documentary evidence clearly warrants it that Catholicism can join in the pursuit of contemporary global justice with full moral integrity."[1] He urged the church as a whole to submit its World War II record to thorough scrutiny by respected scholars.

The Vatican Response: What the Historians Say

The staunchest defense of Vatican activities during the period of the Holocaust, and Pius XII in particular, is to be found in the writings of the long-time Vatican archivist, Fr. Robert Graham, S.J. He spent more than two decades collecting and organizing materials related to the Vatican response to Nazism. In particular he focused on the final year and a half of World War II. Based on his analysis of the documents, now published, he concluded that Pius XII must be judged a "great humanitarian," truly deserving of that forest in the Judean hills that kindly people in Israel proposed to name for him in October 1958."[2]

Graham's argument, to state it succinctly, followed this general course. Though Pius XII felt disappointment over his inability to prevent the outbreak of World War II, he committed himself from its very beginning to the alleviation of human suffering to the fullest possible extent. While Pius's concern extended to all the victims of the Nazis, there is evidence in the materials now collected and available in the official Vatican Acts from this period of his ever increasing predilection for attention to the sufferings of the Jews. While many Vatican actions on behalf of Jews were the direct result of Jewish organizations' requests for assistance (a sign, for Graham, of genuine confidence in the Pope and the Catholic Church), other such helpful actions were initiated solely by the Vatican. Graham argued that there is evidence of an unparalleled amount of communication between the Holy See and Jewish leaders. In the early years of the war, when emigration was still a realistic option in many places, diplomatic pressure was exerted upon countries with close Vatican ties, Spain and Portugal, for example, to issue entry and transit visas to Jews escaping from Nazi-controlled territories. And when the emigration option faded away between 1940 and 1942, the Catholic strategy began to focus on diplomatic protests against the deportation of Jews.

Slovakia serves as a good illustration of this later strategy, according to Graham. When it became apparent in March 1942 that the Nazis intended to forcibly deport some eighty thousand Slovak Jews, the Vatican's diplomatic apparatus moved into high gear. Protests were lodged by papal representatives in Bratislava and by the papal nuncio in Budapest. And when a second round of deportations was announced for 1943, Vatican officials again raised their voices in denunciation of the plan. Finally, says Graham, when it seemed likely that yet more deportations were in the offing in 1944, the Holy See ordered its representatives in Slovakia to approach both the foreign ministry and President Tiso (a Catholic priest) in its name. The representatives were instructed to make clear that "the Holy See expects from the Slovak authority an attitude in conformity with the Catholic principles and sentiments of the people of Slovakia."[3] At the same time it suggested that a joint protest by the Slovak bishops might prove extremely helpful in stopping the deportations. Subsequently, Vatican officials met with the Slovak minister to the Vatican and handed him a formal message that read in part as follows: "The Holy See, moved by those sentiments of humanity and Christian charity that always inspire its work in favor of the suffering, without distinction of parties, nationalities or races, cannot remain indifferent to such appeals."[4]

Graham claimed that the Vatican exhibited particular concern for the Jewish community in its midst, intervening directly with the Nazi authorities for the safety of the Jewish community of Rome and supporting the numerous monasteries and convents that sheltered Jews during those trying times. As one example, Graham cited the intervention of Cardinal Maglione, then the Vatican Secretary of State, who in a private meeting with the Reich ambassador, Ernst von Weizsäcker, in October 1943 strongly protested the special SS raid that had seized more than one thousand Italian Jews for transfer to Nazi death camps in Poland. The cardinal spoke of the pain experienced by Pius XII over this act and over the suffering of so many persons solely because of their race. Graham adds that many of the Jews who were able to escape the raid were taken in by monks and nuns for the remaining months of the Nazi occupation.

Hungary was a particularly noteworthy and successful field of Vatican activity on behalf of Jews, in the eyes of Graham. Prior to 1944 the Hungarian Jewish community had lived in an atmosphere of comparative freedom and security despite the passage of severe antisemitic legislation. The greater part of the Hungarian government had steadfastly refused to relinquish its own Jewish citizens, as well as the Jewish refugees who had fled there from Nazi persecution in Slovakia and Poland. But all that changed when Nazi armies advanced into Hungary in March 1944. The previous leader of Hungary, Admiral Horthy, eventually was replaced by a local government composed mainly of members of the virulently antisemitic Arrow Cross movement. Deportation to Auschwitz in occupied Poland, to Austria for forced labor, or outright massacre within Hungary itself, became an increasingly common fate for Jews residing in Hungary, whether citizens or refugees.

Volume ten of the official Vatican *Acts* from the period contains substantial documentation concerned with the Holy See's central role in the international effort to protect Hungarian Jews. After the Nazi invasion, while Admiral Horthy was still head of state, Papal Nuncio Angelo Rotta communicated extensively with both governmental leaders and Vatican officials in the hope of halting the deportations of Jews. The result was the release of an "open" telegram to Admiral Horthy from Pius XII; it read in part:

> We are being beseeched in various quarters to do everything in our power in order that, in this noble and chivalrous nation, the sufferings, already so heavy, endured by a large number of unfortunate people, because of their nationality or race, may not be extended and aggravated. As our Father's heart cannot remain insensitive to these pressing supplications by virtue of our ministry of charity which embraces all men, we address Your Highness personally, appealing to your noble sentiments in full confidence that you will do everything in your power that so many unfortunate people may be spared other afflictions and other sorrows.[5]

This papal appeal was followed in short order by several other international efforts, including a press campaign in Switzerland and a warning from the British foreign minister, Sir Anthony Eden. The bombing of Budapest was also ordered. These joint efforts initiated by the Vatican intervention resulted in a decision by Admiral Horthy to suspend Jewish deportations. Jewish organizations as well as the War Refugee Board formally conveyed their gratitude to the Vatican, according to Graham, for its crucial role in bringing about this decision by the Hungarian government.

After Horthy was deposed, Rotta found his work on behalf of Jews considerably more difficult. With the assistance of the neutral Swedish ambassador, he arranged for a meeting with the new Arrow Cross leadership. But, as he himself would later relate, his plea for the safety of the Jewish community met with silence. He confessed that he found the Arrow Cross leaders brimming with "fanatical hatred" toward the Jewish community.

The failure to move the new Hungarian government on the Jewish Question did not, however, put an end to Rotta's efforts. He turned to other approaches, principally the issuance of "Letters of Protection"; these seemed to have a measure of success in stalling the deportations of at least some Jews who received them. They proved particularly useful in the case of baptized Jews. These letters, along with similar ones granted by neutral foreign embassies in Budapest, often served as the equivalent of habeas corpus writs for their recipients. In his official report to the Vatican on this endeavor, Rotta claims that some 13,000 such documents were granted under his aegis.

Graham's extensive treatment of the situation in Hungary clearly shows that he regarded this country as one of the prime examples of active Vatican commitment for the safety of the Jewish community. The collaboration of the papal nuncio and Vatican officials in Rome was as intense as possible under very trying political conditions.

Examining Graham's overall argument we certainly see that it makes some important points in support of his contention of a positive papal and Vatican response to the Nazi annihilation of the Jews. On the other hand, definite limitations appear, rendering his conclusions far less solid than he would have us believe.

Because many of Graham's writings have appeared in what maybe described as a "polemical context," that is, they are aimed at diluting the accusation of silence on the Jewish question on the part of Pius XII and his administration, these works often lack the kind of critical analysis that one might legitimately expect from a historian. In one sense Graham ably carried out his assignment. He persuasively demonstrated that simplistic claims about the "silence" of Pius XII do not stand up under the weight of currently available evidence and are likely to become even more problematic as further evidence surfaces. There is little question that Pius and key Vatican officials undertook important initiatives on behalf of all, and not merely Jewish, converts to Christianity.

Let me make it clear, however, that this judgment in no way fully settles the question about the wartime activities of Pius XII and key Vatican officials. Significant questions remain regarding the adequacy and the basic suppositions of Pius's approach. These need a thorough airing by responsible Jewish and non-Jewish scholars. But use of the term "silence," besides being factually inaccurate, degrades the tone of the ongoing investigation and discussion and opens the door to those in both the Christian and Jewish communities who would espouse basically uncritical opinions.

Focusing more specifically on those areas where Graham's materials reveal considerable weakness, the following points stand out: First, he rarely, if ever, questions whether the interventions he brings to the fore were pursued over a longer period or were more in the nature of sporadic efforts. Do the available documents reveal official Vatican persistence in pursuing the issue of Jewish safety and survival, or were Jewish organizations continually forced to renew their appeals to Rome regarding the plight of European Jewry? Only the former stance in my mind would qualify as an indication of a deep, primary policy commitment on the issue. Nor does Graham ever ask whether Pius should have reconsidered his position on certain matters (i.e., his unwillingness to identify Nazi victims by name) in light of the gravity of the situation. In each and every controversial policy decision, Pius XII is accorded the full benefit of the doubt. Those in the Jewish and the Polish community who sustain Pius's judgments are singled out for praise, while the many critics of the Pope in both communities receive a quick dismissal or no mention at all.

Another problematic aspect of Graham's argument is its heavy focus on papal and Vatican activities in the final year of World War II. Graham makes some reference to Vatican interventions on behalf of Jews prior to 1944. But their inclusion serves only to obscure the question of whether in fact the Vatican response was far too slow in coming. His presentation creates this problem by leaving the false impression that the increased activity of the final year had earlier parallels. Uncritical readers might easily reach this misleading conclusion. Regrettably, Graham basically avoids the question of why a more concerted effort to save Europe's Jews took so long to develop in Vatican circles.

Another drawback in Graham's perspective is that his writings convey the impression of rather harmonious collaboration between Jewish organizations and the Vatican *throughout* the period of the war. The subtle message seems to be that criticism regarding the Vatican's response to the Shoah is essentially a postwar phenomenon that ignores the testimonies of Jewish leaders at the time. This again, as we shall shortly see, greatly oversimplifies matters.

Finally, Graham seems little inclined to question the view of the Church that prevailed in Vatican circles during the period and that exercised a decided impact on the shaping of papal social policy. The same holds true for the fairly evident commitment of Pius XII and his close advisors to a defense of the established social order in Europe. This was a course that many other historians view as an important factor muting direct papal condemnation of Nazism for many years, the Nazi movement having been seen, despite its radical human rights abuses, as a bulwark against destruction of social order by the Bolsheviks in particular. Though Pius's personal commitment to defense of this social order appeared to have waned considerably as the war went on (and this may account in part for the Vatican's greater willingness to intervene directly on behalf of Jews), it was only with the election of John XXIII to the papacy and the Second Vatican Council that this commitment was fundamentally abandoned.[6]

For a perspective on the Catholic response to the Nazi period that differs in several major points from that of Fr. Graham, we turn to the testimony of Dr. Gerhart Riegner of the World Jewish Congress, himself an active participant in the organized Jewish efforts to save European Jewry during the Third Reich. His analysis clearly raises questions about several of Graham's claims and shows that considerable research is still needed in a number of areas.

Riegner devoted much of his 1983 Stephen S. Wise Lecture at Cincinnati's Hebrew Union College to a description of Vatican-Jewish relations during World War II as he recalled them from his experiences as an important Jewish representative of the time.[7] The first years of the war were marked by considerable apprehension on the Jewish side. There was great reluctance to seek from Rome assistance for the Jews of Germany and elsewhere. Protestant leadership was seen as much more approachable. This hesitation stemmed in great measure, according to Riegner, from perceived favorable attitudes toward the Third Reich on the part of many German Catholic bishops, as well as what appeared to Jewish leaders to be a basic policy of appeasement on the part of Vatican authorities, particularly after the signing of the Concordat. Other factors that played a role in inhibiting a Jewish approach to Catholic officials were the presence of antisemitism in sectors of Polish Catholicism in the interwar period as well as the seeming ineffectiveness of Catholic protest efforts on those occasions when they were in fact forthcoming. Jewish leaders were also conscious of the Vatican's delicate geopolitical situation, an enclave within a fascist state.

It was not until 1942 that the policy of Jewish organizations on dealings with institutional Catholicism began to change. In large measure this was due to the increasing gravity of the situation in Nazi-controlled Europe and the general feeling among Jewish leaders that every possible avenue had to be explored in the effort to rescue the Jews who faced annihilation. Pius XII now became a special target of Jewish organizational appeals in light of his acknowledged moral authority. Jewish efforts were coordinated through contacts with papal representatives in Switzerland, New York, and London. Some responses did materialize. Particularly important, according to Riegner, was Vatican intervention in Slovakia, where Nazi-leaning

President Tiso (a Catholic priest) relaxed pressure on the Jews for a time after Vatican intervention. But in the final analysis, Riegner's assessment is that little of substance was done with respect to other countries. What steps occurred in Romania seemed more the result of local initiative than Vatican directive. And Rome's reaction to the condition of Jews in the unoccupied sectors of France was much weaker in Riegner's estimation than that of several leading French bishops, particularly Bishop Saliege and Bishop Theas, who in response to Jewish appeals strongly criticized Vichy's anti-Jewish legislation and the deportations in the summer of 1942.

Riegner then turns his attention to an important question that remains basically ignored by Fr. Graham. In March 1942, Riegner assisted in the preparation of a joint World Jewish Congress/Jewish Agency memorandum at the request of the papal nuncio in Bern. This document described in considerable detail the conditions facing Jews in those countries where the Vatican was judged to exercise special influence because of the size of the local Catholic community. Included on this list were Slovakia, Croatia, Hungary, Romania, and unoccupied France. "Strangely," says Riegner, "the detailed memorandum is not reproduced in the collection of documents published by the Vatican on its action during World War II. The collection contains only the letter of transmittal."[8] This represents a critical omission in his mind. For this memorandum clearly demonstrates that the Vatican had been supplied with extensive information about Nazi attacks on the Jews throughout Europe at a relatively early date. When the Vatican first acquired detailed knowledge of the gravity of the Jewish situation certainly is a vital component of any overall assessment today regarding the adequacy of its response to the Shoah.

Another central moment in Vatican-Jewish relations came in autumn 1942. The Vatican received a request at that time from U.S. Undersecretary of State Sumner Welles for confirmation of reports being received by the Allied governments of massive extermination of Jews in Nazi-controlled areas. After some delay and a series of repeated American requests for such confirmation, Cardinal Maglione, then Vatican Secretary of State, responded that the Holy See was not in a position to guarantee their accuracy. Riegner sees this reply as "strange" in light of the briefings that Rome had received from its nuncios about the deportations of Jews from Bucovina and Bessarabia in December 1941, from Bratislava in March 1942, and, in July 1942, from both Paris and Zagreb.

The year 1942 also witnessed a concerted effort by several nations to persuade Pius XII to issue a forthright condemnation of the Nazis for their treatment of the Jews. Included in this coalition undertaking were Great Britain, the Polish government-in-exile, Brazil, the United States, and Uruguay. The motivation for this effort came largely from new revelations about the extent of Jewish suffering made public in London by the World Jewish Congress and the Polish government-in-exile. The Pope eventually did respond to this international appeal in his Christmas radio address of that year. But in rather typical fashion the Jews were not specifically mentioned.

Riegner admits that a first reading of the papal statement leaves the impression of significant courage on Pius's part. But when one places this statement opposite the moving appeals of Polish President Raczkiewicz and others to the Pope, as well as the blunt statement of Cardinal Hinsley of London at a mass protest meeting in

New York in early 1943 in which he explicitly named Jews as primary victims and the Nazis as the oppressors, the fundamental weakness of Pius's stance stands out for Riegner. It is obvious that he does not fully accept the contention of Graham and others that diplomatic reserve on the part of the Pope helped rather than hindered the safety of European Jewry at the time.

The one region where Riegner clearly acknowledges positive Vatican/Jewish collaboration is in Hungary. His recollection of events in this connection parallels in many ways the description offered by Fr. Graham. Fr. John Morley of Seton Hall University has also undertaken further research into the situation in Hungary, focusing especially on 1944–1945. His preliminary conclusion, related in private correspondence, is that the materials existing in various Israeli archives as well as in the Public Records Office in London covering this period tend to compliment the conclusions drawn by Fr. Graham from volume ten of the published Vatican documents. Riegner's own conclusion on the Hungarian situation is stated in the following terms: "On the whole, one can probably say that the Vatican action in Hungary stands out as effective and energetic; it certainly contributed to the saving of many Jewish lives." [9]

Riegner also speaks of certain papal nuncios, especially those in Slovakia and Romania, who apparently undertook numerous efforts to rescue Jews. But the same level of activity is not apparent in other capitals. In this analysis Riegner seems to offer confirmation to the basic thesis advocated by John Morley, to be discussed shortly, regarding untapped possibilities for saving Jews that existed through Vatican diplomatic channels.

Riegner also makes the argument that, especially in the early years of the Third Reich, Catholic leaders tended to focus their rescue efforts on behalf of Jews in favor of those who had received baptism. This was particularly true for the German church. Ernst Christian Helmreich, a scholar fundamentally sympathetic to the church's difficulties in responding to the challenge of Nazism, has looked at this issue. There has also been recent research on internal Reich documents that monitored local church activities throughout the regions of Germany. Both investigative initiatives tend to lend credibility to Riegner's claims on this point. [10]

Overall, Riegner is forced to conclude that Vatican understanding of the full scope of the catastrophe befalling the Jewish community of Europe was very late in coming, if it was ever comprehended at all. Certainly the matter never assumed high priority within the upper echelons of the Vatican. Riegner offers the following personal examples to undergird his contention regarding Vatican misperceptions of the Jewish situation:

> In a long conversation with Msgr. Montini, subsequently to become Pope Paul VI, in October, 1945, in Rome, during which I pleaded with him to help us obtain the return of Jewish children who had been saved by Catholics or Catholic institutions, I was shocked when the Catholic prelate contested the accuracy of my statement that at least 1,500,000 Jewish children had perished in the Holocaust. It took me more than half an hour to explain and justify my statement and for him to accept it. If one of the senior personalities of the Church . . . could take such an attitude in good faith . . . , it seems to me fair to say that high Vatican diplomats never really understood the extent of the tragedy that had befallen the Jewish people. [11]

Without doubt, Riegner has raised some critical points that require further scholarly research and reflection. His recollections would seem to expose important weaknesses in the Graham narrative that need addressing before Catholics today can rest content. If a question is to be raised about Riegner's analysis, it would be his seeming conviction that if the Vatican had spoken out more forcefully and directly with respect to the annihilation of Jews in the public arena, a greater number of Jewish lives would have been spared. We now know from publications such as the wartime memoirs of Cardinal Henri de Lubac[12] that even the indirect language of Pius XII vis-à-vis Jews played a critical role in molding Catholic resistance in countries such as France. And Gunther Lewy, hardly a Vatican apologist relative to the Third Reich period, has insisted that a "flaming protest" by Pius XII almost certainly would have made no appreciable dent in final Jewish death figures, and might well have made matters worse for both Jews and Catholics.[13] So the issue may be far more open to discussion than Riegner would seem to allow.

Having examined two perspectives on Vatican activities during the Nazi era in some detail, we can conclude this section with a brief overview of several other scholarly viewpoints. Fr. John Morley has argued, rather convincingly despite Graham's one-line rejection of his thesis, that the Vatican could have done considerably more to save Jews through its papal nuncios than in fact proved to be the case. In concert with most other historians who have analyzed the period, Morley views the problem as rooted in the basic tone and direction of Vatican diplomacy set by Pius XII rather than in crass papal indifference to the plight of the Jews, Poles, and other victims of the Nazis. Prudence and reserve were the prevailing characteristics of this diplomacy. It studiously tried to avoid "offending" any nation, the Third Reich included. This approach had a straitjacket effect on Vatican diplomacy and did little to distinguish it from the posture adopted by the civil states toward the Third Reich. In fact, on occasion, representatives of the Allied camp spoke more candidly and specifically about Jewish extermination than did the Vatican.[14]

Gerhart Riegner's recollections of the Nazi period, discussed above, would seem to strengthen the force of Morley's basic argument. Even Fr. Graham's own research, when read carefully, shows that most of the initiatives began with a particular papal nuncio, not the Vatican. The possibilities for direct Catholic institutional action differed from country to country. This must be underscored. Hence a measure of caution must be exercised in generalizing from particular areas of some success such as Hungary. Nonetheless there appear to be ample instances of important successes in alleviating the Jewish plight in those countries where nuncios did act and sometimes secured Vatican intervention as well to warrant Morley's more general conclusion.

Michael R. Marrus has joined those whose writings have critically assessed the overall Vatican response to Nazism.[15] He too locates the problem fundamentally in the style of diplomacy that Pius XII had helped to shape during the Depression era as Pius XI's Secretary of State.

Marrus acknowledges the presence of Vatican opposition to racial policies of both Mussolini and Hitler, but he insists that this opposition had more to do with the Christian theology of baptism than it did with concern about the fate of the Jews themselves. Even after the release of the papal encyclical against Nazism in 1937 the

Vatican attempted to prevent an open break with the Third Reich. The primary goal remained, in Marrus's words, "political neutrality and the safeguarding of the institutional interests of the Church in a perilous political world."[16]

The first few years of the war witnessed little Vatican protest against growing Nazi hostility toward the Jewish community, no more in fact than was the case in the 1930s. Catholic representatives spoke generally about the need for justice but remained largely unconcerned about the new antisemitic campaigns being developed by the Third Reich and collaborationist governments. When the murder of Jews began in earnest, says Marrus, the Vatican refused to issue more than the most general of condemnations despite its excellent information on the seriousness of the Jewish condition. It is obvious that Marrus is not persuaded by Graham's argument that, though the Vatican's language was most often general in tone, omitting direct mention of both victim groups and the Nazis themselves, people understood the specific intent of the Holy See's statements.

Marrus joins several other historians in arguing that the root cause of the limited Vatican response was diplomatic style. Vatican documents, he insists, do not indicate any guarded proNazi sympathies or the supremacy of opposition to the USSR. They in fact clearly demonstrate that neither simple hostility nor indifference explains Rome's posture during this critical period. What the documents do establish with reasonable certainty is the dominance of a policy of "reserve and conciliation" under Pius XII, a policy that shaped not only his personal approach but strongly influenced the basic tenor of the Church's diplomatic corps, as well. Marrus puts it this way:

> The goal was to limit the global conflict where possible, and above all to protect the influence and standing of the Church as an independent voice. Continually apprehensive of schisms within the Church, Pius strove to maintain the allegiance of Catholics in Germany, in Poland, and elsewhere. Fearful too of threats from the outside, the Pope dared not confront the Nazis or the Italian Fascists directly.[17]

For Marrus the controlling reality under Pius XII was the preservation of the Church. All else took a backseat.

This same perspective, it might be noted, is shared by another Jewish historian of the Holocaust, Nora Levin, though she attributes somewhat more direct influence to the Bolshevik factor as a principal threat to Catholic survival than does Marrus himself. This priority of Church survival led Pius XII, in Levin's words, to view the Jews as "unfortunate expendables."[18] In the words of Helen Fein, they fell outside the "universe of moral obligation."[19]

To further underscore the predominance of the survival factor over pure antisemitism in shaping the Vatican's response to the Jewish Question, Marrus introduces the issue of the Holy See's reaction to other groups targeted by the Nazis. Here too, he says, the Holy See basically followed a policy of reserve even when it involved strong appeals from Polish bishops to denounce Nazi atrocities against Polish Catholics, as well as in the case of the Third Reich's "euthanasia campaign" and the Italian attack against Greece.

The relations between the Vatican and Poland, as Marrus has indicated, provide a useful parallel study to the question of the Holy See and the Jewish community during World War II. For here there was a staunchly Catholic community that, as historians are increasingly bringing to light, became nearly as critical as the Jews regarding the policy of reserve pursued by papal diplomacy relative to the Nazis.

Polish-American historian Richard Lukas has raised this issue in his writings on the Nazi attack against Poland. He recognizes the practical difficulties the Vatican faced with respect to Poland, in part due to the flight of Cardinal Hlond from the country, which caused great disruption within Polish Catholicism. The cold reception accorded Hlond in Rome by Vatican officials and the Pope himself helped to restore some measure of credibility for Pius XII among Polish Catholics.

Overall, however, Lukas concludes that the balance sheet in terms of Vatican/papal activity on behalf of Poland shows a deficit. This is borne out, according to Lukas, by the concrete negative reactions of ordinary Catholics in the country toward the Pope. "In the face of the persecution of the church of Poland," says Lukas, "the Vatican pursued a timid, reserved attitude."[20] This was likely the result of a constellation of forces—a sentimentality about Poland on Pius' part, a tinge of Germanophilia, and fears that public denunciations would make matters worse for the Poles. It was not until June 2, 1943, that the Pope finally issued the long-awaited statement. And here again, as in the case of the Jews, Pius shied away from direct condemnation of the Nazis.

The 1943 statement, which admittedly did ease Polish-Vatican tensions to some degree, was an effort to counteract the widespread criticism that had grown up within clerical ranks because of the Vatican's seeming hesitancy on the Polish question. There were even some Polish voices calling for the complete severance of relations with the Vatican. The perceived abandonment of Poland on the part of Pius and the Vatican had led to the phenomenon of worshippers leaving church at the very mention of the Pope's name. The Jesuits of Warsaw became so concerned about Catholic loyalty that they published a defense of Vatican activities in behalf of Poland. And Fr. John Morley, who also addresses the Vatican's response to the Nazi attack on Poland and interprets Vatican inaction there as resulting from a certain primacy of the relationship with Germany in Vatican diplomatic circles, relates how Rome explicitly instructed its nuncios on how to counter the mounting dissatisfaction with its approach to Poland.[21]

In his own analysis, Fr. Graham has attempted to respond to the charges against Pius XII relative to Poland. But he concentrates almost exclusively on the 1943 speech and thereafter. And even in this limited context his argument rests on the positive comments of a few representatives of the Polish government-in-exile. It is obvious that a contemporary historian of Poland such as Lukas has not been fully persuaded by this defense.

To close this survey of historians relative to Vatican-Nazi relations, we shall briefly examine the writings of English Catholic historian J. Derek Holmes and an Anglican historian from Canada, John Conway. Besides Fr. Graham, Holmes is among the staunchest overall defenders of the regime of Pius XII. But he presents his position in considerably less polemical fashion. In general he contends that Pius's quiet diplomacy worked far better than many are willing to concede. He appeals, for example, to the remark of an unnamed Israeli consul in Italy who claimed that the Holy See in collaboration with the papal nuncios and regional Catholic leaders assisted in saving some 400,000 Jewish lives.[22]

Yet even Holmes, unlike Graham, is prepared to grant that some major draw-backs existed in Vatican policy. In general, he remains convinced that Vatican officials failed to show sufficient resolve against racist attitudes throughout the Nazi era and Pius XII himself did not exhibit a sufficiently forceful style of leadership with respect to initiatives by local churches. A case in point, says Holmes, is Vichy France. After the Vichy government's ambassador in Rome had inquired of the Vatican whether proposed new legislation concerning Jews would create problems for the Holy See, Marshall Pétain, head of the Vichy government, was able to claim, says Holmes, "unfairly but not without some justification that the Vatican had adopted a careless or even an 'inhuman' attitude."[23]

John Conway shares some of the same cautions as Holmes in his consideration of Vatican policy.[24] He recognizes that Catholic protest was not as strong as might have been anticipated. He attributes this largely to a twofold conclusion on the part of the Catholic leadership elite, both in Germany and in Rome. This conclusion, he argues, was common to the leadership of much of the Protestant Evangelical Church as well, resulting in the growth of an antiestablishment Confessing Church that did confront Nazi policy publicly up to a point. Both the Catholic and Protestant leaderships were convinced that the Christian faithful would abandon the hierarchy if the clergy protested too strongly against the Nazis, and they feared such opposition might open the doors for the emergence in Germany of a liberal, pluralistic society that would threaten their fundamentally conservative social outlook. In their minds the Church's well-being was inevitably tied to the preservation of the old social order in Germany and elsewhere in Europe.

Some Tentative Conclusions

With the above survey of the attitudes of a select number of Christian and Jewish scholars toward Vatican activities during the Third Reich we are now in a position to formulate several tentative conclusions. The first, to repeat a point made above, is that accusations of "silence" against Pius XII and the Vatican are simply unfounded. We must move beyond this code term to a much more nuanced discussion of the issues if we are to gain any insights from our analysis. On the other hand, none of the historians we have examined, whether Christian or Jewish, seemed convinced that Fr. Graham's work, however valuable on the narrow issue of "silence," has resolved all the serious questions at hand.

One conclusion clearly emerges from the research of nearly all the scholars who have examined the question thus far with a measure of objectivity. At the level of the Vatican, Pius had a profound commitment to a "diplomatic" church model. This flowed principally from his desire not only to preserve the Church as an institution but also to ensure continuation of the conservative social order that he and his circle deemed essential for the future health of Catholicism. And this commitment exercised a critical influence on his response to the plight of the Jews, Poles, and other groups who were victims of the Nazis. Behind his "diplomatic" model in practical affairs seemed to lie a fundamental theological understanding of the Church as a "holy and spotless" reality whose true meaning lay beyond this world. It is only in some of the Christmas addresses toward the end of his papacy that we have hints that Pius may have concluded that a totally new social order was now needed, even from the perspective of Church survival.[25] While it would be difficult to prove conclusively, it can at least be suggested that this general shifting of posture on the social order in Europe may have been responsible in part for his enhanced commitment to Jewish and Polish security in the final years of the Third Reich.

Assigning priority to an examination of the Church context of the Vatican's response during the Nazi period provides us with a perspective rooted in historical experience. It is a perspective that can prove extremely valuable as the Church confronts other difficult social situations in the present and the future. I believe that, consciously or not, Catholicism is beginning to learn from the failings of its policy of reserve in the face of the Nazi challenge. This learning is not without some struggle, however. Its recent challenges of unjust political regimes in South Africa, Malawi, the Philippines, and elsewhere, plus the forthright manner in which the February 1989 Pontifical Justice and Peace Commission document on racism condemned apartheid, antisemitism, and anti-Zionism by name[26] attest to decided movement away from the caution so evident during the papacy of Pius XII. While the diplomatic model of the Church has not totally disappeared in Catholic circles, there are now clear signs that the Church is beginning to put it aside as it speaks in a manner that unquestionably carries some measure of risk for its institutional well-being.

The tendency to view certain groups as "unfortunate expendables" in the effort to guarantee the survival of the Catholic community is gradually receding. No doubt this change is due at least in part to the basic theological change in understanding the church-world relationship that emerged from Vatican II's document on the Church in the Modern World.[27] In that perspective there is a sense of a far greater integration between the events of human history and the ultimate purposes of the kingdom of God than was true in Pius XII's fundamental vision of the Church.

A few closing considerations are in order. The first has to do with the question of how great a part traditional Catholic antisemitism played in shaping the Vatican stance toward the Jews during the Nazi era. There is ample evidence to suggest it had considerable impact at least in certain countries. France, Germany, Austria, Poland, and Slovakia, especially, come to mind.[28] At the level of the Vatican the picture is much harder to determine with great precision. Virtually no evidence exists of overt antisemitism at this level, as Jewish commentators such as Riegner have noted. But what subtle impact regional Catholic antisemitism may have had on policy formulation toward the Jews by the Holy See is an issue that awaits further research. This also holds for the private letters and records of personal discussions at the Vatican level—papers that have not been thoroughly examined. At this point, and until new documentation is scrutinized, there appear to be ample documentary grounds for maintaining that traditional Christian antisemitism was not a principal determinant of the Vatican's stance. This thesis does not preclude an argument, let it be clear, that on the regional level antisemitism may in fact have been a significant factor in a local Catholic community's response to the Nazi attack on the Jews.

At this point it must be stressed that if the study of Vatican attitudes is to be pursued with scholarly integrity and brought to finality, responsible scholars must be given adequate access to the relevant Vatican archives. Cardinal Joseph Bernardin of Chicago, in his opening plenary address at the May 1992 meeting of the Vatican-

Jewish International Dialogue held in Baltimore, called for the opening of these archives.[29] His call was substantially repeated in the final communique approved by the participants in that dialogue.[30] It is now incumbent upon scholars and Catholic leaders to join forces in urging the Vatican to implement this recommendation as quickly as possible.

Third, there is need to raise an issue related to the previously made point about the centrality for Pius XII of the preservation of Europe's traditional social order. Several of the papers in the published proceedings of the Historical Society of Israel's 1982 Conference on "Judaism and Christianity under the Impact of National Socialism"[31] clearly show that many Catholics, in Germany especially (but elsewhere as well), perceived the Jews as a threat to their own security and, in some cases, as agents of liberalism and Bolshevism. This seemed to be a far more burning issue relative to Jews than charges connected with traditional antisemitism. While often there was genuine dismay about what was happening to the Jews on the human level, there was also relief that the Jewish community's "subversive" influence on the traditional social order was being removed. Though the case has not been documented and remains one of those unresolved issues that requires further research, it is legitimate to entertain the suspicion that, given Pius XII's high personal regard for the German church where the attitude about the Jewish "erosion" factor was especially strong, it may have had some impact on the overall shape of Vatican policy.

Consensus is beginning to emerge on some points but, on the whole, the research is still substantially incomplete and therefore conclusions must be understood as tenuous at best. We serve neither sound scholarship nor the cause of Christian-Jewish reconciliation with exaggerated charges or attempts to suppress parts of the actual record. A carefully nuanced approach, based on full scholarly access to relevant documentation, is the only approach worthy of the name of scholarship and capable of building a new foundation for Catholic-Jewish understanding in our time.

NOTES

1. Cf. Cardinal Joseph Bernardin, "Tikkun Olam, 'Healing the World,'" *Catholic International* 3/13 (July 1–14, 1992): 610–17.

2. Robert Graham, S.J., *Pius XII's Defense of the Jews and Others: 1944–45* (Milwaukee: Catholic League for Religious and Civil Rights, 1982), p. 34.

3. As quoted in ibid., p. 21.

4. Ibid., p. 21.

5. As quoted in ibid., pp. 29–30.

6. For relevant texts from Pius XII's *Christmas Messages* and John XXIII's *Mater et Magistra* and *Pacem in Terris*, see David M. Byers, ed., *Justice in the Marketplace: Collected Statements of the Vatican and the United States Catholic Bishops on Economic Policy, 1891–1984*, general and document introductions by John T. Pawlikowski, O.S.M. (Washington, D.C.: United States Catholic Conference, 1985), pp. 91–170.

7. Gerhart Riegner, "A Warning to the World: The Efforts of the World Jewish Congress to Mobilize the Christian Churches against the Final Solution," Inaugural Stephen S. Wise Lecture (Cincinnati: Hebrew Union College–Jewish Institute of Religion, November 17, 1983).

8. Ibid., p. 7.

9. Ibid., p. 10.

10. Ernst Christian Helmreich, *The German Churches under Hitler: Background, Struggle, and Epilogue* (Detroit: Wayne State University Press, 1979), p. 364; Otto Dov Kulka, "Popular Christian Attitudes in the Third Reich to National Socialist Policies toward the Jews," in *Judaism and Christianity under the Impact of National Socialism*, ed. Otto Dov Kulka and Paul R. Mendes-Flohr (Jerusalem: Historical Society of Israel and the Zalman Shazar Center for Jewish History, 1987), pp. 251–67.

11. Riegner, "A Warning," p. 11.

12. Cf. Henri de Lubac, *Christian Resistance to Anti-Semitism: Memories from 1940–1944* (San Francisco: Ignatius Press, 1990).

13. Cited in Michael R. Marrus, "The Vatican and the Holocaust," *Congress Monthly* (January 1988): p. 7.

14. John Morley, *Vatican Diplomacy and the Jews during the Holocaust: 1939–1943* (New York: Ktav, 1980), p. 209. In an October 12, 1993, letter to the author, Fr. Morley indicated that his still unpublished research in the archives of Yad Vashem, the Central Zionist Archives in Jerusalem, and the Public Record Office in London seems to support the thrust of the material found in volume 10 of the officially released Vatican documents on the Nazi period regarding Vatican efforts to assist the Jews of Hungary.

15. Marrus, "The Vatican," and idem, *The Holocaust in History* (Hanover, NH: University Press of New England, 1987).

16. Marrus, "The Vatican," p. 6.

17. Ibid., p. 7.

18. Nora Levin, *The Holocaust* (New York: Schocken Books, 1973), p. 693.

19. Helen Fein, *Accounting for Genocide: National Responses and Jewish Victimization during the Holocaust* (Chicago: University of Chicago Press, 1984), p. 33.

20. Richard Lukas, *Forgotten Holocaust: The Poles under German Occupation 1939–1944* (Lexington: University Press of Kentucky, 1986), p. 16.

21. Morley, *Vatican Diplomacy*, pp. 140, 146.

22. J. Derek Holmes, *The Papacy in the Modern World* (New York: Crossroad, 1981), p. 158.

23. Ibid., p. 164.

24. John Conway, "The Churches," in *The Holocaust: Ideology, Bureaucracy, and Genocide*, ed. Henry Friedlander and Sybil Milton (Millwood, NY: Kraus International, 1980), pp. 199–206. See also "The Churches and the Jewish People: Actions, Inactions and Reactions during the Nazi Era," in *Comprehending the Holocaust: Historical and Literary Research*, ed. Asher Cohen, Joan Gelber and Charlotte Wardi (Frankfurt/M., Verlag Peter Lang, 1990), pp. 125–43.

25. On Pius XII's Christmas addresses, see note 6 above.

26. Pontifical Commission "Justitia et Pax," *The Church and Racism: Towards a More Fraternal Society* (Vatican City, 1988).

27. The text of Vatican II's *Pastoral Constitution on the Church in the Modern World* can be found in various collections, including *Catholic Social Thought: The Documentary Heritage*, ed. David J. O'Brien and Thomas A. Shannon (Maryknoll, NY: Orbis Books, 1992).

28. See Kulka and Mendes-Flohr, eds., *Judaism and Christianity*.

29. See note 1 above.

30. See "Statement of the International Catholic-Jewish Liaison Committee," *Origins* 22/2 (May 21, 1992): 32.

31. Kulka and Mendes-Flohr, eds., *Judaism and Christianity*.

40.

DORIS L. BERGEN

The Ecclesiastical Final Solution

THE GERMAN CHRISTIAN MOVEMENT AND THE
ANTI-JEWISH CHURCH

Thanks to fifty years of scholarship, we now know a great deal about the Christian churches in the Third Reich. The courage of those individuals who opposed Nazi brutality, the failure of many church leaders to act decisively in support of Nazism's victims, the cooption of certain groups within German Catholicism and Protestantism—those stories have been told, filled in with detail, and analyzed. Yet a crucial question remains unresolved, a question that is essential if we are to comprehend the role of the Christian churches, their members, and their leaders in the Holocaust. How and in what forms did Christians in Germany and in German-controlled Europe, many of whom supported or tolerated Nazi plans to annihilate the Jews and eradicate Jewish influence, continue to practice their religion, itself an offshoot of Judaism?

Studies of the churches in the Third Reich often start from the assumption that Christianity and Nazism were by definition opposed, that a natural tension between the two had to be overcome before Christians could be Nazis or Nazis Christians. According to this reasoning, Christians who recognized that dichotomy became anti-Nazi resisters; Nazis who acknowledged the mutual exclusivity of the two world views left the church to become its persecutors.

The concept of Christianity and Nazism as polar opposites makes a powerful theological statement. As a means to understand the role of church people in the Holocaust, however, it falls short. As late as 1940, after years of propaganda deriding Christian institutions, over 95 percent of Germans still remained tax-paying members of the established Catholic and Protestant churches.[1] The overwhelming majority of those people never opposed Nazism in the name of their Christian faith. What vision of Christianity enabled them to reconcile devotion to a religion that grew out of Judaism with the imperatives of a regime predicated on brutal antisemitism?

To approach this question, we need to address popular piety and examine what was taught, sung, and read in the congregations. We also need to set aside for a moment the focus on resistance and opposition and look instead for overlap and synthesis. What common ground did Christians find between their religious traditions and Nazi ideas? Which church rituals and practices did they bring into the service of the National Socialist state? Were there limits to their willingness to "deJudaize" Christianity?

This essay addresses these questions by focusing on the German Christian Movement (Glaubensbewegung "Deutsche Christen"). The "German Christians," as members came to be called, were a group of predominantly Protestant lay people and clergy in Nazi Germany who believed that National Socialism and Christianity were not only reconcilable but mutually reinforcing. They aimed to transform the church into a community of blood, the spiritual expression of the racially pure nation. Central to that ecclesiological vision was the quest for an explicitly anti-Jewish Christianity.

The German Christians probably numbered about 600,000 actual members throughout the 1930s and into the Second World War, a small minority in Germany's Protestant population.[2] Many accounts dismiss them as marginal. But while their number was not enormous, it was far from insignificant. After church elections in 1933, German Christians occupied key positions across the country within theological faculties, in regional bishops' seats, and on local church councils. Although members considered it a revolutionary innovation, the German Christian movement was rooted in the culture around it and built on familiar trends in German Protestantism. Moreover, with their self-conscious attempt to fuse Christianity and National Socialism, the German Christians articulated a task that faced every Christian who accepted Nazism as legitimate. Finally, the German Christians, as an extreme expression of pro-Nazi, anti-Jewish Christianity, provide useful insights into the nature of popular piety. Those Jewish elements in Christianity that even this group refused to give up must have been particularly entrenched in the wider religious imagination.

From the inception of the German Christian movement in 1932, members scrambled to appeal to Nazis and to express their devotion to Christian traditions and to National Socialism. To those ends, the German Christians declared war on Jewish influences in Christianity. Becoming more and more daring as Nazi plans for genocide unfolded, they rejected the canonicity of the Old Testament, denied the Jewish ancestry of Jesus, and expunged words like Hosanna and Hallelujah from hymns. The German Christians vowed to remove people defined as non-Aryans from the pulpits and pews of German Protestant congregations. Drawing on precursors that included overseas missionaries, they created an ecclesiology defined by race. Groups outside the movement, such as military chaplains, found themselves echoing German Christian ideals as they pursued their own synthesis of Christianity and National Socialism.

The German Christian offensive against the Jewish roots of Christianity constituted an ecclesiastical counterpart and complement to genocide. This essay traces some forms that assault took in debates about the Old Testament, the New Testament, church music, and so-called non-Aryans in the church. It also explores the relationship between German Christians and mainstream elements in the church by linking the movement to overseas missions and the military chaplaincy. Instead of a fundamental dichotomy between Christianity and Nazism, the German Christians found a synthesis. In their hands, symbols and components of their religious tradition, even those most closely linked to the Jewish origins of Christianity, became weapons in the war against Judaism and Jews.

Blood and Destiny: The German Christian View of Race

The German Christians viewed both Germanness and Jewishness as racial categories. On the basis of race, they decided what would be preached, read, and sung in their services and who could belong to their religious community. They recognized baptism, the symbol and proclamation of church membership, as a pivotal point in their racial policy. Members of the movement denied that baptism changed the status of a former Jew and warned that it allowed alien elements to enter the "Aryan" bloodstream.

Since German Christians sought to fuse church and nation, they tended to blur two contentions inherent in their stance on baptism: baptism could not make a Jew a German, they argued, and by extension, baptism could not make a Jew a Christian. Just as Jewishness for the German Christians was both a religious and a racial category, so German Christianity, its polar opposite, encompassed both a religious and a racial identity. According to the German Christian Reich Bishop Ludwig Müller, people used to believe that "if a Jew was baptized, he was then a Christian. Today we know that you can baptize a Jew ten times, he still remains a Jew and a person whose nature is alien to us, like a Negro remains a Negro and a Chinese a Chinese."[3] A signboard in Lippe (Westphalia) crudely summed up the German Christian view of baptism: "Baptism may be quite useful, but it cannot straighten a nose."[4]

German Christian attempts to create an anti-Jewish church reflected the fundamental illogic of the Nazi definition of Jewishness. On the one hand, Nazi ideology posited Jewishness as a biological fact; German Christians shared that view. But the Nazi concept of Jewishness had religious dimensions, too; by law, the religion of one's grandparents determined one's race.[5]

The assumption that Jewishness resided in religious as well as genetic realities and could therefore be perpetuated via its descendant, Christianity, threatened the German Christians in two ways. In essence, it doomed to failure their goal of creating an anti-Jewish Christian church. Christianity, as German Christians became ever more acutely aware, is intimately and inextricably linked to Judaism, through its scripture, its history, and its ways of conceptualizing humanity's relationship to God. By trying to tear Christianity from its Jewish roots, German Christians set themselves a boundless task they could not accomplish without destroying Christianity itself.

At the same time, the idea that Jewishness could be spread through religion provided inexhaustible ammunition for attacks on Christianity. Nazi theorists, neopagans, and antichurch agitators sneered at Christianity as nothing but diluted Judaism. Their derision egged on the German Christian offensive against Jewish elements in Christianity while putting German Christians on the defensive against the very Nazi worldview they embraced.

But the notion of Jewishness as an intangible spiritual force that had infiltrated Christianity presented opportunities to German Christians as well. It gave them an unlimited sphere of activity in which to prove allegiance to Nazi goals while demonstrating the ability of their form of Christianity to adapt to the demands of its clientele. Moreover, as antisemitic hysteria mounted in Nazi Germany, the attack on Jewish influence in Christianity became for German Christians an area of endeavor guaranteed immune to open opposition. They could point to their anti-Jewish activities as evidence of their loyalty to the Nazi regime; they could silence critics with accusations of treason. Finally, the notion of Jewishness as both racial and religious lent credence to German Christians' own conviction that Germanness too comprised both categories of identity; only Christianity, they maintained, could provide the spiritual content of true Germanness.

War against the Jews: The Old Testament

The Old Testament provided the most obvious target for the German Christians' de-Judaizing fervor. Throughout the 1920s and 1930s, völkisch elements within the Protestant church had assaulted the Old Testament as "too Jewish" for Germans. From 1933 on, German Christians took the lead in that offensive. In June 1933, for example, one man warned that unless the Old Testament were dropped from the Christian canon, it would provide "a constantly open door for the infiltration of Jewish matters and liberal degeneracy."[6] In November, the German-Christian-dominated church government in Schleswig-Holstein limited use of the Old Testament in religious instruction in schools. The binding of Isaac was the first story eliminated as "un-German."[7]

While adherents of the movement agreed that canonicity per se was untenable, they differed as to whether and how portions of the Old Testament might be retained. Reinhold Krause's speech at the movement's rally at the Berlin Sports Palace on November 13, 1933, exposed the extremist position on the Old Testament. Krause, a schoolteacher and leader of Berlin's German Christians, based his attack on the need for the church to appeal to all National Socialists. "Those people need to feel at home in the church," he thundered. To that end, he demanded "liberation from everything un-German in the worship service and the confessions—liberation from the Old Testament with its cheap Jewish morality of exchange and its stories of cattle traders and pimps." If National Socialists refused even to buy a tie from a Jew, he went on, "how much more should we be ashamed to accept from the Jew anything that speaks to our soul, to our most intimate religious essence."[8]

Krause's speech shocked many and sparked a wave of withdrawals from the movement. But he was no anomaly. To the contrary, his words anticipated what, by the late 1930s, would be the definitive German Christian view of the Old Testament.

In the fall of 1935, Hitler's state propagated the Nuremberg Laws, denying citizenship to Jews and codifying a definition of "Jew." Those laws unleashed a new phase in the Nazi assault against Jews; German Christians responded with a harsher tone against the Old Testament. In September, a German Christian speaker in Bavaria ridiculed the Old Testament as a saga of racial defilement. His claim that "Moses in his old age had married a Negro woman," drew boisterous laughter and enthusiastic applause from his audience.[9] A Rhenish pastor quit the German Christian movement in the wake of Nuremberg, appalled by increasing radicalism. The "fight against

Judaism for political and völkisch reasons," he protested, denounced anyone who did not reject the Old Testament as "already 'devoured by Jews.'"[10]

Public antisemitism encouraged heightened German Christian attacks on the Old Testament; in turn, German Christian ideas found resonance in a society that refused membership to those defined as Jews. In late 1936, a Confessing Church pastor described how teenage girls in his confirmation class reacted to a discussion of Jesus's words, "Think not that I am come to destroy the law, or the prophets: I am not come to destroy, but to fulfill" (Matthew 5:17–19). The girls went wild, denouncing "the Old Testament with its filthy stories," the "Jews as a criminal race."[11] It was precisely such attitudes that German Christian pastors and schoolteachers sought to instill in the youth.

By the months following the November 1938 pogrom known as Kristallnacht, leading German Christians decided they needed a more formal organization to express their full participation in Nazi antisemitism and develop an effective defense of Christianity. On April 4, 1939, they got that structure with the founding of the Institute for Study and Elimination of Jewish Influence in German Church Life. From then on, the Institute orchestrated the attack on the Old Testament and its legacy, finding a warm reception especially during the early years of the war. Propaganda that presented the war as mortal combat against "international Jewry" and, after the fall of 1941, deportations of Jews from the Reich, gave new meaning and urgency to German Christian efforts to destroy Jewish influence on the religious front.

Outside the Institute too, German Christians presented the Old Testament as an enemy of the Nazi war effort. In 1941, German Christians in Bavaria proposed a new "celebration of youth" to replace confirmation. In that way, they planned to avoid binding young people to a confession of faith that included the Old Testament:

> We cannot tolerate having our children obligated to that Jewish book of laws, the Old Testament, as the basis of their spiritual life. After all, we all want to cooperate in ensuring that the most inner spheres of German life are free of Jews. Or do you want your children steeped in the doctrines and attitudes toward life of Judaism?[12]

What began as an attempt to separate Christianity from Judaism by banishing the Old Testament became absorbed into a bitter crusade against Jews as German Christian rhetoric merged with the language of genocide. In late 1941, the Thuringian German Christian Julius Leutheuser, writing from the Eastern front, declared the Old Testament and the religiosity of the past to be foes of German Christianity and Germanness. "Behind us is only the decay of a dying epoch," he announced; "our slogan is 'Forward to German faith in God, the secret and power of our German mission.'" For Leutheuser, National Socialist war aims promised a chance to realize the anti-Jewish church: "We call our people to build a National Church, as this final world struggle breaks out, the struggle against Judaism. We now hold the means to strike the weapons from the hands of Judaism for good."[13] From his vantage point on the Eastern front, Leutheuser knew that those "means" involved extermination of the Jews.

Despite bombardment with anti-Jewish tirades in the 1940s, German Christians continued to demonstrate attachment to their religious tradition by using parts of the Old Testament. In 1942, German Christian pastors in Westphalia circulated a list of

Bible readings suitable for wedding ceremonies: one-third came from the Old Testament, all of those from the Psalms.[14] Even a 1943 circular from the National Church group, reputedly the most radical German Christians, cherished bits of the Old Testament. But anti-Jewishness would be the guide in deciding the fate of those Old Testament "gems" in the future people's church. "As a code of Jewish ethics—or rather anti-ethics," one German Christian publicist explained, the Old Testament was unacceptable. But as a piece of religious literature, he continued, it had redeeming qualities:

> The numerous religious treasures that, as religious history can prove, stem from the best Aryan tradition but have been stolen together after the manner of Jewish peddlers and are sprinkled in the Jewish "Old Testament," are to be freed from that unworthy context and released again in their original condition. Their formative power in German popular piety, and German, especially Nordic, art and culture must in no way be underestimated.[15]

Such contorted reasoning suggests German Christians were both eager to add their weight to the Nazi destruction of Judaism and committed to preserving some cultural vestiges of Christianity.

Jesus the Aryan: The New Testament

Once the German Christians drew the Bible into the realm of anti-Jewish criticism, they did not stop with the Old Testament. Rejection of the Old Testament formed the basis for repudiation of scriptural authority in general and provided a criterion for selection within the New Testament. In the drama of Christianity's redemption from Jewish influence, as German Christians construed it, while the Old Testament played the role of the scapegoat that bore away all traces of Jewishness, the New Testament would provide marching orders for an anti-Jewish faith.

The fact that much of the New Testament concerns the theological foundations of Christianity simplified anti-Jewish revision. Antagonistic to considerations of dogma in any case, the German Christians simply excluded such portions from their field of vision and concentrated on those features of the Gospel accounts that informed their cultural identity: Jesus, the manger, and the cross. Instead of progressive radicalization as in the case of the Old Testament, they displayed steadfast consistency on two key points: Jesus was not a Jew, they insisted, and the essence of the Gospel's message was anti-Jewishness.

The German Christians based negation of Jesus's Jewishness on their own presumption of his antisemitism. Jesus, they asserted, could not have been a Jew because he opposed Judaism. This argument formed the core of their Christology and allowed them to preserve the figure of Jesus in their anti-Jewish Christianity. In late 1933, one German Christian offered biblical citations that, he claimed, revealed Jesus's attitude toward Judaism: "A 'murderer,' a 'liar,' a 'father of lies.' It is impossible to reject Jehovah and his Old Testament in sharper terms!" In places, he admitted, the Gospels seemed to suggest the opposite. But those were not the words of Christ, he contended; they were "lies," "Jewishness," the "voice of the Old Testament."[16]

Another German Christian publication advised mothers how to respond when children asked if Jesus were Jewish. They should point out, the author counseled, how "the revolution" opened German eyes:

> We have learned that today the issue is a great struggle . . . between God and the devil. We know now that Jesus was the originator and victor of this gigantic struggle. . . . Because Christ was the "opponent" of the Jews, it is impossible that he himself could have been of Jewish blood and spirit.[17]

The German Christian interpretation of Jesus required minimal alteration to transform an assertion of non-Jewishness into a weapon against Jews and Judaism. As National Socialist attacks on Jews intensified after 1938, German Christians reduced their assessment of what was "genuine" in the Gospel accounts to those fragments that best served an anti-Jewish agenda. In March 1939, a German Christian confirmation examination presented the "German Volk" as the "temple of God," Hitler as Jesus the purifier. That ceremony reflected some effort to preserve Jesus's presence, at least as a symbol. But as the exchange between pastor and candidates reveals, German Christians retained the symbol of Jesus only to use it to sanctify the assault on Jews:

> [Jesus] is no Jew. . . . He was persecuted because he said to the people who considered themselves the chosen ones: God calls pagans, not Jews; God is sick of you chosen people! But why did he not come to the Germanic peoples, this God-man? Why precisely in Judea? He appeared where the enemy was strongest: the Jews are children of the devil and so the offensive had to begin there.[18]

By recasting the central figure of Jesus as antisemitism personified, German Christians turned the New Testament on its head. The heart of its message, they insisted, was not the drama of salvation, but a racial struggle.

German Christians proffered their reinterpretation of the New Testament as a "purification" and "liberation." Reinhold Krause's 1933 speech had demanded removal from the New Testament of an "exaggerated emphasis on the crucified Christ."[19] German Christians took up that challenge, attacking the notion of human sinfulness as a Jewish accretion to the "true" Gospel. In September 1935, a speaker in Kempten (Bavaria) attacked "Jewish-Semitic additions" that "perverted and encrusted" the Gospel. The entire "teaching of sin and grace," he insisted, "was a Jewish attitude and only inserted into the New Testament." The prodigal son, he reminded his audience, had been welcomed home by his father without reprimand for his sins.[20] Concern with sin, a German Christian leader concurred in a 1942 address to assembled women's groups, was a Jewish element to be purged from Christianity.[21]

During the war, the German Christians moved ever further from the text of the Gospels, reducing Jesus to an ally in the war against Jews. A 1939 publication used the language of the apocalypse to sound the call to an anti-Jewish crusade:

> Christ is the idea against Judaism. Therefore, in the world crisis of today, he is—even if unrecognized—the decisive spiritual factor. Christ is the general leading the troops against Jehovah; our age needs him. . . . Jehovah is a force! The world situation shows just how powerful a one. He was triumphant, not only politically and economically in the old

Europe, but above all spiritually. . . . He must be defeated spiritually. That is only possible if all those striving unite under one name. That name is Christ.[22]

But even in their eagerness to use the New Testament to contribute to the Nazi assault on the Jews, German Christians kept something of the Jewish influence of scripture. In April 1944, a German Christian sermon for Good Friday analyzed the crucifixion as a metaphor of war between Christians and Jews: "On the cross we see the most gruesome fratricide. Cain—Israel—murders Abel—Jesus—out of jealousy. Israel's piety, its sacrifices, were rejected by God; the following words applied to Jesus: 'My son, in whom I am well pleased.'"[23] In their eagerness to revamp the New Testament to an anti-Jewish fiat and to throw their weight behind Germany's war effort, German Christians deployed the most powerful imagery available to them. That mental vocabulary included Old Testament narratives.

The Old Familiar Hymns: Church Music

On the basis of a racial imperative, the German Christians overturned Scripture. With hardly a murmur of protest, they abandoned canonicity and mounted an assault on the Old Testament and its legacy. They reinterpreted and eventually rewrote the New Testament to present Jesus as a paragon of anti-Jewishness, their religious ace in the Nazi war against the Jews. Eschewing doctrinal or ethical considerations, German Christians displayed an understanding of Christianity that at heart consisted of an attachment to a handful of symbols and rituals they associated with Christian tradition.

But even in that limited sphere of Christian culture, German Christians encountered evidence of Jewish influence, most notably in church music. On this front, their offensive against Judaism was less intense than in the cases of the Old Testament and the New. It took adherents some time to recognize that racial imperatives impinged here too, and to overcome force of habit when it came to what Germans sang in the church. And even then, while German Christians tinkered with the language of hymns, they never transformed church music itself into a weapon in the Nazi war against the Jews.

Early German Christian events reflected no particular concern about Jewish influence in church music. In June 1933, for example, German Christians met in Dortmund. The program included congregational singing of two familiar hymns that contained what German Christians later decried as Hebraisms. The second stanza of Luther's "A Mighty Fortress" refers to Jesus as "Lord Sabaoth," an ancient title meaning commander of the hosts of heaven; "Oh Come, My Soul with Singing" mentions "Zion" as well as the "God of Jacob."[24] The program provided the standard texts of the hymns, complete with those Old Testament terms.

Rumblings about Jewish influence in church music throughout 1933 suggested the potential for a de-Judaizing assault. At the Sports Palace meeting on November 13, 1933, Berlin German Christian leader Krause, whose proscriptions with regard to the Old and New Testaments proved accurate predictions of subsequent developments, called for transformation of the worship service, including attention to church music:

> We want to worship God in the church, in the congregations, with German words, and from a German spirit. We want to sing songs that are free from all Israelite elements. We want to liberate ourselves from the language of Canaan and turn to our German mother tongue. Only in the German mother tongue can humanity express its prayers, praise, and thanks in the most profound way.[25]

Only in late 1935, after propagation of the Nuremberg Laws, did German Christians begin anything approaching a systematic purge of Christian hymns. The impetus originated high in the movement's ranks, motivated by concern for the church's ability to attract an increasingly antisemitic clientele. Unlike the case of the Old Testament, German Christians expressed a sense of loss in subjecting traditional hymns to considerations of racial purity. Nevertheless, the cause demanded self-denial; according to one member, it was "more Christian to make sacrifice in external forms than through them to kill the spirit and life."[26]

In 1935, the German Christian Wilhelm Bauer published a liturgical guide called "German Christian Celebrations." Bauer decried Jewish influence in church music, complaining, for example, about a draggy musical style that, in his view, was "borrowed from the synagogue." He saved his most detailed criticism for the texts of hymns, contending that it would hardly "contravene the spirit of the Bible or injure the Confession" if the "people of Israel" were replaced with the "people of God," or the "cedars of Lebanon" with the "firs of the German forest."[27] Bauer encouraged musical innovation but did not advocate transforming church music into a weapon against Judaism. His reticence on that score, however, reflected not moral or doctrinal but aesthetic considerations. In the church, he reminded readers, it was "in bad taste" to sing militaristic or folksy kinds of music that "clashed" with the solemn tones of the organ and violated the "hallowed stillness" of the house of God.[28]

Shortly before the war began, Bishop Heinz Weidemann in Bremen coordinated release of a new German Christian songbook, "Songs of the Coming Church" (*Lieder der kommenden Kirche*).[29] It allegedly sold ten thousand copies in the first weeks. Weidemann considered his hymnbook "truly German,"[30] its songs purged of all "Judaisms," including Jewish and foreign words. Most of the hymns included were traditional, although references to the Old Testament had been expunged. The new additions, while often focused more on Germany than on Christianity, did not express explicitly anti-Jewish sentiments. Even the firebrand Weidemann, who showed no compunction in rewriting the Gospel of John into a tirade of hatred toward Jews, appeared bound by considerations of what was tasteful and appropriate in church music.

The largest collection of "de-Judaized" hymns German Christians assembled was a 1941 release named after a familiar hymn: "Holy God We Praise Thy Name" (*Grosser Gott wir loben Dich!*). Containing 339 hymns, a mixture of old and new German material, the book was a product of the Institute for Study and Elimination of Jewish Influence in German Church Life.[31] Here too, the result was a self-consciously conventional hymnbook minus Old Testament vocabulary, not a declaration of war on Judaism in general.

Even in their attacks on so-called Jewish influences in the Old Testament, the

New Testament, and church music, German Christians were committed to preserving certain familiar and powerful cultural artifacts of Christianity. It is significant both as evidence of German Christian commitment to their religious tradition, and as a testimony to the banality of their understanding of Christianity, that notions of taste and appropriateness exercised a much more effective brake on the project of de-Judaization than did any doctrinal or theological considerations. It was in the sphere of church music, far from the core of Christian belief, that the German Christians appeared least eager to complete their ecclesiastical final solution.

Abandoned and Betrayed: "Non-Aryans" in the Church

The German Christians were willing to spare certain aspects of church practice and ritual from the assault of de-Judaization. They demonstrated no such protective instincts toward those people within the church who were defined as non-Aryans. Racial categories formed a wall around the German Christians' ideal church, separating those inside from those outside. The Nazi state's measures against Jews and "non-Aryans" furthered the movement's own goal of creating a racially pure church.

In 1933, the German Christian leadership tried to implement an Aryan Paragraph in the Protestant church that would force all non-Aryan clergy from office. Those efforts foundered on opposition mounted by the Pastors' Emergency League, led by Martin Niemöller. Niemöller himself believed there was some validity in German Christian arguments that the Aryan Paragraph was a necessary response to congregations' prejudices. But, he argued in 1934, for the sake of the confession, the church would have to endure the "disagreeable" racial fact of Jewishness.[32]

German Christians continued to agitate for introduction of an Aryan Paragraph, even after 1939, when institutionalized antisemitism in Nazi Germany more or less ensured de facto implementation of racial exclusion. In the summer of 1939, church offices in Berlin, under the influence of supposedly moderate German Christians, ordered regional churches to collect proof of "descent from German blood" for all pastors and their wives.[33] Only wartime exigencies led to relaxation of that demand in August 1944.[34]

Thus the struggle over the Aryan Paragraph in the Protestant church ended not with a bang but a whimper. Nevertheless, the result was what German Christians had sought since 1933: effective exclusion of non-Aryans from pastoral office in the Protestant churches of Germany. The German Christians could hardly take credit for that outcome. There had never been more than a few non-Aryan pastors; of those, many had left on their own.[35] Nazi policies made sure that people defined as Jews were shut out of German society, while organs of church government, and not only those controlled by German Christians, added their own administrative measures to restrict non-Aryan clergy.

With regard to non-Aryan lay people in the church, the German Christians found their goals of racial exclusion fulfilled almost by default. Like German Christians, many other Protestants referred to converts from Judaism and their descendants as "Jewish Christians" or "baptized Jews." By using those labels, representatives of all camps in the church struggle suggested they too regarded "Jewishness" as an immutable racial fact. Only individual, isolated voices challenged German Christian racism at its roots. That rather broad consensus meant German Christians, having designed a wall of racial exclusion around their ideal spiritual community, could leave much of the construction and maintenance work to other elements within German society and inside the Protestant church.

By the early months of 1939, in the wake of Kristallnacht, German-Christian-dominated regional churches began passing regulations to exclude non-Aryans from the religious community. In February 1939, the Thuringian Protestant church decreed that people defined as Jews under the law could not become members. Pastors were not obligated to perform services for "Jews" already in the church; church rooms and equipment were not to be used for services or sacraments for non-Aryans. Non-Aryan Christians were to pay no more church taxes.[36] The churches in Mecklenburg, Anhalt, Lübeck, and Saxony subsequently passed similar legislation.[37]

The German Christians paced their assault on non-Aryan Christians to match German attacks on Jews. As of September 1941, police regulations forced all people within Germany who were defined as Jews to wear the identifying Star of David. General deportations of Jews to the territory of Poland began in October 1941;[38] those sent to their death included converts to Christianity and their children as well. Just two months later, in December, representatives of seven regional churches, all dominated by German Christians, issued their own proclamation to exclude "racially Jewish Christians" from the church. Leaders of church government in Saxony, Nassau-Hesse, Schleswig-Holstein, Thuringia, Mecklenburg, Anhalt, and Lübeck echoed Nazi charges that Jews had "instigated" the war and placed themselves and their flocks "in the front of this historic defensive struggle." Ever since the crucifixion of Christ, they claimed, "Jews have opposed Christianity." Baptism, they added, changed "nothing about the racial essence of Jews." Therefore, they concluded, "racially Jewish Christians have no room and no rights" in a German church.[39]

Having adopted race as the organizing principle of their project of church renewal, German Christians ended up equating the anti-Jewish people's church with the genocidal German nation. An excerpt from a German Christian publication of April 1944 captures that identity:

> There is no other solution to the Jewish problem than this: that one day the whole world will rise up and decide either for or against Judaism, and will keep on struggling with each other until the world is totally judaized or completely purged of Judaism. We can say with an honest, pure conscience that we did not want this war and did not start this war. But we can proudly profess before all the world—the world of today as well as of tomorrow—that we took up the gauntlet with the firm resolve to solve the Jewish Question for ever.[40]

With that proclamation, German Christians echoed and appropriated the threat of annihilation Hitler had issued on January 1, 1939. Hitler had claimed to be a "prophet" in predicting that the next war would bring the "annihilation of the Jewish race in Europe."[41] Through their quest for an anti-Jewish church, German Christians endorsed and sanctified those murderous dreams for the Thousand Year Reich.

Racial Precursors: Overseas Missions

The German Christians, with their anti-Jewish campaign, represented an extreme position among German Protestants. Yet many components of their racial view were neither unique to them nor unfamiliar to other Germans. Indeed, like National Socialism, the German Christian Movement contained little that was new. Its tenets represented a conglomeration of old and not-so-old ideas drawn from sources that included Martin Luther, Houston Stewart Chamberlain, and the völkisch theologians of the interwar period. The German Christians also traced some of their ideas, in particular their theories of race, to a less obvious source: overseas missions. Recognition of the German Christian debt to missionaries' thinking about race in turn highlights the connections between the movement and more respectable voices in the church.

Since the late nineteenth century, German missions had stressed the need to adapt the Christian message and its presentation to suit each Volk. German Christians took that message as justification for a racially exclusive church. According to one German Christian, missions taught that in "God's order of creation, there is no 'humanity,' rather only German Christians, English Christians, Chinese Christians, and so on."[42] Another German Christian grumbled in 1935 that, "We allow every Negro and every Indian to have a form of Christianity that fits to the life of his soul; only we Germans are supposed to have a Jewish or a Roman style of Christianity."[43]

In addition to legitimizing the racially exclusive church, the overseas mission experience offered an example of racist thinking that could in turn be applied to the Jews. In order to make concrete their view of Jewishness as a racial category, the German Christians compared Jews to the African and Asian subjects of German missionary efforts. By doing so, they transferred the feelings of superiority, fear, and loathing that they experienced toward the foreign "heathens" onto German Jews. In October 1932, the "Gospel in the Third Reich," the official German Christian newspaper, used an analogy to race relations in overseas missions to explain why converts from Judaism could not participate in a German church. "Through baptism," the author intoned, "a Negro who lived in Germany would by no means become a German. It is the same for a Jew." Missions, he continued, "do not eradicate differences among the races." "Just as a baptized Negro becomes a Negro Christian," he concluded, "the Jew will remain racially a Jew; 'only' from the religious point of view will he become a Jewish Christian."[44]

The first Reich Conference of the Student Combat League of German Christians (Studentenkampfbund Deutsche Christen) in August 1933, included a presentation on "Overseas Missions and Mission to the Jews."[45] By linking the two themes, organizers conveyed the message that Jews were as racially "other" as Africans or Asians. By conceding that missions to the Jews might continue under the rubric of overseas missions, the German Christian guidelines seemed to imply that overseas missions were not a potential floodgate to racial defilement; it was no doubt assumed that German missionaries maintained strict sexual separation from the "natives."

German missionaries were by no means completely innocent in the fact that they provided part of the German Christian legacy of race. At least a few prominent mission leaders showed an early interest in the German Christian movement,[46] and even those who opposed it tended to defend an exclusionary view of racial relations. Siegfried Knak, a prominent mission leader, summed up his view of proper race relations with the phrase: "What God has put asunder let no man join together."[47] Eventually, most missionaries and missionary organizations parted ways with the movement, recognizing that the inner logic of German Christianity, with its emphasis on racially and nationally specific religion, doomed the overseas missions endeavor. Nevertheless, German Protestant missionaries did contribute to the German Christian theory of race, linking it to familiar stereotypes and giving legitimacy to the acceptance and promotion of racial distinctions within the community of faith.

The Military Chaplaincy

Historians often dismiss the German Christian movement as inconsequential, absurd, and doomed to fail. Yet a look at the military chaplaincy suggests that the German Christians represented a position shared, at least to some extent, by others in the church who also took on the challenge of fusing Christianity and Nazi ideology. As contrived and illogical as it was, the German Christian stance on race and anti-semitism may have represented the natural outcome of any attempt to blend those two worldviews.

Contrary to common belief, some Protestant military chaplains were outspoken German Christians,[48] although the majority were either indifferent or hostile to the movement. In any case, the nature of their position forced all chaplains to find some way to reconcile National Socialism and Christianity. National Socialism determined the contours of the war effort, even for soldiers who opposed the party and its goals. Christianity, although often in a theologically naive, culturally diluted form, emerged as tremendously important to soldiers under the pressures of battle, injury, and death. As they served those two causes, chaplains willingly or unwillingly reproduced some of the conditions the German Christians envisaged for their racially pure church. For example, military chaplains promoted the goals of the German Christians through the literature they distributed to soldiers. Generally, Protestant chaplains could acquire only two religious publications on anything like a regular basis: the New Testament and the Protestant Soldier's Songbook [*Evangelisches Feldgesangbuch*].[49] German Christians could not claim to have written the New Testament nor were they publicly associated with the Protestant Soldier's Songbook. Yet both pieces of literature bore the marks of their ideas.

Since the early 1930s, in their attacks on Jewish elements in Christianity, German Christians had expressed views on the Old Testament that ranged from ambivalence to emphatic rejection. Incensed by Nazi and neopagan charges that Christianity was simply disguised Judaism, German Christians were eager or at least willing to jettison the Old Testament to show that they shared the rabid anti-Jewishness of National Socialism. Authorities in the chaplaincy and in military offices who chose to make the New Testament the only scripture available for distribution to soldiers did not necessarily accept German Christian views. Most likely they would have defended their decision on the grounds that they needed a scripture cheap enough to be produced in mass quantities and small enough to be carried in a breast pocket. But there are many logical ways to abridge the Bible; a combination of the Psalms and Gospels or selection of familiar passages would be as valid as exclusion of the entire Old Testament. Distribution of the New Testament alone suggests a compromise solution. In this case, the path of least resistance for the chaplaincy, in order to avoid criticism from anti-Christian Nazis, neopagans, or German Christians, reflected exactly the German Christian agenda.

The hymnbook chaplains distributed also reflected the German Christian position. In August 1939, the military office for pastoral care, in conjunction with the Protestant Military Bishop, issued a new Protestant Soldier's Songbook (*Evangelisches Feldgesangbuch*), containing fifty-six hymns and twenty-six songs. The hymns were standard Protestant fare: "A Mighty Fortress"; "Praise to the Lord, the Almighty"; "Silent Night." But they were "purified" along exactly the lines German Christians advocated. None of the hymns mentioned Old Testament figures by name, nor were Hallelujahs or Hosannas to be found. The sole exception was the second stanza of "Silent Night," where the Hallelujah remained. That familiar Christmas carol was probably the only religious song in which the average soldier might have noticed omission or alteration of any stanza but the first.[50] Bremen's Bishop Weidemann noticed with glee that the new songbook, issued in more than two million copies, followed his lead in purging "Jewish elements" from church music.[51] When chaplains distributed the Protestant Soldier's Songbook, they handed out a piece of German Christian propaganda and perpetuated the notion that Christianity and Judaism could and indeed would be separated.[52]

In other ways too the situation in which military chaplains worked reproduced the German Christian ideal of the racially pure church. German Christians dreamed of the church as a community of "pure Germans," devoted to the exclusion of Jews, so-called non-Aryans, and Jewish influence. In effect, the chaplaincy operated under exactly those conditions. Jews were absent among the troops of the Third Reich; the official goals of the war included expansion of Lebensraum for the so-called Aryan race and eradication of Europe's Jews. Chaplains were urged to be vocal in support of those aims.[53] By the mid-1930s, unlike civilian clergy, chaplains themselves were subject to an Aryan clause, requiring that they produce proof that they and their wives were of "Aryan blood."[54] Despite the antagonism of many chaplains toward the German Christian movement, they, perhaps more than any other group, came close to realizing the anti-Jewish church for which German Christians yearned.

This essay began with a question: How and in what forms did Christians in Germany and in German-controlled Europe, many of whom supported or tolerated Nazi plans to annihilate Jews and eradicate Jewish influence, continue to practice their religion, itself an offshoot of Judaism? Study of the German Christian movement and its quest for an anti-Jewish church offers at least some tentative answers. Even the members of this radical group, who twisted and distorted their religious tradition in so many ways, tried to retain some recognizable elements of traditional Christian culture: certain Old Testament narratives, the figure of Jesus, familiar hymns. That willingness to preserve those symbols in turn indicates how deeply embedded they must have been in the religious landscape of Germany. Yet ironically and sadly, even those Jewish elements of their tradition to which the German Christians clung could be manipulated in the service of Nazi genocide. Perhaps equally sobering is the recognition that the German Christian movement, although bold and brash in articulating its positions on race and antisemitism, was not a total aberration, but had ties to more longstanding, respected views within German Protestantism.

NOTES

I am grateful to the Social Sciences and Humanities Research Council of Canada and the Alberta Heritage Foundation for funding the research in German archives on which this essay is based. Some of the material here appears in a different form in Doris L. Bergen, Twisted Cross: The German Christian Movement in the Third Reich *(Chapel Hill: University of North Carolina Press, 1996).*

1. See data from the Ministry of Church Affairs, "Zusammenstellung über Kirchenaustritte und Kirchenrücktritte bezw. Übertritte, ermittelt nach den von den Kirchen veröffentlichten Zusammenstellungen" (no author, 1940, in Bundesarchiv Koblenz (hereafter BA Koblenz), R 79/19.

2. Due to fragmentation within the movement and the loss of membership files, it is difficult to gauge exact numbers of German Christians at any given time. However, German Christians and their opponents generally accepted the figure of 600,000 as a reasonable estimate in the mid-1930s. See, for example, the circular from the German Christian regional office in Dresden, signed Martin Beier, July 9, 1934, "An alle Mitarbeiter der DC!" including reference by German Christian Reich Leader Christian Kinder to the 600,000 members of his organization (Landeskirchenarchiv Bielefeld [hereafter LKA Bielefeld]), 5,1/290,2.

3. "Auszug aus der Rede des Reichsbishofs Ludwig Müller am Sonntag den 21. Feb. 1937 in Gütersloh," no author, Confessing Church report, LKA Bielefeld 5,1/289,2.

4. Quoted in "Propaganda an der Chaussee," no author, in "Schnellbrief für Glieder der Bekennenden Kirche," no. 31 (October 2, 1935), p. 120, LKA Bielefeld 5,1/555,1.

5. Raul Hilberg discusses development of a definition of "Jews" in Nazi Germany in *The Destruction of the European Jews* (New York: Holmes & Meier, 1985), vol. 1, pp. 65–80. A first step was the Interior Ministry regulation of April 1933 that defined as of "non-Aryan descent" anyone with a parent or grandparent of the Jewish religion. As Hilberg points out, that definition was "in no sense based on racial criteria." A definition of "Jews" followed over two years later, but the basis of distinction remained the religious status of the grandparents.

6. A. Bernhardi, "Gedanken zur Glaubensbewegung," sent by its author to the Prussian Minister for Science, Art, and Education, June 27, 1933, pp. 4–5, Bundesarchiv Potsdam (hereafter BA Potsdam) DC-I 1933–1935, pp. 61–62.

7. "Das Alte Testament im Unterricht," no author, unlabeled clipping (November 4, 1933), in LKA Bielefeld 5,1/289,1.

8. Pamphlet, Reinhold Krause, "Rede des Gauobmannes der Glaubensbewegung 'Deutsche Christen' in Gross-Berlin, gehalten im Sportpalast am 13. Nov. 1933 (nach doppeltem stenographischem Bericht)," pp. 6–7, LKA Bielefeld 5,1/289,2.

9. Copy of report signed "Evang.-Luth. Stadtpfarramt, St. Mang.-Kempten," September 20, 1935, p. 2, Landeskirchenarchiv Nürnberg (hereafter LKA Nuremberg), KKU 6/IV. The reference is to the Cushite woman whom Moses had married and who was the subject of strife between Moses and his siblings. God punished Miriam for her rebellion by striking her with leprosy (Num. 12:1ff.).

10. Copy, "Was wollen die rheinishen Deutschen Christen?" no author, n.d., made from a letter announcing his decision to leave the German Christian ranks, sent from a Rhenish pastor to a colleague, in Archiv der Evangelischen Kirche im Rheinland (hereafter AEKR

Düsseldorf), NL Schmidt, no. 17. A copy elsewhere reveals the identities of the correspondents; see copy of excerpts from letter, Loy to Johannes Pack, November 9, 1936, Duisburg-Hamborn, in AEKR Düsseldorf, NL Schmidt, no. 17, pp. 68–69.

11. Pastor Weber to Praeses and Members of the Berlin Fraternal Council ("Bruderrat"), November 9, 1936, Berlin; reproduced in "Beschwerden persönlicher Anliegen und Mitteilungen seitens des Berliner Bruderrates und seiner Mitglieder, Jan. 1936–Dez. 1936," p. 8, Evangelisches Zentralarchiv Berlin (hereafter EZA Berlin) 50/4.

12. Flyer, "Konfirmation? Kommunion?" signed Adolf Daum for German Christians in Bavaria [1941], p. 2, LKA Nuremberg LKR II 246, Bd. IX.

13. Duplicated letter, Julius Leutheuser, "Liebe Kameraden in der Heimat und im Felde!" December 20, 1941, Russia, presumably circulated by the German Christian National Church Union "Informationsdienst," LKA Bielefeld 5,1/295,1.

14. German Christian Pastors' Association, Bielefeld, "Die Trauung," in "Theologischer Arbeitsbrief" (May 1, 1942), p. 2, LKA Bielefeld 5,1/295,1.

15. Hans Schmidt, "Die Nationalkirche als religiöse Erbe und überkommene Verpflichtung für die nach uns Kommenden," circular of the DC Nationalkirchliche Einung Theol. Arbeitskreis (Saarburg/Trier, January 20, 1943), p. 17, EZA Berlin 1/A4/565.

16. Wilhelm Schielmeyer to Reich Bishop Müller, December 1, 1933, EZA Berlin 1/C4/17. Schielmeyer referred to Luke 17:20–21, John 18:36–37, and John 8:44.

17. H. Vogel, untitled piece beginning, "Du Mutter heranwachsender Kinder," in the pamphlet Die deutsche Mutter, ed. Reich Office for Women's Service, Potsdam, [n.d.], p. 7, Collection of the Kirchengeschichtliche Arbeitsgemeinschaft, Kommunalarchiv Minden (hereafter KAG-Minden), loose materials. I am grateful to the staff at the Kommunalarchiv in Minden for permitting me access to these materials.

18. "Bericht über eine 'Konfirmandenprüfung' der Thüringer Deutschen Christen in Berlin-Siemensstadt am 22. III. 1939," LKA Bielefeld 5,1/588.

19. Krause, "Rede des Gauobmannes," LKA Bielefeld 5,1/289,2.

20. Copy of report signed "Evang.-Luth. Stadtpfarramt, St. Mang.-Kempten," September 20, 1935, p. 2, LKA Nuremberg KKU 6/IV. Also copy in LKA Bielefeld 5,1/291,2.

21. Duplicated excerpt from presentation by Hans Hermenau, "Unsere Seelsorge am deutschen Volk," in "Bericht über die Tagung des Frauendienstes Gr. Berlin in Spandau am 27. II. 1942," EZA Berlin 50/600, p. 2.

22. Werner Wein, Das Evangelium jenseits der Konfessionen (Stuttgart: Tazzelwurm, 1939), p. 228.

23. Friedrich Engelke, "Predigtgedanken-Karfreitag," "Theologischer Arbeitsbrief" (April 1, 1944), p. 1, LKA Bielefeld 5,1/295,2.

24. "Ein' feste Burg ist unser Gott," and "Du meine Seele singe." See program entitled, "Wach auf, wach auf, du deutsches Land, du hast genug geschlafen," for meeting of the German Christian Faith Movement in Dortmund, June 22–24, 1933, in LKA Bielefeld 5,1/294,3.

25. Krause, "Rede des Gauobmannes," LKA Bielefeld 5,1/289,2.

26. Report by Tausch, "Entwurf zu einem Propagandadienst der Reichskirchenregierung," May 8, 1935, pp. 1, 3, EZA Berlin 1/A4/93.

27. Wilhelm Bauer, Feierstunden Deutscher Christen (Weimar: Verlag Deutsche Christen, 1935), pp. 47–48.

28. Ibid., p. 44.

29. Lieder der kommenden Kirche, foreword by Heinz Weidemann (Bremen: Verlag Kommende Kirche, [1939]); contains 112 hymns. An expanded version with 186 hymns appeared subsequently: Gesangbuch der kommenden Kirche (Bremen: Verlag Kommende Kirche, [n.d.]).

30. Copy, advertisement from Evangelische Nachrichten (April 23, 1939) for "Die Lieder der kommenden Kirche, hrsg. von Landesbischof Lic. Dr. Weidemann," including quotations from Weidemann's foreword, LKA Bielefeld 5,1/293.

31. In an account of the new German Protestant hymnbook of 1951, a reporter sympathetic to the German Christian cause looked back nostalgically to the 1941 songbook

of that movement, *Grosser Gott wir loben Dich*. In assembling the songbook, he claimed, "careful attention was paid among other things to leaving out foreign and incomprehensible words and replacing them with better ones" (Karl Eichenberg, unpublished manuscript, "Sie waren anders als ihr Ruf. Die Deutschen Christen" [1970s], p. 27, KAG-Minden).

32. Martin Niemöller, "Sätze zur Arierfrage in der Kirche," *Deutsches Pfarrerblatt* 4 (January 23, 1934): 46, LKA Bielefeld 5,1/289,1.

33. Order signed Dr. Werner, Protestant Upper Consistory, to Protestant Consistories in the internal area of jurisdiction, E. O. I 1448/39, July 4, 1939, EZA Berlin 7/1960. Attached are copies of the questionnaires no. 64 IIa for clergy and 65 IIa for spouses. Each is two pages long. The order was linked to the Reich Civil Servants Law of January 1937 (RG Bl. I S.39). The questionnaire itself asked if the individual had Jewish parents or grandparents and requested information on previous religion, if any, of parents or grandparents. Documentary proof was to be appended.

34. The Upper Consistory explicitly patterned its realization of proof of Aryanism requirements on measures adopted by the Ministry of the Interior on September 20, 1943 (RM Bl IV. 1943, sp. 1505).

35. The outspoken and energetic non-Aryan pastor from Bochum, Hans Ehrenberg, for example, was incarcerated in Sachsenhausen in 1938, but his wife managed to secure his release and the family moved to England. Ehrenberg had been active in the Confessing Church but found himself repeatedly pushed to the background and urged to restrain himself by elements in the organization that regarded his non-Aryan status as something of an embarrassment. See Wilhem Niemöller, *Wort und Tat im Kirchenkampf* (Munich: Christian Kaiser, 1969), p. 363.

36. "Thüringens evangelische Kirche schliesst Juden aus," no author, *Deutsche Allgemeine Zeitung*, no. 100 (February 28, 1939), BA Potsdam, Reichlandblatt 1864, p. 145.

37. See the reference to these pieces of church legislation in untitled Confessing Church response to the Godesberg Declaration, [May 1939], EZA Berlin 50/600, p. 30.

38. For a brief summary of these measures against Jews in Germany, see Lucy S. Dawidowicz, *The War against the Jews, 1933–1945* (New York: Bantam, 1986), p. 375.

39. Copy of "Bekanntmachung über die kirchliche Stellung der evangelischen Juden vom 17 Dez. 1941," no. 101, signed Klotsche, President of the Regional Church Office in Saxony; Kipper, President of the Regional Church Office in Nassau-Hesse; Kinder for Schleswig-Holstein; Volk for Thuringia; Schultz for Mecklenburg; Willkendorf for Anhalt; Sievers for Lübeck, in *Kirchliches Gesetz- und Verordnungsblatt*, no. 17 (December 29, 1941): 117–18, EZA Berlin 50/576, p. 40.

40. "Wesen und Entstehung der Judenfrage – Auszug aus einem Vortrag von K. F. Euler," Deutsche Christen Nationalkirchliche Einung, *Informationsdienst*, no. 4 (April 29, 1944), p. 6, EZA Berlin 1/A4/566.

41. See excerpt from Hitler's speech and discussion of its significance in Hilberg, *Destruction of the European Jews*, vol. 2, pp. 393–94.

42. Pastor Ankermann, "Der deutsche Christ und die Heidenmission," *Mitteilungen der Glaubensgemeinschaft Deutsche Christen*, no. 21 (May 21, 1933): 2, LKA Bielefeld 5,1/289,2.

43. "Die angebliche Irrlehre der 'Deutschen Christen,'" circular issued by the leadership of the Reich Movement of the German Christians, no author, May 31, 1935, LKA Bielefeld 5,1/290,1.

44. "Fragekasten," no author, *Evangelium im Dritten Reich*, no. 1 (October 16, 1932): 7.

45. See meeting agenda, "Tagungsplan zur Ersten Reichstagung des Studenten-kampfbundes Deutsche Christen in der Friedrich-Wilhelms Universität zu Berlin vom 7.–10. August 1933," attached invitation signed by Kurt Werner, Reich Organizational leader of the Student Combat League of German Christians, Berlin, July 1933, EZA Berlin 50/631.

46. See, for example, two unidentified clippings, "Heidenmission und Kirchenverfassung," and "'Hakenkreuz und Christenkreuz vereint!'" [1933] LKA Bielefeld 5,1/697,2, that discuss Siegfried Knak, director of the Berlin Missions Society, as an early German Christian sympathizer.

47. Siegfried Knak, *Kirchenstreit und Kirchenfriede beleuchtet von den Erfahrungen der Mission aus*, 2nd ed. (Berlin: Heimatdienst, 1934), p. 22.

48. The total number of Protestant military chaplains varied over the course of the war; Protestant Military Bishop Franz Dohrmann cites a figure of 455; in late 1944, 481 chaplains were in place (Dohrmann's notes, Bundesarchiv, Militärabteilung, Freiburg/Br. [hereafter BA-MA Freiburg], N282/v. 1, p. 163). We do not know how many of those men were German Christians; so far, I have positively identified over fifty chaplains who were adherents of the movement. That preliminary figure computes to more than 10 percent; to double that percentage would still be a conservative estimate.

49. Military authorities ordered large numbers of songbooks but New Testaments were always in shorter supply. The publisher of the *Evangelisches Feldgesangbuch* was E. S. Mittler and Son, Berlin. An order from Army High Command to the publisher in 1941 requested 500,000 copies for a total of RM 25,000. Throughout the war years, High Command contributed up to RM 10,000 annually for religious literature (BA-MA Freiburg, RH 15/277, "Haushaltsangelegenheiten, vol. 4, May 1937–May 1941).

50. "Stille Nacht," *Evangelisches Feldgesangbuch*, p. 59.

51. Weidemann, "Mein Kampf um die Erneuerung des religiösen Lebens in der Kirche: ein Rechenschaftsbericht," [1942] p. 7, BA Koblenz, R 43 II/165, fiche 4, p. 324.

52. In his account of the Protestant Wehrmacht chaplaincy during World War II, former chaplain Schübel recognizes that the 1939 songbook for soldiers was consistent with the ideals of the national Church wing of German Christians. But, he contends, the book was nevertheless useful and valuable to chaplains and soldiers alike. See Albrecht Schübel, *300 Jahre Evangelische Soldatenseelsorge* (Munich: Evangelischer Presseverband für Bayern, 1964), pp. 90–92.

53. As Edelmann instructed supervisory chaplains in 1941, the chaplain "must present this war for German living space as a war that is just before God and as a fight to be rewarded" (Edelmann, "Wesen und Aufgabe der Feldseelsorge," 1941, BA-MA Freiburg, RH 15/282, pp. 22–36).

54. Already in 1936, Army High Command wrote to Military Bishop Dohrmann complaining that two army pastors had not yet completed the paperwork establishing their Aryan blood (OKH to Dorhmann, April 29, 1936, BA-MA Freiburg, RW 12 I/2, p. 26). The first point of the 1940 conditions for employing chaplains stipulated that appointment of a military pastor could occur only if the individual, and his wife if he were married, were of "German or kindred blood" (Edelmann, OKH/AHA/Gruppe S, "Anstellungs- und Beförderungsbestimmungen für Wehrmachtpfarrer" [1940], p. 1, BA-MA Freiburg, N282/v. 8).

Part 9

Jewish Leadership, Jewish Resistance

Few aspects of the Holocaust are more controversial than the behavior of Jewish leadership, most especially the role of the Judenräte, the German-initiated Jewish Councils that presided over the ghetto population. Ghetto diary and memoir writers raised all of the hard questions during the Holocaust. What role did the Judenräte play? Whose interests did they serve? Were they helpful in assisting Jews to survive? Were they guilty of complicity with the enemy? To the German authorities, they were a tool to rule the ghetto. For those interned, they made representations on behalf of Jewish needs to the German rulers; to the Jews they represented and enforced German decrees to do the dirty work for the rulers. The Judenräte were often criticized for freeing up German personnel for other tasks.

Anyone familiar with Holocaust literature knows of the major controversies surrounding the role of Jewish leadership. The debate reached the public more than three decades ago with the publication of two works, Raul Hilberg's *The Destruction of the European Jews* and Hannah Arendt's *Eichmann in Jerusalem: A Report on the Banality of Evil.* Hilberg argued that Jewish responses went through four stages: *alleviation, evasion, paralysis* and ultimately *compliance*:

> Both perpetrators and victims drew upon their age-old experience in dealing with each other. The Germans did it with success. The Jews did it with disaster.

Arendt wrote:

> Wherever Jews lived, there were recognized Jewish leaders, and this leadership, almost without exception, cooperated in one way or another, for one reason or another, with Nazis. The whole truth was that if the Jewish people had really been unorganized and leaderless, there would have been chaos and plenty of misery but the total number of victims would hardly have been between four and a half and six million people.

The essays that follow deal less with the situation in Poland, which is so well described by the late Isaiah Trunk in his definitive work *Judenrat,* than with other aspects of the dilemma of Jewish leadership in diverse countries such as France and Czechoslovakia, as well as in Eastern Europe. While none of the authors addresses the issue directly, these issues loom in the background and serve as the context for each of the articles that follows. What we can see is that the behavior of Jews must also be observed in a country-by-country context.

In "The Armed Jewish Resistance in Eastern Europe: Its Unique Conditions and Its Relations with the Jewish Councils (Judenräte) in the Ghettos," Yitzhak Arad, an Israeli historian of the Holocaust, and former chairman of the directorate of Israel's Holocaust Memorial, Yad Vashem, sets out to understand the place of the Jewish armed resistance units outside the ghettos in their relationship to the non-Jewish partisan movements and to the Judenräte inside the ghettos.

What he discovers in his analysis is striking: unlike the non-Jewish partisan units that fought for life and the liberation of their occupied homelands, Jewish units fought for a choice of how to die, that is to die fighting rather than be taken to gas chambers.

He also argues that the Judenräte in the ghettos did not see the Jewish armed resistance movements as a rival for power but often cooperated with those units by providing people and supplies. It was only when the partisan units began to endanger the lives of the ghetto inhabitants, for instance by smuggling weapons into the ghettos, that the Jewish Councils objected to their actions. Indeed, the partisan units agreed with the basic premise of the Jewish Council policy of trying to extend the life of the ghettos through hard work, in the same way that some Jewish Councils eventually supported the idea of partisan uprising and resistance once the ghetto was in danger of being liquidated.

In "Remembering and Invoking 1789 during the Holocaust: The Trials and Tribulations of French Jews," Richard I. Cohen argues that the political, historical, cultural, and religious baggage with which Jews entered the war was a significant factor in the way they dealt with extreme situations during the Holocaust. The French Revolution shaped French Jewry's political outlook. The true France was revolutionary and embraced the values of "Liberty, Equality, Fraternity." For French Jews, and even for foreign Jews attracted to France, the Revolution was a "new genesis," biblical in its impact. Neither Basel (the site of the Zionist Congress) nor Jerusalem attracted them. The antisemitism of the antirepublican forces, culminating in the Dreyfus affair, did not cause French Jews to consider the antirevolutionary tradition—in which antisemitism figured prominently—as a constant danger in French politics.

Indeed, throughout the early years, Cohen argues, Jews struggled to preserve their trust and belief in the principles of the Revolution and the values of the "true France"—even while the French government embarked on an antirevolutionary and antisemitic course. The break with this perception of France came late—too late—in 1943. The earliest voices, the more shrill and acerbic voices that described the rupture of France with its revolutionary values, were those of Eastern European Jews. It was these Jews who were less attached to the image of revolutionary France and, therefore, more capable of breaking with this long-ingrained perception. Only in the aftermath of the Holocaust did French Jews realize that "the Revolution was over."

In "The Jewish Underground Press in France and the Struggle to Expose the Nazi Secret of the Final Solution," Adam Rayski describes the efforts of the Yiddish underground press, a portion of which was in the hands of Jewish communists, to struggle with the questions of whether or not to inform the French-Jewish community that the Final Solution was taking place in Poland. His observations are both personal and historical. He was a member of the French communist party.

Livia Rothkirchen, "Czech and Slovak Wartime Jewish Leadership: Variants in Strategy and Tactics," depicts the widely divergent behavior of Jewish leadership in the Protectorate of Bohemia and Moravia and in Slovakia. In both countries the behavior of Jewish leadership and the fate of the Jews was related to German plans for the country and the fate of German war efforts.

She argues that the German goal for the Protectorate was to deprive Czechs of their nationhood by strengthening German ethnicity through Aryanization and then to transfer Czech assets into German hands. Thus, the Jews of Bohemia and Moravia came under German jurisdiction, and the confiscation of their property was immediately beneficial to the Germans. In Slovakia, the Jews remained under Slovak jurisdiction.

The behavior of Czech Jewish leadership can be divided into two time periods. From 1939 to 1941, Jewish leaders came together for welfare and self-preservation purposes. From 1942 onward, once the deportations began in earnest, they were compliant. Ironically, the lasting presence of Jews in Prague derives from the initiative of Dr. Karel Stein, who appealed to German authorities to collect historically valuable material and store it in Prague. The SS consented, hoping to make a "museum of the extinct race."

Slovakia's 88,951 Jews formed 3.3 percent of the total population. Its institutions and the community remained under Slovak jurisdiction. At first its institutions developed along familiar lines, with activities based on aid to the needy, philanthropy, vocational training, and emigration. Between March and October 1942, two out of three Slovak Jews, some sixty thousand in all, were deported to Auschwitz and the Lublin area. Yet instead of becoming more compliant, Jewish leadership became more active, more daring. They resorted to bribery and negotiations. They formed an information bureau and intelligence network and thus were among the best-informed Jews in Europe regarding the Jewish fate.

By the fall of 1942, they were in possession of the first written accounts from Majdanek. In 1943, they managed to transmit to the Free World testimonies on Sobibor, Majdanek, and Treblinka, as well as the famous Auschwitz Protocols of 1944, and the request to bomb Auschwitz later that summer. They used overseas contacts to apply pressure against their own deportation.

They even attempted large-scale ransom negotiations. The Working Group (Pracovná Skupina) won time to contemplate wide-ranging rescue operations and presented individual Jews with an opportunity to hide.

41.

YITZHAK ARAD

The Armed Jewish Resistance in Eastern Europe

ITS UNIQUE CONDITIONS AND ITS RELATIONS WITH THE
JEWISH COUNCILS (JUDENRÄTE) IN THE GHETTOS

The response of the Jews in the ghettos of Nazi-occupied Poland and the Soviet Union has yet to be fully explored. With few exceptions, it was mainly in these areas that ghettos were established and mainly there that Jewish armed underground organizations arose.

In order to understand the uniqueness of the Jewish armed resistance, it is necessary to compare its problems of organization and action with those facing the non-Jewish underground and to examine the aims of each.

The main aim of the latter movement was to prepare an underground force that would in due time stage an uprising against Germany and, with Allied help, liberate or participate in the liberation of their countries. All their other activities (sabotage, intelligence, partisan warfare, retaliatory acts) were of secondary consequence. They maintained clandestine contacts and received support, including arms, from their governments-in-exile. Their decisions about when and where to conduct operations of any sort, and especially when and where to start the uprisings, took into account the conditions prevailing under occupation. Among these were the price the local population would pay as a consequence of armed activities, as well as the overall strategic situation in the war. Their aims and activities were supported by large segments of the local populations.

This notion of an armed underground does not apply to the Soviet partisan movement. It did not evolve from the population under German occupation, but was, rather, a part of the Soviet army. Its initiators were individual soldiers or small units that, during the retreat of the Red Army in the first months of the war, had remained in occupied territories, or those who had escaped from prisoner-of-war camps. They later were joined by local people and by regular Soviet military units, NKVD units, or special groups organized by the Communist Party inside the Soviet Union, that parachuted in or otherwise crossed the front line in order to operate in the German rear. The higher staff and the command of this partisan movement remained behind Soviet lines. The partisans' activities were dictated by the Soviet army and its strategic needs without consideration for possible German retaliation against the local populations. The communist resistance movement in occupied Soviet cities does largely correspond to the status of an armed underground. It is appropriate to examine when and under what conditions planned uprisings were to be carried out.

The largest and best organized underground in occupied Europe was the Polish "Armia Krajowa," which numbered approximately 300,000 members.[1] A March 8, 1942, directive from Gen. Wladyslaw Sikorski, the prime minister of the Polish government-in-exile in London, to Gen. Stefan Rowecki, the commander of the Armia Krajowa inside occupied Poland, offers an overview:

> The uprising in our country, in the rear of the German army, can be carried out only in case of full collapse and dispersal of the German forces. If sizeable German forces conduct an organized retreat through the country, an uprising will be impossible because it will have no chance of success.[2]

Rowecki's March 23, 1943, uprising plan, sent to Sikorski on March 22, 1943, confirmed that the "uprising will start when Germany's defeat, either by collapse on the front line, or from inside [Germany], is without doubt. [This] means when there appear clear and increasing signs of Germany's catastrophe."[3] The underground knew that any attempt to stage an uprising against the German army at full strength would be drowned in a sea of Polish blood. Policy notwithstanding, substantial Polish partisan activity—so-called Operation Burza (tempest)—started in the spring of 1944, when the Soviet army reached the pre-September 1939 borders of Poland.

The Polish uprising in Warsaw broke out on August 1, 1944, when Soviet forces were one kilometer from the city, on the opposite bank of the Vistula River. Although both of these Polish military operations were conducted against Germany, their political thrust was against the Soviet Union. The government-in-exile in London and the Armia Krajowa, which was subordinate to the government in London, claimed that the eastern borders of Poland should be as they were before September 1, 1939, that is, western Byelorussia and western Ukraine were to remain part of Poland. However, Moscow regarded these areas as part of the Soviet Union. The aim of Operation Burza was to bring Armia Krajowa units to western Byelorussia and western Ukraine and then meet the Soviet army as established and operating units controlling the area and representing the exiled Polish government. On November 20, 1943, Bor-Komorowski, commander of the Armia Krajowa, ordered that the "Polish commander, meeting the regular Soviet army that enters our lands, . . . should come and present himself as the landlord of this area."[4]

Similarly, the intention of the uprising in Warsaw on August 1, 1944, was that the capital of Poland would be liberated by the Polish people and not the Soviet army. Bor-Komorowski wrote:

> The liberation of Warsaw from German rule by the Red Army without Polish participation would be stressed by Russia as proof that the Polish people are awaiting liberation only by Russia and want to build their future with Russian support, relinquishing their right to a free national existence.[5]

The policy of waiting until the Germans were on the verge of defeat before starting an uprising was adopted by all other underground organizations in Europe.

The uprising in Slovakia began in August 1944 when the Soviet army entered East Slovakia; the uprising in Prague began in May 1945, as Soviet and American troops approached the city and after Hitler's suicide. Germany's policy of harsh retaliation and the virtual impossibility of success in an action not coordinated with the arrival of Allied regular forces dictated the risings everywhere in Europe. Uprisings failed in some places, such as Warsaw, not because of bad timing, but for other, mainly Soviet political, reasons.

The situation of the Jewish armed underground was entirely different from that of its non-Jewish equivalents. The Jewish armed underground, in most of the ghettos, was the continuation of the political underground, which developed from the prewar Jewish political parties. Jews were a minority among the local population and received support neither from them nor the outside world.

In many places, part if not most of the local population collaborated with the Germans against the Jewish population or at least approved of German efforts. Jews were isolated in ghettos and camps, surrounded by walls, barbed wire, and armed guards. Therefore, from the very beginning the conditions for armed resistance were extremely adverse. Moreover, fear of German strength and of retaliation against the civilian population, which prevented the active and continuous struggle of the non-Jewish undergrounds until the moment of Germany's collapse, had still more terrible consequences for the Jews. The Jewish underground knew that even the smallest actions, or German discovery of arms-smuggling into the ghetto, could lead to the immediate execution of thousands of Jews and perhaps even to the liquidation of the ghetto. On the other hand, the Jewish armed underground could not afford to wait for ideal conditions to begin the active struggle against the Nazis. They could not wait for the German collapse and retreat, because the Jews were being systematically murdered while the Nazis were still at the peak of their power. To await German retreat and collapse would be to abandon the idea of armed resistance, because by the time of the collapse, there would be no more ghettos and no more Jews to stage the uprisings. Therefore, the timing of armed resistance and uprisings in the ghettos was not the result of a military evaluation of the situation, which the non-Jewish undergrounds could afford, but was dictated by the very fact that the Jews had nothing to lose.

The question remains, when did the Jews grasp that they were doomed to total destruction and that they had nothing to lose? The realization came only after the majority of the Jews had already been murdered—when in Warsaw, for example, there remained only fifty to sixty thousand Jews out of an earlier population of 450,000. This happened in Vilna (Vilnius) when only one-third of the sixty thousand Jews there remained alive. It happened in the ghettos of Kovno and Białystok after there were virtually no Jews left in the surrounding countryside and part of the ghetto population had been annihilated. Through ruse and secrecy the Germans succeeded in hiding from the Jews the real purpose of the deportations. As a consequence, the Jewish armed underground emerged when the majority of the Jews had already been murdered and only a portion remained in the ghettos. The Jewish masses, from whom the resistance organizations might have derived real strength, no longer existed. This also distinguishes the situation from that of the non-Jewish armed underground, which drew its strength from an essentially intact population and social infrastructure.

In the adverse conditions under which the Jewish underground had to act while the Germans were strong and the Allies far away, the uprisings had a priori, no chance of even partial success. The organizers had no means for rescuing the Jews in the ghetto or even to save themselves.

Specifically, the uprisings in the ghettos of Warsaw, Białystok, and Vilna, and acts of resistance in the ghettos of other cities, took place on the eve of their liquidation, when the Soviet army was hundreds of kilometers to the east. In that situation, the Jewish fighters and their leaders knew that most of them would fall.

This begs the question of the aim of the uprisings. One of the answers reflected in the surviving underground documents is revenge. As the January 21, 1942, agreement of the underground groups to establish the United Partisan Organization (F.P.O.) in the Vilna Ghetto stated, "Resistance is a national act, the struggle of the people for their honor."[6] Another such document from the same city declares, "Better to fall with honor in the ghetto than to be led like sheep to Ponary."[7] A February 1943 meeting of members of the Zionist "Chalutz" movement in Białystok recorded this sentiment: "Only one thing remains for us, . . . to consider the ghetto our Musa Dagh, to write in history a proud chapter of Jewish Bialystok and of our movement."[8] A leader of the Jewish armed underground in Kraków proclaimed, "The Jewish fighters are fighting for three lines in history."[9] Mordechai Anielewicz, Warsaw Ghetto revolt commander, wrote in a letter during the fighting, "The dream of my life has risen to become fact. Self-defense in the ghetto will have been a reality, Jewish armed resistance and revenge are facts. I have been a witness to the magnificent, heroic fighting of Jewish men in battle."[10] The desire to fall fighting and not in the gas chambers was a defining characteristic of the Jewish armed underground. Without hope of liberation or even the option of continued slavery, the Jews fought to choose the way they would die; the non-Jews fought for a way to live.

Partisan warfare is not within the scope of this examination but, given the situation described above, it is necessary to ask why the Jews stayed in ghettos, why they did not leave for the forests. There are a number of answers, some based on ideological factors and some on practicalities. Most of the armed underground organizations in the ghettos were dominated by Zionist youth movements. From their ideological point of view, their place was with their fellow Jews, was to share their fate until the last moment and to rise up and fight for the honor of the Jewish people if and when the conditions were ripe for it. A departure to the forest was to come only after an uprising in the ghetto. A second reason was the lack, in some places, of sizeable forests into which they could escape and take up partisan warfare.

In the vicinity of Warsaw, Kraków, and other areas there were no such forests. But even in places where there were, the partisans could operate and survive only when they had support from the local population. Rarely did Jews find such support. On the contrary, in many places the local population acted against the Jews, for antisemitic reasons or out of fear of German reprisals. The Jews could operate in the forest only if there was a non-Jewish partisan movement that was ready to accept Jews into its ranks. This was the case only in the areas where Soviet partisans were active, and only at a later stage, not earlier than the second half of 1942, by which time most of the ghettos and their inhabitants had been destroyed. In the areas where Polish partisans dominated the forests, the Jews, with few exceptions, could not survive. Nevertheless, for ideological reasons in the Mińsk Ghetto, where the underground was dominated by communists, and for practical reasons in the Kovno Ghetto, the aim of the Jewish undergrounds from the very beginning was to escape to the forests and participate in partisan warfare and not to stage uprisings inside the ghetto.

The armed underground came into being in Kovno at a late stage. There were already Soviet partisans in the forests as well as contact between the underground and the partisans. The chances of continued fighting and survival were better in the forests. New documents recently received from former Soviet archives confirm that Jewish armed resistance took place on a much larger scale than is represented in previously published historical works. There were many Jews among the partisans in the more eastern districts of the German occupied territories. Among lists of partisans found in the Archives of the Central Staff of the Soviet Partisans in Moscow and in the Republican Archives of Ukraine and Byelorussia, there are names of several thousand Jewish fighters. Some of them were commanders of partisan brigades and smaller units, among them officers of the Soviet army who remained in the German rear. Jews, most of whom perished, were also among the leaders and members of the undergrounds of Odessa, Kiev, Minsk, and other cities.

Let us turn now to the relations between the Jewish armed underground and Judenräte. The question is whether the idea of armed resistance and uprisings in the ghetto was the antithesis of or an alternative to the Judenräte's "work for survival" policy, or whether the leaders of the undergrounds may be perceived as an alternative to the official Jewish Councils. Typical Judenräte policy in the ghettos was based on an assumption that the German war economy and the local German authorities needed the remaining Jews as a work force, especially when, at the end of 1941, it became clear that Germany faced a prolonged war. Therefore, if ghetto inhabitants could prove that they were productive, they would prolong their existence, increase their chances of survival, and maybe even live to see the day of liberation.

The hope to keep the inhabitants of the ghetto alive was not opposed by the Jewish underground. On the contrary, the existence of the ghetto enabled the resisters to organize themselves: the longer the ghetto was maintained, the more time they had to plan, to acquire arms, and the like. There were no Jewish underground organizations in places where the Jews were murdered before the establishment of the ghettos, nor where the ghettos were liquidated and their inhabitants murdered a short time after their establishment. It was only in ghettos the Germans left standing because of the need for Jewish labor that underground organizations came into being. The fact that the underground organizations timed the uprisings to coincide with the final liquidation of the ghettos, when the Judenräte's policy of prolonging the existence of the ghettos had ended, proves that the Jewish armed underground tacitly approved of the Judenräte's policy of survival through work. This is what happened in Warsaw, Białystok, Vilna, and other ghettos. For example, in the April 4, 1943, "Comments of the Program" of the Vilna underground, we find the following articles:

1) The F.P.O. will move out into battle when the existence of the ghetto as a whole is threatened. . . .

4) The F.P.O., however, is not a large military force that can enter into a battle of equals with the enemy. It cannot and will not come out in defense of each individual Jewish life.

5) The F.P.O., which is the spearhead of the remainder of the Jewish Community (not only in Vilna) could, by premature action bring about its own premature destruction. . . .
6) This kind of action would be quixotic, a suicidal tactic. Furthermore, Jews might condemn us as provocateurs, and this might cause us to fight against our own brethren.
8) The F.P.O. will move out in such an action when it is estimated that the beginning of the end has come.[11]

On the other hand, most of the Judenräte did not in principle oppose the existence of an armed underground inside the ghetto. Nor were they against staging an uprising at the time of the final liquidation of the ghettos, when it would be clear that the Jews were being taken to their deaths. In many ghettos there were some contacts and an exchange of ideas between the underground leadership and that of the Judenräte.

Specifically, in the Kovno, Białystok, and Mińsk Ghettos which, with the exception of Warsaw and Vilna, had the strongest Jewish undergrounds, the resistance organizations even enjoyed support from the Judenräte. The heads of these councils, Elhanan Elkes in Kovno and Ephraim Barasz in Białystok, were in close contact with the leaders of the underground and had good relations with them until the final liquidation of the ghettos.

In March 1942, the Germans discovered that there was a Jewish underground organization in the Mińsk Ghetto and a communist underground outside the ghetto, and that the Judenrat, headed by Ilia Mushkin, was supporting the two organizations with medicine, clothes, and the despatch of people into the forests to conduct partisan warfare. Consequently, the Germans arrested and executed Mushkin along with the commander of the ghetto police, Ziama Serebrianski. The second chairman of the Judenrat, Moshe Joffe, and the second commander of the ghetto police, Blumenshtok, suffered similar fates. They were executed during the big "Aktion" of July 1942 and accused of inciting the Jews to oppose German orders during that action.[12]

Relations between the underground and the Judenräte were not always ideal. There were contradictions and conflicts, some acute. These occurred when and where the activity of a particular underground was perceived as jeopardizing the existence of a ghetto. The perception of a threat might arise solely within the Judenräte, or it might be the result of a formal warning by the German authorities when the latter discovered that Jews were purchasing and smuggling arms into the ghetto, or when they learned that Jews from the ghetto were escaping to the partisans. As long as the acquisition of arms remained undiscovered by the Germans, the Judenräte did not interfere.

The most conspicuous example of this relationship is that between Jacob Gens's Vilna Judenrat and the underground there. In the spring of 1943 the Germans liquidated some small ghettos that still survived in the eastern part of the General Commissariat Lithuania; several thousand inhabitants were murdered. At that time the partisans became more active in the areas of west Byelorussia, close to Vilna. These two developments caused an increase of underground activity in the Vilna Ghetto, which included arms smuggling and the escape of young people to the forests to join the partisans. The Gestapo discovered these activities and warned Gens of terrible consequences for the ghetto inhabitants should this continue. Gens convened a meeting of leaders of the labor brigades and members of the police and told them:

> A few days ago I was called to the Gestapo and the talk with the commander of the SD ["*Sicherheitsdienst*," or Security Service] there was about the revolvers. I may tell you that he is not at all stupid. He said to me: "From an economic point of view the ghetto is very valuable, but if you are going to take foolish risks and if there is any question of security, I will wipe you out. And even if you get 30, 40, or 50 guns, you will not be able to save yourselves and will only bring on your disaster faster."[13]

At the end of June 1943, when a group of people, including some police patrolmen and even some of officer rank left the ghetto for the forests, Gens told the leaders of the working groups:

> We are faced with the question of leaving for the forest. . . . Why should I not go? Because the question now arises 1 or 20,000! The ghetto exists by virtue of 2,500 strong young men. The rest dance around them. . . . Just imagine if 500 men went out, what would happen then? . . . I put myself in Neugebauer's [commander of the SD] place. . . . I would wipe out the entire ghetto, because a man must be an idiot to allow a nest of partisans to develop under his nose. . . . My interest is to preserve a loyal ghetto so long as it can exist.[14]

Gens was convinced, and to a large extent it was true, that the ghetto (including its women, children, and elderly) existed because it served the Germans as a source of labor. Therefore, if the younger men, who were the main source of that labor, were to leave the ghetto, it would be liquidated. Against this background there were some confrontations between ghetto police and the underground fighters within the ghetto.

A unique event that sheds light on the intricate and crucial relations between the Judenräte and the underground was the Yitzhak Vitenberg affair in the Vilna Ghetto in mid July 1943. Vitenberg was the commander of the F.P.O. and simultaneously a member of the underground committee of the Lithuanian Communist Party outside the ghetto. The German Security Police uncovered this committee and arrested its members. Their investigation revealed that Vitenberg was a member of the committee. The Germans demanded from Gens that Vitenberg be surrendered as a member of the non-Jewish communist underground. The Germans did not know about the F.P.O. and Vitenberg's role as its commander. Vitenberg was arrested by the Jewish police in the ghetto, but he escaped and went into hiding. The F.P.O. refused to hand over Vitenberg. The Germans insisted—either Vitenberg or liquidation of the ghetto. The people of the ghetto supported Gens's demand to surrender Vitenberg. The F.P.O. faced a situation in which they would have to fight the Jews of the ghetto if they wanted to defend Vitenberg. The result was that the F.P.O. and Vitenberg decided that he would be surrendered in order not to endanger the entire ghetto. Vitenberg later committed suicide in a German prison.[15]

In some of the ghettos where small numbers of Jews vital for the war economy still remained after the big extermination action with its transfers to labor or concentration camps, the Germans liquidated the Judenräte. The Germans did not need councils that were composed of Jews who, with few exceptions, both collectively and individually did their best to help the ghetto population in their struggle for survival. In place of the Judenräte the Germans appointed leadership bodies, called by a variety of names, composed mainly of people ready to carry out any German order. These groups were ready to combat the Jewish underground, and even turn over some of its members. In many cases they were not local Jews but refugees, strangers who had recently arrived in the ghetto.

In the ghetto of Mińsk, where the extermination action at the end of July 1942 left only approximately nine thousand Jews out of the nearly 100,000 who had been living there the previous year, the Germans abolished the Judenräte and appointed a "ghetto directorate" with a police department. The groups were called "Operativniki" (Operation Groups) by the ghetto Jews. After the successive execution of the two Judenrat chairmen who had cooperated with the underground, the Germans finally found a group of collaborators, headed by Epshtein, a refugee from Poland. This group of Jews handed over underground members who planned to escape into the forests. In reprisal for their collaboration, some of the Operativniki were caught and executed by the partisans.[16]

Similarly, in Kraków during the action of June 1942, when six thousand Jews were sent to the Belzec death camp, the twenty-four-member Judenrat was liquidated and its leaders sent with the same transports. On June 3 the Germans appointed a new seven-man leadership body called the Commissariat. It was headed by David Gutter, who was not from Kraków and who was ready to do everything the Germans demanded. The Jewish police in the ghetto tracked down underground members and arrested some of them. The hostile attitude this action exemplified was one of the main reasons why the two underground groups there, Hechalutz Halochem and Iskra, decided to transfer their base to the city outside the ghetto. From there they carried out their fighting activities, including the famous attack on the Ziganeria, the German officers' coffeehouse, on December 22, 1942.[17]

But the Operativniki in Mińsk and the Commissariat in Kraców were not and should not be considered Judenräte. They were not the Jewish leadership that enjoyed authority and respect among the ghetto inhabitants. They were criminals ready to do anything in order to save their own lives.

The situation in the Warsaw Ghetto differed from that in other places. There the Judenrat, exercising authority as a Jewish leadership institution, existed from the beginning of October 1939 and ceased to exist with Adam Czerniakow's suicide and the big Aktion of July–September 1942, when about 300,000 Jews were deported, most to the Treblinka death camp, leaving around fifty-five thousand people in the ghetto. During Czerniakow's chairmanship of the Judenrat there was no armed underground in the ghetto, and therefore one cannot examine relations between the two. The formal leadership institution that came into being after Czerniakow's suicide was headed by Mark Lichtenbaum, who had virtually no influence in the ghetto and does not even deserve to be considered a Judenrat representative. The Jewish police and the Jewish managers of the workshops wielded some authority, under strict supervision of the SS, but were not a formal Judenrat.

As time passed, the armed underground, which came into being as a force after the big Aktion, gradually took the leading role in the ghetto. Its position became stronger after some commanders of the Jewish police who had collaborated with the Germans (Jozef Sherinsky, Jacob Leikin, and others) were killed or wounded by the underground. Acts of resistance carried out during the deportations of January 18–21, 1943, and the fact that the Germans stopped this action after a few days, tremendously increased the stature of the underground among the Jews, who believed that the deportation had been halted because of these acts.[18] By the last months of the Warsaw Ghetto, the underground had become the real authority there.

When, on April 19, 1943, the Germans ordered the inhabitants of the ghetto to appear for deportation, the Jews responded instead to the call of the underground to disobey. Some went into hiding and some joined the uprising. They were convinced that the real purpose of the deportation was to send Jews to the gas chambers of Treblinka, as had happened from July to September 1942. They also believed that the strength of the underground was greater than it in fact was, and they hoped that resistance would force the Germans to stop the planned deportation and liquidation of the ghetto, as in January. This earlier experience was the main reason why the Warsaw uprising received widespread popular support, in contrast to the lack of response to calls for uprisings in the ghettos of Białystok in August 1943 and Vilna in September 1943. In those two cities authoritative Judenräte still functioned, which convinced many of the Jews, and it was partly true, that the deportations at that time were to labor camps and not to a certain death.

In summary then, as a rule the Judenräte were neither collaborators nor blind tools in the hands of the German authorities. Neither did the councils assist the Nazis in combating the underground movements. The trend in historiography that identifies the Judenräte as collaborationist institutions is mistaken. First, on two major issues there were no differences of opinion between the Judenräte and the Jewish armed underground in the ghettos: the latter did not oppose the main policy of the Judenräte in prolonging the existence of the ghettos for as long as possible by making the ghetto economically useful to the Germans. Therefore, the time of the uprisings was fixed (and they actually took place in Warsaw, Vilna, and Białystok) when the Germans began the final liquidation of the ghettos. The councils, for their part, did not object to the idea that the underground would rise up and fight when the ghettos were about to be liquidated. When the inhabitants were to be sent to the death camps, it was understood there would be nothing more to lose.

Second, for ideological and practical reasons the Judenräte did not have, did not build, and did not intend to build the tools of force to struggle against the armed Jewish underground.

Third, the clashes between the Judenräte and the underground occurred only in cases in which underground activities, such as smuggling arms into the ghetto or escape to the partisans, endangered the Judenräte's policy of maintaining the existence of the ghettos.

Fourth, the tragedy of this period was that neither the policy of the Judenräte nor that of the underground organizations could affect the ultimate survival of the Jewish masses in the ghettos. Germany's strength and policy were the dominant factors. The result was that some 6,000,000 Jewish people were murdered by Nazi Germany and its collaborators.

NOTES

1. Tadeusz Bor-Komorowski, *Armja Podziemna* (London, 1989), p. 176, and Shmuel Krakowski, *Lechima Yehudit B'Polin neged Hanatzim* (Jerusalem, 1977), p. 21.
2. *Armja Krajowa Dokumentach*, vol. 2 (London, 1973), p. 203; Bor-Komorowski, *Armja Podziemna*, pp. 170–71.
3. *Armja Krajowa*, p. 329.
4. Bor-Komorowski, *Armja Podziemna*, p. 174.
5. Ibid., p. 203.
6. Yitzhak Arad, *Ghetto in Flames* (Jerusalem, 1980), p. 236.
7. Lucy S. Dawidowicz, *A Holocaust Reader* (New York, 1976), p. 335.
8. Ibid., p. 349. Franz Werfel, *The Forty Days of Musa Dagh*. The author, an Austrian Jew, wrote in this historical novel, published in 1933, about the heroic resistance of the Armenians during the massacres carried out by Turkey in 1915. Musa Dagh is a mountain in eastern Turkey.
9. Israel Gutman, ed., *Encyclopedia of the Holocaust*, vol. 3 (Jerusalem, 1990), p. 873.
10. Y. Arad, Y. Gutman, and A. Margaliot, eds., *Documents on the Holocaust* (Jerusalem, 1981), pp. 315–16.
11. Ibid., pp. 435–36.
12. Shalom Cholawski, *Besufat Hakilayon* (Jerusalem, 1988), pp. 116–19, 132, 152, 173.
13. Arad et al., eds., *Documents*, p. 453.
14. Arad, *Ghetto in Flames*, p. 384. SS-Obersturmführer Neugebauer commanded the security police and SD in Vilna.
15. Ibid., pp. 387–95.
16. Cholawski, *Besufat Hakilayon*, pp. 133–34.
17. Yael Peled, *Krakov Hayehudit: 1939–1943* (Ghetto Fighters' House, 1993), pp. 187–88, 197.
18. Yisrael Gutman, *Yehudey Varsha: 1939–1943* (Jerusalem, 1977), pp. 230–31, 319–23, 335–37.

42.

RICHARD I. COHEN

Remembering and Invoking 1789 during the Holocaust

THE TRIALS AND TRIBULATIONS OF FRENCH JEWS

Historiography of the Jewish responses to the Holocaust has struggled to penetrate beyond categoric condemnations of Jewish leaders and organizations on the one hand and apologetic affirmations of their activity on the other. The theoretical constructs presented by Raul Hilberg, Hannah Arendt, Bruno Bettelheim, and others initially provoked tremendous opposition and rancor but gradually proved to be positive catalysts for serious historical research, much more so than their detractors who tried to muzzle any attempt to understand Jewish response and so preserve the "saintly" image of the victims.[1] Nuanced approaches emerged, more concerned with historical understanding than with judgment of the victims; and they allowed many more factors to come into play, not the least of which were the human dilemmas faced by individual Jews. In this spirit, while elucidating some facets of French Jewry's response during the war, this discussion will give special attention to the ways in which memories and images of the past figured in their deliberations and shaped their reading of the unraveling process.

In recent years the theme of history and memory has taken pride of place in historical analysis and has begun to penetrate research on the Holocaust in certain areas. The concern here is with the ways individuals' actions are affected by the memory of an event, or events, which later historians regard as seminal moments in the history of a people or a country. Can we accept H. H. Price's hypothesis in *Thinking and Experience*, in which he claims that "what matters . . . is not what my past actually was, or even whether I had one; it is only the *memories* I have now which matter, be they false or true"?[2] How does the past or memories of it engage an individual in moments of struggle and crisis? What elements of the past and what aspects of memory are incorporated and invoked? Without presenting a theoretical, hard and fast rule for any of these questions, some observations will be suggested relating to French Jewry in the twentieth century, its negotiation with the French historical past, and in particular with the Revolution and the revolutionary tradition.

I would like to offer at the outset a working hypothesis about this approach that challenges a monolithic understanding of Jewish behavior during the Holocaust or at any time during the modern period of Jewish history. The modern state, from the rise of absolutism, enabled Jews to enter into its midst and become engaged in a wide variety of pursuits previously closed to them. This encounter had dramatic consequences for the ways in which Jewish communities in Western and Central European countries developed a sense of belonging to these states and an identity interwoven with a specific country and culture.[3] Invariably, Jews fostered and perceived their experience through the prism of a symbiosis with their native or adopted country, and they regarded their experience as a unique historical development in Jewish history. By and large, Jews developed a singular attraction to that land and its culture and showed a remarkable ability to integrate themselves into the fabric of its life within several generations. Thus, by way of example, Italian or English Jews manifested such a profound sense of belonging and oneness with Italy and England that, when faced with a dramatic moment in their historical development, they tended to dip back into their particular past to draw upon a historical parallel to their situation or, in more tranquil times, to reappropriate from their distinctive past elements from their local tradition.[4] This subconscious, yet also conscious mechanism, served the dual function of giving transient events a historical perspective, mediating the present by the past, and reestablishing a hierarchy of associations that placed the local traditions above all others. The invocation of these paradigms and traditions, as opposed to analogous phenomena among Jewish communities in other countries, was a distinct expression of the sense of uniqueness and pride in the evolution of their experience in that country of origin or newly found homeland. This phenomenon belies the commonly held notion of a universal, collective Jewish mentality with a uniform historical past that independently fashioned the social and psychological makeup of Jewry and, ultimately, its uniform response to the National Socialist reign of terror. Jews under National Socialism showed common characteristic responses, but these should not blind the historian to the many particularistic expressions in different countries—expressions that in part stem from the unparalleled historical developments in those countries. For twentieth-century French Jews, who inherited the words of Abraham Furtado, the president of the Assemblée des Notables convoked by Napoleon in 1806: "Paris will become for us what Jerusalem was for our ancestors in the beautiful days of its glory. . . . Israelites in our temples, French among our fellow citizens, this is who we are."[5] Two major historical developments seem to have shaped their political outlook and historical consciousness—the French Revolution on the one hand and the Dreyfus Affair on the other. These events were neither incompatible nor exclusive and became intertwined with the devotion French Jews expressed toward the Third Republic.[6] The Dreyfus Affair and its variegated associations challenged the priority of the Revolution in the shaping of French-Jewish consciousness in the twentieth century but could not wholly replace it.

To comprehend this phenomenon, a glance at the perceptions of native and immigrant Jews on the eve of the war is necessary. Notwithstanding the gradual acceptance of emancipation ideology across Europe following the Revolution, France, as the innovator of this process, was still heralded as the beacon of freedom. The presence of the revolutionary tradition can best be seen in the way East European Jews, who flocked to France in the interwar period, assimilated it into their perspective of universalism and particularism. Exhibiting diverse forms of Jewish existence, they manifested the possibility of being "heureux comme dieu en France" (happy as God in France). They interpreted the French revolutionary tradition as a gateway to cultural and political uniqueness and, in particular, to an affirmation of Jewish self-expression.[7] An example of this tendency is the way in which Paris became the home for Jewish artists at the beginning of the century, a current that prevailed until the tide of antisemitism in the 1930s curbed their productivity. Recognition of the open cultural ambience is present in many works, but here we will mention two manifest examples. Three years before Hitler came to power in 1933, Mané-Katz, who had immigrated from Ukraine to Paris in 1920, painted his *Homage à Paris*.[8] In the center of the canvas a young, orthodox Jew with flowing side curls is draped in his tefillin and tallith katan as he prays in Hasidic ecstasy; in the background, the sculptured water fountain of the Place de la Concorde and behind it, the Eiffel Tower—symbols of modern France—loom large. A train, representing the speed of modern development, passes between these two French monuments and the city. For Mané-Katz, who like thousands of other East European Jews had flocked to France in the post–World War I period and had received French citizenship only three years before (in 1927), the painting clearly evoked his belief that in the France of the Place de la Concorde and the Eiffel Tower, monuments to different moments in French history, a Jew could wear his distinctiveness even if it clashed with the basic symbols of French society. A contemporary art critic, J.-M. Aimot, commented in 1933 that: "A full and complete understanding of the *Homage à Paris* is possible only with a perfect comprehension of the state of mind so common among young Jews enthralled by the French Revolution—the France of Michelet and Victor Hugo."[9]

Indeed, for Mané-Katz and many East European Jews, Paris was synonymous with the principles of the French Revolution; and several Yiddish writers spoke about their bewilderment on encountering the atmosphere of freedom for the first time—about the experience of sitting on a bench without being disturbed by policemen. Mané-Katz's iconographic depiction of the meeting of two worlds in the spirit of harmony and mutual respect canonized the Revolution as the basis of this encounter. Thus, when antisemitism resurged in French society in the 1930s, individuals and organizations would have to confront the Revolution on its mythic level—they would have to struggle with an aspect of French tradition they preferred to dismiss. But even then, as Jacques Biélinky, an immigrant journalist, would write on the eve of World War II: "It was 150 years ago that France gave a noble example. It showed all of humanity the road of progress under the sign of hope and human dignity." It was to this French tradition that he now looked to bring about the destruction of the "shameful evil that seems to have covered the sun like a veil."[10] This trust in liberal French values was invoked by other immigrant Jews as they witnessed the growing specter of antisemitism.

Jacques Lipchitz, a Lithuanian-born artist who received French citizenship in 1924, understood this intuitively. Commissioned by the Blum government to prepare a sculpture for the Palace of Discovery and Inventions at the Paris World's Fair in 1937, Lipchitz expressed his belief in the power of liberalism to defeat the dangerous tyrant rising in Germany. *Prometheus Strangling the Vulture* united elements from classical, universal culture and French republican tradition to emphasize the need for combined forces to defeat the powerful enemy. Seeing the battle in universal terms,

Lipchitz refrained from using any Jewish symbols and had no desire to present the victim as a Jew. A sculpture at a World's Fair, taking place in the heart of democratic Europe, necessitated the display of established, liberal symbolism.[11] In choosing Prometheus, the mythical Greek figure who as a Titan first opposed his kin and then revolted against Zeus, Lipchitz drew on several attributes later attached to him—fire, light, and science—avoiding the more common one of cunning.[12] But as can be seen, Lipchitz gave Promotheus a republican image by placing a Phrygian cap on his head, knowing full well, as the historian Maurice Agulhon has shown in his studies of Marianne, that the Phrygian cap had become the most constant symbol of liberty in France since the Revolution and that its appearance often sparked heated controversy.[13] The fate of Lipchitz's sculpture was no different. With the close of the fair the sculpture was prominently displayed on the Champs Elysées—an act of much courage on the part of the Blum government in 1937—but within a year it was removed after being seriously damaged. In our context, the significance of Lipchitz's sculpture lies in the way the iconographic revolutionary tradition was incorporated by this East European artist at a moment of crisis in a sculpture unlike any of his previous work. Lipchitz's *Prometheus Strangling the Vulture* embodied the ethos of East European Jews in France during the interwar period: trust in France together with the belief in the necessity of fighting Fascism and antisemitism openly and publicly, with the combined help of Jews and non-Jews. As Lipchitz himself put it, the sculpture was meant to be a warning to mankind to continue its creative work in freedom and to join hands to defeat the evil forces scheming to overcome the world. He, like Mané-Katz, Biélinky, and many others, believed in the French liberal tradition, which they associated with the Revolution, and each one at different junctures of his integration in France, placed his trust in its universalistic message. Here the image of the Revolution, neither memory nor ingrained historical tradition, was at the root of their search for a society that guaranteed universal truths and promised freedom of expression to all.

In the memory and consciousness of native French Jews, the Revolution was not merely a catchword, nor was it referred to simply as equivalent to the process of emancipation or its social derivative, assimilation. The Revolution had a deeper meaning touching on a more primal sensation, that of a new genesis. Just as the French revolutionaries themselves sensed the need at the end of the eighteenth century to begin a new calendar, so French Jews, even after the Dreyfus Affair, spoke of the Revolution as if it had created a new genealogy for the Jews of France, one that included momentous events comparable to those in Biblical history. Its mythic and almost religious quality continued to be invoked in the inter-war period, notwithstanding widespread social change in the community's makeup and the penetration of conflicting ideological currents. Though larger support and appreciation of Zionist aims were manifested, political and cultural Zionism had failed to sway significantly the minds and orientation of French Jews. Rabbinic and lay leaders alike pitted the universalistic principles of the Revolution against the particularistic demands of Zionism and rejected the latter's attempt to turn back the clock of history—Jews and citizenship had become synonymous. "Neither Basel nor Jerusalem"[14] continued to be the hallmark of the established institutions of French Jewry.

Celebrations of the 150th anniversary of the Revolution in the troubled summer months of 1939, when all eyes were focused on the international political scene, allowed establishment Jewish leadership to evoke again its profound trust in the legacy of the Revolution. A remarkable example of this orientation was a commemoration, on June 22, 1939, attended by students of four Jewish schools in the presence of the Chief Rabbi of France, Maurice Liber. Conscientiously worked out to arouse a sense of the magnificence of the revolutionary legacy, the commemoration touched all the nerves of a troubled society. Consisting of both discussions on the universal impact of the Revolution and its implications for Judaism, the commemoration reenacted many of the highlights of the Revolution from the perspective of Jewish life: Abbé Grégoire's famous motion in support of Jewish emancipation, memoranda of Jewish delegations to the National Assembly, and revolutionary songs.[15] One aspect of the program, the reading of "Le Juif errant se présente à L'assemblée nationale" (The wandering Jew appears at the National Assembly), a poem by the nineteenth-century romantic, German-Jewish poet Ludwig Wihl, was somewhat out of the ordinary and it is of particular interest. Since it was the only "foreign" aspect of the conference and the only part of the agenda that did not originate at the time of the Revolution, the choice of poet and poem is highly instructive.

Ludwig Wihl's poem should be read as a reflection on the impact of the Revolution on the eternal condition of Jewish life. Wihl himself took refuge in France after the revolution of 1848; on several occasions, like his idol Heinrich Heine, he found reason to extol French traditions and France's unique attitude toward the suffering Jewish people. Prior to his refuge he had taken up the theme of the "Juif errant" in various poems, stressing repeatedly the Jew's tragic and eternal wanderings through the world and his failure to find a resting place. France and the Assemblée Nationale offered the wandering and persecuted Jew repose and security for the first time in his history.[16] On different layers of association, Wihl and his poetry expressed for the organizers of the commemoration their innermost expectations of the revolutionary tradition, a reaffirmation of France as a haven of refuge and protection. (Whether another aspiration was being intimated by incorporating this rather unknown "foreign" poet into the program [as opposed to a distinguished French or French-Jewish poet]—as a sign of concern for Jewish immigrants who had recently reached France's borders—is difficult to determine but certainly not implausible.) All in all, this community event, on the eve of World War II, highlighted the principles of the revolutionary tradition with which French Jews associated; yet it also gave vent to a certain trepidation in their ranks.[17]

The events of World War II trampled the principles of the Revolution but not their image or their memory. In fact, the direct attack on the revolutionary legacy brought its vision to the forefront of the existential experience of French native Jews, who recurrently invoked it as the authentic French perspective. Though Jewish organizations and individuals had made various attempts to confront the burgeoning antisemitism in the 1930s and at different periods of modern French Jewish history, none of these ever contended (as do historians today) that alongside the humanistic and liberal tradition of the Revolution there existed in France an antirevolutionary tradition, one in which antisemitism figured prominently.[18] In this sense the Dreyfus

Affair, which certainly left a deep impression on French Jewry and contributed profoundly to the reordering of priorities by various individuals, did not shape a new historical outlook that integrated antirepublican tendencies, and French anti-semitism among them, as a constant factor alongside the revolutionary tradition.[19]

The fall of France in May and June of 1940 rapidly unleashed a deep-seated disaffection with the liberal principles of the Third Republic. Measures were quickly taken to undo the revolutionary tradition and replace it with a "National Revolution" that substituted work ("travail"), Family ("famille"), and Homeland ("patrie") as the guiding ideological orientation.[20] Marshal Pétain, an octogenarian and hero of World War I, was called upon to offer France a soothing antidote to the malaise of defeat and disruption. Within a few months, in October 1940, the reinvigorated Vichy govern-ment initiated its anti-Jewish policy, erasing 150 years of emancipation and placing more than 300,000 Jews in a precarious state of limbo.[21]

Jews were faced with a profound inner dilemma. How could they preserve their trust and belief in the principles of the Revolution and obligations to France while Vichy embarked on an antirevolutionary and antisemitic course? What was the efficacy of protesting in the name of the Revolution against a regime that saw itself opposed to it? However, to cast off the revolutionary tradition that had been the core of their historic consciousness with the same speed and easiness with which Vichy did so was to forget that Jews anchored their existence in France on this trust and spirit. Recognition of this inner struggle seems to us a precondition for understand-ing French Jewry's difficulty in uncovering the nature of the new regime and its internal anti-Jewish designs.

Here it is appropriate to reiterate what I emphasized at the outset of this essay. Though we are speaking of 1940, seven years after European Jewry began to live with the Hitlerian threat—the Nuremberg Laws, the Anschluss, conquest of Poland, and so on—the universal Jewish experience, which could have been brought to bear to explain the turn of events in France, is given only a certain weight. Jews of France, as Jews in other European countries, had to mediate between their past history, their sense of belonging and symbiosis with their respective countries, before they could integrate the overall political developments. The Jews of France rarely rushed to conclude that the historic fate and present circumstances were one and the same, and they therefore looked for extenuating circumstances based upon the relationship that existed with the occupied country. For the Jews of France, especially those "de veille souche" (of long native ancestry), this meant cutting through their one-dimensional view of France and its revolutionary tradition.

In the wake of the fall of France but prior to the Vichy anti-Jewish laws, Raymond-Raoul Lambert, editor of the *L'Univers israélite*, the main French-Jewish newspaper during the 1930s, and a leading figure in the efforts to reorganize Jewish attitudes to the refugee crisis,[22] recorded in his private diary:

> French Judaism lives in a particular agony. It accepts suffering like everyone else but dreads a discrimination possibly demanded by the enemy. This fear makes the future for me and my children particularly doubtful. But I still have confidence. France cannot accept everything and it is not for nothing that for more than a decade my parents

blended in her land, and I fought two wars. I cannot imagine . . . life in another climate, a displacement that would be worse than amputation.[23]

But when the infamous antisemitic laws of October 1940 were promulgated, seriously curtailing the rights of all French Jews, Lambert noted: "All my illusions are being destroyed! I do not fear for myself but for my country. This cannot continue, this is impossible. But in history this abrogation of the Declaration of the Rights of Man in 1940 will be recorded as a new revocation of the Edict of Nantes."[24]

Lambert's personal response reveals the nature of his historical consciousness and that of a significant cross section of native Jews. Parallels with the German Nuremberg Laws of 1935 or other "Jewish" tragedies were not made—rather, Lambert invoked, as did Max Hymans, the representative of Indre, in 1942,[25] what was his own historical past and saw the shame of France within the context of its history. The plight of the Jews was viewed within the parameters of France's historic treatment of minorities, as in the case of the expulsion of the Huguenots during the reign of Louis XIV. Seen in this context, the various protests by distinguished figures of Jewish origin and by leaders of the community to French authorities, in which they promised to abide by the laws notwithstanding their anti-French character, illuminate a profound trust that France was not responsible for these laws. The unfolding drama of Jewish life under National Socialism did not seem to penetrate the collective consciousness of native French Jews at this time.

The powerful emotional and historical claim of the Revolution on the minds and imagination of Jews was at loggerheads with the evolution of a new multilevel consciousness that took into consideration the unfolding antisemitic measure. Nowhere was this more apparent than with the historic leadership of French Jewry, embodied in the Central Consistory and its president, Jacques Helbronner.[26] The Consistory was established during Napoleonic days and became an arm of the Ministry of Interior until the separation of Church and State in 1905. Designed to integrate French Jewry into French society, the Central Consistory sought to achieve a balance between its adherence to the Jewish religion and its patriotic affirmation of the French homeland—"Religion" and "Patrie" were its hallowed ideals. In the twentieth century, the Consistory's unique position in French Jewry faced external and internal challenges. No longer wedded to the state, its financial support was severed, while on the home front it confronted the emergence of Zionism and the influx of tens of thousands of immigrant Jews who manifested a whole new political and cultural ethos. Nonetheless the Consistory continued to be seen as the representative organization of French Jewry and it figured prominently in many deliberations in the 1930s regarding the mass influx of refugees. Helbronner, an archetypical "Juif d'État," played a particularly important role in these deliberations, manifesting an undivided loyalty to France. It was a loyalty that historian Vicki Caron has aptly characterized as a "hard-line policy," positing only one solution for the refugees: emigration. Helbronner, a member of the Conseil d'État and vice president of the Consistory, was to be nominated president of the Consistory in March 1941 in its relocated offices in the unoccupied city of Lyon. Choosing the sixty-eight-year-old Helbronner was a clear statement on the part of the Consistory that it preferred the established leadership, apparently well positioned in French administrative circles and with a direct contact to Marshal Pétain. In this spirit, and as anti-Jewish legislation rained down on the community, the Consistory gave Pétain a vote of confidence that went far beyond mere lip service: it promised him the "absolute loyalty and permanent devotion of the French Jews [Français Israélites]" and expressed "their confidence that his sense of justice and goodness will reestablish their honor and dignity as citizens."[27] The following events, in particular the establishment of the Commissariat for Jewish Affairs, the roundup of thousands of foreign Jews, and the creation of a Jewish council (UGIF—Union Générale des Israélites de France) taxed these patriotic declarations but did not put an end to them. Helbronner continued to uphold the position that the law, though contrary to France's traditions and spirit ("our public law") is difficult but that it is the law ("Dura lex sed lex"), and he called on Pétain again and again to intervene to save France from this "humiliation." Thus, in opposing the creation of the UGIF in late 1941, the Consistory rejected the Vichy definition of Judaism that deviated from the contours of Clermont-Tonnerre's historic remarks during the French Revolution and from the Consistory's own self-definition. The Consistory thus remained tied to its prior political course and predisposition.[28] The Consistory leadership was by and large so deeply anchored in this mold that it could not sever itself from the "true France," even if France's legislation was developing in a contradictory way.

Albeit the Consistory's position was complemented by the general attitude of "attentisme" (wait and see) that characterized French society during the first two years of the occupation.[29] An overriding desire to return to normal life figured prominently in this perspective, and it mingled with traumatic memories of World War I and disillusion with the republican ethos. Pétain, and his mystique, evoked deep emotional attachment and provided soothing relief for French society, weary of war and its consequences. The Consistory, wrapped up in the Pétain mystique and similar emotions, but burdened with the decaying status of Jewish life in France, struggled to find a modus vivendi within French society. It continued to view Jews of foreign birth, and their plight, with distant compassion, riding on a definition of French society that mirrored centralistic concepts from the French Revolution. Though the traumatic summer deportations of 1942 provoked genuine protests from leading church figures and riveted Jewish society, the Consistory leadership adhered to its tactics, reasoning and interpreting, while appealing to a higher French code of ethics and behavior. Alongside the expression of deep agony, France's honor continued to figure in these protests even after the occupation of the south,[30] not as mere window-dressing, but as part of the continuing perseverance of the revolutionary tradition. Helbronner, who guided this course in the face of growing opposition, was not blind to Vichy's, and even Pétain's, disingenuous conduct, yet he could not disavow what was more precious to him—the France of liberty, equality, and fraternity. However, the raids and deportations against native French Jews in Marseilles and Lyon in January–February 1943 pecked away at that stance and led Helbronner to warn Prime Minister Pierre Laval that such actions would ultimately bring about a rebellion among those citizens who continued to safeguard the "inheritance of France's loftiness" (patrimoine de noblesse de la France). The raids also led Helbronner to initiate a reconciliation with UGIF for the safeguarding of French Jewry.[31]

These actions were the first symbolic recognition of the existence of a new political order in France. In opening its doors to cooperation with UGIF (South), the Consistory begrudgingly admitted that its heralded symbiosis of religion and homeland was also in jeopardy. A new consciousness was emerging—one that still preserved the spirit of the Revolution but recognized that antirevolutionary forces were threatening its existence. Thus, in the summer of 1943 the Consistory's negative appraisal of the future of French Jewry did not bring it to support illegal activity, nor to counsel direct confrontation with the French authorities, but to accept a more sanguine evaluation of life under Vichy and Nazi occupation. Comparisons with the tragedies of Jewish communities in other Nazi-occupied countries were still not made or intimated but obviously had found a niche in their appraisal of the European context.

The events of the summer and autumn of 1943 in the north and south were critical in bringing about a reversal of the Consistory's policies and its reliance on France. In its protests it no longer continued to hide behind a theoretical smoke screen and spoke openly of the "tragic fate" of more than fifty thousand Jews who had been imprisoned in Drancy and sent to an unknown destination. The tone of the appeals became more shrill and acerbic but at the same time elements associated with the Consistory had already begun to put out feelers to more activist organizations in the community.[32] As was the case in many occupied areas, from Danzig in the 1930s to Warsaw in the 1940s, increased Nazi terror pushed individuals and organizations to pursue a line of action they previously rejected. This is what transpired in France in the autumn of 1943, especially after the arrest and deportation of Helbronner in October. Yet, even as the Consistory negotiated with political factions with which it had never before agreed to meet, and eventually concluded a historic agreement with them (in the form of CRIF, Conseil Représentatif des Institutions Juives de France), it did so in a fashion that guaranteed its unique historical position among French Jewry while retaining an unequivocal statement of allegiance to France.[33] In other words, this realignment seriously revamped the Consistory's traditional banner of religion and homeland but did not override it completely.

The tenacity with which the Central Consistory held to its ideological stance is perhaps an extreme example among the Jews of France but an instructive one. National Socialist oppression and Vichy collaboration could not easily erase the legacy of the Revolution nor distill the "incorrigible patriotism" of these Jews,[34] who personified the ethic of what the political sociologist Pierre Birnbaum has termed "fous de la république" (mad for the republic).[35] Were the Consistory leaders alone? Carole Fink's sensitive biography of Marc Bloch shows how the renowned medieval historian, who in early 1942 asserted adamantly that no anti-Jewish law could change his attachment to France, gradually turned to the Résistance as a way of serving France and proving his undivided loyalty to a country to which his ancestors had been attached for five generations.[36] Like the Consistory with its acquiescent attitude, Bloch and other similarly inclined native French Jews, could thus dialectically manifest that they were indeed French citizens—possibly the true French citizens. At the age of fifty-six and as a father of six, Bloch was certainly not in a prime position to join the Résistance; but as an independent spirit, unchained by eternal devotion to the French state and Republic, yet honoring its eternal values, he was open to the uncertain but challenging contact with France's adventurous spirits. Similar to Raymond Aron, René Cassin, Robert Debré, Simone Weil, and many others, Bloch's "Jewishness" did not figure significantly in this decision. Historians of the French Résistance, and those who have dealt specifically with its Jewish participants, seem to accept a wide range of motivations for joining the growing movement in 1943—from rejection of party politics and the Third Republic's parliamentary regime to strong antifascist and political affiliations; but by and large they follow Robert Paxton's classic analysis in emphasizing a predisposition to opposition in the prewar period as a common denominator.[37] Spanning communists and maverick church figures, Paxton's appreciation of the previous mind-set of an individual or association offers an important perspective for comparing the Consistory's deliberate steps to break with tradition and those of Bloch and kindred individuals. Though sharing a deep commitment to France and its liberal tradition, they differed on the boundaries of this commitment. Often one finds among those who opted for the route to resistance another affiliation that had an impact on the individual's weltanschauung. Bloch, for example, became the champion of interdisciplinary and cross-cultural studies, advocating from the 1920s a nonparochial attitude to the study of the past, France's included; George Friedmann was strongly aligned with the worker's movement; René Cassin with the battle for human rights. The Consistory, on the other hand, was a Jewish organization, wedded to the state and its apparatus even after 1905, and as such, it held on to the basic principle of its existence—the state and its law, the legacy of the Revolution.[38]

The political, historical, cultural, or religious baggage with which Jews entered the war was a significant factor in the way they dealt with the extreme situations they encountered and with the historical memory of the Revolution. Many East European Jews, though less steeped in this legacy, were, as I have indicated, also attracted and attached to it. Yet political activism was a central factor in the lives of many East European Jews in France and it helped loosen their ties to the legacy of the Revolution. As previous research has shown, especially that by Jacques Adler, left-wing politics was definitely such a force. But I would like to pursue briefly a different theme that needs much more serious research: the historical experience of East European Jews and its impact upon their response to oppression and antisemitism.

A historical precedent that suggest the intuitiveness of the East European response to antisemitism can be found in the Dreyfus Affair. Followed closely by East European Jewish newspapers, the affair aroused much anxiety and despair. A mere glance at the Hebrew press in Eastern Europe illuminates a wholly different mind-set than that which we associate with the French Jewish community at the time of the affair. One finds a blunt, bitter reaction from the outset, long before anyone questioned Dreyfus's guilt. Editorials in some of the Jewish newspapers in Eastern Europe left no room for conjecture about who was to blame, and they immediately exonerated Dreyfus of any possible treason. In their estimation, antisemites were at the root of the affair, and they had successfully managed to penetrate even the idyllic world where "the sun of freedom shone." In the words of one of these editorials:

> Was this entire machinery not set up by hostile, villainous, satanic scoundrels who wanted to plunge a Jewish soldier into the depths so that he should be unable to rise

again? Alas, who knows if he was not attacked from afar by one of those anonymous people who are proliferating and multiplying like locusts in France these days, who shot a honed arrow at this unfortunate Jew and also at the entire Jewish people![39]

Other editorials, presaging the vigorous attacks of immigrant Jews on French Jewish leadership during World War II, castigated native French Jews for being blind to the impending danger and behaving as if they still lived in the Garden of Eden. This instinctive sensitivity to the attitude of non-Jews to Jews had become much less common among Jews living in the urban environment in Western and Central Europe but was still very much part of the spiritual and collective baggage that East European Jews carried with them to France and other countries. As one of these immigrants to Paris and a member of the Résistance, Alfred Grant, reiterated in his Yiddish memoirs and in a later interview: "We who had emigrated from Poland as victims of Polish fascism and had fought against Pifsudky's and Colonel Beck's regime will not fail to point out when it is necessary where the major enemy resides."[40] France and the new countries East European Jews inhabited certainly modified the sense of distrust toward the non-Jewish world, but apprehensiveness was not totally dissolved. That is, alongside the trust in France that Lipchitz and Mané-Katz represented, East European Jews seldom possessed a one-dimensional view of France that would grant the revolutionary tradition an exclusive hold over their political and social outlook. This predisposition was to prove significant at the outbreak of war and the occupation of France.

Thus, in the face of growing pressure and antisemitic legislation under Vichy, which had more immediate ramifications for them than for the native French Jews, East European Jews distinguished the prevailing political orientation and disentangled themselves from their expectations of France's humanitarian tradition more quickly then did the native Jews. Moreover, in that many of them were first-generation Jews in France, still closely tied to their native homeland where family members lived in danger, their level of sensitivity to the plight of the Jews in Poland was more acute and immediate than was that of their fellow Jews. This too was part of the weight they carried, and it rose to the surface when their acquired homeland stripped them of their security. National Socialism's threat to Jewish existence, after the fall of Poland and the occupation of several European countries, including northern France, was understood by East European Jews in a broader, more international-Jewish context. Furthermore, France's tradition of humanitarianism and fraternity, which had in their minds withered away in the late 1930s, was no longer regarded as a source of support. From this perspective, and robbed of their belief in the power of the Prometheus with the Phrygian bonnet, they hardly saw any value in turning to the French authorities to repeal the anti-Jewish laws. Instead, activist groups began almost immediately to set up unofficial, clandestine associations to offer basic assistance to a needy community. These original steps would gradually take on a bolder course as the fate of Jews in France deteriorated from year to year. The historical significance of these diverse activities lies not only in their success in saving thousands of lives but in pushing French Jewry's center of gravity away from the acceptance of Vichy toward its rejection.[41]

In emphasizing the way in which the revolutionary tradition was part of the experience of French Jewry, I have purposely avoided suggesting a causal relationship between consciousness of the historical past and action during the war. One can legitimately ask whether this tradition had a direct impact on the behavior of French Jewry during the war and whether the meaning of that revolutionary tradition changed. Our emphasis has been on that tradition as a guarantor of libertarian principles. However, there is room to ask whether there developed a perspective that emphasized its integral spirit of revolt against a decadent regime. This was not the sole factor involved. Yet it appears that there was some correlation between the degree with which one held tenaciously to the eternal nature of 1789 as the promise of freedom and liberty, and the tendency to avoid embarking on an anti-Vichy or anti-German direction. Procrastination and "attentisme" were thus paradoxically encouraged by those who held unswervingly to this image of the Revolution. Interestingly, East European opponents of the regime, résistants, did not claim to be the spiritual heirs to or raise the banner of the Revolution during the war. One combs in vain their manifestos and recollections for such references. Rather, they saw themselves as protagonists and followers of political and ideological agendas that they did not necessarily associate with the Revolution. The legacy of the Revolution was certainly present for French Jewry during the war but stripped of its revolutionary character.

The outcome of the war weighed heavily on French Jewry. The mass deportation of eighty thousand Jews from France and the overall tragedy of European Jewry necessitated a reordering of their structures of belief, support, and memories. Could the Revolution continue to possess the mystique of prewar days? When Mané-Katz was approached in 1946 by members of the Polish-Jewish community in Nancy with a request for a painting for their community hall, he painted a mural of the Warsaw Ghetto insurrection.[42] In the background, buildings are engulfed in flames and smoke, while in the foreground corpses of young and old lie atop each other; in the center of the painting, three dejected figures recalling the past sit beneath a fluttering tallith: an old, bearded, and anguished Jew holding aloft a scroll of the Torah, a young resistance fighter with a gun in his hands, and a solemn, young woman seemingly holding a flag. Facing them in an active fighting position is a man in black, either throwing a rock at the ghetto or struggling with the Angel of Death, who seems to be reaching out to seize a young boy in the forefront. The boy, draped in a shawl (in the colors of the burning buildings) and holding high a book (possibly a prayer book), symbolizes the hope of the future. His gesture and position remind us of the youth in *Homage à Paris*, but without the ecstasy in his face and the optimism of republican ideals. Mané-Katz, who returned to Paris in 1945, found no way to integrate any aspect of French experience or symbolism into this work—no sign of hope was forthcoming from that direction; the boy is alone with his book, surrounded by a cataclysm. The mural also offers a poignant comment on the East European Jews who had commissioned Mané-Katz. They transformed his work into an icon; the mural became the center of the hall, which once bustled with life. The mural reflected a new stage in their historical consciousness, one in which the wounds of the war would supersede all other principles. For them and for many native French Jews "the Revolution was over."

NOTES

Although visual display of a number of works of art accompanied an oral presentation of this material, concerns of space and economy oblige us to rely upon the author's excellent descriptions of those illustrations here. —The Editors

1. Michael R. Marrus, *The Holocaust in History* (Hanover, NH, 1987), pp. 108 ff.; Richard I. Cohen, "Breaking the Code: Hannah Arendt's *Eichmann in Jerusalem* and the Public Polemic: Myth, Memory and Historical Imagination," *Michael* 13 (1993): 29–85.

2. See Henry Habberly Price, *Thinking and Experience*, 2nd ed. (London, 1969), p. 190.

3. Pierre Birnbaum and Ira Katznelson, eds., *Paths of Emancipation: Jews, States, and Citizenship* (Princeton, 1995).

4. David Ruderman, "At the Intersection of Cultures: The Historical Legacy of Italian Jewry," and Mario Toscano, "The Jews in Italy from the Risorgimento to the Republic," both in *Gardens and Ghettos: The Art of Jewish Life in Italy*, ed. Vivian B. Mann (Berkeley, 1989), pp. 1–23, 25–44.

5. Frances Malino, *The Sephardic Jews of Bordeaux: Assimilation and Emancipation in Revolutionary and Napoleonic France* (Tuscaloosa, AL, 1978), p. 103.

6. Pierre Birnbaum, *Les fous de la République, Histoire politique des Juifs d'Etat de Gambetta à Vichy* (Paris, 1992).

7. See David H. Weinberg, *A Community on Trial: The Jew of Paris in the 1930s* (Chicago, 1977); idem, "'Heureux comme dieu en France': East European Jewish Immigrants in Paris, 1881–1914," in *Studies in Contemporary Jewry*, vol. 1, ed. Jonathan Frankel (Bloomington, 1984), pp. 26–54; Paula E. Hyman, *From Dreyfus to Vichy: The Remaking of French Jewry, 1906–1939* (New York, 1979); Nancy L. Green, "La Révolution dans l'imaginaire des immigrants juifs," in *Histoire politique des Juifs de France*, ed. Pierre Birnbaum (Paris, 1990), pp. 153–62.

8. Kenneth E. Silver and Romy Golan, *The Circle of Montparnasse: Jewish Artists in 1905–1945*, Jewish Museum catalogue, New York (New York, 1985), p. 96.

9. J.-M. Aimot, *Mané-Katz* (Paris, 1933), pp. 51–52.

10. Quoted in Jacques Biélinky, *Journal, 1940–1942: Un journaliste juif à Paris sous l'occupation*, ed. Renée Poznanski (Paris, 1992), p. 20. Biélinky arrived in France in 1909, and like Mané-Katz, he became a naturalized French citizen in 1927. His remarks were originally published in *L'univers israélite* in a special issue commemorating the 150th anniversary of the French Revolution (August 25–September 1, 1939).

11. See Silver and Golan, *Circle of Montparnasse*, pp. 51–52.

12. See Gedalyahu G. Stroumsa, "Myth into Metaphor: The Case of Prometheus," in *Gilgul: Essays on Transformation, Revolution and Permanence in the History of Religions* (supplements to *Numen* 50), ed. S. Shaked, D. Shulman, and G. G. Stroumsa (Leiden, 1987), pp. 309–23.

13. The cap, according to Agulhon, "is the symbol most charged with significance, the one whose omission is always significant." See Maurice Agulhon, *Marianne into Battle: Republican Imagery and Symbolism in France, 1789–1880*, trans. Janet Lloyd (Cambridge, 1981), pp. 21–22; idem, *Marianne au pouvoir: L'imagerie et la symbolique républicaines de 1880 à 1914* (Paris, 1989), pp. 106–109.

14. The phrase was coined by Rabbi Zadoc-Kahn, the Chief Rabbi of France during the Herzlian era of Zionism. See Michel Abitbol, *Les deux terres promises: Les Juifs de France et le sionisme* (Paris, 1989), pp. 29–44, 146–58, 195; Michael R. Marrus, *The Politics of Assimilation* (Oxford, 1972). Further discussions of Zionism and French Jewry during the interwar period are found in Weinberg, *A Community on Trial*; Hyman, *From Dreyfus to Vichy*; Catherine Nicault, "La réceptivité au sionisme de la fin du XIXe siècle à l'aube de la seconde guerre mondiale," in *Histoire politique des Juifs de France*, pp. 92–111. All of these authors subscribe to a similar view, with only slight variations of emphasis.

15. Weinberg, *A Community on Trial*, p. 248. See also Robert Sommers, "La doctrine politique et l'action religieuse du Grand-Rabbin Maurice Liber," *Revue des études juives* 125 (1966): 17–18.

16. See Ludwig Wihl, *Gedichte* (Mainz, 1836); Pierre Mercier, *Les hirondelles de Louis Wihl: Poésies allemandes traduites en français* (Paris, 1860).

17. See also *L'univers israélite*, no. 48–49, August 25–September 1, 1939; Weinberg, *A Community on Trial*, which to my mind overstates the case in claiming that the Jews of France continued to look ahead to a messianic future; other expressions of French-Jewish panegyrics to the Revolution are mentioned in Nicault, "La réceptivité au sionisme," p. 111.

18. The book by Joseph Weill, *Contribution à l'histoire des camps d'internement dans l'anti-France* (Paris, 1946), published by the Centre de documentation juive contemporaine (CDJC) in Paris, provides an interesting example of this phenomenon. It follows a line of thinking, common to the founders of the institution designed to collect documentation on war crimes, that regarded Vichy as an aberration and a departure from France's true vocation. Vichy was considered the "anti-France," and thus no explanation is even attempted for the establishment of internment camps on French soil prior to the war. See Richard I. Cohen, "The Fate of French Jewry in World War II in Historical Writing (1944–1983)—Interim Conclusions," in *The Historiography of the Holocaust Period*, ed. Yisrael Gutman and Gideon Greif (Jerusalem, 1988), pp. 161–63.

19. Pierre Birnbaum, *Anti-Semitism in France: A Political History from Léon Blum to the Present* (London, 1992).

20. In stark contrast, Marc Bloch, a medieval historian of Jewish ancestry, chastised his fellow French for having lost a sense of French history. In his *Strange Defeat: A Statement of Evidence Written in 1940* (New York, 1968), p. 167, he attributed the defeat in part to this behavior. Referring to those who are not moved by hearing the account of the Festival of Federation (July 14, 1790), he commented: "I do not care what may be the colour of their politics to-day: such a lack of response to the noblest uprushes of national enthusiasm is enough to condemn them. . . . Unfortunately, the men whose ancestors pledged their faith on the Altar of the Nation have lost contact with the profound realities of national greatness." See also Carole Fink, *Marc Bloch: A Life in History* (Cambridge, 1989), pp. 205–92.

21. See Michael R. Marrus and Robert O. Paxton, *Vichy France and the Jews* (New York, 1981), chapters 1 and 2; André Kaspi, *Les Juifs pendant l'occupation* (Paris, 1991), pp. 56–66.

22. On this important issue see Vicki Caron, "The Politics of Frustration: French Jewry and the Refugee Crisis in the 1930s," *Journal of Modern History* 65 (1993): 311–56.

23. Raymond-Raoul Lambert, *Carnet d'un témoin (1940–1943)*, ed. Richard Cohen (Paris, 1985), p. 71.

24. Ibid., p. 85. See Yerachmiel (Richard) I. Cohen, "A Jewish Leader in Vichy France, 1940–1943: The Diary of Raymond-Raoul Lambert," *Jewish Social Studies* 43 (1981): 292–95; cf. Simone Weil's letter to the Minister of Education in response to the statute in Claude Singer, *Vichy, l'université et les Juifs* (Paris, 1992), p. 237.

25. From February 20, 1942, quoted in Renée Poznanski, "French Jews and Jewish Legislation 1940–1941," *Yad Vashem Studies* 22 (1993): 93.

26. The ensuing discussion is based on the following: Birnbaum, *Les fous de la République*, pp. 471–84; Vicki Caron, "Loyalties in Conflict, French Jewry and the Refugee Crisis 1933–1935," Leo Baeck Institute *Year Book* 36 (1991): 305–38; idem, "Politics of Frustration"; Yerachmiel (Richard) I. Cohen, "French Jewry's Dilemma on the Orientation of Its Leadership: From Polemics to Conciliation, 1942–1944," *Yad Vashem Studies* 14 (1981): 167–204; idem, "'Religion and Fatherland'—The French Central Consistory during the Second World War," in *Shmuel Ettinger Festschrift*, ed. Shmuel Almog, Israel Bartal et al. (Jerusalem, 1988), pp. 307–34 (Hebrew).

27. Meeting of March 17, 1941; see Yad Vashem Archives, 09/30–3; see also YIVO collection, RG 116, section 33. Chief Rabbi Isaïe Schwartz sent a similar letter to all French rabbis and leaders of the community.

28. Helbronner rejected, in a letter to Pétain, any "fictitious connection, racial or ethnic, of foreign inspiration, whose base is insupportable in the spirit of the French legislation and the knowledge of science"; quoted in Birnbaum, *Les fous de la République*, p. 475.

29. This perspective has been slightly challenged by several regional studies, which now tend to see more opposition to Vichy as early as 1941. See, for example, Robert Zaretsky,

Nîmes at War: Religion, Politics, and Public Opinion in the Gard, 1938–1944 (University Park, PA, 1995).

30. See, for example, its vehement protest against the compulsory stamping of all documents with the epithet "JUIF" or "JUIVE"; Protest to Pétain, December 30, 1942, YIVO, RG 116, file 33; and see the deliberations of the permanent section of the Consistory on December 28, 1942), Yad Vashem Archives, 09/30–1.

31. Helbronner to Laval, January 27, 1943, YIVO, RG 116, file 31; Lambert, *Carnet d'un témoin*, pp. 206–15.

32. On the negotiations between Joseph Fisher and the Jewish communists, see Jacques Adler, *The Jews of Paris and the Final Solution: Communal Response and Internal Conflicts 1940–1944* (New York, 1987), pp. 230–31.

33. See Michael R. Marrus, "Jewish Leadership and the Holocaust: The Case of France," in *Living with Antisemitism: Modern Jewish Responses*, ed. Jehuda Reinharz (Hanover, NH, 1987), pp. 380–96.

34. This felicitous phrase is taken from Marrus, ibid., p. 387.

35. Birnbaum, *Les fous de la République*.

36. Fink, *Marc Bloch*, pp. 295–96; Yerachmiel (Richard) I. Cohen, "The Jewish Community of France in the Face of Vichy-German Persecution: 1940–44," in *The Jews in Modern France*, ed. Frances Malino and Bernard Wasserstein (Hanover, NH, 1985), pp. 181–82.

37. See, inter alia, Roderick Kedward, *Resistance in Vichy France* (Oxford, 1978); John F. Sweets, *The Politics of Resistance in France: A History of the Mouvements Unis de la Résistance* (De Kalb, IL, 1976); *Les Juifs dans la Résistance et la Libération* (Paris, 1985); Robert O. Paxton, *Vichy France: Old Guard and New Order* (New York, 1968).

38. See Pierre Birnbaum, "Between Social and Political Assimilation: Remarks on the History of Jews in France," in Birnbaum and Katznelson, *Paths of Emancipation*, pp. 94–127; see also his remark on p. 127: "Jews were numerous in the resistance, once again in the name of the republican state in which they continued to place their hopes and which, after the Allied victory, would restore them to their positions and prestige."

39. *Hamaggid*, 21 Teveth 1895 (Kraków). Quoted in Richard I. Cohen, "The Dreyfus Affair and the Jews," in *Antisemitism through the Ages*, ed. Shmuel Almog (Oxford, 1989), p. 307.

40. Quoted in Maurice Rajfus, *L'an prochain, la révolution: Les communistes juifs immigrés dans la tourments stalinienne 1930–1945* (Paris, 1985), p. 107.

41. Adler, *Jews of Paris*; Cohen, "Jewish Community," p. 204.

42. *Autour d'une synagogue bicentenaire* (Nancy, 1987), p. 29.

43.

ADAM RAYSKI

The Jewish Underground Press in France and the Struggle to Expose the Nazi Secret of the Final Solution

"The Jewish Question will have to be resolved only during the war, since it must be settled without having the entire world erupt in protest."[1]

The silence of the victims before and during their persecution was one of the basic requirements determining the success of the Nazi genocide against the Jews of France. This silence had to be secured by prohibiting, from the beginning of the Occupation, any manifestation of Jewish social and political life, including the press.[2] Before the Jewish "right to live" was eliminated, their "right to speak" was taken away. A little later, the prohibition against owning radios was issued. These were only part of a logical series of decisions aimed at transforming the Jewish community into a mass of individuals having no common organization or plan. Each person was cut off from other members of the community and deprived of forums for decision making and communication. It was, in fact, a community reduced to fragments. This absence of news, communication, and exchange of ideas was felt even more cruelly in the atmosphere of anguish that had become widespread in Paris immediately following the first deportations in March 1942.

Birth of the Underground Jewish Press

In these political circumstances, to claim the right to speak took on, in the eyes of the government, the nature of a challenge, especially because it emanated from persons who, according to Nazi theories, were "subhuman" and "cowards." This was not, however, the main objective of the underground Jewish publications. The Résistance focused on rebuilding social ties among a scattered population. A survey counted more than eight hundred towns and villages inhabited by Jews between 1940 and 1944, and these entities were, as we now know, deprived of any form of social organization. The emergence and circulation of illegal writings proved that, confronted with the cataclysm that was engulfing them, the Jews of France had no intention of submitting passively; there was, somewhere, a leadership of organized persons who continued to reflect on the fate of their community.

The first underground writings appeared in Paris beginning in September 1940, that is, scarcely three months after the arrival of the Germans. They were published by a new resistance organization, Solidarity (*Solidaritet* in Yiddish), which brought together Communist Party members and sympathizers as well as numerous readers of the newspaper *Naïe Presse* (New press), which had been banned in September 1939 following the signing of the German-Soviet Pact. Solidarity's publication was called *Unzer Wort*; beginning in the summer of 1942, it brought out a French edition called *Notre Parole* (Paris) and *Notre Voix* (the South). During this same period, the Parisian branch of the Bund published an issue of *Unzer Shtimme* (Our voice), which ceased publication thereafter, except for one issue published in the southern region in July 1944.

Restoring the old prewar tradition of the "Ligue internationale contre l'anti-sémitisme" (LICA, International League against Anti-Semitism), the leaders of Solidarity founded, in July and August of 1942, the Mouvement national contre le racism (MNCR, National Movement against Racism), to act as a bulwark against racist and antisemitic propaganda. Its main newspapers, *J'accuse* and *Fraternité*, gained a very wide circulation throughout the country by disseminating the truth about Nazi plans for extermination. The underground press in France also included the publications *En avant* and *Jeune combat*, which targeted Jewish youth, whether immigrant or French native, organized under the "Union de la Jeunesse Juive" (UJJ, Union of Jewish Youth).[3]

In prewar France, the richness of the Jewish press in French, Yiddish, Hebrew, Russian, and even German, signaled a highly developed ideological pluralism, in particular among the Jews coming from Eastern Europe. Having remained faithful to their convictions, they had even given themselves the luxury of sustaining three Yiddish dailies, a Zionist, a Communist, and a Bundist paper, as well as numerous weeklies and monthlies. The French Jews, on the other hand, who organized themselves around the Consistory or the Alliance Israélite Universelle (AIU), had published weeklies of a very high quality for a long time. It may be estimated with a fair degree of accuracy that nearly one hundred journalists oversaw the publication of these newspapers and periodicals, not including the personalities of all stripes who participated regularly or intermittently.[4]

This contrast with the prewar situation can be explained by the involvement of some organizations, in particular Zionist organizations, and their leaders in the system of legal existence offered to them in the "Free Zone,"[5] where they had established their offices after the Wehrmacht arrived in Paris in June 1940. Their forced membership in the Union générale des Israélites de France (UGIF) (a sort of Judenrat adjusted to the conditions prevailing in France at that time), where they devoted themselves exclusively to philanthropic activities, led them to renounce any kind of political resistance involvement. Accordingly, their concern for prolonging this state of affairs certainly deferred the choice between legalism and secrecy, with the result that they tied their own hands, in the strict sense of the term.[6]

This panorama, marked by the dominance of Solidarity and MNCR publications, underwent changes beginning in August and September 1943 with the appearance of the Comité uni de défense juive (United Jewish Defense Committee), which emerged from the alliance of all political orientations of immigrant Jews: the general Zionists (liberal), the Poalei-Zion of the left and right, the BUND, and the Union des Juifs pour la Résistance et l'Entraide (UJRE, Union of Jews for Resistance and Mutual Assistance), which succeeded Solidarity in the spring of 1943. The Zionist, socialist, and communist leaders together edited a major newspaper, *Unzer Kamf* (Our struggle), and numerous brochures and tracts in Yiddish and French.[7] In December 1943, the first issue of the Zionist newspaper *Quand Même* appeared. It should also be pointed out that, in 1943, the group Polaei-Zion (leftist) published a bulletin, the *Arbeiter-Zeitung* (Workers' paper).

Furthermore, the explanation of some historians that an underground press was abandoned in a "choice of priorities" does not appear to have any real foundation. Quite the contrary, the impossibility of expression was, in general, very painfully felt, as shown in the editorial in the first issue of *Quand Même*: "Among the many tortures the Nazi leaders and their accomplices inflict on the Jews, that of silence perhaps most strikes at our dignity. To be obliged to be silent, to allow ourselves to be humiliated by degenerate sadists without the opportunity to cry out in disgust, this is the torture of silence we experience in France."[8]

Philanthropy or Political Action?

An important text marking a contrast with the prolonged silence of some elites unfortunately passed unnoticed at the time. It was written by David Knout, a native Russian poet, militant Zionist supporter of Jabotinsky, and right-wing extremist. Only a few months after the occupation of France, he circulated among his friends in Toulouse and Marseille a lengthy notebook entitled *Que faire?* (What is to be done?). To this day, the original notebook has not been found. Nevertheless, Knout mentions excerpts in his memoirs, published immediately after the war.[9]

Knout showed a prophetic perception of the situation: "The Jewish people is threatened as it has never been in its long history. . . . A numberless, powerful enemy is waging *a war* without quarter against us. . . . *The extermination of the Jewish people* is already occurring."[10] At the same time, his text did not spare the leaders of the philanthropic organization, which attributed to charity the status of a survival strategy, thus restating a thought of the great historian, Simon Dubnov: "It is not the philanthropic bureaucratic organizations that will vanquish the misfortunes of our people. You do not fight disasters with offerings, by doing so you teach resignation, that great school of cowardice, to the victims."

Knout proposed the creation of a "revolutionary, national movement, a militant avant-garde of a people that would recover its independence: B'nai David."[11] However, he complained that his idea of armed Jewish resistance was very badly received by the established French Jewish community. Was it for this reason that he took refuge in Switzerland in the summer of 1942? His political colleagues never made his reflections known during the war years.

In underground publishing, the phrase "extermination of the Jewish people" appeared at the end of August 1941 in the "Appeal from Eminent Jewish Personalities of Moscow." Transmitted by Radio Moscow on August 20, 1941, by generals of the army, writers, artists, and others, the appeal revealed that Nazi Germany had undertaken, by means of massacres perpetrated by the famous SS Einsatzgruppen, the total extermination of the Jewish people in territories occupied by the Wehrmacht. The writer David Bergelson ended his speech in Hebrew, citing the words of the Psalmist: "I will not die, but live." At the end of August 1941, *Unzer Wort* and *Notre Voix*, in Paris and Lyon, gave prominent place to the Moscow meeting.

The French Alternative

Beyond its information function, the underground press served as a kind of forum for reflection, a laboratory where the political thought of the Jewish resistance and, ultimately, its strategy, were gradually formulated, the proof that writing promotes thought.

Already in May 1941, an initial, highly significant idea of this strategy appeared in an appeal signed by "A group of Jewish women and children" and addressed to "French opinion" immediately following the first major raid on Parisian Jews of foreign birth, aged eighteen to sixty, mostly Polish nationals.[12]

Denouncing the internments carried out by French police, the women were proclaiming, during that period of public indifference, their confidence in the French of "The Rights of Man and of Citizen": "Join us in our protest, in the name of your glorious past, of your great men such as Voltaire, Victor Hugo, Emile Zola, Jaurès! Once again, a Zola must have his *J'accuse* heard." This appeal thus carried in embryonic form the basic thought that the defense of the Jews should not be practiced in isolation but required alliances with democratic forces, that is, the Résistance.

Searching for a response to the danger, the editors were led to a comparison of the French and Polish situations. In France, the Jewish population was confronted with the same enemy as in Poland. Its forces carried out the same policy of concentration and isolation, but with this difference: in France, these goals could be achieved solely by means of a social and moral ghetto, that is, a *ghetto without walls*, and in particular, a forced union of all Jewish cultural and social organizations in the UGIF.[13] The success of this undertaking presupposed that Jewish leaders would submit to a "return to the ghetto," withdrawal into their own community, and a break with the non-Jewish population.

In the ghetto-prisons of Poland, on the other hand, circumstances offered no alternative or choice, except that of dying with dignity as Jews, especially since the concrete walls surrounding the ghettos were doubled by the wall of hostility or indifference expressed by most Christians. The policy of withdrawal was dictated by actual conditions; accordingly, any survival strategy could be imagined only within the geographical and political boundaries of the ghetto. The basic state of affairs characterizing the French situation, by virtue of the deep roots of humanitarian tradition and of increasingly favorable public opinion toward the Jews, allowed an opportunity to choose between voluntary acceptance of isolation and a refusal to submit to the orders and laws decreed by the Vichy government and the German occupier. The establishment of an overall strategy aimed at defense against deportation ultimately depended on the Jewish resistance's accurate perception of this specific characteristic of the situation in France.

July 16 and 17, 1942: The Survival Strategy Put to the Test

In July 1942 the underground press published a document detailing the means by which one might try to defend oneself against deportation. Until then, newspapers and leaflets had merely repeated endlessly "deportation means death; resistance, life." But this warning was not highly persuasive since no proof could be marshalled to support it. At the beginning of July, Solidarity warned the Jews of Paris of the imminence of a major action: "The enemy is readying a huge raid which, this time, will spare neither women, children, nor the elderly." This leaflet specified with precision what "each Jewish man, woman, and child must do." Jews were instructed not to wait at home: "Take all measures necessary to hide yourselves, and first of all children, with the help of sympathetic French citizens." This call emphasized the relationship between personal survival and the survival of Jewish identity, both of which were threatened with extinction: "Not a single Jew must fall victim to the Nazi beast, each free-living Jew is a victory over our enemy, who must not and shall not achieve our extermination."[14] Although attacked collectively, Jews could defend themselves only as individuals and in isolation. Here lay, in all probability, the entirely unique feature of the "war against the Jews," which was directed, not against an army, but against an entire civilian population; and each person found himself or herself on the front line. Indeed, the front ran through each Jewish household.

Two Historical Turning Points

The historiography of this period seeks, with some justification, to pay tribute to the Parisian people for their active solidarity with the Jews during the terrifying days of July 1942. For there to be *complicity*, the Jews had to stop acting as *objects* and become *active agents* in the drama into which they had been thrown. Documents and witnesses' accounts show that the Parisian Jews reacted sharply and achieved significant results: at least ten to eleven thousand owed their survival above all to their own courage. Several thousand men and women, often accompanied by children, took action, abandoning the passive behavior evident during previous raids.[15] This time surprise was not in the service of the Franco-German staff. An equally important factor regarding the change of behavior among the Parisian Jews was the perception of the threat directed against women and children, for now they realized that work "camps" were not camps at all, since children, the sick, and the old were being sent there. Already, a vague understanding of the true nature of the Germans' plan was being absorbed, even though there was no realization that the deportation of children formed one of its elements.

The most important lesson of this experience was that it was possible to escape deportation. As *Unzer Politik* (Our policy) stated,[16] "Indeed, in August 1942, the threat of deportation is recognized to be a high-priority, dominating threat. . . . There are few people who are not persuaded of the possible success of resistance to deportation." Proof existed that isolation could be defeated, though at a high cost in terms of energy and courage, by placing oneself deliberately "outside the law."

Accordingly, the summer of 1942 did not, as has too often been written, mark only a turning point of public opinion. It was preceded by a radical change of behavior among the Jews.[17] The convergence of these two tendencies is the source of a dynamic that would save nearly three-quarters of the Jewish community in France (i.e., approximately 220,000 out of 300,000).[18]

Illegality, a Condition for Survival

To save their lives, tens of thousands of persons of all ages had to lead an underground existence. They had to eschew the yellow star and identity papers stamped "JEW," find new homes, adopt false identities, work clandestinely—in short, adopt a lifestyle identical to that of the organized Résistance. "Jewish resistance" extended beyond structured organizations to include all illegal Jews, that is, the majority of Jews in France.

This situation was radically new: "The Jews must be sought less in their own homes than in those of the Aryans," states a document from the police, who were forced "to seek out persons no longer wearing the yellow star and living under false names."[19] Because it became increasingly difficult to capture Jews, Helmut Knochen, the German chief of police, was required to prepare for his commandoes very detailed instructions, better suited to the challenging situation.[20]

The underground press published instructions for "vigilance," rules to be followed to avoid giving oneself away:

> Stand firm! Once and for all, abandon your legal dwellings and do not return for any reason. Do not keep your identity papers stamped "JEW." If you have false papers, then keep only your false papers in your pocket. Do not speak Yiddish in public places or in the street. It would be criminal not to take these elementary safety measures, which will enable you to be present at the hour of Liberation.[21]

The newspapers warned their readers about the risks of maintaining UGIF offices and various UGIF centers, where some persons went to seek help or lodging: "These offices are a trap. Those who frequent them will, sooner or later, be arrested and deported. To appear on a UGIF list means continuous surveillance by the Gestapo. . . . We will do everything in our power to rescue you in secret."[22]

Should One Speak of the Gas Chambers?

In the weeks following the major raid of July 16 and 17, 1942, the deportation of children, a previously unthinkable occurrence, was reported. "Drancy is only one step before deportation," stated an MNCR tract. "In fact, children are taken away toward the East in groups of one thousand, under the same conditions as adults. They start by destroying their civil status papers. They shave the head and the genitals of young girls ten, eleven, and twelve years old. They pile them up in weighted railcars."[23] The agonizing question on everybody's lips: What was the real destination of the deportation convoys? Several months were needed before an answer began to emerge.

Continuously searching for information about the deportation sites and attentive to any rumor from the East and, above all, from Poland, the Solidarity leaders in Paris received—in early October 1942—from a resistance member who had infiltrated the Wehrmacht transport division, the incredible news that toxic gases were being used on Jewish deportees. Should this news be reported? One had to know with absolute certainty whether it was true. If it proved to be false, dissemination would be criminal. The argument was frequently raised that a negative reaction could be expected, that people would refuse to believe it. If the news proved true, however, did the journalists have the right to conceal the information?[24]

Gerhardt Riegner, delegate to the World Jewish Congress (WJC) in Geneva in August 1942, was the first to learn of the German plan for complete extermination of the Jewish people. But was it true? The question tortured Riegner and Sagalowitch, president of the Zürich community, during an interminable walk along Lake Geneva. "Finally," said Riegner, "we convinced each other, feeling the chill of death in the soul, that the report had to be considered true. By virtue of my duties, it was my responsibility to transmit the news to the governments of the United States and Great Britain, to persuade them of the reality of the danger."[25]

Finally, on October 20, 1942, *J'accuse* published the news under the title: "Hun torturers burn and asphyxiate thousands of Jewish men, women, and children deported from France." "The news reaching us despite the silence of the mercenary press," wrote the newspaper, "reports that tens of thousands of Jewish men, women, and children deported from France were either burned alive in the lead-shielded railcars or else asphyxiated to test a new toxic gas." *J'accuse* was the first underground publication in France to report the use of gas on Jewish deportees.[26]

Beginning on that day, the search for information about the Final Solution (although this term was still unknown) intensified, becoming a major point of contention between the victims, who had a vital need to know, and the executioners, who elevated secrecy to a weapon in the war against the Jews.[27] Henceforth, the editors of the secret press lived in the shadow of Auschwitz. Attaching crucial importance to the disclosure of the secret, the Jewish resistance in France took part, without knowing it at that time, in the same struggle as Emmanuel Ringelblum in the Warsaw Ghetto, who called this undertaking a "historic mission."[28]

The progress of the crime was matched by the progress of information in the illicit publications. What gradually emerged was a picture of a succession of massacres in the towns, villages, and camps of Eastern Europe. "Savage massacres have been perpetrated by Hitler's forces in the occupied Eastern territories," reported the special bulletin *Atrocités nazies*. "40,000 Jews have been massacred in Riga, capital of Latvia. Thousands of Latvian Jews were deported to an island 15 kilometers from Riga. Thousands of children were torn away from their parents and savagely shot in front of them. In Vilnius, in Svientzany, nearly all of the Jewish population was killed."

On December 25, 1942, under the title "All of Poland a Vast Slaughterhouse for Jews," *J'accuse* reported in telegraphic style the terrible results of the "evacuations" from the Warsaw Ghetto, which had taken place during the summer: "Women, children, the elderly, the sick, were killed. 360,000 human beings were assassinated in the Warsaw Ghetto. The entire world has risen up and proclaimed its hatred of the Nazi murderers. Eleven governments are drafting a writ of accusation. The British Parliament is demanding the supreme punishment for the murderers":

In all of the countries occupied by Germany, Jews are deprived of all human rights, and a horrible process of extermination is being carried out. Poland, in particular, is the theater for this process. Here, tens of thousands of Jews from different occupied European countries have been deported. No news reaches us from these unfortunate people. . . . The undersigned nations report to the world these monstrous crimes against an innocent people, and they have decided to carry out the supreme punishment on all Nazi criminals and on all those who assist them in their plan of extermination.[29]

In January 1943, *En avant!*, the newspaper for youth, confirmed the extent of the massacre with stunning accuracy: "Two million Jews killed in Poland. . . . Out of 400,000 Jews in Warsaw, only forty thousand have remained alive. Everything favors the Nazis in their attempts to achieve their goals: toxic gases, asphyxia in the sulfur chambers, executions, hangings." In May 1943, *Fraternité* spoke of the "gas chambers" for the first time. On August 1, 1943, *Notre Voix* published testimony "from the most reliable source," a truly important event, about the massacres in the Polish camps. The first account came from a Jew from Nice who, after deportation, lived for eight months in the camps in Kosiel (near Auschwitz) and succeeded in escaping. The second was from a Pole, Jan Karski, who, at the request of the Jewish resistance in the Warsaw Ghetto, infiltrated the camp in Belzec (that is, not the famous camp of that name, but Izbica Lubelska), where he saw the massacre of Jewish men, women, and children whom the Nazis had enclosed in railcars filled with lime. Later in London, Karski announced the atrocities to the free world over the radio.

The first issue of *Quand Même* spoke of traditional "Jewish optimism" and encouraged its readers to keep that issue, "in order to be capable of opposing the threat of total destruction." After repeating that, according to the Bible, "the Jews are a stiff-necked people *capable of clinging to this optimism*, it was important to remain confident in the future, because *moral strength will ultimately prevail over just plain strength*. . . . " The solution would come only after the war, when "the true pacification of this world can occur only by virtue of the international settlement of all of the issues touching humanity. Such a settlement must include the Jewish question. . . ." This settlement would entail realization of the Zionist dream, though the paper stopped short of expressing the point explicitly: "How great will be our enthusiasm if we see the youth of the Diaspora join hands in an immense dance on the blessed soil, around a fire of joy in which assimilation, suffering, and fear will have been consumed, to celebrate our truth."[30]

Echo of the Warsaw Ghetto Uprising

The period from May to June 1943 was most certainly an extraordinary time for the Jewish resistance in France. At the end of April, the Solidarity listening posts in Paris and Lyon learned from the BBC that the last Jews in Warsaw were fighting the German troops that had invaded the ghetto, an event as historic as it was tragic. This news was viewed with an emotion that is easily understood and interpreted, above all, since it was a message from the ghetto fighters that the great and glorious Jewish community of Poland was living out its final days. Everything suggested that the Jewish deportees from France were sharing the same fate.[31] The initial reaction of the newspapers *Unzer Wort, Notre Voix, Notre Parole,* and *Jeune Combat* was more emotional than political and attested in particular to the pain and anger of the authors, but also to their desire not to allow the voices of the combatants, whom the Nazis wanted to crush in silence, to be muffled.

"Rise up for the final combat against the Nazi barbarians!" proclaimed *Unzer Wort,*

> Hear the cries of the millions of our brothers tortured in the Polish camps and in the ghettos! Near at hand is the day when Hitler's band will have to account for all of its crimes. This sea of blood will never be calmed, nor will the innocent dead be silent. The specter of defeat haunts the Nazi bandits. It appears to them in the faces of the millions of their victims who rise from their tombs, emerge from the flames and death factories. They spread out like a formidable army, behind them march the living, all of the persecuted, all of humanity, to remove from the surface of the earth all traces of Nazi barbarism.[32]

Fraternité and *J'accuse,* which were intended for the non-Jewish population, published extensive accounts of the uprising, denouncing the Nazi barbarism and glorifying the heroism of the combatants as a glorious example. Other documents reflected on the meaning the rebellion. A declaration published in June 1943 termed the revolt an episode in the history of the Jewish people that represented both continuity and change.[33] On the one hand, the rebellion echoed the era of struggle for the independence of Israel, and, on the other, it broke with the spirit of submission practiced during centuries of exile: "Since the revolt of Bar Kochba, the battle waged by our brothers in Warsaw is the greatest battle in the history of our people."[34] In the newspaper *Unzer Wort* an editorialist stressed the break with the era when martyrdom was heroism: "The uprising also represents the symbol of the new spirit that today animates Jews throughout the world. Yes, to undergo martyrdom, to die for the "sanctification of the Name" (Al Kiddush Hashem) as did our fathers and grandfathers, but in a way different from theirs. . . . Today, Jews die sanctifying the Name, weapons in hand."[35]

The underground press drew from the rebellion lessons for France where, fortunately, it was still possible to save thousands by unifying all of the Jewish forces. This objective led to the creation of the General Jewish Defense Committee (CGDJ, Comité général de défense juive) in June 1943. All of the social and political organizations of immigrant Jews united in this committee around a common program. In the spring of 1944, the CGDJ joined with native-born Jews (represented by the Consistory) to form the Representative Council of the Jews of France (CRIF, Conseil Représentatif des Juifs de France).[36] This date would be one of the most important in the history of Jewry under the Occupation.

Police Repression: Death Penalties!

Police repression, both French and German, of the underground Jewish publications was felt as soon as they appeared. Initially, this job was the responsibility of the Service de surveillance des milieux juifs (Division of surveillance of the Jewish milieux) of the Paris Prefecture of Police. Police agents exhibited a great deal of optimism, since they were persuaded that, after each discovery of a secret printing plant, they had struck a final blow. Accordingly, they were greatly surprised (a fact they did not conceal in their reports) to see tracts and newspapers circulating once again.[37]

The German security service closely monitored the proliferation of Jewish publications. Researchers have found in the archives of the Gestapo in France numerous copies of newspapers and tracts with accompanying letters from units of the Sicherheitsdienst or Security Service (SD) in various cities, in particular Lyon, Bordeaux, and Rennes.

The records of Röthke, Eichmann's representative in Paris, contain, along with the original, the complete translation of issue number 4 of *J'accuse*, dated November 20, 1942, which began *"Ich klage an"* (I accuse), thus suggesting that in Berlin as in Paris, the French Jewish newspapers were being read. It brings some satisfaction to learn today that the Nazis were aware of Jewish resistance and of its disclosure of the secret of the Final Solution. Pétain's cabinet took great interest in the underground Jewish publications, to judge by the place reserved for them in the highly secret "weekly summaries" prepared by the special services. "The Jews are attempting to create a vast movement of solidarity and resistance to support them," observed a report dated March 10, 1943.[38] The dissemination of "prosemitic tracts" was once again reported in April. In a statistical report prepared in December 1943 there was information about the underground Jewish press, for example, *Fraternité*. Under the heading "Tracts Emanating from Jewish Milieux," the following publications were mentioned: *"Qu'est-ce que c'est l'Union de la Jeunesse juive?"* (What is the union of Jewish youth), *"Jeune Juif prends ta place dans le combat!"* (Young Jew, take your place in the struggle), *"A nos frères de l'Union soviétique"* (To our brothers in the Soviet Union), and *"Jeune Combat"* (Youth struggle).[39]

The seriousness of the punishments handed out to the authors, printers, and distributors of illegal Jewish writings (in many cases, death) shows that, for the Germans, the speech of the Jewish resistance was not less to be feared than bullets fired by resistance fighters against the Wehrmacht.[40]

Believe the Unbelievable . . .

Is it possible to assess the impact of underground literature on the attitude of the Jewish population and on general knowledge concerning the death camps? Obviously no opinion poll elucidates the correspondence between the behavior of the Jews and the strategies advocated by the underground press. Nevertheless, the historian is entitled to call attention to this phenomenon. The press doubtless helped to make people strongly aware of the seriousness of their danger; otherwise, would so many Jews have risked "leaping" into the unknown, that is, into a clandestine existence? The failure of the great raid in July 1942 is a perfect illustration of this.

This problem has led to a debate on the subject of what was known and when about the gas chambers. Let us leave out the negationists, the former Nazi leaders, the neo-Nazis, and the friends of Pétain who "knew absolutely nothing" at the time and who still do not know today because they do not want to know.[41] What deserves consideration is the reaction of the deportees and the death camp survivors, who assert with sincerity that they had known nothing beforehand. It is true that no one could think in "pictures." Once the victims had arrived in Auschwitz or other camps and saw the smoking chimneys, abstract ideas passed into ugly reality, a revelatory shock. Anything they might have known was nothing in comparison with what they saw with their eyes.

Here is the entire difference between an unimaginable, abstract piece of information and its comparison with a perceived image, which, paradoxically, nevertheless remains "unbelievable." This reveals the immensity of the effort incumbent on current and future researchers but does not freeze their attention on this unspeakable crime and its perpetrators. It is true that the history of the Jewish people cannot be recounted without tears. However, it must not be "maudlin," in the words of Salo W. Baron. Has the time not arrived to restore to the millions of victims, by means of scientifically rigorous and documented research, their status as combatants who were vanquished during an entirely unequal combat? Through this research, we will serve historical truth and help new generations to conquer the trauma while keeping memory intact.

NOTES

1. Memorandum from "Judenreferent" for Jewish questions, Franz Radenmacher, to the Ministry of Foreign Affairs (AA, Section D III) dated March 24, 1942. Cited in Hans-Jürgen Döscher, *Das auswärtige Amt im Dritten Reich. Diplomatie im Schatten der "Endlösung"* (Berlin: Siedler, 1987), p. 213.

2. The sole publication authorized by the occupying nation, which was subjected to strict censorship, was the weekly (later monthly) *Les informations juives* publised by the UGIF (Union générales des Israélites de France). It encouraged obedience to anti-Jewish decrees.

3. This group of organizations was known in France by the initials MOI (Main d'oeuvre immigrée—section Juive [Immigrant labor—Jewish section]). The MOI was a federation of autonomous organizations having the character of the original nationalities, for example, Jews speaking Yiddish, Italians, Spaniards, Poles, Armenians, etc. It should be noted that the Parisian group, Hashomer Hatsair, had established close ties to the Union of Jeunesse Juive beginning in 1941 by taking part in the dissemination of secret literature and, later, in military activities.

4. The French-American historian, Zosa Szajkowski, estimates the number of Jewish publications in various languages between 1881 and 1940 to be 290, of which 163 were in Yiddish and 108 in French, 4 in Hebrew, 6 in Russian, and 1 in Judeo-Arabic, 1 in English, and 5 in German. Of the 108 French-language periodicals, 64 appeared beginning in 1923, while of the 163 Yiddish publications, 127 (thus more than 75%) also began publication in 1923. This phenomenon is explained by the arrival of masses of Central and Eastern European Jews. As for political orientation, 56 were Zionist (including 35 in French and 21 in Yiddish), 28 Communist, 9 Anarchist, 6 Socialist-Bundist, and 3 Trotskyite. All of the leftist and far-leftist newspapers were written in Yiddish. See Zosa Szajkowski, "Bibliography of the Jewish Press in France and the French Colonies," *The Jews in France*, ed. E. Cherikower (New York, 1942), pp. 236–302.

5. On November 11, 1942, German troops occupied all of France, thus putting an end to the "Free Zone."

6. Thus, for example, the Consistory would twice ask the Ministry of Information for permission to publish a "religious bulletin," but without success. To preserve its legal status permitting the exercise of religion, it abandoned all underground publication. René Meyer, an

influential member of the Consistory and major political figure who late became a minister under de Gaulle, condemned this position: "To save Judaism, it is first necessary to save the Jews."

7. The UJRE technical apparatus made possible these publications in a number of towns having high percentages of Jews in their population.

8. Only page 1 of the first issue has been found; see the facsimile in David Knout, *Contribution à l'histoire de la Résistance juive en France, 1940–1944* (Paris: Editions du Centre, 1947), p. 76.

9. Knout, *Contributions*, p. 142.

10. Ibid. (emphasis added).

11. Knout's idea of an armed formation would be implemented by Zionist revisionist militants (Jabotinsky supporters); paradoxically, they were joined by young Socialist Zionists, and the resulting small resistance group was called the Jewish Army.

12. The men, approximately four thousand in number, were interned on orders from the German Sicherheitsdienst in two camps near Orléans, one hundred kilometers from Paris. A year later, all were deported to death camps.

13. In the occupied zone, the Judenrat, under the name of the Coordination Committee, was established in December 1940. By decree of Pétain on November 29, 1941, it was called the Union générales des Israélites de France (UGIF) in all of France.

14. Published by Solidarity.

15. In his report of July 18, 1942, SS Obersturmführer Heinz Röthke, Eichmann's representative, assessed the result as insufficient: 12,884 persons arrested out of an estimated 29,000. He explained this by "the absence of the effect of surprise." His second observation concerns the "attitude of the French population, who, repeated instances, expressed pity with respect to the Jews arrested . . . particularly toward the children"; CDJC, xxvb–80.

16. *Unzer politik* was a document written in Yiddish and published by Solidarity in August 1942.

17. Pierre Laborie of the University of Toulouse–Le Mirail, known for his research on public opinion in 1940–1944, fully accepts our thesis that the "two turning points are concomitant and integral. Their effectiveness derives from their complementary nature." See Pierre Laborie, "1942 and the Fate of the Jews. What Turning Point Took Place in Opinion?" *Annales* 3 (May–June 1993): 666

18. Two other factors of lesser importance contributed to this result: 1) Berlin's concern not to rush the Vichy government, which was forced to deal with heavy pressure from the Church and public opinion; and 2) the weakened state of the French policy apparatus after Stalingrad, without which the Germans could not undertake massive raids.

19. "Report on Operations to Pick Up the Jews" from the regional Vichy office of the CGQJ (Commissariat général aux Questions Juives) in Toulouse, September 28, 1943 (YIVO Archives, New York).

20. Knochen ordered that the "Jews be tied together by their hands using a long rope." Instructions from Berlin recommended establishing a system of payments to informers for finding "Jews hidden or concealed, if we truly want the territory cleansed of Jews"; April 14, 1944, CDJC, xxxii–56.

21. Tract preserved at the Museum of the resistance in Champigny.

22. Tract signed "Committee for Defense, Region of Marseille," undated (CDJC, xxii–12).

23. Excerpted from *Récit des traitements infligés aux familles juives* (Paris, September 1942).

24. Personal memories of the author.

25. This information was sent to New York and London on August 8, 1942, in a coded telegram from the Consul of Great Britain in Switzerland, who also transmitted a copy to the president of the World Jewish Congress in New York, Rabbi Stephen Wise; interview with G. Riegner in A. Rayski, *Le choix des Juifs sous Vichy: Entre soumission et résistance* (Paris: La Découverte, 1992), pp. 174–75. (It is anticipated that an English-language edition of this book will appear in 1998.)

26. The paper added: "They deny separating women and children, they slander the French intellectual elite, they threaten the princes of the Church, who have sounded the voice of Christian conscience, by asserting that they have merely sent foreign Jews back to their native ghettos. . . ." The paper also denounced the lies the official papers put forth to deceive their readers.

27. Radio monitoring posts, which Solidarity and the MNCR had set up at several sites in Paris and Lyon, constituted the principal source of information. They were able to pick up broadcasts from the BBC (London), Radio Moscow, and Radio Algiers beginning in January 1943.

28. "Our group," wrote Ringelblum, "performed a great historic mission. It warned the world about our fate. . . . We have struck the enemy a fearful blow. We have revealed its satanic plan for exterminating Polish Jewry, a plan it wanted to carry out in silence. We have thwarted its calculations" (Emmanuel Ringelblum, *Chronique du Ghetto de Varsovie* [Paris: Robert Laffont, 1959], pp. 308–309).

29. *J'accuse*, no. 5, December 1942.

30. The *Quand Même* editorial staff sought to deceive the police by giving Geneva as the place of publication. The silence concerning the Zionist program was a part of the same, doubtless illusory course. The second issued proved the last, for the printer was soon arrested.

31. Personal memories of the author.

32. *Unzer Wort*, no. 58, June 15, 1943 (the issue cited belongs to A. Rayski).

33. This document is signed "The Jewish Communists."

34. This analysis has become widespread in the historiography of the uprisings in the Polish ghettos.

35. *Unzer Wort*, Lyon edition, June 1943. These profound and moving words belong to Haïm Sloves, a resistance fighter and editor of the UJRE secret press.

36. In 1994, the CRIF celebrated its fiftieth anniversary. See Rayski, *Le choix des Juifs sous Vichy*, pp. 329–45.

37. General Intelligence Reports (French Secret Police).

38. State Secretariat of War, Cabinet of the Minister, *Highly Secret*, Summary of the Civil Technical Inspections Service (Archives Nationales, Paris, A.G. II-461).

39. Summary Intelligence report, April 19, 1943.

40. Rudolf Zeiler was arrested on October 29, 1941, as he was printing "L'appel aux Juifs du monde entier" (Appeal to Jews throughout the world), which was broadcast over Radio Moscow. After being handed over to the Germans by French police, he was shot on December 19.

Abraham Trzebrucki, 58, was arrested on May 25, 1941, and sentenced on July 5 to five years in prison. On August 27, he appeared once again before the extraordinary court established by Vichy, which sentenced him to death and had him guillotined the next day—a "legal" crime!

Mounié Nadler, writer, poet, and editor of Yiddish newspapers, and Dr. Joseph Burstyn, editor of *J'accuse*, were shot on August 13, 1942.

David Kutner (real name Aron Skrobek) was arrested by French police and handed over to the Germans, who executed him with a bullet to the back of the head at the Stutthof camp, near Strasbourg, in July 1943.

41. During the Barbie trial, the public prosecutor, Pierre Truche, indirectly paid homage to the underground press when he spoke sharply to the accused: "Can Barbie claim that he was unaware of the fate reserved for those he deported, while London radio was already making these camps public and the secret press of the resistance also brought them to public attention?" See Stéphane Courtois and Adam Rayski, *Qui savait quoi? L'extermination des Juifs 1941–1945* (Paris: La Découverte, 1987).

44.

LIVIA ROTHKIRCHEN

Czech and Slovak Wartime Jewish Leadership

VARIANTS IN STRATEGY AND TACTICS

Standard works on Hitler's racial policy have firmly established that victory in the war and the annihilation of Europe's Jewry were parallel aims, the implication being that defensive projects of the Jewish leadership to foil the Final Solution were virtually doomed to failure. In retrospect, however, we may argue that since Nazi extermination policy depended to a certain measure on the fortunes of war, there existed an unknown coefficient—the "time" element. A second factor affecting the modus operandi of the Jewish Councils is the degree of dependence of the "satellite" states upon, and their readiness to cooperate with, Nazi Germany. The diverse sources presently available[1] permit us to assess the stance of the Jewish Councils and their conduct under a variety of conditions, and to differentiate between the countries occupied by Germany and those viewed as "satellites" (e.g., Slovakia, Romania, and Hungary).

The historiography of this subject generally deals with the Judenräte (the way the Nazis handled the Jewish Councils and the way the councils responded) in what may be called "geopolitical groupings." The ruses employed by the Nazi chieftains to deceive East European Jews about their destinations and fate differed in some respects from those employed with the equally doomed deportees from "Greater Germany" (the Altreich, the Ostmark, and the Protektorat). Many of these took the form of verbal obfuscation. As examples of the latter, note the sinister transforming references to "Teresienbad" for Terezín/Teresienstadt Ghetto. It was referred to variably as a "Sammellager" (assembly or even transit camp), as an "Altersghetto" (ghetto for the aged), as a "Prominentenghetto" (ghetto for privileged notables), as the "Musterghetto" (model ghetto), and as "der kleine Judenstaat" (the little Jewish state).[2]

This essay presents two paradigms sui generis discussing the diverse circumstances under which the Jewish communities functioned in 1) the Protectorate of Bohemia and Moravia[3] (which constituted part of the Reich), and 2) in "independent" Slovakia, established by the grace of the Führer under a clerical-fascist regime with an antisemitic agenda.[4]

From the very outset one of the main objectives of the Nazis in the Protectorate was "depriving the Czechs of their nationhood." One of the means for achieving this goal was strengthening the German ethnicity of Bohemia and Moravia through "Aryanization" of Jewish property. Nominally, the Czech president, Emil Hácha, remained in office, as did an "autonomous" Czech government whose acts were completely subordinate to the interests of the Reich. The Landräte—German administrative bodies in all regions and districts—together with the Gestapo quickly acquired control over the Czech administration in the provinces. During the deportations, these agencies were primarily responsible for "cleansing" the Jewish population; Czechs were, as a rule, assigned only minor roles as escorts for the transports and as guards at the assembly points and prisons.

As of July 1939, with the imposition of German jurisdiction over the Jews of the Protectorate, the Jewish Religious Congregation of Prague (JRC) became subject to the exclusive authority of the SS-supervised Central Office for Jewish Emigration (Zentralstelle für jüdische Auswanderung, later renamed Zentralamt für die Regelung der Judenfrage), an outpost of the Reich Security Main Office (RSHA).

In Bratislava, however, it was the Slovak government that executed anti-Jewish measures. Moreover, the Jewish Center (Ústredňa Židov, ÚŽ), set up in September 1940 according to Decree No. 234 of the Slovak Parliament, was under the control of the Central Economic Office (Ústredný Hospodársky Úrad, ÚHÚ), the Slovak equivalent of the Viennese and Prague Zentralstelle. Another body, the "Fourteenth Department" of the Ministry of the Interior, was established a year later to organize the wholesale deportation of the Jews. Eichmann's representative, SS-Hauptsturmführer Dieter Wisliceny, the Adviser for Jewish Affairs (Berater für jüdische Angelegenheiten) acted, as of September 1940, as an intermediary with the Slovak authorities.

For purposes of the present discussion, attempting to demonstrate the crucial impact of internal and external factors upon the strategy of the leadership and the parallel between the Czech and Slovak enclaves seems appropriate. Following the dismemberment of the republic, leaders of various factions of Jewry, both in Prague and Bratislava, joined forces in 1939 to establish united leaderships to struggle for the survival of the communities. This is especially evident in projects such as the organization of "escape routes" and other joint endeavors of Czech and Slovak Jews, mainly Zionist youth groups, tied by twenty years of fruitful cooperation. Secret couriers were dispatched via Bratislava to rescue organizations in Geneva, Istanbul, and Budapest, and in particular to Dr. Jaromír Kopecký, the Geneva representative of the Czechoslovak government-in-exile.

The Jewish Religious Congregation of Prague (ŽNO), 1939–1941

Prior to the Nazi onslaught, the Supreme Council of the Jewish Religious Congregations of Bohemia, Moravia, and Silesia acted as the guiding authority in religious and social spheres. Following the German occupation, the situation changed radically. With the promulgation of anti-Jewish measures, the burden of sustaining the pauperized population fell upon the leadership. Abandoned and isolated, with no avenue of appeal, the assimilationist Czech Jews and the Zionists came to an unwritten truce for a "common effort to save what still could be salvaged."

The development and rapid growth of the JRC have been described by a former representative:

> When the organization was built up in 1939 . . . community work was hardly held to be attractive. In 1939 people were primarily engaged in pursuit of self-preservation and consolidation of their own affairs, eventually with emigration. The organization [later] grew larger and was joined by a number of dedicated people, Zionists and their followers, as well as the activists of the Czech-Jewish Association Kapper.[5]

At this juncture the JRC was led by two assimilationists, Dr. Emil Kafka, the chairman, and Dr. František Weidmann, the secretary. After Kafka departed for London, Weidmann was appointed chairman by the Zentralstelle. Jacob Edelstein, the noted Zionist leader and director of the Palestine Office in Prague, became deputy chairman, assisted by Otto Zucker (for some years JRC chairman in Brno), Franz Kahn, and others. The expanded activities focused on three spheres: welfare, service to the Zentralstelle, and liquidation of Jewish assets. A phenomenon unparalleled elsewhere in occupied Europe was the participation of the intelligentsia on the staff of the JRC. Many of them were lawyers, the first group to be ousted from their positions and thus keen to offer their talents to the persecuted Jewish entity. It is an irony of fate that the elite of Czech Jewry, once regarded as the cream of European society, ultimately became the chroniclers of the community's tragedy.

As emigration became the central issue, the education department launched a large-scale vocational reorientation program to invest the prospective emigrés with new skills in agriculture, handicrafts, industrial arts, inn-keeping, and foreign languages. On November 24, 1939, the new bilingual community weekly *Jüdisches Nachrichtenblatt, Židovské Listy*, made its appearance. Although censored by the Gestapo, it was considered to be the only "free" newspaper available in Prague. (Jews were not permitted to subscribe to or purchase others.) It was edited by Dr. Oscar Singer (later chronicler of the Łódź ghetto), with a number of prominent journalists and public figures contributing regularly: the composer Karel Reiner; the poets Dr. Hanuš Bonn and Jiří Orten; the former editor of the *Berliner Börsenzeitung*, Emil Faktor; the cartoonist Fritz Taussig (Fritta), and others.

The first issue of the weekly announced that aside from emigration, education, and social assistance, youth care was to be the essential task: "Our youth is our future. . . . We have to bring them up so that even under the hardest living conditions we could steadily and courageously fulfill our mission: to preserve our nation."

The editorial in the last December issue, "The Meaning of Jewish Sacrifice" ("Vom Sinn der jüdischen Opfer"), indicated that the Jewish leaders were fully aware of the impending threat to their lives: "Jews in our times must offer their own personal sacrifice. This means not only yielding to the command of love your fellow man but is primarily prompted by the sober instinct of self-preservation." At the same time, a warning was issued to the public "to refrain from any action that might endanger the whole community."

It would not be an exaggeration to claim that, in the wake of the harrowing Nisko experience in October 1939,[6] JRC representatives were among the first to uncover the German intention to destroy the Jews, body and soul. Just prior to the October 1939 episode, the Gestapo in Moravská Ostrava had ordered the registration of the male Jewish population (ages seventeen to seventy) for a "retraining" camp (Umschulungslager). Jacob Edelstein and Richard Israel Friedmann (of the Vienna community) were ordered by Eichmann to "inspect" the Jewish colony to be created in Nisko, occupied Poland (near Lublin). They then traveled with a convoy of fifteen hundred men who, on arriving, were led to a muddy field and ordered to begin building living quarters, without materials or tools. During the first night, Polish gangs attacked the camp: twenty-one Jews were killed.[7]

Upon their return, the two JRC representatives told the German authorities that "no threat of punishment could prevail upon them to lend a hand to this kind of emigration, . . . to have [a] part in this horror."

In December 1939, while staying in Trieste, Edelstein reported his trials and tribulations to Jewish Agency officials Dr. Fritz Ullmann (Geneva) and Eliyahu Dobkin (Jerusalem). In February 1940, lecturing before the Zionist Convention at Geneva, he shocked his listeners with a shattering report about Nisko. Edelstein also confided to his close friends that he and his colleagues, when summoned to Nazi offices, had to endure "indignities, corporal punishments, beatings, and bodily harm." In the years 1939 and 1940, some of the leading figures of the JRC—Marie Schmolka, Hanna Steiner, Jacob Edelstein, Dr. František Friedmann, and Dr. Emil Kafka—were permitted to visit foreign countries. Apart from fund-raising, they were to conduct negotiations with organizations such as HICEM (which united three societies sponsoring Jewish emigration), ORT (Society for Handicrafts and Agricultural Work) and the American Joint Distribution Committee (JDC) to find venues for emigration. Eichmann and associates tried to exploit these trips for their own propaganda purposes.

In March 1941, together with Hans Günther, head of the Prague Zentralstelle, Edelstein and Friedmann were dispatched as envoys to convince the leaders of Dutch Jewry of the advantages inherent in cooperating with the Central Office about to be established in the Netherlands. According to Dutch sources, the "two gentlemen from Prague" acted courageously, using every opportunity to warn the leading members of the Amsterdam community. As Jacob Presser put it: "They sounded the alarm and prophesied, in detail, events that took place at a later date."[8]

Edelstein's missions in 1940–1941 took him to Budapest, Berlin, Upper Silesia, and Bratislava, inter alia, where he conferred with his friends and colleagues on emigration issues. In the summer of 1941, he visited the Łódź ghetto. One may assume that he shared the information gleaned from each of these countries.

The concept of "rescue through work" was espoused by a number of Judenräte: in Upper Silesia, Łódź Ghetto, Białystok Ghetto, Theresienstadt Ghetto, and in Slovakian labor camps. Isaiah Trunk, commenting on this "common strategy," suggested that this course of action might have been the result of views exchanged among members of the Judenräte, who were summoned by Eichmann to his Prague and Berlin offices from time to time.[9] The obvious rationale behind the approach was that the Reich needed Jewish workers to produce goods for the war effort.

Under a decree enacted by the Reich Protector on March 5, 1940, the JRC was given jurisdiction over all communities in the Protectorate and all individual Jews, including 12,680 Jews of "non-Mosaic" faith (i.e., nonpracticing Jews or converts to Christianity), the so-called "'B-Juden." The functions of the JRC were expanded and redefined to include collecting fees and taxes, aiding the needy, gathering statistical data, handling emigration, implementing the orders for forced labor, and assisting deportees. The onus placed on the JRC leadership and the sense of duty felt by those responsible is echoed in the community weekly: "The authority [to be] exercised by this body derives from the competence of the Zentralstelle. The very existence of such an authority is a new [phenomenon] in the history of the Jewish Diaspora. It is the profound wish and the firm hope of the governing body that this authority will be used solely for the benefit of the community." In order to cope with these new functions, a huge bureaucratic apparatus of thirty-two sections with a total of approximately 2,600 employees was established. With German approval, a special fund, endowed by affluent Jews who transferred funds from their personal bank accounts, was launched by Otto Zucker under the slogan "Give! Build! Live!" This made it possible for the JRC to care for needy members of the congregation. During the year 1940, the JRC provided over one million meals in its public kitchens to its pauperized members, five homes for the aged, two orphan asylums, and ten children's homes for a total of nine hundred childred. It ran two hospitals, a dispensary, and a home for the mentally ill. Similar institutions were run in two other major cities: Brno and Moravská Ostrava.

The Deportations (1941–1943)

Nazi Germany's attack on the Soviet Union on June 22, 1941, engendered a new stage in the solution of the Jewish problem. An order issued by Göring, addressed to Heydrich on July 31, 1941, spoke of a "total solution" (Gesamtlösung) to be implemented in all areas under German influence.

Early in September 1941, the JRC was ordered to prepare a statistical breakdown of the Jewish population of the Protectorate by age, labor capacity, family status, health, and the like. The population totaled 88,105 persons.

On September 27, 1941, SS-Obergruppenführer Reinhard Heydrich was appointed by Hitler as Acting Reich Protector, replacing Konstantin von Neurath. His task in Prague was guided by three principal aims: Germanization of the Protectorate, the wiping out of the Czech resistance, and the launching of the Final Solution—the wholesale deportation of the Jews.

In an effort to enlist full cooperation on the part of the JRC, SS officials tightened control, using intimidation to eliminate any obstruction. Prior to the mass deportation, Hanuš Bonn, head of the Emigration Department, and his deputy Erich Kafka were sent to, and subsequently killed at, Mauthausen. (Shortly afterwards, death notices were sent to the community.) The deportation orders were transmitted verbally to the JRC. The Zentralstelle compiled the name lists from the register and had the JRC notify the deportees by way of summons.

At the beginning of the deportations, the so-called Treuhandstelle, dubbed the "Krämer department," was established within the JRC. It employed several hundred skilled workmen to handle the property and valuables left behind and housed in former synagogues or on other Jewish premises. (Items from these stores were eventually smuggled into Terezín by JRC members officially charged with providing some supplies to the ghetto. Funds needed for this campaign came from several Jewish organizations abroad.)

On October 17, 1941, five thousand Jews were dispatched to Łódź; two other transports were sent to Minsk and Riga. The remaining Jews were to be concentrated in Terezín, the former garrison town in the Sudeten area (sixty kilometers northwest of Prague) which had a small number of easily removable inhabitants and could be sealed off and controlled with ready-made housing and barracks. Then, once their numbers had been considerably depleted, they would be sent "to the East."

The Jewish leaders (mainly Jacob Edelstein, Dr. František Friedmann, and Otto Zucker) toyed with the idea of locating the camp in the heart of overwhelmingly Czech populated areas, hoping this might offer a better chance to avert deportation to "the East." The Zentralstelle succeeded in temporarily "pacifying" the concerned leaders with the empty promise that no further deportations were planned from Theresienstadt. Considering the alternatives, Edelstein viewed this development as a "lesser evil." His entire theory of a "race against time" relied on the rescue of the younger generation through the establishment of a self-governing community, engaged in industrial production for the war effort. On November 24, 1941, the first Jewish work detail (Aufbaukommando) arrived at Terezín to prepare living quarters for the prospective inhabitants. The second transport included Edelstein himself and his associates from JRC, who were to constitute the Council of Elders in the ghetto.

Before deportation of the Jews from the provinces began on March 27, 1942, all Jewish religious congregations were dissolved. Each week, transports left for Terezín from Prague, Plzeň, Brno, and other cities. In Prague, under the guidance of Hanna Steiner, teams of pioneer youth group members and scouts assisted the elderly and the helpless to pack their belongings and carry them to the assembly point. By March 16, 1945, 73,608 persons had been dispatched to Theresienstadt (of these, 60,399 were later sent to Auschwitz and other extermination camps).

Upon the initiative of Dr. Karel Stein,[10] who was in charge of the JRC provincial communities, an appeal was submitted to the Zentralstelle to collect historically valuable materials (books, ritual objects, and artifacts) from the vacated communities and to store them on Prague community premises. The SS gave their consent to this scheme, planning to use the collection after the war for a museum of the "extinct Jewish race."

On January 28, 1943, the tenth anniversary of the Third Reich, the Jewish Religious Congregation of Prague, along with its counterparts in Berlin and Vienna, was abolished and replaced by the "Council of Elders" (Ältestenrat der Juden, Židovská rada starších). The outgoing leading officials—Dr. Weidmann, Dr. Franz Kahn, and Richard Israel Friedmann—were deported to Terezín, whence they were later sent to their deaths in Auschwitz. (Weidmann was singled out for "special treatment" and savagely beaten by an SS man at the Bohušovice station before he could even board the train.)

The term of the new heads of the Council of Elders, Salo Krämer and his deputy Herbert Langer, was short-lived. They were replaced (in July 1943) by Dr. František Friedmann and his deputy Erich Kraus, who were to remain in office until the end of the war. The reduced staff of the Council of Elders consisted of officials protected by "Aryan" family ties (arisch versippt); similarly, those individuals left in Prague included Jewish partners in mixed marriages and 1,081 "disputable cases," persons under arrest or in hiding.

Toward the end of 1942, direct contact had been established between the JRC and the newly created, Istanbul-based Rescue Committee of the Jewish Agency, which offered assistance on behalf of the Yishuv in Palestine. Until that time, sporadic messages from the Protectorate were passed to Geneva through the mediation of the Bratislava Working Group and occasionally via Budapest. Two leading figures of the heHalutz organization at the JRC, Lazar Moldovan and Heinz Schuster, were approached by Rudi Schulz, a Gestapo agent (in reality an anti-Nazi), who volunteered for this task and functioned under various aliases. On his subsequent visits to Prague, Schulz forwarded money sent by the Rescue Committee to Moldovan and Schuster; it was slated for the maintenance of Terezín (the money was indeed used to buy food for the ghetto). From an exchange of coded letters, it transpires that one of the aims was to encourage the people behind the bars. "Those fighting for freedom are coming closer to you," reads a message of May 1943. In July, following the deportation of Moldovan and Schuster to Terezín, the contact was again disrupted. In spring 1944, however, the contact resumed during the secret negotiations between the Budapest Vaadah and the SS over the "blood for trucks" deal.

Though acknowledging that some of them "demonstrated the virtues of goodwill and self-sacrifice,"[11] H. G. Adler—the great authority on Theresienstadt— criticizes JRC members for not having disbanded the communities or destroyed the registers and documents. In Adler's view, it was this "failure to act" that led to "terrible entanglement and, ultimately, to ruin." There is evidence that some members of the Council of Elders fully realized that they were being used as tools to carry out the design of the enemy—in Hilberg's words: "being a conduit for orders of the perpetrators."[12] Yet, the question remains: What was their motive in remaining at the helm? Could they have acted differently? In 1980 Erich Kraus, reminiscing about the issue of resignation, wrote:

> Every individual had in the back of his mind [the question of whether to resign his post] whenever a serious decision had to be made: . . . On certain occasions, it was also considered to act collectively. However, it always transpired that this would be a pathetic, unrealistic gesture that could neither slow down developments nor reverse their occurrence. In a certain way the establishment of Terezín and the departure (by Edelstein and the Aufbaukommando) was a quasi act of resignation.[13]

It is important to distinguish between the two different periods. During the first, 1939–1941, while under constant threat and intimidation (suffering indignities and corporal punishment), JRC leaders were still active in various spheres, alleviating the plight of the community as a whole and enabling over twenty-seven thousand to emigrate overseas. All energy was vested in winning concessions, seeking ways to overcome the chaos and misery that engulfed the community.

The situation changed radically during the second stage, 1942–1945, when, in the shadow of incessant arrests, deportation and terror, the leadership was reduced to total compliance. During this period, after all avenues of hope had been closed, they concentrated on salvaging the "precious legacy" of their Jewish heritage, earning them lasting acclaim.

The turn of the tides of war and the approach of the Red Army spurred the Nazis to send off the remaining Jews to Terezín. The tragic circumstances of the last transports are portrayed in a unique report of February 9, 1945, written by Dr. František Friedmann on behalf of the Council of Elders of Prague to SS-Obersturmführer Girczik of the Zentralamt. It pertains to Jewish partners of mixed marriages, the last transport to Terezín. The first part of the report (following standard police briefing formulas) sums up the previous dispatches (January 31 and February 4): the boarding of the train, the number of deportees, the technical difficulties, "discipline," and "mood."[14] The closing paragraph, however, deviates from routine content and wording. Friedmann speaks clearly of the difficulties anticipated during the impending transport of 913 men in two days, on the night of February 11 (during which Council members ordered to assist at the railway station were themselves to be transported). The main problem, however, revolved around the order to transport small "Jewish" children of "Aryan" mothers. The youngsters were to be deported with their Jewish fathers, already separated from their families for more than two years, and complete strangers to their children. All this, Friedmann states, led to panic, hysterical outbursts, and incidents of suicide. The Council was stormed by desperate mothers pleading for their children. Although the closing acknowledges that whatever the difficulties, the transport would be carried out as ordered (ordnungsgemäss abgewickelt), it is the foregoing sentence that stands out as the most stirring "j'accuse." Friedmann bluntly told the Germans: "It is humanly impossible (menschlich unmöglich) to make [the mothers] grasp that such a [Draconian] order had in fact been handed down."

Retropsectively, Erich Kraus observed that "the sheer existence of ŽNO, or ŽRS after 1943, created [sorely needed] venues for self-help—a place to meet and exchange information without being endangered . . . as well as to overcome the total solitude." Karel Poláček, the foremost Czech-Jewish humorist, in a macabre comment explaining the raison d'être of these institutions, made a similar point. While taking inventory of the libraries, he commuted between the various localities and was well acquainted with prevailing circumstances. In a letter of March 21, 1943, Poláček wrote (from Olomouc) to his wife in Prague: "Here I am sitting in the community offices, which are open here, as everywhere, on Sundays: the k'hillah and the cemetery are the only available places of rendezvous left for the Jewish intelligentsia."[15]

Kraus also addressed the "critics and moralists" who deal with this issue today in total disregard of the 1940s' context:

> Perhaps nowadays, in times of [violent] terrorist organizations and hijackings, the situation under which the Jewish organizations functioned and negotiated could be perceived with more insight. How [our] people, bare-handed and totally stripped of their basic rights, were exposed to the wanton despotism of sadists competing among themselves in the exercise of cruelty. The leaders themselves were, in addition, responsible for all the actions undertaken on behalf of the community, without having any chance of appeal, reasoning, or defence. It was not a time for heroic gestures and exalted deeds.[16]

The Dual Role of the Jewish Center in Slovakia

"Independent" Slovakia, established on March 14, 1939, was a clerical state par excellence—a nation of profound Catholic tradition. Approximately 80 percent of Slovaks were Catholics, 14 percent belonged to Protestant denominations. Hence, the Catholic clergy played a significant role in the political life of the state. Dr. Tiso, himself a priest, was the president and leader of the HSĽS, Hlinkova slovenská ľudová strana (Hlinka's Slovak People's Party). (The Apostolic Delegate during the crucial years of the war was Msgr. Giuseppe Burzio, who provided the Vatican with the earliest information on the Nazi extermination policy.) According to the census that took place in Slovakia on December 15, 1940, following the cession of territory to Hungary, the number of Jews dropped to 88,951, that is, to 3.3 percent of the entire population (2,653,654).

Shortly after the Salzburg meeting convened by Hitler on July 28, 1940 (during which the Slovak leaders promised to form a National Socialist regime), a radical change occurred in the situation of the Jews. Two institutions were established whose objective was the solution of the "Jewish problem" in Slovakia.

The Central Economic Office, ÚHÚ, attached to the prime minister's office, was given complete authority to oust Jews from economic and social life and to transfer their property to Aryans, as well as to deprive Jews of basic civil rights and restrict their freedom of movement. As of September 1940, the ÚŽ, or Jewish Center, was the only authority to represent the Jews of Slovakia and to organize their life and thus to transmit the orders of ÚHÚ to the Jews.[17] The ÚHÚ appointed as head of the ÚŽ a Jewish Elder (starosta), Heinrich Schwartz, former head of the Orthodox Community, along with a board of ten functionaries (the Praesidium). The Bratislava headquarters remained in the communal building, located in the center of the city. Branch offices were set up in seven major district towns throughout the country. Several important functions were filled by public figures and leaders of Zionist organizations. Financial resources were derived from the property seized from liquidated Jewish organizations and from taxes imposed on all Jews. The year 1940 saw full "Aryanization" and the total elimination of Jews from social and public life.

Initially the so-called Jewish Central Bureau for the Region of Slovakia (ŽÚÚ, Židovská ústredná uradovňa pre krajinu Slovenska) retained the image of a "philanthropic" institution. Its activity centered on social aid, vocational training, and emigration. Under the pretext of vocational training, all activities of the disbanded Zionist organizations were concentrated in the section for vocational aid. The program not only taught various skills but organized summer camps where the teaching of Hebrew had priority. The courses were also attended by groups of "halutzim," who had escaped from Poland and, after vocational training in Slovakia, had made their way to Palestine.

The anti-Jewish measures introduced in Slovakia beginning in the fall of 1939 were still based on principles of religion. The so-called "Jewish Code" (Židovský Kodex), No. 198/1941, enacted on September 9, 1941, was patterned on the Nuremberg Laws. However, it deviated from the standard model: the president of the Slovak state was authorized to exempt converts and certain other privileged individuals from anti-Jewish legislation. Another article of the Code granted "immunity" to a stratum of skilled professionals (engineers, financial experts, economists, physicians, etc.) who were considered vital to the economy. As a result, these individuals and their families were granted special certificates by various government offices and could thus pursue their professions until fall 1944. Their presence provided the Jewish leadership with an infrastructure helpful in their clandestine and official contacts.

The head of the ÚŽ, Heinrich Schwartz, was arrested on charges of "sabotage" (hindering relocation of Jews from Bratislava to other cities, mainly in eastern Slovakia) in April 1941. Community officials managed his escape to Hungary, where he died in 1943 as a result of injuries suffered during his imprisonment.

The next ÚŽ head appointed by the authorities was Arpád Sebestyén, an "obedient" high school principal with no prior experience in public affairs. The ÚŽ came under the control of Karol Hochberg, head of the Department for Special Tasks, which was created upon Wisliceny's initiative to conduct the "relocation campaign." Hochberg, an opportunist, carried out Wisliceny's orders with alacrity, thereby arousing much apprehension and ill-feeling among the Jewish public.

Sebestyén's term (April 1941 to December 1943) spanned the most fateful period—that of the implementation of the Jewish Code and the deportation of two-thirds of the Jewish population to extermination camps. (Between March and October 1942, 60,000 Jews were sent to Auschwitz or the Lublin area.) The helplessness and submissiveness of the official leadership led, in the summer of 1942, to the formation of the underground Working Group (Pracovná skupina), without parallel in other countries.

The crucial period after the Wannsee Conference—which saw the Slovak initiative to rid the country of its Jewish population, the German-Slovak negotiations over the deportations, and the appeals of the federation of the Jewish communities and rabbis of Slovakia to the Slovak priest-president Tiso, the Vatican, and church dignitaries to thwart the deportations—has been widely discussed in the historiography of the period. The exchange of diplomatic notes between Bratislava and the Vatican, and the demarche presented in February 1942 by Apostolic Delegate Msgr. Burzio to Prime Minister Tuka declaring the intentions of the Slovak government both "inhumane and contrary to Christian principles . . . for the Nazis are sending the Jews to 'certain death' (morte sicura)," have been published in full. (The Vatican's blunt protests against the deportation of Slovak Jews were prompted mainly by awareness that the moral prestige of the entire Catholic Church and its clergy was at stake.)[18]

We shall note here only briefly the inertia and total disregard that characterized the "neutral" stance adopted by the International Committee of the Red Cross (ICRC) in Geneva. New insight into this area was provided when documents, kept until the late 1980s under lock and key by that institution, were finally made accessible to Jean-Claude Favez.[19] It appears that the first alarm signaling that Auschwitz was the destination of the Slovak deportees reached the ICRC from Bratislava (from ÚŽ sources) as early as March or April 1942. On June 9, 1942, the representative of the Slovak Red Cross implored the ICRC to act promptly on behalf of the deportees, stressing that the name list was available at the Jewish Center in Bratislava but adding that "he himself [was] unable to do a thing in this matter." His "moving" appeal "put the ICRC staff into an uneasy position." A month later the Slovak official was coolly reprimanded by Geneva and duly instructed that, in view of the special relationship that existed between Slovakia and the Third Reich, it would be advisable to address the appeals directly to the German authorities.

> You are requesting the ICRC take up the care of these persons, but we have to call your attention to the fact that it is difficult for us to intervene in the sense that you desire. In effect, our role is normally that of a neutral intermediary between two or more belligerents, whereas in the present case, it seems possible for direct contacts to be entered into by the concerned authorities, Slovak and German.[20]

Slovakia, with its numerically insignificant community, occupies a special place on the map of Nazi genocide. Particularly intriguing to historians is the halt in the mass deportations to the death camps between October 1942 and September 1944.[21] Three major factors combined to generate this change: 1) the activities of the clandestine Working Group and its effective contacts with Jewish organizations in the free world and with highly placed Slovak officials; 2) the intervention of the Vatican; and 3) the shift in the local population's attitudes under the impact of the situation at the front.

The Working Group

Also called the "shadow cabinet," the Working Group came into existence in the summer of 1942 as a response to the deportations. Its members, representing the entire spectrum of Jewry, united in a combined effort to save the remnants of the Jewish population in Slovakia and eventually in other Nazi-occupied countries. The active core was composed of Zionists, rabbis, and assimilated Jews: Gisi Fleischmann, Rabbi Michael Dov Weissmandl, Rabbi Armin Frieder, Andrej Steiner, Dr. Tibor Kovacs, and others, some of whom simultaneously acted as members of the ÚŽ. They had staked their hopes on receiving financial assistance from Jewish organizations abroad (the JDC, the Jewish Agency, the World Jewish Congress) with whom they maintained correspondence through the mediation of Nathan Schwalb, the Palestine heHalutz emissary at Geneva. The Working Group cooperated closely with the Budapest-based Committee of Relief and Rescue (Va'ad ha'Ezra ve-haHatzala), which, until March 1944, enjoyed relative freedom.

As a first move, they tried to prevent further transports by bribing the officials responsible both on the Slovak side (Dr. Anton Vašek, head of Department XIV) and on the German side (Hauptsturmführer Wisliceny). The latter was subsequently persuaded to act as a mediator between the Working Group and the SS-chieftains in a project to save the Jewish remnant in Nazi-occupied Europe by payment of ransom. This became known as the "Europa Plan."

Members of the Working Group succeeded in obtaining the support of several Slovak personalities. First and foremost was Jozef Sivák, Minister of Education and Culture, who kept them regularly informed on matters pertaining to the Jewish Question as discussed at cabinet meetings. They succeeded in keeping track of the first Slovak deportees and, through non-Jewish couriers hired for this purpose, smuggled food, clothing, and valuables to various ghettos in Poland. The "headquarters" (Gisi Fleischmann's office) gradually evolved into an "information bureau," processing a constant stream of news from across the border to be disseminated to the outside world. In letters and reports written in special cipher-employing code words in Yiddish and Hebrew, which were transmitted by special messengers and by means of clandestine diplomatic pouches, they unmasked the systematic mass murder in the death camps. They regularly reported on the situation of the Jews of the Protectorate, the Terezín Ghetto, and the fate of the deportees from Austria and Belgium. Attached to their reports were warnings to the Jewish leadership to act immediately, "for time is running out."[22]

By fall 1942, the Working Group was in possession of a detailed account by the first fugitive to make his way back to Slovakia, aided by Polish and Slovak peasants and smugglers, from the Lublin-Majdanek death camp. In early 1943, they also managed to transmit to the free world testimonies on Sobibor, Majdanek, and Treblinka. In May 1944, the now famous Auschwitz Protocols were composed. The Auschwitz Protocols were the first authentic testimony on the annihilation process as described by two Slovak-Jewish escapees, Rudolf Rosenberg-Vrba and Alfred Wetzler, who reached Slovakia on April 24, 1944. The Protocols were dispatched by a special courier of the Slovak resistance to Jaromír Kopecký in Geneva, who transmitted them to the U.S. State Department.

The Vatican

In February 1943, following Interior Minister Šaňo Mach's threat to renew the deportations, a fierce campaign of protest was launched by the Working Group to divert the new peril. The struggle was waged on several levels. The Istanbul-based Jewish Agency Rescue Committee brought the Working Group's alarming appeal to the knowledge of the Papal Nuncio, Msgr. Angelo Roncalli (later Pope John XXIII). The latter's energetic intervention with the Vatican, together with the steps taken by Msgr. Guiseppe Burzio, the Apostolic Delegate at Bratislava, bore fruit. In a note of May 5, 1943, the Holy See intervened in vigorous terms. This time the Slovak government's answer was not long in coming. It stated that in the future "only such Jews would be deported as endangered the state." All Jews who did not participate in the economic process, however, would be concentrated in labor camps set up in Slovakia proper, the rest, that is, those granted certificates of exemption of one sort or another, "could work in their professions without interference and would not be disturbed in their private lives."

The Vatican's firm stand undoubtedly influenced the Slovak Catholic clergy in general and the hierarchy in particular. This change of attitude is even more striking in light of the posture adopted by some of the highest church dignitaries, who lent Tiso qualified support in early 1942. On March 21, 1943, a pastoral letter signed by the bishops was read from the pulpits of all Slovak churches, referring to the lamentable fate of thousands of innocent fellow citizens, "due to no guilt on their part but purely as a result of their descent or nationality."

Throughout 1943 the group concentrated its efforts on providing escape routes for survivors of the Polish ghettos, particularly in the vicinity of Bochnia and nearby Kraków, sending them via Hungary and Turkey to Palestine. (Escape to Slovakia was made possible and preferable by common frontiers bordering on both the General Government, where the Final Solution was carried out, and Hungary, which served as a haven for refugees until the spring of 1944.)[23]

During the "quiet years," the Working Group spared no effort to protect the remaining Jews in the country through a "work strategy." Part of the money received for rescue purposes from the JDC in Switzerland was directed toward satisfying the authorities by increasing productivity in the labor camps of Vyhne, Nováky, and Sered. Some 130 workshops manned by skilled workers were producing textiles, furniture, toys, and chemical products. Other teams were engaged in drainage work and building projects outside the camps. Reich Ambassador Ludin, reporting on developments in Slovakia in the summer of 1943, made a point of referring to these camps as "production centers" and to the fact that the workers enjoyed "far-reaching freedom."[24]

Attitude of the Local Population

While the Slovak public learned about mobile killing units in the occupied Soviet territories from hearsay (occasional reports by soldiers on leave), the higher echelons were briefed officially and in detail on the Nazi extermination policy. Thus Gen. Jozef Turanec told President Tiso in early January 1942 about the tragic fate of Jewish women and their children who were working in the field kitchens of Slovak officers.[25]

In the spring of 1942 Slovaks witnessed daily scenes of mass deportation carried out by the Hlinka Guard and the ethnic German Freiwillige Schutzstaffeln (FS). The cruelty of herding the aged, the sick, and children into railway cattle cars going "east" evoked sympathy. Accordingly, Ludin found it pertinent to report to the German Foreign Ministry in June 1942 that the "deportations became unpopular in large circles of the population."[26]

We should, of course, remember that the most vociferous protests against the deportation came after the German debacle at Stalingrad and the change in the political climate created by the turn of the tides of the war: heavy Slovak losses on the Eastern front and the great number of Slovak soldiers defecting to the Soviets affected many families. The war came close to the borders, and apart from its proximity, Slavophilism and ideological affinity were also at work. Propaganda broadcast by the BBC and the Moscow-based Czechoslovak exile headquarters contributed greatly. Foremost Slovak leaders and highly placed officials began to doubt German victory and think differently about the future of the Slovak Republic. This change was reflected in the increasing number of Slovak citizens willing to come to the aid of Jews.

From January 1944 to September 1944, ÚŽ was headed by Dr. Yirmiyahu (Oscar) Neumann, former chairman of the Zionist Federation in Slovakia and one of the leaders of the Working Group.[27] The fate of the remaining Jews was sealed in September 1944 following suppression of the Slovak National Uprising: Jews were accused of acting as ringleaders. The deportations were renewed and carried out with great efficiency by the German army, aided by storm troopers of the Hlinka Guard. The offices of ÚŽ were closed down, and the last transport from Sered to Terezín left on March 30, 1945.

The Ransom Project

The Europa Plan sheds new light on the moral dilemma that confronted the Jewish leadership in Nazi-occupied Europe and in the free world.[28] It also affords insight into the double-dealing of Reichsführer-SS Heinrich Himmler, the policies of the Allies, and the attitude of the Vatican.

Except for a report written by Dieter Wisliceny in the Bratislava district prison on November 18, 1946, while awaiting trial as a war criminal,[29] only two documents emanating from German sources mention the ransom plan. One, dated November 24, 1942, addressed to Himmler and signed by SS-Gruppenführer Heinrich Müller of the RSHA, refers to a proposal to sell emigration permits to wealthy Slovak Jews, a scheme already in practice in Holland.[30] The aim was to acquire foreign currency to recruit volunteers for Waffen-SS units among ethnic Germans in Hungary. The other document is a memorandum written in December 1942 and signed by Himmler: "I have asked the Führer about the ransoming of Jews in return for hard currency. He has authorized me to approve such cases, provided they bring in genuinely substantial sums from abroad."[31] The dates of these crucial documents coincide with the launching of the Europa Plan and prove that the idea of a ransom scheme was endorsed by the Führer himself.

Previous research on the subject was based primarily on Jewish sources, that is, documentary accounts of the activities of the Working Group, memoirs of some of the dramatis personae, and, most importantly, the Wisliceny report. A minutely detailed account of the Europa Plan and its implications appears in Rabbi Weissmandl's book *Min HaMetzar* (Out of the depths), which includes various documents, the author's own soul-searchings, and some very subjective notes, all informed by the naive assumptions stemming from Weissmandl's blind faith in the ransom scheme.[32] A painstaking chapter on the negotiations between the Working Group and Wisliceny in Yehuda Bauer's *American Jewry and the Holocaust* is written from the vantage point of the JDC's Geneva office, headed by Saly Mayer.[33] A more recent study by the same author deals globally with Nazi-Jewish negotiations.[34]

During the fall of 1942 the Working Group decided that the time had come to proceed from its "Little Plan" for the ransom of Slovak Jews to a "Big Plan" to purchase the lives of all Jews still surviving in the Nazi empire. The big plan called for a ransom payment to "Willy" (Wisliceny) amounting to $2,000,000. The Working Group clung to the hope that it would be possible to raise the needed funds from the JDC, the Jews of Hungary, and also partly from Jews in Slovakia.

Wisliceny is the key figure in the story because it is mainly through his testimony that the whole episode can be authenticated and examined from the German point of view and, thus, the direct involvement of Heinrich Himmler himself ascertained. Wisliceny's *Bericht* contains a wealth of first-hand information. However, the authenticity and historical value of this report are marred by chronological inconsistencies, obviously contrived by Wisliceny to exonerate himself by proving that he had not known about the Final Solution until August 1942.

Saly Mayer's suggestion that the ransom money should not be turned over directly to the Germans but deposited in blocked accounts in the name of the SS leaders at banks in Switzerland until the end of the war elicited harsh criticism in Bratislava. In their desperation, the Working Group could not grasp the stringent Allied currency regulations forbidding the transfer of money to enemy countries for any purpose.[35]

In the end, however, the big plan came to naught. In February 1943, Wisliceny was transferred to Greece to organize the deportation of Jews from Salonica and Macedonia. Yet he made numerous visits to Bratislava and used these occasions to feed the Working Group lies and dubious reports about the plan's progress. Finally, on September 3, 1943, he informed them that he had received personal orders from Himmler to suspend the negotiations because the "general atmosphere was not conducive." On subsequent visits, however, Wisliceny claimed that the Jews had missed a great opportunity by not producing the ransom in time. On the other hand, in his report he placed the blame on Adolf Eichmann.

Our assumption, however, is that Himmler's supposed order to suspend negotiations was caused by a dramatic event that occurred at about the same time: the arrest of Carl Langbehn, Himmler's contact man with the German anti-Nazi resistance, at the Swiss border early in September 1943. The dates of Langbehn's activities (October 1942–September 1943) coincide with the negotiations over the Europa Plan and are, therefore, of primary importance.

The question of whether Himmler's consent to negotiations with the Bratislava Working Group was meant to serve pari passu as an opening for separate peace overtures with the Western Allies remains unanswered. One of the riddles, undoubtedly, is the financial aspect of this "deal." Compared to the enormous amount extracted from applicants in Holland (100,000 Swiss francs per person), the paltry $2,000,000 offered for about one million Jews, only $2 per person, seems most unrealistic.

The second major Nazi objective in negotiating for the ransom of Jews was one of propaganda. The negotiations were intended to influence world opinion in favor of the Germans, to "appease" the Jewish organizations in the free world, and to refute "rumors" circulating in diplomatic circles and in the world press. Perhaps all these considerations were part and parcel of the "hide and seek" tactics in the peace feelers Himmler put out in 1942–1943. Langbehn's arrest in September 1943 ran parallel to Himmler's decision to suspend negotiations with the underground Jewish leadership in Bratislava.

Some of the letters sent abroad by Rabbi Weissmandl allude to changes in the approach of the Nazi chieftains in 1944. Thus we learn of new practices employed by the Nazis in the Czech family camp at Auschwitz-Birkenau: "We were also told that some few thousand inmates were sent off from Theresienstadt to be shipped abroad later; they are not being exterminated there but are waiting there, pending the results of the negotiations."[36]

But neither the turning of the tide in the war, nor the strenuous efforts in 1943 toward a negotiated peace put a halt to implementation of the Final Solution. On the contrary, there is abundant evidence that Himmler himself was anxious to speed it up. Yet, at the same time, he pursued a two-pronged policy.

By spring 1944 (when the so-called "blood for trucks" negotiations were on the agenda in Budapest) Weissmandl had lost some of his former trust in Wisliceny.[37] He now proposed to deal with the SS-chiefs on two distinct levels: "Possibly, even almost certainly, all this is a plot, a maneuver, a gesture of camouflage which they have undertaken *to win our confidence, to undermine our already meager and paltry power to resist them*" (emphasis added). To this end, Weissmandl addressed a letter, dated May 16, 1944, to Jewish organizations abroad, urging them to demand that the Allies bomb the railroad lines leading from Hungary to Auschwitz, thereby stopping the deportation of Jews to the death camp.

It may be assumed that the two-year "gap" was partly the result of the protracted dealings over the nebulous Europa Plan (though Wisliceny kept referring to German "désinteressement"). It nevertheless afforded the Working Group a respite that was used for a wide range of rescue operations. At the same time, the "quiet years" enabled a large number of Jews to go into hiding and thus escape the wave of deportations in the fall of 1944.

Conclusion

In the final analysis, the relentless efforts of the Bratislava Working Group yielded positive results in several areas. However, it is doubtful whether this clandestine organization would have been able to pursue its campaign of alerting the free world and conducting its multifarious activities without the official status as members of the ÚŽ.

The Jewish Center is but one facet of the complex phenomenon of the Jewish Councils. Nevertheless, its experience serves to prove that even under relatively "optimal" conditions, there remained no serious alternative to dilatory tactics in anticipation of the imminent end of the war. Paradoxically, it also permits us to view with greater understanding the constraints that limited the activities of the Council of Jewish Elders in the Protectorate. And finally, the tragic role of this institution defies any facile generalization for, to speak with Ernest Renan, "La vérité est dans les nuances" (truth lies in the nuances).

Note on Historiography

In marked contrast with the corpus of scholarly works on Slovakia, in particular on the Jewish leadership there, there is a paucity of research on the Protectorate. One reason is that the leading personalities of the Jewish Community (Edelstein, Weidmann, Zucker, Kahn, and others) perished at the hands of the Nazis, leaving no personal testimony. Fortunately, the majority of Slovak Jewish leaders survived the war, and thus, aside from the plethora of correspondence clandestinely forwarded to the free world, they were able to write down their reminiscences. The only records by former members of the Jewish Council in Czech lands are Dr. Karel Stein's recorded testimony and the diary of the martyred Egon Redlich (discovered by chance in 1967 and published posthumously), which, however, deals solely with his experiences in Theresienstadt. A modest but most welcome addition, therefore, is Erich Kraus's "Observations," written in 1980 in response to my discussion of the Council of Jewish Elders in Prague.

Most of the research conducted on Czechoslovak Jewry before 1989 has been done in the United States, Israel, and Germany. The main reason for this is the political development of Czechoslovakia after the communist takeover in 1948, and the subsequent subservience to Marxist-Leninist ideological concepts.[38] One of the results was that the Jewish Holocaust was virtually ignored.

A different line has been adopted with regard to the issue of Terezín, most probably due to the international character of this camp, which lent itself to propaganda purposes, especially in the mid-1970s (following the UN Resolution equating

Zionism with racism). The conduct of the Jewish leadership became the central theme of a slander campaign denigrating Jewish martyrdom and vilifying Zionism. Under the slogan "Collaboration of the Jewish Elders with the Nazi Chieftains," the former were accused of, among other things, sacrificing the masses of the population "in order to save their own skins." As of the 1989 "Velvet Revolution," Holocaust literature in the Czech Republic has been enriched by a massive output of diaries and memoirs of survivors, as well as conference papers, adding new vistas of the positive stance of the Jewish leadership.[39]

NOTES

1. On the "blank spots" in research, see my conference paper "Brennende Fragen der Historiographie von Theresienstadt," in *Theresienstadt in der Endlösung der Judenfrage,* ed. Miroslav Kárný, Vojtěch Blodig, and Margita Kárná (Prague: Panorama, 1992), pp. 41–50; see also the note on histography at the end of this essay.

2. Livia Rothkirchen, "The Zionist Character of the 'Self-Government' of Terezín (Theresienstadt): A Study of Historiography," *Yad Vashem Studies* 11 (1976): pp. 56–90; Ruth Bondy, *"Elder of the Jews": Jakob Edelstein of Theresienstadt* (New York: Grove Press, 1989).

3. For the background, see Avigdor Dagan, ed., *The Jews of Czechoslovakia* (Philadelphia: Jewish Publication Society, 1984).

4. Livia Rothkirchen, *The Destruction of Slovak Jewry: A Documentary History* (Jerusalem: Yad Vashem, 1961); Yeshayahu Jelinek, *The Parish Republic: Hlinka's Slovak People's Party 1939–45* (Boulder, CO, 1976).

5. Erich Kraus, "Observations" on the manuscript of my discussion of the role of the Prague JRC and Council of Elders, p. 7.

6. See Seev Goshen, "Eichmann und die Nisko-Aktion in Oktober 1939. Eine Fallstudie zur NS-Judenpolitik in der letzten Etappe vor der 'Endlösung,'" *Vierteljahrshefte für Zeitgeschichte* 29 (1981): 74–96.

7. Moshe Shertok (Sharett), entry of February 2, 1940; see Rothkirchen, "Zionist Character," pp. 67–70.

8. Jacob Presser, *Ashes in the Wind: The Destruction of Dutch Jewry* (London: Souvenir Press, 1968), pp. 343–46.

9. Isaiah Trunk, "Discussion," in *Imposed Jewish Governing Bodies under Nazi Rule*, YIVO Colloquium, December 2–5, 1967 (New York: YIVO Institute for Jewish Research, 1972), p. 83.

10. "Die Juden zur Zeit des Protektorates in Böhmen und Mähren-Schlesien," unpublished manuscript, recorded by Friedrich Thieberger after a series of interviews with Dr. Karel Stein, after the war.

11. H. G. Adler, *Theresienstadt 1941–1945, Das Antlitz einer Zwangsgemeinschaft* (Tübingen: J. C. B. Mohr, 1960), pp. 19–20.

12. Raul Hilberg, "The Judenrat: Conscious or Unconscious Tool," in *Patterns of Jewish Leadership in Nazi Europe 1933–1944: Proceedings of the Third Yad Vashem International Historical Conference, April 1977,* ed. Yisrael Gutman and Cynthia J. Haft (Jerusalem: Yad Vashem, 1979), p. 39.

13. Kraus, "Observations," p. 10.

14. Report addressed to the Central Office for the Solution of the Jewish Question, Yad Vashem Archives, YVA, 0–64.

15. Karel Poláček, *Poslední dopisy Doře,* ed. Martin Jelinowicz (Toronto: Sixty-Eight Publishers, 1984), p. 44.

16. Kraus, "Observations," p. 8.

17. See Livia Rothkirchen, "The Dual Role of the 'Jewish Center' in Slovakia," in *Patterns of Jewish Leadership*, pp. 219–27.

18. For the role of the Vatican, see Fiorelle Cavalli, "La Santa sede contro la deportazioni degli ebrei dalla Slovacchia durante seconda guerra mondiale," *La Civilta Cattolica* 112/3 (1961): 3–18; Livia Rothkirchen, "Vatican Policy and the 'Jewish Problem' in 'Independent' Slovakia (1939–1945)," *Yad Vashem Studies* 6 (1967): 27–53; idem, "The Stand of the Churches vis-à-vis the Persecution of the Jews of Slovakia," in *Judaism and Christianity under the Impact of National Socialism 1919–1945*, ed. Otto D. Kulka and Paul R. Mendes-Flohr (Jerusalem: Israeli Historical Society, 1982), pp. 273–86.

19. Jean-Claude Favez, *Une mission impossible? Le CICR, les déportations et les camps de concentration nazis* (Lausanne: Payot, 1988).

20. Ibid., pp. 269–70.

21. For an analysis, see Livia Rothkirchen, "The Slovak Enigma: A Reassessment of the Halt to Deportations," *East-Central Europe* 10/1–2 (1983): 3–13.

22. See, for example, Letter from Gisi Fleischmann to Saly Mayer, Archives of the Labor Party (Archion Ha'avoda), Tel Aviv, File no. 66.

23. Livia Rothkirchen, "Escape Routes and Contacts during the War," in *Jewish Resistance during the Holocaust, Proceedings of the Conference on Manifestations of Jewish Resistance, April 7–11, 1968* (Jerusalem: Yad Vashem, 1971, pp. 408–14; and idem, "Hungary—an Asylum for the Refugees of Europe," *Yad Vashem Studies* 7 (1968): 127–46.

24. *NMT Trials*, XIII, document N6-4407, p. 31.

25. The trial of Dr. Jozef Tiso before the Bratislava People's Court, Tnl'ud 6/46: the testimony of Gen. J. Turanec; see Ivan Kamenec, *Po stopách tragedie* (Bratislava: Archa, 1991), p. 161.

26. See "Überblick über die Lage der Juden in der Slowakei," Files of the German Foreign Ministry, Yad Vashem Microfilm collection, JM/ AA-K327, Inland II Geheim 57/5 K213012–3018.

27. For details on the background, see Yirmijahu O. Neumann, *Im Schatten des Todes* (Tel Aviv: Edition 'Olamenu,' 1956).

28. Livia Rothkirchen, "The Europa Plan: A Reassessment," in *American Jewry during the Holocaust*, ed. Seymour M. Finger (New York: American Jewish Commission on the Holocaust, 1984), appendices 4–7, pp. 1–20.

29. D. Wisliceny's testimony, Yad Vashem Archives, M-5/36-1.

30. *Eichmann in Hungary: Documents*, ed. Jenö Levai (Budapest: Pannonia Press, 1961), pp. 224–25. Levai erroneously cites Eichmann as the signatory of this document.

31. Quoted in Roger Manwell and Heinrich Fraenkel, *Heinrich Himmler* (London: Heinemann, 1965), pp. 134–35.

32. Michael D. Weissmandl, *Min HaMetzar* (New York: Emunah, 1961).

33. Yehuda Bauer, *American Jewry and the Holocaust: The American Jewish Joint Distribution Committee, 1939–1945* (Detroit: Wayne State University Press, 1981); see also Abraham Fuchs, *The Unheeded Cry: The Gripping Story of Rabbi Weissmandl, the Valiant Holocaust Leader Who Battled Both Allied Indifference and Nazi Hatred* (New York: Mesorah Publications, 1984).

34. Yehuda Bauer, *Jews for Sale? Nazi-Jewish Negotiations, 1933–1945* (New Haven: Yale University Press, 1994).

35. Emanuel Frieder, *To Deliver Their Souls: The Struggle of a Young Rabbi during the Holocaust* (New York: Holocaust Library, 1990); Gila Fatran, *Ha'im Maavak le'Histadrut? Hanhagat Yehudey Slovakia beTkufat haShoah* (Tel Aviv: Moreshet, 1992).

36. Weissmandl, *Min HaMetzar*, pp. 186–87.

37. Ibid.

38. See Livia Rothkirchen, "State-Sponsored Anti-Semitism in Communist Czechoslovakia, 1948–1989," in *Anti-Semitism in Post-totalitarian Europe* (Prague: Franz Kafka Publishers, 1993), pp. 125–36.

39. See Livia Rothkirchen, "Die Repräsentanten der Theresienstädter Selbstverwaltung: Differenzierung der Ansichten," *Theresienstädter Studien und Dokumente 1996*, ed. Miroslav Kárný, Raimund Kemper, and Margita Kárná (Prague: Academia, 1996), pp. 114–26.

Part 10

The Rescuers

Histories of the Holocaust often portray three major actors—perpetrators, victims, and bystanders—without differentiating between diverse types of bystanders, those who were complicitous, those who took no action to help either the Nazis or their victims, and those who assisted the victims. Neutrality is seldom neutral. In the struggle between overwhelmingly powerful Nazis and powerless Jews, neutrality assisted the killers and endangered the victims. Thus, the role of the rescuers was even more important.

The title bestowed on the rescuers by the state of Israel, "Righteous among the Nations of the World," misrepresents the historic reality. Many rescuers were not righteous. For some, the motives for rescue were mixed. To many, rescue was not an act of righteousness but a natural response to people in need. For others, rescue was not altruistic. Payment was received, favors were requested. Still others were rescuers for a time; they offered shelter or a haven until the situation got difficult. In the three essays that follow, the diversity of the rescuers and their motives will be examined. The three scholars are not historians. Nechama Tec is a sociologist, as is Samuel Oliner. They examine the social factors that led to rescue. Eva Fogelman is a psychologist, and she focuses on the personal history of the rescuers. Each approaches history from a different vantage point and each has a personal stake in this history. Both Tec and Oliner are survivors, Fogelman is the child of survivors; all owe their lives to rescuers.

Nechama Tec's contribution, "Reflections on Rescuers," includes discussions of subgroups within the general term "rescuers." Tec's life as well as the lives of her family were protected for more than two years by what she calls "paid helpers." Tec also discusses the fascinating case of confirmed antisemites who also helped Jews, out of guilt, it seems, that their antisemitic attitudes made them responsible for what had happened to the Jews.

But Tec also discusses the altruistic rescue of Jews by Christians and has found in her studies that there were six characteristics and conditions shared by these rescuers: 1) individuality or separateness; 2) independence or self-reliance; 3) an enduring commitment to stand up for the helpless and needy; 4) a tendency to perceive aid to Jews in a matter-of-fact, unassuming way; 5) an unplanned, unpremeditated beginning to a Jewish rescue; and 6) universalistic perceptions that define Jews not as Jews but as helpless human beings.

In the final part of her essay, Tec discusses why she was one of the first scholars to focus on Jewish rescuers of Jews; and she attempts to explain the special characteristics that motivated such rescuers as Oswald Rufeisen and Tuvia Bielski, about whom she has written extensively.

The history of the Holocaust is distinguished not only by the millions who suffered agonizing deaths and the millions who were part of the killing machine, but also by the millions who stood by—who either said no to an opportunity for rescue or who consciously or subconsciously closed their minds and hearts to the horrors occurring all around them.

That is why it is so important to understand those who did say yes and chose to endanger their own lives so that someone else's life might be saved. Eva Fogelman's essay on "The Rescuer Self" is an effort to begin the process of identifying not only the types of rescuers but the factors that helped to direct them. She finds that most rescuers underwent a multiple-stage process of awareness, from the ability to see clearly beyond Nazi propaganda, to interpreting a situation as one in which help was needed.

Once the decision to rescue had indeed been reached, Fogelman argues, a transformation took place within the rescuer and a different self—a rescuer self—emerged, to do what had to be done. Rescuers became different people, although the values that always had been part of them—humanity, religious tolerance, professional concern, and numerous other characteristics—continued to influence the ongoing relationship between the rescuer and those he or she attempted to rescue.

Samuel P. Oliner is that rare rescued human being who can look beyond his gratitude to the rescuer and ask: Why did he or she rescue me? Oliner was rescued by a peasant woman during the Holocaust, while his entire extended family, along with a thousand other Jews in Gorlice, Poland, were killed and buried in a mass grave; he has pursued an answer to his question for nearly two decades. His essay, "Rescuers of Jews during the Holocaust: A Portrait of Moral Courage," is an overview of a project undertaken with his wife and others into the nature of rescue during the Holocaust. Essentially, the study, which involved interviews with more than seven hundred respondents in Poland, France, Germany, the Netherlands, Norway, Italy, Canada, and the United States, was guided by the following questions:

1. Was rescue primarily a matter of opportunity, that is, of external circumstances and situational factors?
2. Was rescue primarily a matter of individual character, of personal attitude?
3. Was rescue a matter of moral values?

Importantly, Oliner found that both rescuers and bystanders were equally aware of the tragedy and the plight of Jews. Yet one sort took action and the other did not. Oliner is also interested in expanding the study of rescuers to Jewish rescuers and other rescuers in other periods of the twentieth century.

45.

NECHAMA TEC

Reflections on Rescuers

In Nazi-occupied Europe, efforts to save Jews signaled an opposition to German policies of Jewish annihilation. Although these efforts endangered the lives of the rescuers, each country under Nazi control had some people who took such risks. Because anti-Jewish measures were introduced in different places at different times with different degrees of ruthlessness, the timing of the appearance of rescuers differed from country to country. More importantly, the efforts required for Jewish rescue also varied with time and place. These variations, in turn, can be traced to a series of interrelated conditions that functioned as special obstacles and barriers.

The most formidable barrier to Jewish rescue was the degree to which Nazi occupying forces controlled the governmental machinery. Where the Germans were in complete control, they were prepared to do whatever was necessary to annihilate the Jewish populations and would brook no interference from any individual or group. Their decision about how much direct control to exert was influenced by their attitude toward the occupied country's Christian population. In the world of Nazi-occupied Europe, policies and controls depended on racial affinities. For example, the Nazis defined the Slavs as subhumans, as only slightly above the racial value of the Jews. In contrast, the highest social rank was reserved for the Scandinavians, who bore a close physical resemblance to the "Aryan" prototype valued by the Nazis. The other Europeans fell somewhere between these two extremes. The Nazis, however, were not always consistent in translating these racial principles into actions. Moreover, a particular kind of policy and control, in a particular locality, could and did change with time.

Another condition affecting Jewish rescue was the level of antisemitism within a given country. Where a strong antisemitic tradition prevailed, denunciations of Jews and their protectors were more common. In addition, in a society hostile to Jews, Jewish rescue by Christians was likely to invite disapproval, if not outright censure, from local countrymen. Also, in areas of pervasive antisemitism, even Christian helpers themselves could be influenced by long-taught anti-Jewish images and values. While engaged in the act of saving Jews, some had to cope with their own anti-Jewish attitudes.

Additionally, the sheer number of Jews within a particular country and the degree to which they were assimilated also affected their chances of rescue. It is easier to hide and protect fewer people. The easier it was for Jews to blend in, the less dangerous it was for others to shield them. Finally, too, for Christian rescuers it would have been easier to identify with those with whom they had more in common. These facts, however, came together in an almost limitless number of combinations.[1]

Practically all publications about those who endangered their lives to save Jews have concentrated on Christian rescuers who extended this protection self-lessly.[2] This emphasis is justified because the overwhelming majority of the Christian rescuers protected Jews without the expectation of concrete reward. Nevertheless, by focusing on this majority we overlook other kinds of rescuers.[3] Ultimately this omission limits our understanding of rescue.

If we concentrate first on the selfless majority of Christian rescuers, we may ask, What characteristics do they share? How do they differ from the others? Some Jews also devoted themselves to the rescue of Jews, although this is a neglected subject of study. Why have Jewish rescuers of Jews been overlooked? Who were these Jewish rescuers and how do they compare to Christian rescuers, particularly those who protected Jews without ulterior motives?

In pursuing these questions I rely mainly on evidence from Poland, a country designated by the Nazis to be the center of Jewish annihilation.[4] Most European Jews were sent to Poland to die. Poland was also a place where the Nazis introduced their measures of destruction early, ruthlessly, and without regard to human cost. As the center of Jewish annihilation, Poland provides the key to understanding the destruction of Jews and to an understanding of Jewish rescue in particular. As a country in which the Holocaust drama was played out in the most gruesome of ways, it can teach us about similar, albeit less extreme, cases.[5]

In regard to the rescue of Jews, a distinction between two types of altruism, normative and autonomous, seems appropriate. Normative altruism refers to helping behavior demanded, supported, and rewarded by others. In contrast, autonomous altruism refers to help that is neither expected nor rewarded by society. Indeed, autonomous altruism may be opposed by society or may involve grave risk to the helper. Society demands that a mother donate a kidney to her child, that a child aid an ailing parent. However, society does not ask its members to sacrifice their lives for strangers, particularly not for those whom society despises. During the Nazi occupa-tion, saving Jews was an act above and beyond the call of duty in that it put the rescuer in conflict with society's values and laws. Christians who, without regard for reward, risked their lives to protect Jews were autonomous altruists.[6] Of the many definitions of altruism, I will rely on one that describes it as behavior "carried out to benefit another without anticipation of rewards from external sources."[7]

Who among the Christians could overcome the seemingly insurmountable barriers to rescue? Who among the Christians was most likely to stand up for the persecuted Jews, traditionally viewed as "Christ-killers," blamed for every conceiv-able social ill? What propelled such rescuers into such a highly dangerous activity? When a large number of these Christian protectors are analyzed in terms of social class, education, political involvement, degree of antisemitism, religious commit-ment, and friendship patterns, they are a very heterogeneous group. But while some characteristics seem to offer partial explanations, none is reliable.[8] Thus, for example, even though belonging to a certain class or espousing certain political preferences might have predisposed an individual toward or away from Jewish rescue, neither alone was strong enough to account for such risk-taking behavior.[9] Only a close-range view of these selfless protectors' lifestyles and behaviors yields a cluster of shared characteristics and circumstances, and this in turn suggests a set of interrelated hypotheses. A selective presentation of findings illustrates these hypotheses.[10]

One of the shared characteristics is individuality or separateness. These rescuers did not quite fit into their social environments, a quality not all of them were aware of. Conscious or not, their individualism appeared under different guises and was related to other shared characteristics and motivations.[11] Being on the periphery of a community, whether one is aware of it or not, means being less affected than others by its expectations and controls. Individuality undermines social constraints and brings a higher level of independence, both of which have important implications. Freedom from social constraints and a high level of independence allow a person to act in accordance with personal values and moral precepts. In short, to the extent that people are less controlled by their environment, they are more likely to be indifferent to whether their moral imperatives conform to societal expectations.

The Christian rescuers I studied had no trouble talking about their self-reliance and their need to follow personal inclinations and values. Nearly all of them (98%) saw themselves as independent. This was coupled with the idea that they were propelled by moral values that did not depend on the support and approval of others. Again and again they repeated that they had to be at peace with their own ideas of right or wrong.

An important part of the rescuers' values was their long-standing commitment to protection of the needy, expressed in a wide range of charitable acts extending over a long period. Evidence for such selfless acts also came from survivors, most of whom described their protectors as good people whose efforts on behalf of the needy were limitless. There seems to have been a continuity between the rescuers' history of charitable actions and their wartime protection of Jews. That is, risking lives for Jews fit into a system of values and behaviors that included helping the weak and the dependent.

However, this link, has limitations. Most disinterested actions on behalf of others may have involved inconvenience, even extreme inconvenience. But only rarely would they have required the giver to risk the sacrifice of his or her own life. Only during the war was there a convergence between historical events demanding ultimate selflessness and the already established predisposition to help.

Maria Baluszko, an outspoken peasant who protected many Jews, said: "I do what I think is right, not what others think is right." At first she resisted telling me that her aid to Jews was an extension of a tradition that involved helping the poor and the destitute. When I touched upon her reasons for rescue, she was at a loss. Then, instead of answering, she asked: "What would you do in my place if someone came at night and asked for help? What would you have done in my place? One had to be an animal without a conscience not to help." Only after a considerable pause did she tell me: "In our area there were many large families with small farms; they were very poor. I used to help them; they called me mother. . . . When I was leaving the place people cried. I helped all the poor, all that needed help."[12]

We tend to take our repetitive actions for granted. What we take for granted we accept. What we accept, we rarely analyze. The constant influence of familiar ideas and habits does not mean that we understand them. What we are accustomed to repeating we don't see as extraordinary, no matter how exceptional it may seem to others; and so the rescuers' history of helping the needy might be in part responsible for their modest appraisal of their courageous actions. This was expressed in a variety of ways. Most rescuers (66%) perceived their protection of Jews as a natural reaction to human suffering, while almost a third (31%), insisted that saving lives was nothing exceptional. Only 3 percent described the saving of Jews as extraordinary.

To this day, Pawel Remba limps from an injury that occurred when he smuggled Jews out of the Warsaw Ghetto during the uprising. For this and other acts on behalf of Jews, he was awarded the Yad Vashem medal. When Pawel and I met in Israel, he categorically denied that he or others like him were heroes: "I would absolutely not make heroes out of the Poles who helped. All of us looked at this help as a natural thing. None of us were heroes; at times we were afraid, but none of us could act differently."

Refusal to perceive the drama of such risky actions was expressed in other ways as well. Some of these Poles omitted from their accounts events that would attest to particularly noble and courageous aspects of their rescues. This tendency is apparent in information collected from matched pairs of rescuers and rescued. One such example is provided by the case of Ada Celka and the girl she saved, Danuta Brill. I interviewed Ada Celka in Poland. A governess by profession, during the war she shared a one-room apartment with her unmarried sister and a handicapped father. In 1942, a Jewish woman, an acquaintance, asked Ada to save her child, a girl of eight. The neighbors were told that she was an orphaned relative. To my suggestion that keeping the Jewish girl must have entailed economic hardships, Ada reacted with a flat denial. She also failed to tell me about other facts that would have enhanced her image.

Only from Danuta, whom I interviewed in the United States, did I learn that Ada had almost succeeded in smuggling Danuta's parents out of a labor camp and placing them with a Polish family on a farm. This, according to the daughter, involved extraordinary efforts. Ada was not an influential person; she had few connections and no money. Her success in locating a peasant family could be ascribed to her willingness to try again and again. But on the chosen day, Ada waited in vain at the rendezvous: Danuta's parents had been already deported to a death camp.

Ada also never bothered to tell me that when food was scarce, which it often was, she fed her handicapped invalid father first, then Danuta. She and her sister ate only if any food was left.

Whereas the Jews were eager to praise their protectors, the rescuers were reluctant to talk about their noble aid. Even those who did spoke modestly. I had to prod before they mentioned things that would put them in a particularly favorable light. They consistently underplayed the risks and sacrifices inherent in their actions. Not only did most helpers deny that their aid to Jews was heroic, they became embarrassed when this was suggested to them. To underplay the heroism of their actions, half of the rescuers emphasized the fears they had experienced. The underlying assumption in such statements was that fears were incompatible with heroism. Felicja Zapolska, one of those who emphasized this fear, felt that "in general, those who helped were sensitive people who tried to overcome their fears. Everyone was afraid, and if anyone says that they were not afraid don't believe it because it has to be a lie." Others denied the exceptionality of their deeds by describing them as expressions of duty, by pushing the dangers into the background, or by depicting them as just another part of a dangerous environment. Some emphasized the great value of saving a life.

Given these matter-of-fact perceptions, it is not surprising that aid to Jews often began in a spontaneous, unpremeditated way. Indeed, 76 percent of the Jewish survivors studied said that the aid they received was given without prior planning, underscoring the rescuers' need to stand up for the poor and helpless.[13] So strong was this need, so much a part of their makeup, that it overshadowed other considerations. When asked why they had saved Jews, the rescuers overwhelmingly emphasized that they had responded to the persecution and the suffering of victims and not to their Jewishness. What compelled them to act was injustice and not the people themselves.

The ability to disregard all attributes of the needy, except their helplessness and dependence, is what I refer to as universalistic perception. Evidence of this perception comes from a variety of sources. One of them is the finding that 95 percent of the rescuers felt they were prompted to help by the need of the Jews. This stands in sharp contrast to the 26 percent who claim to have helped because it was a Christian duty, or the 52 percent whose response was a protest against the Nazi occupation. Clearly, more than one kind of motivation was involved.

Of the Jewish survivors, 81 percent thought that Jewish suffering motivated their saviors to offer protection. Universalistic perception is also indicated by the fact that only 9 percent of the rescuers limited their aid to friends. The rest gave help to all kinds of people, including total strangers. When Jewish survivors were consulted, 51 percent reported that they were protected by strangers and only 19 percent by friends.

This tendency is further illustrated by the case of Dr. Estowski, who was deeply involved in helping others, Jews and non-Jews. He helped both as a member of the underground and as a private citizen. How does he describe his help to Jews? "Whoever came to us, we always managed to help. I felt that it was my duty to help people. It was not because they were Jews. I had a simple obligation to help people. . . . Jews were in a particularly dangerous situation; all of us who were helping were aware of this fact: that because of their difficult situation, they had to be helped the most. After all, a Pole could somehow help himself, but the Jew was in a more horrible situation and could in no way help himself."

In a sense, it was a universalistic moral force that motivated the rescuers, independent of personal likes and dislikes. Some of those I spoke to were aware that to help the needy in general, and the Jews in particular, one did not have to like them. Liking and helping, they knew, did not necessarily go hand in hand. For example, gentle Ada Celka, who expressed a deep compassion for the suffering of others, emphasized the difference between helping and personal attraction when she said: "I would help anyone, anyone who needs help, but this does not mean that I like everybody." In various ways rescuers showed an ability to disregard all attributes except suffering and need.

The altruistic rescue of Jews by Christians that I have studied is partly explained by the meanings and interrelationships of six characteristics and conditions the rescuers shared: 1) individuality, or an inability to blend into their social environment; 2) independence or self-reliance, a willingness to act in accordance with personal convictions, regardless of how these convictions were viewed by others; 3) an enduring commitment to stand up for the helpless and needy, expressed in a long history of good deeds; 4) a tendency to perceive aid to Jews in a matter-of-fact, unassuming way, as neither heroic nor extraordinary; 5) an unplanned, unpremeditated beginning to the rescue of the Jews; and 6) universalistic perceptions of Jews that defined them, not as Jews, but as helpless beings totally dependent on the protection of others.

Not all Christians who helped Jews survive were prompted by altruistic motivations. Both outside evidence and my own survivors' accounts show that some Jews survived mainly because they were able to pay. Indeed, Christian Poles who protected me and my family for over two years fall into the "nonaltruistic" category. For them it was a strictly commercial arrangement.[14] Do those who saved Jews for profit alone belong to the category of rescuers? Yes and no. After all, some of these profit-seeking individuals did save lives. They exposed themselves to the same danger as the altruistic rescuers. Some of them perished in the process.

And yet, we feel uneasy placing them in the same category with the selfless saviors. I refer to them instead as paid helpers, not rescuers. Included in this category are Christians who would not have offered aid without payment. This category contrasts with cases in which payment was accepted but was not the main reason for offering protection.[15]

Beyond their desire for financial gain, what else do we know about the paid helpers? Information about them comes only from Jewish survivors. Christians who saved Jews solely for money refuse to identify themselves as Jewish protectors. Those few who have been identified do not discuss wartime experiences in terms of aid to Jews. None wrote wartime memoirs that describe their help to Jews. Nor did they testify before the many postwar historical commissions that were collecting information. Because of this reluctance, Jewish accounts are the sole, indirect source of information about them.

From this information I learned that paid helpers differ from the rest of Christian rescuers in a variety of ways. Only a few of the paid helpers were individualists. While a substantial proportion of them were independent, none were guided by moral imperatives that required them to stand up for the needy. Whether propelled by hunger or greed, paid helpers were motivated by the desire for tangible rewards; their commitment to the protection of Jews was weak and could easily be terminated by external threats. In fact, unlike the rest of the rescuers, most of those who helped Jews for money eventually came to regret their initial decision, and many in fact discontinued their aid. Some of them mistreated their charges by starving them, demanding more money and sometimes even threatening them with denunciation and death. No such harassment was reported for other rescuers.

The differences between the paid helpers and other Christian rescuers suggest some intriguing conclusions. When their desire for money was fulfilled, the paid helpers saw no reason to risk their lives. At that point, reality, with its threats and dangers, began to reassert itself. But because the helper-helped relationship could not be terminated without serious risk, it often continued. If caught, Jews could tell the Germans who had sheltered them. This could lead to the death of the paid helpers, some of whom inevitably began to feel trapped; some vented their frustrations on the Jews, whom they saw as the source of their fears and apprehensions.[16]

There is also another group of rather ambiguous helpers, a small group of Christian rescuers who were open and avid antisemites. As a rule, they were devout Catholics, intellectuals, often active in rightist political groups. As introspective individuals, during the war, they came to consider themselves responsible for what was happening to the Jews and wanted to repent by helping Jews.

Unlike the altruistic rescuers, the antisemitic rescuers were well integrated into their communities. But they did show a high degree of independence and some of them had a history of standing up for the needy. The rest of the explanatory conditions—the moral compulsion to help the needy, the matter-of-fact view of rescue, and the closely related tendency to diminish its importance—were present both among the antisemitic rescuers and Christians who had selflessly protected Jews.

While there were Jews who selflessly rescued others, as a subject of systematic study they have remained unnoticed.[17] I came to the idea of Jewish rescuers in a roundabout way. In 1978, at the Jewish Historical Institute in Warsaw, I was examining unpublished testimonies of Christian rescuers and Jewish survivors, Christians who had saved Jews and Jews who had benefited from such help. One of these recounted the story of Oswald Rufeisen, a Jewish youth of seventeen when World War II began. He survived by pretending to be half Polish and half German. Through an unusual set of circumstances, Rufeisen became an interpreter and secretary to the head of the German gendarmerie in Mir, a small town in western Belorussia. He wore an SS uniform and carried a gun. Taking full advantage of his official position, Rufeisen saved an entire Belorussian village, a large but unknown number of Russian POWs, partisans, and hundreds of Jews. He armed Jews in the Mir Ghetto and arranged a ghetto breakout. Denounced, Rufeisen escaped, found shelter in a nunnery (where he converted to Catholicism), and yet continued to identify himself as a Jew and a Zionist. His extraordinary experiences as partisan, fugitive, Catholic, monk, priest, and Zionist Jew did not stop with the end of the war.[18]

I was intrigued. Was Oswald Rufeisen a survivor or a rescuer? He fits into both categories. I began to collect information about Rufeisen's life. Only much later, when I actually started to write a book about him, did I become aware that some of the Jewish survivors I had already written about were also helping others.

Why had I overlooked the rescue of Jews by Jews? Did I think that self-preservation, as a basic drive, would take precedence over everything else? Historically Jews have been viewed as victims, and not as rescuers, not as heroes. Had I unconsciously assimilated these perceptions? Had I assumed that victim and rescuer were incompatible roles?[19]

The Nazi designation of all Jews as future victims had to affect popular perceptions. Deprived of all rights, reduced to the most humiliating position, the Jews were already perceived as helpless victims even before their death. And because we believe in the supremacy of self-preservation, we assume that when faced with their own death, individuals will concentrate on their own, rather than others', survival.

Moreover, during the Nazi era the Jews' helplessness overshadowed all other characteristics. Some Christian rescuers saw in their Jewish charges only hunted and persecuted human beings. These rescuers recalled that it was their suffering more than anything else that prompted them to help. Some of these rescuers added that since the Jews were in the worst predicament, they could not help themselves.[20] I myself tacitly accepted the view that those who face overpowering threats are incapable of helping themselves and, by extension, offering protection to others.

Common sense and some available facts tend to support such conclusions. People who are exposed to extreme dangers may be paralyzed into inaction. Whether this occurs is in part contingent on the extent to which they define a situation as hopeless. As a rule, fighting requires hope. Hope tends to fade with grave danger. Danger without hope saps the will to struggle.

Yet, hope also dies reluctantly. For some individuals who are condemned to death even a slim chance of survival turns the wish to live into an all-engrossing passion.[21] During the Nazi occupation many Jews continued to cling to hope. But we have not often considered how hope and a strong desire to live can translate into the determination to protect other victims. On the contrary, we assume that when confronted by personal death, self-preservation overshadows all other considerations.

Oswald Rufeisen's rescue of prospective Nazi victims seems to defy this assumption. It alerted me to the presence of other Jewish rescuers and led me to the study of the Bielski partisans, a forest community that took on the dual role of fighters and rescuers. Though not the only one, theirs was the largest armed rescue operation of Jews by Jews during World War II.

The Bielski partisans and their commander, Tuvia Bielski, belonged to a part of the Jewish population that refused to submit to German terror. They were the rebels. More independent, often endowed with leadership qualities, united in their refusal to become victims, they were at first propelled by the principle of self-preservation. As these rebels continued to elude the Germans, they began to feel more self-assured. When they came to feel personally less threatened, some of them were ready to consider issues beyond self-preservation. Eventually, some of these rebels switched their focus from self-preservation to revenge. Though they knew that death was a real possibility, they opted for revenge through armed resistance. The more successful they were, the more absorbed they became in this near impossible struggle.

But Tuvia Bielski's opposition to the Germans was different. He became absorbed in saving Jewish lives. Feelings of revenge took a back seat. A one-time peasant, resident of a small provincial town, Tuvia Bielski was an unlikely hero. His reactions to the German onslaught were unusual. With his two brothers, Asael and Zus, he became part of a small minority of Jews who refused to become ghetto inmates. Moving to the countryside and forests, they successfully eluded the Germans. They acquired guns and enlarged their group to include more relatives and friends and elected Tuvia their commander. Tuvia argued that the survival of their group depended directly on its enlargement, and hence on bringing more Jews into their camp.

Survival of the expanding group led to feelings of confidence and greater freedom to consider the welfare of others, at first, of family and friends. Further growth led to the rescue of other Jews, Jews who were not necessarily relatives or friends.

Tuvia's concern was further strengthened when in the summer of 1942 the

Germans stepped up their persecutions of Jews. The longer the Bielski unit (otriad) survived, the more involved it became with the rescue of Jews. Charismatic and independent of political ideology, Tuvia made no distinction between different kinds of Jews, the old or the young, the weak or the strong. In time he converted more and more comrades to this open-door policy. Growing support for Tuvia's policy produced new successes.

Though they participated in military engagements against the Germans, preservation of life remained the Bielski otriad's primary mission. Their most significant victory was the rescue of more than twelve hundred Jews, mostly older people, women, and children. The Bielski partisans also fought against local collaborators. Eventually the local population realized that the Bielski otriad would punish those who abused Jews, and this prevented some peasants from dismissing or denouncing their Jewish charges. It also prevented peasants from refusing help and resulted in safer roads which, in turn, encouraged more ghetto escapes.

The Bielski partisans initiated a variety of rescues. Guides were sent into ghettos to help people escape, and scouts searched the roads for Jewish fugitives in need of protection. Most of those collected ended up in the Bielski unit. Some joined other Soviet detachments or found refuge among the local population. In addition, whenever Jewish partisans in Soviet detachments felt threatened by antisemitism, they could count on finding shelter in the Bielski otriad.

The experience of the Bielski partisans and their charismatic leader, Tuvia Bielski, suggests a link between self-preservation and the selfless protection of others. And so, in times of upheaval among the ruins of established society, those who are independent and removed from the mainstream of tradition are likely to see hope where there is none. Threatened by overpowering forces of destruction, those who can see hope will concentrate, more vigorously than others, on overcoming death. Propelled by the need for self-preservation, they struggle to live. When this struggle yields a semblance of success, self-preservation may make room for concern about the welfare of others. Feeding on their own achievement and gaining more support, the protectors and the protected soon come to include anyone who is threatened by destruction and death. Each becomes transformed from prospective victim to prospective rescuer, blurring the distinction between rescuer and rescued. What began as an unrealistic glimmer of hope turns into a chance to survive and a cooperative effort.

In times of crisis, when old, established leaders fail, the uninitiated, the independent, are free of traditional constraints and have the opportunity to develop their leadership skills and their strategies for survival. Though at first they are equipped only with hope and a feeling of self-worth, they soon translate these hopes into actual gains. Success may carry them into a position of leadership and power. Hope, independence, an ability to organize, and the resultant success lead to more opportunities and greater achievements.[22]

My findings about Jewish rescuers suggest that under special circumstances, a victim may become a rescuer and a hero. Now aware of Jewish rescuers, I find them in different contexts. Near the end of 1942, the Polish underground established the Council for Aid to Jews (Zegota) to help Jews escape from the ghettos and find shelter in the forbidden Christian world, to provide them with false papers and, if appropriate, jobs. The second in command of this organization was the Jew Leo Feiner; the secretary was another Jew, Leo Berman. Both were exposed to special dangers but took on perilous duties that benefited other Jews.[23]

Similarly, Hersz Smolar, a leader of the Jewish underground in the Minsk ghetto, known to the Nazis, arranged shelter for injured Russian partisans and initiated a massive Jewish escape into the forest.[24]

The nineteen-year-old Ryszard Axer, an inmate of the Janowska camp, was particularly concerned with the protection of children and the old. And he arranged for escapes in ways that would not lead to reprisals. Ryszard had many opportunities to escape himself but refused because his disappearance would have endangered the lives of remaining inmates. His involvement with plans for an uprising in the Janowska camp was discovered by the Germans. After his arrest, though tortured, he did not reveal any secrets. Axer was murdered before the uprising took place.[25]

My own research as well as the foregoing examples show that though themselves engulfed by destructive forces, some Jews were able to rise above the cruelty of the times to devote themselves to the protection of others. These Jewish rescuers both resemble and differ from the Christian rescuers who selflessly risked their lives to save Jews. Each group demonstrated remarkable individuality and independence. Neither group expected rewards for protecting Jews.

Each group had come to the selfless protection of Jews by different roads. Though persecuted, Christians did not become the main targets of the Nazi policies of destruction. They had more freedom to act on their own behalf and on behalf of others. One might have expected the Christians to feel less obligated toward Jews than toward their own people. Jews belonged to a despised minority and antisemitism promoted indifference to Jewish suffering. Furthermore, Nazi law demanding severe penalties for harboring Jews offered justification for noninvolvement. But in the end, most of these Christian rescuers pushed this menace into the background.

Similarly, some Jews were able to transcend the odds and see to not only their own survival but that of others. The conviction that they were doing the right thing and even the slimmest hopes for success must have helped them remain rescuers.

One difference between Christian and Jewish rescuers lies in the definition of the two forms of altruism mentioned earlier. Whereas the Christian rescuers fit the definition of autonomous altruists, the Jews fit into the category of normative altruists: society expects that a Jew will stand up for a fellow Jew.

Yad Vashem's memorial to Jews who perished in World War II bestows special recognition on Christians who saved Jews under the Nazis. No such special recognition is offered to Jewish rescuers. The decision not to reward Jewish rescuers is based on the assumption that for a Jew to help a Jew was a mere duty, a duty that calls for no special awards.[26]

In this discussion of rescuers I have merely touched on some of the possible issues, raising rather than answering questions. Groping for an understanding of the destruction of European Jews, I concentrate on compassion, altruism, mutual help, rescue, resistance, and survival. I hope that others will pursue the suggested leads, particularly in regard to the complementary but differing roles of Christian and Jewish rescuers.

NOTES

1. See Nechama Tec, *When Light Pierced the Darkness: Christian Rescue of Jews in Nazi-Occupied Poland* (New York: Oxford University Press, 1986), pp. 6–7.

2. Examples of such titles are Eva Fogelman, *Conscience and Courage: Rescuers of Jews during the Holocaust* (New York: Doubleday, 1994); Phillip Hallie, *Lest Innocent Blood Be Shed* (New York: Harper and Row, 1979); Peter Hellman, *Avenue of the Righteous* (New York: Atheneum, 1980); Samuel P. Oliner and Pearl M. Oliner, *The Altruistic Personality, Rescuers of Jews in Nazi Europe* (New York: Free Press, 1988); Kazimierz Iranek-Osmecki, *He Who Saves One Life* (New York: Crown, 1971); Mordechai Paldiel, *The Path of the Righteous: Gentile Rescuers of Jews during the Holocaust* (New Jersey: KTAV/JFCR/ADL, 1993); Alexander Ramati, *The Assisi Underground: The Priests Who Rescued Jews* (New York: Stein and Day, 1978).

3. The emphasis on altruistic rescuers is partly justified. Of the 308 Jewish survivors I studied, 14 percent report they were protected only because they could pay; see Tec, *When Light Pierced the Darkness*, p. 90.

4. For a discussion of methodological issues that touch on the validity of data and the randomness of samples, see Tec, *When Light Pierced the Darkness*, "Postscript on Methodology," pp. 199–206 and notes to those papers, esp. p. 235 notes 10 and 11.

5. Ibid., p. 11.

6. This theoretical distinction has been suggested by David L. Rosenhan, "The Natural Socialization of Altruistic Autonomy," in *Altruism and Helping Behavior,* ed. Jacqueline R. Macaulay and Leonard Berkowitz (New York: Academic Press, 1970), pp. 251–68. See also Macaulay and Berkowitz, "Overview," in ibid., pp. 1–9.

7. Tec, *When Light Pierced the Darkness*, p. 69.

8. Ibid., p. 128; the social heterogeneity of the rescuers is also made apparent in other publications. Two such classic examples are Władysław Bartoszewski and Zofia Lewin, *Ten Jest z Ojczyzny Mojej* (Kraków: Wydawnictwo Znak, 1969); Philip Friedman, *Their Brothers' Keepers* (New York: Holocaust Library, 1978).

9. The present discussion about rescuers follows Tec, *When Light Pierced the Darkness*, pp. 150–93.

10. My idea of individuality and separateness is derived from the concept of marginality as described by Perry London in "The Rescuers: Motivational Hypotheses about Christians Who Saved Jews from the Nazis," in *Altruism and Helping Behavior*, ed. Macaulay and Berkowitz, pp. 241–50.

11. To protect the true identity of the people I interviewed, all the names are fictitious.

12. Some articles describe the rescuers' matter-of-fact attitude toward their help. See, for example, Hubert G. Locke, "Reflections on the Psychology of Rescuers and Bystanders," *Dimensions: A Journal of Holocaust Studies* 7/1 (1993): 8–11. In Eva Fogelman's discussion of moral rescuers, Fogelman talks about their matter-of-fact attitude; see her *Conscience and Courage*, p. 161.

13. Nechama Tec, *Dry Tears: The Story of a Lost Childhood* (New York: Oxford University Press, 1984).

14. For a more detailed discussion of this type, see Tec, *When Light Pierced the Darkness*, pp. 88–98.

15. Ibid., pp. 192–93.

16. Ibid., pp. 99–112; Nechama Tec, "Polish Anti-Semites and Jewish Rescue during the Holocaust," *Proceedings of the Ninth World Congress of Jewish Studies* (Jerusalem, 1986), vol. 3, pp. 181–88.

17. One notable exception is Marion Pritchard, who has been trying to direct attention to Jewish rescuers. See her article "Circles of Caring: An Insider's View," *Dimensions: A Journal of Holocaust Studies* 5/3 (1990): 14.

18. Nechama Tec, *In the Lion's Den: The Life of Oswald Rufeisen* (New York: Oxford University Press, 1990).

19. Nechama Tec, *Defiance: The Bielski Partisans* (New York: Oxford University Press,

1993), p. vii.

20. Tec, *When Light Pierced the Darkness*, pp. 176–77.

21. Tec, *Defiance*, p. 204.

22. Ibid., pp. 204–209.

23. Tec, *When Light Pierced the Darkness*, p. 121.

24. Hersz Smolar, *The Minsk Ghetto* (New York: Holocaust Library, 1989), pp. 52–110.

25. *A Collection of Testimonies about Rysiek Axer, Hero of the Janowska Camp* (Tel-Aviv: privately published, 1990) (Hebrew); Phillip Friedman, *Road To Extinction, Essays on the Holocaust,* ed. Ada June Friedman (Philadelphia: Jewish Publication Society, 1980), p. 312.

26. Mordechai Paldiel, personal communication, Jerusalem, 1984.

46.

EVA FOGELMAN

The Rescuer Self

Rescue of Jews under the Nazis was, in psychological parlance, a "rare behavior." Among a population of 700 million in Germany and the allied occupied countries, the thousands who risked their lives to save Jews and others from Nazi persecution constituted an aberration from the norm. The majority remained passive bystanders; many actively collaborated in the Final Solution.

The diversity among the rescuers[1] of Jews during the Holocaust is enough to dissuade any social scientist from generalizations about motivation. However, systematic analysis of their family backgrounds, personalities, and situations begins to suggest a way of understanding what enabled some people to take extraordinary risks to save the lives of others.[2]

Through the rescuing relationship, the values and innermost core of the rescuer were expressed. That core was nurtured in childhood, came to full expression during the Holocaust, and then continued in the postwar years as an integral part of the rescuer's identity, as, in essence, a rescuer self.

Most rescuers acknowledge that the initial act of such behavior was not premeditated and planned. Whether gradual or sudden, there was little mulling over of the moral dilemmas, conflicts, and life and death consequences involved in the decision to help. The decision to harbor Jews in extremis was often an impulsive response to an immediate situation—the reflection of an integrated self.

The ability to see beyond Nazi propaganda, to strip away the gauze of Nazi euphemisms, and to recognize that innocents were being murdered lies at the heart of what distinguishes most rescuers from the bystanders. It was the necessary first step that made the ensuing rescue activity possible and, in some cases, inevitable. What is disputed among researchers is how one develops this ability to see things differently. Some suggest that awareness of the imminent death of the Jews was a cognitive process that was not influenced by learned values or early socialization.[3] Most, however, emphasize the influence of early experiences, values, and the immediate situation, all of which may have impeded or enhanced the possibility to help.[4]

Bystanders who transformed themselves into rescuers held on to their innate empathy, while others who did not were swept up in a restructured social hierarchy that placed Aryans at the top and Jews at the bottom. Psychologist Daniel Goleman's theory of "psychic obtuseness" is applicable to most people under Nazi terror. People notice certain things (the "frame"); everything else, especially those matters that cause anxiety or pain, are kept from consciousness. We crop our mental picture, says Goleman, and in so doing, ignore clues that indicate that things are amiss.[5]

The work of social psychologists Bib Latané and John Darley on bystander intervention is applicable to the initiation of rescue acts. Latané and Darley delineate a five-stage process by which observers become participants: noticing that something is amiss; interpreting the situation as one in which people need help; assuming responsibility to offer help; choosing a form of help; and, finally, implementing help.[6] Latané and Darley's first two stages—noticing and interpreting—are what I refer to as "awareness."

Becoming a rescuer meant becoming aware of the imminent danger to and probable death of Jews. It was a clear-eyed view—seeing what others did not. It took a determined effort to discover the truth, to be aware. Those who became rescuers made that effort. Their heightened sense of empathy overrode Nazi propaganda and their own instinct for self-preservation. They saw the victims of Nazi persecution as individuals, different, perhaps, but still part of the same human community. They felt empathy: the Jewish plight touched a deeply personal chord.

Interpreting a situation as one in which help is needed is the second stage in becoming a rescuer. While local citizens were aware that Jews were losing their civil liberties, most interpreted this change as temporary, not as fatal, and not necessarily as warranting intervention. Some circumstances were too dangerous or uncertain for bystanders to be of any help. Roundups were carried out quickly, before there was time to think, much less act.

Assuming responsibility is the third and most crucial stage in Latané and Darley's bystander's intervention model. It is the stage from which the final two phases, choosing a form of help and implementing it, logically flow. Psychologist Elizabeth Midlarsky feels that the willingness to take responsibility requires a perception of competency—the view that one can alter events to bring about the desired outcome, whether or not it is objectively true. Other psychologists call this belief in the ability to influence events an "internal locus of control."[7] Samuel and Pearl Oliner's findings in *The Altruistic Personality* support Midlarsky's view: rescuers strongly believed that they could influence events, and this made them feel that what they did, or failed to do, mattered.[8] Rescuers were neither fools nor suicidal. They were not about to offer help unless they felt there was a good chance that they could be effective. They had to have faith in their capacity to assess situations and find solutions. There was seldom time for measured thought, only for quick assessments. Rescuers framed the situation this way: "Can I live with myself if I say no?" Aware that turning down a request for help meant that Jews would die, rescuers weighed the double peril of saying no.

In most cases, transformation from bystander to rescuer was gradual and characterized by an increasing commitment. Most people did not initiate rescues on their own. A friend, an acquaintance, or a friend of a friend came and asked for help. Rescuers thought about the person in trouble, not how their help would endanger them and their family. As one thing led to another they experienced an "upward curve of risk," starting perhaps with smuggling food and messages into a ghetto, then transporting a Jew out of the ghetto, and gradually sheltering the Jew for several years.

Rescuers became outlaws in a Nazi no-man's-land. Their ideas of right and wrong were not widely held. Being isolated was new for them, since before the war, they had been very much part of their communities. Prior to the rescue they tended not to be loners or people who felt alienated from society.[9] But the secret of rescue effectively isolated them from everyone else. Neighbors who suspected people of harboring Jews viewed them as selfish and dangerous because they risked the lives of those around them.

A rescuer's life was intricate and terrifying. A careless word, a forgotten detail, or one wrong move could lead to death. Dutch rescuer Louisa Steenstra recalls that German soldiers arrested the sixteen-year-old daughter of a friend for merely saying "hello" to a resistance man in their custody. Sent to a concentration camp, a guard shot her one hour later for "insolence."

At home strains were often as great. Overnight, dynamics changed as families adjusted to the new "member" being sheltered. The atmosphere could become poisonous if one spouse did not support the other's rescue efforts. Comfortable routines were upset and new patterns had to be developed. Husbands and wives gave up their privacy. Children found themselves sleeping with strangers they had to learn to call brother, sister, aunt, uncle—whatever the situation or the occasion required. "Sibling" rivalries and jealousies developed. Again, core confidence, a strong sense of self, and a supportive situation allowed bystanders to undertake a rescue. But once the decision to help was reached and the rescue began, a different self, a rescuer self, emerged to do what had to be done and to keep the rescuer from becoming overwhelmed by new responsibilities and pressures.

A "transformation" took place. It was not simply behavior that changed. Successful rescuers became, in effect, different people. Psychohistorian Robert Jay Lifton explains the psychological process: when people find themselves in a world that no longer makes sense, their identities—the ways they behave, even notions of right and wrong—no longer seem to fit. They become "de-centered." In an effort to reestablish psychological equilibrium, they have to find new centers, to create new selves.[10] The new self is built on strong moral foundations. It allows the rescuers to do what normally might not seem moral or prudent—including plotting, stealing, lying, taking risks, enduring hardships, putting loved ones in jeopardy, and living in fear—all in the service of setting the world (and their place within it) on solid ground. These actions might not make sense to their former selves, but they become the new essence of rescuers.

Rescue often entailed great risk and anxiety; rescue acts could also unleash strong feelings of guilt (at not being able to do more, at risking one's family in the service of others); rage (at the oppressors); terror and grief (at witnessing atrocities and dehumanization), all of which could induce inner chaos. But it is apparent from my interviews that rescuers have a strong equilibrium. They can withstand intense decentering experiences and the accompanying pain and confusion. As Lifton points out, such experiences can help to recenter people, allowing them to achieve a new mode of flexible psychological coping.

The rescuer self kept the fear of death and the knowledge of Hitler's Final Solution at bay. French pastor and underground leader Marc Donadille summed it up this way:

> On some level we knew [the gassings] were true, incredible as it seemed—but we pushed it to the back of our minds and got on with the daily work of rescuing. It didn't make sense to say to the Jews we were rescuing, living side by side with, in our houses "Hitler is going to kill you all." What haunted us was to save the Jews that were there. We had enough to do to keep them hidden, safe and fed . . .[11]

The rescuer self had to be competent, resourceful, and practical to get through each day. Charges had to eat and shopping for food was a major problem. To avoid arousing suspicion by buying too much food at once, rescuers wandered far afield. In large cities such as Amsterdam this was not a problem at first. Miep Gies, who was buying groceries for seven people hiding above Otto Frank's spice business offices, as well as for herself and her husband, distributed her purchases among several stores. These ruses were not foolproof. One day Gies's local vegetable grocer noticed that she was buying in large quantities. Without saying anything, he began putting vegetables aside for her shopping visits. Months later when she stopped by to shop as usual, he was not there. He had been arrested for hiding two Jews.[12]

Each combination of rescuer, victim, and situation created a peculiar alchemy. Whatever its distinctive traits, the rescuer self that emerged never strayed from the person's basic, humanitarian values, which were solid and unchanging. They were democratic and humane in nature. It was easier, of course, to harbor a person who was likable than someone who was unpleasant or demanding. However, once a rescuing relationship began, it was not easily terminated because of mere personality differences.

The theme of the rescuing relationship was altruism, its product, the creation of a safe harbor in a hostile world. Its basic "contract" ran thus: the rescuer was committed to harboring a Jew—to taking care of daily needs, warning of danger, maintaining a facade of "normal life" behind which there would be safety. The Jew was dependent but was expected to cooperate—making as little trouble as possible, using personal resources to help out in daily life, and staying invisible.

As in any relationship, life strained the original terms. Few if any involved in such relationships could have known in the beginning how long they would go on, or what new demands would be made as other victims needed help, or food ran out, or constant fear created family tension and strange behavior. As each set of expectations was replaced, roles and responsibilities had to be redefined, new problems overcome, and new strategies developed.

Motivation

Rescuers were not a monolithic group. Their initial motivations in large measure defined the essence of who they were. Rescuers saw themselves as helpful, competent people who took on the responsibility of saving Jews. Each had his or her own particular set of reasons.

My research discloses that the motivational category to which a rescuer belonged influenced not only how the rescue was carried out but also the way in which the rescuer self was integrated into postwar life. Assigning each rescuer to one of the ensuing five categories according to his initial motivation was therefore more than sorting piles. On the contrary, an examination of the circumstances and motives that led each to his initial rescuing act pinpointed the salient aspect of the rescuer. It was this aspect—moral, Judeophile, ideological, professional, or of the duty-bound child—that continued after the war as a central part of the inner lives of these individuals, providing tremendous satisfaction and direction.

Sociologist Robert Wuthnow emphasizes the importance of a language for motivation:

> We must have a language that allows us to explain to ourselves and others why we are doing what we do. And in an individualistic society, where caring is sometimes seen as an abnormality, it becomes all the more important to be able to give an account of ourselves. An adequate language of motivation is thus one of the critical junctures at which the individual and the society intersect: being able to explain why is as important to our identity as a culture as it is to our sense of selfhood as individuals.[13]

The very question, "Why did you do it?" evokes discomfort and even annoyance in rescuers. The question challenges an instinctive response that stems from personal integrity, from the rescuer's humanity. Rescuers are often embarrassed with their answers because they are not eloquent or philosophical and because the interviewer may be disappointed at the simple, "It was the right thing to do." "I couldn't have lived with myself if I let this person die." Psychologically, the very word "why" often seems accusatory and puts the rescuer on the defensive. The answer to the question, even if it cannot be formulated verbally by the rescuers themselves, lies buried in the moment of the first act of rescue. Everything up until that act was part of the reason *why*.

Many psychoanalysts believe that rescuers' acts derive from self-centered, unconscious motivations: expressing rage against the Third Reich, for example, or undoing a sense of helplessness. Saving the lives of Jews is perceived as providing rescuers with the narcissistic gratification of outwitting their oppressors or of having someone totally dependent on them. Most analysts would argue that self-gratification rather than altruism underlay rescuers' help. Anna Freud, for one, felt that there was no such thing as altruistic motivation. People who help others do it for personal gratification. Unconscious motivation may have played a role in turning bystanders into rescuers, yet intangibles such as narcissistic gratification and enhanced self-image were small reward when weighed against the vast risks these people undertook.

Sequential analysis of in-depth interviews of three hundred rescuers and more than one hundred and fifty of those they saved readily allows one to categorize initial rescue efforts. Some rescuers were motivated by moral, ideological, or professional ends. Others were admirers of the Jewish people, or they were children who helped their families' rescue. The rescuer self took a quiet pride in its ability to maintain moral integrity, ideological beliefs, professional standards, or humane relationships.

Moral Rescuers

The most prevalent type of rescuer was the moral rescuer; these people, when asked why they risked their lives to save Jews, were most likely to look at the interviewer uncomprehendingly.[14] "How else should one react when a human life is endangered?" some would reply indignantly. Their ideas of right and wrong were so ingrained, so much a part of who they were, that it was as if I had asked them why they breathed.

This clear sense of right and wrong is what child development expert Jean Piaget calls "autonomous" morality. According to Piaget, autonomous morality develops after age eight from both respect for peers' feelings and intellectual advances. Moral decisions are no longer absolute. Justice is a matter of reciprocal rights and obligations, the readings of an inner "moral compass."[15] Eli Sagan takes Piaget's notion a step further, arguing that morality, or conscience, is an independent psychic function that develops in infancy through a caretaker's nurturing and gradually comes to rule supreme. In Sagan's view, conscience reigns not through fear of punishment (or castration, as Freud believed) but through love. A child who receives love wants to give it back. In Sagan's terms, a moral rescuer was simply a person trying to return the love he received as a child.[16]

Moral rescuers, however, were doing more than just reciprocating affection. They had a strong sense of who they were and what they lived for. Their values were self-sustaining, not dependent on the approval of others. What mattered most was behaving in a way that maintained their own integrity; the knowledge that, unless they took action, people would die was enough.

They did not leap at every opportunity to correct wrongdoing. On the contrary, moral rescuers rarely initiated action. Unlike rescuers with other types of motivation (such as people who were propelled by hatred of the Third Reich), moral rescuers typically launched their activity only after being asked to help or after an encounter with suffering and death that reawakened their consciences. For the most part, when asked to help, moral rescuers could not say no.

These rescuers displayed emotional and cognitive types of morality: ideological, religious, and emotional. Ideological morality was based on ethical beliefs and notions of justice. Rescuers with this type of morality acted on a strong sense of right and wrong inculcated since early childhood. A congruence between morality and action was always a part of their lives. They had the ability to stand up for their beliefs; when asked to help, they did. They were more likely than others to be politically involved. Some belonged to socialist, communist, or in a few cases, even nationalist parties.

Religious-moral rescuers described their sense of right and wrong in religious rather than ethical terms. Their morality was based on tenets such as "Do unto others as you would have them do unto you" and biblical precepts about how to live their lives. Religious values such as tolerance were unshakable and permanent. During the war and after, when faced with dire circumstances or morally complex questions, they relied on their faith to see them through.

Spiritual feelings were not limited to those affiliated with traditional religions. A deep spiritual conviction and dedication to the principles and practices of nonviolent action motivated pacifists such as Dutch rescuer Wilto Schortingnius. A registered conscientious objector well before the German invasion, Schortingnius, along with his wife, looked to Mahatma Gandhi and Albert Schweitzer for their inspiration and to their own consciences for motivation. When I asked Schortingnius why he and his wife hid twenty Jews on his farm, his answer was simple: "We feel life is sacred."

Lastly, emotional-moral rescuers felt a compassion for victims of Nazi persecution that compelled them to help. Emotional-moral rescuers were the rarest type among moral rescuers. They helped out of a feeling of compassion and pity. It was not an ideological sense of right and wrong but an immediate and intense emotional response. Theirs was a morality based on caring and responsibility, the same morality that Harvard University psychologist Carol Gilligan celebrated in her groundbreaking book, *In a Different Voice.*[17]

A majority of these emotional-moral rescuers carried out more than five separate rescues. More than any other category, emotional-moral rescuers engaged in rescuing children. Of course, not all of those who rescued children were emotional-moral rescuers, just as not everyone who rescued was motivated by exclusively moral considerations.

Judeophiles

Philosemites or Judeophiles were the second largest category of rescuers I interviewed—people who loved individual Jews or the Jewish people.[18] Some felt affinity toward Jews based on business relationships, intellectual pursuits, social interaction, love relationships, or religious closeness. Many Christians had childhood friends who were Jewish. Others remembered being "shabbos goyim," or non-Jews whose job it was to put on lights, light fires, and perform other minor household tasks for Jews who followed strictly the Jewish injunction not to do any work on the Sabbath. Non-Jewish children often received candy and other treats for their help, and they carried fond childhood memories of Jews.

A surprising number of Judeophiles suspected they were of Jewish descent.[19] Others had been romantically involved with Jews or had been forbidden by their families to continue involvements. In these cases, not only did the love for the lost sweetheart remain, it was extended to the Jewish people in general. Still others thought that they might be the illegitimate offspring of their mother's secret liaisons with Jews.

Closeness to the Jewish people could also come from reading and understanding the Hebrew Bible. Fundamentalist Christians who grew up with stories of the Hebrew Bible felt a love for the ancient people. Some of these Judeophiles had never met a Jew, but when given an opportunity to rescue one, they were more than willing. They felt a religious connection to Jesus, a Jew, or to those people the Hebrew Bible says were chosen by God.

Unlike moral rescuers, most Judeophiles began their rescuing activities by sheltering Jews they knew. Thus, despite centuries-old antisemitic attitudes, particularly in Eastern Europe, it was possible, under the right conditions, for some to overcome their bigotry.

How such relationships resolved themselves differed from person to person and situation to situation. For many rescuers, the relationship brought happiness and meaning to their lives. After the war, some married those whom they had saved; some converted to Judaism; some moved to Israel. Some did all three. For others, the relationship dissolved after the war into a muddle of guilt about not doing enough, of grief over losses, and of rage when their charges were never heard from again.

Relationships were cut off abruptly. Some were severed deliberately; others were torn apart inadvertently by the chaotic conditions of war.

Concerned Professionals

Not all rescuers felt emotional bonds with Jews. In fact members of one group, a group sociologists label "concerned-detached professionals," were drawn into their rescue efforts by virtue of their occupations. They were few, only 5 percent of those I interviewed, but they were a varied and fascinating group. These diplomats, doctors, nurses, social workers, and psychologists did not necessarily love Jews, or even much like them. But they were ideologically opposed to the Nazi regime. When social workers saw that, without help, Jewish families would be split apart and would have to face their deadly destinies alone, they felt obliged to help. When doctors saw men hunted by Third Reich butchers, they made an effort to intervene. And when diplomats saw people of different nationalities stripped of their basic citizenship rights, indeed of their dignity, they felt compelled to act. Unlike moral rescuers, who, through empathy, saw human beings just like themselves, these professionals saw what they were accustomed to seeing day in and day out: clients in trouble, patients in need, strangers in distress.

To be sure, Nazi persecution made cases of Jews more urgent than those of ordinary clients. Rescuing professionals were confident about their ability to help. It was what they were trained to do. They were competent, independent, and dedicated to doing their jobs well. They were also a bit aloof, keeping a professional distance between themselves and their charges, a distance that might seem cold-hearted to a Judeophile. As a result, they did not maintain relationships with those whom they rescued, and survivors most often did not provide testimony for their recognition at Yad Vashem.

As with rescuers in other motivational categories, concerned professionals had a sense of obeying a higher law. Whatever their particular job— social worker, nurse, diplomat—these rescuing professionals applied to the highest ideals of their professions.[20] Nowhere was the determination to uphold professional ideals more apparent than in the case of those diplomats who disobeyed their countries' foreign service directives to save Jews. As diplomats, disobeying home office directives took on added significance. Since the actions of a diplomat were seen as representing the political thinking of his or her country, the Third Reich interpreted it as a deliberate political message.

Network Rescuers

It is axiomatic among sociologists that ideology can only be defeated through group effort. Individual attempts to counteract prevailing beliefs are futile. People for whom Nazism was anathema instinctively knew this. They sought out others who saw the world as they did, felt the same way about it, and wanted to change it. They gathered in political halls, fraternity houses, church basements, and public school classrooms. They met in social welfare offices and hospital staff rooms. They rallied in churches with reputations for humanitarian endeavors, for instance Holland's

Anti-Revolutionary Church and Germany's Confessing Church. And in towns such as France's Le Mazet, Fay, Tence, La Suchere, Montbuzat, and Le Chambon, Italy's Assisi—towns with traditions of harboring the religiously persecuted—they worked together to shelter strangers. They joined in what sociologist Georg Simmel calls "secret societies."[21]

Secret society members were both Jews and non-Jews bound by a common interest or a similar emotional bias. Unlike moral rescuers or Judeophiles, who acted from empathy with others, these rescuers were motivated by fear and abhorrence of the Third Reich's racist and dictatorial policies. Nazism was the very antithesis of the deeply held beliefs and humanitarian values that defined who they were. They felt personally defiled.

Members of the "secret societies" were a strikingly homogeneous group. Most came from business or professional families. Many were young adults who had started their anti-Nazi activities as university students. More than half had attended college or graduate school and all had at least some high school education.[22]

These people were early opponents of Hitler. They passed out anti-Nazi literature, organized protest strikes, and eventually undertook acts of sabotage. They were likely to have shown their defiance of Hitler early on by ignoring the racial laws that prohibited non-Jews from having sexual, social, or business contacts with Jews. Disobeying those laws constituted their first acts of resistance. Their focus was on opposing Hitler, not on saving Jews. Resistance came first. Later, at the urging of Jewish friends and as the plight of the Jews became more desperate, rescue efforts became part of their general resistance.

Some moral rescuers, who started their rescuing relationships in isolation, began to join groups. This gave them resources they needed to continue and provided them with extra ration cards, money, counterintelligence, and hideouts. The sense of being one of many, of belonging to a group, strengthened rescuers' resolve and gave them psychological support. With a group behind them, rescuers felt what Freud described as "an unlimited power and an insurmountable peril." Such psychological support permitted some rescuers to step outside ordinary parameters to lie, steal, and do whatever had to be done to save lives.[23]

While groups gave support and additional resources to their members, they also enmeshed them in a tangle of operations and sometimes conflicting obligations. If caught, rescuers had information to reveal that could jeopardize the lives of others. Danger and urgency drew members into what felt like large enveloping families.

Saving Jews became an all-important, all-consuming task. Rescuers' activities infused their lives with meaning and purpose; theirs was an active defense of values and beliefs. For many, it was an experience so deeply gratifying that they would spend the rest of their lives trying to engage in another compelling act.

Child Rescuers

Like adults, child rescuers had to protect and care for their charges, but there were important differences in their motivations. They were enlisted in a cause; they did not volunteer. Their initial motivation was the wish to please their parents. Children who took the initiative on their own were extremely rare.

The nature of the help varied. One-fourth of the rescuers I interviewed had risked the lives of their children. Half of the latter were involved in passive rescue activity: living in the same house as the Jews their parents hid, or helping elsewhere.[24] All the same, children were subject to risks. If a raid found Jews hiding in their home, children were as likely as adults to be hung, shot, or shipped to a concentration camp. The immediate situation called upon children to become trusted lieutenants in their parents' rescue operations, doing whatever was needed for the job at hand. They became couriers, espionage agents, and guides. They learned to lie convincingly to authorities or feign innocence if caught. Their presence lent even the most dangerous activities an air of guilelessness. Often it was Christian children, rather than adults, who were sent to guide Jews out of ghettos.

Twelve percent of those whom I talked with had become rescuers as children; they ranged in age from five to twenty-one at the time. Many of them attributed their courage to naiveté, a youthful sense of immortality that made their activities seem a lark or a storybook adventure.

Many had ambivalent feelings about their family's involvement in saving Jews. On the one hand, children felt proud that, due to their efforts, lives were being saved. Their work enhanced their self-esteem and gave them a tremendous feeling of competence and importance. Often children were included in the family councils and given a voice in rescue decisions. Parents listened to their concerns and children felt their contributions were valued.

On the other hand, rescue took over every aspect of family life. Other concerns were pushed aside in the face of the daily struggle with life-and-death issues. No matter what troubles or problems a child might have, they appeared insignificant compared to those that faced the Jews. Nevertheless, these children sometimes resented their own loss of center stage. They were angry at their parents for undertaking a task in which they were forced to participate, though they admired them for their altruism. Teenagers were particularly affected. Adolescents depend on support and yearn for approval from their peers. But rescue efforts erected walls that separated them from their friends. They could not be part of the Nazi youth movement, they eschewed antisemitic slurs, and they avoided inviting friends home.

Sometimes the children's sensitivity and conscience outdistanced those of their parents. At other times, the unpredictability of war thrust children into roles their parents had never intended or foreseen, such as caring for those hidden once the parents were caught. The rescuer self thus fostered survived the war. For most, having saved lives was a source of pride and inner satisfaction.

The Postliberation Rescuer Self

Each motivational category incorporated the rescuer self into postwar life in its own way. Moral rescuers continued to channel their altruistic efforts into new situations as they arose. The religious-moral rescuers had little difficulty integrating their rescuer selves into postwar life, continuing to live according to the same Christian principles of compassion and charity they had during the war.

For others, however, rescue and the relationship with Jews were of central importance. These Judeophiles continued to feel a special closeness to Jews. Friendships formed before or during the war continued to play a big part in their lives. For the rest of their lives, Miep Gies and her husband would be known around the world as the would-be rescuers of Anne Frank; and Oskar Schindler would find emotional and financial surety only among his former factory workers.

Among all the groups, concerned professionals experienced the most seamless transition from rescuer to civilian life, continuing their careers after the war. Their professional identities, of which their rescuer self became a part, remained intact. War had not altered their professional outlook. They continued to help people in their usual way.

Diplomats were the exceptions to the concerned professionals' generally smooth entry into postwar life. Aristides de Sousa Mendes and Sempo Sugihara, for example, were drummed out of the diplomatic service for disobeying orders and were ostracized by their countrymen. Raoul Wallenberg was arrested by Soviet liberators as a spy and thrown into jail. He was never heard from again.

While the lack of a personal relationship with their charges generally did not affect concerned professionals, it did make it more difficult for some to integrate their rescuer self into postwar life.

After the war, the fortunates who knew others in their group were better able to heal themselves by confronting the past along with others. By sharing, they overcame neuroses associated with shame for their countrymen, or guilt for not doing more themselves. By talking about what formerly could not be revealed, rescuers made their peace with the past. Their rescuer selves were validated and became part of a collective consciousness.

For others, no such postwar conversation was possible. Some did not get to know others well. The camaraderie engendered by having faced a common danger dissipated, friends drifted away. Most network rescuers continued to be politically active. The same political instincts that made them oppose Hitler compelled them to fight other politically oppressive parties.

Child rescuers seem to have had the greatest difficulty in integrating their rescuer selves into their current lives. Most were *not* too young to understand the terrific risks they had run. Yet their contribution to the family's efforts were rarely mentioned. Some parents downplayed their children's help because acknowledgment was an admission of reckless disregard for their safety. Others felt guilty when their children awoke with nightmares, or continued in the habit of secrecy developed during the war. This habit hindered some adolescents from engaging in intimate relationships and from discussing their problem with their parents.

Conclusion

Each rescuer was unique. Yet research reveals patterns in the ways people became involved in rescue, and these patterns provide useful ideas as to how to nurture humane behavior.

It is not possible to predict who will risk his or her life for total strangers or even loved ones. No single personality type is apparent. However, certain features of family background, values, and personality increase the likelihood that certain people will resist tyranny.

Despite the external differences, there are commonalities in rescuers' upbringing. The most significant link is that most were taught to tolerate people who were different from themselves.[25] The altruism of parents provided role models for future rescuers. Involving the children in helping others enhanced "virtue as a habit." Being taught independence and self reliance as children provided the ego strength to withstand conformity.

Empathy with the victims of Nazi persecution came from several sources: warm, nurturing, and cohesive family environments;[26] discipline by reasoning rather than corporal punishment for misbehavior; a personal separation, loss, or an illness experienced in childhood; group moral support and personal experience of Nazi mistreatment.

The passivity of the majority was crucial to the success of the Final Solution, ultimately implicating the bystanders in the Nazi machinery of death. It is therefore crucial to understand those who did not remain mere bystanders but risked their lives to save the innocent. As this study shows, rescuers were neither angels, saints, nor mythic heroes. They were complex, often contradictory, yet unquestionably flesh-and-blood human beings. They came from all socioeconomic classes, educational backgrounds, and political persuasions; the factors were so diverse that it was not possible to predict who would help.

The rescuers acted humanely for a number of reasons. Some were motivated by religious, ideological, or emotionally based morality. Occasionally the motivation was born out of a transforming encounter with death. Others felt a sense of connection to Jews. Some combined a professional concern for the welfare of innocent victims with cool, professional distance. Some pledged allegiance to an anti-Nazi ideological movement, while others, much younger, obeyed the orders of desperate but committed parents. All possessed deep unconscious needs satisfied through their altruistic behavior. What was basic to all, however, was awareness, courage, and the ability to accept personal responsibility and acknowledge that "these human beings will die if I do not intervene."

Further Research

It will never be possible to predict who will disobey a malevolent authority and become a rescuer. Nonetheless, there is much to be learned from studying the rescuers of Jews during the Nazi period.

The majority of rescuers did not initiate help on their own but were asked by others. Therefore, we need more studies of those bystanders who were asked and refused. This group can teach us what forces impeded rescue behavior. (Anecdotal data and small samples point to the lack of sufficient resources and overwhelming fear.) It would be important to know whether social supports or fundamental personality traits distinguished those who refused from those who felt they could not live with themselves if they let a person die.

Certain people were motivated for religious and moral reasons to "do the right thing," while others with the same convictions remained passive or even became involved in the persecution. Study of different people from the same churches would shed light on how religious beliefs are transformed into concrete action.

Third, the rescuers have much to teach us about developing altruistic communities. Although members of such networks have been interviewed, the technique of network analysis has not been applied to their rescue efforts, which at times even crossed national borders. We need an analysis of the types of networks and their effectiveness or limitations under conditions of terror. This study, and the study of other types of rescuers, can teach us much about human nature, the bystanders' response to inhumanity, and those characteristics that shaped the "rescuer self."

NOTES

1. For purposes of exploring the social-psychological phenomenon of aid under conditions of terror, the focus will be on those non-Jews whom Yad Vashem deems Hasidei Umot Ha'Olam, "righteous among the nations of the world," that is, on those whose acts of rescue that were not performed for external reward.

2. E. Fogelman, *Conscience and Courage: Rescuers of Jews during the Holocaust* (New York: Doubleday, 1994); and idem, "The Rescuers: A Socio-psychological Study of Altruistic Behavior during the Nazi Era," Ph.D. diss., City University of New York, 1987.

3. K. R. Monroe, "John Donne's People: Explaining Altruism through Cognitive Frameworks," *Journal of Politics* 53 (1991): 394–433.

4. Fogelman, "Rescuers" and *Conscience and Courage*; S. P. Oliner and P. M. Oliner, *The Altruistic Personality: Rescuers of Jews in Nazi Europe* (New York: Free Press, 1988); U. Klingemann and J. W. Falter, "Hilfe für Juden während des Holocaust: Sozialpsychologische Merkmale der Nichtjüdischen Helfer und Charakteristik der Situation" (in press); J. Ryeykowski, "Cognitive and Motivational Prerequisites of Altruistic Helping: The Study of People Who Rescued Jews during the Holocaust," paper presented at the Scholar's Roundtable on Altruism under Nazi Terror: Implications for the Post-Holocaust World, Princeton, 1993; D. Rosenhan, "What Qualifies as Altruistic Behavior during the Holocaust?" paper presented at the Scholar's Roundtable on Altruism.

5. D. Goleman, *Vital Lies, Simple Truths: The Psychology of Self-Deception* (New York: Simon and Schuster, 1985).

6. B. Latané and J. Darley, *The Unresponsive Bystander: Why Doesn't He Help?* (New York: Appleton-Century-Crofts, 1970).

7. E. Midlarsky, "Competence and Helping: Notes toward a Model," in idem, *Development and Maintenance of Prosocial Behavior: International Perspectives on Positive Morality* (New York: Plenum, 1984), pp. 291–308.

8. Oliner and Oliner, *Altruistic Personality.*

9. Perry London suggested an element of "social marginality" among rescuers. Their alienation made them more sympathetic to another outside group. See Perry London, "The Rescuers: Motivational Hypotheses about Christians Who Saved Jews from the Nazis," in *Altruism and Helping Behavior,* ed. J. Macauley and L. Berkowitz (New York: Academic Press, 1970), pp. 241–50. Like London, Nechama Tec, in her study of Polish rescuers, *When Light Pierced the Darkness: Christian Rescue of Jews in Nazi-Occupied Poland* (Oxford: Oxford University Press, 1986), found that rescuers stood out within their environment as, for example, an intellectual among peasants or a communist among Catholic believers. But she explains this as individualism that enabled them to stand up for their beliefs. These individualists could stand up to malevolent authority and resist racist norms. I too found rescuers to be independent people. However, the vast majority of rescuers felt a sense of belonging to their community. In my initial interviews of 100 rescuers, only twenty-nine felt they were atypical. This difference may be attributed to the fact that my sample and the altruistic personality study include rescuers from different occupied countries. To be a rescuer in a country known for its antisemitism required a rare individual indeed.

10. R. J. Lifton, *The Life of the Self: Toward a New Psychology* (New York: Touchstone, 1976).

11. See P. Joutard, J. Poujol, and P. Cabanel, eds., *Cévennes terre de refuge, 1940–1944* (Montpellier: Presses Du Languedoc/Club Cevenol, 1987), p. 242.

12. Miep Gies, *Anne Frank Remembered: The Story of the Woman Who Helped Hide the Frank Family* (New York: Simon and Schuster, 1987), pp. 121, 150.

13. R. Wuthnow, *Acts of Compassion: Caring for Others and Helping Ourselves* (Princeton: Princeton University Press, 1991), pp. 49–50.

14. Thirty-two percent of those interviewed for my study, The Rescuer Project, Graduate Center of City University of New York, were coded as belonging to the moral rescuer category. Within that group, 14 percent were ideological-moral rescuers; 12 percent were religious, and 6 percent were emotional rescuers. In general, emotional-moral and religious-moral rescuers were more involved in saving children than ideological moral rescuers.

15. Jean Piaget, *The Moral Judgement of the Child* (New York: Free Press, 1965).

16. Eli Sagan, *Freud, Women, and Morality: The Psychology of Good and Evil* (New York: Basic Books, 1988). Sagan's contention of a separate conscience that limits the superego has informed and influenced my work. His notion of a conscience that passes judgment on the conflicting pulls in the superego is one that I share.

17. Gilligan describes two different moralities based on cognition and affect. Like her predecessor Lawrence Kohlberg, she found that morality can stem from an individual's sense of justice and fairness or from a sense of responsibility embedded in compassion and caring and pity. Unlike Kohlberg, Gilligan does not consider justice a higher morality than caring and responsibility. See Carol Gilligan, *In a Different Voice: Psychological Theory and Women's Development* (Cambridge: Harvard University Press, 1982).

18. The Rescuer Project found that Judeophiles comprised 28 percent of those who risked their lives to save Jews, which ranked them just behind those in the moral rescuer category. Eighty-two percent of those classified as Judeophiles came from apolitical families and some 29 percent of them came from mixed marriages. "Philosemitism," as used by various scholars, is a vague, generalized term, usually applied descriptively to indicate the supposed attitude of specific individuals who, in the opinion of the scholar, benefit or assist Jews. There have been few efforts to examine the term, to offer any detailed definition of it, or to analyze its causes or specific applications. Cecil Roth is unique in suggesting a basis for philosemitism, but he does not discuss what is meant by the term itself. Moreover, Roth's analysis is limited, being concerned essentially with the period in English history when Jews were readmitted to that nation. There has been, in short, no systematic inquiry into the meaning, application, or types of philosemitism. Allan Edelstein of Towson University has undertaken the task of developing a systematic analysis of philosemitism. See A. Edelstein, *An Unacknowledged Harmony* (Westport, CT: Greenwood Press, 1982).

19. The fact that many of the rescuers suspected they had Jewish blood had escaped my attention until Harvey Sarner pointed it out to me. Sarner, a retired California businessman, has dedicated his energies to finding those East European rescuers honored by Yad Vashem and flying them to Israel for the public recognition they deserve. Sarner observed that many of the rescuers he talked with told him they suspected that they had Jewish blood.

20. Professionals who obeyed a higher law, one that involved upholding an oath of office to serve mankind, did not necessarily have to take death-defying risks. In southern France, some gendarmes protected their citizenry and themselves by following their orders to the letter. Before carrying out an arrest, for instance, two gendarmes would go to a local bistro for lunch first. In a loud voice, one might say to the other: "Look Pierre I see here that we have to pick up Max Cohen at Rue Jacob 15." They would continue to enjoy their meal, hoping all the while that someone would pass the word on to Cohen. After lunch, they would go to arrest Cohen, only to be told he had left the day before. They would then place an X next to the man's name. They had fulfilled their assignment. Alas, they had come a day too late to make the required arrest.

21. Georg Simmel, "The Secret and the Secret Society," in *The Sociology of George Simmel*, ed. Kurt H. Wolff (New York: Free Press, 1950).

22. Network rescuers accounted for 22 percent of those I interviewed. The majority had attended college (36%) or graduate school (27%). Over 90 percent of them were involved in more than five rescues, episodes that usually involved helping fifteen persons or more. Forty-one percent rescued one hundred to twenty-five hundred people; 23 percent rescued fifteen to fifty, and 18 percent helped one to seven. Over 90 percent were "professional rescuers" whose full-time occupation was rescuing.

23. S. Freud, *Group Psychology and the Analysis of the Ego* (New York: Bantam, 1960), p. 23.

24. Children of rescuing families who were not involved in rescues are not recognized as Hasidei Umot Ha'Olam.

25. Nechama Tec, who has studied Polish rescuers, recognizes "extensivity" as a universalistic perception of the Jew not as a Jew, but rather as a helpless being needing protection. This value derived from how children saw their parents interacting with "others" in their community, and what they were told if they made derogatory remarks about someone different from them.

26. F. Grossman in *Scarsdale Enquirer*, July 22, 1983 (also *Greenberg Enquirer*, June 17, 1982); idem, "Psychological Study of Gentiles Who Saved Jews" in *Toward the Understanding of Holocaust and Prevention of Genocide*, ed. I. Charney (Boulder, CO: Westview Press, 1984), pp. 202–16.

47.

SAMUEL P. OLINER

Rescuers of Jews during the Holocaust

A PORTRAIT OF MORAL COURAGE

In a seminal, early work on rescuers in Nazi-occupied Europe, Phillip Friedman quotes Sholem Asch:

> It is of the highest importance, not only to record and recount, both for ourselves and for the future, the evidence of human degradation, but side by side with them, to set forth evidence of human exaltation and nobility. Let the epic of heroic deeds of love, as opposed by those of hatred; of rescue, as opposed to destruction; bear equal witness to the unborn generations.[1]

In the early 1960s, Rabbi Harold Schulweis reflected this sentiment when he established the Institute for Righteous Acts,[2] associated with the Judah L. Magnes Museum in Berkeley, California. Its purpose was to direct research on non-Jewish rescuers of Jews in Nazi-occupied Europe, to conduct empirical studies searching out motivations for rescuers' acts, and to apply the information thus gained to education and the teaching of moral character. This important initial step resulted in several studies of rescuers of Jews during the Holocaust. Perry London was among the first of fifty writers we have identified[3] who have concerned themselves with not only gathering stories of bona fide rescuers, but also with explaining their motivations.[4] My research colleagues and I have examined some sixty-five independent variables reported by these authors to explain the motivations for rescue, and we have classified rescuers into eight simplified categories: 1) moral; 2) religious; 3) empathic; 4) principled/autonomous; 5) situational; 6) personality traits; 7) normative; and 8) other. Some of these will be discussed below.

It is beyond the scope of this examination to evaluate critically the various approaches because methodologies vary substantially. Some studies are empirically based; researchers interviewed rescuers in depth and subjected the data to both quantitative and qualitative analysis. Some authors interpreted existing empirical research. Others used broad philosophical and theological approaches, examining the moral climate in which rescue took place. Still others used a historical approach, using archives and describing the events, places, and accounts of rescue. Here I will summarize our findings on the study of altruistic behavior of righteous Gentiles,[5] discuss briefly the newly undertaken research on Jewish rescuers,[6] and briefly suggest possibilities for cross-cultural research that should be undertaken to better understand altruistic behavior.

Our Research and Its Findings

Our research on altruism began in the late 1970s, when I was invited by Seymour Fromer, director of the Judah L. Magnes Museum, to take over the directorship of the Institute for Righteous Acts. In the early 1980s, the American Jewish Committee asked me to undertake a research project on rescuers of Jews. I accepted both invitations for several reasons. First, I myself was rescued in Poland by a peasant woman who risked her life to save me after the extermination of my entire extended family, along with a thousand other Jews, near Gorlice, Poland. The second major reason was my interest in the concept of altruism as an antidote to human indifference. At that time I had begun to teach a course on the Holocaust and antisemitism at Humboldt State University. The content of this course left the students in a state of despair. I thought that including the deeds of rescuers and their moral courage would offer the students some hope that not all people during World War II were perpetrators, victims, or bystanders to human suffering. As Rabbi Schulweis has noted, "If the Holocaust is our nightmare, the rescuers are our hope." Perhaps their deeds will help capture the moral symmetry of human behavior during those dark years. Furthermore, to understand why righteous Gentiles acted the way they did would help us better understand the nature of altruism.

Our study, undertaken by myself, Pearl Oliner, and other colleagues,[7] was guided by the following questions: 1) Was rescue primarily a matter of opportunity, that is, external circumstances and situational factors, and if so, what were they? 2) Was rescue primarily a matter of individual character, of personal attributes, and if so, what were those traits, and how and where were they acquired? 3) Was rescue a matter of moral values?[8] In the course of our study we interviewed more than seven hundred respondents in Poland, France, Germany, the Netherlands, Norway, Italy, Canada, and the United States. A comparison of rescuers, bystanders, and rescued survivors showed that both rescuers and bystanders had opportunities to rescue, and were equally aware of the plight of Jews. While rescuers took action, bystanders, who had similar knowledge, refrained. We may say that opportunity may have facilitated rescue, but it did not by any means determine it.

Of the many reasons for rescue expressed by our respondents, an overwhelming majority of rescuers, 87 percent, cited at least one ethical or humanitarian consideration in their actions. The ethics cited included justice, that is, the persecution of the innocent could not be justified. The ethic that mattered most, however, was compassion.

Most of the offered help was rooted in a need to assume personal responsibility to relieve suffering and pain. Some rescuers felt a particular affection toward Jews they knew.[9] Most felt an obligation toward others in general. Pity, compassion, concern, and affection account for 76 percent of the reasons rescuers gave for the help they extended to strangers. More than 90 percent said that they helped at least one stranger as well as a friend. Typical expressions of rescuers were:

When you see a need, you have to help.

Our religion says we are our brother's keepers.

We had to give help to these people in order to save them, not because they were Jews but because they were persecuted human beings who needed help.

I sensed I had in front of me human beings who were hunted down like wild animals. This aroused a feeling of brotherhood with the desire to help.

I was indignant and aroused against this terrible miscarriage of justice. I couldn't stand by and see innocent people destroyed.

I was always filled with love for everyone, for every creature, for things. I infuse life into every object. For me, everything is alive.

Caring was not a spectator sport. It compelled action. Rescuers assumed responsibility—not because others required them to, but because failure to act meant the abandonment of innocent people. As other rescuers put it:

I couldn't stand by and observe the daily misery that was occurring.

I knew they were taking them and that they wouldn't come back. I didn't think I could live knowing that I could have done something.

Caring attitudes were usually acquired directly from parents. Although parents played a very important role for both rescuers and nonrescuers, significantly more rescuers perceived their parents as benevolent figures.

Values that rescuers learned from their parents also differed significantly from those learned by nonrescuers. Significantly more rescuers made the point that they owed an obligation to all people. We have termed such an orientation "extensivity." The "extensive" predisposition comprises attachment to family in an emotionally healthy way, as well as inclusion of others as deserving of care:[10]

They taught me to respect all human beings.

I have learned logical reasoning and also to be tolerant, not to discriminate against people because of their beliefs or social class.

I have learned from my parents' generosity to be open to people. I have learned to be good to one's neighbor, honesty, scruples—to be responsible, concerned, and considerate. To work and care. But also to help, to the point of leaving one's work to help one's neighbor.

My parents taught me discipline, tolerance, and serving other people when they needed something. It was a general feeling. When someone was ill or in need, my parents would always help. We were taught to help in whatever way we could. Consideration and tolerance were very important in our family. My mother and father could both trust those feelings. My father could not judge people who lived or felt differently than he, that point was made to us.

Significantly more rescuers than nonrescuers emphasized learning the value of helping diverse others. More rescuers felt a sense of responsibility, or even an obligation. Nonrescuers felt themselves exempt. They usually were unaffected by the suffering of others, more detached, and less sensitive to other people's helplessness.

The rescuers' feelings may well have resulted from the perception that they shared fundamental similarities with all of humanity, regardless of social status, ethnicity, race, or religion. A significant number had friends from diverse groups.

Childhood discipline also influenced ethical behavior. Rescuers' parents were more likely to have disciplined them by reasoning and explanation of the consequences of their misbehavior than by verbal or physical punishment, which was common among nonrescuers.

While some of these characteristics help explain why rescuers helped Jews, the picture is a bit more complex. Not all rescuers necessarily possessed all of them. Rescuers' motivations differed with respect to interpretations of moral obligation. Our research identified three categories of rescuer motivation, based on theoretical concepts outlined by Janusz Reykowski.[11] Those rescuers who entered into rescue activity in response to a strongly valued norm, the expectation of a social group, or 'the leadership of a highly regarded authority[12] were termed *normocentric*. Rescuers who responded to an external event that aroused or heightened their sense of empathy were considered *empathic*. Rescuers who behaved according to their own overarching principles, mainly autonomously derived, and who were moved to action by external events that they interpreted as violating human principles, were deemed *autonomous/principled*.

For some rescuers, witnessing arrest or persecution of Jews triggered a response based on the norms of the social group with which they identified and to which they normally looked for moral guidance. Normocentric rescuers' motivations arose not from their connection with the victim but from feelings of obligation to the group or community whose implicit and explicit rules they obeyed. For instance, an Italian priest recalled:

> A monthly meeting of the clergy used to be held in the seminary. After one of these meetings, Bishop Nicolini took Brunacci aside and showed him a letter from the Secretary of State at the Vatican. This letter called upon all bishops to address themselves to the help of Jews, whose safety was becoming increasingly endangered. This, Bishop Nicolini said, was to be held in the strictest confidence.[13]

Thus for the normocentric rescuer, inaction violated the group's rules of behavior. For these rescuers, feelings of obligation or duty were frequently coupled with anticipation of guilt or shame if they failed to act. The norms of their society, its habits and culture, encouraged helping. In the case of Italian military officials, religious leaders, and diplomats, such norms legitimated sabotage of the deportation of Italian Jews. Approximately 52 percent of our respondents were motivated by obligations that fell into the normocentric category.

Empathic motivation expresses feelings of compassion, sympathy, and pity for the person in distress. Reactions frequently contain both emotional and cognitive elements. The following recollection expresses the empathy that motivated rescuer behavior: "It was unbearable to watch a human being in such a state. When they knocked at our door, we helped them and fed them. Not only them, but others soon came—Jews from Bologna."

Empathic reactions are sometimes overpowering feelings that lead people to react spontaneously. Some rescuers could not withstand the grief of seeing other people's agony. In many such cases the direct face-to-face nature of the encounter heightened the impulse to act. Thirty-eight percent of rescuers indicated that they were moved empathically to their first helping act.

People with an autonomously principled motivation interpreted the persecution of Jews as a violation of their own moral precepts. Unlike normocentric motivation, which prescribed a certain group behavior, autonomously principled motivation involved acting on one's own, without requiring permission or outside validation. Such rescuer behavior reaffirmed and applied the individual's personal principles. Even when the actions of the autonomously principled rescuer proved futile, individuals tended to believe that their principles were kept alive so long as people reaffirmed them by acting on behalf of justice. One Italian rescuer denied that rescuing a great number of people was truly remarkable:

> No, no. It was all something very simple. Nothing grandiose was done. It was done simply without considering risk, without thinking about whether it would be an occasion for recognition or to be maligned, it was in effect done out of innocence. I didn't think I was doing anything other than what should be done, or that I was in any special danger because of what I was doing. Justice had to be done. Persecution of the innocents was unacceptable.

Autonomously motivated rescuers felt fundamentally challenged by the abuses they were observing—letting such acts occur was tantamount to condoning them. But only a small minority of rescuers—approximately 11 percent—fell into this category.

These three ideal types are seldom found in any individual case. Elements of empathy were sometimes associated with normocentric considerations, and principled behavior was not necessarily devoid of normocentric or empathic motivating influences. Self-enhancement and fulfillment of personal needs also appeared in several cases. One rescuer, for example, who learned that the women living with her were Jewish, later said that she was reluctant to ask them to leave since her relationship with them was the only affectionate one she had.

Scholars such as Yahil, Zuccotti, A. Ramati, Carpy, Chary, Flender, Friedman, and L. Baron, among others, have addressed the climate in which the rescue of Jews was more likely, usually where social, cultural, and political conditions were conducive to it, or antisemitism was less rampant.[14] Such a climate permitted the rescue, in October 1943, of almost the entire Danish Jewish population, approximately 92 percent, since they could be smuggled into Sweden. The fact that 85 percent of the Jewish population of Italy was rescued is attributed to the general lack of antisemitism and the absence of a sharply drawn distinction between Jews and other Italians.

A variety of explanations for Jewish rescue have been put forward, and many of them are similar. Thus Fleischner concludes that one of the major factors in rescue was compassion for the Jewish victims, as do Kurek, Huneke, Oliner and Oliner, and Tec (1986).[15] Other researchers find that Christian charity or other religious factors help explain rescue, among them Baron, Sauvage, Huneke, Fleischner, Zeitoun, and the Oliners in their latest analysis. Sauvage, Hallie, Fleischner, Kurek, Huneke,

Oliner and Oliner, London, Tec, and Fogelman found that a less specified religious morality underlay the rescue of Jews.[16]

While none of the more than fifty studies of rescue have arrived at a single reason for rescue, nearly all concur that such motivation is most often associated with a particular type of socialization experience and moral climate in which ethical behavior was molded by a significant other, such as a parent. This may help account for the frequently reiterated statements made by rescuers that helping Jews was simply the moral thing to do.

Rescuers were more likely to have an extensive orientation than nonrescuers. They attached themselves to others more readily in responsible relationships and were more likely to do so inclusively. They were more likely to feel closer to their family of origin and to have been taught ethical obligations to others. Rescuers were more likely to feel compassion for suffering and to try to relieve it.

They were more likely to endorse pluralistic and democratic values, to reject ethnocentric stereotypes, and to have had friends from different social and religious groups in their youth. Rescuers were able to identify with people from different social, ethnic, national, and religious backgrounds.

They felt that they possessed personal integrity—that is, they were more likely to perceive themselves as honest and helpful, able to take responsibility, and willing to stand up for their beliefs. Of course they were less inclined to respect unquestioned obedience to authority. By contrast, nonrescuers tended to consider others outside their immediate community as largely peripheral. They were more concerned with their own needs and their own survival. Many paid scant attention to others' troubles. At best their obligation extended to a small circle, from which strangers were excluded.

Jewish Rescuers

While the world should know and record the deeds of those like Herman Graebe, Raoul Wallenberg, Aristide Mendez, Georgio Perlasca, Madam Trocmé, and thousands of others who are less famous rescuers of Jews during the Holocaust, further research is required on Jewish rescuers of Jews.[17] In this regard, Nechama Tec's seminal work *In the Lion's Den* is a welcome trailblazer. But we need more individual narratives of heroic Jewish rescuers; hopefully, they will be recorded while these individuals are still alive. By Jewish rescuers, we mean Jewish individuals or groups who actually hid, rescued, or transported other Jews to safety. We know that Jews were among the partisans and in resistance and fighting movements in virtually every country under Nazi occupation.[18] Historical accuracy demands that we dispel the falsehood that Jews walked liked sheep to the slaughterhouse.

Holocaust historian Lucy S. Dawidowicz has said, "We look at the past through the prism of the present and try to discern the future."[19] A historical myth is a distortion of that prism that is exploited in support of present policies. The image of European Jews passively accepting their fate is one of the most powerful myths of World War II. Historical myths exist because they serve a purpose. The myth of Jewish passivity has served many purposes. To antisemites it has provided proof of the lack of Jewish character, reinforcing the historic stereotype of the passive, cowardly Jew. To the Allies who refused to intervene to halt the extermination of Jews, the myth has served to mitigate guilt; if the Jews themselves were passive, were we really to blame for not intervening?

Faced with the determination of the Third Reich to exterminate them, the European Jews had three behavioral options. First, they could collaborate fully with the Nazis in the hope that by doing so, they could save themselves. Second, they could adopt what Lawrence Baron has called "defensive acquiescence,"[20] hoping that by complying with all Nazi requests, the Nazis would exempt them from destruction. Third, they could choose to resist. The definition of resistance is crucial to understanding Jewish behavior. Raul Hilberg considers resistance to mean only the use of arms.[21] Yehuda Bauer's definition is broader, including "all active and conscious organized action against the Nazi command's policies, or wishes, by whatever means: social organization, morale-building operations, underground political work, active unarmed resistance or, finally, armed resistance."[22] Reuben Ainsztein divides resistance into four types: partisan activities, revolts and underground activities in ghettos, revolts and underground activities in camps, and actions in defense of lives and human dignity.[23]

Resistance for anyone was difficult in the Third Reich, but it was doubly so for Jews, who were scattered among a largely indifferent and frequently hostile Gentile population. The obstacles seemed insurmountable.[24]And yet, many Jews resisted: they fought those who tried to round them up, they escaped to the forests to join the partisans, they revolted in camps and ghettos, they engaged in sabotage, they hid.[25]

Regardless of the particular form resistance took, success was determined by three factors. First, the character and skills of the individuals played a crucial role. Individuals who were assimilated into non-Jewish culture had a better chance of "passing" as Aryan. Courage, the ability to adapt to unforeseen circumstances, physical appearance, and language skills all helped. Second, social environment—that is, the historical attitude of the local population toward Jews—could spell the difference between survival and death. Surviving without assistance from the non-Jewish population was next to impossible. Thus, while 15 percent of Italian Jews lost their lives, the figure is 90 percent for Poland, which had a long tradition of antisemitism and experienced the harsh conditions of German occupation.[26] Jews who attempted to join partisan units were much more successful in the occupied USSR than in occupied Poland. Third, the physical environment also played a role: those who escaped to the forests of Byelorussia had a better chance than those fleeing on the open steppes of Ukraine.

The story of Wilhelm Bachner is an example of the fourth type of resistance described by Ainsztein: the defense of lives and dignity.[27] Bachner saved over fifty persons from the Jewish ghettos of Poland, many of whom survived the war. He did it armed only with his skill, courage, and intelligence.

Wilhelm Bachner was born on September 17, 1912, in the Polish town of Bielsko (German Bielitz). Long a part of the Austro-Hungarian Empire, Bielsko was culturally German, joining Poland only after World War I. Bachner's surname reflected this German heritage as did the fact that he grew up speaking German. Bachner studied engineering in Brno, Czechoslovakia, graduating in 1938. After a short stay in his native city, he went to work in Warsaw in the spring of 1939 and soon married. By then the ghetto had been established.

Hungry and afraid, Bachner slipped out of the ghetto and applied for a position as an engineer with a local German architectural firm that had recently opened an office in Warsaw. He impressed the firm's owner, Johannes Kellner, and before long Bachner was supervising over eight hundred people. He sneaked out over fifty Jews from various ghettos, including his wife—who had to become his "mistress"—and other members of his family and hired them for the firm. The Kellner Firm was under contract with the German railroad (Deutsche Reichsbahn) and was provided with a construction shop on rails (*Bauzug*) that carried its own tools, supplies, food, and sleeping quarters for railroad work crews. Their task was to rebuild destroyed bridges, rail lines, barracks, and railroad stations. Soon after the Nazi invasion of the Soviet Union, Bachner convinced Kellner to open branches in different parts of newly conquered Eastern Europe, most importantly in Kiev. In Kiev Bachner obtained a house, which he converted to a safehouse for Jews he rescued from the Warsaw and Kraków ghettos with the help of his trusted, non-Jewish friend Kazaniecki.

Careful planning and anticipatory action deflected suspicion from Bachner and those Jews he hired as part of the work crews. All of those people were given false identity papers and worked alongside the 750 Poles and Ukrainians under Bachner's supervision. In this manner fifty Jews survived the war on the Eastern Front until Bachner surrendered himself and his crew to the American forces in Germany in 1945.

How and why was this modest man, as well as several of his rescued survivors, able to accomplish this feat? Wilhelm Bachner's success in eluding discovery was due to a complex combination of innate and acquired qualities. For Jews in Nazi-occupied Europe, survival was as much a matter of chance as of skill and environment. Recounting the story of his many brushes with death, Bachner admitted, "If I go through my whole story, it looks like God in heaven had nothing else to do, only to look after Bill Bachner with all his family and with all the Jewish friends he saved."[28]

But growing up in Bielsko meant that he absorbed German culture. He learned Polish as a second language. Bachner's socialization into German culture also gave him a German outlook: "I was used to organizing everything in a perfect, German way," he said, "which was very appreciated by the Germans who were guarding or supervising us."[29] Appearance helped. Though slight in stature, the photo on Bachner's work permit shows a handsome, dark-haired man with a neat mustache. Had Bachner been born with obvious Jewish features, speaking German like Goethe could not have saved him. Dressed in a black leather jacket and boots, discussing construction plans in elegant German, Bachner's Jewish identity was never suspected.

Fast thinking and sheer pluck played a role. In September 1942, shortly after Bachner had brought the last of his people from the Warsaw Ghetto to Kiev, he found himself facing the Gestapo, who, alerted by an informer, showed up at his office, guns drawn, accusing him of hiding Jews. A Jewish crew member, Hania Shane, whom he saved, recalled the incident: "Willie, very calm, was yelling back at them, 'How dare you say this; if you are so sure, why don't you go find them yourselves.' While he was arguing with them and prolonging the heated discussion, my friend Heniek left the office and went to the train station where his crew was working and quietly dispersed the Jewish workers just in case."[30]

But it was character, courage, and his values that motivated Bachner to act. When asked what motivated him to risk his life to rescue others besides his immediate family, Bachner said, "I did it to show—if you are nice to people, God maybe will be nice to you." Bachner's cousin describes their grandmother telling them all that they had the responsibility to do good, and that they would receive their reward in heaven. Bachner himself demonstrated caring for others even after World War II, when he was deeply involved with those whom he had rescued, and even his German boss, Kellner, who only then learned that Bachner and many members of his crew were Jews.

Other Rescuers

We suggest that there is a need to expand the scope of research to prosocial behavior in other contexts and societies. We need to look at diverse types of rescue in contexts where social norms approve the behavior, in contrast to those contexts where it involves acting against prevailing norms. Research needs to collect accounts such as that of Christian Fetteroff, who was stabbed while rescuing a woman who was being mugged in a New York subway. In the hospital, Feteroff explained to a reporter, "What I did makes me a human being. I helped someone who needed help. It wasn't heroic. Until now, I didn't know that everybody wouldn't act the same way."[31]

Since April 15, 1905, the Carnegie Hero Fund Commission has awarded medals and monetary rewards to 7,744 individuals who risked their lives to save individuals who were in great danger. Among the awardees, 8.8 percent were females and 91.2 percent were males, of whom 1,584 (20 percent), received their medals posthumously. Criteria for the award include conclusive evidence that the person risked his or her life in saving, or attempting to save, the life of another person, and the absence of any full measure of responsibility between the rescuer and the rescued (i.e., one doesn't get a reward for rescuing a family member). According to Walter F. Rutkowski, Executive Vice President of the Carnegie Hero Fund Commission, in the fifteen years of his directorship, no systematic research has been done on the Carnegie heroes. This is clearly a fertile area for exploration.

Further research also needs to be done on heroic rescuers who acted in other hostile or disapproving settings, such as the Turkish rescuers of Armenians during the 1915 genocide,[32] and Kuwaiti rescuers of Palestinians after the Gulf War (1991–1992). More work needs to be done on conventional altruists such as hospice volunteers,[33] as well as on inclusively oriented moral communities such as the Bahá'ís,[34] in order to help us better understand goodness, how it comes about, and how it can be fostered. All of the above suggestions could, in our view, shed more light on the nature of altruism and its relationship to rescue and prosocial behavior.

Half a century after the events of the Holocaust, what can we learn from studying rescuers of Jews during World War II? First, acts of heroic altruism are not the province of larger-than-life figures. Rather, they are the *deeds of ordinary people* whose moral courage arises out of the routine ways they live their daily lives—their ways of feeling, their perceptions of what authority should be obeyed, and the models of conduct they learned from parents, friends, or religious instruction.

If we are to empower people to intervene actively in the presence of destructive social forces, then social institutions must also assume that obligation. Schools, clubs, religious institutions, the workplace, and the community in general, should share in the inculcation of moral values, especially in extensive, inclusive orientation. Schools need to rework curricula to include prosocial education as a basic competency along with reading, writing, and arithmetic. They should inculcate not only the obligation to act on behalf of others, they should also explain the consequences of indifference. Rescuers, both Gentile and Jewish, need to appear in the history books as moral heroes who made a difference, thus perhaps correcting the distorted image of humanity brought about by Nazi genocide.

These institutions will need to appeal to the intellect, emotions, and to group norms, emphasizing the obligation not only to the immediate community but to those outside it as well. Such institutions will have to recognize that bonds among people are often created through the experience of caring. Hence, they will need to become caring institutions, especially insofar as they teach the young.

Institutions must be linked to the larger community in an ecological web that facilitates understanding of and promotes universal ethical norms. Such an approach challenges Western thinking, which has traditionally venerated the autonomous individual guided by rationality. But neither autonomous thought nor rationality can guarantee moral virtue. The same, of course, may be said of emotional reactions and empathy, or group norms. The road to virtue is not single but multiple; and we need to study all its paths. Rescuers responded to Jews because to do so confirmed and supported the values of the social group with which they identified most closely. The lonely embattled hero confronting the mob deserves our admiration, but he or she is a rarity. For most people, moral behavior is the consequence of empathy, caring for others, and strong attachment to moral communities that embrace ethical obligations as universally binding.

Should our social institutions fail to acknowledge this they will fail to empower ordinary people with the spirit of altruism. Our need to respond to both local and global concerns in the spirit of altruism is urgent. The concept of the "global village" implies not only the sharing of a single environment but of a single moral community. More than a century ago Emile Durkheim observed that rather than being an "agreeable ornament of social life," altruism is essential for the survival of any society. What Durkheim failed to emphasize, however, and what the research on rescuers demonstrates, is that benefit accrues not only to society as a whole but also to the participants in it. Reaching out to others can be enormously gratifying, persuading the actors to believe in their own potency, their skills, and above all, their humanity. To understand compassion, we need to look at examples of helping in other contexts and cultures, both synchronically, and diachronically. Harold Schulweis has remarked that "goodness is rare but sacred in history; it must not be neglected." To research and understand goodness would prove a valuable legacy for our children.

NOTES

1. P. Friedman, *Their Brother's Keepers* (New York: Crown, 1957).

2. Initially I was involved very briefly with the Institute for Righteous Acts, introducing Professor Frederick Terrien, a sociologist from San Francisco State, to assist Rabbi Schulweis, who served on the first advisory board. Among the first directors were Mrs. Neil Smelser and Perry London. In 1978, I became director of the Institute.

3. See the bibliography in S. P. Oliner and P. M. Oliner, *The Altruistic Personality: Rescuers of Jews in Nazi Europe* (New York: Free Press, 1988), p. 419.

4. Because of the variety of approaches used, meta-analysis of the books and articles of some of these authors in order to arrive at common independent variables explaining motivation proved unfeasible.

5. Altruism is devotion to the welfare of others. Specifically, altruism 1) is directed toward helping others; 2) involves high risk or sacrifice for the actor; 3) is not accompanied by external reward; and 4) is voluntary. Rescuers in the context of the Holocaust meet these criteria.

6. See the recently published book by Samuel P. Oliner and Kathleen Lee, *Who Shall Live: The Wilhelm Bachner Story* (Chicago: Academy Chicago, 1996).

7. See Oliner and Oliner, *Altruistic Personality*, for details on other researchers and methodologies.

8. By values we mean the enduring organization of beliefs concerning preferable modes of conduct and/or states of existence. Another definition is the collective conception of what is considered good, desirable, and proper, or bad, undesirable, and improper, in a culture. Schulman and Mekler define moral values as consisting of empathy, kindness, and responsibility. See M. Schulman and E. Mekler, *Bringing Up a Moral Child* (Reading, MA: Addison-Wesley, 1985).

9. N. Tec, E. Fogelman, L. Baron, D. Huneke, and others, have reported similar findings.

10. On moral heroism and the concept of extensivity, see Oliner and Oliner, *Altruistic Personality*, pp. 249–60.

11. On empathic, normocentric, and principled motivations, see ibid., p. 188; J. Reykowski, "Dimensions of Development in Moral Values: Two Approaches to the Development of Morality," in *Social and Moral Values: Individual and Societal Perspectives*, ed. N. Eisenberg, J. Reykowski, and E. Staub (New Jersey: Lawrence Erlbaum, 1987).

12. As in Denmark, Italy, and Bulgaria, where there were national efforts to rescue Jewish citizens.

13. This chapter includes a variety of rescuers' comments that originally appeared in Oliner and Oliner, *Altruistic Personality*. The identities of the rescuers remain confidential.

14. L. Yahil, *The Rescue of Danish Jewry: Test of a Democracy* (Philadelphia: Jewish Publication Society, 1969); S. Zuccotti, *The Italians and the Holocaust: Persecution, Rescue, and Survival* (New York: Basic Books, 1987); idem, *The Holocaust, the French, and the Jews* (New York: Basic Books, 1993); A. Ramati, *The Assisi Underground: The Priests Who Rescued the Jews* (New York: Stein and Day, 1978); D. Carpi, "The Rescue of Jews in the Italian Zone of Occupied Croatia," in *Rescue Attempts during the Holocaust: Proceedings of the Second Yad Veshem Internationl Historical Conference,* ed. Y. Gutman and E. Zuroff (Jerusalem: Yad Vashem, 1974), pp. 465–525; F. B. Chary, *The Bulgarian Jews and the Final Solution, 1940–1944* (Pittsburgh: University of Pittsburgh Press, 1972); H. Flender, *Rescue in Denmark* (New York: Manor, 1964); P. Friedman, *Their Brothers' Keepers: The Christian Heroes and Heroines Who Helped the Oppressed Escape the Nazi Terror* (New York: Crown, 1957); L. Baron, "The Historical Context of Rescue," in Oliner and Oliner, *Altruistic Personality*.

15. See, for example, E. Fleischner, *Remembering for the Future, Theme 1: Jews and Christians during and after the Holocaust*, International Scholars Conference, Oxford, July 10–13 (Oxford: Pergamon Press, 1988), pp. 233–47; E. Kurek, "The Role of Polish Nuns in the Rescue of Jews, 1939–1945," in *Embracing the Other: Philosophical, Psychological, and Histori-*

cal Perspectives on Altruism, ed. S. P. Oliner, P. M. Oliner et al. (New York: New York University Press, 1992), pp. 328–33; D. K. Huneke, "The Lesson of Herman Graebes' Life: The Origins of a Moral Person," *Humboldt Journal of Social Relations* 13/1–2 (1986): 320–31; Oliner and Oliner, *Altruistic Personality*; N. Tec, *When Light Pierced the Darkness: Christian Rescue of Jews in Nazi-Occupied Poland* (New York: Oxford University Press, 1986).

16. L. Baron, "The Moral Minority: A Review of Psycho-Social Research on the Righteous Gentiles," in *Forty-Five Years After: What Have We Learned about the Holocaust*, ed. A. Berger, F. Littell, and H. Locke (Lewiston, New York: Edwin Mellin, 1993); P. Sauvage, "Ten Things I Would Like to Know about Righteous Conduct in Le Chambron and Elsewhere during the Holocaust," *Humboldt Journal of Social Relations* 13/1–2 (1986): 252–59; D. K. Huneke, "The Lessons of Herman Graebes' Life: The Origins of a Moral Person," *Humboldt Journal of Social Relations* 13/1–2 (1986); S. Zeitoun, "The Role of Christian Community in Saving Jewish Children in France during the Second World War," in *Remembering for the Future: The Impact of the Holocaust and Genocide on Jews and Christians*, ed. E. Fleischner, supplementary volume (Oxford: Pergamon, 1988), pp. 505–25; Oliner and Oliner, *Altruistic Personality*; P. Haille, *Lest Innocent Blood Be Shed: The Story of Le Chambron and How Goodness Happened There* (New York: Harper and Row, 1979); Kurek, "Role of Polish Nuns," pp. 328–33; S. P. Oliner and P. M. Oliner, "Righteous People in the Holocaust" in *Genocide: A Critical Bibliographic Review*, ed. I. W. Charney (London: Mansell, 1991), pp. 363–85; P. London, "The Rescuers: Motivational Hypotheses about Christians Who Save Jews form the Nazis," in *Altruism and Helping Behavior*, ed. J. Macauley and L. Berkowitz (New York: Academic Press, 1970), pp. 241–65; Tec, *When Light Pierced the Darkness*; E. Fogelman, *The Rescuers: A Socio-Psychological Study of Altruistic Behavior during the Nazi Era* (Ann Arbor: University·of Michigan Press, 1987).

17. See Oliner and Lee, *Who Shall Live*.

18. R. Ainsztein, *Jewish Resistance in Nazi-Occupied Eastern Europe* (New York: Barnes and Noble, 1974); N. Tec, *In the Lion's Den: The Life of Oswald Rufeisen* (New York: Oxford University Press, 1990); L. Baron, "The Historical Context of Rescue," in Oliner and Oliner, *Altruistic Personality*; M. Berenbaum, *The World Must Know: The History of the Holocaust Told in the United States Holocaust Museum* (Boston: Little, Brown and Co., 1993); H. Smolar, *Resistance in Minsk*, trans. H. J. Lewbin (Oakland: Judah L. Magnes Memorial Museum, 1966). There are several dozen books and articles about resistance in various parts of Europe. Only a few institutions in the United States, Israel, and Germany were helpful in providing the names of Jewish rescuers: the Moreshet Archives in Israel, the Vidal Sassoon International Center, The Tel Aviv University Wiener Library, Bet Lohamei Haghetaot Ghetto Fighters, the United States Holocaust Memorial Museum in Washington, the Fortunoff Video Archives for Holocaust Testimonies at Yale University, the Technische Universität in Berlin, and the St. Louis Center for Holocaust Studies. In all of these cases only detailed searches can reveal the names of the Jewish rescuers.

19. L. S. Dawidowicz, *The War against the Jews: 1933–1945* (New York: Holt Rinehart and Winston, 1975), p. 341.

20. Baron, "Historical Context of Rescue," p. 35.

21. Raul Hilberg, *The Destruction of the European Jews* (New York: Watts [New Viewpoints], 1973), pp. 660–68.

22. Yehuda Bauer, "Jewish Leadership Reactions to Nazi Policies," in *The Holocaust as Historical Experience*, ed. Y. Bauer and N. Rotenstreich (New York: Holmes & Meier, 1981), pp. 173–74.

23. Ainsztein, *Jewish Resistance*, p. xxvii.

24. Yehuda Bauer, *A History of the Holocaust* (New York: Watts, 1982), p. 247.

25. Berenbaum, *The World Must Know*; Tec, *In the Lion's Den*; J. Semelin, *Unarmed against Hitler: Civilian Resistance in France 1939–1943*, trans. S. Hussert-Kapit (Westport, CN: Praeger, 1993); M. Barkai, ed., *The Fighting Ghettos* (New York: Tower Books, 1962); Smolar, *Resistance in Minsk*.

26. Baron, "Historical Context of Rescue," pp. 25, 44.

27. In 1982 I interviewed Wilhelm Bachner as a rescued survivor. To my surprise we

Part 11

The Survivor Experience

The history of the Holocaust did not end in 1945 with the liberation. It is an unfolding story that continues in the efforts of survivors to rebuild their lives, renew their spirits and document their experiences.

In "We're on Our Way, but We're Not in the Wilderness," Jacqueline Giere describes the experiences of Jews in the displaced persons camps of Germany as instances of a larger survivor-migrant phenomenon. The terms should be defined. Survivors are people who have experienced persecution as members of an ethnic group. Migrants are defined by what they are not: they are neither immigrants nor emigrants. They are in a temporary hiatus—waiting before continuing on to their final destination. They have a past to which they cannot return, and they are not yet at their future home.

When Germany capitulated, more than 10 million foreign nationals were in the country. Most wanted to return home and did so shortly after the collapse of the Reich. Jews had no homes or families to which they could return. They surely did not want to remain in Germany, and there was no country offering them a future.

By the end of 1946, more than 150,000 Jews had moved into displaced persons camps—in part because they had left Poland after the Kielce pogrom, when forty-one Jews were murdered, or they had begun their migration westward from the Soviet Union and Soviet-held territories. Some were survivors of the camps. Their condition was unique; as one of their leaders described it: "We're not alive—we're still dead." Those who survived by hiding their identity were confused about that identity. Partisans were accustomed to the fighting life. For the most part, those who migrated from the Soviet Union survived with their family life intact. They had completed the first part of their emigration. For children, the problem of post-war survival was acute. They had the interrupted education of youngsters and life experience that would have frightened even the most mature of adults.

In each of the DP camps there were theatrical activities, newspapers of diverse sorts and educational programs at all levels—from elementary school to medical school to vocational training. Giere suggests that these diverse activities should be seen as a time line to link both the individuals and the group to a common past, logical present, and probable future. Educational and cultural activities played an important part in helping survivors construct their lives. The newspapers, she suggests, were a bridge between past and present; the theatrical activities were often a photo album of memories. Schools and politics were directly linked to the future. The topology she offers, though directly an outgrowth of the singular experience of Holocaust survivors, may be a model of transition for other victimized groups.

Thomas Albrich's "Way Station of Exodus: Jewish Displaced Persons and Refugees in Postwar Austria" details the role of Austria as the most important transit country for the largest organized clandestine migration of the postwar period. Some 200,000 survivors passed through Austria in the aftermath of the war. The pace intensified immediately after the Kielce pogrom—an event conveying to Polish Jews the insecurity of their return home.

Though between twenty thousand and twenty-five thousand Jews were in Austria at the end of the war, the number dwindled rapidly; only five thousand remained by mid-July of 1945 as Hungarian Jews returned home and the American Jewish Joint Distribution Committee took candidates for Palestine to Italy. By December conditions had settled since three new permanent camps had been established—Bindermichl in Linz, Bad Gastein near Salzburg, and Trofaich in the British Zone. Brichah, the clandestine Palestine-based operation for the migration of Jews to Palestine, was informally running the camps with a skeleton crew of leaders. Money was supplied by Jewish relief organizations. American authorities did not interfere; the British unsuccessfully attempted to infiltrate the group to halt at its source emigration to Palestine.

After the July 4, 1946, pogrom at Kielce, there was a mass flight of Jews from Poland. It overwhelmed the available resources of the occupying Western forces in Austria. The flood continued over the next year notwithstanding the fact that U.S. authorities in Germany accepted forty-five thousand Jewish DPs arriving through Austria. Austria became the critical transit point for this mass exodus; it was an important staging area for those who wanted to use the situation of the displaced persons to press for a Jewish state. The Austrian role remained in effect until well after the establishment of the state of Israel in May 1948.

Albrich indicates that while the early years, 1945–1947, have been well documented, the later years of the displaced persons camps have not. Neither do we know much about the social history of Jewish survivors in Austria, nor do we know much about the tensions between Jews of different countries of origin and diverse political persuasions. Still unexplored is what happened to these transient Jews during their Austrian sojourn.

In "From Illegal Immigrants to New Immigrants: The Cyprus Detainees, 1946–1949," Dalia Ofer details the postwar experience of survivors en route to what was then Palestine. An exact detailing of survivors after the war is not possible, but there are reliable estimates.

Between 50,000 and 80,000 Jews were in Germany after the war; the other large populations were in native countries where they had survived. Approximately 143,000 were in Hungary, almost all of them in Budapest; 400,000 Jews remained alive in the old territories of Romania; the Jews of Transylvania had been killed virtually en masse; 40,000 remained in Bulgaria, which consented to the deportation of Jews from Thrace and Macedonia but not to that of its own Jewish community; 130,000 Jews had survived in Soviet-held territories that had been returned to Poland. After the pogrom in Kielce, Jews fled westward, and by January 1948, 250,000 were in displaced persons camps in the West.

Between 1945 and 1948, many Jews tried to enter Palestine illegally, but most were captured and detained; 51,530 were incarcerated in DP camps in Cyprus. Once the state was established, 373,852 Holocaust survivors entered Israel in its first three years.

Ofer examines the integration of Cyprus detainees into Israel. She reasons that those detained in Cyprus had a better chance to integrate into Israeli society and identify with its visions and concerns. The war did not impede their absorption but rather assisted them, for they were anxious to begin their new lives.

Ofer describes the clash between Israel's ideology of nation building with its emphasis on the collective rather than the individual, and the survivors' understandable desire to find stability, to create a home, a family, to find a good job—personal goals antithetical to Israel's collective orientation.

The Yishuv (pre-1948 Palestinian Jewry) needed to listen to the hopes and desires of the immigrants, yet it could not. Survivors migrated toward the cities, and their economic hopes were facilitated by the shortage of labor in Israel during the War of Independence. Ofer concludes with the early absorption of the immigrants. How Israelis came to perceive survivors and how survivors came to speak of their past once settled in Israel is another story.

In the essay—as in the book of the same title—"Against All Odds: Survivors of the Holocaust and the American Experience," William B. Helmreich attempts to shift the focus of research from pathology to adaptability. He asks, How were survivors able to live again, trust and create a home life, smile and love again? Using the methodology of sociology as well as extensive oral interviews, Helmreich attempts to answer these questions.

One-third of Jewish displaced persons came to the United States; nearly all of the remaining two-thirds went to Israel. Two out of three of the former settled in New York. Unlike previous Jewish immigrants whose migration to the United States meant a break in family ties, many survivors resumed family contacts in this country; their European relatives had been killed and only those family members who had come earlier to America remained.

Helmreich discovered that by 1948 almost no DPs had been deported for any reason and there was almost no criminal activity among this group of immigrants. While there were some instances of family pathology, the overall picture is of love and commitment. He found a tendency for survivors to be overprotective of their children and even more disturbed than nonsurvivors if their children intermarried—they are more mindful of the break with Jewish tradition implied in mixed marriage. They are more reluctant to trust non-Jews. Their children have been as successful as the Jewish children of nonimmigrants. Survivors' children do have a pronounced tendency to enter the helping professions.

Survivors are three times as likely as the general population of American Jews to have visited Israel on at least two occasions. American Jews are more likely to consult mental health professionals than survivors. Most survivors did not become atheists, though they expressed doubts about God's relationship to them. Helmreich lists ten qualities that he found in survivors: flexibility, assertiveness, tenacity, optimism, intelligence, distancing ability, group consciousness, assimilating the knowledge that they survived, finding meaning in one's life, and courage. These, along with good health and good luck, account for the successful adaptation of survivors to America.

As a survivor, Leo Eitinger (1912–1996) had a distinct advantage in analyzing post-Holocaust trauma. He was a trained psychiatrist before he entered Auschwitz, and while imprisoned there, he worked within and in proximity to the infirmaries or hospitals—no word seems quite accurate—inside the death camp. After his liberation, he published many studies of survivors in Norway and in Israel. In "Holocaust Survivors in Past and Present," Eitinger reviews the literature related to survivors.

In studies of Post-Traumatic Stress Syndrome, psychiatrists emphasize that the response of the individual is related to the patient's personality, the nature of the trauma, and the social-psychological interhuman therapeutic situation after the trauma. Eitinger contends that survivors were not a random sample of all the prisoners. They have survived a series of selections, endured the harshest of conditions, and have overcome significant obstacles that mitigated against their survival. Almost all who entered the death camps never left. Those who lived to see liberation were indeed an unusual lot, even if they cannot admit how special they are.

The trauma has been explored by historians and philosophers, and by students of literature and psychology and many other disciplines. The more it is studied, the more we understand the magnitude of the trauma and discover the limitations of our understanding.

Eitinger writes of the post-war situation:

> Danish and Norwegian survivors were relatively best off because they were liberated before the end of the war; they returned to their homes and families and were received as heroes." Other survivors were numbed by their loss; their homes had been destroyed, their families had vanished and they were received with suspicion: "why did you survive when all the others perished?" The awakening was even more painful than the struggle for survival because it was then that they first began to realize the actual meaning of what had happened, it was then they became conscious of the magnitude. Those who returned "home" were confronted with rejection, even pogroms; and those who remained in the camps were treated impersonally.

Eitinger details clinical findings and discusses survivor guilt and Post-Traumatic Stress Syndrome, as well as the early findings of Bruno Bettelheim, who accused the victims of regression and identification with the aggressor. Eitinger's findings lead to different conclusions; thus, he cautioned: "Guilt may be a projection of guilt onto survivors." It may reflect the guilt the clinicians felt toward survivors and toward their own inaction.

Eitinger charted a course for future research—most especially as survivors are entering or have entered old age and the normal process of aging may be intensified by the brutality of their fate during the Holocaust.

We are well aware of the "conspiracy of silence" that existed between survivors of the Holocaust and many of the nations to which they emigrated in the period between 1948 and the early 1950s. Survivors in countries such as the United States and Canada withdrew from efforts at relating their experiences after being told that they had "vivid imaginations." For nearly three decades, most survivors stopped talking about ghettos, deportations, and gas chambers. Much of this has changed since the 1970s and early 1980s, when a new generation of Jews and Christians found reason to listen to survivor voices and as the Holocaust entered the mainstream of American experience.

Of all the places where survivors went to rebuild their shattered lives, the State of Israel should have been the most receptive. But nearly half a century later, many historians have begun to perceive and describe a different kind of reception. Survivors were seen as the remnants of a people who had rejected the message of Zionism and aliyah and had paid a terrible price for it. They were viewed by the Zionist political leaders of Palestine as a tool to be manipulated on behalf of the creation of the Israeli state but at the same time as people who had no intrinsic value or worth to the Jewish nation.

Dina Porat's work is less about the history of the immediate post-Holocaust era in the Yishuv and later in the newly proclaimed State of Israel than about the debate that has developed in Israel in the past decade over Israel's attitude toward the survivors. In "Israeli Society and Recent Attitudes toward the Jews of Europe and Holocaust Survivors," she finds that the debate focuses as much or more on the issue of Israel's post-Zionist critics, revisionist historians who see the creation of Israel as a negative and cynical event and Israel as anti-Arab and as an anti-Holocaust survivor.

In "History, Memory, and Truth: Defining the Place of the Survivor," Dori Laub, writing with Marjorie Allard, discusses the displacement of survivors after trauma. According to Laub, trauma is loss of place: "a home can never be a home again" and an erased relationship can never provide safety. For the survivor, the Holocaust is not past; it did not end with liberation, and time does not heal all wounds. Only the pre-Holocaust world provides a place where the world is whole.

After trauma there are a series of psychological responses, numbing, denial, and survivor guilt. These are the normal mechanisms for dealing with death and have been repeatedly invoked to address survivor experience. To Laub, these are helpful but inadequate. Neither culture nor past experience provides structures for formulating what happened—for the Holocaust is indeed without precedent.

The massive failure of empathy, Laub writes, resulted not just in a negative self-image but in an image of the self as nonhuman, hence with no links to humanity. The crime was not only in killing Jews but in getting Jews to believe they deserved it. For those who endured, the struggle is to get beyond the internalized verdict. To bear witness, Laub writes, "one must live, yet to live one must leave the community of the dead." Thus, the task of testimony is essential for the survivor. The "survivor needed to survive to tell the story, but also told the story in order to survive," Laub declares. We the listeners make the witnessing happen. And the ability to listen with empathy embodies the return of the other, trust in the other.

48.

JACQUELINE GIERE

"We're on Our Way, but We're Not in the Wilderness"

When Germany capitulated on May 8, 1945, more than ten million foreign nationals were in that country: former POWs, former forced laborers, survivors of the death marches, inmates liberated from concentration and work camps. The Allies set about helping them by providing food, clothing, medical support, and shelter. Conditions were not optimal. The country had been heavily bombed, cities lay in ruins, bridges and railway lines were destroyed, and telephone and mail services seldom worked.

The Allies and the UN refugee organization termed these millions who had been brought to Germany against their will "displaced persons" (DPs). The foremost intention of the military and UN administrations was to help the DPs return home. However, most members of the many DP groups had no intention of returning to their former countries. These were the Jewish survivors, mainly from Poland, a few from Czechoslovakia, Hungary, Romania, and the USSR, who felt they no longer had homes in Eastern Europe. Their families had been murdered and their communities wiped out. Their former neighbors had long since taken over whatever material possessions, including living quarters, these former Jewish citizens had left behind.

The Jewish DPs described here[1] spent the years 1945–1949 in the U.S. Occupation Zone of Germany. They came to the American Zone from different backgrounds, they had experienced the war years in different ways and in different places, and they had varying intentions as to their futures. One thing they had in common: virtually none of them intended to remain in Germany.

The majority had lived in Poland between the world wars.[2] There they were a recognized minority, with representatives in the seym, the Polish parliament. Most lived in towns and cities. There they had published Yiddish and Polish-language newspapers and enjoyed classical Yiddish plays performed by professional stage companies such as the Vilna'er Truppe and the Varshever Yidisher Kunst-Teater.[3] Although, for lack of funds, most Jewish children had to attend the Polish elementary schools (powszechny) for secular education, some were able to study at one of a number of Jewish secular institutions, among them the Zionist "tarbut" schools and the "tsisho" schools sponsored by the Jewish labor organization, the Bund.[4] Later, in the Nazi-imposed ghettos, Polish Jewry attempted to continue its cultural life as far as possible; both general and vocational education were offered; illegal pamphlets were published and theater performances given. Later still, musicians and actors even gave recitals or presented short sketches in some of the concentration camps.[5]

At war's end, the relatively few Eastern European Jews who were alive were scattered from Siberia to Germany. By the close of 1946, about 150,000 of them had moved into DP camps and assembly centers in the U.S. Zone in or near Munich, Ulm, Stuttgart, Frankfurt, Kassel, Bamberg, Regensburg, and elsewhere. Of these, approximately 14,500 were children between the ages of six and seventeen. Some had been liberated from concentration camps on German soil or had survived the westward death marches from Auschwitz. Others had fought as partisans or had spent months or years hiding in forests, hiding in peasants' houses, or living in Polish cities with forged so-called Aryan passes. Spring of 1946 brought additional refugees (first called "infiltrees" by military bureaucrats, but later recognized as DPs as well). These were for the most part Polish Jews who, early in the war, had arrived one way or another in the Soviet Union and had spent the following years in Siberia, Uzbekistan, or near the Black Sea. Now their preferred destinations were as varied as their origins. Palestine—in the Yiddish most DPs spoke, Eretz Yisroel—and the United States were first choices, but a number wished to go to France, England, Argentina, Canada, or to other countries.

Decisions about where they would ultimately lead their lives were strongly influenced by forces over which the DPs had little or no control. The newly established communist government in Poland officially welcomed Jews back as an expression of socialist internationalism and expressed a hope that a new Jewish community would establish itself in Lower Silesia. But antisemitism continued to be openly expressed among the general population, and pogroms led most returnees to flee. Germany was considered the "blutike daytshe erd," the bloody soil, the land of murderers. There were Germans who regretted the crimes committed under the Third Reich and German politicians who realized the importance of establishing good relations with Jews in order to effect Germany's reacceptance into the Western world. But memories of mass murder and continued antisemitism led most to refuse a home there. The United States had immigration laws and quotas that made it impossible for more than a few to enter; liberalizing amendments to the law were not passed until 1948. Finally, Palestine was a British mandate, and London had no intention of letting a substantial number of Jews enter the area. Free immigration became possible only when the State of Israel was founded in May 1948.

Decisions as to how the Jewish DPs would lead their everyday lives in Germany were also subject to external control, but here the DPs sought and found ways to cooperate or to coerce the controlling bodies, as needed. The four major organizations involved in daily DP camp life in the American Zone of Germany were the Office of the Military Government for Germany, United States (OMGUS), the United Nations Relief and Rehabilitation Administration (UNRRA), the American Joint Jewish Distribution Committee (AJJDC or Joint Committee), and the Jewish Agency. While OMGUS and UNRRA were responsible for setting up camps and providing basic logistic support, the Joint Committee and the Jewish Agency became involved in many DP projects, offering ideological and financial support or setting limits.

The Jewish DPs

The Jewish displaced persons in the American Zone were not silent survivors. They voiced their opinions and spoke about their experiences; they wrote long articles and delivered articulate speeches about what they expected of life and about what life had done to them. They knew what they wanted themselves to be, and they were painfully aware of what National Socialist oppression and persecution had made of them. Their cultural activities developed within the highly charged atmosphere between these two poles.

In their ideal conceptions, adult DPs were considered "those purified by the smelting pots of the ghettos and concentration camps."[6] The youth comprised the "constructing reservoir" on which the Jewish population in Palestine would be able to draw. Kibbutz Banativ proclaimed: "[Young DPs,] your people is your father, Eretz Yisroel is your mother!"[7] Children were "the pride of the entire Jewish people," "the inheritors of the past and the future for present generations."[8] A teacher found the DP children a consolation "for [my] heart's burning wounds . . . , the sole revenge for past sufferings . . . , the great treasure of a poor people."[9]

The DPs placed high expectations on their group. Women were to teach young people aesthetic behavior "with every word, every gesture and every action. Thus they would fulfill one of the most important national duties."[10] For educators it was a "mitsve," a holy obligation "to erase the mildew [of the past] and raise new, healthy and free Jews."[11] Young people were called upon to hoist the flag of the pioneer movement, which still lay "on top of the ruins of the Warsaw Ghetto."[12] Last, but definitely not least, children were seen as a living monument—to the lost East European culture and to the more than one million Jewish children murdered during the period of the Third Reich.[13]

At the same time, though, writers and lecturers observed their fellow DPs and saw the impact their experience with industrialized mass murder had had upon them. Those who had survived the death camps called themselves "kazetler" (from the German acronym "KZ" for concentration camp—Konzentrationslager). Leo Srole, a UNRRA welfare officer, described them as suffering from symptoms similar to those of combat fatigue.[14] Sama Wachs, editor of the Stuttgart camp newspaper *Oyf der fray*, found them apathetic, lethargic, and incapable of aggressive feelings of revenge: "Considering the deaths of your parents, your brothers and your sisters, no form of revenge, no punishment could ever satisfy you."[15] Zalman Grinberg, who was to become the first chairman of the Central Committee, exclaimed: "We're not alive— we're still dead!"[16]

These survivors mistrusted the world in general and goyim, non-Jews, in particular. Their personalities had become "hard and sinewy"; they saw no reason to feel bound by any kind of law and order.[17] Having suffered from forced labor calculated to work them to death, many now rejected any form of work. They had "an almost obsessive will to live normally again, to reclaim their full rights as free men."[18] Those who had survived as so-called Aryans were used to hiding their Jewishness, while former partisans were accustomed to a hard fighting life.

Jewish DPs who returned from the Soviet Union were different in many ways.

Many more families had remained intact. For them, work had remained the normal basis of everyday life. Having completed the first laps of emigration, they were used to waiting and more confident that the future would evolve as they hoped.

Those in their teens were a constant source of irritation—for DP cultural leaders and educators alike. On the one hand, many youths felt almost intoxicated with the freedoms they had suddenly attained. They had learned to react to "violence with violence and to strength with strength."[19] They had difficulties in settling down to the "boredom" of three certain meals a day and lessons in school. A Youth Aliyah representative summed it up: "A fifteen-year-old often possesses the verbal proficiency of a first-grader in Palestine, the general education of a ten-year-old, and the life experiences of an adult."[20]

Those few children who had survived camps, who had run away from ghettos and lived in dugouts in the woods or hidden on farms, had often never had a chance to learn morals or "bourgeois behavior"; in fact they had not had much of a childhood at all. One teacher reported a conversation with one of his pupils: "'My dear teacher, I killed a man, with an ax,' he told me in about the same tone of voice he would have used if he'd stolen two bowls of soup from the kitchen. 'My dear teacher, if we hadn't have murdered him, he'd have murdered us.'"[21]

Nevertheless, many of these Jewish DPs found ways to try to rebuild their lives. In summer 1945, just weeks after liberation, the Jewish DPs had already begun to build up a community—in spite of the conditions in Germany, in spite of physical and psychological wounds, and in spite of the fact that they were planning on staying only temporarily, for a few weeks, or a few months at most. No one knew at the beginning that their stay in the U.S. Zone would last well into 1948. For some it continued until 1949 or 1950. A few thousand—some who had begun their studies at German universities, some who had established businesses, and some whose physical and psychological wounds prevented moving out—still live in Germany today.

The DPs set up their own rudimentary administration. They held local and regional elections, and they established the Central Committee of the Liberated Jews in the U.S. Zone in Germany, the Central Council, and the yearly Congress of the Liberated Jews in the American Zone, composed of locally elected delegates. Every camp had its own committee supervising offices handling matters dealing with labor, clothing, finances, cultural, and other affairs, and tried more or less successfully to organize life on a local level. Political parties experienced a resurgence and battled one another. While most were Zionist-oriented, they differed about how to realize their goals, the appropriate balance between secular or religious influence, and priorities of action. Supported by mother parties and/or youth groups in the Yishuv (the Jewish settlement in Palestine), they founded kibbutzim and offered "hakhshara"—communal agricultural training—in the hills of Bavaria and on the fields of Hesse. Zionist-oriented DPs sponsored political activities and were in the majority on most camp committees and on the Central Committee as well. (For many DP activists, however, political affiliation was less a commitment to the Zionist ideal of the 1920s and 1930s, with its emphasis on physical work and return to agriculture, than a pragmatic choice: they hoped that one of the Zionist movements would enable them to leave the DP camps as soon as possible.)

Professional and "landsmannshaft" associations (organizations of Jews from the same town or region) were founded, as well as teachers', writers', and actors' unions; and their members fought for better salaries, better lodging, and better working conditions. Cultural activities blossomed, and DPs joined theater groups and wrote for newspapers and journals. An educational system evolved, ranging from kindergarten to university and including elementary schools, middle schools, high schools, teacher in-service training institutes, vocational schools, adult education, and public lectures.

How was this possible? How did the DPs manage in the long run to overcome or sufficiently suppress their traumatizations to establish the rudiments of a society, albeit a society in transit? Certainly, individual social workers, chaplains, U.S. Army officers and representatives from the Yishuv, the Joint Committee, the Jewish Agency, and the Jewish Brigade inspired hope, gave encouragement, or offered enough logistical help to get things going. This made it possible to evolve skeletal structures, which in turn offered fields of action where survivors could regain a sense of living, of doing, and of being. As will become clear, the cultural activities themselves—theaters, newspapers, and schools—played an important role in helping Jewish DPs recover from their past and prepare for their future. American-Jewish, Palestinian-Jewish and international organizations provided theoretical and practical support for these undertakings; OMGUS controlled them, and the Joint Committee, more than any other institution, financed them.

From early postliberation days, the DPs chose to call themselves "She'erit Ha-peletah"—the rest that remained, the surviving remnant.[22] The She'erit Ha-peletah took as their symbol a tree stump from which a tiny leafed branch was sprouting. Cultural activities in the DP camps were a manifest example of the leaves on that branch.

Cultural Activities and Education

DP Theater

Amateur theater groups (dramkrayzn) formed in many of the camps, while most of the professional actors among the DPs joined one of three professional troupes. The largest of these was MIT, Minkhener-[Y]iddisher Teater. Its first and most influential director was Israel Beker, who had fled at war's outbreak from Białystok to Moscow. There he studied theater with Shlomo Mikhoels, head of the Yiddish State Theater and one of the leading Yiddish actors and directors of the time. In 1946, after a stint in Southern Poland, Beker and his young troupe accepted an offer by the Brichah[23] rescue organization to smuggle them into the American Zone of Germany. Soon individual surviving actors joined them, and a year later MIT was the DP Central Theater.

Theater troupes faced many obstacles. At first, they played without scripts, reciting from memory. In the course of time, scripts did arrive and were used by the professional groups; smaller companies had to copy them by hand. Rooms for rehearsals were lacking, as were costumes and stage sets. The actors had to be their own stagehands, setting up sets, taking them down, and often sleeping between performances on stage or in cold buses.

Nevertheless, actors took it upon themselves to "weld anew the torn chain of Yiddish theater."[24] The majority of plays presented on DP stages were classical Yiddish drama (Sholom Aleichem, Avrohom Goldfaden, An-Ski, and others). A number of twentieth-century adaptations completed the repertoires. The plays presented Jewish history and the Yiddish family. Their themes were life and persecution under the Tsars, in the shtetl, during the Inquisition, in the pre-Enlightenment ghettos. The professional troupes traveled throughout the American Zone and reached tens of thousands of Jewish DPs. In 1947, a number of these professionals played roles in one of the first postwar movies made in Germany, *The Road Is Long*. It follows a script written by stage director Israel Beker and tells the story of a Polish Jewish family between 1939 and 1947— life in the ghetto, in a death camp, and in a DP camp. The movie opened on September 1, 1948, in Berlin, and subsequently was shown in Paris, New York, and Tel Aviv. It received enthusiastic reviews everywhere.

The spectators visiting DP theater productions seemed to enjoy themselves. Getting together to watch a play was a joyous occasion. Camp friends and neighbors met to chat, children played in the aisles, adults unpacked picnic lunches, and the audience openly expressed its admiration or its criticism. Some of the plays, such as *Tevye der Milkhiker* or *Shver tsu zayn a Yid*, met with great enthusiasm. Others, such as *Ikh leb*, a story of the Vilnius Ghetto (and a predecessor of Joshua Sobol's play written forty years later) received a cool welcome. One reviewer commented: "It's difficult to measure the gigantic size of a high mountain . . . if you're standing in the foothills."[25] Some presentations were simple musical revues, others, such as *Shlomo Molcho* (written in the 1920s by A. Leyeles, an American Yiddish journalist) were highly intellectual.

While former actors found a field of activity and DP audiences enjoyed the presentations, the Zionist-oriented political parties and quasi-government offices took little or no notice of them. The theater's emphasis on the Yiddish language and on Yiddish plays apparently made it a thing of the past in the eyes of the politicians.

DP Newspapers

Every camp produced a newspaper of sorts. Some consisted of mimeographed sheets or handwritten leaflets like Stuttgart's *Oyf der fray*. A few camps managed to put out multipage, professional productions when former journalists, editors, and academicians joined their staffs. These included *Unterwegs*, published in Frankfurt-Zeilsheim, and *Undzer Hofenung*, published in Eschwege. The *Landsberger Lager-Cajtung*, put out in Landsberg DP camp (near Munich) grew rapidly; a year after its founding, in October 1945, it changed its name to *Jidisze Cajtung* and became one of the main papers in the Zone. In the course of time, journals appeared as well and covered a wide range of topics. *Fun letstn khurbn* was published by the Central Historical Commission, its main purpose being to encourage survivor testimonies. With the *Jüdische Rundschau*, published in Marburg, Polish Jews who had maintained strong connections to prewar Germany established a German-language journal with literary, historical, philosophical, and scientific essays. *Hemshekh* was a literary journal and included survivors' poems, short stories, and reproductions of their art.[26]

Newspaper people faced great difficulties. Where were they to find paper, lead, or Hebrew letters; typesetters, printers, or means of transportation in bombed-out, former Nazi Germany? Although almost all papers and journals were written in Yiddish, for the most part it was "Latinized," that is, written in Roman (instead of Hebrew) letters and spelled according to Polish pronunciation. (This explains certain variations in Yiddish spelling here. "Latinized" titles and names are given as they appeared in the DP newspapers.) This was a hurdle of its own, for several dialects were to be found among the DPs, yet newspaper staffs had to settle for one. Written in Hebrew letters without vowels, Hebrew expressions in Yiddish were "neutral," each dialect reading them as it pleased. However, once the words were written in Latin letters, with vowels, they had to conform to one pronunciation. One of the editors of the *Jidisze Cajtung*, produced in Landsberg DP-camp, complained that the first journalists in Landsberg had been Litvaks, Lithuanian Jews, and had established their dialect as the newspaper's "language." Later journalists, all of them Polish, fought daily to find the correct spelling: "[One of the worst questions is:] '*Szajris-Haplajtu*' or '*Szejris-Haplejto*,' or perhaps in the Sephardic manner, as befits a nationally aware newspaper, '*Szejrit Haplejta*?'. . . The German linotypist is just as embarrassed; he turns to the editor and, by no means arrogantly, asks him in Russian: '*Czto eto takoje Szejrit-Haplejta*?'. . . On top of all of this it's important to realize that the words *Szejris-Haplejto* are in big demand right now. . . . They appear in almost every manuscript."[27]

Newspapers and journals sought to inform and educate their readers. One editor expressed the general goals as follows:

> We want to honor the great inheritance passed on to us by our murdered people.
> We want to build up a new life in which a catastrophe like this will never again be possible.
> We want to weave the melody of our rich history into the workers' song of our future.
> We want to be a bridge between Yesterday and Tomorrow.[28]

Accordingly, newspapers and journals offered information on Jewish history and Jewish holidays. They published reports of life and death in ghettos and death camps. They covered contemporary Jewish life in the world in general and in the DP camps in particular: cultural events, visits by prominent guests, school activities, and political controversies. The larger periodicals reported international events extensively. Most of these publications had special sections on Eretz Yisroel. In the course of time, these sections took on the flavor of national news. Seen as a whole, newspapers seem to have addressed their readers as citizens of Eretz Yisroel temporarily residing abroad. Editorials and essays concentrated on a few basic themes concerning the Jewish past, present, and future. Some described Jewish holidays and related them to the DPs' situation. Some carried satires on DP life—committee behavior, theater audiences, politics in the schools, and so on. Others kept a critical eye on actions and reactions toward Jews internationally and in Germany especially. Some discussed antisemitism, arguing over whether its postwar manifestation was a new development or the "same old hatred of Jews."[29] Many editorials emphasized and explained in detail the necessity for a Jewish state in Palestine.

Regional newspapers had relatively wide distribution, and the Central Committee's paper, *Unzer Weg*, appeared from October 1945 to December 1950. However, there is no way of knowing how much or what sections of the papers and journals DP readers actually read. They certainly used the papers for their immediate purposes, publishing names of relatives they looked for, announcing births and marriages, publicizing coming local events, and commenting on cultural and political activities in letters to the editor.

The central political bodies strongly supported their own Zionist-oriented newspapers. While regional papers such as the *Jidisze Cajtung*, for which people like Dr. Samuel Gringauz, chairman of the Council, regularly wrote could expect a certain amount of support or at least toleration from the Central Committee, most local papers, focused as they usually were on present-day life in the individual camps, had to make do with the help of the Joint Committee or UNRRA.

DP Schools

The school system had to confront obstacles perhaps greater than those of any other cultural agency. For example, practically all materials one would associate with "school learning" were missing. In the beginning there were no notebooks or pencils, no books or blackboards, and no chalk or paper. Sometimes children even had to bring chairs from their living quarters. One teacher reported using a wooden board and aspirin pills as substitutes for blackboard and chalk, while the children wrote their homework on the back of business letters from former German companies.[30]

Moreover, pupils and teachers alike were often poorly prepared for the work required in school education. Most of the children had missed years of schooling or had only limited education in school systems as disparate as those of Poland and Uzbekistan, Siberia and Hungary. In some cases they had been taught privately at home or secretly in the ghettos. Teachers were for the most part idealists or former "madrikhim" (Zionist youth group leaders). Many had no pedagogical training, they spoke different languages—Polish, Yiddish, perhaps a bit of Hebrew—and at first, for lack of books, they had to teach what they could remember from their own days at school. Perhaps most important of all, children and teachers alike had suffered ghetto and concentration camp life (and death), persecution, and the loss of many family members.

In March 1947, the Joint Committee, the Jewish Agency, and the Central Committee formed the Board of Education and Culture in an attempt to standardize at least elementary schooling. Supported by a small group of teachers from Palestine, financial aid from the Joint Committee, and books and school materials from the United States and from the Yishuv, the board gave the schools a curriculum, conducted some in-service training institutes, and provided a bit of infrastructure.[31]

ORT, originally the Russian Society for Handicrafts and Agricultural Work, established vocational schools quite early, but these too suffered from a lack of materials. Pupils in a textile class in Pocking, for example, had "two looms . . . and an old-fashioned spinning wheel . . . , both handmade. The pupils got wool for weaving on the looms by unraveling Wehrmacht leggings."[32] For lack of enough qualified DP teachers, German instructors were often employed, and apprenticeships regularly took place in German factories or small businesses.

ORT offered a variety of subjects, including training in traditional Eastern European Jewish occupations, such as seamstress, tailor, dressmaker, and hatmaker, as well as in modern occupations, such as dress design, dental technology, and even driving. Young people often signed up for courses, but many found life in the German towns more exciting than receiving instruction on lathes and sewing machines: some found dealing on the black market (the prevailing form of economy in postwar Germany) more profitable in the short run than learning English or Hebrew in a classroom. Nevertheless, Jakob Olejski, formerly head of ORT in Lithuania and responsible for its efforts in the Kovno Ghetto, managed to build up in the American Zone a school system that offered several thousand young DPs at least some measure of vocational training.

Adult education was the stepchild of the DP school system. Many attempts were made to offer public lectures, language courses, or vocational refresher courses, but few succeeded over any significant length of time. Individual lectures—on scientific, literary, or political subjects, most delivered from memory—were often received as a welcome interruption in the long days of waiting. And in 1948, after emigration had become possible, courses in English and Hebrew became popular. But for most adults in the uncertainty of the transit situation, returning to school benches for more than an occasional evening event seemed neither attractive nor profitable.

Of all the organized educational efforts, the elementary schools command the most interest, because here the DPs sought to instill their values and ideas in the coming generation. The curriculum included the usual "three R's," and yet it was unusual in one respect. The language ideally to be taught as the "native language" was Hebrew. In practical terms, however, this was often impossible for lack of Hebrew-speaking instructors. History was taught according to the *Tanakh*, the Hebrew Bible, and thus focused on Jewish history in Palestine. And geography was called "Palestinography" and encompassed only the geography of Palestine. Certainly, Zionist youth groups and kibbutzim throughout Europe had always emphasized to their members that learning was necessary in preparation for life in Palestine. In the DP camps, however, an entire society attempted to set up a Palestinian-Jewish school system in Europe.

DP teachers summed up the reasons for this emphasis in their response to an American visitor who had criticized the one-sidedness of the curriculum:

> Maybe it's not good pedagogy to present only one side of a case, . . . but we can't afford such luxuries. The children have nothing, nothing. What should we talk about—the blessings of Poland? They know them. Or the visas for America? They can't get them. The map of Eretz [Yisroel] is their salvation. . . . Indoctrination may not be good for normal children in normal surroundings. But what is normal here? . . . *Auf a krumme fuss passt a krumme shuh.* (A crooked foot needs a crooked shoe.)[33]

The political bodies—central, regional, and local committees—pledged the greatest support to kibbutz schools and after that to the elementary schools. Here they felt they had the greatest chances of achieving a truly Zionist upbringing. While

ORT schools were deemed useful when they taught trades needed in Eretz Yisroel, central political organizations gave little support to adult education courses. Starting in November 1947, the Central Committee did develop a lecturer training program, the "prelegentn-seminar," and the trainees traveled throughout the Zone, giving talks mainly on topics related to life in Palestine. Thus formal educational structures were bound to preparation for life in the land of the DPs' forefathers, a land their people had left two thousand years earlier, a land they themselves had never seen.

The title of a newspaper article on a DP theater production, used as the title of this chapter, sums up the cultural situation very well. Awrohom Browar wrote in the Frankfurt-Zeilsheim newspaper: "We are on our way, but we're not in the wilderness."[34] The DPs were on their way, from Eastern Europe to a new home, presumably somewhere outside Germany, probably outside Europe. But they were not in a barren desert. They built themselves a community and tried to fill their days with the activities of a "normal" life. They often fell quite short of what they intended, but seen in the light of the many obstacles they had to overcome, they nevertheless achieved a great deal.

Theoretical Interpretation

The She'erit Ha-peletah's critical self-descriptions invite the question of how these displaced persons managed to organize themselves into a functioning "society in transit."[35] The empirical research results describe what these Jewish displaced persons actually accomplished. Now the results remain to be interpreted, and it is appropriate to ask how the DPs' activities lent them the resilience that Abraham Peck and Ze'ev Mankowitz have written about elsewhere.[36] Moreover, does the DP experience lend itself to further generalizations? Are there aspects that might be applicable to other groups?

It may seem adequate to interpret DP educational and cultural efforts as typically Zionist and let it go at that. Yet, it is tempting to go beyond this and seek ways to relate the DP experience to educational situations in general. This raises a number of problems that in turn inform a more useful interpretation. The problems can be seen as fields of tension that call for resolution. They consist of three pairs of contradictory concepts: survivors versus migrants, continuity versus change, and uniqueness versus generalization.[37]

Survivors vs. Migrants

The Jewish displaced persons were of two groups—survivors and migrants. The first Jewish DPs were former death camp inmates who had not chosen to be in Germany but found themselves there at the end of the war. About a third of the displaced persons entered the DP camps as "passive" recipients of the offers made to feed, clothe, and house them. Initially, the question of where to go later was to most of them secondary to their own physical recovery. These people were first and foremost survivors. Soon, however, moving on took top priority, and this group began to see itself as a migrant group as well.

The other two thirds of the Jewish DP population entered the American Zone on purpose; from there they hoped to be able to emigrate to Palestine, the United States, or elsewhere. Having left their old homes in Poland or their places of exile in the USSR, these former partisans, deportees, and refugees had already emigrated. With justification, one may call them migrants. Yet they, too, had succeeded in escaping National Socialist persecution—by fighting, fleeing, or hiding. Thus they were survivors as well.

Continuity vs. Change

The second field of tension revolves around concepts of sameness and continuity on the one hand, and adaptation and change on the other. It concerns the Jewish DPs' attempts to establish a community in which both survivors and migrants would be able to participate. It includes questions such as: Which concept of identity was to be fostered? What were educators' and culturally active DPs' motives for trying to establish continuity or bring about change? Were cultural activities meant to conserve a previous status quo in order to repress unpleasant memories of the immediate past? Or did they attempt to place the past on a time line that seemed coherent to the community? Was the community to hold rigidly to a certain life history? Or did it look to its history for guidance and support in facing the unknown to come?

Uniqueness vs. Generalization

The final difficulty in interpreting DP times lies in the contradiction between uniqueness and the attempt to generalize experience. The society of the displaced persons was indeed a unique community in transit—an entire displaced society. Yet, if it was so unique that no comparisons can be made, then one can describe but not interpret it. The DP experience would remain a piece of Jewish history with no further relevance to other transit communities.

Instead, a legitimate interpretation of the She'erit Ha-peletah period lends itself to some useful generalizations based on three assumptions: 1) the Jewish displaced person can be considered a survivor-migrant; 2) for a group of survivor-migrants to actively rebuild their lives, they must establish a community. To this end they must construct their own time line; and 3) education and cultural activities play an important role in constructing this time line.

The Survivor-Migrant

Let us entertain a concept of survivor-migrant that first offers a common denominator for the various members of the transit community. It is a two-part concept. Survivors are people who, as members of an ethnic group, have experienced persecution, extermination, and the resulting traumata and have somehow lived through it all. Examples other than the Jewish DPs include Armenians in Turkey during World War I and East Cambodians under the Khmer Rouge regime.[38]

Migrants, as considered here, are neither immigrants nor emigrants. They are persons who have already left their homes and are temporarily waiting elsewhere before continuing on to their final destination. Migrant sociology has concentrated mainly on the problems of immigrants in their new homes, while adding concepts such as sojourners and working migrants to widen its application. A further concept, that of survivor-migrants, includes the phenomenon of transmigration. It categorizes those fleeing from persecution and living somewhere between their past and their future homelands. The following historical examples illustrate the survivor-migrant concept:

> –Around the turn of the century, hundreds of thousands of Eastern European Jews fled to the United States from Tsarist persecution and pogroms. On their way, many of them spent weeks or months in Berlin and Hamburg, waiting for a chance to continue. (More than 100,000 remained in Germany, many of them in Berlin's "Scheunenviertel".)[39]
> –Many German Jewish school children who fled from Germany after 1933 lived and studied in Kristinehov Boarding School in Västraby, Sweden. The school had been conceived as a transmigratory "waiting room" for the pupils on their way to Palestine.[40]
> –Armenians who flee persecution in Turkey, the former Soviet Union, and Iran often spend one to two years as asylum-seekers in the Federal Republic of Germany. As soon as they are granted asylum, most of them migrate to California, where there is a large Armenian colony.[41]

Time line

If survivor-migrants want to organize themselves into a transit community, they need a time line that connects the individuals and relates them to a supposedly mutual past and future.[42] While a stable community has a common past, a logical present, and a probable future—all forming a more or less continuous time line—a survivor-migrant community seemingly has only the present. Such a "displaced society" evolves ad hoc to mark time and temporarily take care of its members, who now live in a foreign country and have little or no assurance of what the future has in store, and whose actual purpose entails dispersing as rapidly as possible. If the survivor-migrants nevertheless manage to establish their own time line, they will succeed in establishing a functioning community. Such a time line must offer coherence by suggesting a common history. By reifying certain past and present experiences, it offers a form for everyday life and common references for future planning.

Past. By (re)constructing a common past, such a time line offers survivors and migrants a common definition. This past must be sufficiently varied to provide each of the members something to which he or she can relate. (Lawerence Fuchs describes a similar process that he calls "reconfiguration." When immigrant groups arrive in the United States from one and the same country but from different backgrounds, they reconfigure their disparate past experiences to achieve a common—albeit constructed—past identity.)[43] Such a definition of the past must contain positive elements in contrast to recent traumata, and it must suggest ways of fitting individual suffering into the group's life history.

Present-day. The time line gives meaning to actions in the here and now. Everyday life is renewed and old traditions reinstated. Interactions with other groups and cultures help form survivor-migrant identity. Positions become clear inasmuch as historical and cultural alternatives are presented and discussed, absorbed, or rejected. And those who were forced to be objects during the time of persecution can once again become subjects, once again actively taking life into their own hands.

Future. The time line leads from the proposed sameness of past experience into the necessary changes for the proposed future. The path to this future is more than one of pragmatic considerations: Which language, what vocational skills will I need? Nor are ethics alone decisive: To which behavior, to what testimony does my experience oblige me? Above all, survivor-migrants need the spark of an idea that logically—both psychologically and sociologically—extends the time line into the future. It has to combine past and present experience and lead to a goal that seems relevant to life histories. Moreover, the goal must present realms of action and seem actually feasible.

Education and Cultural Activities

Education and cultural activities play an important, perhaps decisive, role in helping survivor-migrants construct their time line. The DP theater, newspapers, and schools are examples.

Theater. Survivor-migrant theater is bound to the past. On stage, the good old (or bad old) times appear anew. Old traditions and values live on in classic plays. But there is more to the theater's significance. For people who have lost everything—family and friends, house and possessions, photos and souvenirs—the theater is a poetry album. It is a collection of words conveying the familiar language, the idioms, and the traditional ideas. Theater is also a photo album, it presents living pictures. It is often the one and only visual connection survivor-migrants have to their former lives.

Newspapers. A DP editor described his paper's function as being a bridge. Perhaps survivor-migrant newspapers are more of a market-place. This marketplace offers three levels of negotiation. Survivor-migrants can write about their experiences and/or read what others went through. At the same time, newspapers put these individual histories into a group perspective and link that again to their people's past. The second interaction takes place among the survivor-migrant groups themselves. Here newspapers and journals offer a forum for arguments and conflicting opinions. On the third level, newspaper photos, reports, and essays allow various cultures to confront one another.

Schools. Schools naturally are oriented to the future. Here is the place where adults not only teach skills but also hope to pass on their dreams and may even see them fulfilled to an extent. This is especially true of survivor-migrant schools. Many of the DPs had lost their own children; Eastern European Jewry as a whole had lost over a million children. Many of these DP children had in turn lost their families. They had been robbed of parents, grandparents, siblings, aunts, uncles, and former friends. For such a group, school becomes a substitute for the family. The family's task of teaching culture and traditions now becomes the school's task. Moreover schools try to develop a monoculturality out of the many, disparate previous experiences the young survivor-migrants have had. Such a monoculturality provides the pupils with a supposed common framework, offers them direction, offers them a certain security within the survivor-migrant community, and presents a common goal for their emigration.

Summary

All of these interpretive attempts cannot disguise the fact that Jewish displaced persons were, indeed, a unique group of survivor-migrants. The industrial mass murder of Jews during the Third Reich remains unique, and academics, writers, and artists continue to struggle with it. Yet it is amazing how quickly and how decisively the survivors began to renew their lives, to build up a community life in transit, and to establish a network of social structures, although they planned to leave "tomorrow," or the day after that at the latest. Was it the Jews' historical advantage, to paraphrase Marx? Was it the almost three thousand years' experience in organizing themselves in the Diaspora? Was it their history of persecution, fleeing, and reconfiguring that enabled them to do so once again? Was it the heritage of social structures of aid to the needy and the sick; of schools and of political bodies that enabled institutions such as the Joint Committee and the Jewish Agency to connect to the DPs immediately? Was it Zionism and the Yishuv, which for decades had been offering a framework? Was it the spark of the idea of a Jewish state, an idea that seemed just out of reach, yet still possible?

Perhaps it was some of all of this that helped the Jewish displaced persons get on their way while waiting in the American Zone of post-war Germany—but definitely not in the wilderness.

NOTES

1. This essay is based on my dissertation, "'Wir sind unterwegs, aber nicht in der Wüste'. Erziehung und Kultur in den jüdischen Displaced Persons-Lagern der Amerikanischen Zone im Nachkriegsdeutschland 1945–1949," Frankfurt University, 1993. Research sources included above all YIVO Record Groups 294.1 and 294.2, the YIVO library (especially the extensive collection of DP periodicals), JDC Archives Record Group 4564, Yad Vashem files M-P/, Zionist Library and Women's American ORT, all in New York City; American Jewish Archives, Cincinnati, Ohio; materials at the Institut für Zeitgeschichte, Munich, and the Stadt- und Universitätsbibliothek in Frankfurt am Main. Survivors, former social workers and former military employees in the United States, Israel, and the Federal Republic of Germany offered additional insights in more than sixty hours of interviews.

2. For information on this period, see Celia S. Heller, On the Edge of Destruction: Jews of Poland between the Two World Wars (New York: Columbia University Press, 1977).

3. For the history of one of the newspapers, see Menakhem Flakhser, "Undser Ekspres: Oygust 1936-September 1939," in Fun noentn ovar, vol. 3 (New York: Alveltlekhn Yidishn Kultur-Kongres, 1957), pp. 361–95. On theater, see Itsik Manger, Yanosh Turkov, and Moshe Ferenson, eds., Yidisher teater in eyrope tsvishn beyde welt-milchomes: Materyaln tsu der geshikhte fun yidishn teater (New York: Alveltekhn Yidishn Kultur-Kongress, 1968).

4. See Miriam Eisenstein, *Jewish Schools in Poland, 1919–39: Their Philosophy and Development* (New York: King's Crown Press, 1950).

5. See, for example, Herman Kruk, "Diary of the Vilna Ghetto," *YIVO Annual of Jewish Social Science* 6/13 (1965): 9–78; Samuel Gringauz, "The Ghetto as an Experiment of Jewish Social Organization (Three Years of Kovno Ghetto)," *Jewish Social Studies* 11 (1949): 3–20; Yanosh Turkov, "Teater un kontsertn in di getos un kontsentratsiye-lagern," in *Yidisher teater*, ed. Manger, Turkov, and Ferenson, pp. 437–515.

6. Jakob Olejski, "Azoj hamert der gojrl an unzer tir," *Landsberger Lager-Cajtung*, no. 10, December 14, 1945, p. 3.

7. Ibid., no. 22 (34), June 28, 1946, p. 9; ibid., no. 33 (45), August 9, 1946, p. 3.

8. *Jidisze Cajtung*, no. 28 (193), April 13, 1948, p. 4; *Undzer Hofenung*, no. 12, May 25, 1946, p. 7.

9. Aron Wider, "Nechome," *Undzer Hofenung*, no. 3 (25), January 31, 1947, p. 5.

10. Pauline Fischer-Sztajer, "Iber die oifgabn fun der Szejrit Haplejta-froj," *Cum Ojfboj*, December 11, 1946, p. 3 (American Jewish Archives).

11. *Unzer Weg*, no. 46, August 28, 1946, p. 3. See also *Undzer Hofenung*, no. 12, May 25, 1946, pp. 7, 18 and the issue of November 22, 1946, p. 5.

12. *Landsberger Lager-Cajtung*, no. 12 (24), April 2, 1946, p. 13.

13. Ibid., no. 22 (34), June 28, 1946, p. 9.

14. Leo Srole, Report, ca. 1946, Institut für Zeitgeschichte, file Fi 01.80, folder 209.

15. Sama Wachs, "Di moral fun unzer tog-teglichn lebn," *Oyf der fray*, no. 2, January 1946, p. 15.

16. Zalman Grinberg, Speech . . . for Political Ex-prisoners in Germany at the Liberation Concert in St. Ottilien on May 27, 1945 (American Jewish Archives). Lawrence Langer, who has evaluated hundreds of hours of survivor testimonies, would agree even today. He calls those who came out of the death camps victims, not survivors, for he sees them as having been dying ever since the Shoah touched them. Lecture given at "Facing History and Ourselves" Summer Institute, Brookline, Massachusetts, August 3, 1993.

17. Koppel S. Pinson, Education Report for Zeilsheim, December 24, 1945, p. 3, in JDC Record Group AR 4564, file 406; Samuel Gringauz, "D.P.'s dercejln G.I.'s," *Landsberger Lager-Cajtung*, no. 41 (53), October 9, 1946, p. 8.

18. Leo Srole, "Why the DP's Can't Wait: Proposing an International Plan of Rescue," *Commentary* 3/1 (January 1947): 13.

19. Letter to the Editor, *Jidisze Cajtung*, no. 64 (132), August 26, 1947, p. 4.

20. Akiba Lewinsky, Bericht über seine Arbeit in Europa, gehalten vor den Mitarbeitern der Jugendalijah, Jerusalem, April 1947, p. 4, in JDC Record Group AR 4564, file 3876.

21. B. Ass, "Die schwere rol fun hajntikn lerer," *Undzer Hofenung*, no. 2, June 14, 1946, pp. 3–4.

22. Time and again the Hebrew Bible chronicles this historical experience of being a surviving remnant, the first reference being in Genesis 32:8. As Jacob prepared to meet his brother Esau, he feared Esau might attack him and his followers and kill them all. Thus he divided his followers into two groups and said, "If Esau come to the one company, and smite it, then the other company which is left shall escape" (ha-makhana ha-nishar lifleta) (*The Holy Scriptures of the Old Testament*. Hebrew and English [London: British and Foreign Bible Society, 1982]).

23. For information on Brichah, see Yehuda Bauer, *Flight and Rescue: Brichah* (New York: Random House, 1970).

24. Israel Segal, "Undzer premyere," Program, August 3, 1946, in Yad Vashem Archives M–1/P–89.

25. Awrohom Gurwicz, "Ojfn weg fun kinstleriszn jidiszn teater," *Undzer Hofenung*, no. 27 (ca. December 1946).

26. *Dos fraje wort* is to be found in the Klau Library, Hebrew Union College, Cincinnati, Ohio; *Oyf der fray*, *Jüdische Rundschau*, certain editions of *Jidisze Cajtung* and *Fun letstn khurbn* are in the Stadt- und Universitätsbibliothek in Frankfurt am Main; *Unterwegs*, *Undzer*

Hofenung, Hemshekh, and most editions of *Landsberger Lager-Cajtung* and *Jidisze Cajtung* are to be found in YIVO Library in New York City.

27. M. Beserglik, "Szejris-Haplejto oder Szejrit-Haplejta? Cum jojwl fun undzer cajtung" (Jo-feljeton un nyt-feljeton), *Landsberger Lager-Cajtung*, no. 40 (52), September 9, 1946, p. 23. The various forms of She'erit Ha-peletah in the quotation are spelled as in the article that appeared in Latinized Yiddish.

28. Samuel Gringauz, "Di brik cwiszn nechtn un morgn (a halb jor 'Lager-Cajtung')," *Landsberger Lager-Cajtung*, no. 13 (25), April 15, 1946, p. 17.

29. Samuel Gringauz, "Di psychologisze wurclen fun neo-antisemitizm: Naje vintn – alte mitlen," *Jidisze Cajtung*, no. 38 (106), May 23, 1947, p. 5; Jakob Olejski, "Nyt neo-antisemitizm nor alter jidn-has (Ojfn smach fun hajntiker wirklechkajt in Dajczland)," *Jidisze Cajtung*, no. 43 (111), June 13, 1947, p. 6.

30. *Undzer Hofenung*, no. 20, December 6, 1946, p. 3.

31. A great deal of information on the Board of Education and Culture is to be found in YIVO Record Group 294.2, especially in the monthly reports (in folder 136) by Philip Friedman, a survivor who worked for the Joint Committee.

32. George S. Wheeler, Report of [Second] Conference at Bad Reichenhall, March 6, 1947, in American Jewish Archives, National Archives files.

33. Marie Syrkin, "The D.P. Schools," *Jewish Frontier* 15/3 (156) (March 1948): 17.

34. Awrohom Browar, "Jidish Teater baj der Szejrit Hachurbn," *Unterwegs*, no. 14, March 28, 1947.

35. Other DP groups—Poles, Ukrainians, Lithuanians—also achieved a certain degree of camp organization, though never to the extent reached by the Jewish DPs. See Mark Wyman, *DP—Europe's Displaced Persons, 1945–1951* (London, 1989).

36. See Abraham Peck, "Befreit und erneut in Lagern: jüdische DPs. Statt eines Epilogs," in *Der Judenpogrom 1938: Von der "Reichskristallnacht" zum Völkermord*, ed. Walter Pehle (Frankfurt/M.: Fischer, 1988), pp. 201–12; Ze'ev Mankowitz, "The Affirmation of Life in She'erith Hapleita," in *Remembering for the Future, Theme 1: Jews and Christians during and after the Holocaust*, International Scholars Conference, Oxford, July 10–13 (Oxford: Pergamon Press, 1988), p. 1114.

37. This theoretical discussion draws upon a number of academic works on migrant sociology, concepts of identity, and theories of survival. Among these are Everett V. Stonequist, *The Marginal Man: A Study in Personality and Culture Conflict* (New York: Russell & Russell, 1961); David I. Golovensky, "The Marginal Man Concept: An Analysis and Critique," *Social Forces* 30/3 (March 1952): 333–39; Robert Zajonc, "Aggressive Attitudes of the 'Stranger' as a Function of Conformity Pressures," *Human Relations* 5/2 (May 1952): 205–16; Paul C. P. Siu, "The Sojourner," *American Journal of Sociology* 58/1 (July 1952): 34–44; Alan C. Kerckhoff and Thomas C. McCormick, "Marginal Status and Marginal Personality," *Social Forces* 34/1 (October 1955): 48–55; Aaron Antonovsky, "Toward a Refinement of the 'Marginal Man' Concept," *Social Forces* 35/1 (October 1956): 57–62; Hartmut Esser, *Aspekte der Wanderungssoziologie* (Darmstadt: Luchterhand, 1980); Pitirim A. Sorokin, *Society, Culture, and Personality: Their Structure and Dynamics* (New York: Harper and Brothers, 1947); David J. de Levita, *The Concept of Identity* (Paris: Mouton, 1965); Lothar Krappmann, *Soziologische Dimensionen von Identität* (Stuttgart: Klett-Cotta, 1982); Bruno Bettelheim, *Surviving and Other Essays* (New York: Random House, 1980).

38. For information on the Armenian genocide, see Margot Stern Strom and William S. Parsons, *Facing History and Ourselves: Holocaust and Human Behavior* (Watertown, MA: International Education, 1982), chapter 11. On Cambodia, see Ben Kiernan, "Poulets sauvages, poulets de ferme et cormorans: la Zone Est du Kampuchea sous Pol Pot," in Camille Scalabrino et al., *Histoire et enjeux: 1945–1985*, Camille Scalabrino et al. (Asie-Debat no. 2) (Paris, 1985), pp. 119–79.

39. See Bertold Scheller, *Die Zentralwohlfahrtsstelle: Jüdische Wohlfahrtspflege in Deutschland 1917–1987: Eine Selbstdarstellung* (Frankfurt/M.: Zentralwohlfahrtsstelle der Juden in Deutschland, 1987); and Irving Howe, *World of Our Fathers: The Journey of the East*

European Jews to America and the Life They Found and Made (New York: Simon and Schuster, 1976).

40. Hildegard Feidel-Mertz, ed., *Schule im Exil: Die verdrängte Pädagogik nach 1933* (Reinbek bei Hamburg: Rowohlt, 1983), p. 104.

41. I owe this information to Udine Eul, "Armenier: ein Volk ohne Land," a term paper written at the Fachhochschule Wiesbaden, winter semester 1989/90.

42. See Jossi Hadar, "Zeiterfahrung und Kontinuitätserleben bei Überlebenden des Holocaust. Eine psychoanalytische Betrachtung," in *"Wer zum Leben, wer zum Tod . . .": Strategien jüdischen Überlebens im Ghetto*, ed. Doron Kiesel, Cilly Kugelmann, Hanno Loewy, and Dietrich Neuhau (Frankfurt/M.: Campus, 1992), pp. 115–30.

43. Lawrence H. Fuchs, *The American Kaleidoscope: Race, Ethnicity, and the Civic Culture* (Hanover, NH: University Press of New England, 1990), p. 22.

49.

THOMAS ALBRICH

Way Station of Exodus

JEWISH DISPLACED PERSONS AND
REFUGEES IN POSTWAR AUSTRIA

In the post-Holocaust Jewish migration in Europe, Austria lay at the crossroads between Eastern Europe and the West, the first destination on the "underground railway" to Palestine. Consequently, Austria developed into the most important transit country in this largest organized clandestine migration of the postwar period.

Between 1945 and 1948, the Jewish displaced persons problem became a major source of discord between the occupying powers in Austria. It constituted a political, social, and economic problem, a test for humanity and—in view of the Middle East— a major bone of contention between the Western Allies and the Soviet Union in the developing Cold War.[1] Last but not least, Jews became the greatest obstacle to putting Austria's postwar ideology—based on the "victim status" of the Moscow Declaration of November 1943—into political practice, because their mere existence served as an ugly reminder of Austria's recent past.[2]

Nevertheless, the more than 200,000 Jewish survivors who transitted Austria on their way to Palestine or other countries have to some extent been neglected in the Austrian historical community.[3] In the past dozen years, the main fields of research in Jewish post-Holocaust history have been Austrian antisemitism,[4] post–1938 emigration and exile,[5] the post–1945 return movement of Austrian Jews[6]—or their refusal to return,[7] the question of reparations or restitution of Jewish property,[8] Jewish post-Holocaust identity and Austro-Jewish relations,[9] and the reconstruction of Jewish life and institutions.[10] Although most of these topics are at least indirectly linked with the Jewish DP problem, no one so far has attempted a synthesis of a history of Jews as part of general Austrian postwar history.

The only study of the Jewish Exodus through Austria between 1945 and 1948, based on records of the occupying powers and Jewish relief organizations, focused on the organizational aspects of the exodus, the Allied DP-system in Austria, the Anglo-American divergence over the emigration of Holocaust survivors to Palestine and the Austrian reaction to the Jewish influx from the East. The "inner view" of the problem was touched upon as far as the Brichah was concerned (Brichah was the organization that directed Jewish Holocaust survivors through various European waystations to Palestine); the same applies to a lesser extent to the social historical aspects of the She'erit Ha-peletah (the "surviving remnant" of Holocaust survivors in Germany, Austria and Italy).[11]

Based on further research carried out in preparation for a social history of the She'erit Ha-peletah in Austria, a mixture of known, reexamined, disputed, and new aspects is presented in this essay. The investigation is divided into three parts: 1) the exodus from Eastern Europe via Austria between liberation and the establishment of the State of Israel; 2) the solution of the Jewish DP problem after 1948; and 3) prospects for future research on the transient Jewish communities in Austria, that is, the Jewish DP camps and their organizational, political, cultural, and social set-up between 1945 and 1955.

The Jewish Exodus from Eastern Europe 1945–1948: A Survey

The fate of Jews in Austria during the final stages of World War II, the death marches from the Hungarian border to Mauthausen and its subcamps between March and May 1945, and the immediate period after liberation are still not well documented.[12] Estimates made shortly after liberation indicate that there were between 20,000 and 25,000 Jews in the western zones of Austria. We have only fragmentary knowledge about the situation in Russian-occupied eastern Austria and in Vienna. In St. Pölten, at the "Institut für Geschichte der Juden in Österreich," a current research project on the fate of thousands of Hungarian-Jewish slave-laborers, who were brought to Austria in late 1944 and liberated by the Red Army in April 1945, should shed new light on the period of liberation and the aftermath.[13]

At the end of June 1945, there were still more than 5,000 liberated Jewish DPs—mostly Hungarians—in Soviet-controlled Vienna.[14] By then, large numbers of Jews had already returned to Hungary, fewer to Poland, Romania, Yugoslavia, and to the West. Between 4,000 and 5,000 had left Austria for Italy on their way to Palestine, many of them with the help of the American Jewish Joint Distribution Committee (JDC), in cooperation with the military. In mid-July 1945, the estimated number of Jews in the three western zones of Austria was down to 5,000, but the numbers were constantly changing due to officially organized and unofficial movements through Austria, especially from Hungary and other Eastern European locations, and from camps in Bavaria en route to Italy.[15] At this stage, most of the remaining Jewish DPs in Austria wished to return to their homes in Poland and Hungary, while some desired to go to Italy for emigration to Palestine and other countries. Many of the undecided eventually would have to "migrate to Palestine if countries in the Western Hemisphere [were not to] open to them within a reasonable time," as one contemporary document predicted. Others, who eventually returned to their home countries, said they were not planning to stay but were "returning simply to find relatives and/or property and then leave."[16]

This period in the summer of 1945—when the military apparently encouraged all DPs (not just Jewish survivors) to leave and Jewish relief organizations were not yet on the spot—warrants some reexamination. Thus far, we have had to rely almost entirely on the views and recollections of the Allied liberators[17]—perceptions that often ran quite contrary to the experiences of those liberated. The survivors' initial joy and relief soon turned into frustration. Very often a lack of sympathetic understanding and of psychological preparation on the part of the occupation forces defined their dealings with survivors. Even in the light of these circumstances, the nature of accusations against the U.S. Army and the generally disquieting reports on the Austrian scene, given by delegates from Austrian camps, at the famous St. Ottilien conference of the liberated Jews in Germany on July 25, 1945, are rather astonishing. Dr. Boris Roisen from Salzburg stated:

> This is not what we expected and hoped for. The atmosphere grows more oppressive from day to day; the Jews do not want to remain in Austria any longer; they wish to get out. Palestine appears to us the only solution. . . . I must repeat that the situation in Austria is not good only because the attitude of the occupation authorities is particularly bad. When we ask for living quarters, they direct us to vermin-infested camps without light . . . and because we would not go there, they deprived us of food. . . . The Austrians are friendly to us and try to help us. . . . The attitude of the occupation authorities must change. . . . Apart from the Hungarian Jews, everyone is waiting for the first opportunity to go to Palestine. There are some 16,000 Jews in Austria, 70% of whom are ready to emigrate to Palestine at once.[18]

Others, like Wolf Reichert, representative from Wels, Upper Austria, speaking for 3,000 Jews liberated from the concentration camp at Gunskirchen, complained about low rations, no outside help, and brutal treatment by the U.S. Army: "To this day, we have received no help from anyone, neither in food nor in clothing. To this day the women who do not associate with the Americans are without decent clothes and without shoes. We have no contact with the outside world."[19]

There were similar reports of bad conditions in other Austrian DP camps, but the situation was even worse for sick Jews remaining in Mauthausen and Gusen, since July part of the Soviet Zone. As they recovered, the Red Army was forcibly transporting them back to Poland. What awaited them was rampant antisemitism. A survivor who had gone to Lithuania and come back to Austria warned: "The problem confronting us today does not concern only the Jews who are in Germany; it is also the burning problem of the whole of European Jewry. You are the pioneers and must blaze a trail for hundreds of thousands of European Jews."[20]

The return to Austria of many of the same Jews who recently had been repatriated to Eastern Europe started in July 1945. Because of this constant influx of refugees— in strictly legal terms they were not DPs—the population of Jews among the DPs increased steadily, both in absolute numbers and in relative proportion. Despite bad living conditions, the Jewish survivors, who had stayed in Austria after liberation, organized their DP camps into well-functioning staging points for transient Jewish refugees on their way to Palestine. This process of the setting up of a network of self-administered Jewish DP camps requires further research. Preliminary results have been published on the early DP situation in the French Zone,[21] and more recently on the major camps in the Linz area, the main staging centers for Jews liberated from the Mauthausen complex.[22]

By the fall of 1945, the Brichah was informally running the DP camps. This well-functioning underground organization built up a network of shelters all along the routes from Poland to southern Italy in order to help the refugees at every stage of their clandestine journey. It was the task of the Brichah to take those Jews heading for Palestine to the coast of the Mediterranean. From there, they were transported illegally by the Haganah (underground army of the provisional government of Palestine) to Palestine, running the British blockade and entering as so-called "ma'apilim." Austria was the ideal center for the work of the Brichah. Taking advantage of the special situation in that country, about 150 people in twenty-five centers worked undercover for the organization as administrators of DP camps and as transport guides for illegal border crossings. They also forged the necessary documents for the refugees. The money needed for bribing border guards and for buying foodstuffs and trucks was supplied by Jewish relief organizations such as the JDC.[23]

It was not until mid-September 1945 that JDC representatives conducted a survey of Jewish life in the three western zones of Austria. The key problems discovered were inadequate supplies, and conflicts between Jews and non-Jews living in the same camps.[24] By December, new permanent camps had been established. The two main camps in the U.S. Zone were Bindermichl in Linz, Upper Austria, with a population of 2,200, and Bad Gastein, Land Salzburg, with 1,250; the largest in the British Zone was Trofaiach, in Styria, with a population of 1,700.[25] The total number of displaced Jews in Austria hovered around 12,500 at that time. In addition, refugees from Poland, Hungary, and Romania en route to Germany or Italy and eventually to Palestine were arriving at a rate of 1,000 a week; the rate of exit from Austria was approximately the same.[26]

By the end of October 1945, the British secret service in Austria was convinced that this was no spontaneous exodus, but that it was financed and organized by elements of the Zionist movement to force the British to revise their Palestine policy. In view of the perceived long-range effects of this exodus on British interests in the Middle East, they made every effort to stop the refugees on their way to Palestine and to uncover the organization behind this smuggling of ma'apilim. Although the activities of the Brichah in Austria were soon understood, the British never succeeded in infiltrating the organization.[27]

The sole result of the British countermeasures in the winter of 1945–1946 was a change in the transit routes through Austria. Before that the refugees had taken the shortest path, from Vienna across the British Zone to Italy. Thereafter, the U.S. Zone of occupation became the preferred initial destination of Jews arriving from Eastern Europe. In the wake of the Earl Harrison Report, which had described scandalous conditions in Jewish DP camps, President Truman had ordered the U.S. Army to give privileged status to Jewish DPs in their area of occupation. The better living conditions and a declared policy of asylum toward these DPs made the American Zone in Austria an ideal staging area for the work of the Brichah.

American authorities in Austria did not interfere in any way with the organization's activities. On the contrary, there was close cooperation between the Army, the JDC, and the Jewish underground in organizing the clandestine movement of Jews through Austria. This action proceeded as follows: Jewish refugees arriving in Vienna first received care and shelter in the U.S. sector of the city. From there, the refugees were taken to special Jewish DP camps in the U.S. Zone. At the same time, the Brichah had to smuggle the same number of refugees out of the zone, either to Germany or to Italy. As a result of this deal, the number of Jewish refugees in the U.S. Zone in Austria remained stable, and the system worked with hardly any problems until early summer 1946. In most cases, the refugees stayed for only a short time—seventy-two hours—before being moved on. An average of 2,000 to 3,000 people a month had to be processed by the Brichah through Vienna via the U.S. Zone to Germany or Italy. The Army's motive behind this deal was not to be burdened with the feeding and housing of additional refugees. Such an arrangement was necessary even if it meant dumping them on the U.S. forces in Germany, who, faced with millions of ethnic German refugees and DPs in their area of control, were not interested in having to care for more Jews. In June 1946, the secret transit system broke down when 6,000 Jews from Poland unexpectedly arrived in Vienna, the first group of what would be a mass flight of nearly 100,000 Polish Jews to Austria.[28]

This "Polish Exodus," triggered by a bloody pogrom in the Polish city of Kielce on July 4, 1946,[29] was the dramatic climax of postwar Jewish migration from Eastern Europe.[30] (In light of new evidence, the collaboration of the JDC with the Jewish underground should be reexamined. American and Soviet interests in the exodus also warrant reinvestigation.) The Kielce pogrom was the signal for most of the remainder of Polish Jewry to leave the country, and the big stream westward, mainly through Czechoslovakia to Austria, began. On their way, many of the refugees were robbed of their last possessions by border guards and professional refugee smugglers. Although the Czech government and Jewish relief organizations took care of the Jewish transients, most arrived in Vienna in a pitiful state. The sheer number of refugees arriving daily—4,000 in a single night in August, for example—was more than the U.S. Army could handle. During August 1946, more than 30,000 Jews were transported to the U.S. Zone, many of them were later transferred to Germany.

At this point, American authorities in Austria had a serious problem on their hands: the permanent DP camps were overcrowded; new camps had to be opened with a capacity to house 18,000 transient Jews at a time.[31] The Brichah was unable to transfer such huge numbers of people to Germany or Italy, and more refugees were due to arrive. In order to maintain their policy of asylum for Jewish DPs, the Americans tried to apply a double strategy: on the one hand, they reached an agreement with the Czech government to limit the daily flow of refugees into Austria to 800, and on the other hand they tried to place 25,000 Jewish DPs in Italy. Under strong British pressure, the Italian government politely turned down this request. Only the U.S. authorities in Germany accepted 45,000 Jewish DPs from Austria in their zone of occupation.

British strategy, at odds with that of the Americans, aimed to stop the transit of Jews all along the route to Palestine. In the fall of 1946, it appeared that such a goal had been reached: for a short time in September, even the Soviets aided the British by sealing off the Austro-Czech border, thereby keeping the Jews from coming into Austria. The French closed their zone to Jewish transients and, with the way into Italy blocked as well, the Americans were isolated. Nevertheless, all British attempts to persuade the U.S. government to change its policy failed. By the end of 1946, a total of 99,000 Jewish refugees had come through the Rothschild Hospital in Vienna, of whom 78,000 were from Poland, 17,000 from Hungary, and 3,000 from Romania.[32] The Jewish DPs, who at first presented just a moral and humanitarian problem, had now become a political factor with increasing weight in the emerging Cold War.[33]

The summer of 1947 saw the arrival of about 30,000 Jews, the majority from Romania,[34] fleeing for reasons similar to those that motivated the refugees from Poland the previous year.[35] But the hopes of these refugees, who reached Austria via

Hungary after a six-week journey on foot, met with disappointment. The American "freeze order" of April 21, 1947, barred their entry into DP camps, the Americans had already closed down their reception centers for DPs in Vienna, the United Nations Relief and Rehabilitation Administration (UNRRA) had ceased its activities, and the International Refugee Organization (IRO) had not yet taken over. Thus there was no institution, apart from the JDC, that felt responsible for the Jews. The Vienna camps—the Rothschild Hospital and three other buildings—were now taken over and run by the JDC. To add to the tragedy, the Soviet authorities closed their zone for the transfer of DPs from Vienna to the U.S. Zone in Upper Austria, and the Brichah likewise refused to help—because these ailing and demoralized people were not regarded as suitable "pioneers" for Palestine.

Living conditions in Vienna became unbearable as more refugees arrived with no opportunity to travel onward. Only after violent demonstrations by the DPs in Vienna did the Austrian government agree to undertake the basic feeding at the rate of 1,550 calories a day for the roughly 10,000 Romanian refugees in the city. The Americans unsuccessfully tried to persuade the other occupying powers to admit Jewish refugees into their respective zones on a proportional basis. The Brichah then decided, for humanitarian reasons, to transfer these unfortunate people illegally into the American Zone, and the Soviet authorities later agreed that 3,000 of the Romanian refugees could cross the Russian Zone to any part of Austria. In the American Zone the Romanians replaced the Polish Jews, who were being smuggled to camps in Bavaria or toward the coasts of the Mediterranean.

The crisis situation in 1947 was marked by two different Austrian responses: on the one hand, the Austrian government pursued a policy of granting asylum to Romanian Jews for humanitarian reasons. On the other hand, the catastrophic situation in Austria regarding the lack of basic necessities led to demonstrations that sometimes turned into antisemitic riots.[36]

Resolving the Jewish Refugee Problem 1948–1955

Research on the period between 1948 and 1955/56 is still very sketchy, presenting far more open questions than answers, especially as far as Israeli activities in Austria are concerned. What can be taken as fact is the important role Austria played as a base for Israeli operations behind the Iron Curtain and as a staging area for emigration of Eastern European Jews to Israel.

In the spring of 1948, the establishment of the State of Israel and the possibility of legal emigration created a new situation and initially sparked high hopes for a speedy solution of the Jewish DP problem in Austria. But Israel's War of Independence and developments in Eastern Europe, such as the coup in Czechoslovakia and the policy of stabilizing communist rule in the Soviet orbit, had deep effects on the Jewish communities in the DP countries as well as in Eastern Europe. When Israel entered the scene, at first getting political support and arms, especially from Czechoslovakia, and successfully negotiating free emigration, the Jews east of the Iron Curtain became pawns in the Cold War.[37] After Soviet goodwill turned into the opposite in 1949, Jews—or Zionists—were made scapegoats in purges and show trials all over Eastern Europe. This is the background that has to be taken into account when looking at the post–1948 Jewish refugee situation and the escalating Cold War.

In the summer of 1948, a number of problems related to the establishment of the Jewish state developed: in June, the U.S. High Commissioner in Austria, Gen. Geoffrey Keyes, was particularly concerned with reports about "recruitment" and "training" for the Haganah allegedly taking place in Jewish camps. While U.S. officials had no objections to "volunteers," they were prepared to take strong measures against coercion and intimidation. According to reports, "a substantial amount of such coercion has taken place." In talks with representatives of the Jewish Agency and "others involved in this work," William Haber, Advisor on Jewish Affairs of the U.S. Army's European Command (Eucom), was able to determine "that excesses, which have occasionally taken place, will not be repeated."[38]

Another major problem in 1948 was the establishment of formal machinery for emigration from Austria to Israel. The problem was complicated since Austria had a sovereign government and military rule was a quadripartite affair. Austria at that time had not yet recognized the State of Israel and, reported Haber, "would probably not agree to do so, unless the United States authorities strongly urged such a course."[39] Therefore, it was impossible to recognize representatives of the provisional government of Israel for the purpose of issuing visas. These legal discussions, involving the Austrians and leading to the establishment of an Israeli consulate in Salzburg, have not yet been analyzed. The same applies to the organization of "legal" emigration to Israel, beginning in the fall of 1948, a time when the Allies put tough restrictions on the "aliyah" (immigration of Jewish people into Israel) of persons regarded as potential soldiers for the Israeli Army. It seems that despite official restrictions, until February 1949, at least the U.S. and French authorities in Austria, as well as the Austrians, turned a blind eye to Israel-bound transports including young men and women.[40]

A "blank spot" in the history of Jewish migration to Austria derives from what might be termed the "Hungarian exodus" of 1948/49. This influx temporarily raised the additional problem of a need for Israeli negotiations with Eastern European governments about mass evacuation of Jews to Israel. At the same time there was underway a clear program of closing down camps in Austria; it was closely coordinated among the U.S. Army, the Israeli immigration authorities, and Israel's representative in Austria, Dr. Kurt Lewin.[41] According to the JDC, about 1,200 DPs were emigrating to Israel each month. That organization believed that, barring any further influx from the East, the problem in Austria would have been met by the end of the year 1949. This prophecy was to be repeated every year until 1955. Looking at the statistics for mid-1949 one can see a definite change in the emigration pattern from Austria: from then on, the majority planned to emigrate to the United States, Australia, and other countries. The "Zionist option" had definitely lost much of its attraction by 1950, when the United States amended its immigration laws.[42] But there remained one group—the 500 hard-core cases with about 1,000 dependents—who still presented a problem.[43] In this final phase, new problems developed between the U.S. authorities, the IRO, and the Austrian government on the question of financing the remaining camps.[44] Due to tighter controls at the Hungarian-Czechoslovak border, the influx of refugees sharply declined in the second half of 1949; and emigration led to a further reduction in the number of Jewish DPs living in Austria—there were 7,700 by the end of December.[45]

The year 1950 marked the end of a number of DP-activities and institutions in Austria: on January 30, the office of the Advisor on Jewish Affairs of Eucom closed, as did the Israeli immigration office in Linz in September. During the year, all Zionist parties dealing with the DPs terminated their activities in Austria and the Central Committee of Liberated Jews was dissolved in October. The process of consolidating camps continued and, apart from the Rothschild Hospital in Vienna, the remaining five Jewish DP camps were taken over by the Austrian government.[46]

In the summer of 1950, the impact of the Korean War on DPs in Austria was felt. The IRO made tentative plans to evacuate refugees from Europe if the crisis became more serious. There was unrest among the Jewish DPs in Austria, and in July 1950 more than 2,000 registered "for immediate emigration" out of fear that "the conflict might develop into a war between the Western democracies and the Soviet satellites."[47] About two-thirds of the remaining DPs wished to emigrate to the United States, Canada, and Australia, while the rest were scheduled to leave for Israel.[48]

According to Israeli sources, since the end of the war a total of about 300,000 Jews from Eastern and Southeastern Europe, or roughly one-third of the surviving Jewish population in those areas, had emigrated abroad via Austria. Of these, 125,000 had already arrived in Israel. Since only 2,000 new arrivals were registered during 1950, the movement of emigrants from Eastern Europe across Austria was expected to come to an end by the close of 1951.[49] About 3,000 had legally emigrated by the end of the year; only 5,000 Jewish refugees were still living in Austria then, and the Western powers continued to give asylum to anyone who made his or her way out of Soviet-dominated Europe.[50]

By the summer of 1952, the number of temporarily resident Jewish refugees in Austria had dropped to 2,000. Nearly 90 percent were recent arrivals, having escaped after 1949 from Iron Curtain countries. The majority of these were strictly orthodox.[51] By now, even the UN High Commissioner for Refugees was convinced that, for orthodox Jews at least, integration into Austrian society was an impossible solution. Since many of them would have had to be counted under the Hungarian quota, they had very little opportunity for U.S. immigration, and their large families made them unacceptable to most other countries. Some emigration opportunities still existed at the beginning of 1953, mainly in South America. At this juncture, looking at the situation of the Jewish DPs in Central Europe from the security viewpoint, the JDC discussed whether it would be its task to interpret for the remaining DPs the "immediate need to take advantage of the haven offered by Israel instead of incurring the risk, by waiting for emigration opportunities in South America and elsewhere, of not being able to leave at all." A JDC representative pointed out that the "JDC in the past has done what it could by way of persuasion and, short of using force, would have to allow present events to speak for themselves."[52]

At the beginning of 1954, about 1,000 Jewish refugees still lived inside and outside camps in Austria.[53] The closing of the legendary Rothschild Hospital in Vienna and of the last Jewish camp in the U.S. Zone of Austria, Hallein in Land Salzburg, marked the official end of postwar DP-operations in that country. With the remaining 130 DPs from Hallein, who had been transferred to the new camp in

Glasenbach near Salzburg (run by the United States Escapee Program), and an additional group at the Asten camp in Upper Austria, there were, in all, about 400 Jewish DPs in the zone and 100 in Vienna. Most of them expected to emigrate to the United States or Britain. Those who could not emigrate were to go into the general Austrian community and eventually be transferred to the existing Jewish community. The JDC thought that its Austrian program "had a very good chance to be liquidated by June 1955."[54]

In February 1955 there were still a few Jewish DPs in the camps at Glasenbach and Asten; they continued to receive free accommodation and a small allowance from the Austrian government. The same applied to needy former DPs living in the community. By the end of Allied occupation in 1955, the number of non-German refugees had dropped at a steady pace to some 33,000, only a few of them Jews. The non-ethnic-German refugees faced a difficult situation; and many of them were still waiting for a chance to emigrate ten years after the end of the war.[55]

Prospects for Future Research

Whereas the Austrian stage of the 1945–1948 exodus from Eastern Europe is fairly well researched, knowledge about what happened in succeeding years is still sketchy. The archival material available regarding Jewish DPs in Austria has so far not been used to its full extent. What is completely missing is a social history of the Jewish survivors in Austria. For practical reasons—basic research seemed to be too costly and time-consuming some years ago—work on these aspects of the She'erit Ha-peletah in Austria was postponed. In the meantime, a new course of investigations has developed in Germany and Israel. These focus more on case studies of individual camps, accentuating social aspects, mentality, and ideology, with a marked trend toward an interdisciplinary approach combining sociology, psychology, and education. Beyond that, the first books with a synthesis of sociohistorical aspects in the widest sense have already been written; one of the pioneering studies is Jacqueline Giere's dissertation on education and culture in the DP camps of the U.S. Zone in Germany.[56]

In light of these more recent developments, the necessity of tackling the socio-historical aspects of the Jewish transient communities in Austria, including the inside view of the survivors' situation, and the internal organization of the She'erit Ha-peletah in Austria, seems obvious. Material on this field of research is located in the archives of the JDC in New York and Jerusalem, of the American Jewish Committee, YIVO, and the United Nations in New York, the World Jewish Congress records at the American Jewish Archives in Cincinnati, and the Central Zionist Archives in Jerusalem.

Probably the most important resource for a sociohistorical project is the collection on Jewish DPs in Austria at the YIVO Institute in New York.[57] This material, which was made available on microfilm at the beginning of the 1990s, documents the reconstruction of Jewish life after the Holocaust, the goals of the survivors and the strong influence of the various factions of the Zionist movement on the life of the refugees. This rich collection from a number of sources enables us to carry out detailed studies of the changing social structure of the She'erit Ha-peletah—age, birth and death rates, marriage, profession, social, and geographical background, health and sexuality—as well as on the political life in the camps, on works-projects, on physical education and leisure activities, on Zionist propaganda and ideology, on education, and on cultural and religious affairs. In addition, special problems of women, contacts among DPs and with the outside world, as well as internal conflicts, can be studied.

Regarding Austro-Jewish relations, even after the Holocaust, antisemitism remained a major factor. Austria, which regarded itself as a victim of Nazi aggression and not as Hitler's accomplice, felt no responsibility for the well-being of the Jewish survivors coming through Austria. In many respects, the Jewish DPs were "ideal" candidates to be scapegoated by the starving Austrian population. In the eyes of the general populace, they enjoyed certain "special privileges," such as better rations and exemption from the duty to work—indeed, they were foreigners and Jews to boot. Utilizing the traditional reservoir of antisemitic stereotypes, a reservoir of bias that had survived Nazi fascism virtually intact, the Jews became the negative showcase example, as it were, the very symbol of the DP per se.[58] Therefore, Jewish DPs served as a propaganda tool for the Austrian government to rid the country of all DPs. How the Jewish DPs perceived Austrian antisemitism remains an open question. Interviews could provide an answer.

Not every conflict between DPs, Allied authorities, and the Austrian population had an antisemitic background. One of the basic problems was an apparent discrepancy in the definition of the mutual situation: whereas the DPs regarded Austria as "enemy territory," the Allies officially treated Austria as a liberated victim of Nazi occupation and the Austrians saw the survivors as "guests in Austria" who should behave accordingly. In addition, until 1948 conflicts existed between Jews and non-Jews in the British as well as American forces regarding the treatment of DPs and the support of illegal movement.

Turning to the social structure of the DP population, one sees a marked progression of changes during the period under study. Most of the survivors who arrived in Austria prior to the summer of 1946 were young and single, and these were the first to move on toward Palestine. Next to arrive were complete families, who had returned from the Soviet Union to Poland and fled to the West in the wake of the Kielce pogrom. Their mobility was impeded by high birth rates on the one hand and a number of older family members on the other. The Romanian exodus of 1947 brought a different type of refugee to Austria, often with different experiences regarding the Holocaust and a different social and psychological background. These differences commonly led to discrimination with regard to their chances of being helped by the Brichah.

After spring 1948, new problems were caused by selective emigration, even to the State of Israel: the first, and often only, priority was given to the young and healthy. By 1950, apart from newcomers, only the hard-core cases were left. How were these people and their families looked after in Austria? Who took responsibility and what kind of special institutions were run for these survivors? Although MALBEN,[59] an organization of institutions for the care of handicapped immigrants in Israel, helped to solve this problem in the 1950s, many families had to stay in Austria for much longer than planned and eventually decided to settle there for good. In order to understand the changing pattern of emigration from Austria, we have to look into the social and educational background of the refugees at different stages of the exodus. For example, the Hungarian exodus from late 1948 until mid-1949 brought well-educated, urban, middle-class types, who often planned to stay in Austria, at least until they could find an opportunity to go to the United States. Israel was an option few of these latecomers favored.

A second collection of outstanding importance as a resource for sociohistorical research is the so-called Wiesenthal Collection at Yad Vashem, which covers the period from 1945 to 1952. Because of Simon Wiesenthal's functions and interests, it contains material on a wide variety of issues untouched thus far. Of special importance are records dealing with the activities of the Central Committee of Liberated Jews in Austria and those dealing with the activities of individual camp committees, for example, organizing elections. Issues discussed in the Central Committee ranged from religious problems to setting up "courts of honor" for dealing with Jewish collaborators. In August 1946, the Central Committee even voted for a seven-point catalogue that addressed itself to the Protection of Jewish Honor (zum Schutze der jüdischen Ehre),which, among other things, required that every election candidate supply an autobiography signed by at least two witnesses.[60] These documents give us a closer look at the biographical background of the DP leadership in Austria. Apart from everyday problems, such as rations, camp elections, and political quarrels, interesting issues were, among others, claims against Austrian companies to pay wages for slave labor, and attempts to install Jewish survivors as commissioners in charge of formerly Nazi-owned companies.

In addition, the Wiesenthal Collection documents relations of the Central Committee with the JDC, the Austrian administration, and the U.S. authorities in Austria. A preliminary study of the minutes of the Central Committee reveals a number of developments similar to those in Germany. The name Central Committee in no way reflects actual power; important decisions on the situation of the DPs and the running of the camps were made outside the Committee by the U.S. Army, the JDC, the Brichah, and representatives of the Jewish Agency. The Central Committee essentially had to follow orders. Individual camp leaders and camps had their own interests and made their own policy. Simon Wiesenthal, for example, set up the "Self-aid of the Jewish Former Concentration Camp Inmates in Upper Austria," which often carried out a program parallel to that of the Central Committee. It engaged in, among other things, the erection of a monument in Palestine in memory of the Jews who had died in the camps of Austria.[61] Uncoordinated initiatives led to internal quarrels among members of the Central Committee. Time was wasted, for example, on the design of a letterhead, while other people engaged in politics for the sake of making politics, thereby developing all the habits of professional politicians, and in later years often gained material advantages from their functions.

The Wiesenthal Collection is also of special value regarding the years after the establishment of the State of Israel, a period that deserves considerable attention: the DPs were confronted with the question of restitution and indemnification, the closing of camps, the termination of the activities of the IRO, and the step-by-step reduction of JDC's relief work. From the correspondence it becomes obvious that serious changes took place in the organization of the DP population, that by 1950 the fighting Zionist elements had already left the country, that the State of Israel eventually lost a great deal of interest in the people staying behind.

Our third main resource for a social history of the transient communities is the JDC Archives in New York and Jerusalem, which provide, among other things, statistical material on key data that go well beyond "counting calories." Further documentary materials are located in the records of the Jewish Agency at the Central Zionist Archives in Jerusalem. These materials deal with various aspects of Zionist propaganda in the camps as well as with questions related to emigration.

In this connection, topics related to the political ideology and political identity of the survivors should be reexamined.[62] Looking at Austria, there are at least some doubts as to the general Zionist outlook of most of the survivors. The horrors of the Holocaust did not create a common Jewish identity per se and Jewish survivors were not a homogeneous group; there were important differences in cultural background, past experiences, and future outlook. Evidence exists of disputes along "national" lines between Hungarian and Polish Jews,[63] of distrust among various groups in the camps, and of discrimination, for example, by the Brichah against the Romanian refugees in 1947.

The apparent wish of survivors to go to Palestine was based to a great extent upon a lack of alternatives—according to Yehuda Bauer, only about one-third of the 250,000 would have resisted the temptation of going to America[64]—and was strongly influenced by Zionist propaganda and even coercion. A few examples should demonstrate the questionable basis for the claim that more than 90 percent of the survivors favored the Zionist solution as an answer to Europe and the Holocaust.

The survey made for the Anglo-American Committee of Inquiry at the beginning of 1946—with a multiple-choice questionnaire—has so far been misinterpreted and has not been critically analyzed: all the standard reasons for Jews leaving Eastern Europe and refusing to go to their previous homes are known. Only twenty-one DPs out of 5,000 in the U.S. Zone in Austria mentioned their Zionist attitude as a reason for not returning.[65] In addition, we have known for some time about massive manipulation of questionnaires by "emissaries from Palestine" (shlichim) working in the camps.[66] This fits the picture of the general attitude of relief organizations dealing with the survivors: when Jacob L. Trobe of the JDC, at the end of October 1945, urged "psychological rehabilitation," the World Jewish Congress (WJC) made its attitude clear: "We do not want to give the Jews in D.P. camps community life, the semblance of normal living. Jews should not be made to feel comfortable in Germany. This would thwart the necessity of immediately transferring them to Palestine."[67]

In the summer of 1947, David Bernstein of the American Jewish Committee (AJC), referring to JDC policy in Germany, stated: "There has, in effect, been a conspiracy of silence to keep DPs ignorant of their chances in any country but Palestine, and JDC bears some part of the responsibility for this."[68]

After the establishment of the State of Israel, one would expect that the appeal of Zionism would peak. Kurt Grossmann of the WJC stated in May 1948: "On the occasion of the visit of the Anglo-American Commission in Austria in 1946, 90 to 95% of the DPs expressed their willingness to go to Palestine. This figure has changed recently." By then, 25 percent of the DPs had registered for thirty-eight different countries, and the rate of potential emigrés to Israel was dropping further. To overcome this situation, it was admitted that a substantial amount of coercion was taking place in Jewish camps in connection with the recruitment and training for the Haganah.[69] These reports put in question the general enthusiasm of Jewish DPs to emigrate and fight in Israel.

Most historians have thus far just repeated the propaganda of DP leaders in various contemporary articles in American Jewish publications, apparently written to support fundraising drives in the United States. The same applies to DP camp newspapers, which seem to have been more of a propaganda tool than a mirror of DP community life since they were funded—and often run—by interested parties. Why did so many of these prominent pro-Zionist DP leaders, such as Josef Rosensaft, Zalman Grinberg, or Simon Wiesenthal, either emigrate to the United States or stay on? Oral history interviews regarding the DP experience and emigration might provide new answers and alter commonly held beliefs.

As regards Austria, it has become necessary to deal with the problem of integration or nonintegration of ex-DPs into the reestablished Jewish communities. Even at this early stage of research, it seems that remnants of the "old" assimilated Jewish community in Austria did not press for the integration of Eastern European Jews; to the contrary, rejection of, and even hostility toward Eastern European Jews had a long tradition in Austria. As during the years after World War I, Austrian Jews again feared a new outbreak of antisemitism, triggered by the appearance, language, and behavior of orthodox newcomers, that would endanger their own desired assimilation and social standing. The JDC, too, put pressure on the refugees to move on, preferably to Israel, by denying financial help to newcomers refusing to live in camps and planning to settle down in Austria.[70] Population statistics reveal a shocking imbalance: whereas between 1945 and 1953 more than 200,000 ethnic German refugees were naturalized, only twenty-three Jewish DPs were granted Austrian citizenship.[71]

Despite these adverse circumstances, Jewish survivors remained in Austria. We do not yet know exactly how many former DPs actually stayed and for what reasons. We should attempt to find a pattern regarding a specific biographical background of these people, for example, their personal fate during the Holocaust, nationality, age, social or educational background, and so on.

As a first step in this direction and as a basis for further research, there are plans to publish a handbook documenting most of the sixty-seven Jewish DP camps that existed in Austria between 1945 and 1954, when camp Hallein was closed.[72] While there are a growing number of case studies on individual camps in Germany,[73] comparable studies of Austrian camps are rare. Therefore, a number of works on individual camps in the U.S. and French zones are underway at the universities of Innsbruck, Salzburg, and Vienna; the research is based mainly on archival sources of units of the U.S. occupation forces in Austria and the material of Jewish relief organizations.[74] A similar project on the British Zone will be carried out in the near future.

The ultimate attempt must be to place the entire Jewish exodus in a broader European context—in a political as well as a geographical sense. A closer look must be taken at the postwar situation of Jewish communities behind the Iron Curtain and the political implications of relief work in Central and Eastern Europe as well as its impact on Jewish communities. At the same time, Israeli policy toward the Soviet bloc has to be related to Western interests in the remnant of Eastern European Jewry in light of the Cold War. The same applies to Eastern European policy toward the Jewish minority and Zionism from the late 1940s onward. For this purpose, it will be necessary to overcome existing language barriers and establish closer relations with Polish, Czech, Slovak, Hungarian, and Romanian scholars in this field. First attempts in this direction have already begun in Austria as regards Hungary. Since the Jewish survivors were a European phenomenon, research should be a common enterprise with a comparative approach.

NOTES

1. For a brief summary of the occupation period 1945 to 1955, see Thomas Albrich, "Zwischenstation des Exodus: Jüdische DPs und Flüchtlinge nach dem Zweiten Weltkrieg," in *Asylland wider Willen: Flüchtlinge in Österreich im europäischen Kontext seit 1914*, ed. Gernot Heiss and Oliver Rathkolb (Vienna: Jugend und Volk, 1995), pp. 122–39.

2. Thomas Albrich, "'Es gibt keine jüdische Frage.' Zur Aufrechterhaltung des österreichischen Opfermythos," in *Der Umgang mit dem Holocaust: Europa—USA—Israel*, ed. Rolf Steininger in collaboration with Ingrid Böhler (Vienna: Böhlau Verlag, 1994), pp. 147–66.

3. First mentioned in the mid-1970s by Karl Stuhlpfarrer; see "Antisemitismus, Rassenpolitik und Judenverfolgung in Österreich nach dem Ersten Weltkrieg," in Anna Drabek et al., *Das österrreichische Judentum: Voraussetzungen und Geschichte* (Vienna: Jugend und Volk, 1974), pp. 141–64.

4. John Bunzl and Bernd Marin, *Antisemitismus in Österreich. Sozialhistorische und soziologische Studien* (Innsbruck: Inn-Verlag, 1983); Hilde Weiss, *Antisemitische Vorurteile in Österreich? Theoretische und empirische Analysen*, 2nd ed. (Vienna: Wilhelm Braumüller, 1987); Ruth Wodak et al., *"Wir sind alle unschuldige Täter": Diskurshistorische Studien zum Nachkriegsantisemitismus* (Frankfurt/M.: Suhrkamp, 1990); Werner Bergmann, Rainer Erb, and Albert Lichtblau, eds., *Schwieriges Erbe: Der Umgang mit Nationalsozialismus und Antisemitismus in Österreich, der DDR und der Bundesrepublik Deutschland* (Frankfurt: Campus Verlag, 1995).

5. Erika Weinzierl and Otto Kulka, eds., *Vertreibung und Neubeginn: Israelische Bürger österreichischer Herkunft* (Vienna: Böhlau, 1992); *Jüdische Schicksale: Berichte von Verfolgten*, ed. Dokumentationsarchiv des österreichischen Widerstandes (Vienna: Österreichischer Bundesverlag, 1992); Adi Wimmer, *Die Heimat wurde ihnen fremd, die Fremde nicht zur Heimat: Erinnerungen österreichischer Juden aus dem Exil* (Vienna: Verlag für Gesellschaftskritik, 1993).

6. F[riederike] Wilder-Okladek, *The Return Movement of Jews to Austria after the 2nd World War: With Special Consideration of the Return from Israel* (The Hague: Martinus Nijhoff, 1969); Christoph Reinprecht, *Zurückgekehrt: Identität und Bruch in der Biographie österreichischer Juden* (Vienna: Braumüller, 1992).

7. Dorit B. Whiteman, *The Uprooted: A Hitler Legacy* (New York: Plenum Press, 1993) (translated into German by Marie-Therese Pitner as *Jüdische Lebensgeschichten nach der Flucht 1933 bis heute* [Vienna: Böhlau Verlag, 1995]).

8. Robert Knight, *Ich bin dafür, die Sache in die Länge zu ziehen: Wortprotokolle der österreichischen Bundesregierung von 1945–52 über die Entschädigung der Juden* (Frankfurt/M.: Athenäum Verlag, 1988); Albert Sternfeld, *Betrifft: Österreich: Von Österreich betroffen* (Vienna: Loecker, 1990); Brigitte Bailer, *Wiedergutmachung—kein Thema: Österreich und die Opfer des Nationalsozialismus* (Vienna: Loecker, 1993).

9. John Bunzl, *Der lange Arm der Erinnerung: Jüdisches Bewusstsein heute* (Vienna: Böhlau Verlag, 1987); Ruth Beckermann, *Unzugehörig: Österreicher und Juden nach 1945* (Vienna: Löcker, 1989); Robert S. Wistrich, ed., *Austrians and Jews in the Twentieth Century: From Franz Joseph to Waldheim* (New York: St. Martin's Press, 1992).

10. Helga Embacher, *Neubeginn ohne Illusionen: Juden in Österreich nach 1945* (Vienna: Picus Verlag, 1995).

11. Thomas Albrich, *Exodus durch Österreich: Die jüdischen Flüchtlinge 1945–1948* (Innsbruck: Haymon Verlag, 1987).

12. Benedikt Friedman, *"Iwan hau die Juden!" Die Todesmärsche ungarischer Juden durch Österreich nach Mauthausen im April 1945* (St. Pölten: Institut für Geschichte der Juden in Österreich, 1989); see also chapters on death marches and liberation in Gordon J. Horwitz, *In the Shadow of Death: Living Outside the Gates of Mauthausen* (New York: Free Press, 1990), and the TV documentary "Totschweigen" (1994) by Margareta Heinrich and Eduard Erne.

13. Eleonore Lappin, who is working on this project, delivered a paper titled "Prozesse der britischen Militärgerichte wegen nationalsozialistischer Gewaltverbrechen an ungarisch-jüdischen Zwangsarbeitern in der Steiermark" at the Österreichische Zeitgeschichtetag in Linz, May 1995 (it has now been published in *Österreich – 50 Jahre Zweite Republik: Österreichischer Zeitgeschichtetag 1995*, ed. Rudolf G. Ardelt [Innsbruck: Studien-Verlag, 1997], pp. 345–50). In addition, see Szabolcs Szita, "Die Todesmärsche der Budapester Juden im November 1944 nach Hegyshalom-Nickolsdorf," *Zeitgeschichte* 22, no. 3/4 (1995): 124–37.

14. IK Jahresbericht, December 30, 1946; World Jewish Congress Papers (hereafter WJCP), H 43/Austria 1946, American Jewish Archives (hereafter AJA).

15. Reuben Resnik, JDC St. Gallen, to Moses Leavitt, JDC New York, July 19, 1945; AR 4564/855, Joint Distribution Committee Archives (hereafter JDCA), Reuben Resnik, JDC, to Joseph Schwartz, JDC, July 20, 1945; AR 4564/195, JDCA.

16. Ibid.

17. Robert H. Abzug, *Inside the Vicious Heart: Americans and the Liberation of Nazi Concentration Camps* (New York: Oxford University Press, 1985).

18. Minutes of the business session of the Conference of the Liberated Jews in Germany, St. Ottilien, July 25, 1945; WJCP, A 75/2, AJA.

19. Ibid.

20. Ibid.

21. Thomas Albrich, "Tirol, Transitland des jüdischen Exodus 1945–1948," *Sturzflüge* 5 (1986): 137–48; and idem, "Zur Kontinuität eines Vorurteils: Die ostjüdischen Flüchtlinge in Vorarlberg nach dem Zweiten Weltkrieg," in *Antisemitismus in Vorarlberg: Regionalstudie zur Geschichte einer Weltanschauung*, ed. Werner Dreier (Bregenz: Vorarlberger Autorengesellschaft, 1988), pp. 250–86.

22. Michael John, "Displaced Persons in Linz. 'Versetzte Personen' und fremdsprachige Flüchtlinge in der Nachkriegszeit," in *Prinzip Hoffnung: Linz zwischen Befreiung und Freiheit*, ed. Willibald Katzinger and Fritz Mayrhofer (Linz: Stadtmuseum Linz-Nordico, 1995), pp. 213–29; Adina Stern, "Nur weg von Österreich! Die Linzer Durchgangslager für jüdische Flüchtlinge," in ibid., pp. 271–86.

23. For details, see Yehuda Bauer, *Flight and Rescue: Brichah* (New York: Random House, 1970); Aba Gefen, *Unholy Alliance* (Jerusalem: Y. Tal, 1973); Ephraim Dekel, *B'riha: Flight to the Homeland* (New York: Herzl Press, 1973).

24. James P. Rice to Reuben Resnik, Report on Steiermark and Upper Austria, October 4, 1945; AR 4564/161, JDCA.

25. Melvin Goldstein, JDC Paris, to JDC New York, February 22, 1946; AR 4564/161, JDCA.

26. Distribution of Jewish DPs: 6,000 in the U.S. Zone, excluding Vienna; 3,500 in the British Zone; 500 in the French Zone; and 2,500 in Vienna. Robert Pilpel, JDC, Memorandum to Hyman, Sobel, Leavitt, December 10, 1945; AR 4564/161, JDCA.

27. This and the following discussion of the beginning of illegal infiltration from the late summer of 1945 until the spring of 1946 is based on Albrich, *Exodus*, pp. 37–97.

28. Israel Gutman, "Juden in Polen nach dem Holocaust 1944–1968," in Steininger, ed., *Der Umgang mit dem Holocaust*, pp. 265–76.

29. Michael Checinsky, "The Kielce Pogrom: Some Unanswered Questions," *Soviet Jewish Affairs* 5, no. 1 (1975): 57–72.

30. The following on the "Polish Exodus" is based on Albrich, *Exodus*, pp. 98–145.

31. Report for American Zone Operations, JDC for August 1–31, 1946; September 10, 1946; AR 4564/161, JDCA.

32. Internationales Komitee, annual report, December 30, 1946; WJCP, H 43/Austria 1946, AJA.

33. Idith Zertal, "Verlorene Seelen: Die jüdischen DPs und die israelische Staatsgründung," *Babylon. Beiträge zur jüdischen Gegenwart* 5 (1989): 88–102.

34. The following discussion of the "Romanian Exodus" is based on Albrich, *Exodus*, pp. 146–79.

35. Jean Ancel, "She'erit Hapletah in Romania during the Transition Period to a Communist Regime, August 1944–December 1947," in *She'erit Hapletah, 1944–1948: Rehabilitation and Political Struggle*, ed. Yisrael Gutman and Avital Saf (Jerusalem: Yad Vashem, 1990), pp. 143–67.

36. Margit Reiter, "'In unser aller Herzen brennt dieses Urteil.' Der Bad Ischler 'Milch-Prozess' von 1947 vor dem amerikanischen Militärgericht," in *Politische Affären und Skandale in Österreich: Von Mayerling bis Waldheim*, ed. Michael Gehler, and Hubert Sickinger (Vienna: Thaur Kulturverlag, 1995), pp. 323–45.

37. Documents related to emigration from Eastern Europe are published in *State of Israel, Documents on the Foreign Policy of Israel*, vols. 1–7 (Jerusalem 1981–1992).

38. William Haber, Adviser on Jewish Affairs Eucom, to A. C. A. Liverhant, American Jewish Conference, June 17, 1948; AR 4564/161, JDCA.

39. Ibid.

40. Mordechai Ben-Ari, Immigration Office for the State of Israel in Austria, Salzburg, Summary of immigration activities in Austria, August 1948–January 1949, January 18, 1949; S 6/6067, Central Zionist Archives (hereafter CZA).

41. Harry Greenstein, Adviser on Jewish Affairs of the U.S. Army's European Command (Eucom), Report on Austria, May 11, 1949; AR 4564/161, JDCA.

42. Leonard Dinnerstein, *America and the Survivors of the Holocaust* (New York: Columbia University Press, 1982).

43. Notes of New York JDC Staff Meeting, June 6, 1949; AR 4564/197, JDCA.

44. Harry Greenstein, Adviser on Jewish Affairs Eucom, Report on Austria, May 28, 1949; AR 4564/194, JDCA.

45. Bundesministerium für Inneres, Gesamtaufstellung der in Österreich befindlichen DPs und Flüchtlinge, November 1, 1949; Bundesministerium für Auswärtige Angelegenheiten, II pol-49, K 104, GZ. 80.697-pol/50, Österreichisches Staatsarchiv, Archiv der Republik, Vienna, Austria.

46. Ernst Stiassny, WJC Vienna, to Siegfried Roth, WJC London, August 4, 1951; WJCP, H 48, Austria 1949–52, AJA.

47. Robert S. Marcus, AJC, to Gerhard Riegner, WJC, August 11, 1950; WJCP, B49/1, AJA.

48. For the 1950s, see Thomas Albrich, "Der Traum von 'Amerika'. Jüdische Flüchtlinge 1950–1957," in *Österreich in den Fünfzigern*, ed. Thomas Albrich, Klaus Eisterer, Michael Gehler, and Rolf Steininger (Innsbruck: Österreichischer Studienverlag, 1995), pp. 95–117.

49. *Austrian Information*, published by the Information Department of the Austrian Consulate General, New York, September 11, 1950; WJCP, B 73/XCIX, AJA.

50. AJC, "The Jews of Europe and North Africa. A Report of Trends and Developments, July–November 1950"; AR 4564/3593, JDCA.

51. JDC Paris, "The Jewish Neo-Refugees in Austria," October 9, 1952; AR 4564/197, JDCA.

52. JDC Paris HQ, Meeting of Department Heads, February 5, 1953; AR 4564/3453, JDCA.

53. *ISKULT-Presse-Nachrichten*, January 25, 1954.

54. JDC Paris HQ, Meeting of Department Heads, January 21, 1954; AR 4564/3452, JDCA.

55. Yvonne v. Stedingk, *Die Organisation des Flüchtlingswesens in Österreich seit dem Zweiten Weltkrieg* (Vienna: Wilhelm Braumüller, 1970), pp. 29–30.

56. Jacqueline Giere, "'Wir sind unterwegs, aber nicht in der Wüste.' Erziehung und Kultur in den jüdischen Displaced Persons-Lagern der amerikanischen Zone im Nachkriegs-deutschland 1945–1949," diss. Frankfurt University, 1993.

57. MK 492, YIVO Institute for Jewish Research (YIVO).

58. For the attitude of the Austrian population toward Jewish DPs, see Albrich, *Exodus*, pp. 180–93.

59. Hebrew abbreviation for "mosdot letipul be'olim nachshalim."

60. Minutes of the Central Committee for Liberated Jews in Austria, September 11, 1946, M-9/26, Wiesenthal Collection, Yad Vashem.

61. Self-aid of the Jewish Former Concentration Camp Inmates in Upper Austria to United Jewish Appeal, New York, March 8, 1948; AR 4564/161, JDCA.

62. As a brief introduction, see Abraham J. Peck, "Befreit und erneut in Lagern: jüdische DPs. Statt eines Epilogs," in *Der Judenpogrom 1938: Von der "Reichskristallnacht" zum Völkermord*, ed. Walter Pehle (Frankfurt/M.: Fischer Taschenbuch Verlag, 1988), (published in English as *November 1938: From "Reichskristallnacht" to Genocide* [New York: Berg, 1991]), pp. 201–12.

63. As an example, see the statement by Simon Wiesenthal, Minutes of the Central Committee for Liberated Jews in Austria, September 11, 1946, M-9/26, Wiesenthal Collection, Yad Vashem.

64. Yehuda Bauer, "The Brichah," in *She'erit Hapletah, 1944–1948,* ed. Gutman and Saf, p. 55.

65. See Allied Commission Austria (British Element and U.S. Element), Combined Report, February 14, 1946; FO 945/383/6 c. Public Records Office, London.

66. Giere, "'Wir sind unterwegs, aber nicht in der Wüste,'" p. 124, quoted from Ze'ev Zachor, "She'arit ha-pleita ke-goram politi," in *Machanot ha-girush be-kaprisin*, ed. P. Hillmann (Yad Tabenkin, 1987), p. 24.

67. Robert Serebrenik, WJC, to Arieh Tartakower and Leon Kubowitzky, WJC, October 29, 1945; WJCP, H 11/JDC Correspondence 1945–1947, AJA.

68. David Bernstein to John Slawson, AJC, July 14, 1947; AJC, GEN–12, box 78, Joint Distribution Committee General 47–56, RG 347, YIVO.

69. William Haber to A. C. A. Liverhant, American Jewish Conference, June 17, 1948; AR 4564/161, JDCA.

70. Harold Trobe, JDC Vienna, to Joseph Schwartz, JDC Paris, December 28, 1948; AR 4564/197, JDCA.

71. U.S. Embassy, Vienna, to Department of State, Report on Present Refugee Problem, April 2, 1953; RG 59, 863.411/4–253, National Archives, Washington D.C.

72. For a list of Jewish DP camps in Austria, see Thomas Albrich, "Die fehlende Innensicht: Überlegungen zu einer Alltags-, Mentalitäts- und Sozialgeschichte der jüdischen Displaced Persons in Österreich," in *Österreichischer Zeitgeschichtetag 1993*, ed. Ingrid Böhler and Rolf Steininger (Innsbruck: Österreichischer Studienverlag, 1995), pp. 59–61; of the sixty-seven camps currently known, forty-five were in the U.S. Zone (including Vienna), ten in the British Zone, seven in the French Zone, and five in the Soviet Zone (only for a short period after liberation).

73. The pioneer study was presented by Juliane Wetzel, *Jüdisches Leben in München 1945–1951: Durchgangsstation oder Wiederaufbau?* (Munich: Kommissionsverlag Uni-Druck, 1987).

74. The first results are a number of MA theses: Bernadette Lietzow, "Green Shelter 106. Das Lager für jüdische DPs in Enns 1946–1948. Eine Fallstudie," University of Innsbruck, 1995; Katrin Oberhammer, "Der Staat Israel begann im 'Wiesenhof,' Tirol als Transitland des jüdischen Exodus 1945–1949," University of Innsbruck, 1996; Christine Oertel, "Jüdische DPs in der amerikanischen Besatzungszone unter besonderer Berücksichtigung der Lager in Wien," University of Vienna, 1996; Norbert Ramp, "Österreich und die jüdischen Flüchtlinge 1945–1951," University of Salzburg, 1996.

50.

DALIA OFER

From Illegal Immigrants to New Immigrants

THE CYPRUS DETAINEES, 1946–1949

Unlike other national movements, Zionism faced a preliminary task: restoring Jews to the historical land of Israel, which it viewed as their true homeland. "Illegal immigration," a term used by the British to describe clandestine entry in defiance of the immigration laws, was central to Zionist settlement of British-Mandatory Palestine from the movement's early years. The number and social composition of illegal immigrants varied over time. In the early stages it consisted of self-selected groups who prepared themselves for life in Palestine in organized youth movements; other illegal immigrants came from the Jewish petite bourgeoisie in Poland. As a mass movement, illegal immigration began at a time when the majority of the participants were persecuted Jews who had fled their countries of origin. Immigration was concentrated in two periods: 1938–1940 and 1945–1948. The major cause for the growth of the movement was Nazi policy in 1938–1940 and its consequences.[1] From 1945–1948, illegal immigration was a response to British policy toward Palestine.

I shall discuss here only some seventy thousand illegal immigrants during the post–World War II period, most of them survivors of the Holocaust and among them a great number from the displaced persons (DP) camps in Germany and Italy. The term "Holocaust survivor" as used here includes all Jews who were in occupied Europe and who suffered directly from Nazism. Among them are Jews living in countries allied or collaborating with the Nazis (e.g., Romania, Bulgaria, Hungary, Slovakia, and Croatia), and the Jews who managed to escape to the Soviet Union during the war and were repatriated to Poland in 1945–1946. This defines the Zionist understanding of who was a survivor and also conforms to the definition expressed by most survivors themselves in their writings, public declarations, and private correspondence.[2]

It is very difficult to determine the number of survivors. At war's end, there were an estimated fifty to eighty thousand in Germany, but many died in the first month after liberation. There were a large number of survivors in Eastern Europe and the Balkans: some 400,000 in Romania; 143,000 in Hungary; 40,000 in Bulgaria; and, after repatriation from the Soviet Union, some 130,000 in Poland. The movement of Jews from country to country and their concentration in Germany and Italy in 1946 and 1947 brought the number in DP camps in Germany to some 250,000 by January 1948.

After many years of immigration restrictions under the British Mandatory Government in Palestine, the Provisional Government of the new state of Israel ended all restrictions on the immigration of Jews to the country in May 1948. The following three years are known in the literature as the "years of mass immigration." The Jewish community in Palestine, which had numbered some 670,000 in May 1948, received 717,923 immigrants in those three years, among them 373,852 Holocaust survivors. The number of immigrants per 1,000 people living in Israel was 236 in 1948 and 266 in 1949, a huge number when compared with other immigrant countries: in 1913 the figure was 12.1 for the United States, 38.4 for Canada, 38.3 for Argentina, and 7.7 for Brazil.[3]

Early mass immigration into Israel reflected the policy of free and unrestricted immigration that was a basic tenet of Zionism and corroborated the desire of the new state to populate areas gained during the War of Independence, including that deserted by Arab refugees. Of the 778,946 immigrants to Israel between 1946 and 1953, 48.6 percent were Holocaust survivors; between 1946 and 1948, 85 to 95 percent of the 162,914 immigrants were survivors. In 1949, the percentage declined to 52.1, falling still further thereafter.[4]

The immigration of some 200,000 Holocaust survivors to Israel took place while the country was fighting a war of survival. In spite of the Israeli government's preference for able-bodied immigrants of military age, immigration was neither restricted nor selective: Jews from all walks of life came, most from the DP camps. Both the war and its cessation had a significant impact on the absorption of the new immigrants.

Archival documents, contemporary newspapers, oral testimonies, and other literature can shed light on the preparedness of both the new immigrants and the veterans to adapt to their new situation; the influences of past experiences on the process of their absorption; and the way both groups saw themselves, each other, and their roles in the absorption process.

The Cyprus Detainees

A significant subgroup among the survivors were the 51,530 deported to Cyprus. From August 13, 1946, the British deported for detention in Cyprus thousands of illegal immigrants, many of whom had actually reached Palestine. From November 1946 until May 1948, these detainees were permitted to enter Palestine at a rate of 750 per month, that is, they made up half the total quota of 1,500. During 1947 and 1948, special quotas were allotted for pregnant women, mothers with babies, and the elderly. Cyprus detainees constituted 67 percent of total immigration between November 1946 and mid-May 1948, and almost 40 percent from May to September 1948, the peak months of the War of Independence. The group included all categories of Holocaust survivors. Sixty percent of these detainees had been in the DP camps; the others came from the Balkans and other East European countries. A very small group from Morocco was also processed through Cyprus.[5]

In 1947, the Cyprus detainees made up 55 percent of total immigration (12,128 out of 22,098)—between January and April 1948, 63 percent (10,853 out of 17,165), and between July and September 1948, 30 percent (12,795 out of 42,835). Most of the Cyprus detainees immigrated in a rather short period immediately before and after the establishment of the Jewish state. Only the last group of some 10,000 immigrants, the majority of military age, reached Israel in February 1949. They had been detained in Cyprus by the British, after which they all immigrated and many joined the Israeli armed forces.[6]

The Cyprus detainees were highly motivated to get to Palestine; they became a symbol of the dedication of the survivors to create a new life for themselves in Israel; and the Jewish community in Palestine, the Yishuv, acknowledged their efforts. The British deportations from Haifa had been a painful experience for many. The encounter between the Palestine "veterans" (a third had been in the country for less than a decade) and the Cyprus detainees illustrates why Israel made such an enormous absorption effort.

The Cyprus detainees, who represented the illegal immigrants among the survivors of the Holocaust, had excellent prospects for being integrated into Israeli society and for identifying with its vision. Like most survivors, they were strongly motivated to return to normal life and appreciated the opportunity to work and establish a family. Their experiences during and after the war proved anything but an impediment to their absorption. Their self-perception as activists—people who took their fate into their own hands, especially through the "Gar'inim" or youth groups planning a collectivist life on kibbutzim—prepared them to confront all difficulties. However, the long months of detention in Cyprus were difficult. These months had weakened their trust in the intentions of the Yishuv's leadership to end their homelessness but reinforced the dependency of the immigrants on this leadership. The small but steady flow of immigration certificates permitted cautious optimism. And the regular arrival of new immigrants to Cyprus proved that the Yishuv was not going to give up on immigration. Yet it increased the number of people in the camps expecting a certificate.

The first steps toward absorption in Palestine/Israel were characterized by much frustration and disappointment and gave rise to many anxieties based on survivors' past experiences. It is difficult to follow precisely the fate of Cyprus detainees as a subgroup after their arrival in Israel; and this causes a methodological difficulty, although much information can be drawn from the general data on immigrant survivors for the same period.[7]

Demographic Profile of Immigrants, Holocaust Survivors, and Cyprus Detainees

Holocaust survivors as immigrants can be divided into two groups with somewhat different demographic attributes: a) immigrants of the years 1946 to May 14, 1948; and b) immigrants of the years from May 15, 1948 to 1953. The age distribution of immigrants was as follows:

1946–May 14, 1948		May 15, 1948–1953	
Age	*Percentage*[8]	*Age*	*Percentage*[9]
0–4	5.3	0–4	10.4
5–19	33.5	5–19	15.8
20–39	49.9	20–39	38.0
40–59	8.2	40–59	26.8
60+	3.1	60+	9.0

The demographic attributes of the detainees in October 1947 were as follows:

Age	*Numbers*	*Percentage*[10]
0–4	619	3.5
5–12	141	2.3
13–18	2,961	16.8
19–35	11,334	64.3
36–50	1,759	10.0
51+	538	3.1

The Cyprus detainees' profile was closer to that of group a) immigrants, with 80 percent between thirteen and thirty-five years of age. The number of the elderly and the very young was relatively small, although it is worth noting that 2,200 babies were born on the island. Of the 8,000 young people between ages twelve and eighteen, 6,000 had lost both parents.[11] While both groups consisted primarily of people of working age, group b) included more of the old and very young: this resulted from the large numbers of families from Eastern Europe and the Balkans who came to Israel after the establishment of the state when the voyage was no longer dangerous or illegal. The gender distribution of the immigrants reflects hesitation by women to undertake the strenuous illegal voyage:

	Males	*Females*[12]
	(as a percentage)	
1946–1948	55.3	44.7
1948–1953	49.3	50.7
Cyprus	66.0	33.0 (rounded)

No records indicate the formal educational levels of the Cyprus detainees; however, those characteristics of Holocaust survivors in general placed them below Palestine veterans but above immigrants from Islamic countries. The educational levels of Holocaust survivors above the age of fourteen in June 1954 (expressed as a percentage) are as follows:[13]

	No School	*Attended Elementary School*	*Graduated Elementary School*	*Graduated High School*	*Higher Education*
Males	2.6	33.1	41.2	18.3	4.8
Females	6.3	31.9	40.6	19.2	2.1

The educational levels of Palestine veterans (countries of origin in Europe and America), above the age of fourteen (expressed as a percentage) are as follows:[14]

	No School	Attended Elementary School	Graduated Elementary School	Graduated High School	Higher Education
Males	1.0	17.7	37.7	33.4	10.2
Females	4.8	16.3	40.4	33.4	5.1

The Cyprus group appears to have been the least educated. Reports of the emissaries from Palestine/Israel stressed the lack of basic skills such as reading, writing, and arithmetic. But their testimonies stressed the desire of the detainees to learn and their willingness to study. One of the major problems was the shortage of teachers at all levels.[15] In July 1947, teachers from Palestine established the Rothberg Seminar for adult education in Cyprus (called "the open university" by the detainees) and graduated 1,800 students during the year and a half it operated. However, in Cyprus there was no vocational education such as that which had played an important role in the DP camps in Europe. The ORT (Organization for Rehabilitation through Training), established in 1880 to spread artisanal and agricultural vocations among Jews, did not open a workshop in Cyprus. Neither did 'Amal, the vocational system of the labor union Histadrut, which was established in 1946. The lack of vocational education reflected both the interest of the Yishuv and the Joint Distribution Committee (JDC) in assuring that the detainees on the island would want to move on as soon as possible, as well as the attitude of many emissaries, especially from kibbutzim, that the immigrants would learn on the kibbutz. Since the establishment of workshops was expensive and required long planning, this attitude also suited other organizations. The immigrants, however, demanded that workshops be opened, and they complained about the lack of opportunity to learn a vocation or to work.

We have no details about the occupational structure of the Cyprus detainees. However, information is available about the immigrants of 1947, of whom 67.7 percent (13,352 out of a total of 19,702 registered by the Jewish Agency) had been Cyprus detainees.[16] Only 35 percent (3,401 persons of working age) registered as having an occupation. In comparison, among the other 6,350 immigrants that year (all Holocaust survivors), 59 percent of those of working age registered an occupation.

Many of the Cyprus detainees were too young to have had an occupation and, since they had not been able to study during the war years, they were now trying to gain some skill. Of the young adults, some had learned vocations in the Nazi forced labor camps or in the Soviet Union; for many, however, these skills were connected with painful memories that led them to despise their "professions."

If we look at the previous occupations of Holocaust survivors as a whole during the years from 1948 to 1952, the approximate percentages for males (and females, in parentheses), are as follows: 43.8 percent in crafts and industry (46.6); 9.8 in technical and white collar occupations (20.2); 12.8 in trade and sales (1.8); 13.2 in clerical jobs and administration (16.9); 4.8 in construction (0.3); 4.5 in transportation (0.2); 4.4 in agriculture (3.1); the remaining 6.5 percent unskilled. The percentage of individuals in agriculture and white collar professions was lower than among the veteran Palestinian community. Immigrants from Islamic countries had a higher representation (22.4%) in trade and sales and a lower proportion (0.6%) in technical and white collar professions. These structures of occupational experience gave the survivors some basic tools for finding their way in the new Israeli economy, although many had to change their profession or take special training courses offered by the state.[17]

All of this information reflects the influence of the war. Demographically, the greatest losses were suffered by children and the elderly. The large numbers of very small children (to age four) was a reflection of the vitality of the survivors and their will to reproduce (the birth rate in the DP camps in Germany was 41 per 1000).[18] The large number of orphans in Cyprus and the relatively large numbers of children aged five to eighteen among group a) immigrants indicated the priority given by the policymakers toward these groups through Youth Aliyah, a special institution established in 1934 to bring German youth to Palestine. After the war, Youth Aliyah became the most important rescue organization for orphans and children. During the years 1946–1948, Youth Aliyah and Cyprus detainees accounted for well over half the total number of new immigrants.

Some 90 percent of the Cyprus detainees were organized into political parties or youth movements connected to various kibbutz movements. This provided a network of connections and a support group, both of which were very important in assisting their integration into Israeli society and politics. Overall, the Cyprus detainees were typical of Holocaust survivors, new immigrants to Israel, and new participants in the Israeli labor market in general.

Self Perception of the Cyprus Detainees

Kopel Pinson described the DPs in Germany as "a marvelous example of a society without an elite."[19] Nahum Bogner applied this perspective to the Cyprus detainees.[20] The Yishuv, too, considered them a special group, having selected them to participate in illegal immigration. It is very difficult to draw a group profile regarding the self-image of the immigrants. The variations between individuals were many and extreme. However, the sources reveal a low level of self-esteem. Although the illegal immigrants consisted of a partially self-selected group among the survivors, the majority belonging to Zionist youth movements and determined to shape their own fate, they generally were self-critical and looked up to the emissaries and veterans of the Yishuv.

One of the first emissaries to reach Cyprus, in November 1946, was the teacher Aharon Zeev from Tel Aviv. After serving for three months, he returned to Palestine in January 1947, six months after the deportations to Cyprus had begun, and reported on the situation to the Executive Committee of the Histadrut, one of the central institutions involved in immigration and absorption. In relation to the self-image of the detainees he said,

> When I had a free half hour, I used to walk in the camp and talk with people. One day a person introduced himself in the following way. You should know comrade Zeev, that I am a liar, and if somebody will tell you that I am a murderer, you should believe it; if somebody will tell you that I am robber and a thief you should believe it! As to myself, you may believe me only if I told you that I am scratching all the time.

"He wanted to tell me," continued Zeev to explain the strange declaration, "that he was not cured from scabies. However, many introduce themselves in this fashion and in their naiveté they believe that this is the truth."[21] Zeev predicted it would be difficult to change this poor self-image, for the detainees had a deep feeling that their experiences had left negative marks on their character.

In the opinion of the psychiatric team that visited the camps in the summer of 1947, a particularly difficult period for the detainees, the arduous physical conditions in Cyprus reenforced this image and strengthened the detainees' anxiety about facing a return to "normal working life." The dreariness of everyday life in the Cypress camps resulted from the difficult physical environment and the unwilling idleness of more than 85 percent of the detainees: "Idleness is one of the most serious problems of the refugees. Some of them are profoundly fearful that further enforced inactivity will seriously diminish their ability and capacity to work in the future."[22] Other hardships were the constant standing in line, and in particular the shortage of water, an essential in the hot Cyprus summer. This caused considerable aggression and hostility among detainees:

> Drinking water is tepid, often quite warm; on several occasions it was seen to be steaming as it flowed from the tap of the water tank. Only the physically strongest and most aggressive internees in the camp manage by sheer force to reach the tap, as long as the supply lasts, and have water. It is not surprising therefore to hear the internees say "water on Cyprus is mixed with blood."[23]

The bulletins of the youth movements and cultural life in detention generally reflected internees' anxieties about their future life in Palestine/Israel. These included harsh criticism of their own lifestyle with its tense human relations, distrust, and spiritual emptiness, an ambivalent image of the community in Palestine, and criticism of the Yishuv for neglecting them and losing interest in their plight. None of this, however, negated widespread admiration for the values and sense of community that detainee society demonstrated. The art exhibitions and theater performances usually portrayed the risky attempts to enter Palestine illegally, the difficulties of life in the Cyprus camps, and the heroic images of the new life awaiting them in Palestine. Only a few works related to the war, the ghetto, or lost family. In the opinion of the emissaries and the psychiatric team, this demonstrated the desire to negotiate the unsettling transition from life behind barbed wire to an open society.[24] Many lacked a realistic view of life in Palestine and therefore had false expectations. The members of pioneering farm collectives had more information about life on the kibbutzim, but many did not join and others left the kibbutzim shortly after arrival. Some counted on the support of relatives already in the country. The majority, however, even those formally belonging to a political movement or party, had little accurate information about jobs, housing, primary assistance, or other aspects of life in Palestine. The Jewish Agency (JA), the body that represented the Zionist movement in Palestine and that constituted the executive and bureaucracy of the Yishuv, intended to settle them in agricultural villages away from the "big cities," but this represented for them the threat of continued isolation, even in the new homeland.[25]

Yet it would be wrong to view the detainees in Cyprus as a passive, noncreative group. They were able to organize an internal order, there was very little criminal activity in the camps, and they were determined to control the process of immigration to Palestine/Israel on their own. The intention to ensure that those who arrived in Cyprus first also would leave first reflected a firm commitment to fairness. Mothers with young babies, pregnant women, the sick, and the old, all had to accept this principle. By the fall of 1948, when only some 10,000 detainees remained, mostly single men or families of military age whom the British did not permit to leave the island for political reasons, a strong resistance to British policy manifested itself in the form of riots and organized marches out of the camps. Several hundred escaped with the help of emissaries of the Israel Defence Forces (IDF).[26]

The detainees suffered from a strong sense that they were losing precious time: they had been on the brink of escaping DP status but now were captive again. Those who reached Cyprus from the Balkans had not experienced DP camp life before and found the forced idleness very hard. Being close to Palestine/Israel did not necessarily ease their situation but often the contrary—being so near and yet so far produced feelings of despair and the suspicion that they were being neglected.[27]

Veterans' Perceptions of New Immigrants and the Cyprus Detainees

Aharon Zeev's report emphasized the misconceptions of the Yishuv about detainees. Zeev cited the false expectations that he brought with him on his first visit to Cyprus, images fashioned by newspaper reports in Palestine. Zeev compared the detainees' longing for Palestine with a person suffering unbearable thirst. As for the detainees, who had almost reached Palestine, their present plight and the remembrance of past suffering were salved only by concentrating on the wish to reach their goal. In spite of all the difficulties, Palestine was still their most hopeful possibility. They were looking for a way of life that would liberate them from their personal anguish and allow them to live in a community that would understand and shelter them.

However, their feelings did not derive from any ideology or philosophy. The future of the Jewish people and their need for a homeland were not key to the understanding of the internees' motivations. Thus, the Histadrut and other groups of the Yishuv should not have expected them to be pioneers. Rather, the Yishuv needed to listen to the immigrants and appreciate the fact that stability, a home, a family, and a good job were their principal requirements; they had lacked these for too many years.[28]

Giora Yosephtahl, in charge of absorption at the Jewish Agency (JA), described the survivors in all their complexity. They were very lonely and needed a community to lean on; however, they were also individualistic and cherished their freedom. They were tired of living according to strict regulations as they had for years in the camps, but they did not know how to be alone and how to use their time creatively. The mentality of the survivors, Yosephtahl explained, was "I am deserving because of my past": the Yishuv, the Jews, humanity in general owed them. However, this should cause neither disappointment nor misunderstanding of the positive human potential of the immigrants.

Whether Yosephtahl was right or wrong, the attitude of the veterans toward the survivors could be characterized as the opposite: it was the survivors who were obligated. Once they arrived in Israel they were supposed to enlist in the task of "nation-building," joining the veterans to pave the way for future immigrants.[29] The survivors were expected to embrace the country right away and treat early hardships as unavoidable first steps in the absorption process. Although the issue of understanding the special emotional situation of the newcomers was widely discussed, the basic attitude of many veterans did not change; they were sure that they knew what was best for the immigrants.[30] Many veterans reacted to the difficulties of the new immigrants by averring, "when we came to the country, things were more difficult." Theirs was a patronizing attitude that overlooked the individuality of the immigrants and viewed them merely as a cohort of undifferentiated recruits to be transformed into true pioneers: if immigrants integrated successfully, this would demonstrate that the veterans had done a good job. Some extreme examples of this attitude were found in labor movement newspapers and speeches at kibbutz conventions, and they revealed a very low opinion of the survivors, in particular the survivors of the death camps, and a self-assurance that "we had to transform this dust of men into a new Jewish community; it was an enormous task fraught with many difficulties."[31]

Another major gap between the veteran and the survivor lay in their differing personal and communal memories. While the veteran related tales of his pioneer years in Palestine as part of his efforts to familiarize the new immigrant with the "Zionist experience," the survivor was often unfamiliar with such approaches, resented being preached to, and sometimes suspected the authenticity of the narrator's adherence to the principles he avowed. While the veteran had been safe in Palestine during the war years, the survivor carried painful memories of that period that were almost impossible to share with anyone who had not been there.[32] Therefore, stressed Yosephtahl, the veterans needed to have faith in the desire of the survivors to recover and return to normal life and should give up attempting their ideological recruitment. Survivors should be talked to personally and intimately and their points of view accepted.[33] Some veterans were sufficiently tolerant and enlightened to offer to return to the immigrants after they had a year or two to settle down, and only then to try to persuade them to adopt a particular ideology.

The greatest sensitivity was demonstrated toward the youngsters of Youth Aliyah and the younger orphans among the children. Their teachers and tutors expressed sympathy and compassion, though they too were often very judgmental and exercised the educator's prerogative to mold their students.[34]

Goals of the Cyprus Immigrants

When the Cyprus detainees finally arrived in mandate Palestine they were eager to start a "real life." Nonetheless, most had to spend more weeks in detention camps there because of the British system of distributing certificates. Immigrants who arrived after May 15, 1948, were taken to immigration centers where the Jewish Agency accommodated them for a number of weeks and took care of all the administrative tasks. For many immigrants the situation was confusing; many had no practical plans and waited for the Jewish Agency to guide them. Only then did some realize that they were not ready to make the important decisions. The advice of the relatives and friends who visited them in detention helped many to grasp the alternatives available.

Even for those who were part of a political movement affiliated with the kibbutzim, not all decisions were easy. The spartan life of a collective settlement did not look so romantic when closely scrutinized. Friends and relatives were often not encouraging, and the rules and regulations of the collective life looked similar to those of the camps from which they had just been released. Many immigrants were hesitant about going to remote places in Galilee or the Valley of Jezreel, preferring the big city. There they could get lost in the crowd and not be observed too closely by the community. They would be the masters of their own movements and could engage in their own private pursuits.[35] It was not easy to break with a group that had supported one after the war and in detention, but nevertheless many decided to go it alone, helped only by the financial support they received from the absorption section of the JA: Israeli £12 and some basic equipment, including a bed, a mattress, blankets, and sheets.

The Cyprus Immigrants in the Cities

One important form of assistance was the location of housing in special immigrant homes where four single persons shared a room or a family of three got a room to itself. The JA also found rooms in private homes for the new immigrants and paid the rent for the first six months. Health insurance was provided by the Histadrut—Kupat Holim—or by Hadassah hospitals (supported by the American Zionist women's organization). Meanwhile the new immigrants needed to find work; agencies of the Histadrut guaranteed them at least a few working days every month.

These facilities became available only at the end of 1946 and became more organized in 1947 as absorption received more attention in anticipation of a substantial influx of Holocaust survivors. This special attention reflected the awareness in the Immigration Department that this was not selective immigration and that the newcomers had neither capital nor savings. Nonetheless, the JA wanted the absorption to progress according to its general economic and social goals. Thus, it directed people to agriculture and construction and influenced their choice of where to live. However, except when it concentrated loans and investment in particular areas, it had to take into account the constraints of the local labor market, which offered more jobs in larger cities and established villages. There was a great housing shortage: although the World War II ban on private construction was partially eased in 1947,[36] the JA could initiate construction only where the Jewish National Fund possessed nonagricultural land, which in many cases was far from existing centers of employment.

The new housing policy and loan systems to encourage employers to take on more workers were inadequate to prevent a rise in unemployment as demobilized soldiers joined 1,500 new immigrants per month seeking work.[37] Many felt that the new immigrants from Cyprus deserved better, and they were given some preferential treatment in labor and housing.[38] Morale among those responsible for absorption was very low; Yosephtahl complained about the inefficiency of the JA and other organizations and that decisions and plans were not implemented once agreed; he also felt that the general public was not interested.[39]

There were considerable differences between the manner of absorption of immigrants in cities and towns and in smaller places such as moshavoth—villages that mixed private agriculture and small-scale industrial activity. Both economically and socially, life was easier in the city, especially until the end of 1948. The moshavoth offered mostly seasonal agricultural work, which was new to most immigrants and physically very difficult for all of them, in particular during the long hot season when most of the work had to be done: only strong young men and women could accept these jobs. The immigrants wanted a profession, and while they sought work in industry or—to a lesser extent—construction that offered some promise of security, agriculture was not considered a suitable vocation.[40]

In the small moshavoth, the new immigrants were concentrated in special housing and isolated from the farmers and their families; the only contact was through work. When the number of immigrants increased, the absorption of large numbers posed a problem for the veteran population of the moshavoth and the new immigrants sensed the resentment of the community. On the other hand, the work of voluntary organizations such as Working Mothers and the Women's International Zionist Organization (WIZO)—who handled childcare services, lectures, Hebrew classes, and immigrant/veteran contacts—was facilitated by the concentration of the immigrants, as was that of the clubs set up by the Histadrut and, later, the Ministry of Education and Culture.[41] After September 1948, when the number of immigrants per month climbed to more than 10,000 (reaching a peak of 35,000), the problem became more acute as new immigrants were settled in recently abandoned Arab towns and villages with no local resident veteran Jewish community.

Since most Cyprus detainees did not have a profession, they were more willing to begin with agriculture and other manual work during a transition period and were spared having to change occupations, unlike many of the Holocaust survivors who came later from Eastern Europe or immigrants from Islamic countries.[42] Some went to special training courses offered by the Histadrut, while many young women studied nursing and childcare in courses at the hospitals. They were provided with room and board, which was a great advantage. The need for professional welfare workers increased with the mass immigration, giving them good job prospects.[43]

The minority of the Cyprus immigrants who had a white collar profession, and those who had a high school education and knew Hebrew, found work in schools, immigrant camp operations, medical services, and other absorption-related fields.[44] Those Cyprus immigrants who arrived prior to May 1948 enjoyed the advantage of being more settled when mass immigration started in September.

Employment reports from the end of 1948 show that the demand for labor was very strong. The War of Independence then being fought meant that many new workers were required to maintain or expand industrial and agricultural production and to provide social services. The labor market offered a variety of jobs to skilled and unskilled workers, and immigrants were ready to accept almost any job, to the satisfaction of the Histadrut executive, which admitted that "this immigration is good from the work point of view; all our fears were unfounded—the people want to work."[45] However, the fluctuations in the labor market were many, and as early as March 1949, worries were expressed about the large number of workers who would be looking for new jobs after the end of the citrus season. Meanwhile, the number of immigrants per month in early 1949 averaged 25,000 (the 25,000 in transit camps in March were not even included in those statistics).[46]

Housing problems eased considerably during the summer and fall of 1948, when buildings in the Arab towns and villages became available after Arabs either fled or were deported. Some 55,000 rooms in cities and towns came under the control of the state by March 31, 1949. A large number of rooms, damaged during the fighting, had to be repaired. These became the housing for the immigrants of 1948–1949. By the end of April 1949, 89,781 new immigrants were housed in towns and villages that had been deserted, 52,000 in Haifa and Jaffa. (The total number settled in Tel Aviv, Jewish Haifa, and the moshavoth was 10,921; in the collective villages [moshavim] and kibbutzim, 4,959.)[47] Even so, by the spring of 1949 this source of housing was also exhausted; in May 1949, more than 60,000 new immigrants lived in transit camps, where many remained for a long time.[48]

Many of the Cyprus immigrants used their special status to settle in Haifa and Jaffa. There the prospects of finding work were greater and the veteran community offered greater chances for integration.

Reactions on the Kibbutzim to the Selection of City Life by New Immigrants

"All the immigrants wanted was to get to Tel Aviv" complained one of the members of the executive of the Histadrut.[49] He expressed a disappointment that many members of kibbutzim shared. The kibbutzim had entertained great hopes that Holocaust survivors (and in particular the Cyprus detainees) would join their movement in large numbers. The population of these collectives had increased considerably by the end of World War II, by 259 percent between September 1944 and September 1945 alone (from 13,606 to 35,260), when the kibbutzim accounted for some 6 percent of the population of the Yishuv[50] (they had constituted about 5 percent at the beginning of the war). By September 1947, 7 percent of the population lived on kibbutzim—45,041 people—but by 1950, this figure fell to 5.5 percent, representing a total of 57,810 out of 1,202,993 people; the decline was apparent from the beginning of 1947. The majority of the small but constant flow of Cyprus detainees (750 per month) confounded expectations when they chose not to join the kibbutzim; among other immigrants the percentage was even smaller.[51]

During 1947 and 1948, the labor movement in general and the kibbutz movement in particular grew alarmed. While 9 percent of the new immigrants went to kibbutzim in March 1947, only 5.5 percent did so in April, 6 percent in May, and still fewer in 1948.[52] This greatly disappointed that part of the Yishuv elite drawn from the labor movement and the kibbutzim, especially leaders of illegal immigration operations and heads of missions to the DP camps in Europe. Meanwhile, many kibbutz members were involved in the underground defense forces (in particular in the select Palmach unit); the kibbutz movement hoped to replace them with new immigrants. Leaders of the Histadrut were disappointed that only a third of the new immigrants joined the union. They too had hoped that a larger proportion of the newcomers would work in agriculture.[53] Only with difficulty did all of them come to understand that many immigrants lacked ideological commitment or an understanding of the importance of agriculture to a viable Jewish society; that those who left the Soviet Union rejected what seemed a new version of the kolkhoz; that to immigrants from Romania, who detested the policies of the Communist Party there, the kibbutz seemed too much like communism.[54]

But the kibbutz and Histadrut leaders still were not ready to give up hope for a change, and they conceived of new ways to recruit more immigrants. Some centered on better educational work in the Diaspora; this seemed especially important in Cyprus, where the number of potential "joiners" appeared largest. It was also suggested that certain immigrant groups be assigned to specific kibbutzim; again, Cyprus seemed a good place to start this scheme.[55] Direct contacts with new immigrants arriving in the transit camps were also viewed as important: kibbutzim envisaged sending special envoys to look for those who had been affiliated with the movement in the past and to present to young families the advantages of life on the collectives. They expected that as the absorption became more difficult and the number of immigrants waiting in transit camps grew, the kibbutz movement would be perceived as a more attractive option.[56]

The kibbutzim themselves changed. New immigrants were offered fifty-two working days for the study of Hebrew and other subjects, they were granted special travel days to see the country and meet relatives, and social and cultural activities were designed for them. Kibbutz members were encouraged to open their homes and create a friendly environment for the newcomers. Veteran kibbutzniks often found the new demands on them difficult: as one activist said at the kibbutz general assembly, "We like the immigration but we don't like the immigrants."[57]

The collective settlements had been involved in the fighting since the beginning of the War of Independence; the number of casualties was high and the burden on the members heavy. As more people were recruited into the IDF, the contribution of the new immigrants to the kibbutz economy became crucial, and few of the special arrangements endured. Many immigrants found the situation difficult, especially since they could not follow developments because they were unable to read a newspaper or understand the radio. However, while some felt alienated and isolated, others became more dedicated and involved. Moreover, with the easing of the general situation after July 1948, they shared the pride of having been part of a community that overcame the difficulties of the war.[58]

During 1947, 12,128 Cyprus detainees immigrated, 55 percent of all immigrants. In November 1947, the Cyprus detainees represented 43 percent of total immigration and 18 percent of them went to kibbutzim. In December 1947, 11.8 percent of the 2,244 immigrants from Cyprus went to the collectives, a total of 266 people. From January 1948 their share grew. No wonder the kibbutzim saw the Cyprus detainees as an ideal source of manpower.

Conclusion

Any conclusion about the transition of the Cyprus detainees from illegal immigrants to immigrants in Israel has to examine the integration of the immigrants into the IDF. Another vital topic that merits special attention is the integration of Youth Aliyah, though that subject is beyond the scope of this discussion.

As has been suggested, Holocaust survivors in general and the Cyprus detainees in particular were integrated into the Israeli economy rapidly. The younger the immigrant, the more easily he or she adapted; although many did not have a profession, they succeeded in entering the labor force and starting vocational training. They adapted to the spartan lifestyle that characterized Israel during the 1950s.

The most difficult period of mass immigration to Israel started in the spring of 1949 and continued for several years. The number of immigrants continued to be high and the tension between the absorption authorities, the immigration department of the JA, and the government mounted. Not until 1952 did the number of immigrants decrease, remaining low for the next four to five years. By 1961, Israel's population had reached almost two million, including 870,000 immigrants (43% of the total) who arrived after May 1948. Of that number, 397,295 were Holocaust survivors. The census of 1961 provides much data that might be relevant to an evaluation of the absorption of the immigrants, but it does not permit us to sort out the Cyprus immigrants, since they are listed only by country of origin and they are thus swallowed up in the "Europe-America" group.

NOTES

For a related discussion, see Dalia Ofer, "Holocaust Survivors as Immigrants: The Case of Israel and the Cyprus Detainees," Modern Judaism 16 (1996): 1–23.

1. On the issue of illegal immigration ("Ha'apalah" or "Aliyah Bet" in Hebrew), see Dalia Ofer, *Escaping the Holocaust: Illegal Immigration to the Land of Israel, 1939–1944* (New York: Oxford University Press, 1990).

2. For Holocaust survivors, the subgroup they belonged to was very important; the "kazetler" (from the German for concentration camp), the partisans, the ghetto fighters, and the Asians (those repatriated from the Soviet Union) all had radically different war experiences. However, the experience of surviving was common to all, along with a sense that the experience would in some way or the other motivate their future.

3. Moshe Sicron, *Immigration to Israel 1948–1953* (Jerusalem: Falk Center for Economic Research, 1957), pp. 26–27 (in Hebrew) .

4. Sicron, *Immigration*, statistical supplement, pp. 2, 20, 23. The percentages in succeeding years were, in 1950, 49.8; in 1951, 28.6; in 1952, 26.2; and in 1953, 19.6 percent.

5. David Scha'ari, *The Cyprus Detention Camps for the Jewish Illegal Immigrants to Palestine 1946–1949* (Jerusalem: Hasifriah hazionit, 1981), appendix, table 16, pp. 364 (in Hebrew); Nahum Bogner, *The Deportation Island: Jewish Illegal Immigrant Camps on Cyprus 1946–1948* (Tel Aviv: Am Oved, 1991) (in Hebrew).

6. The number is based on a report from Famagusta by Rabbi J. Schreibum (representative of the Immigration Department of the Jewish Agency), October 21, 1948, Central Zionist Archive (CZA) S6\4326; Sicron, *Immigration*, statistical supplement, pp. 2, 20; Scha'ari, *Cyprus Detention Camps*, appendix 16, p. 364.

7. In December 1947 two illegal boats, *Pan York* and *Pan Crescent*, arrived in Cyprus with

15,000 illegal immigrants from Romania. The demographic characteristics of these immigrants, more normal than that of the previous detainees, influenced the overall demographic structure. This further justifies the use of general absorption data to characterize Cyprus detainees. See Zeev Zachor and Venia Hadari, *Ships of State* (Tel Aviv, 1981).

8. Sicron, *Immigration*, statistical supplement, p. 11, table 17A.

9. Ibid., p. 46, table 7.

10. Scha'ari, *Cyprus Detention Camps*, p. 300.

11. Ibid., pp. 299–300. The birthrate in Cyprus was 30.8 per 1000, slightly lower than in the DP camps but still very high. In 1947, when the average number of detainees was around 13,000, at least 124 weddings took place. See ibid.

12. Sicron, *Immigration*, statistical supplement, tables A13 and A23; Bogner, *Deportation Island*, p. 221.

13. Don Patinkin, *The Israeli Economy in the First Decade* (Jerusalem: Falk Center for Economic Research, 1960), p. 27 (in Hebrew). See also Moshe Sicron, "Mass Immigration, Its Characteristics and Influences: Immigrants and Transit Camps," *Idan* (1988): 31–52 (in Hebrew).

14. Patinkin, *Israeli Economy*, p. 27, table 4. The veterans referred to are those living in Israel since before May 1948.

15. "Psychiatric Report" Cyprus, June 27–September 18, 1947, pp. 12–14; Joint Archive Jerusalem (JAJ), Cyprus A file 78 (henceforth "Psychiatric Report").

16. "Jewish Immigration to Palestine 1947," the Statistical Department of the JA, Israel State Archives (ISA), Ministry of Labor, Gimel g/5366/186.

17. Sicron, *Immigration*, statistical supplement, p. 76, table 97A. I use the figures given for 1948–1952 under the heading "Europe/America."

18. M. Dvorjetski, "Holocaust Survivors in Israel," *Gesher* 1 (1956): 83–114.

19. Kopel S. Pinson, "Jewish Life in Liberated Germany," *Jewish Social Studies* 2 (April 1947): 101–26.

20. Bogner, *Deportation Island*, p. 231.

21. Haganah Archives (HA), 4608.

22. "Psychiatric Report," p. 11.

23. Ibid., p. 11.

24. Ibid., pp. 13–14; Bogner, *Deportation Island*, pp. 58–61, 222–29.

25. Ibid., pp. 227–28; Labor Archives (LA), Executive Meeting, April 23, 1947.

26. Bogner, *Deportation Island*, pp. 304–19; Scha'ari, *Cypress Detention Camps*, appendix 9, pp. 343–44; 'Iidth Zertal, "Invisible Souls," *Studies in Zionism* 14 (1989): pp. 107–26 (in Hebrew) .

27. A view of Cyprus quoted from a song of the detainees by Morris Laub in June 1947, in a meeting of Youth Aliyah workers in Palestine: "I don't care to stay in Cyprus since Cyprus is almost the land of Israel" ('*Alim* [a bulletin of Youth Aliyah in Palestine/Israel] [June 1947], pp. 22–24). He repeated this view in a meeting of JDC's country directors in April 1948. This attitude was common among workers at the time and continued to be the myth. The psychiatric team questioned this hypothesis.

28. HA, 4608.

29. Kibbutz Meuhad Archive (KMA), 47/6/7, March 2, 1947, General Assembly of the Kibbutz Gvat.

30. Adah Fishmann, who was in charge of absorption in the Histadrut, talk at the Executive Meeting, April 23, 1947, LA.

31. *Hapoel Haztair* (newspaper of the main labor party, Mapai, that headed the government), January 11, 1949, and March 2, 1948; a different style of patronage was expressed in the women workers' newspaper, *Devar Hapoeleth*, February 5, 1948, calling for the hosting of older immigrants in private homes during the first stages of absorption to ease the lack of housing and allow them to observe the simple and healthy lifestyle of Palestine; see also ibid., February 2, 1948.

32. *Zror Micktavim* (a paper of the Kibbutz Meuhad movement), March 14 and June 27, 1947.

33. Ibid., June 27, 1947.

34. Numerous records describe youth in the different schools and organizations of the kibbutzim, villages, and towns; *Devar Hapoeleth*, February 5, 1948; *Aliyah* (a quarterly on Youth Aliyah), November 1947–January 1948; and KMA, 1-b/8/39a, Protocol of the Secretariat, April 26, 1950.

35. CZA, Protocol of the Executive of the JA, June 1, 1947: discussion about unemployment and the Cyprus immigrants, "A Report on Cyprus"; KMA, 1-b/7/9/ Protocol of the Secretariat, August 31, 1947; ibid., 1-b/8/35a, February 16, 1949.

36. For a comprehensive report on the building situation in Palestine-Israel, see Dr. Ernest Lehman, JAJ, Malben files, 111/1/2, November 1948.

37. "A Report on the Immigrant Housing Projects," CZA S13/65, March 1948.

38. *A Special Planning Report on Housing Construction for the Immigrants from the Camps in Cyprus and Others*, CZA S13/65, December 21, 1947.

39. The issue was raised at a number of meetings of the Histadrut executive, in particular that of April 23, 1947 (see the speech of Adah Fishmann), and of November 12, 1947 (see Yosephtahl).

40. *Devar Hapoeleth*, July 7, 1947.

41. LA, Protocol of the Histradut Executive Committee, April 23, 1947; *Devar Hapoeleth*, July 7, October 14, and December 17, 1947. For an expression of the veterans' resentment of the choices made by the new immigrants, see Izhak Koren in *Hapoel Hatzayir*, March 2, 1948: "The big immigration from Cyprus should be the first warning to us that we cannot give free choice in absorption matters to the tens of thousands of new immigrants."

42. "Jewish Immigration to the Land of Israel 1947," (Information of the Statistical Department of the JA) June 6, 1948, ISA, Gimel g/5366/186 (in Hebrew).

43. Oral testimony of Yehudah Pearst, Oral History Division, Institute of Contemporary Jewry, Hebrew University of Jerusalem, Mass Immigration Project, 3442.

44. Oral testimony of Israel Raviv (Ravschzinski), ibid., no. 3460.

45. Mr. Frumkin, LA; PHE, November 11, 1948.

46. LA PHE, March 16, 1949.

47. *Report on the Action on the Property of Missing Arabs*, ISA, Prime Minister's Office, March 31, 1950 (in Hebrew); Gimel g/5440/210/OS (1582). For the number of immigrants who were settled in the deserted places, see JAJ, Malben, 111/1/2, "Report on the Activities of the Absorption Department, 1 September 1948 to 30 April 1949."

48. Giora Yosephtahl, "Report on the Situation of Housing to May 1949," CZA S 57/129, December 6, 1948 (in Hebrew). Idem, "Possibilities and Needs for the Absorption of Immigrants to February 1949," December 1948 (in Hebrew). Zvi Herman to the executive of the JA, S 41/247, April 23, 1949. On the number of immigrants in the transit camps and conditions there, see JAJ, Malben, 111/1/2, "Report on the Activities of the Absorption Department, 1 September 1948 to 30 April 1949."

49. LA, PHE, April 23, 1947.

50. The immigrants during this year came from parts of Europe that were being liberated. The war in the Balkans ended in August 1944, and so immigration from there increased. Jewish refugees who reached Spain and Portugal during the war arrived in Palestine, as did refugees from southern Italy.

51. Sources for the numbers include Ze'ev Tzur, *Hakibbutz Hameuhad Beyishuvah Shel Haaretz*, vol. 2, 1939–1949 (Tel Aviv, 1982), p. 184; Sicron, *Immigration*, statistical supplement, pp. 3, 23; David Horowitz, *The Israeli Economy* (Tel Aviv: Am Oved, 1954), p. 175 (in Hebrew).

52. LA, PHE, April 23, 1947, Yosephtahl report; A. Reichman, "In the Field of Absorption," *Zror Micktavim*, June 27, 1947. For a more elaborate discussion of the integration of Holocaust survivors in the kibbutzim and Histadrut, see Hannah Yablonkah, *Foreign Brothers: Holocaust Survivors in the State of Israel, 1943–1952* (Jerusalem: Yad Ben Zvi, 1994) pp. 62–70, 79–109 (in Hebrew).

53. KMA, 1/6/5, Kibbutz Assembly in Gvat, March 2, 1947, Ben Gera's speech; KMA, 1/3/II, the seventeenth convention of Hakibbutz Hameuhad, October 18–24, 1949, conclusions on immigration and absorption. The preference for agricultural settlement was also in the

interests of the JA and the government of Israel, which needed to supply more food and to utilize large areas of cultivated land that had been deserted by Arabs who fled during the War of Independence.

54. Many sources confirm these arguments, for example, Aharon Reichman, "Problems of Absorption," a lecture before the kibbutz committee, *Zror Micktavim* (1947), pp. 269–76, and others at the same meeting. The immigrants from Cyprus are referred to as one of the most important groups of immigrants for the kibbutzim; see Ze'ev Meinrat, "Immigration and Absorption," *Zror Micktavim* (1950), pp. 93–103; LA, PHE, November 3, 1948.

55. Brackah Rechtman, on the issues of absorption in the kibbutz assembly, November 6, 1948, KMA 5/12/3.

56. In 1948 the kibbutzim absorbed some 4,500 new immigrants, in 1949 the number was 8,072. The growth of the numbers did not correspond with growing immigration ("Report on the Absorption of Immigrants in the Kibbutzim," February 2, 1949, and March 1, 1950, KMA 2/3/1).

57. Brackah Rechtman at Hakibbutz HaMeuhad assembly, November 6, 1948, KMA 5/12/3.

58. KMA 1-b/8/35, kibbutz secretariat, August 15, 1948; "Report on Immigration and Absorption to the General Assembly of the Kibbutzim," *Zror Micktavim* 14 (October 18–24), pp. 93–103.

51.

WILLIAM B. HELMREICH

Against All Odds

SURVIVORS OF THE HOLOCAUST AND THE
AMERICAN EXPERIENCE

Introduction

In looking at the research on the postwar adaptation of Holocaust survivors who
came to North America, the focus until recently was overwhelmingly on their
problems and pathology. One reason for this was that the case studies and interviews
reported on were most often drawn from the files of people who had been treated by
mental health professionals. The question was: Could one generalize from these
findings to all or most survivors? Whatever their psychological problems, these were
people who had communities in which they participated and to which they contributed, both before and after the war. What a travesty if the predominant lasting image
of them were to be that of the emaciated figures they were when they emerged from
the camps. After all, it was the Nazis who were responsible for their condition. To
render a correct picture, it would be necessary to chronicle the achievements of the
newcomers.

All of us are familiar with works such as Irving Howe's *World of Our Fathers* and
Moses Rischin's *The Promised City*, both of which tell of the migration and subsequent
experiences of Jews who came to the United States between 1881 and 1920. But
where is the equivalent "World of Our Fathers" book about the post–World War II
immigrants? A link in the chain of Jewish history is missing.

Almost everyone goes through crisis or tragedy at some point in his or her life.
Here were people who had gone through terrible experiences of a magnitude that
most of us, thankfully, have never experienced. How did they do it? How were they
able to learn to live again, trust and hope again, smile and laugh, and even feel love
again? How does one pick up the pieces and go on? The answers to these questions
have broad applicability to the problems that face all human beings. This is the
pragmatic and most important reason for investigating and sharing the story of
achievement against the odds.[1]

The Early Period

Between 1946 and 1953, almost 140,000 known Holocaust survivors arrived
in the United States. New York City was the major point of entry, but many also
landed in Boston, San Francisco, New Orleans, Baltimore, and even Galveston,

Texas. The largest number came after the passage of the Displaced Persons Act on June 2, 1948, which allowed for up to 205,000 displaced persons to enter the United States.[2] On June 16, 1950, President Truman signed into law a second bill, increasing the number of refugees to be granted entry to 415,744. In addition, nearly 37,000 refugees immigrated to Canada.[3]

Approximately one-third of the Jewish DPs went to the United States and the remaining two-thirds went on aliyah to Israel. The reasons for choosing America varied. For many survivors America offered a chance to *resume* ties with family members who had emigrated from Europe before the war. Others moved to the United States because the wartime ordeals they had undergone had so sapped their energies that they could not seriously consider becoming pioneers in a new land. Forty years later one immigrant remembered: "I felt I went through such a terrible war, and conditions in Israel were very tough. My uncle here said: 'You can always go to Israel from America.'"[4]

Many survivors also viewed America as a place where they could fit in and put the past behind them. Its size and diversity seemed to offer anonymity within a framework of tolerance. Moreover, many Jews had not been raised in Zionist homes and did not feel drawn toward the idea of a homeland. Conversely, there were survivors interested in aliyah who were not given priority by those making such arrangements because their prewar backgrounds indicated a lack of commitment to Zionism.

Typically, immigrants were met at the pier by representatives of the Hebrew Immigrant Aid Society (HIAS) and the United Service for New Americans (USNA), who assisted them with customs, baggage-handling, medical concerns, and transportation. Ultimately, more than $37,000,000 was spent by the organized Jewish community on refugee aid.[5] Notwithstanding the extensive involvement of organized Jewry, the larger American Jewish community viewed the survivors with considerable ambivalence. The newcomers frequently were seen as loud, demanding, and boorish, observations that often masked many American Jews' sense of guilt about not having done enough for European Jewry during the war. At the same time, many Americans felt duty-bound to help their brethren who had suffered so much.

The survivors, in turn, appreciated the assistance rendered but often felt it was given grudgingly and that the Americans looked down on them. In fact, many refugees reported that American Jews appeared uninterested in learning more about their coreligionists' experiences in the concentration camps. Most painful, perhaps, was the suspicion harbored by at least some Jews here that those who outlasted the camps survived because of what they did to others. One woman survivor recalled: "I thought, 'You must tell the world about what happened. How else will they know?' But I saw, when I came here, that some people thought, 'How come you're alive and the others are dead? Must be *you* killed them, not Hitler.'"[6]

By the end of July 1949, arrivals under the 1948 DP act had been resettled in 334 communities in forty-three states, usually with the help of either HIAS or the USNA or both.[7] The USNA took on a large number of the more difficult cases. The geographical distribution pattern remained fairly constant until 1953, with about two-thirds of the refugees remaining in the New York metropolitan area and the remaining one-third taking up residence in the rest of the country, mostly in communities with substantial Jewish populations.

The arrival of this wave of Jews had consequences for the State of Israel, created in 1948. Passage of the DP act in that same year clearly affected worldwide Jewish immigration patterns. No one knows how many thousands of Jews would have opted to turn to a more easily accessible Israel had America kept its restrictive policies intact. The same holds true for the amended DP act of 1950, which opened the gates to the United States even wider.[8]

Another important issue was the effect Israel's emergence as an independent nation had on fund-raising on behalf of the survivors in America. The Jewish community as a whole was not as well endowed then as it is today, and these twin emergencies strained resources to the breaking point. Supporters of each cause complained that their own priority needs were receiving inadequate funding. Which position prevailed, in which communities, and why is a subject that warrants full investigation by historians.[9] The answer would, among other things, greatly enhance our understanding of how American Jewry viewed the importance of establishing the State of Israel as opposed to helping Jews in need.

Key factors in the survivors' successful adaptation were the individual community's attractiveness and response, and here there was considerable variation. Washington, D.C., was cited as generally unhelpful, refusing to accept difficult cases, while Denver was described in glowing terms as "extremely cooperative." Atlanta and Miami repeatedly were unwilling to take in Sabbath observers or those with serious medical problems. San Antonio was described as a "difficult sell" to immigrants because of its hot climate, and Milwaukee as a good community but one that faced periodic staff shortages. Of course, the assessments of these cities may well have changed from year to year.[10]

Some survivors selected certain cities because relatives resided there, but in most instances their decisions resulted from efforts by the agencies to persuade them that living somewhere other than New York City had clear benefits: low crime rates, friendly people, and the like. In fact, most agency leaders felt that the immigrants would be more motivated to Americanize if forced to interact with other Americans. There was also an unspoken hope that spreading the refugees amongst the various communities would create an impression of a group that could blend well in the idealized "American melting pot." As matters turned out, these assumptions were largely correct. Looked at from the vantage point of more than four decades, it seems clear that those who went to smaller communities acculturated faster, while those who remained in the larger centers tended to cling to the old ways. On the other hand, large numbers of refugees left the outlying communities to which they were sent. The relative lack of Jewish cultural and religious life and the isolation from their fellow survivors were often too much to bear, especially in light of all they already had gone through.

The formidable nature of the task facing the agencies in the resettlement of a traumatized population should not be underestimated. While most of the survivors presented little difficulty to themselves, their sponsors, and hosts, thousands of immigrants experienced severe stresses. Many had marital problems, partly because a number of those marriages had been hastily contracted after the war, often in the DP camps. Even in cases where the couples had been married earlier, the strains of the war years often created difficulties within the relationship. The agencies frequently made strenuous efforts to straighten out such matters. In one, not altogether atypical case, a caseworker made twenty-one phone calls and wrote several letters in an attempt to locate a refugee's relative.[11] On the whole, the agencies responded heroically to what was a massive responsibility.

Still, the agencies were far from perfect. Their most common mistakes consisted of thoughtlessness in matching new arrivals with appropriate communities, or a lack of empathy on the part of staff members. But sometimes they made tragic errors with consequences that resulted in destroyed lives and even death. Given the agencies' desire to be portrayed in the best possible light, it is surprising that any of these unfortunate occurrences ever came to light.

One of the most grievous stories concerned a woman admitted to a Philadelphia hospital for treatment of a neurosis, a hand-washing compulsion. A partial lobotomy was performed. Afterwards, in the course of her stay in the hospital, the Immigration and Naturalization Service became aware of what a United Service for New Americans file described as a "racket." Various persons had come from a Latin American country under the pretense of seeking treatment. In reality, it was a ruse to gain admission to the United States. When the INS learned of this, they attempted to interview the woman, who had immigrated from Germany, to learn what she knew of the situation at the hospital. After the hospital initially decided to let her appear, officials changed their minds, saying she "had not responded to treatment." Instead, a second lobotomy was performed which, at least incidentally, postponed her ability to testify. In the file, the woman's father describes her as having once been a "'perfectly normal, strong, highly educated girl' until she was in a concentration camp." While the NCJW was not directly involved in the hospital's decision, it knew that a second operation had been decided upon, and it chose, for whatever reason or reasons, not to actively intervene in the situation.[12] More than anything, the story highlights how powerless the refugees often were, still unfamiliar with the country and with their rights, in determining their fate.

Even during this early period, the survivors were seen as a success story. The evidence from the social work journals and HIAS documents indicates that most were able to function well consistently. They obtained employment, raised families, and were involved in their communities. There were, it is true, thousands who could not adapt, and their memory will forever haunt those who knew them. Still, the words of Maj. Abraham Hyman in 1951, Adviser on Jewish Affairs to the Armed Forces in Germany, best sum up the situation at the time:

> In evaluating what [the refugees] achieved in a brief span of a few years, we may err only on the side of understatement. The self-restraint they exercised during their period of waiting, the resilience they displayed in picking up the threads of their lives, and the determination they showed in collectively asserting the right of a Jew to a country of his own, entitle them to a position of honor in the history of the Jewish people and in the history of mankind.[13]

By 1948, almost no DPs had been deported for any reason. On the average, they required but six months to become settled and find employment. Their children had excellent school records. Most were not supported by public agencies, and none were known to have been on public relief.[14]

Most striking, perhaps, is the almost complete absence of any criminal behavior among the survivors, or of juvenile delinquency among their children. Where are the Lepke Buchalters, Arnold Rothsteins, and Dutch Schultzes among the children of the survivors? The files, scholarly literature, and popular journals of the day contain no hint of such activity.[15] Those Americans who were hostile to the idea of immigration after the war, and there were many, would have liked nothing better than to find evidence that the immigrants were ne'er-do-wells.[16]

Economic Adaptation

The common pattern among the immigrants was a series of menial jobs until the individual finally succeeded in establishing himself. As Joseph Bukiet, a successful real estate developer, recalled:

> I arrived Friday and on Sunday I read in the *Tog* that they're looking for a furrier. I had learned this after the war. I started working. After this I got jobs doing cushions. I was a machine operator, too. I must have had seven jobs right away. I changed jobs so often because I wanted to improve myself and also because the jobs didn't pay much.[17]

While many found employment with the help of friends and relatives, the agencies often played a major role in this area, providing job training, funding, and special services.[18] In addition, certain Landsmanschaften (home-town societies) tried to help their fellow townsmen. As a matter of pride, many newcomers were reluctant to accept financial assistance and when they did, they repaid their loans as soon as possible.

The survivors encountered numerous obstacles in securing employment, the most prominent of which was their lack of education. Based on the random sample interviewed for this project, more than half never graduated from high school. Of those who did, only about one in five went on to attend college. Of those who went to college, about half earned a degree, with a significant number of them continuing on to graduate or professional school. Besides the interruption of the war itself, the immigrants' age when they arrived here and their lack of proficiency in English also impeded their job opportunities and performance. In addition, there were health problems and the need to learn new trades. Probably a majority of the survivors changed their line of work after the war. Their willingness to do so in order to advance gave rise to the following joke: "When J. J. registered for a visa to Canada, he called himself a furrier. Two weeks later he received an affidavit from America, certifying that he was a shoemaker. So the question was: 'What do you mean, you are a furrier and a shoemaker?' He replied: 'I used to make shoes from fur.'"[19]

Survivors also encountered antisemitism. In response, there were those who changed their names and others who fought back. Some, like Lola Shtupak, simply left their jobs:

> I worked on a machine in a clothing factory, twelve to fourteen hours a day. I used to come home, I couldn't move my hands. I was dead. And they were so antisemitic. The forewoman was Italian and she bothered me and made my life miserable so that I couldn't take it anymore. Finally, after a few months, I said to myself, the only way is to get married and get rid of this job because otherwise I'm not gonna survive here.[20]

Let us turn our attention to how survivors perceived work itself. Because they had been unable to work during the Holocaust, many of these people literally venerated labor. In addition, hard work for wages was frequently therapeutic because it allowed them little time to think about the past. Later, as a way of demonstrating how hard they had worked once given the opportunity, many survivors often noted how few vacations they had taken over the years. Only in unguarded moments did some admit that free time frightened them. Since the health of many individual survivors tended to deteriorate more rapidly than that of persons who had not undergone such tribulations, one would, under ordinary circumstances, have expected them to retire earlier than others commonly did. Yet the data show that they continued full-time work for as long as their American-raised counterparts.

Another crucial issue was independence. More than controlling one's destiny, many a survivor felt that, in the final analysis, he or she could trust only himself. Even when such an individual entered a partnership, it was usually with another survivor. Generally, most survivors were also aggressive in their business relationships and, in interviews, traced that behavior directly to the need to survive and rebuild after the war. On the other hand, some were passive and displayed a dulling of affect, or inability to express emotion.[21]

Many survivors saw the income derived from work as conferring upon them a special obligation to give generously to Jewish causes, especially to Israel- and Holocaust-related activities. Others were even able to enter occupations that allowed them directly to connect their employment to their wartime travails. Fred Terna, for example, was incarcerated in Theresienstadt, Dachau, and Auschwitz from 1941 until the end of the war. In America, he carved out a career as an artist, and many of his works combine biblical themes with what happened during the Holocaust.[22] Cantor Isaac Goodfriend recounted how he persuaded a temple hiring committee to engage him, explaining that his Holocaust suffering would make him more sensitive to the prayers themselves.[23]

Did the survivors succeed by conventional standards of measurement? By 1953 the USNA could say that, to its knowledge, fewer than 2 percent of those Jews who had come to the United States since 1945 required financial assistance and of these, nearly all were either aged, sick, or physically disabled.[24] A study in Cleveland found that while two-thirds of the survivors had unskilled jobs upon arrival, that percentage was reduced to one-third only five years later. On average, they also earned the same amount of money as native Cleveland residents.[25] Today, the largest number of survivors are clustered in the semiprofessional (business) or managerial categories, followed by the semiskilled, crafts, and sales/clerical categories. There are very few executives or unskilled workers among them.[26] The difference in income between them and American-raised Jews is not significant. Moreover, survivors and American-raised Jews are equally likely to own their own homes. When one considers their suffering and lack of educational opportunities, these figures are truly remarkable.

The Family

Although there is pathology within many survivor families, the overall picture is one of great love and commitment. Most survivor families are surprisingly normal when one considers what the parents lived through. Starting with the parents, the divorce rate among survivors is lower than among their American coreligionists. In 1989, forty-four years after the war, about 82 percent of survivor couples were still married, only 9 percent had divorced, and the remainder of the marriages ended due to the death of one of the partners.

That the survivors decided to have children after the war represents an affirmation of life and hope for the future despite the catastrophes that befell them. The decision, however, was often arrived at only after a good deal of agonizing.[27] Some wondered if, after all of their suffering, they would truly be able to feel love for their children, while others revealed their apprehensions about the world they lived in by giving their offspring Gentile first names.[28] Usually, however, a belief that they should replace those who were lost overrode such considerations. In fact, the birth rate among survivor families is higher than it is among American-raised Jews.[29]

Survivors tend to be overprotective and quite concerned about the importance of education for their children, even more so than typical Jewish parents. They also use material possessions as tangible expressions of love. Barbara Fischman Mevorach, a child of survivors raised in Brooklyn's Borough Park section, vividly remembered her mother's attitude in this regard: "She used to buy me the nicest clothes in Bunnyland [an expensive local shop]. But I didn't want them because no one else in my class had such expensive clothes. It was too much and it embarrassed me. I recall how it was torture for me to go to that store."[30]

Like other parents, survivors complained about their children. They were disrespectful, stayed out late, watched too much TV, and the like. Still, certain areas stood out. The "gruene" (the green ones) as they were called, were painfully aware that they lacked the finesse and basic knowledge of their American counterparts and were sensitive to the subject when it was brought up by their children. One survivor, the owner of a fabric shop, spoke candidly about his feelings on the matter:

> I was talking with my son about investments and he said to me: "How do you know so much? You know all these things and you don't even know how to read English. . . ." Maybe I'm not so educated but I know what is going on and I'm interested. The children think that because I never went to college I don't know anything. I said to them: "I never went to school here. Can you imagine how much I'd know if I went through two grades here?"

For religiously observant survivors, remaining religious was crucial. One Orthodox rabbi's daughter received a master's degree in social sciences, but for him the achievement was completely overshadowed by her decision to cease being observant:

> She got a degree in social work and then she wanted to analyze herself and became irreligious. This was the worst thing that happened to me since the war ended. She was my youngest; I figured I'll get "naches" [pleasure], I'll see a future, but somehow, she became completely out of her mind.

He blames the daughter's university education for what happened.

Of all the issues that disturb the survivors, none is as troubling as interfaith marriage. This is so for several reasons. First, marrying out of the faith is seen as breaking with Jewish tradition and history, or even leaving it altogether. Second, there is the feeling by many survivors that the decision to marry a Gentile may be an attempt to hurt the parents. In fact, that is sometimes the case. Finally, survivors, because of their experiences, often find it hard to trust Gentiles in general and are therefore likely to find accepting them into their family particularly problematic.

Being a child of survivors presented another set of problems. Many felt acute discomfort about their parents' accents, language difficulties, styles of dress that marked them as newcomers, and their lack of status.[31] Most of all, they suffered from relative poverty compared to American Jews. One son of survivors painfully reflected on his bar mitzvah: "It was an open house party, not in a hall. We borrowed three hundred dollars. We gave back the money. My friends? I couldn't invite my friends. I was embarrassed."[32]

An important issue in the literature is the degree of pathology exhibited by children of survivors. Some studies have reported a greater incidence of psychological problems, others have asserted the opposite.[33] Very few, however, have been based on random samples. One important exception is the work of John Sigal, a psychologist, and Morton Weinfeld, a sociologist. Their extensive research shows that children of survivors, when compared to a control group, are no different in terms of guilt, hostility, sadness, and passive-aggressive behavior.[34] At the same time, there is no denying the validity of actual cases of pathology as reported by mental health professionals.

Some very good novels have been written by those who have grown up in survivor families, but some of the most dramatic works have appeared in film. In *Kaddish*, Yossie Halevi Klein, a Jewish writer raised in America and now living in Jerusalem, writes about his loving relationship with his father, Zoltan. He also describes his recurring nightmare of being chased and killed by Nazis on Coney Island's boardwalk while uncaring bystanders continue eating cotton candy. He characterizes the 1981 World Gathering of Holocaust survivors as the symbolic passing of the torch from parents to their offspring. By contrast, in *A Generation After*, resentment is expressed by one son in a family at the "guilt trip" transmitted from parents to children, while a second son views his parents with awe and forgives them "for the pain they have caused me." A third film, *Breaking Silence*, examines the dynamics of a second generation therapy group and focuses on the problems of having survivor parents.[35]

Generally, survivors' children seem to have done quite well occupationally and educationally. They achieve at about the same level as most American Jews, differing only in a tendency to enter the helping professions.[36] The in-depth interviews also suggest that they may be more likely to have attended elite universities. Finally, they have positive self-images as Jews, displaying little hostility toward Judaism and little self-hatred.[37]

Social Organization and Communal Involvement

Survivors, by and large, seek out each other. They frequently live in the same neighborhoods, vacation at the same resorts, and attend the same synagogues, often sitting next to each other as well. This is hardly surprising, for the intensity of their experiences strengthens the bonds of friendship that they either had before the war or developed afterward. One way in which the gruene developed these ties was through the Landsmanschaften. In cases where such groups were founded before the war, they became members and eventually officers, often breathing new life into organizations that had become moribund because the earlier generation of members had become Americanized.[38]

The strength of the survivor community is most clearly apparent in the causes that its members take up, and in how they do so. Chief among them is Israel. Survivors are more than three times as likely as American Jews to have visited Israel twice or more. Many survivors believe that the postwar sympathy generated for Jews was at least partly responsible for the creation of the state. They also see Israel as a refuge against persecution and often are enamored of the stereotypical image of the proud fighting Jew that Israel represents to so many people in the world. These are among the reasons Israel is very dear to the survivors.[39]

Survivors are, of course, involved in Holocaust memorial matters. The commemorative dinners, the monuments built, and the museums established, all serve to further their purpose: to perpetuate the memory of those who died and to ensure that people do not forget what happened to both the dead and the survivors. This enhances group solidarity and provides the survivors with a generally healthy way of coping with tragedy and mourning their losses.[40] And, understandably, survivors are also heavily involved in combating antisemitism.

Coping with Long-Range Effects

"If you've been through Auschwitz and you *don't* have nightmares, then you're not normal," one survivor told me. If we think of survivors as happy, perfectly well-adjusted individuals, then they do not fit the criteria that some people would use to define normalcy. If, on the other hand, our definition encompasses individuals who get up and go to work in the morning, raise families, and participate in a range of social and communal activities, then, as already has been discussed, survivors are not only "normal" but highly successful.

But what about their psychological adaptation? One measure of psychological health is whether or not one feels a need to seek professional help for one's problems. Remarkably, our quantitative survey of a group of randomly selected Holocaust survivors and another group of American-raised Jews found that the Americans were actually *more likely* than the survivors to have sought assistance. About 31 percent of the Americans were in this category, compared to only 18 percent of the survivors. This clearly runs counter to the prevailing image of the survivors as chronically depressed, anxious, and even paranoid.[41]

Even the 18 percent figure may overstate the case somewhat if we are talking about the need for therapy. Clearly a person who saw someone because he or she was required to do so in order to receive reparations or because the HIAS asked him to do so upon arrival in the United States is not in the same category as someone being treated for serious psychological difficulties. On the other hand, survivors may resist seeing someone because they do not want to admit that they need to, or that the Nazis were able to inflict such damage upon them.[42] In addition, survivors, the majority of whom come from a traditional Jewish background, may simply not believe in the validity and efficacy of therapy. Against this, we must consider the likelihood that those survivors who really needed help and sought it did so out of desperation or were compelled to do so by relatives and/or friends. When all is said and done, the 18 percent figure is low enough to justify further investigation. This was, after all, a severely traumatized population.[43]

Notwithstanding that a large majority of survivors have apparently done well in a psychological sense, there is no denying that thousands fared poorly, requiring extensive treatment. Most of the research supports the view that the traumatic effects can be deep and long-lasting, even for those who seem to have "recovered" from them.[44] The most common symptom is nightmares, with most saying, however, that it has not impaired their ability to function in day-to-day affairs. Others suffer from a variety of symptoms, including depression, anxiety, a dulling of affect, difficulty trusting others, and, overall, a worldview that gives everything a coloration or tinge that is best captured in the following poem, penned by a survivor:

> A survivor will go to a party and feel alone.
> A survivor appears quiet but is screaming within.
> A survivor will make large weddings, with many guests,
>   but the ones she wants most will never arrive.
> A survivor will go to a funeral and cry, not for the
>   deceased, but for the ones that were never buried.
> A survivor will reach out to you but not let you get
>   close, for you remind her of what she could have been
>   but will never be.
> A survivor is at ease only with other survivors.[45]

Religiously, most survivors did not become atheists, but the number of believers decreased.[46] Their doubts center more around the nature of God's relationship to them than around His existence. Their reasons for believing may be categorized as follows: belief in God based on personal experience; general theological explanations; identifying with the contemporary Jewish community; preserving linkages to tradition and to their prior European-Jewish lifestyle; and a richer, more rewarding way of life.

Based on a number of studies, survivors appeared to be reasonably satisfied with their lives.[47] The research done for this project indicates ten factors that best explain why those survivors who were able to rebuild their lives succeeded in doing so: flexibility, assertiveness, tenacity, optimism, intelligence, distancing ability, group consciousness, assimilating the knowledge that they had survived, finding meaning in one's life, and courage. In addition, many survivors benefited from good health and a healthy dose of good luck.

It should be emphasized that there is no way of knowing with certainty to what extent, if any, these traits contributed to survival during the war. In most instances, victims were not in control of their destinies. Millions were swept up and hurled to their deaths by a giant killing machine that indiscriminately annihilated them. That survivors and those who ultimately did not survive acted on their own behalf in certain cases simply proves that most human beings will do all in their power to live when given the chance to do so. The survivors themselves attribute their ability to outlast the Nazis primarily to chance. In part, their postwar traits may have emerged because they successfully internalized the very fact that they had prevailed over nearly impossible circumstances.[48] Based on the interviews, the survivors are not remarkable people. Rather, they are an example of how remarkable people in general can be.

Areas for Further Research

Our knowledge about the postwar lives of the survivors is truly at a low level, and a number of areas could and should be explored. To this end, one should be aware of several valuable existing collections:

One very extensive collection is the Hebrew Immigrant Aid Society (HIAS) papers at YIVO. While materials pertaining to the organization are available on microfilm, thousands of individual case files are stored away in boxes in another building. The New York Association for New Americans (NYANA) and the American Jewish Joint Distribution Committee also possess a comparable number of case files; when these documents are made available they will be of great interest to scholars.

The United Service for New Americans (USNA) files are also accessible on microfilm at YIVO. A portion of the collection contains minutes of the organization's meetings and related materials, but most of it consists of a state-by-state account of what happened to the survivors in each of the communities to which they were sent. The discussions are primarily centered around the adjustment problems of the new arrivals and on how they were received by each community. While they were used for this project, it was possible to go through only a portion of the collection; much more work remains to be done. A further resource is a portion of the National Council of Jewish Women Service to the Foreign-Born archives, currently housed at Yeshiva University. The materials contain much important information, are in excellent condition, and have not yet been carefully scrutinized. Still another significant collection is that of the Jewish Welfare Board, currently housed at the American Jewish Historical Society. Because of the enormous amount of archival material, researchers will, naturally, have to make decisions on which collections or portions of collections deserve the most attention.

Then there are the newspapers of the period, in particular the *Forward*, whose "Bintel Brief" continued to appear through the 1946–1953 period, during which most of the survivors came to the United States. The letters that appeared there have not been systematically examined and the same could be said of the many articles about the survivors that appeared in the other Yiddish newspapers of that era and of the German-language *Aufbau*.

There are many collections of oral history, of varying quality, detailing the experiences of survivors; the number of such testimonies grows each year. At this very moment, someone, somewhere, probably is taping an account of his or her survivor parents' lives, and the discussions often touch upon what happened after the war. One hopes that these tapes eventually will be scrutinized by Holocaust researchers. Parenthetically, it is important that those in possession of many of these tapes transcribe as many as possible, because as those in the field know, few people have the time and patience to listen to them. In written form they are far more likely to receive the attention they deserve. At the same time, it is important to preserve the tapes, not merely as a safeguard against transcription errors, but because the inflections, emphasis on certain points and words, and the sheer emotions and drama of what happened can best be captured when one listens to the survivors themselves.

Written transcripts of the 170 interviews I conducted for this project are housed in the Oral History Department and Archives of the United States Holocaust Memorial Museum (USHMM), Yad Vashem, Hebrew University's Oral History Library in the Institute of Contemporary Jewry, and the Museum of Jewish Heritage. In addition, the USHMM Archives has a full collection of the interviews on audio tape. The material is available on a limited basis to qualified researchers.

The only topic that has been investigated until now has been the pathology of survivors, with hundreds of articles and numerous books on the subject. Even here, there has been an underemphasis on the psychological strengths of survivors, but that is changing. Space does not allow for a full presentation of the many possible areas of research, but some of the more important are briefly outlined here. First, research should be conducted on which survivors went to Israel and which came to the United States and Canada—and why. And, of course, such work could also touch on the much smaller, but still substantial, groups of survivors who settled elsewhere in the world.

To fully understand this, a complete demographic breakdown would have to be provided for those who entered each country, comparing factors such as age, health, religious affiliation, country of origin, socioeconomic status, and how they spent the war years. We would need to know whether they were positively influenced by Zionist ideas before the war, what Jewish/Zionist organizations they belonged to at the time, whether they had relatives in Israel, Europe, and America, and so forth. All this would have to be done for *each year* of the postwar era. Clearly, decisions to take up residence in Eretz Israel before or after 1948 were likely to have involved different calculations. Ideally, this breakdown would be supplemented by in-depth interviews. Only then could general and reliable conclusions be drawn about the survivor communities in Israel and in the West.

There is also a need to undertake comparative studies of the survivor populations living in the West and in Israel. This is because the postwar experiences have differed in a number of important ways. For Israeli survivors there was the cathartic effect of fighting the enemy instead of running, cowering in fear, and the humiliation that typified the wartime experiences of most survivors. In addition, survivors in Israel immediately became members of a majority, as opposed to a minority culture. Finally, even as new arrivals, they were not seen as an intrinsically different group because large numbers of immigrants both preceded and followed them. Some work is already being done on this, most notably by Dalia Ofer, who has demonstrated that Palestine-born Jews viewed the survivors in particular ways when the latter arrived in Israel in the late 1940s. Among the areas that could usefully be examined are how the survivors fared in the larger cities, such as Tel Aviv and Haifa, as opposed to small communities, moshavim, and kibbutzim; whether there were any differences relating to country of origin; religious attitudes and practices; attitudes towards Sephardic

Jews and vice versa; views and opinions regarding Arabs; economic and cultural impact on Israel, and so forth.

Work on the postwar survivor community generally has not even progressed to the point where the survivor population is differentiated according to the groups that comprise it (except, of course, for those studying its pathology). One may examine males and females, religious and irreligious, Eastern Europeans and Western Europeans (not to mention individual countries), urban and rural backgrounds; wealthy, middle class, and poor; and geographical distribution throughout areas of resettlement. All this and more should be done and could yield fascinating results.

Turning to the United States, it would be of considerable interest to compare the economic patterns of the survivors with similar information about those of earlier generations of Jewish immigrants. Those who went to America between 1882 and 1917 were far more likely to be members of the working class, while those who arrived in the post–World War II era were more apt to be small-business entrepreneurs. Why this was so was a function of both the nature and composition of each immigrant generation and of the opportunities available in the United States for each group at the time of arrival. Interviews with survivors might focus on these questions as well as on why their families did not immigrate earlier to America. Was it due to their economic position in Europe, or were there religious considerations? At this point we simply do not know. There should be a focus on the extent to which the Holocaust itself affected the economic patterns of the Jewish community in general, and this has not been done.

It is known that survivors contributed much to Jewish life in America. They invigorated it and redirected its focus. But the precise impact has not been measured. A systematic effort should be made to do so in terms of their contributions to the growth and development of Jewish communities and institutions. For example, how much of the money that went into the building of synagogues, Jewish day schools, and support for Israel came from the survivor communities? We know that they were responsible for much of the increased emphasis given the Holocaust and for the building of Holocaust memorials and research centers, but we know little about their effect on other aspects of Jewish life. How did their involvement in synagogues and temples, for example, influence the direction taken by those congregations? What was their influence, respectively, upon the Orthodox, Conservative, and to a lesser extent, Reform movements? How did their views on Jewish education shape and redirect policies made on both local and national levels? In short, no one has really examined the broader question of where the American Jewish community would be today had this wave of immigrants not landed on these shores.

And then there are the children of survivors. With respect to the points made above, the two groups really cannot be separated. Survivors' children populated the synagogues and Jewish schools; now that these children are adults, their actions frequently reflect the beliefs and values of their parents. A wealthy child of survivors gives the money for a Jewish community center or buys $4,000,000 worth of Israel Bonds. This is clearly part of the larger picture, representing, as it does, the *legacy* of the survivors.

In general, far more research ought to be conducted on the impact of the Holocaust on the children of survivors. Studies exist, but future examinations should be performed with samples that are truly random and nonclinical. Only then will we know whether the case studies and journalistic accounts are accurate.

There are many narrower issues that also could be usefully examined. For example, it would be interesting to know whether or not survivors who were saved by Gentiles have attitudes towards Gentiles generally different from those of survivors who did not have such experiences. Also, it is important to understand whether or not such suffering increases or decreases tolerance toward others who are victimized and what factors influence such attitudes. Another related question would be how the experiences of survivors have affected those around them, particularly friends and relatives. There is room for considerable work on how the agencies' treatment of the survivors might have influenced their subsequent adaptation to life here. Studies could also be done on how the media's treatment of survivors has affected their own interpretation and internalization of the experience, and vice versa.

In truth, there are literally hundreds of topics that could be pursued in these areas. In any case, it is imperative that such work commence as soon as possible because time is running out. In a few years the survivor generation will be gone and with it will go the opportunity to interview firsthand those who went through one of history's most awful periods. We need to know more, much more. In the 1930s, during the Depression, interviews were conducted with ex-slaves in the African American community. It was seen as a last chance to learn firsthand what they had gone through. About 140,000 survivors migrated to the United States after the war and rebuilt their lives there. How they did so contains important lessons for us all. Should we do any less in regard to this latter group?

NOTES

1. The methodological approach used here is multifaceted. The files of the Hebrew Immigrant Aid Society (HIAS) and the United Service for New Americans (USNA) have been examined. These include minutes of meetings, social worker reports, presentations at conventions, correspondence, and other material. The caseworker files of the National Council of Jewish Women (NCJW), which interviewed thousands of refugees, have also been evaluated. Oral history collections focusing on the postwar experiences of the survivors have also been perused. These include the collections of Yad Vashem, the American Jewish Committee, the Fortunoff Video Archives for Holocaust Testimonies at Yale University, and that of the Brooklyn Holocaust Center (now housed at the United States Holocaust Memorial Museum). Newspapers of the period in question, such as the *Forward*, *Aufbau*, and the *Jewish Examiner*, have been evaluated. Finally, 170 survivors from a range of backgrounds were interviewed in depth and an additional 211 randomly selected survivors were surveyed and compared with a random control group of 295 American-raised Jews.

2. Walter H. Waggoner, "DP Admission of 200,000 Is Voted by Senate 63–13," *New York Times*, June 3, 1948, pp. 1–2; Anthony Leviero, "President Scores DP Bill, but Signs," *New York Times*, June 26, 1948, p. 1; "Truman's Statement on Refugee Bill," *New York Times*, June 26, 1948, p. 1.

3. Anthony Leviero, "Truman Signs Bill Easing DP Entries: 415,744 Get Refuge," *New York Times*, June 17, 1950, p. 1; Joseph Kage, "Canadian Immigration: Facts, Figures and Trends," *Rescue* (Fall 1953): 8. See also Harold Troper, "Canada and the Survivors of the

Holocaust," in *She'erit Hapletah, 1944–48: Proceedings of the Sixth International Yad Vashem Historical Conference*, ed. Yisrael Gutman and Avital Saf (Jerusalem: Yad Vashem, 1990), pp. 261–85.

4. Interview with Samuel Halpern, February 14, 1988.

5. "$37,000,000 Spent to Resettle D.P.'s," *New York Times*, January 15, 1950, p. 30. Some other organizations that helped the newcomers were the Jewish Agriculture Society, Agudath Israel, and the Workmen's Circle.

6. Interview with Frieda Jakubowicz, April 16, 1988.

7. Morris Zelditch, "Immigrant Aid," *American Jewish Yearbook* 51 (1950) (Philadelphia: Jewish Publication Society, 1950), pp. 195, 198.

8. Yehuda Bauer, "The Brichah," in *She'erit Hapletah, 1944–48*, ed. Gutman and Saf, p. 55; David Wyman, "Refugees and Survivors: Reception in the New World," *Simon Wiesenthal Center Annual*, 2 (1985): 193–203; Leonard Dinnerstein, *America and the Survivors of the Holocaust* (New York: Columbia University Press, 1982), p. 115.

9. Dinnerstein, *America and the Survivors*, p. 115.

10. Displaced Persons Program/Communities/Quotas/Community Quota Status Report for General Settlement, September 30, 1948, United Service for New Americans Folder, CJFWF, Agency Files, Box 20 (American Jewish Historical Society).

11. National Council of Jewish Women (NCJW) Papers, Box 55, File 48L854.

12. USNA Papers, File 469.

13. "DP Problem near Finale, Report Shows," *Jewish Examiner*, October 16, 1951, p. 6. Yehuda Bauer drew the same conclusion, observing in 1989 that "the real heroes of the story were the survivors. . . . Had it not been for the determination of the survivors, no JDC [Joint Distribution Committee] would have made any difference"; see *Out of the Ashes: The Impact of American Jews on Post-Holocaust European Jewry* (Oxford: Pergamon Press, 1989), p. xxv; see also pp. 38–39.

14. Maurice R. Davie, "Immigration and Refugee Aid," *American Jewish Yearbook* 49 (1947–1948) (Philadelphia: Jewish Publication Society, 1947), pp. 212–22; Maurice Davie, "Immigration and Naturalization," *American Jewish Yearbook* 51 (1950) (Philadelphia: Jewish Publication Society, 1950), pp. 127–33.

15. Contrast this with the situation at the turn of the century. See Jenna Weissman Joselit, *Jewish Crime and the New York Jewish Community, 1900–1940* (Bloomington: Indiana University Press, 1983).

16. "Captain Eddie Says 'Bar Immigrants,'" *Jewish Examiner*, March 7, 1947, p. 9; "Immigration Is 'Racket of Racial, Religious Groups, American Legion Commander Tells D.A.R.," *Jewish Times*, May 30, 1947, p. 8.

17. Interview, December 5, 1989.

18. Lyman Cromwell White, *300,000 New Americans: The Epic of a Modern Immigrant-Aid Service* (New York: Harper & Bros., 1957), p. 185.

19. Helen Epstein, "A Study in American Pluralism through Oral Histories of Holocaust Survivors" (New York: William E. Wiener Oral History Library of the American Jewish Committee, 1975; unpublished report), p. 24.

20. Interview, April 28, 1989.

21. There is a vast literature on the psychological effects of the Holocaust. See, for example, S. A. Luel and P. Marcus, eds., *Psychoanalytic Reflections on the Holocaust* (Denver: Holocaust Awareness Institute and Ktav, 1984); Callman Rawley, "The Adjustment of Jewish Displaced Persons," *Journal of Social Casework* (October 1948): 316–21.

22. Interview, February 15, 1990.

23. Interview, May 19, 1989. For a book-length account of a survivor-cantor's experiences, see Matus Radzivilover, *Now or Never: A Time for Survival* (New York: Frederick Fell, 1979).

24. "USNA Correspondence to CJFWF, 1953," CJFWF, Agency Files, USNA Folder, American Jewish Historical Society.

25. Helen Glassman, *Adjustment in Freedom: A Follow-up Study of 100 Jewish Displaced*

Families (Cleveland: United HIAS Service and Jewish Family Service Association, 1956), pp. 45–46.

26. There were also no differences in the occupational patterns of New York and out-of-town survivors. Another follow-up study of survivors identified a similar configuration of only a small percentage of professionals. See Lore Shelley, "Jewish Holocaust Survivors' Attitudes toward Contemporary Beliefs about Themselves," Ph.D. diss., Fielding Institute, 1984, p. 94.

27. On this general point, see Robert Jay Lifton, *Death in Life: Survivors of Hiroshima* (New York: Random House, 1967), p. 505.

28. See Dorothy Rabinowitz, *New Lives: Survivors of the Holocaust Living in America* (New York: Avon, 1976), p. 143.

29. The rate was 2.14 versus 1.88 and is statistically significant.

30. Interview, December 18, 1990.

31. Helen Epstein has described it beautifully in *Children of the Holocaust: Conversations with Sons and Daughters of Survivors* (New York: Putnam, 1979): "They could not find the right words. The wide, bright, sprawling fan of their experience snapped shut among people who spoke English. They were forced into a groping that changed the nature of what they had to say, that made them appear helpless, that distorted what they were. They became outsiders" (p. 146).

32. Those children born immediately after the war were perhaps more apt to have "suffered" in this way. By the time the second or third child was born, the parents had been here longer and usually could afford a more lavish affair.

33. For an excellent summary and critique of these works, see Norman Solkoff, "Children of the Nazi Holocaust: A Critical Review of the Literature," *American Journal of Orthopsychiatry*, 51, no. 1 (1981): 29–42. See also Aaron Hass, *In the Shadow of the Holocaust: The Second Generation* (Ithaca: Cornell University Press, 1990), pp. 32–36.

34. See John J. Sigal and Morton Weinfeld, *Trauma and Rebirth: Intergenerational Effects of the Holocaust* (New York: Praeger, 1989); Morton Weinfeld and John J. Sigal, "The Effect of the Holocaust on Selected Socio-Political Attitudes of Adult Children of Survivors," *Canadian Review of Sociology and Anthropology* 23, no. 3 (1986): 365–82.

35. Peggy Kaganoff, "The Second Generation Comes of Age," *National Jewish Monthly*, April 1985, p. 22.

36. For more on the reasons for this, see Hass, *In the Shadow of the Holocaust*, p. 45.

37. See Ilana Kuperstein, "Adolescents of Parent Survivors of Concentration Camps: A Review of Literature," *Journal of Psychology and Judaism* 6, no. 1 (1981): 7–22. A study of Christian immigrants from Estonia also found a high level of ethnic identification among the immigrants' children that came about because the parents made a conscious effort to instill pride of heritage in their offspring. See Mary Ann Walko, "A Sociological Study of the Estonian Community of Lakewood, New Jersey: Patterns and Ethnic Maintenance between Parents," Ed.D. diss., Rutgers University, 1983, p. iii.

38. See Michael R. Weisser, *A Brotherhood of Memory: Jewish Landsmannschaften in the New World* (New York: Basic Books, 1985); Hannah Kliger, "In Support of Their Society: The Organizational Dynamics of Immigrant Life in the United States and in Israel," *American Jewish Archives* 42, no. 2 (1990): 33–53.

39. For an explanation of how the Six Day War affected the survivors, see Judith Miller, *One, by One, by One* (New York: Simon & Schuster, 1990), pp. 222–23.

40. For a perceptive analysis of the underlying basis for this view, see Abraham J. Peck, "The Lost Legacy of Holocaust Survivors," *SHOAH* 3, nos. 2–3 (1980): 33–37.

41. See, for example, Paul Matussek, *Internment in Concentration Camps and Its Consequences* (New York: Springer-Verlag, 1975); Martin Bergmann and Milton E. Jucovy, eds., *Generations of the Holocaust* (New York: Basic Books, 1982); Joel E. Dimsdale, ed., *Survivors, Victims and Perpetrators* (Washington, D.C.: Hemisphere, 1980); Henry Krystal, ed., *Massive Psychic Trauma* (New York: International Universities Press, 1968); Leo Eitinger, *Concentration Camp Survivors in Norway and Israel* (London: Allen & Unwin, 1961).

42. Norman Linzer, "The Holocaust and Its Survivors," in *The Nature of Man in Judaism and Social Work* (New York: Federation of Jewish Philanthropies, 1978), pp. 90–91.

43. Similar results were found among respondents who attended a national gathering of survivors. Only 10 percent received regular counseling and an additional 13 percent received "some counseling." Those who sought such counseling were found (by scaling tests) to have greater psychological problems. Boaz Kahana et al., "Predictors of Psychological Well-Being among Survivors of the Holocaust," in *Human Adaptation to Extreme Stress: From the Holocaust to Vietnam*, ed. John P. Wilson et al. (New York: Plenum Press, 1988), pp. 171–92.

44. See, for example, Eva Fogelman, "Intergenerational Group Therapy: Child Survivors of the Holocaust and Offspring of Survivors," *Psychoanalytic Review* 75, no. 4 (1988): 619–40; Dori Laub, "Holocaust Survivors' Adaptation to Trauma," *Patterns of Prejudice* 13, no. 1 (1979): 17–25.

45. Cecilie Klein, *Sentenced to Live* (New York: Holocaust Library, 1988), p. 141.

46. This was borne out in the in-depth interviews carried out for this study. See also Reeve Robert Brenner, *The Faith and Doubt of Holocaust Survivors* (New York: Free Press, 1980).

47. This was confirmed by the data gathered for this project. See also Barbara Stern Burstin, *After the Holocaust: The Migration of Polish Jews and Christians to Pittsburgh* (Pittsburgh: University of Pittsburgh Press, 1989), p. 160; Shelley, "Jewish Holocaust Survivors' Attitudes," p. 262.

48. For more on how people overcome adversity, see Aaron Antonovsky, *Unraveling the Mystery of Health: How People Manage Stress and Stay Well* (San Francisco: Jossey-Bass, 1987); Jerome Kagan, *The Nature of the Child* (New York: Basic Books, 1984).

52.

LEO EITINGER

Holocaust Survivors in Past and Present

Introduction: The Situation in the Camps

The conditions in the concentration camps have been described by Jews and non-Jews, by survivors and by those who did not survive. As a survivor myself I do not feel objective enough to give a dispassionate description of the prisoners' lives. Let me therefore quote an author remote from direct involvement, the non-Jewish Australian psychiatrist F. Hocking:[1]

> The existence in the camps was a constant state of humiliation, degradation, hunger, over-crowding, cold, pain, terror, lack of sleep, beatings, infestation with fleas and lice, the threat of death, and the knowledge that family, friends and fellow Jews were being exterminated. Resistance was virtually impossible, because, like all starving people, they were apathetic and passive—something long known to the less scrupulous slave-owning communities. Prolonged severe undernutrition may result in irreversible brain damage [and] permanent personality changes. It is probable that, as well as producing its own psychiatric symptoms, starvation "sensitizes" individuals to the effects of other types of stress, so that it lowers the threshold of stress tolerance. The prolonged horror of concentration camp existence has been described as the most stressful situation which human ingenuity could devise. As it has been estimated that one person survived of every six hundred of those imprisoned in concentration camps, it would seem that chance was the biggest factor in survival, although a strong mental and physical constitution would surely have been a necessary prerequisite.

In spite of Hocking's objectivity—or because of it—I am painfully aware that intellectual descriptions, explanations, and research are by no means sufficient to make anyone understand what Auschwitz and other annihilation camps were for the inmates. How is it possible to feel the anguish and agony of victims standing naked in front of the gas chambers, or the fear of going through a selection by the SS doctor in a camp hospital? How is it possible to feel the sufferings of those who were not murdered immediately after their arrival in the camps, but had to slave during weeks or months until they, too, succumbed, to be killed off and replaced by new victims? How can I expect that anyone will really understand the hunger that ravaged the inmates, bringing them not only to the limits of human behavior, but also beyond them, as when a prisoner, formerly a high-ranking official, a highly intellectual person, fell to his knees and licked—yes, licked like a dog—a few drops of soup that had run out of the soup kettle?

How can I convey what it meant to live literally in the shadow of the chimneys of the crematoria and their steady stream of smoke, which became fatter and darker and more threatening every time a new transport arrived? That happened nearly every day. And every day one could see hundreds of the killed and thousands of the barely living, maltreated prisoners in the most hopeless conditions and situations.

How can one understand oneself and how can one get someone else to understand the survivors' hunger and thirst, desperation and hopelessness, suffering and ordeals, but also waiting and hoping, anticipation and dreams? Even if our fantasy must remain insufficient, one has to try. Otherwise no one but the survivors themselves would understand the situation from which the survivors started.

The Liberation Period

Dr. Collis,[2] who was with the troops that liberated Bergen-Belsen, concludes his most dispassionate but nevertheless extremely striking account by confessing: "This . . . brief preliminary report of Belsen camp to give the medical profession in Britain some idea of the medical problems involved . . . is a complete understatement." And then he continues:

> The problem of what to do with these forsaken . . . souls is immense, but one which if not tackled and solved will make all our efforts a mere waste of time, for then it were kinder to have let them die than to have brought them back to mere existence and more sufferings in a hostile world, where they no longer have even a hope of being able to compete in the struggle of the survival of the fittest, and must inevitably go down.

After the liberation, millions of prisoners, forced laborers, and other inmates of Nazi camps tried to reach their homelands again. But the European countries involved in World War II were depleted of resources, and many were disorganized. Nevertheless, there were substantial differences. The ex-prisoners experienced these perhaps more than the rest. In the countries where the economic situation was extremely difficult, interest in treating nonpsychotic psychiatric disturbances was minimal. The Danish and the Norwegian survivors were relatively best off, because they were liberated before the end of the war and brought to non-occupied Sweden by the Red Cross.[3] When the war was over, they returned to their homes and families and were received as heroes with flowers and flags. Even the Danish Jews were liberated from Theresienstadt and brought home in the famous "white buses" together with the other Danish ex-prisoners.

The fate of the other Jewish survivors was far more difficult. When their hour of liberation came the majority were far too weak to move or even to reflect on what was happening. For the majority, awakening from the nightmare was perhaps more painful than the captivity itself. It was then that they first began to realize, although not yet fully—the whole emotional reaction took place much later—the actual meaning of the goodbyes on the railway ramp upon arrival at the camps. Actually, it did not take many days before a new prisoner got to know, in some way or other, about the fate awaiting those members of the family who had not come to the camp from the transport. In the majority of cases, however, the ability to react was already so reduced, the psychic anaesthesia so developed, that new impressions apparently had no effect. For most, the area of interest was very rapidly reduced to primitive self-preservation, the mere battle for existence, represented by a bowl of soup and a crust of bread. Neither the outer world, the course of the war, nor the fate of others appeared to have meaning in the daily life of the prisoners. Everything seemed unreal, as in a nightmare. The reality confronting the individual after the liberation was therefore very painful, and apart from the somatically improved situation, it was almost worse than the dream from which they had just awakened. They became suddenly aware of the full weight of their isolation, the lack of purpose and meaning in their life.

The newly released prisoners had no one left, there was nowhere for them to go, they were completely through with their old lives, and they hadn't the faintest idea what they could do with the new life so unexpectedly granted them. Most remained in the camps. New international organizations took care of them. The efforts of these organizations must not be belittled in any way. However, the individual person was, as yet, of very little importance to them. Indeed, the individual still had no right to decide for himself, to determine his own fate. The "displaced persons" were brought before boards from various countries who decided whether or not to receive them. Many of the Jews, however, had no desire to be dependent on others' decisions; they would not live "on charity" any longer, so they tried to make their way to Palestine, where they expected to find a solution to all their problems. Some were admitted, but the majority were stopped by the British and put into yet other internment camps on Cyprus. Only when the State of Israel was established did it become possible for all to start a new life there.

Ex-prisoners who returned to their hometowns were often confronted by rejection, hate, and in some cases, as in Poland, with persecution and even pogroms. Their homes were frequently in ruins, and the possibility of finding a new means of existence minimal. They were often the only survivors of a large family, now isolated, without any basis for contact with hostile neighbors who showed no understanding of their plight. They themselves were not capable of understanding their new circumstances, so different from the world of which they had dreamed. Thus Israel seemed the place designated by fate as a solution to all their difficulties and problems.

Scientific Studies of the Survivors

Scientific studies were needed to describe life in the concentration camps and the short and long-term reactions to concentration camp survival. The background of my first study on so-called health care in Auschwitz was the fact that I was a medical doctor who knew both typing and the German language and was allowed to work in the office of the prisoners' sick bay. I thus got to know what really was going on in this field in Auschwitz. These experiences became the topic of my first paper on concentration camp prisoners.[4] It was a factual report which, in spite of its very "dry" and nearly emotionless description, was so incredible that I myself, as I read printer's proof, found it necessary to add a postscriptum stressing that it contained no exaggerations.

During the stay in the camps one of the problems that was nearly always considered as soon as it became possible to raise oneself above the daily worries was: What will the future bring? How will people who suffer so incredibly be able to adapt to the world? And will the world understand? The experience was, however, too near and too painful for psychiatrists to study the problems of the survivors immediately. The approach had to be slow.[5] But all Norwegian refugees who came in contact with psychiatric institutions during the first ten years after the war were studied.[6] All of them had been either forced laborers or concentration camp inmates. While working with them I learned that listening to, trying to understand, and helping them was good therapy for a psychiatrist-survivor.

And then in 1957 it was my good fortune to become a member of a medical-psychiatric-psychological team whose task it was to study ex-prisoners. We were asked to judge as objectively as possible the connection between war experiences and actual disability and to decide what action to take. Since then I have not been able to abandon the question of survivors. I have interviewed and studied survivors from nearly all European countries living in Norway and Israel; I have examined the morbidity and mortality of all the Norwegians who were in concentration camps outside Norway during the war; and I have followed the few Norwegian Jewish survivors, practically from the day of their arrest until now, over fifty years after the liberation. The members of this team have published three monographs on the different aspects of the topic[7] as well as dozens of articles.

The First Findings

Of the survivors examined in Israel,[8] 80 to 90 percent had lost the majority of their close relatives—parents, siblings, husband or wife, and children. Not one had not lost at least one near relative, and three out of four had lost their entire family. The psychotraumatic influence of losses such as these on the survivors can hardly be overstated, particularly in view of the very close-knit ties of the Jewish family. It might, of course, be suggested that these findings are not typical, but this is not the case. In Norway, a tiny group of eleven were the only Jewish survivors of nearly seven hundred deported.[9] Six of the eleven were the sole surviving members of their immediate families. The most extreme case was that of a man who had lost his parents, four brothers, and three sisters in Auschwitz. Some of the family members of the other five in this group of eleven had survived, but again, not one among them had not lost at least two close relatives. Two surviving brothers, for example, had lost their parents and four siblings.

The fate of the survivors in Israel was not an easy one. In the first years after the establishment of the state the situation there did not permit any discussion of concentration camp experiences, and practically speaking, this continued to be the case until the Eichmann trial in 1961–1962. Many survivors felt a certain inability to fill their positions in new or surviving families adequately, to be mother, wife, or provider; they felt their personality had changed, felt old and indifferent, like a corpse that could walk about but was still a corpse. They felt unable to enjoy the company of other people, unable to talk freely to anyone, unable to live a normal life because of all the memories. One comment I'll never forget should be recorded here as typical of many survivors: "How do you think that I can be the same as before the war when I am the only one, absolutely the only one left of eighty-five members of the family I was with in the ghetto."

Not all survivors felt strong enough to go to Israel. Others had relatives or friends in the United States. Thus, another major stream of survivors went overseas. We need to mention briefly the research in Europe and the United States, in which a characteristic and nearly stereotypical pattern emerges. In the first twenty years after the war, it was mainly the somatic morbidity and the social difficulties of the survivors that dominated the papers. The French literature,[10] the first to deal with survivor problems, described the chronic asthenia and premature aging. The Danish clinical investigations[11] are comprehensive, dealing with somatic, social, and psychiatric aspects. But even there, weight loss plays a central role. The Dutch[12] and Norwegian investigations[13] that followed reflected comprehensive somatic, social, and psychiatric aims but still tended to be dominated by organic findings, including those of brain damage. The American literature has just the opposite focus: these descriptions of the late after-effects focus only on the psychological symptoms.[14] Niederland,[15] who renamed the Scandinavians' "concentration camp syndrome" the "survivor syndrome," summarized it as a mixture of reactive chronic depression and anxiety syndrome with ongoing survivor guilt; the guilt in particular is felt as both a constant depression and a constant fear manifested in vigilance and paranoic reactions.

Later Findings

A 1971 review by Hoppe[16] of psychiatric studies of survivors (summarized in appendices 1 and 2) showed that it was not easy to be diagnosed and judged by psychiatrists. Meerloo[17] makes a similar point in regard to survivors applying for restitution:

> During the past years, I have examined and re-examined several survivors of extermination camps who were nominees for monetary compensation by the West-German government for damages suffered during the Hitler regime. As I listened with horror to their tales of years of persecution and torture in prisons and concentration camps, I was sometimes just as infuriated by the prejudiced course of previous medical examination in deciding on the amount of damage related to the traumatic years.

In several instances an elaborate internal and neurological examination was thought to be sufficient (seeking the physical results of abuse), that is, no thorough psychiatric interview was considered necessary. Usually the patient was sent home with some parting remark such as: "I'm sorry, I cannot diagnose any bad result from your concentration camp stay sojourn." It was no easier to be judged by a medical doctor than a psychiatrist!

But why was it mainly American psychiatrists who were able to find "bad results" of the sojourn in the camps while the Europeans found mainly somatic disorders? It was not, of course, because these Jewish survivors had been less maltreated than, for instance, the Danish or Norwegian. The contrary was the case. The reason is that the Jewish prisoners who survived were an extremely select group: they had passed through repeated selections—in the ghettos, on arrival in the camps, at medical inspection, in the sick bays, at every transfer from camp to camp, and on innumerable occasions. Practically everybody with any sign of physical disease had been eliminated. When the end of the German Reich was very close, the prisoners—mainly the

Jewish ones—were subjected to new transfers, meaningless and senseless journeys, the infamous death marches. These often lasted for weeks, right up to liberation by the advancing Allied Forces. The death toll of these marches was horrifying. The weak, the sick, those unable to march on, were shot dead on the spot. Many died even after liberation.

Thus the Jewish ex-prisoners who, against all odds, survived the war are such an extremely select group that any statistics, any discussions, that do not take these factors into consideration must therefore come to incorrect conclusions. The question of restitution was made rather difficult by the state of German psychiatry immediately after the war. In 1958 Venzlaff[18] described in detail German attitudes toward post-traumatic states, dividing those states into three groups, none of which promised any right to compensation. He added a fourth group, patients who had been exposed to such long-lasting terrorization that their psychological changes should justify compensation. He called these "changes of personality provoked by life events." His work and that of a few others[19] first influenced the rigid German compensation laws concerning psychogenic reactions; there is reason to believe that Norwegian studies contributed to the same effect.

The controversial struggle for compensation, along with negative reactions of third parties, made the survivors feel abandoned by the world, misunderstood, sold out. Elie Wiesel[20] described these feelings in his emotional, even harsh essay of 1975, "A Plea for the Survivors." A short excerpt must suffice here:

> No sooner were the survivors among you than you began to question and criticize. Fierce discussions and debates took place in newspapers, magazines and drawing rooms. . . . Why did the victims march to the slaughterhouse like cattle? Why this and not that? The height of irony and cruelty: the dead victims needed to be defended, while the killers, dead and alive, were left alone. Then the question became more brutal, the heckling more brazenly offensive: Why did you survive? Why did you remain alive, you and not another? Was it because you were more cunning? Or hardier? More tenacious? More selfish? Questions and insinuations that sickened us. We could only repeat over and over again: You do not understand, you cannot understand. You who were not there will never understand. . . . At that point their tone became even more accusatory. They accused us, often by implication, of having willingly endured the concentration-camp experience, perhaps even of having brought it upon ourselves. . . . They accused us of making a public show of ourselves, of having commercialized our experience. Suddenly the roles were reversed. While people who had not lived through it took the liberty of saying, writing, showing whatever they chose on the Holocaust, its survivors found themselves forced to explain themselves, to justify themselves. The real accused? The survivors. They were placed in the position of having to defend their honor and that of the dead.

Survivors experienced certain problems as especially hurtful, painful, and stigmatizing. The one-sided description of their behavior in the camps that Elie Wiesel alluded to was preceded by incorrect interpretations already given before the end of the war.[21] Bruno Bettelheim was interned for a relatively short time in Dachau and Buchenwald. He obviously had no access to the secret underground movements in these camps. However, he did "find" that the main psychic mechanisms employed by the inmates were regression and identification with the aggressor. In 1943, at the peak of mass murder in the death camps, Bettelheim felt "objective enough" (as he himself writes) to publish his observations, though these had very little to do with the extermination camps. Unfortunately his paper was published in a well-known journal and has been quoted and requoted by countless authors with little knowledge of the camps who could therefore take Bettelheim's descriptions as a sort of biblical truth. The theories of "regression" and "identification with the aggressor" remained in the literature like ghosts difficult to exorcise; though refuted time and again, they serve some unconscious need and will thus probably continue to haunt the literature.

In her review of Dina Wardi's *Memorial Candles: Children of the Holocaust*, Natasha Burchardt writes, "At one conference I attended in Germany, the discussion of 'identification with the aggressor' had deteriorated to the point where it was being glibly proposed that there was 'no difference' in the psyches of the persecutors and their victims." Burchardt recalled the disdain Primo Levi expressed for this notion in *The Drowned and the Saved*:

> I do not know, and it does not much interest me to know, whether in my depths there lurks a murderer, but I do know that I was a guiltless victim and I was not a murderer. I know that the murderers existed, not only in Germany, and still exist, retired or on active duty, and that to confuse them with their victims is a moral disease or an aesthetic affectation or a sinister sign of complicity; above all, it is precious service rendered (intentionally or not) to the negators of truth.[22]

Still, identification with the aggressor *was* employed by some prisoners. This was made possible by the fact that the SS guards delegated some of their unlimited power to certain well-selected prisoners. But any shift of the regime in the camp, any transport to another camp or subcamp, resulted in the dethronement of these "superprisoners," often with drastic or even fatal results. Identification with the aggressor, as far as it occurred, was thus a negative coping mechanism, potentially leading to the destruction of those involved, and—in the case of some survivors—to deep pathological changes of personality.

The inmates of the camps were neither angels nor aggressors but simply human beings. Based on several hundred interviews with both Jewish and Norwegian survivors, we may say that prisoners who were completely isolated from their families, deprived of all contact with groups to whom they were related before the war, people who were completely overwhelmed by the notion that they had nobody and nothing to struggle or to live for, were those who most easily succumbed. Prisoners able to stay with members of their prewar peer groups, to help others, and to get help, resisted best.

The next stigma came from the survivors' internal "guilt feelings." They *had* to feel guilty because they survived, they had to feel guilty because they did not march against the SS, did not revolt, did not fight the Nazis, did not commit suicide. Others felt guilty because their unconscious death wishes against their parents had been fulfilled in the camps. Many a survivor wondered, Why me and why not my brother? They communicated the small self-reproaches one can hear in many interviews: "If I had done this or that or if I had not done this or that, perhaps he or she would have lived today." These small daily self-reproaches, known to everybody, are not specific

in their losses, their unique sociopsychological and interhuman relationships, and not merely the scientific persuasion of the authors, can explain most of the differences of the findings published.

Undeterred by psychiatrists' findings, many survivors found coping mechanisms for life in their new surroundings; many found their place in the new societies, and they give the impression that they have integrated their massive traumatization into their psychic functioning and the new reality of the present. The individual survivor's desire to become once again an active part of a family, to be a member of a community, to belong and to create, must not be underestimated. However, many intrapersonal difficulties are often repressed, not resolved. Studies that uncover subconscious material demonstrate clearly that the scars are present and that they may influence the psychic life of former prisoners. Studies during the past few years demonstrate this very clearly, though only a few of them can be mentioned here.

H. Dasberg[27] published a review in 1987 in which he describes the renewed interest in the Holocaust and its victims generated in Israel by a new generation's willingness to reexamine the past. Both social and developmental changes, and the reaction to the "conspiracy of silence" (which perhaps was stronger in Israel than other places), contributed to a growing demand that the plight of the victims not be ignored. Dasberg finds continuous threats to the psychological well-being of survivors and their families and that their plight has been misunderstood for too long, resulting in the lack of a nationwide framework to provide psychosocial support. There has been, furthermore, a collusion between the survivors' own denial, the reticence of many third parties to listen to them, and the misunderstandings of over-identifying therapists.

Dasberg also discusses the problems of what he calls the "erstwhile child survivor": Dutch studies demonstrated that child survivors were the most vulnerable age group. Most of them, however, had not been studied until thirty or forty years after the liberation. Some studies were written in a rather optimistic vein, much as those of Judith Hemmendinger,[28] or the interviews done by Sara Moskowitz.[29] Dasberg demonstrated that child survivors are a socially successful but at the same time highly vulnerable group, especially as they approach middle age. The younger the age of persecution and separation from parents, the higher seems the risk for later problems.

Robinson and coworkers in Jerusalem[30] interviewed extensively two nonclinical groups of elderly child survivors. Both groups were basically well adjusted and revealed that they still suffer from symptoms belonging to the concentration camp syndrome; death camp survivors suffered more than those subjected to less extreme forms of persecution. We must not forget these facts when learning of the social successes of individual Holocaust survivors.

Present Problems and Future Work

Are new methodological approaches necessary to broaden the scholarship in this field? Before trying to answer this question it is necessary to stress that there are two main roads to the problems of survivors: research and emotional counseling. What do we need in order to produce better research? First of all a better differentiation of the kinds of traumatization and better operational descriptions of the difficulties encountered in postwar life. It is important to differentiate between the difficulties caused by migration and their psychological effects on the one hand and the late effects of persecution on the other. Only large-scale comparative studies will bring us meaningful results. The theoretical understanding of these problems is probably of less importance for the relatively few still living survivors than for more recently traumatized refugees. To better understand children and youngsters (not only Jewish) with mental health problems and adaptation difficulties, it would be important to understand the influence of the parents' traumatization. More detailed research would help us reduce the ill-founded generalizations that have often proven disastrous for objective judgment.

The second main road is better psychosocial help for survivors and their families: there are still many who need it. Organizations such as Amcha in Israel and ESRA in Germany, which offer help to survivors are struggling—as improbable as it might appear—with very sub-stantial economic difficulties. This should not be the case.

We must not forget that in spite of all efforts and all social achievements, the survivors' psychic wounds hurt and sometimes reopen. The strength to deny or fight old memories diminishes during serious diseases or when vitality is reduced by other causes, for instance old age. But while many survivors continue to exhibit increased vulnerability to stressful situations, they may also show a greater sensitivity toward fellow humans, a greater capacity for empathy, and a greater appreciation for the higher values in life. Their psyche is thus complicated and full of contradictory feelings, their lives are still full of unresolved problems.

For a survivor it is not always easy to accept one's past and to reach inner harmony. The lives of several authors demonstrate this clearly. Primo Levi committed suicide many years after his liberation, so too Jean Améry, Paul Célan, and Jerzy Kosinski. They and many others could no longer stand life. Everything they had gone through had become meaningless. They died of what Primo Levi had called "survivors' disease."

What exactly is this "survivors' disease"? To put it simply: the survivors who committed suicide did it because they could neither understand nor accept that the world easily forgot what happened in the Nazi camps. All those who hoped that the Holocaust had changed both the world and mankind had to learn that nothing and no one had changed. The world continues as if the death of fifty million human beings, the industrial slaughter of six million Jews, of two million children, had never taken place. Ex-prisoners—poets and writers who wanted to shake the world out of its indifference and lethargy by telling what had happened in the camps—felt lost, felt betrayed by this same world that did not want to be told, did not want to listen, did not want to understand. After years of vain efforts they gave up.

Elie Wiesel knows also that it is not easy to be a survivor. His main conclusion is perhaps expressed best in his essay on the two sages Hillel and Shamai.[31] These two disagreed in practically everything. But both understood that it is not man's privilege to choose the time or the place of his birth, but that it is his privilege to give his life a direction—and a justification. "And each of us must do likewise. This applies particularly to my generation," says Elie Wiesel. "None of my contemporaries knows why he is alive—or rather, why he has survived, why he and not someone else. For us every moment is a moment of grace and wonder—we and we alone can give it meaning."

Nevertheless, the daily life of many survivors is characterized by isolation: they are refugees, old people, survivors of a period nearly everybody else wants to forget. The latter have more than enough to think about. For the former it is more than enough to worry about, more than enough to not be listened to, to not be understood, to be distrusted and misjudged, and they fall into despair and depression.

Survivors of Nazi concentration camps have their share of problems. With the passage of time health deteriorates, strength is reduced, and mental capacities dwindle. Traumatic experiences return with reinforced strength. Survivors are of course in need of help for all their somatic ailments but still more for their psychological isolation, their feeling of having lost their anchorage in the world and in humanity. If we manage to reverse this tragic evolution by establishing at least the traces of real interhuman relationships and reducing the deep existential isolation, then we have made an important step—perhaps not bigger than the first step on the moon, but surely more important for a fellow human being, because it reduces the total sum of suffering in this world—and this is the most important task for all of us.[32]

APPENDIX I

Symptoms Described	Author	Year
Neurological causes of asthenia	Farkas & Szokodi-Dimitrov	1957
Chronic reactive depression (depression caused by up-rooting)	Strauss	1957
Premature break in the life pattern (*vorzeitiger Knick in der Lebenslinie*)	Kolle	1958
Change of personality due to traumatic life experience (*lebensbedingter Persönlichkeitswandel*)	Venzlaff	1958
Neurosis of the outlawed, of extermination, etc. (*Neurose der Geächteten, der Vernichtung*, etc.) A scale of anxiety and personality disorder	Bensheim	1960
Hypochondrial preoccupation, loss of productivity, inadequate control of thinking, affective manifestations, depressive and aggressive tendencies	Raveau	1960
Organic brain damage	Eitinger	1961
Neurological findings	Klimková-Deutschová	1961
Chronic depression with organic features	Kluge	1961
Living corpse appearance, survivor guilt, depression, feeling of being persecuted or hated	Niederland	1961
Traumatogenic anxiety syndrome (nightmares, brooding preoccupation, and fantasies concerning the past, dreams of revival of murdered family members, survivor guilt) Disturbed affects and personality structure	Trautmann	1961
Lack of self-esteem	Hoppe	1962/68
Chronic reactive depression	Hoppe	1962/68
Chronic reactive aggression	Hoppe	1962/68

Symptoms Described	Author	Year
Psychosomatic symptoms	Hoppe	1962/68
Chronic melancholia (defect of an adynamic nature)	Kluge	1963
Irritability, disturbed memory, shortened span of attention, affective instability	Müller-Hegemann & Spitzner	1963
Impaired attention and recent memory	Paul	1963
Predominantly somatic and predominantly emotional disturbances	Eitinger	1964–67
Chronic or persisting identity diffusion	Koenig	1964
Obsessive symptoms and depressive paranoid syndrome	Maller	1964
Reduced memory fixation	Sager	1964
General rapid fatigue	Thygesen & Herman	1964
Psychosis Permanent damage	Von Baeyer, Haefner Kisker	1964
Psychosomatic disorders, Social isolation, Uprooting—depression without depression	Lederer	1965
Shortened lifespan (1 year CC = 4 years civil life)	Richet & Mans	1965
Survivor syndrome	Niederland & Krystal	1966/68
Acute stress syndrome (*Akutes Belastungssyndrom*)	Venzlaff	1966
Permanent psychotraumatic disorders	Paul & Herberg	1967
Primary disorders: Anxiety, nightmares, high irritability; Secondary disorders: Depression, withdrawal	Haefner	1968
Dissociative reactions with repeated traumatic experiences	Jaffe	1968
Predominantly emotional disturbances	Ström	1968

APPENDIX 2

Psychodynamics	Author	Year
Representation of individual experience apart from the collective representation of events	Venzlaff	1958
Will-to-meaning	Frankl	1959/61
Decompensation of neurotic mental structure	Cremerius	1960
Enforced association and fusion of incomparable concepts— projected onto any authority	Engel	1962
Loss of security in inter-personal relationships	Kisker, Von Baeyer Haefner	1963
Survivor-guilt cannot be given up because of "forgetting the murdered," forgiving the persecutors	Chodoff	1963/69
Depth of depression depends on extent of narcissistic regression and diffusion of libidinal and aggressive instinctual drives	Hoppe	1962/63
Atrophy of instinct	Maller	1964
In contrast to depressed survivors, inmates who developed chronic reactive aggression and hate-addiction were protected from unconsciously relating to their torturers as parental figures by a firm ego-ideal and by shame, pride, and the idea of having a mission. The aggressive survivor permanently externalizes a part of his superego and fights against representatives of the externalized negative conscience. The aggression creates new guilt feelings, especially if the survivor's hate addiction turns against his own family members.	Hoppe	1964/66/68
Double-bind	Kanter	1968
Masochistic personality changes in survivors (slave personality, etc.). Compensation for shame and humiliation of persecution	Krystal	1968

Psychodynamics	Author	Year
Impairment of social status: psychic damage	Luthe	1968
Survivors' guilt-ridden fear of emotional closeness and guilt-ridden fantasies and dreams demonstrate a marked ambivalence toward their lost love-objects, who failed to protect them from persecution, as well as sadistic fantasies on an oral-incorporative level	Niederland	1968

NOTES

1. F. Hocking, "Human Reactions to Extreme Environmental Stress," *Medical Journal Australia* 52 (1965): 477–82.

2. W. R. F. Collis, "Belsen Camp: A Preliminary Report," *British Medical Journal* (1945): 814–16.

3. N. M. Apeland, *Fra Aulaen til Buchenwald* (Stavanger: Otto Flor, 1945); P. Helweg-Larsen, H. Hoffmeyer, J. Kieler, J. H. Thaysen, P. Thygesen, M. H. Wulff, "Famine Disease in German Concentration Camps. Complications and Sequelae," in *Acta Psychiatrica Neurologica Scandinavica* (Copenhagen: Ejnar Munchsgaard, 1952), supplement 83; K. Hermann, "Die psychischen Symptomen des KZ Syndroms. Versuch einer pathogenetischen Schätzung" (The psychic symptoms of the concentration camp syndrome. An attempt at a psychopathogenic evaluation), in *Gesundheitsschäden durch Verfolgung und Gefangenschaft und ihre Spätfolgen*, ed. M. Michel (Frankfurt/M.: Röderberg Verlag, 1955), pp. 41–47.

4. L. Eitinger, "Sykehusbehandlingen i Konsentrasjonsleiren Auschwitz" (Hospital treatment in Auschwitz concentration camp), *Tidsskr Norske Lägeforen* 65 (1945): 159–61.

5. L. Eitinger, "Skolebarnas Boligforhold i Bodø og Skoleprestasjoner," *Sosialt Arbeid* 21/22 (1947): 108–12, 144–52.

6. L. Eitinger, "The Symptomatology of Mental Disease among Refugees in Norway," *Journal of Mental Science* 106 (1960): 947–66.

7. L. Eitinger, *Concentration Camp Survivors in Norway and Israel* (The Hague: Martinus Nijhoff, 1972; first published by the Norwegian Research Council for Science and Humanities, 1964); A. Ström, ed., *Norwegian Concentration Camp Survivors* (Oslo: Universitetsforlaget; New York: Humanities Press, 1968); L. Eitinger and A. Ström, *Mortality and Morbidity after Excessive Stress* (Oslo: Universitetsforlaget; New York: Humanities Press, 1973).

8. Eitinger, *Concentration Camp Survivors.*

9. L. Eitinger, "Jewish Concentration Camp Survivors in Norway," *Israel Annals of Psychiatry and Related Disciplines* 13/4 (1975): 321–34.

10. C. Richet and A. Mans, *Pathologie de la déportation* (The pathology of deportation) (n.p.: A.D.I.F. des Alpes-Maritimes et de la Principalité de Monaco, 1958); R. Targowla, "Die neuropsychischen Folgen der Deportation in deutschen Konzentrationslagern. Syndrom der Asthenie der Deportierten" (The neuropsychological sequelae of the deportation to German concentration camps. The syndrome of asthenia in the deportees), in *Gesundheitsschäden*, ed. Michel, pp. 30–40; L. F. Fichez, *L'etio-pathogénie et la thérapeutique de l'asthenie et de la senescence premature* (The etio-pathology and the treatment of asthenia and premature aging) (Bucharest, 1964).

11. Helweg-Larsen et al., "Famine Disease"; Hermann, "Die psychischen Symptomen des KZ Syndroms."

12. J. Bastiaans, *Psychosomatischen gevolgen van onderdrukking en verzet* (Psychosomatic sequelae of persecution and resistance) (Amsterdam: Noord-Hollandsche Uitgervers Maatschappij, 1957).

13. Eitinger, *Concentration Camp Survivors*; Ström, ed., *Norwegian Concentration Camp Survivors*; Eitinger and Ström, *Mortality and Morbibity*; E. A. Løchen, "Psychometric Patterns," in Ström, ed., *Norwegian Concentration Camp Survivors*, pp. 132–55; A. Lönnum, "Om KZ-Syndromet" (On the concentration camp syndome), *Nordisk Medicin* 69 (1963): 480–84; idem, "Neurological Disorders," in Ström, ed., *Norwegian Concentration Camp Survivors*, pp. 85–123.

14. P. Chodoff, "Psychiatric Aspects of the Nazi Persecution," in *American Handbook of Psychiatry*, vol. 41, ed. S. Arieti (New York: Basic Books, 1975), pp. 932–46; K. R. Eissler, "Pervertierte psychiatrie?" (Perverted psychiatry?), *Psyche* 8 (1967): 533–75; K. D. Hoppe, "The Psychodynamics of Concentration Camp Victims," *Psychoanalytic Forum* 1/1 (1966): 76–85; H. Krystal, "The Late Sequelae of Massive Psychic Trauma. Theme of the First Studies of Concentration Camp Survivors," Second Wayne State University Workshop on the Late Sequelae of Massive Psychic Traumatization, Detroit, 1964.

15. W. G. Niederland and H. Krystal, "Clinical Observations on the 'Survivor' Syndrome," in *Massive Psychic Trauma,* ed. Krystal, pp. 327–48.

16. K. D. Hoppe, "The Aftermath of Nazi Persecution Reflected in Recent Psychiatric Literature," *International Psychiatry Clinics* 8 (1971): 169–204.

17. J. A. M. Meerloo, "Neurologism and Denial of Psychic Trauma in Extermination Camp Survivors," *American Journal of Psychiatry* 120 (1963): 65–66.

18. U. Venzlaff, *Die psychoreaktiven Störungen nach entschädigungspflichtigen Ereignissen* (Psychological disturbances as reactions to traumatizations that entitle to restitution) (Berlin: Springer Verlag, 1958).

19. W. R. von Baeyer, "Erlebnisbedingte Verfolgungsschäden" (Damage caused by experienced persecution), *Nervenarzt* 32/12 (1961): 534–38; E. Kluge, "Über die Folgen schwerer Haftzeiten" (On the sequelae of severe incarceration), *Nervenarzt* 29 (1958): 462–65; K. Kolle, "Die Opfer der nationalsozialistischen Verfolgung in psychiatrischer Sicht" (The victims of the National-Socialist persecution in the light of psychiatry), *Nervenarzt* 29 (1958): 148–58.

20. E. Wiesel, *A Jew Today* (New York: Vintage Books, 1978), p. 242.

21. B. Bettelheim, "Individual and Mass Behavior in Extreme Situations," *Journal of Abnormal and Social Psychology* 38 (1943): 417–52.

22. N. Burchardt, "The Long Shadow of the Holocaust," *British Journal of Psychiatry* (1993): 1–6; citing P. Levi, *The Drowned and the Saved* (New York: Summit Books, 1988), pp. 48–49.

23. Y. Danieli, "Therapists' Difficulties in Treating Survivors of the Nazi Holocaust and Their Children," Ph.D. diss., New York University, 1981.

24. E. A. Rappaport, "Survivor Guilt," *Midstream* 27 (1971): 41–47.

25. A. Antonovsky, B. Maoz, N. Dowty, H. Wijsenbeek, "Twenty-Five Years Later: A Limited Study of Sequelae of the Concentration Camp Experience," *Social Psychiatry* 6/4 (1971): 186–93.

26. M. Rosenbloom, "The Holocaust Survivors in Late Life," in *Gerontological Social Work Practice in the Community* (New York: Haworth Press, 1985), pp. 181–91.

27. H. Dasberg, "Psychological Distress of Holocaust Survivors and Offspring in Israel, Forty Years Later: A Review," *Israel Journal of Psychiatry and Related Sciences* 24/4 (1987): 243–56.

28. J. Hemmendinger, "A la sortie des camps de la mort: Reinsertion dans la vie" (Coming out of the camps: Return to life), *Israel Journal Psychiatry and Related Sciences* 18/4 (1981): 331–34.

29. S. Moskovitz, *Love Despite Hate: Child Survivors of the Holocaust and Their Adult Lives* (New York: Schocken Books, 1982).

30. S. Robinson and J. Rapaport et al., "The Late Effects of Nazi Persecution among Elderly Holocaust Survivors," *Acta Psychiatrica Scandinavica* 82 (1990): 311–15; S. Robinson, M. Rapaport, J. Rapaport, "Child Survivors of the Holocaust," *Echoes of the Holocaust* 1/2 (1993): 24–30.

31. E. Wiesel, *Sages and Dreamers* (New York: Summit Books, 1991), p. 174.

32. L. Eitinger, "The Aging Holocaust Survivor," *Echoes of the Holocaust* 1/2 (1993): 5–12.

53.

DINA PORAT

Israeli Society and Recent Attitudes toward the Jews of Europe and Holocaust Survivors

The attitudes of Israeli society toward the Jews of Europe during the Holocaust, and especially to those who survived it, are a sensitive and a painful issue in Israel's public life. Long lists of public debates, documentaries, and memoirs show how that society has sought to describe and analyze these attitudes and the changes they have undergone. During the summer of 1995, the debate reached a new peak of intensity, and two opposite opinions were contrasted more sharply than ever before. According to one argument, Holocaust survivors were cared for after being liberated from the camps so that they could ultimately serve as voters and cannon fodder in Israel. Yet, upon their arrival in Israel they were received with contempt and accusations. As a result, they retreated into themselves for many years. According to the second argument the former interpretation is nothing but a lie, planted in Israeli discourse by "post-Zionists" in order to support their claims against Zionism and the state it established. In fact, this line of reasoning continues, following their liberation, survivors were taken care of wholeheartedly as suffering brothers and were received in Israel with sympathy and an extended hand, as much as the meager resources the Yishuv and the fledgling state would allow. The silence of the survivors was essential in order for them to regain their mental strength and to rebuild their personal lives.

Needless to say, these two opinions highlight contradictory images of Israeli society and of the moral character of the Jewish inhabitants of the state. In other words, the controversy goes far beyond the specific issue of Holocaust survivors to the most basic questions concerning the establishment of the state and its values.[1]

The controversy has found expression in public debates, art, literature,and journalism, but actual research on attitudes toward survivors has barely begun. Therefore, the vehemence of the debate reflects actual needs, not academic or statistical findings. Though two opinions stand at the core of the controversy, the prevailing one, the one believed more accurate by most of the Israeli public, is the critical one: attitudes toward the Jews of Europe and those survivors who came to Israel during the 1940s and early 1950s are a source of disgrace to Israeli society. It was only after the Eichmann trial in 1961–1962, this opinion continues, that these attitudes began to soften; and one can point to a gradual process of change from contempt and criticism to empathy and identification during the 1970s and 1980s. This chronology of attitudes is, again, a kind of "common knowledge" in Israeli society.[2]

Yet without trying to argue which is the historically correct opinion, two assumptions should be presented: first, in the 1990s Israeli society has reached a point of reconciliation in its relationship to the Jews of Europe and to the survivors. Regardless of the debate as to how the survivors were received fifty years ago, there is no doubt today that survivors and their families are part and parcel of Israeli society. The sources that support such an assumption are speeches in 1992 by Ehud Barak (then the IDF [Israel Defence Forces] Chief of Staff) on formal Holocaust Memorial Day occasions; the recently expressed (1991) and published (1992 and 1995) credo of a well-known Israeli author, Hanoch Bartov, once a young soldier who met the survivors upon liberation from the camps; and the monologue of a survivor, lawyer Avraham Tory, during the Gulf War (1991), a time when Israelis compared their ordeal with the Second World War.

Our second assumption is that these texts demonstrate unshaken respect and empathy for Jews victimized by the Nazis, though their writers and speakers knew full well that until recently the opposite opinion predominated in Israel. Why did they express these long-held feelings so forcefully in the 1990s and not before? What are the recent changes in Israeli society that led them—and others—to speak out?

On April 7, 1992, Holocaust Memorial Day, a delegation of eighteen representatives of the IDF headed by Ehud Barak visited Auschwitz. "There is something symbolic, a kind of a circle closing, in the fact that I am here today as the IDF commander," Barak said, words echoed by the others: Jewish and Zionist helplessness during the Second World War was now seen as a bygone part of history. Some of the participants were sons and grandsons of survivors, or relatives of murdered Jews; few were born in DP camps or even lived through the Holocaust as small children.[3] In that respect these representatives symbolized the blend in Israeli society between the general population, whether the native born or immigrants from all over the world, and the survivors' living families, who now constitute about a sixth of the total number of Jews living in Israel.[4]

Ehud Barak's speech in Auschwitz deserves analysis. It should be emphasized that Barak wrote it himself, deliberately defining and formulating his thoughts on the issue, knowing full well that the visit, the first by Israeli soldiers in uniform to the death camps, would later serve as both symbol and point of reference for Israeli media and for Israeli youth. The speech, addressed to all IDF soldiers and commanders, opened with the surprising statement that "we, the first generation of redemption . . . find it difficult to understand the scope and meaning of what happened" in Auschwitz, thus contradicting a prevailing opinion in the Yishuv, and later among the Israeli public, who thought they had a basical understanding of the events of the Holocaust. This understanding seemingly gave them the right to pass severe judgment on European Jewry—and hence on the survivors—and consider those who did not engage in fighting against the Nazis, for the most part passive cowards.[5] When Barak openly admitted the difficulties in grasping the immensity of the Holocaust and its implications, he also undermined the right to judge.

He then went on to make it clear that the Jewish communities in Europe had been cornered and could not do much to rescue themselves: familiar laws and values were turned upside down by insane governments, endorsed by "modern science" and "modern methods of organization"; the leading figures of that government fanatically fixed their mind on wiping out Jewish life, "while . . . not . . . even one government [was] willing or capable of defending or sheltering them." Thus, again, Barak reversed an opinion held in postwar Israel that the Jews in Nazi-occupied Europe should have and could have defended themselves physically and heroically, and failed to do so because of reasons originating in their diaspora nature and history.[6] The speech brought the issue to an opposite conclusion: nothing is wrong with the Jewish people, and self-accusation, for which Jews have a special gift, misses the real reasons that caused the catastrophe. Forsaken by all governments, including the Allies, by millions who knew yet kept quiet, while hundreds of thousands of others actively collaborated with the Nazis, lacking any military or political support, Jews had no way of escaping the machinery set in full motion against them. They therefore could not be blamed, and their alleged stereotypical character traits or unique history had nothing to do with what happened. "Heavens and humans kept silent" in the face of the tragedy—the aggressors and the bystanders were responsible, not the victims.

Thus, the soldiers were asked to face and accept two major principles: their limited comprehension of the event, and the helplessness of the Jewish people at that time. This restraint on the powers of judgment is difficult for Israeli society to accept. The essence of Zionism, which is, after all, the active attempt to change Jewish history, prevents, at least ideologically, an empathetic attitude toward helplessness.

Barak then addressed the Jews of Europe as "our deceased brothers." He spoke of his colleagues and himself as the generation of national revival that grew up "under this blazing light," as Amos Oz defined the Israeli experience. "We, who did not stand in your place," Barak said (a reference to the Mishna in Aboth 2:4, "condemn not your fellow man until you stand in his place"), "know that we are, therefore, unable to criticize you." Once again, he censured the rush to judgment as unfair. No one who did not experience the Holocaust may be permitted such a liberty.

He asserted that "we are proud of your struggle to preserve the human image in the Devil's domain." In fact, the preservation of the human image as another, more personal, and daily expression of bravery during the Holocaust had been considered in Israel time and again as no less respectable than organized fighting. Preserving the human image had even become a sort of code word, signifying the masses of Jews who could not engage in fighting, because circumstances did not allow for it.[7] Yet those in Israel who praised personal courage expressed in daily activities did not overcome, at least not until the 1980s, the more widely accepted line that saw active resistance as the only correct answer to Nazi brutality. The persistence of this view is illustrated by the attacks leveled at the poet laureate Nathan Alterman who, on Holocaust Memorial Day of 1954, published a poem entitled "The Day of Revolt and the Rebels," which equated all kinds of bravery as equally respect-worthy and emphasized that the ghetto fighters themselves recognized them as such: the fighters understood that only a few and only the young could follow them and therefore did not condemn those who did not. Passages from his diary, written forty years ago, in which he elaborated on the possibilities and motivations of Jewish fighting, raised a fresh public debate about the meaning of bravery when the diary was published in 1991.[8]

In the 1992 speech at Auschwitz, preservation of the human image in all possible forms is not merely a legitimate source of pride, no less important than fighting, but also juxtaposes Jews with Nazi evil, for Jews are the bearers of human and humane values. Only then did Barak speak of resistance: "We are proud of the expressions of resistance and struggle, as limited as they were." Organized fighting was for decades considered in Israel the essence of Jewish reaction in the Holocaust, a theme in speeches, conferences, educational material, and public conversation. The 1953 "Yad Vashem" law, called the "Holocaust and Heroism" law,[9] reflected the desire to balance armed struggle with this multifaceted daily resistance. Historically speaking, this was impossible because "Holocaust" signified the experiences and death of nonfighting Jews, by far the vast majority, while "heroism" defined the rebels and fighters, a small minority. Still, the law defined nine categories, one being the "Righteous among the Nation," that is, Gentiles who selflessly rescued Jews. The remaining eight categories fell into two equal groups of four. One of these embraced those who fought in Allied armies; those who fought in the underground in forest and town; those who fought in the ghettos; and those who sought to make their way to Palestine to fight for the liberation of Israel. The other group of four categories included all the others—the vast majority—trapped by the Germans, whose only opportunity for resistance was the daily struggle to preserve human dignity. Needless to say, such a division, as if the two halves were of equal weight, distorted the historical reality, in which fighting was a possibility only for a few and the fate of most Jews in the countries allied with or occupied by Nazi Germany was marked by roundups and deportations and death.

Barak concluded with utmost respect: "The IDF salutes your ashes."

Barak's comments indirectly connected the Holocaust and the establishment of the State of Israel, though it was not the disaster as such that brought about the rebirth of a Jewish state. Indeed, the Holocaust was an obstacle, because millions who could have come to build a Jewish state were no longer alive when the war was over in 1945. Yet the realization of what happened and the shocking meetings with survivors and ghetto fighters intensified the struggle to achieve national goals after the war.[10] The experience of the Jews of Europe was an indirect reason for the establishment of the state, a source of motivation and energy to build and defend it.

Then Barak addressed another lesson of the Holocaust: that Israel must be strong enough to maintain a sovereign political existence and wise enough to understand that strength alone will not guarantee such sovereignty; only a triangle of strength, justice, and political wisdom will suffice.

The struggle against Holocaust deniers, neo-Nazis, and antisemites, wherever they are, should go on, he averred, despite the fact that the antisemitic political tools prepared against the Jews were ripe before Zionism was ready with an answer. The IDF had come to Auschwitz "fifty years too late," the latter statement arousing severe criticism against Barak, as if he had been saying that a Jewish state could have prevented the Holocaust, or that the IDF was some invincible Entebbe-style rescue squadron.[11] Barak answered that "fifty years too late" was a metaphor meaning that had the Zionist tools been ready before those sharpened by antisemitism, and had a Jewish state emerged before the Second World War, even a small and still fragile one, history could have been different; today, certainly, no one can attempt a mass killing of Jews.[12] Again, Barak's analysis has to do with history and not with the faults of European Jewry or with any comparison between the survivors and the Israeli public.

This was indeed a surprising speech, resulting from a deliberate decision to plant these points of view as a national historical truth, regardless of the sway of the opposite opinion over the majority. As Barak later said, "I tried to . . . bring out the essence of the only possible relation to the Jews of Europe and their survivors."[13] Barak pointed out that a) no one has the right to judge the Jews of Nazi Europe; b) it was a well-rooted but wrong axiom that had Israelis been there, they would have proved proper fighters; c) *any* person subjected to the preparatory measures of the Nazis, aimed at humiliating, dehumanizing, and defeating the individual, would have had to struggle very hard just to keep his human identity from being taken from him; d) Israeli society, fighting for its existence during the late forties and the fifties, chose, with correct intuition, lessons and symbols of heroism from the Holocaust, because they were needed at that point of time in Israeli history. But this mythology, rooted for too long in the collective memory, cast a shadow on the Jews of Europe and the survivors, as if they had some genetic flaw.

Coming back from Auschwitz, Barak added at another ceremony in Israel:

> The survivors still walk among us, aging with time, but still haunted by nightmares and memories from "the Other Planet" and the revolts in the ghettos. We are the last generation to know them in person, which means that in our very generation the experience of the Holocaust will shift from a personal one into historical consciousness and collective memory. Therefore we should, as ordered every Passover night, regard ourselves as if we, each one of us, were forced to dig a pit with his brothers, and be shot into it; as if his own baby and wife were smashed before his very eyes, and his sister used for years by the SS; as if he were pushed into the gas chambers to be strangled to death, or forced to untangle the dead and take them to be burnt; as if he survived—in all kinds of places and ways—alive, with a heavy conscience, haunted by the sights, smells, and memories, waking up sweating even decades after the crematoria fires were extinguished, feeling that he is the last of the survivors, carrying the cry for revenge which can never be satisfied, and the never-ending demand to remember and not to forget or forgive.[14]

This emotional piece expresses sympathy and identification in Jewish and human terms. Zionism had not managed to save its followers from the fate of European Jews by bringing them to the Land of Israel in time. Here the speaker actually goes against the concept that since Zionism is the correct solution, superior to any other in modern Jewish history, whoever chose to stick to it is by definition superior to others. Instead he advocated another notion—that Jews shared and share one common fate.

Moreover, when one says that Jews survived in all kinds of places, and in all kinds of ways, one says that they survived by sheer chance and luck, and that their personal character traits or the way they behaved toward their fellow Jews had little to do with their survival. It has been said in Israel that the survivors were hard and mean and that they held out at the expense of the more righteous.[15] But survivors themselves are haunted by pangs of conscience. They relive the past constantly, and torture themselves asking what is it they could have done, or wondering whether it is their fault that their families were killed and they spared. They cannot be blamed for anything, says Barak. They are like you and me.

Let us examine now another text, published in the winter of 1992, by the writer Hanoch Bartov in a literary magazine as a reaction to a long-standing accusation. Bartov's text bears the title "There Is No Truth in the Libel about Our Indifference to the Holocaust";[16] the "our" refers to Israeli-born authors and poets, often called "the generation of the State" or "the Palmach generation"—those who were born in the early twenties, fought in the War of Independence, and began writing during the first years of the state.

"I have an urgent inner need to join this repetitious tiresome discussion on the role played by the Holocaust in the self-awareness and the literary work of my generation," wrote Bartov, "though I know, that there is very little chance to bring forth our truth."[17] Having kept silent for so long, Bartov finally answered because the poet Nathan Zach claimed, again, that "the generation of the State" had no awareness of the Holocaust and would have suppressed their Jewish identity altogether had it not been for the Holocaust. This was a vicious libel, sold for years to a new generation, against an entire generation for expressing no feeling for the extermination of the Jewish people in their writings, and for concentrating "all our efforts on our tiny provincial Eretz-Israeli Pupik" (belly button).

Pretending to be older than his seventeen years, Bartov volunteered for service in the Jewish Brigade in 1944 and sent home letters describing his experiences. It was only later that the full meaning of these experiences became clear to him. The letters describe the first Yom Kippur the Brigade celebrated outside the Land of Israel, as if it were "a truly Jewish army"; Bartov describes the Jewish ghetto in Rome, the feelings of pity its children aroused, and his desire to take revenge. Having learned in Italy in 1945 about the murder of his relatives in Poland, he does not cry, because comfort would not be found in tears: only the blood of German men, women, and children would be an expiation for Jewish blood. He knows full well that such revenge, taking the life of the innocent as well, is "a horribly extreme conclusion." But he is not alone. In one of his letters he lists all those yearning for revenge: the dead Jews; the survivors; the Jews in Palestine, expecting the Brigade to fulfill this duty; most of the soldiers themselves; and the non-Jewish soldiers of the British army who, certain that the Brigade would take revenge, were already telling stories about its dark deeds.

When the order came to move from Italy into Germany, in July 1945, the organ of the Jewish Brigade, *Bama'avak* (In the struggle), published "13 commandments" that each soldier swore to abide by:[18]

> Remember your six million brothers.
> Cling to the hatred for the butcher of your people for generations.
> Remember you are a messenger of a people in struggle.
> Remember, the Brigade in Germany is a Jewish occupation army.
> Remember, our appearance in Nazi Germany, with our flag and insignia, among
>   members of the German people in their own country is in itself a revenge!

Remember your mission: the rescue of Jews, immigration to Palestine, a free
   homeland.
Your duty is dedication, loyalty, and love to those who survived the sword and the
   camps.

In the 1990s Bartov presents these commandments as proof of the soldiers'
identification with the survivors and the soldiers' desire to share the survivors'
decisions as to what the national priorities should be after the war. Although this is
amply documented, and the motive of revenge occurs and recurs in Jews' last
testaments, letters, and writings on prison walls as well as in the Yishuv press,[19] the
postwar question of whether or not to actually kill Germans, which ones, how many,
and how, proved very complicated. Since this subject does not fall within the scope
of our discussion, let us confine ourselves to pointing at expression of feelings of
revenge as a way of being part of the saving remnant and its wishes, and to Bartov's
way of emphasizing it today as a refutation of the prevailing opinion.

To their great disappointment, the Brigade soldiers were not sent to Germany
after all. They halted at the Italian-Austrian border, where they met thousands of
survivors, coming southward from all over Europe on their way to Palestine. "This
new wave [of survivors] elevated our morale, encouraged us, and gave taste to our
life. We met our finest destination, finer than any we could think of. We met with
brothers rescued from hell. And not only met them—full help was rendered to
them—food, clothing, and encouragement," Bartov writes home. He does not go into
details, because the soldiers gave both from their own resources and from what they
could take ("organize" in the slang of the time), legally or not, from British army
warehouses. Yet he promises that "our boys, soldiers from the Brigade, are writing the
finest page in the history of the Hebrew Yishuv." He describes in detail encounters
with survivors, whose average age is the same as his, seventeen, and the horrors they
kept repeating: "Our boys are so shocked . . . they do not stop thinking about [the
survivors]."[20]

Bartov realized that this exceptional summer had accompanied him his entire
life, entered into the stories he wrote, and turned him, the Petach-Tikva born
(Petach-Tikva is a symbol of the first Zionist settlements, surrounded by orange
orchards) into a Jew by choice, not only birth. This choice, to realize he is first of all
a Jew, made him a Zionist; and being a Zionist made him an Israeli. He was not "born
from the Sea," as author Moshe Shamir depicted the local Sabra, born without
national historical roots, the son of nature's elements. Bartov rejected this concept: "I
am not the mythological Sabra," he concluded. His encounter with the remnants,
realizing they were his brothers, forced him to this inner choice, following which "I
came back another man, I came back a Jew."[21]

In 1993 he went on to say that there had never actually been any real distinction
between the Israeli-born generation and the newcomers, before or after the Holocaust. There never was a deeply rooted alienation of Israeli from Diaspora, because
the vast majority of the Yishuv had always consisted of newcomers, who themselves
spent no more than a few years in Palestine before a new wave of newcomers arrived.
This was all the more the case in 1948, when half the population consisted of brand-
new arrivals, half of them survivors. It was only on an ideological plane that Zionism

rejected the "Diaspora" Jew. In reality, Zionism consisted of these very same Jews. According to Bartov, identification with survivors was therefore only natural.[22]

Why did Bartov publish these pages only in 1993? The letters had been with him since the war. He had indeed integrated them into his stories, so that they had not really lain waste in his drawers. Was it only the provocation that he felt when reading the words of Nathan Zach? Time and again he had heard the same accusations leveled at his generation, of not being sensitive enough, of not writing in time about the great catastrophe, of being too involved in Eretz Israeli matters. Perhaps he had not challenged these accusations because he knew that "there is very small chance to bring forth our truth." But if so, why bring it up so forcefully in 1993?

His answer, to which we will return, is that Israel in the nineties is a different place than it had been before; and the change in attitude toward the survivors could only now be fully presented: "In Europe of summer 1945 we met the remnants of European Jewry... and witnessed such a total Jewish and human destruction that we in fact should have despaired of any hope that a Yishuv of 600,000 Jews would ever establish a state of its own, perhaps even despair of any Jewish future at all."[23] But now, forty-five years after its establishment, the journey toward national independence seems to have been completed. Israeli society no longer needs "the mythological Sabra," because it no longer needs to struggle for its very existence.[24] Feelings long suppressed would find their way out; it was time to reject the libel against the first generation and decide once and for all that "either we are Jews who are here because of a common past, fate, and dream, together responsible for the present and the future—or there is nothing for us to look for here."[25]

As if to support Bartov's words, two books were published during that same year, A Living Bridge,[26] and The Encounter, the protocols of a meeting of survivors, Brigade soldiers, and historians that took place in 1991.[27] The meeting was initiated by the original soldiers, who had long claimed that the original encounter had never been fully acknowledged. Falling between two enormous events—the Holocaust and the War of Independence—the years between 1945 and 1948 had never been properly treated in the historiography, and the moral and practical support they had rendered to the survivors had been forgotten. But that encounter had "affected each of us personally, and had an impact on the character of the state [...] its values and preferences, and its relations with Jewish communities abroad," wrote ex-president Chaim Herzog, himself a former officer in the British army.[28] During the 1991 meeting the six survivors confirmed that the very appearance of the Brigade in liberated Europe, where the survivors felt lost and aimless, was "the strongest, the greatest, and the most important event that could happen to us," for it gave them a direction, a sense of renewed dignity and self-respect.[29]

Our third source is the minutes of a conversation with a Holocaust survivor during the Gulf War, on February 1991. The conversation took place on his initiative. Mr. Avraham Tory called me, worried about my safety and well-being. His words shed light on relations between the survivors and those parts of Israeli society for whom the Holocaust is not a personal memory. He noted the resemblance between the Second World War and the Gulf War, the way Israeli society, especially nonsurvivors, reacted to it, and the way survivors felt.[30]

He did echo a certain public consensus in Israel during January and February 1991 regarding the many similarities between the wars: the association the gas masks raised again between the killing of Jews and gas, was strengthened by newly revealed information that the gas was supplied to Iraq by German mega-companies. Such companies had financed Hitler's rise to power. "There is no new Germany," claimed leading Israeli commentators, post-Nazi Germany merely hid its old hostility to the Jews behind a fake pacifism. Saddam Hussein was compared to Hitler: the same cruelty, the same unpredictable disregard for logic or interest, the same indifference to the suffering of their own people, the illegal annexation of territory, even their fortified bunkers. The coalition organized against Iraq, the largest since World War II, reminded the Israeli press of the World War II Allies; and President George Bush spoke about two worlds, the democratic and the totalitarian, fighting each other again. The Palestinians in Judea and Samaria, dancing on their roofs at the sight of missiles falling over Tel-Aviv and Ramat-Gan, brought back the memory of Poles glad to see the Warsaw Ghetto burning. The American soldiers, operating the missile batteries in Israel, were the righteous of the nations. And most important of all, the passive role played by Israel in the Gulf War was a reminder of the situation in which Jewish communities in Nazi-occupied Europe were cornered: Israeli society found itself in a position awkwardly similar to that of the Jews of Europe, and the question of former attitudes toward them was a central issue during those weeks.[31]

The reaction of Israeli society to this war struck the survivor and many of his friends. The new, "in," Americanized way of talking and exhibiting one's feelings and fears, shared by many Israeli youngsters, was seen by survivors as a kind of dandyism of spoiled children. People brought up between the wars, or during the Nazi period, cherished self-discipline and strict education. Moving down to Eilat, as many young families did during the Gulf War, or transferring the family to Jerusalem and commuting there daily, seemed to go against Zionism:

> we, the survivors, are the true Zionists of today, because we know it means standing up against fears, against those who attack you, and it certainly means never abandoning your place in Israel, come what may. We know, more than Sabras, more than newcomers from other countries and situations, the value of a Jewish state, in itself and as a compensation for former Jewish helplessness. Each of us witnessed such horrors and suffering, both as a result of a gigantic world war and of the anti-Jewish Nazi policies, that now a few bombs that destroyed a few buildings here and there, or being confined to your place for just a few weeks, and in your own country, seem to us a children's game.[32]

In his book, *Shoa in the Sealed Room*, the historian of ideas Moshe Zuckermann brilliantly analyzed the Israeli press and its reference to the Holocaust during the Gulf War. His findings show that our survivor had an observant eye. Though there was no uniform reaction of Holocaust survivors, and though some survivors reacted very emotionally (up to and including closing themselves in their rooms with food that could suffice for a year), a survey then revealed, to the surprise of many, that "Holocaust survivors and their families show the lowest level of anxiety compared to other groups in the population."[33]

Moreover, following the war, psychologists began questioning psychological theories developed since the mid-seventies regarding the effect of the Holocaust on survivors and their families. After some thirty years of minimizing the mental effect of the Holocaust, the tide turned in the mid-seventies, and a flood of research and treatment reports caused an "over generalization causing factors of behavior, not necessarily connected to the Holocaust [to be] attributed to it." Psychology researcher Amichai Levi ascribed this "professional historic error" to the consensus in society at large, which the psychologists and historians reflected. Could it then be, asked Nizan Yaniv, Levi's colleague, that the Gulf War brought about a new professional historic mistake, a continuation of the first, and that the mental impact of missiles on the general population and on the survivors was overemphasized?[34]

The younger generations who had not witnessed a large-scale war, let alone a Holocaust, and did not know what to expect, were more vulnerable to fears and wild imaginings. The unknown is worse, especially when the collective national history exerts a deeper influence than has been anticipated. The descriptions of the Holocaust in Israeli education and public life took their toll in the war, when the inner fears previously instilled in persons "who were not there," as the local expression for nonsurvivors goes, came forth. Constant comparisons to the Second World War increased these anxieties. "In normal times historical images are domesticated, and in times of crises they go wild," wrote historian Saul Friedlander.[35] "There is no proportion between the level of fear . . . and the reality that nourished it," observed a younger historian, Yechiam Weitz.[36]

Not only did the survivors show strength, they were proud for the first time of being ahead of the rest. They were "those who were there," who knew all there was to know about gas and bombing and shattered buildings and insecurity. They could not be frightened again by trifles: "I will never wear a mask"; "I lost my ability to be afraid"; "Hitler did not wipe me out, and a Pisher (wimp) such as Hussein certainly will not." Suddenly, being a survivor was an advantage, and survivors did not fail to emphasize this. Moreover, Israel's leaders, despite having an air force eager to attack the H–3 zone in place of the Allies, decided that it was in Israel's interest to let others defend it because of political constraints. This was outright proof that passivity is not necessarily an outcome of Diaspora characteristics. It was simply a calculated measure that has to be taken in certain situations, regardless of the eagerness to act otherwise.

"Yes, It Happened to Us as Well," was the title of a newspaper article published ten days after the war started:[37]

> Our attitude to the Jews murdered in the Holocaust, an attitude of hard-hearted vanity mixed with insecurity and anxiety, changed considerably. It became more sober, human, and soft, a lot less 'Israeli,' a lot more 'Jewish.' The certainty that 'it will not happen to us' has turned into a realization that 'it did happen to us. . . . In this respect, the recent events are one more step in the process of changing our attitude [to] . . . the Jewish reaction in the war. The Jews of Europe took from us, perhaps finally, the status we assumed we deserved, the status of judges sitting, cold and distant, on the high bench, issuing a verdict on millions of Jews.

And the main point:

> Now we cannot escape the conclusion that it is hardly conceivable that a public under stress would react with heroism. Such a reaction is open only for an elite, and it does not

come immediately. . . . The present events will accelerate the process of reconciliation with a past, in which fear was not dandyism—it was a fear of real death.

Let us return now to the question of timing: Why is it that Barak and Bartov and Tory spoke louder and clearer than ever before, or indeed for the first time? And why were the two books initiated by ex-Brigade soldiers with introductions written by President Herzog only recently published? Some of the reasons for the change in Israeli attitudes to the survivors have already been mentioned:

–The more complicated wars in the Middle East became, the more the complexity of the situation in Nazi-occupied Europe became understandable and empathy toward other Jews in distress increased.
–Following the Yom Kippur War a process of self-examination encompassed the history of Zionism since its very beginning, including the Holocaust.
–The de-heroization in post–World War II Western culture reached Israel as well: from the collective to the individual, from the ideological to the material, from the hero to the man-in-the-street. Therefore, more interest was taken in the plight of survivors as individuals and not only as representatives of a community or a nation.
–Social and political changes in Israel also contributed to the change. Ben-Gurion's ideas of "statehood" that required a new generation, heroic and victorious, and secular socialism, also looking for a new man, were gradually replaced by a growing tendency to return to Jewish roots and thereby to the culture of the Jews in the Diaspora, including Europe during the Holocaust.
–The more Israel became an established fact, and the more the peace process developed following the many wars, the less important became the need to cling to heroism as a focus of symbolism and education. In other words, the thorns needed to protect Zionism at its beginnings, and needed to foster a new clear-cut Israeli identity, could be softened.
–With the passage of time, survivors, one out of four in the local population at the beginning of the fifties, grew again, with their families, to about a sixth of the population.[38] Moreover, it seems that this group is one of the strongest in society, having recovered, integrated, rebuilt their lives, and contributed to "postcatastrophic Zionism." When the "each person has a name" ceremony took place in the Knesset on Holocaust Memorial Day of 1995, most of the country's leadership stood there, either to commemorate relatives, or as survivors, such as Supreme Court President Aharon Barak, once a child in the Kovno Ghetto; or Shevach Weiss, Speaker of the House, who spent two years in hiding; or Chief Rabbi Israel Lau, once a child in Buchenwald. The list was long and impressive. The ceremony celebrated the transition from the collective to the individual with regard to the Holocaust: each of the six million had a name, and those names that are known should be read aloud.

Many of the above mentioned reasons are not a product of the nineties: they explain an evolutionary process which has only recently matured. Yet there is another major development in Israel in the 1990s: post-Zionism. This phenomenon, a local derivative of postmodernism, neither resembles the self-criticism that followed the

Yom Kippur War nor continues the ongoing debate about the history of Zionism. It is different, as sociologist Moshe Lisak put it, because it is an outright ideological attack intended to present Israel as born in sin and based on antagonism toward Arabs, toward the Diaspora Jews, toward newcomers. A state built on such immorality has no right to exist. Among the many sins that post-Zionists pinpoint are the attitudes of the Yishuv, and later Israeli society, toward the Jews of Nazi-occupied Europe and the survivors of the Holocaust: politics and national manipulation motivated the effort to bring the survivors to Israel, they were needed to create Zionist myths and justifications, but they did not count as persons, and their own needs were coldly ignored.[39]

Let us raise the possibility that the texts we have dealt with are reactions to post-Zionist attacks. Their subtexts carry clear messages. Barak admits that a mythology of heroism was needed in the first years of the state to build a new image. Never promoted cynically, present-day Israel can afford to do without it, implying a more correct attitude to the survivors. Bartov, with no official position, was free to speak more openly and less elaborately: "Who forgot? Who ignored his own flesh and blood? Who did not remember, and who did not write?" he painfully asked a group of students.[40] He wants to present his generation as that which met the survivors and carried them home "on their shoulders,"[41] fought the War of Independence, and opened the country for the flood of refugees from Muslim countries. It was a generation with positive values, sensitive, dedicated, ready to sacrifice. The state it built was based on solid foundations, said Herzog. The moral base of the state and its Jewish solidarity were shaped by the Holocaust and the encounter with the survivors; to say the opposite is to distort the historical truth.

The confrontation between the post-Zionists and their opponents is perhaps the most important debate in this debate-ridden society. Our sources may be insufficient as a basis for generalizations. But the feeling that the basics of life in Israel were being attacked is common to all of them. No one can tell now, in the middle of the 1990s, how far the post-Zionist impact will reach, or how far the opposition will go to defend the foundations of their beliefs. But as far as one can say now, it seems that the small group of post-Zionists will face strong opposition because they attack the existential foundations, the raison d'être, of Israel.

NOTES

All works cited are in Hebrew.

1. The following are but a few examples from the 1990s: *A Broken Cloud*, a documentary by film director Orna Ben-Dor Niv, 1992; and Irit R. Kupper, *The Gate of Immigration* (Tel Aviv, 1991), a memoir. On August 7 and 14, 1995, Israeli TV broadcast the documentary "The Seventh Million: The Israelis and the Holocaust," based on Tom Segev's book of that title (Jerusalem, 1991). The two-part documentary was followed by an exceptionally stormy debate, the two opposite opinions being most sharply presented by author Yehudit Hendel and poet Haim Guri.

2. On this "common knowledge," see Gershon Shaked in *Leshon Hamarot* (The language

of the sights), a 1994 TV documentary series on Hebrew literature reflecting the history of the country. See also Hanna Yablonka, *Foreign Brethren* (Jerusalem, 1995).

3. *Bamachane* (In the camp, the IDF soldiers monthly), April 15, 1992, pp. 22–25.

4. About 330,000 survivors reached Israel between 1948 and 1953. In order to assess their numbers today, and the size of their families, one should take into consideration that about 77,000 survivors left the country between 1946 and 1956, that some passed away, some never married, many married other survivors, and that survivors have generally a small number of offspring. Taking these factors into consideration, the survivors' families today number about 800,000, or a sixth of the Israeli Jewish population (about 4.8 million). Between the two world wars, 350,000 immigrants came from Europe to the land that became Israel. Most lost the majority of their families. Together with the new members of their families in Israel, and the survivors' families, they constitute 35 percent of the current Jewish population in Israel. Calculations are based on Benjamin Gil, *Pages of Immigration: 30 Years of Immigration to Palestine, 1919–1949* (Jerusalem, 1950); annual publication of the central bureau of statistics, 1950, pp. 29–37, and 1951, pp. 24–30; Moshe Sikron, *Immigration to Israel, 1948–1953*, Special Series of the Falk Project, no. 60 (Jerusalem, 1958), p. 23; *Central Bureau of Statistics, Census Series* (Jerusalem, 1961), no. 13, table 3; *Hebrew Encyclopedia* (Jerusalem, 1957) vol. 6, pp. 667–70; Meir Dvorzecki, "The Survivors in Israel," *Gesher* 2/1 (Jerusalem, 1956), especially pp. 85–88, based on data collected by the Ministry of Health and the Kupat-Holim (public health care) stations.

5. See the introduction to poet Haim Guri's book on the Eichmann Trial, *Mul Ta Hazechuchit* (Facing the glass cell) (Tel Aviv, 1962), and his credo expressed on August 7, 1995 (see note 1 above).

6. Ya'acov Robinson, *Vehaya He'akov Lemishor* (And the crooked shall be straight) (Jerusalem, 1967), written in response to Hannah Arendt and Raul Hilberg, who expressed such opinions in 1961.

7. See especially debates in the Knesset regarding a suitable date for Holocaust Memorial Day, for example, the discussion on April 12, 1951. See *Divrei Haknesset* (minutes), Jerusalem, meeting 250, vol. 9, p. 1656.

8. Nathan Alterman, *Between Two Roads: Selections from a Diary*, ed. Dan Laor (Tel Aviv, 1989).

9. The Yad Vashem "Holocaust and Heroism Remembrance Day Law" of 1953, Articles 1 and 3B.

10. The most famous example is Haim Guri's poem, "Min Hadleika Hahi" (From that fire), first published in *Sefer Milhanot Hagetaot* (Tel Aviv, 1996), p. 696.

11. See Yehuda Bauer in *Ha'aretz*, April 28, 1992.

12. I interviewed General Barak on April 17, 1992, following publication of his speech.

13. Ibid.

14. April 29, 1992, at Masua, a center for the study and commemoration of the Holocaust in Kibbutz Tel-Yitzhak. Thanks to Ayala Ben-Naftali, the director, for the text.

15. See, for example, David Ben-Gurion in a Mapai Center meeting, July 22–23, 1949, Labor Party Archives 24/49 and *Ha'aretz*, September 28, 1945, p. 3.

16. Bartov spoke to master's degree students of mine and of Dan Laor at Tel Aviv University on December 23, 1991. His testimony was published first in *Eton 77*, nos. 144–45 (January–February 1992), and then in *I Am Not the Mythological Sabra* (Tel Aviv, 1995), pp. 26–36.

17. Ibid., p. 26.

18. Ibid., pp. 31–32.

19. See Levi Arye Sarid, "The Nakam [Revenge] Organization: History, Image, Deeds," *Yalkut Moreshet* 52 (April 1992): 35–43, on the desire for revenge.

20. Bartov, *I Am Not the Mythological Sabra*, pp. 33–34.

21. Ibid., pp. 34–35.

22. Ibid., "Here, On This Mountain" (on Mount Scopus), pp. 336–37 and note 4.

23. David Ben-Gurion, chairman of the Jewish Agency Executive during the Holocaust,

said time and again: "Without European Jewry there is no Zionism and no Yishuv." See Dina Porat, "Ben-Gurion and the Holocaust," in *David Ben-Gurion: Politics and Leadership in Israel*, ed. Ronald W. Zweig (London, 1991), pp. 145–70.

24. Bartov, *I Am Not the Mythological Sabra*, pp. 334, 341.

25. Ibid., p. 34.

26. Mordechay Naor, *A Living Bridge* (Tel Aviv, 1993), so entitled because the survivors crossed a river in northern Italy over the backs of the Brigade soldiers.

27. *The Encounter: Jewish Liberators and Survivors Meet in the Wake of World War II* (Tel Aviv, 1993).

28. Ibid., pp. 7–8.

29. Ibid., p. 30 (Supreme Court Judge Moshe Beisky, a survivor).

30. Conversation with Avraham Tory, February 1991. To verify his claims I spoke to twenty-five other survivors; all agreed wholeheartedly.

31. See Moshe Zuckermann, *Shoah in the Sealed Room: The "Holocaust" in the Israeli Press during the Gulf War* (Tel Aviv, 1993), especially chapters 6 and 8, for comparisons between World War II and the Gulf War.

32. Conversation with Tory.

33. Zuckerman, *Shoah*, p. 116.

34. Nizan Yaniv, "Is There a Mental Impact of the Gulf War?" *Mirkachton* (supplement to *Ha'aretz*), July 10, 1995, p. 10.

35. *Davar*, February 15, 1991.

36. *Davar*, January 25, 1991.

37. Ibid.

38. See note 4 above.

39. For a sound summary of post-Zionism, see Dan Michman, "The Smashers of Zionism," *Mimad* 5 (August–September 1995). Sociologist Moshe Lisak wrote "On the Sin We Sinned in Establishing the State," *Davar*, June 18, 1994.

40. See note 16 above.

41. See Nathan Altermann, *The Seventh Column* (Tel Aviv, 1948), p. 121. The expression, "they carried their people on their shoulders," referred to the Ha'apala, Yishuv's illegal transfer of survivors to shore from 1945 to 1948.

54.

DORI LAUB WITH MARJORIE ALLARD

History, Memory, and Truth

DEFINING THE PLACE OF THE SURVIVOR

The Non-Place of the Survivor

This examination deals with the role of clinical *listening* in survivor testimony; it is about testimony itself, its promises and its hazards. It is also about the formulation of the essence of the survivor experience and thus attempts to define a place for the survivor.

We speak of the need to *create* a place for the survivor because, from a psychologically experiential perspective, such a place has never yet existed. The nature of massive trauma and the persistence of its effects preclude such a place. This is true for three times: for the past, when the survivor's experience was contemporaneous with the event; for the present, when it is dealt with as memory; and for the future, where it will be part of the mosaic, a legacy still unfolding.

Trauma is about having lost one's place, both in the reality of life and in the context of a dyad, of a relationship to an "other" who offers an empathic presence. Facing the executioner, one had no place. One had no existence. The executioner relentlessly proceeded no matter how strong the plea for life. In the face of this negation of one's place, one's right to live—of life itself—all connection to the world and all relation to humanity was lost. Jean Améry, a survivor of Auschwitz who was tortured by the Gestapo, observed:

> Trust in the world includes . . . the certainty that the other person will spare me . . . that he will respect my physical and metaphysical being. . . . The expectation of help, the certainty of help, is indeed one of the fundamental experiences of human beings. . . . But with the first blow . . . against which there can be no defense and which no helping hand will ward off . . . *[one] can no longer feel at home in the world.*[1] (Emphasis mine)

It is interesting to note the pivotal text in Genesis where Paradise is lost once the threshold of knowing is crossed. This text provides us with a paradigm both for the experience of trauma and for the experience of exile from oneself. Once the threshold of knowing good and evil is crossed (and it is "evil" and not "good" that is being newly discovered), the garden is no longer one's place. A much more precarious and painful existence lies ahead. In the same view, a home can never be a home again after trauma, and an erased relationship can never provide safety. When asked which country he considered his home, Claude Lanzmann, a resistance fighter during the war and the director of *Shoah*, replied, "My film is my country."[2] His reply indicates that it is only in the retrieval of memory and in the creation of testimonies that the place can be reclaimed. Without this witnessing there is a repeated and continuous wandering from place to place, and no place can be home without truth being established.

Thus, the task at hand is to define a place for the survivor in history, in memory, in present life, and in future aspirations. The question to be addressed is how one embarks on this arduous journey. How can survivors and their witnesses accomplish this? What can scholars from different disciplines, and in particular clinicians trained to be listeners, contribute to this arduous pursuit of historical truth, which is the only authentic route through which one can re-find a place, rebuild a home.

Displaced People, a History not Locatable

In his essay "Memory and Monument," James E. Young outlines the significance of aspects of the physical layout of Yad Vashem in Jerusalem: in the exhibition, the visitor has to leave one room, which recounts the history of the Jewish people in Europe until 1942, in order to reach another room, which houses the exhibit on the death camps. This physical dislocation from one room to the next marks the rupture that the Holocaust represents in the traditional chronology of the Jewish people, as well as its challenge to the very notion of historical chronology.[3] The deaths of six million people can be recorded only as a break in history, as a gap in understanding and in the continuation of time that cannot be bridged. The devastation is marked only by an absence, by this rupture that cannot be bridged.

The Holocaust exists both inside and outside history. It exists as part of the world's history, as a reality we cannot ignore, yet it exists also as a challenge to our understanding of history, to any belief in progress or civilization. The character and magnitude of the crime defies any attempt to locate it within any one place or time. It is a crime without a statute of limitations, whose repercussions on the lives of survivors and their children, on the future of the world itself, continue to be spelled out today. The Holocaust exists as the unassimilable core of Western history. Once the Holocaust happened, once the threshold of that kind of massive destruction was crossed, derivatives and re-crossings of that threshold can occur again and can model themselves after Holocaust events. In these terms, we can think of the "ethnic cleansing" in Bosnia as an aftermath of the Holocaust, as a derivative, however distorted. While it is important not to draw parallels too directly, or to see similar events as exactly alike, these more recent atrocities justifiably evoke a sense of déjà vu. As atrocities against humans and against the essence of civilization continue to be perpetrated around the world, the tragedy of failed empathy and the reverberations of the Holocaust continue to play themselves out in our culture's conscious and unconscious traumatic memory.

By definition, the Nazi crime of genocide—the crime against humanity—against the essence of what it is to be human—is itself a crime perpetrated against the existence of the past and the possibility of a future. There were to be no traces of the crime left, no traces of the bodies burned, no traces of the thriving Jewish life that had existed for generations. There was to be no future for the Jewish people. All continuity was to be broken, all places were to be destroyed.

As a clinician, my observation is that psychologically, experientially speaking, the Nazi verdict remains in effect. To the survivor the Holocaust is not "past," it did not end at "liberation"; time does not "heal all wounds." The executioner's verdict was not lifted, it was merely postponed. "We were reprieved dead men," Filip Müller says in Lanzmann's film *Shoah*,[4] a section of which deals with the Sonderkommando; and that sense of reprieval, never fully owned, continues in survivors' vague yet compelling sense that they are living on borrowed time in a state of suspended, shared execution.

Just as the future seems impossible to the survivor, so too the past seems impossible to return to. In the attempt to resurrect an empathic tie, the survivor turns inward to prewar memories, for that is the "only place he knows of where a whole, hale world exists." Yet this attempt at self-healing through remembering will be seriously compromised in the survivor by the fact that neither selective remembrance nor selective repression works after massive psychic trauma. No matter how persistent the attempt at recapture, that benevolent past will always be associated with the circumstances of its destruction and loss. This is because the enormity of the evil overburdens and outweighs the ego's reservoir of positive imagery and prevents the separation of positive from negative images. The event, therefore, not only retroactively affects the past, but it proactively contaminates all previous and subsequent events, compromising the healing ability of post-traumatic experience. The imagery of genocide remains indelible, unassimilated, and paralyzing; it continuously intrudes upon the survivor's thoughts.

Even the physical places bear the contamination of this genocide, of a verdict still in operation. Europe today, and in particular Eastern Europe, remains a site of massive death. Among the empty fields and the desecrated synagogues and Jewish homes are the traces of a crime intended to destroy the very principle of life. These are the "non-places of memory."[5] They are empty, they reveal nothing of what has occurred in their midst. The markers are almost all ideological abstractions, giving no hint of the identity of the families, children, men, and women who died there. They act mostly as erasures, as foreclosures to knowing. The physical places of Auschwitz, Birkenau, Babi Yar, Bergen-Belsen are almost as "Judenrein" as the perpetrators themselves wanted,[6] and the *presence* of Jews in Europe is marked mostly by an *absence*, by a lack of place.

The Jewish survivor exists only as an abstraction in these national memories, as a statistic, or as an ideology. The survivor's experience has no place in the myth of the French as a nation of "fighters for the Résistance," of the Poles as martyrs for the socialist cause, or in particular of the Germans as a people on which a tyrannical regime was inflicted. There is no place for personal history, for personal testimony in these myths of national memory. There is only an endless forgetting. It is only in the intimacy of the personal testimonies of Jewish survivors that the richness, the authenticity of a deep subjective historical truth emerges, a truth that can be found nowhere else, and is often at odds with formal historical accounts.

When Elie Wiesel told Ronald Reagan before the president's visit to Bitburg: "That place is not your place," his words, as Geoffrey Hartman noted, resonated with a meaning beyond themselves. If the president of the United States can so betray history, if the country can show such an eagerness to forget, then "this place," the United States, is also not the survivor's place, and can never be.[7]

The Loss of Place: Locating the Trace

For Holocaust survivors, the shadow cast by the Nazi verdict of annihilation is not limited to a specific time and place. It extends into the future, haunting the present and determining the structure of life. It is as though this experience, that can be neither known nor represented, has profoundly and irrevocably transformed one's identity, and the rest of one's life becomes engulfed in painfully missing what one was and what one has lost, in a futile attempt to return to that sense of place through one's own life and the lives of one's children. There is no grave for the children and grandchildren to visit, nothing to mark the unbearable loss. "I did not bury my family in Auschwitz," says one survivor, "I left them there." Her words testify to the impossibility of closure that is the survivor's destiny. Her words speak as well of the loss of home, of an exile from which there can be no return. The loss of place is a loss of home, an alienation of self, a loss of language itself that speaks of more than just having lost one's "native tongue." It is the loss of the very foundation of identity, the very basis of self. Home represents order, security, and trust. "Home is the land of one's childhood and youth," Améry states; "whoever has lost it remains lost himself."[8]

This loss of place has its outer signifiers in the physical states of the survivor—in the deportations, the displaced person's camp, the statelessness, and the out-of-placeness that defined and still defines the survivor's existence. Yet it has its most powerful manifestations in the survivor's own self-observing comments of feeling dead, of not believing the reality of what happened, and of perpetually feeling estranged, distant, and "other." The testimony is to an *absence*, to an event that has not yet come into existence because the person who lived through it does not know it and does not grasp it. For us, as listeners, it is a question of listening through the train of silence to the black hole of knowledge, to the wordless reenactment of this historical event that continues to evolve beyond the silence.

In the field of psychoanalysis, a myriad of psychological mechanisms related to the experience of facing death and of surviving—such as numbing, denial, derealization, freezing, survivor guilt—have been repeatedly invoked to address various stages of the survivor experience. Yet these theoretical mechanisms, while helpful, are inadequate. While events have been and are perceived by the survivor at a certain level, the degree to which they become an inner mental representation and, therefore, a *real* memory, remains very much in question. Because of the radical break between trauma and culture, victims often cannot find categories of thought or words to contain or give shape to their experience. That is, since neither culture nor past experiences provide structures for formulating acts of massive destruction, survivors cannot articulate trauma even to themselves. A great deal of witnessing, and self-witnessing, with the help of an empathic listener, is currently taking place—a radical process of evolving knowledge that spans generations, as evidenced in the proliferation of memoirs and other writings that began only recently, almost fifty years after the event. It is a process that takes place across the boundaries of time and our traditional modes of understanding and that requires a rethinking of the relationship between history, trauma, and place.

Failed Empathy and the Loss of the Internal and External Other

In all situations, people take a certain amount of empathy for granted. In the concentration camps, this basic assumption was disproved. The sadistic and bureaucratically sanctioned killing that characterized the Nazi genocidal system depended on the severance of this psychological basis for life, of the connection between "I" and "you." The Nazi belief system defined the Jewish race as a different species; it sanctioned the radical negation of the other. An empathic response was absent not only from the Nazis but from the bystanders and Allies as well (i.e., from society at large). A hitherto unimaginable nightmare crossed the threshold into reality.[9]

When people prove to be evil on such a massive scale, the survivor retains the memory of a *deficit*—of a compromise of the very possibility of an empathic dyad. Faith in the efficacy of communication dies, and intrapsychically there may no longer be a *matrix of two people*—self and resonating other. Such a life experience throws into question not only empathy and human communication, but also ultimately one's own humanity. As Primo Levi told us, "part of our existence lies in the feelings of those near to us. This is why the experience of someone who has lived for days (or for years) during which man was merely a thing in the eyes of man, is a non-human experience."[10] Confronted by this massive failure of empathy, life appears only as an endless dying or as a long struggle to rid oneself of the image created by the perpetrator—*not a negative self-image but an image of the self as non-human and hence with no links to humanity.* In this context, we quote the interpretation made by a psychoanalyst to a survivor patient: "Hitler's crime was not only the killing of the Jews but getting the Jews to believe that they deserved it." At the center of the victim's survival is the enigma of having *survived*, of having somehow lived beyond the internalized verdict, yet still feeling its weight upon one's life. It is the enigma of a life that cannot be claimed, of a survival that cannot be owned.

The natural outcome of the radical failure of empathy is a profound loneliness that consumes one's internal world representation. To be a survivor is to be utterly and unbearably alone. It is to suffer the feeling of "being the last person on earth," as it is expressed by Simon Srebnik in Lanzmann's film, to be a witness to a devastation that can be recorded only as an absence, as the impossibility of connection. The survivor's dread of remembering is linked to the fear of "discovering again that he is alone in the world—that the world has gone and is always going away from him."[11] Despite the need to rebuild the link to the "other," to repair the empathic dyad that the failure of empathy destroyed, the survivor often finds himself unable to connect to this new and alien world that he or she is supposed to "belong" to. As a survivor, he belongs among this world of the living. Yet as a victim he feels himself connected only to the dead. The survivor survives only as an impossible "I," absolutely alone, without any feeling of a "thou" who could be addressed. "After Auschwitz," states

Jean Améry, "I was a person who could no longer say "we" and who therefore said "I" merely out of habit, but not with the feeling of full possession of myself."[12]

In *Shoah*, Filip Müller speaks of this irrevocable loss of community. A worker in the Sonderkommando, he sees the Czech family transport in the gas chambers and decides that life is no longer worth living, that it is "meaningless." He attempts *to take his place* with his countrymen, but some of the women recognize him and push him out: "One of them said: 'So you want to die. But that's senseless. Your death won't give us back our lives. That's no way. You must get out of here alive. You must bear witness to our suffering, and to the injustice done to us.'"[13]

Müller's survival is possible only through expulsion from the community, an expulsion that carries with it overtones of an expulsion from a family, with the women—the mothers, the caretakers—pushing him out to save him from a death that is "senseless" in order to live a life that seems to him equally "senseless." Similarly, later in the film, Rudolf Vrba speaks of his decision to leave the community in Auschwitz for which, as a resistance leader in the camp, he felt "co-responsible at the time," in order to "inform the world" of what was happening.[14]

That Müller and Vrba must leave their community in order to bear witness illustrates the central paradox of the act of witnessing. To witness, one must live. Yet to live, one must leave the community of the dead, the "we" that makes communication and dialogue possible. Where does one find the "thou" to address, the response to one's own testimony? The voices that call to the survivor—the voices with whom he can share most of what is alive to him—are the voices of the dead, the voices that must be left behind.

Thrown into a future he or she cannot own, into a world that cannot or will not understand, the survivor feels encircled by his isolation. Survivors described coming to new communities after the war that did not offer means for sharing, telling, or even memorializing their experiences. The public silence was often paralleled by private silence in the individual, personal encounters. One survivor recalled how one day while putting her little boy to bed he asked, "How did Grandpa and Grandma die?" When she explained they had been murdered, he asked, "You mean like cowboys and Indians, bang, bang?" Horrified at the inability of the listener to comprehend the enormity of her loss, and at the gap between listener (son) and survivor, she resolved never to speak of her experiences again, at least not until her son was old enough to comprehend. "How do you convey the loss of an entire world?" she asked us.

Similarly, Chaim Guri's film *The Eighty-First Blow* portrays a man who narrates the story of his sufferings in the camps only to hear his audience say: "All this cannot be true, it could not have happened. You must have made it up." This denial by the listener inflicts, according to the film, the ultimately fateful blow, beyond the eighty that a man, in Jewish tradition, can sustain and survive. The absence of an empathic listener, or more radically, the absence of an *addressable other*, an other who can hear the anguish of one's memories and thus recognize their realness, annihilates the story and destroys the survivor once again.

Fearful of this mortal eighty-first blow, of another devastating betrayal and failure of empathy, many survivors choose silence and isolation and stop trying to connect to a life that seems so impossible to live. Intense experiences and feelings need to be avoided because the individual is so helpless to deal with them. In this void, the self—its cohesiveness over time, and its ability to integrate and make sense—eventually suffer, and the vulnerability to external experience and to internal emotion increases. One feels too brittle, too vulnerable to partake of life.

One survivor we interviewed poignantly summarized the sense of loneliness that has suffused his life since the war:

> In Auschwitz I still had the feeling of protectiveness as long as my father was standing behind me in the same commando. And there was suddenly an emptiness there once he was gone. . . . We were a big family, perhaps 60 people. . . . Wherever we went there were relatives. There is nothing there . . . an . . . emptiness. No more the home one had before. . . . And there is no longer the connection . . . the linkage is gone. I live now in a Jewish community with all the Jewish traditions—but nevertheless I live in an exile, estranged. . . . As if from one day to the next a chasm opened into which everything fell. . . . A wall of fog remained, through which I cannot penetrate. . . . I have no true friends. One can talk of everything with one's wife in a good marriage and I have a good marriage . . . and the wife tries to be there in my loneliness and my sadness. . . . But this cannot quite work because one still has a corner in the depth of one's heart where another cannot come close, not even one's wife . . . because this violent ending of one's youth, this violent extinguishing of a whole period that still lies before one's eyes, cannot be replaced—not even by one's own wife. . . . The absolute worst that happened to the one that survived is the feeling that he is totally isolated in this world. He stands totally alone. He had nobody—nobody near him in the good days and not in bad days. . . . When I talk about it I do not feel understood although I recognize the effort of those who try to understand me. . . . I can never feel protected enough to feel as a child again, feel unburdened enough to feel close. . . . This joy, this uninhibited joy, I must say I have no more.[15]

The form of other people is present, but the inner connection is difficult to experience.

The Haunting of the Present: Dislocation and Intergenerational Disconnection

Frequently, the survivor feels that if only he or she can get things as they were before, he or she will be able to experience a sense of putting things back in order. Toward that end, and in the effort to combat the deadness, the survivor searches for a new other who can be seen as a reincarnation of the caring companion who has been lost. Children, with their promise of rebirth, similarities to dead relatives, and the ability to rekindle a sense of trust and attachment often provide examples of construed opportunities for return of the beloved past. Every Jewish child born after the war is a "miracle," proof that Hitler's victory was not total.

Yet, the need to refuse Hitler a "posthumous victory," to evade the despair of the "second," or "continued" Holocaust, often consumes and distorts the survivor's relationship to his or her own child. There is no place for the child to be simply a child; it must be a "miracle," a denial of the past. In the words of one survivor, "I have children, I have a new family. But I can't take full satisfaction in the achievements of my children today because part of my present life is my remembrance, my memory of what happened there, and it casts a shadow over my life today." The shadow of the executioner continues to haunt the survivor and structure his relation to others. The traces of the first Holocaust shape survivors' reactions to subsequent losses, which likewise are experienced as totally devastating and without recourse.

This phenomenon of the "second Holocaust" is not limited to the first generation's experience; it exists as well in the world of the child of survivors. It exists in the anachronistic hold that the past claims upon the child's present, and in the child's continuation of the parents' death sentence by not allowing him or herself, whether through fear or loyalty, to live.

It is the child who finds himself compelled to experience more fully, or even amplify, the parents' suppressed feelings. The child echoes what exists in his parents' inner world; his inner reality thereby reveals the indelible marks left by the events of their time.

Nadine Fresco writes of the legacy that survivors pass on to their children. Her data comes from interviews with eight children of survivors:

> 'Then Papa and I got married and then you were born.' Before that 'then' was the gaping vertiginous black hole of the unmentionable years.

> Born after the war, because of the way they sometimes replaced a child who had died in the war, the Jews I am speaking of here felt their existences as a sort of exile, not from a place in the present or future, but from a time now gone forever, which would have been that of identity itself.

> They transmitted only the wound to the children, to whom the memory had been refused. . . . The silence formed like a heavy pall that weighed down on everyone. Parents explained nothing, children asked nothing. The forbidden memory of death manifested itself only in the form of incomprehensible attacks of pain.[16]

The children of survivors and their contemporaries were both more heavily burdened (from early in their lives) and less constrained from giving expression to their parents' conflicting emotions. Their distance from the experience itself, as well as the compelling quality of their heritage, make them inevitable spokesmen for it. It is the children who inherit the loss of place, the empty circle, and the ceaseless struggle to define oneself, to rebuild a home. In the words of one child of survivors, "I am a prisoner of an empty space."

For the children of survivors, the legacy of trauma is often experienced as a compelling force that determines their life but that has no conscious content. It is like a center of gravity for the direction or course that the individual's life takes, as the following case of a child survivor indicates:

> A young man was in a stalemate with analysis because of the spectacular book he wanted to write but could not. His mother was a survivor of Auschwitz. She considered herself to be the greatest sculptor in the world, while he considered himself the greatest writer. For both of them, this illusion had a life-saving quality. When the additional meaning of his grandiosity was clarified and allowed to make sense within its original Auschwitz context—in Auschwitz one would have to be special in order to have *any* hope for survival—the son could then proceed not only with the writing of the book, which was not spectacular, but also with his life.
>
> His personal response to this clarification was interesting. He told the story of the

oyster: as a wonderful creature, creating the pearl—a product of artistic beauty. It is a sculptor (like his mother). Yet at the center of the pearl is a grain of sand, around which the pearl forms. He commented: "The grain of sand that I am built around is Auschwitz."

Later in his analysis, the patient spoke of his emotional distance in relationships. He wondered if this distance was his father's distance from the family. His father had no place. But why did his father have no place? Was Mother ultimately the one who could not allow for a place to exist and was Father's distance simply his acquiescence in Mother's flight from intimacy because for Mother intimacy, being at home, meant pain. When talking of her family, all of which was killed in Auschwitz, she would say: "I can never speak it. I can never speak to you from that place. I can speak to you around it, about it."

The patient continued: "when I think of her talking to us this way, I imagine my brother and myself as being little kids and saying to one another 'If she cannot say it, we are really alone.'"

For the children of survivors, the "wound without memory,"[17] the empty circle that is transmitted without words, may take place as the very shape of their lives—as a sense of terror, woundedness, and loss that defies all comfort and resists all interpretation and understanding. Children of survivors may feel doomed to accept the delusional verdict of their inhumanity and fatedness in life and come to believe that they would have no chance if they tried to fight it.

For example, one man—we shall call him Isaac—relinquished in his twenties the hope to have a family and a career of his choice. He seemed to be following in the footsteps of his father, an Auschwitz survivor married to another survivor and divorced by that woman when Isaac was six years old. Isaac's father never recuperated from this "second Holocaust," this loss of the family he had built after his first one had been destroyed. Father felt, and indeed was, condemned by his ex-wife and her new husband. He made only a few attempts to rebuild the link with his two boys and it was only near the end of his life, after he had remarried to a woman who wrote children's stories, after he had begun a new life, that he was able to connect with the younger son, who had in the meantime himself married and had grandchildren for the bereaved father. Isaac, the older of the two boys, remained alienated from his father throughout the remainder of the latter's life. He was even too late, by only a few hours, in arriving at his father's death bed.

In spite of external successes, Isaac's life continued in the grip and in the shadow of the verdict of not having a life that his father had accepted and that his mother had both decreed and lived herself, through her own shadowy, absent emotional existence. Unable to commit to family life, having relinquished his childhood dreams of a career in art, he feels himself burdened by the legacy of disconnection and placelessness that his parents have left him.

What is striking in Isaac's experience is that his very distance from the Holocaust—the fact that he is not a survivor of the events themselves—seems to give him not more of a memory but *less*: "Children of survivors have much less than their parents. . . . My father had a past to recapture, but I have nothing."

His mother was a complete absence except for the times that she would hit him when he was growing up. It was a blank space, but this absence exerted intense power. It drew all other life into it, swallowed it up. It was like the black hole in which everything vanishes. What could life or the Nazis have done to her to make her like this? *His own view of life and absence of possibilities were simply a continuation of that very absence of his mother from life.*

The break and missed encounters in Isaac's life exceeded their individual ramifications and became the very elimination of the concept of the family in his memory and in his anticipation of the future: "I have no memory of a family," he says, "and I cannot create a family myself. . . . The Holocaust destroyed the idea of the family, it condemned it to nonexistence. . . . To create a family," he says, "would be like reinventing the wheel; I have no model for one, no memory of one."

The power of the Empty Circle is in its perpetuating itself, its emptiness and black hole, and in its paralyzing any effort for life. Unless this is interpreted to the patient as the experience of a repetition of the fate incurred at another time or by another generation, the patient will not take crucial steps in life and will continue to live as helplessly as he faced the mass murderers. The patient will continue to live in a world in which families and lives have no place, and within a time they themselves do not own.

It is only through an active claiming of one's own life, of one's own place, that the verdict can be lifted and life resume. It is only when the child can come into his or her own identity separate from the survivor parents and freed of the burdens of historical events, that the child can liberate both himself and his parents. The children of survivors must find their own way, in Isaac's words, "to live with the despair" created by the black hole of trauma. They must search and define their own place. When Isaac could accept this, he was indeed, for the first time in his life, able to fall in love with a woman with whom he intended to build a family.

Testimony: Inscribing the Other

Toward the end of her interview at the Fortunoff Video Archives for Holocaust Testimonies at Yale, one woman survivor stated: "We wanted to survive so as to live one day after Hitler, in order to be able to tell our story."[18] In listening to testimonies, and in working with survivors and their children, I came to believe that the opposite is equally true. The survivors needed to survive not only so that they could tell their story, they also needed to tell their story in order to survive. The urge to bear witness, to create knowledge in an audience via one's testimony, is intended ultimately to create knowledge in oneself from which life can proceed. The experience of failed empathy (of being abandoned by those turned persecutors, by bystanders, and ultimately by one's own internal other) is at the heart of the survivor's intolerable and overwhelming sense of aloneness; it structures the survivor's need to find a good other who can combat this sense of aloneness and who can refigure the survivor as a human being who has a place in the world. The listener embodies the return of the other. Thus, the latent meaning of the desire to bear witness is reparation of the impaired dyad in the imagined or attempted act of communicating. The wish is to reinvent the responsive other through testimony so as to reconstitute the self as *one who is heard*.

Accordingly, while survivors *wanted* to live one day longer than the war in order to tell, they *needed* this telling in order to go on living, for telling confirms who they are. The performative act of testimony that reinvents and reimagines the other also reconstitutes and restores the self. We, the listeners, make the witnessing happen. Bearing witness to a trauma is, in fact, a process that includes the listener. For the testimonial process to take place, there needs to be a bonding, the intimate and total presence of an *other* in the position of one who hears. Testimonies are not monologues; they cannot take place in solitude. The witnesses are talking to *somebody*, to somebody they have been awaiting for a long time.

Thus, it is the role and the responsibility of the listener—whether the listener be a family member, an interviewer, or a therapist—to be the empathic and responsive witness whom the survivor so desperately searches for. The listening stance of the other can alienate and depersonalize; or it can rehumanize by revealing a totally present, passionate listener who is interested, affected, and responsive to what he or she hears. Only the latter can help turn narrative into memory and prevent retraumatization. We recall a patient whose traumatic account moved his therapist to tears. Later he confessed that it was the therapist's crying with him that had broken through his unbearable loneliness.

The need is for a passionately present yet noninterfering listener, for a listener who respects the silence of the witnessing itself. The listener must identify him or herself as one who can precisely recognize and *meet* the victim's silence, who can recognize and meet around the black hole, the empty circle of the experience of trauma. What emerges from testimony, from this place of meeting, is a narrative that both listener/analyst and patient have been waiting for, a place of truth. It is as though the phantasmagoric sides to the experience have been conquered in a more human, comprehensible way, and the painful can now emerge and keep its place, thus making the circle whole.

In essence, it is a progression from interpretation of fragmentary, defensive reenactments—a personalized, arrested state of "possessedness" by trauma—to a knowing of the realness of trauma that has occurred in a specific time and place, that allows one to negotiate a place for trauma vis-à-vis one's life so that it can become part of the flow of life, and thus allow life, in turn, to be more whole again.

Trauma and Art: The Crisis of Truth

The survivor's struggle to communicate is depicted in the poetry and prose of Paul Celan, who likened poetry to a handshake: it is a form of sharing and mutual recognition that asserts the integrity of relation and personal memory. An "urge to reach some 'other' obsessed Celan, some *du* (which is 'thou' or 'you')—the word occurs in [four hundred] of his poems . . . which come to us terse and compelled, seeking a listener, an other, seeking recognition."[19] At the same time, however, Celan's poems almost defy that which they seek. Celan's hermetically sealed poems, which seem to invite dialogue, also by their very opaqueness, criticize and thwart it. That is because after the Holocaust, although the survivor may yearn for or even invite dialogue, the survivor cannot assume it. The efficacy of communication and of intersubjectivity is no longer a given. Accordingly, Celan also likened poetry in his "Bremen Speech" to "a dialogue . . . a message in a bottle, sent off in the (not always greatly hopeful) belief that it may somehow wash up somewhere, perhaps on the shoreline of the heart." Poems are then an address, a movement en route toward "something open, inhabitable, an approachable you, perhaps an approachable reality," a search for a place that perhaps cannot ever be found.[20]

Paul Celan committed suicide in 1970 by jumping into the Seine. His death and his art testify both to the burdens and the complexities of speech. In the core of trauma is the empty circle, an absence undefinable and unrepresentable, the "black hole." When there is no internal dialogue, there is no narrative and therefore no representation. It may very well be that the core of trauma does not lend itself to recall, analysis, or representation because the experience itself extends so far beyond the parameters that define human experience. Anyone crossing these boundaries of the unspeakable cannot necessarily return.

The reader of Paul Celan's poems is held captive, a perennial audience who can never fully finish with the text and move on, a position hauntingly similar to the placeless, timeless state of the survivor, who is trapped in a past that is hauntingly ever present, defeating any attempts to fully master or be done with it. Yet ultimately, the poems themselves gesture through their very opaqueness and confusion to a truth which lies beyond representation, beyond the silence imposed by Celan's death. Demanding constant reinterpretation, they insist upon an engagement of the reader, an engagement that is constructed in the space between words, in the space between poet and poem, between reader and text.

The silences of Paul Celan's poetry are echoed in the absences of Claude Lanzmann's film *Shoah*. In the film there is nothing to see. The camera circles the abandoned barracks in Auschwitz, the wildflowers that overrun Birkenau, the empty fields of Chełmno. . . . "It's hard to recognize, but it was here," Simon Srebnik, a survivor, says at the beginning of the film. "Yes, this is the place. . . . There were two huge ovens, and afterward the bodies were thrown into these ovens and the flames reached to the sky." "To the sky," Lanzmann repeats, and the camera moves upward to the pale blue sky, silent and empty.[21]

This moment is an important one. Something happens. The camera pans the landscape, beautiful and silent, empty, haunted by the ghosts. It testifies to an absence and to a horror that cannot be represented but that are received by the viewer. The memory exists not in the empty fields but in the words that animate the place, that haunt the silence. It is there, in the words, *the telling*, and in the reenactments, *that the place of the survivor exists*. It is there, in the space created by testimony, a human space, that truth resides.

Where does one find a home for the homeless? A place for the displaced? A present for the dislocated? After the destruction of the Second Temple, the Jewish people no longer had a physical home. It was the sages' relentless engagement, generation after generation, for millennia, with the ancient texts, the unquenchable thirst for learning and for knowledge that provided sustenance to the Jewish people, a spiritual home and eventually a return to its physical homeland. In Exodus 25:22 God instructs the people to build an ark of the covenant and to place at its four corners four cherubim standing facing "man to his brother." It is there in the space created by these cherubim, in the emptiness between them, that God "will dwell." It is there in the space not created by representation, but created within the absence marked out and gestured at by the cherubim, in the silences between words, that God exists. It is in this space, a space defined as a human space, man to his brother, one to the other, in the space defined by the empathic response, the reflection of self to other, that Truth resides.

The Return of Memory: Defining a Space

In the last few years we have witnessed a proliferation of Holocaust-related books, museums, monuments, and conferences. The child survivor organization came into existence with thousands of members all over the world. In Israel, AMCHA addresses the psychological and social needs of thousands of survivors and their children.

It is a phenomenon that is hard to understand or explain, but it is undeniably related to this vital need to testify for the purposes of survival. A new enriched truth emerges from a variety of sources. How can we ensure that this is not a transitory phenomenon that passes like a fad? How can we protect what is valuable in this new emerging truth so that it can remain an integral part of our lives? It is our duty to ourselves and our children to be open and responsive to these very unique and special times. The ugly forces of oblivion have gained strength in recent years. A single conference, no matter how enriching, even if it is followed by a publication, does not ensure that this truth will continue to be sustained. This truth poses difficulty to knowing. A place needs to be created—a space both physical and human—in which this truth can continuously be remade, rediscovered, and relearned. It is only through such personal rediscovery that one comes to own it.

The United States Holocaust Memorial Museum is such a place. It creates a locus for Holocaust studies and places the United States in the forefront of recognizing the responsibility of future generations to remember and to bear witness. Yet, the creation of this museum carries with it an enormous burden of responsibility. The physical building is only half the idea of the "place"; it still requires the presence of students, scholars, and listeners, in order to animate it, to make it a true place of meeting, of witnessing. Today, we face a challenge to our abilities to listen and to act.

The need to create a place of meeting carries with it the responsibility to accept all of the challenges and burden that such a place entails. A new international, interdisciplinary group for the study of genocide, violence, and trauma, composed of professionals in the United States and abroad, is now reaching far beyond academia to accrue knowledge that can be directly applied to major issues affecting survivors' daily personal, communal, and political life. The impetus for this work comes from the recognition of the need for an interdisciplinary approach to these issues, where the different disciplines of history, philosophy, the social sciences, psychiatry, psychology, literature, film, and law can meet with one another and dialogue can take place. At Yale this process of interdisciplinary work has already begun to take place through individual research, classes, and conferences, often focused around the resources of Yale's Fortunoff Video Archives for Holocaust Testimonies. The idea behind the creation of a Trauma Center is to carve out a lasting home for this work, to give it a consistency and authority that it has previously lacked.

It is interesting to return here to the pivotal text of Genesis where the place in Paradise is lost once the threshold of knowing, or knowing trauma, is crossed. A physical home can never be a home again after trauma, and perhaps an erased relationship cannot provide safety. Lanzmann's statement, "my film is my country," takes us one step farther. It indicates that it is in the retrieval of memory and the creation of testimonies that the place can be reclaimed. Without it, there is a repeated and continuous wandering from place to place, and no place can be home without truth being established. It is interesting that in the creation of the Trauma Center, a place and a home is the most essential step and the most difficult one, too. It is as though the creation of the Center is in itself addressing trauma, attempting to build its antidote, and only through such a place—geographical, institutional, but most of all, as a community of scholars, a human place—*that trauma can be appropriately addressed.*

NOTES

1. Jean Améry, *At the Mind's Limits: Contemplations by a Survivor on Auschwitz and Its Realities*, trans. Sidney Rosenfeld and Stella P. Rosenfeld (Bloomington: Indiana University Press, 1980), pp. 28–29, 40. The original German-language edition was published in 1966.

2. Fortunoff Video Archives for Holocaust Testimonies, Yale University, T700, Claude L. (1986).

3. James E. Young, "Memory and Monument," in *Bitburg in Moral and Political Perspective*, ed. Geoffrey Hartman (Bloomington: Indiana University Press, 1986), p. 111.

4. Claude Lanzmann, *Shoah: An Oral History of the Holocaust* (New York: Pantheon Books, 1985), p. 68.

5. Claude Lanzmann, "Les non-lieus de mémoire," in *Au Sujet de Shoah: Le film de Claude Lanzmann*, ed. Bernard Cuau (Paris: Beilin, 1990), p. 280. The description has an overt legal implication in the original French-a memory without "lieu," without a venue for trial.

6. See Young's discussion of monuments in Europe in Hartman, ed., *Bitburg in Moral and Political Perspective*, p. 106.

7. See Geoffrey Hartman's discussion of Reagan's visit to Bitburg in Hartman, ed., *Bitburg in Moral and Political Perspective*, p. 5.

8. Améry, *At the Mind's Limits*, p. 48.

9. For a lengthier psychoanalytic discussion, see Dori Laub and Nanette Auerhahn, "Failed Empathy: A Central Theme in the Survivor's Holocaust Experience," *Psychoanalytic Psychology* 6 (1989): pp. 377–400.

10. Primo Levi, *Survival in Auschwitz*, trans. Stuart Woolf (New York: Macmillan), p. 156.

11. Patricia Joplin, personal communication, 1986.

12. Améry, *At the Mind's Limits*, p. 44.

13. Lanzmann, *Shoah*, p. 165.

14. Ibid.

15. Translated from the German.

16. Nadine Fresco, "Remembering the Unknown," *International Review of Psychoanalysis* 11/4 (1984): 418–19, 421.

17. Ibid.

18. Fortunoff Video Archives for Holocaust Testimonies, Yale University, T58, Helen K. (1979).

19. John Felstiner, *Paul Celan: Poet, Survivor, Jew* (New Haven: Yale University Press, 1995).

20. Paul Celan, "Bremen Speech," address given on acceptance of the Literature Prize of the Free Hanseatic City of Bremen, in 1958.

21. See the discussion of this scene in Shoshana Felman and Dori Laub, M.D., *Testimony: Crises of Witnessing in Literature, Psychoanalysis, and History* (New York: Routledge, 1992), p. 221.

CONTRIBUTORS

THOMAS ALBRICH is Assistant Professor of History at the Institute of Contemporary History, University of Innsbruck, Austria. He has been a teaching fellow at Tel Aviv University and a research assistant at the Wiener Library, London. He is the author of *Exodus durch Österreich: Jewish Refugees in Austria, 1945–1948; In the Bombing War: Tirol and Vorarlberg 1943–1945*; and a number of articles on Jewish history and postwar Austrian history.

MARJORIE ALLARD was a Raoul Wallenberg Scholar at The Hebrew University, Jerusalem, in 1994–1995; she is now a student at Yale University Law School.

JEAN ANCEL has been a research fellow at the Avraham Harman Institute of Contemporary Jewry, The Hebrew University, Jerusalem, and a staff researcher on the history of Romanian Jewry at Yad Vashem. He has published numerous articles on the history of Romanian Jewry during the Holocaust; a multivolume set of documents concerning the fate of Romanian Jewry during the Holocaust; he has co-compiled a bibliography of the Jews in Romania and coedited a volume on the historical record of Romanian Jewry.

YITZHAK ARAD is the former Chairperson of the Directorate of Yad Vashem, the Holocaust Martyrs' and Heroes' Remembrance Authority of Israel. He taught at Tel Aviv University for over a decade and was also a guest professor at Yeshiva University. He is the author of numerous articles and several books on the Holocaust, including *Ghetto in Flames: The Struggle and Destruction of the Jews in Vilna in the Holocaust*, and *Belzec, Sobibor, Treblinka: The Operation Reinhard Death Camps*. He is now engaged in research on the Holocaust in the Nazi-occupied territories of the Soviet Union.

WALTER ZWI BACHARACH is Professor of General History and a member of the Board of the Leo Baeck Institute, Jerusalem. He has published numerous scholarly articles and several books, including *Racism—The Tool of Politics: From Monism to Nazism* (in Hebrew); *Modern Antisemitism* (in Hebrew); and most recently, *Anti-Jewish Prejudices in German-Catholic Sermons* (in English).

DAVID BANKIER teaches Holocaust Studies at the Avraham Harman Institute of Contemporary Jewry, The Hebrew University, Jerusalem. He has also held visiting professorships at the universities of London, Capetown, Colorado, Mexico, and São Paulo. In addition to a large number of articles on contemporary Jewry, antisemitism, and Nazi policy, he is the author of *The Germans and the Final Solution: Public Opinion under Nazism* and of a recent volume published in German, *Die deutsche Öffentlichkeit im NS Staat*.

OMER BARTOV is Associate Professor of History at Rutgers University. He has also held appointments at Harvard and Princeton Universities as well as an Alexander von Humboldt Fellowship. He is the author of *The Eastern Front 1941–45: German Troops and the Barbarization of Warfare; Hitler's Army: Soldiers, Nazis, and War in the Third Reich*; and *Murder in Our Midst: The Holocaust, Industrial Killing, and Representation*.

YEHUDA BAUER has been Jona M. Machover Professor of Holocaust Studies at the Avraham Harman Institute of Contemporary Jewry, The Hebrew University, Jerusalem, since 1977. He was, until 1995, Chair of the Vidal Sasson International Center for the Study of Antisemitism and editor of the journal *Holocaust and Genocide Studies*, which is published under the auspices of the United States Holocaust Memorial Museum. He is the author of a large number of volumes on the Holocaust and related topics, including a three-volume history of the American Jewish Joint Distribution Committee and a volume entitled *Jews for Sale?: Nazi-Jewish Negotiations, 1933–1945*. He is currently Chair of the International Center for Holocaust Studies at Yad Vashem.

MICHAEL BERENBAUM is President and Chief Executive Officer of the Survivors of the Shoah Visual History Foundation. He was Project Director of the United States Holocaust Memorial Museum during its creation, then served as Director of its Research Institute. He was Hyman Goldman Adjunct Professor of Theology at Georgetown University.

Among his publications are *After Tragedy and Triumph: Modern Jewish Thought and the American Experience* and *The World Must Know.*

DORIS L. BERGEN is Assistant Professor of History at the University of Notre Dame. She is the author of *Twisted Cross: The German Christian Movement in the Third Reich.*

RANDOLPH L. BRAHAM is Distinguished Professor Emeritus of Political Science at the City College and the Doctoral Program at the Graduate Center of the City University of New York. He is also the Director of the Rosenthal Institute for Holocaust Studies at CUNY. He is the author or editor of numerous books and articles dealing with comparative politics and the Holocaust. In 1981 his two-volume study, *The Politics of Genocide: The Holocaust in Hungary*, was selected for the National Jewish Book Award.

RICHARD BREITMAN is Professor of History at American University. He is editor-in-chief of *Holocaust and Genocide Studies.* He has written a number of books on various aspects of the Holocaust, including *Breaking the Silence*, with Walter Laqueur; a volume dealing with Eduard Schulte, the German who divulged the secret of the Final Solution; *American Refugee Policy and European Jewry, 1933–1945*, with Alan Kraut; and most recently, *The Architect of Genocide: Himmler and the Final Solution.*

CHRISTOPHER R. BROWNING is Professor of History at Pacific Lutheran University. He is the author of numerous scholarly articles and several books in the field of Holocaust Studies: *The Final Solution and the German Foreign Office*; *Fateful Months: Essays on the Emergence of the Final Solution*; *The Path to Genocide*; and *Ordinary Men: Reserve Police Battalion 101 and the Final Solution in Poland.*

RICHARD I. COHEN is Professor of Jewish History at The Hebrew University, Jerusalem. He is the author of *The Burden of Conscience: French-Jewish Leadership during the Holocaust*; *The French Revolution and Its Historical Impact*; and *Jewish Icons: Art and Society in Modern Europe.* He is editor of several works, including the wartime diary of Raymond-Raoul Lambert, *Carnet d'un témoin, 1939–1943*; and coeditor, with Vivian B. Mann, of *From Court Jews to the Rothschilds: Art, Patronage, and Power, 1600–1800.* He is the author of numerous essays on French Jewry during the Holocaust and on Hannah Arendt's *Eichmann in Jerusalem* and the subsequent controversy. He has taught at the Jewish Theological Seminary, Wesleyan University, and Yale University.

ANNEGRET EHMANN is Director of the Education Department and Deputy Director of the memorial Haus der Wannsee-Konferenz in Berlin. She has published articles on nine-teenth- and twentieth-century German and Jewish History. From 1986 to 1988 she conducted research on the role and fate of the so-called Mischlinge/non-Aryan Christians, an analysis of the theories of racial mixing and Nazi racist population policy, at the Center for Research on Antisemitism at the Technical University, Berlin. She is coauthor of "Human Beings as Objects of Human Genetic Research and Policies in the Twentieth Century" and "Racist and Antisemitic Traditions in Nineteenth- and Twentieth-Century German History."

LEO EITINGER (1912–1996) was Professor Emeritus of Psychiatry at the University of Oslo. He was a pioneer in work with Holocaust survivors, attempting to help them overcome the many difficulties of enduring the "concentration camp in the individual" long after the individual left the concentration camp. His many publications include *Concentration Camp Survivors in Norway and Israel; Psychological and Medical Effects of Concentration Camps: A Research Bibliography;* and *The Anti-Semitism in Our Time—A Threat against Us All.* He was honored with several prizes, among them the Bergen-Belsen International Award and the "Free Word" Honorary Prize. He was decorated Commander of the Royal Norwegian Order of St. Olav.

MARK A. EPSTEIN is an international business consultant in Washington, D.C. In addition, he has worked in the economics division of the German Foreign Ministry and the international division of the Federation of German Chambers of Congress and Industry. He has served as Executive Director of the Union of Councils for Soviet Jews and as a staff member of the U.S. Congress. He has taught at the University of Washington, the University of Munich, and the Foreign Service Institute of the U.S. Department of State. Before leaving academic life, he published numerous articles and reviews and coauthored a volume on sixteenth- and seventeenth-century Ottoman documents on Balkan Jewry as well as a volume on Ottoman Jewish communities in the sixteenth and seventeenth centuries.

EVA FOGELMAN is a social psychologist and a licensed psychologist and supervisor in private practice. She is a senior research fellow at the Center for Social Research, Graduate Center of the City University of New York, and Co-Director of Psychotherapy with Generations of the Holocaust and Related Groups at the Training Institute for Mental Health. She is the author of *Conscience and Courage: Rescuers of Jews during the Holocaust;* writer and coproducer of *Breaking the Silence: The Generation after the Holocaust;* and coeditor of *Children during the Nazi Reign: Psychological Perspective on the Interview Process.* She is a founding director of the Jewish Foundation for Christian Rescuers, now called the Jewish Foundation for the Righteous, a project of the Anti-Defamation League of B'nai B'rith.

JÜRGEN FÖRSTER is affiliated with the Research Office of Military History at Potsdam, Germany. He has taught at Arizona State and Ohio State Universities and in 1993 was a Lady Davis Visiting Scholar at The Hebrew University, Jerusalem. He is the author of *Stalingrad: Event, Influence, Symbol* (in German and Russian), and numerous articles on World War II.

HENRY FRIEDLANDER is Professor of History in the Department of Judaic Studies at Brooklyn College of the City University of New York; in 1996 he was Ruth Meltzer Senior Fellow at the Research Institute of the United States Holocaust Memorial Museum. In addition to articles on the historiography of the Holocaust, the Nazi concentration camps, and postwar war crimes trials, he is the author of *The German Revolution of 1918* and *The Origins of Nazi Genocide: From Euthanasia to the Final Solution;* he is coeditor of *The Holocaust: Ideology, Bureaucracy, and Genocide,* seven volumes of the *Simon Wiesenthal Center Annual,* and the twenty-six-volume documentary series, *Archives of the Holocaust.*

HUGH GREGORY GALLAGHER is an author and public affairs advisor. Previously, he spent a year at the White House during the Johnson administration and nearly a decade on Capitol Hill. While there he conceived and drafted the language of the first national disability rights legislation. In 1995 he was awarded the Betts Prize for lifetime achievement in improving the quality of life of disabled people, and in 1996 he received an honorary doctorate from John Jay College, City University of New York. He is the author of several books, including *FDR's Splendid Deception and the Role of the U.S. Senate in Foreign Policy Decisions,* which was nominated for a Pulitzer Prize. In 1990 he published *By Trust Betrayed: Patients, Physicians, and the License to Kill in the Third Reich.*

JACQUELINE GIERE is an educational consultant at the Fritz Bauer Institute, Study and Documentary Center on the History and the Impact of the Holocaust, Frankfurt am Main. Her publications include a photographic documentary, Jacqueline Giere and Rachel Salamander, eds., *Ein Leben aufs Neu: Das Robinson-Album / DP-Lager: Juden auf deutschem Boden 1945–1948;* she is editor of the volume *Die gesellschaftliche Konstruktion des Zigeuners: Zur Genese eines Vorurteils.*

DANIEL JONAH GOLDHAGEN is Associate Professor of Government and Social Studies at Harvard University and is also an Associate of the Minda de Gunzberg Center for European Studies at Harvard. He is the author of *Hitler's Willing Executioners: Ordinary Germans and the Holocaust.*

GÜNTER GRAU is a member of the Institute for the History of Medicine at Humboldt University, Berlin, and a member of the Executive Committee of the Society for Sexual Research, Leipzig. Among his publications are *And This Love Too: Theological and Sexual Contributions to Homosexuality; Aids: Illness or Catastrophe?* (in German); and, with Claudia Schoppmann, *A Hidden Holocaust: Lesbian and Gay Persecution in Germany 1933–1945.*

JOHN A. S. GRENVILLE is former Professor of Modern History and head of the Department of Modern History at the University of Birmingham, England (1969 to 1994); he is now Professorial Research Fellow at the postgraduate Institute for German Studies at the same university. He has also held visiting professorships in France, Germany, and the United States. He is the author of numerous articles on the history of international relations, German history, and documentary film. In addition, he has published several books dealing with themes as diverse as the reshaping of Europe, 1848–1878; the foreign policy of Lord Salisbury; studies in American diplomacy, 1863–1917; and recently, a history of the world in the twentieth century. He is editor of the highly respected Leo Baeck Institute *Year Book*, and his research interests now center on the question of the relations of Jews and Germans in the twentieth century, with a focus on the city of Hamburg.

PETER HAYES is Professor of History and German and Alfred W. Chase Professor of Business Institutions at Northwestern University. He is the author of *Industry and Ideology: IG Farben in the Nazi Era*, which won the Biennial Book Prize of the Conference Group for Central European History. He is also the editor of *Lessons and Legacies: The Meaning of the Holocaust in a Changing World*, an Anisfield-Wolf Book Award winner, and *Imperial Germany*. He is currently working on a book dealing with German big business and the persecution of the European Jews between 1933 and 1945.

WILLIAM B. HELMREICH is Professor of Sociology and Judaic Studies at City University of New York Graduate Center and City College of New York. He is the author of numerous books, among them *The World of the Yeshiva* and *Against All Odds: Holocaust Survivors and the Successful Lives They Made in America*.

RAUL HILBERG taught in the Department of Political Science at the University of Vermont until his retirement. His principal work, *The Destruction of the European Jews*, has appeared in several editions and translations. He is also the author of *Perpetrators Victims Bystanders* and *The Politics of Memory*.

GORDON J. HORWITZ is Associate Professor of History at Illinois Wesleyan University. He is the author of *In the Shadow of Death: Living Outside the Gates of Mauthausen*.

EBERHARD JÄCKEL has been Professor of Modern History and Director of the Institute of History at the University of Stuttgart since 1967. His many books include: *Hitler's World View*; *Hitlers Herrschaft*; *Umgang mit Vergangenheit*; and *Das deutsche Jahrhundert*. Two of his recent essays have appeared in English translation as *David Irving's Hitler: A Faulty History Dissected*.

STEVEN T. KATZ is Professor of Religion and Director of the Center for Judaic Studies at Boston University. He is the editor of the journal *Modern Judaism*. He is the author of a large number of scholarly articles and numerous works on Jewish mysticism, anti-semitism, and Jewish thought, including *Post-Holocaust Dialogues: Critical Studies in Modern Jewish Thought*, and the prize-winning first volume of the projected three-volume study, *The Holocaust in Historical Context*.

ROBERT KESTING (1946–1997) was Senior Archivist at the Research Institute of the United States Holocaust Memorial Museum. For over four years Dr. Kesting worked at Suitland, Maryland, to identify, survey, and catalogue for the Museum Holocaust-related information located in National Archives record groups. In 1992 he received Congressional recognition for his achievements. He published widely, and his Holocaust-related articles appeared in *Polish American Studies*, *Polish Review*, and the *Journal of Negro History*. Dr. Kesting served as Records Management Officer for the United States Holocaust Memorial Council and Museum until his untimely death in 1997.

STEFAN KÜHL, sociologist and historian, is a management consultant for the Gesellschaft für interdisziplinäre Technikforschung, Technologieberatung und Arbeitsgestaltung in Berlin. He is the author of *The Nazi Connection: Eugenics, American Racism and German National Socialism* and *Die Internationale der Rassisten: Der Aufstieg und Niedergang der internationalen Bewegung für Eugenik und Rassenhygiene im zwanzigsten Jahrhundert*.

DORI LAUB is Associate Clinical Professor in the Department of Psychiatry at Yale University. He is coauthor of numerous articles and of the volume *Testimony: Crises of Witnessing in Literature, Psychoanalysis, and History*. He was the cofounder of the Holocaust Survivors' Film Project and a pioneer in developing what later became the Fortunoff Video Archives for Holocaust Testimonies at Yale University.

RÜDIGER LAUTMANN is Professor of General Sociology and the Sociology of Law at the University of Bremen, Germany. Among his many books are *The Study of Society and*

Homosexuality; Equalizing Gender and Legal Reality; Constraints to Virtue: The Social Control of the Sexualities; Homosexuality: Handbook of the History of Research; and *The Homosexual and His Audience* (all in German).

PAUL A. LEVINE completed a two-year term as Director of the Raoul Wallenberg Professorship in Human Rights, Department of History, Rutgers University, then returned to Sweden, where he continues his research into Swedish diplomacy and Raoul Wallenberg's role in Budapest. He is the author of *From Indifference to Activism: Swedish Diplomacy and the Holocaust, 1938–1944.*

FRANKLIN H. LITTELL is Professor Emeritus of Religion at Temple University and was, from 1973 to 1993, Adjunct Professor in the Institute of Contemporary Jewry of The Hebrew University, Jerusalem. In 1970 he cofounded the Annual Scholars' Conference, which continues to be a major center of academic research and discussion on issues of interfaith relations and the Holocaust. Professor Littell is the author or editor of numerous books and countless articles on themes such as religious liberty, persecution, and genocide. His book *The Crucifixion of the Jews* was perhaps the first discussion of the Holocaust from a Christian point of view.

LOUISE LONDON worked for several years as a legal aid lawyer in London specializing in immigration law. She then turned to research on history at the University of London. She has lectured in British history at Royal Holloway College, University of London, and on Holocaust studies at Queen's University of Canada and University College London. She has published several articles dealing with Jewish refugees and British immigration policies during the Holocaust and on the entry of Nazi war criminals and collaborators into the United Kingdom. Her study *Whitehall and the Jews: British Immigration Policy, Jewish Refugees and the Holocaust, 1933–1948* is forthcoming.

MICHAEL R. MARRUS is Dean of the Graduate School at the University of Toronto and a fellow of the Royal Society of Canada. He has published a number of books on the Holocaust, and his 1981 volume, *Vichy France and the Jews*, coauthored with Robert Paxton, received a National Book Award. He is perhaps best known for his award-winning volume *The Holocaust in History*, which has been translated into French, Polish, Italian, and Japanese.

GUUS MEERSHOEK is a researcher at the International Police Institute of the University of Twente. He is currently doing research on the Amsterdam police during World War II, and he has published articles and designed an exhibition on the subject.

MEIR MICHAELIS is Professor at the Institute for Contemporary History at The Hebrew University, Jerusalem, and has also served as military historian on the Israeli General Staff, as a visiting professor at London University, and as a visiting fellow at St. Antony's College, Oxford University. He is the author of numerous journal articles, and his book *Mussolini and the Jews* has been published in English, Hebrew, and Italian. The Italian version won the prestigious Premio Acqui Storia prize in 1983. He is currently preparing the volume on Italy for Yad Vashem's multivolume history of the Holocaust.

SYBIL MILTON is an independent historian affiliated with the Independent Experts Commission: Switzerland–World War II and the Wannsee Conference memorial in Berlin. She served as Senior Historian of the United States Holocaust Memorial Museum and its Research Institute from 1988 to 1997 and as Director of the Archives of the Leo Baeck Institute from 1974 to 1984. Her books include the coedited volumes *The Holocaust: Ideology, Bureaucracy, and Genocide* and *Genocide: Critical Issues of the Holocaust*; seven volumes of the *Simon Wiesenthal Center Annual*; and the twenty-six-volume documentary series *Archives of the Holocaust*. She also coauthored *Art of the Holocaust*, which received the National Jewish Book Award in the Visual Arts. She has published numerous articles about Nazi Germany and the Holocaust, including discussions of the use of photographic evidence as historical documentation; women and the Holocaust; the politics of postwar memorials; the problems of memory and archival access to the records of Nazi Germany and the Holocaust; and the fate of Sinti and Roma in Germany and occupied Europe between 1933 and 1945. Her most recent book is *In Fitting Memory: The Art and Politics of Holocaust Memorials.*

HANS MOMMSEN is Professor of Modern European History at the Ruhr University, Bochum.

He has also taught at Princeton, Harvard, the University of California–Berkeley, Georgetown, Syracuse, and The Hebrew University, Jerusalem. He is the author of numerous volumes on German history, including *The Labor Movement and the National Question; From Weimar to Auschwitz; The Rise and Fall of Weimar Democracy*; and *The History of the Volkswagenwerk in the Third Reich.*

BENNO MÜLLER-HILL is Professor of Genetics and Director of the Institute of Genetics at the University of Cologne. He has been a research fellow at both Harvard and Indiana Universities. He is the author of *Murderous Science: Elimination by Scientific Selection of Jews, Gypsies, and Others, Germany 1933–1945* (first published in German), and of a number of essays on genetics and psychiatry in the Nazi era.

DALIA OFER is Max and Rita Haber Professor for Holocaust Studies, Avraham Harman Institute for Contemporary Jewry, The Hebrew University, Jerusalem, and the head of the Vidal Sasson International Center for the Study of Antisemitism. Her book *Escaping the Holocaust: Illegal Immigration to the Land of Israel, 1939–1944*, won the 1992 Jewish Book Award. Her book in Hebrew, *Derech Baiam, Aliyah Bet Bitkufat Hashoah*, received the 1992 Ben-Zvi Award. Her most recent volume (coauthored with Hannah Weiner) is *Dead End Journey: The Tragic Story of the Kladovo-Sabac Group*. She has published many articles on Zionism, the Holocaust, and everyday life during the Holocaust. With Lenore Weizman, she is currently editing a book on women in the Holocaust.

SAMUEL P. OLINER is Professor of Sociology at Humboldt State University, Arcata, California. He is founder and Project Director for the Altruistic Personality and Prosocial Behavior Institute and founding editor of the *Humboldt Journal of Social Relations*. He is author of *Embracing the Other: Philosophical, Psychological, and Historical Aspects of Heroic Altruism*; coauthor with Pearl Oliner of *The Altruistic Personality: Rescuers of Jews in Nazi-Occupied Europe* and *Toward a Caring Society: Ideas into Action*; coauthor with Kathleen Lee of *Who Shall Live: The Wilhelm Bachner Story*; and coeditor with Phillip T. Gay of *Race, Ethnicity and Gender: A Global Perspective*.

JOHN T. PAWLIKOWSKI is a Servite Priest and Professor of Social Ethics at the Catholic Theological Union. He has written extensively on the relationship of the Holocaust, antisemitism, and Christian theology. Among his many books and articles are *Cathechetics and Prejudice; The Challenge of the Holocaust for Christian Theology*; and *Christ in the Light of the Christian-Jewish Dialogue*. He is a member of the Advisory Committee on Catholic-Jewish Relations, National Conference of Catholic Bishops, and a member of the United States Holocaust Memorial Council. In 1986 he received The Righteous among the Nations Award from the Holocaust Memorial Museum in Detroit, and in 1989 he received the Raoul Wallenberg Humanitarian Award for Distinguished Contributions to Religion.

ABRAHAM J. PECK is Executive Director of Holocaust Museum Houston and former Director of the American Jewish Archives. He was a special consultant to the Director of the United States Holocaust Memorial Museum. He is the author of *Radical and Reactionaries: The Crisis of Conservatism in Wihelmine Germany*; coeditor of *Queen City Refuge: An Oral History of Cincinnati's Jewish Refugees from Nazi Germany*; and editor of *American Jewish Archives, Cincinnati: The Papers of the World Jewish Congress, 1934–1950*, two volumes in the twelve-volume series *Archives of the Holocaust*.

FRANCISZEK PIPER has been employed in the Department of Historical Research at the Auschwitz-Birkenau State Museum since 1965 and now heads that department. He is the author of several monographs about the Auschwitz satellite camps and the employment of Auschwitz prisoners and has led research on the methods of extermination of prisoners (including the use of gas chambers) and on the numerical results of that extermination.

DINA PORAT is Senior Lecturer in the Department of Jewish History and Head of the Project for the Study of Antisemitism at Tel Aviv University. She has written numerous articles on various aspects of the Holocaust and antisemitism. She is the author of *The Blue and the Yellow Stars of David: The Zionist Leadership in Palestine and the Holocaust, 1939–1945*, which explores the efforts made by the Jewish community in Palestine and its leadership to rescue the Jews in Nazi-occupied Europe. She also edited the original Hebrew version of Abraham Tory's *Surviving the Holocaust: The Kovno Ghetto Diary*. She is presently writing a biography of Abba Kovner.

EDITH RAIM is currently with the Haus der Geschichte in Bonn, Germany. She taught German and European history at Durham and Liverpool Universities from 1991 to 1995. Her study of the Kaufering complex of concentration camps, subcamps of Dachau, was published in German in 1992.

ADAM RAYSKI left Poland in 1932 for Paris, where he became a full-time journalist working for the *Neie Presse*, a left-wing Yiddish daily newspaper. From July 1941 until the end of World War II, he served as national secretary of the Jewish section of the French Communist Party and was the head of the most important French Jewish organization, Union des Juifs pour la Résistance et l'Entraide, in which he played a major part in Jewish survival in France. His publications as a historian include *Les choix des juifs sous Vichy*.

LIVIA ROTHKIRCHEN was for many years, until her retirement, a researcher at Yad Vashem and editor of *Yad Vashem Studies*. She is coeditor of *The Catastrophe of European Jewry*. In 1973 she received the Max Nordau Prize for History in recognition of her outstanding scholarship on a wide range of topics, from *The Destruction of Slovak Jewry* to works on Vatican attitudes toward the plight of Slovakian Jewry and the role of Jewish leadership in the Protectorate of Bohemia and Moravia during the Holocaust. Her recent studies include "State Antisemitism in Communist Czechoslovakia, 1948–1989" and "Spiritual Resistance in Terezín."

CHARLES W. SYDNOR, JR., is President and CEO of the Central Virginia Educational Telecommunications Corporation. He is both a historian and a filmmaker, and his film research and script for the documentary *Adolf Hitler: 1889–1945* received the 1978 James Harvey Robinson Prize of the American Historical Association for the outstanding audio-visual creation produced by an American historian. He is also author of *Soldiers of Destruction: The SS Death's Head Division, 1933–1945*, as well as a number of articles dealing with the history of the SS. He has also served as an expert witness for the Office of Special Investigations of the U.S. Department of Justice and was an affiant in the case against John Demjanjuk.

NECHAMA TEC was Senior Research Fellow at the Miles Lerman Research Center for the Study of Resistance at the United States Holocaust Memorial Museum and is Professor of Sociology at the University of Connecticut, Stamford. She is the author of several books and numerous articles and has lectured extensively both in the United States and abroad. Since 1977 she has conducted research on compassion, altruism, resistance to evil, and the rescue of Jews during World War II. Her book *Defiance: The Bielski Partisans* won the 1994 International Anne Frank Special Recognition Prize in Switzerland. In 1995 it was awarded the First Prize for Holocaust Literature by the World Federation of Fighters, Partisans, and Concentration Camp Survivors in Israel. The book has been translated into Hebrew and German and has been optioned for a movie.

GERHARD L. WEINBERG is William Rand Kennan, Jr., Professor of History at the University of North Carolina at Chapel Hill. He has also taught at the universities of Chicago, Kentucky, and Michigan, and he has directed the American Historical Association's Project for Microfilming Captured German Documents. He is the author of numerous articles in both American and German journals and many books. Among his best known are *Hitler's Zweites Buch*; *Germany and the Soviet Union, 1939–1941*; *A World at Arms: A Global History of World War II*; *The Foreign Policy of Hitler's Germany*; and *World in the Balance: Behind the Scenes of World War II*. His most recent work is *Germany, Hitler, and World War II: Essays in Modern German and World History*.

SUSAN S. ZUCCOTTI has taught at Columbia University, Barnard College, and New York University. She is the author of several articles and of *The Italians and the Holocaust: Persecution, Rescue and Survival*, which received a National Jewish Book Award and the Premio Acqui Storia, Opera Prima award in Italy, and of *The Holocaust, the French, and the Jews*.

INDEX